The
INTERNATIONAL CRITICAL COMMENTARY
on the Holy Scriptures of the Old and New Testaments

GENERAL EDITORS

G. I. DAVIES, F.B.A.
Emeritus Professor of Old Testament Studies in the University of Cambridge
Fellow of Fitzwilliam College

AND

C. M. TUCKETT
Emeritus Professor of New Testament in the University of Oxford
Fellow of Pembroke College

FORMERLY UNDER THE EDITORSHIP OF

J. A. EMERTON, F.B.A., C. E. B. CRANFIELD, F.B.A. and G. N. STANTON
General Editors of the New Series

S. R. DRIVER
A. PLUMMER
C. A. BRIGGS
Founding Editors

A CRITICAL AND EXEGETICAL COMMENTARY

ON

ECCLESIASTES

BY

STUART WEEKS

Professor of Old Testament and Hebrew, Durham University

IN TWO VOLUMES

VOLUME 2

Commentary on Ecclesiastes 5.7–12.14

t&tclark
LONDON • NEW YORK • OXFORD • NEW DELHI • SYDNEY

T&T CLARK
Bloomsbury Publishing Plc
50 Bedford Square, London, WC1B 3DP, UK
1385 Broadway, New York, NY 10018, USA
29 Earlsfort Terrace, Dublin 2, Ireland

BLOOMSBURY, T&T CLARK and the T&T Clark logo are trademarks of
Bloomsbury Publishing Plc

First published in Great Britain 2022

Copyright © Stuart Weeks, 2022

Stuart Weeks has asserted his right under the Copyright, Designs and Patents Act,
1988, to be identified as the Author of this work.

All rights reserved. No part of this publication may be reproduced or transmitted
in any form or by any means, electronic or mechanical, including photocopying,
recording, or any information storage or retrieval system, without prior permission in
writing from the publishers.

Bloomsbury Publishing Plc does not have any control over, or responsibility for, any
third-party websites referred to or in this book. All internet addresses given in this
book were correct at the time of going to press. The author and publisher regret any
inconvenience caused if addresses have changed or sites have ceased to exist, but
can accept no responsibility for any such changes.

The NewJerusalemU, GraecaU and TranslitLSU fonts used to print this work
are available from Linguist's Software, Inc., PO Box 580, Edmonds,
WA 98020-0580 USA.
Tel (425) 775-1130. www.linguistsoftware.com

A catalogue record for this book is available from the British Library.

A catalog record for this book is available from the Library of Congress.

ISBN: HB: 978-0-5676-6654-3
       ePDF: 978-0-5676-6655-0

Series: International Critical Commentary

Typeset by Trans.form.ed SAS
Printed and bound in Great Britain

To find out more about our authors and books visit www.bloomsbury.com
and sign up for our newsletters.

For my mother, Moyra Weeks

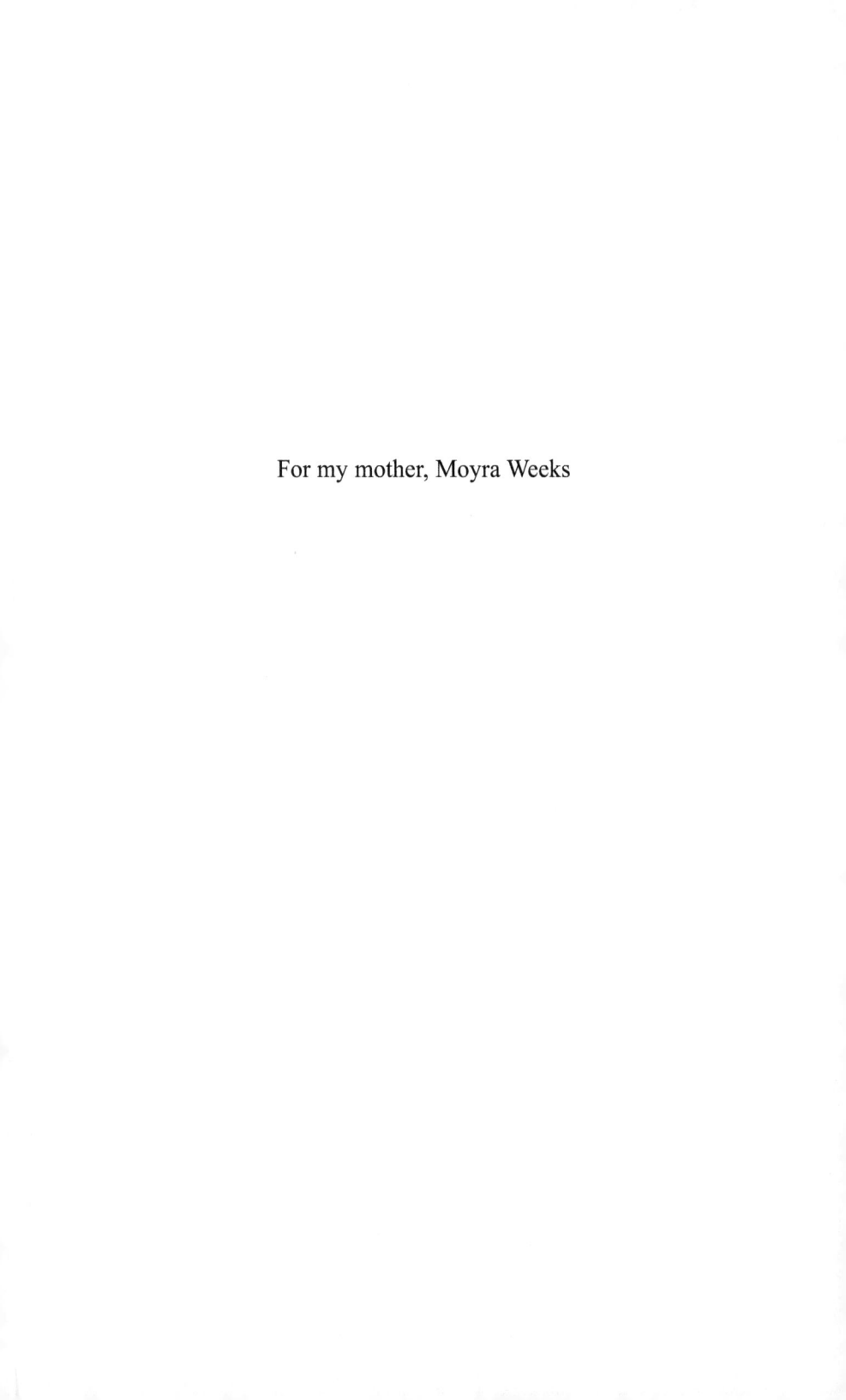

CONTENTS OF VOLUME 2

General Editors' Preface	ix
Preface to the Second Volume	xi
A Paraphrase	xv
Additional Bibliography of Works Cited	xxiv
Additional Abbreviations	xlv

INTRODUCTION TO 5.7–6.9 (ET 5.8–6.9):
WEALTH, LONG LIFE AND FULFILMENT   1
   5.7-11 (ET 5.8-12)   6
   5.12-19 (ET 5.13-20)   32
   6.1-2   63
   6.3-6a   72
   6.6b-9   92

6.10-12: THE LIMITS OF BEING HUMAN   118

INTRODUCTION TO 7.1-22:
SAYINGS   140
   7.1-6   145
   7.7   164
   7.8-12   174
   7.13-14   192
   7.15-22   202

INTRODUCTION TO 7.23–8.1:
QOHELET'S SEARCH FOR WISDOM   228
   7.23-24   234
   7.25   252
   7.26   269
   7.27–8.1   286

INTRODUCTION TO 8.2-9:	
POWER AND POWERLESSNESS	323
8.2-5a	327
8.5b-9	340
INTRODUCTION TO 8.10-17:	
INVISIBLE JUSTICE	357
8.10-13	359
8.14-15	381
8.16-17	387
INTRODUCTION TO 9.1-12:	
DEATH AND LIVING	396
9.1-3b	402
9.3c-6	418
9.7-10	436
9.11-12	447
INTRODUCTION TO 9.13–10.3:	
WISDOM AND FOLLY	456
9.13-18	459
10.1	475
10.2-3	485
10.4-10c: BAD LEADERSHIP	491
10.10d-15: WISE AND FOOLISH SPEECH	515
10.16-19: INACTION	535
10.20–11.6: OVER-CAUTION	551
11.7–12.2: LIVING MINDFULLY	575
12.3-8: DEATH	601
12.9-14: EPILOGUE	659

GENERAL EDITORS' PREFACE

Much scholarly work has been done on the Bible since the publication of the first volumes of the International Critical Commentary in the 1890s. New linguistic, textual, historical and archaeological evidence has become available, and there have been changes and developments in methods of study. In the twenty-first century there will be as great a need as ever, and perhaps a greater need, for the kind of commentary that the International Critical Commentary seeks to supply. The series has long had a special place among works in English on the Bible, because it has sought to bring together all the relevant aids to exegesis, linguistic and textual no less than archaeological, historical, literary and theological, to help the reader to understand the meaning of the books of the Old and New Testaments. In the confidence that such a series meets a need, the publishers and the editors are commissioning new commentaries on all the books of the Bible. The work of preparing a commentary on such a scale cannot but be slow, and developments in the past half-century have made the commentator's task yet more difficult than before, but it is hoped that the remaining volumes will appear without too great intervals between them. No attempt has been made to secure a uniform theological or critical approach to the problems of the various books, and scholars have been selected for their scholarship and not for their adherence to any school of thought. It is hoped that the new volumes will attain the high standards set in the past, and that they will make a significant contribution to the understanding of the books of the Bible.

G. I. D.
C. M. T.

PREFACE TO THE SECOND VOLUME

Current constraints upon UK academic research have made it necessary for me to publish the two volumes of this commentary separately, and the first appeared while I was still bringing this second to completion. Although I have not felt driven to revise my views fundamentally on any of the issues that I discussed in the Introduction to that first volume, I have since had more time to consider some of the later passages relevant to those issues, and a careful reader may detect some subtle changes in emphasis or precision. In ch. 10, for instance, I think there is rather more thematic coherence than I had previously allowed, and I have slightly refined my ideas about Qohelet's relationship with wisdom at the end of ch. 7. On more minor points, I have revised my understandings of 5.10 (as cited in the notes to 2.21) and 5.15 (see the Introduction, 23). There are no changes, however, that I feel obliged to register as major corrections to what I said before, and the only significant thing to add is that, as I anticipated, Peter Gentry's Göttingen edition of the Greek text has now been published. My first volume was already in production when I got my hands on a copy, but I have been able to revise my notes for the second in the light of Gentry's finished text, and would draw attention to the very full account of the Greek text, and of the versions dependent upon it, that he offers in his own introduction.[1]

---

[1] The edition also includes a significant number of new hexaplaric readings, especially for σ´, from sources that were unavailable to Field and Marshall (notably the tenth-century catena ms 788). Amongst the additional information that these provide for the text treated in my first volume are: the Greek for the reading of θ´ and σ´ at 1.5 (καταντῶν, not Field's retroversion ἐπαναστρέφει); further Greek for readings from σ´ preserved in Latin (1.6, 13) and in Syriac (1.9; 5.6); new readings for σ´ (esp. 1.7, 14; 2.1, 5, 11, 17, 23; 3.15, 18, 19; 4.6, 8), and for α´ (1.15; 3.11, 22); and unattributed readings (3.18; 4.1). None of these really affects any points made in my discussion, but it is worth noting that the new reading of σ´ attested at 2.1 makes it highly likely that σ´ was in fact the source for Jerome's understanding in V, and many of the new readings overall affirm the influence of σ´ on V. The readings at 2.11 and 2.23 are very interesting in themselves. At 2.21, ms 788 attributes the reading οὗ to α´ and σ´, which is relevant to the text-critical question around Gentry's reading ὅ τι, and in 3.16 it identifies τῆς δικαιοσύνης as the reading of all the Three, not just α´.

To the bibliographical works listed on page 1 of my Introduction, we can also now add the valuable D.J.H. Beldman and R.L. Meek, *A Classified Bibliography on Ecclesiastes* (London & New York, 2019), which covers the period 1900–2015.

On the text more generally, I summarized in a note on p. 124 the various points at which I had felt it necessary in the first volume to depart from the readings of the Masoretic text, and, for the sake of completeness, it might be helpful to add a similar note here.[2] It would be fair to say, I think, that I have continued to find less good cause for emendation of the consonantal text than have many other commentators. At the same time, though, work on this second volume has only tended to strengthen my opinion that the Masoretes' pointing, and perhaps in particular their division of the text, often reflects early interpretations that were out of step with the probable intentions of the author. At times, this has pushed subsequent understandings down some very particular channels, but the same can be said also of readings drawn from the ancient translations. The broader lesson to be learned is not about the fallibility or otherwise

---

[2] Where 4QQoh^a is preserved, I have often preferred the readings that it attests or implies to those of M: 5.14 כיא for כאשר; 5.15 גם for וגם; 5.16 כעס (see the note) for וכעס; 6.3 הנפל ממנו for ממנו הנפל; 6.8 כמה (= כמו) for כי מה; 7.2 שמחה for משתה, and מאיש for מלשמוע, and נערת for נערות 7.5; twice, בבית for בית 7.4; סוף כל for כל סוף שמע; 7.6 גם זה (found also in some later manuscripts) for וגם זה; 7.19 תעוז (cf. G) for תעז. I have followed the readings that I take to be reflected in G (sometimes also in other versions) at: 5.8 על כל (cf. σ′, T); בכל for בכל; 5.15 כי לעמת for כל עמת; 5.16 וחלי (all witnesses except M) for וחליו; 6.4 הולך for ילך; 7.12 בצלה for בצל; 7.14 וראה ביום for וביום רעה ראה; 7.26 ומוצא אני אתה ואמר for ומוצא אני; 8.10 וישתבחו (found also in some later Hebrew manuscripts) for וישתכחו; 8.17 האדם for אדם; 9.1-2 ולבי ראה הכל לפניהם הכל כאשר לכל (cf. σ′) for הכל לפניהם הבל באשר לכל, ולבור את for ולרע (cf. Hie, V, S); 9.5 ידעו for יודעים; 9.10 ככחך for בכחך; 9.14 מצור (cf. σ′) for מצודים; 10.3 הכל for לכל (cf. Hie, T); 10.10 והוא לו פנים (attested as an 'eastern' reading) for והוא לא פנים; 10.16 עיר for ארץ; 10.17 a verbal form from בוש for בשתי; 11.5 אין for אינך; 12.5 וגם (cf. σ′) for גם; 12.6 וירץ for ונרץ. In 7.25, I would read כסלות וסכלות or כסלה וסכלות, which is less certainly reflected in G, for כסל והסכלות, while in 5.9 and 10.1, I have proposed reconstructions that draw on the readings of both M and G. In 12.6, I have tentatively followed σ′ with many others, reading ינתק for ירחק. In 7.27, I divide the consonantal text not as אמרה קהלת, but as אמר הקהלת, with G and most scholars, and in 12.5 not as חתחתים, but as חת חתים or חת התתים, with α′. Only in three places have I proposed readings reflected directly in none of the ancient versions: 8.2 אפי for אני פי (which is widely acknowledged to be corrupt); 8.10 קרבים ובאים מקום (the first part of which includes a common emendation) for מאת ומאריך for ומותו מאריך; and 8.12 קבורים ובאו וממקום.

of all these earlier, very able scholars, but about the impossibility of separating this book's textual history from its history of reception and interpretation.

As before, I am very grateful to the sharp-eyed Duncan Burns for his valuable help at the production stage, but I should like to express my particular gratitude once again to Graham Davies. As editor of the series, he has engaged in great detail with my manuscript, saving me from various errors and howlers, but also contributing many interesting and stimulating ideas of his own. He has influenced my understanding of 12.6-7, in particular, but the commentary as a whole has benefitted from his wisdom and learning at many points, and I am greatly in his debt. This volume will be the last published under his editorship, as he is stepping down after holding the role since 2004, and after breathing new life into the Old Testament section of the series. The great amount of work that he has done is largely hidden from plain sight, but I know that his insights have informed all the volumes that have appeared during this time. He has commissioned a number of others, some of them now well-advanced, so as I have the honour of taking over the editorship myself, I shall continue to benefit from his endeavours.

Durham, December 2020

A PARAPHRASE

There is a long tradition of paraphrasing Ecclesiastes, and some distinguished writers have tried their hand over the centuries. Before my effort here is judged against those standards, I should explain at once, therefore, that this paraphrase is offered as a matter of practicality, rather than as a literary endeavour. In a commentary of this nature, it can be difficult to see the wood for the trees, and this is, as much as anything, an attempt to provide an overview. Since the translation elsewhere has had to be tied closely to the original, it can at times be nearly as unclear as that original. Here I have tried to convey more lucidly what I think it is that Qohelet is saying and, to some extent, how I think the different discussions fit together. Obviously, that means coming down on one side or the other where different readings are possible, and this paraphrase is also much more speculative than the commentary itself. I have found writing it helpful as I have gone along, though, and offer it in the hope that others may find it useful too.

1.1-11
Qohelet said:
It's all smoke and mirrors.
 Life is hard work: what does anyone get to take away from it? Humans enter, and then swiftly leave, a world that never changes: things move around here—the sun, the wind, and all the rivers—but they never truly finish what they're doing. Nothing is really new, even when we say it is: things just get forgotten. What can we take from a world like that, or bring into it?

1.12–2.11
Back in the day, I set out to think about what we do. Is God giving us a bad deal by making us live? Looking around, everything seemed like that: for us, it's all just broken and costly. That led me to think about thinking itself. I'd worked hard to become as wise as anybody, but when I looked into being wise rather than stupid, I realized it was painful and frustrating. Then I considered pleasure, but that seemed to me then to be just another illusion, and pointless.

In the end, I settled down for a proper investigation, and contrived to live a remarkable life—building a business that would last, living in luxury off the profits, becoming as rich as I'd been wise, and denying myself nothing I wanted. If there was anything to get out of life, I was going to find it. I enjoyed it all, but in the end, I rejected all I had accomplished. There was nothing real for me in it: just smoke and mirrors, and trying to catch something I couldn't.

2.12-26
Two things in particular worried me after this. I'd been busy being wise, but now I couldn't see the point: I was still going to die like all the idiots out there—a fact I seemed to have forgotten when I invested so much effort into wisdom, because we do forget. And then, what about whoever it is that ends up following me, and their contribution? My business didn't seem so good anymore, when I realized that someone else will get it all. I put work and thought into that business, but they'll get it for nothing, even if they're a complete fool—and the same can happen to anybody: even if they have half killed themselves with the work of building up a business, it can all go to someone who never did a thing. So, when someone's running their business and having fun, it doesn't mean they've done anything to deserve it. The idea that God only makes his favourites wise and lets them have fun, getting the sinners to prepare it all for them—well, that's just deluded.

3.1-15
When anything happens, it's the right thing—God wouldn't make it happen otherwise. So, what's the point in having people do everything? God makes people work, and he gives them a sense of some bigger picture, but they have no idea where it all fits into what he's doing, and there's no real value gained by using them. I did see that God at least pays them: other people can get the sort of pleasure that I'd found in my own work, and this is a wage, of sorts. In the end, though, it's God's world: nobody could change what he's done—even if they weren't too afraid to try—so it won't ever change, and if anything serious does need doing, God will do it himself.

3.16-22
Anyway, thinking about humans, I saw that they're all mixed together, the bad with the good: I'm sure God will decide who's who, when it's the right thing. Humans cannot distinguish, though, even when it comes to telling themselves apart from animals, because all they can see is that both die the same, and they have no idea whether they even have different spirits. When we've no way to know what happens when we're gone, the best we can do is enjoy what we're doing.

4.1-16
I also saw that humans rob each other, and the victims are left with no-one even to comfort them: with such bad things going on in the world of the living, I thought the dead were better—and the not-yet-born better still.

And I saw that when people immerse themselves in work, it just cuts them off from other people. They're chasing an illusion: it's better to keep one foot out the water.

I saw another illusion like it—the person who works endlessly and joylessly for the sake of nobody but themselves (was that me?). That's a bad deal. If there's enough to go around, there are practical benefits anyway to working and living with someone else.

Even if they start out dirt poor, a wise child is always going to be better than any wealthy and powerful idiot who hasn't improved with age: poor kids can get rich, but old, rich idiots have been poor their whole life. All the same, I looked at everyone out there with the children that will replace them one day, and I thought of all the ones that came before, and of all the ones coming later, who will feel nothing for them, and it seemed like a lot of pointless trouble.

4.17–5.6
If you're dealing with God yourself, be careful. Only fools keep offering sacrifices, just in case they've sinned, and you don't need to start jabbering in the temple just because you think God's there: he's a long way away, and you can pick your words. If you do make a vow, though, don't try to wriggle out of your promises: he's not *that* far away. Careless talk can ruin you, and it's when there are lots of dreams and talk that you should be most afraid of God.

5.7–6.9

Now, wealth. Don't be fooled by all those government officials, each supervised by the next: they're not really there to stop the poor getting robbed, because in any civilized country they are all reporting to the real king—profit! Those who love money can never get enough of it, and when there's more money, there are more to spend it too. The rich have a boundless appetite, and it's others who have to feed them.

We're all like a man who had put his money somewhere safe, for when it was needed, but then lost it in a bad deal, so that when he did need it, he had nothing. He's going to leave the world as naked as the day he was born, able to take nothing away from it, and will meantime live off his anger. He'd be better off without that anger, enjoying what he has left, for as long as he has left. We've had a bad deal too, but if God has given us wealth to enjoy, and the capacity to enjoy it, this is the only pay we are going to get from him, and we should take it.

There's something far worse: having all that wealth, but not being able to enjoy it, because God is saving it for someone else. Long life, too, is pointless if there's no pleasure in it—even a stillborn child, with no life at all, is better off: the stillborn might never see the light, but it's the person with no joy in life who has to spend their many days in the dark. In the end, we are all going to the same place, and someone who has nothing but their need, has nothing to live for. It's deluded to choose constant yearning over satisfaction with what we have.

6.10-12

Our place in the order of things is already fixed, and nobody classed as human can achieve anything by arguing with some greater power, except maybe a lot of pointless hot air. Nobody really knows what's good for us, with our short, deluded lives, and nobody can explain what the future holds beyond us. We can't change how things are run, or understand what we should do, either for ourselves or to shape the future.

7.1-22

Speaking of the future, if the reputation we leave behind were really valuable, then that would mean the day we die must be more important than the day we're born, and we should look to that future, spending our time at wakes, not weddings—isn't it good for us to be unhappy, after all? So, if the mind of someone wise is like a house in mourning, and the idiot's like a house in celebration, then we should prefer getting lectured at by the wise to being sung at by the idiot. But those idiots laugh a lot too, even when they're doomed—isn't this just more smoke? Can't the wise be made to look stupid?

When ends are better than beginnings, we should also be patient, and wait to see how things turn out—it's the idiots who keep their anger close to hand. Wisdom is not about glorifying the past: even if it's sheltered by old money, what we get from it is survival in the present.

One way or another, these sorts of ideas make us focus on the future, but humans can't sort out what God has distorted. Rather than looking forward the whole time, we should enjoy things when times are good—and when they are not, realize that God has made bad times to match the good ones, to stop us predicting what the future will hold.

Things do not always work out the way we think they should: the good can be killed by being good, and the bad can just keep going—so, practically, don't be too good or too wise, even if it's more obviously dangerous to be too bad or too stupid. So long as you fear God, you should be able to get away with a bit of both. Remember that wisdom is helpful, but not always as helpful as other things, and that nobody is actually good all the time—and don't base your behaviour on other people's opinions of you.

7.23–8.1

I originally set out to make my investigations using my wisdom, but we seem to have become estranged. So, I went to look for her, to find a blueprint for living, and to learn what makes being stupid wrong. If I'd found her or Folly, I planned to tell them to their face that they are nothing but a trap for the unlucky—but although I met a lot of women while I looked, I never did. What I found instead is that, even if God made humans uncomplicated, humans, like me, go looking for a lot of plans to live their lives. Is anyone really the wise man I'd thought myself to be? Or does anyone possess any powers of analysis at all? Being wise makes you clever, but makes you cautious too.

8.2-9

When you are in a court with a king, you have to watch out for his anger, be careful about the promises you make to him, and be ready to run if he says something frightening—because nobody is going to stop him. All you can do in that situation is avoid any risk by doing everything the king says.

What someone wise knows is that there is always going to be a moment of reckoning for everything. Knowing that something bad will happen, but not what or when, just makes it worse. There's nothing we can do about it anyway.

I could tell all this just from looking at what happens to humans when it's only other humans exercising power.

8.10-17

When the issue is divine power, then the problem is that humans cannot really know what God (unlike the human king) actually wants them to do. To be sure, I know that things should be okay for those who fear him, but when the wicked seem to get away with it for ages, and even get praised for their piety, it is not surprising that people start to imitate them. It's misleading when good or bad people are not seen to get what they deserve, but when I realized that, then all I could suggest was that we just get on with enjoying our lives. When I'd given a lot of thought to wisdom, what I also realized is that God has contrived to prevent humans from knowing what he has contrived, however hard they look, so when the wise say they'll find out, well, they won't.

9.1-12

Actually, this goes further. Everybody is under God's control, and because all anyone can see is that the same thing happens in the end to everyone, they cannot work out which of the choices that others make are good, and which bad. They make things worse by ignoring the dead, whose lives might have held lessons, because it's more appealing to keep company with the living—and so the dead, and their choices, are forgotten.

The only sensible thing to do is to go and get on with enjoying life—you're only anyway doing work that God has set you. Live well, and throw yourself into whatever you find yourself doing: there will be nothing to do or to worry about in the underworld.

In the end, it is not just the wicked who don't always get what we think they deserve: the strong and the wise are all subject to circumstance. And when it comes to enjoying life, remember that humans never know how long they have left: we're already in the hunter's trap, and we're just waiting to die.

9.13–10.3
Getting back to wisdom. Within the world itself, it has always seemed powerful, and capable of great things—but it's also vulnerable: people in charge forget about it, or cannot hear it above the din. It's better than stupidity, at least (although, frankly, neither will be much use when we're dead), and someone who's stupid makes the fact obvious to all.

10.4-10c
(If you ever get the urge to take charge yourself, by the way, stay seated. In this world I've seen things turned upside down, apparently by whoever is in charge getting things wrong. Even the most unlucky, accident-prone of individuals can end up with power.)

10.10d-15
Anyway, the point of wisdom is what we can get from it—if we can get those things without it, there's no need for it. One advantage is obvious when it comes to speaking: wise people win friends when they talk, while idiots destroy themselves (although it doesn't seem to stop them). It is true that the wise cannot explain the future, but the stupid cannot even tell you the way to the city without becoming tiresome.

10.16-19
Speaking of cities, they have a problem when their ruler is just a vassal, and their ministers have nothing better to do than start supper as soon as they get up: better a land with a king free to act. Likewise, even when it comes to simple maintenance of a house, laziness is damaging, but total inaction worse. There is a cost attached to doing nothing, which may be greater than the cost of acting—as when people deny themselves the pleasure of a party because they are worrying about the bill.

10.20–11.6

Over-reaction can be as costly as inaction, even though, in a dangerous, unpredictable world, you might feel the need to take absurd precautions—like giving up what you have for fear of losing it. What will happen will happen, and those who spend their time watching for the right moment will never accomplish the things they're trying to guarantee: nobody can predict the future, and, when it comes to what God plans, we're like babes still blind in the womb. We should deal with the unpredictable by covering all bases—through constant action, not through the sort of caution that surrenders any chance of accomplishment.

11.7–12.2

Besides, that gets us out into the sunshine, which we should enjoy while we can—remembering that there is a lot of darkness ahead for each of us. What's coming is just more smoke, but we are the young, who should enjoy their youth and follow their dreams, even if they should know too that God will make his own judgments about them, and who should enjoy the carefreeness that comes with the illusion of youth, even as they should know they are just God's creatures—during the good times, before the bad times come, and while the light still returns.

12.3-8

Death leaves a lasting mark on the living, stunning and terrifying them, but nature still flowers and fruits regardless, even as each human moves from the house where they died to the house where they will spend the rest of time—broken before their baubles are broken, and stripped even of the flesh and breath that had been lent only for a lifetime.

It's all smoke and mirrors.

12.9-14

Qohelet hasn't mentioned that he was a writer, crafting all these words. The wise men like him, who write books like this, use sharp and painful words to get under your skin and push you about like sheep. Now you've experienced that from this one writer, I wouldn't bother reading any others: there's no end of books to study, but it will wear you out. That's enough words. Just fear God: all any human has, or needs, is the fact that they're accountable to him for everything they do.

ADDITIONAL BIBLIOGRAPHY OF WORKS CITED

As in the first volume, works marked with an asterisk are cited by author's name alone, or by author and date where that is necessary to avoid confusion. Other works are cited by short title. Citations are *ad loc.* unless otherwise specified in the text.

Aaron, D.H., 'Shedding Light on God's Body in Rabbinic Midrashim: Reflections on the Theory of a Luminous Adam', *HTR* 90 (1997), 299-314.

Ackroyd, P.R., 'Two Hebrew Notes', *ASTI* 5 (1967), 82-86.

Aitken, J.K., *No Stone Unturned: Greek Inscriptions and Septuagint Vocabulary* (CrStHB 5; Winona Lake, 2014).

Althann, R., 'Ellipsis in Psalm 9,19, Qohelet 11,5 and Esther 2,1', in A. Vonach and G. Fischer (eds.), *Horizonte biblischer Texte. Festschrift für Josef M. Oesch zum 60. Geburtstag* (OBO 196; Göttingen, 2003), 91-98.

Anat, M.A., 'הקינה על מות האדם במגילת קהלת' = 'The Lament over Human Death in the Book of Qohelet', *Beth Mikra* 15/43 (1970), 375-80.

Anderlini, G., 'Qohelet 5,7-8. Note linguistiche ed esegetiche', *BeO* 37 (1995), 13-32.

Andrews, S., 'Ecclesiastes 7:1-19', *Int* 55 (2001), 299-301.

Assmann, J., 'Der schöne Tag. Sinnlichkeit und Vergänglichkeit im altägyptischen Fest', in W. Haug and R. Warning (eds.), *Das Fest* (Poetik und Hermeneutik 14; Munich, 1989), 3-28.

Asurmendi, J., 'Power in Qoheleth and the Prophets', in N. Calduch-Benages (ed.), *Wisdom for Life: Essays Offered to Honor Prof. Maurice Gilbert, SJ on the Occasion of his Eightieth Birthday* (BZAW 445; Berlin; Boston, 2014), 132-44.

Athas, G., 'Qohelet in His Context: Ecclesiastes 4,13-16 and the Dating of the Book', *Bib* 100 (2019), 353-72.

Auwers, J.-M., 'Problèmes d'interprétation de l'épilogue de Qohèlèt', in Schoors (ed.), *Qohelet in the Context*, 267-82.

Backhaus, F.J., 'Der Weisheit letzter Schluß! Qoh. 12,9-14 im Kontext von Traditionsgeschichte und beginnender Kanonisierung', *BN* 72 (1994), 28-59.

Bady, G., 'L'Ecclésiaste chez Jean Chrysostome', in L. Mellerin (ed.), *La Réception du livre de Qohélet* (Paris, 2016), 149-61.

Bain, D., 'Audience Address in Greek Tragedy', *The Classical Quarterly* 25 (1975), 13-25.

Baltzer, K., 'Women and War in Qohelet 7:23-8:1a', *HTR* 80 (1987), 127-32.

Barclay Burns, J., 'Some Personifications of Death in the Old Testament', *IBS* 11 (1989), 23-34.

Barolín, D., 'Eclesiastés 8:1-8: Consejos para leer entre líneas', *Cuadernos de teología* 20 (2001), 7-22.
Barr, J., 'Philology and Exegesis: Some general remarks, with illustrations from Job', in C. Brekelmans (ed.), *Questions disputées d'ancien Testament: méthode et théologie* (BETL 33; Gembloux, 1974), 39-61.
Barton, G.A., 'The Text and Interpretation of Ecclesiastes 5:19', *JBL* 27 (1908), 65-66.
Bauer, U.F.W., 'Kohelet in Distanz zu Eschatologie und Apokalyptik', *ZAW* 131 (2019), 563-76.
Baumgärtel, F., 'Die Ochsenstachel und die Nägel in Koh 12 11', *ZAW* 81 (1969), 98.
Bauschatz, J., 'The Strong Arm of the Law? Police Corruption in Ptolemaic Egypt', *The Classical Journal* 103 (2007), 13-39.
Beal, T.K., 'C(ha)osmopolis: Qohelet's Last Words', in T. Linafelt and T.K. Beal (eds.), *God in the Fray: A Tribute to Walter Brueggemann* (Minneapolis, 1998), 290-304.
[Beard, J.R.], *The People's Dictionary of the Bible* (London, 1847).
Beentjes, P., '"Who is like the Wise?" Some Notes on Qoheleth 8,1-5', in Schoors (ed.), *Qohelet in the Context*, 303-15.
Berger, B.L., 'Qohelet and the Exigencies of the Absurd', *BibInt* 9 (2001), 141-79.
Bernstein, H.G., *Quaestiones nonnullae Kohelethanae* (Breslau, 1854).
*de Bèze (Beza), T., *Ecclesiastes: Salomonis concio ad populum habita, de vita sic instituenda, ut ad veram aeternamque felicitatem perveniatur* (Geneva, 1588). ET *Ecclesiastes, or, the Preacher* (Cambridge, 1593).
Bianchi, F., 'Qohelet 10,8-11 or the Misfortunes of Wisdom', *BeO* 40 (1998), 111-17.
—, '"Un fantasma al banchetto della sapienza?" Qohelet e il libro dei Proverbi a confrontò', in Bellia and Passaro (eds.), *Il Libro del Qohelet*, 40-68.
Boda, M.J., 'Speaking into the Silence: The Epilogue of Ecclesiastes', in Boda, Longman, and Rata (eds.), *The Words of the Wise*, 257-79.
de Boer, P.A.H., 'A Note on Ecclesiastes 12:12a', in R.H. Fischer (ed.), *A Tribute to Arthur Vööbus: Studies in Early Christian Literature and its environment, Primarily in the Syrian East* (Chicago, 1977), 85-88.
Bordreuil, P., and A. Caquot, 'Textes en cunéiformes alphabétiques découverts en 1978 à Ibn Hani', *Syria* 57 (1980), 343-73.
Börner-Klein, D., 'Transforming Rabbinic Exegesis into Folktale', *Trumah* 15 (2005), 139-48.
Brin, G., 'The Significance of the Form mah-ṭṭôb', *VT* 38 (1988), 462-65.
Brindle, W.A., 'Righteousness and Wickedness in Ecclesiastes 7:15- 18', *AUSS* 23 (1985), 243-57.
Bronznick, N.M., 'כי העשק יהולל ויאבד את־לב מתנה (Eccles. 7:7)', *Beit Mikra* 52 (2007), 91-94, 8*-9*.
Bruns, J.E., 'The Imagery of Eccles 12:6a', *JBL* 84, (1965), 428-30.

Brunsell, S., *Solomons Blessed Land: A sermon upon Ecclesiastes X.17. Preached before an extraordinary assembly at Newark upon Trent, May 29. 1660. Being the birth-day of our soveraign lord Charles II. King of Engladnd* (sic), &c. (London, 1660).

*Budde, K., 'Der Prediger', in E. Kautzsch (ed.), *Die Heilige Schrift des Alten Testaments* Vol. 2 (3rd edn; Tübingen, 1910), 384-403.

Bühlmann, A., 'Qoheleth 11.1-6 and Divination', in T.E. Klutz (ed.), *Magic in the Biblical World: From the Rod of Aaron to the Ring of Solomon* (JSNTSup 245; London, New York, 2003), 55-65.

*Bullock, W.T., 'Ecclesiastes', in F.C. Cook (ed.), *The Holy Bible, According to the Authorized Version (a.d. 1611) with an Explanatory and Critical Commentary and a Revision of the Translation, by Bishops and Other Clergy of the Anglican Church: Vol. IV* (London, 1873), 619-63.

Busto Saiz, J.R., 'Estructura métrica y estrófica del "Poema Sobre la Juventud y la Vejez": Qohelet 11,7-12,7', *Sefarad* 43 (1983), 17-25.

—, 'בוראיך (Qoh 12,1), reconsiderado', *Sefarad* 46 (1986), 85-87.

Butting, K., 'Weibsbilder bei Kafka und Kohelet. Eine Auslegung von Prediger 7,23-29', *Texte und Kontexte* 49 (1991), 2-15.

Buzy, D., 'Le Portrait de la vieillesse (Ecclésiaste, XII, 1-7)', *RB* 41 (1932), 329-40.

*—, 'L'Ecclésiaste', in *Proverbes. Ecclésiaste. Cantique des Cantiques. Sagesse. Ecclésiastique* (La Sainte Bible 6; Paris, 1946), 189-280.

Caird, G.B., 'Towards a Lexicon of the Septuagint I', *JTS* 19 (1968), 453-75.

Carasik, M., 'Syntactic Double Translation in the Targumim', in E.M. Meyers and P.V.M. Flesher (eds.), *Aramaic in Postbiblical Judaism and Early Christianity: Papers from the 2004 National Endowment for the Humanities Summer Seminar at Duke University* (DJSS 3; Winona Lake, 2010), 217-31.

*Castelli, D., *Il libro del Cohelet volgarmente detto Ecclesiaste: tradotto dal testo Ebraico con introduzione critica e note* (Pisa, 1866).

Cathcart, K.J., 'Notes on Micah 5,4-5', *Bib* 49 (1968), 511-14.

—, 'Micah 5,4-5 and Semitic Incantations', *Bib* 59 (1978), 38-48.

Ceresko, A.R., 'The Function of Antanaclasis (*mṣʾ* "to find" // *mṣʾ* "to reach, overtake, grasp") in Hebrew Poetry, Especially in the Book of Qoheleth', *CBQ* 44 (1982), 551-69.

Chango, P-M.F., *L'Ecclésiaste à la confluence du judaïsme et de l'hellénisme: deux siècles d'histoire des études comparées du Qohelet et des vestiges littéraires et philosophiques grecs* (CahRB 93; Leuven, 2019).

Choi, J.H., 'The Doctrine of the Golden Mean in Qoh 7,15-18: A Universal Human Pursuit', *Bib* 83 (2002), 358-74.

Christianson, E.S., 'Qoheleth the "Old Boy" and Qoheleth the "New Man": Misogynism, The Womb and a Paradox in Ecclesiastes', in A. Brenner and C. Fontaine (eds.), *Wisdom and Psalms* (The Feminist Companion to the Bible, Second Series 2; Sheffield, 1998), 109-36.

ADDITIONAL BIBLIOGRAPHY OF WORKS CITED   xxvii

*le Clerc, J. (Clericus), *Veteris Testamenti Libri Hagiographi: Jobus, Davidis Psalmi, Salomonis Proverbia, Concionatrix & Canticum Canticorum* (Amsterdam, 1731).
Clifford, R.J., 'Another Look at Qoheleth 7,23-29', *Bib* 100 (2019), 50-59.
Cohen, A., 'Studies in Hebrew Lexicography', *AJSL* 40 (1924), 153-85.
*Cohen, J. ben A. [Moidz], ספר דברי חפץ הוא באור על קהלת = *A Book of Valuable Words: a commentary on Qohelet* (Vilnius, 1864).
Cook, E.M., *Dictionary of Qumran Aramaic* (Winona Lake, 2015).
*Cowley, A.E., *Aramaic Papyri of the 5th Century B.C.* (Oxford, 1923).
Cox, C., 'When Torah Embraced Wisdom and Song: Job 28:28, Ecclesiastes 12:13, and Psalm 1:2', *Restoration Quarterly* 49 (2007), 65-74.
Crenshaw, J.L., *Defending God: Biblical responses to the problem of evil* (New York, 2005).
Dahood, M.J., 'An Allusion to Koshar in Ezekiel 33,32', *Bib* 44 (1963), 531-32.
—, 'Hebrew–Ugaritic Lexicography I', *Bib* 44 (1963), 289-303.
—, 'Canaanite Words in Qoheleth 10,20', *Bib* 46 (1965), 210-12.
—, 'Hebrew–Ugaritic Lexicography VIII', *Bib* 51 (1970), 391-404.
—, 'The Independent Personal Pronoun in the Oblique Case in Hebrew', *CBQ* 32 (1970), 86-90.
—, 'Three Parallel Pairs in Eccl. 10:18. A Reply to Prof. Gordis', *JQR* 62 (1971), 84-87.
—, 'Ugaritic-Hebrew Parallel Pairs', in L.R. Fisher (ed.), *Ras Shamra Parallels: The Texts from Ugarit and the Hebrew Bible. Vol. 1* (Analecta orientalia 49; Rome, 1972), 71-382.
—, 'Northwest Semitic Texts and Textual Criticism of the Hebrew Bible', in C. Brekelmans (ed.), *Questions disputées d'ancien Testament: méthode et théologie* (BETL 33; Gembloux, 1974), 11-37.
—, 'Phoenician-Punic Philology', *Orientalia* 46 (1977), 462-75.
—, 'Review of *Die Partikeln des Ugaritischen 2. Teil* by K. Aartun', *Or* 51 (1982), 281-83.
D'Alario, V., 'Between Misogyny and Valorization: Perspectives on women in Qoheleth', in C.M. Maier and N. Calduch-Benages (eds.), *The Writings and Later Wisdom Books* (The Bible and Women; Atlanta, 2014), 93-107.
—, ''Chi ama il denaro non è mai sazio di denaro…" (Qo 5, 9). Povertà e ricchezza nel libro del Qohelet', *RivLSE* 25 (2019), 54-75.
Debel, H., 'What about the Wicked? A survey of the textual and interpretational problems in Qoh 8,10a', in H. Ausloos, B. Lemmelijn, and M. Vervenne (eds.), *Florilegium Lovaniense Studies in Septuagint and Textual Criticism in Honour of Florentino García Martínez* (BETL 224; Leuven; Paris; Dudley, 2008), 133-50.
—, 'When It All Falls Apart: A Survey of the Interpretative Maze concerning the "Final Poem" of the Book of Qoheleth (Qoh 12:1-7)', *OTE* 23 (2010), 235-60.
Delekat, L., 'Zum hebräischen Wörterbuch', *VT* 14 (1964), 7-66.

Delitzsch, Friedrich, *Die Lese- und Schreibfehler im Alten Testament, nebst den dem Schrifttexte einverleibten Randnoten klassifiziert* (Berlin, 1920).
Dell' Aversano, C., 'משפט in Qoh 11:9c', in A. Vivian (ed.), *Biblische und Judaistische Studien (Fs. P. Sacchi)* (Frankfurt am Main, 1990), 121-34.
DeRouchie, J.S., 'Shepherding Wind and One Wise Shepherd: Grasping for Breath in Ecclesiastes', *SBJT* 15 (2011), 4-16.
Dickie, M.M., 'An Analysis of the Lucianic Recension of the Greek Ecclesiastes', (Ph.D. diss.; Southern Baptist Theological Seminary, 2013).
Döderlein, J.C., *Scholia in Libros Veteris Testamenti Poeticos Iobum Psalmos et Tres Salomonis* (Halle an der Saale, 1779).
Dohmen, C., 'Der Weisheit letzter Schluß? Anmerkungen zur Übersetzung und Bedeutung von Koh 12, 9-14', *BN* 63 (1992), 12-18.
*van den Driesche (Drusius), J., *Annotationes in Coheleth* (Amsterdam, 1635).
Driver, G.R., 'Studies in the Vocabulary of the Old Testament IV', *JTS* 33 (1931), 38-47.
Dulin, R., '"How Sweet Is the Light": Qoheleth's Age-Centered Teachings', *Int* 55 (2001), 260-70.
*Duncan, J.A., *Ecclesiastes* (Abingdon Old Testament Commentaries; Nashville, 2017).
Dunham, K.C., 'Intertextual Links between Deuteronomy and Ecclesiastes as a Pointer to Qohelet's Positive Message', *JESOT* 6 (2020), 34-57.
*Durell, D., *Critical Remarks on the Books of Job, Proverbs, Psalms, Ecclesiastes, and Canticles* (Oxford, 1772).
Eitan, I., *A Contribution to Biblical Lexicography* (Contributions to Oriental History and Philology 10; New York, 1924).
Ellermeier, F., 'Die Entmachtung der Weisheit im Denken Qohelets. Zu Text und Auslegung von Qoh 6, 7-9', *ZTK* 60 (1963), 1-20.
Ember, A., 'The Pluralis Intensivus in Hebrew', *AJSL* 21 (1905), 195-231.
Emerton, J.A., 'The Meaning of *šēnā'* in Psalm CXXVII', *VT* 24 (1974), 15-31.
Engelhardt, E., 'Der Epilog des Koheleth', *TSK* (1875), 287-330.
Enns, P., 'כל־האדם and the Evaluation of Qohelet's Wisdom in Qoh 12:13 or "The 'A is so, and What's More, B' Theology of Ecclesiastes"', in H. Najman and J.H. Newman (eds.), *The Idea of Biblical Interpretation. Essays in Honor of James L. Kugel* (JSJSup 83; Leiden & Boston, 2004), 125-37.
Eppenstein, S., *Aus dem Kohelet-Kommentar des Tanchum Jeruschalmi (Cap. I - VI): mit Einleitung und Anmerkungen* (Berlin, 1888).
Estes, D.J., 'Seeking and finding in Ecclesiastes and Proverbs', in K.J. Dell and W. Kynes (eds.), *Reading Ecclesiastes Intertextually* (LHBOTS 587; London & New York, NY, 2014), 118-29.
Ewald, H., Review of F.W.C. Umbreit, 'Die Einheit des Buches Koheleth' (*TSK* 30, 7-56), *Jahrbücher der Biblischen Wissenschaft* 8 (Göttingen, 1856), 174-75.

ADDITIONAL BIBLIOGRAPHY OF WORKS CITED   xxix

Fassberg, S.E., 'The Shift from *qal* to *piel* in the Book of Qoheleth', in G. Geiger (ed.), Ἐν πάσῃ γραμματικῇ καὶ σοφίᾳ. En pāsē grammatikē kai sophiā: *Saggi di linguistica ebraica in onore di Alviero Niccacci, OFM* (Studium Biblicum Franciscanum 78; Milan, 2011), 123-27.
Fisch, H. (ed.), *The Holy Scriptures* (Jerusalem, 1992).
*Fischer, J. [Piscator], *In Ecclesiasten Salomonis commentarius* (Herborn, 1612).
Fishbane, M.A., *Biblical Interpretation in Ancient Israel* (Oxford, 1985).
Fitzgerald, A., 'Hebrew *yd* = "Love" and "Beloved"', *CBQ* 29 (1967), 368-74.
Fontaine, C.R., '"Many Devices" (Qoheleth 7.23–8.1): Qoheleth, Misogyny and the *Malleus Maleficarum*', in A. Brenner and C. Fontaine (eds.), *Wisdom and Psalms* (The Feminist Companion to the Bible, Second Series 2; Sheffield, 1998), 137-68.
Forti, T., 'The Fly and the Dog: Observations on Ideational Polarity in the Book of Qoheleth', in R.L. Troxel, K.G. Friebel, and D.R. Magary (eds.), *Seeking Out the Wisdom of the Ancients: Essays offered to Honor Michael V. Fox on the Occasion of his Sixty-Fifth Birthday* (Winona Lake, 2005), 235-55.
—, '"בעל הלשון" הצירוף למשמעות :לחש לו אין אשר הנחש ועל לנחש הלוחש על ,הלחש על בקהלת י, יא', *Shnaton* 18 (2008), 43-56. Author's English title: 'The Charm of the Snake Charmer and the Snake with No Charm—Towards the Meaning of בעל הלשון in Ecclesiastes 10:11'.
—, 'Of Snakes and Sinners: An Intertextual Reading of *baʿal Ha-Lashon* in Ecclesiastes 10:11 in Light of *ʾish Lashon* in Psalm 140:12[11]', in K.J. Dell and W. Kynes (eds.), *Reading Ecclesiastes Intertextually* (LHBOTS 587; London & New York, NY, 2014), 84-93.
Fox, M.V., 'Aging and Death in Qohelet 12', *JSOT* 42 (1988), 55-77.
Fox, M.V., and B. Porten, 'Unsought Discoveries: Qohelet 7:23–8:1a', *HS* 19 (1978), 26-38.
Fredericks, D.C., 'Chiasm and Parallel Structure in Qoheleth 5:9–6:9', *JBL* 108 (1989), 17-35.
—, 'Life's Storms and Structural Unity in Qoheleth 11.1–12.8', *JSOT* 16 (1991), 95-114.
Freedman, D.N., 'The Broken Construct Chain', *Bib* 53 (1972), 534-36.
Frendo, A., 'The "Broken Construct Chain" in Qoh. 10,10b', *Bib* 62 (1981), 544-45.
Fries, H.J., '"Freue dich, doch bedenke…" – letzte Worte eines Weisen. Überlegungen zu Koh 11,9-12,7', in M. Häusl and D. Volgger (eds.), *Vom Ausdruck zum Inhalt, vom Inhalt zum Ausdruck: Beiträge zur Exegese und Wirkungsgeschichte alttestamentlicher Texte: Festschrift der Schülerinnen und Schüler für Theodor Seidl zum 60. Geburtstag* (Arbeiten zu Text und Sprache im Alten Testament 75; St. Ottilien, 2005), 101-120.
Galling, K., 'The Scepter of Wisdom: A Note on the Gold Sheath of Zendjirli and Ecclesiastes 12:11', *BASOR* 119 (1950), 15-18.

García Bachmann, M., 'A Study of Qoheleth (Ecclesiastes) 9:1-12', *International Review of Mission* 91 (2002), 382-94.

Garrett, D.A., 'Qoheleth on the Use and Abuse of Political Power', *TJ* NS 8 (1987), 159-77.

—, 'Ecclesiastes 7:25-29 and the Feminist Hermeneutic', *CTR* 2 (1988), 309-21.

Géhin, P., *Évagre le Pontique: Scholies à l'Ecclésiaste* (Paris, 1993).

Gelio, R., 'Osservazioni critiche sul *māšāl* di Qoh. 7,5-7', *Lateranum* 54 (1988), 1-15.

Gentry, P.J., 'Special Problems in the Septuagint Text History of Ecclesiastes', in M.K.H. Peters (ed.), *XIII Congress of the International Organization for Septuagint and Cognate Studies Ljubljana, 2007* (SBLSCS 55; Atlanta, 2008), 133-53.

—, 'Issues in the Text-History of LXX Ecclesiastes', in W. Kraus, M. Karrer, and M. Meiser (eds.), *Die Septuaginta – Texte, Theologien, Einflüsse. 2. Internationale Fachtagung veranstaltet von Septuaginta Deutsch (LXX.D), Wuppertal 23.-27. Juli 2008* (Tübingen, 2010), 201-22.

*—(ed.), *Septuaginta: Vetus Testamentum Graecum. Auctoritate Academiae Scientiarum Gottingensis editum. Vol. XI, 2 Ecclesiastes* (Göttingen, 2019).

Gerleman, G., 'Adam und die alttestamentliche Anthropologie', in J. Jeremias and L. Perlitt (eds.), *Die Botschaft und die Boten: Festschrift für Hans Walter Wolff zum 70. Geburtstag* (Neukirchen-Vluyn, 1981), 319-33.

*Gerson, A., *Der Chacham Kohelet als Philosoph und Politiker ein Kommentar zum biblischen Buche Kohelet, zugleich eine Studie zur religiösen und politischen Entwicklung des Volkes Israel im Zeitalter Herodes des Grossen* (Frankfurt a.M., 1905).

Gilbert, M., 'La Description de la vieillesse en Qohelet XII 1-7 est-elle allégorique?', in J.A. Emerton (ed.), *Congress Volume, Vienna, 1980* (VTSup 32; Leiden, 1981), 96-109.

*Gill, J., 'Ecclesiastes, or the Preacher', in *An Exposition of the Old Testament... Vol. IV Containing Psalms, the Latter Part, Proverbs, Ecclesiastes, and Song of Solomon* (London, 1765), 512-87.

Ginsberg, H.L., 'Koheleth 12:4 in the Light of Ugaritic', *Syria* 33 (1956), 99-101.

Godman, W., בֶּן חוֹרִים *Filius Heröum, the son of nobles. Set forth in a sermon preached at St Mary's in Cambridge before the University, on Thursday the 24th of May, 1660, being the day of Solemn Thanksgiving for the Deliverance and Settlement of our Nation* (London, 1660).

Gordis, R., 'A Note on Yad', *JBL* 62 (1943), 341-44.

—, 'The Asseverative Kaph in Ugaritic and Hebrew', *JAOS* 63 (1943), 176-78.

Gorton, L., 'From Hebrew to Greek: Verbs in Translation in the Book of Ecclesiastes', *Open Theology* 2 (2016), 405-23.

Gray, J., *The Legacy of Canaan: The Ras Shamra texts and their relevance to the Old Testament* (VTSup 5; Leiden, 1957).

Greenfield, J.C., 'Lexicographical Notes I', *HUCA* 29 (1958), 203-38.

ADDITIONAL BIBLIOGRAPHY OF WORKS CITED   xxxi

Gude (Gudius), G.F., and P.C. Schultz (Schultzius), *Disputatio philologica qua sensum oraculi Salomonis, Coheleth V, 7* (Leipzig, 1723).
Gurlitt, J.F.K., 'Zur Erklärung des Buches Koheleth', *TSK* 38 (1865), 321-43.
*Hahn, H.A., *Commentar über das Predigerbuch Salomo's* (Leipzig, 1860).
Harmer, T., *Observations on Divers Passages of Scripture* (2 vols.; 2nd edn; London, 1776).
Haupt, P., 'On the Book of Ecclesiastes, With Special Reference to the Closing Section', *JHUC* 10 (1891), 115-17.
—, 'A New Hebrew Particle', *JHUC* 13 (1894), 107-8.
—, 'Babylonian Elements in the Levitic Ritual', *JBL* 19 (1900), 55-81.
—, 'Assyr. *lâm iççûri çabâri*, "Before the birds cheep"', *AJSL* 32 (1916), 143-44.
—, 'Crystal-Gazing in the Old Testament', *JBL* 36 (1917), 84-92.
*Heim, K.M., *Ecclesiastes: An Introduction and Commentary* (TOTC 18; Downers Grove, IL & London, 2019).
Helsel, P.B., 'Enjoyment and its Discontents: Ecclesiastes in Dialogue with Freud on the Stewardship of Joy', *JRH* 49 (2010), 105-16.
*Henry, M., *An Exposition of the Five Poetical Books of the Old Testament; viz. Job, Psalms, Proverbs, Ecclesiastes, and Solomon's song. Wherein The Chapters and Psalms are sum'd up in Contents, the sacred Text inserted at large, in Paragraphs, or Verses, and each Paragraph, or Verse, reduc'd to its proper Heads, the Sense given, and largely illustrated With Practical Remarks and Observations* (London, 1710).
Henslow, G., 'The Carob and the Locust', *ExpTim* 15 (1904), 285-86.
Hilbrands, W., and J. Kosiol, 'Kohelet als Frauenfeind? Eine kanonische Perspektive auf Koh 7,25-29', in T. Arnold, W. Hilbrands, and H. Wenzel (eds.), *Herr, was ist der Mensch, dass du dich seiner annimmst? (Psalm 144,3): Beiträge zum biblischen Menschenbild: Festschrift für Helmuth Pehlke zum 70. Geburtstag* (Witten, 2013), 83-96.
Hillers, D.R., and E. Cussini, *Palmyrene Aramaic Texts* (Baltimore and London, 1996).
Hölemann, H.G., 'Die Epiloge des Predigers Salomonis und des Evangeliums Johannis', in *Bibelstudien: Zweite Abtheilung* (Leipzig, 1860), 25-88, 187-89.
Hollinshead, J.K., '"What is good for man?": An Exposition of Ecclesiastes 7:1-14', *Bibliotheca sacra* 170 (2013), 31-50.
*Holmes, R., and J. Parsons, *Vetus Testamentum Graecum cum variis lectionibus* (5 vols.; Oxford, 1798-1829).
Homan, M.M., 'Beer Production by Throwing Bread into Water: A New Interpretation of Qoh. XI 1-2', *VT* 52 (2002), 275-78.
Horrocks, G., '*Ouk 'Ismen Oudén*: Negative Concord and Negative Polarity in the History of Greek', *JGL* 14 (2014), 43-83.
Horton, E., 'Koheleth's Concept of Opposites: As Compared to Samples of Greek Philosophy and Near and Far Eastern Wisdom Classics', *Numen* 19 (1972), 1-21.

Huehnergard, J., 'Asseverative *la and Hypothetical *lu/law in Semitic', *JAOS* 103 (1983), 569-93.
Hummel, H.D., 'Enclitic Mem in early Northwest Semitic, especially Hebrew', *JBL* 76 (1957), 85-107.
Hurowitz, V.A., 'ABL 1285 and the Hebrew Bible: Literary Topoi in Urad Gula's Letter of Petition to Assurbanipal', *State Archives of Assyria Bulletin* 7 (1993), 9-17.
Hurvitz, A., 'The History of a Legal Formula: *kōl ʾašer-ḥāpēṣ ʿāśāh* (Psalms cxv 3, cxxxv 6)', *VT* 32 (1982), 257-67.
—, בית־קברות and בית־עולם: Two Funerary Terms in Biblical Literature and Their Linguistic Background', *Maarav* 8 (1992), 59-68.
—, 'רֹאשׁ־דָּבָר and סוֹף דָּבָר: Reflexes of Two Scribal Terms Imported into Biblical Hebrew from the Imperial Aramaic Vocabulary', in M.F.J. Baasten and W.Th. van Peursen (eds.), *Hamlet on a Hill: Semitic and Greek Studies presented to Professor T. Muraoka on the Occasion of his Sixty-fifth Birthday* (OLA 118; Leuven, Paris, Dudley MA, 2003), 281-86.
Ingram, D., '"Riddled with Ambiguity": Ecclesiastes 7:23-8:1 as an Example', in Boda, Longman, and Rata (eds.), *The Words of the Wise*, 219-40.
Irwin, W.A., 'Ecclesiastes 8:2-9', *JNES* 4 (1945), 130-31.
Jarick, J., 'Theodore of Mopsuestia and the Interpretation of Ecclesiastes', in M.D. Carroll R., D.J.A. Clines, and P.R. Davies (eds.), *The Bible in Human Society: Essays in Honour of John Rogerson* (JSOTSup 200; Sheffield, 1995), 306-16.
Jeffers, A., *Magic and Divination in Ancient Palestine and Syria* (Leiden & New York, 1996).
Jones, S.C., 'Qohelet's Courtly Wisdom: Ecclesiastes 8:1-9', *CBQ* 68 (2006), 211-28.
Joosten, J., 'Materials for a Linguistic Approach to the Old Testament Peshiṭta', *JAB* 1 (1999), 203-18.
Jost, R., 'Frau und Adam (hebr. *ʾādām*). Feministische Überlegungen zur Auslegung von Kohelet 7,23-29', in E.S. Gerstenberger and U. Schoenborn (eds.), *Hermeneutik - sozialgeschichtlich. Kontextualität in den Bibelwissenschaften aus der Sicht (latein)amerikanischer und europäischer Exegetinnen und Exegeten* (Exegese in unserer Zeit. Kontextuelle Bibelinterpretation aus lateinamerikanischer und feministischer Sicht 1; Münster, 1999), 59-67.
Joyce, P.M., 'The Poor Wise Man and the Cacophony of Voices', in R.S. Sugirtharajah (ed.), *Wilderness: Essays in Honour of Frances Young* (LNTS 295; London & New York, 2005), 101-5.
Kaiser, O., 'Determination und Freiheit beim Kohelet/Prediger Salomo und in Der Frühen Stoa', *NZSTR* 31 (1989), 251-70. Reprinted in his *Gottes und der Menschen Weisheit. Gesammelte Aufsätze* (BZAW 261; Berlin & New York, 1998), 106-25.
Kautzsch, E., 'Die sogenannten aramaisierenden Formen der Verba ע״ע im Hebräischen', in C. Bezold (ed.), *Orientalische Studien Theodor Nöldeke zum Siebzigsten Geburtstag (2. März 1906)* (2 vols.; Giessen, 1906), 2:771-80.

ADDITIONAL BIBLIOGRAPHY OF WORKS CITED   xxxiii

Kedar-Kopfstein, B., 'Semantic Aspects of the Pattern *qôtēl*', *HAR* 1 (1977), 155-76.
King, P.D., *Surrounded by Bitterness* (Eugene, OR, 2012).
Klein, E., *A Comprehensive Etymological Dictionary of The Hebrew Language for Readers of English* (Jerusalem, 1987).
Koenen, K., 'Zu den Epilogen des Buches Qohelet', *BN* 72 (1994), 24-27.
*Köster, F.B., *Das Buch Hiob und der Prediger Salomo's nach ihrer strophischen Anordnung übersetzt: nebst Abhandlungen über den strophischen Charakter dieser Bücher: Gebrauche bey akademischen Vorlesungen* (Schleswig, 1831).
Kottsieper, I., 'Die Bedeutung der Wz. *ṢB* und *SKN* in Koh 10,9', *UF* 18 (1986), 213-22.
Kotzé, Z., 'Jung, individuation, and moral relativity in Qohelet 7:16-17', *JRH* 53 (2014), 511-19.
Kovacs, D. (ed.), *Trojan Women, Iphigenia among the Taurians, Ion* (Loeb Classical Library 10; Cambridge, MA, and London, 1999).
Kramer, J., and B. Krebber, *Didymos der Blinde. Kommentar zum Ecclesiastes (Tura-Papyrus). Teil IV: Kommentar zu Eccl. Kap. 7-8,8* (PTA 16; Bonn, 1972).
Krammer, I., '"Wer anderen eine Grube gräbt, fällt selbst hinein" Ben Sira als Tradent eines bekannten Sprichwortes', in R. Egger-Wenzel and I. Krammer (eds.), *Der Einzelne und seine Gemeinschaft bei Ben Sira* (BZAW 270; Berlin & New York, 1998), 239-60.
Kraus, M., 'Christians, Jews, and Pagans in Dialogue: Jerome on Ecclesiastes 12:1-7', *HUCA* 70/71 (1999), 183-231.
*Kravitz, L.S., and K.M. Olitzky, *Kohelet: A Modern Commentary on Ecclesiastes* (New York, 2003).
*Kroeber, R., *Der Prediger. Hebräisch und Deutsch* (Schriften und Quellen der alten Welt 13; Berlin, 1963).
Kruger, H.A.J., 'Old Age Frailty versus Cosmic Deterioration? A Few Remarks on the Interpretation of Qohelet 11,7–12,8', in Schoors (ed.), *Qohelet in the Context*, 399-411.
Krüger, T., '"Frau Weisheit" in Koh 7,26?', *Bib* 73 (1992), 394-403.
—, '"Wertvoller als Weisheit und Ehre ist wenig Torheit" (Kohelet 10,1)', *BN* 89 (1997), 62-75.
—, 'Meaningful Ambiguities in the Book of Qoheleth', in Berlejung and van Hecke (eds.), *The Language of Qohelet*, 63-74.
Kselman, J.S., 'Semantic-Sonant Chiasmus in Biblical Poetry', *Bib* 58 (1977), 219-23.
Kuhn, G., *Erklärung des Buches Koheleth* (BZAW 43; Giessen, 1926).
Kutler, L., 'A "Strong" Case for Hebrew Mar', *UF* 16 (1984), 111-18.
Kynes, W., 'Follow Your Heart and Do Not Say It Was a Mistake: Qoheleth's Allusions to Numbers 15 and the Story of the Spies', in K.J. Dell and W. Kynes (eds.), *Reading Ecclesiastes Intertextually* (LHBOTS 587; London & New York, 2014), 15-27.

Labuschagne, C.J., 'The Emphasizing Particle *GAM* and its Connotations', in *Studia Biblica et Semitica. Theodoro Christiano Vriezen qui munere professoris theologiae per XXV annos functus est, ab amicis, collegis, discipulis dedicata* (Wageningen, 1966), 193-203.

Laiblin, W.L., *De Rectitudine Hominis Primaeva Secundum Oraculum Sacrum Ecclesiast. Vii, 30* (Tübingen, 1753).

Lange, A., *Weisheit und Torheit bei Kohelet und in Seiner Umwelt* (Europäische Hochschulschriften 433; Frankfurt a.M. & New York, 1991).

—, 'Eschatological Wisdom in the Book of Qoheleth and the Dead Sea Scrolls', in L.H. Schiffman, E. Tov, and J.C. VanderKam (eds.), *The Dead Sea Scrolls Fifty Years after their Discovery: Proceedings of the Jerusalem Congress, July 20-25, 1997* (Jerusalem, 2000), 817-25.

Lasater, P.M., 'Subordination and the Human Condition in Ecclesiastes', *The Journal of Religion* 100 (2020), 75-102.

Lavoie, J.-J., 'Bonheur et finitude humaine. Étude de Qo 9,7-10', *ScEs* 45 (1993), 313-24.

—, 'Étude de l'expression בֵּית עוֹלָמוֹ dans Qo 12,5 à la lumière des textes du Proche-Orient ancien', in J.-C. Petit et al. (eds.), *Où demeures-tu? La maison depuis le monde biblique: en hommage au professeur Guy Couturier à l'occasion de ses soixante-cinq ans* (Montreal, 1994), 213-26.

—, 'Un Éloge à Qohélet (Étude de Qo 12,9-10)', *LTP* 50 (1994), 145-70.

—, 'Vie, mort et finitude humaine en Qoh 9,1-6', *ScEs* 47 (1995), 69-80.

—, 'Temps et finitude humaine: Étude de Qohélet IX 11-12', *VT* 46 (1996), 439-47.

—, 'La Philosophie politique de Qohélet 9,13-16', *ScEs* 49 (1997), 315-28.

—, 'La Philosophie comme réflexion sur la mort: Étude de Qohelet 7:1-4', *LTP* 54 (1998), 91-107.

—, '"Laisse aller ton pain sur la surface des eaux." Étude de Qohélet 11,1-2', in Berlejung and van Hecke (eds.), *The Language of Qohelet*, 75-89.

—, 'Ambiguïtés et ironie en Qohélet 12,11', *Theoforum* 38 (2007), 131-151.

—, 'Ironie et ambiguïtés en Qohélet 10,16-20', *SR* 37 (2008), 183-209.

—, 'Qohélet 12,12 ou l'autocritique ironique', *LTP* 66 (2010), 387-405.

—, 'Avantage et limites de la sagesse. Étude de Qohélet 7,11-12', *EstBib* 71 (2013), 367-92.

—, 'Ambiguïtés et désir en Qohélet 6,7-9', *Théologiques* 22 (2014), 179-215.

—, 'Le Sage et l'insensé. Étude de Qohélet 7, 5-7', *RevScRel* 88 (2014), 1-26.

—, 'Ironie et ambiguïtés en Qohélet 10,2-3', *ScEs* 66 (2014), 59-84.

—, 'Force meurtrière et imperfection humaine: Étude de Qohélet 7,19-20', *LTP* 71 (2015), 57-78.

—, 'Qui est comme le sage? Étude de Qohélet 8,1', *Theoforum* 46 (2015), 89-118.

—, 'Quoi de nouveau sous le soleil ? Le Dieu de Qohélet', *Theoforum* 47 (2016), 105-32.

—, 'Sagesse de cour royale et sagesse universelle: Étude de Qo 8,5-6', *Theoforum* 48 (2018), 207-34.

—, '"J'ai vu des méchants…": Un Texte illisible? Étude de Qohélet 8,10', *LTP* 75 (2019), 75-106.
—, 'Les Pièges de la femme et les ambiguïtés d'un texte: Étude de Qohélet 7,26 dans l'histoire de l'exégèse juive', *SR* 49 (2020), 165-92.
Leahy, M., 'The Meaning of Ecclesiastes 10:15', *ITQ* 18 (1951), 288-90.
—, 'The Meaning of Ecclesiastes 12:1-5', *ITQ* 19 (1952), 297-300.
Leanza, S., 'Eccl 12,1-7: L'interpretazione escatologica dei Padri e degli esegeti medievali', *Augustinianum* 18 (1978), 191-208.
Lohfink, N., 'War Kohelet ein Frauenfeind? Ein Versuch, die Logik und den Gegenstand von Koh., 7,23 - 8,1a herauszufinden', in M. Gilbert (ed.), *La Sagesse de l'Ancien Testament* (BETL 51; Leuven, 1979), 259-87.
—, 'Kohelet und die Banken: zur Übersetzung von Kohelet V 12-16', *VT* 39 (1989), 488-95.
—, 'Qoheleth 5:17-19 – Revelation by Joy', *CBQ* 52 (1990), 625-35.
—, 'Deuteronomy 6:24: לְחַיֹּתֵנוּ "to maintain us"', in M. Fishbane and E. Tov (eds.), *"Shaarei Talmon" Studies in the Bible, Qumran, and the Ancient Near East Presented to Shemaryahu Talmon* (Winona Lake, 1992), 111-19.
—, 'Grenzen und Einbindung des Kohelet-Schlußgedichts', in P. Mommer and W. Thiel (eds.), *Altes Testament: Forschung und Wirkung: Festschrift für Henning Graf Reventlow* (Frankfurt am Main, Berlin, Bern, New York, Paris, Vienna, 1994), 33-46.
—, 'Les épilogues du livre de Qohélet et les débuts du canon', in P. Bovati and R. Meynet (eds.), *Ouvrir les Ecritures. Mélanges offerts à Paul Beauchamp à l'occasion de ses soixante-dix ans* (Lectio Divina 162; Paris, 1995), 77-96.
—, 'Zu einigen Satzeröffnungen im Epilog des Koheletbuches', in Diesel et al. (eds.), *"Jedes Ding hat seine Zeit…"*, 131-47.
—, 'Der Weise und das Volk in Koh 12,9 und Sir 37,23', in N. Calduch-Benages and J. Vermeylen (eds.), *Treasures of Wisdom: Studies in Ben Sira and the Book of Wisdom. Festschrift M. Gilbert* (BETL 143; Leuven, 1999), 405-10.
—, 'Jeder Weisheitslehre Quintessenz. Zu Koh 12,13', in I. Fischer, U. Rapp, and J. Schiller (eds.), *Auf den Spuren der schriftgelehrten Weisen. Festschrift für Johannes Marböck anlässlich seiner Emeritierung* (BZAW 331; Berlin & New York, 2003), 195-205.
Loretz, O., '"Frau" und griechisch-jüdische Philosophie im Buch Qohelet (Qoh 7,23–8,1 und 9,6-10)', *UF* 23 (1991), 245-64.
Lowth, R., *Isaiah. A new translation: with a preliminary dissertation, and notes, critical, philological, and explanatory* (London, 1778).
Luria, S., 'Die Ersten werden die Letzen sein', *Klio* 22 (1929), 405-31.
Lux, R., 'Der "Lebenskompromiß"–ein Wesenszug im Denken Kohelets? Zur Auslegung von Koh 7,15-18', in J. Hausmann and H.-J. Zobel (eds.), *Alttestamentlicher Glaube und Biblische Theologie. Festschrift für Horst Dietrich Preuß zum 65. Geburtstag* (Stuttgart, Berlin, Köln, 1992), 267-78.
Macintosh, A.A., *A Critical and Exegetical Commentary on Hosea* (ICC; Edinburgh, 1997).

McKane, W., *Proverbs: A New Approach* (OTL; London, 1970).
MacNamara, L., 'How the Wind Blows? God's Role in Human Origins and Humanity's Response: Qoh 11,5', *BN* 152 (2012), 67-86.
Magarik, L., 'Bread on Water', *JBQ* 28 (2000), 268-70.
Manniche, L., 'Ancient Scent—An Evaluation of the Sources', in C. Leblanc (ed.), *Parfums, onguents et cosmétiques dans l'Égypte ancienne* (Memnonia, Cahiers supplémentaires 1; Cairo, 2003), 81-89.
Margoliouth, D.S., 'Ecclesiastes VIII.10, and Incidentally Parts of VI.3 and VIII.9', *The Expositor* Ninth Series 1 (1924), 94-102.
Margoliouth, G., 'Ecclesiastes xii. 8-14', *ExpTim* 35 (1923), 121-24.
—, 'Qoheleth (Ecclesiastes) VII.7', *Theology* 8 (1924), 228-29.
Martin, J. de, 'Explication lxxxviii. Explication litterale & morale des trois premiers versets du onziéme chapitre de l'Ecclesiaste', in *Explications de plusieurs textes difficiles de l'Ecriture Sainte, qui, jusqu'à présent, n'ont été ni bien entendus ni bien expliquez par les commentateurs, avec des règles certaines pour l'intelligence du sens littéral de l'ancien et du nouveau Testament. Ouvrage enrichi d'antiques gravées en taille-douce... Première partie* (Paris, 1730), 304-13.
Maussion, M., 'Qohélet vi 1-2: "Dieu ne permet pas..."', *VT* 55 (2005), 501-10.
May, H.G., 'The Two Pillars before the Temple of Solomon', *BASOR* (1942), 19-27.
Mazzinghi, L., 'Qohelet tra Giudaismo ed Ellenismo. Un'indagine a partire da Qo 7,15-18', in Bellia and Passaro (eds.), *Il Libro del Qohelet*, 90-116.
—, 'The Divine Violence in the Book of Qoheleth', *Bib* 90 (2009), 545-58.
—, 'Esegesi ed ermeneutica di un libro difficile: l'esemplo di Qo 8,11-14', in J.N. Aletti and J.L. Ska (eds.), *Biblical Exegesis in Progress: Old and New Testament Essays* (Analecta biblica 176; Rome, 2009), 173-207.
—, '"Dieu te convoquera en jugement": Qo 11,9c, un texte "intrus"?', *BN* 185 (2020), 99-111.
Meek, T.J., 'Translating the Hebrew Bible', *JBL* 79 (1960), 328-35.
Melton, B., 'Solomon, Wisdom, and Love: Intertextual Resonance between Ecclesiastes and Song of Songs', in K.J. Dell and W. Kynes (eds.), *Reading Ecclesiastes Intertextually* (LHBOTS 587; London & New York, NY, 2014), 130-41.
*Mendelssohn, M., מגלת קהלת: עם באור קצר ומספיק להבנת הכתוב על פי פשוטו (Berlin, 1770). German translation in M. Mendelssohn and J.J. Rabe, *Der Prediger Salomo: Mit einer kurzen und zureichenden Erklärung nach dem Wort-Verstand zum Nuzen der Studierenden* (Anspach, 1771).
*le Mercier, J. [Mercerus], *Commentarij in Salomonis Prouerbia, Ecclesiasten, & Canticum Canticorum* (Geneva, 1573).
Michel, D., 'Vom Gott, der im Himmel ist (Reden von Gott bei Qohelet) (1)', *ThViat* 12 (1973), 87-100.
—, 'Zur Philosophie Kohelets: Eine Auslegung von Kohelet 7,1-10', *BK* 45 (1990), 20-25.

Milik, J.T., R. de Vaux, and P. Benoit (eds.), *Les Grottes de Murabba'ât* (DJD 2; Oxford, 1961).
Miller, G.D., 'Attitudes toward Dogs in Ancient Israel: A Reassessment', *JSOT* 32 (2008), 487-500.
Mizrahi, N., 'Qohelet 6:5b in Light of 4QQoh[a] ii 2 and Rabbinic Literature', *Textus* 21 (2002), 159-74.
Moore, G.F., 'The Caper-plant and its Edible Products, with Reference to Eccles. XII, 5', *JBL* 10 (1891), 55-64.
Müller, A.R., 'Qoh 12,6: Die Ambivalenz des menschlichen Lebens', in C. Karrer-Grube, J. Krispenz, and T. Krüger (eds.), *Sprachen—Bilder—Klänge. Dimensionen der Theologie im Alten Testament und in seinem Umfeld. Festschrift für Rüdiger Bartelmus zu seinem 65. Geburtstag* (AOAT 359; Münster, 2009), 171-81.
Müller, H.-P., 'Das eblaitische Verbalsystem nach den bisher veröffentlichten Personennamen', in *La Lingua di Ebla: Atti del Convegno Internazionale (Napoli, 21-23 Aprile 1980)* (Naples, 1981), 211-33.
—, 'Weisheitliche Deutungen der Sterblichkeit: Gen 3,19 und Pred 3,21; 12, im Licht antiker Parallelen', in *Mensch—Umwelt—Eigenwelt. Gesammelte Aufsätze zur Weisheit Israels* (Stuttgart, 1992), 69-100.
Munnich, O., 'Traduire la Septante: Ecclésiaste XII, 1-8', *Lalies: actes des sessions de linguistique et de littérature* 3 (1984), 105-11.
*Münster, S., קהלת: *Ecclesiastes iuxta Hebraicam veritatem per Sebastianum Munsterum translatus, atque annotationibus ex Hebraeorum rabinis collectis, illustratus* (Basel, 1525).
Muraoka, T., *A Greek-English Lexicon of the Septuagint: Chiefly of the Pentateuch and the Twelve Prophets* (Louvain, Paris and Dudley, MA, 2002).
—, *A Syntax of Septuagint Greek* (Leuven, Paris and Bristol, CT, 2016).
Murison, R.G., 'The Almond', *ExpTim* 16 (1905), 334-35.
Murphy, P.R., 'Petronius 71.11 and Ecclesiastes 12:5-6', *The Classical Weekly* 45 (1952), 120.
Murphy, R.E., 'On Translating Ecclesiastes', *CBQ* 53 (1991), 571-79.
Nebe, G.W., 'Qumranica I: Zu unveröffentlichten Handschriften aus Höhle 4 von Qumran', *ZAW* 106 (1994), 307-22.
Nel, P.J., 'Remember the "Spring" of your Youth: The Vanity of Male Power in Qohelet 12', *OTE* 21 (2008), 149-60.
Neubauer, A., *The Book of Tobit. A Chaldee text from a unique MS. in the Bodleian library, with other Rabbinical texts, English translations and the Itala* (Oxford, 1878).
Niccacci, A., 'Qohelet o la gioia come fatica e dono di Dio a chi lo teme', *LASBF* 52 (2002), 29-102.
Niehr, H., *Herrschen und Richten: die Wurzel špṭ im Alten Orient und im Alten Testament* (Forschung zur Bibel 54; Würzburg, 1986).
Nötscher, F., 'Zum emphatischen Lamed', *VT* 3 (1953), 372-80.

xxxviii ADDITIONAL BIBLIOGRAPHY OF WORKS CITED

*Odeberg, H., *Qohælœth: A Commentary on the Book of Ecclesiastes* (Uppsala & Stockholm, 1929).
Ogden, G.S., 'Qoheleth IX 17–X 20: Variations on the Theme of Wisdom's Strength and Vulnerability', *VT* 30 (1980), 27-37.
—, 'Qoheleth IX 1-16', *VT* 32 (1982), 158-69.
—, 'Qoheleth XI 1-6', *VT* 33 (1983), 222-30.
—, 'Qoheleth XI 7–XII 8: Qoheleth's Summons to Enjoyment and Reflection', *VT* 34 (1984), 27-38.
—, 'Translation Problems in Ecclesiastes 5:13-17', *BT* 39 (1988), 423-28.
*Ogden, G.S., and L. Zogbo, *A Handbook on Ecclesiastes* (UBS handbook series; New York, 1997).
Osborn, N.D., 'A Guide for Balanced Living: An Exegetical Study of Ecclesiastes 7:1-14', *BT* 21 (1970), 185-96.
Pabst, I., '"Ehe die bösen Tage kommen...": zum Verständnis von Alter im Schlussgedicht des Koheletbuchs (12,1-8)', in *Zeit wahrnehmen. Feministisch-theologische Perspektiven auf das Erste Testament* (Hedwig-Jahnow-Forschungsprojekt; Stuttgarter Bibelstudien 222; Stuttgart, 2010), 153-82.
Pahk, J.Y.S., 'The Significance of אשׁה in Qoh 7,26: "More Bitter than Death is the Woman if She is a Snake"', in Schoors (ed.), *Qohelet in the Context*, 373-83.
—, 'Women as Snares: A Metaphor of Warning in Qoh 7,26 and Sir 9,3', in N. Calduch-Benages and J. Vermeylen (eds.), *Treasures of Wisdom: Studies in Ben Sira and the Book of Wisdom. Festschrift M. Gilbert* (BETL 143; Leuven, 1999), 397-404.
—, 'A Syntactical and Contextual Consideration of *'šh* in Qoh. IX 9', *VT* 51 (2001), 370-80.
—, 'The Role and Significance of *dbry ḥpṣ* (Qoh. 12:10a) for Understanding Qohelet', in A. Lemaire (ed.), *Congress Volume Leiden 2004* (VTSup 109; Leiden & Boston, 2006), 325-53.
Palm, A., *Qohelet und die nach-aristotelische Philosophie* (Mannheim, 1885).
Pardee, D., 'The Semitic Root *mrr* and the Etymology of Ugaritic *mr(r) // brk*', *UF* 10 (1978), 249-88.
Parpola, S., 'The Forlorn Scholar', in F. Rochberg-Halton (ed.), *Language, Literature, and History: Philological and Historical Studies Presented to Erica Reiner* (American Oriental Series 67; New Haven, 1987), 257-78.
*Patrick, S., *A Paraphrase upon the Books of Ecclesiastes, and the Song of Solomon, with Arguments to Each Chapter, and Annotations Thereupon* (London, 1685).
Paul, S.M., 'Psalm 72:5—A Traditional Blessing for the Long Life of the King', *JNES* 31 (1972), 351-55.
Perles, F., *Analekten zur Textkritik des Alten Testaments* (1st edn, Munich, 1895; 2nd edn, Leipzig, 1922).

*Philippson, L., 'קהלת Ecclesiastes. Prediger', in מקרא תורה נביאים וכתובים *Die Israelitische Bibel. Enthaltend: Den heiligen Urtext, die deutsche Uebertragung, die allgemeine, ausführliche Erläuterung mit mehr als 500 englischen Holzschnitten. Dritter Theil: Die Heiligen Schriften (Leipzig, 1854), 703-52.

Pinker, A., 'The Doings of the Wicked in Qohelet 8.10', *JHebS* 8 (2008), art. 6.

—, 'The Advantage of a Country in Ecclesiastes 5:8', *JBQ* 37 (2009), 211-22.

—, 'Qohelet 6:9—It Looks Better than it Tastes', *JJS* 60 (2009), 214-25.

—, 'A New Approach to Qohelet 11:1', *OTE* 22 (2009), 618-45.

—, 'On Sweetness and Light in Qohelet 11:7', *RB* 117 (2010), 248-61.

—, 'On Cattle and Cowboys in Kohelet 5,9b', *ZAW* 123 (2011), 263-73.

—, 'An Interpretation of Qohelet 5:17-19 Based on Intertextuality Considerations', *BeO* 53 (2011), 65-86.

—, 'The Ligature עו = ש in Qohelet 6.3', *BT* 62 (2011), 151-64.

—, 'A New Interpretation of Qohelet 10:10', *OTE* 24 (2011), 173-91.

—, 'A Reconstruction of Qohelet 10,15', *BN* 149 (2011), 65-83.

—, 'Qohelet's Nuanced View on Matrimony: A New Interpretation of Qohelet 11:9-12:1a within its Pedagogical Milieu', *ABR* 59 (2011), 13-30.

—, 'Qohelet's Views on Women—Misogyny or Standard Perceptions? An Analysis of Qohelet 7,23-29 and 9,9', *SJOT* 26 (2012), 157-91.

—, 'Qohelet 9:3b-7 – A Polemic Against Necromancy', *JJS* 63 (2012), 218-37.

—, 'The Structure and Meaning of Qohelet 8,5-7', *BN* 153 (2012), 63-88.

—, 'On the Meaning of זעקת מושל in Qohelet 9:17b', *BBR* 22 (2012), 493-503.

—, 'Aspects of Demeanour in Qohelet 8:1', *OTE* 26 (2013), 401-24.

Piotti, F., 'Il rapporto tra ricchi, stolti e principi in Qoh. 10,6-7 alla luce della letteratura sapienziale', *ScC* 102 (1974), 328-33.

—, 'Osservazioni su alcuni paralleli extrabiblici nell' "Allegoria della Vecchiaia" (Qohelet 12,1-7)', *BeO* 19 (1977), 119-28.

—, 'Osservazioni su alcuni problemi esegetici nel libro dell'Ecclesiaste (Studio II): il canto degli stolti (Qoh. 7,5)', *BeO* 21 (1979), 129-40.

—, 'Osservazioni su alcuni problemi esegetici nel libro dell'Ecclesiaste: Studio III', *BeO* 22 (1980), 243-53.

—, 'La relazione tra מדע e מלך in Qo 10,20. Problemi linguistici ed esegetici', *BeO* 49 (2007), 79-101.

—, 'Le teorie Aramaica e Fenicia a confronto in Qo 8,8', in F. Aspesi, V. Brugnatelli, A.L. Callow, and C. Rosenzweig (eds.), *Il mio cuore è a oriente לבי במזרח: studi di linguistica storica, filologia e cultura ebraica dedicati a Maria Luisa Mayer Modena* (Milan, 2008), 349-64.

*Preston, T., קהלת: *The Hebrew Text, and a Latin Version of The Book of Solomon called Ecclesiastes; with Original Notes, Philological and Exegetical, and a Translation of the Commentary of Mendlessohn from the Rabbinic Hebrew. Also a Newly Arranged English Version of Ecclesiastes, with Introductory Analyses of the Sections; to which is prefixed a Preliminary Dissertation* (London & Cambridge, 1845).

Qimron, E., and J. Strugnell (eds.), *Qumran Cave 4: V: Miqṣat ma'aśe ha-torah* (DJD 10; Oxford, 1994).

ADDITIONAL BIBLIOGRAPHY OF WORKS CITED

Rainey, A.F., 'A Study of Ecclesiastes', *CTM* 35 (1964), 149-57.
*Rambach, J.J., 'Notae uberiores in Ecclesiasten Salomonis', in J.H. Michaelis (ed.), *Uberiores Adnotationes Philologico-Exegeticae In Hagiographos Vet. Testamenti Libros: Volumen Secundum* (Halle a.S., 1720), 827-1042. Originally presented as a dissertation in 1716.
Reese, J.M., *Hellenistic Influence on the Book of Wisdom and Its Consequences* (AnBib 41; Rome, 1970).
*Reichert, V.E., and A. Cohen, 'קהלת Ecclesiastes: Introduction and Commentary', in A. Cohen (ed.), *The Five Megilloth: Hebrew Text and English Translation with Introductions and Commentary* (Soncino Books of the Bible; London, Jerusalem, New York, 1946), 102-91.
Reines, C.W., 'Koheleth VIII, 10', *JJS* 5 (1954), 86-87.
Rey, J.-S., 'Knowledge Hidden and Revealed: Ben Sira between Wisdom and Apocalyptic Literature', *HeBAI* 5 (2016), 255-72.
Richter, H.-F., 'Kohelets Urteil über die Frauen- Zu Koh 7,26. 28 and 9,9 in ihrem Kontext', *ZAW* 108 (1996), 584-93.
—, 'Kohelet—Philosoph und Poet', in Schoors (ed.), *Qohelet in the Context*, 435-49.
Riesener, I., 'Frauenfeindschaft im Alten Testament? Zum Verständnis von Qoh 7,25-29', in Diesel et al. (eds.), *"Jedes Ding hat seine Zeit..."*, 193-207.
Rindge, M.S., 'Mortality and Enjoyment: The Interplay of Death and Possessions in Qoheleth', *CBQ* 73 (2011), 265-80.
Rodríguez Gutiérrez, J.L., '"Mientras hay vida hay esperanza" Las pequeñas y firmes esperanzas diarias en Qohélet', *RIBLA* 39 (2001), 74-81.
Rose, M., 'Verba Sapientium Sicut Stimuli', in D. Knoepfler (ed.), *Nomen Latinum. Mélanges de langue, de littérature et de civilisation latines offerts au professeur André Schneider à l'occasion de son départ à la retraite* (Université de Neuchâtel Recueil de travaux publiés par la Faculté des Lettres 44; Neuchâtel - Genève, 1997), 209-18.
Rubin, A.D., 'The Form and Meaning of Hebrew *ʾašrê*', *VT* 60 (2010), 366-72.
Rudman, D., 'Woman as Divine Agent in Ecclesiastes', *JBL* 116 (1997), 411-27.
—, 'The Translation and Interpretation of Eccl. 8:17a', *JNSL* 23 (1997), 109-16.
—, 'The Anatomy of the Wise Man. Wisdom, Sorrow and Joy in the Book of Ecclesiastes', in Schoors (ed.), *Qohelet in the Context*, 465-71.
Rudolph, W., 'Review of G. Kuhn, *Erklärung des Buches Koheleth*', *TLZ* 52 (1927), 224-26.
Rüger, H.P., 'Hieronymus, die Rabbinen und Paulus. Zur Vorgeschichte des Begriffspaars "innerer und äußerer Mensch"', *ZNW* 68 (1977), 132-37.
*Sacchi, P., *Ecclesiaste* (Nuovissima Versione della Bibbia dai Test Originali 20; 2nd edn; Rome, 1976).
Salters, R.B., 'Text and Exegesis in Koh 10:19', *ZAW* 89 (1977), 423-26.
Salvaneschi, E., 'Memento vivere (Qohélet 12,1-8)', *La Rassegna Mensile di Israel* 56 (1990), 31-59.
Salvesen, A., *Symmachus in the Pentateuch* (JSSM 15; Manchester, 1991).

Sandoval, T.J., and D.B.E.A. Akoto, 'A Note on Qohelet 10,10b', *ZAW* 122 (2010), 90-95.
Saracino, F., 'Ras Ibn Hani 78/20 and some Old Testament Connections', *VT* 32 (1982), 338-43.
Sargent, L.G., *Ecclesiastes, and Other Studies* (Birmingham, 1965).
Sawyer, J.F.A., 'The Ruined House in Ecclesiastes 12: A Reconstruction of the Original Parable', *JBL* 94 (1975), 519-31.
Schäfer, D., '"Hebraeorum Hippokrates rei medicae peritissimus fuit": Über die Rezeption der pseudosalomonischen Metaphern zum Greisenalter (Koh. 12,1-6) in der frühneuzeitlichen Medizin', *Medizinhistorisches Journal* 35 (2000), 219-50.
*Schelling, J.F., *Salomonis Regis et Sapientis quae supersunt eiusque esse perhibentur omnia ex Ebraeo Latine vertit notasque ubi opus esse visum est adiecit...* (Stuttgart, 1806).
*Schmidt, S., *In librum Salomonis Regis Hebr. Koheleth, Graec. & Latin. Ecclesiastes dictum, Commentarius in quo cum textu Hebraeo, versio eius, analysis, paraphrasis, annotationes et loci communes exhibentur* (Strasbourg, 1691).
Schoeps, H.J., 'Symmachusstudien III: Symmachus und der Midrasch', *Bib* 29 (1948), 31-51.
Schoors, A., 'A Third Masculine Singular *taqtul* in Biblical Hebrew?', in Walter T. Claassen (ed.), *Text and Context. Old Testament and Semitic Studies for F.C. Fensham* (JSOTS 48; Sheffield, 1988), 193-200.
—, 'Bitterder dan de dood is de vrouw (Koh 7, 26)', *Bijdragen* 54 (1993), 121-40.
—, 'Theodicy in Qohelet', in A. Laato and J.C. de Moor (eds.), *Theodicy in the World of the Bible* (Leiden & Boston, 2003), 375-409.
Schöpflin, K., 'Political Power and Ideology in Qohelet', *BN* (2014), 19-36.
Schüle, A., 'Evil from the Heart: Qoheleth's Negative Anthropology and its Canonical Context', in Berlejung and van Hecke (eds.), *The Language of Qohelet*, 157-76.
Schulte, A., 'Zu Koh. 5,7 u. 8', *BZ* (old series) 8 (1910), 388-89.
Schwab, G.M., 'Woman as the Object of Qohelet's Search', *AUSS* 39 (2001), 73-84.
Schwienhorst-Schönberger, L., 'Via Media. Koh 7,15-18 und die griechisch-hellenistische Philosophie', in Schoors (ed.), *Qohelet in the Context*, 181-203.
—, 'Vertritt Kohelet die Lehre vom absoluten Tod? Zum Argumentationsgang von Koh 9,1-6', in I. Fischer, U. Rapp, and J. Schiller (eds.), *Auf den Spuren der schriftgelehrten Weisen. Festschrift für Johannes Marböck anlässlich seiner Emeritierung* (BZAW 331; Berlin & New York, 2003), 207-19.
—, '„Bitterer als der Tod ist die Frau" (Koh 7,26). Zum Argumentationsgang von Koh 7,25-29', in K. Kiesow and T. Meurer (eds.), *Textarbeit: Studien zu Texten und ihrer Rezeption aus dem Alten Testament und der Umwelt Israels: Festschrift für Peter Weimar zur Vollendung seines 60. Lebensjahres. Mit Beiträgen von Freunden, Schülern und Kollegen* (AOAT 294; Münster, 2004), 443-55.

—, 'Buch der Natur. Kohelet 12,5 und die Rückkehr des Lebens', in F.-L. Hossfeld and L. Schwienhorst-Schönberger (eds.), *Das Manna fällt auch heute noch. Beiträge zur Geschichte und Theologie des Alten, Ersten Testaments: Festschrift für Erich Zenger* (HBS 44; Freiburg, 2004), 532-47.

Scott, N.E., 'An Egyptian Bird Trap', *Bulletin of the Metropolitan Museum of Art* 35 (1940), 163-64.

*Scott, R.B.Y., *Proverbs. Ecclesiastes* (2nd edn; AB 18; Garden City, NY, 1965).

*Segal, B.J., *Kohelet's Pursuit of Truth: A New Reading of Ecclesiastes* (Jerusalem, 2016).

Sekine, S., 'Qohelet als Nihilist', *AJBI* 17 (1991), 3-54.

Seow, C.L., '"Beyond Them, My Son, Be Warned": The Epilogue of Qoheleth Revisited', in M.L. Barré (ed.), *Wisdom, You are my Sister. Studies in Honor of Roland E. Murphy, O.Carm., on the Occasion of his Eightieth Birthday* (CBQMS 29; Washington, 1997), 125-41.

—, 'Qohelet's Eschatological Poem', *JBL* 118 (1999), 209-34.

Serrano, J.J., 'I Saw the Wicked Buried (Eccl. 8, 10)', *CBQ* 16 (1954), 168-70.

*Sforno, O. ben J., באור שיר השירים וקהלת = *A Commentary on Song of Songs and Qohelet* (Venice, 1566).

Shead, A.G., 'Ecclesiastes from the Outside In', *RTR* 55 (1996), 24-37.

—, 'Reading Ecclesiastes "Epilogically"', *TynBul* 48 (1997), 67-91.

Shemesh, Y., '?ומוצא אני מר ממות את האשה' (קהלת ז, כו)—האומנם מצויה שנאת נשים במקרא' ("I find woman more bitter than death" (Ecclesiastes 7:26): Is there Misogyny in the Bible?')', *Shnaton* 19 (2009), 77-101.

Sherwood, Y., '"Not with a Bang but a Whimper": Shrunken Apocalypses of the Twentieth Century and the Book of Qoheleth', in C. Rowland and J. Barton (eds.), *Apocalyptic in history and tradition* (JSPSup 43; London, 2002), 229-51.

Shields, M.A., 'Re-Examining the Warning of Eccl. XII 12', *VT* 50 (2000), 123-27.

Shnider, S., and L. Zalcman, 'The Righteous Sage: Pleonasm or Oxymoron? (Kohelet 7,16-18)', *ZAW* 115 (2003), 435-39.

Simian-Yofre, H., 'Conoscere la sapienza: Qohelet e Genesi 2–3', in Bellia and Passaro (eds.), *Il Libro del Qohelet*, 314-36.

Slemmons, T., 'Ecclesiastes 12:1-13', *Int* 55 (2001), 302-4.

Smith, M.S., *The Early History of God: Yahweh and the Other Deities in Ancient Israel* (2nd edn; Grand Rapids & Cambridge, 2002).

Sneed, M., 'A Note on Qoh 8,12b-13', *Bib* 84 (2003), 412-16.

Solmsen, F., 'The Vital Heat, the Inborn Pneuma and the Aether', *JHS* 77 (1957), 119-23.

Sozzi, G.O., and A.R. Vicente, 'Capers and caperberries', in K.V. Peter (ed.), *Handbook of Herbs and Spices* (Cambridge, 2006), 3:230-56.

Spieckermann, H., 'Jugend—Alter—Tod: Kohelets abschließende Reflexion: Koh 11:7-12:8', *VT* 70 (2020), 193-208.

Spronk, K., 'Prediker in de *Nieuwe Bijbelvertaling*', *ACEBT* 21 (2004), 103-15.

ADDITIONAL BIBLIOGRAPHY OF WORKS CITED   xliii

Staples, W.E., 'The "Vanity" of Ecclesiastes', *JNES* 2 (1943), 95-104.
—, 'Vanity of Vanities', *CJT* 1 (1955), 141-56.
Strack, H.L., *Prophetarum Posteriorum Codex Babylonicus Petropolitanus* (St Petersburg, 1876).
Szubin, H.Z., and B. Porten, 'Royal Grants in Egypt: A New Interpretation of Driver 2', *JNES* 46 (1987), 39-48.
Taylor, C., *The Dirge of Coheleth in Ecclesiastes XII, Discussed and Literally Interpreted* (London & Edinburgh, 1874).
—, 'The Dirge of Coheleth', *JQR* Old Series 4-5 (1891), (4) 533-549; (5) 5-17.
Thomas, D.W., 'A Note on בְּמַדֻּעֶךָ in Eccles. X.20', *JTS* 50 (1949), 177.
Thompson, J.A., 'Translation of the Words for Locust', *BT* 25 (1974), 401-4.
Todd, J.E., 'The Caper-Berry (Eccles. xii. 5)', *Journal of the Society of Biblical Literature and Exegesis* 6 (1886), 13-26.
Toledano, E.R., *State and Society in Mid-Nineteenth-Century Egypt* (Cambridge, 2003).
Tomson, P.J., '"There is No One who is Righteous, Not Even One". Kohelet 7,20 in Pauline and Early Jewish Interpretation', in Berlejung and van Hecke (eds.), *The Language of Qohelet*, 183-202.
Torrey, C.C., 'The Question of the Original Language of Qoheleth', *JQR* 39 (1948), 151-60.
Tov, E., 'Scribal Features of Two Qumran Scrolls', in *Textual Criticism of the Hebrew Bible, Qumran, Septuagint. Collected Essays, Volume 3* (Leiden & Boston, 2015), 368-386.
Toy, C.H., *A Critical and Exegetical Commentary on the Book of Proverbs* (ICC; Edinburgh, 1899).
*Tremellio (Tremellius), I., and F. Du Jon (Junius), 'Ecclesiastes', in *Bibliorum Pars Tertia, Id Est, Quinque Libri Poetici, Latini recens ex Hebraeo facti, brevibusq[ue] Scholiis ad verborum interpretationem rerúmque methodum pertinentibus illustrati ab Imm. Tremellio & Franc. Junio. Libri tertii tomi. Ijob. Psalmi. Proverbia. Ecclesiastes. Liber Canticorum* (vol. 3 of *Testamenti Veteris Biblia Sacra*; Frankfurt a.m., 1579).
Tsukimoto, A., 'The Background of Qoh 11:1-6 and Qohelet's Agnosticism', *AJBI* 19 (1993), 34-52.
Vajda, G., 'Ecclésiaste XII, 2-7 interprété par un auteur juif d'Andalousie du XIe Siècle', *JSS* 27 (1982), 33-46.
Vall, G., 'The Enigma of Job 1,21a', *Bib* 76 (1995), 325-42.
Van der Wal, A.J.O., 'Qohelet 12,1a: A Relatively Unique Statement in Israel's Wisdom Tradition', in Schoors (ed.), *Qohelet in the Context*, 413-18.
Van Leeuwen, R.C., 'Proverbs 30:21-23 and the Biblical World Upside Down', *JBL* 105 (1986), 599-610.
Varela, A., 'A New Approach to Eccl 5:8-9', *BT* 27 (1976), 240-41.
Verde, D., 'Standing on the Shoulders of Giants: On the Crucial Role of "Testimony" in Biblical Wisdom Literature and in the Book of Qoheleth in Particular', *LS* 41 (2018), 359-76.

Vignolo, R., 'La scrittura di Qohelet e la sua ricezione canonica alla luce della sua cornice editoriale (1,1-2.3; 12,8.9-14)', *Teologia* 35 (2010), 184-221.

Viviers, H., 'Nie 'n kans vat of 'n kans vermy nie, maar alle kanse benut! 'n Sosioretoriese waardering van Prediker 11:1- 6', *Verbum et Ecclesia=Skrif en Kerk* 18 (1997), 365-79.

Vogels, W., 'Performance vaine et performance saine chez Qohélet', *NRT* 113 (1991), 363-85.

Waldman, N.M., 'The *dābār raʿ* of Eccl 8:3', *JBL* 98 (1979), 407-8.

Watson, W.G.E., 'The Unnoticed Word Pair "eye(s)" // "heart"', *ZAW* 101 (1989), 398-408.

Weißflog, K., 'Worum geht es in Kohelet 8,10?', *BN* 131 (2006), 39-45.

Whitwell, C., 'The Variation of Nature in Ecclesiastes 11', *JSOT* 34 (2009), 81-97.

Whybray, R.N., 'Qoheleth the Immoralist? (Qoh 7:16-17)', in J.G. Gammie, W.A. Brueggemann, W.L. Humphreys, and J.M. Ward (eds.), *Israelite Wisdom: Theological and Literary Essays in Honor of Samuel Terrien* (Missoula, MT, 1978), 191-204.

Willan, E., *Beatitas Britanniae, or, King Charles the Second, Englands beatituded as preached to the incorporation of the honour of Eay, in the county of Suffolk, March 31, 1661, being the Lords Day before their election of Burgesses, and the week before the choice of knights for the county* (London, 1661).

*Williams, A.L., *Ecclesiastes in the Revised Version with Introduction & Notes* (CBSC; Cambridge, 1922).

Witzenrath, H., *Süß ist das Licht: Eine literaturwissenschaftliche Untersuchung zu Koh 11,7-12,7* (Münchener Universitätsschriften Katholisch-Theologische Fakultät. Arbeiten zu Text und Sprache im Alten Testament 11; St Ottilien, 1979).

*Wolfe, L.M., *Qoheleth (Ecclesiastes)* (Wisdom Commentary 24; Collegeville, 2020).

Wright, A.G., 'Ecclesiastes 9:1-12: An Emphatic Statement of Themes', *CBQ* 77 (2015), 250-62.

Zahavy, T., *The Talmud of the Land of Israel: A Preliminary Translation and Explanation. Vol. 1 Berakhot* (Chicago Studies in the History of Judaism; Chicago & London, 1989).

Zehnder, M.P., *Wegmetaphorik im Alten Testament: Eine semantische Untersuchung der alttestamentlichen und altorientalischen Weg-Lexeme mit besonderer Berücksichtigung ihrer metaphorischen Verwendung* (BZAW 268; Berlin & New York, 1999).

Zimmer, T., *Zwischen Tod und Lebensglück: eine Untersuchung zur Anthropologie Kohelets* (BZAW 286; Berlin, 1999).

ADDITIONAL ABBREVIATIONS

ABL	Harper, R. F. and L. Waterman, *Assyrian and Babylonian letters belonging to the Kouyunjik Collection of the British Museum* (14 vols.; Chicago: 1892–1914).
AJBI	*Annual of the Japanese Biblical Institute*
AnBib	Analecta biblica
ASTI	*Annual of the Swedish Theological Institute*
BT	The Bible Translator
CahRB	Cahiers de la Revue biblique
CJT	*Canadian Journal of Theology*
COut	Commentar op het Oude Testament
CTR	Criswell Theological Review
HBS	Herders Biblische Studien
HeBAI	*Hebrew Bible and Ancient Israel*
IBS	Irish Biblical Studies
ITQ	*Irish Theological Quarterly*
JAB	*Journal for the Aramaic Bible*
JGL	*Journal of Greek Linguistics*
JHS	*The Journal of Hellenic Studies*
JHUC	*Johns Hopkins University Circulars*
JRH	*Journal of Religion and Health*
JSNTSup	Journal for the Study of the New Testament Supplement Series
JSSM	Journal of Semitic Studies Monograph
LNTS	Library of New Testament Studies
LS	*Louvain Studies*
NRT	La Nouvelle Revue Théologique
NETS	Pietersma and B.G. Wright (eds.), *A New English Translation of the Septuagint and the Other Greek Translations Traditionally Included Under That Title* (Oxford & New York, 2007).
NIV	New International Version
NZSTR	*Neue Zeitschrift für systematische Theologie und Religionsphilosophie*
RivLSE	*Rivista di Letteratura e di Storia Ecclesiastica*
RTR	Reformed Theological Review
SBJT	Southern Baptist Journal of Theology
ScC	La Scuola Cattolica
TOTC	Tyndale Old Testament Commentaries
ZNW	Zeitschrift für die neutestamentliche Wissenschaft und die Kunde des Urchristentums

Introduction to 5.7–6.9 (ET 5.8–6.9): Wealth, Long Life and Fulfilment

(5.7 ET 5.8) If it's extortion of the poor and depredation of what's rightful that you see in the province, don't be surprised at the situation. For above everyone high up, there is someone higher standing watch, and higher ones above them, (5.8 ET 5.9) but profit from a land is above everyone, king of any cultivated ground. (5.9 ET 5.10) No-one who loves money will ever have enough money, so will whoever loves a lot of it be satisfied by any yield? This, too, is an illusion. (5.10 ET 5.11) The more prosperity there is, the more there are to consume it—and what aptitude does anyone with a claim to it have, except for looking on with his eyes?

(5.11 ET 5.12) Sweet is the sleep of an underling, whether it's a little or a lot that he eats, but finding satisfaction for a rich man leaves him no chance to sleep.

(5.12 ET 5.13) There is something painfully bad I have seen beneath the sun: wealth was being kept for its owner, against a time of trouble, (5.13 ET 5.14) but that wealth was lost in some bad deal. Then he fathered a son, but was completely empty-handed. (5.14 ET 5.15) For he emerged from the womb of his mother naked: he will go on again as he came—and he will take up nothing in his business which can go in his hand. (5.15 ET 5.16) This too is painfully bad, that exactly as he came, so shall he go—and what lasting gain will there be there for him who would work in the wind? (5.16 ET 5.17) Also, for all his days he will feed in darkness, off great resentment, pain, and anger. (5.17 ET 5.18) Look, what I have seen to be good, is that it would be best to eat and drink and find happiness in all his business, at which he will work beneath the sun for the limited duration of his life which God has given him. For that is what is his.

(5.18 ET 5.19) Also, every person to whom God has granted wealth and property, and to whom he has given the power to take enjoyment from them, to take up what is his, and to take pleasure in his business—this is a payment from God, (5.19 ET 5.20) for he will not give much thought to the length of his life when God busies him with the joy of his heart.

(6.1) There is something bad which I have seen beneath the sun, and it is a lot for humans to deal with: (6.2) a man to whom God may grant wealth, property, and prestige, and he lacks nothing for himself that he might crave; but God does not give him the power to take enjoyment from them, as some quite different man is going to enjoy them. This is an illusion, and it is a terrible pain.

(6.3) If a man has children a hundred times, and lives many years, and the days of his years are going to be a lot, while his self is not satisfied by his good fortune, then, even when it has no proper burial, I say that a miscarried child is better off than him. (6.4) For he has come in illusion and walks in darkness, and by darkness will his name be covered, (6.5) while it never saw or knew sunlight—it would be easier for it than for him, (6.6) even if he lived a thousand years twice over, but never found happiness.

Is it not to just the one place that everybody's going? (6.7) When all a person's work is for their mouth, and also the self is not fulfilled, (6.8) then, like the wise man's advantage over the fool, what is there for a poor man in knowing that he will go on among the living? (6.9) What is in front of one's eyes is better than a hunger that just goes on. That too is an illusion, and wishing for the wind.

Qohelet's lengthy discussion here falls into several parts. He begins in 5.7-11 with statements about the insatiable desire for wealth which holds in its power even—or perhaps especially—the rich, and leads to extortion from the poor. In 5.12-19, he turns to the case of a man who has lost his wealth when he most needs it, leaving him empty-handed and liable to a life subsequently filled with resentment. I take this case to be a sort of metaphor for the position of humans more generally in the world—the reference to a 'bad deal' picks up the vocabulary of 1.13. Qohelet suggests that it would be best for the man to enjoy what life he has, and extends this also to those who have wealth, and who have the capacity to enjoy it. The man may depart his life just as empty-handed as when he entered it, and that is ultimately going to be true for us all: his loss merely pre-empts a loss that every human will experience. Taking pleasure in life is a compensation granted by God, that may prevent him from brooding upon his ruin, and us from worrying about our mortality.

In 6.1-2, however, this more cheerful idea is qualified by the observation that not everybody will be granted that power to find pleasure: Qohelet points to another instance of a man who has everything he could want, but who is denied by God the ability to enjoy his good fortune, because it is destined to be enjoyed by somebody else. The point here is probably not that the man will actually be stripped of what he has, but simply that the pleasures to be found in it are reserved for whoever else it is that will eventually acquire it—that fortune is not actually his to spend, even though he might seem to own it. The issue is pursued in 6.3-6a, where long life rather than great wealth becomes the focus: the miscarried child, who has never seen a moment of life outside the womb, is better off than someone who lives thousands of years without seeing a moment of happiness.

These ideas are brought together in the final verses, 6.6b-9, which ask 'are we not all headed for the same death?' Much earlier (in 2.13-15) this meant that the wise man had no discernible advantage over the fool, so now, similarly, what good does it do somebody to know that they will keep living when their life is a life of poverty? That is, a life marked by effort without fulfilment.

The final conclusion employs expressions that are a little obscure to us, but Qohelet's general point is probably that the enjoyment of life is more important than the endless perpetuation of our needs and desires. If our quest to meet those needs is what defines our living, then we are being driven by an illusion, and looking for a fulfilment that we can never achieve: it is better that we take what is before us than that we just keep going like that. This brings the discussion back, in some ways, to the insatiability of greed, with which Qohelet began, and if there is any single theme that runs throughout, it is that the human desire to accumulate wealth or property is a source of unhappiness not just to those who are the victims of the greedy, but to those who can never find satisfaction in what they already have. This desire is also, of course, pointless: whatever happens, we will be left with nothing when we die, so we can throw away our lives in pursuit of more, but will still end them the same way as everyone else. Although the conclusion of the discussion returns to points with which it started, it also lays the ground for some of the ideas that will become prominent in the next chapter, and particularly the notion there, which Qohelet seems to both espouse and reject, that we should be looking not to the present but to the future.

As commonly in the book, the Hebrew is often very tricky in the course of this discussion, and the precise meaning debatable at many points. The context of the discussion as a whole, moreover, is very important for understanding the particular elements of it, which are sometimes open to misinterpretation if considered in isolation. Indeed, the very way in which he links the themes of wealth and longevity here is important for understanding Qohelet's attitude to both. There is, to be sure, some element of a social critique in his initial remarks about the effects of a human greed for profit: no adequate protections can be built in to any society, when every society is effectively ruled by profit (although that idea, I think, effectively excludes the common claims that he is addressing problems specific to Ptolemaic rule; so, e.g., Asurmendi, 'Power in Qoheleth and the Prophets', 135). It becomes clear very swiftly, however, that his concern is actually with the relationships between individuals and their wealth, which can lead them to frustration or even despair. As he shifts to talk about longevity, he also brings into focus another key issue here, that good fortune, whether measured in gold or years, is useless, and perhaps worse than useless, if it is not matched by a capacity to find pleasure in life. We are all in danger of rushing onward throughout our lives, driven only by the prospect of the next meal or the next deal, when the truth is that we will each end up in the same place, as impoverished as everybody else. All that can really make one life better than another is a willingness, if we are able, to enjoy what we do and what we have—although some people, Qohelet suggests, may be fated never even to accomplish that.

Qohelet talks about 'eating' elsewhere (2.24, 25; 3.13; 4.5; 8.15; 9.7; 10.16, 17), but Provan (126) notes a particular concentration of the verb in 5.10, 11, 16, 17, 18, and 6.2, and describes it as 'the key word in the whole section'. The repetition is indeed striking, especially since these verses employ metaphorical references to 'consuming' property or life alongside the literal references to eating food that are characteristic of Qohelet's other usage. I doubt that the author's intention, as Provan supposes, is simply to emphasize the importance of what goes into our mouths after focusing in the previous verses upon the words that come out of them, and we should also note in 6.2, 3, 7, 9 the concentrated use of a noun which has, amongst its various implications, a nuance of hunger and appetite (for reasons discussed below, I have translated it variously as 'self' and 'hunger'). There is not a single, simple image here, but the vocabulary ties Qohelet's discussion of greed and desire to ideas of physical need and consumption, depicting the human relationship with wealth and property in terms of gratifying a physical, visceral need, and these ideas come to the surface at various points (most notably 5.11 and 6.7).

5.7-11 (ET 5.8-12)

(5.7 ET 5.8) If it's extortion of the poor and depredation of what's rightful that you see in the province, don't be surprised at the situation. For above everyone high up, there is someone higher standing watch, and higher ones above them, (5.8 ET 5.9) but profit from a land is above everyone, king of any cultivated ground. (5.9 ET 5.10) No-one who loves money will ever have enough money, so will whoever loves a lot of it be satisfied by any yield? This, too, is an illusion. (5.10 ET 5.11) The more prosperity there is, the more there are to consume it—and what aptitude does anyone with a claim to it have, except for looking on with his eyes?

(5.11 ET 5.12) Sweet is the sleep of an underling, whether it's a little or a lot that he eats, but finding satisfaction for a rich man leaves him no chance to sleep.

Commentary

As did the discussion in ch. 4, this short series begins in 5.7-8 with a statement by Qohelet about extortion, but extortion proves again not to be his real theme: such extortion arises from a limitless desire for wealth that corrupts the very system which should protect the poor, and the following verses dwell on the inability to fulfil the need of the rich for wealth. In 5.12, Qohelet will then turn to a problem that is almost the opposite: the unexpected loss of wealth by a man who is left destitute, which exemplifies some of his broader concerns, and leads him into a discussion about enjoyment of what one has. While 5.7-11 covers the last of the topics explored in the survey of human dealings that began in ch. 4, therefore, it also provides a transition to the rather different reflections in ch. 6.

I take Qohelet's first point in 5.7 to be that the exploitation of the poor in the province *should* be surprising when there is such strict regulation, with every official at every level watched over by a superior. The problem is that the real ruler of this system is profit, and a desire for money can never be satisfied by what is produced.

The connection of the last two verses to this theme is complicated by the double problem that we do not understand some key expressions in 5.10, and that both 5.10 and 5.11 are ambiguous, but there may be a basic continuity here. The first of these verses presents an issue parallel to that in 5.9: it is not just the case that individuals remain satisfied by nothing, but also that the numbers consuming it grow in line with any increase of property, either leaving its true owner no better off, or contributing nothing themselves. This could be understood as a free-standing saying, and usually is. In that case, the point is probably that any business or household grows in line with its prosperity, so that there is no net gain, and no real reason to achieve such growth. Although he has already passed judgment on the love of money as 'vapour', however, I am inclined to think that Qohelet still has in mind at this point the extortion with which he began this discussion. The difficulty, then, is not just that those seeking a profit are insatiable, but that the more there is to be gained, the more there are to take it.

5.11 is more probably to be read as separate, but it does pick up directly the point made in 5.9, as a further statement that the rich can find no satisfaction. If it is actually the underling who is kept awake here (see below), then the verse also picks up the initial theme: it is the poor who suffer as the result of endless greed. In any case, though, Qohelet's overall point is that the desire for wealth undermines proper social order because it is built into it, and will always do so because such desire has no limit.

5.7-8 (ET 5.8-9)] While many commentators take 5.9–6.9 as a block, these verses are normally treated separately, and, indeed, are commonly separated from each other—principally, perhaps, because their meaning has been much disputed.[1] Many earlier commentators saw a promise of divine judgment in the last part of

---

[1] Given that they clearly concern money and that not every commentator separates them, it is curious, all the same, that Fredericks does not consider their relationship with 5.9–6.9 in his 'Chiasm and Parallel Structure', which, very much in the fashion of its time, finds an elaborate chiastic structure in those verses. While it draws out elements of continuity in the language, that analysis is far from compelling, but if we do want to isolate 5.9–6.9 on structural or other grounds, then 5.7-8 should be considered at least to be an introduction to those verses. There is a useful recent summary of opinions about the structure in Lavoie, 'Ambiguïtés et désir', 185-89.

5.7, with its suggestion that there is a power still higher than these humans, while most recent ones have tended to believe that the multi-tiered bureaucracy described in this verse is depicted as the source of oppression in itself—with some identifying very specific historical circumstances for such a situation.[2] Both readings do raise questions about why Qohelet should think that we might be 'surprised', or why he should use the normally positive verb for 'stand watch over' if he is trying to imply something altogether more negative—Garrett, 'Use and Abuse', 165, has to conclude, for instance, simply that he 'betrays a certain (justifiable) cynicism: the more people are involved, the greater the probability for wrongdoing'. The more significant problem, however, is that they make it almost impossible to understand the following verse, 5.8, in any way that is sensible or relevant. The RSV's rendering, 'But in all, a king is an advantage to a land with cultivated fields', is by no means the only understanding that has been offered, although it represents a popular choice, but to obtain even that sense—which is unsatisfactory and verging on the absurd—requires something of a stretch. Other readings sometimes rely on understanding things that are unsaid: Varela, 'New Approach', notably turns the words into two claims by the officials: '(And they will tell you that) all of this means progress for the country, (and that) the king is servant of the land!' (241). It might feel less awkward to import so much if anything in the text actually suggested that we were supposed to

---

[2] D'Alario, 'Chi ama il denaro', 60, is only one among the most recent studies to observe that Qohelet refers to a Ptolemaic financial system 'basato su una gerarchia di poteri in virtù della quale nessuno era tenuto a rendere conto del proprio operato', 'based on a hierarchy of power, by virtue of which nobody was required to account for their work'. Ptolemaic administration is discussed at length in Sneed, *Politics of Pessimism*, Chapter 3, and the way it functioned in Egypt has been the focus of much modern research; Qohelet's general point here may well reflect popular resentment of taxation and tax-farming, with a perception that the poor were being fleeced. Assumptions, though, that this system was in fact corrupt have not passed without challenge (see especially Bauschatz, 'Strong Arm of the Law'), and Qohelet's complaint is, anyway, not against any particular crushing bureaucracy, but against what he considers the universal problem of a state draining money from its population—even when it might appear to offer safeguards through administrative oversight and policing. If he is referring to the Ptolemaic administration, then he seems even to be conceding that it is not malign in intent, and merely unable to resist the inevitable: the system is not the problem, or the cause of the problem, but it is also not the solution that one might expect it to be.

take it this way, and such readings are a mark of scholarly desperation: Gordis is by no means the only commentator to regard 5.8 as 'an insuperable crux'. That may very well be true, if we insist that it should be read as free-standing after assigning a particular sense to 5.7. It is not really difficult at all, however, to read this verse with the previous one, and the two in combination provide a clear introduction to the theme of wealth that follows.

5.9 (ET 5.10)] The connection of this verse to the preceding two is less certain, but 'yield' retains a strong agricultural connotation even when the Hebrew word is used more generally. That forges a link to the previous discussion and suggests that we are dealing here not with a completely new point, but with an elaboration of the first one: the desire for a profit leads to extortion because such a desire can never be sated. The text is difficult in the second part of the verse, and probably requires emendation, but the general sense is clear and undisputed. Such desire is a 'vapour', perhaps, because it involves an aspiration that can never be fulfilled, rather than because it is bad in some more general way.

5.10 (ET 5.11)] The precise implications of this verse depend more on the way we contextualize it than on the terms it uses. The consumption to which the first part refers is probably not something in itself that Qohelet regards as intrinsically bad: in 6.2-3, indeed, it is the inability or failure to consume what one has, and to be sated by one's prosperity, that he condemns. It is not clear, moreover, that those who are doing the consuming must be behaving improperly, and the comments are not expressed explicitly in terms of money bringing 'only a crowd of greedy friends and hangers-on who swallow it up' (Whybray; D'Alario, 'Chi ama il denaro', 62, speaks of parasites) or of it 'disappearing because it attracts others who will try to take it for themselves' (Fox). It is too easy, perhaps, to align what is said here with the sort of sayings found in Prov 14.20; 19.4, 6 (as does, e.g., Fischer, *Skepsis*, 61). If this is about a household, though, Qohelet could as readily be thinking of a growing family as of 'hangers-on' (Jerome thinks in terms of servants), and there is nothing, furthermore, to suggest that he has in mind someone who is (or would otherwise be) exceptionally wealthy—he has just been talking, after all, about farmers, or those who work on the land. Read simply by itself, therefore, Qohelet's point is merely that growth in prosperity tends to be cancelled out by a corresponding growth in those who depend on it. If we take the saying with what has preceded, on the other hand, then the point is ultimately similar, but Qohelet is painting a very different picture, of prosperity that is eaten away by profiteers.

In either case, though, it is difficult to be certain that we have properly understood every nuance of the verse, because it involves both a word (expressed here by 'aptitude') and an idiom ('looking on with his eyes') that we know only from elsewhere in the monologue, and we largely have to guess at their implications. Although the traditional understanding, moreover, is that the actual owner gets to enjoy nothing of his own possessions, and is left merely to look on, the word commonly translated 'owner' can be read as either singular or plural, and very often implies connection of a sort other than possession. It is possible, therefore, broadly to understand either 'and what is its owner fit for other than to look on?' or 'and what aptitude have those consuming it shown, except for looking on?'. I think the latter is more likely to be the sense intended, and that Qohelet is talking about the lack of actual contribution from those who enjoy the wealth (perhaps evoking the ideas he explored in ch. 2). I have tried in my translation, though, to preserve the ambiguity of the original.

5.11 (ET 5.12)] The second part of this verse is commonly read as a statement that the rich man is kept awake either by concerns over his wealth or by the fullness of his stomach, and this is contrasted with the ability of a servant to sleep well however much they have eaten. That apparent contrast already points up, however, the difficulty of such readings. If the issue is the rich man's worrying about his possessions, then the question of how much the servant ate becomes completely irrelevant, and can only obscure the contrast: it is the servant's lack of responsibilities, not his diet, that gives him a good night. If the issue actually is diet, on the other hand, or at least if diet is being used to epitomize something more general, then what the servant ate *is* relevant, but so is the quantity. If the text said 'The servant sleeps well even though he eats little' then we would have a proper contrast with the rich man who sleeps badly, and a warning against the consequences of a surfeit. As it is, though, the explicit statement that the servant sleeps well even if he has himself eaten a lot suggests that, in effect, it is only by virtue of being wealthy that the rich man is kept awake by his food—Qohelet would be claiming that only the rich, in other words, get indigestion. The problem is rarely even noted, but the contrast between the two men makes this saying much more complicated than the proverbs with which it is sometimes compared (see especially Lavoie, 'Le Repos', 339-42, who adds the French-Canadian 'bon dîneur mauvais dormeur', 'good diner: bad sleeper').

For this reason, and for others discussed in the notes, it seems unlikely that Qohelet was originally talking about the rich man's 'surfeit' at all—whether we understand his wealth or his diet by that—and probable that the Masoretic vocalization of the text misrepresents the original purpose. The author most likely intended not the rare 'surfeit', but a relatively common word that refers to satisfying one's hunger, and Qohelet's point would then be that the rich man, unlike the servant, is kept awake by his desire to find an elusive satisfaction. The text could also be read, in fact, to suggest that it is the servant who is kept awake, not by his own needs—he'd be happy to sleep however much he ate—but by those of the rich man, which cannot be met: that reading would give a good connection to 5.7-8 in terms of the poor suffering for the greed of others (and it would also, perhaps, offset what Wolfe sees as a problematic romanticization of poverty). The ambiguity is apparently again original, but even if we do not take the text that way, the servant/rich man distinction makes another specific social point: the man driven by greed here is the one who already has money.

Notes

5.7 (ET 5.8) extortion] On the meaning of עשק, see the note at 4.1.

5.7 (ET 5.8) the poor] Lit. 'a poor person'. The plural forms in S and V are translational: M, G, Hie, T all read a singular, and Kamenetzky, indeed, would delete the seyame in S as secondary, making that singular too.

5.7 (ET 5.8) depredation] גזל is linked with עשק in Lev 5.21 (ET 6.2); Ezek 18.18; 22.29; Ps 62.11 (ET 62.10); indeed, Isa 61.8 is the only place that the noun appears in biblical Hebrew without עשק. The cognate verb is also used on a number of occasions with עשק (cf. Lev 5.23 [ET 6.4]; 19.13; Deut 28.29; Jer 21.12; Mic 2.2), but it seems likely that the nouns are virtual synonyms, with גזל emphasizing slightly more, perhaps, the actual removal of something. Like עשק, it is not a general term for oppression.

5.7 (ET 5.8) what's rightful] Lit. 'justice and rightness'. משפט וצדק occur together also in Ps 119.121, where the psalmist, professing fear of God's judgments, claims that he has 'done justice and rightness' and pleads not to be given over to his oppressors (לעשקי). As Fox observes, the accentuation, and the consequent pointing of the conjunction as וָ, indicate the close connection of the nouns in the Masoretic understanding (cf. GKC §104 g; J-M §104 d), and he takes them as 'a hendiadys equivalent to *mišpaṭ ṣedeq*, "righteous judgment" or "just due"'.[3] At the very least, they should probably be considered together, although Rashi offers one interpretation that understands 'and if you see צדק coming to the city'—that is, apparent divine favour. The similar language in Isa 10.2 suggests that Qohelet may be talking about the removal or subversion of legal protections against extortion. If they form a fixed expression, that might also explain their construction with גזל, which is pointed as construct in M: classically, Hebrew prefers to avoid the use of multiple *nomina recta* with a single *nomen regens* except where they have such a connection (see GKC §128 a, n. 3)—although this is not a hard-and-fast rule, and there are many late exceptions (see J-M §129 b).

Graetz declares that the construct simply cannot be used to express theft of something in this way, and inserts מקום to read 'Raub (an der Stätte) des Rechtes und der Frömmigkeit', 'robbery in the place of justice and righteousness'. The basis of his objection is unclear, especially since he seems to find no problem with the preceding עשק רש. It is possible, though, that he was not the first reader to find the expression difficult. S, curiously, reads ܘܕܝܢܐ *wdyn'*, equivalent to ומשפט, and has no equivalent for וצדק, giving 'humiliation of the poor and theft and judgment'. The first variation is found also in T ודין, so may reflect a Hebrew variant with a conjunction, rather than a miswriting of ܕܕܝܢܐ *ddyn'*, and in S it probably led to the second, since צדק sits uncomfortably in such a list (T has to present the situation as a juxtaposition of extortion with charity, which raises a question about the divine will). The conjunction is unlikely to be original, and probably arises from a failure or reluctance to recognize the construct relationship.

Vinel, 'Le Texte Grec', 298-99, suggests that the vocabulary here offers a link to the story of David and Mephibosheth, noting that the particular combination of terms is not common, and pointing to 2 Sam 8.15, where David administers 'justice and righteousness'; the term שדה, she observes, is found here and also in the subsequent 2 Sam 9.7-8. The idea is unpersuasive, since שדה itself is far too common to be suggestive of a specific link, while 2 Sam 8 uses not משפט וצדק, as here, but the similar, far more frequent משפט וצדקה. When G translates both perfectly regularly, it is hard to see any basis for the idea of a specific or deliberate echo in either the Greek translation or the Hebrew original.

5.7 (ET 5.8) the province] Or 'a province': the Greek renderings vocalize במדינה without the definite article of M. T has בקרתא, 'in the city', which

---

[3] Galling 1969 similarly takes them as a hendiadys, although previously, in 1940 and in 'Kohelet-Studien', 284 n. 2, he proposed the deletion of וצדק.

probably reflects the semantic shift of מדינה in Aramaic from 'province' or 'country' to 'city', perhaps *via* references to the administrative centres closely associated with provinces. S ܒܡܕܝܢܬܐ *bmdynt'* reproduces M, but should possibly likewise be read as a reference to the city. Hebrew was not immune to this shift, and the biblical distinction between עיר and מדינה has to be explained at the beginning of Esther Rabbah. Indeed, the Midrash to this verse strikingly offers an interpretation of the setting as Rome. It is interesting, therefore, both that G chooses to use ἐν χώρα, which might simply mean 'in a land' (cf. Hie *in regione*), but could also mean 'in (the) countryside', and that we have an anonymous hexaplaric reading ἐν πόλει, which Marshall attributes to σ', and which has found its way into Origenic manuscripts of G. It is difficult to know precisely what מדינה would have signified to the original author, but although we should probably see a reference here to a situation which involves the province as a whole, 5.8 and 5.9 do introduce agricultural references that seem to locate the heart of that problem in the countryside.

As well as its reference to Rome, the Midrash offers a wordplay involving Gehinnom's 'judgment on him (the oppressor)'—בו דינה for במדינה—and Seow suggests quite independently, although not wholly persuasively, that a similar wordplay was actually intended: מדינה is etymologically the 'place of jurisdiction' where justice is being violated. Kugel, 'Qohelet and Money', 37, speculates, indeed, that this is not a matter of wordplay but of the author's intended meaning, and that the text might originally have read מדין. Ogden rather differently uses the supposed origin to suggest that what is meant here is 'in a (specific) legislative district'.

5.7 (ET 5.8) surprised] Scholars who see a reference to God in the last clause (see the note below) also commonly see this as an exhortation not to worry about what is happening, and Krüger, 'Meaningful Ambiguities', 64-67, although he does not see such a reference, does think nevertheless that there is an ambiguity here: we should not be *frightened* (because the system is robust), or we should not be *surprised* (because the system is corrupt). The verb תמה, to be sure, refers to being taken aback by something when it is encountered, and so can be associated with surprise, astonishment or panic in different contexts. There is no reason to suppose, however, that it can actually connote the sort of ongoing worry or concern (perhaps engendered by a surprise) that might justify a reading in terms of 'do not worry' or 'do not be frightened'. If there is an ambiguity here, it lies not in the vocabulary, but in the potentially different ways that an audience might react to the description of the officials, and I doubt that this is deliberate.

5.7 (ET 5.8) situation] Perhaps more lit. 'matter' or 'thing'. On חפץ, see the note at 3.1.

5.7 (ET 5.8) for] I have translated כי as explanatory, but it could be read as concessive here: 'although (כי) גבה above גבה stands watch...yet (ו) profit...'. For analogous uses of כי concessively with a subsequent conjunction, see, e.g., Isa 54.10; Ezek 11.16.

5.7 (ET 5.8) everyone high up] Lit. 'a high man'. The adjective גבה literally means 'high' or 'lofty', and the idea of God as 'most high' has shaped some interpretations: T talks of God, mighty over the highest heavens, watching humans, and Rashi of the 'highest over the high' waiting to mete out retribution, which is similar to Jerome's understanding. Although to be 'high' or 'low' might seem to us an obvious metaphor for social station, the cognate verb is not, in fact, used very often of achieving or maintaining power and status (cf. perhaps Isa 52.13 and more certainly Job 36.7; 40.10), and only in Isa 5.14-15 and Ezek 21.31 (ET 21.26) does the adjective itself even possibly have that connotation (see also the commentary at 10.5 on 'heights'). It is never used, moreover, to describe official, as opposed to social rank, and as Kugel, 'Qohelet and Money', 35, rightly points out, therefore, biblical usage offers no basis for translations like the 'high official' of RSV.

Kugel's own interpretation involves associating the references here with the later Hebrew uses of a verbal stem גבי or גבה to connote the collection of payments or taxes, and he sees the passage in terms of 'payment-takers' seeking bribes. Seow, who finds this approach attractive, adds that גבי is attested in Aramaic texts from the Persian period, where it has a specific reference to tax-collection. That sense cannot wholly be excluded here, but as Kugel acknowledges, it is difficult to derive the subsequent גבהים from anything other than גבה, 'high': we should expect גבים from the stem that he proposes (cf. Schoors, *The Preacher* II, 311), and explaining or emending גבהים adds a significant level of complexity. Seow adopts the translation 'arrogant one(s)', from an established sense of גבה, especially in uses connected to one's heart, face or eyes (e.g. 2 Chr 26.16; Pss 10.4; 101.5; 131.1: note also the famous גבה רוח, 'haughty spirit', of Prov 16.18; cf. Eccles 7.8), and he says that by this he means 'anyone who is of higher socioeconomic or political status than the ordinary person'—but that is not what 'arrogant' means, and this unnecessarily introduces a nuance of attitude whilst trying to smuggle the poorly attested connotation of 'high status' in through the back door.

What we can reasonably say is that the notion of 'height' or 'elevation' here accords with the image of each גבה watching the next from above (see the next note), and that the terminology may have been driven by this imagery rather than by any specific use of גבה to represent a particular class or status: Qohelet paints a picture of individuals each standing high enough to look down upon the next, and the lowest, perhaps, at least high enough to look down on everybody else. These people presumably *are* officials or supervisors of some sort, but it is unlikely that Qohelet is actually describing them as such explicitly.

5.7 (ET 5.8) there is someone higher standing watch] The Hebrew says literally 'A high man from above a high man (is) standing watch'. In general, the versions support M's vocalization of the text here, although G renders שמר as an infinitive φυλάξαι, apparently understanding '(there is) a superior…to stand guard'. This text is often, however, perceived to be problematic, most notably because, although שמר על does occur in the sense 'watch over' (cf. 1 Sam 26.16; Job 14.16; Prov 6.22), שמר does not usually take a following מעל, and if the first גבה is the subject, moreover, then the verb stands very late in the clause. Some commentators have also found a problem in the inconsistency between מעל here and עליהם in the next clause, and a number have been inclined, accordingly, either to emend מעל to על, by deleting or detaching[4] the מ—which might also open up the possibility of understanding this as an expression of plurality, 'superior upon superior' (cf. Kugel, 'Qohelet and Money', 36)—or to emend עיליהם to מעליהם (so, e.g., Ginsberg, who reads וגבה מעליהם).

I doubt, however, that these issues present any real obstacle to accepting the text as it stands. The preposition does not simply mark the object of שמר, and the verb is being used intransitively, with מעל marking the position of the first גבה relative to the second. This is what has determined the word-order: Qohelet is stressing that each stands watch above the next, rather than that they are watching over each other (which is an obstacle both to the interpretation of, e.g., Hitzig and Fox, that they are protecting each other, and to the idea of, e.g., Rashbam, Delitzsch, that they are watching to take advantage of each other). In fact, although מעל often means 'from upon', it can connote 'above, looking down', as when it is used to explain how Ezra could be visible to all the people as he read out the Law (Neh 8.5), and in 2 Kgs 25.28 and Esth 3.1 it is used of indicating status by setting someone's seat above those of others—a usage which, perhaps, involves a similar nuance. Although I take there to be a comparison implicit in the statement here, it is unlikely that, as Ogden suggests, the -מ is itself being used to express the comparative: for that, it would not be attached to על.

The participle of שמר is used commonly to mean 'a watchman' (e.g. Isa 21.11-12; Ps 127.1), so it is possible that Qohelet is evoking the image of watchmen in towers or upon the walls of a city (cf. Isa 62.6), and Gordis translates 'each guardian of the law is higher than the next'. It can also be used, however, to mean 'keeper', of those who have a particular responsibility toward, or control over something (e.g. 2 Kgs 22.14; Neh 2.8, Esth 2.3), raising the possibility that these individuals are simply 'in charge'. In interpretations of the verse as a promise of divine judgment, שמר is sometimes taken to refer to God (and cf. Ogden's interpretation, discussed below), but Gordis wrongly attributes that view to Ewald and Delitzsch.

There are no grounds on which to emend the verb, e.g. to the niph'al נִשְׁמָר, which Siegfried adopts and takes in the sense 'sich vor jemandem in Acht nehmen', 'be on one's guard against somebody'. Seow seeks to detach it by re-dividing שמר וגבהים as שמרו גבהים, and translating 'an arrogant one is above an arrogant one, (and) arrogant ones have watched over them all'.

---

[4] So, e.g., Anderlini, 'Qohelet 5,7-8', 14-17, tries, without any foundation at all, to take the מ as an enclitic mem, displaced from the end of the previous word.

Realistically, though, this requires not only a different division of the consonants, but the insertion of a new conjunction before his שמרו.
5.7 (ET 5.8) and higher ones above them] Lit. 'and high ones (are) above them', or 'and high ones (stand watch) over them'. The plural cannot imply a superlative, as Ogden asserts (unconsciously following a long tradition of earlier interpreters),[5] but there is an implicit comparison here. σ' καὶ ὑψηλότεροι ἐπάνω αὐτῶν, 'and higher ones above them', makes that comparative force explicit, while α' and θ' change the sense by reading μετ' αὐτούς, 'besides them', for G ἐπ' αὐτούς, 'over/upon them'. The reading *excelsior* in Hie is comparative, and may have been influenced by σ' in that respect, but it is also singular, and as Marshall points out, there are no attestations of a singular ὑψηλότερος for σ' in any of the Greek manuscripts (*contra* Field): Jerome is, in fact, reading גבהים as a reference to God (although he takes a different approach in V *eminentiores*). This remained quite a common interpretation of the verse well into the nineteenth century, with scholars such as Geier, Ewald 1837 ('der persische König der Könige', 'the Persian King of Kings') and Delitzsch seeing here a plural of excellence or majesty (cf. GKC §124 g-k; J-M §136 d-e), or an intensive plural (GKC §124 e; J-M §136 f; the case is still made in Ember, 'Pluralis Intensivus', 209-10, which sees וגבהים עליהם as a theological gloss.). Stuart summarizes the sentiment as: 'When inferior magistrates are oppressive...do not regard this as a perplexing, inexplicable, and hopeless matter. An appeal lies to a higher court...but if the matter still goes on adversely there, then remember for your comfort that there is *One Superior to all*, who will bring all into judgment.' Ogden steers a similar course, and although he neither makes an explicit connection with God nor fully explains how he parses the syntax of the verse, he takes its sense to be: 'despite the abuse of justice, one should not be duly concerned, because the one who preserves justice [Ogden takes this to be the force of שמר] is actually the more highly exalted one. He is in fact the most exalted one, this being the force of the plural *gebōhîm*. He stands above those who oppress the poor and ravage society.' Such interpretations do not wholly depend upon reading the plural as singular, and Rashi thinks in terms of divine agents, but they understand the verse to offer reassurance, and hinge on the meaning of אל תתמה, on which see the note above.

[5] So, e.g., Tremellio and Du Jon (Tremellius and Junius) in 1579 noted *plurale pro singulari superlativo*, although they also see a reference to the Trinity. For the complicated publication history of their commentary, see Weeks, *The Making of Many Books*, 20-22; I have consulted the 1580 edition published by Harrison in London. De Groot justifies the rendering as a superlative by claiming that terms which we would understand as intensive plurals are, in fact, abbreviated forms, so that אלהים, for example, stands for אלהה אלהים, and חכמות for חכמת חכמות; correspondingly, we should understand גבהים here as גבה גבהים (although that would still not strictly be a superlative: see my note on 'complete illusion' at 1.2). This is ingenious but unconvincing.

5.8 (ET 5.9) but profit from a land] Galling 1969 tries to turn the whole verse into a question by adding מה at the beginning, but there is no justification for this addition. The reading ויתרון is not in doubt—although some manuscripts of S omit the conjunction and/or replace ܝܘܬܪܢܐ *ywtrn'* with ܝܘܪܬܢܐ *ywrtn'*, 'inheritance', through metathesis—but the significance of the term depends very much on the way in which we understand this notoriously difficult verse.

For a start, it is unlikely that יתרון ארץ means 'a profit/advantage for the land', although it is often taken that way: see the notes on 'from the worker' at 3.9 and 'for the wisdom' at 2.13. It is Qohelet's habit to use a simple construct, as here, when he is talking about the gain *from* something, and to use -ל when he is talking about the gain *to* something, and although it is conceivable that here, as in 2.13, the usage is complicated by questions of determination, S and T, at least, have both probably understood 'from', and none of the other ancient versions contradicts that understanding. The scope of ארץ here is uncertain: it commonly designates 'land' in the sense of 'a country', or other political unit, but it is also used of land in other contexts, referring in Exod 23.10 and Lev 19.9, for example, to land that is to be cultivated and from which a harvest is to be gathered. It is noteworthy, indeed, that ארץ and שדה stand in parallel in Ps 78.12 and Jer 12.4, which both apparently present שדה as a subset of ארץ, so we should be wary of imposing upon them any strong distinction of type. Since Qohelet is going to use agricultural terminology later in this verse and the next, but has established a political and judicial context in the previous verse, both senses may be in play: he is talking about the profit to be extracted from a country (or province), but that profit will come principally from what is produced in each שדה. *HALOT* proposes speculatively that ארץ here should be emended to ערץ = עריץ, 'tyrant'.

In a recent article that suggests extensive reference to Ptolemaic politics in the book, Athas, 'Qohelet in His Context', 367, accepts the sense 'from a land', but renders: 'Though the increase of a land should be for all, a king is served by a country'. He explains that his translation of the initial conjunction as concessive is derived from the contrast that he sees here between what 'should' happen and what 'does' happen, but that contrast is only achieved by taking the conjunction as concessive, and is not indicated otherwise by the Hebrew. It is sometimes easiest to translate -ו as 'although', but it is not used as a way to introduce concessive clauses.

5.8 (ET 5.9) is above everyone] Or 'over everything'. M בכל should probably be understood as 'in everyone / everything' (hardly 'for all people', as Bartholomew proposes; cf. also Athas, *loc. cit.*). It is doubtful, however, that this is the original reading, and the ancient witnesses are divided. M is supported by S, Hie, and θ' ἐν παντί (which is found in Origenic manuscripts of G, and assigned to Origen by ms 252). The Targum, on the other hand, has על כולא, and G* was almost certainly ἐπὶ παντί (the reading also of σ'), reflecting a Hebrew על כל (see especially Gentry, 'The Role of the Three', 174-77, who notes that Rahlfs' ἐν παντί was based on a single, strongly hexaplaric manuscript). V is paraphrasing, but the basis of V *insuper*, 'moreover', is probably also ארץ על כל (Jerome uses *insuper* to render עליו in Lev 6.5). In any case, the combined witness of T and G is sufficient to establish beyond reasonable doubt that we are dealing with two early variants of the Hebrew text, one with ב- and the other with על.

Goldman prefers על כל to the בכל of M for reasons that rest upon specific interpretations of each, and a somewhat subjective characterization of M's reading as ideological. The Greek does seem to give a better sense, however, especially if we read it as a continuation of the previous verse, to which it is, after all, linked by a conjunction. McNeile, 70, recognizes that 'ὁ ἐπὶ παντί ἐστι...refers to the grades of officials in *v.* 7', but does not note T and assumes that the reading is secondary: 'A scribe was apparently influenced by the foregoing ἐπάνω and ἐπὶ, and thought of the king as the climax in the series of officials' (159). We would be taking the principle of *lectio difficilior* to the point of absurdity, however, were we to discount the reading of G because it gives a much better reading than M, and we would have also to find a quite different explanation for the reading in T, which clearly does not interpret the text this way. I take G and T to be based on a more original text in which על כל does indeed follow מעל and על in the previous verse: one superior is above another, there are more superiors above them, but יתרון ארץ על כל הוא, profit from the land comes above everyone—which is why Qohelet can go on to describe it as 'king'.

G itself can be understood in similar terms: 'and the surplus of the land is over everyone/everything, king of the worked field', while σ' καὶ περισσότερον ἐπὶ τῆς γῆς ἐπὶ παντί αὐτός ἐστι βασιλεὺς τῇ χώρᾳ εἰργασμένῃ probably means 'and much more on the earth, he is over everyone/everything, a king for the land that is worked'—although it is not clear who or what is supposed to be the antecedent for αὐτός. T reads, 'and the advantage from the gain(s) of the cultivation of the land is above everything', meaning it is the most important thing.

Most previous commentators follow M בכל (perhaps because, at least amongst recent commentators, Rahlfs' reading—along with his division of the text in line with M, cf. Vinel—has meant that the alternative in G has not been recognized widely), and Schoors, *The Preacher* II, 5-6, collects a long list of proposed translations, many of which impute rare or wholly unattested meanings to the preposition, or to the expression as a whole: there really is no basis on which to understand בכל as meaning 'all things considered', for example, and if we translate it properly as 'in all', we cannot take that to imply 'all in all'. Anderlini, 'Qohelet 5,7-8', 17-18, goes so far as to canvass the possibility that K*ethîbh* היא here should be taken as a neuter pronoun equivalent to זאת, so that we can read 'all this'—a reading that has little to commend it except its recognition of the difficulties—and adds an even less plausible suggestion (19-21) that the ב- should be read as comparative. Much earlier,

Gude (*Disputatio*, 13) tried to suggest that it must mean 'for', so that the text could express a worthy sentiment about the profit being due to everyone, rich or poor. Even those solutions that are credible lexically tend to offer a poor or redundant sense: is Qohelet really trying to say, for instance, that a king, agriculture, or whatever, is profitable 'in all respects' (cf. Fox, Backhaus) or 'under all circumstances' (cf. Wildeboer)?

Seow attempts to cut the knot by interpreting כל not as 'every', but as a derivative from the root כיל or כול, 'measure', and he renders 'the advantage of land is in its yield'; this requires, however, not only that the word could mean 'yield'—a sense listed for none of its cognates in other languages—but also that we append a suffix pronoun to read בכלה. If we are not to resort either to emendation or to the outermost reaches of the lexica to explain some perfectly common words, then M probably has to mean 'and profit from the land (is) in everything/everyone'. This makes enough sense in itself to explain the emergence of the reading בכל in place of על כל: M probably reflects an interpretative hyper-correction that conveys the gist but misses the precise point of Qohelet's metaphor, and instead of setting profit at the apex of the system, portrays it as pervasive.

I read the pronoun (or copula) with this clause, as probably do all the versions except S and V (although the latter is paraphrasing so broadly that it is hard to tell), making this a tripartite non-verbal sentence of the common form subject (ויתרון ארץ)–predicate (על כל)–pronoun (cf. J-M §154 I; this is also the way in which, e.g., Whitley construes the text). Since the subject יתרון is usually taken to be masculine (although it is not demonstrably so in biblical usage, unless we read הכשיר at 10.10—see the notes there—or take the identification as 'king' here to affirm that gender), the *Qᵉrê* הוא offers a smoother reading than the *Kᵉthîbh* היא. Whether we should take it to have been the original reading, however, is a slightly different matter: היא could conceivably refer to ארץ, which is feminine, but only if that noun were somehow read outside the construct relationship with יתרון, and it has a good claim to be the *lectio difficilior*. Schoors, *The Preacher* I, 34 recognizes the same basic structure, but extends it to the whole verse, and claims that יתרון ארץ is the predicate, with מלך לשדה נעבד as the subject, so that the order is predicate–pronoun–subject, and the sense something like 'a king for cultivated ground is a profit of the land'. That is the other common form of such nominal sentences, and many commentators construe the verse this way, but it is by no means, as Schoors implies, the only option, and it unnecessarily creates significant problems. To take the order as subject–pronoun–predicate as does, e.g., Fox ('And the advantage of a land in all regards is <in every worked field [?]>') presents the difficulty (amongst others) that such an order would be highly unusual.

My own reading takes the verse as a whole to represent, in fact, an extended form of the normal subject–predicate–pronoun construction, in which the basic statement is supplemented with an additional description of the predicate. Such further specification is not uncommon: see, e.g., Deut 4:24 'For YHWH your God is a devouring fire, a jealous God'; Exod 32:16 'the writing was the writing of God, carved on the tablets'. Literally, therefore, I am reading 'profit from the land, it (is) above everyone, a king…'. The recent translation by HCM is superficially similar ('And the profit of land—he is over everything, a king…'), but they understand a reference to the king getting the profit—something like 'And (in relation to) the profit of land, he is over everything, the king…'.

5.8 (ET 5.9) king of any cultivated ground] Lit. 'a king for countryside/a field (that) is tilled'. The point is that profit is king wherever there is a profit to be made—most notably, perhaps, in the agriculture that fuels the economy, but it is possible that by שדה נעבד Qohelet is making a distinction not between town and country, but between land that is used and land that is unused by humans. Haupt talks of 'a civilized land' here, and Qohelet could indeed be saying that profit is king wherever there is civilization.

The Hebrew מלך לשדה is indefinite, and the article in G τοῦ ἀγροῦ εἰργασμένου probably translational (despite the usual fidelity of the translator when it comes to articles): I take the reference to be to 'any given land', not land in general or some specific plot of land. שדה is open land, or a piece of land, that is not necessarily used for agriculture—Esau is 'skilful at hunting, a man of שדה' (Gen 25.27)—although it can be used of land which has been farmed or, more broadly, of the agricultural land around or belonging to a city (e.g. 1 Chr 6.41 ET 6.56). Where we find the niphʻal of עבד in biblical usage, on the other hand, it is used solely of preparing ground for sowing, or perhaps more generally of cultivating land and the plants grown in it (Deut 21.4; Ezek 36.9, 34; cf. the uses of the qal in, e.g., Gen 2.5, 15; Deut 28.39; Isa 30.24):[6]

---

[6] This tells against the proposal of Schulte, 'Zu Koh. 5,7 u. 8', who would understand 'ein König für ein geknechtetes Reich', 'a king for an enslaved kingdom'. That sense is not unattractive in context, but it is unlikely that it would have been expressed using these words. Zimmermann, 'Aramaic Provenance', 37-38, also tries to find a different sense for the verb, but by proposing that it renders an Aramaic משתעבדא. He cites *b. Baba Meṣiʻa* 73b for the proper sense, and translates 'even a king is dependent on a field'. The talmudic passage that he cites describes the more complicated situation of land that is 'in service' to the king for taxes (those who pay them are allowed to consume produce from it), and on the previous folio 73a the term also appears with reference to land 'in service' (leased) to sharecroppers. This is a technical usage, related to leases, liens and other forms of temporary possession, and if that sense were really in play, it would mean that the king is temporarily owned by, or for the sake of a field—some way from the idea of his depending on it for income. In fact, the Aramaic term is used in one version of T here, where the text talks of it being proper even for the king to be made to serve as a servant for his field, which tends to suggest that the Aramaic Zimmermann proposes simply would not have conveyed the meaning he wants.

we are dealing with farming, therefore, rather than the countryside in some more general sense. HCM speak of 'arable land'.

The construction is curious: the versions (except perhaps T) have probably taken נעבד to be a participle, but the consonants can alternatively be read as a third-person singular qatal; since it is in pause, moreover, even the vocalization in M allows it to be read as qatal (which is how it is parsed in BDB, *HALOT*), so that the expression may literally be either 'tilled land' or 'land it has been tilled'.[7] If we read it that latter way, it is probably to be understood as an asyndetic relative clause (GKC §155 f; J-M §158 a), which is how I have translated it, and this is equivalent to the participle if שדה is the subject. The sentence can also be read less naturally, though, with יתרון as the subject, and the niphʿal treated as a simple passive, meaning '(profit) is served as king in any field'—although both readings amount to the same thing.

It is much more difficult to construe the verb with מלך as subject, but there have long been attempts to do so, often in pursuit of an assertion that the country benefits from a king who takes an interest in agriculture: this is apparently how T read it, and Delitzsch notes that such a reading is taken for granted by Rashi, Ibn Ezra and others. Among more recent commentators, Hertzberg, translates 'ein König, der dem Ackerland dient', 'a king who serves the farmland', and Gordis likes 'for even a king is subject to the land'. Whitley, who shows a somewhat greater awareness of the obstacles to reading the verb that way, argues from the use of the niphʿal as a middle voice in later Hebrew that נעבד can mean 'is served', or 'benefits'—although to achieve 'a king benefits from the land' he then has implausibly to read -ל in the sense 'from', in support of which he can cite only its use in certain temporal expressions; this interpretation is, nevertheless, accepted by Longman.

Seow avoids the possibility of taking the king as subject by re-dividing the text in such a way that מלך disappears: ויתרון ארץ בכלה ואם שדה לכל נעבד.

Although he does not adopt it, Piotti, 'Osservazioni su alcuni problemi I', 178, thinks that the idea of dependence could be implied in the Hebrew itself, *via* the notion of being 'in service to': I doubt that is true, but the key point, in any case, is that the use of the Hebrew verb in connection with land makes it difficult to overlook the normal sense.

[7] Richter, 'Kohelet', 447, goes in a completely different direction, reading the verb as first-person plural, 'for him [the king] must we till', an interpretation that leads him also to emend לשדה to לו שדה. Another odd solution is offered by Bühlmann, 'Thinking in Greek', 107, who believes that the intended voice of נעבד must be active, referring to 'a king who works for agriculture', and that the verb is in the niphʿal (which makes it appear passive) because it has been influenced by technical usage of the Greek deponent verb ἐργάζομαι. Krüger notes the interesting translation offered in H. Fisch (ed.), *The Holy Scriptures* (Jerusalem, 1992), which takes neither the king nor the land as subject, but which does require the verb similarly to be understood as active: 'he who tills a field is a king'.

This he takes to mean: 'the advantage of land is in its yield, that is, if the field is cultivated for [its] yield', adopting the meaning 'yield' for כלה and כל (see the previous note). Fox also disposes of מלך, but by emendation rather than re-division: מלך לשדה becomes בכל שדה, 'in every cultivated field', by which he understands: 'a country that has all of its fields cultivated has an advantage over others. Far better for a country to be thoroughly agrarian rather than to be burdened with a stratified and self-serving bureaucracy.'

Disconnecting 'king' from 'land' in a very different way, Haupt and Barton take לשדה נעבד to be epexegetical of the preceding ארץ: a country will profit from having a king, that is, if it is a certain type of country. Pinker thinks that שדה נעבד is simply part of a gloss, כל שדה נעבד: Qohelet himself declared that 'the advantage of a country in everything is a king', to which somebody else wrote a rejoinder in the margin: 'each field is fully cultivated'; when the gloss found its way into the text, the כ of כל dropped out after מלך.[8] Galling, 'Kohelet-Studien', 284 n. 2, emends to לשר ולעבד, so that there is a king 'for prince and servant'. Setting aside any other objections to these readings, they all seem to offer a sense that is, by Qohelet's standards, extremely dreary and feeble, and that offers no very adequate explanation of, or response to, the issues raised in the previous verse.

5.9 (ET 5.10) No-one who...will ever] Lit. 'One who...will not'. In the light of passages like Prov 12.1; 17.9; 21.17; 22.11, there seems little reason to suppose that אהב כסף must be a calque on some Greek term like φιλάργυρος or φιλόπλουτος, as suggested by, e.g., Lohfink. The problem is not just that such uses probably precede the Hellenistic period (so Chango, *L'Ecclésiaste*, 81), but that this is a perfectly natural Hebrew usage.

5.9 (ET 5.10) so will whoever loves a lot of it be satisfied by any yield?] Lit. 'and who loving (it) in great quantity will be filled by a harvest?' The text as it stands is difficult. We would expect to find a verb before תבואה, and in the absence of that verb, it would be reasonable to supply the preceding לא ישבע: it is more than awkward, however, to supply just ישבע for an existing לא. That לא, furthermore, is not reflected in G, which does, however, have a pronoun in the same position, variously attested as αὐτῶν or αὐτοῦ. There is no equivalent for that pronoun in M, and it is tempting, therefore, to suppose that it somehow corresponds to לא: McNeile (143, 159) speculates, accordingly, that G* was αὐτῷ for לו, an interpretation of an original לוא. Euringer, very differently, thinks that there was originally an οὐ in G, reflecting לא, but that it dropped out after αὐτοῦ.

There are strong grounds for supposing, however, that G* was αὐτῶν (which, as Goldman suggests, is probably because the translator read בהמונם, understanding it to have a plural suffix pronoun); it is unlikely, on the other

---

[8] Pinker, 'The Advantage of a Country in Ecclesiastes 5:8'. Although his solution is unconvincing, Pinker does offer one of the best summaries of scholarship on this text, and a good analysis of the problems.

hand, that G ever had an equivalent to לא.⁹ This casts doubt on the originality of that לא, which is anomalous in M, and has provoked implausible efforts elsewhere to read תבואה as a verb: an attempted derivation from בוא is reflected in T לעלמא דאתי, 'for the world to come', in an anonymous hexaplaric reading [δ]ώρα ἐν πλήθει [ο]ὐκ ἐλεύσεται, 'gifts will not come in plenty',¹⁰ and, more recently, in Gordis' reading 'it will not come to him'. S ܠܐ ܢܓܕ܂ܘ܂ܗ܂, *lʾ nqdywhy*, Hie *non fruetur eis* and V *fructus non capiet ex eis* all similarly translate the clause as though it has a verb here, but are probably rendering freely or guessing, rather than attempting a direct translation of תבואה.

Since Qohelet elsewhere uses מי as an interrogative rather than an indefinite pronoun (except in 9.4), we should probably not, in fact, expect a negative particle here: this is most likely a rhetorical question. M, therefore, has a לא which is stranded and redundant, while G has an αὐτῶν for which there is no antecedent.¹¹ Goldman's solution is to relocate the final מ from the presumed בהמונם of G's source-text to the beginning of the next word, taking it as comparative, 'and the one who loves wealth more than the harvest, this too is vanity', which is awkward and does not give a good meaning. I think it is more likely that both M and the source-text of G go back to a text that had ימלא in parallel with ישבע (so, similarly, 1.8; cf. Pss 17.14; 107.9; Ezek 7.19), and that this was mis-divided (probably under the influence of the preceding clause) to give בהמ(ו)נם לא → לא בהמונים, which, if the plural is not written *plene*, has the faults of both G and M. In M, the mysterious final מ has been eliminated, whilst in G the redundant לא has been removed, but the original

---

⁹ There is, correspondingly, no textual basis for Whitley's reconstruction לא לו תבואה, 'has no gain', for which we should, anyway, expect a construction with אין, not לא. Mutius notes that the discussion of this passage in *b. Makkot* 10a presents a text (in Goldschmidt's edition) where לו stands in the place of M לא, and is interpreted accordingly. Although Mutius connects this with G, it is probably a secondary reaction to the awkward לא. See Mutius, 'Eine talmudische Textvariante'.

¹⁰ On the basis of translation technique, this is assigned by Marshall to σ' or θ'. The margins of ms 252, where this reading is found, have been clipped for binding, so that some characters from the marginal readings have been lost (photographs are available at the Biblioteca Medicea Laurenziana website, where the manuscript is Plut.8.27). As Marshall notes, traces of the δ are visible, however, and the reading is not in doubt. Since attributions are usually set above the readings and somewhat inset in this manuscript, it is unlikely that any attribution has been lost this way.

¹¹ The translator has probably attempted to make sense of his text as a suggestion that nobody has ever loved a single product when there are many of them. This does not stand directly in parallel with the preceding thought, and probably motivates also the reading of the verb as qatal, rather than as a second participle. Apart from V, which paraphrases, the other versions prefer to match the first verb, and we may note the participial καὶ ὁ ὑπεραγαπῶν, 'the one loving excessively', of σ' (cf. Gentry).

text would have read ומי אהב בהמון ימלא תבואה, '(he who loves money will not be sated by money,) and who, loving בהמון, will be filled by תבואה?' Since it would not involve the assumption that the error occurred in a text written *plene* but was found by G in a text written defectively, it is marginally simpler to suppose that the reading was מלא rather than ימלא: this would give a similar sense, but offer a worse parallel to ישבע. Intriguingly (but probably coincidentally), Theodulphian manuscripts of V (cf. the Introduction, pp. 144-5), have here *auarus non impletur pecunia et qui amat diuitias fructus non impletur ex eis*, 'the greedy man is not filled by money and whoever loves riches is not filled with the fruit from them', which replaces the normal V *capiet* ('reap' fruit) with a second 'filled'; see BM Add ms 24142, f. 137v; Kongelige Bibliotek, NKS 1 2°, f. 35r; Württemburgische Landesbibliothek HB II, 16, f. 109v; Paris, BnF, lat. 9380, f. 179r.

S, Hie, V see a reference to loving wealth here, but the verb אהב does not elsewhere take an object with ־ב, and in the absence of any other examples, it is doubtful that we can simply extrapolate such usage from the use of the preposition after verbs like חפץ and חשק (as, e.g., Barton, McNeile 70, Seow suggest). We must either delete the ־ב of בהמון as a dittograph (so, e.g., Gordis, Fox, Whitley, *BHS*), or read the word as an adverbial expression, and the latter suits the sense: המון can be used of wealth, but it does not mean 'wealth' *per se*, either in biblical or post-biblical Hebrew (that meaning is achieved in S and T by reading the Aramaic ממון, which may either have emerged as a variant in the Hebrew tradition or have been adopted individually by each translator, but is, in any case, *pace* Graetz, clearly secondary). Rather, the noun המון nearly always indicates a crowd or the sort of noise made by a crowd (sometimes metaphorically, of rain, waves, wheels etc.). It is used of wealth in Ezek 29.19; 30.4, where it represents the booty collected from Egypt, and in 1 Chr 29.16 of the resources collected for re-building of the temple, but the point in those passages is that these are heaps of goods, and that is probably the sense in Isa 60.5, where it refers to the produce of the sea. The use in Ps 37.16, where המון means 'a lot', contrasted with 'a little', reinforces the fact that it connotes not value but quantity.[12]

I take אהב, therefore, to have an implicit כסף as its object here (as it did explicitly in the previous clause), and בהמון to be a qualification: whoever loves money never has enough, and whoever loves *a lot* ([money] in great quantity) is certainly not going to be satisfied with a תבואה. This is apparently the way that it is understood by G, which translates ἐν πλήθει, and probably also by T in a double translation ממון יתיר, 'excessive wealth'.

---

[12] As observed in Pinker, 'On Cattle and Cowboys in Kohelet 5,9b', 265-66. Pinker is also right to emphasize (267) the agricultural reference of תבואה. We do not, however, need to follow him in emending בהמון to בהמות, and translating 'who loves cattle would not be sated with crops'.

The following תבואה is often translated as though it, too, were a general term for wealth or gain, but it has a basic reference to the harvest or to produce from agriculture, and although this can be extended figuratively to other sorts of product, it generally retains that connotation: cf. Prov 8.19, where it represents what is gained from wisdom, but still stands in parallel with 'fruit'. The problem portrayed in 5.7 is explained in two stages: there is misrule because ultimately power is controlled by profit, and because the desire for money can never be satisfied by whatever the workers produce.

5.10 (ET 5.11) The more there is…the more there are] Lit. 'with the increasing of…(those consuming it) increase', or possibly 'when there is much of…'. According to M, the Hebrew uses forms from the verb רבה in both places, but unless G ἐν πλήθει, 'in plenty' (cf. S, Hie, V), is interpretative or an unusually free rendering, the translator may have read ברב, as McNeile, 23, suggests, rather than the initial infinitive ברבות (cf. 1.18; 5.2; 5.6; 11.1); hexaplaric manuscripts restore the verbal form as πληθυνθῆναι (ms 253 πληθῆναι). I think it is more likely, however, that the translator has simply vocalized רבות differently and taken it as a noun or as רַבּוֹת, 'many'; cf. T כד סגיעא טיבותא, 'when goods are many'; V *ubi multae sunt opes*, 'where riches are many'.

5.10 (ET 5.11) prosperity…consume it] For similar uses of אכל, cf. 5.18 and 6.2, and on the role of the verb in the current discussion, see the commentary. Qohelet uses טובה also in 4.8; 5.17; 6.3, 6; 7.14; 9.18. Although it may indeed be used of prosperity or for the material good things in life, Qohelet tends to use it to express peace or contentment, and in none of these places does he refer to 'goods' (as, e.g., RSV translates here), which is not the normal sense of the word. In this context, some reference to material rather than spiritual prosperity seems to be required (cf. Krüger, 'Das Gute', 53-54), but the point is probably not simply that any accumulation of possessions will disappear or be divided up by a flood of people. In 6.3, where הטובה is also presented as something that can be consumed (cf. Job 21.25), Qohelet clearly believes that the man should have found satisfaction (his appetite should have been sated) in his good fortune, and it is doubtful that he understands the consumption of טובה to be inherently a bad thing.

Rahlfs has τῆς ἀγαθωσύνης here, but the article (which is the reading of α′ according to ms 252) is barely represented in the manuscript tradition. G seems, in fact, to have read טובה, without the article of M (cf. Goldman): this is more in line with Qohelet's usage elsewhere (the article appears only in 6.3), so I think it is probably original—although it does not affect the sense whether we read an article or not.

5.10 (ET 5.11) what aptitude does anyone with a claim to it have] Lit. 'what aptitude (is) for its owner/someone laying claim to it'. Regarding the problems around the sense of כשרון, see the note at 2.21. Gordis suggests that the issue here is 'What value is there in superior ability for the owner?', but that makes מה do a lot of work, and there is anyway no good reason to suppose that כשרון refers to ability, or that, as is more commonly asserted, it connotes the owner's 'reward'—although S ܕܝܠܗ ywtrn' makes it equivalent here to יתרון.[13] As usual, G renders with ἀνδρεία (cf. Hie *fortitudo*), and σ' has ἀνδραγάθημα.[14] I have understood the noun in 2.21 and 4.4 to indicate aptitude in the context of work. Here, the point might alternatively be that there is nothing which the owner 'is able to do' in these circumstances except watch, which is essentially the traditional interpretation, but that is a rather different meaning: the constraints upon the owner, on such an understanding, arise from external circumstances rather than from personal abilities or motivations, which seem to be integral to Qohelet's uses of the noun elsewhere. If we are to retain any consistency in the way we understand this noun, then we need to consider the possibility that Qohelet is not talking about a constraint on the original owner, but saying that each person who consumes the prosperity does so without having possessed any aptitude themselves other than for looking on. That understanding could be reached by reading בעליה as plural: with a suffix, בעל often takes a construct form בעלי, which is indistinguishable from the plural form, and if the singular suffix pronoun on the subsequent עיניו points to בעל here, and not the plural בעלים, that pronoun could itself be taken as distributive. We could also, more simply, just understand the whole expression that way: 'what aptitude is there for each/any בעל...?'.

Although Gentry, 'Role of the Three', 167, describes G's rendering of לבעליה with τῷ παρ' αὐτῆς here as 'a clever one, accomplishing both formal and functional equivalence at the same time', the use of παρά to represent בעל when it has a suffix pronoun is a peculiarity of the G translation of Ecclesiastes: cf. also 5.12; 7.12; 8.8; 12.11 (contrast 10.11, and ὁ ἔχων in 10.20, where there is no suffix, but see the notes there), and note that the translator uses παρά with the genitive only to translate בעל (although it is used comparatively with the accusative in 2.9 and 3.19). σ' here has the more conventional τῷ ἔχοντι (var. σχοντι) αὐτό, 'to the one having it' (which has influenced

---

[13] There is a widely attested variant ܕܗܘܘ ܟܫܝܪ *whwt kšyr'*, which uses the Syriac cognate of כשרון, and means in Syriac 'it is the success/prosperity': Lane, 'Lilies', 489, describes this as 'a translation according to consonants rather than meaning', and Kamenetzky, 198, has no doubt that it is secondary. Quite independently, Sacchi would read יתרון in M rather than כשרון, which, he claims, makes no sense.

[14] Although ἀνδραγάθημα is regularly used for 'manly deeds', the two words ἀνδρεία and ἀνδραγάθημα are distinguished in the grammatical treatise Περὶ ὁμοίων καὶ διαφόρων λέξεων (traditionally attributed to Ammonius Grammaticus, but now generally taken to have been originally the work of Herennius Philo in the first or second century CE) on the following basis: ἀνδραγάθημα μὲν γάρ ἐστιν, εἰ καὶ τὴν ψυχικὴν ἀρετὴν ἔχει μαρτυροῦσαν· ἀνδρία δὲ δύναμις ἐπαινουμένη; that is, ἀνδραγάθημα refers to the possession of spiritual excellence, ἀνδρεία to laudable power.

the ἔχοντι αὐτήν found in hexaplaric manuscripts of G); cf. Hie *habenti illa*. On the face of it, G more naturally means 'he who is owned by something', than 'he who owns it': as MM notes, οἱ παρ' αὐτοῦ is widely used in the papyri of those who represent or are associated with somebody (not of the somebody who is represented; see also Gwynn, 'Notes', 119-20), and expressions like τὰ παρ' αὐτῆς (Mk 5.26) indicate what is possessed, rather than what possesses.

The translator is probably rendering in this way because he recognizes the broader uses of בעל to indicate close connection rather than possession (see the note at 10.11). That requires imputing to παρά the sort of usage that we find in the English 'man *of* arms' or 'bird *of* prey'. For any translator, בעל can be a tricky term, since it frequently indicates a variety of commitments to, or associations with something, rather than simply ownership or mastery of it (as in 8.8, for example, or Prov 1.19; 17.8). The 'owners' of 'good' in Prov 3.27-28, indeed, are apparently not those who actually hold the money or goods in their possession, but those to whom they are owed or promised. If the G translator has indeed been 'clever' here, it is not least by preserving the ambiguity of the Hebrew. I am inclined to do the same. In 5.12, Qohelet will shortly use בעל to describe a man whose 'ownership' of money consists not in his tangible possession or control of it, but in the fact that it is kept for him by a bank or some such, so that he has a claim on it comparable to that of the 'owners' in Prov 3.27. That is not, of course, precisely what is envisaged here, but it does suggest that a tax-collector, say, might consider himself the בעל of monies owed, just as much as would the man who owed the tax, and that the scope of the term here cannot be confined simply to the holder or originator of the wealth concerned.

5.10 (ET 5.11) except for] As Goldman notes, G usually renders כי אם with εἰ μὴ or ὅτι ἐάν (ἀλλ' ἢ is used nowhere else, and ἀλλά itself, indeed, is curiously absent from the Greek version of Ecclesiastes), while Rahlfs' ὅτι ἀλλ' ἢ is derived principally from hexaplaric manuscripts. It is unlikely, therefore, that the better attested variant ὅτι ἀρχὴ simply arose from a corruption of ΑΛΛΗ to ΑΡΧΗ, as Euringer suggests (cf. Klostermann, *De libri Coheleth*, 59), and Goldman takes it to be G*; cf. Gentry, 'Role of the Three', 168. Goldman himself takes this ὅτι ἀρχὴ to have resulted from a misreading of אם as אם, which appears in Ezek 21.26 in the phrase אל אם הדרך בראש שני הדרכים (cf. Gentry's apparatus). That, however, is very unlikely indeed. The passage in Ezekiel is talking about a place where the road forks, and uses an idiom אם הדרך, 'mother of the way', to describe that place: אם by itself just means 'mother', and nowhere else presents any equivalent to ἀρχή. The Greek version of Ezekiel, incidentally, uses ἐπὶ τὴν ἀρχαίαν ὁδὸν for אל אם הדרך, and ἐπ' ἀρχῆς there represents בראש.

It is improbable, moreover, that the translator would have ignored the familiar expression כי אם without a good reason to do so, especially when the resulting ὅτι ἀρχὴ τοῦ ὁρᾶν ὀφθαλμοῖς αὐτοῦ makes little obvious sense, and has hardly been driven by the desire to find a particular meaning in the verse. McNeile, 143, suggests, on the face of it more plausibly, that the *K*ᵉ*thîbh* ראית has been misread as ראשית. In that case, however, the presence of τοῦ ὁρᾶν requires that the source-text must also have contained the *Q*ᵉ*rê* ראות, and the absence of an equivalent to אם has to be explained (McNeile thinks it 'was ousted by the following אא' in the text with ἀλλ᾽ ἤ, but offers no explanation for its absence in manuscripts with ἀρχή): the suggestion ἀρχή = ראשית from ראית is much less straightforward, therefore, than a first glance would suggest. There is no tidy answer, but it seems likely that the problems pre-date the Greek translator, and that he read כי ראש ראות, or כי ראשית ראות, a text that had been corrupted somehow in transmission. One possibility, close to McNeile's suggestion, is that ראית had been introduced before ראות, as a correction or in order to preserve both variants, and became entangled with the אם. In any case, it is unlikely that G presents a better reading here than M.

In S we find a significant variant ܡܛܠ ܕܡܢ ܪܝܫ (ܗܘ) ܓܐܐ ܣܘܐ ܚܙܝܬ ܒܥܝܢܝ *mṭl dmn ryš(y) ḥzyt b ʿyny*, 'for what is first/best of seeing with the eyes', which Lane, 'Lilies', 483, sees as a conflation of phrases from 1.14 and 2.14, but which is probably based on the version of G with ἀρχή. On the other hand, σ' εἰ μὴ μόνον is probably just 'a reinforced translation of M', as Goldman puts it, and θ' εἰ μὴ τοῦ ὁρᾶν is what we would expect G to have read were it rendering the same text as M.

5.10 (ET 5.11) for looking on with his eyes] Lit. 'the sight/seeing of his eyes'. Neither the *K*ᵉ*thîbh* ראית nor the *Q*ᵉ*rê* ראות appears elsewhere in biblical Hebrew as a substantive (although Montgomery, 'Notes', 243, identifies ראית with the רית in line 12 of the Mesha inscription, which apparently means something like 'a spectacle'). The former can, however, be read as רְאִיַת, the construct form of a noun ראיה or ראייה, found in later Hebrew with a range of meanings (including 'sight', 'seeing', 'glance'); the latter can be read רְאוֹת, which is the infinitive construct of ראה, and this is almost certainly how G and θ' τοῦ ὁρᾶν understand it (cf. Yi, 20), treating עיניו as an accusative of respect. This is the pointing applied to the *Kethîbh* in M at Isa 42.20, where the same *Qerê* / *Kethîbh* occurs, rather than the רְאוּת suggested by the pointing here, which is probably intended to retain the *Kethîbh*'s construal as a noun (Mᴸ, incidentally, omits the circellus for the note in both places, perhaps because in both places ראית lies at one end of the line, immediately next to the note). It is harder, though, to judge the original basis either of the verbal forms used in Hie, V, T, or of the substantives in S and σ' θεωρία ὀφθαλμῶν αὐτοῦ, 'sight/ seeing of his eyes'. Goldman takes ראות to be original (and intended to be read as an infinitive), using criteria that are more stylistic than strictly text critical. Schoors, *The Preacher* I, 35, on the other hand, opts for ראית, but compares the two forms as substantives (in accordance with the pointing of M), without apparently asking whether the infinitive has a better claim than either noun. Other commentators, such as Seow, have made their choice simply on the basis of the sense that they prefer, and there really are no other strong grounds for a decision.

In terms of the meaning, it is difficult to ignore the very similar expression, מראה עינים, which occurs in 6.9 and 11.9, and which is discussed in the notes to 6.9. It is also possible, however, that the different form here actually distinguishes this occurrence from those others, and the link may be no more than that both expressions employ a redundant reference to seeing 'with eyes'.

5.11 (ET 5.12) sweet is the sleep] On 'sweet', see the note at 11.7. Rashbam reads שנת as the construct form of שָׁנָה, 'year', taking this as a reference to the farm labourer's year. The ambiguity is exploited elsewhere in Jewish exegesis (not least by Rashi), and probably lies behind T's complicated account here, in which both death (sleep) and length of life (years) figure prominently.

5.11 (ET 5.12) underling] Lit. 'the one who serves' or 'the slave/servant'. M reads a participle but G τοῦ δούλου has apparently vocalized as a noun הָעֶבֶד; cf. the La *serui* of Ambrose, *De Nabuthae*, 6.29. The readings of σ' and θ' are more problematic: following Field, Goldman takes the Syrohexaplaric annotations to suggest that they support G here (cf. Salters, 'Textual Criticism', 58), but Gentry, 'Role of the Three', 169-71, argues persuasively that they in fact read the participle τοῦ δουλεύοντος, with the hexaplaric Greek manuscripts. It is perhaps from σ' that Jerome has derived the participial Hie, V *operanti*. S could be read as either noun or participle. *BHQ* prefers to read the noun, with G, but the consonantal text is simply ambiguous, permitting either reading with no significant difference to the sense. It is naturally tempting to assume that the term refers to someone who works directly for the rich man, but the verb can be used of working generally, not just in domestic service (e.g. Gen 2.5; Exod 5.8), and the noun of subordinates in all sorts of positions (e.g. 2 Kgs 24.1, 10).

5.11 (ET 5.12) whether it's a little or a lot that he eats] Lit. 'if a little and if a lot he will eat'. The fact that the amount eaten by the underling is explicitly described as irrelevant makes it difficult to identify the contrast as between moderation and over-indulgence.

5.11 (ET 5.12) finding satisfaction for a rich man] Lit. '(reaching the point of *or* providing) satiation for a rich man'. M והשבע לעשיר is pointed as two nouns, commonly translated as 'the satiety of the rich man' or similar, and usually taken as the subject of what follows. Also with nouns, σ' reads ἡ δὲ πλησμονὴ τοῦ πλουσίου οὐκ ἐᾷ καθεύδειν, 'but the satisfying of the rich man does not permit sleeping', which probably underpins Hie *et saturitas diuitis non sinit eum dormire* (V is similar; cf. Cannon, 'Jerome and Symmachus', 193). The πλησμονὴ from this has been picked up in hexaplaric manuscripts, but G* has two verbs instead: καὶ τῷ ἐμπλησθέντι τοῦ πλουτῆσαι οὐκ ἔστιν ἀφίων αὐτὸν τοῦ ὑπνῶσαι, 'and for one who is filled by being rich, there is none letting him sleep' (cf. Ambrose, *Explanatio XII Psalmorum*, 1.28.4: *etsi quis satiatus fuerit diuitiis non est qui sinat eum dormire*, 'though whoever would be sated with riches, there is no-one that will allow him to sleep').

Goldman claims 'probably G misunderstood the rather rare form of the [first] noun', and Gordis speaks of it 'failing to recognize the late genitive construction of השבע לעשיר', but it might be fairer to suppose that the translator of G approached the text with an awareness of certain problems: (1) The noun שָׂבָע, as it is pointed in M, occurs otherwise only in Prov 3.10 and a number of times in Gen 41, always with the sense 'plenty' (of crops), and is not an obvious way of talking about wealth more generally. G has accordingly understood the adjective וְהַשָּׂבֵעַ, 'and the sated one' (cf. Yi, 25), which supplies a better counterpart for the servant who has eaten, in the corresponding clause. (2) Classically, -ל is used in place of a simple construct to express the genitive when the *nomen regens* must be marked explicitly as indeterminate and the *nomen rectum* is determinate (cf. GKC §129; J-M §130). Here, השבע is patently not indeterminate, and it would have been perfectly possible for Qohelet to have used the construct. To account for the -ל, therefore, G understands לעשיר as a hiph'il infinitive construct of עשר (so too Yi, 20), with syncopation of the initial ה (לְעַשִּׁיר; for the syncopation, see the note 'get...into trouble' at 5.5). In doing so, it manages to avoid reading an exceptional genitive construction, of a type never used elsewhere in Ecclesiastes, and it is interesting to note that S retains the -ל here, apparently also rejecting a reading as genitive.

In the end, however, G does not itself adequately explain the -ל of לעשיר, since this preposition is not used elsewhere to mark a source of satisfaction or satiation, and the point here is clearly not about being 'too sated to be rich' (see the note on 'too sated for seeing' at 1.8). The difficulties can also be overcome in other ways. Rather than שָׂבָע (the vocalization of which in M may be intended to imply that it is the rich man's 'plenty' that keeps him awake), it seems likely that the author intended the more common שֹׂבַע to be read: this refers specifically to the satisfaction of hunger (although it is used metaphorically at Ps 16.11), and fits the context much better. To eat לשבע is to eat until one is full (Exod 16.3; Lev 25.19; 26.5; Ps 78.25) or until one's appetite is satisfied (Prov 13.25), while one's שבע is the point at which one has eaten enough (Deut 23.25 ET 23.24; Ruth 2.18).

This is, in fact, close to the sense of the noun πλησμονή used by σ', which BDAG defines as the 'process of securing complete satisfaction, satiety esp. w. food and drink', and I think that σ' has properly understood Qohelet's point here: it is not a full stomach that is at issue, but the quest to fill a rich man's stomach, and so to bring him to an elusive state of satisfaction. Correspondingly, השבע לעשיר is not a genitive construction, but means either 'satiation in the case of, or from the viewpoint of the rich man' or 'satiation provided for a rich man'. The word-order, perhaps, marginally favours the latter, which would mean that Qohelet is talking not about the rich man filling himself, but about the worker trying to satisfy the rich man: he would sleep well himself whatever he ate, but trying to provide satisfaction 'to a rich man' leaves him no chance to enjoy that sleep. I have tried to leave both possibilities open in the translation.

5.11 (ET 5.12) gives him no chance to sleep] Qohelet uses constructions with אין quite commonly (cf. Schoors, *The Preacher* I, 151), and generally in the form (*subject*) + אין + *suffix* + *participle*, with the subject, or the suffix that picks it up, acting as protagonist of the participle. So, 4.17, for example, is talking about the fools who offer sacrifice כי אינם יודעים, 'because there is not them knowing' = 'they do not know', and in 1.7 we read about the sea, 'and there is not it filling' = 'it does not fill'. Here matters are complicated by the fact that if the suffix on איננו picks up השבע, the natural subject, then the sense demands that the suffix on לו has to have a separate, human referent, since it is not השבע that will be deprived of sleep. Strictly, this could be either the servant or the rich man.

G's previous construal makes it impossible for the translator to understand the Hebrew in the way just outlined: for him, השבע *is* the rich man. He therefore treats איננו as impersonal and equivalent to אין. In doing so, he may have been influenced by the use of נוח in the qal with impersonal constructions at, e.g., Job 3.13; Isa 23.12, but he has more probably just been forced down this route by his understanding of the verse as a whole. It is unlikely that he actually found אין in his source-text, although had he done so, this would have been a further reason to adopt that understanding.

The hiphʻil of נוח is most often used of 'leaving', as in 2.18 and 10.4. It can very rarely have the sense 'give leave to (do something)' (Ps 105.14 = 1 Chr 16.21 is the clearest example), but it is not a general word for 'permit', and there is still a strong sense of 'leaving someone alone to', or 'giving them a chance to do something' (cf. Judg 16.26).

5.12-19 (ET 5.13-20)

(5.12 ET 5.13) There is something painfully bad I have seen beneath the sun: wealth was being kept for its owner, against a time of trouble, (5.13 ET 5.14) but that wealth was lost in some bad deal. Then he fathered a son, but was completely empty-handed. (5.14 ET 5.15) For he emerged from the womb of his mother naked: he will go on again as he came—and he will take up nothing in his business which can go in his hand. (5.15 ET 5.16) This too is painfully bad, that exactly as he came, so shall he go—and what lasting gain will there be there for him who would work in the wind? (5.16 ET 5.17) Also, for all his days he will feed in darkness, off great resentment, pain, and anger. (5.17 ET 5.18) Look, what I have seen to be good, is that it would be best to eat and drink and find happiness in all his business, at which he will work beneath the sun for the limited duration of his life which God has given him. For that is what is his.

(5.18 ET 5.19) Also, every person to whom God has granted wealth and property, and to whom he has given the power to take enjoyment from them, to take up what is his, and to take pleasure in his business—this is a payment from God, (5.19 ET 5.20) for he will not give much thought to the length of his life when God busies him with the joy of his heart.

Commentary

From the problems that arise from wanting wealth, Qohelet turns now to the related but very different problem of losing wealth. He begins with an example of something that he claims to have seen: a man who had money but has lost it. Not all the details are undisputed (and the text is very difficult in places), but it seems that this man had been saving the money for when he needed it, and lost it just at the point when that need actually arose, leaving him destitute but with a son to raise. He is left to go on no better off than when he was born, and Qohelet predicts that the rest of his days will be dominated by a consuming resentment. He suggests that it would be better for the man instead to get on with his life and to find happiness in what he does. This leads him to a more general statement, that those who have been given wealth and the ability to enjoy it should do so: this is their payment from God, and it will leave them too busy being happy to worry about their own mortality.

The story itself functions as a sort of parable, and enables Qohelet to move through a series of issues. The first bad thing that he identifies is apparently the loss itself, but this is followed by the problem that the man will show no profit for all that he had achieved—and this exemplifies Qohelet's broader concern about the human inability to turn a profit from life, allowing him to make statements that can be read in those terms. In addition, however, the man is going to be miserable, and it is this last problem that provokes a positive reaction: such unhappiness can and should be avoided. As Qohelet generalizes from this, he picks up the ideas of 2.24; 3.12-13, 22, although they are specifically applied now to those who have wealth. In doing so, he implies, perhaps, that the man should have enjoyed his wealth while he had it, as well as that he should enjoy what he can now, but 5.18-19 also provide a transition to what will be his next topic: the situation of those who have wealth without enjoyment.

The relationship between the story and the more general points that Qohelet wishes to make is somewhat strained at times. Essentially, the man of the story experiences prematurely what will happen eventually to everybody: his loss returns him to the state in which he was born, with a successor but nothing to show for his work, which is how all humans will find themselves at death. It is important that his loss be premature, because his state of deprivation is then visible, in a way that a loss at death is not. This leaves a period after his loss and before his death, however, which others will not have. Qohelet fills this by suggesting both that the man will continue to live in his state of deprivation—were he to restore his fortunes, the whole point would be spoiled—and that he will be profoundly unhappy. This provides a useful transition to the theme of happiness, but it changes the role of the man: he can no longer strictly represent everybody, since not everybody will experience continued deprivation in their life, or have the space to reflect on what they have lost. If there is some more general equivalent, it is perhaps to be found in the potential resentment that humans might feel at the rather different 'bad job' or 'bad deal' imposed on them by God (1.13). In any case, though, the difficulty shows not that the story is supposed to be read in some other way, but that it is designed to offer pegs from which Qohelet can hang his observations, not as a strict allegory of human life.

The way that he approaches the issues throughout this discussion, and not merely in the story, leads Qohelet to talk about them in a curiously specific way. The man's circumstances make him untypical, but when he finally moves on, Qohelet does not enlarge his recommendations to encompass all of humanity, and turns instead to the particular case of those humans with wealth and property (perhaps a tiny minority of the population at the time when the book was written). This is an important reminder that, although 5.17 has brought him back to the issue of finding pleasure in what one does, the context here is still a discussion of wealth and of the problems associated with it. Although they do not draw in issues of divine favour, comparable to the ideas that Qohelet rejected earlier in 2.24-26, vv. 18-19 do not attribute wealth to personal merit but to divine action: in a world where humans essentially act out roles assigned to them by God, some will necessarily be rich. This is not portrayed as a reward, and in 6.1-6 Qohelet will emphasize in the strongest terms that this is not necessarily even a good thing for them. That is because, as 5.18 indicates, the assignment of wealth does not in itself entail the ability to enjoy that wealth (which is also assigned by God, but apparently separately). The ideal, of course, is what Qohelet portrays here: wealth and a capacity for enjoyment of wealth, but this is an ideal from which most people will in practice be excluded, because they lack one or other, or else have been granted neither. Although the closing verses here are relevant to all humans in terms of the principles they imply, they do not enunciate a policy that all humans can follow.

5.12 ET 5.13] Although it is widely suggested that his wealth itself somehow harmed the man (cf. RSV 'riches were kept by their owner to his hurt'), the Hebrew more probably means that the riches were kept 'for (a time of) his harm'—i.e. for a time when he might be in trouble. It is neither the wealth itself nor his retention of it that harms the man, but his loss of it, and his reaction to that loss.

5.13 ET 5.14] 'Bad deal' here is the same expression used in 1.13 to ask whether God has given humans a 'bad job' to do, and in 4.8

to characterize Qohelet's experience of working for nobody. The link with 1.13, in particular, seems likely to be a deliberate hint that Qohelet is using this story to address bigger issues, should anyone have missed the point. In any case, though, the expression seems to imply engagement in a task that proves unprofitable: we are not told the nature of this venture, nor whether the man himself was responsible for its failure, and it is unlikely that Qohelet wants to place any emphasis here on the vicissitudes of life. There certainly seems little justification, moreover, for trying to place this common experience, so very generally described, in a particular socio-economic context (as, e.g., Fischer, *Skepsis*, 64-65), or to specify more precisely what has gone wrong (Lohfink, 'Kohelet und die Banken': see the notes).

5.14-15 ET 5.15-16] The situation has resulted from the man's loss of his wealth, and the wording is strongly reminiscent of Job's famous declaration in Job 1.21, 'Naked I came from my mother's womb, and naked shall I return there; YHWH gave, and YHWH has taken away; blessed be the name of YHWH'. In Hos 2.5 (ET 2.3), there is a similar threat to strip someone naked and to 'make her as (on) the day she was born', so Qohelet may be drawing on a familiar image of personal ruin.[1] Not least for that reason, we should probably not, as some commentators suggest, take the reference to birth here as an indication that the subject is the new-born son, rather than the man. Qohelet's point is not that the son will live a life of poverty, or even, more simply, that he will receive no inheritance, but that the man himself has been returned to the state in which he was born, with nothing to show for his life so far. The son is introduced, I

---

[1] The reference to nakedness recurs in Philo, *De specialibus legibus* 1.295: γυμνὸς μὲν γάρ θαυμάσιε ἦλθες γυμνὸς δὲ πάλιν ἄπεις, 'for naked, O fine one, you came, but naked again you will leave', where it is a reference to all human life. More generally, Sir 40.1 describes the course of a human life in terms of emergence from the womb through to a 'return'. Qohelet avoids the puzzling claim in Job, that the dead in some sense return to the womb, which is discussed in Vall, 'The Enigma of Job 1,21a'. Vall (334-35) sees the 'naked' return in terms of Job remaining in his torn garments or stripped of the flesh with which God has clothed him (Job 10.11), but if there is an established imagery at work in all these passages, it may be that Qohelet actually draws out the original point—that the dead lose everything, even the clothes off their back. We should probably not strive too hard to reconcile this idea with actual burial practices.

think, at least in part to make the situation seem even worse—this is a man who now has family responsibilities, but lacks even the resources that he put aside for less predictable contingencies. In view of his earlier attitudes, though, it is possible that Qohelet is trying also to make clear that having a child does not count toward the things that we might take with us when we go.

Further complications emerge as the account goes on, and when Qohelet predicts that penury will be the constant state of the man, we could reasonably start to object: there will presumably be opportunities for that man to replace what he has lost, so how on earth does Qohelet know that this will be so? The oddness of this claim is only highlighted, furthermore, by the fact that Qohelet states it as a prediction, when he could easily just have made it part of the report—'I saw a man lose all his money and the rest of his life was spent in misery'. This is a consequence of (and an indication of) the story's symbolic or exemplary character, which has become more explicit by this point: Qohelet is extrapolating, from the man's experience of loss, the future fate of all humans, and this requires him, within the constraints of the story, to talk about the future situation of the man himself. The point is driven home by 5.15, which repeats the claim of 5.14, but in rather different terms—picking up the language of human coming and going from 1.4, paraphrasing the programmatic question of 1.3, and generalizing the statement away from the man who *did* work to encompass anyone who *would* work. While the second verse seems initially just to duplicate the claims of the first, therefore, it actually becomes a statement of life as a whole. What happened to the man is indicative of what will happen to all humans: he lost his money prematurely, to be sure, but his situation is now that which everyone will face eventually, when they depart the world as naked as when they came, and their work proves to have been 'in the wind'—all blown away.

At the beginning of 5.14, I have followed the reading of 4QQoh[a], which has 'for' where later texts and versions have 'just as'. Syntactically, this simplifies what would otherwise be a complicated and redundant double comparison (see the notes), but it does require some explanation itself. I take Qohelet to be introducing his statements about the man's 'nakedness' initially as an explanation or expansion of his claim that he is empty-handed: his poverty is not just a consequence of his loss, but is a return to the natural state with which he began, and will end, his life.

5.16 ET 5.17] The text is very difficult here, and probably corrupt, so although the general sense is plain, it might be unwise to place too much weight on any of the details. Qohelet is apparently not continuing the description of the previous verse, or suggesting that every human will have spent their days in misery before they die, but is instead beginning a new point. Having spelled out the fact that the man has been returned to the state in which he was born, and drawn from that statements about the ultimate fruitlessness of life, he now turns to a prediction that the man will not just be poor, but will also be profoundly unhappy and resentful: he depicts him in darkness, sustaining himself with his grievances. This will lead Qohelet to a response that again has implications for everybody, but it seems likely that this new point remains anchored in the story, rather than that he is predicting such extraordinary unhappiness for everybody: what marks the man out from others is that his loss is premature, so that he will have time to grieve for it, while most people will be stripped of everything only when they die. As Qohelet will indicate shortly (6.4; cf. 11.8), darkness is something that awaits everybody, so the man's premature loss is matched in part, perhaps, by a premature experience of death—although actual death will involve none of the emotions that he feels here.

5.17 ET 5.18] The vocabulary echoes 3.13 very strongly, so although Qohelet is making a recommendation that is superficially directed at the man—who should not nibble at his anger in the dark, but feast and find happiness in his work under the sun—it is clear that he has returned to the ideas expressed there about what all humans should do (cf. Enns, 'Evaluation', 128-33). This verse also pulls in, however, the notion of pleasure as a 'portion' ('what is his'), which Qohelet associated more specifically with the pleasure of work in 2.10 and 3.22, and a reminder of human mortality, expressed in terms similar to those he used in 2.3. A lot of important threads are being drawn together here, therefore, and this is Qohelet's fullest statement so far of his ideas about the way human life should be lived.

5.18-19 ET 5.19-20] When Qohelet moves explicitly away from the man of the story, he implicitly extends the recommendation of the previous verse to cover a different group: those who possess wealth and the power to enjoy it. This is, of course, teeing up for the next story he will tell, of a man unable to enjoy his wealth, but it reintroduces an idea with which 2.24-26 had engaged: the capacity of humans to take pleasure in what they have is not entirely under the control of humans themselves. Indeed, the language used here has a legal ring to it: God may grant humans the right to take advantage of what they have while it is in their possession, without giving them true ownership of it (what a lawyer might call 'usufruct': see the notes). As the story that follows will show, he may also withhold that right—although Qohelet never clarifies the grounds on which he might choose to grant it or not. Once again echoing 3.13, the double dispensation of property and of the capacity to enjoy it is described as a gift, or more properly a payment from God. Verse 19 has attracted much discussion, not least because many commentators have been unhappy with the implication that God offers happiness almost like a narcotic. That does seem, however, in fact to be more or less Qohelet's contention: joy is a reward from God because it keeps humans from thinking too much about the limited span of their lives.

Notes

5.12 (ET 5.13) something painfully bad] In accordance with normal usage, רעה חולה is most naturally read as 'something bad (that is) sick': a noun followed by a participle. T בישותא מרעיתא, S ܟܘܪܗܢ ܕܒܝܫܬ *kwrhn' dbyšt'*, σ' νόσος κακή, Hie *languor pessimus*, and V *infirmitas pessima* all, however, translate the expression as though the word-order were reversed and treat חולה as a substantive to get 'a bad sickness', although no such noun is attested elsewhere with that sense. G ἀρρωστία, 'sickness', furthermore, not only takes חולה as a substantive, but seems not to render רעה at all. When exactly the same expression occurs again in 5.15, G has πονηρὰ ἀρρωστία, which now reflects רעה, while S, Hie, V, all retain their reversal of the words and reading of חולה as a substantive, despite using slightly different vocabulary.

It is difficult to know how much of this is simply a matter of translation or interpretation. In the case of חולה, it is possible that (as McNeile, 144, suggests) all these versions actually read חלי in both the verses where חולה appears, with חולה itself only arriving late in the textual tradition as an interpretative replacement, and *BHQ* suggests restoring that word here. Since חלי is masculine, however, and used with רע at 6.2, it is difficult to see why the versions would then have construed רעה as an adjective in agreement with it. We should have to assume that, finding themselves apparently confronted by two substantives that lacked any connecting particle, and that could not be linked in a construct relationship, the versions each then read them as a sort of hendiadys without a conjunction, with 'an evil, a disease' becoming 'an evil disease'. Because it is no less hard to see why the versions did not simply read חולה as a participial attribute of רעה rather than as a substantive, I agree that it is unlikely they found the same text that we have in M, but emendation to חלי is clearly not a straightforward solution. It seems no less likely that the versions found some corrupt or orthographically irregular form like חוליה, and took it to be a neologism, or that they actually found the two words transposed, which, in this syntactical context, might equally persuade them to take רעה as an adjective, and הולה as a substantive.

As for the absence of an equivalent to רעה in G, it is highly likely either that רעה was lacking in the source-text, or that the word used to translate it dropped out early in the transmission of G. Goldman prefers the former, and suggests, indeed, that רעה is secondary in the Hebrew text, arising as a harmonization with 5.15. Against that, we might note that the expression is introduced in this later verse by גם זה, which would more naturally imply that Qohelet is referring back to a previous רעה חולה than that he is introducing a worse type of חולה. It is also worth observing that Qohelet uses רעה by itself in these sorts of expressions at 6.1 and 10.5 as well, while he never uses חלי or חולה alone or unqualified: if this verse originally had only one term, therefore, we should expect it to have been רעה. I think it is easier to suppose more simply that רעה had dropped out of G's source-text through homoioteleuton than to view it as secondary. This second problem in G does add weight to the suspicion that things have gone wrong with the text here at some point, and the relatively easy reading of M could well be an interpretative restoration, which has been implemented at 5.15 also. It is very possible, even likely, that the other versions read something different.

As regards the meaning of the expression, Gordis sees a transferred epithet: 'a sick evil' = 'a sickening evil', but it is not clear that this sort of language is ever used elsewhere: people are not generally 'made sick' by something that appals them, although the use of נחלו in Amos 6.6, to express the sort of feelings that people should experience confronted with 'the ruin of Joseph', does come close. As Whitley observes, the nearest analogies are in uses of the niphʻal participle to express the severity of wounds in Jer 10.19 and 14.17, to which we may add Jer 30.12; Nah 3.19: from these, it seems that the verb can be used, at least in the niphʻal, to provide a sort of intensification (see also the note 'a terrible pain' at 6.2). Along with Qohelet's liking for רעה, that is probably the best reason for preferring M's reading to any of the plausible alternatives, but it is also true that none of those alternatives would yield a radically different sense.

5.12 (ET 5.13) kept…against a time of trouble] Lit. 'kept…for his trouble'; this is generally taken by the versions and subsequent commentators to suggest that it was his wealth that somehow got the man into trouble.

Hertzberg even renders it as a sort of proverb: 'Reichtum, wohlbewahrt, wird zum Schaden dem, der ihn hat', 'Wealth, well-kept, will wound the one who has it'—a translation that, as Gordis points out, is quite impossible. The trouble inherent in wealth is not, however, an issue in the story that unfolds, and the sense here is more probably that of the expression found in 1 Sam 9.24, where למועד שמור לך is used of food 'kept for you until the appointed hour'; here the money is kept for its owner until he should be in trouble—in England we would say that it has been set aside 'for a rainy day'—and the -ל on לרעתו is temporal, not an expression of consequence. Ogden, 'Translation Problems', 425, remarks that 'the most likely sense here is that the prepositional phrase…indicates the potential disaster against which the owner hopes to defend', and the Good News Bible translates, rather more loosely but with the same sense, 'people save up their money for a time when they may need it'. The problem, it turns out, is that the man loses it anyway, and so is unable either to enjoy it while he has it, or to use it when he needs it.

The readings of the Three are all preserved, but there are some variants and disagreements: α' is εἰς πονηρὸν αὐτῷ, 'for a hurt to him' (the variant αὐτοῦ in ms 252 is an adaptation to G). σ' is given as κακία αὐτοῦ, 'his misfortune', by Field and Marshall on the basis of Syh, but Gentry prefers κακὸν αὐτῷ, 'a wrong to him', identifying the Syh reading with an unattributed reading in ms 539. This manuscript, which alternates hexaplaric readings with scholia by Evagrius, has the readings of both α' and σ', neither attributed (see the photograph at gallica.bnf.fr/ark:/12148/btv1b100379726/f2 9), and Géhin, *Scholies*, which includes a list of the hexaplaric readings in its appendix, makes the same identification (180). θ' is εἰς κάκωσιν αὐτοῦ, 'for his suffering/mistreatment'.

5.12 (ET 5.13) for its owner] On the rendering in G, see the note on 'its owner' at 5.10. Marshall argues that a reading τῷ ἔχοντι αὐτὸν ('for him who has it') found in the text of Origenic manuscripts is hexaplaric, and consistent with the translations of בעל by σ' elsewhere. It appears actually to be an adaptation of σ': in Gentry's edition a similar reading from ms 788, ὑπὸ τοῦ ἔχοντος αὐτόν, 'by him who has it', is now explicitly attributed to σ'. Despite much discussion, it does not really matter whether the -ל on לבעליו means that the money was retained *by* the owner, as that latter reading supposes (so also, e.g., Crenshaw, Seow, Fischer, *Skepsis*, 57; see Schoors, *The Preacher* I, 199) or *for* him (so, e.g., Gordis, and the analogy in 1 Sam 9 supports this view). Lohfink, in 'Kohelet und die Banken', however, has developed an elaborate interpretation of the story in which the man's wealth is invested in a bank, with the result that it then gets caught up in the collapse of that bank. This rests heavily on an interpretation of ביד in the next verse as a technical term meaning 'on deposit', but as Seow demonstrates in his discussion of that verse, even if the term does have that technical sense in the Aramaic documents cited, which is far from certain, it is used very commonly without any such nuance. To be sure, Qohelet may have some such circumstance in mind, but he is characteristically hazy about the details, and there is a risk of reading in more information than is actually offered.

5.13 (ET 5.14) but] The initial conjunction is often seen to be explicative (by, e.g., Delitzsch, Seow), providing an explanation here for a claim in the last verse that the man kept the money to his detriment.

5.13 (ET 5.14) lost] G reads a future tense: 'that wealth will be lost', and this seems to be the understanding of T also. They have presumably read ואבד with waw conversive, perhaps under the influence of the subsequent references to the future.

5.13 (ET 5.14) bad deal] The expression ענין רע is the same one used in 1.13 and 4.8, where I rendered it as 'bad job'; see the note at 1.13. The term is rather broad, and here probably does not refer to the employment of the man. Equally, it need not indicate specifically that he lost his money in the course of business, although that is probably the implication of σ', which is attested as ἐπὶ ἀσχολίαν κακήν (cf. τὴν ἀσχολίαν τὴν πονηρὰν in 1.13). According to Syh, α' and θ' agreed with G here.

5.13 (ET 5.14) completely empty-handed] Lit. 'and there was not anything in his hand'. The suffix on בידו can refer in principle either to the father or the son, but Gordis suggests that it is a phonetic misspelling of בעדו meaning 'for him' (i.e., the son; in addition to his commentary, see Gordis, 'A Note on Yad', which examines the supposed phenomenon more generally). I doubt that, in view of the references to carrying away in the next verse, and understand the hand in question here to be the father's. There is no basis for Longman's rendering 'to leave him' (that is, as an inheritance for the son), while on Lohfink's supposition that this is a way of talking about money 'on deposit', see the note on 'for its owner' in the last verse. G renders with a double negative, οὐκ ἔστιν ἐν χειρὶ αὐτοῦ οὐδέν, which properly gives the sense 'there is nothing in his hand' (on the post-verbal use of οὐδείς etc. in such constructions, see Horrocks, 'Ouk ῎Ismen Oudén', 44).

5.14 (ET 5.15) For] M כאשר can be used with a variety of meanings, and Qohelet uses the word both temporally, perhaps with some nuance of 'whenever' (e.g. 4.17; 5.3), and correlatively (e.g. 11.5) to mean 'as' or 'like'; cf. Schoors, *The Preacher* I, 144. In principle, therefore, the sense of M here could be that the man was empty-handed 'when' his son was born, although none of the versions has opted to translate it that way. If we are to take it correlatively, however, it is not clear whether the clause is to be compared with what has preceded it (he is as empty-handed as when born naked), which seems clumsy and is commonly avoided, or with what follows (he will go as naked as when born): if the latter, then we run into the problem that ישוב ללכת is correlated already with כשבא, which would give the redundant 'as he was born—so he will go—as he came.'

The issue is either greatly complicated or entirely resolved by the fact that 4QQoh[a] (frag. 1, 1) clearly reads כיא after the last word of v. 13, and presumably, therefore, at the beginning of this sentence. That reading is curious in itself: the scribe of this manuscript prefers not to break words across lines, and these characters stand at the end of a line, with plenty of blank margin to their left: this suggests that they should be a word in themselves, rather than just the start of a word which continued on the next line. The spelling כיא for כי is commonplace at Qumran, so that would seem the obvious way to take the text here. The scribe of 4QQoh[a], however, also shows a preference in 6.4 and 7.6 for the spelling כי, without an א, so it seems at least awkward, on the face of it, that he should have written כיא just here. There is no other reasonable explanation for the כיא, however, and such inconsistencies are found elsewhere. For instance, 1QH[a] XII has כי in line 20, swiftly followed by כיא in line 22, with both spellings used elsewhere in the manuscript and כי twice corrected to כיא (XII, 5; XX, 21). Indeed, Tov, 'Scribal Features', 371-72, shows how their preferences for one spelling or the other help to distinguish the work of two scribes on 1QIs[a]—but also that both scribes used both forms variably. The fact that 4QQoh[a] uses כי elsewhere, then, does not at all prevent us from reading כיא as כי in the manuscript here.

If we do so, however, then we should also note that, if something else followed at the beginning of the next line, and the manuscript originally had כיא אשר (perhaps an error for כאשר) or כיא כאשר, then the text missing on that line (the shortest preserved from the column) must have been quite compact for there to have been space for that extra word. This tells against the supposition that the כיא is a plus which was originally followed by כאשר, as Goldman believes (following Nebe, 'Qumranica I', 312). Ulrich, in DJD, and Puech, 'Qohelet a Qumran', 146, both reconstruct the text instead with כיא where M has כאשר. Simply counting is a very crude measure (although the variable size of spaces in the manuscript means that even a more precise measurement of the letters would be little better), but the other lines in the column suggest that there are likely to have been about 31-35 characters and spaces altogether in this line, while the reconstructions without כאשר have a total of 32. The characters required for כאשר are all broad, and, with a space to be considered as well, even אשר would be a very tight fit. It is not wholly impossible that כיא is just a plus, therefore, but it is very much more likely that the manuscript had כיא instead of, not as well as, the כאשר of M.

It is possible, of course, that both this reading and that of M are corrupt versions of a different original, like כי איש יצא. Without speculating so much, however, it seems easier to understand the כאשר of M and the ancient translations as a secondary, facilitatory development, under the influence of the subsequent כשבא and the construction in 5.16, than to explain כיא as derived from a corrupt כאשר. While the problem cannot be solved with any certainty, and although the weight of the witnesses is on the side of M, the much earlier date of 4QQoh[a] must also be an important consideration, and I consider its כיא more likely to be original. This deals with the issue noted above, that we seem to have too much correlation in these clauses, and if we were instead to follow M, then, in order to avoid that, we probably should have to take its כאשר with what precedes: 'he was completely empty-handed, just as he emerged from the womb of his mother; naked, he will go on as he came'. If we wished to read כאשר כיא, that construal would become impossible, and we should have to accept the redundancy, however ugly it may seem. I have treated the כי itself as explanatory, although it could plausibly be understood here as emphatic.

5.14 (ET 5.15) he] The reference to birth so soon after the declaration that the man has fathered a son raises the further possibility that Qohelet is actually talking about the son in this verse, and Gordis, for example, sees a chiastic structure in the text, with vv. 12 and 15 referring to the father, vv. 13 and 14 to the son. Ogden, 'Translation Problems', 426-27, sees two different situations in 12-13a and 13b-15a, and understands this verse to mean 'Just as a child is born without possessions, he departs the world in the same state'. Other readings, which switch abruptly between father and son—as when, e.g., Krüger, HCM, consider the possibility that at the end of this verse the father is taking from his own work to put into the hand of his son—tend similarly to arise not from strict contextual constraints, but from a desire to find a greater role for the son than is explicitly granted by the text. Such readings cannot be excluded in principle, and I shall argue below that in 6.4-5 Qohelet will use a similar ambiguity to force an initial misreading of the text: it is conceivable that he is attempting something similar on a more limited scale here, by juxtaposing fatherhood and birth. I am not convinced, however, that such a device would really serve any purpose in this context, and it is manifestly simpler to suppose that the son is mentioned simply as an additional complication, with the father acting as subject throughout.

5.14 (ET 5.15) naked] As Fox points out, the accents in M encourage us to read ערום with ישוב ללכת, but T has taken it with יצא מבטן אמו, and it seems possible that the slightly curious position of the word (preserved in the other versions) is intended to encourage us, or permit us, to read it with both clauses.

5.14 (ET 5.15) go on again] Lit. 'go back to going'. ישוב ללכת may be read either as a construction of שוב with an infinitival complement (GKC §120d; J-M §102g; 177b), which is the more natural reading, or as 'he will return going/turn round to go' (cf. 1 Kgs 12.24; 13.17). When the expression is picked up again in the next verse, Qohelet uses just ילך.

T makes this an explicit reference to death, and it is commonly understood that way. It is difficult, indeed, wholly to ignore the fact that שוב appears also in the similar Job 1.21, where it means 'return' and certainly does refer to death, so anyone reading the passage in terms of human fate, or even as a direct reminiscence of Job, is naturally likely to find ישוב ללכת evocative of death. Vall, 'The Enigma of Job 1,21a', 339-40, goes so far as to argue that the language has been formulated deliberately to echo Job, while eliminating Job's problematic reference to returning 'thither', as if to the womb of his mother. In Job 1.21, however, there is no following infinitive to give a second verb, and when Qohelet uses שבים ללכת in 1.7 to refer to the continuous flow of rivers into the sea, it is clearly not a simple return, but a return in order to go or a continuation of going (whatever process we understand him to have in mind there). Insofar as Qohelet is still talking about the man here, rather than about humans more generally, I take his point to be that, having lost what he had, the man is now back to the point where he started, and must go on as naked as when he was born: it is what follows that turns this into a prediction about his whole life. The 'returning' in that is closer to an idea of reversion (cf. ישובו לעשות in Neh 9.28, where the people 'go back to doing' evil after a break), and Lohfink, 'Kohelet und die Banken', 492, offers the understanding 'Wie er aus dem Schoß seiner Mutter herausgekommen ist, nackt muß er von neuem seinen Lebensweg beginnen—genau so, wie er herausgekommen ist', 'As he is come from the womb of his mother, naked he must begin his life anew, in just the same way as he came out'.

5.14 (ET 5.15) he will take up nothing] Lit. 'and he will not pick up anything'. G renders with a double negative as in the previous verse, but by seeking to imitate the word-order of the Hebrew in οὐδὲν οὐ λήμψεται, creates an expression with a pre-verbal οὐδὲν that would more properly mean 'he picks up something'. The expression does not strictly involve double negation in the Hebrew, as D'Alario, 'Chi ama il denaro', 64, supposes. The book uses the verb only here and in v. 18, which probably refers back to this verse.

5.14 (ET 5.15) in his business] M בעמלו. The preposition here has been described variously as a *beth pretii* (e.g. Gordis, Seow, HCM) or as instrumental (e.g. Barton, Fox), while Dahood ('Canaanite-Phoenician Influence', 191) and Whitley both argue that it means 'from' (so also, e.g., Longman). 'From' is perhaps the term that we would normally use (and that is the way that σ' and V translate both this and the בעמלו of 8.15), but that is not strictly the sense of the preposition here.

On the meaning of עמל see the note at 2.11. Although, e.g., Fischer, *Skepsis*, 57, speaks here of 'seiner Arbeit Lohn', 'the wages of his work', the expression does not refer simply either to labour or to wealth: Qohelet is not talking about what the man might gain by working or might keep back from his earnings, but about the ultimate impossibility of his finding anything *in* what he has built up that he can keep. The image is of picking something up in the course of business and retaining it—so that ultimately it goes with you when you leave.

5.14 (ET 5.15) which can go in his hand] Although Driver, 'Problems and Solutions', 228, thinks that the pointing of the verb in M is a *'forma mixta'* which permits the reading of either hiph'il or qal, it is usually taken to suggest that ילך should be read as hiph'il (perhaps a hiph'il jussive without a jussive implication), '(which) he might take'; cf. V. However, G, Hie, S, and σ' ὃ συναπελεύσεται appear all to have read the qal, שֶׁיֵּלֶךְ, 'which might go'.² Goldman rejects the view of Euringer, that T also read the qal, although it is possible to read its paraphrase here as an attempt to capture readings of both the hiph'il and the qal (he has nothing 'to carry' to the world where 'he is going').³ Salters, 'Textual Criticism', 58, accuses these versions of taking 'the easy way out' by reading the qal (is it their duty to adopt a less natural reading?), and Seow thinks that they are anticipating ילך (qal) in the next verse. Whatever the merits of the hiph'il over the qal in terms of sense, however, it is hard to see why the author would have used (or a scribe introduced) the defective writing ילך here if he wished to prevent the more natural reading as qal, especially when he was going to use the same writing for the qal in the next verse (contrast the writing יוליך for the hiph'il in 10.20). Unless this defective spelling is itself an early corruption, it is more likely that the qal was intended. It is not clear, furthermore, either why Gordis thinks that it is impossible to read the qal without deleting בידו (as Ehrlich), or why he feels that בידו must modify מאומה, but his rendering 'nothing that he can take in his hand will he carry off for his toil' flies in the face of the Hebrew word-order.

5.15 (ET 5.16) This too] M וגם זה. The initial conjunction is supported by S (although there is a variant without it), Hie, and T, but V does not render any of the expression, and G uses καί γε not only here and in 7.6 (the only other place where גם זה has such a conjunction), but everywhere else that M has גם זה, so it is difficult to tell whether it has read the conjunction or not. The conjunction is lacking in 4QQoh[a] (frag. 1, l. 3), however, both here and at 7.6. This brings the reading of those verses into line with the normal usage of the book, but that fact can be used as an argument both for and against its originality. For much the same reason, we should probably not put too much weight on the absence of the conjunction in a few of the manuscripts collated by Kennicott: they could simply be conforming to the normal usage.

I am inclined, all the same, to take the view of Seow that the conjunction is secondary, albeit more tentatively. I cannot agree with Schoors, *The Preacher* I, 133, however, that Lauha is right to see the גם here as purely emphatic, and

---

² In Hie *ut uadat* the relative -ש has also been understood to express purpose, most likely on the basis of G ἵνα πορευθῇ, although G itself probably uses ἵνα merely to substantivize the clause ('take nothing...that might go'; see the note 'achieved their fear' at 3.14).

³ Goldman also suggests that the reading of σ', ὃ συναπελεύσεται, 'which will depart together with him', takes עמלו to be the subject, presumably so that the reference would be to the man's עמל ceasing to exist at the same time that he does. Gentry, however, has now supplied from ms 788 the first part of the σ' reading: καὶ ἀπερχόμενος οὐδὲν ἀρεῖ τοῦ μόχθου αὐτοῦ, 'and departing he will pick up nothing from his labour'. It is clear from this that οὐδέν is in fact the subject, and, if the reading is complete, then the idea of accompaniment may be no more than an interpretation of בידו similar to that found in V *nihil auferet secum* (which may, indeed, have borrowed it from σ').

it is not merely 'a summing up and a confirmation' of the preceding verses: the רעה חולה of v. 12 was what happened to the man, while this second רעה חולה is what will happen.

5.15 (ET 5.16) painfully bad] See the note at 5.12.

5.15 (ET 5.16) that exactly as he came] M reads כל עמת שבא, which is widely taken to be an Aramaism analogous to the דכל קבל ד- used here by T (so, e.g., Barton). Schoors, *The Preacher* I, 146-47, follows e.g. Gordis and Whitley, however, in stressing that, although there is a 'structural affinity' with that Aramaic, the expression is actually good Hebrew if understood properly not as כל עמת, but as כ-ל-עמת (כְּלְעֻמַּת).[4] The argument in favour of this reading is that עמת is not used without an initial ל-, and with it forms a sort of compound preposition that can be used to express similarity, to which כ- has here been added. As Goldman points out, this understanding goes back to Qimḥi, and before him Ibn Ghiyyat, but it is open to the objection of Hertzberg (voiced also earlier by Delitzsch) that the כ- is effectively redundant if we construe the expression that way.

Noting a number of ways in which it differs from the habits of the translator elsewhere, McNeile, 160, writes of G ὥσπερ γὰρ παρεγένετο οὕτως καὶ ἀπελεύσεται, 'for as he came, so also will he depart', that the 'whole clause savours of' σ', and, whatever the truth in that, it is undeniably surprising to find here γάρ, 'for': that word occurs nowhere else in the translation. This γάρ, however, does signal that, whichever translator we are dealing with, he read כי in his source-text, and the reading is supported by both Hie and S (although both are probably dependent on G itself here: S even uses the Greek loanword ܓܝܪ *gyr* = γάρ!). Schoors takes this as support for his view that we should read כ-לעמת, on the basis that these versions must have read כי לעמת (which he presumably takes to be an error, although he does not explain how the י appeared). Goldman argues more plausibly and simply, however, that M is derived from the misreading of an *original* כילעמת as כולעמת. In any case, כל is unlikely to be original, which is enough in itself to stand in the way of Levy's proposal, drawing on the thirteenth-century commentary of Joseph ben Tanhum Yerushalmi, to read it as the subject: 'Jeder muß gehen, so wie er kam', 'everyone must go, just as he came' (see Eppenstein, *Aus dem Kohelet-Kommentar*, 26).

5.15 (ET 5.16) and what lasting gain will there be there for him who would work in the wind?] Or possibly 'for the wind', which is how I understood this in the Introduction (23)—but see below. An article is widely attested in G before περισσεία αὐτῷ, but is likely to be a secondary improvement to the style; αὐτοῦ is also well attested in place of αὐτῷ, which is the

---

[4] Gordis, 'Translation Theory', 107, suggests that the present vocalization in M is a result of influence from the Aramaic, although it might potentially be more precise to say that the vocalization is a product of the way the consonantal text had come to be written, perhaps under Aramaic influence.

basis for Barton's suggestion that G read יתרונה, and McNeile's (144), that it read יתרונו, but this too is likely to be secondary in G. σ' has τί οὖν περισσὸν αὐτῷ μοχθήσαντι εἰς ἄνεμον, 'what advantage is there, therefore, for him who is working into the wind?' (the last two words are from ms 788, and extend the reading reported by Field and Marshall; cf. Gentry). This broadly supports M: the οὖν is probably interpretative, but is imitated in Hie, V *ergo*. For לו שיעמל, S has ܒܟܠ ܕܥܡܠ *bkl d'ml*, 'in all that he has done', which echoes references elsewhere to 'all one's work' (cf. 1.3; 2.19, 22; 3.13; 5.17), and may reflect a misunderstanding or variant reading of μοχθεῖ.

Both G and σ' have εἰς ἄνεμον for לרוח, which might simply be a consequence of translation technique in G, but more probably reflects a particular understanding in both: the Greek expression suggests labouring into an opposing wind (cf. Nicander, *Theriaca*, 268-70, and Aratus, *Phainomena*, 154-5, which both use it in a maritime context); the *in uentum* of Hie and V can bear the same meaning. That is not a way in which the original is usually understood, but the Hebrew preposition is not normally used in the same way that we talk about working *for* a wage, and the only clear parallels to the expression are in 6.7, where work is 'for' the mouth, and Prov 16.26, where עמל ל- is used of 'working for' someone. This led Staples to suggest, in 'The "Vanity" of Ecclesiastes', 97, that Qohelet is saying 'it is the spirit that impels man to toil, and it is the spirit that receives the benefit of that toil'. As Schoors points out, we would expect 'work for *his* רוח' in that case, but some similar idea seems to have informed T, which talks precisely about working 'for his spirit'. If we prioritize the other uses of עמל ל-, then we probably do have to think broadly in these terms, or at least conceive the man to be working on behalf of, or as though employed by 'wind' in some more general sense. That does not fit especially well with Qohelet's other figurative uses of 'wind', which is elusive and unpredictable in the monologue, but is not a symbol of nothingness—although that is the way most commentators treat it here (sometimes speaking as though Qohelet is talking of the work as simply *being* wind). We might do better, in fact, to follow the example of the Greek and Latin versions, and to consider instead the significance of לרוח, which can just mean 'in the wind' (Gen 3.8), but is used at Jer 13.24 of chaff being carried 'on the wind' and in Ezek 5.2 of scattering hair 'into the wind'. The imagery is then one of work blown away—something that people will try to avoid in 11.4-6, where sowing seeds stands as a symbol for human activity in general. The Midrash Rabbah here interprets in terms of a profit for God (as at 1.3), but notably sees the reference to wind as a reference to winnowing. Very differently, Heim thinks that, after the allusion to digestion in 5.11, 'wind' here is flatulence.

Although RSV translates 'that he toiled for the wind', the verb here is yiqtol, and seems unlikely to refer to the man's past activities. The sense, moreover, does not accord with the future 'going' of the man, and it is not clear that Qohelet is really talking about the man in particular here at all. It is probably simplest to see the question here as distinct from the story and almost parenthetical: Qohelet's purpose is to draw an analogy between the man's losses and the futility of anyone working in the wind.

5.16 (ET 5.17) Also, for all his days he will feed in darkness] On my translation, see the next note. Barton declares that 'The MT of the verse is obviously corrupt; a translation of the present text is impossible'; that is an overstatement, but the text certainly presents significant difficulties, and several different forms of the first part are attested. (1) M^L here reads גם כל ימיו בחשך יאכל, and that reading is supported by Hie, V, T. (2) In G, however, we find καὶ ἐν πένθει instead of יאכל (Rahlfs wrongly omitted the ἐν—see Goldman, and Gentry, 'Role of the Three', 155-56), which probably reflects a source-text that read ובאבל, 'in mourning', or possibly ואבל, 'and mourning' (this is considerably easier to understand as a graphical variant of אכל, but ב may have been added on the basis of the previous word).[5] S has both ܐܟܠ ʾkl (= M יאכל) and ܘܒܐܒܠܐ wbʾblʾ (= G καὶ ἐν πένθει), although it places the latter later in the list (see the next note), so it reflects the readings found in both M and G. (3) Miletto notes in several Babylonian manuscripts the reading ילך for יאכל; this would give the sense 'he will walk in darkness', and it appears to have been the reading found by the Midrash and by Ibn Ghayyat as well (see Loevy, *Libri Kohelet*, 23).[6] There are no early witnesses, however, and the reading seems likely to have arisen after metathesis of the כ and ל.

The Qumran evidence further complicates the issues. 4QQoh^a 1, 5 (frag. 1) has just כעס, with a torn edge preceding it. There is space between the כ and this edge, and right on the edge there is a trace of another letter (slightly more of which seems to be visible in PAM M40.607 than in later photographs). Since the tear slopes diagonally downward to the right beneath this trace, there is also a considerable amount of the surface preserved beneath it, and this is blank. The trace is evidently, therefore, from a character whose body must have been some considerable distance from כעס for the rest of it to have been lost, and it almost certainly belongs to the preceding word. Further weight is lent to that supposition by the fact that the כ itself has been written over part of another character, probably marking a false start to a new word, and 4QQoh^a better supports a reading כעס (cf. Sacchi) than M וכעס. It does not seem, however, that this כעס was preceded immediately by יאכל, or any

---

[5] This explanation for the -ב appears to be more or less what Seow is trying to propose, but he confuses the issue by suggesting that the καὶ πένθει of Codex Venetus (and Rahlfs) might have been the original reading of G: if G* was indeed καὶ πένθει, then the addition of ἐν would have to have been an inner-Greek phenomenon.

[6] See also Ratzabi, 'Massoretic Variants', 104, and Lavoie and Mehramooz, 'Le Texte hébreu et la traduction judéo-persane', 501-2, which note the reading in later manuscripts that may preserve earlier Babylonian readings, as well as Kennicott and de Rossi.

form from that stem: the scribe of this manuscript characteristically writes a very tall ל, and there is enough space preserved beneath the line above that we should expect to see the top of it had any ל been written less than about half a dozen characters away from כעס.[7] We must assume, therefore, that the text of 4QQoh[a] differed significantly here from that read by both M and G, although it also offers no support for the later Babylonian reading.

The difference between the majority reading יאכל in M, and G καὶ ἐν πένθει forces us to construe this part of the verse very differently in each—although neither can be read easily. G has to be taken as a non-verbal clause with πᾶσαι αἱ ἡμέραι αὐτοῦ as subject, 'indeed, all his days (are) in darkness'. M is verbal, and either takes כל ימיו as an adverbial expression of time with יאכל used intransitively, 'also he will eat in darkness for all the days of his life' (so Hie, V, cf. T) or takes כל ימיו as the object of the verb: 'also he will consume all the days of his life in darkness' (for such a metaphorical use of אכל, cf. v. 18). Earlier critical commentators (including Barton, who lists many others) were inclined to emend M on the basis of G, but M is easier syntactically, whichever way we read it, and it is also simpler to explain the emergence of G's reading אבל in the context of the list that follows than to explain M as an alteration of G (although, in an attempt to balance the scales, Goldman does try, unconvincingly, to make a case that 'revisers of the proto-M text' might have resisted associating mourning with the 'foolish businessman' here, when it is associated with wisdom in 7.2, 4; the case would be stronger were there any indication that Qohelet regarded this man as foolish, rather than unfortunate).

Dahood, 'Phoenician Background', 272-73, suggests a very different approach, taking יאכל as an aph'el imperfect of כלה, with which he compares Job 36.11, יכלו ימיהם, 'they complete their days', and Ps 90.9, כלינו שנינו, 'our years come to completion'. As Whitley points out, though, the aph'el is not otherwise used in Hebrew, so its presence here would require considerable justification. יאכל will be discussed further in the next note.

There has not generally been so much debate about בחשך, but Kugel, 'Qohelet and Money', 38-40, expressing dissatisfaction with a common interpretation of the verse, that the man's poverty or miserliness obliges him to eat his meals in darkness (a very reasonable objection when it comes to any meal eaten before sunset), points the word with śin for the šin of M, and notes the nominal form in Isa 14.6 from a verb חשׂך that is commonly used of restraint in the Bible, and can later have a specific nuance of being sparing with money. The point would then be that the man eats not in darkness, but sparingly. As Kugel himself notes, the same suggestion had already been

---

[7] See the notes in Ulrich, '4QQoh[a]', 222. Puech, 'Qohelet a Qumran', 146, would restore יואכל בחושך, which would be a reversal of the words in M. This problem also excludes, of course, Driver's proposal (see below) to emend וכעס to ולו כעס.

made independently by Ehrlich and Zer-Kavod. This is ingenious, but perhaps as overly literal-minded as the interpretation that it seeks to replace. M points בחשך with a definite article which is not reflected in G. On determination of the word in Ecclesiastes, see the note at 2.13.

5.16 (ET 5.17) off great resentment, pain, and anger] Although it is pointed as a verb וְכָעַס in M, the other versions have all apparently read וכעס as a noun, וְכַעַס, and they show no knowledge of the suffix ו- on וחליו. On the face of it, S also has a longer list:

ܘܒܪܘܓܙ ܣܓܝ *wbrwgz' sgy"* corresponds to M וכעס הרבה, G καὶ θυμῷ πολλῷ.

ܘܒܗܡܬ *wbhmt'* (1st) also corresponds to M וכעס (cf. 1.18; 7.3; 11.10).

ܘܒܐܒܠ *wb'bl'* corresponds to G καὶ ἐν πένθει.

ܘܒܟܘܪܗܢ *wbkwrhn'* corresponds to M וחליו (without the suffix), G καὶ ἀρρωστίᾳ.

ܘܒܗܡܬ *wbhmt'* (2nd) corresponds to M וקצף.

Of these, the second and third are lacking in one manuscript (7g2), the third in another, and the last in a significant number of witnesses (probably because it repeats the second). It seems likely that the list was originally shorter: the third has been introduced from G, probably secondarily under hexaplaric influence (although Janichs, *Animadversiones*, 9, takes it as original, and decisive evidence of dependence on G), and Kamenetzky, 198, thinks that the second came with it, as the catchword to which the gloss was attached; Lane, 'Lilies', 482, also suggests that these have not been omitted in 7g2, but added elsewhere as a gloss, or (less plausibly) a double translation. If we discount these, and retain only numbers 1, 4, and 5, then S has the same list as the other versions. Kennicott notes one Hebrew manuscript (his 109, which presents many variants) in which a longer list is also to be found: for וקצף it has וכסף וקצף. Driver, 'Problems and Solutions', 229, would link the additional word with the Aramaic כסוף, 'shame', but it could have arisen as a phonetic error for the following word. In any case, it is most unlikely to be original.

As in Hie and to a lesser extent V, a preposition -ܒ (*b-* equivalent to ב-) has been added in S for translational reasons to each item, and this is indicative of the greater problem here, which is how the members of the list relate to each other and to the verse as a whole. By adding a preposition, these versions effectively align the items with בחשך, so that the man is eating or spending his days not only 'in darkness', but 'in' a series of conditions: many modern commentators (e.g. Whitley, Seow, Fox) adopt the same understanding, with the preposition of בחשך governing the remaining terms, even though it is difficult to adduce any clear parallel to such an extension across more than two items (and Gordis points to many more coherent lists in which the preposition is nevertheless repeated); see my notes at 7.25. G probably has to be read similarly, even though the prepositions extend only to πένθει and the other nouns are expressed with a simple dative: the man's days are '*in* darkness' and '*in* mourning', then '*with*' much anger' etc.

By pointing כעס as a verb, M breaks the material into shorter sections—the man eats in darkness and feels great anger—but leaves a difficult וחליו וקצף at the end. Sacchi emends speculatively to a verbal form וחלה, but Gordis, Lauha, and more recently Schoors, *The Preacher* I, 153, take וחליו as a nominal clause in itself, with the suffix serving as the predicate, giving a sense 'sickness is his, and anger': this is ugly, if it is even possible, and it is difficult to see why the writer would have inflicted such a difficult reading when (as Delitzsch pointed out long ago), such an expression would really require וחלי לו. Delitzsch's own option, however, to read simple exclamations here (O his sickness! etc.), seems no less a counsel of despair. As an alternative to the difficult construals in both M and G, Hitzig makes the interesting suggestion that כעס should be read as a second object of יאכל, so that the man consumes all his days *and* his great anger, an idea that suffers not so much from the absence of any clear parallels to such a metaphor, as from the problem that it seems to mix two different metaphors of consumption—using up time and feeding off resentment. Were we to read וחלי(ו) וקצף as a hendiadys, this suggestion could perhaps be adapted, and the text taken to mean that the man feeds in darkness off both great resentment and angry pain. Driver, 'Problems and Solutions', 229, also reads כעס as a noun, but thinks that לו must have fallen out from an original non-verbal clause: ולו כעס הרבה, 'and much anger (will be) his'.

As for וחליו, the absence both of any echo in the versions and of corresponding suffixes on the other nouns here point to the final ו being a simple dittograph, and even Rashi regards it as redundant, so although it can have some claim to be the more difficult reading, it should probably be deleted. Puech, 'Qohelet a Qumran', 147, says that it cannot be restored in 4QQoh[a] (presumably for reasons of space, since the text is missing there).

In short, then, the first part of this verse presents problems of textual variation, while the second part has a string of words that have been related to each other, and to that first part, in a variety of different ways—none of which is without difficulties. If we are to retain the consonantal text of M precisely as it stands, then probably the simplest way to construe it is in terms of the man devouring his days in darkness, with the resentment, pain and anger serving to specify the days or the darkness. This is one of two ways in which Driver, 'Problems and Solutions', 228-29, thinks that the text can be construed (although Driver then less plausibly links the text to an Arabic idiom, whereby 'consuming one's life' means 'getting very old').[8] It is not very satisfactory, though, principally because such a string of specifications would be unusual,

---

[8] Driver's preferred alternative is to read כל ימיו as an 'accusative' of time and יאכל as 'elliptical' for יאכל להמו, 'he shall eat his bread', which he takes to mean 'he shall live'. Amos 7.12 does suggest that such an expression could connote 'spend one's life', but it is much less likely that the verb alone could do so, and Driver's suggestion that there is a similar ellipsis in Job 21.25 takes the metaphorical usage in that verse too literally.

to say the least. None of the established variants, moreover, offers a significant improvement, or points the way clearly towards a better text (except probably in respect of וחליו). Some minor improvements to the sense might be possible through small emendations (such as reading a niphʻal כעס יאכלו for וכעס יאכל; cf. Ezek 23.25 באש תאכל) or different vocalizations (such as taking הרבה as a main verb), but these take us largely into the realm of speculation.

I think the best approach here is to take seriously the fact that the next verse will itself refer to eating, happiness, the sun, and days of one's life: the elements of what Qohelet suggests as best for the man are probably intended actually to stand in contrast with what he predicts here, and, in that case, we should not dismiss out of hand the traditional understandings that the man is eating in darkness, and that he is doing so 'for all his days'. This allows the terms that follow to act as objects of the verb, and the only syntactic obstacle to reading them that way is the conjunction on כעס, the originality of which is thrown into question by 4QQoh[a] (see the previous note). That text suggests that there may also have been some other changes to the Hebrew, but it is not difficult to suppose that the author intended here a slightly grotesque, metaphorical portrayal of the man.

5.17 (ET 5.18) Look, what I have seen to be good, is that it would be best] For 'is that it would be best', the Hebrew is lit. 'that (it is) fine'. הנה is not a verb and it cannot, strictly speaking, take an object, so if we are to follow the accents Qohelet must be saying not 'look at what I have seen' but 'look, what I have seen (is): …'; cf. Fox, 'here is what I have seen'. Qohelet uses ראיתי אני similarly in 2.24 to express a conclusion that he has reached. Here S follows the pronoun with ܩܗܠܬ *qwhlt*, 'Qohelet', which clarifies (rather unnecessarily) the identity of the speaker, and probably originated as a gloss, maybe recalling 7.27. σ' paraphrases with ἐμοὶ οὖν ἐφάνη, 'therefore it appeared to me' (cf. V *hoc itaque mihi uisum est*). Many commentators, however, prefer to disregard the accents of M and read טוב with the first clause: 'look, what I have seen to be good', and this opens the possibility of splitting the otherwise awkward טוב אשר יפה into two components, '…(seen to be) good, that (it is) fine…', with אשר introducing an object clause (so Whitley, Seow; cf. Schoors, *The Preacher* I, 139). Conscious of the accents, Niccacci, 'Qohelet o la gioia', 65-66, opts for 'è buono il fatto che è bello che (uno) mangi e beva', 'it is good that it is fine that one eats and drinks', which does this in a very slightly different way (not taking טוב directly with ראיתי אני), and offers a very slightly different sense, but all such readings can be justified with reference to the טוב אשר constructions used in 5.4 and 7.18 (even if those are followed by verbal clauses).

In G, however, טוב אשר יפה is read as a single expression, ἀγαθόν ὅ ἐστιν καλόν, 'a good thing which is fine' (cf. Hie *bonum quod est optimum*), which is undoubtedly an awkward way to take it, although Delitzsch, Gordis, and others point to עון אשר חטא in Hos 12.9, which is similar if one follows the M pointing and reads חטא as a noun (in fact, the Greek there, and many commentators, do not). A number of scholars have seen a reference in the Hebrew טוב אשר יפה to the Greek ideal of καλὸν κἀγαθόν; indeed, Graetz (in his appendix on 'Graecisms', 181), remarks on the clumsiness of the verse if we do not see such a reference. It should be noted, however, that G's rendering does not demonstrate any specific awareness of such a connection (it used καλὰ for the only other occurrence of יפה, in 3.11, and generally uses ἀγαθός for טוב, so these are simply the terms we would expect for this Hebrew), and many other scholars have observed that the Hebrew would be a more convincing calque on the Greek if it reversed the terms and used a conjunction rather than אשר (S actually uses a conjunction here, although more probably to ease the awkwardness than, as Kamenetzky, 218 n. 1, suggests, to reflect the Greek).[9] This has driven some to look elsewhere in Greek: Ranston, *Ecclesiastes and the Early Greek Wisdom Literature*, 34, notes an expression τερπνὸν ὁμῶς καὶ καλόν in Theognis, which seems even further from the Hebrew, and Fox is struck by the phrase ἀγαθόν ὅτι καλόν, which Braun, *Popularphilosophie*, 54-55, identifies in Plato and elsewhere (cf. Palm, *Qohelet*, 17). It is one thing, however, to say that Qohelet might be imitating a famous Greek expression, and quite another to seek more obscure parallels in Greek literature.

Gordis takes טוב אשר יפה as an idiom, equivalent to 'fit and proper', and Fischer, *Skepsis*, 58, takes the use of טוב with another adjective to express intensification ('ein echtes Glück', 'a really good thing'), comparing Zech 9.17 and Ps 133.1, although those are expressed very differently. Lohfink, 'Qoheleth 5:17-19', even treats it as superlative: this is 'the supreme good'. In the absence of any close parallels that would justify those understandings, however, it is simpler to deal with the clumsiness of the phrase by supposing that it is not in fact a phrase at all, but parts of two clauses (cf. HCM).

On the sense of יפה, see the note at 3.11. Approaching much the same place as Lohfink from a different direction, I have borrowed Hie *optimum* to translate it here, as I take Qohelet to be saying not that these actions are inherently admirable, but that they are the best option available.

5.17 (ET 5.18) to eat and drink and find happiness] On ב- ראה טובה, see the notes at 3.13. טובה rather than טוב is also used in the similar expression at 6.6, and especially in the light of e.g. 6.3; 7.14, I take it to have a nuance of contentment (cf. the note 'giving up happiness' at 4.8). Similar sequences of verbs are found in 2.24; 3.13; and 8.15.

---

[9] It is important to observe that the Greek is used in quite a fixed way, to the extent that καλοκἀγαθός could eventually be treated as a single word (it can have the nuance 'gentleman[ly]'; see, e.g., *Letter of Aristeas*, 3). The simple proximity of the two terms, therefore, might not have evoked any automatic recognition of the cliché.

Ben Naphtali is reported to have pointed לֶאֱכוֹל with *metheg* under the ו where ben Asher puts it under the ל (see Lipschütz). On the orthography, the Masoretic note in M[L] observes that there are thirteen occurrences of the infinitive written *plene*, and lists of the passages are found elsewhere. Ginsburg, *Massorah*, 4:61, notes, however, that one such list in the fourteenth-century Harley ms 5710, identifies instead the occurrence in 6.2, and the *plene* writing of the infinitive there is attested in several of Kennicott's manuscripts.

5.17 (ET 5.18) all his business at which] The suffix is very commonly translated as 'one's' or similar, taking Qohelet to be making a general point about how everyone should act; cf. the additions V *quis*, 'somebody', and T לבני נשא, '(good) for humans'. No new subject has been introduced, however, and since the following verse extrapolates the advice explicitly to every human, it seems more likely that Qohelet is still, strictly, talking about the man who lost his money, and about what he should do, or should have done. The expression בכל עמלו שיעמל תחת השמש is the same used in 1.3. On the meaning of עמל, see the note at 2.11.

The complicated construction of the verse, with a second relative clause beginning here, and a third to follow, is presumably what underlies the rare omission of an ’*athnaḥ* in this verse: Delitzsch supplies a list (reproduced by Barton) of other verses where the structure has made it difficult to impose a break.

5.17 (ET 5.18) the limited duration of his life] Lit. '(during) the number of the days of his life'; similar expressions are used in 2.3 (see the note there) and 6.12. M *K*ᵉ*thîbh* חיו is an alternative form of the חייו found at 8.15 and presented as the *Qerê* here. This form appears in the same expression ימי חיו at 2 Kgs 25.30 and Jer 52.33; and 4Q226 frag. 7, 3, while Sir 41.13 appears to play on that expression when it says טובת חי ימי מספר, 'the goodness of life is for numbered days'. In 2 Sam 18.18 בחיו likewise appears as *K*ᵉ*thîbh*, with *Qerê* בחייו, and we also find חיו in 1QS I, 1 (לחיו); III, 1; 4Q257 III, 2. The Masoretic note to this text describes חיו as a defective spelling (חסן[ר]; cf. also Ginsburg, *Massorah*, 4:383-84), and it seems to have been used interchangeably with חייו (כל ימי חיו in Jer 52.33 is followed in the very next verse by כל ימי חייו): we should be very wary, then, of assuming that these are instances of the noun in the 'singular' rather than the normal 'plural' form חיים (so apparently HCM, although they go on to speak of חיו as the 'fully-written form'). Although found in Sir 41.13, as noted, the singular is not generally recognized in biblical usage outside another set expression (usually rendered 'as X lives'; e.g. Job 27.2). On the treatment in *BHS*, see the Introduction, p. 188.

A hexaplaric reading ψήφῳ (for G ἀριθμὸν, 'number') is assigned to σ' by Field on the basis of the attribution in ms 248, but is probably α'; cf. Marshall, and Gentry, 'Role of the Three', 160. It does not convey any noticeably different sense or nuance here.

5.17 (ET 5.18) which God has given him] Galling, 'Kohelet-Studien', 288 n. 1, deletes the clause, which he considers to have been drawn in from the next verse. Isaksson, *Studies*, 84, wonders whether the verb expresses 'a past decision concerning the predestined life span of a human being (= English perfect tense) or just the present fore-ordaining will of God (= English present tense)', to which the short answer is surely that it 'expresses' neither in particular, and can be translated no less legitimately as 'gives'. Obviously, a tense has to be picked in translation, but the very ambiguity tells against there being any intention here specifically to promulgate or deny the idea that the length of an individual's life is pre-ordained. As Schoors, 'Theodicy', 385, points out, the idea stated is simply that one's lifespan 'completely depends on God and is within his control', but it is not clear even that this idea is a key point here.

5.17 (ET 5.18) what is his] Lit. 'his portion'. See the note at 2.10.

5.18 (ET 5.19) Also, every person to whom] Schoors observes that BDB includes the use of גם here amongst the adversative uses (cf. also Schoors, *The Preacher* I, 132), and remarks that 'Nowhere else in scholarly literature have I found this idea and it is certainly mistaken'. The author of the hexaplaric ἀλλὰ καί, 'but also', which Field assigns to α', but which Gentry, 'Role of the Three', 160, plausibly attributes to σ',[10] presumably does not count as a scholar, but Schoors has overlooked the assertions of Ellermeier, *Qohelet I.1*, 274-75, 291, and of Isaksson, *Studies*, 121, who both take גם in that way here. Isaksson's understanding is admittedly confusing: following a suggestion by Labuschagne (in 'Emphasizing Particle', 199), he claims that 'The particle *gam* in this case signals "a statement expressing an obvious fact"', but translates 'However, even this, that…'. Seow's characterization of גם as 'rhetorical', on the other hand, seems belied by his further observation that the contents of this verse form, in effect, a second object to the ראיתי…טוב of the previous verse. I take it to have some nuance of 'likewise': what Qohelet has said about the man in the previous verse relates to a broader point about all humans.

The resemblance of this verse to 3.13, which is also structured with an anacoluthon and has similar content, is important for our reading and reconstruction, and in both verses there are significant doubts about the reading of an article in G before ἄνθρωπος. I doubt that the article is original here in either the Hebrew or the Greek traditions: see the note at 3.13. In G, it is notably confined almost entirely to the hexaplaric, *O*-group of manuscripts, and is presumably accepted by Gentry and Rahlfs on the basis that the translator would have found it in his source. That text-critical consideration poses a significant obstacle to the idea of HCM, that כל האדם constitutes a special expression, meaning 'the whole (portion) of man'. This is not far from my own understanding of the phrase at 12.13, although I do not regard it there

---

[10] Cf. Barthélemy, *Les devanciers d'Aquila*, 27, where the resemblance to Symmachus is used as an argument against Aquilan authorship of the α' readings.

as an ellipsis (for כל חלק האדם), which seems implausible and unnecessarily complicated. Here, their reading leads HCM to understand 'the whole portion of man is that God has given...'. Seow's understanding of אשר, that it introduces a further thing that Qohelet has seen, leads him similarly to deny that it qualifies כל האדם, and to render 'Indeed, to all people God has given...', which in turn likewise implies that this verse is talking about all humans, not just any to whom God has granted certain things. Seow's is already a difficult reading to sustain when at least one relative clause with אשר has already intervened (אשר נתן לו), but, by implying that *all* humans have been granted wealth *and* the power to enjoy it, both readings introduce an unnecessary contradiction to 6.2, which will shortly deal in similar terms with humans who have been granted such things *without* that power. The Midrash is surely right to observe that Qohelet is not talking here about everyone.

Schoors prefers a reading of the clause as a subject clause, with כל האדם in anticipation, which is subsequently resumed by זה; this would mean literally 'anyone, that God gives them...is a gift of God', and is essentially the reading of both Ellermeier, *Qohelet I.1*, 290-91 ('auch der Fall, daß Gott einem Menschen...gibt', 'also in the case that God gives to a man'), and Isaksson, *Studies*, 120-21, although the latter makes this an absolute statement, 'that God gives man'—so we are not dealing with cases where God does this, but the fact that God normally does this, as a general rule. Isaksson must again deal with the problem of 6.2, which he regards as presenting exceptions to that rule, and I doubt that his understanding can be sustained. It does draw attention, however, to the problem that Ellermeier and Schoors are importing an element of conditionality. Such conditionality seems necessary in context, but is difficult to find in the text itself unless one reads אשר here simply as the introduction to a relative clause qualifying כל האדם. This is the least convoluted understanding of אשר, even if one is forced then either to understand '(as for) every person', or to accept a subsequent disjointedness much later in the verse.

5.18 (ET 5.19) property] נכסים is a loanword, which can be traced back to Sumerian, but travelled *via* Akkadian, and probably *via* Aramaic, where it is used both of possessions and of land, rather like the English 'property'. In Hebrew, it is used in the plural, and the rare biblical uses elsewhere are confined to late texts: Josh 22.8; 2 Chr 1.11, 12. Qohelet uses it again in 6.2, where it is followed, as on both occasions in 2 Chr 1, by וכבוד, but there is no particular reason to assume that it can only naturally be used in the expression נכסים וכבוד, and that we should therefore insert וכבוד here (cf. *BHS* and Galling 1940), as some manuscripts listed by de Rossi have done.

5.18 (ET 5.19) to whom he has given the power to take enjoyment] The verb שלט was used in the qal at 2.19; for its background, see the note there. Here and in 6.2 it is used in the hiphʻil of giving somebody the power to 'consume', i.e. 'enjoy', what they possess; elsewhere, the hiphʻil is found only in Ps 119.113, of giving or taking power over someone. Szubin and

Porten, 'Royal Grants', 47, see in this usage a striking parallel to the legal language of royal grants, in which the right to use something granted may be given without any surrender of the donor's title to it—*usufructum*, in other words, but not ownership. Rudman, *Determinism*, 144-59, examines the usage in great detail, and emphasizes the aspect of delegation that is involved in such ideas. I am not persuaded by his claim that Qohelet uses this terminology to describe a sort of free will, or exemption from determinism, but it may be true that it connotes an authority that is constrained by the greater authority that grants it.

G uses ἐξουσίασεν, and the same verb at 6.2, which is awkward because it usually means 'have power', not 'give power'. The object of that verb, what one has power over, is expressed using the genitive, which may explain attestations among the Greek witnesses of the following pronoun in the genitive singular and plural, but the strongest rival to the accusative αὐτὸν (adopted by Gentry) is the dative singular αὐτῷ. This, in fact, is the form for which the manuscripts show an overwhelming preference in 6.2, and McNeile argues that it is the original reading in both verses. We should certainly anticipate some consistency in such usage, and the dative is the case that we should expect if G understands the verb in a special sense of 'giving power to'. While it might be suggested that 6.2 has influenced the dative variants here, a good case could also be made that the accusative represents correction toward M, and I am inclined to agree with McNeile.

For the use of אכל, cf. 5.10, and also, of course, 6.2.

5.18 (ET 5.19) from them] M ממנו is singular, apparently treating עשר ונכסים as though it were a single entity; cf. G ἀπ' αὐτοῦ and T. Hie and V, however, have *ex eis*, while S has variants with both the singular and the plural (which Kamenetzky, 198, prefers). We cannot exclude the influence again of 6.2, where the singular is more defensible, but the evidence is not strong enough to compel emendation to the plural here. As Fox points out, the preposition is widely ignored by translators, but is used partitively here: Qohelet is taking care not to be understood as saying that the person will use up what they have.

5.18 (ET 5.19) take up] Pinker, 'Qohelet 5:17-19', 72 n. 27, suggests that we should perhaps translate 'increase his portion', granting 'an extension of the meaning "lift up, elevate" for נשא'. That is well beyond the scope of the verb, however, and there is probably a deliberate contrast here with v. 14, since these are the only two places where Qohelet uses it.

σ' reads interpretatively, καὶ ἀπολαῦσαι τῆς μερίδος αὐτῶν, 'to enjoy/ get the benefit of their share', but it is not clear where the plural αὐτῶν has come from.

5.18 (ET 5.19) what is his] Lit. 'his portion'. See the note at 2.10.

5.18 (ET 5.19) in his business] De Rossi notes several manuscripts with בכל עמלו, presumably under the influence of the previous verse (cf. also 1.3; 2.22; 3.13).

5.18 (ET 5.19) payment from God] See the note at 3.13.

5.19 (ET 5.20) For] Lohfink treats the initial כי as introducing a specification of the divine מתת, giving the sense 'it is God's gift *that*…', and Schoors, *The Preacher* I, 104-5 accepts this as a strong possibility, although he also allows the alternative understanding of כי as emphatic (so Seow, 'indeed'; Schoors describes Lauha's similar 'fürwahr' both as 'emphatic' and as 'asseverative'). Especially in the light of 3.13, I doubt that Lohfink's reading is strictly accurate: the nature of the gift in both 3.13 and 5.18 has been specified already in the first half of each verse, albeit using deliberately broken syntax. The usual reading here, however, gives a similar sense: the granting of both wealth and the power to enjoy it is a gift or payment from God *because* it offers the benefits outlined here.

Gordis adopts a more radical approach to deal with both uses of כי in the verse, taking the first part of the verse to provide an explanation of v. 17, and the second part an explanation of v. 18. This would not be unlike the way I have suggested that the two occurrences of כי in 4.14 should be read, referring individually to the youth and the king, but in 4.13-14 the distance between the first statement and its explanation is considerably less, and the difficulty here is illustrated by the very fact that Gordis feels obliged to render the text in the order 17, 19a, 18, 19b 'for the sake of clarity' in his translation.

5.19 (ET 5.20) he will not give much thought to the length of his life] Lit. 'days of his life'. In 11.8, Qohelet uses similar language: ויזכר את ימי החשך כי הרבה יהיו, 'while being mindful of the days of darkness, that they will be many.' It is natural to suspect, therefore, that he is speaking about much the same thing here, and Gordis, citing Ibn Ezra, suggests, for example, that we might read 'let him remember that the days of his life are not many'—which would literally be 'not many, let him remember, (are) the days of his life', with לא הרבה in anticipation. Ginsburg translates, 'He should remember that the days of his life are not many', and cites a line of Jewish commentators in support, from Rashi up to Philippson in his own time.

G οὐ πολλὰ, lit. 'not many' (perhaps, 'not many times'), rejects or ignores that understanding, in favour of an idea that the man's thinking is 'not much', rather than that his days are 'not many'. So too do Hie *non enim multum* and V *non enim satis*, along with a rendering (first noted in Géhin, *Scholies*, 29-30) that Marshall attributes tentatively to σ': οὐ γὰρ ἐπὶ πολὺ μνημονεύει τὰς ἡμέρας τῆς ζωῆς αὐτοῦ, 'for he does not much think about the days of his life'. S effectively leaves the matter open by simply imitating the Hebrew, but the very loose rendering by T here does come closer to Gordis, envisaging a man who thinks about how many of his days will be good or bad. Gentry, 'Propaedeutic', 153, furthermore, argues (against Field) that α' and θ' read οὐ πολλάς, which is also widely attested as a variant in the G tradition, and which would likewise make the adjective agree with τὰς ἡμέρας τῆς ζωῆς αὐτοῦ. Seow suggests that the Masoretes are trying to point in that same direction by putting a disjunctive accent on הרבה. The difficulty is, that in order to say what he says in 11.8, Qohelet may use similar words, but he also uses a very different construction: even if we were to conscript the initial כי here, and assume that some equivalent to יהיו can be taken as implicit, the position of יזכר would still make it very difficult to read a direct parallel here. In the light of the preceding sentence, it may very well be that we should understand Qohelet to be talking about diversion from the brevity of life, rather than from life itself, but the text does not say that directly, and לא הרבה is better taken as an adverbial expression qualifying יזכר.

The verb itself can mean 'recall' or 'remember', but is best not translated that way here: Qohelet's point is clearly not that the man will be unable to remember the days of his life. Seow further urges, though, that we should take the sense as injunctive rather than indicative—'he should not' rather than 'he will not'—arguing that the indicative would be counter-factual, since many people clearly do brood over their lives. Fischer, *Skepsis*, 58, similarly wants to read the verb as jussive. Such arguments miss the point, however, that this verse is talking not about all humans, but about those described in the previous verse, to whom God has granted possessions and the capacity to enjoy them. Accordingly, there is a conditionality here, which will be drawn out in the following verses. In terms of the grammar, moreover, Fischer has to make a case that negation with לא here, rather than with the אל that we should expect for the injunction he proposes, must be a late feature—there are few clear parallels—and it is hard to see why the author should have chosen to obscure that sense by using לא rather than אל.

5.19 (ET 5.20) when] Lit. 'for'.

5.19 (ET 5.20) busies him with] M מענה has attracted a great deal of discussion. It is most often connected with the verb, ענה = 'be occupied' (III ענה in *HALOT*; II ענה in BDB), used earlier in 1.13 and 3.10 where the form is לענות, a qal infinitive. On the sense there, see the note at 1.13: it is used with reference to undertaking the work that God has given humans to do. G περισπᾷ αὐτὸν ἐν εὐφροσύνῃ καρδίας αὐτοῦ, 'occupies him in the joy of his heart', clearly makes that connection (it uses περισπᾶσθαι at 1.13 and 3.10), as does the reading ὅτι ὁ θεὸς ἀσχολεῖ αὐτὸν περὶ τὴν εὐφροσύνην τῆς καρδίας αὐτοῦ, 'for God engages him concerning the joy of his heart', attributed to σ' (who used ἀσχολεῖσθαι at 1.13). These renderings have a plus, αὐτὸν, 'him', which corresponds to nothing in M, but Hie *deus occupat in laetitia cor eius*, 'God occupies in the joy of his heart', and V *deus occupet deliciis cor eius*, 'God occupies his heart with delights' (1.13 *occuparentur* in both; 3.10 *occupentur* in Hie), affirm the same connection even without that plus.

T, however, talks loosely of divine decrees, and may not render the verb directly at all, while the obscure S ܡܥܢܐ *mʿnʾ* is effectively, as Kamenetzky, 218, observes, just a transcription of the Hebrew, and may suggest that the translator was unsure what it meant. Very many subsequent commentators have preferred to associate מענה here with the more common verb ענה = 'answer' (I ענה in *HALOT*, BDB), so that God is portrayed as responding to humans, or evoking a response within them. Some scholars, furthermore, stretch the sense of that verb very considerably: Levy looks at such odd usages as Gen 41.16 and 1 Sam 9.17 to suggest that it means 'reveal oneself', while Gordis reaches even further to come up with a wholly implausible '*provides* him with the joy in his heart'.

Although he swiftly rejects it, Backhaus, *Den Zeit*, 194, reminds us that there is also another verb ענה = 'be wretched' (II ענה in *HALOT*; III ענה in BDB); this is widely attested in the pi'el (which, like the hiph'il indicated by the pointing here, could also generate a participle with -מ) in the sense 'oppress', more dubiously in the hiph'il, 'humiliate'. Schoors, *The Preacher* II, 431, observes that Luzzato tried to understand ענה that way in this verse by seeing a reference to the way God can ruin even the prosperous,[11] and Pinker notes Sforno's similar effort, much earlier, to find a claim that it is just when one is rejoicing in success that God afflicts humans with anxiety; Pinker himself adopts the view that there is an affliction here, which lies in the way that God 'tantalizes' humans through their enjoyment of what is a fleeting experience ('Qohelet 5:17-19', 75-76).

So far as I am aware, no very recent commentator has tried to find here the remaining[12] ענה = 'sing' (IV ענה in *HALOT*, BDB), even though that too is attested in the pi'el, and would give a nice sense. It was an interpretation not unknown, however, to earlier commentators, such as Rashbam and Köster ('Weil Gott [ihn] singen macht in seines Herzens Freude', 'because God makes [him] sing in his heart'). Lohfink, rather questionably, tries to bundle this verb together with I ענה = 'answer',[13] but he does also raise a rather wider question about the extent to which 'Qoheleth and his readers had the same feeling for distinct homonymic roots as we have' or might rather 'perceive one single word with sometimes very different meanings' ('Qoheleth 5:17-19', 630). This enables him to develop an interpretation of the verse that sees it as evocative, on the one hand, of the discussion about what is good for humans in 3.10-15, where ענה was used in the sense of occupation, but also provocative, because by using ענה now in the sense 'respond', it introduces an idea that joy 'must be something like divine revelation': 'it means one does not have to meditate on death, that is, one does not have to exercise the "fear of God"... When we experience joy at least in one small moment, we come in touch with that sense of things which normally God alone sees' ('Qoheleth

---

[11] Luzzatto, 69. The introduction to Luzzato's commentary, not listed in Schoors' bibliography, was published in the previous, 1860 volume of the same journal, 15-16, 17-25.

[12] *HALOT* and BDB have only four each, but it may be noted that *DCH* distinguishes no fewer than thirteen separate entries for ענה.

[13] Lohfink, 'Qoheleth 5:17-19', 626 n. 8. *HALOT* observes that IV ענה is 'not always clearly distinguishable from I ענה!', but that is more a matter of determining the sense in particular contexts than of blurred boundaries in the actual usage, and although it is possible that the verb in this meaning originated in some special use of I ענה, there are cognates in Syriac and Arabic that tell against this.

5:17-19', 634). This is such a radical idea, he concludes, that as early as the time of the G translation, 'people were looking around for another possible meaning of the word' ('Qoheleth 5:17-19', 635). There are many difficulties with this proposal, but the most important for our present purposes is its reliance on a semantically improbable assumption that, having been guided by 3.10 to the reading ענה = 'be occupied', readers would then somehow also recognize ענה = 'answer' in the verse. Lohfink's protestations about the blurred lines between homonyms do raise some genuine and important issues, but this particular claim savours of what James Barr famously called 'illegitimate totality transfer'.

Much the same is true of the claim by Backhaus, *Den Zeit*, 194-95, that the expression here faces, as it were, in two directions, with the more positive 'respond' matching what precedes, the more negative 'occupy' what follows. It is by no means impossible or even improbable that Qohelet would use ambiguity or a play on words, but such devices rely upon there being an ambiguity in the context, not merely upon the fact that words can mean more than one thing, and to say that a word can have different senses when read in different contexts is not to say that it contains all those senses when read in just one. Here, the clear resonance with the earlier verses 1.13 and 3.10 surely links מענה closely to those verses, and to the use of ענה in those verses, while nothing is introduced that would induce readers suddenly to think also, or instead, of ענה = 'answer' (unless they shared the theological sensitivities of later commentators, and felt the need to cast around for some other meaning).

The further objection that no hiph'il of ענה = 'answer' exists[14] which could give rise to the form מענה is not quite the knock-down argument that Schoors, *The Preacher* II, 99, 431 takes it to be: the same objection could be levelled against ענה = 'be occupied', which occurs nowhere else in the hiph'il, and, if we are not averse to minor emendation, then McNeile, 72, points out that the problem of the hiph'il form can anyway be resolved by deleting the -מ as dittographic (cf. the proposal ענה in *BH¹*). Although it is true that ענה = 'answer' is so common that the use of an otherwise unknown hiph'il might therefore be strange enough to discourage the reading of מענה from that verb, and that ענה = 'be occupied' is much rarer, it is also true that there are established nouns מענה with senses corresponding to each verb that could have guided readers in either direction.[15]

---

[14] Schoors says that a hiph'il of I ענה does not occur elsewhere in the Bible, and this is probably true. BDB offers nothing but this passage, and the handful of potential hiph'ils listed by *HALOT* at Job 20.3; 32.17; Prov 29.19 are probably all to be explained in a different way. As Goldman points out, there are, in fact, very few other uses of any ענה in the hiph'il stem: he notes only 1 Kgs 8.35 = 2 Chr 6.26 and Prov 15.1 (where in fact the substantive מענה is surely to be understood).

[15] On the basis of the vocalization, in fact, Rashi reads the word as the noun 'answer' found in, e.g., Job 32.3, 5. This being ענה, there are of course, other nouns with the consonants מענה, and although it is unlikely that anyone ever read

Although the linguistic data do lean in that direction, it is the link with 1.13 and 3.10 that makes ענה = 'be occupied' the more natural reading here. If we take the verb that way, then we should observe also that in both those other verses it takes an indirect object with ב- (which may itself constitute an argument for the reading; cf. Whitley). Translations like the RSV 'occupied with joy in his heart' are ambiguous, in that they make it possible to read the 'with' as an expression of circumstance (as though people were working 'with a smile on their face'), and Hie *occupat in laetitia cor eius*, V *occupet deliciis cor eius* goes so far as to make 'heart' the object, with V treating the ב- as instrumental—a construal that Haupt has commended.[16] The Hebrew suggests, however, that the joy itself is the object of attention for the humans concerned.

Commentators are divided over the possibility that there was originally a direct object also, as attested in G, σ' and S. It would not accord with the translation technique of G to have added its αὐτὸν, and there is no reason to suppose that this arose secondarily in the G tradition, so it probably represents a variant reading in the source-text, which McNeile, 144, takes to have been ענהו, and Goldman מענהו (which is advocated also by Sacchi). Goldman believes this to be the original reading, and thinks that the suffix was omitted as 'a spontaneous reaction' to a reading of the verb as the much more common pi'el of II/III ענה = 'be wretched', which would give the difficult sense 'God oppresses him with/in the joy of his heart'. That supposition does indeed rely on the existence of a very trigger-happy copyist, because omission of the pronoun does nothing to relieve the difficulty, and if it was indeed original, then the pronoun is more likely to have been lost through a simple graphic error. The reading without the pronoun is more awkward (and Barton, 'Text and Interpretation', 66, goes so far as to suggest, indeed, that 'the chief difficulty in the passage was created by the falling out' of the ו). This leads many to see it as a facilitatory addition (so, e.g., Seow), but Fox (cf. also Murphy, 'On Translating Ecclesiastes', 579) is probably right to remark that in this context the pronoun may anyway have been implicit—although the need to read it may be signalled as much by לבו as by the first half of the verse. If we take it to be neither original nor implicit, Qohelet is presumably making a general statement, 'God occupies with the joy of one's heart'.

---

a reference to a 'lion's den' here (cf. Amos 3.4; Nah 2.13, etc.), Pinker, 'Qohelet 5:17-19', 75 n. 33, does pick up on a highly original interpretation of the verse in Jacob Cohen's commentary (fol. 18b/ p. 36). This relies on the מַעֲנוֹתָם ($Q^e r\hat{e}$ מַעֲנִיתָם), the furrows made by a plough, in Ps 129.3 (cf. 1 Sam 14.14) to achieve an understanding that God sets a limit to the length of life by making חריץ וגבול, 'a rut and a boundary', for one's days.

[16] Haupt, 'Babylonian Elements in the Levitic Ritual', 71. It is not clear that Jerome actually read בשמחה instead of בשמחת, as Haupt suggests, and his rendering may simply be facilitative (cf. Delitzsch, Euringer).

6.1-2

(6.1) There is something bad which I have seen beneath the sun, and it is a lot for humans to deal with: (6.2) a man to whom God may grant wealth, property, and prestige, and he lacks nothing for himself that he might crave; but God does not give him the power to take enjoyment from them, as some quite different man is going to enjoy them. This is an illusion, and it is a terrible pain.

Commentary

Having introduced the idea in 5.18 that both wealth and the capacity to enjoy wealth are given by God, Qohelet now briefly paints the picture of another individual, who has been given the wealth but not the capacity. There is no real back-story here in the way that there was for the other man in 5.12-17, but the situation is presented as similarly terrible. The reasons why it is so bad are not explained directly, and even when 6.3-6 goes on to develop the theme in a slightly different way, Qohelet emphasizes the lack of positives in such a situation, rather than spelling out the nature of the negatives. From that point of view, it is important to read the statements here in context. 5.7-11 emphasized problems that arise from wealth, both for its possessor and for others, and the positive portrayal of it in 5.18-19 made its value contingent on the ability to enjoy it. Without that ability, and the contentment that it can bring, wealth retains its destructive aspects.

6.2] The addition of the information that 'some quite different man is going to enjoy them' creates a significant complication, and Qohelet leaves the statement so vague that we cannot say for sure even whether the man is supposed to lose his wealth to another while still alive or merely pass it on: commentators have long explored both possibilities. Although the Hebrew reads most naturally, moreover, as a statement that enjoyment is withheld from the man *because* somebody else is going to enjoy it, we cannot wholly exclude a simple contrast: the man finds no enjoyment, but somebody else does.

It is reasonable to assume here, though, that this information is germane to Qohelet's central point. A simple contrast would take us away from that point, since it really does not matter whether anybody else might enjoy the property just so long as the man cannot. A statement of deprivation—that somebody else will take or acquire the man's property—is more plausible in that respect, but it will become perfectly clear in the following verses, if it is not already, that Qohelet believes that the failure to enjoy property results from something other than the simple loss of it. To imply that the man's inability to enjoy what he has results simply from the fact that he no longer has it is either to narrow the point to a very specific sort of case, or else to distort it altogether. The most likely sense, I think, is tied up with Qohelet's determinism. Although he does not discuss it in his notes, Gordis renders the expression here as 'for some stranger is destined to consume it', and such a sense would explain the lack of specificity here. Qohelet is not talking about the mechanism by which God withholds capacity from the man, but about the reason why he does so: the property is going to be enjoyed by somebody else, and the man's role is merely to hold it—he is, as it were, merely keeping it warm for a later owner. This is similar to the idea in 2.26, that some people are given the task of accumulating wealth solely for the benefit of others, and although Qohelet was critical of the broader claims expressed there about worthiness, he is apparently able to accept this possibility.

Of course, this constitutes a theological problem in itself: humans may be put in this position deliberately by God for reasons that have nothing directly to do with them. As Lavoie, 'Quoi de nouveau', 124, puts it, 'l'agir divin n'est justifié par aucune considération éthique', 'the divine action is justified by no ethical consideration'. Lavoie correspondingly sees a discreet critique of any retributive theology that might associate this misfortune with human behaviour rather than divine will, and this corresponds to Qohelet's insistence elsewhere on happiness as something 'given' by God. Schwienhorst-Schönberger speaks similarly of a 'disguised critique' ('versteckte Kritik'). I am not sure that it is so very veiled or discreet, in fact, and this verse only picks up the more explicit rejection of such ideas in 2.26. It highlights once again, though, the tension between Qohelet's determinism and his insistence upon the reality of divine judgment, and indicates that this judgment is not always, if ever, manifested in the lives and capacities of individuals. So far as we can tell, he sees it principally as something that affects the length of life, but even then it can be overridden by other divine purposes—and this will become an important consideration in chs. 7 and 8.

Notes

6.1 something bad which] Many late manuscripts lack אשר, and a smaller number additionally or alternatively have חולה after רעה (see de Rossi). Both variants bring the text closer to 5.12 יש רעה חולה ראיתי, and they are generally viewed as secondary attempts to align the texts (we may recall that Goldman sees רעה as secondary in 5.12, which would make the influence mutual). This is most likely true of חולה, for which there is no support in the versions; it is more difficult to say whether or not אשר is original, however, since most of the versions translate the relative expression in the same way in both passages, and would probably have done so whether they found אשר or not (T is the exception: in line with the majority reading of M, it has -ד or די here, but no relative pronoun in 5.12). If אשר is original, the variation from the earlier verse may be euphonic, to break up the sequence רעה ראיתי.

6.1 a lot for humans to deal with] Lit. 'much upon the human'. In his commentary and in V, Jerome renders רבה...על האדם with *frequens apud homines*, 'common among humans', and this reading with a plural has probably been influenced in part by σ' παρὰ τοῖς ἀνθρώποις, as Marshall observes. Many modern commentators (including, e.g., Gordis, Ogden) have likewise seen a reference here to frequency rather than to gravity—despite the fact that this is clearly not the sense of the similar רבה עליו in 8.6—but many others have taken the use of על in the expression to indicate that Qohelet is referring to something which 'weighs heavily upon' humans (as, e.g., Schoors puts it); a third possibility mooted by Levy, that this is a comparative expression, something 'bigger' or 'stronger than the human', is generally (and rightly) rejected.

Exodus 23.29 is widely cited in the debate, because it contains a threat that רבה עליך חית השדה, 'the wildlife of the land will become much on you', which presumably means in context that wild animals will multiply if the land is left deserted, and become a problem for the incoming Israelites. Less often noted is Gen 34.12, where Shechem begs Jacob and his sons to demand of him ('make much upon him') whatever they like by way of a bride-price for Dinah: הרבו עלי מאד מהר ומתן. To be sure, in both these passages, the challenge that is potentially to be faced involves quantity, and the same may be true in 8.6. The other uses do not suggest that the reference here is to a suffocating weight, or that we should accordingly place great emphasis on the על. Quantity is not the same, however, as frequency, and even in the case of Exod 23.29 we are not required to suppose that the threat means specifically 'there will be many animals amongst you'; indeed, that reading becomes very difficult when we appreciate that the passage is talking about the multiplication of animals in the absence of any humans. In fact, the expression seems strictly to connote neither frequency nor weight, but rather a quantity or amount with which humans may (or may be expected) to struggle to cope—in Qohelet's usage, something which threatens to 'overwhelm' them. It is possible that something of this is implied also in the expression רעה רבה at 2.21.

6.2 a man to whom] It is tempting to speculate that יש has dropped out here before איש, and the verse is commonly translated as though it were present. G, Hie, V translate איש with nouns in the nominative followed by relative clauses, and probably understand it in this way: '(there is/may be) a man to whom…'. None of the versions, however, actually offers grounds to emend M's rather convoluted construction, in which no main clause appears until after a lengthy relative clause or clauses, and, although the general sense is not in doubt, it is difficult to say precisely how the parts fit together. Ellermeier, *Qohelet I.1*, 292-95, points out that the subsequent זה הבל cannot refer to the man here, but must relate to the situation that is being described. Accordingly, he takes the preceding clauses of this verse to stand in apposition to the statement in the last, and the initial איש is then taken to be in anticipation of these clauses, standing in a different grammatical relationship with each. On that understanding, the construction is:

There is something bad…
    a man:
        that God grants to him…
        that he has everything
        that God does not grant to him…
This is הבל.

There is a certain elegance to this construal, and it has, in general terms at least, won considerable support among subsequent commentators. Against it, the fact that the verse is obviously intended to stand in parallel with 5.18 makes it difficult to construe איש אשר יתן לו האלהים here quite differently from כל האדם אשר נתן לו האלהים there, and I have noted above that it is difficult to read אשר נתן לו in 5.18 in the same way, as the beginning of a nominalized clause with כל האדם in anticipation. If we do so, 5.18 must mean that God grants to *every* human both possessions and the power to enjoy them, an idea that contradicts both the common experience that most humans are not wealthy, and the statement here in 6.2 that God may prevent such enjoyment in particular cases: there is no indication of conditionality in 5.18 if the אשר does not mark a relative clause qualifying כל האדם, and so we should expect the אשר here likewise to qualify איש. We might also suggest that the use simply of conjunctions on the subsequent ואיננו and ולא ישליטנו seems weak if their clauses are supposed to play the role that Ellermeier proposes.

A different analysis is offered by Backhaus (in 'Die Pendenskonstruktion im Buch Qohelet', 7-8), who believes that there is in fact a relative clause qualifying איש and marked by אשר, but that this extends only as far as וכבוד, where God ceases to be the grammatical subject and the syntax shifts from a verbal to a non-verbal clause. Correspondingly, איש stands in anticipation of ואיננו, although it might be more accurate to say, as Backhaus does not, that on this understanding it is not just איש, but the whole expression איש אשר יתן לו... וכבוד that stands in anticipation. This is less elegant but also less problematic and artificial than Ellermeier's reading, and I have adopted it here.

It may be that we should indeed understand יש at the beginning, but I am more inclined to think that the איש and his situation are supposed to be construed loosely as a second object of ראיתי in 6.1, which specifies the רעה: roughly, 'there is something bad which I have seen (and it's a serious problem), a man who may be granted wealth, but he may not be granted the power to enjoy it himself'.

6.2 may grant] Where 5.18 used אשר נתן לו, this verse now has אשר יתן לו, and a little later ישליטנו will replace the השליטו of 5.18. This change of tense generally passes without remark, and the verbs are often translated, indeed, as though they were identical in both verses. Isaksson, who has a special concern with such issues, argues (*Studies*, 121-23) that the difference lies in the scope of the verses: 5.18 talks about the '"normal" state of affairs' (121), whilst 6.2 talks about the possibility that this may not always come to pass, and the philosophical problem that this raises: 'in 6:2 the actuality of such cases of misfortune under the sun is considered with open eyes, which accounts for the use of a PC form (*yitten*) in this passage' (123). In the broader context of his study (cf. 130-33), what this means is that Isaksson understands the form of the verb here to imply that Qohelet considers the situation, although exceptional, to be real rather than purely hypothetical. Following a similar line, Fischer, *Skepsis*, 67, emphasizes that Qohelet is talking about an exceptional or borderline case, which is not supposed to obscure the general message outlined previously. However, this all reads too much into the usage, I think. Although Isaksson may be right to emphasize that the issue at stake is not the fate of individuals so much as the general principle that enjoyment may be withheld, it is more likely that the tense of the verb here is different from that in 5.18 because the verse explains (and so is governed by the perspective of) the problem declared in 6.1: for the humans that are confronted by it, the difficulty lies not in what might have happened in the past, but by what will or may happen to them.

6.2 wealth, property, and prestige] Lit. 'wealth and property and prestige'. Two of the three nouns here were used in 5.18: for the meaning of נכסים, see the note on 'property' there. With the addition of כבוד, the list now matches that in 2 Chr 1.11, 12, where these things are promised to Solomon, and it may be a cliché representing all that one could wish for in terms of physical prosperity, although it is not clear, if so, why the third term should have been omitted in 5.18. Schoors suggests that there is 'a subtle reference to

Solomon' here, and if that is indeed the intention, then the difference might be a no less subtle attempt (by the author or some later hand) to identify Solomon as the sort of man described here, rather than in 5.18.[1]

As regards the meaning of כבוד, commentators have traditionally been divided between 'honour' or 'prestige' (the normal sense of the word) and 'wealth' or 'abundance' (a sense that appears to be demanded in some passages, e.g. Isa 10.3), but 'wealth' has had the upper hand in most recent studies. After reviewing earlier commentators, Salters ('Qoh 6_2', 283-84) accepted the argument of Ginsburg, that since the items listed here serve subsequently as the object of לאכל and יאכלנו, then כבוד must be something that can literally be 'consumed', which points to 'wealth', and he drew attention to a parallel, although problematic, usage in Isa 61.6. This conclusion is widely cited, but it does rest on the supposition that אכל is in some sense still a live metaphor, and that it has not taken on a broader sense 'enjoy'. Levy makes the stronger argument, cited by, e.g., Schwienhorst-Schönberger, that it would be harder for a man to enjoy another man's honour than to enjoy his wealth, although this too is susceptible to the point that prestige, as opposed to reputation, can quite readily be taken over or inherited—as I daresay any aristocrat would affirm. Both arguments are logical, but also, perhaps, too pedantic, especially if עשר ונכסים וכבוד, which serve collectively as the object of אכל (to the extent that a singular pronoun refers back to them in each case), are considered as a package. From that point of view, and if we are to indulge in such nit-picking, then it is also worth asking just what sort of physical wealth could be represented here by כבוד that has not already been covered by עשר or נכסים. Fox helpfully talks of it as 'the prestige attendant upon wealth', and I take that to be the more natural sense here.

6.2 he lacks nothing] The author's use of constructions with אין has been touched on already in notes at 1.7 and 5.11: he favours the sequence *subject* + אין + *suffix* + *participle*, and whether we parse חסר as a verbal participle (cf. G οὐκ ἔστιν ὑστερῶν, 'he is not lacking'; σ' οὐκ ἀναλίσκει εἰς ἑαυτὸν, 'he does not use up for himself') or as an adjective, that is essentially the construction here, so the literal sense is '(the man) is not lacking for himself from anything' (the -מ of מכל is partitive). The sense may be similar to ומחסר את נפשי in 4.8: see the note there. The understanding of the text as an impersonal construction, reflected in Hie, V *nihil deest animae*, 'nothing is lacking', takes איננו as simply equivalent to אין, with a pleonastic suffix, and some earlier scholars often made an appeal to Gen 30.33; 39.9 in support of such a reading (cf. Ginsburg, who considers it an option), although it is unlikely to be correct. Joüon, 'Notes philologiques', 421, would actually emend to אין,

---

[1] Maussion, 'Qohélet vi 1-2: "Dieu ne permet pas…"' uses this as the basis for associating the passage here with 2.1-26, and Qohelet's failure there to enjoy his wealth.

and is followed by Galling 1940. It is sometimes difficult to tell whether that construal underpins certain other translations (e.g. Levy, 'es fehlt ihm', 'it is lacking for him'; Schwienhorst-Schönberger 'so dass es seinem Verlangen an nichts von allem, was er sich wünscht, fehlt', 'so that there lacks for his desire nothing of all that he wants'). The point is more significant than it may seem, because fulfilment of the נפש is to become an important issue in the next few verses: Qohelet is saying that the man has everything he could want for his נפש, but not that the נפש itself has everything that he or it wants.

6.2 himself] The term נפש (which we have encountered already in 2.24 and 4.8) is notoriously difficult to translate, or even to define, and its use here will take on a more appreciable significance in the subsequent verses. It is difficult to express the connections between these verses in English, however, and it is surely the case that this initial use would most naturally be understood here simply in its common sense 'oneself' (cf. σ′ εἰς ἑαυτὸν, and the remarks in Salters, 'Qoh 6_2', 284). There is probably also, however, some implication of an appetite that demands satisfaction, and for that connotation of נפש, see the note at 6.3, below.

6.2 that he might crave] The subject of the (masculine) verb is sometimes taken to be the נפש (so, e.g., Ginsburg), even though נפש is explicitly feminine in vv. 3 and 7. Joüon, 'Notes philologiques', 421, again followed by Galling, goes so far as to propose that the feminine תתאוה be read in place of יתאוה. It is true that this verb often takes נפש as its subject, but there are no text-critical grounds for emendation, and it is probably true, as Gordis remarks, that 'The entire clause cannot mean "he lacks nothing his soul desires"...for this directly contradicts his [Qohelet's] theme'.

Ben Naphtali is reported to have pointed אשר here with *metheg* under the ש (see Lipschütz).

6.2 the power to take enjoyment from them] See the corresponding notes at 5.18, and, on the spelling of לאכל, the note at 5.17. As in that verse, the singular suffix pronoun on ממנו probably refers collectively to the things that the man has been given, but could conceivably here refer instead to the 'everything' which the man might have craved. It is noteworthy, however, that although G renders כל as a plural, it too has a singular pronoun, so is not reading the text that way; cf. likewise σ′ ἀπὸ πάντων ὧν ἂν ἐπιθυμήσῃ οὐδὲ δίδωσιν αὐτῷ ἐξουσίαν ὁ θεὸς τοῦ φαγεῖν ἀπ'αὐτοῦ, 'from all things that he would desire and God does not give him the power to consume from it' (this is partly retroverted from Syh, but ms 788 gives more in Greek than was available to Field and Marshall).

6.2 as] Commentators understand כי here variously as explicatory—which is the most common sense of the word—or as adversative (the majority view), and this difference of opinion is reflected in the ancient versions: contrast G ὅτι ἀνὴρ ξένος, 'because a foreign man', with σ′ ἀλλὰ ἄνθρωπος ἀλλότριος, 'but a strange man' (followed by Hie *sed uir alienus*, V *sed homo extraneus*). Since neither can be excluded, it is not possible to say for sure whether the man is unable to enjoy what he has *because* someone else enjoys it, or whether somebody else will go on to enjoy it despite the fact that he has failed to do so. It is correspondingly uncertain whether we are supposed to envisage the property actually being removed from him for the benefit of somebody else, whilst he lives, or simply passing to somebody else at his death (cf. 2.18-19). S in fact adds ܡܢ ܒܬܪܗ *mn btrh*, 'afterwards', to the account of the foreigner enjoying the property, and T spins a long story about the man dying childless and his property passing to a stranger that his widow has married, but these are speculative interpretations. The vagueness is reminiscent of 5.13, where the point was not how the man lost his money, but simply that he did, and here, similarly, the issue is not how this other man's inability to enjoy his wealth was actually manifested.

6.2 some quite different man] איש נכרי is literally 'a foreign man', but it is not uncommon for נכרי to be used in an extended way to express the idea of someone or something completely different; cf. Prov 27.2, 'Let a stranger praise you, and not your mouth; (better still) a נכרי, and not your (own) lips'; Prov 27.13; Isa 28.21 (I have discussed such uses in more detail elsewhere: see Weeks, *Instruction and Imagery*, 199). It is not necessary, therefore, either to insist that the man has lost his property to agents of a foreign power (Krüger sees a reference to the Ptolemaic tax system), or to find some other specialized sense for the term. At the beginning of the clause, G ὅτι preserves the common, causal implication of כי that was probably intended here, while σ' ἀλλὰ ἄνθρωπος ἀλλότριος gives a more specifically adversative sense—'*but an alien man*' (cf. *sed* in Hie, V).

6.2 is going to enjoy] The reading καταφάγεται is attributed to α', σ', and θ' (and found as a variant in G), and the use of this verb may suggest an understanding that the second man was considered not to be enjoying the property, but to be consuming or devouring it; cf. V *uorabit*, in contrast with the previous *comedat*. On the attribution, see Marshall.

6.2 This is] De Rossi notes that a significant number of later manuscripts read גם זה, rather than just זה (cf. also Miletto and the Codex Graecus Venetus). This is supported by none of the ancient witnesses and it probably reflects assimilation to Qohelet's more common usage. Many manuscripts of G similarly have καί γε τοῦτο, and are probably themselves assimilating to the common usage in G.

6.2 a terrible pain] M חלי רע is clearly related to the similar expression רעה חולה at 5.12, 15: on the text-critical problems that surround that term, see the note at 5.12. The reversal of the words here offers a simpler reading, with חלי as a noun followed by an adjective רע, but it compounds a suspicion that these terms have become entangled, and perhaps confused in the course of transmission. Hie uses *languor pessimus*, 'a very bad weakness', in all three places (and is probably following σ' νόσος κακή, 'bad disease', in 5.12, at least), but G has ἀρρωστία πονηρά, 'grievous sickness' (5.12 ἀρρωστία; 5.15 πονηρὰ ἀρρωστία), V has *magna miseria*, 'great misery', (5.12 *infirmitas* *pessima*; 5.15 *miserabilis prorsus infirmitas*), and T has מרעא בישא, 'evil sickness' (5.12, 15 בישותא מרעיתא) which at least affirm that they all probably read this variation. S is complicated because two variants are found: ܒܪܝܘܬܗ *krywth* and ܒܪܝܗܘܬܐ *kryhwt'*, 'grief' and 'illness', which could each be equivalent to חלי, but there is no equivalent for רע (at 5.12 S previously had ܒܗܘܢܐ ܕܒܝܫܬܐ *kwrhn' dbyšt'*, 'a disease of evil', and at 5.15 ܒܗܘܢܐ ܒܝܫ *kwrhn' byš'*, 'disease, evil'); Kamenetzky, 219, suggests that it may have been omitted as superfluous, but that seems unlikely.

Qohelet's use of חלי / חלה is confined to 5.12–6.2 (note the appearance also of חלי in the difficult 5.16), suggesting that he is using the terms as one of several ways to bind this material together, and that is probably why וחלי רע הוא appears here as an addition to the normal זה הבל.

6.3-6A

(6.3) If a man has children a hundred times, and lives many years, and the days of his years are going to be a lot, while his self is not satisfied by his good fortune, then, even when it has no proper burial, I say that a miscarried child is better off than him. (6.4) For he has come in illusion and walks in darkness, and by darkness will his name be covered, (6.5) while it never saw or knew sunlight—it would be easier for it than for him, (6.6a) even if he lived a thousand years twice over, but never found happiness.

Commentary

This is probably not a continuation of the previous example, and his interest in the enjoyment of prosperity actually leads Qohelet away, finally, from the topic of wealth itself. The man described here (variously identified as Cain and Ahab in the Midrash) has superficially good fortune of a different sort, with many children and a long life, but he is not explicitly wealthy. Qohelet plays off the man's longevity and fatherhood to develop a complicated comparison with a miscarried child, who has no life at all: such a child is better off than a man who finds no satisfaction in his good fortune, however long that man might live. Because he deliberately intertwines his descriptions of the man and the child, the comparison is difficult to follow at points, but the key issue seems to be that the (non-)existence of the child is an easier experience than a long life lived without happiness.

6.3] 'The days of his years are going to be a lot' is difficult, but the situation envisaged appears to be that of a man who has not only lived many years, but still has many years to go. This is one of a number of reasons to reject what was, until recently, an almost universal assumption that Qohelet is talking about the man himself lacking a burial, rather than the child. That reading is easier to achieve from the Hebrew, although there are some grounds to suspect that the text has been changed, in fact, to favour it (see the notes). In terms of sense, however, it is extremely awkward, and even Fox, who retains this understanding, concedes that it 'has perplexed the commentators, for it seems odd that Qohelet would place so much weight on the formality of burial, as if that could somehow compensate for a life of joyless toil'. Even if we acknowledge that the lack of a burial might exacerbate the pointlessness of the man's life or indicate that others took no joy in him, it would be a distraction from the issue here, and Gordis, who would vocalize the text differently (see the notes), comments quite correctly that this clause 'reduces the sentence to nonsense'.

The situation has become more complicated in recent years, but orthodox Judaism has traditionally imposed no period of mourning for stillborn children, and the expectation has generally been that they will be buried without formal ceremony in unmarked graves (cf. Kravitz and Olitzky, 58, 61). At least when it comes to early miscarriages, this expectation is common outside Judaism as well. It is impossible to say just what the practices would have been in the original context of the book, but Qohelet is more probably saying that the child received no proper grave or burial than that it was actually left above ground, and the point is, accordingly, that its existence received no recognition or memorialization.

It is not clear whether the 'anyone who has not yet come into existence' of 4.3 is actually an unborn child or a simple rhetorical figure, but in 11.5 Qohelet will evoke the image of still being in the womb as an analogy for human ignorance, and he has used emergence from the womb naked to make a point in 5.14. All this rests on a more fundamental and widespread presentation of human life as a sort of interval between womb and grave—one that is not always welcomed (cf. Job 1.21; 3.11, 16; 10.18, 19; Ps 58.9 [ET 58.8]; Jer 20.17-18). The miscarried child here presumably would have been born, even if it was born dead, so, strictly speaking, Christianson, 'Qoheleth the "Old Boy"', 130, which plays off the imagery in 5.14, is probably wrong to suggest that its rest consists of *staying* in the womb. In Job 1.21, though, Job talks of 'returning', and in Jer 20.17-18 the womb actually becomes the grave, so the presentation in general does imply an association between the two, if not actual identity. Despite the brief physical appearance of its corpse in the world, therefore, the stillborn can be envisaged here as passing effortlessly from one to the other, almost without a break and with little change in its condition. This idea serves Qohelet's broader agenda, which may be why he returns to aspects of it so often, and it appears more widely in contexts where the value of living is questioned—but it is also, accordingly, a rather positive way of envisaging both miscarriage and mortality.

6.4-5] Just as most commentators have taken it to be the man who had no burial in the last verse, so most recent ones have taken vv. 4-5 to be a description throughout of the child (with Fox providing a prominent exception: he takes them to be talking throughout about the man). Alongside some earlier commentators, I take the position to be more complicated. In 6.4 Qohelet uses language appropriate to the child, but ultimately reveals himself to be talking about the man, since a miscarried child would probably not have had a 'name' to cover (whatever the connotations of that expression here—see the notes). We have to be cautious about the extent to which statements in 6.4 might have been thought apt as descriptions of a miscarried child, but this verse probably seeks to transfer the negative aspects of the child's fleeting existence to the man and then reverse the audience's expectation. The effect is not unlike the type of joke that runs 'What is the difference between a lawyer and a shark? One is a dangerous predator, the other a fish.' In any case, though, the point is not simply to describe one of the two or to provide a contrast between the man and child, but to show that they are fundamentally alike: the different phases of the man's existence are characterized as much by darkness and 'vapour' as is the child's non-existence. If 6.5 continues to consider the man and child together, then the man does not (metaphorically) get to see the sun, just as the child (literally) does not do so. What distinguishes them, ultimately, is that the man has to experience this existence while the child does not, and so it is the child who has the easier (or more 'restful') time of it—which makes the truth of 6.6 self-evident. That this is a man with a particular experience of living makes the claim here narrower than that of 4.2-3, and Qohelet is not condemning all living. Peterson, 'Coming into Existence', brings both passages, however, into a productive dialogue with the ideas of the modern philosopher David Benatar, who argues that the potential for suffering always makes coming into existence a harm. It is interesting to compare also the disagreement between the schools of Hillel and Shammai reported in *b. ʿErubin* 13b, over the question of whether it would have been easier for humans had they never been created. Braun, *Popularphilosophie*, 118, sees a similar comparison with stillbirth in Euripides, *Trojan Women*, where Andromache in lines 640-41 declares κείνη δ', ὁμοίως ὥσπερ οὐκ ἰδοῦσα φῶς, τέθνηκε κοὐδὲν οἶδε τῶν αὐτῆς κακῶν, 'that girl, just as though never having seen light, has died and knows nothing of her troubles'. We shall note later some connections between this speech and 9.5-6, and the similar language of 'seeing light' is interesting, but Andromache is actually claiming that death is the same as non-existence—in line 636 she declared τὸ μὴ γενέσθαι τῷ θανεῖν ἴσον λέγω, 'I say that not being born is the same as dying'—and stillbirth is not involved. The comparison, then, is arguably closer to that in 4.3, but Andromache does go on to say in line 637 that τοῦ ζῆν δὲ λυπρῶς κρεῖσσόν ἐστι κατθανεῖν, 'dying is better than living painfully', which is close to the theme here, even if Qohelet never commends death itself. Direct influence seems unlikely, but similarities with this passage do suggest that Qohelet is drawing on themes, ideas, and maybe even language, that might have been more widely familiar in Hellenistic literature and culture.

Notes

6.3 a man] The indefinite איש of M is affirmed by G, S, and gives no grounds for supposing that Qohelet is talking about the same man as in 6.2.

6.3 has children a hundred times] The expression is straightforward, with the cardinal מאה specifying how many times the man has become a parent (see the similar 1 Sam 2.5, and cf. GKC §134 r; J-M §102 f; §142 q).

The hiph'il of ילד does not demand an explicit object (e.g., Gen 5.3), but T supplies בנין, 'children', and some witnesses to Hie, V similarly add *filios* or *liberos*; Hitzig does not appear to suggest an emendation in line with these, as Barton claims, and certainly no emendation is necessary (although see the next note). The verb may have been used, rather than a simpler statement that he had a hundred children, because Qohelet's concern here is to emphasize not the man's good fortune in possessing so many children, so much as his age and patriarchal status. Indeed, if this is a second case, distinct from that in the previous verse, Qohelet is not concerned at all with the man's material prosperity, but only with his longevity. The reference to his fatherhood also, however, sharpens the contrast with the stillborn child, and implies expectations about his posterity (see the note on 'his name will be covered' at 6.4).

6.3 lives many years] In the otherwise identical expression at 11.8, Qohelet uses הרבה rather than רבות; cf. דברים הרבה in 5.6 and 6.11, also in the epilogue ספרים הרבה at 12.12. However, רבות / רבים is also found in 7.22, 29; 10.6, so although the inconsistency of usage is curious (and although G uses the same ἔτη πολλά both here and in 11.8), there are no grounds to insist that one or the other formulation must originally have been used throughout.

In order to avoid repetition between this clause and the next, Joüon, 'Notes philologiques', 421-22 (cf. Galling 1940), conjectures that שנים has displaced an original בנים, and that the text originally read מאה בנים ובנות רבות—'a hundred sons and many daughters'—which is attractive, but improbable.

6.3 and the days of his years are going to be a lot] It is difficult to take M ורב שיהיו ימי שניו simply to mean 'and the days of his years are many' or as a specification of what has preceded, as in the RSV 'so that the days of his years are many'. This is partly because, if it is an adjective, (the singular) רב ought to agree with (the plural) ימי שניו (which leads a number of scholars to emend it to רבים), partly because the -ש on שיחיו seems redundant (it is hardly iterative of אם, as e.g. Barton, Crenshaw conjecture, and -ש nowhere expresses the sort of concessive idea that Gordis favours), but partly also because the whole idea seems repetitive and superfluous.

There is no need to emend ימי שניו to ימי חייו, as does Graetz (with the subsequent support of Zapletal; that phrase is preferred in 6.12; 8.15; 9.9). The expression 'days of one's years' is itself unusual but not without parallel: ימי שני חיי is found in Gen 25.7 ('these [are] the days of the years of the life of Abraham which he lived') and 2 Sam 19.35 (ET 19.34; 'How many the days of the years of my life [remaining], that I should...'); apart from those, there are several occurrences in Gen 47.8-9, after Pharaoh asks Jacob 'How many (are) the days of the years of your life?', and Jacob's reply includes two uses of ימי שני חיי, and one reference to ימי שני מגורי, 'the days of the years of my sojourning'. That last is the only occasion, apart from this verse, when the phrase is not followed by חיי, and it is clear that ימי שני is a fixed expression most commonly used to describe periods of life (up to a particular point, after a particular point, or in total). This tells quite strongly against attempts to understand its use here differently, such as Krüger's otherwise ingenious suggestion (picked up by Schwienhorst-Schönberger), that Qohelet is talking about the man living as many years as there are days in a year (cf. the 365-year lifespan attributed in Gen 5.23 to Enoch, who was not himself buried).

It makes it difficult also to explain the singular רב as distributive, and to translate as 'each day of his life is long' (the way in which Prov 28.16 is perhaps to be understood). Seow adopts a drastic solution by parsing (and re-vocalizing) וְרַב as וְרָב, a third-person singular weqatal from ריב, which is taken to mean 'he complains that the days of his years will come to pass'. This gives a poor sense in context, however, and it is highly unlikely that ריב can mean 'complain' in that way. G offers what is probably the best reading, by taking רב as the noun רב (cf. Yi, 25, 360; Ehrlich also favours reading M this way): καὶ πλῆθος ὅ τι ἔσονται ἡμέραι ἐτῶν αὐτοῦ, 'and a lot is what the days of his years will be'. If that is not simply a restatement of the fact that the man lives many years, then it is perhaps a way of saying that he still has many years to go: were it intended just to stand in parallel with the previous statement, the sentiment could have been expressed more simply (and surely less awkwardly) using a non-verbal clause, and in a context where the yiqtol is already in use to express a durative condition after אם, the use of the relative isolates יחיו from the syntax of the protasis and allows it to express a prospective aspect of its own (we may recall the explicitly future character of שיהיו in 1.11). G itself draws the distinction earlier: it rendered יוליד with the aorist subjunctive γεννήσῃ, but has since used future indicatives, and probably takes all but the first clause to refer specifically to the man's future.

I have translated accordingly, albeit with limited confidence. I am not persuaded by any of the various other readings that have tried to deal with the awkwardness of the clause through emendation, or by taking component parts in an exceptional way. The earliest example is T's attempt to avoid the tautology by taking רב in a different sense: the man will spend his days בשולטנותא ורבנותא, 'in rule and power'. The translator is apparently reading רב as 'chief', although this word, as Ginsburg points out, only appears in titles meaning 'chief of', or 'head-'; the word-order tells against Zer-Kavod's suggestion that T might have understood the following -ש to be an abbreviation for שלטון, although this is congruent with his own suggestion that it actually is an abbreviation for שלום. Rashi claims, rather differently, that the clause says the man will *have* much throughout the days of his years ('much' being a sufficiency of all sorts of goodness), and Durell in 1772 reached a similar destination down a different path by suggesting that 'if instead of שיהיו we read שיהו, which word is used in 1 Sam xiv.34, and translated HIS SHEEP, which may here be taken for SUBSTANCE in general, we shall not only avoid the Tautology, and remedy the Defects of Construction, but find a Sense much more suited to the Context'. As Ginsburg comments drily, 'This requires no refutation'. With no less ingenuity, Pinker (in 'The Ligature עו = ש in Qohelet 6.3') has proposed that the -ש is an error arising from the writing of עו as a ligature, so that the text originally read ורב עז יהיו ימי שניו, which he renders 'and enjoy power all the days of his life' (although it would literally be 'and much of might will be all his days'). Leaving aside technical questions about word-spacing, and about whether a scribe would actually have used such a ligature in this context, this is certainly attractive in terms of its simplicity, but the supposed original is far from elegant, and lacks any explicit expression of possession: we should at least expect לו. All of these suggestions add some further enhancement to the quality of the man's life, but although the previous verse might well lead us to expect some such statement here, it is quite impossible to draw that meaning from the text. It seems likely, in fact, that in this verse, unlike the last, Qohelet's focus is solely on the man's longevity, which will form the point of comparison with the stillborn in the following verses.

6.3 while his self is not satisfied by his good fortune] Lit. 'and/but his self is not satisfied by the good'. נפש can be associated with the physical appetite of a person, and so Prov 27.7, for instance, contrasts נפש שבעה with נפש רעבה, the sated נפש which will reject even honey, with the hungry נפש that finds sweetness even in what is bitter, while Ps 107.9 talks of God sating the thirsty נפש and filling the hungry נפש with what is good. Other examples include Deut 12.20; 14.26; Mic 7.1; Prov 13.25. By extension, the נפש can also be used more generally of what one desires (e.g. Job 23.13; Ps 10.3). Especially given the use of שבע here, that sense must surely be in play,[1] but Qohelet clearly does not intend us to understand simply that the man spends his many years with an empty stomach, or unable to obtain anything that he might want or desire, so the specification מן הטובה is crucial. The problem does not lie in the fact that the man has no satisfaction of any kind, but that he does not derive his satisfaction 'from (partitive מן) what is good'. The thought is similar to 4.8, where Qohelet speaks of depriving a נפש of טובה (see the note there). It is true that Qohelet associates טובה with eating and drinking in 5.17, but there it is also something found in work, and he does not just mean fine food or drink. Although Qohelet is at one level working with the image of a hunger that must be sated, therefore, he is also talking about the needs of the נפש in its more general sense—the person or self, with all its needs and desires.

It is difficult to know how much weight we should place on the fact that Qohelet uses an article with טובה only here: in 5.10 the article is probably secondary (see the note there), and the uses at 4.8; 5.17; 6.6; 7.14; 9.18 are all certainly indefinite. Krüger ('Das Gute', 56) suggests that we should deduce from it a reference to the man's own material possessions, citing J-M §137 f, 'the Hebrew article is sometimes equivalent to the possessive pronoun of our languages' (among many examples, see, for instance, Judg 4.15, where המרכבה is not just any chariot, but clearly Sisera's own). I am not persuaded that material goods, as such, are in focus here—unless we link it to the preceding verses, this passage is talking about children and long life, rather than possessions—but I think it probably is true that the article specifies the man's circumstances, as they have just been described, rather than some more general concept of 'what is good'. S, Hie, V, T all render interpretatively in these terms with a plural.

6.3 then, even when it has] The traditional understanding of this clause is as a further description of the man, contrasting his fortune with a failure to get a proper burial, and this is reflected explicitly in T, and, earlier, in σ' ἀλλὰ μὴ δὲ ταφῆς εὐπορήσῃ, 'but he attains no burial' (see Gentry). I

---

[1] A helpful survey of the usage in Zimmer, *Zwischen Tod und Lebensglück*, 9-13, emphasizes this sense throughout Qohelet's usage. G* here is taken by Gentry to be οὐ πλησθήσεται (Rahlfs preferred οὐκ ἐμπλησθήσεται; see the note on 'is not filled' at 6.7), but θ' οὐ χορτασθήσεται plays up the aspect of physical hunger and satiation—the verb is used of filling animals (and later humans) full of food.

follow, however, the suggestion of Crenshaw, later re-iterated by Murphy and adopted also recently by Schoors, that וגם קבורה לא היתה לו refers to the miscarried child, and not to the man. The difficulties involved in the more common reading are illustrated by the many earlier attempts to get around it (helpfully reviewed in Michel, *Untersuchungen*, 144-47), and it is undoubtedly the case that Crenshaw's reading offers a better sense.

There are also, though, some more technical considerations. Amongst the issues that led Hitzig to reject the clause altogether was its use of the qatal היתה, which fits awkwardly into a context where the protasis of the condition has so far used yiqtol forms (תשבע, יהיה, יוליד). This is undoubtedly original: S, like σ', brings the verb into line with the others, but the reading of M is affirmed by G ἐγένετο, and while Jerome blurs the issue in the lemma to his commentary (*fuerit*), he does use the perfect *fuit* in the text (Gentry, 'Role of the Three', 157, takes that to be La).[2] This presents a strong argument in favour of Crenshaw's position, because it represents not only a syntactic break, but a break in the sense: the construction of the Hebrew condition with the yiqtol implies that the man is alive (or yet to live), and if it is read in that context, the qatal has then to be understood as a sort of future perfect (hence Jerome's *fuerit*) or perfective, neither of which is very satisfactory.[3] It seems more likely that the shift of tense was supposed to signal both the arrival of the apodosis to the condition and the switch to a subject who is not alive.

The two factors that seem principally to have inhibited this reading are the use of וגם at the start of the clause, and the fact that לו has to be read not as a reference to the man, as would be more natural, but as an anticipation of the deferred subject הנפל, while the subsequent suffix-pronoun on ממנו still does refer to the man. These are serious considerations, even if it is not impossible

---

[2] It is worth noting that we do possess another rendering by Jerome of this verse (and part of the next): in his commentary on Ephesians, book 3, discussing Eph 6.1, he translates: *si genuerit uir centum, et annos plures uiuerit, et multi fuerint dies annorum eius, et anima illius repleatur bonis, et sepultura non sit ei: dixi melius est super eum abortiuum quia in uanitate uenit et in tenebris nomen eius operietur et quidem solem non uidit.*

[3] Isaksson, *Studies*, 84, uses the presumption of a reference to the man to claim that היתה 'must be regarded as referring to present time, or possibly to the future… the whole context demands that the man be regarded as living, his death without burial being looked upon as the end point of his life… Therefore, the *hāyᵉtā* cannot have a preterite meaning.' He also cites with apparent approval the remark of Podechard, that 'Après une série d'imparfaits, היתה exprime un fait présent et durable', 'after a series of imperfects, היתה expresses a present and lasting fact'. It is not clear how this is supposed to work within the framework of the conditional clause. In Seow's interpretation, which takes the man to be complaining that he has no burial site, the tense is explained in terms of the man not having yet secured such a site; apart from the more general objections to that reading, this seems a particularly odd thing for him to be worrying about when he could presumably deal with it straight away.

to suppose that הנפל has been deferred for provocative effect, or, in principle, to grant וגם the concessive force implicit in Crenshaw's translation (as Schoors notes; cf. also his *The Preacher* I, 134). Without any immediate indication that the subject has changed, however, there is nothing apart from the change of tense that might alert readers to take וגם that way, rather than in its more common additive sense, and most clearly have not, so whilst both the syntax and the sense push us toward taking the miscarried child as subject, the word-order and the use of וגם encourage us to think still of the man.

In fact, I shall argue below that the next verse, 6.4, refers to the man, and if that is indeed the case, then the word-order here may have been influenced by a desire to separate a statement about the stillborn from that subsequent statement about the man, and to prevent them from being read as a single sequence about either. In the text as it stands, however, the result has been that it is read too easily as a continuation of the preceding statements about the man. This may be a simple miscalculation on the part of the author, who has obscured the sense by over-engineering the order, but it is interesting to observe that the four words preserved from the end of the verse at the top of col. II on 4QQoh[a] do, in fact, show a different order (see below). There, the position of ממנו after הנפל relieves the difficulty of taking each suffix-pronoun to have a different reference even before the new subject has been introduced. That in itself tips the scales considerably, but, although the interpretation does not depend on emendation, I suspect that if the bottom of the preceding column had been preserved, we should have discovered also that an אם has dropped out after גם in the textual tradition on which our later versions are based (cf. the similar concessive construction with וגם אם in 8.17).

6.3 proper burial] Ginsburg says that 'קְבוּרָה invariably means a *burial-place*, a *grave*, a *sepulchre*' (see also, e.g., Margoliouth, 'Ecclesiastes VII.10', 96-97), but Gordis that it means 'proper, dignified, burial', and commentators seem resolutely divided over whether the word refers to the place where somebody is buried or to the act / occasion of burial. Schoors has recently come down rather curiously on the side of the latter by arguing from the morphology of the word—'nouns of the type קְטוּלָה are abstract or action nouns…"grave" would be קֶבֶר'—but, as he himself notes, קבורה is clearly used with both senses in biblical Hebrew (compare, e.g., Gen 32.50 with Jer 22.19), and whatever might have been its *original* meaning is a matter of no relevance for the interpretation of this verse. On the whole, in fact, the biblical and epigraphic evidence (see Seow on the latter) point to 'grave' as more common, but the fact that the author has chosen this word, which can have either meaning, indicates how little it matters here, and should caution us against any interpretation that depends on one sense or the other.

6.3 I say] Not 'I said'. As Isaksson, *Studies*, 84-85, points out, the way the story has been set up as a present or future condition prevents us from taking אמרתי as a report of something that Qohelet had said in the past (as at, e.g., 2.1-2).

6.3 miscarried child] The term appears otherwise only in Job 3.16 and Ps 58.9 (ET 58.8), which both refer to the נפל never having seen the light. It describes a foetus that has been aborted or miscarried, and so has never lived outside the womb. As noted above, 4QQoh[a] II, 1 reads הנפל ממנו rather than M ממנו הנפל. I take this to be original, but the fact that the later versions all support the word-order of M indicates that the words were swapped at an early stage of transmission. *BHS* claims that it is G which inverts the order here, but, although this reversal is actually found in the Coptic tradition based on a G source (cf. Gentry), that is probably a typographical error—𝔊 for 𝔔.

6.3 better] As elsewhere in such statements, G renders טוב literally as 'good' (ἀγαθὸν), but σ' βέλτιον, 'better', is imitated by Hie *melius*, V *melior*.

6.4 for he…(6.5) it…] Most recent commentators take 6.4-5 to be talking throughout about the נפל, with Fox presenting the only significant challenge to the modern consensus by taking the subject of both verses to be the man. It is certainly true that 6.5 seems to be talking about the stillborn when it says that 'it never saw the sun': this is a feature attributed to stillbirths elsewhere (see the note above). I think it is more probable, however that 6.4 is referring to the man of the preceding verses (cf. Kugel, 'Qohelet and Money', 40), and I take the structure here to be similar to that of 4.14, which is quite commonly read in terms of two parallel statements (see the note there), each picking up as its subject one of the two individuals compared in the preceding 'better than' statement. In that verse, the structure is marked by כי and גם כי, while here we have כי and גם: the גם functions, I think, to establish the parallel, although it could be considered adversative.

Fox concedes that 'this sentence could describe either the stillbirth or the unfortunate man, an ambiguous fact that is itself ironic', and it is indeed possible that there is a degree of deliberate ambiguity until late in 6.4, to give a reversal of expectation. Qohelet's purpose here is to show that the existence of the man is just like the existence of the stillborn, except that it requires more effort, and so he speaks of the one using terms that could describe the other. As Kugel, 'Qohelet and Money', 40, puts it: 'It is precisely to elaborate the comparison with the נפל that the dispossessed's existence is described in these stark, stillborn-like terms'. Some older commentators, indeed, have suggested that the verse actually refers to both the man and the stillborn (so, e.g., Patrick '…this makes the clearest sense; if in the next Verse…we suppose that he compares these two together').

The degree of ambiguity, however, depends largely on what reading we adopt for the second verb (see the next note), and also partly on the way that we believe Qohelet and his audience might have thought about a foetus that never lives outside the womb: in what sense does it 'come' or 'go', if it is not born alive? There is a danger here of imposing our own knowledge and expectations because, as 6.5 very clearly suggests, the נפל does not really have any existence in the world 'under the sun' at all. As Fox points out, though, the clearest indication that we are dealing with the man in 6.4 lies in the reference to 'his name' at the end of the verse. There is no reason to suppose either that the meaning of that term has become so diluted that it indicates just the memory of someone's existence (see the note below), or that miscarried foetuses were usually named in the ancient world.

6.4 has come...and walks] Or 'has come...and goes'. The reading of 4QQoh[a] is complicated here (see the Introduction, 127-30). Having written כי בהבל בה ובחושך at the end of the first line in col. II, the scribe has initially skipped to the second בחושך and written שמו, omitting the clause that in M reads ובחשך ילך. The mistake was obviously not caught at once, but when he did realize what had happened, the scribe deleted שמו in line 2, leaving a large smear of ink, and wrote a correction in the top margin of the scroll, above cols. II and III. This appears to read הלך ובחושך שמו, although much of the ink has been lost from the first character and some of the uppermost traces possibly belong to an initial parenthesis ')', matching the better-preserved '(' at the end of the correction; see the careful and accurate description by Ulrich, 224. As will be evident from the writing בחושך, 4QQoh[a] tends to use plene spelling, and הלך is likely, therefore, to have been understood by the scribe as a qatal form, 'he went', in parallel with the preceding בה (= M בא). The ילך of M, on the other hand, supported by S, places the verb in parallel with the following יכסה (which is preserved in that form by both M and 4QQoh[a]), and this makes it difficult to read it as a 'generalizing present' (Fox): contrasted with the qatal בא, it more naturally connotes a future tense. Accordingly, M and S should be read 'he came...he will go...his name will be covered', while 4QQoh[a] reads 'he came...he went...his name will be covered'.

The situation is further complicated by G, which uses three tenses here: ἦλθεν...πορεύεται...καλυφθήσεται, 'he came...he goes...his name will be covered' (for πορεύεται, cf. Hie *uadit* [var. *uadet*], V *pergit*; a variant πορεύσεται affirms M and is hexaplaric). As McNeile, 144, suggested long ago, πορεύεται implies that G read a participle rather than the ילך of M, and Goldman aligns the reading of G with that of 4QQoh[a], speculating that G read הלך but vocalized it as a participle 'in preparation for the impf. at the end of the verse'. That is surely less likely, however, than that it would have paired הלך with בא and read both as qatal, and there is no reason to suppose that G would have felt some need to interpose a present tense somehow to mediate between the past tense of בא and the future of יכסה, which is what Goldman seems to be suggesting. Indeed, it is difficult to conceive of any good reason for G to have used the present πορεύεται unless the translator had been confronted with an explicit writing הולך in his source-text.

There are, therefore, three possible readings ילך, הלך and הולך, and any judgment between them will necessarily involve a consideration of what we take to have been the original sense, since there are significant exegetical consequences. If 'coming' and 'going' are ways of talking about the beginning and end of individual existence (as in 5.14; cf. 1.4), or at least about the beginning and continuation of existence, then M ילך must apply to the man (who is alive) rather than to the stillborn, which is, by definition, already dead. T, which supports M, takes this on board, and affirms that the verse is talking about the man's coming into 'this world' and departing into 'that world' (i.e., the world to come). G's reading הולך may likewise refer to the man, but it could also describe the stillborn, since both could be said to come into existence and then to pass their existence in darkness. If it is read as qatal, the הלך of 4QQohª, on the other hand, tends more strongly to favour the stillborn as subject of the verb, since it, unlike the man, has certainly come and gone.

We should also consider, however, not just their sense, but the ways in which the variants could have arisen. If it is secondary, M ילך could have arisen either in an attempt to align it with יכסה, since both follow בחשך, or as a way to make the subject of the verb more explicitly the man. Similarly, the הלך of 4QQohª could have arisen under the influence of בא, as an attempt to specify the stillborn as the subject, or through a defective writing of the less ambiguous הולך. It is difficult, on the other hand, to see how G's presumed הולך would have arisen as a variant, when it introduces a form and tense that is parallel to neither of the other verbs, and offers no clear direct identification of the subject. It is harder, in other words, to see how we would have got הולך, rather than ילך or הלך, as a secondary reading, and that makes it less likely to be secondary. On the reasonable assumption that plene spelling was available to the author, it is most probable, therefore, that he wrote an explicit participle הולך. If so, the shifts from qatal to participle to yiqtol are hardly accidental, and it seems no less probable, therefore, that they are supposed to suggest three different periods of time, as implied by G: the man or the נפל has been born in הבל, and spends a life in darkness, while memory of them will ultimately be swallowed up in darkness.

6.4 in illusion] Motivated by a sense that the subject would originally have been explicit, Joüon, 'Notes philologiques', 422, suggests that בהבל is secondary: the original text had כי הנפל בחשך בא, and בהבל supplanted הנפל after בחשך dropped out. This is picked up by Buzy (to whom Schoors attributes it), but is speculative and highly implausible.

The sense of the expression בהבל בא has been much discussed, especially with respect to the meaning of the preposition. Meek, 'Translating the Hebrew Bible', 331, proposes that we should translate 'comes as a sorry thing and departs in darkness', which is close to Jenni's suggestion (*Die Präposition Beth*, 83), that we are dealing with a *beth essentiae* (cf. GKC §119 i; J-M §133 c): the subject 'kommt als Nichtigkeit', 'as a nothing'. A number of other commentators translate in these or similar terms (so, e.g., Lohfink, 'als Windhauch kam sie', 'as a breath it came'), and these translations naturally conform both to the common assumption that it is the stillborn child whose 'coming' is being described, and to various beliefs about the meaning of הבל in this context. Something very similar occurs in Ps 78.33, the only other biblical occurrence of בהבל, where RSV, for instance, renders 'So he made their days vanish like a breath, and their years in terror'.

That verse presents the same obstacle as this, however: just as in Ps 78 we should think hard before rendering בהבל as 'like a breath' when the parallel בבהלה clearly does not mean 'like terror', so here it seems a considerable stretch to read 'comes *as* הבל but goes *in* darkness'. It is true both that the subsequent third use of -ב ('by darkness') will involve a different use of the preposition, and that Jenni is willing to tolerate the difference (cf. his p. 211). The problem is not, however, just that these are different uses of the preposition—and we should be wary of demanding consistency in respect of nuances present only in languages other than Hebrew—but that the different uses actually imply different syntax in each clause, with the -ב introducing a predicate in the first, but an adverbial expression in the second. Although the use of *beth essentiae* cannot, of course, be excluded as a theoretical possibility, it seems unlikely therefore that the context would have encouraged any reader to take בהבל that way. The same consideration, of course, tells against Dahood's suggestion that -ב here means 'from', a possibility that is anyway open to criticism on other grounds.[4]

Schoors insists, citing *HALOT*, that after a verb of motion -ב must mean 'into', so that הבל is the situation into which the stillborn, as he takes it to be, enters. In fact, BDB is better on this, pointing out correctly that after such verbs the preposition more normally means 'through', either in the sense of travelling 'through' a land (e.g. Gen 12.6; 13.17) or of passing 'through' an entrance or gateway (e.g. Isa 62.10), which is probably similar to the idea of going 'under' the shelter of a roof in Gen 19.8. It seems more likely, however, that -ב here has nothing to do with the motion *per se*, and simply indicates a state or condition, as when ולך בשלום indicates going 'peacefully' in 1 Sam 29.7. This is probably how the expression was understood by Symmachus, who renders μάτην γὰρ ἦλθεν, 'for he came vainly', with an adverb (cf. V *frustra*). There is a danger that we over-specify the translation to suit our interpretation, and I am happy to maintain the breadth of potential meanings by translating 'in', like all the ancient versions, although I take the probable implication to be linked to the uses of הבל in 6.12; 7.15; and 9.9, where it characterizes human life.

6.4 in darkness[1]] On the determination of חשך, see the note at 2.13. When the fool walks 'in darkness' in 2.14 (where the qal participle is used, as probably here), the point is that, unlike the wise man, he does not know what lies ahead. That may be an implication here, but such ignorance has not been emphasized so far as a theme in this story. The point is rather that, even though it is the stillborn who has never seen the sun, it is the man who

---

[4] See Dahood, 'Northwest Semitic Texts and Textual Criticism of the Hebrew Bible', 11, where a translation of 6.4 in these terms is presented simply as an epigraph to the article; the idea is attacked by James Barr on p. 49 of the same volume, in his essay 'Philology and Exegesis'. On the general issue of such usage in Hebrew, see the note on 'in any of' at 1.3.

experiences darkness, and it is difficult to ignore the recent use in 5.16, where darkness represents a less intellectual state of frustration and resentment, or to overlook the link with 'seeing good' in 6.3: it is darkness that prevents him from seeing. Kugel would again point *śin* rather than *šin* here (see the note at 5.16), understanding the point to be that the man will die בְּחֹשֶׁךְ, 'in penury', and seeing a play on the subsequent בַּחֹשֶׁךְ, 'in darkness'. He links this story to the preceding account of the man who has been dispossessed, but I see no reason to suppose that the man in question here has been materially impoverished. In principle, there might be an ambiguity in the consonantal text here, but in practice it seems unlikely that any reader would have been driven by the context to read בְּחֹשֶׁךְ, and the evidence that it could actually mean 'in penury' is anyway rather slight.

6.4 his name will be covered] Qohelet will use שֵׁם, 'name', again in 6.10 and 7.1. In the latter, it seems primarily to connote reputation, and in the former to express a label or identity. Barton claims that here it is effectively equivalent to זֵכֶר, but although it is true that the two terms are sometimes found in parallel (cf. Job 18.17; Prov 10.7), they do not have the same meaning. It also difficult to see any basis for the statement of Murphy, seconded by Schoors, that 'Covering the name with darkness...is idiomatic for non-existence or death; the name is the person'. Ginsburg, at least, is quite frank about his reasons for taking שֵׁם not to mean name: 'That it is here *memory*, and not "name," is evident from the fact that, being an untimely birth, it had no name given to it'; it seems likely that the same motivation, an identification of the subject as the stillborn, underpins other attempts to find a different sense.

Used in the context of dying and posterity, שֵׁם can, in fact, express something more than just the identity or reputation of an individual. In 2 Sam 14.7, the loss of an only son will deprive a man of שֵׁם וּשְׁאֵרִית, 'name and remnant', an idea found also in Isa 14.22, with Isa 56.5 conversely promising perpetuation of a 'name' even to eunuchs who will have no children. Such passages refer not merely, if at all, to the preservation of memories about a person, but more profoundly to a heritage that individuals hope to pass on, through their descendants or otherwise: their 'name', in this context, is their posterity, and the mark that they continue to make upon the world. Linking it to the stillborn, Schoors himself paraphrases the expression here as 'it has no name'; the unmistakable implication of the text, however, is that the subject of the clause must have a name, in order for that name to be covered or concealed. Qohelet does not say that it will be eliminated or cut off, but if the reference is to the man, then the prediction is that he will achieve no perpetuity through his many children—an idea that is wholly in accord with Qohelet's statements elsewhere (cf. 1.11; 2.16). This is the fate of all humans, and is not linked to the man's particular inability to take pleasure. Rather, it emphasizes that nothing about the man's existence, even his posterity, makes it more meaningful or worthwhile than that of the stillborn.

6.5 saw or knew] Lit. 'saw and knew'. I take M לא ידע in parallel with לא ראה, so that both verbs have שמש as their object. This reading was favoured by the Masoretes, judging by the accents, and has been adopted by many commentators, including recently, for example, Fox and Schoors (although the former takes the verbs to be nominalized: 'he who did not see or know'[5]). It takes account of the fact that these two verbs are often found together in parallel like this (e.g. Deut 11.2; 1 Sam 12.17; 14.38; 23.22-23; 24.11; 25.17; 26.12; 1 Kgs 20.7, 22; Neh 4.5; Isa 41.20; 44.9; Jer 2.19; 5.1), to the extent that they have been characterized as forming a hendiadys (see Mizrahi, 'Qohelet 6:5b', 161-63), and in combination they usually indicate an awareness or understanding of something through observation of it. Others such as Seow, however, take the usage of ידע to be absolute: the stillborn firstly did not see the sun and secondly 'did not know', with the implication that it had no consciousness or awareness. That is an attractive interpretation: when it is used absolutely with a negation, however, the verb expresses ignorance, not a lack of consciousness, and generally has a pejorative edge (as in the examples cited by these scholars from Isa 44.9, 18; 45.20; cf. also Isa 1.3; 56.10; Pss 73.22; 82.5), which would seem inappropriate here.

That neither construal seems entirely natural, mostly because of the position of שמש, is affirmed by the various ancient and modern attempts to find a different reading. The ἀνάπαυσιν of α' and θ' suggests that both have taken נחת to be the object of ידע, despite the problems that this causes for the treatment of לזה מזה. Perhaps guided by the same unease, as well as by a determination to preserve 'saw the sun' as a set phrase for 'lived', Fischer, *Skepsis*, 71 n. 76, supplies a separate object for ידע, supposing the text originally to have been ורעה לא ידע. It is probably not the case, however, that G went down the same path as α' and θ'. *BHQ* supposes G* to have been ἀναπαύσεις (accusative plural), but G more probably had ἀνάπαυσις (see Gentry, 'Role of the Three', 172-73): that nominative singular is supported by Hie *requies*, which Gentry takes to be La, and there is no reason for the translator to have used a plural form. G originally left ἀνάπαυσις τούτῳ ὑπὲρ τοῦτον as a non-verbal clause, 'rest (is) to this more than that', and the variant ἀναπαύσεις may have arisen as an orthographic one—McNeile, 160, sees simple itacism—but it more probably suggests that some scribe fell into the trap that the translator of G had avoided, and tried to make ἀνάπαυσις the object of ἔγνω. On the very different readings of σ', V, T, see below.

6.5 sunlight] Lit. 'sun'. This is the only place in the book where שמש is used without an article, and the absence is confirmed both by G and by

---

[5] It is not clear that this nominalization (which Schoors calls 'far-fetched') is a necessary element of Fox's interpretation: it enables him to suggest that in some technical sense the man is the subject throughout, at the cost of supposing that most of the verse anticipates לזה, but no reader would have taken it that way, and it seems less plausible than accepting a simple switch of subject.

4QQoh^a. Such usage is relatively unusual elsewhere in biblical Hebrew, and, outside particular expressions, is often associated explicitly with references to the light or heat of the sun: cf. 2 Sam 23.4; Job 8.16; Isa 49.10; 60.20; Jer 31.35; Ezek 32.7; Joel 2.10; 4.15. Ps 58.9 (ET 58.8) is particularly striking, because it refers to the נפל אשת בל חזו שמש, 'a stillborn of a woman, that has not seen sun' (cf. Job 3.16, 'a hidden stillborn…children that have not seen light'). This is rather like the way we can speak in English of 'getting some sun'. We should not put too much weight on the distinction (and the article notably is present in 11.7, when Qohelet sets 'seeing the sun' alongside a statement about light), but if there is such a nuance here, then it more effectively picks up the references to darkness in the previous verse.

Schoors expresses a not uncommon idea when he claims that 'The expression undoubtedly means "to live", and the participle in 7:11 refers to "the living"' (see, similarly, Ginsburg). It is true, to be sure, that Qohelet does use contrasts between light and darkness to talk about living and dying, but that is not the principal point of the reference in 7.11 to 'those who see the sun', and it is doubtful, even if we take into account the similar usage at Ps 49.20 (ET 49.19), that we can extrapolate some fixed expression from the three places, each contextually very different from the others, in which Qohelet refers to seeing the sun, let alone that it is a Graecism, as some scholars have suggested (most notably Palm, *Qohelet*, 19). Heim, who reads 'under the sun' throughout the book as a cypher for living under Ptolemaic occupation, thinks that the language here points to the man being a collaborator, the stillborn 'a cryptograph for those who oppose foreign rule, ideologically, through passive resistance or as actual resistance activists' (114). All else aside, when Heim goes on to speak further of 'resistance fighters' and 'partisans', it is not clear what context of Jewish insurgency he envisages during the late third-century, which is the period to which he dates the book.

6.5 it would be easier for it than for him] Lit. 'repose (is) for this one rather than this one'. Before this point, some commentators insert וגם קבורה לא היתה לו, from 6.3 (whilst I do not agree with it, I'm also not sure why Schoors characterizes this as is a 'weird suggestion').

On the meaning and form of נחת, and of the reading נוחת in 4QQoh^a here, see the note 'repose' at 4.6. According to Syh, for G καὶ οὐκ ἔγνω ἀνάπαυσις τούτῳ ὑπὲρ τοῦτον (see above), σ' has the very different καὶ οὐκ ἐπειράθη διαφορᾶς ἑτέρου πράγματος πρὸς ἕτερον, 'and he has not experienced distinction between one deed and another'.[6] This appears in its entirety as a

---

[6] There is some confusion over the reading of σ', since Field gives ἀνάπαυσιν as the reading for α', σ', and θ' on the basis of a Syrohexaplaric note. It is presumably this that gives rise to claims such as that of Crenshaw, who says that 'Symmachus construes *naḥat* (rest) with the verb *yādāʿ*. Those who read on, however, discover that Field also attributes the reading given here to σ', still on the basis of the Syrohexapla. The key to understanding the apparent contradiction

plus in two distinct groups of G manuscripts, so we can be confident about the original Greek. It has a counterpart in T ולא ידע בין טב לביש ולמבחן בין עלמא הדין לעלם אוחרן, 'he knew not (how to distinguish) between good and evil or to tell this world from the next', and one or both of these interpretations has surely also informed the reading of V, *neque cognouit distantiam boni et mali*, 'he did not know the difference between good and evil',[7] which probably does not rest directly on a fresh reading of the Hebrew. It seems likely that both T and σ' lacked נחת in their source-texts: there is no equivalent to the word in their translations, and the fact that neither struggles with its other occurrences, in 4.6 and 9.17, makes it unlikely that this is just a matter of (mis)interpretation.

In the note at 4.6, I cited *b. ʿErubin* 13b (mentioned also in the commentary, above), which asks whether it would have been easier for humans not to have been created, and which uses the mishnaic idiom נוח לו ל-. This is used more broadly in statements claiming that 'it would have been easier/better for someone had…', and Delitzsch (followed by Euringer) supposes that T and σ' have read נחת ל- as equivalent to that idiom. Even had they known it, however, it is not clear why T and σ' should have understood that here. Furthermore, the idiom does not mean 'what is better' in some more abstract way, as Delitzsch implies, so had they done so, they would simply have understood 'knew it would be easier/better for this one than that'.[8] Their actual renderings, by contrast, are all about knowing how to make distinctions between things, not about what is easier or better (note especially T's second attempt, which is about recognizing different worlds). The elaborations are much more probably an attempt, in fact, to take לזה מזה as an object or adverbial expression, qualifying ידע and implying that the verb refers to distinguishing one thing from

---

lies in the fact that these notes differentiate the readings of the Three in various respects from those of Origen (who here had ἀναπαύσεις). As Marshall observes, the first note indicates that all three have a singular form in contrast to Origen's plural; the second then specifies more closely what it is that σ' actually does read (and, in accordance with the first note, I have construed διαφορας as genitive singular rather than accusative plural).

[7] Cannon, 'Jerome and Symmachus', 194, and Gentry, 'Role of the Three', 173, recognize the influence of σ', but it is hard to overlook the more precise correspondence of *boni et mali* to T טב לביש, than to σ' ἑτέρου πράγματος πρὸς ἕτερον, and Jerome may have been relying on a Jewish tradition of interpretation (so Ginsburg). It seems doubtful, on the other hand, that we should link these readings with S ܢܝܚ ܠܗܢ̈ܐ ܛܒ ܡܢ ܕܠܗܢ̈ܐ *nyḥ lhn' ṭb mn dlhn'*, which inserts 'good' ('quiet for this one is good rather than for that'), probably in an attempt to clarify the sense (although in fact it somewhat changes it).

[8] There is a helpful survey of the rabbinic usage in Mizrahi, 'Qohelet 6:5b', 163-65, where it is pointed out *inter alia* that the use of מן to express 'better for… than' in such sayings appears to be very late, so would not have been used to parse מזה here.

another; each translator has then supplied their own specification of what those things might be. It is not clear how (the certainly original) נחת or נוחת would have dropped out, unless it is because a scribe's eye slipped in a long sequence of three-letter words, but it is difficult to imagine that any translator would have attempted such a reading had it not done so, let alone that both T and σ' would both have made the attempt independently.

Whatever its relevance to those renderings, however, I think it probably is true that the later נוח לו ל- is broadly equivalent to Qohelet's נחת ל- here, and reflects the same idea, that what is more restful for somebody is correspondingly easier for them: the point is that neither the man nor the stillborn truly experience light, but for the stillborn it is a simple absence, while the man has to experience darkness instead, throughout a long life and beyond. The stillborn is not being said to have more 'satisfaction' (Gordis, basing himself on a misreading of *b. 'Erubin*), and even the idea that it has 'repose' suggests something more positive than the context implies. Whether the stillborn enjoys the repose of death (which Backhaus, *Es gibt*, 218, takes to be the ironic implication here) depends on whether Qohelet believes it actually to possess a grave and a place in the afterlife—which, on my reading of the text, he probably does not.

As Ehrlich noted, the construction is similar to תקוה לכסיל ממנו in Prov 26.12, and it has not generally been regarded as problematic. Mizrahi, however, claims (in 'Qohelet 6:5b', 160) that it 'is enigmatic, and requires some kind of completion (who is the agent? what is the action or state of things?)'. His solution is to read the נוחת of 4QQoh[a] as a participle from נחת, with the sense 'descending', and לזה מזה as a reference to the stillborn's descent *to* the darkness of the underworld *from* that of the womb, which he compares with 3.20-21 (*from* dust...*to* dust). Mizrahi does not offer a translation, but he presumably understands 'it never saw or knew sun, descending from this (darkness) to that'. His reading finds some support, as he notes, in Sir 30.17, where ונוחת עולם is set in parallel with וילרד שאול, and Mizrahi thinks that an original reference to descent is also echoed in the midrash to this passage, which tells a parable about a man disembarking ('going down') from a ship.

That last point, I think, stresses too much a minor aspect of the midrashic story, in which the issue is that the man sees but has no more enjoyment of things than a man who stayed on the ship, although it is not impossible that the midrash is acknowledging the resemblance of roots. In the case of Ben Sira, it is similarly possible that some play is in the mind of the writer, but it is not difficult to see 'eternal rest' as a consequence of, rather than an equivalent to, 'descent to the underworld'. By saying (170) that 'Ms B (*prima manu*) contains two parallel formulations of Sir 30:17', Mizrahi seems to suggest that the text has something like a double rendering, but it is not clear what that could mean in the context of the Hebrew text itself, and there is no reason to see anything more than commonplace parallelism. The main objections to this suggestion, however, are that it seems unnecessary (the reason that Schoors rejects it), and that it removes the explicit rationale for Qohelet's claim that the stillborn is better than the man.

6.6 even if] For M ואלו, 4QQoh^a II, 3, reads אם לוא. At first glance, this might appear to be a reversal of the sense, because although it only otherwise appears in biblical Hebrew at Esth 7.4, the meaning 'if' or 'in the case that' is well-established for אילו / אלו in mishnaic usage (cf. at 4.10), while אם לא more typically means 'if not' (a sense that would force us to take the stillborn as the subject; e.g. Num 5.19).[9] These are probably, however, just two related expressions, or even variants of what is essentially the same expression, used respectively to present an open condition and a condition that has not been or cannot be fulfilled ('If it had been the case that...', 'Were it possible that...', etc.). Accordingly, the לוא of 4QQoh^a is not the negative לא (as it commonly is in that manuscript), but the לו / לוא used for this purpose in earlier Hebrew texts. That expression אם לוא probably lies behind the difficult אם לא of Ezek 3.6, and its development is discussed at some length in Schoors, *The Preacher* I, 136-37, although it remains difficult to establish the extent to which the combination of particles and the contraction to אלו were influenced by Aramaic or other usage. Observing Masoretic characterizations of the form as 'defective', Ginsburg, *Massorah*, 4:89, suggests that it was understood to be a contraction of אי לו, analogous to ואילו in 4.10, which would in turn suggest an interpretation of the latter as conditional.

I do not take this to be aposiopesis, or the beginning of a broken construction in which the protasis is replaced by a question (as, e.g., Seow), but a continuation of what has preceded: the stillborn is in a better position than the man, even if that man goes on to live thousands of years, so long as he remains unable to find pleasure. Accordingly, I doubt that yet another individual has been introduced, as Ogden suggests (we would at least need an explicit subject like איש to introduce him).

6.6 he lived] As we might expect (cf. GKC §159 l–m, x–y on the biblical usage of אלו / לו / לוא), אלו is generally followed by the qatal in the protasis, as here, and it is the syntax of the condition rather than considerations of tense that have governed the form of the verb. Qohelet is not stating that the man is now

---

[9] As Schoors notes, Castelli did suggest that the stillborn continues to be the subject in 6.6, and that Qohelet envisages the possibility that, had it not died, it might have found itself in the same position as the man (do not all go to the one place?). This is an interesting idea, which both incorporates the last part of the verse and saves a further switch of subject here, back to the man, while Castelli himself emphasizes that it seems better to read the text this way than to suppose lazy repetition on the part of the author, so long as it can be done 'senza sforzare il testo', 'without forcing the text'. The fact alone, however, that we have to take as read some equivalent to 'if he had not died' does seem to place that text under considerable strain, and Castelli's reading seems significantly to weaken Qohelet's argumentation.

dead, but projecting an implausible future, in which the man has achieved an incredible lifespan. The purpose is not to repeat the point made already in 6.3, but to emphasize that there is no limit on its validity: the scales will never tip in favour of the man, however long he continues to live. The form of חיה attested in both M and 4QQoh[a] (II, 3) is unusual, and we should expect יה, which is normal in biblical usage: חיה appears elsewhere only with an initial waw, and in a limited number of places; Schoors, *The Preacher* I, 99, accepts as original Ezek 18.23; 33.11; Esth 4.11; Neh 9.29, which all have consecutive וחיה, and which are all late (cf. also J-M §79 s, especially n. 1).

6.6 a thousand years twice over] As Barton and others have pointed out, the expression אלף שנים פעמים probably does not mean just 'two thousand years', although it is often translated that way. In biblical and in later Hebrew, פעם is used in the dual or with numerals to indicate the number of times that something happens or is done (e.g. זה פעמים, 'it is twice now that...' in Gen 27.36; 43.10; פעמים ארבע, 'four times' in Neh 6.4). As with the English 'times', the sense can involve multiplication rather than simple repetition, so the people are to be supplemented by 'a hundred times' their existing number in 2 Sam 24.3, or made 'a thousand times as many' in Deut 1.11, but this is not simply a way in which multiples of numbers are expressed: Qohelet seems to be saying that the man will live a thousand years twice, not that he will live twice-a-thousand years. G χιλίων ἐτῶν καθόδους, which Gentry, 'Role of the Three', 160, translates as 'Even if he lived recurrences of a thousand years', does not reflect the dual of M. Likewise, α' has (καὶ εἰ ἔζησεν) χίλια ἔτη καθόδους (although the citation of the reading is unusual in the manuscripts; see Marshall, Gentry, 'Role of the Three', 166), and these readings open up the possibility of an even longer lifespan (cf. Ibn Ezra, who understands the text to mean a thousand thousands). The plural and dual forms of the Hebrew are identical, of course, in the consonantal text, and the dual is only implied by the absence of a numeral. S, Hie, V, T all agree with M.

6.6 but never found happiness] Lit. 'and did not see good'. See the note 'eats, drinks and finds good' at 3.13; the fact that 'the good' is not located here in any particular activity, and the use of טובה instead of טוב (as at 5.17) probably make no appreciable difference to the sense, which is clearly the antithesis of the failure to be sated by what is good in 6.3. Although 'seeing good' carries particular connotations for Qohelet, the idea may be linked to the imagery of the man 'walking in darkness' (6.4). Ginsberg's idea, that we should read the verb here as from רוה has already been mentioned (see the note 'and you must see' at 2.1): it does make some sense in this context, but is hardly necessary.

6.6B-9

(6.6b) Is it not to just the one place that everybody's going? (6.7) When all a person's work is for their mouth, and also the self is not fulfilled, (6.8) then, like the wise man's advantage over the fool, what is there for the poor man in knowing that he will go on among the living? (6.9) What is in front of one's eyes is better than a hunger that just goes on. That too is an illusion, and wishing for the wind.

Commentary

Qohelet uses some complicated analogies to make his point here, which can be clarified by taking them in a different order. The prospect for a poor man is of a life lived in constant hunger, which will eventually deliver him to the same place as those who have experienced no such need—just as, Qohelet reminds us, he observed in 2.13-15 that the wise man and the fool meet the same end, rendering wisdom pointless. There is, correspondingly and similarly, no benefit for that poor man in knowing that his life will continue: he is going to suffer without gaining anything that he would not have got anyway. The insatiable rich, back in 5.7-11, and more recently the man in 6.3-6, who can find no satisfaction from his fortune, are people who work to feed themselves, but never quench their appetite: anyone in this position is intrinsically like the poor man, facing a future of constant hunger, from which they will ultimately gain nothing. Survival without satisfaction is a delusion, and we should look to what is before us at the moment, rather than to any such future. In short, it is pointless to want to keep on living, if there is pain or effort but no fulfilment in that living.

6.6b] As the division of the verses suggests, 6b has traditionally been seen as the conclusion to Qohelet's comparison in 6.3-6, but it does not belong there. This issue played no role in that comparison, and it was not because the man was going to the same place as the stillborn that his many years of life were useless, but because he saw no pleasure in all those years. The association of this statement with what precedes it, rather than with what follows, has been motivated by the references to burial and darkness in 6.3-5, and the Targum illustrates one of the interpretations to which this has given rise: the man will go to Gehenna along with all the other sinners if he has not devoted his long life to study and good works. It seems likely that the Masoretic punctuation reflects a tradition which understood the text in some similar way, but modern efforts, driven by that punctuation, seem sometimes no less forced. For example, according to Fischer, *Skepsis*, 71-72, Qohelet's whole point has been to declare that human existence is only ever a longer or shorter journey to death, with happiness contingent on the will of God, while Seow takes him to be saying that 'if one does not enjoy good when one is able, then there is no difference between the living and the dead'—which is not what the previous verses have been saying.

In fact, Qohelet uses this question here not as a way to epitomize his statements so far, but in order to mark the summarizing character of what follows by referring back to points that he made earlier. Its language, of course, is strongly reminiscent of 3.20, and more loosely of 2.13-15, which is the passage that he will pick up in 6.8, and Qohelet's intention seems to be to present his more recent claims as building upon conclusions that he reached earlier. The sheer futility of a life lived without satisfaction rests not upon the immediate problems caused by greed or deprivation, but upon the fact that no gain can ultimately be achieved by the dead from any life. Perpetually to defer satisfaction, by always wanting more, will in the end be to lose any possible benefit, precisely because the world is, Qohelet claims, the way he described it earlier. The question also, though, sets up a theme of movement that will be continued in 6.8 and 6.9, using the same verb. I have translated it in those places as 'go on', but there is an image throughout 6.6b-9 of humans processing through life, as it were, towards death, and this is the movement that Qohelet will ascribe to the poor man and the self.

6.7] There is no explicit 'when...then' in the Hebrew, but if this were a general statement that everybody works only for their mouth, without fulfilling their appetite or their 'self', then it would be difficult to reconcile it with the fact that Qohelet has only just finished talking about a man whose inability to satisfy his self was presented as exceptional (cf. 6.3). Qohelet might be picking up that reference and talking about a world in which we were all like that, but I think it is more straightforward to see this as an expression of the condition or circumstance to which the following questions are addressed.

Lavoie, 'Ambiguïtés et désir', 190, makes the point that mouths are not only about food, and argues that Qohelet is talking not just about survival here, but also about the pleasure and happiness that can be achieved *via* the mouth. I do not disagree, to the extent that Qohelet evokes an image of people feeding themselves potentially for many reasons, but it is important not to erode the contrast between intention and effect which is at the heart of his comment: whether they are eating because they are hungry, or tickling their palates with a fine wine, these people are depicted as failing to achieve some more significant satisfaction.

Lavoie also picks up (193-94) an idea that the mouth and self in question here can be read not as those of the person, but those of the place to which all people are going—Sheol, which is sometimes personified and described in terms of its insatiability (e.g. Prov 27.20). This offers an intriguing and brutally nihilistic image of humans working ultimately only to feed death, and the text is arguably ambiguous in this respect. It is less clear, however, that this ambiguity was intended by the author, and few commentators, ancient or modern, have actually taken it that way—not least because Qohelet has been talking for some time, and with no ambiguity, about human satisfaction, so that the context gives a strong steer toward the normal interpretation.

6.8] The question here has caused great difficulties to interpreters, for reasons identical to those surrounding the fools in 4.17: the Hebrew appears on the face of it to be saying that the poor man knows *how* to do something. This has naturally led many to suppose that his 'going' or 'walking' must have some special significance, and this has not just inspired such renderings as the RSV's 'And what does the poor man have who knows how to conduct himself before the living?', but also provoked many attempts to contrast or associate the poor man with the wise man. As in the earlier verse, I think it is simpler in this context to suppose that Qohelet is using the Hebrew expression not with its typical sense of 'know *how*', but with a prospective reference: the poor man 'knows *that he is going to*'. What he knows is that he is going to 'keep going', or, in the light of 6.6, 'keep walking' among the living but towards death. It is possible that the sense was originally clearer, although it is difficult to interpret the evidence from Qumran, which points to a text that may have differed in some respects.

Much recent commentary has focused upon the idea that Qohelet is attacking here, or at least referring to, a fashion for associating poverty with piety in the post-exilic period, which would permit 'poor' to be seen as something at least comparable to 'wise'. Without prejudice, however, to the question of whether there actually was some particular association (which we shall touch on in the commentary to 9.14-15), the real issue is whether the 'poor man' actually has to be aligned with the 'wise man' here, when it seems unlikely that 'the living' are correspondingly a counterpart to the 'fool'. If anything, moreover, it is the reference to the wise man and the fool that seems problematic: wisdom has played no part in the discussion up to this point (and Qohelet has only mentioned it once in passing, at 4.18, since the end of ch. 2), while economics, one way or another, have been on Qohelet's mind since 5.7. As he winds up his discussion of wealth, in other words, we might fully expect Qohelet to use the vocabulary of poverty here, but a reference to wisdom seems quite out of place.

As is often recognized, the claimed lack of distinction between the wise man and the fool evokes 2.13-15, where Qohelet had earlier already established, in very similar terms, that their common fate gives no advantage to the wise man. In the light of that, I think we should read the first part of the verse not as an attempt to broach a new and different topic, but as a way of laying a foundation for the second: the continuation of a life in poverty is as pointless as Qohelet found his wisdom to be. This is true even if we follow the Masoretic text, which juxtaposes two rhetorical questions, 'what is the advantage of the wise man over the fool?', and 'what is there for the poor man...?'. That is best understood here, I think, loosely in terms of 'we know the answer to the first question, and the answer to the second will be the same'. However, in one of the manuscripts from Qumran we find a reading that can be understood as drawing a more explicit analogy, and that is the direct basis of my translation here (see the notes). On this understanding, Qohelet does return to the topic of wisdom, which is about to become very important in the next chapter, but he does so by drawing it in almost incidentally to his current discussion.

I have expressed some scepticism that 'poor' here is being used in relation to contemporary associations of poverty with piety, but there is probably some figurative aspect to its use, all the same. To be sure, the question that Qohelet asks could be understood simply in specifically economic terms: what is the point in continuing to live (presumably in hardship), when one has none of the things in which pleasure might be found (at least in the eyes of the materialistic Qohelet)? That would be adding something new to what has been said already, however, and the initial context supposed in 6.7 suggests that Qohelet is looking beyond simple poverty, toward an impoverishment that arises from some basic absence of fulfilment. To be 'poor' here is not simply to lack goods or money, but to find no fundamental satisfaction in what one does have. In the broader context, indeed, we are probably supposed to understand that even the wealthy may be poor in this sense, and, although the vocabulary is different, the idea is not dissimilar, perhaps, to that in 4.14, where the old and foolish king will always be, in some sense, poorer than the poor, wise child. That is not to say that 'poor' does not mean 'poor', however: Qohelet is using the deprivations of poverty as a figure for the absence of fulfilment.

6.9] When the same verb has already been given prominence twice already, in 6.6 and 6.8 (where the same unusual form of the infinitive was employed), it is unlikely that we should assign a wholly different sense to the 'going' of the self here. Beyond that, however, we are left at something of a loss, because we do not know for sure what either 'the seeing of the eyes' or 'the going of the self' would have signified to the original audience. We encountered an expression similar to the first in 5.10, and the same expression that is used here will occur again in 11.9. In all its uses, but especially the last, it is likely (but not certain) that Qohelet uses this image to refer to taking pleasure in some way, perhaps involving attentiveness to the world around or to what is in front of us. The 'going of the self' is less likely to be an established idiom, but the word for 'self' can have a range of connotations, including 'life', 'appetite' or 'desire': commentators have correspondingly seen many possible meanings here, ranging from death to the 'wandering of desire'—largely according to their understanding of the context.

Matters are made no easier by Qohelet's further remark that 'this too is vapour', which serves a structural function by bringing the current discussion to an end, but which also requires an explanation: is the 'vapour' the claim that has just been made, in which case Qohelet may be being critical of that claim (as seemed to be true in 2.26), or is he referring back more generally? It is hard to be sure, because of this, even whether the first part of the verse is expressing a sentiment compatible with his preceding remarks, or an idea with which he disagrees.

It is very difficult, then, to say anything useful about this verse with any confidence. So far as we can tell, though, the most natural sense of the first part is something like 'what one sees is better than continuing hungry', or, by extension, 'better to take what you see than to go on yearning for something' (cf. Gordis: 'Better a joy at hand than longing for distant pleasures')—and this has been a popular understanding among commentators ancient and modern. If it seems too self-evident, we should perhaps understand it either in terms of seizing what we have rather than holding out for more ('a bird in the hand is worth two in the bush'), or as an admonition against letting our needs become more important to us than the fulfilment of those needs. In either case, the sentiment seems entirely in line with Qohelet's beliefs elsewhere that we should seize life and live it to the full, so the idea is unremarkable in the context of the book as a whole. It appears, however, more precisely in a context where Qohelet has been talking for some time about people who seem unable to do just this, and whose 'hunger' will inevitably continue, so its relationship with this context is more complicated: people should be acting on this advice, but many will not, and some perhaps cannot. The 'vapour' lies, perhaps, both in the delusion of those who spurn or defer satisfaction, and in the illusion, implicit in the advice itself, that it is always easy just to choose such satisfaction.

Notes

6.6 Is it not to just the one place that everybody's going?] I have tried in the translation to reflect the word-order of the Hebrew, which emphasizes the singular destination, rather than the fact that everybody is going there. This question relates to what follows, and correspondingly כל is a reference to all humans, not simply (as many commentators assert) to 'both' the man and the stillborn.

G* is εἰς τόπον ἕνα τὰ πάντα πορεύεται, which takes כל as 'everything' ('to one place, everything goes'; cf. Hie, V *omnia*), but there is a well-attested variant εἰς τόπον ἕνα πορεύεται τὰ πάντα, which McNeile, 144, took to be original, and to reflect a similar reversal in the Hebrew, הולך הכל. Although we cannot exclude the possibility of a Hebrew variant (and the transposition would be an easier error in Hebrew than in Greek), an early date for it is not affirmed by 4QQoh[a] II, 4, which has the same order as M, and it seems likely to have been the variant in G itself, perhaps originally just a stylistic improvement, which has influenced the order in S ܗܠܟܝܢ ܠܐ ܗܘܐ ܠܐܬܪܐ ܚܕ ܐܙܠ ܟܠ *dlm' l' hw' lḥd 'tr' 'zl kwl'*. In Hie, V, Jerome's *properant*, 'hasten', adds the notion of everybody rushing to the grave, and another, very well-established G variant, the future πορεύσεται, 'will go', seems likely also to be interpretative.

6.7 When all a person's work] There is no conjunction in the Hebrew, but I take this verse to establish the situation in which the questions of the next verse will apply (cf. 1.8 for a similar case; also, e.g., Job 9.24; 34.29), so that it is, in effect, an unmarked conditional sentence. It seems unlikely that, having specified the particular case of a man ונפשו לא תשבע in 6.3, just four verses later Qohelet will be declaring of humans generally that הנפש לא תמלא, and this drives many commentators to see האדם not as generic, but as a reference to that man, although they do not explain why Qohelet does not accordingly still describe him as איש. It is simpler to suppose that האדם is generic, while the situation is not. On the article, see the note 'every person' at 3.13.

S ܕܗܒܠܐ ܐܢܫܐ *kl d'ml 'nš'*, 'all at which man labours' is odd, and, if it is original, suggests that עמל has been taken as a verb. On the sense of the Hebrew noun, see the note at 1.3; Foresti, '*'āmāl* in Koheleth', 429, takes it to mean 'income' here, and that broadly in the sense, inasmuch as Qohelet envisages working in order to earn a living, rather than scavenging directly for food here, but it is hardly necessary to spell that out.

6.7 for his mouth] S continues its strange rendering here with ܒܦܘܡܗ *bpwmh*, '(all at which a man works is) *in* his mouth'. It does seem plausible (*contra* Euringer) that this is based on a variant reading in the Hebrew or Greek sources, and it may be a need to accommodate the reading that has driven the curious translation of כל עמל האדם as well (see the previous note): the translator did not want to say that a person's actual work is in their mouth. The Latin tradition heavily favours *in ore* here (cf. Hie and V), which could be derived from a similar variant, since if it were just a slightly free rendering of G εἰς στόμα we should really have expected the accusative, *in os* (cf. V at, e.g., Ps 40.4 ET 40.3). The simplest explanation would be a corrupt reading in the Greek tradition, but no such reading is attested in the extant manuscripts, and it is quite possible that the Syriac and Latin traditions each independently assimilated to the more common 'in (one's) mouth'.

Luther made the interesting suggestion, based on the use of לפי הטף in Gen 47.12 (cf. Exod 12.4), that לפיהו is being used similarly here as a way of indicating proportion. This deserves more consideration than it is usually given, but it is doubtful that we can extrapolate from those passages, which refer specifically to the distribution of food, a more general idea of doing things proportionally, let alone the idea that Qohelet is saying each human works in accordance with their ability to do so. No less importantly, it is difficult to ignore the literal sense of פיהו when it stands so close to נפש. In origin at least, the נפש could be not just the self or the appetite, but also physically the throat or gullet, and there are indications that this sense persisted (e.g. Pss 69.2 ET 69.1; 105.18). That offers not only some opportunity for writers to play upon the different meanings (as probably, for instance, in Prov 3.22), but also a clear connection with the mouth (cf. Ps 63.6 ET 63.5). What Qohelet presents in this verse, therefore, is a sort of paradox: people work to fill their mouths, but this doesn't fill their throats—or rather, it fails to meet the needs of their נפש. Coming so soon after 6.3, with its similar reference to the נפש, this is probably not intended to suggest that their appetites are insatiable, as is occasionally suggested, but to depict the same sort of problem as in that verse: there are humans who work to meet the pressing needs of their body, while failing to fulfil a less obvious need inside themselves, and so their survival means no more than did the prosperity of the man who could not enjoy it, or the longevity of the man who found no satisfaction.

A number of commentators have observed helpfully that the verse shares with Prov 16.26 a linking of both the mouth and the נפש with work (עמל). That saying declares that 'a worker's נפש works for him, because his mouth puts pressure on him', in other words that the worker is motivated by his appetite, and Qohelet may be drawing on an established idea that work is motivated by hunger, expressed in these terms. The connection between נפש and the mouth, however, has led some interpreters in a very different direction. Ackroyd, 'Two Hebrew Notes', 84-85, suggested in 1967 that the pronoun on פיהו refers back not to האדם but to the 'place', of the last verse, i.e. Sheol, and translated 'All man's trouble is simply for its (Sheol's) mouth, but even so (its) appetite is not satisfied'. This was picked up rapidly by Dahood (in 'Hebrew–Ugaritic Lexicography VI', 368; 'Hebrew–Ugaritic Lexicography VIII', 395), who added the further suggestion that נפש here is 'throat' or 'maw', and this version has been adopted by Lauha and Lohfink. The idea is not inherently implausible: Sheol is proverbially hungry (e.g. Hab 2.5), and Isa 5.14 connects פה with נפש to talk about Sheol swallowing the population of Jerusalem, so such a reference would be by no means isolated. There are significant obstacles, however. Seow's objection (to what he regards as 'a tantalizing possibility') is that we should expect the 'place' to have been named if it was going to be personified this way (although Dahood takes the 'one place' to be a specific allusion), and Murphy comments quite rightly and perhaps decisively, that, 'Although all this is possible philologically, the idea of Sheol consuming human *toil* is peculiar': it is more typically people themselves that are to be swallowed (cf. also his 'On Translating Ecclesiastes', 577-78). Whilst the reading does provide a way, furthermore, to integrate 6.7 into its immediate context—a task which has driven many commentators to despair—it fails to achieve a broader congruence with the context, and involves a sudden leap from discussions of longevity to the personification of an avaricious death.

6.7 and also] It is interesting to compare this verse with 1.7, where all the rivers flow into the sea, and the sea is not filled. There the two statements are linked by a simple conjunction, but here Qohelet uses וגם, and it is not clear whether that implies any difference of meaning or emphasis. The discussion about וגם here, however, has been hindered by a lack of terminological clarity. Schoors complains that 'critics translate the particle as an adversative: "but, and yet, *et pourtant*", but they parse it as a concessive', while Ellermeier, *Qohelet I.1*, 250 observes similarly, that to explain it as concessive but to render it as adversative (as, for example, Barton does) just obscures the issue completely: 'Adversativ- und Konzessivsätze sind eben nicht dasselbe!', 'adversative and concessive clauses are simply not the same!' In this case, the difference is essentially between reading 'but his נפש is never filled' (adversative: the statements are contrasted) and 'even though his נפש is never filled' (concessive: humans keep eating despite the fact that they find no satisfaction).

The confusion has been provoked largely, I suspect, by the fact that concessive uses of גם are widely acknowledged, but claims that it can be adversative are disputed, so although most commentators adopt the adversative sense, they tend to justify it in terms of the concessive. The reason that the claims are disputed offers, in fact, the strongest reason to reject an adversative sense here, even though it has been advocated so often (albeit in the guise of a 'concessive'): if גם can be adversative, examples are so rare (*pace* Gordis, 222, and Lavoie, 'Ambiguïtés et désir', 191, who consider it common in this book) that it is unlikely any reader would have taken the particle this way unless the context left them no choice, which is not the case here. Ellermeier, in *Qohelet I.1*, 250-51, rejects his own earlier reading of וגם as adversative in 'Die Entmachtung' (2, 20 'und dennoch'), and points out that if we are to insist on an adversative sense, then it can be obtained from the conjunction alone, although the גם would tend then to make the meaning 'all work is for the mouth, but *even* the נפש is not filled'. He also considers the possibility that Qohelet is simply presenting two sayings, linked by וגם: '"All work is for the mouth" and furthermore "The throat is never filled"', but himself settles for a (true) concessive sense. Despite the fact that he cites Ellermeier for his description of the clause as 'concessive', Fox translates the verse adversatively, as 'All a man's toil is for his mouth, but the appetite is never filled', showing that the terminological confusion remains alive and well (although Schoors and Seow have described their similar renderings of גם accurately as adversative).

At the risk of compounding that confusion, I think that two further possibilities should be considered. The first is that גם here is emphatic, and is being used in the way that it is sometimes used with personal pronouns to mean, e.g., וגם אני 'I, for my part' (Amos 4.6; Mic 6.13). In Neh 5.8, this is used to draw a sharp contrast 'We have bought…(but) you, for your part, sell'. My own preference, however, is for a second, which is linked to my construal of the verse as a whole, and is part of the reason for that understanding: this takes וגם to be used here in its most obvious and common additive sense, simply to present the second of two associated conditions: when it is the case that all human work is for the mouth *and also* the case that the נפש remains unsatisfied, then human life is not worth living—everybody is going to die, and nothing is gained, whoever one is, from a life without satisfaction. I take the combination of conditions to be important: Qohelet probably understands all or most humans to be working in order to feed themselves, and the problem arises only for those who do this but find no satisfaction. The reading of the verse as conditional does not depend on reading וגם this way, but this is the simplest understanding of וגם, and it supports that reading.

S has avoided the problem—by accident or design, it has no equivalent to גם—but of the other ancient versions, only V renders it as adversative. None explicitly reads it as concessive, and 4QQoh[a] affirms M וגם, so there is, therefore, no text-critical support for Ginsberg's speculative emendation of גם to אם.

6.7 the self] As Bertram, 'Hebräischer und griechischer', 38-39, has pointed out, G's translation of נפש with ψυχή, 'soul', although more or less compelled by its translation technique, leads it to express a very particular, spiritualized sort of sentiment here ('the soul will not be satisfied'), and any English translation of the word risks a similar problem (although Bartholomew, among others, seems happy to run that risk). For the difficulties, and for some of the various senses of נפש in play, see the notes at 6.3 and earlier in this verse. In short, the context and proximity to 'mouth' emphasize the physical aspects of נפש more than was the case in 6.2 and 6.3: it is the human throat and appetite, which need sustenance (as in Prov 16.26). The verse plays on these aspects, but the meaning is not, of course, confined to them, and although he is using the imagery of hunger or appetite, Qohelet is not literally worrying about humans who work to eat but remain hungry, but about those who, like the men of the preceding verses, lack satisfaction at a deeper level. The neutral 'self' captures very little of this, but does at least avoid putting the emphasis in the wrong place. In particular, the very common translations in terms of 'appetite' or 'desire' imply, I think, a sort of frustration that is not central to what Qohelet is saying: the issue for him is not that people have some conscious difficulty fulfilling needs which they know they have, but that the joylessness of their lives robs those lives of meaning.

There is no possessive pronoun on נפש, in contrast to the preceding פיהו, and the absence is affirmed by 4QQoh[a], G, Hie, T. There is an equivalent to 'his' in some manuscripts of G and Hie, however, and the G variant may have influenced the appearance of an equivalent in S and V also, if it is not simply a facilitation. Many modern translations and commentaries likewise supply a second 'his', and the use of the article gives an excuse to do so: it is clear that not just any נפש is intended, but *the* נפש of someone working for their mouth (so, e.g., Lauha; cf. J-M §137 f 2). The absence of the suffix does deserve some notice, however, and it is not enough just to claim with Dahood, 'Hebrew-Ugaritic Lexicography VI', 368, that the article 'is meant to balance stylistically the suffix' (whatever that may mean), or to compare the similar instance at 7.1, which is text-critically problematic in this respect: neither actually offers an explanation. My own suspicion is that Qohelet uses no suffix because, unlike the mouth, the נפש he is talking about is not strictly that of האדם conceived generically, but that of anyone who finds no satisfaction in the work that everybody does (see my comments on גם, above). There has been a shift from the general to the particular, in other words, and so a suffix would have no direct antecedent: 'when everybody works for their mouth, and the נפש (of anyone doing so) is not filled'.

6.7 is not fulfilled] Lit. 'will not be fulfilled'. θ' uses οὐ χορτασθήσεται, 'he will not be filled (with food)', which Theodotion used for לא תשבע at 6.3; this probably represents an interpretative linking of the two passages rather than a variant reading with תשבע in his source, but it also, as Bertram, 'Hebräischer und griechischer', 39, observes, retains a connection with the physical appetite, which is implicit in the Hebrew but absent from the more general G οὐ πληρωθήσεται. A G variant οὐκ ἐμπλησθήσεται, found in the hexaplaric *O*-group of manuscripts, has more of that nuance, and is often used of food in particular. In fact, this is the verb (ἐμπίμπλημι) that Gentry himself took G to have used in renderings of לא תשבע or לא ישבע at 1.8 and 4.8 (and for השבע at 5.11), but not at 5.9 or 6.3, where he prefers forms from πίμπλημι (although Rahlfs, we may recall, preferred ἐμπλησθήσεται at 6.3, where that is more widely attested as a variant). For מלא, the translator uses forms from, or terms closely related to, πληρόω, except at 1.7, where there is no significant rival to ἐμπιμπλαμένη, and 8.11, where the translation is a contextual ἐπληροφορήθη. This degree of flexibility makes it difficult to use translation technique as a guide to the proper reading in each place (and the reading at 6.3 seems particularly uncertain), but, if its origins are not in one of the other translations, the variant here is likely an assimilation to 6.3. T supplies a specific object of satisfaction ('with eating and drinking'), as do Theodulphian manuscripts of V, which have *non implebitur bonis*, 'will not be filled with good things' (cf. 6.3); this matches the tense of M and G (contrast the majority reading *impletur*, 'is filled').

6.8 then, like] Lit. just 'like'. M has כי מה, but 4QQoh[a] II, 6 reads כמה, which we should usually understand as 'how much?'. It is unlikely that this is simply a matter of orthography,[1] and matters are further complicated by

---

[1] Muilenburg, 'A Qoheleth Scroll', 25, writes: 'It seems likely that here we have a preservation of Phoenician spelling in the omission of the *mater lectionis*, especially significant since the scribe usually employs the fuller form elsewhere (*ky* or *ky᾽*)'. It is the very fact, however, that the fuller form is employed elsewhere

Lavoie, 'Ambiguïtés et désir', 180, understands him to be suggesting 'how much!', not 'how much?', which is a sense found often in Aramaic and in the Hebrew of Qumran and later, but which would seem out of place here). If כמה is indeed secondary, and M original, it would seem more likely that it has been provoked somehow by the difficult כי, which many modern commentators have themselves found awkward. That כי certainly does not mark a cause or explanation, but Ginsberg seems to have conscripted no followers for his proposal to move the word to the next verse, and most have seen it as simply emphatic ('what indeed...?', or some such), with a few claiming implausibly that it is adversative, despite the lack of any previous negation: see Schoors, *The Preacher* I, 105.

It may certainly be the case that if we are to read כי here, then it has very little force, as in some other places, like 1 Sam 26.18; 28.13; Zech 9.17, where כי מה seems effectively equivalent to מה alone (note also similar uses of מי כי, e.g. at 7.13; Jer 15.5), and although 'emphatic' can cover such cases, there is little actual emphasis involved.[3] The understanding of σ' is intriguing, however: its τί οὖν περισσόν, 'what advantage then?' (for the Greek expression, see, e.g., Acts 21.22; Rom 6.1), apparently reflects an understanding of כי as marking a consequence, or perhaps even an apodosis, as it often does in expressions like כי עתה (e.g. Num 22.29) and כי אז (e.g. Job 11.15); see J-M §168 s, and especially Schoors, 'The Particle כי', 250-51. σ' takes the question as a problem that arises from and in the circumstances outlined in the previous verse, but whether or not we could take the connection to be marked explicitly depends on whether or not we are willing to grant that כי might have been understood to have a consecutive force outside such expressions, when clear examples are rare (Isa 7.9 is the best known instance).

The problem with כי in the text as it stands is not acute, and we could legitimately treat כי מה as equivalent to מה, but there is a broader issue that I have addressed in the comments above: the reference to the wise man and fool has little obvious place here except as an analogy for the statement about the poor man which will follow. In that case, it seems worth returning to the כמה of 4QQoh[a], which could reasonably be read not as 'how much?', but as a writing of כמו, the very word that Hebrew uses to express such analogies. The Aramaic equivalent is often written that way, and if the scribe has not been influenced by that, then he may have been swayed by the use of ה to write the third-person masculine singular suffix pronoun, which is a spelling found quite commonly even in Masoretic texts; on the use of ה for -ō / -ô at Qumran, see Reymond, *Qumran Hebrew*, 159-60. After some hesitation, I have adopted that reading. Matters of context aside, it is easier on balance, I

---

[3] If אשר, in the מי אשר of 6.12 is being used similarly (see the note there), then it is possible that this usage is related not so much to emphasis as to the use of כי and אשר to mark object clauses or indirect speech.

the other versions, among which only T ארום מא מותר איח, 'for what surplus/ advantage is there (to the wise man)', and Hie *quid enim est amplius*, 'for what is more (for the wise man)' (of which V *quid habet amplius [sapiens]*, 'what has the wise man more', is probably a looser version), support M clearly and directly.

Although the ὅτι τίς that is found in many manuscripts of G (and that was adopted by Rahlfs) could indeed be a rendering of M, the Syrohexapla indicates that the τίς in that reading was put under asterisk by Origen—it is a hexaplaric addition, in other words, drawn from the version of α' or θ' (for both of whom ὅτι τίς is indicated), and intended to bring the Greek into line with the Hebrew; see Gentry, 'Role of the Three', 177-80. Gentry himself argues not only that the strongly attested ὅτι (without τίς) is earlier, but that it was supposed originally to be read as ὅ τι (to give the sense 'whatever surplus'). This latter point seems a little strained, even if we do not insist that the expression ought then to agree in gender with περισσεία (Gentry notes the existence of many exceptions), or resist the temptation to wonder just how the translator would have distinguished ὅ τι from the more common ὅτι in his text. If we at least permit the possibility, however, then ὅ τι would translate מה, while ὅτι would render כי. In neither case does G directly support M as a whole, therefore—but it does not necessarily contradict it. Reading ὅτι, McNeile, 144, assumed that G must have found כי מותר for כי מה יותר in its source-text; this is more plausibly, however, a matter of an early error within the Greek tradition itself (a possibility that McNeile acknowledges), with an original τι dropping out after ὅτι: if the translator read כי מה, then we should expect G* to have been ὅτι τι, and we saw a similar case of τι probably falling out after ὅτι in 2.22.[2] It seems likely that S ܡܛܠ ܕܐܝܬ ܝܘܬܪܢܐ ܠܚܟܝܡܐ *mṭl dʾyt ywtrnʾ lḥkymʾ*, 'for there is an advantage for the wise man', is derived from a text of G with just ὅτι, although it may also have been influenced by 2.13 (as Kamenetzky, 219, insists).

Matters may be a little messy, then, but the evidence of G and S offers no strong grounds in itself either to discount the reading of M, or to prefer the כמה of 4QQoh[a]: at most, it raises the faint possibility of a variant text in which מה (or less probably כי) was lacking. Goldman suggests that 4QQoh[a] 'is an attempt to give an advantage to the חכם', an idea that I do not quite understand, unless he means that the use of כמה rather than מה allows that the wise man might have *some* advantage, rather than none at all (apparently also puzzled,

---

which makes this unlikely, and Lavoie, 'Ambiguïtés et désir', 180, is rightly sceptical both of that idea and of the alternative suggestion by Puech, 'Qohelet a Qumran', 149, that the scribe has simply omitted a letter in error.

[2] Euringer, in fact, suggested along the same lines that τίς dropped out after ὅτι in some manuscripts through a graphical error, although that slip is less likely than the loss of τι. I think that τίς itself is secondary, and imported as a hexaplaric correction, but that it actually replaced an original τι that had been lost earlier.

think, to explain how מה כי arose as a hypercorrection to create a parallel to the following מה, than how כמה might have replaced it (unless as a very careless error)—and the attestation is, of course, very early.

6.8 better off] Qohelet uses יותר rather than יתרון here and in 6.11, suggesting that the issue at stake is not that of 'profit' as he usually understands it; the idea of personal advantage is also picked up in 6.11 and 7.11. Elsewhere, he uses יותר to speak of excessive or unnecessary wisdom in 2.15 and 7.16, and it is used rather differently in the epilogue (12.9, 12); this is closer to the only other biblical uses in 1 Sam 15.15 and Esth 6.6, and to later usage.

6.8 What is there for] Or perhaps 'what (advantage) is there for'. M מה ל- is literally 'what for'; cf. σ' τί δὲ τῷ πτωχῷ, 'but what for the poor man'; Hie *quid pauperi*; T ומאן אית ל-. Most manuscripts of G, however, have διότι, 'because'. This was the reading favoured by Rahlfs, but it seems likely that διότι arose as an error early in the transmission of the Greek, and that G* was in fact διὰ τί, 'why' (see Gentry, 'Role of the Three', 180). Through a relatively simple graphical slip, perhaps under interpretative influence, most of the G tradition has turned the second question into a statement. Despite the fact that διότι is the reading even of the hexaplaric Greek manuscripts, the text of Syh here has ܡܛܠ ܡܢܐ *mṭl mn'*, which renders διὰ τί. Its note, therefore, that the readings of α' and θ' are the same as those of the hexaplaric text (unlike the reading of σ'), suggests that α' and θ' also had διὰ τί (cf. Marshall).

It is not absolutely necessary to suppose (as do, e.g., Kamenetzky, 219-20, 236, and McNeile, 145) that the translators must have used a Hebrew text with למה rather than מה ל- in order to come up with διότι or διὰ τί. Gordis showed long ago that מה + ל- + participle in later Hebrew means 'why should someone do something?', and we can grasp the equivalence through such English expressions as 'what (is in it) for someone to?'. That is probably how M is to be understood here, and it saves understanding a second, implicit יותר—although, especially if we understand an analogy between the two ideas here, it is not difficult to do so. It is mildly surprising, however, to find not just G, but also α' and θ' rendering so much according to sense rather than wording, and leaving σ', remarkably, as the only literal translation. It is very possible, therefore, that a variant text with למה existed and served as the basis for most of the Greek translations.[4] If so, it is hard to say whether למה or מה ל- is more likely to have been original. McNeile supposes למה to have been a

---

[4] Kamenetzky, 219-20, takes this to be the basis of S ܠܡܢ *lmn'* as well, and it seems likely that the translation does indeed reflect either למה or an uncorrupted διὰ τί. On the basis of the following ܕ *d*, Lavoie, 'Ambiguïtés et désir', 181, argues that it must actually be equivalent to διότι, and although instances cited in Payne Smith do not suggest that this absolutely excludes the normal interrogative sense, he has a point that the Syriac does not read most naturally as just 'why?'. The construction may suggest, however, not that the translator understands 'because'

corrupt form, which appeared, perhaps, partly as the result of the preceding ל in הכסיל. Ellermeier, on the other hand, takes G to preserve a fragment of the original text in this respect, and offers a radical reconstruction of the Hebrew as למה אני יודע, 'why do I understand?', turning it into a question that Qohelet asks of himself, comparable to that in 2.15.[5] If the putative למה was original, however, it offers no basis for further 'corrections' of the text, and if it was secondary, then it may have come into existence more as a clarification or stylistic improvement than as an accidental corruption. Whether we read למה or מה ל-, the sense is much the same.

V *et*, T ומאן, and σ' δέ all introduce a conjunction before the second question, but as Goldman observes, this is a facilitation, and is unlikely to reflect an original Hebrew variant.

6.8 a poor man in knowing] Lit. 'poor man knowing': I understand the sense to be 'why should the poor man know', as suggested by Gordis (see the previous note).

For the verb, M has יודע, which G translates using a main verb οἶδεν, in accordance with its use of διὰ τί / διότι (see the last note). Hie *nisi scire* reflects a different idea, 'what is there for the poor man *except* to know', which also underlies T אילהין. This is partly interpretative, suggesting that the knowledge is the poor man's only possession, or that to know is the only course open to him, but it may have been provoked also by a knowledge of the vocalization that led M to point לעני with the article (a vocalization affirmed by G and T as well), while the corresponding יודע is indefinite—we should have expected היודע (cf. GKC §126 u; J-M §138 a; the current mismatch goes some way beyond any normal irregularity in Qohelet's use of articles, cited by Lavoie, 'Ambiguïtés et désir', 183, in defence of the M pointing). Of course, the simplest way around this difficulty is to vocalize לעני without the article, and that is probably what we should do (as, e.g., Barton suggests), but it was not unreasonable for the versions to have anticipated an article in לעני after that of הכסיל and to have taken the indefinite יודע as an indication that the participle was not just to be read as a simple attribute of עני.

Some commentators have gone down the same path as Hie and T, albeit in a more radical way. Burkitt, 'Is Ecclesiastes a Translation?', 25, supposes that, 'The advantage of the wise man over the fool, seeing that their fates (according to our author) are so much alike, should consist in some saving or excepting

(which is a difficult sense to extract from the Syriac), but that he has taken a מה or τι as indefinite instead of interrogative, and understood something like 'in respect of whatever it is that the poor man knows'.

[5] Ellermeier, 'Die Entmachtung', 12-15. This reading is adopted by, e.g., Galling 1969; Lange, *Weisheit und Torheit*, 135, and is probably what underlies the suggestion of Loader, which draws out the significance: 'The best reading is probably that the Preacher refers to himself here, asking why he is making all this effort to find out how he must conduct himself in life'.

clause', and he accordingly replaces מה לעני with מבלעדי, 'except', an emendation that has since been advocated by Scott and, apparently independently, by Fischer, *Skepsis*, 73, as well. Other proposals to emend the text have been no less explicitly based on a desire to find a better connection with the first part of the verse, and so Budde, for instance, would read לעשיר מן העני, 'to the rich over the poor', and Hertzberg (followed by Ginsberg) would replace מה לעני יודע with מהעני ליודע, giving a chiastic 'what is to the wise man over the fool, over the poor man, (what is) to him who knows…'; this is picked up by Ginsberg in his 'Supplementary Studies', 45, and in his commentary. Galling 1940 makes the poor man insightful (see below), and reads מהלך for להלך, so that the question asks what advantage he has over one who goes.

Rather more scholars have tried to do this, however, whilst leaving the text as it is, and either viewing the construction as elliptical, or taking particular words to have a special meaning. When Ginsburg says that 'מִן, from the first clause, must be supplied before יוֹדֵעַ', allowing him to read 'what the poor man over him who knoweth', it is not clear whether he is suggesting an emendation or not,[6] but Plumptre, who also favours that solution, sees it explicitly as a matter of ellipsis. Ginsburg himself notes the ellipsis in the interpretations of Rashi and Rashbam, who respectively understand Qohelet to be asking what the poor man has less than a rich man or less than the wise. Of course, suspicions of ellipsis are not always driven by a desire for symmetry in the verse, and much more recently Seow (after toying with the idea that יודע should be emended to וידע) has taken מה לעני יודע to be elliptical for מה לעני שיודע or מה לעני כי יודע, 'what is there for the afflicted that they should know?'.

When it comes to finding special meanings, a few scholars have focused on the second מה here and taken it differently from the first, as an indefinite pronoun supplying the answer to the first question, rather than beginning a second. This reading was proposed by Durell in 1772, who translates '(for what hath the wise more than the fool?) that which the poor hath who knoweth &c.' Apparently unaware of Durell, Aalders argues the case for such a reading at some length, and renders, 'Datgene, wat ook de arme bezit', 'that which the poor man has too', i.e. the knowledge of how to live. Strobel simply translates, 'Was der Arme hat, der weiß, das Leben zu meistern', 'What the poor man has, the knowledge of how to master life', but is clearly following the same interpretation. This is a very interesting approach, in fact, and, in the absence of any evidence that we are actually dealing with poetry here, there is little force in Schoors' objection that 'the parallelism seems to favour a second question instead of an answer'. It is undoubtedly harsh, however, to read each occurrence of מה differently like that.

---

[6] The same is true, of Bernstein, *Quaestiones nonnullae Koheletanae*, a little earlier, where we are told simply, 'Addatur enim oportet מִן', 'For מן must be added' (21 n. 15), although the other instances that he supplies for comparison suggest that Bernstein has ellipsis in mind.

More commentators have paid attention to the עני יודע, and Ibn Ezra, for example, takes the participle as descriptive, so that the poor man stands in parallel with the wise man, and the question is, essentially, 'why should the intelligent poor man walk…?'; similarly Ewald 'der verständige Dulder' (the intelligent sufferer), Galling 1940 'der einsichtige Arme' (the insightful poor man) and Lohfink 'dem Armen, auch wenn er etwas kann', rendered in the ET of his commentary as 'the poor, however perceptive'. Whitley reaches much the same destination by a different route, connecting עני with the root ענה, 'answer', then progressing rapidly and speculatively through the senses 'answer', 'answer effectively', and 'a shrewd and intelligent speaker', until he arrives at 'the intelligent man who knows…'.

A different approach simply imbues עני with a sense that sets it better in parallel with חכם, and Kroeber declares that '"Der Arme" gibt keinen Sinn. Es geht nicht um eine Tugend aus der Not, sondern um ein Verhalten aus der Einsicht', '"The poor" makes no sense. This is not a matter of making a virtue of necessity, but about a behaviour based on insight.' He accordingly translates עני as 'der Zurückhaltende', 'one who is restrained', justifying the translation by reference to the use of an expression ענה את נפש in Lev 16.29 and elsewhere to mean fasting, or some other form of ritualized self-deprivation. Of course, it is questionable whether ענה can have that sort of reflexive sense without את נפש, and Lauha, reasoning in a similar way to Kroeber, is on slightly firmer ground when he argues that we are dealing here with the sort of humility, rather than strict economic poverty or oppression, that is frequently associated with עני in the Psalms (e.g. 72.2). Adopting the same understanding, but contextualizing it rather differently, Michel sees an attack on such an 'Armenfrömmigkeit', a 'piety of poverty', and this interpretation has been supported by, e.g., Krüger, Schwienhorst-Schönberger, Lavoie ('Ambiguïtés et désir', 200-201), and Köhlmoos—it is arguably the dominant interpretation at present. Although Michel claims that the context makes this clear, however, it only does so if one brings certain assumptions to the reading of the verse, and it could be said, indeed, of all these many and varied attempts to emend or to re-interpret מה לעני יודע, that they arise not from any great difficulty inherent in the expression, but from ideas about the verse as a whole, or from interpretations of the words that follow.

6.8 that he will] Or 'how he will'. The use of the infinitive construct with ל- after ידע was discussed in the note 'they have no idea when' at 4.17, and I canvassed the possibility there that Qohelet was using the construction to mean 'know that one is going to' rather than with the sense 'know how to' found at 4.13. Which is appropriate here depends in large part on the way we understand the subsequent clause.

6.8 go on among the living] 4QQoh^a may not reflect the same text as M here. Verse 8 began on line 6 of col. II, and was preserved clearly up to the מ of מן, with the ן broken at the edge of the fragment. Since we know the width of the column from earlier lines, we can use a rough count of characters to work out that line 7, which lies at the bottom of fragment 1 and is badly damaged, should begin with יודע or להלך. The traces, however, do not fit: most of the characters are too fragmentary or damaged to permit reconstruction, but what is left of them probably represents two words, each containing a ל, with its distinctive upright preserved in the space above the line. In neither word is the ל the first character, and the instances are too far apart for us to read the two as one word להלך: Ulrich in DJD transcribes as ל∘∘ ∘ל∘∘. 4QQoh[a] most likely had additional or alternative text here, which is probably beyond recovery. Puech, 'Qohelet a Qumran', 149-50, reads הל]ך אושלו, and reconstructs a preceding שידע in place of M יודע: on that reading, the text must have meant something like 'what (is there) for the poor man who knows, but that he does not walk...'. I doubt, however, that this can be sustained in its entirety—there is insufficient space for the ש in Puech's ושלוא, and the traces do not suit the א. There is a strong possibility, I think, that the 'additional' text here is actually just an error, partially erased, like that with which the scribe began the second line of the same column (five lines above this). If so, it is hard to exclude the possibility that a text identical to M has simply vanished off the edge, after the deletion, but Puech may be right that the final traces are of הלך (or הלוך), where M has להלך. In that case, 4QQoh[a] would simply lack the preposition, which would not require us to understand it very differently (perhaps 'that he is going on' rather than that 'he will go on').

As for M itself, there is at least one potential ambiguity in להלך נגד החיים, since החיים can be read as 'life' (so G, S, Hie, V, Codex Graecus Venetus; cf. 2.17; 6.12; 9.9; without the article at 9.9; 10.19) or as 'the living' (M, T; cf. 4.2, 15; 9.5 and probably 9.4). Two manuscripts noted by Kennicott enforce the former sense, replacing נגד with דרך to read 'the way of life' (cf. Jer 21.8). There is also one grammatical curiosity, which lies in the fact that Qohelet uses the strong form of the infinitive (להלך) here and in the next verse, but the weak form ללכת elsewhere (1.7; 5.14; 7.2; 10.15); it is particularly striking that 10.15 uses that form after ידע, but it is hard to say whether there any distinction of sense is intended, or if the differences, for that matter, are even original. The other ancient versions present no significant problems, although G has translated נגד using κατέναντι, and Hie (perhaps on the basis of La) rendered that in turn with *contra*, so that, through a sort of translational game of whispers, Jerome has found himself with a poor man who walks 'against' life, which does not really fit his interpretation—hence, presumably, the very different and theologically interpretative V *ut pergat illuc ubi est uita*, 'that he might go there, where there is life'. The Targum talks similarly of the man knowing how to walk amongst the righteous in Eden.

Those issues aside, no single word of the clause presents any great difficulties, but taken together they are something of a mystery: we may well be dealing with an idiomatic expression, as Gordis points out, and without knowing the meaning of that idiom, it is difficult to know in what particular sense we should take each of the words. The best clues are offered by נגד,

which we encountered earlier in 4.12. In that verse, I suggested that it was being used to imply alignment or association with people (see the note 'stand before him'), and it most commonly indicates action or location in the presence or sight of others. Used this way, it can have the implication that what is נגד someone is known to them (e.g. Ps 31.20 ET 31.19; Prov 15.11), and something done נגד the sun, in 2 Sam 12.12, is the opposite of something done secretly. When it is used with objects and places, נגד indicates 'before', 'in front of', 'opposite' or 'in line with', and this is the implication on those rare occasions when it is used as a preposition with verbs of motion (cf. Josh 3.16), although it can also be found with suffix pronouns used reflexively, meaning '(to go) straight ahead' (e.g. Josh 6.20; Jer 31.39; Amos 4.3).

None of this favours such translations as Gordis' 'knows how to meet life' or 'face the living', because נגד is all about position, alignment or visibility, not about engagement, and to walk נגד someone would be to walk in their sight, not to walk facing them. The same is not true of מנגד ל-, which occurs in Judg 20.34 and Prov 14.7, and which implies movement toward something from a position of disengagement with it, but there is no good reason to suppose that the uses of that expression can throw any direct light on the uses of נגד itself, so Fox's idea that we are dealing here with leading people or getting along with them, based heavily on his own interpretation of Prov 14.7, has no secure foundation. Some translations seem more or less to disregard the attested meanings of נגד altogether: Provan, for instance, talks of 'walking well through life' and Seow of 'going along with life' (an idea approved by Schoors). In this respect, the traditional understanding that the clause means to go 'before' or 'in the presence of the living' is greatly to be preferred, and is in line with many other instances of נגד, although I suspect that, as in 4.12, there may be some more specific implication of association (and there is also, perhaps, some connection with the expressions about the living and dead in the very difficult 9.3-4).

If that is the location of the 'going', however, we can only guess at its nature, and so it is surprising to find little direct discussion of the matter among commentators. The idea that ידע ל- with the infinitive must mean 'know how to' has undoubtedly exercised a strong influence here, however, and many translations correspondingly assume that הלך must involve some sort of expertise; hence, for example, RSV's 'knows how to conduct himself'. Of course, it is true that the verb is very often used in contexts where it expresses behaviour, and this can hardly be disconnected from the common image or metaphor of walking a particular path, or following in the footsteps of a particular person.[7] In such uses, however, הלך is essentially neutral, and

---

[7] See, for instance, Zehnder, *Wegmetaphorik*. It is interesting to note that a few manuscripts are reported by Kennicott and de Rossi to have here an interpretative דרך החיים, 'the way of life', for נגד החיים.

does not in itself connote behaviour that is good or bad. Accordingly, it is not used that way absolutely, without additional qualification, and it does not mean 'behave' in some more abstract way. Equally, the qal does not usually mean 'walk around' or 'go about' in some general sense, like the piʿel (cf. 4.15) or, more often, the hithpaʿel. I take the sense rather to be something like 'go on' (as, e.g., Gen 15.20): the poor man knows that he will go on amongst the living, or perhaps knows how to go on amongst them, and this sense will be picked up in the next verse. The meaning overall, then, is that there is no benefit in knowing how to carry on living, or in knowing that one will carry on living, when life itself offers no benefit—as is true, in Qohelet's view, for the 'poor man'.

In this respect, I have changed my mind since I suggested in *Ecclesiastes and Scepticism*, 98, that the verb indicated 'departure' in the sense of dying, largely because I have come to doubt that the going of the נפש would be understood that way (see below), but also partly because I think a reference to a continuation of life in poverty fits better in the context. Understood in terms of death, or knowledge of death, these verses question the usefulness of a wisdom that gives us consciousness of our mortality, which is compatible with ideas elsewhere in the book, but a reference to the continuation of life gives a more immediate relevance.

6.9 What is in front of one's eyes] It seems likely that מראה עינים, lit. 'sight/seeing of eyes', is another idiom, and Qohelet says something similar in 11.9, when he talks about walking בדרכי לבך ובמראי עיניך, 'in the ways of your heart and in/with the sight of your eyes'. The context there is complicated, because the statement lies between a call to be happy in one's youth and a warning that one will be judged, but the parallel with 'ways of your heart', in particular, suggests that Qohelet is talking about living in a way that fulfils one's needs and desires—a topic close to the subject-matter of 6.1-9.

The meaning of מראה is important, and is often misrepresented. Barton, for instance, claims that it is the 'power of seeing', and he cites as evidence for this the discussion at *b. Yoma* 74b, which has been picked up by a number of other commentators—probably because it is mentioned in Jastrow, *Dictionary*, which glosses one of the uses there as 'the pleasure of looking at one's wife'. The passage in question is, in fact, a discussion of this verse, which is cited first to support an assertion that the blind continue to eat without ever getting satisfied by their food, and a claim that one should therefore eat only in daylight. A secondary comment (the one picked up by Jastrow) then adapts the expression, and suggests טוב מראה עינים באשה יותר מגופו של מעשה, which probably means 'better the sight of the eyes on a woman rather than the act itself', or that looking at a woman (with pleasure or desire?) is better than actually doing anything about it. This affirms that מראה can mean 'seeing' in later Hebrew, but not that it can mean 'vision', 'the ability to see' or 'the sense of sight' (the example is also too particular and its meaning too unclear to sustain the claim of Schoors, presumably based on Jastrow, that מראה עינים

can connote 'enjoyment' in rabbinic Hebrew). Biblical usage is generally more restrictive still: Seow claims that מראה עיני refers to the faculty of vision, citing Lev 13.12 and Isa 11.3, but both those passages, in accordance with most other uses of מראה, are talking about what can be seen (cf. G ὅραμα here), and the noun refers most commonly, in fact, not to the scope of what can be seen, as in those passages, but to the appearance of something, or to what is actually seen (cf. especially מראה עיניך in Deut 28.34, 67).

This certainly encourages an interpretation of the verse in terms of being content with what we see rather than what we desire (cf. V *melius est uidere quod cupias quam desiderare quod nescias*, 'it is better to see what you desire than to long for what you know not'; T: טב ליה לגברא למחדי על מא דאית ליה, 'it is better for a man to rejoice over what he has'), and that understanding has been adopted by many interpreters, with Gordis putting the strongest modern case for it. As Luther summarizes it, the text means, 'utere praesentibus et noli vagari cupiendo', or in the English version, 'use the thynges thou hast, and let not thy witte wander about coveting of that'—he compares the dog in Aesop, who drops his meat trying to catch his own reflection. The meaning has been interpreted as almost the reverse, however, by Symmachus, whose version is attested in two forms: the first, found in the manuscripts and Syh, reads βέλτιον προβλέπειν ἢ ὁδεύειν αὐταρεσκείᾳ, 'better to look forward than to travel with the desire to satisfy oneself'; the second is a citation by Evagrius, βέλτιον πρὸς τὸν (var. τὰ) μέλλοντα βλέπειν ἢ ἐπὶ τοῖς παροῦσιν εὐφραίνεσθαι, 'better to look to what is coming than to rejoice in what is present' (see Géhin, *Scholies*, 146-47).[8] The latter is probably, in fact, a paraphrase of the former (as Marshall notes), rather than a direct citation. Evagrius does not present Symmachus' understanding as a contradiction to his own interpretation here, that it is better to be guided by knowledge of God than by the desires of the spirit; that knowledge is superior to more perishable pleasures. Jerome similarly explains the view of Symmachus as 'melius est iuxta sensum cuncta agere, qui animae est oculus, quam uoluntatem cordis sequi', 'it is better to act in all things according to reason, which is the eye of the soul, than to follow the will of the heart'.[9] For Symmachus, in other words,

---

[8] We might expect τὸν μέλλοντα to mean 'the one who is coming', but Evagrius draws out no christological or similar ideas. If this is the original reading, we are probably supposed to supply a noun such as χρόνος or αἰών: the variant τὰ μέλλοντα refers more straightforwardly to future events; cf. Wisd 8.8; 19.1.

[9] Verde, 'Standing on the Shoulders', 367, glosses the expression as 'knowledge', which seems to indicate a similar understanding, and to be derived from his discussion of 'seeing' as a cognitive process in the book (365-66). I think that this discussion blurs some important distinctions, and if we were indeed to understand the expression in terms of such usage, it would really have to refer to the observation of phenomena or apprehension of facts, not to whatever knowledge might be acquired in such ways.

this is a call not to take pleasure in what one has, but to take care about where one is going. If he is right, then we would perhaps need to consider the 'sight of your eyes' in 11.9 to be part of the warning about judgment ('walk in the ways of your heart, but with your eyes open'), and the potential ambiguity in that verse means that it cannot be used straightforwardly to resolve the issue here. My interpretation, however, broadly accords with the traditional one, not that of Symmachus, although the latter does align the verse with themes that will become important in ch. 7.

6.9 than a hunger that just goes on] Lit. 'than going of a self' or 'than a self going'. Where M has מהלך נפש, pointed as an infinitive construct, G reads ὑπὲρ πορευόμενον ψυχῇ with a participle, 'than one going in/for spirit'. Yi, 274-75, points out that G does not always translate the Hebrew infinitive with a Greek infinitive in such constructions (see, e.g., ἀκροάσεως for משמע in 1.8), and claims that we cannot say whether the translator read the participle or the infinitive here. It is important to note, however, that just a few verses later, in 7.2, G does use the infinitive πορευθῆναι in what would seem to be a similar position (although there are some complications); the use of πορευθῆναι in the last verse, moreover, shows that the translator has not simply been confused by the use of the strong form הלך, which is found there as here. It is possible that G read מהולך rather than מהלך, but more probable that the translator has vocalized or simply translated מהלך as a participle to accord with a particular understanding that נפש is not the subject of the verb here (hence the dative ψυχῇ). This is adopted in turn by Hie *super ambulantem in anima*, and both most naturally mean 'than one going/walking in mind/ spirit'. T נפש בסיגוף ההוא לעלמא דייזיל מאן, '(it is better for a man...) than that he go to that world with affliction of נפש', also avoids making the נפש the subject, as does σ' (see the previous note), although the latter does employ an infinitive ὁδεύειν. S, however, by rendering the Hebrew infinitive with a noun, ܗܠܟܬܐ *hlkt'*, 'going' or 'movement' (of the נפש), affirms the pointing in M, and takes נפש as the subject.[10] It is doubtful that the differences between the versions in this respect actually reflect any textual variants, but they do, with the exception of S, display a strong tendency to take the subject of the verb as indefinite, and to take נפש as a sort of adverbial accusative. This may have been influenced by a perception that, in the preceding clause, 'seeing of eyes' means, in practice, 'seeing *with* the eyes', so this clause should mean 'going *with* the נפש'. That construal is implicit in some more modern understandings also, such as Strobel's rendering 'das Wagnis des Lebens', 'the risking of life'. Strobel wrongly supposes that we can deduce a meaning 'risk one's life'

---

[10] Kamenetzky, 220, notes the use of the same noun to translate שרעפים in Ps 139.23, but although modern scholars commonly understand that rare Hebrew word to connote 'disquieting thoughts' (*HALOT*), it seems not to have been taken that way by early translators, and G there uses τὰς τρίβους. We should probably not, therefore, imbue ܗܠܟܬܐ *hlkt'* with any such significance here.

for נפש הלך from החלכים בנפשותם, 'those who went at the risk of their lives' in 2 Sam 23.17, or וילך אל נפשו, 'he went for the sake of his life' in 1 Kgs 19.3: נפש always takes a preposition in such phrases, which can involve other verbs (see similarly Gen 19.17; Prov 7.23; Lam 2.19; 5.9). It is difficult in principle, however, to exclude a reading of הלך נפש which treats נפש not as the subject, but as an accusative of limitation (cf. GKC §117 ll; J-M §126 g, and compare G, θ' τοῦ ὁρᾶν ὀφθαλμοῖς αὐτοῦ for ראות עינים in 5.10)—indeed, one of the best known instances of that construction involves נפש at Gen 37.21, where לא נכנו נפש means 'let us not strike him (as to) life', that is, 'let us not kill him'.

Such readings are also motivated by the problem that it is difficult to see in what way a נפש itself might 'go'. Ginsberg (in his commentary and in 'The Structure and Contents of the Book of Koheleth', 142) deals with the problem of מהלך simply by emending it to ממלוא, so that this becomes about fulfilment of the נפש. His claim is that 'going' has just intruded from the previous verse, but there is no versional support, and the graphic dissimilarities would make this more than a simple slip, so we cannot avoid מהלך that easily. A few commentators see a reference to 'departure of the נפש', that is, death, and Whybray suggests a sense 'that life should be enjoyed to the full because it is at the very least preferable to the inevitable onset of death', while Whitley paraphrases 'better the pleasure of the moment than the departing of life'. Whether or not that makes good sense here, it is not clear that 'going of the נפש' is a way that Jewish writers would normally have spoken about death. To be sure, in Gen 35.18 Rachel's נפש is 'going out', and the implication is that her life-force is ebbing; likewise, in 1 Kgs 17.21 Elijah prays for the נפש of the dead child to return. In principle, therefore, the departure of the נפש is an idea that could be associated with death, but in practice נפש is never used with הלך that way. In the account of Rachel's death, indeed, the expression is immediately glossed with כי מתה, presumably because it did not carry that implication by itself; when the speaker's נפש 'goes out' in Ct 5.6, it seems to mean no more than that she is thrown into a state of panic. It is important to note, moreover, that the verb used there is יצא: it is unlikely that הלך could carry the same connotation of 'exiting' or 'leaving' the body. People may sometimes be said to 'go on their way' when they die, using הלך, although even then rarely, if ever, without further specification of their destination, see, e.g., 2 Sam 12.23; 1 Kgs 2.2; Ps 39.14 ET 39.13; Job 10.21; 1 Chr 17.11, with a possible exception in the difficult 2 Chr 21.20.[11] There is no reason, however, to suppose that

---

[11] Qohelet does use הלך several times in connection with death, and Whitley, following Galling 1969, lists 3.20; 5.14; 6.4; and 9.10. In none of these places, however, is הלך used without either a specification of the destination ('one place', 'Sheol'), or an accompanying idea of 'coming', which portrays life as a matter of arrival and departure. This does not indicate that 'הלך means "to go hence (to death)"'.

their נפש would be said to do the same in such terms. The meaning 'death' here cannot wholly be excluded, but the idea of a נפש departing at death is probably more obvious to later readers, conditioned by discourse about the 'soul', than it would have been to a contemporary audience, and it is notably not a possibility picked up in the ancient versions.

Galling 1940 and Pinker, 'Qohelet 6:9', take נפש as 'throat': Galling understands 'than that the throat goes' to mean 'als daß die Kehle gierig ist', 'than that the throat is greedy'; while Pinker sees a contrast between what something looks like and how it tastes when it 'goes in the throat'—which would surely require a preposition, even if it made any sense in context. Most commentators who reject the sense 'life' here, however, have preferred to take the meaning of נפש to be 'desire' or 'appetite', which leads to several different understandings. For Ellermeier ('Die Entmachtung', 18) הלך נפש is searching with wisdom, of which Qohelet speaks elsewhere, and he translates (20) 'als daß man weiter *fragt*', '(better that one enjoys what comes before the eyes) than that one keeps on *questioning*'. This is wholly speculative, and driven by a broader interpretation of the passage, but it is picked up and mangled by Lange (*Weisheit und Torheit*, 135-36), who notes that 'seeing of the eyes' in 11.9 is an expression for taking joy in life, and because הלך נפש must be its antithesis, according to him, claims 'Daraus läßt sich schließen, daß das "Wandeln der Näphäsch" einen Prozeß weisheitlicher Betätigung umschreibt', 'thereby it can be concluded that the "wandering of the נפש" must describe a process of wisdom activity'—he is unwilling to be as precise as Ellermeier, but he loses the implication of 'desire (to know)' inherent in the latter's interpretation, and offers no proper argument at all to replace Ellermeier's broader framework. Very differently, but characteristically, Zimmermann, 27-28, sees the issue as sexual desire: sexual experience ('seeing with the eyes') is better than the loss altogether of such desire. All else aside, it might be possible to discern an association with romantic, if not sexual desire in the uses of נפש at Ct 1.7; 3.1-4 (although that is not what the term itself means there, and it is hard to identify any other passage that would suggest such an implication), but 'seeing' would surely indicate something more voyeuristic than physical in the context of sexual engagement (as in *b. Yoma* 74b), while the use of the verb for loss or departure runs into the same problems encountered by translations in terms of death.

Going back much further, for Graetz ('als Schwinden des Leibes', 'than dwindling of the body') and Renan ('que de s'exténuer', 'than to enfeeble oneself'), the issue here is abstinence, or starvation of the self, and Qohelet is commending enjoyment over asceticism. A number of slightly earlier commentators, most explicitly Heiligstedt, took הלך to have an aggressive nuance here (Heiligstedt himself associates that with the use of the strong form הלך rather than לכה), and compared it both with the Latin verb *grassari*, which can imply movement with a violent intention, and with such passages as Exod 9.23; Ps 73.9, 91.6, where the verb seems indeed to imply something more than movement. This is the *impetus animae appetentis*, the 'impulse of the longing soul', which Ginsburg describes as 'ever dissatisfied with what it has, and always running after that which it has not'. Delitzsch protests that הלך can only have this nuance with particular subjects and in particular forms, and prefers to compare the Latin *erratio*, 'wandering', so that the implication here is of an unsatisfied נפש, seeking fulfilment in a less directed way.

Various of these understandings are drawn together in a widespread modern assumption that the saying is to do with a 'longing' on the part of the נפש, which is itself frequently interpreted in terms of 'fantasizing' (Crenshaw) or 'dream' (Schoors)[12]—although Fox sees the image as of a desire so intense 'that it is as if his soul had left his body and gone after what it covets'. Wright commented of the earlier discussion that, 'The attempt...to draw a distinction in meaning between the various forms in use of the verb הָלַךְ is somewhat too subtle'. It did have the considerable merit, though, of actually enquiring into the meanings of הלך, and Delitzsch's objections to Heiligstedt *et al.* do bring into focus the important point—which we have touched on already in respect of its use for dying—that the various nuances of the verb beyond 'going' are heavily dependent upon context. It is probably untrue, in fact, that הלך can mean 'go out' or 'go after' (without a specific object), as Fox implies, and it is questionable, at the very least, whether the verb in the qal can mean 'wander': that is a role, as we observed in the notes to 6.8, adopted principally by the hithpaʿel, and sometimes the piʿel—the noun הֵלֶךְ, cited by Delitzsch in support of his position, is found only in 2 Sam 12.4, where it refers to somebody travelling through, not wandering, and in 1 Sam 14.26, where (if original) it refers to the dripping or flow of honey. If הלך ever could have these meanings, it would have to be as part of some idiomatic usage with נפש (attested nowhere else and now unknown to us), or through some other specification in the immediate context.[13]

---

[12] D'Alario, 'Chi ama il denaro', 69, even claims equivalence between הלך נפש and the idea of an ὁρμή τῆς ψυχῆς, which she cites from Marcus Aurelius (presumably *Meditations* 3.16) and characterizes as 'il fantasticare, l'andare dietro ai sogni', 'daydreaming, going after dreams'. This is not really the sense of that concept, which is used in Stoicism rather of impulses and instincts subject to the power of human reason (and is also typically found in the plural): הלך, moreover, can hardly bear the sense of impulsion that is conveyed by ὁρμή.

[13] It follows that I am uncomfortable with Seow's suggestion, that הלך נפש has a double meaning, referring both to death and 'to the voracious appetite of those who are discontented with their lives', not only because I doubt that either sense gives a natural reading of הלך, but because if the context is open enough to permit both readings, then it is too open to indicate either one in particular. For a potential parallel to a conventional usage, Krüger points to ῥεμβασμὸς ἐπιθυμίας in Wisd 4.12, which is commonly understood as the 'wandering of desire' and which is also noted by Schoors. Lavoie, 'Ambiguïtés et désir', 204-5, rightly doubts that ῥεμβασμὸς is likely to be modelled on a form from הלך, and more

The only guidance offered by that context here is that the 'going of the נפש' is different from (but not necessarily the opposite of) the מראה עינים, and that does not much narrow the scope. If we look back a few words further, however, to the end of the last verse, we do again find the same unusual form of the infinitive, הלך, and it is not unreasonable to suppose that the use in that verse should offer a basis for our understanding of it here. I argued above that in 6.8 the reference was to continuation, and I take that to be the basic sense of the verb here as well, with this verse following up the implications of the last (and it is interesting to note in passing that *b. Yoma* 74b, also discussed above, likewise understands הלך here in terms of continuation—the blind *go on* eating their food because they cannot see it). A continuation in this context could be a continuation of 'life', which is the issue in 6.8, or of 'appetite', which is the issue in 6.7, and is perhaps implicit in 6.8's reference to a poor man. Maybe נפש has been used because it can refer to both, and so draw the two together, but I take Qohelet to be explaining 6.8 rather than simply summarizing or repeating himself.

6.9 illusion...wishing for the wind] See the corresponding note at 1.14. Unexpectedly, S here has ܕܢܦܫ *dnpš'*, 'of the נפש' for רוח, but a variant ܕܪܘܚ *drwḥ'*, 'of the wind/spirit', is also found, and Kamenetzky, 220, is probably correct to consider this original: a scribe still had ܕܢܦܫ *dnpš'* in his head from earlier in the verse.

generally denies that the verb is ever likely to have meant 'wander'. He himself prefers 'pursue' (and an ambiguous reference to death), but the passage he cites in support, Ps 131.1, is pointed as pi'el in M, and it has indirect objects marked with -ב: it seems unlikely that sense would be understood without such strong markers from the context.

6.10-12

The Limits of Being Human

(6.10) When whatever exists has already been named, and that which is human been recognized, then it cannot argue with a power greater than itself, (6.11) since if there were a lot of words making a lot of hot air, what advantage would there be for the human?

(6.12) Who knows what is good for the human in life? The days of his life of illusion are finite, and he spends them as a shadow: who is going to explain to the human what will be after him beneath the sun?

Commentary

Loretz talks of the material in these verses as 'a compilation of four sayings...which should not be forced into a logical connection with each other',[1] and Whybray speaks of 'a loose group of sayings', claiming that 'they do not appear...to have a single unified theme'. Most commentators have been more inclined to see a basic coherence here, and to recognize the verses as a unit, but the relationship between this unit and the material around it has been described in many different ways. Fox, for example, represents what has traditionally been the majority position when he calls it a 'conclusion', but Seow describes it as 'a theological introduction' to a section that will extend to 7.14, Backhaus (*Den Zeit*, 260-62) treats it as a unit that (with 8.16-17) frames a new section, Crenshaw calls it 'a transitional unit', and Gordis regards it as 'an independent passage', whilst noting close links with what has

---

[1] Loretz, *Qohelet und der alte Orient*, 230-31 n. 63: 'eine Zusammenstellung von vier Maschalen (Qoh 6, 10a; 6, 10b; 6, 11a; 6, 11b (?) 12), die nicht in einen logischen Zusammenhang zu zwingen sind'.

preceded. A case can be made for any of these, but the very fact of so much disagreement highlights the absence of direct connections with the material that comes immediately before and after. Once we start reaching further afield for links, it is easier to find them, but harder to evaluate their significance: is it better to connect the last part of 6.12, for instance, with 3.22 or with 7.14, when both express the same idea? If it is relatively easy, moreover, to find connections with 6.12, the same can hardly be said of 6.10-11, which are congruent with Qohelet's thought in other passages, but which express an idea that is addressed directly nowhere else in the book.

As many commentators note, the Masoretic count usually takes 6.10 to be the beginning of the second half of the book (although see the notes at 7.1), and even if the author was not himself counting words, he may well have been conscious of reaching a halfway stage in his composition. The first half of ch. 7, moreover, will be composed in a style that Qohelet has not used up to this point, with a long series of short sayings evocative of the sentence literature which dominates much of the book of Proverbs, and this marks a significant break with what has gone before. I am inclined to think, therefore, that 6.10-12 are intended to act in part as a structural device, which indicates a change of style and direction. The verses do not directly pick up the discussion that has immediately preceded them, and do not function simply as an introduction to what will follow straight after them—and to that extent they are a sort of interlude. More generally, though, questions about the human capacity to comprehend and to control are going to play an increasingly important part in the second half of the book, with wisdom coming to the forefront of Qohelet's concerns for the first time since ch. 2, and these verses herald that change of theme as much as they introduce the shift in style.

Two issues are addressed. The first, in 6.10-11, concerns the status of humans in relation to what is more powerful than them. This status is fixed, and makes it impossible for them to put their point of view at the same level: this would result in mere 'vapour', and be of no benefit to them. The reference is probably not to contending directly with God, or fighting against him, but to humans questioning his decisions or setting up their opinions as equal in value. The last verse, 6.12, turns to the limits of knowledge: humans have no way to know either what is good for them while they live, or what will happen in the world after their limited lives have ended. Together, these points describe the place of humans in the world: they have no say in how it is run, and no understanding either of what they should do for themselves or of what the future will hold for their successors. It is against the background of these ideas that Qohelet will begin ch. 7 with statements that seem initially much more sanguine about the idea of preparing for the future, and about the importance of wisdom, and they prepare us both for the significant qualifications that he will go on to introduce, and for his subsequent focus on wisdom—although he notably does not actually use that term yet here. If 6.10-12 are supposed to stand out from the text and mark a break, therefore, it seems likely that they are also supposed to set the scene for what follows.

Some commentators have gone further, in fact, and suggested that ch. 7 begins with an attempt to address the questions raised here, pointing in particular to the numerous repetitions in 7.1-14 of the word 'good', which is central to the first question of 6.12. Lavoie, 'La philosophie comme réflexion', 96, even speaks of 7.14a providing a final answer to that question (although Ogden and Zogbo more plausibly claim that it answers the second). While I agree that 7.13-14 pick up the themes here, however, the intervening verses have little to do with them, and the prominence of 'good' is a result largely of ch. 7 containing many 'better than' sayings (which are literally 'good [more] than' sayings in Hebrew).

6.10] Qohelet has already talked about 'whatever exists' in 1.9 and 3.15, where his emphasis was on the continuity of the world. The emphasis here is different, but the point rests on an assumption of such continuity: everything that has come into existence has been 'given a name' already—and this, by implication, will not change. Much has been written about the significance of naming here, but the most natural understanding is that everything possesses an identity. Qohelet does not say who gave those identities (the verbs are passive), but correspondingly, everyone who is human has already been recognized as such, and their human identity precludes them from a particular sort of engagement with anything more powerful.

In this context, many commentators have wondered if Qohelet is making a direct reference to 'Adam', whose name is the Hebrew word for 'human', and some weight is lent to that idea by his use of that single word here, rather than his preferred expression 'children of the human'. The usage may be driven by the context, however, since nobody is *named* 'child of the human', and if there is an allusion, we should not put too much weight on it. Although the corresponding 'someone/something more powerful' presumably includes God, it could also in principle refer to any number of supernatural or angelic beings, and Qohelet does not pin it down, perhaps, because he is trying to talk in terms of the way abstract classes relate to each other. This impersonal way of putting things manages to avoid any statement that the human relationship with God is set by God's attitude to humans: it arises rather from the way in which everything in the world is set up. One consequence, of course, is that all humans fit into the same category, and so there can be no exceptions. Precisely what they are precluded from doing is uncertain, but it is doubtful that Qohelet is talking about humans fighting or contending with God in some general way: there is a legal nuance of challenging God in court or of setting their opinions alongside his.

6.11] 'Hot air' here is actually *hebel*, 'vapour', but in this context it also surely represents the hot air generated by too much talking, and Qohelet is playing on the literal meaning of the word—a play that is impossible to reproduce in translation. There may be a similar device in Jer 23.16. This verse is presented as an explanation for the previous one, and should not be read simply as a general statement that speech gives rise to vapour, leaving humans no better off. Qohelet's concern is not with some general uselessness of speech, but with the futility of human attempts to match or challenge what is more powerful: words spoken in that context can have no effect, and offer no benefit. The interpretation has rightly fallen out of favour, but many earlier commentators (discussed in the notes, below) saw this not just as a general statement, but as a statement about 'things' rather than 'words' (the Hebrew term can in principle mean either). On that reading, Qohelet is saying that there are many things in the world that give rise to vanity, or to a sense of vanity—hence the Authorized Version's 'Seeing there be many things that increase vanity, what is man the better?'. This, of course, would give the verse considerable prominence as an epitome of the book as a whole, but it ignores a connection to the previous verse that is explicit in the Hebrew, and rips the statement out of context.

6.12] Qohelet has already used 'who knows?' questions at 2.19 and 3.21: here, as there, the question is rhetorical, implying that 'nobody knows', and something similar will be said later in 8.1. 'The days of his life of illusion' will also be echoed by similar expressions in 7.15 and 9.9, and the 'limited number' of those days has been mentioned in 2.3 and 5.17. Again, the image of being taken to see what comes after has already been used in 3.22, and the notion that people cannot know what comes after will appear again in 7.14. This verse is full of ideas and expressions found elsewhere in the book. It is not surprising to find, therefore, that Qohelet will refer to living life as a 'shadow' again in 8.13, where it will clearly indicate the brevity of the wicked person's life. Accordingly, although the context makes it attractive to see 'shadow' as a metaphor for ignorance, as have several recent commentators (and correspondingly perhaps to read '*in* shadow' with the Greek), that later use makes such a sense unlikely here: shadow is not uncommon as an image for human transience in biblical literature, and Qohelet is employing it conventionally as such. What is most striking, perhaps, is the very strong connection that he makes between such transience and the limitations on human knowledge—which themselves involve, of course, not knowing what will happen after we are gone (as in 3.22 and 7.14). For Qohelet, humans are not ignorant simply because the secrets of the world are concealed, but because the limited spans of their own lives prevent them from seeing the bigger picture of which those lives are only a tiny part.

Notes

6.10 When whatever...and...then] Lit. 'whatever...and...and'. G renders the first clause as the protasis of a conditional sentence (see the next note), and that may not be incorrect; we do not have to label it as such, however, to see that there is intended to be a logical connection between the sequence of statements that could only be rendered very weakly in English (as in Greek) by 'and'.

6.10 whatever exists] On the indefinite use of מה, see the note on 'whatever' at 1.9. On each of the four occasions when M has מה שהיה (1.9; 3.15; 6.10; 7.24), G renders it differently and apparently contextually (cf. Yi, 92), opting here for what Euringer sees as the elegant εἴ τι ἐγένετο, 'if something happened' (perhaps to be read as a gnomic aorist, 'if something happens'). S takes כבר with this verb, and renders interpretatively ܡܕܡ ܓܕܫ

ܡܕܡ ܡܢ ܩܕܝܡ *mdm dhw' mn qdym*, 'something which has existed from of old' (with a variant ܡܢܕܪܝܫ *mndryš*, usually 'again' but perhaps here 'from the beginning', for ܡܕܡ ܡܢ ܩܕܝܡ *mn qdym*); the use of ܡܕܡ *mdm* rather than ܡܐ *m'* (as in 1.9; 3.15) probably reflects the influence of G τι. T מא דהוה simply reflects M, and it is Jerome's readings that are curious: Hie *quid est quod futurum est* and V *qui futurus est*. Both seem to reflect מה שיהיה (compare his rendering of 1.9, where *quid est* = מה, not מה שיהיה)[2] and the tense is not driven simply by Jerome's own primary interpretation in christological terms: a secondary interpretation that he reports is also made to refer to the future. *BHQ* does not note the discrepancy, but with no trace of such a reading in the Greek tradition, there is a strong possibility that Jerome found שיהיה as a variant in his Hebrew source. It is very unlikely but not impossible that this is original (with M representing alignment to 3.15): that would give a specific sense of predetermination here, and fit well with 6.12—but those may be the very reasons that such a variant arose.

As I remarked in the notes at 1.9, there is no strong distinction between past and present in Qohelet's use of שהיה, and he employs it to talk about everything that has come into existence. I take his point to be that once anything has appeared in the world (as has everything, presumably, given his earlier statements about the world), then it has been labelled and will always be recognized for what it is. The text could also be translated 'when whatever has existed has been given a name', but the question of tense is an issue that relates to the translation of the Hebrew, not to the scope of the Hebrew itself. שהיה certainly cannot, on any grounds other than interpretative, be restricted here to a past reference 'what was' (as Schellenberg would like, or as Zimmermann believes it to be as the result of an error).[3] It is also, perhaps, a translational issue to suggest that the common rendering 'happens' or 'happened' gives a misleading sense here, but it is an issue that has significant exegetical consequences. Fox remarks that,

---

[2] In 1.9, Hie has *quid est* (מה) *quod fuit* (שהיה) *ipsum* (הוא) *quod erit* (שיהיה), and V is the same, except with *quod futurum est* (שיהיה) for *quod erit*. In 3.15, Hie has *quid est* (מה) *quod fuit* (שהיה) *ipsum quod est* (הוא), or possibly כבר הוא: see the note at 3.15) *et quae* (ואשר) *futura sunt* (להיות) *iam* ([2]כבר) *fuerunt* (היה); V, more loosely, *quod factum est ipsum permanet* (מה שהיה כבר הוא) *quae* (ואשר) *futura sunt* (להיות) *iam* ([2]כבר) *fuerunt* (היה). In both verses, Jerome is close to the Hebrew, although in 1.9 his text also corresponds to that of his earlier revision of La—see the note there.

[3] Schellenberg, *Erkenntnis*, 106, tries to see a distinction in 6.10-12 between human knowledge of the past and of the future, which requires her to insist on a past tense ('Was war') here. Zimmermann, 107, thinks that his Aramaic translator has mistakenly read a present-tense דְּהוּא as a past tense דַּהֲוָא.

hayah is better translated "happen" than "be," since Qohelet is not speaking of the simple existence of things. *Mah yihyeh* (v. 12b) does not refer to the future existence of beings or things, as if it were important to know that a certain person or a certain building, for example, will exist in the future.

This is certainly true, but if the Hebrew verb can be used both of events and of existence, the same is not true of the English. A translation like 'What happens has already been given its name, and that what a human being is, is known' (Schoors) favours those who see a reference to predetermination here (see below), but it slants the Hebrew in a particular direction by importing a specific reference to events that is absent from שהיה and, I think, undermines the point that is being made. This is another case where we have to make a distinction in English that is not present in the Hebrew, and it does not negate any continuity between vv. 10 and 12 to suggest that the same verb in each case needs to be rendered slightly differently.

It is possible also to go too far in the other direction, however, and I very much doubt, especially in the light of Qohelet's uses of מה שהיה elsewhere and of מה itself here, that we should see a reference only to humans in particular from the outset of the verse, as does Schwienhorst-Schönberger, 'Was jemand auch ist, schon längst ist er bei seinem Namen genannt', 'even what someone is, long since has he been called by his name'; cf., e.g., Plumptre 'What he is, long ago his name was called'. It is not only humans that have been named, but it is because everything has been named that the identity of what is human is known.

6.10 has already been named] Lit. 'has already been called its name'. Schoors rightly rejects a strange translation by Gerleman (in 'Adam und die alttestamentliche Anthropologie', 329) which parses the verbs as first-person plural (presumably taking נודע to reflect a misunderstood נדע) and takes כבר as a substantive, to read 'Was gewesen ist, nennen wir mit dem Namen "Schon längst", und wir wissen…', 'What has happened, we name "long ago already", and we know…'.

It is not clear why Power declares קרא שם to be a Graecism: the expression is a very common way of talking about the bestowal of a name (upon people, places, and animals, amongst other things), and sometimes of a new name (e.g. Isa 62.2; 65.15). To take a few examples, this expression is used in Gen 2.19-20 when Adam famously gives names to all the animals (God does the same for the stars in Ps 147.4), and he names Eve this way in 3.20; it is used a little later of Cain naming a city (4.17), and God similarly gives the name אדם to humans in 5.2. In the passive, the expression can alternatively be used of a name being perpetuated or called out because it is famous (Gen 48.16; Deut 32.3; Ruth 4.11, 14), but it also sometimes has the sense of being called by the name of another. It is generally used this way to indicate that people or things belong to God (they are 'called by his name'); see, e.g., Jer 7.14 (the temple); Dan 9.18-19 (Jerusalem and the people); Amos 9.12 (nations); Jer 15.16 (prophet); in Isa 4.1, however, it is used of women wishing to take a man's name through marriage. For the active counterpart of this latter expression, however, Hebrew uses קרא בשם, 'call *by* name', and when God calls somebody by name (בשם), he is claiming them as his (Isa 43.1, and cf. God's calling of Cyrus by name in 45.3-4); there is probably a similar idea at work in Exod 31.2, where God calls Bezalel by name (בשם) and fills him with skills for the construction of the tabernacle. Again, God is not the only possible subject: cf. Ps 49.12 ET 49.11. Confusingly, the same expression, with -ב is used frequently also of calling on a deity (e.g. Gen 26.25; 1 Kgs 18.25-26), and קרא שם without the preposition is used once that way in Lam 3.55. The expression with the preposition is used a third way in Josh 21.9, where certain 'named' cities are to be given to the Levites (הערים האלה אשר יקרא אתהן בשם, 'these cities which it will call by name', i.e. which will be listed by name below); in its literalness, this is similar to Esth 2.14, where Esther waits for her name to be called (ונקראה בשם), and Isa 40.26, where God calls out the stars בשם, as though at a rollcall.

In the present verse, we have the passive without the preposition, and so at first glance it might seem likely that we are dealing with somebody or something being called by the name of another. There is, however, no antecedent other than מה שהיה for the suffix pronoun on שמו, and there is also no preposition which might permit us to derive this from the expression קרא בשם. Correspondingly, there is no good reason to associate this use either with passages where נקרא שם or קרא בשם are used in a context of choosing or appointing people, or with those rarer instances where they are summoned by name. There has been a certain muddying of the waters by some commentators in this respect. Seow, for example, talks of 'the idiom *qārā' (bĕ)šēm* "call by name"', as though the preposition made no difference to the sense, and then claims that it 'means roughly the same thing as Akkadian šumam nabû "to call the name" = "to appoint, designate, choose"', as though קרא שם and קרא בשם between them had any such sense in more than a tiny minority of cases. If we consider all the other usage, it seems most likely that Qohelet is talking simply about everything having been 'given its name', not designated the agent or possession of another, and not summoned by name. Furthermore, although we might extrapolate from this an idea that everything has been given a role to go with its name, there is no more explicit claim of that here than in, say, the account of Adam naming the animals.

The limitations of the Hebrew have not, however, prevented some grand and confident claims. Schoors, for example, declares that 'The connotation of "give a name" is "preordain"', but the verses that he cites in support of this (probably following Lauha) consist solely of God's naming of created items in Gen 1, his calling out of the stars in Isa 40.26, and the calling by name of

Israel and Cyrus in Isa 40.26 and 45.3. It might be objected that קרא is used without שם in Gen 1, and that in all the other cases קרא בשם, with the preposition, is employed, but whether or not we accept their relevance to the meaning of the expression here, not one of these examples has anything to do with preordination. To be sure, determinism is an important aspect of Qohelet's thought, but I see no reason to suppose that it is an issue for him here, and the lack of differentiation in tense between the verbs tells against that being his intention (unless we adopt our reading from Jerome). The point is rather that, in a world where the identity of everything is already established, no human can hope to transcend the limitations of that identity.

6.10 and that which is human] In Esth 3.4, it is said that Mordechai הגיד להם אשר הוא יהודי, 'had told them that he was a Jew', and in 1 Sam 18.15 Saul sees אשר הוא משכיל, 'that he (David) is succeeding'. After ונודע, a verb of perception, we might expect אשר similarly to introduce a clause specifying what is known, and that would lead us to take אשר הוא אדם to mean 'that he is a man'. Unfortunately, there is no identifiable 'he', unless we follow Schwienhorst-Schönberger and others in seeing מה שהיה as the antecedent of הוא, an idea that is improbable on other grounds (see above).[4] Gordis (followed by Zimmerli) tries to get around this by seeing the הוא as anticipatory, and the clause as equivalent to ונודע אשר האדם לא יוכל, 'it is known that the man will not be able to'. As Fox has shown, however, this is impossible: in constructions like ודעו חטאתכם אשר תמצא אתכם, 'know your sin, that it will find you out', which Gordis cites from Num 32.23 as an analogy, the word in anticipation (חטאתכם) serves as the object of the main verb, and is not put after אשר. Gordis is right, however, to point out that אשר הוא אדם cannot mean 'what man is'—a translation that has often been adopted—because that would require מה, not אשר.[5]

---

[4] Lohfink similarly has 'Was auch immer jemand war...es war erkannt, daß er nur ein Mensch sein wird', 'Whatever someone was...it was known that he was only a man'. That understanding of שהיה does not seem possible anyway, but the antecedent disappears altogether in the ET of his commentary: 'Whatever has occurred it was already called by name. It was also perceived that each one is only human.'

[5] This remains a popular translation, despite the difficulties, which is at least in part because the ambiguities surrounding the English 'what', and many of its equivalents in other languages, have led to a great deal of confusion. Schoors illustrates this confusion by first accepting the point that 'אשר is not the normal pronoun introducing an indirect question', and then, however, putting forward a translation that seems indistinguishable from what he has just rejected, 'that what a human being is, is known'. From his explanation 'that the relative pronoun אשר contains its antecedent in itself', I think that he means we should understand strictly 'that-which (אשר) a human being is it (הוא אדם)'—cf. Delitzsch, whom he cites in support, *id quod homo est*. Although it swaps subject and predicate, this is not essentially different from my own understanding. To move from 'that

That limits our options to taking אשר הוא אדם as a relative or substantivized clause, serving as the subject of נודע, and this would make the literal sense 'that which (it) is a man is known'. The construction is not very pretty, perhaps because the concept is not very simple, but I think this is probably the intended reading, and it is the way that G seems to have taken it.[6] What Qohelet is saying in a rather convoluted fashion, then, is that since everything has an identity, everything that is human will be recognized as such, or, to put it another way, no human will be taken for anything else.

The awkwardness has inspired a number of proposals to emend the text or to read it in another way. Fox makes the speculative suggestion that the conjunction should be moved from ולא to אדם, effectively making אדם the subject of יוכל. The emendation is less straightforward than it sounds, however, because the word-order of the next clause would be strange, and Fox admits that it would give a better correspondence to other uses of לא יוכל, (e.g. 8.17, לא יוכל האדם) were one simply to place אדם after the verb and read ולא יוכל אדם (a suggestion made already by Ginsberg in his commentary and in 'Supplementary Studies', 47-48, and independently by Loretz, *Qohelet und der alte Orient*, 231 n. 63).[7] Fox also renders the remaining אשר הוא as 'what it is (is known)', which raises the familiar objection of Gordis, that we might have expected מה. Dahood, in 'Canaanite-Phoenician', 208, likewise moves אדם to the next clause, but he also deletes an א as a dittograph and reads ונודע אשרהו, which he interprets as 'its destiny was known', largely on the basis of the Ugaritic *aṯyrt* (later, in 'The Independent Personal Pronoun', 89, he achieves that sense without emendation by taking הוא as genitive). This is accepted by Scott, and Seow elaborates it further, taking ונודע to be a qatal rather than a participle, then retaining אדם and understanding אשרהו to have a suffix that is proleptic of it: this gives him 'the course of human beings is known'; this version has been accepted by Miller. These manoeuvres would be more attractive were there some evidence that אשרהו could actually have the required sense in Hebrew, but it is hard to find any such meaning in the only comparable usage at Prov 29.18.

---

which he is' to 'what he is' in the translation, however, is to move from the proper provenance of אשר in such contexts to that of מה; cf. 11.5 הרוח דרך מה יודע אינך. There is a difference between 'what thing it is' and 'what it is', which Delitzsch himself compares to the difference between *quod* and *quid* in Latin, and which corresponds to distinctions between identity and nature. Bartholomew more explicitly makes a similar move.

[6] Understanding καὶ ἐγνώσθη ὅ ἐστιν ἄνθρωπος to indicate 'what is a man', not 'what man is'—contrast the way G handles that sense in 11.5 γινώσκων τίς ἡ ὁδός.

[7] Whitley would simply take אדם with the next clause, and treat the ו of ולא as asseverative, which gives a (very forced) sense, 'man cannot indeed'. So, similarly, Crenshaw, who describes the position of אדם as a matter of *casus pendens*.

6.10 been recognized] M points ונודע as a participle, but only V amongst the other ancient versions differentiates it in tense from the preceding נקרא, and this suggests that it has been read by the others as the much more common niph'al perfect (see Yi, 249-50, on the reading of G). As is recognized in Seow's emendation (see the last note), it gives a better correspondence with the previous verb to vocalize in this way, and it is the more natural reading. If the writer had explicitly intended to change the tense, he would have done so in a way that was not invisible in the consonantal text, and I think it is more probable that the M reading is interpretative.

The word is taken by Zimmermann as yet another error of translation, whereby the noun חכים has been misunderstood to be a passive participle from the verb חכם: his translation of the supposed original reads, 'and the most learned man, because he is mere man, cannot struggle with…'. Whilst this gives quite a nice sense, it attributes even more stupidity than usual to Zimmermann's poor translator.

6.10 then it cannot] Lit. 'and he/it cannot'. Unless the verb is being used impersonally ('it is not possible', cf. Exod 10.5), the subject must be the preceding אשר הוא אדם, whatever it is that has been identified as human: without actually disconnecting it from the preceding clause, as do Fox and others (see above), it is difficult to make אדם itself the subject (having done so, though, Fox himself takes it to mean just 'one' here). It is also very unlikely that the verb is consequent upon ונודע, with a sense 'known…*and that* he cannot' (on Gordis' attempt to achieve this by reading הוא אדם in anticipation of the verb, see above).

6.10 argue] G κριθῆναι μετὰ probably has the forensic sense of pursuing a legal case against somebody (cf. 1 Cor 6.6), and that is picked up explicitly by V *in iudicio contendere*. In biblical usage, however, the verb דין does not elsewhere mean 'contend' in the qal (although it is found once in the niph'al at 2 Sam 19.10, where it seems to indicate general discontent or strife), and it does not take עם. It is generally used, in fact, of judging or upholding the rights of others, and involves no element either of competing with somebody else, or of pleading one's own cause. It is possible that we should retain this normal biblical sense, and understand the verse as a warning that humans cannot set themselves up as judges alongside or in company with someone more powerful, which would make 6.10-11 a statement about human pretension. Hie *non poterit iudicari cum fortiore se*, 'he will not be able to be judged with one stronger than him', goes some way down this path, with Jerome explaining in his (christological) interpretation that a man cannot compare himself with God.

Commentators have generally preferred, however, to follow G and V in seeing a reference to some sort of challenge or dispute. There is some justification for this to be found in later Hebrew, but only in very much later Hebrew. Seow points to midrashic and talmudic uses of the verb with the sense 'argue with, quarrel, dispute', but in the passages that he cites (*m. ʿEduyyot* 1.10; *b. Sanhedrin* 17b) it retains a technical legal sense: the expression is used for arguing about the interpretation of the Law (and, again, is not found with עם used to indicate an opponent). It is only when we reach texts like the Midrash on 2.8, for example, where the Queen of Sheba's verbal and intellectual jousting with Solomon is מדיינת עמו בחכמתה ובשאלותיה, that we find a more general sense. The verb there is in the piʿel, and it is tempting to suppose that that stem was originally intended here; the quite common use of the derived nouns מדון and מדין to refer to quarrelling or disputes suggests at least that, even if the qal seems to have been restricted to 'judging', some such connotation was attached much earlier to the verb in other stems. It is unlikely on the basis of any available evidence that לדין could connote fighting or resisting in some more general or physical way, but if Qohelet does not have in mind an actual argument or debate, he may be talking about 'arguing the toss', as we would say in Britain—disputing or protesting uselessly against decisions long since made.

6.10 a power greater] Lit. 'someone/something strong (more than it)'. M^L has a *Kᵉthîbh*, usually vocalized שֶׁהֲתְקִיף, and a *Qᵉrê* שֶׁתַּקִּיף; the latter simply appears in the text of some late manuscripts (see, e.g., Baer, 81), and in the early Or 9879 it is the *Kᵉthîbh*, with a circellus but no extant Masoretic note—the bottom of the page with much of the Masorah is missing.[8] Both are connected with תקף, which we encountered as a verb in 4.12, where it connoted overwhelming strength. Here the *Qᵉrê* can be read as the relative -שׁ with an adjective תקיף, not attested elsewhere in biblical Hebrew, but known from Aramaic and occasionally found later in Hebrew, meaning 'strong' or 'powerful'. This is compatible with the understanding of the versions, that the reference is to somebody strong.

Presumably on the basis of the *BHS* apparatus, Schoors claims (in his commentary and in *The Preacher* I, 36) that 'Some manuscripts have the variant הַתַּקִּיף', and asserts that G and V are based on this: so far as I am aware, however, this reading appears in no manuscripts, and Goldman says explicitly that התקיף is not directly attested. *BHS* appears simply to have invented such attestation. Where we do find the form, is in Gordis' plausible suggestion that the more mystifying *Kᵉthîbh* arose from a conflation of two variants, שתקיף, which is now the *Qᵉrê*, and a *hypothetical* התקיף, which would be the same word with an article rather than -שׁ (of course, the word should have one or

---

[8] It is likely that the Masorah offered some form of the observation recorded in Ginsburg, *Writings*, that the western reading has the writing with ה as *Kethîbh*, the writing without as *Qerê*, while the eastern has the form without as both *Kethîbh* and *Qerê*. This note is not found in M^L, as Bar-Asher claims in Garr and Fassberg, *Handbook*, 207 (and I do not know how he has supposedly established the readings of the Aleppo Codex here and in 10.3). On the Masoretic treatment, see also Ginsburg, *Massorah*, 4:282.

the other, but not both). The versions could all render either of those variants, although S and T may slightly favour שתקיף, and it is only the appearance of the anomalous ה in the K*ᵉthîbh* that might lead us to suppose that התקיף ever existed at all.⁹ Other suggestions for the form of the K*ᵉthîbh* שהתקיף include the idea that it is essentially the same as the Q*ᵉrê*, with ה as a vowel-letter,¹⁰ that it is an abbreviation of an original שהוא תקיף,¹¹ and that it might be from the otherwise unattested hiph'il stem of the verb (so Herzfeld, and the idea is given serious consideration by, e.g., Delitzsch and Goldman). Stuart makes the enjoyably preposterous suggestion that the ה is not superfluous, but that 'It may be read and pointed שֶׁהַתַּקִּיף, i.e. *him who is the mighty One, the Almighty,* of course with the article'; it is not clear what he makes of the subsequent ממנו on that reading. In any case, the Q*ᵉrê* is to be preferred, and is affirmed in the text of many manuscripts.

G renders with τοῦ ἰσχυροῦ ὑπὲρ αὐτόν, lit. 'strong beyond him', but the comparative ἰσχυροτέρου ('stronger') appears in a significant number of manuscripts (cf. Hie *fortiore*) and as an unattributed marginal gloss: Marshall plausibly takes it to be hexaplaric, and argues that it is probably the reading of σ' (but possibly that of θ', or of both).

6.11 since if there were] Although it is sometimes treated as emphatic (cf. Schoors, 'Certainly there are'; Seow 'indeed'), there is no good reason not to take the initial כי as causal, providing an explanation for the previous statement. If that is the role of this verse, however, then it would make little obvious sense simply as a general statement. A number of modern commentators, therefore, have seen a conditional sentence here, although they generally do not see the כי itself as a conditional particle, but treat כי as causal and the condition as unmarked. So, for instance, Fox translates 'For (if) there are many words', and Galling 1969 as 'Denn, wo viele Worte sind, da...', 'For, where there are many words, there they...'. I think this is the correct approach, and it is consonant with Qohelet's occasional use of יש to posit hypothetical situations (as we have seen already in 1.10; 2.21; 4.8).

---

⁹ Kamenetzky 220 suggests that S ܚܕ ܡܢ ܕܐܬܩܦ *'m mn dtqyp,* 'with whoever is strong(er)', reflects the K*ᵉthîbh* שהתקיף, presumably on the basis that ܡܢ *mn* might reflect the article, but -ܕ ܡܢ *mn d-* may simply be a rendering of -ש.

¹⁰ So Ginsberg, 'Supplementary Studies', 48. This is similar to the view of Euringer and McNeile, 73, that the K*ᵉthîbh* is an old writing, and that the Q*ᵉrê* omits the ה to prevent the word being read as a hiph'il. See also Bar-Asher in Garr and Fassberg, *Handbook*, 207-8, who notes the use of ה as a vowel letter representing *segol* after -ש in Tannaitic manuscripts and inscriptions. Preston takes the contrary viewpoint that the ה 'crept in' because the word was taken wrongly as a hiph'il.

¹¹ See especially G.R. Driver, 'Once Again Abbreviations', 79, but the suggestion goes back to his father, S.R. Driver, in *BH¹*; it is followed cautiously by Whitley.

The scope of the condition is generally, however, restricted to the first two clauses, with יש דברים הרבה serving as the protasis, מרבים הבל as the apodosis, to give a sense 'if there are many words, they make much הבל'. This is awkward with the participle, and although it does not significantly alter the sense, I take the final question, מה יתר לאדם, to be acting as the apodosis. Fox rightly rejects Ginsberg's idea that יש is simply emphatic, noting that uses like that in Gen 24.42 always occur with a pronominal predicate, and only in particular constructions.

6.11 many words] As is well known, דברים has more than one meaning, and Odeberg in 1929 was still keen to emphasize that either 'words' or 'things' offered a legitimate reading of דברים הרבה, as more recently have Reichert and Cohen, and Sicker. Within mainstream scholarship for more than a century, however, דברים has been taken almost universally to be a reference to words, rather than things, although there has been a significant amount of discussion about what particular words are meant, and how, correspondingly, they might increase הבל.

The other ancient versions support 'words', but T, while retaining a certain ambiguity, talks of פתגמין, with which a man might engage himself (מתעסק בהון), which leans toward 'things'. At least from the Midrash and Rashi onward, moreover, there has been a long line of scholars who prefer that understanding, and this includes not only such notables as de Groot, Geier, Patrick, le Clerc, Rosenmüller, Knobel, Ginsburg, Hengstenberg, and Tyler, but also the translators of the Authorized Version. This has been, historically speaking then, an extremely influential interpretation, and it should not be rejected merely out of hand or out of habit. Hengstenberg takes 'things' in a very particular way, and sees here a statement that the wealth and property of the rich turn out to be illusory, which runs into the problem that Qohelet talks about such things elsewhere without using דברים, but the more common interpretation in terms of 'things' is a general one, in which הבל arises or increases from human preoccupation with things that are worthless. Patrick speaks of the 'many things…that adde to the natural uncertainty which attends all worldly enjoyments', and Zöckler, much later, sees a reference to the way in which all the vicissitudes of life strengthen within each of us a perception of the world's vanity. Gerson, later still, understands the point to be that the lack of human satisfaction addressed in previous verses only intensifies as worldly things increase. Very differently, Bullock notes that the halfway point in the book has just been crossed, and sees this verse as a reference backward to the many things already rejected as הבל by Qohelet—which is an attractive reading, if we are willing to disconnect it from the preceding verse.[12]

---

[12] It is interesting to note that Michaud, although he understands 'words', rather similarly sees a reference *forward* here, to 'les proverbes qui vont être cités et critiqués'—the sayings which Michaud believes Qohelet is about to cite in order to subject them to his own critique; see Michaud, *Qohélet et l'hellénisme*, 171.

It is the very link with that verse through כי, however, that makes 'words' more plausible here, as well as the possibility that Qohelet is playing on the idea of הבל as the 'air' produced by speaking: the context sets us up to understand this verse not as a sudden and free-standing reference to the multiple sources of הבל, but in terms of the argument just mentioned (cf. the explicit link in V *uerba sunt plurima multa in disputando habentia uanitatem*, 'there are many words having much vanity in disputation'). A marginal scholion, noted by Marshall in two Greek manuscripts, takes this idea in a slightly different direction: these many words are 'those of the heterodox'.

Seow rightly draws attention to the sound of the Hebrew: although it is not strictly alliteration, there is strong consonance in דברים הרבה מרבים הבל.

6.11 making a lot of] G πληθύνοντες rightly renders מרבים as a participle rather than turning it into a main verb: the point is not that the number of words is in proportion to the amount of הבל ('many words make much'), but that there is no advantage in 'many words which are making much'.

6.11 what advantage] Rahlfs reads τί περισσὸν, which is the majority reading of G, but that is also the (retroverted) reading of σ', and, largely on the basis of translation technique, Gentry, 'Role of the Three', 180-83, argues that G* was probably the much less well-attested τίς περισσεία, which he adopts in his own edition. This argument has some limited strength when it comes to affirming περισσεία, if we allow that in 6.8 and 7.11 G shows some preference for using that term to render יתר when it stands before -ל, although it uses περισσός elsewhere (2.15; 7.16; 12.9, 12). As we saw in the note on 'then how' at 6.8, however, τίς περισσεία in that verse is certainly not original, and Gentry's own arguments favour reading τί there, so consideration of technique may support περισσεία, but does not really favour τίς. The main reason for Gentry's opposition to Rahlfs on this point is that it is easy to see how τίς περισσεία might have become τί περισσὸν under the influence of σ', but harder to see what might have motivated a change in the other direction. It is not difficult to suppose, however, that the programmatic 1.3 (τίς περισσεία τῷ ἀνθρώπῳ ἐν παντὶ μόχθῳ αὐτοῦ) might have exercised an influence on copyists here, and so although Gentry's proposal cannot be excluded, there is no very compelling reason to overrule the strong manuscript support for τί περισσὸν. The sense is much the same in either case.

Kamenetzky, 220, supposes that S has understood יְתֵר rather than יֹתֵר, and although it is not clear why he believes this, it is tempting, in fact, to suppose that יְתֵר was intended not only here, but also in 6.8 and 7.11, the other places where the word has a substantival rather than adverbial or prepositional sense. The plene writing יותר at 6.8 stands against that, however, and is supported by 4QQoh[a].

The most significant issue arising from the ancient translations here is Jerome's understanding of מה יתר לאדם as part of the series of questions that follow in the next verse, rather than as a single consequence of the 'many words' (it is not impossible that G and S shared this understanding, although

T makes a clear link to what precedes). In V, this leads to a very specific, interpretative understanding, *quid necesse est homini maiora se quaerere*, 'what need is there for a man to inquire about things greater than him?',[13] but Hie *quid est amplius homini*, 'what more is there for a human?', stays close to the wording of G and M, while understanding the question as part of a string of human limitations. It is hard to exclude completely the possibility that this is what the author originally intended. The only comparable use of יתר / יותר in 6.8, however, does not suggest that it can be used in some very general way, as an equivalent to יתרון or with reference to matters 'beyond' one, but that it refers specifically to advantage in a particular situation, a sense that would be out of place in the next verse.

6.12 who knows] As we observed at 6.8, the force of כי often seems to be muted before מה and מי, so although the versions reflect the כי (G ὅτι τίς; Hie *quis enim*; S ܡܛܠ ܕܡܢܘ *mṭl dmnw*; T ארום מאן; σ' τίς γάρ; cf. V *cum*), כי מי here may mean little more than simply מי—although the כי might possibly serve to show that this verse does not mark a new start. On the expression מי יודע, see the corresponding note at 2.19.

6.12 what is good] The absence of τί in some manuscripts of G is taken by McNeile, 145, to indicate an early Hebrew variant in G's source-text, presumably lacking מה. Although the other versions affirm M in this respect, it is conceivable (although not necessary to suppose) that σ' τίς γάρ οἶδεν ὃ συμφέρει ('who knows what benefits') might also be derived from a text without מה,[14] and it is also true that the loss of τί is hard to explain as an inner-Greek development, as opposed to a slip of the pen—so McNeile may have

---

[13] In pursuit of his metrical reconstruction, Zapletal used V to reconstruct a stich parallel to מה יתר לאדם and based on Sir 3.20: שידרוש רב ממנו. Barton similarly believed that Jerome was translating an earlier reading, although he speculated that 'the words are an ancient gloss supplied to relieve a supposed abruptness in the sentence'. There is no other equivalent to מה יתר לאדם in V, however, and it is clear that Jerome is interpreting that text, not translating a plus (although Podechard suggests that he has indeed taken his inspiration from Sir 3.20).

[14] The full reading of σ' for this verse (largely retroverted) runs: τίς γὰρ οἶδεν ὃ συμφέρει τῷ ἀνθρώπῳ ἐν τῇ ζωῇ ἀριθμοῦ ἡμερῶν ζωῆς ματαιότητος αὐτοῦ ἵνα ποιήσῃ αὐτὸν <σκέπην> ὅτι οὐδὲ εἷς ἐρεῖ τῷ ἀνθρώπῳ τί ἔσται ὀπίσω αὐτοῦ ὑπὸ τὸν ἥλιον, 'For who knows what benefits the human in life for the number of the days of his vain life that he might make it <a shelter>, for no-one will tell the human what will be after him under the sun'. Field supplies σκέπην, arguing that ܡܛܠܠ *mṭll*, 'booth, shelter' (which is the rendering of צל attested for σ' at Ct 2.3, and cf. σκέπει attested in Greek at Eccl 7.12), must have dropped out of the Syrohexaplaric text before the following ܡܛܠ *mṭl*. It is interesting to note, however, that Jerome's account of σ' in his comments on 8.12 omits any reference to shadow or shelter, and, although unlikely, it is not impossible that the word was absent from the outset in Symmachus' translation of both verses, or lost from it very early in the course of transmission.

a point. Qohelet would then be speaking rather as he does in 2.3 and 8.15, not about 'anything that might be good' for humans, but about their 'good' in some more general way—it could be argued, indeed, that this is more typical of the way he expresses himself. The evidence for the reading, however, is very slight, and the G variant more likely a simple error.

Brin's short study ('The Significance of the Form mah-ṭṭôb') of the seven places in which the expression מה טוב occurs (Judg 9.2; Job 34.4; Ps 133.1; Prov 15.23; 16.16; Eccl 6.12; Mic 6.8) shows considerable variety, and although it is certainly true that in Mic 6.8 the expression refers to divine expectations of human behaviour and that in Job 34.4 it is aligned with משפט as a description of the decision that Elihu calls upon those present to make, Brin is probably right to group the usage here most closely with Judg 9.2, which also has a following -ל, and which deals with an issue of practical advantage. In any case, there is no reason to suppose that this is a general philosophical question.

6.12 in life] Many manuscripts of G, and of versions that depend on G, have ζωῇ αὐτοῦ, 'his life' (cf. V *in uita sua*; S ܒܚܝܘܗܝ *bḥywhy*), where Rahlfs and Gentry have just ζωῇ. Whether this reading arose in Hebrew or Greek, it seems probable that it did so as a facilitation, or in assimilation to what follows, and that M represents the earlier Hebrew reading, without 'his'.

6.12 The days of his life of illusion are finite] The ancient versions and modern commentators alike have been inclined to read מספר ימי חיי הבלו as an adverbial expression of time, qualifying what has preceded, so that the sense is something like 'what is good for the man in life for the number of days of his vain life'. To be sure, Qohelet has used similar expressions that way already in 2.3 and 5.17, but to understand the expression the same way in this context not only makes it repetitious, leaving בחיים redundant,[15] it also strands the subsequent ויעשם כצל—forcing translators to see that clause as a parenthetical addition, which they then have to translate awkwardly as a relative clause (e.g. RSV 'which he passes like a shadow') or by introducing some other notion like 'seeing that', which overloads the conjunction, especially in the light of the אשר that follows (for a discussion of approaches, see Ellermeier, *Qohelet I.1*, 172). It seems simpler and tidier to see מספר in this instance as a substantival predicate indicating a small or limited quantity (see, e.g., Gen 34.30; Deut 33.6 Ezek 12.16 for that sense) rather than just a number, and Marshall, incidentally, notes in ms 252 an explanatory gloss along those lines: ἐπὶ σπανίου, 'scarce', for G ἀριθμὸν ἡμερῶν. Qohelet is not here assuming, but explicitly stating the limits of human life.

Expressions similar to ימי חיי הבלו will be used again at 7.15 (בימי הבלי) and 9.9 (ימי חיי הבלך): the construct state is probably being used attributively, to express quality (cf. GKC §128 p; J-M §129 f)—although see the note at 7.15.

---

[15] This, and perhaps the influence of 7.15, may have contributed to the absence of חיי in some later manuscripts; cf. de Rossi.

6.12 and he spends them] G's aorist ἐποίησεν is explained by Yi, 163, as an attempt to retain a temporal distinction between this clause and the subsequent מה יהיה אחריו, which leads the translator to avoid the future tense with which he would usually translate the yiqtol. This seems forced, as does his alternative explanation, that ויעשם was read with waw consecutive: on the one hand, there is nothing to have prevented the translator using a present tense, as he sometimes does for the yiqtol, and so avoiding the oddness of the aorist here; on the other hand, nothing in the context suggests the sort of narrative sequence that would favour a consecutive form. It seems much more probable, in fact, that G read a variant ועשם instead of M ויעשם. In this respect, most of the other versions affirm M, but McNeile, 145, is probably right to suppose that S ܘܥܒܪ *w‛br*, although it is most likely a corruption of ܘܥܒܕ *w‛bd* (so McNeile; Kamenetzky, 199), agrees with G. In any case, M is probably original here, although the extent to which the past tense makes any sense at all depends on the meaning we assign to the expression. There is no text-critical basis for Sacchi's proposed אשר יעשם.

The object of the verb is also difficult to pin down in G: the better manuscript witnesses tend to support αὐτά here, rather than the αὐτάς adopted by Rahlfs and Gentry (cf. Hie *faciet eas*). That latter reading makes the reference explicitly to the 'days', and ἐποίησεν αὐτάς most naturally means 'he spent (those days)', since the verb can be used of spending time in Greek. It is not so clear what αὐτά would refer to, unless it be a generalizing 'these things', but it is possible that the translator would have adopted such a rendering if he were aware that עשה, unlike its Greek counterpart, is not generally, if ever, used elsewhere of 'spending' time, with a period or expression of time as its direct object. It is true that Jastrow, *Dictionary*, lists 'to spend time' as a meaning of עשה in rabbinic Hebrew, and a lot of commentators have pounced on this, but a scrutiny of his examples shows very quickly that, although עשה can indeed mean to 'spend time' in an absolute way, it cannot take an expression of time as a direct object—in other words, it cannot mean 'to spend an hour/day/year', and to get that sense one has to say 'עשה *for* x years'. Ruth 2.19 is often cited also, but even if עשה means 'spend time' there at all ('work' seems more likely in the context, cf. Whitley), then it is again being used absolutely. In principle, then, ויעשם should not mean 'and he spent them (the days of his life)', and I suspect that the translator of G was aware of this.

In practice, however, it is difficult to see what else it could mean in this context,[16] and that consideration has led many commentators to suppose,

---

[16] If Field's restoration is correct (see the footnote above), then Symmachus' interpretation apparently tries to take בצל or כצל as a secondary object: he will make 'it' (the number of his days, or the good) a protection. Even if this is possible, it does not make any obvious sense. Other commentators have dealt with the problem by retaining the sense but emending the text. Renan declares

quite plausibly, that we are dealing with a Graecism here. Seow, defending a Persian-period dating, points to the comparable use of *iri* in Egyptian: examples from Late Egyptian or Demotic would be more apt, perhaps, than the much earlier Middle Egyptian instances that he adduces, but it is not clear in any case what he is trying to accomplish. The Egyptian usage does not demonstrate in some general way that 'there is nothing distinctly Hellenistic about the expression. No Hellenistic influence can be established on the basis of this idiom', as though its existence means that 'make' can be used for 'spend (time)' in any language. At best, it demonstrates that there are other potential sources for the usage here, but if we have no evidence for other Egyptian influence on Qohelet's language, it is hard to see why we should discount Greek as a much more likely source. Differently, Chango, *L'Ecclésiaste*, 54, speculates that this usage might have arisen through uses of the verb to connote 'celebrating' a feast (Exod 12.48; 31.16), but concedes that Greek influence remains a strong possibility.

6.12 as a shadow] Qohelet uses צל in four places, each time with a preposition. Here, M has כצל but G ἐν σκιᾷ reflects בצל (the other ancient versions all support M; we may also note that G does not reflect the article indicated by the pointing in M); for the two uses in 7.12, M has בצל twice, while G appears to reflect בצל followed by כצל; finally, in 8.13, as here, M has כצל but G reflects בצל. This degree of confusion is attributable in part, of course, to the close graphical similarity of בצל and כצל, but the issue is not merely one of scribal error: copyists were reading any ambiguously written בצל or כצל in accordance with their understanding of what the context demanded. For that reason, it is important to note that כצל appears in a number of other places as a way of depicting human transience: see, e.g., 1 Chr 29.15, 'as a shadow are our days on the earth'; Ps 102.12 (ET 102.11), 'my days are like a lengthening shadow'; Ps 144.4, 'his days are like a passing shadow'.[17] In contrast, בצל is used elsewhere almost exclusively of the shelter or protection offered by someone or something: see, e.g., Gen 19.8; Pss 17.8; 36.8 (ET 36.7); 91.1; Isa 30.2, 3—this would appear to be the way it is used in 7.12.

that ויעשם cannot be retained, and proposes that ויעבדו (a misprint for ויעברו?) or something similar must be read. Taking an approach that is not dissimilar, perhaps, to that of σ′, but as part of a broader re-interpretation of the text here, Ginsberg, 'Supplementary Studies', 48, argues for emendation to ויעשה or ויעשנו, so that the object of the verb would be the 'good' that a human is to 'do' during their life, and a similar approach was suggested earlier by Tur-Sinai in 'Dunkle Bibelstellen', 280. See further below.

[17] Such usage tells against Seow's supposition that כצל might mean 'as in shadow' here, which enables him to accept the sense of G without actually emending M. When a second preposition is omitted with -כ, the meaning is always strongly indicated by the context. T, incidentally, does not support G here, as he suggests.

Goldman, largely following Hertzberg, argues that Qohelet is actually using 'shade' in a different way here, to indicate ignorance, and that an original בצל has been displaced by copyists assimilating to the familiar uses of כצל to depict transience. That is an attractive idea, and Schoors has recently subscribed to it in his commentary (although many of his comments on the passage seem still to depend on his previous acceptance of כצל; cf. *The Preacher* I, 148); it is certainly possible that some such understanding underpins G, if the text has not simply been assimilated to 7.12 or 8.13. Against it stand, however, the important considerations that צל is simply not used elsewhere in Hebrew as a metaphor for ignorance, that to be בצל is elsewhere always a good thing, and that for Qohelet to be claiming that humans live their lives בצל would fit awkwardly with his image of them living 'under the sun' (which will be reiterated in the very next clause). Without wishing to discount the originality of the book in terms of its imagery, it is important to take account both of the existing connotations of צל, and of the ways shade is likely to be regarded in a hot climate: if we were to read בצל with G, then the implication would probably have been that humans live their short lives protected by their ignorance of what is to come, and that does not seem likely to be Qohelet's intention.

Although כצל seems preferable, however, I doubt also that Qohelet is trying to portray the 'days' of human life here as a shadow: the text reads more naturally as a portrayal of the human, as in, e.g., Job 14.2. If the metaphor is to be linked to what follows, then we might say that the human lives briefly like a shadow under the sun, with no knowledge of what will follow when it has gone.

A denial of that sense is the starting point for one of several attempts to understand צל in quite different terms here, each of which appeals to Aramaic in some way. Without saying why, Zimmermann declares that '"to spend one's days as a shadow" is conceptually impossible', which leads him to suggest that his translator read as מטלל, 'shelter', a word that was actually some form of טלל, 'play', so that the original sense would have been 'so that he could spend his days as if at play'. With a pinch more plausibility but a further level of complexity, Ginsberg suggests that כצל אשר is actually a poor rendering of מטל די, 'because', which was misread as 'shelter' under the influence of the context, with an original מצל then becoming כצל through scribal error. See his *Studies*, 27-29; 'Supplementary Studies', 48. The most thoughtful such suggestion is made in Wise, 'A Calque'. Without resorting to any idea that the book has actually been translated from Aramaic, Wise observes that בטלל, the Aramaic equivalent of בצל, undergoes a shift of meaning from 'owing to the protection of' or 'with the help of' to 'because of' or 'on account of', and suggests that Qohelet is employing a calque of the Aramaic in that latter sense. We shall return to Wise's suggestion at 7.12 and 8.13, but we may note Wise's own observation on 6.12 that 'in truth here the Hebrew text could make sense without postulating the calque' (256-57). The proposals of Ginsberg and Wise would give a sense similar to that proposed much more straightforwardly by Tur-Sinai: see the next note.

6.12 who²] 4QQohᵃ once again raises some difficult questions. After 6.8, which lay at the bottom of the second column on the largest fragment (fragment 1), the text breaks off and something like four lines are missing altogether. The column continues, however, on fragments 3-6, which fit together to form another substantial block of text. The second line of this new block contains the beginning of 7.1, and before that a single ש: this is most likely the final character of השמש, the last word of 6.12. The traces on the first line should also belong to 6.12, therefore, and Ulrich reconstructs the last two visible characters on that line as the י׳ of יגיד: at the very least, there is a *yod*. The problem lies in the fact that traces of two further characters precede that word, and one of those is almost certainly ש; the other is more ambiguous,[18] but Ulrich reads it as a final ם, and reconstructs here [שׁם̇]י̇[. Obviously, this does not correspond to the text of M, and traces of another character, about two character-widths before the ש, make it awkward even to read שם as the end of ויעשם.[19] Although the spacing for the break between words would be slightly tight, the traces that Ulrich reads as a final ם are also compatible with the initial/medial form of that letter, and I think it is more probable that we should, in fact, reconstruct שׁ[י'] י̇[גיד here, making this one of several instances where 4QQohᵃ has ש- for M אשר. Puech, 'Qohelet a Qumran', 148-50, adopts this reading.

Whether we read שמי or מי אשר, however, the sense is difficult to pin down. Tur-Sinai, 'Dunkle Bibelstellen', 280, suggested that in both 6.12 and 8.13, צל is in fact an error for של, and that we should read the conjunction באשל, which Qohelet uses at 8.17. The meaning of that conjunction is not wholly straightforward itself, but in 8.17 it appears to express consequence, so here it would mean something like 'on account of which', and the question would be presented as a logical consequence of the previous statements. Tur-Sinai's suggestion requires emendation of ויעשם as well as of צל (see above), and would be a little too speculative even if it gave a good sense. As it is, though, it is open to the same criticism as Lauha's proposal to take אשר by itself with a similar meaning (cf. Gen 11.7): even if we allow that the 'shadiness' of human life is connected to the limits of human perception (which, I have suggested, it is probably not), the inability of anybody to predict the future is not a result of that shadiness.

---

[18] The trace consists of a horizontal line at the baseline of the text, with a slight upward turn at the left: it lies at the edge of the fragment and most of the character has been lost altogether. The trace cannot be from the ר of אשר.

[19] Those traces do not fit ו or י. Ulrich's further observation, that it is difficult to make the text of M fit the space available, has to be qualified by a recognition that, with a gap of unknown size after fragment 1, it is difficult to know just how much space actually is available.

Most commentators (and most of the ancient versions) take the relationship to be the other way around, and understand אשר as causal, although it is not really any easier to see how any of what has been said so far in the verse follows from the implications of the final question. Of course, it is possible that Qohelet is claiming a logical relationship where none actually exists, but it is interesting in this respect to compare Deut 3.24, the only other occurrence of אשר (or ש) before a question with מי, where it is also difficult to establish the relationship between that question and what precedes. As with כ before מה and מי in Qohelet's usage, I suspect that the word in this position serves more to introduce the question than to convey a specific connection to what has gone before, and I have accordingly left it untranslated. S, which has no equivalent here, may have pursued the same policy, although Kamenetzky, 201, believes that -ܡܛܠ ܕ *mṭl d-*, 'because', has dropped out after ܬܠܠ *ṭllʾ*.

6.12 is going to explain] Or 'will inform'. Qohelet uses מי יגיד also in 8.7 and 10.14, both of which also assert human ignorance of the future; cf. מי יביאנו לראות in 3.22. The expression appears in 1 Sam 20.10 and Job 21.31 as well, but does not appear to be a fixed way of talking about such ignorance. It is difficult to say here whether Qohelet is talking simply about future events, or about something closer to an explanation of what will unfold: the hiphʿil of נגד can be used of providing information, but also of expounding dreams, riddles and mysteries (e.g. Gen 41.24; 1 Kgs 10.3; Judg 14.12; Dan 2.2; Job 11.6). That latter nuance, however, fits the context of 8.7 very well, and prevents a simple tautology in 10.14, so I have translated accordingly in all three places.

6.12 after him] On אחריו, see the corresponding note at 3.22.

Introduction to 7.1-22

Sayings

(7.1) Better is fame than fine unguent—and the day of death than the day of one's being born.

(7.2) Better to go to a house of mourning than go to a house of celebration, since this is the whole end of a human, and one who lives will take it seriously.

(7.3) Better is vexation than laughter, for an unhappy face cheers the heart.

(7.4) The heart of wise men is a house of mourning, and the heart of fools a house of celebration: (7.5) better to hear rebukings from a wise man, than to hear singing from fools.

(7.6) For like the sound of sticks beneath the skillet, such is the laughter of a fool.

This too is an illusion.

(7.7) For extortion discredits a wise man, and crushes the generous heart.

(7.8) Better is the end of an account than its beginning,

> better long of spirit than lofty of spirit.

(7.9) Do not rush in your feelings to get angry, for anger lives in the lap of fools.

(7.10) Do not say 'What has happened, that the old days were better than these?', for it is not wisdom that has led you to inquire about that. (7.11) Wisdom is good with inherited property, but an advantage to those who see the sun. (7.12) For in its shade, that wisdom is in the shade of that money, but it is a profit from knowledge that the wisdom may sustain its possessor.

(7.13) Behold the achievement of God: who can straighten what he has bent? (7.14) On a day of good things, live the good life, but think about a day of bad things: God has made this as well, to match the other, so that a person may never discover anything after him.

(7.15) I have seen both, in my days of illusion: there may be a righteous man who perishes through his righteousness; and there may be a wicked man who lasts long through his wrongdoing.

(7.16) Do not be very righteous, and do not show yourself wise more than needs be: why give yourself a shock?

(7.17) Do not be very wicked, and do not become an idiot: why die when it is not your time?

(7.18) It is good that you grab this, and do not hold your hand back from that, for someone who fears God will get away with both.

(7.19) Will wisdom come to the aid of a wise man more than would ten men of authority who are in the city?

(7.20) For there is no person so righteous on earth that he can do good and not sin.

(7.21) Also, do not apply your mind to all the words that people say, in case you hear your servant being rude about you: (7.22) for your mind knows also the many occasions when you too have been rude about others.

Qohelet has jumped rapidly between topics sometimes, and as well as offering us scattered aphorisms almost from the outset, has already admonished us several times in 4.17–5.6. With the series of matching 'better than' sayings that begin ch. 7, however, he now switches for the first time to the looser style of composition that we associate with ancient sayings-collections. Within the series that runs to 7.22 (not without interruption), we can identify certain blocks of material. 7.1 uses a saying about the importance of one's reputation at death (which makes dying more important than being born) to introduce further sayings in 7.2-6 that associate the wise with mourning, and commend seriousness above laughter; 7.8 similarly prefers ends to beginnings, but the next two verses now draw conclusions from that about patience and nostalgia. In 7.15, Qohelet interrupts the series with a personal observation, but extrapolates from it a series of admonitions in 7.16-18: since the righteous and wicked may not receive the longevity or early deaths that each deserves, we should steer a course that neither exposes us to the surprising fate of the righteous who die early, nor incurs the expected death of the wicked and foolish. There is a certain coherence across, as well as within, these short blocks: each is, in its own way, initially concerned with 'ends'.

It is much harder, however, to establish any broader coherence. There are some textual problems around 7.7, but both that verse and 7.20 are presented as though they were explanations for the advice that immediately preceded each, even though they have no obvious connection with it—and 7.20 looks as though it belongs with 7.16-18, rather than after 7.19. The advice in 7.11-12, 13-14, and 21-22 is all internally coherent, but no piece connects directly with any other or with the longer blocks, while 7.19 seems so decontextualized that it is hard to fathom its purpose. It seems likely, in fact, that we are supposed to read all of 7.19-22 as a sort of follow-up to 7.16-18: we should not be too wise because wisdom has limits, nor too righteous, because nobody is always righteous, and we should not let the reactions of others deter us from the safest course. Perhaps 7.13-14, furthermore, set the scene for 7.15, with their reference to the mystery of God's activity, and his responsibility for both good times and bad. The format of the series does not lend itself to explicit connections, but even if we permit ourselves to make them anyway in those cases, it is hard to see how 7.11-12 can be connected to 7.10 by anything more than the catchword 'wisdom'. While it is possible that some clearer original coherence has been obscured by disruptions to the text or by clumsy interpolations, it seems likely that much of this is deliberate: Qohelet adds his own touches (a *hebel* declaration in 7.6, a personal observation in 7.15), but is broadly adopting the style associated with compositions that are inherently more atomistic and miscellaneous than is most of his discourse. If this looked more coherent, it would look less like a sayings-collection, and so, apparently in order to evoke that literature, the author is striking a balance.

Formally, there is perhaps a little more coherence, although that should not be overstated. Gordis (supported in this by Osborn, 'Guide', 186) talks about 'a prose heptad, a collection of seven utterances', each beginning with the word for 'good/better' (vv. 1, 2, 3, 5, 8, 11, 14), but even if we allow a little looseness in that respect ('good' is the *second* word of v. 14), there are other sentences interspersed here, some containing the same word in another position, some not containing it at all. The idea is developed productively by Fischer (*Skepsis*, 90-96), who speaks more generally, and less problematically, of 'good' serving as a sort of catchword across the sequence, alongside some other words. I would not myself wish to push even that too far, however, and if there is anything that holds this material together, it is a certain oddness, that is neither strictly formal nor thematic.

We shall look in more detail below at the advice itself, but I have already drawn attention in the Introduction to the way in which 7.2-6 appear to commend wisdom while actually making it look less attractive than folly. A pre-occupation with one's reputation at death, furthermore, seems more than a little at odds with Qohelet's concerns about living life—and that peculiarity may extend as far as 7.8. Unsurprisingly, a number of commentators have speculated that Qohelet is citing and commenting upon existing sayings, which do not necessarily express his own views, although there is not a great deal of agreement about what belongs to whom. There is, I think, a certain truth to this, inasmuch as Qohelet clearly says some things that he does not mean, but he also appears not actually to disown them at this point, and it is difficult to see some clear reaction against the views of others—it is also hard to find any real parallels elsewhere to some of the views against which he is supposedly reacting. It seems more likely that there is something closer to parody here, and that Qohelet's efforts to present advice in a conventional way, and to commend the wise, are actually used as a device by the author to highlight the growing gap between the positions Qohelet has developed, and the ideas that a more conventionally wise man (or perhaps an unusually ascetic one) might have been expected to hold.

It is not clear how conscious of all that Qohelet himself is supposed to be, but the saying in 7.11-12 comes across as unashamedly cynical, and by the time we reach 7.13-18, where he abandons the sayings format for a while, Qohelet's own distinctive ideas and observations are reasserting themselves (although some scholars think that he is continuing to cite and comment upon established sayings in 7.13-14; cf. Michel, 'Qohelet-Probleme', 100-101; *Untersuchungen*, 111-12). If he began the chapter with commendations of wisdom that made it sound a miserable business, and with an emphasis on looking to the long term, Qohelet sounds increasingly more like himself as he rejects the possibility of knowing anything about that long term, and suggests that neither righteousness nor wisdom should be pursued without limit at the cost of one's own wellbeing. When he closes with three final sayings in 7.19-22, these question the relative value of wisdom, doubt the possibility of complete righteousness, and, in a stark reversal of 7.1, suggest that we should not be too concerned with what other people say about us. The monologue is building up to a point, immediately after the end of these sayings, when Qohelet will confess that he has found himself distant from the wisdom with which he set out, so it should not be surprising if 7.1-22 depict what seems to be his changing relationship with wisdom and with more commonplace ideals. The interesting thing is that the author appears to be attempting this without resort to an explicit memoir (although that is to follow), but by using the advice that Qohelet himself offers to illustrate his growing alienation.

7.1-6

(7.1) Better is fame than fine unguent—and the day of death than the day of one's being born.

(7.2) Better to go to a house of mourning than go to a house of celebration, since this is the whole end of a human, and one who lives will take it seriously.

(7.3) Better is vexation than laughter, for an unhappy face cheers the heart.

(7.4) The heart of wise men is a house of mourning, and the heart of fools a house of celebration: (7.5) better to hear rebukings from a wise man, than to hear singing from fools.

(7.6) For like the sound of sticks beneath the skillet, such is the laughter of a fool.

This too is an illusion.

Commentary

The string of sayings in 7.2-6 revolves around a central contrast between two images: a household that is in mourning, and one that is feasting or celebrating a family event (see the notes on 7.2). Qohelet advises that it is better to visit one than the other, and then transfers this advice to a different context: our earliest source suggests that he identifies the mind of the wise with the house of mourning and the mind of the fool with that of feasting, so that it is better to visit the former, and hear the rebukes of the wise, than to visit the latter, where one will hear only the laughter of fools. In subsequent sources, this comparison has mostly been lost, because the hearts of the wise and the fools are now said to be 'in' each house, with an implication that the wise think about death, the foolish only about having fun. The advice about listening to each then becomes a more general statement, that one should listen to those pre-occupied with death rather than those who seek to enjoy themselves. All this is introduced by a beautifully crafted aphorism, which is virtually a word-unit palindrome in Hebrew—*ṭôb šēm miššemen ṭôb*, literally 'good name than-oil good'. If this suggests that one's reputation is worth more than famously expensive fine oil (cf. 2 Kgs 20.13; Prov 21.17), then what immediately follows is likewise sensible (not shocking or absurd, as sometimes suggested): a reputation is something that one can possess when one dies, but not when one is born (cf. *b. Berakot* 17a). If this is the aspect of death upon which the wise are supposed to focus, or which they in some way represent, then Qohelet's advice here is arguably conventional at heart: one's efforts should be directed toward that deathbed reputation. It is difficult, however, not to become uneasy quite quickly as one reads this advice (cf. Murphy, 'On Translating Ecclesiastes', 576). Is such an idea remotely compatible with Qohelet's views that we need to live life to the full, that nothing after death really matters to us, and that the future beyond us is unknown? There is nothing to suggest, moreover, that the celebrations disparaged here are excessive or in any way unrespectable—the language used is that found elsewhere for weddings and other family gatherings—and there is also no clear reason to suppose that Qohelet is limiting his comments to issues of reputation (about which he shows no concern anywhere else, except when he rejects its importance in 7.22). What he depicts is, on the one hand, a wisdom characterized by morbidity and rebuke, and, on the other, a folly that is bursting with celebration, singing and laughter. Even if that laughter belongs to people who face imminent destruction, like sticks on a cooking-fire, the life of a 'fool' here seems much more attractive than that of the wise.

Qohelet finishes with a very ambiguous characterization of all this as *hebel*. Does the illusion lie on the part of the foolish? As he has already made clear, their fate will be that of the wise, and all that distinguishes them here is their willingness to celebrate the pleasures of life—to be houses of celebration, rather than of mourning. In the broader context of Qohelet's ideas, it is actually the wise who seem to be getting the worse deal in these verses, and if there is an illusion anywhere, it is surely in the idea that a constant pre-occupation with death can achieve anything if it does not lead to a better enjoyment of life. Qohelet may just be having another 'bah, humbug' moment, but the implications of what he is saying, along with the portrayals of wisdom and folly, may well lead us to suspect that he is not merely serving as a caricature here, but is either being set up by the author, or himself actively parodying the ideas that he presents as advice (and, e.g., Michel, 'Philosophie', 24-25, accordingly suggests that he is citing the views of others).

Verse 3 is important in this respect, because it sheds the imagery for a moment to lay bare the central claim—that displeasure is better than laughter—and to offer a justification for it. This claim uses the same term that Qohelet used in 1.18 for the bad effects of wisdom, and that he has subsequently used in 2.23 and 5.6 of those who have suffered for their work or because of their circumstances; it represents an emotion that he will reject, furthermore, in 7.9 and 11.10, and it seems extraordinary that he should commend it here. The justification, moreover, can only reasonably be read in one of two ways, given the normal uses of the Hebrew terms: either one is cheered up by wearing a sad expression, or, less likely, one is cheered up by seeing the sadness of others. The first seems simply paradoxical, while the second seems to revel in a sort of *Schadenfreude*, suggesting that the wise enjoy mourning because of the pleasure they derive from the grief around them—which would be simply detestable.

If we are willing to overlook the common usage of the Hebrew, then Qohelet could be saying that a sad face 'corrects' or 'improves' the mind, so translators and commentators have long sought to find a link here to the 'rebukes' that follow in v. 5, and a general sense that one will be made better by the displeasure of others. Even were that not intrusive here, however, it hardly provides a reason for *anger* being better than laughter: the corollary would have to be that one should make the wise angry in order to get rebuked, not merely that one should heed their stern advice. Fox suggests that the paradox which arises when we read the words in their natural sense must force us to put some such unnatural construction upon them, but it seems simpler to suppose that the paradox is the point. The person who commends the sort of wisdom described here is the sort of person who says, 'I enjoy being unhappy', and we are invited to evaluate the advice accordingly.

7.1] 'Oil' can be used in food (e.g. Ezek 16.13) or as fuel for a lamp (e.g. Exod 25.6), but many of the biblical references are to its cosmetic use: oils and fats (rather than alcohol) were the basis of ancient perfumes, and fragrant oils were used on the skin and hair, both by women (e.g. Ct 1.3; 4.10; Esth 2.12), and by men (e.g. Ps 133.2)—Qohelet will refer to the practice in 9.8. In the light of what follows here, it is interesting to note both the suggestion in 2 Sam 14.2 that mourners would not have used oil in this way, and the quite common association of anointing oils with feasts and banquets (e.g. Ezek 23.41; Amos 6.6; Ps 23.5): in Egyptian iconography, participants at such events are commonly depicted as being anointed, or with symbolic cones of scented fat on their heads, representing their perfumed state (see, e.g., Manniche, 'Ancient Scent', and the illustrations in Assmann, 'Der schöne Tag').

Loader sees a metaphor here, based on the image of life as a lamp (cf. Prov 13.9; 20.20): that would give a closer parallel to the second part of the verse, but even were such imagery common enough to be presumed, it seems doubtful that oil valuable enough for this saying to work would be wasted in lamps. Others have noted associations with anointing at births, or the use of oil in funerary rites (so, e.g., Vílchez Líndez), but there is a danger, I think, of reading more into the reference than is there. While it is not unlikely that the precious oil foreshadows references to celebration in the verses that follow (as Lavoie, 'La philosophie comme réflexion', 100-101, argues), oil was used too widely for us to affirm any specific implication. For the purposes of the saying, furthermore, 'oil' is simply a valuable commodity, and the Hebrew term for 'oil' gives a play on words with the term for 'fame'; anything more is gravy for the author, and we can only guess whether he intended it.

Lohfink picks up, I think, the proper link between the two parts of the verse. We are not being invited simply to suppose (as do, e.g., Ogden, 'The "Better"-Proverb', 501-2, and Hollinshead, 'What is good for man?', 38-39, citing Eaton) that just as the claim in the first part is true, so must be the claim in the second (whether it follows or not), but to recognize that the importance of reputation is at the time of death, not the time of birth. Osborn, 'Guide', 187, paraphrases: '"Your reputation is more important than your money!" Therefore, the day you die, after you have proved your good name, will really be more important than the day you were born'. Of course, this does not fit with many of the things that Qohelet says elsewhere, as Lavoie (*loc. cit.*) is swift to point out. Lavoie notes also the more complicated interpretation in Vogels, 'Performance vaine', 383, which associates these verses with a negative pole in Qohelet's thought, and with ideas of a 'non-life' to which death may be preferred, but himself concludes eventually that the concern here is with reflection on death: it is by thinking about death that we understand the realities of our condition, and come to appreciate life.

In general terms, that is not an uncommon interpretation of what Qohelet is saying in 7.1-4 as a whole, but it renders 7.1a almost irrelevant: a pretty saying about something at best loosely related to such ideas. Since that interpretation also draws heavily on what I take to be a secondary form of the text in 7.4, I think it is easier simply to accept that Qohelet is expressing in this verse an opinion that sits uneasily with ideas that he holds elsewhere about human forgetfulness of the dead (see especially 1.11; 4.16; 9.3-5), which would logically render any posthumous reputation irrelevant. If he does indeed suggest here that 'It is our death that will ultimately measure the meaning of our life' (Andrews, 'Ecclesiastes 7:1-19', 300), this is absolutely not his position elsewhere. The opinions in 7.2-3 will likewise seem odd in view of his ideas elsewhere about happiness, and the advice in 7.5 will seem at best optimistic when he turns to look at wisdom in more depth. As I have noted above, moreover, it is hard not to read these verses without some sense that it is the fools, superficially condemned by them, who are living life in a way that better accords with Qohelet's own ideas elsewhere than do his pronouncements at this point. I doubt that we are dealing with something so simple as the citation and rejection of ideas held by others, or even, explicitly, with the ironic *reductio ad absurdum* that Lohfink identifies. There are no other grounds, moreover, for excising any of the difficult materials as secondary, which some commentators have been inclined to do. Qohelet's parroting here of more conventional-sounding themes, set within the conventional framework of a sayings-collection, seems rather to be building toward the crisis that he will experience later in this chapter in relation to his own wisdom, and it is most likely an original aspect of the way in which the development of his character is being presented.

7.2-3] When it is used in Jer 16.8, the expression 'house of celebration' probably refers to a wedding-feast; 'celebration' is used several times of formal feasts in Esther, and in later literature is a common word for family events (as Seow notes). Although the Targum speaks of a wine-tavern here, and many commentators have been inclined to think in similar terms, there is no reason, therefore, to associate the vocabulary specifically with anything frivolous or disreputable.[1] The point is, essentially, that it is better to attend wakes than weddings, since the living should take to heart the fact that they will die.

I have adopted here the Qumran reading 'whole end' rather than the 'end of every human' attested in the later texts and versions: the word-order in 4QQoh^a was slightly different, but the general sense is similar. Qohelet is concerned elsewhere that the living turn their backs on the dead (9.3-4), and 11.8 affirms that we should bear death in mind even as we take pleasure in life. If the idea in 7.2 is unexceptionable, however, the way it is pursued is curious: 7.3 does not deal with the contemplation of death, but with the benefits of vexation and sorrow for their own sake, while 7.4 will use 7.2 as a way to promote listening to the wise—not specifically for their wisdom, but in order to endure their rebukes. Commentators have often observed that the term used here for 'vexation' was used back in 1.18 to describe an effect of wisdom, but Qohelet did not use it there as something for which wisdom was to be commended, and he has since used the same term very negatively in 2.23 and 5.16. In the latter, it is something specifically to be avoided, and Qohelet is about to deprecate it again in 7.9. Nothing he says elsewhere might lead us to suppose that he sees any benefit in it. The expression at the end of 7.3, moreover, is used elsewhere very much in association with the sort of pleasure to be experienced from eating a good dinner—Qohelet is not saying that an outward sadness corrects or disciplines us, but, improbably, that it cheers and relaxes us.

The whole thrust, then, seems to be that, if we want to cheer ourselves up, then we should hang out at wakes, make ourselves as angry and miserable as possible, at least on the outside, and get ourselves told off a lot. These are not views expressed generally in

---

[1] Christian interpretations in such terms may have been shaped in part by G's use here of the term πότος, which can describe both reputable (Gen 19.3) and disreputable (1 Pet 4.3) circumstances, and the subsequent La *potus* (Augustine *de Ciuitate Dei* 17.20; cf. Vaccari, 'Recupero', 117), or *potatio* (Leanza, 'Le tre versione', 92). Bady, 'L'Ecclésiaste', 153, notes several patristic citations which talk instead about a 'house of laughter' (cf. Holmes Parsons), and although it is far from certain that these reflect the existence of a variant reading with γέλωτος, as he suggests, they do attest to the pervasiveness of a particular understanding.

ancient advice literature, which, in its own various ways, tends to be no less concerned with happiness than is Ecclesiastes. It is not even really recognizable as a parody of opinions known from other literature, and seems more simply to be an extension to extremes of commonplace ideas about the benefits of discipline and taking life seriously. Although commentators have usually been inclined to take it at face value, it at least verges on the absurd to a modern eye, and we have no good reason to suppose that the original audience would have found it any less strange.

7.4-5] Here the Qumran reading is again different from that of the much later texts and translations: it presents the hearts of the wise and foolish not as being *in* houses of mourning and joy, but as themselves being houses, which we can visit. Picking up the imagery of 7.2a, the point then is that one should visit the mind of the wise and not that of fools, and so, as 7.5 goes on to say, hear rebukes and not songs. The later versions instead pick up the idea in 7.2b, that one should take death seriously, and depict the wise as doing so—which makes perfectly good sense, but loses the connection with the next verse. The difference in the Hebrew is slight, *bbyt* rather than *byt* in each place, and the longer form may have arisen either after a scribe failed to recognize the metaphor, or in an attempt to clarify it (see the notes).

7.6] 'Sticks beneath the skillet' is alliterative, and probably a play on words in the Hebrew (*hsyrym tḥt hsyr*), while also, perhaps, conveying something of the hissing and crackling sound that is implied (so, e.g., Bartholomew). The 'laughter of the fool' (*śḥq hksyl*) is also alliterative, and perhaps intended to match that sequence, while Heim suggests that *hsyr* picks up *šyr* ('singing') from the previous verse.

Notes

7.1 Better is fame] שם means 'name' or 'reputation', but as in the similar Prov 22.1, it is implicitly a particular sort of reputation here. T, V, some manuscripts of S, and σ′ (ἄμεινον ὄνομα ἀγαθὸν ὑπὲρ μύρον εὐῶδες / μύρου εὐωδία, 'better a good name than fragrant ointment') all add a word for 'good' to draw out an implication that it is a 'good reputation' (the less paraphrastic G does not, as Fox mistakenly suggests, although it is cited with

152   ECCLESIASTES

an added καλόν by John of Damascus). That may indeed be the point. Most other such uses of שם by itself actually involve, however, an idea of renown— 'great fame' rather than 'a reputation for being good' (e.g. Deut 26.19; 2 Sam 23.18; Ezek 16.14-15). Whether we want to talk of 'reputation' or of 'fine reputation' here and in Prov 22, therefore, we should not suppose that there is a specific commendation in either place of a reputation marked by blamelessness or virtue.

Some manuscripts (cf. Ginsburg, *Writings*) claim that this is the halfway point of the book, or the halfway point by verse-count. That claim would be valid were we counting chapters instead, but it pre-dates the application of chapter numbers to Hebrew texts, and is probably a simple error, rather than the product of some earlier variation: M[L] has 222 verses, which puts the halfway point between 6.9 (the 111th) and 6.10 (the 112th). In any case, though, some manuscripts and editions also enlarge the ט that begins the verse, perhaps as a result of this perception. Ginsburg, *Massorah*, 4:39-40, finds this enlarged ט included in six of the ten Masoretic lists of such letters that he collates, and notes that it is also mentioned at the end of a list in the fourteenth-century BM Add. 15250, where it is said that אית דאמרי, 'there are some who say' the ט should be enlarged here.

7.1 than[1]] Kselman, 'Chiasmus', 221, notes that the play on words would be even better if the preposition were unassimilated to give טוב שם מן שמן טוב, and it is interesting to wonder whether the saying was, in fact, originally phrased that way.

7.1 of one's being born] The use of the niphʻal infinitive avoids the ambiguities that surrounded ללדת in 3.2, and the expression here is similar to that in Hos 2.5 כיום הולדה, 'as on the day of her being born'. The suffixed ה- picks up a specified subject in that passage, however: the wife/mother who is serving as an image of Israel. Here we have in M יום הולדו, by contrast, a suffix pronoun with no obvious antecedent. There is no equivalent to this pronoun in many manuscripts of G, and in Syh (cf. also ms 788) the pronoun is under asterisk and assigned to α', indicating that Origen did not find it in his text, but borrowed it from Aquila's translation to fit the Hebrew. S also lacks a pronoun, and may have been influenced by G in this respect, while Hie, on the other hand, does have a pronoun but may have been influenced by Jerome's reading of the Hebrew. V lacks a pronoun, but may be paraphrasing. It is difficult to say what has happened definitively, but it is hard to see any reason why the pronoun would have appeared secondarily in the text of M, and so it is probably original (although the restoration of the ו on 4QQoh[a] in DJD is highly speculative). It was eliminated as puzzling and redundant either in the source-text of G or in at least some early manuscripts.

If we accept the pronoun, then it has to be understood as a sort of impersonal 'one's', and there is a similar usage at 3.12 (see the note 'one's life' there). That raises a question, however, about the absence of a matching suffix pronoun on מות, and either Qohelet is allowing the one pronoun to do double duty (perhaps for rhythmic or euphonic reasons), or he is, less probably, drawing a distinction between the two days: the day of the death of anyone is better than the day of one's own birth.

7.2 a house of mourning…a house of celebration] Or, in the second part, 'a house of feasting'. In 7.4, בית אבל is paired with בית שמחה, but M here pairs it with בית משתה, an expression known from Jer 16.8. In Jer 16.5, the prophet has been prohibited from entering the בית מרזח, which is usually understood to be the house where a feast of mourning is taking place, and 16.7 bans breaking bread for the mourner, or offering a 'cup of consolation'. In 16.9, God promises that he will do away with the voice of joy (שמחה), and links this specifically to the idea of a wedding. Sitting between the references to funerals and weddings, 16.8 could belong to either image, but the point is probably that the children mentioned in 16.1-2 are themselves to be food: *funeral-feasts* for them are to be avoided, and *wedding-feasts* will never happen. In Esth 9.17, 18, 19, 22, משתה and שמחה are again linked: a יום משתה ושמחה, 'a day of feasting and joy', is depicted there as a formal gathering and celebration by the Jews, who send food to each other (cf. Neh 8.10, 12), and both terms are found commonly in rabbinic literature referring to celebrations, especially of family events. It would be a mistake, therefore, to assume that a בית משתה or a בית שמחה would be just any house of celebration, or even something like a pub: Qohelet is talking about household gatherings linked to sad or happy occasions. Noting rabbinic descriptions of the celebrations around circumcision, Levy suggests Qohelet has that in mind, and it would give a good match with the death/birth contrast of 7.1, but it seems unlikely that anything so precise is intended.

The reading of the second term is slightly complicated by the fact that some manuscripts attest an alternative המשתה, with a definite article, presented either as the $K^e th\hat{i}bh$, with משתה as $Q^e r\hat{e}$, or as $Q^e r\hat{e}$ with משתה as $K^e th\hat{i}bh$.[2] With or without an article, though, M משתה is backed by all the ancient translations, and there was no reason to doubt this reading until the discovery of 4QQoh[a]. The first letter of the word has been lost in that manuscript, but there is little doubt that it read שמחה, as in v. 4, rather than משתה. As we have seen, the terms are closely connected in this sort of context, so the use of one rather than the other has no great impact on the sense, but it is difficult to say for certain which is original. Fox claims that the Qumran version has simply substituted a

---

[2] Ginsburg, *Writings*, presents a Masoretic note that the writing with the article is the $K^e th\hat{i}bh$ of the eastern tradition, and that without is the $Q^e r\hat{e}$; cf. his *Massorah* 3:71; Baer, 81; and the Introduction, p. 190. T-S D1.15, 2v 12, simply gives המשתה as the eastern reading, without reference to a $Q^e r\hat{e}$ (contrast its treatment of 9.9). Origenic manuscripts of G have an article before πένθους (= אבל) and πότου (= משתה), and it is possible that these represent correction towards a Hebrew text with articles in both places. Kennicott, however, notes some nine later Hebrew manuscripts with an article on משתה, and only one with an article on אבל.

synonym (which could, of course, as easily be said of the text from which M is derived), and various scholars have seen an assimilation to v. 4 (so, e.g., *BHQ*; Salters, 'Textual Criticism', 56). The words are graphically similar, however, and there are no real grounds to suppose that the variation has resulted from anything more than a simple error (and it is worth noting that Kennicott lists two manuscripts which will read משתה for שמחה in v. 4, an error found also, it seems, in the source-text of Codex Graecus Venetus). If there was a deliberate change, then it should also be said that, since v. 4 is clearly referring back to this verse, any scribe who consciously assimilated משתה to שמחה would have had good reason to do so: if original, the difference between the verses is hard to explain. In the end, without strong reasons to prefer either reading on other grounds, we need to give proper weight to the relative antiquity of 4QQoh[a], which is significantly older than any of our other sources. If it offers the original reading, however, then this was clearly extinguished early in the course of transmission.

7.2 than to go] G ἢ ὅτι πορευθῆναι, lit. 'than that to go', is supported by S ܓܠܡܐܙܠ ܡܢ *mn dlmʾzl*. McNeile, 161, tries to show that the unexpected ὅτι is a graphical error that arose in the transmission of the Greek, but his suggestions are unconvincing, and Goldman may be right that it is rooted in a reading משלכת. Goldman himself compares מאשר in 3.22, which has a comparative sense 'than that', but the construction with a yiqtol in that verse is quite different from the use of an infinitive here, which would not need -ש or אשר, and so the proposed Hebrew is as meaningless as the Greek. It seems likely that this is just an error: a ש has been introduced after מ because the scribe's eye, perhaps, has drifted to the subsequent משתה. Variants with παρὰ τὸ and ὑπὲρ τοῦ in place of ἢ ὅτι are both attested for G, the former in hexaplaric manuscripts where it may plausibly represent a correction toward the Hebrew, rather than an independent attempt to mend the text—which is accomplished more simply in many other manuscripts (and citations) by omitting the ὅτι.

The verb is missing altogether in Hie, which is strange: we have the La associated with Jerome for this verse, and that includes *quam ire*, 'than to go'.[3] Because it is redundant, strictly speaking, the verb is missing in many citations of the Greek, and Jerome leaves it out in V, probably for that reason. In Hie he usually sticks closer to his sources, however, and it seems more likely that it has dropped out during transmission of his commentary than that he omitted it himself.

---

[3] *Melius est ire in domum luctus quam ire in domum potationis, quia hic finis omnis hominis; et qui uiuit uiuit ad cor suum.* See Berger, 'Notice', 140; Leanza, 'Le tre versione', 92. La is also cited in Augustine *de Ciuitate Dei* xvii, 20: *melius est ire in domum luctus quam ire in domum potus*; see Vaccari, 'Recupero', 117.

7.2 since] G καθότι may reflect באשר, rather than M באשר (cf., e.g., McNeile, 145; *BHQ*), and is probably supported by S. See the note 'when' at 4.17.

7.2 this is the whole end of a human] Or 'the end of every human'. There is again a difference between M and 4QQoh[a], with the other ancient versions supporting M הוא סוף כל האדם. In 4QQoh[a], the pronoun is reconstructed by *DJD* as ה[ו]אה (although, it should be noted, the ו is barely visible, if at all). The spelling הואה is familiar from other manuscripts at Qumran (see Reymond, *Qumran Hebrew*, 158), and is not the result of carelessness, as Goldman suggests. This is important, because his claim that it 'points to a rather careless copy at this point' is the only apparent reason that Goldman offers for dismissing the further reading כול סוף: where M and the versions have 'the end of every human', 4QQoh[a] has 'the whole end [of the human]' (or just possibly 'the whole end [of every human]'). This is clearly a more difficult reading than M סוף כל האדם, which includes the very common כל האדם, so although the latter could easily be considered a facilitation, it is hard to see how כ(ו)ל סוף האדם would have arisen naturally, and it has a better claim to be the earlier reading.

On the originality or otherwise of the article in G παντὸς τοῦ ἀνθρώπου, 'every human', see Gentry, 'Relationship', 73. It is unlikely that the translator found כל אדם (whether the text is original or not), and correspondingly unlikely that he used παντὸς ἀνθρώπου. Gentry also discusses the attestations in Syh of a plural for the noun in α' and of a singular (like G) in θ', and shows (73-5) that these accord with the translation techniques of each elsewhere.

7.2 one who lives] Qohelet tends to use the plural חיים for 'the living' when he wants to talk about them collectively (4.2, 15; 6.8; 9.4, 5), and this is normal in biblical Hebrew. The construction with the singular here may have a different nuance, therefore—perhaps 'while one is alive one should'.

7.2 will take it seriously] The Hebrew of M means literally 'will give/put to his heart', and seems odd because it lacks an object for the verb. Seow cites as analogies the rather different expressions at Isa 42.25 and 57.11, which use שים על לב, 'put on one's heart', but although these have no direct object either, it is not clear that they can be used to shed light on the expression here (any more than can the similar expressions with שים and אל at 2 Sam 13.33; 19.20). Qohelet elsewhere uses נתן לב ל-, 'give one's heart to', in 7.21, apparently meaning 'pay attention to', but that is different again, and when, in 9.1, he does use the same expression נתן אל לב as here, it is with an object (את כל זה). In short, there are expressions that look a bit like this which can be used without an object, but there is no reason to suppose that to be true of this expression.

It is interesting to find, then, that G has δώσει ἀγαθὸν, 'will put *good* (into his heart)', although '*good*' is omitted by Rahlfs. The support for that reading is very limited outside the G tradition itself, however: there is no object in σ' καὶ ὁ ζῶν προσέξει τῇ διανοίᾳ, 'and the living will bear in mind' (translated into Latin by Jerome as *et qui uiuit, respiciet ad mentem*), in Hie *et qui uiuit dabit ad cor suum*, 'and he who lives will give to his heart', or in the La *et qui uiuit uiuit ad cor suum*, 'and who lives, lives at his heart' (which is, admittedly, probably faulty). V and T both paraphrase, but in different ways, neither of which involves 'good', so it looks very much as though ἀγαθόν or טוב has simply been borrowed from the start of the next verse to supply an object in G or its source-text, where there was perceived to be a need for one. Unfortunately, as most of the text is missing, 4QQoh[a] cannot help here, although its reading was clearly not significantly longer than that in M. If we are not dealing with some idiomatic usage, however, or with an expectation that the audience would simply supply the object from context, then it is possible that a suffix pronoun 'it' has been lost from ייטן early in the course of transmission.

7.3 vexation] See the note 'exasperation' at 1.18.

7.3 for an unhappy face cheers the heart] Lit. 'for by badness of face a heart becomes good'. The opposition of רע and ייטב is not an opposition of 'good' and 'evil' here: these are two idioms known from elsewhere. The first, רע פנים, is used at Gen 40.7 and in Neh 2.2, on both occasions to ask people why they are looking unhappy. Prov 15.13 uses ייטב with פנים to express the opposite idea of a cheerful face, but with לב the verb is commonly associated with eating, drinking, relaxing, or enjoying hospitality, to the extent that this may be a primary implication (cf. Judg 19.6, 9; 1 Kgs 21.7; Ruth 3.7; there is a similar usage of the hiphʿil in Judg 19.22, but a different implication the qal in Judg 18.20). Qohelet will turn the expression round in 11.9, where it is the heart that is the subject (see the note there on 'be good to you'), but here he talks, in effect, of a sad face having the same effect as a good dinner. If it is not just an error, the writing ייטבלב as a single word in 4QQoh[a] perhaps reflects the status of the expression as a familiar idiom.

σ′ is attested as ὅτι δι' ἀηδίαν (var. διὰ ἀηδίας) προσώπου βελτίων ἔσται διάνοια, 'for through unpleasantness of face, a mind will be better', which Jerome paraphrases as *per tristitiam quippe uultus, melior fiet animus*, 'for through sadness of face, the mind becomes better'. In G, καρδία, 'heart', dropped out of at least a part of the manuscript tradition, leading Origen to restore it from α′ and θ′, which is why it is under asterisk in Syh: the loss was probably through haplography (cf. Gentry), since καρδία is repeated as the next word at the beginning of v. 4. The La text published by Berger reads *melius est sapientia cum iracundia quam risus, quia in malitia uultus letificat cor*, 'better is wisdom with irritability than laughter, for in badness of face it delights the heart', which has probably drawn in 'wisdom' interpretatively from the next verse. V interprets in a slightly different direction: by sadness of face *corrigitur animus delinquentis*, 'the mind of the offender is corrected'. Both, however, apparently understand the 'bad face' to be that of someone offering reproof, and this is not entirely unlike the interpretation in T, where divine sadness leads to a punishment that will provoke the righteous to prayer.

In light of the idiomatic uses of the qal with לב, it is not clear how readily the verb could naturally connote the ideas of 'correcting', 'amending' or 'improving' the heart which the Targum and Jerome adopt—and which underlie many modern readings too (e.g., in various ways, Podechard, Fox, Eaton). The hiphʿil does in fact, though, have some such sense occasionally in connection with 'ways' and 'deeds' (e.g. Jer 26.13; 35.15), and since we could vocalize ייטב as hiphʿil, the consonantal text is arguably ambiguous in this respect. Rudman, 'Anatomy of the Wise Man', 467-68, defends this interpretation without going down that route, however, and by pointing instead to the ways in which Qohelet associates sorrow with wisdom elsewhere. The point then is that sorrow improves the mind by inducing wisdom. Even were that a plausible understanding of the verb in the qal with לב, however, it fudges the association: in 1.18, the only really relevant passage, it is wisdom that induces sorrow, not *vice versa* (and 2.23, which he also cites, has nothing to do with wisdom).

7.4 is a house...a house] Or 'is *in* a house...*in* a house', although that is probably a secondary reading. In M, G, Hie and La,[4] the hearts of the wise and the fools are respectively *in* houses of mourning and celebration. Where M has בבית אבל, however, 4QQoh[a] has בית אבל; it is difficult to be sure that it also had בית שמחה where M has בבית שמחה, as the broken edge of the manuscript lies immediately before the second בית. There is at least, however, no sign of the long tail which the scribe uses with ב, and which commonly stretches under the next character, so בית is more probable than בבית. This reading presents the two houses as metaphors for the hearts of the wise and fools, to be understood in connection with what has gone before and what will follow: just as you should go to a house of mourning, so you should go to the wise, who offer rebukes; the foolish only offer song, like the house of celebration.

In M, the suggestion is apparently rather that the wise think on the house of mourning, and the fools on the house of celebration, which offers a link to v. 2, but not to v. 5. This does not represent a standard usage in biblical Hebrew, where the engagement of the mind with something can occasionally be expressed with -ל (see the notes at 10.2), but -ב is only used contextually with a verb (e.g. Zech 10.7). M itself, therefore, has to be read as a sort of implied metaphor or as a pregnant expression. The Qumran reading is not only early, therefore, but no more inherently complicated. It also finds some potential,

---

[4] The La reads *cor sapientium in domo luctus et cor insipientium in domo epularum*, 'the heart of wise men (is) in the house of mourning, and the heart of fools in the house of banquets'; this is cited identically in Augustine *de Ciuitate Dei* xvii, 20. Hie *cor sapientium in domo luctus et cor insipientium in domo laetitiae* simply substitutes 'of joy' for the reference to dining. T, incidentally, interprets the first בית as the Temple, over which the wise mourn, but the second as a house of scoffing and dining in which the fools are to be found.

albeit very slight, support in an unexpected quarter. S here reads ...ܒܒܝܬ ܐܒܠܐ ܒܝܬ ܚܕܘܬܐ *bbyt ʾblʾ...byt ḥdwtʾ*, with a preposition *b-* on the first *byt* in all but one of the manuscripts (albeit that is the important ms 12a), but only on the second in two manuscripts. Although Kamenetzky, 199, is keen to read a preposition in both places, it is hard to make a strong case for the second, and while it is not unlikely that we are dealing simply with a coincidental error in the Syriac, it is also conceivable that the verse reflects the influence, at least in part, of a Hebrew text without prepositions. If this is tenuous but intriguing, we should certainly not make too much of V *cor sapientium ubi tristitia est et cor stultorum ubi laetitia*, 'the heart of the wise is where sadness is, and the heart of the fools where joy', but Jerome's paraphrase steers the text in rather the same direction as 4QQoh[a]. If the Qumran reading is original, which I consider likely, בבית has probably appeared through a misunderstanding of the expressions as locative, perhaps because the houses were literal houses in v. 2, or just possibly *via* an explicatory כבית in each place, which turned the metaphors into similes.

7.4 and the heart] The conjunction is missing from a number of G manuscripts, and some use the more elegant καρδία δέ in place of καὶ καρδία. It is asterisked in Syh, indicating that Origen restored it in his text, and marked as the reading of the Three.

7.5 rebukings from] The noun גערה can indicate 'rebuking' rather than just a single rebuke (it is set in parallel with מוסר, 'instruction', in Prov 13.1). Correspondingly, it is normally used in the singular even when some implication of plurality is present, so the clearly written plural גערות of 4QQoh[a] is striking and anomalous (although no more actually 'incorrect' than is 'rebukings' in English). I tend to think that this plural is original, and that 'rebukes' or 'rebukings' were intended, rather than 'rebuking', but such usage is otherwise unattested even at Qumran: the גערתכה of 1QH[a] xviii, 18 and 4QShir[b] frag. 52, 7 is compatible with the normal, singular usage. The singular of M is also supported by all the other ancient versions, and offers a better parallel to the singular שיר in the corresponding clause. On the other hand, חכם and כסילים do not correspond in number, while if the plural was not, in fact, ever normally used, then it is hard to explain the Qumran reading except as a very odd slip of the pen: if they were unfamiliar with גערות, no scribe would have misconstrued the familiar גערת as a defective writing of that word. The likeliest explanation is that the author used the noun abnormally and for effect, to create a heightened contrast between a plurality of rebukings by one wise man, and a single act of singing by multiple fools. In that case, M simply reflects an early assimilation to the standard usage, which has lost that contrast while otherwise making little difference to the sense.

7.5 than to hear] M מאיש שמע is supported by all the versions except V, which paraphrases (although T possibly vocalized the verb differently: see below). However, it means 'than one/a man hearing', or 'than one/a man who hears' (cf. Prov 21.28), and cannot have the sense 'than that one/a man should hear'—even though some such sense is commonly asserted or assumed.[5] In principle (although it is hard to find any actual analogy), we could have a comparison between 'a man who hears the rebuke' and 'a man who hears the song', just as we would more conventionally find a comparison between 'hearing the rebuke' and 'hearing the song'. What we have here, however, is an unhappy mixture of the two, in which 'it is better to hear the rebuke of a wise man than a man who hears the song of fools'. It is doubtful that this makes any sense, unless we understand something like 'than (to be) a man who hears', or take the point to be, improbably, that we should listen to a wise man who rebukes rather than to someone who listens to fools (an interpretation found among the versions: see below). Attempts to explain why Qohelet should express himself in this way, moreover, have generally involved claiming that the construction emphasizes a distinction between the subjects: the one who hears rebuke is not the one who hears song (so, e.g., Delitzsch; McNeile, 74). It is hard to discern, though, how this is different from the case in any other 'better than' saying with verbal clauses, and the explanation carries little conviction. If we do accept it, however, then it also effectively excludes understanding an infinitive—'than (to be) a man who hears' simply makes this a choice for the listener. When Lavoie, 'Le Sage et l'insensé', 15, adds the suggestion, furthermore, that the two different forms of the verb are supposed to draw out the different senses hearing = obedience and hearing = perception, it is difficult not to feel that commentators are scraping the bottom of the barrel.

The difficulty of what he rightly describes as 'a lopsided comparison between an action ("to hear") and a person ("a man hearing")', leads Fox to propose that we should emend מאיש שמע to משמע, with an infinitive that matches the לשמע of the first part. What he does not note is that we already have a similar reading in 4QQoh[a]. At the righthand of col ii, line 19, the initial מ has been lost, and the scribe has had to write the ש above the line after omitting it, but considerations of space put it beyond reasonable doubt that the text originally read מלשמוע (without a preceding מאיש), matching the previous לשמוע, and the text is reconstructed that way by both Ulrich in DJD and Puech, 'Qohelet a Qumran', 148, 152. Only very small traces of ink are visible in a lengthy gap that then follows before the subsequent שיר, and a word has probably been erased deliberately here after the ink was dry. Puech thinks that word might have been the מאיש of M, but מאיש only has any place

---

[5] In pursuit of his belief that odd uses of איש in passages like Isa 46.11 reflect a hitherto unacknowledged meaning, Gelio argues that it serves here as a relative pronoun, so that מאיש is equivalent to מאשר or -מש. All else aside, it is questionable whether such a construal would permit the translation he offers; 'meglio dare ascolto alla riprensione del saggio più che all' adulazione dello stolto', 'it is better to listen to the reproof of the sage rather than to the flattery of the fool'. See Gelio, 'Osservazioni', 6-8, 15.

here if we assume that the scribe originally wrote a garbled version of M and then corrected it to something quite different from M. It seems more likely that he initially wrote the wrong object, perhaps repeating that of the first clause. In any case, 4QQoh[a] probably reads 'better to hear rebukes [of a wise man than] to hear a song of fools', and removes the lop-sidedness of M. Is it simply, however, a facilitation, to give what Seow calls 'a syntactically smoother reading'? Lavoie, 'Le Sage et l'insensé', 2, is likewise in no doubt that the preposition has been added to smooth the syntax, and that M should be retained as the more difficult reading.

It is difficult to judge whether the relative ease of the reading in 4QQoh[a] tells for or against its authenticity (and the principle of *lectio difficilior* has to be applied with great care), but it is certainly possible that there has been some assimilation. In 7.2, ללכת was picked up by מלכת, not מללכת, and if this is the original reading (the word is unfortunately lost in 4QQoh[a]), then לשמע might equally have been picked up by the משמע that Fox proposes, which would make the ל of 4QQoh[a] a minor assimilation to the preceding verb. On the other hand, it is also possible, of course, that the ל dropped out anyway in the form of the text from which M is derived: not only is this ל redundant, but *lamed*s more generally were, perhaps surprisingly, amongst the letters most commonly omitted in error, at least by the scribes of the Qumran manuscripts (see Reymond, *Qumran Hebrew*, 32).

If M is secondary, though, how did משמע become מאיש שמע even without the ל? A purely graphical error would have involved not just the reduplication of ש but also the introduction of at least one other character that is not found in the immediate area—and although prothetic alephs are found in the orthography of the Qumran texts, particularly after prepositions and other particles, instances are relatively rare (Reymond, *Qumran Hebrew*, 151-53). If this is an error, the best explanation is probably that it was phonetic: the scribe has said to himself *miš-* and written *m'išš-* because elision of א in the vernacular language could lead to forms like היש for האיש (Reymond, *Qumran Hebrew*, 77-87), and he is unconsciously hyper-correcting—a little as though I were to read 'there' and write 'they're'. Some other error, though, like the simple duplication of the ש, might equally have initiated a more deliberate process of 'correction'.

T may be somewhat enlightening here, firstly because it speaks not of a man 'listening', but of a man going 'to listen', which probably suggests that the translator read לשמע or construed שמע as an infinitive (which leads him to frame the advice within a contrast between sitting to study and going to hear song). We may contrast this with Hie *melius est audire correptionem sapientis super uirum audientem carmen stultorum*, 'it is better to listen to the rebuke of a wise man than to a man who hears the song of fools'—which shows that Jerome clearly understood a participle. T also, though, sets the גבר חכימא, 'the wise man' (elsewhere T generally uses just חכימא for 'wise man'), explicitly in parallel with the גבר דאזיל למשמע, 'a man who goes to listen', and in this respect corresponds to Hie: both appear to have been influenced by an understanding of the Hebrew that found a contrast between שמע or איש שמע and חכם. It is hard to know whether such understandings have been driven by a text like M, or whether the text of M arose in the light of them, but there is at least a fair possibility that M developed not as the result of an error, but as a deliberate 'clarification' of a reading like משמע, which seems to have been understood in different ways, in favour of a particular construal.

Especially given that 4QQoh[a] has clearly been checked and corrected at this point, on the other hand, then מלשמוע is unlikely to be an error created by the scribe himself, and if it, and not M, is the text at fault, then some still earlier copyist's eye would have to have skipped from one ש to the next before the introduction of ל through assimilation. It is impossible to be sure, but given the relative dates of attestation and the difficulties of explaining satisfactorily the mismatched clauses in M, I am inclined to prefer the Qumran reading here, even though it might be slightly more readily explicable as an error than is M. Unless we are missing some special nuance in M, however, the choice of one reading over the other does not greatly affect the sense.

7.5 singing from fools] Or 'a song of fools'; I think 'singing' is more likely in context, and שיר apparently has that sense in passages like 1 Chr 25.6; Ps 137.3. More radically different is the proposal of Zimmermann, who suggested ('Aramaic Provenance', 24) that 'singing' or 'song' is not a good match for 'rebuke', and reflects a mistranslation from Aramaic: the reference should be to 'praise'. Gordis, 'The Original Language of Qohelet', 72 (cf. also his 'Translation Theory', 112), responded by noting the semantic links between the two ideas, and proposing that שיר itself should actually be rendered 'praise' here (as it then was in his commentary), while allowing the possibility that this might be an Aramaism. Dahood, 'Canaanite-Phoenician', 210, also observed a number of places where songs are songs of praise, and the point has been reiterated more recently in Lavoie, 'Le Sage et l'insensé', 19. The issue has also been picked up and treated at much greater length in Piotti, 'Osservazioni su alcuni problemi II', which concludes rightly, I think, that 'singing'/'song' is actually the intended sense. The saying is continuing the imagery of celebration from the previous verses, and the whole question only arises from too atomistic a reading of the text. It is a secondary point, but I doubt also that שיר can ever mean 'praise': singing, to be sure, is often depicted as an element of praising, but it always refers to praise in song. One could as well claim that 'song' must mean 'love' in English, because we have so many 'love songs', and there is a confusion between content and form at work in this discussion.

7.6 For] M כי is supported by 4QQoh[a], σ' (see below), Hie, V, T. There is no equivalent in many manuscripts of G, however, or in some manuscripts of S, which may have been influenced by G in this respect. Syh suggests that Origen placed ὅτι under asterisk, not finding it in his Greek text, but restoring it to fit the Hebrew, and it is likely that it was absent from the source-text of

G: see Gentry, 'Special Problems', 134-35, which sets out the evidence in detail. The attestation at Qumran tells in favour of the word, and it may have been lost in G's source-text simply as an error caused by the following -כ. It is also possible, though, that it has been introduced secondarily, to give a slightly forced link to the preceding verse (where songs, not laughter, are strictly the issue—although Joüon, 'Notes philologiques', 422, would simply emend שחק to שיר, to overcome that discrepancy and enhance the alliteration; he thinks שחק was originally in 7.7).

7.6 like the sound...skillet] σ' is attested as διὰ γὰρ φωνὴν ἀπαιδεύτων ἐν δεσμωτηρίῳ γίνεταί τις, 'for on account of the voice of the ill-informed, one is put in prison'. The reading is affirmed by Jerome, who translates it as *per uocem enim imperitorum uinculis quispiam colligatur*, 'for by the voice of the inexperienced, one is tied in bonds', and then paraphrases this as *ad uocem talium praeceptorum magis auditor innectitur, dum uinculis peccatorum suorum unusquisque constringitur*, 'at the voice of such teachers, the hearer becomes more tangled up, while each is tied by the bonds of his sins'. Field remarks that it is scarcely credible that Symmachus came up with such a perverse translation of such clear Hebrew, and he has a point: הסירים seems to have been rendered as though from סור or סרר, and הסיר connected with the בית הסורים found in 4.14 (probably not with the Aramaic סיר as sometimes claimed: that can refer to threads or to armour, but not to chains). At the least, he may have read ו in some of the places where M has י, and he probably read בקול, not כקול: I doubt that Symmachus read the Hebrew as a nominal clause, as Marshall suggests, or understood 'The place of prison (is) in accordance with the voice/sound of the uninstructed'. Probably the crux of the matter is his reading of תחת, which has perhaps been read as תהיה, or some other form of היה/הוה, to yield γίνεταί τις. It is possible that some otherwise unknown interpretation lies behind the rendering, but it seems more likely that Symmachus had only a corrupt or illegible copy of the Hebrew at this point, than that he was attempting exegetical gymnastics. Schoeps, 'Symmachusstudien III', 43, is speculating wildly, moreover, when he supposes that Symmachus is extending the statement to embrace some particular personal experience.

7.6 such is the laughter] The text of Syh has 'likewise *also* the laughter of fools', placing the 'also' under asterisk. There is a ∞ s above the word, which identifies it as the reading of σ', and a marginal note affirms that the word was absent from α' and θ', as well as from G. This should all suggest that a conjunction was borrowed by Origen from σ' to match a word in the Hebrew (a conjunction or גם / וגם) that was lacking in his text of G, and it is very plausible that σ' had the οὕτως καὶ γέλως assigned to it here by Marshall and Gentry (we may recall that in 5.15, the only place where G itself has οὕτως καὶ, McNeile, 160, suspected the influence of σ'). The problem is that there is no corresponding word attested anywhere in the Hebrew text tradition that might have led Origen to make this addition. Marshall suggests that Origen was using the asterisk abnormally, adding a word so as better to bring out the sense of the Hebrew, and he notes a similar case at 4.6, where the asterisk plausibly marks a clarification of the syntax. The addition here, however, does not obviously accomplish the same, and it is possible that some error is involved, either in the transmission/characterization of the reading or, more fundamentally, in the Hebrew found by Origen.

7.6 fool] G has the plural 'fools', which is supported by S, and possibly by σ' (the index for a reading equivalent to ἀπαιδεύτων is set here in Syh: Goldman and Marshall take it to be a misplaced reference to part of the reading discussed in the note above on 'like the sound...skillet', but Gentry retains it here). Other witnesses, including 4QQoh\ support the singular of M, and the plural has probably arisen through assimilation to the כסילים of the previous verse.

7.6 This too] Where M^L has וגם זה, 4QQoh\ has just גם זה. See the corresponding note at 5.15, where there is a similar disagreement. Since they generally render גם and וגם the same way, it is difficult here, as there, to gauge the support of the other versions for M (and Lavoie, 'Le Sage et l'insensé', 4, is too quick to declare that G and S affirm M), but many manuscripts of T likewise have no conjunction this time. The variation persists in the tradition. Miletto notes two Babylonian manuscripts which also have just גם, and a later instance in a Persian manuscript is observed in Lavoie and Mehramooz, 'Le Texte hébreu et la traduction judéo-persane', 502. Because the Van der Hooght text used by them itself has no conjunction here, the readings collected by Kennicott and de Rossi reflect manuscript support for M^L, and it is hard to quantify the prevalence of גם זה, let alone the extent to which readings in the later Hebrew tradition may have been influenced by T. Qohelet generally uses his formula without an initial conjunction, so assimilation to the normal form might have influenced its omission here, but that evidence cuts both ways, and in the absence of any good reason to reject it, the reading גם should probably be preferred as the earliest attested. The reading we adopt, though, makes no real difference to the sense.

7.7

(7.7) For extortion discredits a wise man, and crushes the generous heart.

Commentary

There are a lot of problems here, and the meaning is very uncertain. In the first place, it is very possible that some text has been lost before this saying: it begins in Hebrew with a word that commonly (though not always) means 'for' or 'because', but commentators have struggled to find any clear connection with the preceding 7.6. Many scholars were already persuaded, therefore, that it originally explained some lost statement or admonition, even before the discovery of 4QQoh[a] at Qumran. That manuscript presents significant difficulties at the appropriate point, but clearly had something between 7.6 and 7.7. The problem is that this something may have been no more than deleted text in a place where the scribe is trying to make good more than one error, and if there was anything else there, it is beyond reconstruction. If it is not just an unfortunate coincidence that the manuscript is such a mess precisely at the point where it could have solved a long-standing problem, then it is possible that existing problems contributed to the scribe's difficulties, and that those problems emerged very early.

The sense is also difficult. The RSV has 'Surely oppression makes the wise man foolish, and a bribe corrupts the mind', but the feminine noun 'bribe' does not agree with the masculine verb 'corrupts', and so the Greek translation, for instance, takes 'oppression' (or more properly 'extortion') to be the subject throughout. On the RSV construal, moreover, 'the mind' is literally '*a* mind', and so strictly should not take the object-marker that it has in the Hebrew: this is not usually employed for indefinite objects. Of course, there are exceptions to that usage, just as subjects sometimes exceptionally disagree with verbs, but the construction of the verse undoubtedly presents problems. The vocabulary is no more straightforward, and the various understandings that have been offered tend to depend on understandings of that construction. So, for instance, RSV's 'bribe' translates a word used once elsewhere in connection with gains made dishonestly (Prov 15.27), but it is really a very general word for gifts or giving (despite the assertion of Bartholomew that 'it refers to a bribe and not just any gift'). The sense 'bribe' has been assigned here only because it has been taken to stand in parallel with 'extortion' (and some of the ancient versions have connected it with a quite different term). The first verb might conceivably mean 'make foolish', but other uses suggest that it more probably refers to making someone look foolish—so the presumed parallelism does not really justify translating the second verb as 'corrupts': its normal reference is to destroying something, or letting it slip away (as at 3.6; cf. 9.18). These and other difficulties will be explored in the notes. Suffice it to say here that, in the absence of any clear guidance from the context, it is hard to say for certain what the verse means.

The other passages where Qohelet speaks about 'extortion' are 4.1 and 5.7, which mark the beginning of new discussions. He never follows up on it as a theme, however, and 4.1 functions largely to paint the world as an unhappy place, while 5.7 leads into the topic of greed for money. When we hear about extortion in the book, therefore, it seems we can expect to embark upon a new theme but not to hear much about extortion. Reflecting on his experience of writing hard-boiled pulp fiction, Raymond Chandler famously observed that 'the demand was for constant action and if you stopped to think you were lost. When in doubt have a man come through a door with a gun in his hand.'[1] It may be that our author treats extortion in much the same way, simply using it from time to time as a device to re-boot Qohelet's discourse with a dramatic protest or lament. In that case, it is not, perhaps, a great problem that this verse has no obvious connection with 7.1-6. However, 4.1 and 5.7 do have some relevance to what *follows* them, so it is interesting to note that in much later Hebrew we find a noun *mtynh*, which is cognate with a number of Hebrew and Aramaic terms which indicate 'taking one's time', and are often associated with care or diligence. If *mtnh* here

---

[1] 'The Simple Art of Murder', *The Saturday Review of Literature* April 15, 1950, 13-14. Not to be confused with another, better-known essay, first published in 1944 under the same title.

were not a 'gift' but a writing of that noun, then Qohelet could be talking about the damage done by too much deliberation or, more probably, about extortion discrediting the wise man and crushing the 'diligent heart'—which would give a link to the issue of patience in the sayings that follow. Tempting though it may be to find such a connection, however, there is just too little evidence that a noun with such a sense existed early enough, and even later it was very rare.

The translation offered above is arguably the most 'natural' reading of the text as it stands, insofar as it enforces the rules of syntax and assigns their normal meanings to each word. If it is also the correct reading, then it almost certainly implies that some text has been lost: this is half a saying, at most, and it is difficult to see how it might follow from 7.6, perhaps as an explanation or elaboration of the *hebel* declaration there. Unless we are simply missing some nuance, our text is very probably broken at this point, and the damage may involve more than just a loss. We can only speculate about the original context, but I doubt that Qohelet was admonishing against extortion, as is sometimes assumed: the point seems rather to be that extortion is stronger than both wisdom and generosity of spirit. If we do want to take the verse as complete and free-standing, on the other hand, then probably the best translation would be something like 'While extortion discredits a wise man, it is giving that crushes a heart', with a contrast between 'taking' and 'giving', and perhaps the implication that, while taking by force demeans even a wise man, because he is helpless in the face of brute power, it is to give without such compulsion that truly demoralizes. The Hebrew word used for 'gift' or 'giving' here, however, is sometimes used of allowances made to children by their parents (e.g. Gen 25.6; Ezek 46.16), and is also used in Esth 9.22 of alms given to the poor, so a reading in such terms might alternatively refer to receiving such a gift: it can be demeaning to be forced to give, but far worse to be dependent, and forced to receive.

It should be emphasized, finally, that although the Hebrew text that we have is very early, and is more or less the text upon which the ancient translations seem to have been based, the Qumran evidence tends to affirm the strong possibility not only that this text is incomplete, but that it is corrupt. One of the two words that can be read on 4QQoh[a] corresponds to nothing in our text, and is not implausibly restored by the editor as meaning 'and twists'. The proper position of that word is uncertain, and the problems make it hard to say anything much more about the Qumran reading as a whole, but our awkward Hebrew may very well not be an accurate reflection of what the author originally wrote. In that case, our attempts to make sense of it may not simply miss whatever point was intended, but import quite different ideas.

Notes

7.7 For] Or 'while'. The complicated situation in 4QQoh^a at the top of col. III is outlined in the Introduction (127-30).[2] Essentially, it is possible that the manuscript originally contained material for which there is no equivalent in M or the ancient translations, but the scribe has been forced to make a significant correction at that point, and the text is in a mess. This makes it difficult to tell even whether any words are actually missing, let alone what they might have been—a situation made all the more frustrating by the fact that some scholars suspected a loss of text here long before the Qumran manuscripts were found: 7.7 simply does not seem to follow logically from 7.6, or to relate to it in any way that might be expressed using כי.[3] This is

---

[2] To the discussion there, it is worth adding that Puech, 'Qohelet a Qumran', 152-53, would reconstruct the traces around the כ visible on the first line as כיא מקרה, noting the appearance of this sequence in 3.19 and 9.3. Some of the traces here are apparently of a line beneath the marginal correction above, which delineates the top and top-right corner of the column: Puech's supposed כ seems to come from that, and the other traces are too slight either to affirm or deny his reconstruction, which is highly speculative. The writing here has probably been erased deliberately, anyway, and it would be wrong to assume that it can be used to reconstruct some missing text.

[3] Delitzsch discusses the numerous efforts to establish a relationship between 7.6 and 7.7 that were current in his own day, before concluding that 7.7 must represent the surviving two stichs of what was originally a four-stich saying, with the first two stichs saying something along the same lines as Ps 37.16 or Prov 16.8—he also suggests that כי גם זה הבל in 7.6 was added to try to make a link after the text had been lost. S.R. Driver picked up the suggestion of a loss in *BH*, while *BH*³, and *BHS* later imitated also Delitzsch's suggestion that כי גם זה הבל should be deleted. These editions did not content themselves with suggesting that text might have been lost, but actually offered the text of Prov. 16.8 as though it were being proposed as an emendation, perhaps because Delitzsch himself had presented a text reconstructed illustratively along those lines. The points need to be distinguished, however: the probability that text of some sort has been lost is quite high; the probability that this text was the same as Prov 16.8 is close to negligible—Qohelet nowhere else uses material found also in Proverbs.

probably why, of course, Jerome simply fails to translate כי in Hie and V, although it is represented in the other versions.

That problem in itself cannot *force* us, however, either to conclude that text has been lost or to push for some tenuous link with what precedes, and, as noted in the commentary, it is striking that twice previously (in 4.1 and 5.7) Qohelet has marked a break and fresh start with sayings that talk about extortion but lead on to something quite different. With that in mind, we should recall that כי does quite often connect its clause to a main clause that follows, rather than to anything that has preceded, and this may have been its function here whether or not any preceding text has been lost. The nature of such connections is often far from clear cut, and such uses are variously described as causal, conditional, temporal or concessive—Aejmelaeus, 'Function', helpfully groups them together as 'circumstantial' to reflect the fact that they are not really distinct from each other, even if they may require distinct translations according to context. Should we want to read the verse as free-standing, then, we could treat כי here as introducing a circumstance or concession, and although it tells a little against it, the use of a conjunction to connect the second clause does not preclude such an understanding (cf. Isa 54.10; Ezek 11.16).

7.7 extortion] On the general sense of עשק, see the note at 4.1. There are no text-critical grounds for emendation of the word here, either to עשר, as originally suggested by Ewald,[4] or to שחק, as Ehrlich would prefer: the former tries to find a better parallel to the subsequent מתנה in 'wealth', the latter seeks a link to the preceding verse through 'laughter' (and is considered sympathetically by Fischer, *Skepsis*, 87; the suggestion is made independently in Joüon, 'Notes philologiques', 422). T, however, has probably vocalized the word differently as a participle, so that the wise man can be confronted with an opponent.

More significant questions surround the precise implication, rather than the reading. BDB suggests that the noun here is used not of the *act* of extortion, as elsewhere in the book, but to describe the *proceeds* of extortion, just as we might speak colloquially of 'paying blackmail' with reference to the money demanded: Lev. 5.23 (ET 6.4), and perhaps Ps 62.11 (ET 62.10) are offered as potential analogies. That would give the financial parallel to מתנה that Ewald has not been alone in seeking, but it is questionable whether the word actually has that sense in the passages cited: Lev 5.23, the more plausible example, could as easily be speaking of 'making restitution' for the crime (see, e.g., Num 5.7 for that use of שוב in the hiph'il), while Ps 62 is surely speaking of reliance on extortion as a source of income. They are certainly a poor basis for supposing any yet more extended sense, such as the 'dishonest money...a bribe to judges', which Fox, among others, understands here.

---

[4] First during his review of Umbreit, in his *Jahrbücher der Biblischen Wissenschaft*, 175, then subsequently in the 1867 edition of his commentary.

Driver, 'Problems and Solutions', 229, has offered a different understanding of עשק here as a reference to 'slander' or 'calumny', and it is certainly true that the cognate verb can be used of making false accusations in Syriac. His appeal to G συκοφαντία and Hie, V *calumnia* here, however, would be more persuasive were it not for the fact that those same renderings were used at 4.1 and 5.7, where it is unlikely that either the translator of G or Jerome actually understood such a sense (see the note at 4.1).

7.7 discredits a wise man] For הלל generally, see the note at 1.17. In the poʿel, the verb appears also in Isa 44.25 and Job 12.17, where it apparently refers to discrediting individuals who claim authority (diviners, judges), and a similar sense is probable in Ps 102.9 (ET 102.8), where it is associated with taunting or belittling. In the poʿal, it was used in 2.2 to say something about pleasure, in parallel with a statement of its uselessness, and all these references make it very doubtful that the verb can imply actual maddening, or the transformation of the wise man into a fool. They seem instead to suggest that Qohelet is talking about extortion discrediting the wise man, or making him seem impotent or unimportant—T speaks accordingly of the oppressor 'making fun' of the wise man (although the text is difficult there). So similarly, Garrett, 'Use and Abuse', 167.

The other versions have struggled: G περιφέρει simply reflects its characteristic understanding of הלל, which was discussed at 2.2, and the πλανήσει attributed to α′ likewise corresponds to Aquila's use of the noun πλάνησις elsewhere, so that they envisage respectively deranging or misleading the wise man.[5] Jerome's *conturbat*, 'troubles', in both Hie and V, is either an interpretation of σ′ θορυβήσει (which is again in line with the σ′ renderings elsewhere: Jerome understood the cognate noun to mean 'tumult' at 2.2), or a guess from context. S simply replaces this verb with the second one, so that it reads ܡܘܒܕ...ܘܡܘܒܕ *mwbd...wmwbd*ʾ, 'is ruinous to...and is ruinous to'. None of the versions has taken it this way, but we should note that the consonantal יהולל could also be vocalized as from the puʿal of הלל, which is used in Prov 12.8 of being praised or commended: DJD restores a form from עוה in 4QQohᵃ (see below), which is also found in that verse.

However they have understood it, almost all commentators have taken חכם to be the object of the verb, but Gelio, 'Osservazioni', has offered a very different reading of the verse that takes it instead to be the subject, and he understands the sense to be that 'a wise man nullifies ("vanifica") oppression and annihilates ("annienta") a violent heart'. Setting aside the extraordinary

---

[5] Marshall and Gentry attribute πλανήσει to θ′ here as well, following ms 252. Two other manuscripts attribute it to α′ only, and Syh to α′ and σ′. As Marshall notes, the attribution to σ′ is clearly wrong (Syh has confused the readings of σ′ and θ′), but, if the attributions are reliable, it appears that θ′ rendered words from the root variably, sometimes in agreement with G (1.17; 2.2), sometimes with α′ (2.12; 7.7).

word-order that it presupposes, the principal objection to this as an overall construal is the lack of correspondence in form between העשק and את לב מתנה, which are supposed to stand in parallel as objects on that reading. More specifically, though, even if we are willing to accept his construal of מתנה (see below), we could probably at best only find a statement here that a wise man 'mocks' extortion, or makes it look foolish, which would be a curious sentiment.

7.7 and crushes the generous heart] Or possibly 'and/but it annihilates a heart, a gift', meaning 'it is a gift that annihilates a heart'. Muilenburg and Ulrich restore ויעוה, 'perverts' or 'twists', in 4QQoh[a], at the point where M has ויאבד: see the Introduction, 128. This has been inspired in part by Prov 12.8, so of course it fits well with an understanding that the לב is being corrupted, but neither the restoration nor the proper place of the traces in the text is certain, and if we are to read this word at all, it may be as part of the text missing before 7.7. The Qumran reading is intriguing, especially since יהלל appears in Prov 12.8 as well (see above), but it has added a further complication to a sentence that already has more than enough.

With G and some other ancient versions (see below), I take לב to stand in a construct relationship with מתנה, so that it is like the לב מרפא of Prov 14.30. This avoids the problem that, if we take מתנה separately, it has to be the subject of יאבד, with which it does not agree. 'Heart of a gift' would not mean much, but מתנה can be used of 'giving' in a more abstract sense (cf. Deut 16.17), and in Prov 19.6 the expression איש מתן, which uses a closely related noun, apparently refers to 'a generous man'. It is a reasonable supposition, therefore, that לב מתנה might mean 'a generous heart' (and the first interpretation of מתנה in the Midrash seems to understand it in terms of serving the needs of the community). The expression as a whole, therefore, should stand as the object of the verb, governed by את: this is potentially problematic, in that it is undetermined, but, even if we do not go so far as to take the ה as a writing of the third-person suffix pronoun -ו and the noun itself correspondingly as מתן (see below), determination may be implied either by the abstraction, or, conversely, by taking the heart as that of the wise man (cf. GKC §117 d; J-M §125 h). The problem would not be solved by taking לב alone as the object.

G construes the syntax in this way, but understands εὐτονία, 'vigour', rather than 'giving', and this meaning seems to have been accepted by α' and θ', as well as by Jerome, who uses *cor fortitudinis*, 'heart of strength', in Hie and *robur cordis*, 'strength of heart', in V. It is often suggested that the translators have tried to find a connection with the word מתנים, 'loins', but, although loins can obviously be strong (e.g. Prov 31.7), that term has no particular association with the sort of vigour implied by εὐτονία, and the Hebrew noun is always used in the dual: it would be curious if G had rejected 'gift' or 'giving' in favour of such a strange and loose translation, and remarkable if α' had done so also. The same versions that have 'vigour' also have a possessive pronoun (*his* vigour), however, so that G reads τὴν καρδίαν εὐτονίας αὐτου, lit. 'the heart of his vigour', or 'his heart of vigour'—both presumably meaning 'his vigorous heart'. This might be an attempt, as Goldman supposes, to read the ה on מתנה as an abnormal writing of the masculine suffix pronoun at the end of a noun מתן (cf. GKC §91 d), which Whitley and Driver ('Problems and Solutions', 229) take, in fact, to be the proper understanding. If they were not driven that way by some tradition of reading or interpretation, the mysterious rendering by these translators of מתנה as a whole, however, raises the possibility that G, α' and θ' actually found something different in their text: if so, that is most likely to have been מתניו, which they would have been forced both to construe as from מתנים and to take as metaphorical. Unless לב מתנים is an otherwise unknown idiom, such a reading is unlikely to be original. Jerome certainly knew the reading מתנה (see below), but probably took it as a writing of/error for מתניו in the light of G.

T also takes עשק to be the continuing subject, but reads לב and מתנה in apposition: the wisdom of the wise man's heart, or the Torah which it contemplates, is understood to be 'a gift'. Some modern commentators similarly follow what seems to have been G's understanding of the structure, but are happy with neither 'gift' nor 'vigour'. So, for instance, Driver, 'Problems and Solutions', 230, and Whitley both try to find a link with the mishnaic adjective מתון, מתונה, connected with the Aramaic מתן, 'be slow' or 'wait', which itself refers not to strength but to a carefulness or caution, often associated with patience and diligence, and this sense has been commended more recently by Bronznick, 'Eccles. 7:7'. The same association is already commended in one interpretation offered by the Midrash Rabbah, which talks of מתנה being 'written' (כתיב) as מתונה, but probably implies merely that it can be read as a defective spelling of that word (cf. Ginzberg, 'Die Haggada', 34; the expression would be unusual in that sense, however, and we cannot exclude the possibility of a reference to an otherwise unattested variant). Graetz had already suggested similarly that מתנה was an abstract noun meaning 'deliberation', if it was not in fact an error for מתן, (another word for giving or gift, which would, however, agree with the verb). Jastrow notes a noun מתינה, which has precisely that sense, although it is attested only once, in Genesis Rabbah (and in a citation of that midrash by Yalkut Shimoni). A translation along these lines offers an attractive sense and a fit to context, but it is hard to be sure that any noun with such a sense existed early enough, and even in much later Hebrew it seems to have been extremely rare.

Rather differently, Margoliouth, 'Qoheleth (Ecclesiastes) VII.7', proposes that מתנה should be read as a hiph'il participle from the verb תנה, meaning a 'teacher', but the verb is rare in Hebrew, and Margoliouth can only cite any such sense for its Aramaic cognate. Rose, *Rien de nouveau*, 395, independently makes a similar case, although he prefers the pi'el, and faces the same objections. Gelio, 'Osservazioni', 13-15 takes a different approach again. Noting how often עשק appears in parallel with ינה, 'oppress', he takes מתנה to be a participle from a causative form of that verb, and understands the sense to be that 'a wise man destroys oppression and annihilates a violent heart'. Of course, this requires an explanation for the ת, and Gelio would class מתנה here among the supposed instances of a Hebrew verb with an infixed t. The existence of any such forms is controversial, however, and tends to be posited on the basis of phenomena in related languages. It would seem extraordinarily negligent of any author, furthermore, to use what must have been at best a very rare verbal form to express a common enough idea, when there were alternatives that would have avoided confusion with a much more familiar noun. This is a point that could be levelled in a more general way against all the alternative readings of מתנה, although it is also true to say that an association with patience, if we were to follow Graetz et al., would offer the only obvious link to the surrounding context that can be identified among any of the renderings commonly proposed for this verse.

Other translators have preferred to accept or to overlook the disagreement in gender between ויאבד and מתנה, and to treat מתנה as the subject, which is probably the reading indicated by the Masoretic accents. This underpins renderings like that of the RSV, but is not confined to modern translations. According to Jerome, σ' actually included the Hebrew word in transliteration (*matthana*, presumably ματθανα): the translation 'gift' attached to that by Jerome is probably not his own gloss, and Gentry notes in ms 248 a reading θεοδώρητον, 'gift from God', which is assigned to σ' but mistakenly attached to the next verse. In any case, however, Jerome suggests that Symmachus took the sense to be that bribes blind even the wise—although the fact that he included a transliteration might be taken to indicate that he did not consider the sense straightforward. S probably took the same path originally, although there are variants within the tradition that turn 'gift' into 'giver' or 'givers': this may be because of an understanding (based on Syriac usage) that ܫܘܩܝ *'šwqy'* means not 'extortion', but 'calumny' or 'false witness', which is ruinous 'to whoever gives it' (so Lane, 'Lilies', 489).

Were we to go down the same route as M, σ' and S, we could in fact embrace the disagreement in gender between ויאבד and מתנה as a clue to the sense of the verse, rather than simply ignore it. It is true that, as J-M §150 k puts it, 'the feminine is sometimes neglected' (cf. GKC §145 o [a]), and we may be dealing with no more than a display of that neglect, but sentences such as this can also be constructed with the uninflected verb serving to give a sort of temporary, impersonal subject before the presentation of the actual subject, which correspondingly receives a certain emphasis. So in Ps 124.5, for example, we can understand a climactic 'then it would have been raging waters that went over our נפש', rather than just a virtual repetition of the preceding clause to give 'then the raging waters would have gone over our נפש'. This clause can similarly be construed 'and it will destroy a heart, a gift', and the word-order, with the subject placed unusually at the end, would favour such a reading.

If it was indeed the author's purpose to put such an emphasis on the subject, or at least to avoid a strict correspondence in word-order with the preceding clause, then his motive may have been to indicate that we are dealing not with synonymy but with contrast: extortion may do *this*, but it is a gift that does *that*—and, by implication, it is the gift that is actually more dangerous. Precisely what is being said, however, depends on our understanding of the various terms, and the lack of context is unhelpful in this respect. The association with extortion might well lead us to suppose, for instance, that מתנה is a 'bribe' rather than just a 'gift' (although the two concepts may not have been so distinct in the author's mind as they are in ours), but it is worth noting that the noun is only used with that specific nuance in Prov 15.27: elsewhere it always refers to gifts or offerings, and if the author wanted to make a clear reference to bribery here, שחד would have been a more obvious choice. We could think of the association with extortion in another way, however, as the representation of opposites—'taking forcefully' contrasted with 'giving willingly'.

Whatever we take to be its subject and object, the sense of the verb is also hard to pin down. We encountered the pi'el of אבד in 3.6, and will meet it again in 9.18: in neither place does it possess simply its common force of 'destroy', and in the former, it refers to letting something go, while in the latter it may have the force of rendering something useless or cancelling it out. Perhaps our best clue, however, lies not in those uses of the pi'el, but in the occurrence of לב (twice) with the qal of אבד in Jer 4.9. There the expression is applied to the rulers but stands in parallel with statements that the priests נשמו and the prophets יתמהו—those are terms that refer to being horrified, astonished or stupefied, and the context is one of helpless demoralization. When applied to a heart, then, we might expect a causative form of the verb correspondingly to connote leaving someone utterly demoralized.

In the end, then, we have two options for reading the text as it stands. If we take העשק as the subject throughout the verse, then 7.7 states that extortion discredits the wise and, in some sense, demoralizes the לב מתנה, perhaps a mind that would usually be inclined to giving (or, just possibly, patience). The point then would most likely be that wisdom and the לב מתנה, whatever it is, look ridiculous in the face of extortion. It is a lot more complicated to take the second option, and read a separate subject in each clause, but if we do so, then the sense most easily justified is that the taking of money discredits a wise man, but it is the giving of money which truly demoralizes.

7.8-12

(7.8) Better is the end of an account than its beginning,

better long of spirit than lofty of spirit.

(7.9) Do not rush in your feelings to get angry, for anger lives in the lap of fools. (7.10) Do not say 'What has happened, that the old days were better than these?', for it is not wisdom that has led you to inquire about that. (7.11) Wisdom is good with inherited property, but an advantage to those who see the sun. (7.12) For in its shade, that wisdom is in the shade of that money, but it is a profit from knowledge that the wisdom may sustain its possessor.

Commentary

It is more difficult to find any continuity in these sayings than in the preceding vv. 1-6, but there is a thread of sorts. 'Better long of spirit than lofty of spirit' in 7.8b appears to commend patience or due caution over recklessness (see the notes), and so fits well with the sentiments in 7.9, which link hasty anger with being a fool. If we take these as a guide to the rest, then it is not hard to see 7.8a as a similar commendation to patience. The point is presumably not that the end of any saying or matter is necessarily better than its start, but, in this context, that it is better to wait for the outcome of something than to react instantly. 7.10-12 is more difficult, and perhaps more nuanced, but its point seems to be that wisdom should be all about living, and continuing to live, in the present (cf. Bianchi, 'Un fantasma', 56), not about seeking reasons for perceived differences between that present and some idealized past: its benefits are pragmatic, not explanatory.

7.8] The contrast may not simply be between initiation and conclusion: the 'beginning' and 'end' can refer to early and later stages of something, or to what happens at the outset and what happens afterwards. The 'better than' form is similar to that of 7.1, and the thought arguably somewhat similar also.

7.9] The Hebrew does not imply that the anger dwells inside fools, as RSV 'lodges in the bosom of' and similar translations might suggest, but more probably means that fools either clutch it to their chests or hold it ready in their clothing (we might say that they have it in their pocket).

7.10] There are three sayings in Proverbs that use the same 'Do not say' formulation to warn against making a false or unwise declaration (3.28; 20.22; 24.29), and it is used in divine commands at Deut 9.4 and Jer 1.7. It is only in Ben Sira, however, that we find a number of sayings that are strongly reminiscent of what Qohelet says here (5.3-6; 11.23-24; 15.11-12; 16.17), and that give grounds for supposing that he is employing a familiar admonitory style.

7.11-12] This is often seen as a frankly cynical statement, that wisdom is useful just so long as there is some money to go with it (the various sayings that elevate wisdom *above* wealth, like Prov 16.16, are saying something very different, and do not make this a 'traditional wisdom value', as suggested by, e.g., Murphy and Zimmerli). Some cynicism may indeed be present, but the Hebrew term used for 'inheritance' here almost always refers to land or property, and Qohelet's point is probably not just that wisdom requires a financial cushion. Rather, there is a mutually beneficial relationship: wisdom, to be sure, will enjoy protection—expressed here in terms of protection from the sun—but it will also be a source of profit, by way of the knowledge to be gained from possessing it.

Read simply in those terms, it is less clear how this saying is supposed to relate to the context in which it stands, beyond picking up the reference to wisdom that has just been made in 7.10: Qohelet is not going to return to such matters until late in ch. 9, and he is not self-evidently explaining any of the sayings that have preceded in 7.8-10. If he is not just throwing out a one-liner, however, then we should probably pay attention not just to the issue of protection that is raised explicitly in 7.12, but also to the mentions of inheritance and of 'those who see the sun' in 7.11. That latter corresponds to expressions in 6.5 and 11.7 where Qohelet refers literally to seeing sunlight, but where he also gives that idea a strong association with being alive (see likewise Ps 49.20 [ET 49.19], and cf. 58.9): it is not a way that he refers elsewhere simply to people or humans. One aspect, of course, will be picked up in 7.12, where the sunlight is contrasted with shade, but it is tempting to suppose that an emphasis on living is important here as well—especially when 7.12 will also refer to the preservation or perpetuation of life. In that case, we are dealing, perhaps, with a certain ambivalence towards sunlight, both as a source of heat and as a symbol of life, but also more clearly with an affirmation that, although wisdom might itself benefit from wealth accumulated in the past, the advantages that it offers are for those living in the present—and it will help them continue to do so. Read in conjunction with 7.10, the point would then seem to be that even when wisdom has been cultivated in the shelter of old money, it will always focus on the present, not the past.

7.12] There is significant confusion in the text here: see the notes.

Notes

7.8 better[1]] For the majority G reading ἀγαθὴ, 'good' (agreeing with ἐσχάτῃ, 'end'), Origenic manuscripts have ἀγαθόν, 'a good thing', which is the word used by G in the second half of the verse. When Syh says that α' and θ' are 'like Origen', it probably means that they too read ἀγαθόν (see Marshall); since they seem to have used an adjective in agreement with the subject in the second half (see below), that might imply that they read a neuter noun here, like the τέλος of σ' (see the next note), but Muraoka, *Syntax*, §20 ea, points to other uses of neuter adjectives with masculine and feminine nouns (including at 7.26), and we should probably just understand literally '(is) a better thing than'.

Those translators seem to be taking their cue from the Hebrew here. Since אחרית is feminine, we might expect טובה, so there is a similar mismatch of gender in the use of טוב. Delsman, 'Inkongruenz', 36, lists this as one of numerous exceptions in the book to the normal rules of agreement in Hebrew, and J-M §148 a notes it as a rare exception to the more specific rule that attributive adjectives should agree with the substantive they describe. The other examples that J-M gives (excluding one from 10.1, which I think is to be construed differently) are from Ps 119.72; Prov 15.17; 17.1: these are all 'better than' statements, and it seems likely that the conventional form of 'better than' sayings has weighed more heavily in each case than the grammatical requirements; we shall encounter another case in 7.26. The disagreement here, therefore, may exemplify something more widespread, and when Qohelet uses the correct טובה חכמה in 7.11, just after this, it is notably *not* in the context of such a saying.

7.8 end] Or 'outcome'. In combination with ראשית, אחרית is used to talk about the end of something (e.g. Deut 11.12), but also about its future (e.g. Job 8.7), and the noun can have a more general reference to outcomes, results, or the latter phases of something (Job 42.12). Qohelet uses it in connection with speech again at 10.13, where he is talking about the beginning and end of the fool's speech, and the intended sense here is probably much the same, as most of the ancient versions recognize. A rather different interpretation, however, seems to be offered by σ' βέλτιον τέλος λόγου τῆς ἀρχῆς αὐτοῦ, 'better the fulfilment/outcome of a word/thing than its beginning'. On the reading and attribution, see Marshall, who also discusses (363-64) the faulty or misplaced attribution to σ' of θεοδώρητον/-οι rather than βέλτιον, which was mentioned in connection with the last verse. The choice of τέλος might suggest that Symmachus took Qohelet to be commending accomplishment, but he may alternatively have understood the saying in rather the same way that I do.

G's ἐσχάτη is odd: as noted already, this is feminine, as at 1.11 and 10.13, and it is the neuter form of the adjective that is usually used as a substantive. The feminine might have been used to match the gender of the Hebrew, but this is probably not, in fact, just an *ad hoc* calque on the Hebrew, either here or in a further use at Dan 11.29. There are substantive uses of the feminine to refer to a good 'outcome' or 'result' in the oracular *Sortes Astrampsychi* (in the initial question 37, then the responses at 4.1; 21.4; 23.5; 31.9; 33.10; 40.3; 62.8; 70.6; 96.2; 99.7), and in 40.3, the outcome may be good but short-lived, so the reference is clearly to the outcome of *undertakings*, not to the ultimate fate of the enquirer. The *Sortes* are commonly dated to the second or third century CE, so this usage, which gives a particular nuance, may well have been current at the time G was composed. Vinel's suggestion, that the feminine is used specifically by the G translator to provide a matching contrast with ἀρχή, does not fit 1.11, but it is not impossible that this has influenced his choice of word.

7.8 an account] Qohelet generally uses דבר to talk about words, not things or matters, but that sense cannot be excluded, and is preferred by most commentators. There is a similar ambiguity in some of the ancient translations, but Jerome clearly backs a reference to speech in Hie and V, interpreting it in those terms in his commentary, while T leans toward 'matter' (and Jerome reports his Hebrew teacher's comments as being about a *negotium*, 'an affair' or 'a matter').

The plural λόγων, 'words/things', is strange in G, not only because all the other versions have the singular, but also because it is picked up by a singular possessive pronoun αὐτοῦ, 'his' or 'its': we have to understand the Greek text as something like 'the end of words is good beyond his/one's beginning', since the pronoun is masculine and cannot agree with ἐσχάτη. If this is indeed the original reading (the singular is attested in some manuscripts), then the translator might conceivably have found דברם in his text, produced by dittography of the מ that follows (e.g., McNeile, 145; Salters, 'Observations on the Septuagint', 169; Goldman), and read it as דברים—although that does not really deal with the pronoun. It is more likely, I think, that he has used a plural interpretatively to make it clear that Qohelet is talking not about a word or a specific matter, but about a speech or account (cf. Hie *sermonis*, V *orationis*), with the plural understood collectively (enabling it to be picked up by the singular pronoun). In context, I think this is probably the correct understanding.

7.8 better[2]] As for the first 'better' (see above), the readings of the Greek translations are complicated. Marshall argues that α' and θ' had ἀγαθός, in contrast to the ἀγαθόν of G. It is not clear, however, why G itself should not have used ἀγαθός in agreement with μακρόθυμος, when it previously used ἀγαθὴ in agreement with ἐσχάτη. It seems likely that some confusion has entered the manuscript tradition at an early point.

7.8 long of spirit] Or perhaps 'length of spirit'. The expression ארך אפים is used commonly to talk of God being 'slow to anger' (e.g. Exod 34.6), but it means literally 'long of nostrils' (אף, 'nose', is used more generally of anger). The same expression is used sometimes of humans (Prov 14.29; 15.18; 16.32), and in Prov 25.15 we find it with the cognate noun, so that ארך אפים there implies 'patience' or 'cool-headedness'. With אף rather than אפים, in Jer 15.15 ארך אפך is similarly 'your patience'. The expression that we have here in most manuscripts, however, is not ארך אפים, but ארך רוח, literally 'long of spirit'.[1] This is not attested elsewhere in biblical Hebrew (although in Job 6.11 the comparable אאריך נפשי is set in parallel with איחל, and so has something to do with waiting), but in Sir 5.11 we do find היה ממהר להאזין ובארך רוח השב פתגם, 'be swift to listen, but answer with a long spirit', which seems to suggest that ארך רוח refers to 'deliberation', or the willingness to be slow in doing something.

War-horses are described in 1QM vi, 12 as ארוכי רוח, 'long in spirit', and this is usually translated as 'unrelenting', but since it immediately precedes references to their maturity and training, some similar notion of patience or restraint would not be inappropriate to the context. In Aramaic, we find אריך רוח used to render ארך אפים in, e.g., Targum Neofiti Exod 34.6, but a similar expression occurs in line 4 of 4Q550, where we have ארכת רוחה די מלכא. Cook, *Dictionary of Qumran Aramaic*, 24, takes this to mean 'the king was patient'. It has been translated in many ways, however, and the context does not commend that sense: whatever the king was doing or feeling, it leads immediately to the reading before him of his father's books, and we are perhaps dealing with the familiar motif of a 'bored' king.

For both Hebrew and Aramaic, therefore, we have evidence that 'length of spirit' was a familiar concept, but the range of uses does not suggest that ארך רוח means quite the same as ארך אפים: it is not the quality of being slow

---

[1] In fact, ארך אפים is attested in BM ms 2333, although it may be just an assimilation there to the more common expression; cf. Ratzabi, 'Massoretic Variants', 104, and note the other attestations in Kennicott, de Rossi.

to anger, so much as the quality of avoiding haste (and the king in 4Q550 has perhaps had slowness thrust upon him). It may be that it is familiarity with ארך אפים that has led most of the versions to read both ארך and גבה here as adjectives, so that Qohelet is talking about one type of person being better than another. Each could as well be vocalized as a noun, 'length' and 'height', and this is how they have been read by S, ܢܓܝܪܘܬ ܪܘܚܐ *ngyrwt rwḥ*', 'length of spirit' (which *does* mean 'patience' in Syriac) and ܪܡܘܬ ܪܘܚܐ *rmwt rwḥ*', 'height of spirit'.

7.8 lofty of spirit] Or perhaps 'loftiness of spirit'; see the previous note. Unlike ארך רוח, the expression גבה רוח does appear elsewhere in biblical Hebrew, set in parallel with גאון in Prov 16.18: 'before a crash, exaltation, and before a stumbling, height of spirit'. That verse is about pride, and is more familiar, perhaps, in the Authorized Version's 'Pride goeth before destruction, and an haughty spirit before a fall'. In the next verse, however, גבה רוח is picked up by its counterpart שפל רוח: 'Better low of spirit with the poor than to share out the plunder with the proud' (Prov 16.19). Here and in Prov 29.23; Isa 57.15, 'low of spirit' seems to refer not to virtuous, elective humility, which would be the simple opposite of arrogance, but rather to the misery and broken spirit of the impoverished—and this suggests that 'high of spirit' correspondingly implies a state not just of arrogance, but of something close to what we mean by 'high-spirited' in English. In that case, the imagery of Prov 16.18 is more nuanced: something high and proud is smashed down (cf. שבר in Isa 30.14), and something else trips over when it proceeds with reckless arrogance. That sense would also suit the context here very well, and get around the apparent difficulty that patience and pride are not natural alternatives: the saying would then, in fact, be commending deliberation and self-restraint over a careless or arrogant self-confidence.

σ′ ὑψηλοκάρδιον, 'high-hearted', loses the distinction, or perhaps seeks a different nuance, by aligning the expression here with the high-heartedness of Prov 16.5 (that reading is now slightly contradicted by ms 788, which has just καρδία for σ′ here). In several manuscripts of G, on the other hand, the sense has become obscured because the initial letters ΜΗΟ of 7.9 have been duplicated to create a faulty reading πνεῦμα τιμῆς, 'spirit of honour' in place of πνεύματι.

7.9 Do not rush in your feelings] Lit. 'in your spirit/breath'. G manuscripts 161 and 248, both important witnesses for hexaplaric readings, each have two notes here which are described by Marshall. The first reads ἐπὶ στόματί σου, 'on your mouth', the second διὰ λόγων σου παροργίσαι, 'to provoke anger by your words'. In 161, the first is attributed to σ′ and the second is anonymous, but in 248, it is the other way around. Marshall is certainly right to suppose that the second is actually the reading of σ′ (for M לכעוס ברוחך, G ἐν πνεύματί σου τοῦ θυμοῦσθαι, 'in your spirit to become angry'), and he may well be right that ἐπὶ στόματί σου is simply a scholion that recognizes a link with 5.1, where the pi'el of בהל is also used with the sense of hastening. The scholion also, however, draws attention to the distinctiveness here of σ′, which understands רוח to be a reference to speech, probably *via* its common use for 'breath', but perhaps with an eye to passages like Neh 9.30 or Zech 7.12, where 'spirit' is associated with prophetic speech. The only other of the ancient translations that may have such an understanding is T, which renders ברוחך directly with בנפשך, but which then goes on to add a contrast between speech and silence. Furthermore, σ' uniquely understands לכעוס to be transitive—'provoke anger', rather than 'be angry'—perhaps by taking a defectively spelled לכעס to be pi‘el. This presumably reflects an understanding that Qohelet sees anger not as the mark of a fool, but as something that will be received by fools in a particular way.

Its paraphrastic character means that σ' has to be used with some caution, but Symmachus is generally a good interpreter, and his reading here recognizes a difficulty that more modern commentators have been inclined to overlook: רוח can be used to describe mood (e.g. 1 Kgs 21.5) or feelings (unleashed too easily by the fool in Prov 29.11), and so may be associated with anger (cf. Judg 8.3; 2 Chr 21.16; Prov 16.32), but it does not, like לב or נפש, describe the location of those feelings—the רוח *is* the anger, not just the place where the anger resides. Accordingly, things are very rarely 'in' the רוח, and the ב- in ברוח normally has an instrumental sense, except where it is constructed with a particular verb or verbal concept (Prov 16.32; Eccl 8.8; Mal 2.15, 16). Of the few exceptions, two involve a 'share in' (2 Kgs 2.9) and a 'fracture in' a רוח (Prov 15.4), so only 1 Chr 28.12 and Ps 32.2 seem to involve a use that might be compared to what we would have here if Qohelet were talking about 'anger in the spirit'.

The former is talking about the content of David's plans for the Temple, and is probably to be understood as 'what he desired'; in the latter, ברוחו רמיה is strikingly translated in the Septuagint text as ἐν τῷ στόματι αὐτοῦ δόλος, 'guile in his mouth', not 'guile in his spirit', reflecting an understanding of ברוח similar to that shown here in σ'. There are good reasons, therefore, why Symmachus should have been reluctant to understand a reference here to anger 'in your spirit', and like the translator of Ps 32.2, he has been led to suppose that spirit here must be breath or speech. We need not follow him, but it would clearly be sensible to avoid introducing a new notion of emotions residing 'in' the רוח, and I take it to be the haste, not the anger itself, that Qohelet associates directly with the רוח: when it comes to one's feelings, one should not rush to let them become angry.

7.9 to get angry, for anger] We have already encountered the noun כעס several times (1.18; 2.23; 5.16; 7.3), and it will occur again in 11.10. The noun has a broader scope than 'anger' (see the note at 1.18), but the less common verb, found alongside the noun here, is almost always used in that sense (Ezek 32.9 is a likely exception). We should probably translate in such terms, therefore, but given the way he has used the noun elsewhere, Qohelet may be talking about frustration and resentment rather than simple rage.

7.9 lives in the lap] The translation 'in the bosom of' adopted by, e.g., the RSV, allows an understanding that the anger somehow resides inside the fools, but חיק is not a way of talking about the heart or inner self (*pace* Schoors, who claims such a sense but adduces no examples). Rather, it refers either to the part of the body against which lovers or children are held in an embrace, or to a fold in the clothing above the waist (cf. Prov 6.27), in which the hands may be wrapped or objects held (Prov 16.33 speaks of lots being cast into it). The image may be of fools clutching anger to themselves (cf. Job 23.12), but בחיק more probably implies that they keep it close and ready. The verb is used of settling or resting, but can also have an implication of waiting quietly for something (1 Sam 25.9; Hab 3.16). A variant in some manuscripts of S, found also in Theodore of Mopsuestia's text, suggests that the anger of fools rests in their laps, rather than anger resting in the laps of fools; cf. Jarick, 'Theodore and the Text', 372-73.

7.10 What has happened] מה היה is used in Exod 32.1, 23 and Lam 5.1 of 'what has happened' to (-ל) someone, but in 1 Sam 4.16; 2 Sam 1.4, מה היה הדבר means literally 'how was the matter?', equivalent to the English 'how did it go?'. These different uses illustrate an ambiguity that HCM observe here: the following sentence, substantivized using -ש, either stands in apposition to a מה that is being used as an interrogative pronoun ('what has happened, that the former days…?'), or serves as the subject of a clause in which מה is being used adverbially to mean 'how?' or, in effect, 'why?'. G, Hie, S all apparently take מה as a pronoun with the sentence in apposition, but the more awkward adverbial understanding probably underpins α' διὰ τί, 'on account of what (has it happened)'—there is, at least, no evidence elsewhere for an actual textual variant למה, which would be the only other natural basis for such a reading—while V *ne dicas quid putas causae est quod*, 'do not say "what do you think is the reason that"', seems to be more loosely along the same lines.

T finds a third way, treating the מה as an indefinite, not interrogative pronoun: מא הוה מן קדמת דנא טב, 'whatever was of old is/was good', and goes on to express no doubt that the past was, in fact, better; this understanding has probably driven its construal. Judging by the strong statements about continuity that he made in ch. 1, Qohelet himself probably does not believe that the past in general was better (or worse) than the present, even if there might be better and worse times from a human perspective. It is apparently his intention here neither to make that point, however, nor specifically to contradict the notion of a better past that is presumed by the question: on any reading, this would be a convoluted way to make such points. Rather, Qohelet warns against the very asking of that question, with its concomitant assumption that there must be an underlying cause or explanation.

7.10 it is not wisdom that has led you to inquire about that] For the literal sense, see below. Of the other ancient versions, only T supports M

במחכמה directly:[2] G ἐν σοφίᾳ, 'in wisdom', appears to reflect a source-text with בחכמה, and is matched by S ܒܚܟܡܬܐ *bḥkmtʾ*; Hie *non enim sapienter* adopts the same paraphrase as σ' οὐ γὰρ φρονίμως, 'for not wisely'. It is easy to see why מחכמה might have been replaced or paraphrased, since the expression is without parallel in the biblical sources and does not give a straightforward sense. If only for that reason, it is probably the original reading, but precisely what nuance Qohelet intends to give by using it is unclear. Seow compares several verses in which somebody speaks 'out of' something, but in those the something is always a place (e.g. Amos 1.2, 'YHWH roars from Zion'), which is hardly comparable. The notion of origin is extended somewhat in later Hebrew to embrace causation, and Jastrow, *Dictionary*, cites examples of מן used to describe the original causes 'from' which subsequent events have come, but, again, those do not really match what we have here. It might be better to look to places like 2 Sam 3.37, where the preposition is used to express in a very concise way that Abner's assassination was not 'from' the king, in the sense that he had neither ordered nor willed it, or Judg 14.4, where Samson's wish for a Philistine wife is 'from' God, in the sense that he has put the thought in Samson's head. It is that sort of sense that presumably lies behind the more common use of מן to express the agent with passive verbs. On that reading, Qohelet's point would be that such a question is not driven by wisdom.

The verb שאל itself is normally used of actually asking questions, and even in places like Deut 13.15 (ET 13.14) it probably means 'ask around', rather than 'investigate' in some more general way. We should note also, however, a use of the verb that was to become more common in later Hebrew, but appears already in passages like Exod 3.22; 2 Kgs 4.3; and Zech 10.1. In this usage, שאל means not 'ask (a question)', but 'ask (for something from someone)', and it is used of begging someone for a gift or for the loan of something. Naturally, מן is used to indicate the someone 'from' or 'of' whom the request is made. Taken that way, Qohelet's words would mean something like 'you have not got this by asking wisdom for it'—or, at least, they would if the 'this' could be taken as a direct object. The last phrase, however, makes that impossible, and if the verb is indeed supposed to be read in these terms, then Qohelet must be using it absolutely.

Turning to that last phrase, we should note first that M על is supported by the other versions, and that there are no grounds for emendation, however tempting that might be. When used of questioning, שאל is more commonly construed with -ל, which can indicate both the topic of the question and the person to whom it is addressed, as in, e.g., Gen 43.27 וישאל להם לשלום, 'and he enquired *of* them *about* (their) health'. Correspondingly, we find שאל נא לימים

---

[2] The reading מן is preserved only in BM ms Or. 1302; in other manuscripts of T (and therefore in many editions) it has been displaced by על, which is an obvious error caused by the proximity of על דנא.

ראשנים, 'ask now concerning the former days', in Deut 4.32, a verse that is rather similar to ours. In Neh 1.2 and Isa 45.11, however, על is used to indicate the topic. If that is the intention here too, then it is difficult to say whether this is simply a 'later' usage, as implied by Podechard and Whitley, but equally clear that Schoors, *The Preacher* I, 193, is strictly wrong to suggest that the construction would be equivalent to the use of the verb with a direct accusative: Qohelet would not be saying 'ask this', but 'ask about this', and זה would be the topic of the question, not a reference back the question itself, מה היה. Although it is taken as such in the paraphrastic V, the other versions maintain the distinction explicitly (S even has 'these', although that is presumably under the influence of the previous plural pronoun). If we retain the usual biblical senses of שאל, then, Qohelet would have to be speaking of 'asking about this, motivated by wisdom' or, less probably, of 'borrowing from wisdom in this matter'. There are later uses of the verb with an implication of 'discussing' or 'suggesting' (cf. Jastrow, *Dictionary*), but the general sense seems clear, whatever the precise understanding that we adopt.

7.11 with inherited property] נחלה: refers almost exclusively to land in biblical usage. There is a helpful survey in Lavoie, 'Avantage et limites', 379, which grants it the slightly broader sense of material wealth, and I have also opted to retain a certain ambiguity in my translation, but we should not think more generally of 'an inheritance' in modern Western terms. The money to which Qohelet will go on to refer in the next verse is more probably income generated from an estate than the actual substance of the inheritance.

S ܡܢ ܡܐܢܝ ܙܝܢܐ *mn mʾny zynʾ*, which probably means 'more than implements of weaponry', is close to the statement at 9.18, where wisdom is said to be better than 'weapons of war'. Even though in that verse S itself uses the more common ܡܢ ܡܐܢܝ ܩܪܒܐ *mn mʾny qrbʾ* (cf. Deut 1.41; Judg 18.11, 16, 17), therefore, it is likely that a recollection of the thought there has displaced whatever was the original translation here (so, e.g., Euringer; Kamenetzky 201), perhaps after the text had become damaged or corrupt. In any case, although McNeile, 75, suggests that the translator might have linked נחלה with חיל, and others have thought that he might be rendering the obscure נחילה: attested only at Ps 5.1 (so, e.g., Ginsburg, Whitley, Lavoie, 'Avantage et limites', 368), it is difficult to view the existing text of S as a rendering at all of the Hebrew reflected in the other versions.

Although the remaining versions are consonant, we do find some variation in the G tradition: κληροδοσίας, which is most probably original, has been displaced in many manuscripts by the more common κληρονομίας. In modern Greek, κληροδοσία is used of legacies and inheritance (as much earlier was κληρονομία), but uses elsewhere in Greek biblical translations at, e.g., Ps 78.55 and 1 Macc 10.89, refer rather differently to the distribution of land, and although the modern meaning is attested in patristic literature (cf. Lampe), it is difficult to know at what point that became a familiar sense. It is correspondingly hard to say whether the translator meant to indicate 'inheritance' more generally, or was influenced by the association of נחלה with land in the biblical texts, and tried to give a more technical nuance.

In any case, G and all the other ancient versions (except S, as it stands) take Qohelet's point to be that wisdom is good 'along with' an inheritance. Many modern commentators, on the other hand, understand his meaning to be that wisdom is 'as good as' an inheritance (Whitley, Seow), or more commonly 'like' an inheritance. At 2.16, I noted that the similar attempt to understand 'along with' there rested on a questionable assertion that, essentially, the use of עם to imply collocation means that we can take it also to imply comparison. Here again, it is not impossible that Qohelet intends to say that wisdom 'stands alongside' an inheritance, meaning that it is comparable to one, rather as 2 Chr 14.10 and 20.6 speak of nobody standing alongside God to help or withstand. Such uses of the preposition, however, are so unusual and so dependent on clear indications from the context, that we can hardly see that as the natural or most obvious meaning here, and if the writer wanted unambiguously to make a comparison, he could easily have used -כ (Lavoie, 'Avantage et limites', 380-81, suggests that he is, in fact, being deliberately ambiguous, but even then I am not sure what is supposed to point the audience towards this relatively obscure, similizing sense alongside the more obvious associative one). If there is something in the language or context to lead us away from 'together with', then it has been missed by all but one of the ancient versions, by the Midrash and by earlier commentators, none of whom understand Qohelet to be comparing wisdom with an inheritance here, even though the various readings of -כ instead of -ב with צל in the next verse (on which, see below) have led some of them to see a comparison with money there.

That said, S, among its various idiosyncrasies here, renders using ܡܢ *mn*, 'than', instead of 'with', so that the point becomes neither that wisdom is good *with* an inheritance, nor that it is good *like* an inheritance, but that it is *better than* an inheritance. This is actually commended by Kugel, 'Qohelet and Money', 40 n. 21, who thinks that a similar sense is required for עם in 2.16, while Hertzberg aims to achieve the same by reading מעם on the basis of S (so, similarly, Galling 1969, although he sensibly does not cite S). Beyond even the efforts to find a comparison, this seems simply an attempt to insist on a particular meaning, whatever the text might say, and it should be obvious that S here is a safe witness neither to the text nor to the possible meanings of the Hebrew.

As it is in English, the implication of 'good with an inheritance' in the Hebrew is most naturally that inheritance provides a benefit or enhancement to wisdom, and Hollinshead, 'What is good for man?', 48, offers no evidence for his claim that Qohelet is talking here about the possibility of an inheritance itself being destroyed if used without wisdom. Not dissimilarly, Heim takes the point to be that wisdom 'will help people keep their property to pass on to their posterity', which forces עם to mean something almost like 'when it comes to', or 'for the purposes of'.

7.11 but an advantage to] Or 'and/while an advantage to': I have translated with 'but' in this verse and the next to draw out what I perceive to be a distinction in each verse: wisdom benefits from past profits, but the profit it offers in itself is for the present; wisdom is protected by money, but offers a protection of its own. In neither case is there an actual contrast: this is more a case of 'on the one hand…on the other'.

On Qohelet's use of יותר, see the note at 6.8. Joüon, 'Notes philologiques', 423, would read זה יותר, as a sort of positive counterpart to Qohelet's refrain of זה הבל. There is no basis for this, or any obvious problem with the text as it stands, although Joüon claims vaguely that the conjunction creates problems. On the spelling, Ginsburg, *Massorah*, 4:486, describes a Masoretic note that presumes the reading here to be plene (ויותר), and in 7.16 to be defective (cf. Baer, 64); both readings are found by Kennicott.

7.12 in its shade, that wisdom is in the shade of that money] The use of the article with חכמה has been discussed in the note at 1.13. It is not absolutely impossible that Qohelet is referring to 'wisdom' in a general way, but it is more likely that the article on החכמה, if original, points anaphorically to the wisdom of the preceding verse: the wisdom that is in shade would then be the wisdom that comes along with an inheritance, not just wisdom in general. It is just possible that the ה is actually to be explained differently (see below), but I have translated it as anaphoric, and taken the corresponding הכסף in the same way (cf. my notes on the use of הכסף at 10.19).

The various readings of בצל or כצל in 6.12 were discussed in the notes to that verse; we have similar problems here (and will encounter the issue again at 8.13). M reads בצל…בצל, but G seems to have read בצלה…כצל, while Hie, V seem, on the face of it, to reflect כצל…כצל. It is probable, however, that Jerome is following σ′, which Field restored as ὅτι ὡς σκέπει σοφία ὁμοίως σκέπει τὸ ἀργύριον, 'for just as wisdom shelters, so likewise does the money shelter', on the basis of Greek witnesses to most of the words, along with renderings of the whole by Syh and Jerome; ms 788 now suggests that we should read καθάπερ rather than ὡς, and there is strong support for ὡς rather than ὁμοίως, but the overall sense is not in doubt. This seems more likely to be a paraphrase than a witness to an actual variant text, although Goldman treats it as such in his lengthy discussion of the problems (cf. also McNeile, 145-46). Something similar may be true of S and T. In the former, ܡܛܠ ܕܛܠܠܗ ܕܚܟܡܬܐ ܐܝܟ ܛܠܠܗ ܕܟܣܦܐ *mṭl dṭllʾ dḥkmtʾ ʾyk ṭllʾ dksp'*, 'for the shade of wisdom is like the shade of money', might represent a Hebrew …צל כצל, but can plausibly be construed as an interpretation based on G (or on the same Hebrew text used by Jerome and σ′, if we follow Goldman). With בטלל twice, on the other hand, the Targum has probably read the same text as M, and simply taken the statements to stand as a comparison as though one or both had -כ ('just as a man may find shelter in the shadow of wisdom, so he may find shelter in the shadow of money').

The real choice, then, seems to be between the readings of M and G: the other versions simply reflect a desire to equate or compare the protection offered by wisdom with that offered by wealth. From this point of view, it is important to consider the fact that G has not only read כצל where M has a second בצל, but that it has also found a possessive pronoun after the first, which is key to its understanding of the text. There can be little doubt that this pronoun was in G's source-text, but it is commonly assumed that a בצלה appeared there in place of a בצל through duplication of the following ה on החכמה (so, e.g., Salters, 'Observations on the Septuagint', 169). Of course, it is no less simple to suppose either that it actually dropped out of the tradition because of that same following ה, surviving only in the witness of G, or, less probably (given the article in G—although not, interestingly, in σ') that it has moved from the end of one word to the beginning of the next. The pronoun does, moreover, supply an effective link between vv. 11 and 12 without self-evidently having been designed to do so. In this respect, I think G is probably original. As it stands, however, the broader G ὅτι ἐν σκιᾷ αὐτῆς ἡ σοφία ὡς σκιὰ τοῦ ἀργυρίου, 'for in its shade the wisdom is like money's shade', expresses an idea that wisdom can only offer a protection comparable to that offered by money when it is itself protected by an inheritance. This offers an explanation for why wisdom might be best with an inheritance, but that explanation is itself odd: it seems to envisage that by being *in* the shade of inheritance, wisdom can somehow become *like* the shade of wealth.

If G is awkward, though, M is almost unintelligible. Efforts to read the two phrases with בצל in parallel result in understandings like 'wisdom (is) in shade, money (is) in shade', or 'wisdom (is) shade, money (is) shade' (with a *beth essentiae*, as, e.g., Lavoie, 'Avantage et limites', 385, which is also the understanding behind Niccacci's less plausible identification of each as 'true shade' in 'Qohelet o la gioia', 69). These are commonly parsed to create the sort of analogy seen by Jerome, '(just as) wisdom (is) shade (so) money (likewise) is shade', or 'wisdom is in shade (just as) money is in shade', or '(to sit) in the shade of wisdom (is the same as to sit) in the shade of money' (Zimmerli), or 'in the shadow of wisdom (means as much as) in the shadow of money' (Michel, 'Qohelet-Probleme', 93; *Untersuchungen*, 101). It will be obvious that such understandings require us to read in a great deal, without much help from the context. This has undoubtedly influenced a number of recent commentators to prefer the כצל reflected in G to the second בצל of M, and by further omitting the possessive pronoun of G in line with M, Goldman, for example, restores a text בצל החכמה כצל הכסף that might mean 'being in the shade of wisdom (is) like being in the shade of money'—if we do not consider it too much of a stretch to make the two phrases the subject and predicate of a non-verbal clause.

I agree that neither M nor G offers a good text by itself, but take the original to have been בצלה החכמה בצל הכסף, with the probable sense '(wisdom is good with an inheritance because) in its shade, that wisdom (is) in the shade of money'. This is only one ב/כ confusion away from the likely source-text of G, which I think has been influenced by the desire to find an analogy between wisdom and money; it is also almost identical to M, where the first ה has probably dropped out accidentally before the second.

The difficulties have offered fertile ground for those scholars who suppose the original to have been written in Aramaic. Zimmermann, 'Aramaic Provenance', 30, suggests that participles from the Aramaic verb בטל, 'cease', have been misinterpreted as ב-טול, 'in shadow', and this idea is picked up in Ginsberg, *Studies*, 22-23, which substitutes final forms and paraphrases 'when the wisdom goes, the money goes'. Of course, this attributes no less stupidity than normal to the presumed translator, although it is, admittedly, one of the most ingenious cases adduced for the translation theory. In fact, although it is very rare in a Hebrew context, בטל does appear in 12.3, and Gordis explores (but rejects) the possibility of taking בצל in each case as a simple error. No less clever, but no more plausible, is the suggestion of Dahood, 'Canaanite-Phoenician', 209-10, according to which the second -ב in M is an accidental reminiscence, to be deleted, and the first a case of *beth essentiae*. Noting an Ugaritic expression read as *ẓl ksp* by Gordon, who himself suggested a link with this passage, Dahood then uses this as the basis for a translation, 'The sheen of silver is the protection of wisdom', and claims that Qohelet is deliberately playing on two different senses of צל. The complexity of all that might strain credulity even were the reading and sense of the Ugaritic more certain, but the simplicity of Tur-Sinai's proposal ('Dunkle Bibelstellen', 280), to take both instances of בצל as erroneous writings of בעל, is no more compelling. Whitley, who supports this latter, translates, 'he who possesses wisdom possesses money'. The scope for confusion between צ and ע in the square script makes the error plausible, but there is no trace of the reading in any of the ancient versions, and it is not clear what would have led a scribe who found בעליה at the end of the verse to introduce references to shadow elsewhere if he found an ambiguous writing. We shall touch on the suggestion again in the next note.

I noted at 6.12 the suggestion of Wise, 'A Calque', that בצל may be used in the book as a calque on a use of 'in shadow' in Aramaic to mean not just 'owing to the protection of' and 'with the help of', which are natural extensions of the literal sense, but more generally 'because (of)'. With respect to this verse, Wise claims (256) that 'with the help of' offers the most appropriate sense—and this is the sense also that he establishes most securely for the various Aramaic texts that he examines. I think the suggestion is quite plausible, but it does not change the sense, implying merely that Qohelet is using 'in shadow' not as a live metaphor, but as a familiar expression connoting assistance or protection.

7.12 but it is a profit from knowledge that the wisdom may keep its possessor alive] On the literal sense, see below, and on my translation 'but', see the note at 7.11. G, S, and T read יתרון דעת החכמה as a construct chain serving as the subject of the verb; the vocalization in M would permit but does not require this construal (and the accents point a different way; see below). In Hie *et quod plus est scientia sapientiae*, Jerome retains 'knowledge from wisdom', while treating ויתרון as an adverbial 'and what is more', but in V he construes the text quite differently as *hoc autem plus habet eruditio et sapientia quod uitam tribuunt possessori suo*, 'in this, however, learning and wisdom have more, that they give life to their possessor'. This apparently paraphrases '(there is) an advantage of knowledge (and) wisdom, (that) they...', which is not a plausible reading of the Hebrew (Ginsburg calls it 'a mutilation of the text').

In this case, at least, Jerome is not following σ', which is only partially attested as ἡ σοφία διασώσει τοὺς ἔχοντας αὐτήν, 'wisdom will save those who have it', but which seems to be in line with the interpretation that is probably indicated by the Masoretic accents, and that has long established itself as the most popular among commentators. In the RSV's version, this reads 'the advantage of knowledge is that wisdom preserves the life of him who has it'; cf. a little differently, Michel, 'Qohelet-Probleme', 93 (*Untersuchungen*, 101), where it is construed as, 'the profit of knowledge (lies in the following:) wisdom keeps its owner alive'. Such readings rest on a supposition that החכמה תחיה בעליה is being identified as the יתרון דעת. The grammatical assumptions are rarely spelled out, but unless the identification is supposed to be achieved by simple juxtaposition, then presumably החכמה תחיה בעליה has to be taken as a substantivized verbal clause ('*that* wisdom preserves'), the substantivization of which is unmarked in the Hebrew (so, e.g., HCM). More directly, Joüon, 'Notes philologiques', 423, finds a similar construction, but would read וחכמה and then simply replace תחיה with a substantive תחית, so that 'knowledge and wisdom' are the 'bringing to life' of those that possess them. Needless to say, that is entirely speculative. The usual formulation does not require any such emendation, but the fact that the text was not read this way by many of the ancient versions does draw attention to its difficulties—most notably the lack of any clear signposting to identify the construction, and the presentation not directly of the profit offered by wisdom (cf. 7.11), but of profit from knowledge. That expression, furthermore, is not determined, despite the various translations noted above, which makes it difficult to take החכמה תחיה בעליה as defining *the* profit from knowledge.

Sitting closer to G's construal, Bianchi, 'Un fantasma', 58, achieves a somewhat different understanding by taking דעת as an infinitive construct interrupting the construct chain יתרון חכמה. The notion of a 'broken' construct chain is rooted in the observations of Freedman, 'The Broken Construct Chain', but Bianchi cites more directly the suggestion of Frendo, 'Broken Construct Chain', about 10.10, suggesting that he understands the meaning here to be 'knowing is the profit from wisdom'. This proposal potentially addresses the principal objection to reading a construct chain, which is that the verb תחיה is feminine and יתרון is usually taken to be masculine (that gender is confirmed if we read הכשיר as a main verb in 10.10; see the note there). In a chain of three items where two are feminine, however, it would not be very surprising if the normal rules of agreement were not applied strictly (cf. GKC §146 a; J-M §150 n), and the versions that read a construct chain must either have been willing to overlook the disagreement, or else found a reading תחיה—the current תחיה could itself have resulted from the proximity of the feminine nouns. Neither of these explanations is entirely satisfactory, but both are better than resorting to an exceptional fracture of the construct relationship: even if we allow the various examples that have been adduced (and most are far from straightforward), this is a much rarer phenomenon than disagreement, and the particular version of it advocated by Frendo and Bianchi, which creates non-verbal clauses out of the interrupting and interrupted elements, is especially problematic (see the notes on 10.10).

Kugel, 'Qohelet and Money', 43-44, also tries to avoid the grammatical disagreement, but does so by taking הכסף ויתרון together as a single expression, 'money and payback', which then leaves דעת החכמה as the feminine subject of תחיה; he paraphrases the sense as 'he who acquires wisdom acquires money and payback'. The objections of Lavoie, 'Avantage et limites', 388—that this ignores the M accents and was understood by none of the ancient versions— carry only limited weight in themselves, but it is true that we should not overlook the refusal of readers, ancient and modern, to adopt what seems, on the face of it, a straightforward construal that overcomes a grammatical problem. One good reason is the absence of an article on יתרון to match that on הכסף, which would be odd if they are supposed to stand together, and another, perhaps, the absence of any conjunction or particle to indicate what would then be the relationship between the last clause and the rest. The more important point, though, is that 7.11 has said that wisdom is an advantage (ויתר) to the living, and readers have clearly expected to find here a specification of what that advantage (ויתרון) is.

Kugel's broader construal does actually offer such a specification: it depends upon the suggestion by Tur-Sinai and Whitley (see above), which enables him to understand 'whoever has wisdom, has money and profit: the knowledge from wisdom keeps whoever has it alive'. This is neat, but it is founded on a highly speculative emendation, and it does not fit well with 7.11 unless, as does Kugel, we read a declaration there that wisdom is 'better' than an inheritance. There are too many problems, then, simply to accept the proposal as it stands, but it does seem worth considering separately the very specific suggestion that הכסף ויתרון should be taken together, which would solve our grammatical issue and get rid of what seems an unnecessarily clunky construct chain. It would be by no means impossible, I think, to read 'For in its shade, that wisdom is in the shade of the money and profit, (while) the knowledge from that wisdom may keep its possessor alive'. The mismatched determination and absence of a conjunction before דעת remain troubling, however, and if we were to adopt this as the intended reading, then we would have to accept also that the text has most likely been adjusted slightly in line with attempts to read it differently.

Overall, then, there are no solid grounds for emendation, and the text as it stands here can be read in two different ways. One, represented in G and elsewhere, involves accepting a grammatical disagreement, and, realistically, all attempts to get around that problem require us to emend. The other, indicated by the accents in M, avoids that issue, but forces us to find quite a complicated, unmarked construction. Neither is really satisfactory, and I have a strong suspicion that the text would originally have been clearer, but if we are to deal with what we have, then we should probably follow M to avoid the disagreement, and I have translated accordingly. On this reading, the literal sense is 'profit of knowledge (is) (that) the wisdom may keep its possessor alive', and it is possible that the nuance might be 'profit from knowledge is such that wisdom may...'.

7.12 may sustain] There is some shifting of ground in these verses, and we should not insist upon absolute consistency. All the same, 7.16 will shortly imply that Qohelet probably does *not* believe that wisdom will necessarily preserve the wise, whatever he is saying here. Since a translation 'will keep' would introduce a note of certainty in the English that the yiqtol does not always convey in Hebrew, and so impose a contradiction more direct than might actually have been intended, I have rendered in a way that leaves the matter more open—at some risk of going too far the other way.

As regards the sense of the verb, Lavoie, 'Avantage et limites', 389-90, offers a detailed review of the usage in order to rebut the various claims that Qohelet is talking about giving or restoring life here, as opposed to preserving it, or allowing it to continue. Such nuances cannot be excluded altogether— the verb has quite a wide range—but they do not seem appropriate to a context where a comparison is being made with the protection offered by shade. Going further, Lohfink, 'Deuteronomy 6:24', reviews a range of passages to suggest, quite plausibly, that the piʻel of חיה can have a particular implication of taking responsibility for the maintenance of somebody—not just keeping them alive, but providing them with the necessities of life—and he suggests that such a sense is in play here. I think he is probably right, and the context here might well lead us to suppose that wisdom offers something continuous, corresponding to the protection from the inheritance, rather than simply stepping in to avert danger at particular moments, or 'letting' the wise live. For similar usage, Lohfink notes Deut 6.24; Jer 49.11; Pss 33.19; 41.3 (ET 41.2); Neh 9.6.

7.12 its possessor] Or 'possessors'. On the number and use of בעל here, and the rendering τὸν παρ' αὐτῆς in G, see the note at 5.10, and the discussion in the corresponding note at 8.8, where the construction is similar. As often with this term, it is difficult to give a good correspondence in English: the reference is probably not just to 'ownership' (despite σ' διασώσει τοὺς ἔχοντας αὐτήν, 'will preserve those having it'; cf. Hie, V, and note also the plural) but to close association, and we could even translate, perhaps, 'one/ those who is/are characterized by it'. The feminine suffix pronoun refers to the wisdom or the knowledge, not the profit.

7.13-14

(7.13) Behold the achievement of God: who can straighten what he has bent? (7.14) On a day of good things, live the good life, but think about a day of bad things: God has made this as well, to match the other, so that a person may never discover anything after him.

Commentary

7.13 is obviously reminiscent of 1.15, although the 'bending' here is explicitly identified as the work of God. If a criticism of him seems to be implied by any expectation that things should be straight, not bent, that is rapidly offset by the next verse. Speaking more specifically about times, this declares that God has made (or makes) days which we would consider both good and bad, and his activity, therefore, may be perceived not as malign, but as neutral. It is unlikely, however, that in the last part of 7.14 Qohelet is actually suggesting explicitly that God's actions protect him against criticism—an understanding shared by several commentators, which is attractive but hard to derive from the Hebrew.[1] It is also difficult

---

[1] Lasater, 'Subordination', 101, claims more generally that 'For Qohelet, God simply is not a moral agent', and that the book lacks any interest in theodicy, or in a justification of divine action as compatible with human moral judgments. This lack, for Lasater, arises in large part from the fact that the very notion of justifying God has its roots in much more modern ways of thinking about 'universally valid, law-like, "rational" principles to which any moral agent is enjoined' (100), but even Crenshaw, who discusses biblical theodicy at great length in his *Defending God*, is forced to conclude that Qohelet offers 'no defense of divine justice' (169), and has to resort to the idea of an 'indirect theodicy' in Ecclesiastes, whereby God is protected from condemnation because humans can know too little about his conduct. Backhaus, *Den Zeit*, 382, speaks similarly of God standing outside the scope of the rational argumentation that would be a prerequisite for a rational theodicy, and Schoors, 'Theodicy', whilst claiming that theodicy is 'a towering problem' for Qohelet (375), thinks that Qohelet considers any solution to that problem to be concealed by 'the unfathomable mystery of God' (409).

to claim that Qohelet is portraying God's activities here as naturally and inevitably involving things that will be perceived sometimes as bad by humans. Although a number of other interpretations have also been put forward, he is not proclaiming merely that we have to take the rough with the smooth, and his point actually seems to be that, by making good times and bad, God somehow prevents humans from discovering what is to come.

It is the difficulty of understanding how that is supposed to work which has motivated attempts to find another, less obvious sense—Murphy, 'On Translating Ecclesiastes', 573, declares that 'there is no connection between this action and human ignorance as its alleged result', and this leads him to adopt the rather speculative suggestion of Burkitt (discussed in the notes), which finds a whole new sense for 'discover...after' here. The connection becomes clearer, however, if we look back to the points that Qohelet made in 7.8-10. The issue is not that outcomes are concealed by the neutrality of God's actions, but that the situation to be perceived at any one time tells us nothing about the situation that will prevail at some later point—just as Qohelet suggested in 7.10 that we should not try to judge the present against the past, without knowing the future. On a small scale, God's action results in the fact that the quality of no single day tells us what the next will be like (which is why we should enjoy the good ones while we can). At 3.22, though, and especially 6.12, 'after him' seems to have implied 'after his death', and some such implication may be likely here: Qohelet is talking about the hiddenness of the future course of the world on a grander scale, which is merely epitomized in the impossibility of predicting each day on the basis of the last.

The Hebrew probably implies that this human ignorance is a purpose and not a byproduct of God's actions in creating different times. This is a stronger statement of Qohelet's belief that God deliberately conceals his activities than was 3.11, 14, although he will make a similar point at 8.17, and it is difficult to know how much we should read into it. Reduced to the absurd, Qohelet's claim might seem to imply that all history is geared to a concealment of divine purpose, or we might suggest alternatively that the claim itself is a sort of paradox, displaying human knowledge of the divine activity designed to prevent such knowledge. It might be wiser, though, not to press the matter too far, or to claim that the good and bad times both occur *only* because God wishes to curtail human insight into the future. Although he has begun with a call to consider God's actions, Qohelet's interests here, as elsewhere, are not in discerning the motives of God so much as in establishing the situation of humans.

7.13] Pinker, 'The Principle of Irreversibility', argues that here and in 1.15 Qohelet's chief concern is with the fact that things cannot be reversed, because it is in the nature of the world, as it has been created by God, that things will move ever onward. Correspondingly he understands that the 'he' here is not God, and that the question is asking 'who can restore what one deforms?' (402). That is not a natural reading of the text, and I doubt that it suits the context, which is going to introduce the idea of God making days (Pinker sees the verse as stand-alone, so that does not concern him). He probably is correct, though, that we should not think of 'bending' and 'straightening' simply in terms of creating and correcting problems, and the issue here is that humans cannot alter what God has enacted. It is because we can change nothing that, although we should accept the good, we should not simply reject the bad, but consider its significance.

Most of the ancient versions understand the reference here to be to people, not things, although they variously describe the condition of these people. Symmachus talks of them as 'cut short' or 'punished' by God, and Jerome of them being 'overturned', but G talks of deformation, and they probably all draw this understanding ultimately from something like the interpretative tradition presented in the Targum. According to this, God has distinguished some individuals, by giving them physical characteristics such as blindness, lameness, and curvature of the spine—and nobody but God can alter those characteristics. The Hebrew itself can certainly be read that way, and the approach is of interest for the evidence it offers into understandings of physical impairment. It has not, however, proved popular among modern commentators, largely because there seems no place here for such a remark, whereas the idea of God bending *things* can be connected with what follows.

7.14] Jerome notes an interpretation that makes this verse much more conventional: we should do good now, in the good times, so that in the evil day of judgment we may be free simply to look on (as the wicked are punished). This is the understanding of Rashi, and Ginzberg, 'Die Haggada', 35, notes that a similar interpretation is attributed in Jewish sources (the Pesikta and Midrash Rabbah) to R. Aḥa, leading him to wonder if the *ecclesia* in which Jerome claims to have heard it expounded was actually a synagogue rather than a church. Jerome, in any case, though, rejects this reading.

Notes

7.13 achievement of God] As at 5.5; 8.17; and 11.5, G (cf. Hie, V) has plural τὰ ποιήματα, 'the works', where M has singular מעשה. σ' is attested by Jerome as *disce opera dei, quia*, 'learn about the works of God, for', and *opera* is also plural. Although possible, it is less certain here than in 5.5 that this represents a Hebrew variant, and it may be interpretative or translational; see the note at 5.5, and the very similar case discussed at 8.17.

Here, as in 8.17, the expression is followed by כי, and the usage in that verse suggests that the particle there is specifying the achievement. Likewise here, we should probably understand the literal sense to be 'the achievement of God, that...', but this is awkward in English unless we change the subsequent question to a statement that 'no-one can straighten' (cf. σ', V, below), and so I have left כי untranslated. It is sometimes understood differently as an emphatic 'surely' or 'indeed' (so Schoors).

7.13 who can straighten what he has bent?] The vocabulary is similar to that of 1.15, which described not the achievements of God, as such, but all the achievements achieved beneath the sun: on the sense, and on the rendering of לתקן by Hie *adornare*, see the corresponding notes there; G here uses κοσμῆσαι (contrast ἐπικοσμηθῆναι at 1.15), and so has a clearer sense of 'setting in order'. The most interesting feature of the versions, though, has been addressed in the commentary, above. While Jerome gives the reading of σ' in Latin as *nemo poterit corrigere, quod ille imminuit*, 'no-one will be able to set right what he has impaired', the Greek ὃν ἐκόλασεν is preserved separately for *quod ille imminuit*, and that verb has a more precise sense of 'cutting short' or 'punishing'. This suggests that Symmachus, like T and like Jerome himself in the body of his commentary, understands Qohelet to be referring specifically to *people* affected by God, which is an idea found also in La, Hie, and G τίς δυνήσεται τοῦ κοσμῆσαι ὃν ἂν ὁ θεὸς διαστρέψῃ αὐτόν, 'who will be able to set straight anyone whom God deforms (him)?'.[2]

---

[2] La is attested here as *quoniam quis poterit ornare eum quem deus euerterit*, 'for who will be able to commend/adorn him whom God has overthrown', and probably provides the basis for Hie *quoniam quis poterit adornare quem deus peruerterit*, 'for who will be able to adorn him whom God has overturned'. See

S makes the sense passive (and this is perhaps an error inspired by 1.15), but ܠܡܢ ܕܡܕܘܕ ܗܘ *lmn dmdwd hw*, 'whom he is made crooked', also takes the reference to be to people, not things more generally. This understanding finds one particular expression in V (perhaps inspired by σ'; cf. Cannon, 194): *quoniam nemo possit corrigere quem ille despexerit*, 'for no-one can correct him whom he has despised', but a rather different one in T, which takes the verse to be talking specifically about people who are marked out in the world by their various sorts of physical impairments (including curvature of the spine, which is probably what has provoked this interpretation). Such understandings broadly correspond to the treatment of 1.15 in T, Hie, V, although T there viewed 'crookedness' in terms of rebelliousness.

7.14 day of good things] The expressions here are lit. 'day of goodness' and 'day of badness'. The terms טובה and רעה could embrace, e.g., notions of prosperity (e.g. 5.10), benefit (e.g. 9.18) or pleasure (e.g. 4.8), and their opposites, but the scope of each is so wide that it would be wrong to confine the reference to any particular such idea: these are really just days or periods during which whatever good things happen or persist seem to outweigh any bad things, or *vice versa*. In some Greek and Coptic sources, this phrase is read with the previous verse; see Gentry, and Diebner and Kasser, *Hamburger Papyrus Bil. 1*, 290-91.

7.14 live the good life] Lit. 'live in good' or 'be in good'. A similar sense for בטוב is found in Job 21.13; 36.11, where one 'completes one's days in good'; cf. also Pss 25.13; 103.5; Prov 11.10. For M היה, G, and α', θ' according to Syh, have clearly read חיה, which is rendered as ζῆθι, 'live'. This is more in line with those other uses of בטוב, although M is supported by the other ancient versions, including σ' *in die bono esto* (ἔσο) *in bono diem uero malum intuere*, 'in the good day be in good, but think about the bad day' (the verb is attested in Greek, the rest offered in Latin by Jerome). As Euringer observes, however, the sense is much the same whichever reading we follow.

7.14 but think about a day of bad things] Lit. 'and/but look into a day of badness', but there is an alternative reading, 'and in a bad day, look!' The text of G offered by Rahlfs, καὶ ἐν ἡμέρᾳ κακίας ἰδέ, 'and in a day of badness, look', is based on Syh and the Origenic manuscripts. Most manuscripts of G have καὶ ἰδε ἐν ἡμέρᾳ κακίας ἰδε, 'and look in a day of badness, look'. Euringer and Goldman, among others, suggest that this is a conflation of two renderings, each of which placed ἰδέ in a different position, and on that reckoning G* was probably καὶ ἰδε ἐν ἡμέρᾳ κακίας,

Berger, 'Notice', 40; Leanza, 'Le tre versione', 93. Commenting on the next verse, however, Jerome apparently cites this as *quis poterit adornare* quod *peruerterit deus*, 'for who will be able to adorn *what* God has overturned'; the manuscripts offer no evidence that this is simply a textual error, and Jerome is perhaps generalizing the point.

with the second ἰδέ appearing through assimilation to a text that had the order found in M. Given the preference of G for retaining the word-order of the Hebrew, it seems likely that the translator read וראה ביום רעה rather than the ובים רעה ראה of M, and it is not impossible that knowledge of such a reading also informed the understanding in σ′ (noted above), although the order in σ′ itself matches M.

Hertzberg 1963 raised another possibility, that the double G reading καὶ ἰδὲ ἐν ἡμέρᾳ κακίας ἰδέ is not a conflation of two Greek renderings, but is, rather, based on an original Hebrew text in which רעה had originally appeared twice (presumably וראה ביום רעה רעה), but on the second occasion had become corrupted to ראה (וראה ביום רעה ראה). That original text would then have meant something like 'and consider, on an evil day, evil', which gives a better parallel to the first clause. However, even allowing that there is probably some wordplay between רעה and ראה, which may have affected the word-order, we would expect וראה ביום רעה רעה for a sentence with that sense.

Both explanations of the Greek involve an assumption that a Hebrew text with וראה ביום רעה existed, and the formal difference between this and M is striking (even if, in principle, both could be understood in the same ways). It is difficult to say whether the parallel word-order of the two clauses in M is an argument in favour of or against its originality, and Goldman, in fact, prefers the earlier position for the verb: he understands the original admonition to have been 'be content with a day of badness', or 'consider being content with a day of badness'. That, however, implausibly imbues ראה with a sense that it nowhere else seems clearly to possess and if we were to go for that order, then the text would have to mean either 'look, on a bad day', or 'examine a bad day' (on the significance of ב-, ראה, see the note at 2.1). The reading in M could then plausibly be considered a disambiguation in favour of the former, as well as an alignment with the first clause, while it is difficult to see how the וראה ביום רעה suggested by G might have emerged as a variant: it is not a simple copying error, and, whichever way we understand it, this wording takes the clause out of alignment with the first. Such considerations suggest that Goldman has quite a strong text-critical case here, even if his subsequent interpretation seems forced.

Other factors are more difficult to assess. M is not usually considered awkward at this point, but read in parallel with the first clause, it is commonly taken to mean 'on a bad day, look', with the verb used absolutely. The translator or some early tradent of S (which reads it that way) was apparently disconcerted enough by the lack of an object or כי clause after ראה that they felt obliged to supply an object ܢܦܫܟ *npšk*, 'yourself', which is found in many manuscripts (and which makes bad days a time for self-examination). On the other hand, V *malam diem praecaue*, 'beware in advance of the evil day', adopts the day itself as an object to avoid reading the absolute. The usage is not grammatically problematic, but is unusual enough to have provoked such concerns.

In the end, the real question here is: were ביום טובה and ביום רעה originally supposed to stand as parallel temporal clauses, which is the direction in which the word-order of M most strongly points, or was ביום רעה intended to be the indirect object of ראה, which is the likely implication of G's source-text? One reading gives us, literally, 'in a good time, live in good, and in a bad time, look', the other, 'in a good time live in good, and look into a bad time'. There is nothing much at stake in terms of the overall sense, and the evidence is not overwhelming in either direction, but I am inclined to agree with Goldman that the second is more original, and to think that the author set out not only to play on the sounds of רעה and ראה, but on the various meanings of ביום :ב-. רעה looks like ביום טובה, but syntactically ראה ביום רעה corresponds instead to היה בטוב. A misunderstanding of this has probably led to a 'clarification' in the tradition behind M, with the verb moved so that the two types of day can each stand at the head of a clause. If the order in M is original, on the other hand, it is just possible that the sense suggested by G, 'look into a bad time', was anyway indicated by the expectation of an object for the verb (which is probably what underpins V), and by the implication of the following clause, that the bad day is, in any case, what is to be considered.

7.14 as well] There is no reason to suppose that גם here is emphatic, as e.g., Seow and Goldman suggest, although the suggestion leads them to different translations. The point is surely just that the bad day has been made 'as well as' the good one, and this is similar to the associative usage that we find in, e.g., Ct 7.14. Very few manuscripts of G have a σὺν to reflect the את that follows, and BHQ uses that absence to justify deleting the את. The representation of σὺν in those few manuscripts, however, is unlikely to have been a secondary development, and Gentry considers it G*, so the grounds for deletion seem weak.

7.14 to match the other] Lit. 'in correspondence with that'. לעמת is generally used to express the correspondence or alignment of one thing with another. So, for instance, it is used of Shimei in 2 Sam 16.13 when he walks along a bank, tracking David as he moves on the road below, just as the wheels track the creatures in Ezek 1.20. In Lev 3.9 it is used of cutting meat parallel to the spine, and in Exod 38.18 the dimensions of the screen 'correspond' to those of the hangings. As we saw earlier, Qohelet probably used the term to express the precise correspondence between the man's coming and going at 5.15 (see the note there). It is doubtful that it ever means something so vague as 'close to', although that translation is offered in the lexica, and there is no evidence at all that it can mean 'just as', or 'as well as', which Schoors suggests here. Sir 33.14-15 uses [זה] זה לעמת to indicate the relationship to each other of things that God has made in pairs: evil and good, death and life, sinners and the godly (the Hebrew text is fragmentary, but corresponds to the Greek). Qohelet's meaning is probably similar here: the good and bad days form a matching pair, each corresponding to the other. Compare σ' καὶ γὰρ τοῦτο ἀνάλογον τούτου ἐποίησεν ὁ θεός, 'for God has made this an analogue of that'.

7.14 so that] Qohelet uses על דברת, which we encountered in 3.18, although it had a rather different sense there; we shall encounter it again in the difficult 8.2. With the following -ש, it corresponds to the Aramaic על דברת ד- used in, e.g., Dan 2.30, and this supports the view that it expresses purpose, or less probably consequence. Some scholars prefer to read it as causal, and that sense cannot be excluded altogether, but it is hard to see what Qohelet would then mean here: while God might make matching days as part of the deliberate obfuscation to which 3.11 refers, it is not clear why he would make them in response to human ignorance. σ' ὑπὲρ τοῦ μὴ εὑρεῖν ἄνθρωπον, 'so as to avoid a human finding', probably gets it right (Jerome cites this as *ut non inueniret homo*), but see the next note.

On each occasion when על דברת is used in the book, G renders it in terms of speech, and such translations are, strictly, in line with the translation technique of G. Here, however, περὶ λαλιᾶς, 'about speech', makes so little sense that the translator might seem genuinely to have misunderstood the expression, and his translations in 3.18 and 8.2 offer no affirmation in themselves that he was familiar with it. Those words are followed, however, by ἵνα, 'so that', and if (as seems likely) this translates -על דברת ש-, not just -ש, then we might be dealing with a double translation. The translator resorts rarely to these, so were that indeed the case, it might indicate not just an understanding of the expression's proper sense, but an awareness of interpretations based on finding a secondary implication in דברת. It is striking, from that point of view, that T here elicits a reference to speech by introducing an idea of God acting 'to admonish' (לאוכחא) humans. It would be hard to claim, however, that G itself explicitly imposes any such interpretation, and the text here merely means something like 'God has made this one corresponding to that one concerning/with regard to speech, so that the human might not find'—which is vague and confusing in itself, but keeps open the option of a secondary interpretation. I doubt we should identify any similar manoeuvre in 3.18 or 8.2: the sense required here, 'so that' (see the note at 3.18), would very plausibly have been familiar to the translator from its use in the Aramaic text of Daniel, but that sense would not fit the context of those other verses, and he apparently did not know the sense 'concerning' that is adopted for them by most modern commentators.

Hie *ad loquendum*, 'for speaking', is based on G, and probably understands it to suggest that God has contrived days evocative of each other when humans come to speak of them: any complaint about one day is therefore offset by praise for another (which suits Jerome's broader understanding of the verse); Jerome maintains that understanding in V, but drops the explicit reference to speech. S also mentions speech, but seems simply to be following the Hebrew (or less probably G) verbatim.

7.14 anything after him] σ' κατ' αὐτοῦ μέμψιν, '(so that a human may not find) against him a ground for complaint', is imitated in V *ut non inueniat homo contra eum iustas querimonias*, 'so that a human may not find against him just complaints' (cf. Cannon, 194). This understanding has probably not arisen simply from a construal of דברת in terms of speech, but from an interpretation of 'find anything' as 'find anything against'. This gives a nice sense, and although it is not compatible with any normal meaning of אחריו in Hebrew, Burkitt (in 'Is Ecclesiastes a Translation?', 24) has suggested that it is also the intention here of S ܕܠܐ ܢܫܟܚ ܒܪܢܫܐ ܡܕܡ ܒܬܪܗ *dlʾ nškḥ brnšʾ mdm btrh*, which is literally 'so that the human will not find something after him'. He argues that the Syriac expression ܐܫܟܚ ܒܬܪ *škḥ btr*, lit. 'find after', means to find someone guilty or responsible, so that S here would in fact mean just what σ' supposes the Hebrew to mean. This, he goes on to claim, is also the intended sense: an expression in Aramaic, in his view the original language of the book, corresponds to the Syriac usage, but has been rendered too literally in the Hebrew.

Setting aside the question of Aramaic translation into Hebrew, which is Burkitt's main interest, the general claim has some force, although it is questionable whether 'find something after somebody' would have been understood widely even in Syriac to mean 'find a charge against somebody' without explicit contextualization, let alone in other forms of Aramaic.[3] Furthermore, S always elsewhere uses ܒܬܪܗ *btrh*, 'after him', for אחריו (3.22 and 6.12) and ܐܫܟܚ *škḥ*, 'find', for מצא (3.11; 7.24, 26-29; 8.17; 9.10, 15; 11.1; 12.10), so this is precisely how we would expect it to render the Hebrew here: the translator might conceivably have understood the original in terms of the Syriac idiom, but there is no indication that he is trying to impose that sense. Unless the idiom was used more widely in Aramaic, moreover, then it is unlikely to be the basis for the translation in σ', and that more probably rests on a reading of מאומה as מאום, a spelling of מום, 'blemish', 'fault', found in Job 31.7 and Dan 1.4 (so, e.g., Podechard, Seow).[4]

---

[3] In the Old Syriac text of Lk 23.14, which Burkitt offers as his prime example, Pilate's ܡܕܡ ܠܐ ܐܫܟܚܬ ܒܬܪܗ *wmdm lʾ ʾškḥt btrh*, 'and I have found nothing after him', does indeed mean that he has found no charge that will stick from among those laid against Jesus, while in the next verse ܡܕܡ ܕܫܘܐ ܠܡܘܬܐ ܠܐ ܐܫܬܟܚ ܒܬܪܗ *wmdm dšwʾ lmwtʾ lʾ ʾškḥ btrh* similarly means 'and nothing deserving of death has been found after him'. In other examples, however, from the Peshitta texts of Dan 6.4; Jn 19.4; and Acts 28.18, 'charges' or 'evidences' are mentioned specifically, so although it is clear that 'find after' can be used of finding something to charge someone with, it is only really in the Old Syriac that it seems to have this force without the explicit use of an appropriate noun.

[4] A different, more complicated explanation is offered by Schoeps, in 'Symmachusstudien III', 43-45, who notes the citation of this verse in *b. Ḥagiga* 15a by the 'heretical' R. Elisha ben Abuyah (known as אחר; he was the teacher of R. Meir, who was mentioned in the Introduction [192 n. 212], for his love of Greek tunes). That citation is used to justify an assertion that God has created the wicked as well as the righteous, Gehenna as well as Eden, and that every person begins life with a share in each of the latter, gaining or losing each share as they become more wicked or righteous. Schoeps reads this as gnosticism, and the translation by Symmachus as an apologetic reaction against such ideas. Both claims are a

Burkitt's observations have been taken in a different direction by some other scholars. For Burkitt himself, the Hebrew accidentally reflected an Aramaic original, but his examples of the Old Syriac usage appeared a year later in the commentary by Williams, who proposed (differently, and apparently independently) that they illustrated an idiom to be found in both Syriac and Hebrew, which had been understood correctly by σ'. Odeberg subsequently took both Burkitt and Williams to be making the same claim, and accepted the idea of a Hebrew idiom 'find fault' in his own commentary. Later, Driver, 'Problems and Solutions', 230, raised the same possibility again; it has been accepted by, e.g., Whitley, and has been explored more recently in Schoors, *The Preacher* I, 118-19, although it is ultimately rejected by Schoors in his commentary. The most that can be said in response to this idea is that, if such an idiom did indeed arise in Hebrew (whether independently of the Syriac or connected to it through some lost link elsewhere in Aramaic), then this is the only place that we find it, and an interpretation in those terms is accordingly hard to justify.

Even ignoring the Syriac usage altogether, however, some commentators have found it possible still to seek a reference to God in the suffix pronoun of אחריו. Sargent, perhaps unconsciously, echoes a theme in some early Jewish exegesis of the passage when he insists that 'The last clause may best be understood if "Him" is applied to God: man cannot go beyond or behind God's ways and find any basis for criticism of His actions'—an interpretation that Schoors, *The Preacher I*, 119, finds 'very attractive'.[5] Since commentators do not normally find a similar reference when אחריו is used in 3.22 and 6.12, such readings are clearly driven by considerations of context rather than consistency of usage: it is harder to see the creation of good and bad days as a way to conceal the future than as a way to conceal God's actions. If we go down that route, however, the pronoun really has to refer not actually to God but to his 'ways' or some such, making the expression more awkward than at first it seems.

---

stretch, but the passage includes R. Meir's interpretation also (God created hills as well as mountains, rivers as well as seas), and nicely illustrates the way in which decontextualization of the words permitted the rabbis to see a much more general reference here to the nature of creation.

[5] In a way that is reminiscent of σ', Rashi observes here that the human 'will find nothing after him to complain about the Holy One', which may likewise be connecting מאומה with מאום, but which is more probably just an extrapolation from his understanding that the suffix pronoun on אחריו refers to God; a similar understanding leads Rashbam to suggest that humans will find out nothing about God beyond his righteousness and justice, and this is a theme found elsewhere in Jewish interpretation of the passage (see the citations in Williams).

7.15-22

(7.15) I have seen both, in my days of illusion: there may be a righteous man who perishes through his righteousness; and there may be a wicked man who lasts long through his wrongdoing.

(7.16) Do not be very righteous, and do not show yourself wise more than needs be: why give yourself a shock?

(7.17) Do not be very wicked, and do not become obtuse: why die when it is not your time?

(7.18) It is good that you grab this, and do not hold your hand back from that, for someone who fears God will get away with both.

(7.19) Will wisdom come to the aid of a wise man more than would ten men of authority who are in the city?

(7.20) For there is no person so righteous on earth that he can do good and not sin.

(7.21) Also, do not apply your mind to all the words that people say, in case you hear your underling being rude about you: (7.22) for your mind knows also the many occasions when you too have been rude about others.

Commentary

It is in these verses that Qohelet seems to offer his greatest provocations to orthodoxy: the righteous may be killed by righteousness, so we should not ourselves be too righteous—or wise—and nobody is so righteous that they never sin. Commentators have been inclined, understandably, to offer qualifications to the claims, and to see Qohelet as speaking about self-righteousness, or about excessive attachment to unnecessary religious practices and outward forms. No such qualifications are offered in the text itself, however, and it is hard to pair such specific understandings with the wrongdoing and wickedness of which Qohelet also speaks.

At one level, we must allow that Qohelet is counselling a sort of realism. It is undeniably true that what is right may not always be what is safe, and that claims around punishment of the wicked can often ring hollow. Qohelet will return to the latter point in 8.10-15, when he identifies the problem that condemnation may be deferred, and a little later in 9.2 he will emphasize his confidence that all humans are going to the same end, including both righteous and wicked. Although he does not spell out his presuppositions here, therefore, we may say with some confidence that Qohelet's advice about righteousness and wickedness is based on two considerations: that actions do not attract immediate reward or punishment, but that any reward or punishment will occur before one dies. Accordingly, there can be no reward for an action, however righteous, that has already led to one's death, and compensation for any suffering may be deferred for a long time. On the other hand, the wicked are not a model to emulate: they will be punished in the end, and die before their time, and anyone who thinks they will get away with it is wrong. If we are to be judged eventually and in the round for our actions (as everyone must be, presumably, if no-one is wholly righteous), a little wickedness may be offset, but it is dangerous either to be very wicked, or to take risks for the sake of being righteous.

Of course, Qohelet's calculations here are not those of everybody. In particular, he shows no interest in the idea of doing what is right *because* it is right, or in avoiding evil on principle, so that here, as often, he seems unusually pragmatic and materialistic. This applies less, of course, to his treatment of wisdom and folly alongside righteousness and wickedness, and although the advice against excessive wisdom is, in its way, no less provocative, it is in line both with the experience recounted in 2.15 and, more broadly perhaps, with the suggestions of the epilogue in 12.11-12. After all that, however, it is still somewhat surprising that 7.18 offers fear of God as a path to survival—an idea that Qohelet will present again in 8.12-13. His point is probably not that piety will make up for any behaviour, or that we are judged on faith and not actions—even though such ideas might naturally be attractive to some modern Christian readers, and even though they might offer some relief to the tension between Qohelet's determinism and his insistence on the reality of divine judgment. Especially in the light of the way he discussed interactions with God early in ch. 5, it seems more likely that Qohelet is talking about the influence of such fear on our behaviour: we should not endanger ourselves for the sake of being righteous, but if avoidance of divine anger is always a factor in our decisions, then we will generally end up acting in our own interests. To put that another way, Qohelet is not interested here in the morality of actions, as such, but pragmatically concerned with the divine response to them.[1]

Two sayings stand out in all this. In 7.19 Qohelet either praises or disparages wisdom: it is not entirely clear which, but the point seems out of place in either case, and it is difficult to see how the next verse might be serving as an explanation for it. A number of commentators have accordingly sought to move the saying, and Fox, for example, places it after 7.12. The issue raised in 7.21-22, on the other hand, seems not just out of place, but wholly irrelevant. Sitting in between them, 7.20 has caused fewer concerns, because it more clearly does relate to what has just been discussed. It does not follow from the statements and admonitions that precede it, however, and I think that we have to treat 7.19-22 as a sequence of sayings that are unrelated to each other, but each offer a different sort of comment on what has come before, picking up a separate aspect. So, we should not be too wise, and wisdom is not that powerful anyway; we should not be too righteous, because, anyway, nobody is righteous all the time (and God cannot therefore expect it). More generally, if we behave as Qohelet suggests, then we shall be judged by others, and must learn to shrug that off. I would not want to press any of those connections too far, however: although he has actually grouped much of it around themes, Qohelet has presented his material so far in ch. 7 largely in the style of a sayings collection, and these last few points emphasize that character before he returns to memoir in 7.23.

---

[1] Lasater, 'Submission', 89, puts this in rather different terms: fearing God 'involves adopting a stance distinguishable from ethical principles of righteousness and wickedness'; the fear itself is to be understood as a posture of subordination. Speaking later about 8.12-13, he notes the situation of 'fearing God' in 'considerations of how to respond properly to authority, which, on its own, Qohelet may not deem an essentially moral issue, but a more strictly relational one', and describes it as 'a matter of acting in accordance with what someone is as a human creature, and therefore a subject, of God' (91-92). This is, I think, a very helpful way of understanding Qohelet's presuppositions, which squares both with the declarations of 6.10-11, and with Qohelet's more general ideas about humanity working for God.

7.15-18] The Hebrew of 7.15, literally 'in his righteousness' and 'in his wrongdoing', can suggest that these things happened to the righteous and wicked *while* they were righteous and wicked (making it clear that they had not ceased to be what they were), or that their righteousness and wrongdoing were the instruments of their fates (so that they are, in some way, killed or preserved *by* their actions), or, indeed, that things happened *in spite of* their qualities. The Hebrew leaves open all these options (see the note), and we have to understand what Qohelet is claiming retrospectively, after we have seen where he is going with the issue. From that perspective, I take his initial observation to be in fact that the righteous can be harmed *by* their righteousness: righteous actions are not always inherently safe, whether they involve climbing a tree to rescue a cat, or fighting for a worthy cause. This is recognized, of course, in the important later Jewish principle of פיקוח נפש (commonly rendered as *piquach nefesh*), which prioritizes the preservation of human life above obedience to most laws, and the concomitant allowance that one 'may transgress and avoid being killed' (יעבור ואל יהרג; see, e.g., *b. Sanhedrin* 74a). The wrongs of the wicked, conversely, could be understood as beneficial to them, perhaps in defence of their own lives or prosperity, but the fact that Qohelet will go on to associate wickedness with death probably implies that he intends 'there may be a wicked man who lasts long *even in* his wrongdoing'. In any case, though, if someone ignores the first observation in particular, and relies heavily on their righteousness or wisdom to protect them, they may be in for a nasty surprise. Correspondingly, I am inclined to think that 'righteous' and 'wicked' are understood in quite a general way. It is sometimes suggested that such vocabulary (and the 'fear of God' that follows in 7.18) would have been associated especially with adherence to the Law, and such a connotation is indeed possible (cf. 12.13)—but it is questionable whether it would ever have been confined to such a reference.

Qohelet's response to his observations has provoked much reaction. He begins with a blunt admonition not to be very righteous, and then goes on to warn against demonstrating 'excessive' wisdom. The pairing itself deserves attention, not least because wisdom itself was not mentioned in 7.15, where Qohelet said nothing about the wise suffering through their wisdom, and he is leveraging his observations about righteousness and wickedness to talk in parallel about the rather different phenomena of wisdom and folly.[2] In 7.16, he also talks about them in different ways, with the simple 'do not be very righteous' followed by a warning in which the form of the verb used probably connotes not 'being' wise but demonstrating wisdom—or even showing it off—and in which 'very' is replaced by 'excessively' or 'pointlessly' (echoing the language of 2.15). In part the differences are probably stylistic, and 7.16-17 uses a chiastic structure which is hard to reproduce in English ('do not be...do not...do not...do not be...'—many commentators see this as just part of a very complicated structure, although they differ over details). We may note also that the advice against being or becoming a fool is not qualified by 'very' or 'excessively' at all. There probably is some implicit acknowledgment, all the same, that simply 'being' very wise does not pose the same risks as being very righteous, since wisdom is expected to identify dangers, not lead one to defy them in pursuit of principle.

This in itself makes it unlikely, I think, that we can think of wisdom and folly as the primary topic of these verses, despite various efforts to deduce from the structure, presentation or content, that Qohelet has no real concern with ethics here (helpfully summarized and rejected in Choi, 'Golden Mean', 358-60). Such efforts tend to discount the difficulty of Qohelet's warning against righteousness, but it seems that, if anything, wisdom and folly are piggy-backing on a discussion about righteousness and wickedness here, not *vice versa*, and they do not fit entirely comfortably either with the initial observation in 7.15 or with Qohelet's conclusion in 7.18. They do, however, suit very well the broader context of this chapter, with its concerns about wisdom, which is probably why Qohelet has drawn them in here. Righteousness and wickedness, on the other hand, correspond to a theme that is prominent in the sort of advice literature from which Qohelet has borrowed his format for much of ch. 7. Prov 10.2, for instance, claims that righteousness delivers from

---

[2] There is little reason to suppose that the righteous and the wise are equivalent for Qohelet, as, e.g., Lavoie, 'Force meurtrière', 74-75, suggests. When they appear together later in 9.1, it is because righteousness and wisdom are presented there as the two motivations that might lead humans to evaluate different behaviours with a view to adopting them, not because they are synonymous. The two qualities both appear frequently in Hebrew advice literature, and they are not unrelated in such texts—but they are also not usually equated.

death (while the treasures of wickedness offer no benefit), and the next verse that God prevents the righteous from starving; in that chapter, similar ideas are expressed also in vv. 6, 16, 24, 25, 27, and 30, with other sayings expressing the same sentiments in different terms. That concentration is untypical, perhaps, but the point is reinforced across the following chapters as well, that righteousness leads to life, and wickedness to death, and it is this point that Qohelet flatly contradicts here. The issue crops up also in other, related literature, and is a major theme of Ps 37; without speculating too precisely about the texts the author might have known, it seems worth noting, indeed, that even Qohelet's observation in 7.15 finds a counterpart in Ps 37.25, where the psalmist famously claims never to have seen the righteous forsaken. In short, then, 7.15-18 confront a claim about righteousness that is very common in some of the literature that Qohelet has been imitating in ch. 7: these verses reject, or at least heavily qualify that claim, and take the opportunity also to draw in wisdom—effectively undermining the assertion of 7.12, just a few verses earlier, that wisdom itself sustains life.

The advice that Qohelet actually offers has generally been characterized in either of two ways: he is admonishing the audience against excessive, perhaps false pretensions to righteousness and wisdom (sometimes associated with particular groups or religious movements), or he is commending moderation, and the steering of a course between the extremes of righteousness and wickedness, wisdom and folly. Both interpretations are old, and both are represented in Jerome's commentary, which summarizes the first neatly in terms of recognizing somebody to be *plus iustum...quam iustum est*, 'more proper than is proper', and which explicitly links the second to philosophical ideas. Both also have their modern advocates, with Whybray, in particular, arguing strongly for the first (in 'Qoheleth the Immoralist'), and a number of other scholars taking the verses specifically to embody the Greek idea of a 'golden mean' (see, e.g., Schwienhorst-Schönberger, 'Via Media').[3]

The first relies heavily, however, on imbuing certain terms here with particular connotations. Whybray has to claim, for instance, that 'righteous' must mean 'someone who calls themselves righteous',

---

[3] Brindle, 'Righteousness and Wickedness', 243-51, offers an overview of the scholarship, and see also Kotzé, 'Jung, Individuation, and Moral Relativity', 511-12.

via a very questionable argument (see the notes), and while it is true that the form of the verb used for being wise here can be more about displaying than possessing the attribute, it does not in itself insinuate that the display is of something unreal. The interpretation is appealing to scholars who, for one reason or another, struggle to accept that Qohelet might actually be deprecating righteousness, but it reads into the Hebrew an implication that simply is not there, and (as Whybray himself appreciates) makes it impossible to read 7.16-17 as a continuation of 7.15, despite the obvious links between them.[4]

It is harder to say whether Qohelet is advocating the pursuit of moderation as such, although that interpretation fits more readily with his actual words. Again, there is a danger of reading too much into the warning against 'excessive' wisdom: the qualification 'very' for righteousness and wickedness, along with the complete absence of a qualification for 'fool', do not point strongly toward him having some ideal level in mind for all of these qualities. When he generalizes in 7.18, furthermore, Qohelet shows no apparent interest in moderation or in finding some balance, but seems to suggest rather that the best course is to seize upon one thing or another without regard to whether it is righteous, wicked, wise, or foolish, and to rely instead on fearing God. Whether or not it is true that Qohelet views righteousness and wickedness as poles between which something else may lie, rather than as absolutes between which one must choose (cf. Schwienhorst-Schönberger, 'Via Media'; Mazzinghi, 'Giudaismo ed Ellenismo', 106; Chango, *L'Ecclésiaste*, 56), his language is not that of compromise or mediation, but of eclecticism (so Lohfink, who talks also of a 'situation ethics'). There may be some compatibility, then, with ideas about a golden mean, but, as Fox observes, Qohelet does not talk about mid-points or moderation, and is highly unlikely to be expressing that idea deliberately.[5]

---

[4] For Lux, 'Lebenskompromiß', who follows a similar line, the chiastic structure of 7.16-17 is used to define the particular types of 'righteous' and 'wicked' who are affected in 7.15 as the excessively self-righteous and foolishly wicked. This seems very contrived in any case, but it is still not apparent how such an interpretation then deals with the problem of the wicked man who prolongs life.

[5] Horton, 'Koheleth's Concept of Opposites', helpfully sketches the differences between what Qohelet says and the ideal mean as it is classically set out

A similar idea about fearing God will be propounded in 8.12-13, where God-fearing is contrasted with wickedness, but Qohelet again expresses confidence that those who fear God will be alright. It is difficult to get to the bottom of what he means by this (and, as often, how it is supposed to fit in with his determinism), but it seems likely that Qohelet is advocating a certain pragmatism as more important than conformity to categories or principles: people may have to make self-interested choices, but they will survive if they factor God's likely reaction into their calculation of self-interest. Although the Midrash to 7.17 is a little obscure, moreover, it probably draws out a point that is vital to understanding how this works: any single choice can have immediate consequences that are good or bad, and may affect God's attitude, but God's judgment will be based on the accumulation of our choices. If we do something bad one day because it protects us, it may still be outweighed by the good that we have chosen to do on other days. The righteous suffer because God does not arrive instantly to punish or protect—which is precisely the issue that Qohelet is going to confront in ch. 8—but the positive side to this is that our misdemeanours will not instantly destroy us. The sensible path is to try to stay on the right side of God, in order to defer or avoid the long-term destruction that will come from not doing so, but in the meantime to do whatever it takes to avoid the short-term destruction which can render his judgment irrelevant. To spell this out, then, righteousness can bring immediate danger, and wickedness immediate security—but wickedness and folly are both ultimately punished. We should behave as well or badly as each situation requires, to keep ourselves alive, and so should avoid whatever extreme righteousness or excessive displays of cleverness might endanger us in that situation, as well as the extreme wickedness that will weigh heavily in any divine judgment, and the folly that is intrinsically dangerous. We should also always bear in mind that God will judge us—a consideration that will incline us to be good overall, and enable us to avoid forgetting the danger that his judgment poses when we are faced with more obvious problems.

by Aristotle. I doubt, though, that his alternative portrayal of Qohelet's thought is really sustainable. According to this, Qohelet seeks to understand the world in terms of concepts that can be paired and treated as linked or as opposites, but that presentation has at least as much to do, I think, with the conventions of parallelism in Hebrew composition as with any particular way of seeing the world.

If this is indeed the logic behind Qohelet's advice, then that advice is perhaps not so radical as it first seems. Schwienhorst-Schönberger, 'Via Media', 190, draws attention to the interesting situation described in Mal 3.13-21 (ET 3.13–4.3), where the wicked put God to the test and get away with it, so that there is a problem distinguishing between the righteous and wicked. The names of the God-fearing are then written in a book for God, who promises that they will be spared, and the wicked punished at a future time. Qohelet shows no interest in eschatology, as such, and maybe envisages any coming divine action in a different way, but this is very much the same problem of deferred judgment that he addresses here and in ch. 8. However we date the texts (and Schwienhorst-Schönberger sees them as almost contemporary), it is plausible that this problem was quite widely recognized, and that Qohelet is merely carrying to their logical conclusion a set of assumptions that would have been shared by others.

Compressed into a stylized sequence of warnings and questions, though, the nuances are not immediately obvious, and that is probably deliberate: these verses lay the foundations for the crisis that Qohelet is about to face. By connecting wisdom to the issues around righteousness and judgment, the author has contrived to bring his character to a point where he seems to have moved far beyond the curious conventionalism with which the chapter started, and to be imposing serious qualifications on the value both of righteousness, so central to some Hebrew advice literature, and of wisdom itself.

7.19] The first word of the Hebrew has a prefix that can be read in the consonantal text either as a definite article or as the marker of a question. It is commonly read as the former, but 'wisdom' as a general phenomenon is rarely '*the* wisdom' in Hebrew, and I read this verse as a question expressing doubt: if one is in danger, being very wise (cf. v. 16) is probably not going to offer as much help as would having some powerful human support. That support appears to be envisaged in terms of influence and authority, rather than brute strength. If we read an article instead, then Qohelet is affirming that, actually, wisdom is better—which is not impossible, but sits less comfortably with his qualifications of wisdom elsewhere. Heim takes an article to be indicating that Qohelet is talking about '*this* wisdom', that is, the wisdom that he has commended in the previous verses. I am not sure that the precise figure of ten has any significance here: the point is just that this is a substantial group—and, in a general sort of way, it may not be entirely a coincidence that this is the size of the *minyan*, the quorum that would later be required for certain religious activities. Efforts have been made, however, to find a specific historical reference (and there is a useful survey in Vattioni, 'Due note', 157-61). On the face of it, the most plausible of these is adduced by Gordis, who speaks of 'the δέκα πρῶτοι, who governed Hellenistic cities, including largely Jewish cities such as Tiberias (Josephus, *Vita* 13 and 57), perhaps even Jerusalem (*Ant.*, XX, 8, 11)', and a number of other commentators have made this connection. *Vita* 13 and 57, in fact, refer to 'the ten leading men of the council' of Tiberias, who are left to look after some valuable furniture, and *Antiquities* to a delegation of ten leading members of the community. It is not clear in either case that the groups constitute an official body, rather than a group constituted *ad hoc* out of some larger body, but the references do again, at least, suggest a fondness for the number 'ten' in such contexts. Lavoie, 'Force meurtrière', 70-71, rejects this and various other suggestions, in favour of the view that ten here is just a round number, connoting 'a lot'—and he may well be right to do so.

7.20] If 7.19 was talking about the limitations of wisdom, this verse talks in a rather different way about the limitations of righteousness, or perhaps more specifically about the limitations of humans who might aspire to be righteous. In doing so, it injects a note of realism, and suggests that the advice Qohelet has offered is, practically speaking, what everybody is doing anyway: even the most righteous of humans cannot sustain that righteousness on every occasion, and will sometimes opt for something sinful. Kotzé, 'Jung, Individuation, and Moral Relativity', offers a Jungian analysis that is targeted principally at the advice itself, but that highlights the importance within analytical psychology of the individual integrating and embracing the different aspects of the self; Helsel, 'Enjoyment', looks at similar issues from a Freudian perspective. Qohelet is no psychologist, but there is an implicit acceptance in this context that everyone will have good and bad sides, whatever the balance between them, that to strive for perfection is unrealistic, and, consequently, that we need not only to acknowledge the mixture of motives that may drive us, but to recognize more consciously that this works positively to our benefit.

As Lavoie, 'Force meurtrière', 76-77, emphasizes, this is not the only biblical passage to express a sentiment of this sort: Ps 143.2 suggests that no human is righteous in God's sight, while 1 Kgs 8.46 has Solomon, no less, declare that 'there is no human who does not sin'. The latter (repeated in 2 Chr 6.36) is particularly close to 7.20, although shorter: especially if the associations of Ecclesiastes with Solomon are original, it is not impossible that there is a conscious allusion here. Qohelet may, though, simply be elaborating a familiar idea, just as we might declare that 'nobody's perfect'. Tomson, 'Kohelet 7,20', suggests that Rom 3.10 is a mash-up of this verse and material from Ps 14.1-3, which is possible, but difficult to demonstrate: if he is right, this is one of few places where Ecclesiastes has plausibly exercised any influence on the New Testament (and the scarcity of such parallels might itself be an argument against making a link here).

7.21] The reference is apparently to overhearing a servant or slave complaining about their master or mistress—which offers a further insight into the social status of the audience that is presumed here.

7.22] The point is probably that we should not read too much into the sort of mutinous mutterings that we might hear if we follow Qohelet's advice in the preceding verses, since we know how little our frequent complaints about others really mean. The tradition, however, does not speak with one voice here (see the note). The Greek text has become entangled with Aquila's version in the manuscript tradition, but both reflect a Hebrew source slightly different from M, in which the point is apparently that we should not pay too much attention to the words of others, because if we hear our servant complaining about us, then that will hurt our heart over and over. I have preferred to follow the majority M text in my own translation, but this is another place where different readers of the book over the centuries will have encountered rather different messages.

Notes

7.15 both] Or 'everything'. With many commentators, I think it is more likely here that את הכל refers cataphorically to the two situations that follow, than that Qohelet is declaring himself to have seen literally everything. It is also possible, though, that the sense is something like the world-weary English 'I have seen it all (so nothing can surprise me anymore)', as, e.g., Crenshaw, 'Quantitative', 2, suggests.

7.15 my days of illusion] Qohelet used ימי חיי הבלו, 'the days of his life of illusion', at 6.12, and at 9.9 will speak of ימי חיי הבלך, 'all the days of your life of illusion'. It is not clear why he uses the shorter ימי הבלי here, unless it is because he is not talking about the whole span of a life, as in those verses, but only about his time up to the present, or about a previous period of his life. In each place, G characteristically retains the order of the Hebrew, and here talks about ἡμέραις ματαιότητός μου, 'days of my illusion' (α' probably did much the same, judging by the ἀτμοῦ μου, 'of my vapour', that has been preserved), rather than about 'my days of illusion'. This leads Salters, 'Observations on the Septuagint', 171, to complain that the translator has been willing to sacrifice the sense in pursuit of his translation technique, since he had surely recognized the Hebrew construction. However, we should allow, firstly, that, although they found a wider audience subsequently, translations in this style were probably supposed originally to be read in circles with some understanding of common Hebrew usages (not least to facilitate reading the otherwise incomprehensible uses of σὺν), and, secondly, that the Hebrew is, strictly speaking, ambiguous. 'Days of my vanity' would actually be a perfectly natural translation here, and is discouraged principally by the longer usages elsewhere, in which ימי חיי is less likely to mark the span of an individual's הבל.

7.15 through his righteousness...through his wrongdoing] Various different renderings are possible because the preposition -ב has many different meanings. It can be used to indicate circumstance, of course, and sometimes the context demands a sense 'even in this circumstance'. So, for example, in Lev 26.27, אם בזאת לא תשמעו means 'if you do not listen (even) in these circumstances' (cf. Deut 1.32; Ps 27.3; Isa 9.11 ET 9.12; Ezek 16.29—most of these use בזאת), and לא יאמינו בי בכל האתות in Num 14.11 means 'will they not believe me (even) amidst all the signs' (cf. Isa 47.9). Such uses are strongly determined by context, however, and 'in spite of' is not an inherent sense of the preposition. Many commentators have nevertheless understood the context here to demand such a sense, and taken Qohelet to be saying that the righteous person perishes *despite* their righteousness. If that is the intended sense in both places, then it relieves a certain tension between the comment about the wicked surviving, and the subsequent advice that wickedness leads to death, as Piotti, 'Osservazioni su alcuni problemi III', 246-48, argues—but it also leaves the subsequent advice to avoid being very righteous without any obvious basis, as Hertzberg points out.

It may be, alternatively, that בצדקו has been included merely to make it clear that the righteous person did not suffer only after ceasing to be righteous, or slipping up in some way (and so is essentially temporal or circumstantial). It is also possible to take the -ב as instrumental: righteousness is to be treated with caution because it can itself bring trouble—and in 1 Macc. 2.37, the Jews who refuse to fight back on the sabbath speak of dying 'in their innocence', but could as well be claiming to die because of it.[6] This interpretation is favoured by a number of commentators, and it seems to have been adopted, at least in the second part, by σ', which is (partly retroverted from Syh in that second part) τῇ δικαιοσύνῃ αὐτοῦ...και ἔστιν ἄδικος μακρόβιος διὰ τὴν κακίαν αὐτοῦ, '(through) his righteousness...and there is an unjust man long-lived on account of his wickedness' (ms 788 now affirms Field's retroversion κακίαν, discussed at length by Marshall). The other ancient versions stick to 'in' (including α' ἐν δικαιοσύνῃ αὐτοῦ...μακρύνων ἐν πονηρίᾳ αὐτοῦ, 'in his righteousness...prolonging in his wickedness'), and none interprets the preposition adversatively/concessively as 'in spite of'.

Amidst the various arguments, it is important to remember that this is a translational issue: the Hebrew leaves open all these possible meanings, and the implications we find will of necessity reflect our understanding of the relationship between the different elements at play here. Correspondingly, of course, the way we render the preposition should not drive that understanding. Nor, indeed, should any fetish for consistency, and I think the logic at play over the next few verses probably demands that we understand 'by/because of his righteousness' but 'in spite of his wrongdoing'. Like the original audience, however, we can only understand this logic as the text unfolds, so I have adopted a translation that is, I think, as neutral as possible (although it leans toward the causal).

Jerome reports a Jewish interpretation that identifies the righteous and wicked in this verse and at 8.14 with the sons of Aaron in Lev 10 and King Manasseh.

7.15 lasts long] The verb is used reflexively with לו in 8.12 and with ימים as its object in 8.13, but appears to be used absolutely here, as in, e.g., Prov 28.2, so the sense is not so much of actively prolonging his days, as simply of enduring. On the absolute use, see Paul, 'Psalm 72:5', 352 n. 9, which discusses this passage. This is the sense of S ܕܓܪ d'gr, 'who endures', which Gordis, 140, considers to be an inner-Syriac error for ܕܓܕ d'gd, from ܢܓܕ ngd, 'stretch out, prolong', although he does not say why.

---

[6] Although he accepts this understanding, Dahood, 'Qoheleth and Northwest Semitic Philology', 358-59, speaks rather of a causal usage for the preposition, identifying possible instances in Phoenician and Aramaic. 'Causal' may indeed be more accurate than 'instrumental' here, but Piotti, 'Osservazioni su alcuni problemi III', 244, notes analogous uses in biblical Hebrew, e.g., Gen 18.28; Neh 10.1, and we need not look so far afield.

7.16 be very righteous] The subsequent יותר has an implication of excess, but הרבה (which Qohelet uses often) does not, and there is no linguistic justification for the 'overmuch' of RSV, or similar translations in other versions and commentaries. Before acknowledging this, Whybray, 'Qoheleth the Immoralist', 191-96, makes much of the fact that Qohelet uses אל תהי צדיק here, rather than the simple verbal expression אל תצדק, and claims that this must mean 'do not be a צדיק'. Since there is no defined group of צדיקים, he goes on, this must in turn imply 'do not be a self-styled צדיק', allowing him to understand the admonition in terms of avoiding self-righteousness—a sense that many commentators have sought to find here. The logic of the last jump is questionable in the extreme: if anyone called a צדיק must of necessity be open to criticism as 'self-styled' and 'self-righteous', then much of the Hebrew Bible needs re-interpretation, and that is a problem that confronts any reading of this verse in terms of self-righteousness. More immediately, though, Qohelet's avoidance of the verb צדק is very simply explained: that verb, which is not especially common, rarely if ever means 'be righteous' in a general way (Job 15.14 and 22.3 are among the few potential exceptions). Rather, it means 'be in the right', and if Qohelet advised אל תצדק, then he would be saying 'do not be in the right', instead of 'do not be righteous', which is a very different matter. Add to this the fact that אל תהי צדיק provides a stylistic balance with אל תהי סכל in the next verse—which could not be expressed using a verb—and there seems no good reason to seek some hidden or implicit meaning.

Other attempts to get around the perceived difficulty of the verse tend to involve simple assertion. Seow suggests, for instance, that the expression is equivalent to אל תצטדק in Sir 7.5, which he claims has the sense 'do not flaunt your righteousness' (although the hithpaʻel could just as well mean 'try to prove your innocence', as in Gen 44.16). If that is what he wanted to say, however, then it is not clear why Qohelet should not simply have used the hithpaʻel, and the construction here is not some sort of periphrasis for that form. There is no basis for supposing that Qohelet is saying or implying anything here other than 'do not be very righteous'—which is precisely how his words are understood in all the ancient translations except T (which introduces יתיר, 'excessively', to match the יתיר [= M יותר] later in the verse) and perhaps σ', which uses πλέον, apparently to give a sense 'become ever more righteous'.

7.16 show yourself wise] The hithpaʻel of חכם is used by the new king of Egypt in Exod 1.10 to characterize his plans to keep the Israelites in check, and means something like 'deal shrewdly' or 'show one's self clever in one's dealings'. This is probably how it has been understood here by G μὴ σοφίζου, 'do not devise cleverly' (which has perhaps given rise to the odd, interpretative *ne quaeras*, 'do not ask questions' of Hie). In Sir 10.26, however, the Hebrew verb is set alongside boasting, and אל תתחכם לעבר חפצך must mean something like 'do not show off your wisdom when you are conducting your business', while in 32.4 the verb is used of showing one's cleverness at the wrong time while at a banquet. It can mean, then, 'show intelligence' or 'show off intelligence', and Qohelet presumably uses the hithpaʿel rather than the qal because he is advising a limit on the demonstration rather than on the acquisition of wisdom.

7.16 more than needs be] Lit. 'much' or 'excessively', but note 2.15 למה חכמתי אני אז יותר, 'why was I pointlessly wise back then', where the force of יותר was to suggest not that Qohelet's wisdom was excessive in some way, but that it was redundant, ultimately offering him no advantage over the fool. On the spelling, see the note at 7.11.

7.16 why give yourself a shock?] Or 'be shocked'. On the translation of למה as 'lest' in G, S Hie, V here and in the next verse, see the note on 'why' at 5.5.

The verb שמם is used in the qal of being abandoned or isolated, but also of being shocked by someone or something. Here it is usually thought that we are dealing with a hithpaʿel in which the preformative ת has been assimilated (GKC §54 c; J-M §53 e), although תשומם has also been parsed as from a rare hippaʿel stem (see Schoors, *The Preacher* I, 45)—and the disappearance of the ת might be no more than the consequence of a scribal error.[7] In its other biblical uses (Isa 59.16; 63.5; Ps 143.4; Dan 8.27), the hithpaʿel has a similar, perhaps intensified, meaning (Dahood, 'Canaanite-Phoenician', 210-11, adduces a parallel use in Phoenician), and this is reflected in G ἐκπλαγῇς, 'be panic-stricken', Hie and V *obstupescas*, 'be stupefied', and S ܬܬܡܗ *ttmh*, 'be amazed'; σ′ simply elaborates it slightly in ἵνα μὴ ἀδημονῇς περισσῶς, 'lest you be excessively amazed', which either read יותר with this clause or translates it twice. I take this to be the proper understanding, although I have given the form some reflexive force in my translation.

With תצדי ית אורחתך, 'lay waste your ways', however, T imputes to the verb an implication of destruction, and this sense is preferred by a number of commentators and translators (cf. RSV 'destroy yourself'), largely, perhaps, because it offers a closer parallel to תמות in the next verse. That is to miss the point, I think, that premature death is what the wicked and foolish may expect, but that it is likely to come as a surprise to anyone who has invested heavily in their own righteousness or wisdom. More importantly, though, it requires of the verb a sense that, as Podechard emphasizes, it simply does not seem to possess elsewhere, except possibly in the famous expression שקוץ משומם / שקוץ שמם, 'abomination of desolation' of Dan 11.13; 12.11 (cf. Dan 8.13; 9.27). Parsing the verb as hippaʿel rather than hithpaʿel opens up

---

[7] If so, we probably need do no more than restore the missing ת, but Perles, 'Miscellany', 130-31, notes Sir 11.33 תשא למה מום עולם, 'why should you bear a lasting injury?', and wonders if the text here was originally למה תשא מום, 'why bear an injury', corrupted after the omission of the א as a matter of orthography. This is an attractive and plausible suggestion, which deserves to be mentioned more often, but it is speculative, and the text is not seriously problematic as it stands.

the theoretical possibility of a different sense, but it is arbitrary to use this as an excuse to impose one, and does not justify adopting the popular translation (cf. Piotti, 'Osservazioni su alcuni problemi III', 251-53). There may indeed be an implication of destruction here, but the actual reference is to the reaction such destruction will provoke.

7.17 do not be very wicked] S offers an explanation ܕܠܐ ܐܬܣܢܐ ܣܓܝ *dlʾ tstnʾ sgy*, 'so that you may not be very hated'. This has no counterpart in any other version, although it is possible that it was inherited from a Greek or Hebrew source (cf. Kamenetzky, 221). It is unlikely to be original, not least because this verse seems to have been structured to match the last, and it breaks the symmetry, but it is difficult to explain how it arose except, perhaps, as an explanatory gloss.

7.17 obtuse] On סָכָל, see the note at 2.19. G's use of σκληρός, 'hard', to translate סכל is unexpected and very difficult to explain. It is probably an error for ὀχληρός, 'troublesome' (although that has been displaced altogether from the manuscript tradition here), and the untypical rendering suggests that its source-text may have differed from M in some way; see the note at 7.25.

7.17 when it is not your time] α' renders בלא עתך as πρὸ τοῦ καιροῦ σου, 'before your time', and that is clearly the proper sense (the reading is attributed unambiguously to α' by Syh, Field, Marshall, but to σ' in Gentry's edition—this is presumably a typographical error, since he cites Syh in support). There are similar expressions in Job 15.32; 22.16; Sir 30.24, and the first of these uses יומו rather than עתו, while the last refers to premature old age rather than death. We should probably not place too much emphasis, therefore, on the use of עת in relation to death here, or on the idea of some 'proper time' for dying.

7.18 It is good that] The construction here is similar to that used in 5.4, but without the comparative -מ (which makes it difficult, I think, to share the view of Ogden that this is 'a "Better"-proverb'). The clauses introduced by אשר act as the subject of a non-verbal sentence, with טוב as predicate.

7.18 you grab] On the Masoretic pointing of תאחז, see GKC §68 b, J-M §73 f. The initial א is usually quiescent, and the verb treated as weak, but on a few occasions, as here, it retains its pronunciation, and the verb is treated as a strong verb with an initial guttural (cf. Judg 16.3; 1 Kgs 6.10; contrast, e.g., 2 Sam 6.6). Ginsburg, *Writings*, notes a few late manuscripts and printed editions with *šewa* rather than *ḥaṭep-segol* under the א, but the pointing as a strong verb is largely consistent. See also Schoors, *The Preacher* I, 92-93. Ginsburg further notes that many manuscripts and early printed editions connect אשר to the verb with *maqqeph* (cf. Baer, 64).

7.18 this…that] Commentators have identified each זה variously with the righteousness, wisdom, wickedness, and folly mentioned in the preceding verses, but Qohelet is either encapsulating them all into two broad categories, or, I think more probably, speaking loosely of 'one thing and another', rather as we use 'this and that' in English to denote a variety of things; cf., e.g.,

Ps 75.8 (ET 75.7).[8] V *bonum est te sustentare iustum*, 'it is good thing for you to uphold the just', is in line with Jerome's exegesis in his commentary, and is wholly interpretative.

7.18 do not hold your hand back] The את of אל תנח את ידך is absent from a number of manuscripts in the Babylonian tradition and elsewhere (see Miletto; Ratzabi, 'Massoretic Variants', 105; Lavoie and Mehramooz, 'Le Texte hébreu et la traduction judéo-persane', 502), while many other late manuscripts, noted by Kennicott and de Rossi, have a plural ידיך, 'your hands'. No את is used when Qohelet employs the same expression in 11.6, and many witnesses again have a plural there: it is difficult to assess how far the two passages may simply have exerted an influence on each other in the course of transmission, but no significant distinction of sense is involved.

There is a very different problem in the G tradition, where most manuscripts have μὴ μιάνῃς, 'do not defile (your hand)'. It has generally been thought that this is a corruption of μὴ ἀνῇς, 'do not loosen', resulting from dittography which led to ΜΗΜΗΑΝΗC (cf. McNeile, 162), read as a spelling of ΜΗΜΙΑΝΗC (cf. Euringer, 86). This is plausible, and μὴ ἀνῇς is taken to be the original reading by both Rahlfs and Gentry, but no manuscript of G actually has this reading in its main text: three give it as an unattributed marginal reading, and Syh attributes it to θ′. Those witnesses that do not have μὴ μιάνῃς, principally hexaplaric manuscripts, have μὴ ἀφῇς, 'do not release', which Syh attributes to α′ and σ′; this reading probably also lies behind the *dimittas* of Hie (which Rahlfs uses to justify μὴ ἀνῇς in his text). Vinel retains μὴ μιάνῃς, and Goldman wonders whether it might not, in fact, be original in G, and the result of a faulty source-text: he points to the rendering of הזניח by ἐμίανεν in 2 Chr 29.19. That possibility cannot be excluded, but the conventional explanation is somewhat easier. An early displacement of μὴ ἀνῇς in the G tradition does mean, however, that readers of the Greek were generally confronted by a very different admonition.

7.18 for] A few commentators translate כי as emphatic or adversative here, disconnecting the following clause in a way that enables a sense 'even if they do both, the God-fearing will still...' (cf. Mazzinghi, 'Giudaismo ed Ellenismo', 105). If that were the intention, however, the use of כי would be positively misleading, and most scholars rightly understand it to be introducing an explanation.

---

[8] Shnider and Zalcman, 'The Righteous Sage', are right to emphasize that Qohelet would not generally equate wisdom with righteousness. Their own conclusion, that these two qualities themselves constitute the 'this and that', has been advocated from time to time down the ages, and is not so 'arbitrary' as Schoors suggests. It requires, however, both that we treat v. 17 as an almost parenthetical qualification, and that the grasping recommended in this verse involve some implicit limitation—one should be keeping merely 'a grip on the fundamental principles of basic morality' (438)—which is hardly indicated by Qohelet's choice of vocabulary.

7.18 someone who fears God will get away with both] Or possibly 'with everything': see below. In the qal, the verb יצא is normally used intransitively of 'going out', and the fact that it appears to take את כלם as a direct object might make one suspect, on the face of it, that this is actually a hiphʿil ('take/ send out', later 'exclude'), wrongly vocalized in M.[9] The hiphʿil, however, does not yield any obviously meaningful sense in this context, and that is why both the ancient versions and modern commentators have tried to make sense of the verb in the qal. As it stands (see below), G does this by taking 'everything' as something like an accusative of respect: the God-fearer ἐξελεύσεται τὰ πάντα, 'will go out in respect of all things'. σ' is similar, but uses a transitive verb: ὁ γὰρ φοβούμενος τὸν θεὸν διεξελεύσεται (var. διελεύσεται) τὰ πάντα, 'the one fearing God will pass through all things'; Hie *qui timet deum egredietur omnia* can be understood in the same way. Of the other versions, S seems strangest at first glance: ܢܩܦ ܠܟܠܗܝܢ *nqp lklhyn* means 'will stick to all of them'. As is usually recognized, however, ܢܩܦ *nqp* is an error for ܢܦܩ *npq*, 'go out' (see, e.g., Kamenetzky 201; Euringer 86), and the real outliers here are V and T.

The former has *nihil neglegit*, 'neglects nothing', which is probably just an interpretative paraphrase. The latter, however, has נפיק ית ידי חובת כולהון, lit. 'eludes the hands of the duty of all of them', which is the Aramaic form of a rabbinic expression יצא ידי חובתו, perhaps 'escape the clutches of one's obligation', used of discharging commitments. Like that of V, this reading gets around the difficulty that Qohelet seems to be advocating actions then immediately saying that the God-fearing will avoid them, and it is an understanding picked up by Rashi and Rashbam, which has been popularized among modern commentators by Gordis in particular. He translates 'he who reverences God will do his duty by both'. It is commonly understood that this expression has been abbreviated in *m. Megillah* 2:1-2, where יצא and לא יצא are used of the man who succeeds or does not succeed in fulfilling his obligation when reading out the Megillah (so, similarly, 19b:2; see also, e.g., *m. Roš Haššanah* 3:7; 29a:2-5; 32b:24; *m. Berakot* 2:1, 3; *m. Pesaḥim* 115b:6, and compare the use of Aramaic נפיק in *b. Berakot* 53b). The image involved, however, is one of being held to a task until released by accomplishing it properly, and the יצא means, in effect, 'he can go now!', not 'he has done it'. It should also be noted that the expression is used in very specific contexts, in a very specific way. Even if we allow that it might have been known to the earlier writer of Ecclesiastes, it is a considerable stretch to suppose that he would—or could—have used it in this context to express some general sense of doing one's duty. Connecting יצא here with that usage, furthermore, only exacerbates the problem of את כלם. In its long form, the mishnaic expression requires a genitive construction, and in its short form it is used absolutely: the

---

[9] Note the variant יוציא attested in Loevy, *Libri Kohelet*, 23, which has likely been provoked by this expectation.

verb has not simply become a way of saying 'fulfil', and it still cannot take a direct object.[10]

That leaves us only with the option, then, of understanding את כלם as something other than a direct object. It is important first, though, to note that the reading itself is uncertain. As we have seen, G here has just τὰ πάντα, which shows no reflection of the suffix pronoun in M: for את כלם in 2.14 and 9.11, G has τοῖς πᾶσιν αὐτοῖς, with a separate pronoun. There is, similarly, no recognition of the pronoun in σ', Hie or V, although it is rendered in S and T. If G had just read את הכל, however, then we should have expected σὺν τὰ πάντα, as in 3.11; 7.15; 10.19; and 11.5: a simple τὰ πάντα is, instead, consistently the way it renders הכל without את (1.2, 14; 2.11, 16, 17; 3.19, 20; 6.6; 9.1; 12.8). It seems very likely, then, either that there existed a variant Hebrew text which read יצא הכל, or that G is corrupt. The former is more probable, since the only evidence of the latter is an alternative reading, σύμπαντα ταῦτα, which dominates the hexaplaric manuscripts, but which seems likely to be an assimilation toward a text like M (although Syh ܢܦܩ ܟܠ ܡܕܡ *npq kl mdm*, 'goes out [of] everything', supports τὰ πάντα). Within a significant part of the G tradition, the reading τὰ πάντα has led to a further development, whereby it has been taken as the subject of the verb, and φοβούμενος has become φοβουμένοις, so that the text reads 'everything goes out to those fearing God'.[11] It is possible that G's source-text was pushing in a similar direction, and trying to understand 'if he fears God, each will escape', but, especially in that case, the reading is likely to be secondary: either הכל or את כלם has arisen as a deliberate facilitation, not a simple error, and it is difficult to see why anybody would have changed הכל to the much more difficult את כלם of M.

In the end, then, we have to reckon that the text originally read את כלם, but that the את is functioning either as a preposition or to mark an accusative of respect or specification. Seow favours the former, and paraphrases accordingly: 'the "fearer of God" will venture forth in life with both righteousness-wisdom and wickedness-folly', while Lasater, 'Subordination', 86, thinks of going forth 'with' the two admonitions in 7.16-17. Whether or not the verb can convey that sense, however, the preposition would connote assistance or companionship in such a context: its scope is not as wide as the English 'with', and it is doubtful that this could imply setting out 'equipped

---

[10] Crenshaw makes the strange claim that the mishnaic usage is found in Sir 38.17, ושית אבלו כיוצא בו, lit. 'make his mourning as going out in him', but this must be understood in terms of the more fragmentary Sir 10.28, where כיוצא בך must mean something like 'befitting to yourself', in a passage that deals with giving oneself due credit. The expression כיוצא ב- is used to express likeness or similarity in rabbinic Hebrew; cf. the Aramaic כד נפק ב-.

[11] See especially Gentry, 'Hexaplaric Materials', 14-15. McNeile, 121 n. 1, wonders if a scribe had been influenced by Rom 8.28.

with'. Unless we are to allow some sort of personification of the qualities or sayings, therefore, the established prepositional uses probably do not offer a good sense here. There is, to be sure however, something of a grey area in which it is difficult to know whether את is acting as a preposition or as a marker, and I, like G, take Qohelet to be saying that the God-fearer will escape 'in respect of' both this and that. The point is not that they will avoid doing either, but that they will avoid perishing when they do either, and Qohelet is making a statement along the same lines as in 8.12, where the context is very similar.

7.19 will wisdom] The use of the article with חכמה was discussed in the note at 1.13, where I observed that the noun rarely takes an article unless there is a reference to some specific wisdom, rather than to wisdom in general. Here, it is difficult to understand החכמה as an anaphorical reference back to some wisdom that has previously been mentioned, as at 7.12. I take the -ה to be interrogative, in fact, rather than a definite article, which means that Qohelet is expressing doubt rather than affirming the power of wisdom, and this makes it significantly easier to understand the place of the verse in its current context. Because the H of G Η ΣΟΦΙΑ can be read as an article ἡ or as the interrogative ἤ, the Greek, consciously or unconsciously, preserves the ambiguity in this respect of the consonantal Hebrew—which weakens the (anyway questionable) protest of Lavoie, 'Force meurtrière', 58-59, that the reading as interrogative is impossible because none of the versions has taken the text that way.

7.19 come to the aid of] M תעז is from עזז, 'be strong', and is supported by S, Hie, V, and by a reading ἐνισχύσει τὸν σοφόν, 'will strengthen the wise man', which is attributed to α' in two manuscripts, but which Marshall suspects is σ'. In 4QQoh[a], however, we find תעזר, 'help', which is supported by G, mentioned in the body of Jerome's commentary, and probably understood by T (where Joseph's wisdom 'aids' him in becoming wiser than his ten brothers). Both readings are certainly old, but this is the earliest reading attested, and is undoubtedly the better one, despite Goldman's virtual presupposition that it is secondary.[12] In the first place, it is easier to explain the loss of an ר as a simple error than the introduction of an ר as a deliberate change to the sense. In the second, עזר ל-, with the meaning 'come to the aid of' is a common and well-established idiom (e.g., 2 Sam 21.17; 2 Kgs 14.26; Job 26.2), but if we read תעז (and especially if we follow Goldman in vocalizing it as hiphʻil to mean 'make bold', or, in 'Le Texte massorétique', 89-91, 'make presumptuous'), then the -ל of לחכם has to be explained in some other

---

[12] In *BHQ* and 'Le Texte massorétique', 91. The Qumran reading is also questioned, more thoughtfully and less categorically, in Salters, 'Textual Criticism', 56. Salters says that תעזר 'was found in some Hebrew MSS before the scrolls were discovered', which would be extremely interesting, but there is no mention of such a reading in any of the normal sources.

way. It is sometimes understood by scholars who adopt this approach as a rare marker of the accusative, although Dahood, 'Phoenician Background', 274, takes it as comparative ('wisdom is stronger *than* the wise man'). The best explanation in such terms is probably that of, e.g., Krüger (wisdom is stronger *for* the wise man), which makes the strength of wisdom something merely asserted by those who possess it (and I shall argue that -ל has such a force in 9.4), but even this is somewhat awkward. For that reason, the reading might perhaps be described as the *lectio difficilior*—which is the basis on which it is preferred by Lavoie, 'Force meurtrière', 59—but it is not really so in text-critical terms, and the problems do not make תעז, which is easier to explain as an error, a better reading than תעזר, which fits more easily the syntax of the sentence.

Lavoie also rejects Goldman's vocalization of M's תעז as hiph'il, proposed in *BHQ*, in favour of retaining the qal and reading it as transitive (as have Gordis and others), citing Ps 68.29 and Prov 8.28—both of which, however, pose problems in that respect. Goldman has subsequently elaborated his suggestion ('Le Texte massorétique', 89-91), observing that the hiph'il has a particular nuance of impudence, and proposing that the text was originally critical of the wise, whose wisdom makes them more arrogant than the governors of a town. Of course, if we retain M and go down either path, the -ל remains difficult. Seow's attempt to address that problem, by having the verb mean 'be cherished' so that wisdom is valuable 'to' the wise, rests on an unconvincing appeal to Arabic.

7.19 a wise man] M vocalizes לחכם without an article, but '*the* wise man' is understood by G and by the hexaplaric reading mentioned in the last note. In S, many manuscripts have marked the noun with *seyame*, making it plural.

7.19 than would ten men of authority] Lit. 'than ten men of authority': the point of comparison is between wisdom and these men, not between them and the wise man (which is why שליטים has no -ל). We shall discuss the noun itself at 10.5. Suffice it to say here that it expresses the possession of authority and influence (not physical strength), and so can be used of rulers or people granted authority in a particular area (cf. Gen 42.6), but can also be used of having power more generally. Qohelet's point is presumably not that these ten would charge out in a group to help the wise man in a fight, but that ten individuals well-placed in the centre of power can offer him much support. Duncan makes the attractive but speculative suggestion that מעשרה שליטים has been wrongly divided, and should be read as מעשר השליטים, 'than the wealth of the rulers'. While this is by no means impossible, the very use of שליטים does seem to imply that the comparison is with a source of power rather than wealth (so far as those things are separable).

Note that 4QQoh^a appears to have read -ש after this phrase, rather than אשר. There are no stylistic or other grounds upon which to determine which reading is earlier, and it makes no difference to the sense, but when 4QQoh^a is around a thousand years older than our earliest manuscripts of M, it seems curious to default to the M reading in such cases, as Lavoie, 'Force meurtrière', 59, proposes we should.

7.20 For] The כי is often taken as explicatory, but commentators have naturally tended to translate it according to their understanding of the relationship between this verse and those around it, with some preferring to give it an emphatic or asseverative force. I have translated it as explicatory, but doubt very much that it is supposed directly to explain or justify either the preceding 7.19 or any particular one of the statements and admonitions which came before that. See the commentary.

7.20 there is no person so righteous...that] Lit. 'a person is not righteous...who/that'. Although the general sense is clear, the construction is not. Many commentators offer a translation along the lines of the RSV's 'there is not a righteous man on earth', which effectively ignores the אדם in M אדם אין צדיק, or treats the text as though it said אין אדם צדיק (which is the order adopted by S, V, T and La).[13] This is sometimes justified by the claim that אדם has been moved forward for emphasis, or to give a sense 'as for humans' (see, e.g., Lauha)—although we might reasonably expect Qohelet actually to say 'humans' or '*the* human', if that were indeed the case. We probably need rather to understand, as Schoors suggests, that אין is functioning here to negate a nonverbal clause rather than to state non-existence, and this is how the text has been understood by G, Hie. Without wishing to claim that the subsequent אשר (-ש again in 4QQoh[a]) is actually serving as a final conjunction, I take it to have some nuance of consequence here: if the clauses that it introduces were simply an elaboration or definition of what it means to be righteous, Qohelet would effectively be denying the existence of any righteousness. That is, of course, a possible reading, and is how some prefer to understand the text; Lasater, 'Subordination', 88, for instance, compares the condemnation of humanity in Pss 14.1-3; 53.2-5. Qohelet speaks freely about the innocent or righteous, however, in 3.17; 8.14; and 9.1-2, just as he has very recently in 7.15, and we could only really reconcile that usage with an absolute denial here by understanding צדיק as though with scare quotes and some special connotation (such as 'there is no *truly* righteous person, who...'). That comes to much the same as reading 'so righteous...that'.

7.21 do not apply your mind to] Qohelet uses the same expression, lit. 'give your heart to', at 1.13, 17; 8.9, 16, always in connection with investigating or examining. In 8.9, indeed, it appears to have this sense even without

---

[13] The understanding may have been influenced by 1 Kgs 8.46 (כי אין אדם אשר לא יחטא). For the La, note Augustine, *In Euangelium Ioannis Tractatus Centum Uiginti Quatuor*, xcv, 2, *non est iustus in terra qui faciet bonum, et non peccabit*, which Vaccari, 'Recupero', 117, takes to be based on Jerome's revision, and Cassian *Collationes* xxiii, 5, 1 *quia non est iustus homo in terra qui faciat bonum et non peccabit* (it is cited again identically in xxiii, 18, 3).

an associated verb, so it is unlikely that Qohelet here means simply 'do not take them to heart' or even 'do not listen to them'. Rather, the point is presumably that one should not enquire into them too closely. G has μὴ θῇς καρδίαν, 'do not set your heart', but a more literal μὴ δῷς, 'do not give', is attested in hexaplaric manuscripts and widely elsewhere, and is likely itself to be hexaplaric.

7.21 all the words which people say] Lit. 'they say': this is an impersonal construction, which could also be translated as passive 'all the words that are said'—and that is, in fact, the approach taken by σ' ἀλλὰ μηδὲ (var. μὴ δὲ) πᾶσι τοῖς λαλουμένοις παράσχῃς τὴν καρδίαν (var. τῇ καρδίᾳ) σου, 'but do not to all that are said put forward your heart (var. in your heart)'. In the Hebrew, imitated by that reading in σ', this clause is placed before the admonition not to set one's heart, and there is perhaps a nuance 'when it comes to all the words that are said, do not set your mind to them'.

G here is πάντας λόγους, 'all words': Rahlfs' πάντας τοὺς λόγους, 'all *the* words', has little support among the witnesses. Correspondingly, the translator probably found לכל דברים in his source-text. It is also likely that he found אשר ידברו רשעים, 'that the wicked say': the manuscript evidence is more divided on this point, but λαλήσουσιν ἀσεβεῖς, 'the impious say', is widely attested, and is supported by T, as well as by S, making it unlikely that the subject has simply been supplied by the G translator (as Salters, 'Observations on the Septuagint', 172, suggests). It seems likely that the noun has been supplied to give the verb a subject, rather than that it is original, but it carries the implication that 'your servant' must be one of the wicked, which was presumably not intended.

7.21 in case you hear] Or 'so that you do not'; an earlier generation would have said 'lest', covering both senses, and the Hebrew probably has a similar range. This is one of the relatively rare places, however, where most translators and commentators have found it difficult to deny that the construction with אשר must have some implication of consequence or purpose; even Holmstedt, who is very reluctant ever to grant it that meaning, supposes that אשר here serves for למען אשר, a usage that he regards as late ('The Grammar of ש and אשר in Qohelet', 305-6; cf. *Relative Clause*, 368).

An alternative, advanced by Lohfink and Michel, and subsequently accepted by Schoors, takes אשר instead to mean 'because'. The point would then be that those who hear only flattery should not put too much faith in it: they are never going to hear their servant being rude about them. Attractive though that interpretation might be for this verse, however, it not only requires that the next verse be understood as a concessive 'even though you know that you have been rude about others' (which is not impossible, see below), but it also forces אל תתן לבך to mean something like 'have confidence in' or 'place weight on'—and that is not the sense of the expression elsewhere. S avoids committing itself to any interpretation, by simply ignoring אשר.

7.21 being rude about] The pi‘el of קלל, used here and in the next verse (and also at 10.20), can have a literal sense of 'cursing' (cf. 2 Sam 17.43), but often probably means no more than saying bad things to or about somebody (e.g. Judg 9.27-29). It is used in Prov 30.10 of a servant's response to somebody who has complained about him to his master. σ' uses λοιδοροῦντος here, and in 7.22 has καὶ σὺ ἐλοιδόρησας ἄλλους. This is a good translation: the Greek verb is used of abusing or reviling somebody, but sometimes without any implication of actually insulting them—in colloquial English we might use 'have a go at'.

7.22 for...also] The sense of the initial כי גם has been much discussed. As we saw in the note on 'even' at 4.14, there is no reason to suppose that the combination of words has any particular implication, and it is not a way in which Qohelet elsewhere expresses a concession. Since both words can have a range of meanings, therefore, translations have tended to match the various ways in which commentators have understood the different elements of 7.21-22 to fit together. On any reckoning, however, the גם here seems awkward, and this is perhaps another point in favour of the reading in G (see below): if the subjects are different in each clause, the two uses of גם in the verse may be intended to evoke a correspondence, rather like that between גם המה and אני גם in Isa 66.3-4.

7.22 for...many occasions when] Or very possibly 'for many times he will hurt your heart, as'. Rahlfs gives G here as ὅτι πλειστάκις πονηρεύσεταί σε καὶ καθόδους πολλὰς κακώσει καρδίαν σου, 'for very often will he wrong you, and many times will he mistreat/distress your heart', and Gentry reads the same, but with καί <γε>. There are variations on this, but the G tradition as a whole presents a reading in which the text that appears as פעמים רבות ידע in M seems to have been read with ירע rather than ידע, and translated in two different ways (Kennicott, incidentally, notes the same reading ירע in his ms 1). The variation between the two translations suggests, of course, that two different translators are involved, and it has long been recognized that what we have here is most likely a conflation of two different versions (although Salters, 'Observations on the Septuagint', 170, apparently attributes both readings to the G translator as a double rendering). What is not so clear is how we should disentangle them, identify their sources, and reconstruct the original G. The only other Greek version that has been preserved directly is ὅτι πρὸς πλεονάκις (var. -νακης) καιροῦ πονηρεύσεται (corrupt var. πορευσεται) καρδία (var. -διαν) σου, which is attributed to σ' by Field, but to α' in the manuscripts and by Marshall (following Gentry, 'Role of the Three', 186-87). This version is likewise based on a reading with ירע, and means 'for at a frequency of occasion your heart will wrong you' or 'he will wrong your heart'—the initial πρὸς πλεονάκις καιροῦ (where πρὸς = גם), is very ugly, and that in itself lends weight to the supposition that this is Aquila's work. The resemblance of this version to the first part of the text in G, however, which is enhanced in the hexaplaric manuscripts by the presence of καιροῦ as well, suggests that it may have been the basis for that part,[14] and we may note also that κακώσει in the second part corresponds to G's rendering of לרע in 8.9 as κακῶσαι. In other words, it looks very much as though ὅτι πλειστάκις πονηρεύσεταί σε has been derived from a hexaplaric reading, and καθόδους πολλὰς κακώσει καρδίαν σου from the original form of G. McNeile, 163, accordingly concludes that G* was ὅτι καί γε καθόδους πολλὰς κακώσει καρδίαν σου. Gentry's reconstruction in his article (187) is identical, except that he would read the nominative καρδία σου, as would Goldman, who sees the accusative καρδίαν as the result of influence from the previous verse. Gentry translates the verse 'For, in fact your heart will cause harm many times so that even you cursed others'. I think myself, though, that McNeile is more probably right here: reading ירע, the translator has reasonably taken Qohelet's point to be that the servant has spoken badly about his master, and either the servant or the fact (now) upsets him: רע לב or לב רע is a way of talking about sadness or upset (Neh 2.2; Prov 25.20), and 'being upset' is expressed with לב and the qal of רעע in Deut 15.10 and 1 Sam 1.8, so it would not be strange for ירע לב (with the verb read as a hiph'il) to mean 'he/it will make (someone) unhappy' or 'upset them' (cf. the use of the Greek verb at, e.g., Acts 14.2). It should also be noted that the only important manuscript among the very few that have the nominative is Codex Vaticanus, which is not always the most reliable witness to G* in this book. Gentry appears to have come around to the same view in his edition, which has the accusative. That edition also reconstructs καί <γε> from the conjunction that joins the two variants, which seems tenuous, and since there is no equivalent in α' either, it seems unlikely that the translator found the first גם in his source here.

We have, in any case, two different texts and understandings. In the sourcetext of G (and possibly that of α' also), 7.22 initially picks up the last part of 7.21, and the point is that one should avoid hearing one's servant being rude, because he could prove often to be hurtful. In M and the other versions, 7.22 more loosely justifies or qualifies the advice offered in 7.21 as a whole: one should not get into what other people say and risk encountering one's servant

---

[14] The only use of πλειστάκις elsewhere in the Greek tradition appears to be at Ps 119.164 (Greek 118.164), where Field notes a mention by Theodoret of its use by 'some people' for שבע, 'seven times', but quotes with approval the doubts of Schleusner that this is a citation of any translation, rather than a reference to the understanding of certain commentators. It is not clear to me how McNeile, 163', deduces from this note a possible link with θ', which evokes a faint echo in Gentry's discussion (above). We find πλεονάκις used for רבות פעמים at Ps 106.43 (Greek 105.43), and elsewhere for רבת in רבת צררוני (Ps 129.1-2, Greek 128.1-2). Neither term, therefore, has a strong association with any particular translator, but πλειστάκις could reasonably be considered a tidying-up of πρὸς πλεονάκις καιροῦ.

being rude, because of one's awareness of being rude about others many times. If we look only at the first part of the verse, then G seems to offer the tighter and more cogent reading, and it also explains the very strange word-order, which in M seems to imply that the heart will be knowing on many occasions, rather than that one has insulted others often.

It is much harder, however, to understand the last part of the verse in G, and its correspondence to the first. The ὅτι ὡς of most manuscripts here is generally, and plausibly, taken as an error for ὅπως (so Rahlfs, Gentry; cf. Gentry, 'Role of the Three', 184-85), which the translator sometimes uses elsewhere to render אשר, and which is found in some witnesses. This is then followed, however, by an aorist indicative, rather than the subjunctive of, e.g., 8.12. That is not an obvious way to form the analogy supposed by NETS 'as, indeed, you have cursed'—which is roundly rejected by Muraoka, *Syntax*, §29 c (iv)—but it is more difficult to say what it actually does mean. Similar uses in 2 Macc 7.22; Luke 24.20 (and other, non-biblical instances noted by MM) suggest that such a construction would typically be used of knowing *that* something had happened, and the translator may be intending it to be read as pregnant: 'he/it will upset you (recalling) how you yourself cursed others'. It is tempting to speculate, indeed, that his translation tries to embrace both the Hebrew variants 'harm' and 'know', without explicitly reproducing the latter. The sense here is uncertain, however, and, the previous textual problems make it difficult anyway to rely too much on G. Accordingly, I have based my translation on M, even though I suspect that G reflects a reading which is at least as old.

7.22 you] As often, what is presented as the $Q^e r\hat{e}$ in M^L is found in the main text of many manuscripts, including several in the Babylonian tradition (see Miletto). *BHS* points the $K^e th\hat{\imath}bh$ אתה as the feminine אַתְּ, but it is probably to be vocalized אַתָּ: this spelling is found also at 1 Sam 24.19 (ET 24.18); Ps 6.4 (ET 6.3); Job 1.10 and Neh 9.6, always with אתה as $Q^e r\hat{e}$, and should be regarded as an orthographic variant rather than as an error. See also the note at 5.3.

Introduction to 7.23–8.1

Qohelet's Search for Wisdom

(7.23) All this I had ventured through wisdom; I had said 'Let me be wise!' But it has been far from me: (7.24) whatever had been has been far away, and deep, deep down—who can find it?

(7.25) My heart and I turned away, to know and to explore, and seek wisdom and a plan, and to know the wrongness of folly, and obtuseness and mindlessness. (7.26) If I found her, I would say, 'More bitter than death is this woman, she who is all nets, and her heart dragnets, her hands fetters. Whoever seems right to God will escape from her, while one who is wrong will be trapped in her.'

(7.27) Look at this: I met (says the Qohelet) one woman after another, in order to find a plan, (7.28) which my self still sought and I did not find. I met one person from every thousand, but I met no woman $^{7.29}$ who stood apart $^{7.28}$ among all these. (7.29) Look at this: I found God made each person uncomplicated, and it is they themselves that have sought a lot of plans. (8.1) Is anyone really the wise man? And does anyone know how to interpret something that is said? A person's wisdom will light up their face, but the strength of their face will be dimmed.

This is widely, and not without reason, regarded as one of the most difficult parts of the book. The serious problems that arise directly from the text and language have been compounded both by issues around the attitudes seemingly displayed by Qohelet towards women (at least as implied by certain common interpretations of the text), and by the determination of many commentators to read his statements here in terms of a quest to find some superior form of wisdom, which will enable him to understand how the world works. These concerns have motivated various different attempts to find more in the text than, I think, is there, but they have also tended

INTRODUCTION TO 7.23–8.1   229

to pull the elements of it apart, despite the language of 'seeking' and 'finding', or 'meeting', that runs throughout 7.23-29.

To understand the context, it is important to recognize that Qohelet is drawing here on an established set of imagery, which connected wisdom and folly with women by personifying them as female (the Hebrew noun for 'wisdom' is feminine, which was probably one of the starting points for this). The imagery is best known from Proverbs 1–9, where it may well have made its first appearance, and that work depicts wisdom and her counterpart (who is usually called the 'strange' or 'foreign' woman, but who is ultimately 'folly' in Prov 9) as rivals for the attention of the uneducated. Both offer attractive invitations, but while one can promise genuine advantages, the other is dangerous, and to follow her is to court disaster. The difficulty lies in telling them apart, and this is a key concern in Proverbs 1–9 itself. Later authors, however, were more concerned with the women themselves than with that problem or with the relationship between them, and although we find both characters in subsequent literature, they are never again paired (at least in the texts as we have them), and wisdom is, as one might expect, much more prominent.

The text of 7.25 is probably damaged, and we do not know precisely what Qohelet is trying to do after his confession in 7.23-24, but it does certainly involve looking for wisdom, apparently with a view to finding a plan or calculation of some sort, and it may involve the investigation of folly as well. What follows is, I think, a literary conceit that exploits the established imagery by taking it literally. Since wisdom and folly are women, supposedly waiting out there to be found, Qohelet sets out to encounter one or both of them (perhaps with his heart as a companion or chaperone) by meeting lots of women. He has a prepared speech, which is probably appropriate for either, describing her as something that traps men in her—it is only by the grace of God, as it were, that any might escape. This description has some very slight points of contact with the 'foreign woman' of Proverbs 1–9, which have often been noted, but what worries Qohelet here is not a woman who might lead him into danger, but one who might hold him in her grip—and with whom, perhaps, he already has some familiarity. He does not spell out what the consequences of being trapped in this way might be, but following so soon after the advice in 7.15-18, the point is most probably that this imagery entails choosing between one of the women and the other, and so the sort of absolute commitment to either wisdom or folly that he has just decried. To be caught up by either is to be deprived of the freedom to steer a course between them, which he has himself been granted by the dissolution of his own close relationship with wisdom.

In any case, Qohelet does not get to use his speech except to us because, despite meeting many people, he does not find a woman who stands out from the crowd, whether it be as wisdom or folly. What he takes away from the experience instead, and offers as his real discovery, is that searches such as his own are not something that God sets humans to do, but something with which humans complicate their own existence: we do not have a duty to go looking for wisdom or for ways to work things out, and it is our own responsibility if we do so.

This fable (I hesitate to call it a narrative or memoir) falls after a long series of sayings and observations which, in different ways, have raised doubts about the value of wisdom, or have suggested that life involves finding balance and compromise more than a winning formula. It will be brought to an end by a difficult but very interesting saying in 8.1, the point of which seems to be that wisdom does indeed offer insight and an enlightenment of sorts, but at the same time undermines whatever within us is impulsive or self-confident—in turning up one light, it turns down another. As this implies, Qohelet is not actively against wisdom, but, once again, his attitudes towards it are complicated. The rhetorical questions that precede this saying in 8.1 do not preclude the possibility of wisdom, but wonder whether anyone is really wise in the way that Qohelet had once considered himself to be, or really possesses even the sort of academic insight that might be associated with wisdom. Shortly afterwards, moreover, the knowledge that he will attribute to the wise is seriously circumscribed in 8.5b-9, by limitations that are inherent in all human knowledge, and when he returns to the subject of wisdom in 8.16-17 it will be to conclude that, by God's design, any real understanding of what happens in the world remains inaccessible to humans, whatever the wise may claim.

Although other preoccupations eventually take over, this part of the book retains the strong concern with the drawbacks and limits of wisdom that has been visible since 7.1, and the particular role of 7.23–8.1 in this discussion is to detach wisdom from the vision of Proverbs 1–9, in which she is a woman waiting to show us the way we should follow, in order to align ourselves with the will of God. For Qohelet, wisdom is an entirely human activity, which many people undertake, but which is neither something that God has intended us to do, nor something that will bring us closer to understanding him. His closing questions and comment in 8.1 are very difficult, but probably both damn wisdom with faint praise, and suggest that nobody really conforms to the ideal of the wise man.

To deal with problems in 7.28, commentators have resorted for many centuries to an understanding that Qohelet was claiming never to have found a *good* woman—an idea that can be tied to the description in 7.26, if that is taken to be a description of every woman. Even before such statements about women became quite unacceptable to modern readers, however, that understanding provoked concern in various quarters, and it has long led to a characterization of Qohelet as misogynistic (and, of course, to many attempts to defend him against that charge).[1] Such a reading is, I think, wholly untenable,

---

[1] Garrett, 'Feminist Hermeneutic', is probably the most striking modern example, and brings to the surface some of the less obvious influences on the scholarship, and in particular the discomfort that scholars he calls 'radical Christian feminists' (310) provoke in certain quarters. Reading the passage in the light of Gen 3, and presuming the influence of personal experience on Qohelet's claims, Garrett understands it to be a brutally honest description of what Qohelet has observed to be the way most men feel about their domestic relationships. This is not 'wrong or incorrect' (318), but represents only one side of such relationships, which could be supplemented by a woman's take on her situation: 'nothing brings out the sinfulness of humanity more thoroughly than the marriage relationship'—though it is possible to find friends of one's own sex (if only one in a thousand). I doubt that Qohelet is cleared of misogyny by taking the text this way as an outpouring of irrational male resentment, although the reading is actually quite close, in fact, to the interpretation in Fontaine, 'Many Devices', which we shall consider with respect to 7.26, and which Garrett would doubtless regard as 'radical'. This and other modern efforts are discussed very helpfully in Christianson, 'Qoheleth the "Old Boy"', 110-21, while Backhaus, *Es gibt*, 272-81, looks in detail at some of the key German-language research. To the studies covered in those works, we might add Hilbrands and Kosiol, 'Kohelet als Frauenfeind?', which sees allusions to the Solomonic background, but seems to acquit Qohelet of misogyny principally on the grounds that to condemn female seductiveness is actually to condemn male weakness. Shemesh, 'More Bitter Than Death', takes a very different tack, by accepting the misogyny of Qohelet, but denying that this is a view typical of the biblical literature.

and I doubt, accordingly, that Qohelet is actually saying anything negative about women as a sex, directly or indirectly.

It might be possible to detect sexism of a rather different sort, and the original imagery in Proverbs 1–9, which many have associated with 7.26, is itself at least open to such a charge: it was aimed at a male audience who could identify with the rival attractions of 'good' and 'bad' women, and relies at points on male responses to the portrayals of such women. It is not clear that even those elements are present, however, in Qohelet's allusions to the imagery. The woman of 7.26 has none of the erotic overtones of the foreign woman in Proverbs, and it is not obvious even that men are supposed to be drawn to her by physical or romantic attraction—unless her 'heart', unlike Qohelet's own, is supposed to be an organ of love and not of thought (a common supposition, which surely says more about the attitude to women of commentators and their cultures than about the original author's views).[2]

The woman in that verse is a trap, or a collection of traps, in which people, and not necessarily men in particular, can become caught: she catches them with her mind and holds them with her hands, not by fluttering her eyelashes at them, or even by speaking seductively (the preferred method in Proverbs, e.g. 2.16). Her sole purpose, moreover, seems to be to hold them, and there is no suggestion that she is leading them to their death; even the idea that she is trying to trap them in marriage is something that interpreters read into, not out of the text.[3] Many disparaging things were said about

---

[2] Wolfe will not absolve Qohelet of misogyny 'just because' he is employing personifications or metaphors, and says that his words 'exude the misogynistic aura of the culture in which they were composed'. There may be truth in that, as also in her complaint that 'our contemporary context continues to assist in making these metaphors effective', but the example she cites, of even the 'progressive' NRSV translating 'foreign woman' in Proverbs using terms like 'loose' and 'adulteress', is actually another instance of interpreters forcing their own stereotypes on to the text: such translations turn what was originally a very specific—albeit xenophobic—allusion to apostasy (see my *Instruction and Imagery*) into a more general depiction of folly in terms of a female sexuality that is dangerous because it is outside male control. Such scholarship has not so much enabled the metaphors as conscripted them.

[3] The passage is famously cited in the fifteenth-century *Malleus Maleficarum*, where it is interpreted in terms of voracious female sexual desire, which is in turn taken to be the reason for the prevalence of witchcraft among women, more than men. Wolfe helpfully includes a translation of the relevant section (124-26).

women in the ancient world, and many are still said, if usually more *sotto voce*: it would not be astonishing to find such statements here, therefore, but I do not think they are present, nor even that Qohelet's presentation strongly exhibits the specifically male perspective that characterizes Proverbs 1–9.

7.23-24

(7.23) All this I had ventured through wisdom; I had said 'Let me be wise!' But it has been far from me: (7.24) whatever had been has been far away, and deep, deep down—who can find it?

Commentary

Much earlier in the monologue, Qohelet spoke quite often of his own wisdom: he claimed to have possessed a great deal of it (1.16), to have used it as an important tool in his investigations (1.13; 2.3), and even to have retained it throughout his lengthy experiment with work and wealth (2.9), although he also observed more generally the pain that wisdom can bring (1.18), and questioned the real value of his having been so wise (2.13-15). He has not, however, mentioned his wisdom for a long time—indeed, not since the end of his direct reflections on his work in ch. 2—and so its reappearance as a tool here, surely in an echo of 1.13, takes us back to a much earlier stage of Qohelet's discourse. In the next verse, 7.25, he will evoke another early interest (cf. 1.17; 2.12), and if he is not actually returning to where he started, Qohelet is at least revisiting his earlier concerns (similarly, Clifford, 'Another Look'). In doing so, he also returns, I think, to the memoir through which he had presented those concerns, and talks once more about his experiences at a specific time, or rather, perhaps, at a specific point on his intellectual journey.

If we acknowledge the general resemblances of theme and vocabulary between the first part of 7.23 and 1.13 and between 7.25 and 1.17, then we should not forget that the intervening 1.16 presented Qohelet's claim to have become wiser than any in Jerusalem before him. Qohelet now talks again about his wisdom, and reminds us that he had undertaken his examinations with the intention of using his wisdom, but where 1.16 spoke of accumulating wisdom, the corresponding material in 7.24, and the last part of 7.23, speak instead of a distancing: Qohelet confesses that he now finds wisdom, and that past, impossibly distant. This seemingly leads him in the following verses to change direction, and to embark upon a quest which includes a search for wisdom, and which is broadly equivalent, perhaps, to the lengthier experiment which he undertook in ch. 2. It is less clear, though, precisely what the context for all this is supposed to be. Why, most importantly, does Qohelet suddenly now assert that he cannot be wise, when he has led us to believe earlier that he was already supremely wise?

Many commentators have tried to resolve the apparent contradiction by assuming not that Qohelet himself has changed, but that he aspires to become wise in a different way, which will enable him to understand the world. His declaration, 'Let me be wise!', read as a fresh intention and not a recollection, would then signal his desire to upgrade his wisdom, and what follows would describe his failure to achieve that new sort of wisdom. There is no indication in the Hebrew, however, of any such distinction between different sorts of wisdom, even if anything he had said so far suggested that Qohelet might believe in the possibility of such superior insight. This is an idea that arises solely from a need to address the contradiction, and it introduces further, unnecessary complexity to Qohelet's already ambivalent beliefs about wisdom. We shall look at this interpretation in more detail below, but it is clearly simpler to suppose, with other commentators, that the issue here is not a change in the nature of the wisdom at stake, but a change in the relationship between Qohelet and wisdom.

Qohelet's recognition of this change has not come out of the blue. To be sure, it is a long time since he lamented in 2.15 his previous, naïve accumulation of wisdom, but ch. 7 has already raised further questions about the attractiveness and value of wisdom— to the extent that Qohelet's alienation from wisdom can hardly be unexpected. He may have set out back in 1.13 to be wise, but we are probably supposed to understand that there have been changes in his own ideas or perceptions, which have affected his relationship with wisdom. Jerome has a nice interpretation here in terms of the way Qohelet has come to feel: the more he sought wisdom, the less he found it, until he was *in media demersum caligine, tenebris ignorantiae circumdatum*, 'bogged down in the midst of obscurity, hemmed in by the shadows of ignorance'.[1] Qohelet still *wants* to be

---

[1] Jerome also finds, perhaps tongue in cheek, an analogy in his own experience that may strike a chord with any student of Ecclesiastes: *qui eruditus fuerit in scripturis, quanto plus scire coeperit, tanto ei in his cotidie oritur maior*

wise, but the very application of his wisdom has led him to a point where he does not *feel* wise. Qohelet himself, however, characterizes the situation only in terms of distance and depth, and as he slips into the imagery of searching for wisdom as a woman, he seems even to imply that it is wisdom who has distanced herself from him. In any case, the change is apparently permanent. Although the epilogue describes him as wise in 12.9, Qohelet will never again speak of his own wisdom.

7.23] Qohelet's statement that he wished to be wise (a single word in Hebrew) is most immediately associated with a claim that 'he ventured all this with wisdom'. The problems are discussed in the notes, but there is some debate both about what 'all this' refers to, and what 'venturing' it might mean—although it is highly unlikely that the Hebrew could mean Qohelet has tested or validated his conclusions using wisdom, as many commentators would like. It is also difficult to impose some distinction of tense upon the verbs, which might enable us to understand that Qohelet is talking about using wisdom in the past, and only encountering a problem when he declares his intention to be wise again. The most plausible reading sets both verbs in the past, as a recollection of Qohelet's much earlier ambitions: he is re-stating the programme which first led him to look at 'all this', that is, at the many issues that have arisen from those initial enquiries. What follows is expressed using non-verbal clauses, with no direct indication of tense, and could potentially, even most naturally, be read as a claim that wisdom had always actually been distant. That seems unlikely to be the intention, however. Qohelet has made very clear his understanding that he was wise when he began, even to the point that this wisdom caused him problems. Equally, though, he is probably not just saying that the disappearance of his wisdom is sudden and recent. The vagueness of tense allows the suggestion that Qohelet has discovered, or come to acknowledge, a change that may have occurred some time before, or over a period of time—perhaps more in the way he has come to perceive his wisdom than in any actual alteration of that wisdom. I have tried to represent this so far as

obscuritas, 'as for anyone who has become learned in the scriptures, the more they begin to know, the more the obscurity that they encounter in them every day'.

possible in the translation: the original says literally 'I ventured...I said...it/she far from me'.

For scholars reluctant to see a development in Qohelet's character or ideas, all this sits in tension with his earlier claims to have been wise, and, as I have noted already, many commentators have long supposed that he must be talking here about a different sort of wisdom, one which in some way transcends whatever more mundane variety he already possessed. Especially in the light of the way the next verse is commonly understood, this wisdom is widely taken to be a special sort of wisdom that might permit one to understand the workings of the world, and Gordis talks about '*hokmah par excellence*, as against practical Wisdom'. Qohelet is also sometimes understood simply to be appreciating that the wisdom he had believed himself to possess was flawed or unreal. Murphy expresses both possibilities, claiming that Qohelet came to 'realize that he was not truly wise or did not possess the wisdom he sought for', while Fox and Porten argue that he introduces a new definition of wisdom in terms of what it cannot attain ('Unsought Discoveries', 28).

Such attempts to resolve the contradiction, however, only introduce greater complexity and raise further questions. To be sure, Qohelet spoke in 1.16 of increasing his wisdom beyond that of others, and so would presumably accept that there might be different degrees of wisdom—but that is not at issue, and he is not talking here about becoming 'more wise'. It is also true that we sometimes find the term 'wisdom' used to describe purely technical skills in other literature: it can be important in other contexts to recognize that not every instance of 'wisdom' is a facet of the same phenomenon. What we do not find elsewhere in Ecclesiastes, however, or anywhere else in biblical literature for that matter, is the notion of some special wisdom *par excellence*, which can be applied successfully to philosophical or cosmological questions in a way that 'ordinary' wisdom cannot. Nothing that Qohelet has said or will say, furthermore, leads us to suppose that he would at any stage have accepted the possibility either of such special wisdom or of 'normal' wisdom permitting humans to understand the workings of God or the world. The later verse 8.17 is especially interesting in this respect, because it describes a failure of 'the wise man' to discover the work of God, despite his stated intention to do so. There is no suggestion there that the man's wisdom is of an inferior sort, or that he is the wrong sort of wise man—indeed, the fact that he is *the* wise man implies that Qohelet is talking about any or all wise men, or at least about an archetypal wise man, and, accordingly, that *no* wisdom can accomplish this task, whatever others might claim. Any objection, furthermore, on the grounds that 8.17 might only represent Qohelet's opinion after his own experience of failing to find 'true' wisdom, has to confront the fact that the verse echoes the language and ideas expressed already in 3.11: we have no reason to suppose that Qohelet ever, at any point after his initial investigations, believed the hidden workings of God or the world to be susceptible to any human analysis, or that he would consequently have sought a true or enhanced wisdom that might allow him such access.

Equally, any idea that Qohelet is simply recognizing the flawed or inadequate character of his own wisdom has to explain his earlier, unqualified claims to have been unusually wise, and any explanation that does not resort to the idea of some superior type of wisdom has instead to introduce a notion of different perspectives into the monologue, as though it were like a diary, reflecting his outlook as it changed over time. It is one thing, however, to say that the Qohelet of the monologue looks back at the naivety of his younger self, and traces the changes that have been induced by his experience, but quite another to suggest that the monologue itself embodies these changes, and offers us without differentiation the views of Qohelet at different points of his journey. The possibility that he might actually have been wise, but failed successfully to apply his wisdom is similarly belied by the clear statement of 2.9, that it remained with him through at least the first part of his investigations. It seems much simpler to resolve the apparent contradictions not by assuming that Qohelet was trying somehow to upgrade his wisdom, or that he considered himself never truly to have been wise, but by supposing that he is recognizing a change that took place in the course of his experiences and reflections—that his wisdom did not, in other words, continue to remain with him. His subsequent search will suggest, of course, that he regrets this, and wishes still to be wise, but like the sayings about wisdom which have preceded, it will also display a certain ambivalence.

7.24] The Greek version reads a comparison here, so that Qohelet is going on to say that wisdom proved not only elusive, but more elusive than anything that has ever existed. Most modern commentators, however, prefer to follow the Hebrew, which more probably preserves the original reading at this point, and which is naturally understood to describe 'whatever is/has been' also as distant—and buried so deep as to be unreachable. Despite some differences of opinion about whether he is referring to the past or the present, moreover, most commentators are also united in the opinion that Qohelet is talking in one way or another here about the inaccessibility of the world to human enquiry, and that this is being presented as the basis of his stated inability to be wise. Qohelet found himself unable to be wise, in other words, because a proper understanding of the world is beyond not just his reach, but that of everybody.

This reading, of course, reinforces the view of many, that the sort of wisdom to which he aspired in v. 23 must have involved just such a capacity to understand the world, and Fox, strikingly, discusses this verse almost entirely on the basis of 8.17. Such an interpretation suits very well my own understanding of Qohelet's ideas, and there can be no doubt that he regards the workings of the world as beyond the reach of human knowledge. This is an awful lot, however, to read into a text here that refers nowhere to the work of God, requiring us to find in the expression 'whatever is/has been' a sense that it has possessed in none of its several uses so far, and a reference to what Barton calls 'the true inwardness of things, the reality below all changing phenomena'. To assign such a special implication here is to say, in effect, that 'I cannot find something' must be able to mean the same as 'I cannot discover the cause behind something'. Equally, though, if we are to avoid reading an absurd statement that 'everything is out of reach' without resorting to such an equivalence, then Qohelet's point has to be taken in context as a description of his own perception and predicament. Accordingly, I take the statement here to be less far-reaching: Qohelet is saying that his past, in which he identified himself as a wise man, now seems irrecoverable.

Notes

7.23 All this I had ventured] S ܟܠܗܝܢ *klhyn*, Hie *omnia haec*, V *cuncta* may each have followed the plural of G, πάντα ταῦτα, 'all these things', where M has כל זה, 'all this'; a plural τούτων is also attested (in Greek) for σ'. That rendering accords with the tendency of G to treat כל as plural (as in, e.g., 1.2, 16), but we might contrast the singular renderings of כל זה in 8.9 (καὶ σὺν πᾶν τοῦτο εἶδον, 'and I saw all this') and 9.1 (σὺν πᾶν τοῦτο ἔδωκα εἰς καρδίαν μου, 'I put all this in my heart'), which are the only other places in the book where the expression occurs. The plural ἐπὶ πᾶσι τούτοις, moreover, reflects the Hebrew plural על כל אלה in 11.9, so we cannot exclude the possibility that G (and perhaps some of the other witnesses) found a variant כל אלה here too. If the plural is simply interpretative, then G perhaps wishes to clarify what the translator believes the 'all' to consist of.

That is not entirely clear, since כל זה does not necessarily point either forward (to what Qohelet is about to discuss) or backward (to what he has discussed already). Fox and Porten, 'Unsought Discoveries', 27, observe the parallels between this verse and 1.13, where Qohelet is talking about 'everything which is done beneath the heavens', and suggest that, analogously, he is talking here about 'all the matters examined so far in Qohelet's search', which is plausible, if perhaps too precise, but the two uses of כל זה itself in 9.1 apparently each indicate, respectively, what has preceded and what is to follow. Despite a lot of discussion on the subject, we probably cannot determine the reference of the phrase here simply by judging the usage elsewhere. The context is not entirely unhelpful in this respect, and it is important to note that Qohelet will declare himself to be turning to something else very soon afterwards in 7.25, making a 'forward' reference awkward. Much depends, though, on what we understand the verb here to mean.

To get one textual problem out the way first, the reading of σ' is attested in one manuscript as τούτων ἐπειράσθη ἐν σοφίᾳ, literally '(all) of these things he was tested in wisdom', but ἐπειράσθη (found also as the faulty επειρασθ in another ms) is almost certainly an error for the first-person ἐπειράσθην ('I was tried/tested'), which Marshall and Gentry claim to be the reading of ms 252 (and Field affirms that Nobilius read this also). From the photograph at the Biblioteca Medicea Laurenziana website, however, it is clear that the note on that manuscript (fol. 283r) says ἐπειράθην (which is the reading Field gives himself). This most probably means, 'I tried/tested', since, unlike πειράζω, πειράω is commonly used, in effect, as a deponent verb. The variations ἐπειράσθην / ἐπειράθην may simply be an interesting manifestation of the way in which the two verbs were entangled, and we could plausibly read the former as active anyway, but the direct attestation of ἐπειράθην means both that we do not need to assume that Symmachus took the sense of נסיתי to be passive (or read some other form of the verb), and that we can avoid this assumption without resorting to an emendation, or to a slightly forced reading of ἐπειράσθην. All that said, the evidence does leave open the possibility that Symmachus intended 'I was tried/tested', and there may have been a reason for this.

If the reading of the verb is secure its precise significance is not, and it presents a difficulty here that has received little attention. This lies in the fact that נסה is not clearly used elsewhere of evaluation or validation in a general way, and is applied almost exclusively to God or to people. In typical cases, the Queen of Sheba 'tests' Solomon with questions in 1 Kgs 10.1, or God 'tests' Abraham in Gen 22.1, and the purpose of such tests is usually to establish something about the character, ability, or trustworthiness of the subject (compare the uses of the noun נסיון in Sir 4.17; 6.7). This is not achieved simply by scrutinizing them, and נסה describes a process that requires a response or reaction—indeed, it may involve nothing more than observing a reaction, as when God leaves Hezekiah alone in 2 Chr 32.31 to test him by seeing what he will do in a particular situation. Sir 37.27 speaks of testing one's נפש, to see what is bad for it and to be avoided. In English, we might better translate this regular usage in terms of 'setting a test for', rather than just 'testing'. It is interesting, in this respect, to observe that even when it is a change in their diet that is actually the subject of a test in Dan 1.12-15, it is Daniel and his companions who are themselves said to be tested: biblical (and later) Hebrew seems strongly disinclined to use the verb with a more general sense of evaluating things that cannot act or respond. The verb is, to be sure, found twice without an explicit object. The first time is in 1 Sam 17.39 where David might be claiming that he has not 'tried out' his armour, but is more likely saying that he is not 'experienced' in wearing it (see the note at 2.1 on that usage). The second is in Judg 6.39, where Gideon asks to make one (more) test with (-ב) the fleece. The sense there is much the same as that found quite commonly when the verb is used of people putting God to the test (e.g. Num 14.22; Isa 7.10-12), and God may be implicitly the object if the use is not simply absolute. In the light of usage elsewhere, then, we do not expect this verb to be used of 'testing' something like 'all this', because 'all this' cannot be evaluated in the way that נסה usually requires when it refers to testing. If σ' actually was supposed to be read as passive, it may have been such considerations that led Symmachus to suppose that it must be Qohelet himself being tested.

The verb can, however, have at least one other connotation (associated with the niph‛al in *HALOT*, although the forms are identical to the pi‛el), and in Job 4.2 הנסה דבר אליך is usually understood in terms of Eliphaz 'venturing a word', which accords with the uses in Deut 4.34 and 28.56, where נסה takes a following infinitive, and the meaning seems similarly to be 'venturing' or 'trying' to do something. In English, this seems a big leap of meaning, but 'test' and 'attempt' are not so strongly differentiated in all languages, and it is interesting to observe that G πάντα ταῦτα ἐπείρασα could itself in principle be understood here either as 'I tested all these things' or 'I made an attempt at all these things'; there is a similar ambiguity in Jerome's *temptaui*. It is possible too that we are dealing with a more extended sense of the verb than is attested elsewhere in Hebrew, and the cognate Aramaic נסי does, in fact, possess a potentially rather broader meaning. This is attested rarely, and mostly in Syriac, but in b. ʿAbodah Zarah 15a, for example, the mishnaic prohibition on selling large cattle to gentiles is understood in terms of the possibility that a Jew might end up breaking sabbath regulations if a buyer on the eve of sabbath wished to 'test-drive' his prospective purchase before assuming ownership. In short, the general usage of the verb makes it very unlikely that Qohelet is claiming simply to have evaluated the qualities of 'all this' through testing, but do permit an understanding that he 'ventured' or 'tried all this out'.

Only Hie *et dixi* attests a conjunction before אמרתי, and the Hebrew does not demand a sequence 'I tried...then I said': the verbs are set in parallel and probably should be read in parallel, so that Qohelet's 'trying out' does not precede his declaration, but is aligned with it, or even specified by it. Arguably, indeed, we are pushed towards such a reading by the content: Qohelet is more naturally stating a desire to be wise when he wants to do something involving wisdom, than using wisdom before stating that desire. If we take the clauses together in this way, though, the statement that Qohelet used wisdom is difficult to reconcile with the subsequent declaration that 'it is/ was far from me', whether we take the 'it' to be 'all this' or wisdom. We must either take נסיתי to connote 'I was going to try out', which is not a sense that would naturally be attributed to the qatal, or, more simply, set the actions in different time-frames, so that the use of wisdom and the absence correspond to different points in Qohelet's journey.

Given the difficulties around the use of the verb for testing things rather than people, it is not impossible that Qohelet is talking about his process of enquiry, but far more likely that נסה is being used to describe the way he 'attempted' or 'ventured' that process. He does not 'venture all this' in quite the way that Eliphaz ventured a word, and is more probably using the verb in the way that it is elsewhere used with a following infinitive. If so, there may strictly be an ellipsis involved, but only to the extent that we might say 'I tried that' when we mean 'I tried doing that', and there may also be some implication that the action is at least mildly risky or daring, since that seems to be a nuance present in other such uses of the verb.

7.23 with wisdom] The -ב has generally been taken as instrumental, which would suit the probable allusion to 1.13 and which is the understanding I adopt here. Interpretative issues have provoked less justifiable translations in this case as well, though, with many scholars deducing from the context that, if Qohelet merely aspires to be wise, he should not already be testing things 'with wisdom'. Lauha accordingly translates 'im Blick auf die Weisheit', 'with a view to wisdom', and Thilo 'um Weisheit darinnen zu finden', 'in order to find wisdom in it'. The former appeals to GKC §119 l, which deals, however, with the special use of the preposition in expressions like 'trust *in*' or 'rejoice *in*', and hardly provides a basis for the more general sense that Lauha wants. Thilo sees an analogy with 1.13, where he understood לתור בחכמה in terms of scouting something out, but for the objections to that understanding, see my note there.[2] Even were it the case that תור sometimes took an object with -ב, the (different) verb here already possesses an object, כל זה, which has no preposition, and it is difficult to see what syntactic function any of the scholars who take this approach are actually attributing to בחכמה.

Whybray says casually that 'the test really amounts to a test *of* (conventional) wisdom', however we read the preposition, and Krüger wants to have it both ways by saying that wisdom is both the instrument and object of the test (so similarly Pinker, 'Qohelet's Views on Women', 178, which declares 'חכמה is both method and objective'). Lohfink's understanding, 'in all ways I tried having knowledge', presents a multitude of problems, from which we might single out the facts that he appears to have transferred the preposition to כל and that כל זה can neither mean 'all ways' nor, given the singular, refer to any separate 'ways' that are still to be mentioned. All such efforts, however, seem determined to deduce from the context a statement that is simply not present in the sentence, where it would be extremely unnatural, if not impossible, to take חכמה as the object of נסיתי.

In the light of the problems that surround the precise sense of the verb, however, the role of בחכמה does require some explanation: as we saw in the last note, it is unlikely that Qohelet was talking about some mental evaluation of 'all this', so to speak of חכמה simply as the instrument of his actions is potentially misleading. It may better to think in terms of an accompanying circumstance, so that the sense is almost adverbial and Qohelet is saying that he was, or was trying to be wise while he did what he was trying to do. It is just possible, however, if we were to insist on some notion of testing, that the preposition could be taken as a *beth essentiae*, so that Qohelet would be 'testing all this *as* wisdom' (cf. בכסף in Isa 48.10—'[I have refined you but not] as silver').

As for the nature of the wisdom, the vocalization in M implies an article, 'by *the* wisdom'. The readings of G are mixed, but most manuscripts have ἐν τῇ σοφίᾳ, so support M; σ' ἐν σοφίᾳ does not. The determination of חכמה was also discussed in the note at 1.13. Here, of course, the consonantal text leaves

---

[2] Hertzberg makes the same connection in his 1932 commentary, and expands on it in the 1963 edition. Although it is put rather differently, and without specific reference to 1.13, a similar supposition seems to have influenced Schellenberg (in *Erkenntnis*, 150), who renders 'mit der Weisheit', 'with wisdom', but stresses in a footnote that this should not be understood as instrumental. She compares the German expression where 'einen Versuch machen mit (something)' does not refer to a test which 'uses' that something as a method, but to a test in which that something is the object of investigation. This is rather like the English 'experiment with' in the sense 'experiment on', but it is doubtful that Hebrew possesses a similar usage.

the question open, and it is interesting that both M and G understand the noun to be determined even though the context does not seem to demand it: both have likely been influenced by the החכמה a few verses earlier in 7.19 (on which, see above). We can certainly not, however, read into the determination the sort of significance that Gordis sees. He takes it to indicate that Qohelet is distinguishing here and in 1.13 wisdom *par excellence*, but we should note that, all else aside, this is at best a distinction being made by those vocalizing the text: unless the article was unsyncopated, it would have been invisible in the original.

7.23 Let me be wise!] M vocalizes אחכמה as a cohortative form, which is indicated in the consonantal text by the paragogic ה-. This form has probably been read by the other versions, and although G σοφισθήσομαι, 'I shall be/become wise', is a simple statement, there is a volitive nuance in Hie, V *sapiens efficiar*, 'May I be made wise' (if we take the verb as subjunctive), and the more paraphrastic σ' ὑπέλαβον σοφὸς γενέσθαι, 'I undertook to be/become wise'. Ginsberg wishes to vocalize differently as אֶחְכְּמֶהָ, with a suffix pronoun referring back to 'all this' and a sense 'I know it'; that reading would be more plausible were the qal of the verb normally used transitively (cf. Seow), and Ginsberg has to blame his translator from Aramaic for the peculiar usage. Many commentators have asserted, on the basis of the context, that Qohelet must be talking about being wise in some particular way, but we have no reason to attach any such specific connotation to the verb or the form of the verb here. Qohelet has already used the same verb in 2.15 to talk about his 'excessive' past wisdom, in 2.19 of the wisdom that has served him in his work, and in his discussion of wisdom and righteousness in 7.16, so he certainly does not reserve it for references to some more general or universal wisdom: if such a nuance is to be sought, it must be in the context, not the lexicon.

Schoors states curiously that 'If it is correct to understand "wisdom" here as "knowledge", the verb אחכמה also means "I want to understand"'. In some very broad sense that might be true, but it should be observed both that הכמה does not mean 'knowledge', even if it is often associated with knowledge, and that the verb חכם is never used of 'understanding' something—even the transitive forms refer solely to making people wise. To the extent that 'I want to understand' implies that there is 'something' which Qohelet wants to understand, it is a misleading paraphrase: אחכמה can have no implicit object. So far as the language used here is concerned, Qohelet is doing no more than declare that he wishes to possess precisely the same quality that he already claimed to have possessed in 2.15 and 2.19.

There have, of course, been some attempts to resolve the tension by speculative emendation. *BH³* suggested simply omitting אמרתי אחכמה as secondary, and Galling's 1940 commentary replaced אחכמה with את החכמה אקה, which he translated as a declaration that Qohelet was going to 'summarize wisdom'.

7.23 it has been far] In G and S, the last clause is generally taken with what follows, and included within 7.24. M vocalizes רחוקה as an adjective, and is followed in this respect by S. However, G ἐμακρύνθη and T איתרחק suggest that both translators read a verb here, as most probably did Jerome (Hie *ipsa longius facta est*, 'it has become further'; V *ipsa longius recessit*, 'it receded further').[3] *BHQ* prefers that, and commends the verbal form רָחֲקָה as part of a broader interpretation of the passage which favours G. This reading requires, of course, that the ו in רחוקה should have arisen as a *plene* writing of רחקה when the word was already (mistakenly) understood to be an adjective. If the original consonantal text was indeed רחקה, however, like the source-texts of G and T, then either reading would have been quite possible, and there is no very great distinction of sense.

Goldman's broader interpretation, which underpins the recommendation in *BHQ*, is set out at length in Goldman, 'Le Texte massorétique', 80-85, and rests on the belief that there is an image here of wisdom 'fleeing' out of Qohelet's grasp. The verb, however, never has such a meaning. Although in certain contexts it may refer to people becoming progressively more distant as they wander away or follow something else (e.g. Jer 2.5), when the verb refers to an action taken with deliberation, rather than simply to location, then it generally connotes holding oneself back or 'away' from someone or something—so in Prov 19.7, for example, the poor man calls out to the friends who are avoiding him, but when the text says that he 'pursues them with words' it does not mean that they were actually taking to their heels to get away from him. There is, in fact, no particular reason to see movement or deliberation of any sort here, and, on the face of it, Qohelet's statement resembles the uses of the verb in, e.g., Isa 59.11; Lam 1.16. Perhaps the most striking parallel, however, is Deut 30.11, where the commandment is לא נפלאת הוא ממך ולא רחקה הוא, 'not too hard for you and not too far from you': this passage, of course, uses the adjective in parallel with a term used frequently to indicate difficulty.

Whether we read a verb or an adjective may be a matter of little consequence, but in the light of the next verse it is important to note that the form is feminine, matching the pronoun היא. This fact is rarely noted by modern commentators, who perhaps share the assumption of Ehrlich that it is simply a 'neuter'. Those scholars who have sought an antecedent usually agree with Schoors, that 'The feminine pronoun היא refers to "wisdom", which is implicitly present in the context, viz. in the verbal phrase "I want to be wise"'. Goldman notes, similarly though less lucidly, that 'The subject חכמה

---

[3] This may not be an independent reading of the Hebrew. Cassian *Collationes* viii, 25, 5, gives La (with adaptations to context) as *longius fiet a nobis magis quam erat et alta profunditas quis inueniet eam*, 'it will become further from us more than it was, and a deep depth, who may find it?', so Hie is likely following it closely here.

is present through a wordplay in the cohortative אחכמה', and this point was made as long ago as 1525 by Sebastian Münster, who remarked that רחוקה *est adjectiuum fœm. gen. quia & sapie(n)tia Hebræis est fœm. gen.*, 'רחוקה is a feminine adjective because wisdom in Hebrew is also feminine'. That is very plausible, is probably the way in which the versions took it, and is most likely correct. We should not dismiss out of hand, however, the possibility that Qohelet is referring to כל זה, which can itself be read as feminine in his usage, and is pointed as such in M, while in principle, at least, the antecedent could also be the חכמה of בחכמה. It is much less likely that, as Heim supposes, the reference is to יתרון: this term has not appeared since 7.12, and is nowhere explicitly feminine (see the note 'is above everyone' at 5.8). The ambiguity means that there are several slightly different ways in which what Qohelet is saying could be understood, but none seems to offer a better sense. If the antecedent is indeed 'wisdom', then, in view of what follows, a case could be made for rendering the pronoun as 'she' here.

7.24 whatever had been has been far away] The readings of M and G diverge significantly. M takes רחוק to be the beginning of a new sentence, and construes it as the predicate of a clause in which מה שהיה is the subject—hence 'whatever has been (is/was) far'. G, on the other hand, takes רחוק to be an intensification of the previous רחקה: καὶ αὐτὴ ἐμακρύνθη ἀπ' ἐμοῦ μακρὰν ὑπὲρ ὃ ἦν, 'and it/she was far from me, further than what was'. It is highly likely that this reflects a source-text with משהיה instead of מה שהיה: that difference is what allows G to find a comparison (G almost certainly did not just read 'an additional *mem*', as Longman suggests, because we would then expect to find a τί, reflecting מה). M is supported by T כל מא דהוה, 'everything which was', and G is supported by Jerome's *magis quam erat*, 'more than it was', in Hie and V.

The place of S ܝܬܝܪ ܡܢ ܟܠ ܕܗܘܐ ܪܘܚܩܐ *ytyr mn kl dhw' rwḥq'*, 'more than anything which has existed (was) the distance', is more difficult to determine. Goldman thinks that it had a source מכל מה שהיה, with רחוק transposed to the end, but ܟܠ *kl*, 'anything', is absent from many manuscripts, and Kamenetzky, 199, is probably right to think that it appeared secondarily. The odd word-order suggests that S probably tried originally to express a sense that 'its distance from me is more than the distance was', which is likely to have been derived from G (or from a Hebrew text that had משהיה, like G's source-text); ܟܠ *kl* could reflect a correction towards the מה of M if it is not just a facilitation. In any case, S probably does not attest to the existence of a third reading מכל מה שהיה in Hebrew, and we have essentially to choose between מה שהיה and משהיה.

Two factors seem especially important here. The first is the possible meanings of שהיה, which G would have to have read without מה, and which Goldman believes to connote 'anything that has ever come into existence'. This is certainly how Qohelet uses it in 1.9; 3.15; and 6.10—but on each of those occasions it appears in the phrase מה שהיה, and it is the מה which gives the sense 'anything', just as the כל gives the sense 'everyone' in the expression מכל שהיה at 2.9. The only place where the book uses שהיה otherwise is at 12.9, where the expression is difficult, but the meaning clearly not 'anything that has ever come into existence'. It is very doubtful that it can have such a sense without מה or כל,[4] and even G itself does not try to find that meaning here: correspondingly, if we read משהיה, as BHQ recommends, we are left struggling to find either a referent for the -ש or a justification for the use of שהיה in place of מה שהיה. The second consideration is the shift of gender between רהוקה in the last verse and רחוק here (followed, of course, by the subsequent עמק). If we are to find the sort of continuity between 7.23 and 7.24 that a comparison would require, we should expect the gender to remain constant. G, however, represents רחוק by the adverbial μακράν, which allows it to avoid (evade?) specifying the gender of the subject, and raises the suspicion that it found the same masculine form attested in M. Goldman would like to get round the problem by treating the Hebrew in the same way, so that רחוקה...רחוק would mean something like 'flee away...far away': he does not, however, offer any other examples of רחוק (or עמק) being used adverbially in that fashion, and his reading depends on the problematic assumption that the verb has the strong connotation of movement which would justify such adverbial qualification.

It is much easier, then, to assume that G reflects an attempt to create a comparison (most likely in the Hebrew manuscript tradition), than to take it as original: construed as an independent non-verbal clause, M presents no lexical or syntactic difficulties, while G requires us to make a number of awkward suppositions.

It is not difficult to see, though, why G or its source might have taken the approach that it does. In 7.23, Qohelet spoke merely of wisdom being distant from him; if we read a new sentence in 7.24, however, he seems to be making a claim that anything or everything is distant and deep. This not only changes the subject but also seems absurd if it is supposed to be taken as a general statement of reality—we can all reach out and touch *something*. Especially in light of the word-order, however, it is really not possible to make the Hebrew mean 'whatever is distant' and then take that as an object of the later מי ימצאנו, to give 'who will find what is distant (and deep)?'—which, as Schoors observes, is the understanding of the Dutch *Statenvertaling*'s 'hetgene dat verre af is en zeer diep, wie zal dat vinden?'('whatever is far off and is very

---

[4] This tells against the attempt of Frydrych, *Living under the Sun*, 158, to read משהיה with G (or 'the versions', as he puts it misleadingly), but understand '(distant) from that which is', which he supposes also to be close to the sense of S. That sense is not impossible, but this would not correspond to the way Qohelet expresses such ideas elsewhere.

deep, who can find it?), and also, we might note, of the AV's 'That which is far off, and exceeding deep, who can find it out?'.[5]

Schoors himself, however, entangles his discussion of that approach with his examination of a rather different interpretation, which has proved more popular among very recent commentators (although it is by no means new),[6] and which places weight on the tense of היה to suggest that מה שהיה is a reference specifically to the past. Krüger, for example, translates 'Fern ist, was war', lit. 'it is far away, what was' (or in the ET, 'That which was, is far away'), taking the sense to be that past events are too far and deep to be comprehended; the same translation is used by Schellenberg, while Köhlmoos opts for 'fern ist, was geschah', 'what has happened is far away'. This avoids

[5] Other attempts to construe M differently have enjoyed some popularity. In his commentary, Luther translated *longinquum est, quidnam est? profundum est profundum, quis inveniat ipsum?*, 'It is far off, what is it? It is a deep deep, who may find it?', which takes מה to be an interrogative pronoun matching מי, but offers, among other problems, no explanation for the -ש. This appeared in his Bible as 'Es ist ferne; was wird's sein? und ist sehr tief; wer will's finden?', and presumably underpins the Geneva Bible's 'It is farre off, what may it be? and it is a profound deepenesse, who can finde it?'. Ewald in 1837 was still reading 'fern ist, was es sei? und tief tief: wer wird's finden?'. Ginsburg's ingenious 'Far remaineth what was far, and deep, deep! who can find it out?', on the other hand, is achieved by supposing that the repetition of עמק shows that רחוק must likewise have been repeated originally and omitted through brachylogy (the sort of usage that allows the greeting 'good evening!' to become just 'evening!'). On his reckoning, what we have is an abbreviated version of רחוק הוא מה שהיה רחוק, but it is not clear how all that would have been understood from רחוק מה שהיה unless this were somehow a very familiar expression. Ginsburg does not acknowledge the debt, but this understanding goes back at least as far as Herzfeld in 1838 ('Fern bleibt, was fern war, und tief das Tiefe', 'What was far remains far, and the deep, deep'), who observes that the verse has 'great conciseness'. Subsequently, Levy read 'Fern ist, was (fern) war und tief, (was) tief (war)', 'What was (far) is far and (what was) deep, deep', and the understanding persists into Galling's 1940 commentary, which has 'Fernes "bleibt fern" und Tiefes "tief"', 'the far remains far and the deep, deep'.

[6] Schoors himself notes that Geier supported it in 1730 (*remotum est id, quod fuit*, 'whatever was, it is far away'), but Rambach had *illud, quod fuit* more than ten years before that, citing van den Driesche and de Groot, who both likewise rendered *remotum est id, quod fuit* in the first half of the previous century. De Groot, in fact, thinks that there are separate references here to the past, which is distant, and the future, which is deep—a view that was also expressed by de Bèze at the end of the sixteenth century. Without trying to track it back further, we may note all the same that Rashbam's interpretation, although generally in rather different terms, does include a temporal element, as also, perhaps, does that of Rashi.

the apparent absurdity of the statement, and perhaps brings what Qohelet is saying into line with the ideas of 1.11, but does not get around the problem that such a claim would seem to mark a sharp break with the previous verse. In order to understand how the obscurity of the past might be connected with Qohelet's failure to be wise, commentators who adopt this approach have accordingly tended to think in terms of a past that is the foundation of the present. This has been put in different ways. Gill, long ago, understood Qohelet to be saying, 'That which has been done by God already, in creation and providence, is out of the reach of men, is far from their understandings wholly to comprehend or account for; and likewise that which is past with men, what has been done in former ages, the history of past times, is very difficult to come at'. Krüger talks about a critique here of wisdom claims to an understanding that is rooted in creation or in a longstanding tradition—but that is really just a different contextualization of much the same understanding. If a reference to the past is actually to be understood in such terms of a past that shapes the present, then the position of those scholars who read 'whatever was' here is not substantially different from that of the many other modern commentators who prefer a generalized present, 'whatever is' or 'whatever happens', and who likewise usually believe that Qohelet is talking fundamentally about the human inability to understand what is *really* going on. If מה שהיה had the same sense here, moreover, as elsewhere in the book, then it could incorporate notions of both past and present (see the note on 'will be…is' at 1.9), reducing the choice between 'whatever is' and 'whatever was' to an almost entirely translational problem.

The difficulty that the statement seems absurd may be overcome simply by accepting that it is not supposed to be a general statement about reality, but relates specifically to Qohelet's personal inability to be wise. I take it indeed to be past tense, but the reference to be much more limited, so that Qohelet is contrasting his own, wise past with his present, and we might almost paraphrase 'whatever used to be the case'. It is interesting in this respect to note that Vinel translates G μακρὰν ὑπὲρ ὃ ἦν as 'loin de ce que j'étais', 'far from what I was'. She offers no justification, and the rendering of ὑπέρ as simply equivalent to the preceding ἀπό is certainly open to challenge. We may also observe both that the translator is unlikely to have found a first-person verb in his source, and that ancient readers seem to have been reluctant to take the Greek that way (although ἦν can, of course, be first- or third-person). However, Vinel's idiosyncratic rendering does draw out, apparently by accident, precisely what I think Qohelet was actually getting at.

Ginsburg, *Writings*, and Baer, 65, note that the lost Hillel codex reportedly pointed מה here as מֶה, and according to Ginsburg, *Massorah*, 3:131, it used that pointing at 6.10 also.

7.24 and deep, deep down] Lit. 'deep, deep' (possibly meaning 'very deep down' or 'deeper and deeper'): the issue is not that it has depths, but that it lies deep—see below on the sense. M points this as two adjectives, so sees a simple repetition of the same word; on the *paseq homonymicum* used to divide them, see the note at 1.6. G, on the other hand, reads βαθὺ βάθος, 'a deep depth', which suggests that it has vocalized one occurrence as a noun, the other as an adjective; this is also the understanding behind Hie, V *alta profunditas*. T is paraphrasing, but ורז...ורז suggests that it may have read two nouns. These are all matters of vocalization, although S, strikingly, has ܪܘܡܩܐ ܕܪܘܡܩܐ *w'wmq' d'wmq'*, 'and the depth of the deeps' (or 'the deepest deep'). Kamenetzky takes this to represent a Hebrew וְעֹמֶק עֲמָקִים, but it is more likely just an interpretation of G, or possibly an independent reading of ועמק עמק in similar terms.

The reading of G has probably been motivated, as Goldman suggests, by the desire to find a referent for the suffix pronoun on the verb that follows (מה שהיה is not available because G has read משהיה, see above), but Goldman himself, who considers משהיה original, apparently takes it also to be the correct reading. If we do not read משהיה, however, then the vocalization of M is preferable, and not just because it is simpler.

Words from the root עמק in Hebrew generally indicate depth more often than profundity—position, as it were, rather than volume. So Prov 18.4, for example, is not saying that the words of a man's mouth are profound when it describes them as deep waters, but depicting them as the sort of water for which one has to dig a well, in contrast to the stream of water that flows freely from wisdom. In Prov 20.5, similarly, the image is not of deep water, but of water that has to be drawn up from a depth. The usage can be extended to describe holes (cf. Prov 22.14; 23.27) or, in Ezek 23.32, a cup that goes down a long way, but the point here is most likely not that מה שהיה is 'unfathomable', or 'a depth too deep to plumb', in the sense of being too profound to comprehend, but that it is 'deep down', with an implication that it is buried too deep to find (cf. Ps 64.7 ET 64.6). In any case, it is things that are deep down which are difficult to find, not depths themselves (except, perhaps, in Job 12.22), but if we were to vocalize one עמק here as a noun, it would become the natural referent of the suffix on ימצאנו, displacing מה שהיה as in G, and Qohelet would be speaking of finding a depth. In order to retain the probable sense of the passage, in other words, we have to follow M and vocalize both uses of עמק as adjectives.

The repetition may mark a 'superlative', as Gordis, Seow and others claim, although they seem actually to be referring to the sort of rhetorical intensification described as an occasional function of repetition in GKC §133 k (which itself explicitly differentiates this usage from the expression of, and periphrases for the superlative). On that very common understanding, Qohelet is saying that it is 'very deep', but we could equally point to Deut 28.43 as evidence that he means 'deeper, ever deeper', and I have elected simply to keep the repetition, which picks up the pairing of רחוק רחוקה and רחוק.

7.24 who will find it?] A rhetorical question with מי of the sort used elsewhere in the book (e.g. 6.12; 7.13); it means, effectively, 'nobody can find it', and the attestation of ὃ οὐδείς for σ', indeed, probably reflects a rendering with the sense 'which nobody will find' (see Marshall; the subsequent verb is not attested but was probably εὑρήσει). The verb מצא will play a prominent role in the remainder of ch. 7, and it is worth noting at this point that Qohelet always uses it in its normal senses of 'finding', 'discovering' or 'encountering'. There are places like 3.11 and 8.17 where the verb is used in connection with intellectual endeavour, but those involve an idea of humans 'discovering' secrets or mysteries, and the verb does not mean 'comprehend' or 'understand' even in those contexts (see the notes at 3.11 and especially 7.26), let alone here, *pace* Krüger.

The masculine suffix pronoun is odd if it is supposed to refer to the preceding היא, or back to wisdom, and although both Gentry and Rahlfs take the neuter αὐτό to be G*, it is not surprising that a significant number of Greek witnesses have a feminine pronoun αὐτήν here, to match the likewise feminine αὐτὴ that corresponds to היא in G. This was probably the reading both of Origen (cf. Syh) and of La (cf. *eam* in the citation above from Cassian). As Goldman indicates, this feminine αὐτήν reflects an interpretation in terms of finding wisdom, which is an understanding sought by many commentators too. The rest of Goldman's discussion is rather confusing, since he insists on talking about the Greek text in terms of the Hebrew suffixes. When he says that 'The m. sfx., well attested in the ancient mss., would refer to the עמק', I assume that he is talking about the neuter pronoun αὐτό referring to the neuter βαθὺ βάθος—even though αὐτό is actually rather sparsely attested in the Greek tradition: no Hebrew manuscripts, so far as I am aware, read anything other than ימצאנו. Whatever has happened in the Greek, though, this Hebrew obliges us to take מה שהיה, and not היא, as the referent of the pronoun. I do not see why that should be considered problematic unless one insists that what is distant should be consistent throughout, but Pinker, 'Qohelet's Views on Women', 179, wants to see the נו- as a ligature for ם-, and read the pronoun as masculine plural, referring to the distance and depth. Apart from the fact that this gives an odd sense ('find' no more means 'measure' in Hebrew than it means 'understand'), it seems wholly unnecessary.

7.25

(7.25) My heart and I turned away, to know and to explore, and seek wisdom and a plan, and to know the wrongness of folly, and obtuseness and mindlessness.

Commentary

When Qohelet 'turned away' in 2.20, it was to cease caring about his business, after the anger and disappointment to which his own reflections had given rise. This is potentially a similar moment, following the recognition of his alienation from wisdom, although the language here also continues to echo the earlier, more optimistic intellectual enquiries of 1.13 and 1.17 (Ingram, 'Riddled with Ambiguity', 227, helpfully sets out the resemblances with 1.17 in a diagram). With his heart accompanying, he sets out to do something different, and the content of that enquiry must be related to what he will talk about in 7.26-29: indeed, he speaks of 'seeking' here, and of a 'plan', both of which will be key terms in those verses. Although we might reasonably hope, however, that this verse would therefore throw some light on what follows, it presents problems of its own. The most obvious of these lie in the second half, where numerous small issues with the text suggest that it may be corrupt, and any original point lost to us. As it stands, Qohelet seems to be promising enquiries there into matters that find little obvious echo in vv. 26-29, some of which he has investigated before, but there is evidence that he originally declared himself to be seeking to know wisdom and folly, each along with things that were associated with them (see the notes).

The first half of the verse is less difficult, but hardly more enlightening. Much hinges on the meaning of the word which I have translated here as a 'plan', and in 7.27-29 Qohelet will have more to say about the seeking and finding of the same thing by himself or others. Most commentators have long taken him to be saying by this that he is setting out to establish some sort of account or reckoning of the world, which would make this verse a response to his failure in 7.23-24, if those verses are also read in that way. This understanding depends, though, on granting to the Hebrew word here a connotation of being a 'special type' of plan, reckoning or calculation, just as commentators saw a 'special type' of wisdom in the last verses. Nowhere here, however, does Qohelet either specify such a particular meaning for these words or, for that matter, make any explicit effort actually to discover anything about the world or God's intentions for it. If this is what other humans in 7.29 are said to be attempting when they too 'seek' plans or reckonings, then there is, likewise, no clear indication of it in 7.26-28.

Notes

7.25 My heart and I turned away] Lit. 'I turned away, I and my heart', or less probably, 'I went around, I and my heart'. Qohelet used וסבותי אני earlier in 2.20, where the verb had the sense of turning around or away. Here, G ἐκύκλωσα and Hie *circuiui* probably have an implication more of encircling or going around something, which picks up the different and less common use of סבב found in 1.6; 9.14, and perhaps 12.5. That is also the literal sense of the verb in the hexaplaric reading περιώδευσα πάντα, 'I went around all things' (attributed to α′ in two manuscripts, but most plausibly to σ′ in ms 252; see Marshall). Jerome offers more context for this, however, translating σ′ in full as *pertransiui uniuersa sensu meo, scire, et disserere et inuestigare*, 'I passed by everything in my mind, to know, and to discuss, and to investigate', which makes it clear that he takes the Greek verb here to have an intellectual nuance, occasionally attested elsewhere, of reviewing or surveying. This undoubtedly influenced Jerome's own later rendering in V: *lustraui uniuersa animo meo ut scirem et considerarem et quaererem*, 'I have surveyed all things with my mind that I might know, consider and seek out'.

All of these renderings, along with S ܐܬܟܪܟܬ ܐܢܐ *'tkrkt 'n'*, 'I went around', understand Qohelet to be talking about further investigation, but the more likely nuance of the Hebrew is that he is turning from one thing to another, so that although the verse follows from 7.23-24, it also signals a discontinuity in Qohelet's own actions (so Hitzig: having found nothing good on one path 'somit schlägt er einen andern ein', 'he accordingly follows another'—which captures something of the image). At least σ′ and V may have been influenced, furthermore, by the relationship that they perceive between Qohelet and his heart here: *sensu meo* and *animo meo* both seem to suggest a reading בלבי, 'in/using my heart', instead of the ולבי, 'and my heart' of M. That בלבי is apparently presumed by Ibn Ezra and is actually found in a substantial number of later Hebrew manuscripts (see especially de Rossi), perhaps in part, at least, under the influence of T בליבבי, which itself supports בלבי (although G, S and Hie all support M); it also conforms more closely to Qohelet's usage elsewhere, since we find אני בלבי at 2.1, 15 (twice); 3.17,

18. In all of those other places, however, Qohelet is speaking 'in' his heart, and it is unlikely that he is 'turning' in his heart here: as Euringer suggests (see also Goldman), it is probably only interpretations of his statement as a reference to intellectual activity that have given rise to the reading בלבי, and it may not even be a very ancient variant, let alone a witness to the original reading. There are certainly no good grounds to emend to בלבי, as McNeile, 75, proposes, or to read לתור בלבי לבקש with Sacchi, let alone to delete the whole expression, as Galling 1940 wished to do, or to substitute ונתון לבי לתור for ולבי לדעת ולתור, following the suggestion of *BHS*, which is picked up by Longman. Richter, 'Kohelets Urteil', 587, adapts this to read ונתון לבי לדעתו לתור, taking לדעת to be original, but the subsequent conjunction to be a misplaced suffix—an emendation that is marginally less radical but seems no less arbitrary, even if it suits Richter's poetic scansion of the text.

If ולבי is indeed original, as seems likely, then Qohelet seems almost to be describing his heart (or mind) as a companion, as when he 'conversed with' it in 1.16 (cf. perhaps 9.1) and set it to a task in the following 1.17 (cf. 8.9, 16)—the strategy is investigated at length in Holmstedt, 'Syntactic Encoding'. The grammar might seem a little awkward if we expect to find a first-person plural verb here, and not a first-person singular (cf. Gen 41.11, אני...ונחלמה והוא), but it is not actually problematic. Hebrew can 'add' a subject, as in, e.g., Gen 32. 7 (ET 32.6), where Esau is הלך לקראתך, 'coming (sing.) to meet you', וארבע מאות איש עמו, 'and four hundred men with him', but the more important consideration is that when a verb precedes multiple subjects, it may agree with all of them or with just the first (cf. GKC §146 f; J-M §150 q). 1 Kgs 17.15 is slightly complicated by different *Qᵉrê* / *Kᵉthîbh* readings of the pronouns, but 'she, he, and her household' are all covered there by an initial third-person feminine singular verb (ותאכל), and see also, e.g., Gen 9.23, ויקח שם ויפת; Num 12.1, ותדבר מרים ואהרן. It is legitimate to ask whether, in syntactic terms, the subjects really are 'subjects' of the verb, and Holmstedt prefers, using the terminology of generative linguistics and drawing on some earlier work in this area, to speak here of 'I' picking up 'the null *pro* syntactic subject of the verb' and adding 'my heart' (14). However we analyse the phenomenon, though, we most naturally render the verb in such cases with a form that encompasses all the 'subjects'.

Although he has been followed by Seow and has more recently reiterated the view in his own commentary, Schoors, in *The Preacher* I, 154, greatly over-complicates the matter by citing Pss 3.5; 44.3; Isa 26.9 as parallels to the construction here, and referring to J-M §151 c. The construction involved in those passages and discussed by J-M is quite different: it consists of agreement between the verb and a suffix attached to a part (or to the voice) of a person, as in Isa 26.9, נפשי אויתיך, which is literally 'my נפש, I yearn for you', but has to be understood as '(With) my נפש I yearn for you'. That is a rare device, moreover, which seems to be confined to poetry, and it never involves a conjunction (there are no genuinely separate subjects). Here, where we have

אני ולבי functioning as two subjects of a verb and linked by a conjunction, it would seem unnecessary to suppose that סבותי is actually agreeing simply with the suffix on לבי (which might associate our text with that other construction).

Qohelet, then, is turning away from what he was doing in 7.23-24 in order to do something else, and he portrays his heart as his companion in this new endeavour. Is there any additional nuance? D'Alario, 'Between Misogyny and Valorization', 97, notes the use of the verb in 1.6, where there is an implication that the wind does not just turn, but ultimately turns back, and sees a 'rotary' movement here 'a metaphor for the human mind occupied…with a pitiful but unavoidable quest, which forces it to return to the same topics'. Without going so far, it is hard to ignore the apparent evocation of earlier vocabulary in what follows (cf. especially 1.13, 17; 2.12), and there is a possibility that Qohelet is talking not just about turning away, but about turning away and going back to the issues with which he had begun his investigation. In 1.6, however, the act of returning is described using שוב, not סבב, and when turning to go back is involved, the two verbs are paired also in Jer 41.14: it seems unlikely that סבב can convey that nuance by itself, and if Qohelet is indeed turning 'back', then that is implicit in the allusions, not explicit in the verb.

7.25 to know and to explore, and seek] The first two infinitives in the sequence לדעת ולתור ובקש have a prefixed -ל, while the third does not, and this difference is reflected in the probable G* τοῦ γνῶναι καὶ τοῦ κατασκέψασθαι καὶ ζητῆσαι, 'to know, and to spy out, and seek', which correspondingly avoids using τοῦ before the last verb. S ܠܡܕܥ ܘܠܡܣܥܪ ܘܠܡܒܥܐ *lmd' wlms'r wlmb'* probably just reflects an effort to impose consistency (as in T), either independently or under the influence of one of the numerous Greek manuscripts that have similarly added τοῦ. It is difficult to evaluate the reading of σ', which is cited by Jerome but only partly preserved in Greek: *scire, et disserere* (καὶ διαθρῆσαι) *et inuestigare*, 'to know and to examine and to investigate'. However, since it is more natural to smooth over such differences than to create them, as Euringer observes, it seems very likely that the absence of a third -ל is original.

It is harder, though, to say what, if anything, we should make of the distinction. Syntactically, it does not prevent us from reading all three verbs in parallel, but stylistically it does raise the possibility that the third is to be taken differently in some way, and that we are dealing with a signal that indicates how the text is to be read.[1] We should also observe that Qohelet has not so

---

[1] Schoors, citing Aalders, notes that in Hos 2.20 (ET 2.18) a sequence has עם before every member but the last, and refers to J-M §132 g for the opinion that prepositions need not be used consistently with every element of an enumeration. J-M itself also cites Hos 3.2 and 2 Kgs 13.23. In the first of those, however, the sequence is interrupted and the omission quite natural, while in the second the patriarchs are probably to be regarded as a group with which God has made a

far used בקש to describe his own enquiries, and that the verb does not usually possess such a sense in Hebrew, so is not a natural companion to דעת and תור. Without the conjunction on ובקש, it could be read as the object of those verbs, making Qohelet's investigation an exploration not of wisdom and חשבון, but of the human search for those things—which would fit very well with what he claims to find in 7.29, where humans בקשו חשבנות רבים. The text-critical problems created by early efforts to construe this verse in different ways will become very clear in what follows, and it would not be unreasonable to question the originality of this conjunction. I doubt, however, that it is necessary to do so.

As the text stands, it would be possible to achieve a similar sense by taking the conjunctions to be paired ('to know and to explore both the search for wisdom and a חשבון'), but that seems forced, and the differentiation of בקש may indicate no more than that there is some sort of break here for emphasis: Qohelet is going to know and explore (in a more general way)...but then specifically to *seek out* wisdom and a חשבון—which would suit the fact that Qohelet has previously used prepositions to mark the object of תור in 1.13 and 2.3, and explain the subsequent need for a resumptive לדעת. Riesener, 'Frauenfeindschaft', 206, similarly takes the conjunction as explicative, highlighting בקש as a keyword. To that extent, there might even be an allusion to the exhortation to seek insight in Prov 2.4, as Estes, 'Seeking and Finding', 125, suggests (although I am not persuaded by the various other allusions to Proverbs that he finds in these verses).

7.25 wisdom and] Although he does not translate it as such, Schoors describes the alliterative חכמה וחשבון as a hendiadys, following Whybray, and says that '"wisdom obtained by investigation" is a good rendering of the word pair' (cf. also Murphy). Michel, *Untersuchungen*, 235, talks similarly of the expression as a 'compound' ('Verbindung') and of חשבון as a special type of wisdom—an opinion that has been re-iterated by Seow—and Crenshaw speaks even more broadly of חשבון constituting 'the substance of human thought, the sum total of all knowledge', when it is 'coupled with' wisdom. Schwienhorst-Schönberger, 'Bitterer als der Tod', 447, expresses a similar idea in rather different terms when he claims that the ו- must be understood not as coordinating, but as specifying, so that in effect this means 'חכמה i.e. חשבון'. Of course, whether we treat the pairing of the nouns in such a way will depend in part on how we understand חשבון, and whether, consequently, a hendiadys or compound expression would make good sense here—which my own understanding leads me to doubt. There is a more compelling reason to avoid such a synthesis, however: if חשבון merely qualifies a חכמה that is being sought, then it is difficult to see why it is the חשבון alone that is sought in 7.27

covenant (as suggested by J-M in the following note). This does not mean, of course, that such omissions can never occur, but we should be clear that they are not so commonplace as to be ignored easily. See also the note at 5.16.

(and חשבנות in 7.29), while there is no further direct mention of חכמה in the rest of the chapter. While it might be possible to see a reference here to a חשבון that is characterized by wisdom, the context makes it unlikely that Qohelet is talking about a wisdom that is characterized by חשבון.

7.25 a plan] Pointed as חֶשְׁבּוֹן (cf. Jerome's transliteration as *esebon* in his commentary on 7.27-29), the word חשבון usually occurs as a geographical name ('Heshbon') in M, but it obviously bears a different sense in Eccl 7.25, 27 and 9.10. Here, in the first of these uses, it is paired with חכמה, and in 9.10 it is one of the things that is said to be missing in Sheol—alongside action, knowledge and wisdom—so it appears to be associated with an intellectual activity. Qohelet 'seeks' one here, and one is sought in 7.27 too, with some implication that it is difficult to find. Since humans also 'seek' the חשבנות to which Qohelet refers very shortly afterwards in 7.29, it seems reasonable to suppose that the noun in that verse is simply a plural form of the same noun חשבון (in a context where the plural is required), even though M points it as though from an unattested singular חִשָּׁבוֹן, using the vocalization found in the only other biblical occurrence of חשבנות, at 2 Chr 26.15 (cf. 1Q27 1 II, 2 [ת]חשבוֹנוֹ).

G notably renders the חשבון of 7.27 and the חשבנות of 7.29 using forms of the same word (λογισμόν, λογισμούς), although it does use a different term (ψῆφος) at 7.25, and, unless we imbue the vocalization in M with great interpretative significance, it does not seem that any of the ancient versions observed the clear distinction of sense between חשבון and חשבנות that is emphasized by some modern commentators.[2] If people can seek חשבנות רבים, though, then they can also seek a particular חשבון, so, despite its association with intellectual activity and with wisdom in 7.25 and 9.10, the term probably does not refer to an intellectual quality directly comparable with wisdom (the adjective in 7.29 prevents us, of course, from taking חשבנות as comparable to the חכמות of, e.g., Prov 1.20; Ps 49.4 ET 49.3, which is plural in form but not

---

[2] Note especially Schoors, *The Preacher* II, 446-47, who claims that commentators who treat the terms together are overlooking 'the peculiar vocalization' of חשבנות in M, and who goes on to suggest that 'in the present context and with the particular vocalization' this term in 7.29 may have a much broader sense. The point about context is questionable, in light of the similarities with 7.27, but the observations about vocalization can only indicate at most an issue in the traditional or Masoretic interpretation of this verse, rather than a matter of authorial intention, and there may be no more involved than an assimilation to the pointing in 2 Chr 26.15. Seow notes more sensibly that 'We do not know if the word is correctly vocalized in this passage', but the simple fact is that the author had no way to impose any permanent distinction between חֶשְׁבּוֹן and חִשָּׁבוֹן, if they even really existed as separate words, and we could only legitimately suppose that readers would have been led to understand חשבנות as distinct if we had any reason to believe that this form of the plural was specifically associated with a different noun—which the occurrence in 1Q27 tells against.

meaning). It also seems unlikely that חשבון represents something that can only exist in one true form, like 'the explanation of the universe' or some such: in 7.27, where we might expect to find even a concept like חכמה determined, חשבון lacks a definite article, and it is clear that what Qohelet seeks is '*a* חשבון', not '*the* חשבון'.

Beyond that, however, it becomes harder to pin down the sense—not because we have no evidence, but because the evidence points in several different directions, and different understandings of the word have been influenced by separate semantic developments from the root. As is often noted, the cognate Ugaritic *ḥtbn* is used to head lists or accounts of inventory (e.g. RS 15.062 line 1; 18.024 line 1), and the Aramaic חשבן can be used in the same way (see especially TAD C3.28, 79 line 79 = Cowley, no. 81, line 1); in a later bilingual text from Palmyra תגרא לכל די עלל לחשבן is equivalent to ὅσα εἰς ἐμπορείαν φέρεται, and apparently refers to the application of tax to miscellaneous items (only) at the point when they enter a merchant's 'inventory' or 'stock' to go on sale.[3] At least in these languages, therefore, חשבון could be used to mean a list, or enumeration of the elements that belonged to something or someone, and the sense may be similar in 1QS vi, 20, where the possessions and earnings of an initiate are ascribed בחשבון בידו, which apparently refers to a list of things that are his, and not the community's.

In less clear-cut contexts, it can be difficult to distinguish this sense from uses of the term to indicate calculation or computation, which move a little beyond observational counting or listing (cf. in Aramaic 4QEnGiants[b] ar [4Q530] i, 4, בחשבון שניא, 'according to the reckoning of the years'; 1QapGen ar vi, 9, the calculation of the number of jubilees in a lifetime). Something of this latter understanding is found also in rabbinic usage, where the noun appears in the context of presenting financial accounts for settlement,[4] and is

---

[3] CIS 3913, the Tariff of Palmyra: see conveniently PAT 0259/C3913 line 115 in Hillers and Cussini, *Palmyrene Aramaic Texts*, 62. Hillers and Cussini raise the possibility in their glossary (367) that the expression here means 'on account of' (a rare sense attested for על חשבן in Syriac and possibly in another Palmyrene text), but this seems unlikely in context.

[4] Delitzsch equates 'giving' (נתן) a חשבון in mishnaic Hebrew with the New Testament usage of λόγον ἀποδιδόναι, which is found in, e.g., Mt 12.36. The Greek expression, which came to mean 'give an account of oneself (in the face of judgment)', is indeed matched occasionally, although only in much later Jewish texts: Midrash Qohelet itself speaks twice at 12.1, for example, of everyone being destined ליתן before God דין וחשבון, 'to present before him a case and account' (of themselves; cf. *Pirkei ʾAbot* 3:1). In Aramaic, the Targum Pseudo-Jonathan to Gen 3.19 has the promise made to Adam similarly include a claim that he will rise למיתן דינא וחושבנא על כל מה דעבדת ביום דינא רבא, 'to present a case and an account concerning all that you have done, on the great day of judgment'. This is not so very different from more everyday uses, however, as when Moses gives a חשבון to the Israelites in the Midrash Rabbah to Exod 38.21, and he is just literally

used metaphorically in *b. Baba Batra* 78b of balancing the immediate losses and gains incurred by obedience to the law against the ultimate rewards and punishments. This is described as חשבונו של עולם, lit. perhaps 'the calculation/ accounting of temporal matters' (not an account of the world or of human affairs, as Jastrow, *Dictionary*, suggests); a little later, the wicked are said to claim that this has ceased to exist when they deny God's existence.[5]

presenting the accounts on completion of the Tabernacle, or when חשבון is used in *b. Megillah* 31a to describe the 'reckoning' of readings from the Torah, against which individual readings are checked off. The financial usage is copiously illustrated in *b. Šabbat* 150 a-b, which discusses the accounts that may and may not be dealt with on the sabbath. The broader context is of speech on the sabbath, and the discussion is illustrated with examples of people stating their expenditure to those who are supposed to pay them, which make it clear that the subject-matter here, and the sense of the term חשבון מחשבין, is not the calculation of accounts or the balancing of books, but the presentation of expenses for settlement. This usage fits well with the notion of a דין and חשבון that is to be presented to God: humans will have to itemize and justify their activities in order to earn their due recompense. There may have been some more complicated developments or extensions of the 'invoice' connotation. In *b. Gittin* 14a we are told about a group of workers who do a חושבנא with each other and discover that one of them has five staters too much, which is duly handed over to their employer—only for that worker then to do his own חושבנא and discover that he did not, after all, have too much. It is not entirely clear what is going on here, but the workers are apparently trying to square their own claims for payment with a sum that has been paid to them collectively. Rather than seeing a specific technical meaning, though, we should perhaps take the Aramaic to be expressing a vaguer sense that the workers were 'doing their accounts', or some such.

[5] That same passage subsequently uses a wordplay, based on מחשבון ('from Heshbon') in Num 21.28, to claim that a fire will go out from those who 'do the sums' (מחשבין) and consume those who do not. This seems to be the basis for claims that חשבון is being used with reference here to a day of 'reckoning', and Seow talks of this passage describing 'an accounting of the world on the day of judgment...that is, a reckoning of the fate of the good and the wicked'. Although there is indeed a reference at the end to a coming judgment of the wicked, however, חשבון does not characterize either that judgment or its basis (here or, to the best of my knowledge, anywhere else): it is used not of a way in which God distinguishes good from bad or determines the fate of each, but of a calculation that has been made by the righteous; unlike the wicked, they perceive that their ultimate gains have to be factored in to any accounting of purely temporal gains and losses (cf. Levy, *Wörterbuch*). The whole passage, in fact, is a midrashic treatment of Num 21.27-30 which plays extensively on the place-names and on Heshbon in particular, so its usages are rather forced: its חשבונו של עולם is a product of its exegesis, and probably not a reference to some widespread concept. I can only assume that Schoors too has this passage in mind, when he claims in a similar way that 'The commercial meaning in MH often receives a figurative sense, as

Elsewhere, חשבון refers to numbers and, perhaps, to arithmetic: in *b. Bekorot* 5a, Moses is defended against the charge that he might not be 'good with numbers' (בקי בחשבונות) because of an apparent inconsistency in the sums between Exod 38.26 and 27. The sense is probably similar when *b. Baba Batra* 9b speaks of small donations combining to become a great 'number' or 'amount' (לחשבון גדול). This is not a 'sum total', since that idea is generally expressed in other ways (cf. בכלל in the passage from *b. Bekorot*), and since the context is not really one of addition but of combination or accumulation: analogies are offered with links in mail-armour and with threads in clothes to make the point that small things can make up something greater than themselves while remaining small.

In the Aramaic and later rabbinic uses of חשבון, then, we find references to enumeration, to computation, and to numbers, along with a particular use to describe the presentation of financial accounts for settlement. It is difficult to know, however, which of these would have been familiar to the author of Ecclesiastes or his readers. Whatever the original associations of the root with counting, in fact, terms derived from חשב in earlier, biblical Hebrew are rarely linked directly with numbers or accounting, and apart from some legal discussions in Lev 25 and 27, it is only 2 Kgs 12.16 (which has a similarly technical reference) that shows any clear use of the verb חָשַׁב in that sense. This may be in part a product of the subject-matter in our texts, but they refer much more commonly either to estimation and evaluation, or to planning and invention (sometimes in the form of craftsmanship), while the associated noun מחשבה is used of thoughts, plans and schemes.

Although a certain technical or commercial usage undoubtedly persisted, moreover, it is clear that such usage was not behind most of the early appearances of חשבון itself outside Ecclesiastes. In 2 Chr 26.15, the term חשבנות מחשבת חושב, perhaps literally 'devices of the devising of a deviser', describes what were apparently fixed-mount artillery weapons, set on the walls of Jerusalem to fire stones or arrows against potential attackers. This does not imply that Qohelet may be alluding to the human construction of artillery in 7.29 (as Lohfink, 'War Kohelet ein Frauenfeind', 286, very curiously suggests), but it does tie the noun firmly to the more common uses of the verb. Elsewhere, Sir 9.15 (where חשבון stands in parallel with סוד, 'confidential speech') seems to be making the point that one should be careful to share one's conversations or confidences only with the wise, while the context of Sir 27.5 suggests that the testing of a man על חשבונו is a reference to what he says when he

applied to moral accountability, punishment and reward'. He offers no references, and might alternatively be speaking of the 'accounts' that must be given to God by individuals, which we considered in the last note. In either case, however, 'often' would be an overstatement, and the claim wrongly implies that השבון has itself acquired a connotation of 'holding accountable' or 'judging', which is patently not true.

speaks, through which the cultivation of his mind can be perceived (with the implication that his חשבון could be good or bad). In both cases, the Greek translator has opted to use διαλογισμός, which refers to judicial decisions in Hellenistic Greek (see MM) and develops a broader sense of 'idea' or 'plan' in NT usage, while in neither place would 'accounting' be appropriate. Chronicles uses the noun in a context of invention, therefore, and Ben Sira in relation to the content of speech, but the usage of חשבון in both works seems to associate it more with the products and designs of human intelligence than with the reckoning or calculation of something external to the self. The notion of 'plans' more generally is found in Aramaic in 4QNoah ar (4Q534) I, 9-13, where both the hero and his opponents will have (controversial but unspecified) 'plans'.

Matters are more complicated in 1QH^a IX, 29, where the context describes a divine creation of speech, and the references to measurement might lead one to think in terms of calculation or accounting, but לחשבונם there probably indicates that utterances are brought out 'in accordance with the plans for them'; this is true also in 4Q254^a where, if חשבון has correctly been restored in the second line, then it apparently describes the list of measurements that follows as 'the plan of manufacture' of Noah's ark, rather than as an account of its components. Both texts, accordingly, seem to understand a חשבון to be something like a 'blueprint' or 'schedule'.

The only early use that potentially associates the noun with the technical, financial use of the cognate verb is in the first half of the difficult Sir 42.3, which is often interpreted in terms of making financial settlements or keeping accounts with companions—a sense lent weight by the reference to the division of inheritances in the second part of the verse, and perhaps an early example of the use for 'expenses'. Even though this meaning becomes very important in later Hebrew, therefore, it seems neither to have been the principal meaning of חשבון in most earlier texts, nor typically to have been extended outside specific references to financial settlements.

In short, then, חשבון is used in various times and places of inventories, of invoices, of computation more generally, of invention and inventions, of the expression of ideas, and of plans. Some or all of these senses doubtless co-existed in some contexts. This is a wide field, but the context and Qohelet's usage can help us to narrow his meaning: it seems unlikely, for instance, that people are seeking inventories or accounts of expenditure, even in some broad, metaphorical sense, and it is not clear that one could really 'seek' (as opposed to 'improve') the way of talking mentioned in Sir 27.5—for better or worse, everyone already has that. If Qohelet wants an invention or a blueprint, furthermore, it is not clear what he wants it for, and if he is speaking about plans in some specific way, then he would surely want more than one—if it is some great, over-arching plan for the world that people are looking for, on the other hand, it is not clear why that should always be 'a' plan, or how it could exist in multiple forms.

Especially given the association here with wisdom, I think the understanding of חשבון most compatible both with Qohelet's usage and with the meanings attested elsewhere must lie in the sphere of plans and calculations that people make about their own lives—about just how righteous it is sensible to be, for instance—and this would accord well with a common use of the cognate verb חשב to talk about the way in which people try to make plans for themselves (cf. especially Prov 16.9). On that understanding, when people seek a חשבון, what they are seeking is a way to take stock of what confronts them, and work out what to do. These are ideas associated with חשבון elsewhere, although they are not easily captured by any single word in English.[6]

Many interpretations of חשבון here have been guided, however, by other considerations. As we have already noted, G uses ψῆφος in 7.25. This refers to a pebble or small piece of stone, and in some other contexts the term is connected with voting, for which such pebbles might be used; this forms the basis of Vinel's translation ('suffrage'), but it is unlikely in this context that the translator had that use in mind. Here, it more probably means a 'number' (as in, e.g., Rev 13.18): small pebbles were used on ancient counting-boards in much the same way as beads are used on an abacus—which is how terms like 'calculation' came ultimately to be derived from the equivalent Latin word *calculus*. It is not clear what sort of 'number' the translator might have thought that Qohelet was looking for, but the rendering suggests that his own understanding of חשבון was, at least initially, in the sort of numerical terms attested for later rabbinic Hebrew (possibly influenced also by the appearance of actual numbers in 7.27-28)—and that he may himself have found the use of the word here puzzling.

G switches in subsequent verses to a different term, λογισμός. Since this can refer to calculations, it is not clear that the translator has entirely moved on from the idea that numbers are involved. This use of λογισμός, however, both in G and in the other Greek translations, opened the interpretative door much wider, because the term can be used to talk not just of calculation, but of thinking and reasoning in much more general or abstract ways. Consequently, Jerome's later discussion of the usage, for example, offers a range

---

[6] Schwab, 'Woman', understands the noun broadly in these terms, but notes also that Qohelet uses it only in contexts where he talks also about women. He deduces that it refers specifically in the book to romantic relationships, and that it is such a relationship that Qohelet seeks here. Schwab himself pursues this idea, unconvincingly, in terms of Solomon's relationships: it might work better, perhaps, as a reference to Qohelet's desire for a relationship with wisdom (with which חשבון is more closely associated in both 7.25 and 9.9-10). In the end, however, even though he tries to link them by talking about amorous 'intrigues', the main difficulty with Schwab's proposal is that what he wants חשבון to mean here is just too far from any other known uses of the word.

of translations using Latin terms that permit both a literal understanding in terms of calculation, and an extended or abstracted understanding in terms of reasoning or cogitation, so that humans can be depicted as using their rationality to seek a rationale, or to develop their own thoughts about the world.[7] Many modern commentators have followed a similar route, sometimes drawing in the commercial Aramaic usage and exploiting a similar breadth of meaning in terms like 'reckoning' or 'accounting'. This leads to an understanding that what Qohelet seeks is, in fact, some underlying rationale for his observations of the world. Seow, for instance, defines חשבון as 'an intellectual accounting, that is, an explication…of the events in the universe' which 'probably includes activities that approximate what we call "philosophy"'— and while this would be a reasonable description of λογισμός, it goes so far beyond any use of חשבון attested elsewhere that we could hardly speak even of it being an extended, abstracted or metaphorical sense.[8] So far as we can tell, any ancient reader who did not see a reference to a plan, blueprint or number here would have taken Qohelet to be seeking an inventory, a calculation or a settlement of debt—not looking to conduct an audit of the world.

7.25 and to know] Jost, 'Frau und Adam', 63-64, interprets the text as saying that Qohelet set out to find one thing (wisdom in the form of the results of investigations), only in the end to find another (wickedness etc.). The repetition of לדעת is striking, to be sure, but, as the text stands, the infinitive is still subordinate to the initial סבותי and stands in parallel with at least the

---

[7] Jerome comments at 7.27 that, although all the Greek translators render *esebon* with (the accusative) λογισμόν there, which he imitates using *numerus* ('number'), the ambiguity of the Hebrew word would also permit Latin translations like *summa* ('sum' or 'the sum [of everything]'), *ratio* ('reckoning', 'calculation', or '[the mental faculty of] reason'), and *cogitatio* ('thinking' or '[the mental faculty of] thought'). He also illustrates the proposed diversity of meaning himself in the lemma to his commentary, by using *ratio* at 7.25, *numerus* at 7.27, and *cogitatio* at 7.29 (in the plural) and 9.10—in the Vulgate these become *ratio* everywhere except 7.29, where he resorts to a paraphrase based on σ'.

[8] Fox suggests that, on the contrary, the 'semantic range' of חשבון is 'well reflected' by λογισμός, claiming that it 'refers to both the process of reckoning and the solution reached', but offers no evidence that it ever has either sense elsewhere. He does, however, cite with approval the opinion of Machinist in 'Reflections', who understands Qohelet to be using the term with a high level of abstraction (170-71), and sees his usage as part of an effort to develop a new technical vocabulary for discussions of this sort (172). Of course that is a possibility, but to argue for such a sense on the basis of a context that does not *demand* such a sense is to risk circularity: Machinist uses his understanding of חשבון to interpret the very texts from which he then formally derives that understanding— and in doing so, of course, also applies the concepts from Greek second-order thinking which then enable him to find such second-order thinking throughout the book.

preceding ולתור ולדעת: we would expect a new main verb here, to give the sort of sense that Jost wants. I do wonder myself, though, whether the original intention was for לדעת not to stand in parallel with the previous infinitives, but to specify the nature of the חשבון that Qohelet seeks—perhaps a plan for knowing the wrongness of folly etc. The conjunction tells against that, however, and is supported by all the witnesses, while such a reading would more or less compel us to understand 7.26 as a description of wisdom.

7.25 the wrongness of folly, and obtuseness and mindlessness] There are several problems here, making it difficult, and perhaps impossible, even to establish what text we should be reading. It may be helpful to describe these individually.

(1) רשע may be vocalized as רֶשַׁע, 'wickedness', or רָשָׁע, 'a wicked man': the proper vocalization has to be deduced from context, and M's tradition has opted for 'wickedness' (as have Hie, V, S, T), but G for 'wicked man'.

(2) The word כסיל means 'fool', but the related noun כסל does not mean 'folly': everywhere else (when the reference is not to 'loins') it means 'confidence' (cf. Pinker, 'Qohelet's Views on Women', 180), and although that confidence may be misplaced (as in Ps 49.14 ET 49.13), the term is not in itself pejorative. The meaning 'folly' is never found in Aramaic or in later Hebrew, moreover (except just possibly, in 4Q300 [4QMyst^b] 1, ɪɪ, 2, where כסלכמה, 'your כסל', appears in a context where both false teachings and a lack of understanding are involved). If like M, therefore, we read כֶּסֶל here, the context pushes us to take it in a sense that is otherwise never clearly attested. G ἀφροσύνην apparently does this (although we shall return to its reading), but S, T, Hie, V all have 'fool' instead of 'folly', and have either read כסיל or taken כסל to be a writing of כסיל.

(3) It is difficult to establish the original equivalent to והסכלות in G. There are particular problems in G at 1.17, discussed in the note there on 'mindlessness and obtuseness', but the translator consistently renders the noun elsewhere with ἀφροσύνη (2.3, 12, 13; 10.1, 13). Here, however, if he found the same words and word-order that we find in M, he must have used ἀφροσύνην for כסל (or however he read that word) instead, leaving the equivalent to הסכלות as one of two words barely attested elsewhere in Greek: σκληρίαν, presumably 'hardness', or ὀχληρίαν, 'annoyance'; these are graphically very similar (ϹΚΛ-, ΟΧΛ-), and one probably arose as an error for the other. The reading ὀχληρίαν is much more common, and Aitken, 'Rhetoric and Poetry', 66-67, notes both its early attestation and the appearance of the word in a first-century BCE papyrus (which also, interestingly, uses περισπασμός, another unusual term favoured by G). As we saw earlier, the adjective σκληρός, related to σκληρίαν, is found at 7.17 where M has סכל (itself, of course, related to סכלות); there is no rival to σκληρός in the manuscript tradition for that verse, except an obvious error σκηρος, and it is doubtless that fact which led Rahlfs to take σκληρίαν as G* here (Gentry had σκληρός in 7.17, but has ultimately opted for ὀχληρίαν here). However,

σκληρίαν is an incomprehensible rendering of any form from כסל—σκληρός usually renders קשה, as we might expect, and the only basis on which G might have used it for כסל would be the phonetic resemblance between the two (so Vinel at 7.17)—a potential last resort if the translator did not actually understand the word. Since he translates it without difficulty elsewhere, it is clear that he did know the sense of כסל, and this makes it likely that we should read not σκληρίαν / σκληρός here and in 7.17, but ὀχληρία / ὀχληρός: the former was preserved by almost all manuscripts in this verse, but the latter almost completely extinguished in 7.17, where the more common word σκληρός is less obviously inappropriate. Just as he prefers ἀφροσύνη for סכלות, however, so the translator of G also consistently prefers ἄφρων for כסל elsewhere (2.19; 10.3, 6, 14). That presents him with a difficulty here, because he uses ἄφρων for כסיל as well (2.14-16; 4.5, 13, 17, etc.), which he treats as a virtual synonym of כסל. If he felt constrained by the context to understand כסל (or whatever he read) as 'folly' then it is not surprising that he should have used ἀφροσύνη for that, and might then have had to reach for a different translation of סכלות. The idea that ὀχληρία might be a sort of 'back-up' translation for סכלות, to be sure, though, is not entirely borne out by its use in 7.17, where there is no obvious reason for G not to have used ἄφρων for כסל, while the very term ὀχληρία seems an unlikely synonym for ἀφροσύνη. Given the translator's preference for consistency, and the scope for confusion between terms with כסל and with כסל (although the later Hebrew manuscript tradition is remarkably consistent in this respect), we may reasonably wonder whether M and the source-text of G were identical in every respect.

(4) In any case, G (and α')[9] almost certainly did not read the article that M has on הסכלות, but strangely on no other word; cf. the note on 'the obtuseness' at 2.13. The presence or absence of this article constrains the ways in which we can understand the relation of the last two words in particular. Pinker, 'Qohelet's Views on Women', 180-81, simply deletes it so that he can read a construct: 'to know the wickedness of self-confidence and the stupidity of unruliness'. This is attractively simple, and might explain why the nouns are not in their usual order (see below), but is speculative, and does not offer any particular improvement to the sense in context.

---

[9] In the midst of all the other complications surrounding the text of G in the next verse, 7.26, there is a striking addition καὶ εὐφροσύνην πλάνας found in hexaplaric manuscripts and in a correction to Codex Sinaiticus (εὐφροσύνην = ἀφροσύνην; cf. the note at 2.3). πλάνας / πλάνη has long been known as a part of the α' reading (it renders הוללות; on the various Greek translations of that word, see the note at 1.17), and Goldman's deduction, that the plus in fact reflects the fuller reading of α' for this verse, has now been confirmed by the reading of ms 788 given by Gentry as καὶ ἀφροσύνην καὶ πλάνας, as also has his observation that the α' rendering of הסכלות therefore includes no article.

(5) At least in the Greek tradition, and possibly more widely, the development of the text may have been influenced by readings of the next verse, 7.26, which require a feminine referent for an 'it' or 'her' that Qohelet claims to have seen—סכלות and הוללות are the closest candidates.

(6) Finally, the last word, הוללות, has no conjunction in M^L or other early witnesses to M, and this absence is reflected in Jerome's translations also.[10] De Rossi lists, however, a significant number of later Hebrew manuscripts which do read והוללות, and a conjunction is reflected also in G, S, and most manuscripts of T. It is difficult to say whether the conjunction has been omitted to facilitate the reading of a separate clause (see below), or added on the assumption that the list continues—although we should note both that the same nouns are joined by a conjunction elsewhere, in 1.17 and 2.12—a fact that might be taken either for or against the originality of a conjunction here—and that in those verses they appear in reverse as הוללות ושכלות / הוללות וסכלות (although cf. 10.13).[11]

This variation in respect of the conjunction, in fact, has been much more influential than it sounds. The early Masoretes, likely vocalizing a text that had no conjunction, seem to have read the last two words as a non-verbal clause ('[know that] סכלות is הוללות'), and to have understood רשע כסל accordingly as another such clause equating two abstract nouns: Qohelet is, therefore, looking to know that 'wickedness is folly and the obtuseness is confusion'.[12] The translator of G sees instead a list, in which only one of the components, כסל, lacks the conjunction expected in such lists. Goldman suggests that he

---

[10] Hie *imprudentium errorem* and V *errorem inprudentium*, 'the error of the imprudent' suggest that Jerome attempted to read a construct relationship between the words, which the article on הסכלות makes impossible in M. Since Jerome himself seems to reverse the sense, however, and to take one noun improbably as a reference to people, he is most likely aware of that, and his contortions cannot be used to deduce further that his own Hebrew text must have lacked the article. The reading of σ' for הוללות is attested as ἔννοιαν θορυβώδη, 'confused thinking', and Goldman thinks that this likewise suggests the absence of a conjunction. Such notes, however, usually contain only the information necessary to distinguish the reading from the base text with which it is compared, so the absence of a καὶ is not determinative, and may even suggest that σ' shared that reading with G.

[11] It seems more likely that the conjunction arose or was removed as an attempted facilitation than that it came about simply through a mistaken transposition of ה and ו in הוללות which turned it into והללות, as Euringer suggests. He is right, though, to say that it would be unlike the translator to make such a change himself, so whether the conjunction is secondary or original, it was almost certainly in G's source-text.

[12] This is the understanding in Codex Graecus Venetus. I am not sure why Goldman, who considers the article on הסכלות secondary, takes it to betray M's intention to read a non-verbal clause: the absence of an article on the corresponding הוללות would seem to make that reading less, not more straightforward.

has accordingly taken רשע כסל as a construct chain, but reversed the normal sense (he has hardly misconstrued it, as Euringer claims) to get ἀσεβοῦς ἀφροσύνην, 'the folly of an impious man'—which could then be considered as a single item (the word-order indicates that he did not find כסל רשע). Alternatively, he may be trying to deal with רשע by making it the source of knowledge: 'to know of/from an impious man: folly, and…and…'. T does much the same, but without the reversal: understanding כסיל rather than כסל, it can talk about חובת שטיא, 'the sin of the fool'. S has followed G, and Jerome has also adopted G's perception of a list here: finding a text without a conjunction on the last word, however, he has resorted to dealing with הסכלות הוללות in much the same way that G dealt with רשע כסל.

Subsequent commentators have likewise tended to parse the text either as two clauses, following the majority M reading, or as a list, broadly following G but usually taking רשע כסל as two separate items: thus Seow, for example, has 'to know wickedness to be foolishness and folly to be irrationality', while Fox reads 'to understand wickedness, stupidity, and folly, <and> madness'. Of these, the second is the lesser evil, both because it is difficult to establish that 'know x y' could mean 'know *that* x *is* y' without a כי,[13] and because the equation of סכלות with הוללות seems either pointless (if Qohelet's pairing of them elsewhere suggests that they are virtual synonyms anyway) or to run against Qohelet's understanding (if that pairing suggests instead that they are distinct).

In any case, there are many variations on both readings, of course, but most commentators acknowledge the text to be difficult, and few find a pleasing sense in either. We may observe, furthermore, that although these construals deal with the overall shape, they do not in themselves address such problems as the meaning of כסל or the anomalous determination of סכלות. There is a strong possibility, in fact, that the text is irrecoverably corrupt (Galling 1940, for example, simply deletes it all—for once with some justice), and that errors or misunderstandings of the author's intention have eventually left it buried too deep beneath accumulating 'clarifications' for us to retrieve it.

In fact, though, I think that we can take one or two steps toward restoration. In light of points (2) and (4) above, it seems probable that what the G translator found here was רשע כסלות וסכלות והוללות, or רשע והוללות וסכלות,

---

[13] GKC §117 ii takes this as one of only three instances of a second object with a *verba sentiendi*, used of knowing something 'to be' something: the other examples are Gen 7.1 ('seen you righteous') and Isa 53.4 ('reckoned him smitten'). These are not, however, good parallels to the sense proposed here: each uses an adjective or participle attributively, not a substantive. It would be a real stretch for the verb to cover two such constructions, both expressing equivalence, and if we were to insist on this sense then we should probably have to construe the text as something analogous to direct rather than indirect speech—'to know "wickedness (is) folly" and "foolishness (is) confusion"'.

with a noun interpreted correctly as a form connected to כסיל (but perhaps written defectively). The anomalous article in M would then most likely be a secondary error ותו → וה or הו → וה. The latter is simpler, but כסילות is at least attested directly in Prov 9.13, where it may have been coined to provide an אשת כסילות parallel to the חכמות of 9.1.[14] In either case, the rarity of the word may have contributed to the misreading, but itself suggests an allusion to that passage—and if so, Qohelet is declaring here a dual quest to know Wisdom (and the planning that goes with wisdom), but also to know Folly (and the bad qualities associated with her, paired as elsewhere in the book, although with the usual order reversed to allow the pleasing כסלות וסכלות or וסכלות כסלה). If the Greek preserves a better reading in this respect, furthermore, I think this tilts the balance slightly towards viewing the conjunction on והוללות as original, and that also suits the easier reading of the terms as a list. I have translated accordingly.

I have some suspicions about רשע, which is universally attested, but which has no direct counterpart in the statement about seeking wisdom. It is tempting, in particular, to wonder whether the word might, in fact, be an error for רשת, 'a net', which would make 7.26 more explicitly a description of folly, or whether Qohelet actually spoke originally about an אשת כסילות himself. If the term is original, on the other hand, then the intention may have been for it to stand as a pair with folly, as in 7.17, where Qohelet admonishes against being wicked or a fool. In this context, that would favour the M interpretation of the word as 'wickedness', and perhaps imply also that another conjunction has been lost—this time without trace. With no actual evidence to go on, however, I have retained the text as it stands here, and translated it as a construct 'wickedness of folly'.

---

[14] Riesener, 'Frauenfeindschaft', 205, does not emend, but takes the article on הסכלות to indicate that there is a deliberate allusion here to the אשת כסילות of Proverbs. This would be plausible, though a little tenuous, were we to retain the text as it stands, but she does not address the problems raised by כסל.

7.26

(7.26) If I found her, I would say, 'More bitter than death is this woman, she who is all nets, and her heart dragnets, her hands fetters. Whoever seems right to God will escape from her, while one who is wrong will be trapped in her.'

Commentary

The Hebrew is ambiguous: on the more obvious understanding, adopted by the ancient versions, Qohelet calls the woman 'bitter', but he can also be understood to be calling her 'strong' (see the notes). On the interpretation advocated here, that makes little substantial difference, but this verse is more commonly read as a statement about women in general (Lohfink, 'War Kohelet ein Frauenfeind', 279, describes it as the sort of thing men say among each other—'locker-room talk', perhaps),[1] and in that case, 'strong' obviously offers a more positive evaluation, even if the association with death remains sinister. That reading, in fact, is difficult for other reasons, even if we do not take Qohelet to be talking specifically about wisdom or folly: the construction of the Hebrew is unusual (again, see the notes), but he is probably at most then talking just about the sort of woman 'who is nets', etc., not all women.

Before 'more bitter', or 'stronger', the Hebrew text here has only the awkward 'and finding I': the fuller reading of the Greek establishes the context of what Qohelet is saying, and is more likely to be original. It is not entirely clear, though, whether Qohelet is referring to wisdom or to folly by 'her', and if that is not just a product of the textual disturbances at the end of the last verse, then he may be leaving the matter open deliberately (and perhaps by 'her' we should understand 'either one of them'). Many commentators,

---

[1] Lohfink actually develops a rather complicated explanation for this and the following verses, in which Qohelet disproves the idea that women are stronger than death through observations of human mortality. The idea that Qohelet is citing a popular saying or opinion is also associated with Michel, *Untersuchungen*, 225, 236.

however, have seen a particular connection with the figure of the 'foreign woman' in Proverbs 1–9, and interpretations of the verse have often been shaped by understandings of that other figure, either as an immoral woman or as a personification of folly (Seow, and Riesener, 'Frauenfeindschaft', are among the most notable representatives of this position in recent scholarship).

Although I think the imagery of Proverbs 1–9 does underpin Qohelet's account here, however, the direct points of contact with that woman in Proverbs are limited. To be sure, she is associated there with death (Prov 5.5; 7.27; 9.18), and the young man who is unwise enough to follow her is once described as being like an animal led to slaughter, a goat skipping into a snare (perhaps—the text is corrupt), or a bird rushing into a trap (Prov 7.22-23). The woman presented here by Qohelet, however, is not described in terms of luring people to their deaths, and she attempts none of the invitations and seductions associated with the foreign woman of Proverbs. Rather, she is simply a trap herself, who binds fast anyone who is caught in her, and Krüger (in his commentary and in 'Frau Weisheit', 401-3) has made the important observation that in Sir 6.24-31 it is not folly but personified wisdom who binds her followers in chains and fetters—the depiction of wisdom in that chapter more generally is as a harsh, demanding discipline. I think Krüger is right to suggest that Qohelet sees wisdom in similar terms and could be talking about her here, although I think it is no less likely (especially in view of the list in 7.25) that he has deliberately portrayed the woman in terms that could be understood to indicate either wisdom or folly, and could be applied to both.[2] In that case, then the last part of this verse, which uses the same language of seeming 'right' or 'wrong' to God as 2.26, can be read as a cruel

---

[2] In an interesting discussion of these verses, Ramond, 'Y a-t-il de l'ironie', 635-36, suggests that Qohelet's search for wisdom and folly introduces no criteria by which to distinguish them, and that in effect he finds them both the same: 'in each case the object of his research is bitter, the woman a trap'. Simian-Yofre, 'Conoscere la sapienza', 327-31, also suggests that both women are involved here, but with folly more clearly distinguished as a trap on the difficult path to seeking wisdom: Qohelet avoids the trap but does not ultimately find wisdom himself. Without committing herself to the interpretation, Wolfe suggests that the application of '"Strange" Woman' language to Wisdom would be 'yet another radical move for Qoheleth, essentially collapsing Proverbs' dichotomy' and 'providing yet another challenge to the wisdom tradition'.

reversal of the idea rejected in that verse, where wisdom was given to those who seemed right: Qohelet claims now that it is the fortunate who escape her, as well, perhaps, as folly. More directly, though, there is an evocation here of the attitudes expressed earlier in 7.16-18: wisdom and folly both trap those who are not allowed to avoid them, and those who actually do enjoy divine favour will pass between them, caught by neither.

The woman here has sometimes been understood in other symbolic terms, but those commentators who have not taken her to be wisdom or folly have generally understood this to be a more literal description, in which she represents either a particular type of woman (a way in which the 'foreign' woman of Proverbs is also often understood), or women in general. Of course, if this is the case, then whatever the grand plans were that Qohelet announced in 7.25, what he actually finds is apparently irrelevant to them, and much more limited in scope—Fox and Porten, 'Unsought Discoveries', 30, acknowledge the 'bathos'. The Targum, all the same, weaves an account of a bad and lazy wife, while most interpreters have been even less specific, and many have seen an attack on women as a sex, often noting (occasionally with altogether too much relish) other ancient sources critical of women.

Setting aside the questions that arise from 7.28, in which a further criticism of women is also often perceived, it is interesting to ask, though, what exactly the woman here is supposed to be doing that is wrong. She does not, in fact, act at all, and although our understanding of the way she functions as a trap may be affected by the way we understand the various nets and snares to work, there is no direct implication that she goes looking for men or seduces them, let alone that she damages them in any way after catching them. To be sure, the outlook for trapped animals was not healthy, but the text here refers to bonds as well, and capture seems to be the issue, rather than an imminent, subsequent death—so we should be wary of reading in ideas such as that 'the description of woman as a snare in Qohelet may represent the possible reality of certain women leading men to death' (Pahk, 'Women as Snares', 398-99). To the extent that she is a woman, moreover, and not just a trap, this woman is never said to be adulterous, immoral or personally problematic in any way, and Qohelet's characterization of her as 'bitter' or 'strong' seems to be derived wholly and simply from the fact that she is, in some sense, a trap.

Other aspects of the presentation, in fact, lead Rudman, 'Woman as Divine Agent', 418, to declare that 'she cannot be deemed "wicked" as such since her whole *raison d'être* is to perform God's will by punishing those who have sinned' (a perception that leads Ogden, rather differently, to deduce that she must be 'a figure for premature death', although it is not clear what Qohelet's meeting her would then entail). That is less clear cut than Rudman assumes, given the questions it raises about agency and determinism (cf. Isa 10.5-7). All the same, though, it is hard to see the details here as evidence that Qohelet is talking specifically about a human woman who is 'bad' in some more general way, and, if we were to insist upon rejecting any link with established figures of wisdom or folly, then they would point rather towards him talking about all women, and disparaging any relationships between men and women.

Fontaine, 'Many Devices', 149-50, accordingly associates this passage with a tradition of advice about women: 'That young male students should be warned of the "wiles" of females for whom the only hope of status and fulfilment offered them by patriarchal culture is in the capture, acquisition and annexation of the unwary male who cannot escape their machinations: this is surely the stock in trade of patriarchal pedagogy'. Apart from the passages that relate specifically to the 'foreign' woman in Proverbs 1–9, though, there is little or nothing to suggest that this was a common theme in ancient advice literature, however offensive modern readers might find some of the other things said about women (or, more often, said selectively about women—as though there were no difficult male partners [cf. Prov 21.9, 19; 25.24], or philandering men [e.g. Prov 22.14; 30.20]). That may be because the historical context was actually somewhat more complicated (with arranged marriages likely to have been more common than individual seductions), or it may be because the 'pedagogy' was actually reluctant to condemn women for 'acting in accordance with the messages their culture has sent', as Fontaine puts it. In any case, it is hard to find any evidence to support a suggestion that women simply seeking marriage were regularly perceived as somehow hunting or trapping men. Indeed, whatever we make of the social attitudes and circumstances that undoubtedly constrained women, the efforts of, say, Ruth, or of Tobit's relation Sarah, seem, if anything, to be portrayed with some admiration elsewhere in Jewish literature. I doubt, therefore, that we can see even a reference to some widespread male pre-occupation with being trapped into marriage, let alone a specific offence on the part of the woman.³ Some commentators have seen the supposed dissonance as a prime example of Qohelet's tendency to contradict himself (see especially Berger, 'Exigencies', 161-62), but the facts that Qohelet views relationships between men and women in positive terms elsewhere (9.9), and that he seems neither to be talking here about a particular sort of 'bad' woman, nor referring to some conventional image of marriage as a trap for men, seems to be a strong argument in itself for seeing the woman as symbolic—or rather, perhaps, for following the Greek reading with 'her', which identifies her explicitly as either wisdom or folly.

Notes

7.26 If I found her, I would say] Lit. 'Finding her, I will say'; I take the original text to have been ומוצא אני אתה ואמר, and the last two words to have been lost in M but preserved in G (cf. Goldman). To begin with the sense, though, Jerome's translation in V, *et inueni*, 'and I found', is echoed in many modern translations: it suits the apparent context in which Qohelet turned to seek something and then found something. M ומוצא, however, does not readily lend itself to an interpretation in terms of a simple past tense, but has to be read as a participle. In Hie, Jerome himself accordingly rendered it *et inuenio ego*, 'and I find', which matches G καὶ εὑρίσκω ἐγώ, and it seems more likely that the past tenses of S and T are an adaptation to context, like V, than that they reflect a different Hebrew text. Ecclesiastes uses a participle with a following pronoun like this also in 1.5; 3.21 twice; and 8.12, always expressing continuous action in the present.

Although that sense does not seem appropriate here, it is more generally true that the participle does not naturally express the past, and when contextualized in the past, expresses durative, or less often, frequentative action (J-M §121 f), not a simple aorist. This leads Isaksson (*Studies*, 65)

---

³ How this passage was regarded later is another matter. In *b. Berakot* 8a, it is claimed that Israelites would ask a newly married man whether his wife was מצא or מוצא, that is, the 'benefit' of Prov 18.22, or the bitter woman of this verse. Lavoie, 'Les pièges', 174, notes this as just one reference among many in his very rich account (169-85) of the literal and symbolic ways in which the woman has been identified and understood in Jewish exegesis, which go far beyond the options I explore here. As well as a bad wife or immoral woman of one sort or another, she has been variously identified as the personification of particular phenomena, such as sorcery, heresy and Gehenna, and Lavoie observes that the verse has commonly served as a vehicle for misogyny, even if such implications have sometimes been resisted.

to understand 'Time after time I have found', and Schoors to translate 'I continually find'. Such translations are more easily justified as renderings of the participle than is 'I found', but they do run into problems of sense, as we shall see in a moment: מצא cannot really refer to a repeated action in this context (unless Qohelet is talking about repeatedly encountering someone). We are, moreover, stuck with מצא. M vocalizes the verb וּמוֹצֶא, rather than וּמֹצֵא, but this probably just marks a wider tendency to confuse *lamed-aleph* with *lamed–he* verbs, rather than any particular understanding (see Schoors, *The Preacher* I, 98-99, and cf. the note 'one who is wrong' at 2.26). While it is possible in principle to construe the form not as a qal participle of מצא, but as a hiph'il participle of יצא—a reading adopted by Ibn Ezra, who cites the מוצא of Ps 135.7, and advocated more recently by Whitley (who does not offer a translation)—it is difficult to see, however, that this yields any better meaning, and the other occurrences of 'seeking' and 'finding' in the immediate context make it less natural.

The conventional reading of M is usually along the lines of 'I found more bitter than death the woman' (RSV), which attributes to מצא a nuance of understanding, rather than specifically of discovery. This is a simple shift in English, where we can 'find the coffee too hot', for instance, and Greek can do something similar with εὑρίσκω in the sense 'find that'. Especially in the later biblical books, the Hebrew verb is sometimes used similarly (e.g. 1 Chr 20.2; Neh 9.8; Dan 1.20), but always in the context of discovering a quality in someone or something that one has encountered or acquired: the usage does not stretch to statements of habitual opinion, like the English 'I find it remarkable that', and there is no evidence that the verb ever has some more general cognitive sense of 'grasping' or 'comprehending' a fact.[4] We observed in the last verse, moreover, that the sense 'see something *to be* something' for a verb of perception without כי or an equivalent is unusual, even if such usage is marginally better attested with a noun + adjective, as here, than with two nouns. The late uses of מצא, though, commonly employ just such a

---

[4] Such a sense is proposed for the verb here in Ceresko, 'Function of Antanaclasis', 562-63, 566, but the analogies that Ceresko proposes are unpersuasive. It is true that in Prov 2.5 דעת אלהים תמצא, 'you will find the knowledge of God', stands in parallel with אז תבין יראת יהוה, 'you will understand the fear of YHWH', and that מצא appears a number of times in similar contexts. In such appearances, however, it is always used in connection with a noun like 'wisdom' or 'knowledge'—never absolutely—and the sense is not that one may 'grasp the meaning of knowledge, or 'understand understanding'. This is simply a particular use of מצא in its broader sense of 'achieving' or 'attaining' something that has been, or should be sought, and such uses in association with terms that express knowledge do not indicate that the verb itself has acquired that implication. When Qohelet uses מצא of a 'discovery' in 7.29, the sense is, again, not that he has grasped the meaning of something but that he has uncovered a truth—which is perhaps a way we could take it here in 7.26 as well.

construction, presumably because they are derived from the more basic idea of finding something in a particular condition, or someone engaged in an activity (e.g. 2 Kgs 19.8). This should in itself caution us against viewing the verb as a general verb of perception, even in such usage, and it indicates the limited scope of what Qohelet could be saying here if we follow M—which is essentially that he discovered the woman to be bitter. That sits uncomfortably, of course, with the frequentative or continuous connotations of the participle, since the implication would have to be that Qohelet kept making the same discovery, or that he was constantly engaged in making it ('I keep discovering the woman to be bitter'). The sense of the verb makes it hard to claim that he is simply expressing a continuously held opinion or understanding, while its form makes it hard to claim that he is talking about something he once discovered.

It is not impossible that Qohelet is saying, extremely concisely, that his every encounter with a/the woman results in the same discovery, and that is probably how we have to understand M. In the light of these difficulties, however, the text-critical questions that arise from the reading of G become extremely interesting. Rahlfs did not include it in his text, which is why, perhaps, it has been so neglected by modern commentators, but all witnesses to that tradition in fact have αὐτὴν after καὶ εὑρίσκω ἐγώ, so that Qohelet is saying 'and I find it', or 'her'. As observed in the notes to 7.25, some then add καὶ εὐφροσύνην (= ἀφροσύνην) πλάνας, or καὶ εὐφροσύνη (= ἀφροσύνη) πλάνα, which is probably derived from Aquila's rendering of 7.25. That addition leaves Qohelet saying 'and I find it, and merriment (= folly), errors', and both those pluses provide 'find' with a further object (if it is not the result of an error, the gloss from α' was likely intended to specify this object more precisely by reference to the previous verse, rather than to identify the woman with Folly in Prov 1–9, as Schoors, 'Bitterder dan de dood', 123, suggests).

A significant number of other witnesses instead have καὶ ἐρῶ after αὐτὴν, while many of the same ones follow the gloss from α' with an aorist καὶ εἶπον or καὶ εἶπα, a reading reflected in the Coptic witnesses also. If we omit the gloss, which is generally acknowledged to be secondary, Qohelet is saying, 'I find it and will say', or 'I find it and said': Gentry takes the former to be original, and G* to have been καὶ εὑρίσκω ἐγὼ αὐτὴν καὶ ἐρῶ.[5] Goldman shares this belief, and takes the Greek to reflect a Hebrew text ומוצא אני אתה ואמר in G's source-text. The shorter reading of M is supported by Hie, V, S (which lacks an equivalent to M אני) and T, while Syh has αὐτὴν under an obelus that it attributes explicitly to Origen, indicating that he found no equivalent in his Hebrew text.

---

[5] This represents a change from his position in 'Hexaplaric Materials', 15-16. As Goldman suggests, καὶ εἶπον would appear to be a correction, although it was probably the reading of the Hexapla.

If M were to represent the earlier text, then the Hebrew reflected in G could have arisen, as Goldman and McNeile, 163, suggest, in part through a process that began with an accidental reduplication of the characters in the following word מר: some scribe would subsequently have tried to make sense of the resulting אנימרמר as מר ואמר אני. However, even apart from requiring a scribe who would rather add two characters than delete two obviously incorrect others, this does also need us to consider the presumed אתה (or whatever αὐτὴν renders) to have been a separate, later addition, motivated by a desire to connect Qohelet's 'finding' here with his 'seeking' in the preceding verse. Since it would not be difficult to make a much simpler case for the two sequences of מר in an original text having caused a scribe's eye to jump, this is not a place where the priority of one reading over the other is wholly self-evident without resort to the context. As we have already seen, M's reading is not straightforward in terms of the sense or syntax of ומוצא, and G's alleviates this by providing both a direct object and a second verb. It is interesting to observe, moreover, that Schoors is only the latest of several commentators who try to get around the problems by turning מר into the beginning of a saying or quotation—which is essentially what G accomplishes.[6] If it is secondary, therefore, the reading reflected in G might be the result of a similar facilitatory calculation, rather than just an error.

I think, however, that it is most likely original, and that something like ומוצא אני אתה ואמר makes much more sense both in and of the context. In particular, it allows us to take ואמר as the main verb here, introducing what follows, and to avoid trying to take the participle either as a simple present or as an expression of continuous or repeated action, neither of which gives a good sense. When it is followed by another verb like this, it is natural, in fact, to take מוצא instead as specifying a circumstance in which Qohelet would speak (cf., e.g., Job 41.18; 2 Kgs 7.2, 19), which would suggest that we are dealing with an asyndetic conditional clause, marked as such by the very use of a participle. The most probable referent for the pronoun is wisdom, the first item for which Qohelet was planning to search (although it is possible that the difficult second part of 7.25 once contained a different referent), and if his subsequent description is indeed directed at her (see the commentary), it is not surprising that the gloss from α' was added in parts of the Greek tradition, changing the reference to folly. It is hard to know what the original translator made of the text, but εὑρίσκω and ἐρῶ give a strange and inappropriate sense if they are both read as indicative (which led to the substitution of εἶπον): it is not impossible that, without venturing to add a

---

[6] This is an aspect of Lohfink's interpretation, noted above in the commentary. Michel, *Untersuchungen*, 225, likewise offers the translation, 'Ich finde (also immer wieder die Ansicht), bitterer…', 'I find (again and again the view expressed that) more bitter…'. Although, to be sure, this approach gives some weight to the form of the participle in M, it is driven principally by interpretative concerns.

conditional particle, the translator intended εὑρίσκω to be read as subjunctive, and himself saw a conditional expression here (as I think happened at 9.14; see my notes there). In any case, the more significant problems arose in the text from which M is derived, which preserved the participial form of the first verb, but lost the two other words that made sense of it—a change which left readers scrabbling to relate מוצא to a sentence it was never intended to govern.

I would not want to press the point, but, if there is indeed a reference in these verses to the imagery of Prov 1–9, then it is interesting to observe that a similar construction with the participle of מצא is used in connection with personified wisdom at Prov 8.35 (מצאי מצא חיים, 'someone finding me finds life'), and this is arguably an expression characteristic of that work (cf. 4.22, finding teachings, and 8.9 knowledge). If there actually is any reminiscence of that verse here, then there is also a contradiction of it in the characterization of the woman here as stronger or more bitter than death. More generally, Prov 1–9 also uses similar language of seeking and finding wisdom in 1.28; 3.13; 8.17, while her dangerous counterpart is not sought herself, but seeks and finds the youth in 7.15. That might tilt the scales very slightly towards identifying the woman in question here as wisdom.

7.26 More bitter than death is this woman] Or 'stronger'. The meaning of מר is contested, since it is now more widely recognized that, as Dahood suggested, the word can have the sense 'strong' in Hebrew, and this meaning is preferred by Whitley.[7] It also seems to have been picked up in medieval Jewish exegesis (not least in the Midrash Rabbah), as Schoors shows, but most modern commentators have preferred to understand 'bitter', which was also the understanding of the ancient translators (on such usage, cf. the note 'sweet' at 11.7). Many, like Crenshaw, point to the association of מר with death in 1 Sam 15.32, although 'strength' might be read there also, and some to Sir 41.1, which provides a more definite witness to 'bitter'. However, the 'bitterness' of the strange woman, herself associated with Sheol in Prov 5.3-5, as is also widely noted, provides the most compelling evidence for that understanding in this context. Seow wonders, in passing, whether both meanings might be intended, and it does seem very likely that the text is deliberately ambiguous: if a knowledge of Prov 5 might have pushed an audience towards 'bitter', the subsequent description is one that, as Dahood argued persuasively, places much more emphasis on the woman's strength.

---

[7] The case for 'strong' in this verse was made originally in Dahood, 'Qoheleth and Recent Discoveries', 308-10, although Dahood himself cited C.H. Gordon's observations on Exod 1.14 and Judg 18.25. Pardee's attempt (in 'Semitic Root') to deny the existence of that sense in Hebrew was itself countered by Kutler, 'A "Strong" Case', a few years later, and the meaning has been accepted by *DCH*.

The rejection of 'strong' on the basis that 'immortality is imputed to woman, which is absurd in the literature of both the ancient Near East and Ugaritic' (Loretz, 'Poetry and Prose', 183) rests on a very literal-minded reading in terms of the woman being able to overcome death—although it is true that some advocates of that translation have taken it in such a way. 'Stronger than death' perhaps acknowledges, rather, that death proverbially has its own snares and bonds (Pss 18.4-5 [ET 18.5-6]; 116.3; Prov 13.14; 14.27; 21.6—Barclay Burns, 'Personifications', 23-25, connects the imagery here and in 9.12 with longstanding traditions of Death as a hunter), but Ct 8.6 also uses the strength or savagery of death as a point of comparison ('love is as mighty as death, passion as relentless as Sheol'): if 'strong' is intended, at least as a possible understanding, then the expression is probably comparable to our saying 'hotter than hell', rather than a claim that the woman can fight off her own mortality.

More generally, the construction of the sentence as a comparison is not in doubt, and the fact that מר does not agree in gender with האשה does not make it impossible to read it this way: we encountered a similar case already in 7.8, and J-M §148a suggests that comparative clauses furnish many of the relatively rare exceptions to the rules of agreement. Although we might also expect the elements to be in the order 'bitter/strong—the woman—more than death' (compare, e.g., 7.1), death has been moved forward, probably not, as Seow suggests, simply for emphasis, but because this order permits both the alliterative expression of מר ממות and the direct attachment to the woman of the lengthy relative clause that describes her. G πικρότερον reproduces the mismatch of gender between מר and האשה—maybe not deliberately (although see Muraoka, *Syntax*, §20 ea), but under the influence of the following θάνατον; it is corrected to the feminine in many manuscripts.[8]

A potentially greater problem arises from the fact that we find here את האשה, not האשה, and the את would classically mark the noun as the object of a verb. This would not be difficult were we to take האשה as the direct object of ומוצא, but we have already seen good reasons not to do so, and Schoors ties himself in knots by trying to take האשה both as the subject of a sentence in direct speech and as an accusative governed by ומוצא. Since G represents it in σὺν τὴν γυναῖκα, furthermore, the את cannot be dismissed as a secondary

---

[8] It is likely that the Syh note here, claiming that the reading of the Three is 'likewise', refers to this question of gender; ܒܗ ܒܕܡܘܬܐ *bh bdmwtʾ* (corresponding to the Greek ὁμοίως, which is how Field renders it) is used commonly in these notes to indicate the affinities of each translator where there are known variants. Gentry, 'Hexaplaric Materials, 15-16, concludes that the Three probably had the feminine here, 'like' the lemma before the scholiast, but unlike the text of Origen. Lavoie, 'Les Pièges', 168, apparently misunderstands the note in Field when he claims that they actually read the word ὁμοίως instead of πικρότερον / -αν, and considered the woman comparable to death (cf. also p. 187 n. 16).

clarification of the structure in M following the loss of text: this reading pre-dates that loss. The role of את becomes increasingly more complicated in late biblical Hebrew, however, and while the use of the particle to mark the subject of clauses does not become positively common until mishnaic Hebrew, biblical instances are not especially rare. Quite what nuance it has in such cases is a matter of dispute, and J-M §125 j is surely right to reject the idea that it is simply emphatic. In this context, its use may have something to do with the expression of the relative that follows, and I suspect its principal functions are to identify 'the woman' as the 'her' Qohelet has found, and to prevent her from being understood as 'woman', in the sense 'any or every woman'—an ambiguity present in האשה that is relevant to much subsequent discussion of this passage. This would put the usage close to such instances as Ezek 43.7 ('[this is] the place of my throne and the place of the soles of my feet, where [אשר] I will dwell'); Zech 7.7 ('[are] not [these] the words which [אשר]…'); and perhaps Hag 2.5 ('[this is] the word which [אשר]'). In such passages, as J-M observes, את clearly functions almost as an alternative to using a demonstrative pronoun, 'this' or 'these'. It is probably not a coincidence that in all those cases the noun marked by את is qualified by a relative clause with אשר, and the sense something like 'this, the x which…', so we may be dealing with a well-established usage.

7.26 she who is all nets] Lit. 'who/that she is nets'. The word אשר here is discussed at length in Pahk, 'Significance', which notes (377) the different translations of it as relative and causal, associated with interpretations of what follows as descriptions either of a particular type of woman ('the woman who…'), or of women in general ('woman, because…'), but concludes, on the basis of Qohelet's views elsewhere, that it should actually be understood as conditional (383: 'the woman, if she is…'; cf. also his 'Women as Snares', 398). There are a few places, to be sure, where אשר has to be translated that way (e.g. Lev 4.22), although, as often when it functions in effect as a conjunction, the sense in all those places is clearly determined by the immediate context, and the word itself may be doing little more than substantivizing the clause that follows: it is not inherently a conditional conjunction, any more than it is a final one (cf. Ruth 3.1). We may reasonably ask here, therefore, whether the *immediate* context (rather than a reading of the book as a whole) demands that rendering, and may note that nobody other than Pahk has felt compelled to take it that way—although, if we do, the result is surely much the same as just reading a relative pronoun.

In fact, M אשר היא מצודים has the same form as, e.g., אשר היא טובה לך in Ruth 4.15, where the אשר introduces a nonverbal clause, 'she (is) good for you', and I have translated in the way that the clause in Ruth has to be understood. Although in this verse it may also be constructed with the preceding את האשה (see the last note), that usage is not unusual or inherently problematic, and if it seems odd that the woman is equated with a plural noun, then we may observe that the same is true subsequently of her (singular) heart. It is probably a discomfort with the equation, nevertheless, that gives rise to the reading of a singular noun in great swathes of the G tradition, and elsewhere—along with, perhaps, a desire to simplify the image.[9] That is unlikely to be the intended sense of the original, even though Seow justifies his translation of the nouns with a singular 'trap', 'net', by referring vaguely to 'the plural of complexity'. It is difficult to say whether in any case the plural is being used to represent a singular concept, but that is unlikely to be true of all (and even Seow allows 'fetters'). The imagery as it stands is presumably intended to suggest that the woman can trap more than one person at a time.

Gordis remarks that the accents in M tie מְצוֹדִים to the following word rather than to הִיא, but the witness of the accents does not actually oblige us to read a *casus pendens*, 'she: her heart (is) nets and snares, her heart fetters'. That reading has been adopted by many translators and commentators, but only by T among the ancient translations. If there is any difficulty at all in the expression here, it lies in the fact that we might expect another body part to match the subsequent heart and hands, rather than a description of the woman as a whole ('What could it have been?' asks Baltzer, 'Women and War', 128, 'And has it been omitted deliberately?'). This led Perles to make the clever suggestion that the text originally read אֲשֻׁרֶיהָ, 'her steps, feet', employing the same noun used in, e.g., Ps 17.5; if it also had אשר as a relative, then this perhaps dropped out through haplography.[10] This hardly seems necessary, however,

---

[9] The reading of the singular θήρευμα in place of θηρεύματα is investigated in Gentry, 'Relationship', 75-77. Gentry concludes, against Field, that the evidence of Syh points to Origen and θ' having had θηρεύματα, but α' a different word, which means that an unattributed hexaplaric gloss παγηδεύματα (= παγιδεύματα, probably baited traps) found in ms 252 must probably be α', which therefore also had a plural. Hie *laqueus*, specified in V as *laqueus uenatorum*, 'a noose used by hunters', does have a singular, and V, at least, is probably based upon σ' δίκτυον θηρευτικόν, which is a 'hunting net'. It is possible that S ܗܡܐ ܨܝܕܐ ܘܡܨܝܕܬܐ ܗܝ, ܒܠܗ dhy ʾytyh pḥʾ wmṣydtʾ lbh, lit. 'who she is a trap, and a net her heart', has inherited its singular ܦܚܐ pḥʾ from the variant in G, but it also uses a singular for the subsequent ܘܡܨܝܕܬܐ wmṣydtʾ. As Kamenetzky points out, a comparison with the renderings in 9.12 suggests the further complication that the nouns here have actually been reversed—more probably a development within the S tradition than the reflection of a different source-text. It is tempting to wonder whether the use of the construction with ܐܝܬ ʾyt + suffix, which is common in later texts but relatively rare in the Peshitta (Joosten, 'Materials', 213-14, notes only fourteen instances) is also a mark of such development, although it does occur again in 8.13.

[10] Perles, 'Miscellany', 131; *Analekten*, 18, 28. Dahood, 'Phoenician Background', 275-76 (cf. 'The Independent Personal Pronoun', 89-90), was later to argue that this sense could be achieved without emendation, by reading אשר as a defective spelling of the plural אשרי and taking the pronoun to be used in the genitive. As Whitley points out, though, the text uses suffix pronouns for 'her' heart and hands, so even were the use of an independent pronoun in this way plausible, it is not clear why it would be used only here.

especially when the versions support M in this respect. Baltzer answers his own questions by proposing that the text was originally supposed to be read with שדיה, 'her breasts', which would have offered alliteration and a rhyme with ידיה: this was either deleted as a result of later prudishness, or never actually stated by Qohelet, but merely implied by allusion to passages like Ct 8.9-10. Of course, that is very speculative, and it also depends on a particular understanding of מצודים as 'walls' (on which, see below).

The word מצוד is rare, in fact, and we shall consider at 9.14 the problems raised there by מצודים. Either because of textual errors or because there genuinely were different forms and homonyms, it has become hard to separate terms connected with the two very different fields of hunting and fortification, or to identify which is which in various texts—and we may note that when Qohelet talks of a net used for fishing in 9.12, it is the form מצודה that is used. Such difficulties make it impossible for us to be as specific as we might like to be, given that the nature of the nets is potentially important for the imagery: the θηρεύματα of G and θ' may not suggest implements of any sort,[11] while the παγιδεύματα attributed to α' are snares or traps into which the prey may fall. Jerome's *laqueus* and σ' δίκτυον θηρευτικόν, on the other

---

[11] The term θήρευμα is never found elsewhere in connection with nets or other implements used in hunting or trapping. In Plato, *Laws* 823b, θηρεύματα simply means 'hunts', while similarly Euripides, *Iphigenia in Aulis* 1162, σπάνιον δὲ θήρευμ' ἀνδρὶ τοιαύτην λαβεῖν δάμαρτα claims 'It is a rare *catching* for a man to take such a wife'. This appears to be the sense of the singular in the Greek of Lev. 17.13; Jer. 37.17. In light of the other usage, readers would have been unlikely to understand 'nets' or some such from the Greek. It is conceivable that the G translator has treated the noun as though it were ציד, or has perhaps tried to derive it directly from צוד, but מצודה in all its biblical uses elsewhere could be taken to connote 'catching' or 'custody', rather than an actual implement, so the translation is plausibly based on a lexical understanding in those terms, rather than a purely contextual interpretation. All the same, Didymus is interesting on this passage. He stresses that θήρευμά ἐστιν, οὐ θηρευόμενον, 'she is hunting, not what is hunted', adding that δυνατὸν δὲ καὶ τοῦτο εἰπεῖν, ὅτι μετέρχεταί τις τὴν κακίαν, οὐχ ὡς ἥμερόν τι, ἀλλ' ὡς ἄγριον θηρίον ἐπισπώμενον ἑαυτῷ, 'it is possible to say that one goes after evil not as something tame but as a savage beast drawing (one) toward itself' (Tura codex p. 227, 1.18-21). Just as מצודה seems to refer to 'prey' in Ezek 13.21, but to nets elsewhere, the Greek θήρευμα can refer not just to hunting but to what is caught, as in Strabo, *Geography* 15, 3 οὐχ ἅπτονται δὲ τῶν θηρευμάτων οἱ παῖδες, 'The youth do not eat the *game*', and the image in Didymus is of hunting a creature that wants to be hunted, in the expectation that it will turn the tables on its hunter. Given the subsequent, problematic statements about the woman's hands which may have inspired such understandings (see below), it is very possible that the G translation reflects a similar idea, that those who seek her correctly see what they are doing as a hunt, without realising that is they who are the hunted (cf. *NETS*, 'the woman who is hunted prey').

hand, probably imply active hunting: in his commentary, Jerome speaks in terms that suggest lassoing and dragging away, while in Xenophon's *Cynegeticus*, 2.5, δίκτυα are hayes, or hay-nets, into which animals are driven by dogs.

In some recent studies, the questions around מצוד have given rise to some very different ways of understanding the text—most clearly exemplified, perhaps, in Lohfink's understanding that the woman is actually being described as like the siege-towers (or whatever they are) that appear in 9.14. In his work more generally, that is connected with the references to male militarism, and the broader interpretation that he draws out in 'War Kohelet ein Frauenfeind'. Jost, 'Frau und Adam', 64, also picks up uses of the vocabulary in contexts of war or conflict, to suggest, differently, that Qohelet is alluding negatively to 'militaristic' women like Deborah and Jael. The interpretation of Butting, 'Weibsbilder', 9, is more in line with conventional readings of the passage as misogynistic, and perceives Qohelet to be claiming that certain women effectively wage war, like invading kings but in the sphere of private life, against the 'male part of creation'. We shall encounter some related questions at 9.14, and in particular those arising from the common use in depictions of sieges of imagery from hunting and trapping—which adds a further dimension of complexity to the lexical and textual problems. I am strongly inclined to doubt, though, both that any of the vocabulary here would have been perceived primarily as military, and that the original audience would have made an association between the different contexts in which hunting imagery could be used: if they did, there is no sign of it in the ancient versions. The connection with 9.14, moreover, rests largely on what is probably a textual error in the Hebrew in that verse—an issue that is well known, but is largely overlooked in these interpretations.

7.26 and her heart dragnets] As observed in the last note, there is no very good reason to link the preceding מצודים with חרמים here, and identify the woman's heart as both. It is difficult, however, to know what, if anything, might have distinguished the two terms in the mind of the author: חרם is a more common word, but is used likewise of nets employed by hunters and fishermen (e.g. Mic 7.2; Ezek 26.14). In Ezek 32.3 and Hab 1.15 we do find some indication of the way such a net might be used, corresponding to G's use of σαγῆναι, a term that can refer to nets which are used to catch all the fish in an area of water: BDAG describes 'a large net hanging vertically, with floats on the top and sinkers on the bottom', while MM talks of 'a large "dragnet"... generally worked by two boats, which separate and then draw it in a sweep to the shore'. We shall examine how G construes this within the sentence in the next note.

Although we have encountered the 'heart' often already in the book, it is perhaps important to emphasize in this context that it does not have the romantic connotations in biblical use that hearts possess in modern Western culture. Accordingly, there is unlikely to be any specific nuance here that she is trapping men through loving them or making them love her.¹² The sense is more likely to be that she is, as it were, constantly fishing with her mind for victims.

7.26 her hands fetters] Or perhaps 'in her hands, fetters'; see below. The suggestion of *BHS*, that we should read an initial conjunction here, has no support from the versions, but the text is not without problems. Most strikingly, it seems likely that G* was the well-attested δεσμὸς εἰς χεῖρας αὐτῆς, rather than the δεσμοὶ χεῖρες αὐτῆς which Rahlfs prefers and which matches the normal understanding of M. According to this rendering, her hands are not bonds, but 'a bond (is) on her hands'. T also understands the woman's hands to be tied, as does S, in a rather complicated reading, and Jerome tells us that α' similarly read *uinctae sunt manus eius*, 'her hands are bound' (the Greek is not preserved). Although supported by the vocalization in M, by the nominative αἱ χεῖρες of σ', and by Hie *uincula manus eius* and V *uincula sunt manus illius*, the sense 'her hands are fetters' was clearly not favoured by all of the ancient versions, and in the Midrash Rabbah the woman is compared to a chained bitch, snapping at people as they pass in the street.

---

¹² Schoors claims, on the contrary, that 'the heart...can only mean the seductive love with which she seeks to trap men', but presents no analogous use of 'heart' in Hebrew. He does, however, cite with approval (although not acceptance) the suggestion of Fitzgerald that ידיה ('repointed' to the singular) might refer to love in this verse, and sometimes elsewhere, rather than to hands. See Fitzgerald, 'Hebrew *yd*', 369. This is not, in any case, one of Fitzgerald's more plausible examples, but it rests on the parallel with לב, and so also itself on an undemonstrated assumption that the heart must have had a special association with romantic love. The heart was, of course, associated with all sorts of things in the ancient world, including emotions, but the special connection of the heart with love or romance with which modern Western readers are familiar (and which they are, perhaps, inclined to read into the text here) is not a commonplace of ancient literature, and there is no reason to suppose that an ancient reader of Hebrew would have made this connection in particular. In the Song of Songs, where romantic and erotic feelings make up much of the subject-matter, לב appears only three times, and, although 8.4 associates it with love, in none of these is it identified as the source of romantic feelings. The closest we come to that is perhaps in Ct 4.9, where RSV renders the pi'el of the related verb לבב as 'you have ravished my heart', but where the actual sense has been much debated, especially since the qal in Job 11.12 must mean something quite different. In Prov 1–9, where we also find the topic, לב is used of the strange woman in 7.10, but it is doubtful that the reference to her 'guarding her heart' has anything to do with her romantic inclinations, and it is probably contrasting her hidden mind or intentions with her less guarded appearance; the many uses elsewhere in those chapters refer always to the heart as the centre of thought, not love. It is interesting to speculate whether scholars would so freely have found romantic rather than intellectual associations here, were the heart in question that of a man, not a woman.

This different understanding may not be unrelated to the interpretation of מצודים in G, which I noted above, but the connections made to the context are varied. T and S (which is very difficult) qualify the purpose of the binding. T understands the woman to be a bad wife, the binding of whose hands is just a way of saying that she does no work with them. As the text stands, on the other hand, S resorts to a double rendering of the subsequent טוב, so that she has 'bound her hands from what is good', but since this involves a simple repetition of ܡܢ ܓܐܒ *mn dtb*, it is probably a secondary attempt to solve the problem (which, according to Kamenetzky, 199, also caused ܐܣܘܪܝ *'srt* to be substituted for an original ܐܣܪܐ *'sr'*).

Jerome's report of α' offers a clue to one reason for these readings: Aquila seems to have taken אסורים as a passive participle from the verb אסר, 'bind', rather than as the noun attested in Judg 15.14 (so, e.g., Euringer, Marshall). This is a slightly awkward construal, because יד is usually feminine (although cf. Exod 17.12), but the noun אסור is, admittedly, very rare, and on its only other probable appearance in Ecclesiastes, at 4.14, it was in the form הסורים, with the א elided. It would not be surprising if α' got it wrong in this instance, and such a construal may lie behind the readings of S and T as well. G is harder to interpret. Although Euringer suggests that the translator was working with the same consonantal text as M, simply interpreting it in a different way, this is highly unlikely—both because of the contextual constraints and because this translator does not insert prepositions just as he pleases. Other scholars have concluded that G found אסור בידיה in its source-text, which would explain the singular δεσμὸς as well as the introduction of εἰς. For McNeile, 146, this reading arose when the final character of אסורם (written defectively) was misread as a ב, although Goldman, while eventually coming down on the side of M, observes that this error could easily have happened the other way around, with an originally singular אסור becoming plural under the influence of the preceding plurals.

For my part, I think it is pertinent that Judg 15.14 uses על and not -ב when it is talking about the bonds and cords 'on' Samson's arms and hands (cf. Ezek 3.25; 4.8): it is not at all clear that אסור בידיה would naturally be used in Hebrew to talk about the bond 'on' somebody's hands rather than one that was 'in' them, so if אסור בידיה is indeed what the G translator found (which seems likely), he may have misunderstood it. It is quite possible either that the author originally presented an image of the woman holding chains 'in her hands' ready for use on her victim, which was subsequently brought into line with the image of her heart as snares, or, alternatively, that the text was adjusted to give that sense through some failure to understand the image and/ or as the result of a copying error. I too tilt towards M in the end, however, while acknowledging that I am persuaded by the very desire for consistency that might have suppressed the variant attested in G.

7.26 Whoever seems right...one who is wrong] The expressions used here are similar to those in 2.26, which were discussed in the commentary on that verse. The text of σ' is attested as ὁ ἀρεστὸς τῷ θεῷ ἐκφεύξεται αὐτήν ὁ δὲ ἁμαρτωλὸς ἁλώσεται, 'the one pleasing to God will escape her but the wrongful one will be caught', which is close to V *qui placet deo effugiet eam qui autem peccator est capietur*, and has probably influenced it; G and Hie are closer to the Hebrew. Note that חוטא here is vocalized in M^L with *ṣere*, as we should expect, and not with the *segol* found at 2.26; 8.12; 9.2, 18 (which arises from treating it as a *lamed–he* verb; see the Introduction, 160-61), despite the fact that מוצא has just been vocalized with *segol* at the start of the verse.

7.26 trapped in her] Although nearly always translated 'by her', it is unlikely that בה can imply 'she catches him': -ב is used with passive constructions primarily, and perhaps exclusively, to express the instrument of action, rather than the agent (J-M §132 e would exclude even cases like Deut 33.29, where the people are saved ביהוה, but YHWH is being portrayed as a shield and sword). Since the woman is not obviously being used as an instrument by somebody else, the best way to understand the preposition is in terms of the overall imagery: people are caught *in* her as they might be caught in a net or snare. The verb, in fact, is commonly used of trapping, and note, e.g., Isa 24.18; Jer 48.44 where ילכד בפח refers to being caught *in* a trap, or similarly Job 36.8.

7.27–8.1

(7.27) Look at this: I met (says the Qohelet) one woman after another, in order to find a plan, (7.28) which my self still sought and I did not find. I met one person from every thousand, but I met no woman [7.29]who stood apart [7.28]among all these. (7.29) Look at this: I found God made each person uncomplicated, and it is they themselves that have sought a lot of plans. (8.1) Is anyone really the wise man? And does anyone know how to interpret something that is said? A person's wisdom will light up their face, but the strength of their face will be dimmed.

Commentary

I take vv. 27-28 to be an account of the search on which Qohelet embarked in v. 25. Looking for wisdom or folly, and after telling us what he would say if he met them, Qohelet now speaks of meeting many women in succession, and finding none of them who stood out as the personification that he is seeking. If he does not find what he was actually looking for, however, he does share a discovery that he made: humans go in search of many ways to bring order to their lives and decisions, but that is something that they do for themselves, not because God has made them that way. If that discovery arises from the failure of his search, then Qohelet may be denying the idea promoted by, for instance Proverbs 1–9 and Ben Sira, that wisdom has been set in the world for humans to find as a way of aligning their lives to God's will. On what is, though, the only occasion that Qohelet talks about engaging with anyone except his heart, perhaps the most important point is simply that he finds his fellow humans human, and to be seeking much the same as him.

The difficulties presented by these verses are notorious, however, and previous interpretations, although often differing significantly from each other, have tended to be in very different terms. Verse 27 and the first part of v. 28 are commonly viewed as a description of the way in which Qohelet undertook an altogether more intellectual quest, adding one observation to another in an attempt to find an overall total or understanding. The second part of v. 28 is then taken as a claim that Qohelet never found any good woman, although, on some readings, he may have found a few good men. After that, v. 29 is read, finally, as a statement that humans have departed, presumably in a bad way, from the state of virtue or simplicity in which the first human was created, and many Christian readings, in particular, have associated it with the idea of a 'Fall'. Of course, it may be obvious at a glance that such interpretations, taken overall, assume v. 27 to be wholly parenthetical: if it is talking about Qohelet's methods, then it interrupts his discussions of women in vv. 26 and 28. Less obvious from some translations, however, is the extent to which key words have to be supplied, or taken to have meanings that they do not usually possess elsewhere, in order to achieve these readings.

Scholars are not normally inclined, of course, to view as good practice what is, in effect, the insertion of words and changing of meanings, and the fact that such readings have become so established in these verses cannot be put down wholly to the fact that they go back a long way—although that has been, I think, an important factor. The most significant difficulty for commentators has been that neither of vv. 27-28 seems to have all the words that it needs to make sense. That difficulty arises, however, because of the way in which the text has conventionally been divided at two points, and those divisions, I think, are themselves the consequence of interpretative presuppositions. Qohelet is often accused of misogyny on the basis of what is said here, and I do not doubt either that the conventional reading is misogynistic, or that many attitudes prevailing at the time the book was written would be considered hostile to women by modern readers. It is very likely, on the other hand, that the misogyny usually found here has been imposed upon the text by early translators and interpreters, who have divided it in a way that is unnatural, and that creates significant problems. It is probable that they did so at least in part because they did not understand (or perhaps wish to engage with) the broader context of the passage, but, equally, it is clear that they were not reluctant to find statements disparaging of women, or to impute such sentiments to Qohelet. What is more surprising is that their readings, although clearly forced, have passed largely unchallenged.

Those issues aside, the most noticeable influence on interpretations of these verses continues to be the conviction of many interpreters, already touched on several times above, that Qohelet must be seeking big ideas and making big claims here, so that almost everything he says becomes a grand pronouncement. In fact, I doubt that anything here really has that character, and even the observation in v. 29 seems more to puncture the pretensions of his quest than to claim anything important about humanity: what he saw in all those encounters was neither the work of God nor some symptom of a deep malaise, but just a lot of people each trying to do the same as him, and find a way to get by. The closing questions and statement in 8.1 relate this back to the issues with which he began, as Qohelet comes to doubt the very possibility of anybody actually being the wise man he had formally considered himself to be, and the desirability of wisdom itself.

7.27] This verse is not very complicated, at least by the standards of the book. It begins with the same words found at the beginning of 7.29 (very literally, 'look this I have found'), which I take to mean, 'look at this: I have found...', but which is often construed as 'look at what I have found'. That construal creates some complications for reading 7.29, but it positively wreaks havoc here, by removing from consideration the verb that governs the sentence as a whole. If we reject it, then Qohelet straightforwardly recounts, after quoting his own intended speech to wisdom, how he went on to encounter woman after woman, in search of what he had earlier set out to find. If we accept it, on the other hand, then we are left with a clause that simply but obscurely declares 'one thing/woman to one thing/woman to find a plan'. It would not seem difficult to choose between those construals, but two considerations in particular have driven commentators to adopt the more difficult reading. The first is that Qohelet, in the next verse, will apparently declare that he has met no woman, making it hard to accept that he could be talking here about meeting many women. That objection rests on a problem in 7.28, which we shall discuss below. The second factor is the insertion here of 'says the Qohelet', which falls after 'I have found', and seems to affirm the otherwise problematic reading 'look at what I have found'.

This insertion poses its own problems: as it stands in the Hebrew text, it involves a division of its words that make the verb feminine ('says she, Qohelet') and, although that division was probably not intended, it raises interesting questions. I doubt, nevertheless, that the insertion itself is secondary—it seems likely that the author is using it to mark a return to the monologue itself, after Qohelet's speech-within-a-speech. Even if it is original, however, there is a strong case for suggesting that it should be ignored, at least in syntactic terms: this is a parenthetical observation by the author, not part of the sentence itself. It is not clear just why the author should have positioned it precisely where it is (always assuming that it occupied that position from the outset), but there are parallels to such interruption (see the notes), and it seems likely that the positioning was intended to achieve some emphasis or effect. I suspect the author was trying to draw out the distinction between what Qohelet hoped to find, in 7.26, and what he claims, disappointingly, now actually to have found—'look, I found…just ordinary woman after ordinary woman, not that special woman'. In any case, though, 'says the Qohelet' should not be treated as a sort of punctuation, breaking the second part of the sentence off from the first.

When the sentence has been treated as broken that way, then the almost fragmentary character of the second half has provoked some creative exegesis. In particular, translators and commentators since at least the time of Symmachus have been conscious of the fact that the term translated 'plan' here could be used in connection with numbers and calculations, leading to a popular understanding of the words as a subordinate clause: 'Look at what I found…(by adding) one thing to another to find a plan'. This is open to various objections, among them the facts that the word for 'plan' does not mean 'sum total', and that Hebrew does not use the preposition found here for addition (where English adds one thing *to* another, Hebrew adds one thing *on* another). The greatest and most obvious difficulty, however, is that it involves importing, or at least understanding, a verb 'adding' that simply is not present in the text or context. That interpretation has fed a modern appetite to find some grand intellectual quest in these verses, and has been influential upon ideas about Qohelet's epistemology and processes of thought. It creates significantly greater problems, however, than does reading a simpler statement about meeting women.

7.28] My translation here rests on a division of the text that runs counter to the Masoretic punctuation and the understanding of other, earlier readers. My reasoning is explained in more detail in the notes, but briefly, the word *lbd* (roughly 'alone', or 'by oneself') is not a conjunction, and when it is not being used in a prepositional construction, it always follows the word that it qualifies. Just in itself, therefore, the normal usage of that word would not encourage us to read it, exceptionally, as the first word of a new sentence in 7.29, which is where Masoretic texts place it, rather than as the last word of 7.28. Doing so creates the additional problem that 7.28 then has Qohelet make an improbable declaration, not that he has encountered no woman who stands out among the many humans he has met, but that he has encountered no woman at all. The Masoretic punctuation nonetheless demands just such a division, and it reflects an understanding that not only underpins the ancient translations as well, but has also come to dominate subsequent interpretation of these verses.

This understanding, that Qohelet must mean somehow that he found no woman worthy or virtuous enough to meet some unspecified standard, is epitomised in *b. Gittin* 45a, where R. Ilish is said to have thought that he had found a contradiction to 7.28 in the example of R. Naḥman's daughters, who were apparently so righteous that they could stir a hot pot with their hands (although they turned out later not to have been so praiseworthy, so there was no real exception). It is also represented in Jerome's commentary, which cites Vergil (*Aeneid* 4.569-70) to explain this verse: *uarium et mutabile semper femina*, 'woman is ever a fickle and inconstant thing'. Jerome backs this up with a reference to the γυναικάρια, of 2 Tim 3.6-7, the 'little ladies' who are laden with sins, driven by their various passions, always learning about something, but never able to get so far as knowing what is true. It is impossible to say how far back this interpretation goes, but it seems clear that early readers found in the text here an affirmation of prejudices that were surely widespread. In the Targum and the Midrash Rabbah, the interpretation is more nuanced, and placed in specific historical contexts. The idea persists into those sources, however, that Qohelet is talking about finding, or failing to find, people who are worthy in some way, and it is this understanding that has shaped the division of the text in the early versions: it has no place for *lbd*, which is accordingly consigned awkwardly to the next verse.

This is, perhaps, merely an extreme example of the ancient tendency to lift passages out of their immediate context—leaving a word behind, in this case—to make some point quite unrelated to the original concerns of the text. It is also an illustration of the extent to which the Masoretes and ancient translators were willing to be guided by such traditional understandings and usages, even when these created problems. The persistence of this reading into more modern commentaries has naturally led to a certain amount of discomfort, and in recent times has provoked strong criticism of Qohelet and the book: if the text really were disparaging women that way, it would indeed be a striking display of misogyny. Even in the early eighteenth century, Matthew Henry felt obliged to observe of Qohelet here that, 'Doubtless, this is not intended as a Censure of the Female Sex in general, 'tis probable enough, that there have been, and are more Good Women than Good Men…but he only *alludes* to his own sad Experience'. This discomfort has not proved sufficient, however, to embolden any widespread challenge to the Masoretic punctuation, even though the resulting oddness of *lbd*'s use in 7.29 has often been observed.

The issue with *lbd* aside, however, the traditional interpretation faces the very real problem that there is no actual mention of worthiness here, and nothing in the surrounding context to suggest that such a notion should be read into the text. In English, we can talk about 'finding' something good or bad, so that 'find' can express an evaluation or become almost synonymous with 'consider' ('I find it strange that', 'I found her good company'). To the extent that the corresponding Hebrew word can be used in the same way at all, however, that use is much more restricted, and there is no reason to suppose it can have the particular connotation 'find worthy': the term is more specifically used of encountering or discovering. It was probably not the apparent absurdity of Qohelet saying that he met no woman which initially drove a reading in such terms, because reading the expression with *lbd* removes that absurdity. More likely, the interpretation was driven by an understanding that, earlier in the verse, Qohelet was claiming to have 'found' one person in a thousand, taken to mean that he found someone with rare qualities (much as we might speak of someone being 'one in a million'), which is how Jerome explains it. On that understanding, the failure to find a woman would have to mean, correspondingly, that no woman possessed such qualities.

I take Qohelet's claim actually to have been that he met one person in every thousand (a significant number, even allowing for smaller ancient populations, but more realistic than claiming to have met everybody), and failed to find among so many the incarnation of wisdom or folly as a woman that underpins the imagery in Proverbs 1–9.[1] The language of seeking and finding probably has nothing to do with evaluation, but it is quite strongly reminiscent of the language used by lovers seeking each other in the Song of Songs (e.g. Ct 3.1-4), and if that resemblance is deliberate, then Qohelet further alludes loosely to the imagery of Proverbs 1–9 by speaking of himself as a man looking for wisdom or folly as though for a lover.[2]

Matters are further complicated by questions around the distinction of sexes here, which are discussed in the notes. Once *lbd* had been pushed out of the reckoning, 7.28 seemed to state that Qohelet had found one person, but not found any woman—with the implication that the person must therefore have been a man. Jerome does not pursue this implication, but he translates the text in those terms, and there have long been efforts (including even alterations of the text in some Greek manuscripts) to find a more explicit statement

---

[1] I think that the device here involves a deliberate confusion of the symbolic with the real: for effect, the author has Qohelet take literally the existing presentations of wisdom and folly as women who can be found in the street, and speak of meeting actual people. It is possible, though, that he is instead accepting and building upon that symbolism, so that the claim is to have met many potential 'wisdoms', without finding any that stood out as *the* wisdom described in Proverbs and elsewhere. That latter reading is potentially very fruitful, and might perhaps correspond to the idea of multiple human plans in the next verse. I think the more neutral 'person' here tells against it, however: a maintenance of the symbolism would surely require the 'wisdoms' all to be women.

[2] Clifford, 'Another Look', 53-55, has argued recently that this language marks a division between remarks about personified folly in 7.26, and a quest for personified wisdom in 7.27-28. It is true that Wisdom speaks of a time when men will seek her in Prov 1.28, and there are references to 'seeking' and/or 'finding' her in 3.13; 8.17, 35, while in Prov 7.15, conversely, it is the 'foreign woman' who seeks out and finds the youth. Both figures are presented as potential lovers in Prov 1–9, which may itself draw on the language of love poetry, and, although both actively solicit male company, it is Wisdom who explicitly wants to be sought out. If our author is drawing directly on Prov 1–9, then 7.28 likely does refer to Wisdom (although I doubt that 7.26 refers to Folly so clearly as Clifford supposes), but it is important to recall that the imagery was picked up and adapted by others, so it might be unwise to presume that we can interpret Qohelet's words through reference to the specific nuances of Proverbs itself. Clifford goes on to suggest, very implausibly I think, that Qohelet rejects any quest for personified wisdom, after posing as someone on just such a quest, because he has never found a woman to be a useful conversation partner among the many he has had.

distinguishing men from women here. Combined with a particular understanding of what 'finding' might mean, this would facilitate an interpretation of Qohelet's words as saying that he found one man in every thousand to be worthy in some way, but no women. It is highly unlikely, in fact, that the Hebrew should be understood that way: Qohelet uses a neutral term 'person' or 'human' here where he could easily have said 'man'. Again, though, without *lbd* the text becomes awkward, and it is unsurprising that, once the second part had been seen as a statement about women in general, the verse as a whole should have come to be interpreted as distinguishing the sexes.

7.29] Qohelet repeats the same expression that he used in 7.27, this time to announce not whom he had met, but what he had actually discovered. His conclusion is not syntactically difficult, but we are faced with problems in the vocabulary. On the one hand, he declares, God made people (probably the people he had met in the last verse, but possibly 'humanity' or even 'Adam') in a certain way; on the other, he observes, they, like him, have set out to find 'plans' for themselves, perhaps each seeking, or finding, different ones. Our difficulty lies in the fact that *ḥšbwn*, translated here as 'plan', can actually have a wide range of meanings, none of which, however, correspond clearly to the idea that God has made the human *yšr*—a term we normally translate as 'upright'. It has suited certain theological tastes to see here a reference to the decline of humanity: from a state of perfection when they were created, humans have descended to seeking out their own schemes or devices (and this verse has sometimes been used to make the case for that decline in a way that Genesis does not—see, e.g., Laiblin, *De Rectitudine Hominis*). It is far from certain, however, that Qohelet even intends any criticism of humanity, and he has not depicted his own quest for a *ḥšbwn* as some act of depravity: in the preceding verses, it seems to have been connected rather with his quest for wisdom.

The issue is more probably, in fact, that God intended human existence to be more straightforward than humans themselves will permit it to be, and that their quests for some understanding of what is happening, or of what they should do, introduce a complexity to their lives that lies outside the scope of divine intentions. It is possible even to understand the text as saying that they act as they do *because* of the way that God made them, and Qohelet's intention is probably not to imply that they are doing something bad, or contrary to the divine will. The emphasis in his observation seems instead to be on the fact that these quests are human, not divine initiatives. In that case, it is tempting to wonder whether Qohelet is engaging here too with the sort of claims made in Proverbs 1–9, where personified Wisdom puts herself forward as a way to align oneself with God's will, and deliberately solicits human attention. Whether the author presents him this way consciously or not, Qohelet depicts a very different situation, in which that figure of wisdom is nowhere to be found, and humans rush around seeking their own answers, on their own initiative.

The idea that humans over-complicate their lives picks up a strand of thought in the book that was most obviously explicit in 2.15, when Qohelet questioned his own accumulation of wisdom, but which was visible also in his treatments of work, wealth and greed. It will inform his advice in 9.7, and is clearly related both to Qohelet's own concerns about excessive caution in ch. 11, and to the epilogue's impatience with complexity in 12.13-14.

8.1] This verse has been seen both as the end of the preceding sequence and as the introduction to what will follow (there is a helpful summary of opinions in Lavoie, 'Qui est comme le sage?', 99-100). Fox and Lohfink, indeed, themselves defy the Masoretic punctuation at this point, by breaking it in two: they take the initial questions to pick up 7.25-29, and to imply that nobody can really be wise or know anything, but take the second part of the verse to introduce 8.2-9, so that it is to be understood in the context of the royal court. I have considerable sympathy for that approach, but where we put the verse, and whether we treat it as one unit or two, depends essentially on what we take it to mean.

That is a greater problem in the second part of the verse than in the first, since the apparent contrast that Qohelet draws involves two idioms, and we do not know for sure the meaning of either. On the basis of similar expressions elsewhere, however, he is probably saying that wisdom enlightens a person intellectually on the one hand, but on the other lessens their capacity to act without hesitation or consideration—what we might consider the pros and cons of thoughtfulness. In the first part, there is some ambiguity, and his questions could possibly be read as acclamation of the wise man (although surely also, in that case, as ironic after what has preceded). They more probably, however, express Qohelet's doubt that there really is any such person as the archetypal wise man that he has talked about previously, or that anybody really has insight into anything—the second question uses a technical expression associated with identifying the hidden meanings of texts or visions, and that might accordingly exemplify the sort of claim associated with those deemed wise. As a whole, therefore, the verse wonders first whether, in this world of humans all searching for their own answers, anyone really has them, and then whether the intellectual enlightenment offered by wisdom is not at least offset by the uncertainty and indecision that it engenders (a theme that will be developed in the first part of ch. 11). When Qohelet returns to what wisdom offers, at the end of 8.5, his point will be that what constitutes wisdom is principally an understanding of the limits set upon what humans can know or do.

These issues are going to be picked up, then, and matters of consideration and decisiveness will not be irrelevant to what follows more immediately in 8.2-3. Even if it facilitates a transition to the next topic that way, though, I think that the most immediate purpose of this verse is to round off Qohelet's account of his quest. He began this account by recalling his own intentions to use wisdom and be wise, realizes that he has not succeeded in this aim, and then finishes it with the understanding not just that everybody is in the same boat, but that wisdom itself may be a mixed blessing.

Notes

7.27 Look at this:] Qohelet will use ראה זה again shortly, in 7.29, but it was also, in 1.10, the expression that he put into the mouth of someone claiming to have something new. In the latter, we can read ראה זה followed by a non-verbal clause, or a free-standing imperative ראה followed by a non-verbal clause structured זה...הוא (see the note there). In 7.29 ראה זה מצאתי (the same expression as here) will be followed by אשר. In both verses, ראה זה can be taken as an independent expression, and in 7.29, indeed, it would be awkward to construe ראה זה מצאתי as 'Look what I have found', because we would have to read an asyndetic relative (or a relative clause with זה itself serving as a relative pronoun, if we were to follow the suggestion Dahood, 'Phoenician Background', 276-77, makes for this verse), immediately followed by a clause with אשר. That meaning has long established itself as the most common translation here in 7.27, however, probably because 'says the Qohelet' breaks into the sentence after מצאתי. If those words are treated as a new clause that must be considered within the structure of the sentence overall, then they leave מצאתי without an explicit object, and interpreters have looked to זה to fulfil that function, which results in, e.g., S ܚܙܝ ܗܢܐ ܕܐܫܟܚܬ, *ḥzy hn' d'škḥt*, 'see this that I have found'. The difficulty of reading the other uses of ראה זה in that way, however, is itself a strong indication that אמרה קהלת should be treated as parenthetical, which is what its sense would anyway suggest. As I shall discuss below, this makes another object available for מצאתי, and the fact that another verb has otherwise to be conjured up for this object offers a further strong indication of the structure here.

Whether the other occurrences can also be used to suggest that the זה must refer forward to what follows, as Ginsburg claims, is another matter: as it happens, I think that in each case it does (if we read it as the object of the imperative), but I doubt that that is inherent in the wording rather than the context, or that ראה זה could never be used to refer back (which is how, e.g., Fox and Porten, 'Unsought Discoveries', 31, take it). In any case, even if something more specific was in view at 1.10, the force of the expression here and in 7.29 is probably little more than 'Look here'.

7.27 I met…one woman after another] If we do not read 'Look at what I have found', then מצאתי needs an object, as already noted, while the subsequent אחת לאחת needs a verb to govern it: taking אחת לאחת as the object of מצאתי meets both needs. We shall look at the intervening אמרה קהלת below, but may treat it as irrelevant to the underlying construction of the sentence, and look at אחת לאחת first. What we can say with reasonable certainty about this expression is that it refers to 'one…another': this is quite a common use of אחד…אחד (e.g. 2 Sam 12.1; Job 41.8 ET 41.16). The form here is feminine, moreover, and so, without any other feminine substantive in sight, we are dealing either with one woman and another, or with one thing and another— as Jerome observed, and many commentators since, Hebrew can use the feminine effectively as a neuter, and this understanding seems to be reflected in σ' ἓν πρὸς ἕν (G μία τῇ μιᾷ retains the feminine).

Beyond that, matters become more complicated. Because they have linked מצאתי to זה, commentators generally have to understand another verb here, the most popular supposition being that Qohelet is 'adding' one thing to another to find a 'sum'. This has been the basis of much discussion about Qohelet's thinking and methods, but is very unlikely to be the meaning of the phrase. As we have seen, חשבון does not mean 'total', and so although by adding things one might conceivably perform a חשבון, in its sense 'calculation', one does not 'find' a חשבון by doing so. More importantly, Hebrew almost exclusively expresses the addition of one thing to another by using על not -ל: see, with a verb of addition, e.g., Deut 4.2; Lev 5.16; 2 Sam 4.2; Isa 38.5; Jer 36.32 (אל appears once with יסף in 2 Sam 24.3); more generally Gen 28.9; Ps 69.28. It would probably not be surprising to find -ל used in such a context, since it has such a wide range of uses, and BDB does describe addition as a 'rare' use of -ל—although it offers only a handful of examples (including this verse), not one of which is both clear and persuasive. It would be astonishing, on the other hand, if an author used ־ל rather than על in an expression like this with an expectation that his readers would *understand* addition to be implicit. Indeed, the very fact that ־ל can be used in so many ways makes the supposed elision of a verb all the more puzzling.

Our best clue to the proper sense here, I think, is the use of the similar לאחד אחד in Isa 27.12. The image in that verse, applied to the gathering of the people, is one of hand-threshing grain on a small scale, not a threshing-floor (cf. Ruth 2.17), probably beating the ears with a stick to release the seeds (Isa 28.27), and then picking those up individually: correspondingly, the implication is that the people will be gathered 'one by one', 'one after another', or 'one at a time'—perhaps even with some nuance that this will be a laborious process. If we are willing to dispense with the need for an imaginary verb by taking מצאתי to govern אחת לאחת, then Qohelet is talking about 'finding' people or things individually or in succession—one at a time.

For those who insist on seeing a revelation of his thought-processes here, then this might be understood in terms of his using successive discoveries to build towards what he is seeking—which would make this merely a way of putting the notion of addition on a more secure footing. I do not take that, however, to be the point here. Qohelet has just spoken about 'finding' a woman in the previous verse (with מצא there having its common implication of 'meeting' rather than discovering), and although the next verse presents problems of its own, there is no reason to doubt that he refers there also to his encountering, or rather his failure to encounter a woman. It does not seem problematic, therefore, to think that here too he is talking about encountering women, and to read אחת לאחת as 'one (woman) after another'.[3] This not only conforms better to the context than 'one thing after another', but actually avoids inserting a sudden, short-lived change of direction into that context.

Given that the text as it stands seems to make sense, there is no good reason to emend אחת לאחת, and no versional support for doing so. All the same, Pinker, 'Qohelet's Views on Women', 183-84, prefers to read אחת לא חתה, and understands Qohelet to be saying that he found one woman who was 'unafraid to discover an original thought'. Whether or not such an idea would be expressed that way, the emendation is speculative and unnecessary.

7.27 says the Qohelet] There have been various attempts, some very complicated, to explain why at this point, and this point alone, the monologue is interrupted to remind us that Qohelet is speaking. I doubt, however, that too much should be read into the words. If they are original, and if we follow the Greek in 7.26, as I have proposed, then their most likely function is to mark an end to Qohelet's direct 'speech within a speech' in that preceding

---

[3] So, similarly, Gill, who does not read מצאתי with אחת לאחת, but says nevertheless that 'the sense is, examining women one by one, all within the verge of his acquaintance'. This sense is also considered by Kravitz and Olitzky.

verse, and a return to the monologue itself—the author had no resort in quotation marks. The specific position of אמרה קהלת is striking, however, and there is no obvious reason, at least in terms of the general sense, why it should not have preceded ראה זה. Since אחת לאחת, furthermore, does not mark the beginning of a new thought, then however we construe the text, this makes the words feel intrusive. We should consider the slight possibility that אמרה קהלת originated as a marginal gloss identifying the previous verse as direct speech by Qohelet: the point at which such glosses are drawn into the text may be determined more by line-breaks in a manuscript copy than by any considerations of sense. Much more probably, however, the positioning is a deliberate device used by the author, and it is not without parallel.

In, e.g., 2 Kgs 20.17-18; Isa 1.18 and Jer 11.11, a reference to the speaker speaking appears at neither the beginning nor the end of direct speech, and there is clearly no unbreakable rule that says it must. Judg 5.23 shows how the positioning of such references can be used for effect: אורו מרוז אמר מלאך יהוה ארו ארור ישביה, lit. 'Curse Meroz, says the angel of YHWH, cursing curse its inhabitants'. In none of these is there an actual interruption to the syntax, and the reference is placed between clauses, but we do find such interruptions in Gen 3.3, where the prepositional phrase precedes its verb and is separated from it by אמר אלהים; in Exod 5.16, where a direct object is involved (ולבנים אמרים לנו עשו, lit. 'and bricks—they are saying to us—make!'); and in Isa 48.22 (אין שלום אמר יהוה לרשעים), where 'says YHWH' simply interrupts a statement constructed with אין ל-. The non-verbal phrase נאם יהוה is also used parenthetically, interrupting the syntax, in Jer 1.19. Such usages are not so common that we can readily make generalizations either about their purpose or about any constraints upon their use, but in the instances we have, the device seems to employ the separation created by the parenthetical insertion to evoke anticipation or place the emphasis on one element of the clause ('there is no peace!…at least for the wicked')—a sort of stylistic drum roll.

In any case, it is well known that the form of אמרה קהלת presents a problem in itself: the verb אמרה is third-person feminine, while Qohelet is usually considered to be male. This problem is usually (and correctly) resolved by the simple expedient of moving the ה from אמרה to קהלת and construing the text as אמר הקהלת, 'the Qohelet says': that brings the text into line with G εἶπεν ὁ ἐκκλησιαστής, which has a corresponding definite article.[4] There is

---

[4] Of the other versions, S translates as though it simply found אמר קהלת, and Hie, V are indeterminate, since Latin has no definite article. T may show an awareness of the reading with an article in its otherwise unnecessary specification 'said Qohelet, who is called Solomon, the king of Israel' (cf. 12.8). Perhaps surprisingly, אמרה קהלת seems to be found consistently in the Hebrew tradition, and de Rossi denies that any manuscript has אמר הקהלת. Likewise, there is no $Q^e r\hat{e}$ (in any manuscript, so far as I am aware) supporting the emendation, as Wolfe, lxv, supposes.

grammatical support elsewhere in the text for the portrayal of Qohelet as male (see the Introduction, p. 241 n. 19), so we cannot simply suppose that Qohelet is actually a woman, and correct the אמר הקוהלת of 12.8 instead (as Perry, *Dialogues*, 178, suggests). If it is easy to fix such an apparent mis-division of the text, however, it is a little harder to understand how it happened and persisted, which leads, e.g., Provan, 29, to insist that the reading must be original, and a number of scholars to think that this must be a deliberate device. So, Ingram, 'The Riddle of Qohelet', 501, suggests that it is an attempt to compound the mystery surrounding Qohelet's identity, and Heim thinks that Qohelet is playfully switching gender to amuse his audience, while Hengstenberg famously saw an incarnation of wisdom in the person of Qohelet here, designed to counter the description of the foreign woman. This last is a view that Hilbrands and Kosiol, 'Kohelet als Frauenfeind?', 87, rightly describe as 'Überinterpretiert', 'over-interpreted', but it is not improbable that the many references to women and the feminine in this context inhibited correction of the error among scribes, who could themselves have suspected some such hidden allusion, just as some modern commentators have seen a sort of instability in the gender of Qohelet, expressed also in the 'feminine' form of 'Qohelet' itself—see, e.g., Koosed, *(Per)mutations*, 83-4; Wolfe, lxvii. This is an issue, though, that can probably not be separated from broader questions about the use of an article with the epithet (which I discussed in the note at 1.1), and it is difficult to attribute the reading specifically to authorial design.

7.27 a plan] Although חשבון is commonly translated here as '*the* sum', '*the* reckoning', or similar, it lacks a definite article, as we noted earlier. This absence is affirmed not only by G τοῦ εὑρεῖν λογισμόν, but also by σ' ἐν πρὸς ἓν εὑρεῖν λογισμὸν, which is attested in Greek but wrongly attributed to α' in some manuscripts (see Marshall; Jerome affirms that G and all the Three had the noun λογισμὸν itself). It accords both with the similar absence in 7.25 and with the mention of many חשבנות in 7.29. S marks the noun here as plural with seyame, but Kamenetzky, 202, is surely right to see this as secondary.

7.28 which] The reading of σ' continues further, but lacks any equivalent to אשר in the Greek manuscripts. Marshall argues that ὃν must have dropped out through haplography after λογισμὸν, and accordingly presents it as <ὃν> ἔτι ζητεῖ ἡ ψυχή μου καὶ οὐχ εὗρον, '[which] my soul still sought and I did not find'. There are, however, some other inconsistencies between the versions here: M is supported by G, Hie, V, but S ܘܬܘܒ *wtwb* has just a conjunction, and although T דעוד does have a relative -ד, it is preceded by an explicit statement that what Qohelet still sought was not the preceding חשבון, but פתגם אוחרן, 'another thing', or 'something else'. It is very possible that a variant reading without אשר is actually reflected in σ', and that S, T represent different attempts to make sense of it, but the evidence does not point clearly that way.

If there are slight signs of disturbance here, however, there is no versional support for the otherwise attractive proposal by Perles (in *Analekten*, 33) and Ehrlich, picked up more recently by Fox, that we should read אשה, 'woman', instead of אשר.[5] For Fox, at least, that suggestion is motivated by a perception that, as he puts it, '*Ḥešbon* is not what Qohelet failed to find, because in the next sentence he says that he did find a *ḥešbon*'—which would leave אשר without an antecedent. Such concerns have more commonly led some commentators to a reading that is reflected in the verse-division and in the Masoretic punctuation, whereby אשר is understood as 'that which' or 'what' his נפש sought, so that Qohelet is saying, in a slightly convoluted way, 'What I sought but have not found is…', and the whole clause points forward. So Murphy, for instance, has 'what my soul has always sought without finding (is this): …' (so similarly, e.g., Schwienhorst-Schönberger, 'Bitterer als der Tod', 448-49). I do not see the problem, however, at least as Fox states it: Qohelet never claims to have found a חשבון, even in Fox's own translation, and Fox himself later suggests that he did not. Unless we quietly insert a conjunction, as does Ginsburg, it is manifestly simpler and more natural to ignore the Masoretes and read אשר as introducing a relative clause that qualifies חשבון.

7.28 my self still sought and I did not find] In the G tradition, ἔτι ἐζήτησεν, 'still sought', which corresponds to M עוד בקשה and was almost certainly the original reading, has disappeared and been replaced in most manuscripts by just ἐπεζήτησεν 'sought after' (some have ἐξεζήτησεν, 'sought out', or other variations). Vinel rejects the ἔτι, but there can be little doubt that ἐπεζήτησεν has resulted from a graphical confusion between ΕΤΙ and ΕΠ, transforming ἔτι into a pronominal prefix, and something similar has happened in the transmission of the σ' reading, where ἔτι ζητεῖ has been displaced by ἐπιζητεῖ or its equivalent in all but one of the witnesses.

The two readings are interesting in another respect, in that they reflect two different understandings of the tense here: is Qohelet saying that his נפש still 'sought' a חשבון at the time to which he is referring, or that it still 'seeks' one at the time he is speaking? In V, perhaps under the influence of σ', Jerome uses the present-tense *quaerit*, 'seeks', but in Hie he used the perfect *quaesiuit*, which matches the sense of G, and may be La. This uncertainty persists into modern translations and commentaries, which take the statement in both ways, but despite Isaksson's claim that 'the most natural translation is the present-tense one' (*Studies*, 91), it is not really a matter that can be resolved simply by reference to the Hebrew verbs, which can be read either way, and the context does not seem to give a strong steer.

---

[5] Perles sees the error as the result of an abbreviation אש, and I cannot locate the suggestion in the later 1922 edition of his work, which makes much less of supposed abbreviations more generally. Fox, on the other hand, sees a graphical error resulting from confusion between ה and ר.

The meaning of עוד in this context is relevant to the question, but it too is disputed. Fox, like others, claims that "*Od* = "continually," as in Gen 46:29; Ruth 1:14; Ps 84:5', and notes also what he takes to be a similar use in 12.9. We shall return to that claim when we reach 12.9, but in the verses that he cites, which are the only ones where עוד is commonly granted this sense, it may be allowed, at least, that the expression apparently qualifies actions that people keep on doing because they will not or cannot stop. That sense would not be inappropriate here, but it is difficult to see why we should prefer it to the much more common meaning 'still' or 'yet', which also works well in this context. Doing so potentially turns Qohelet's search into a life-long quest, which is probably why it attracts those commentators who see Qohelet's actions in terms of some great search for meaning, but the more basic sense of the text here is that his encounters continue because none provides what he is seeking. Differently, Pinker, 'Qohelet's Views on Women', 184, takes Qohelet to be saying 'when for more [with respect to the finding in v. 27] <I> asked myself, I did not find'. This is ugly, and it is doubtful either that אשר could be used for 'when' and עוד for 'more' in the ways that Pinker would like, or that the sentence as a whole could reasonably be construed to mean 'When I asked for more, I could not find'—even if we allowed the exceptional usages.

With reference to such questions, and to the sense of the relative clause as a whole, it may be helpful to note the very similar language in Ct 3.1, where the woman declares, 'I sought (בקשתי) him whom my נפש loves: I sought him (בקשתיו) but did not find him (מצאתיו)'. As Melton, 'Solomon, Wisdom, and Love', 136-37, observes, there are a number of places where Qohelet's seeking stands comparison with the theme of seeking a lover in Song of Songs, and the links with Ct 3.1-4 are particularly striking. Seow suggests, very plausibly I think, that there is a deliberate allusion here, and that 'the motif of seeking and not finding belongs to the language of a lover's pursuit'; see, similarly Hos 2.7.[6] Setting aside such broader issues, though, the fact that

---

[6] Fox and Porten ('Unsought Discoveries', 34-38) draw comparisons also with Gen 37.15-17, 32, and 1 Sam 9.1–10.27, seeing elaborate combinations of 'seeking' and 'finding' as 'a set of key words which functions to develop a theme, structure a unit, and trace a theology' (34). In the stories of Joseph and Saul, 'Man seeks one thing but finds something quite different because God controls his destiny' (37), and Qohelet is led to frustration and the discovery merely that 'woman is a misfortune', when what he sought was a much broader understanding. The idea seems to be that biblical literature attests to a rhetorical or narrative motif in which searches are frustrated or diverted, with an implication that divine determination may be involved. The reading of the Joseph story seems a little forced, but seeking and finding probably is used as a narrative device in the account of Saul looking for his father's asses. I am not sure, though, that anything is accomplished by bundling these disparate accounts together, and

this other text uses the same forms of the same verbs to tell what is undoubtedly a story set in the past tense would seem to put the onus on those who would see a present tense here, to demonstrate any reason why we should consider that 'the most natural translation'.

It is a different point, but the appearance in Song of Songs of the נפש draws attention to its use here too, which has received little recent attention (although Riesener, 'Frauenfeindschaft', 196, 201, does pick up on it). We may well be reminded of the association between נפש and desire that we encountered earlier in the book (see the note at 6.3), and, even if it is not a specific reference to love poetry, Qohelet's use of the noun here gives his search a colouring that is not really intellectual (despite such translations as Schoors' 'my mind'). As the contrast between בקשה נפשי and ולא מצאתי shows, נפשי is also almost used as a synonym for 'I, me' here, and I have not tried to give it any strong connotations in the translation, but Riesener is surely right to suggest that the links to love poetry reinforce the associations here with the imagery of Proverbs 1–9, which also draws on the language of seeking and finding.

7.28 I met one person from every thousand] Lit. 'one person from a thousand I met'. Although Rahlfs omits it, all manuscripts of G have a conjunction here before 'person': καὶ ἄνθρωπον ἕνα ἀπὸ χιλίων εὗρον, '*and I met one person from a thousand*'. This is supported by none of the other versions except those, like La,[7] which are derived from G, but it is likely to be G* and to reflect a variant in the source-text. It makes little difference to the sense, but is not compatible with, e.g., Schoors' rather forced attempt to see here a saying which Qohelet is affirming. The text itself otherwise presents no problems, although Shields, *The End of Wisdom*, 188, has proposed (against the witness of all the ancient versions) that we should delete the verb as secondary—a suggestion that greatly simplifies the sentence, but that correspondingly raises questions about how מצאתי might have come to be added. The issues that have been more generally debated are rather the meanings of מצאתי itself, and of אדם.

These arise as issues out of the broader problems presented by Qohelet's statement as a whole, the point of which has long puzzled commentators. Jerome's influential reading is expressed concisely: *et cum uix paucos de uiris bonos inuenerim, ita ut de mille unus potuerit inueniri, mulierem bonam omnino inuenire non potui*, 'and while I barely found a few good among men,

---

thereby subsuming the more specific resemblances between our passage and Song of Songs. Fontaine, 'Many Devices', 152, sees in those resemblances 'yet another play on the Solomonic royal fiction'.

[7] Jerome's La here is *et hominem unum de mille inueni et mulierem in his omnibus non inueni*; cf. Leanza, 'Le tre versione', 93. Elsewhere, in *Aduersus Jouinianum* 1, 29, Jerome cites the passage identically but without the conjunction: his other citations from the book in that passage, however, show similar slight variations, and he is probably citing from memory or paraphrasing a little.

so that one from a thousand could be found, I was unable to find any good woman'. To get that from the text, however, it is necessary not only to find a contrast between men and women here, but to assume that the Hebrew is even more compact, with 'good' understood, or the sense 'find (someone) good' taken to be inherent in the verb. It is interesting to note that an interpretative ἄνδρα, 'man', has displaced ἄνθρωπον, 'human', in a few corners of the G tradition as well, most notably in the 'Lucianic', *L*-group of manuscripts (see Dickie, 'Analysis', 70). Didymus (Tura papyrus 231.2) reports that [πολλὰ ἀντί]γραφα 'ἄνδρα' ἔχει 'γυναῖκα δὲ ἐν πᾶσιν τούτοις οὐχ εὗρον', '[many co]pies of the text have "man", "but a woman among all these I did not find"'—which strengthens the point with a δὲ, 'but', which is absent from the manuscript tradition (see Kramer and Krebber, *Didymos der Blinde IV*, 118-19).

The question of a male/female contrast remains a legitimate debate, and it is true, of course, that אדם and אשה represent different genders in, e.g., Gen 2.22, where they are Adam and Eve. Adam, however, also represents humanity as a whole, before the species is split into sexes. As is often pointed out, moreover, if we read אדם in the sense 'male' here, then it is difficult to assign it the inclusive sense 'human' or 'person' in the next verse, in order to avoid excluding women from Qohelet's general statement there. The possibility that אדם *might* mean 'male' is difficult to dispute (although also difficult to demonstrate for biblical Hebrew). It is no less difficult to dispute the fact, however, that if Qohelet had such a contrast in mind, he could easily have used איש, while it is unclear what other than אדם he could have used if he wanted to say 'human' and specifically not to say 'man'—his favourite בני האדם, or the singular בן האדם would hardly do in this context. A reading in terms of men/women, then, has not just to prove the possibility of that sense, but to explain the choice of a word that does not make it clear, and the apparent re-application of that word to a broader sense 'human' in the very next verse. That reading also runs into the lesser difficulty that, subsequently, Qohelet will talk about not finding a woman בכל אלה. If the 'one' in a thousand that Qohelet is talking about are all men, then אלה obviously does not refer to that subset, and so must refer to the original thousand, but in that case, we would expect מכל אלה, to match the first construction.

As for 'finding good', there is no reason to suppose that מצא can be used with the specific implication 'find something to be good',[8] so even if we assume that ישר from the next verse is somehow being foreshadowed (as, e.g., Ginsburg claims), it is difficult to take the expression that way. If that sense

---

[8] For such a sense, Levy compares the Greek εὑρίσκω, and this analogy has sometimes been cited by subsequent commentators. Levy supplies no source or references, and the Greek verb is very common, so I should not like to claim that it *never* has such a meaning. If it does, though, this seems to have eluded the major lexica.

is doubtful, a more general cognitive implication is almost certainly to be rejected, despite, e.g., the efforts of D'Alario, 'Between Misogyny and Valorization', 103, to suggest that this is about the impossibility of finding a result if we try to investigate a woman (a reading that is self-evidently problematic for other reasons too), or of Gorssen, 'La cohérence', 312, to claim that Qohelet is talking about understanding the conduct of men and women. Some commentators have correspondingly tried to transfer the ellipsis to the nouns, so that אדם and אשה take on the sort of special nuance that *Mensch* can have in Yiddish, but there is, again, absolutely no evidence for such usage elsewhere. On the surface, Qohelet is simply claiming to have met one person in every thousand, and there is no reason (other than the difficulty that his statement presents for particular interpretations) to suppose that the audience would have recognized any more specific claim below this surface.

The ingenious reading of Richter, 'Kohelets Urteil', 589, avoids these difficulties, taking אדם as 'human' and assigning its usual sense to מצא, but achieving, nevertheless, a very different meaning overall. Richter takes Qohelet (or actually a later editor speaking as Qohelet) to be saying that what his נפש *had* sought and not found was one person in a thousand, but he has now found a woman, so that he has not made all his discoveries by himself. This involves parsing the text rather differently, of course, and introducing distinct time periods. It also, though, requires a specific minor emendation (or re-division of the text): Richter reads מצאתיו אשה rather than מצאתי ואשה, and translates: 'Ich habe ihn gefunden: eine Frau', implying 'I have now found them (i.e., that person I was seeking): a woman'. This change, of course, is crucial—the interpretation is not possible without it—but the lack of versional support for it presents less of an obstacle than do the lack of fit with the immediate context (Richter understands this to be part of a secondary addition) and the awkwardness of the construction that is presupposed (I am not sure that his reading is actually self-contradictory, though, as Zimmer, *Zwischen Tod und Lebensglück*, 128, supposes).

Finally, it is hard to find a close biblical analogy to the expression 'one from a thousand'. Judg 20.10, which uses מאה לאלף and similar expressions, employs -ל because it is talking about conscripting a hundred 'for' every thousand, although the partitive use of מן, as found here, can be illustrated more generally by, e.g. Gen 6.19 'two out of every sort'. The same expression as here is found, however, in 11QT^a (11Q19) LVIII, 13 (alongside אחד מן המאה מן הכול, 'one hundredth of the whole') and LX, 4 both of which use אחד מאלף for 'a thousandth'—a share of spoils. It appears also in Sir 6.5/6.6: אנשי שלומך יהיו רבים ובעל סודך אחד מאלף, 'may the people on good terms with you be many, but just one in every thousand be a member of your inner circle', and Schwienhorst-Schönberger, 'Bitterer als der Tod', 452, tries unconvincingly to find a broader connection with Sir 6, where he sees a model of male friendship from which women are excluded: the connection is likely to be no more than linguistic, however, and Ben Sira is not talking about some particular social phenomenon of the 'one in a thousand' friend. In Jerome's commentary, and often elsewhere, Qohelet is taken to be claiming that he actually did find one man or person, out of a thousand, who conformed to some particular requirement. I take the point more probably to be that he encountered a lot of people—we would say one 'in' every thousand—but the uses in Ben Sira and at Qumran suggest that the same expression would have been used either way. It is not this phrase, but the scope of the verb that makes Jerome's understanding less likely.

Baltzer, 'Women and War', 130-31, claims that 'thousand' should be taken in a technical sense, so that Qohelet finds no woman in 'the army', implying that war is the responsibility of men; this is then tied to an interpretation of חשבנות in 7.29 as 'weapons of war', and the implication of the whole passage taken to be that it is not women who are deadly, as men might suggest, but men themselves. The idea is picked up in Leithart, 'Solomon's Sexual Wisdom', 453-56, which emphasizes the notion of Qohelet leading his male audience on with misogynistic claims before reversing them, and Jost, 'Frau und Adam', 64-66, argues along similar lines, but speaks less specifically of a lethal militarism, and more of an oppressive mode of male rule, supported by a type of wisdom that is attacked here. Although very clever, this approach lays altogether too much weight, I think, on the occasional use of a few terms here in military contexts, and neglects important elements—not least Qohelet's stated quest for a חשבון, which fits badly with the proposed interpretation of חשבנות. It is far from clear, moreover, that 'thousand' would have been recognized as a contemporary military term by the time the book was written: that sense is generally confined to stories of Israel's distant past, and often overlaps with more general references to clans or tribes; it is fairly unusual, in any case, and was probably never just a way of referring to the military.

7.28-29 but I met no woman who stood apart among all these] Lit. 'and a woman in all these I did not meet apart'. As I spelled out in the commentary, I think that the key to understanding what Qohelet is saying here lies in the word לבד, which has traditionally been placed at the beginning of the next verse and so tended to fall out of consideration. This expression is quite commonly found with a following מן, meaning 'apart from', and מלבד is similar;[9] with suffix pronouns it has the sense 'alone' or 'by oneself' (לבדו in Gen 2.18 is a good example). Outside those constructions, it is more rarely used of things that are set apart or separately. So in Exod 26.9 and 36.16, it apparently refers to curtains hung separately (as opposed to folded?), in Zech 12.12-14 to the mourning of families and the wives of families in separate acts of mourning, and in Judg 7.5 to the 'setting apart' or 'marking out' of the warriors who lapped the water like dogs. The particular nuance in those passages is not, it seems, the amount of physical or temporal distance between

---

[9] That may be the sense also of the only example with a following על in Ezra 1.6, although there is a nuance of addition there as well, and of לבד בך in the difficult and possibly corrupt Isa 26.13.

the entities, but the fact that there is such a distance, so that they are distinct and unjoined to others.

As has frequently been observed, on no other occasion in biblical Hebrew, or elsewhere, is לבד used in the way that it has to be read with 7.29, where it is usually taken to introduce a main clause and to mean 'Only, look at this', or 'however' (Schoors); noting this, Fox can offer only the speculation that it is being used uniquely as a calque on the Aramaic לחוד, which can be used that way (as it apparently is here by T). Rather than resort to explaining the usage as unique or as an otherwise unparalleled borrowing, however, it seems better to observe that when לבד stands by itself elsewhere, it always stands *after* whatever it is qualifying (rather like the English word 'alone'), which means that it is more natural to try to take it here as a qualification of what has preceded—Qohelet's extraordinary statement that he found no woman. Whether it makes sense for him to be saying that he found no woman 'apart' depends, of course, on one's understanding of the context more broadly, but if we think that he is looking for a woman who is wisdom (and/or folly), then it would not seem problematic for him to be saying that he found no woman who 'stood out' or was distinct from everybody else he met (בכל אלה...לבד) in the way that one might expect her to be. That reading, of course, relieves us of the need to find some other, implicit quality of 'goodness' elsewhere in the statement, and it seems much less forced than taking that route.

This suggestion is not entirely without precedent. Ingram, 'Riddled with Ambiguity', 234, has proposed similarly, for example, that 'if the (late) verse divisions are ignored לבד may be read with לא מצאתי, which would be more in keeping with its use elsewhere in the Hebrew Bible', but because he takes Qohelet to be talking about 'things', he translates 'I did not find this alone' (and the insight does not feed consistently into his subsequent presentation of the ways the text could be understood). A comparable line is pursued also in Richter, 'Kohelets Urteil', 589, who, however, understands Qohelet to be saying that he did not make his discoveries by himself (because Richter thinks that he *had* found a woman: see above on 7.27). Bartholomew, on the other hand, has sought a similar sense without re-division of the text: he thinks that Qohelet has encountered Folly in 7.26, but speaks here of missing Wisdom, characterized as 'a woman'. That broader understanding might be possible reading לבד here, but it seems a considerable stretch to find, just in an undetermined אשה, a reference to Wisdom in particular.

It is important to note, of course, that the Greek sources here seem to back the division of the text in M: G πλὴν means 'but' or 'nevertheless', although it often just starts a new topic, and α', σ' μόνον is being used adverbially, 'only'. The same is true of the other ancient translations. Despite the difficulty of the usage, therefore, and the problems that this division creates for understanding 7.28, the reading of M appears to be underpinned by a solid and early tradition of interpretation—probably founded in the more basic understanding that Qohelet is making general statements about women—that was willing to override those problems.

7.29 Look at this: I found] Qohelet is playing on the different uses of the verb: he did not successfully 'meet' or 'find' a חשבון or the woman he sought, but he did 'discover' something as a result of all his encounters, and מצאתי refers to the statement that follows.

We have already touched on the construal of the sentence in the note on 'look at this' at 7.27. S ܚܙܝ ܗܢܐ ܕܐܫܟܚܬ ܕܥܒܕ ܐܠܗܐ, *ḥzy hn' d'škḥt d'bd 'lh'*, 'see this that I have found, that God made', takes ראה זה מצאתי to contain an asyndetic relative clause 'this (that) I found', then takes אשר as a verbal complement or conjunction. G ἰδὲ τοῦτο εὗρον ὃ ἐποίησεν ὁ θεός, 'see this: I found what God made', instead construes אשר itself as a relative pronoun, while T has חמי דין אשכחית דעבד יײ, 'see this: I have found that God made', which takes אשר as a conjunction, but reads no relative clause. Curiously, the readings of Jerome do not reflect ראה at all (we would expect *ecce*): Hie *solummodo hoc inueni quia fecit deus* and V *solummodo hoc inueni quod fecerit deus* both mean just 'only, I found this, that (V what) God made'. This cannot be the influence of σ', as one might normally expect, since (μόνον) ἴδε ('only, look') is attested as the reading of both α' and σ', but it is probably not simply a matter of free rendering, as Euringer suggests. *Ecce* is also missing when Jerome cites the verse elsewhere in *Aduersus Iouinianum* I, 29 (*PL* 23, 262) as *uerumtamem reperi quod fecit deus*, 'nevertheless, I found out what God made': this is much closer to G and is probably La, so it may suggest that Jerome found no equivalent to ראה in his Latin sources, and chose not to restore it on the basis of the Greek or Hebrew, perhaps because it seemed redundant or repetitive.

There is a significant degree of variety in all this among the versions, despite the probability that all were working with the same Hebrew. Although the different renderings do not change the sense very much, they do reflect the absence of any consensus among the translators about precisely how the syntax was to be understood. I have suggested already that ראה זה מצאתי is unlikely to contain a relative clause, but it is unlikely also that the subsequent אשר should be understood as relative: the attempt by G to take it that way creates a very awkward structure and unnatural sense for the sentence as a whole ('I found what God made: man upright. And they…'). The אשר could be read as a conjunction with מצא, 'find *that*', were we willing to treat מצא, against other usage, as a verb of cognition or perception, and perhaps Qohelet is using it very loosely that way. I think it is more probably, however, to be taken simply as nominalizing what follows, rather as אשר nominalizes a clause to act as the subject of a non-verbal sentence in 5.4: the distinction may be clearer to us than it would have been to the author. In any case, Qohelet's statement about God and humans is effectively presented as the object of מצאתי.[10]

---

[10] In 'The Grammar of שׁ and אשר in Qohelet', 307, and *The Relative Clause in Biblical Hebrew*, 380, Holmstedt explains the אשר of 7.29 as standing in apposition to the זה, which would make this comparable to the construction in 9.1 ('[saw]

7.29 God made each person uncomplicated] Especially in connection with עשה, Qohelet's use of האדם here has led most commentators, from an early date, to see a specific allusion to creation, and perhaps even to Genesis itself—an idea that lends itself, of course, to the very common interpretation of Qohelet's discovery in terms of something like the Fall. It is important to bear in mind from the outset, however, both that אדם (which appears quite commonly in the book, often just referring to individuals rather than humanity) has only just been used in the previous verse, where there was certainly no reference to creation, and that the links between עשה and creation in Ecclesiastes are tenuous at best: see the note 'he has made everything' at 3.11. In the same note, I also considered the comparable construction of עשה in את הכל עשה יפה בעתו, and we saw then that it typically refers not to 'making something as something' but to 'making something become something'. Pinker, 'Qohelet's Views on Women', 185, sees a reference to something else in Genesis—the appointment of Adam to rule over the animals and his wife— and vocalizes ישר as a yiqtol form from the verb שרר, so that God made man to rule. It is highly unlikely, however, that עשה could have been constructed with a yiqtol to give such a sense. Pinker then takes המה to refer to women, who elude this male rule, but while it is not grammatically impossible that the pronoun might refer to women, given the late Hebrew usage in particular, it is hard to believe that an author would have relied on a masculine pronoun to represent the feminine if his point was specifically to distinguish between men and women.

It is not impossible that Qohelet is talking in this verse about God having made a humanity that was in possession of some particular quality at the point of their creation (so, e.g., Schoors, 'Theodicy', 379), but if we jump to that interpretation, it is not because the text forces us to do so. So let us pretend, for a moment and for the sake of argument, that there is no book of Genesis. In that case, the most straightforward way to understand האדם would be with reference to the preceding אדם (the article functioning anaphorically): Qohelet would then be saying something about each of the people he met. I prefer that reading because it offers a clear reason for the use of a singular form, but if

all this, *that*') and, if we accept his reading of 8.11 and 8.12, to the relationship between the initial אשר in each of those verses and the זה of 8.10 ('this, too, is הבל, *that*...[and] *that*...). Schoors, *The Preacher* I, 138, claims similarly 'the אשר-clause explicates the pronoun זה' here and in 9.1. This implies, however, that זה is itself governed by מצאתי in 7.29, and the construction there would have to be the much more complicated 'See this (that) I have found, *that*', with אשר standing outside an asyndetic relative clause, in apposition to the pronoun qualified by that clause, but acting simultaneously as a complement to the verb that constitutes that clause and so stands within it. This could not be excluded as an analysis of the text, were there any other compelling reason to find a relative clause in it, but I doubt that it is a natural reading, and S is the only ancient version to take it that way.

we take it alternatively to be 'the human' in general, that makes little difference to the sense: in either case the statement is, essentially, that 'God makes (or made) each person ישר', in much the same way that he makes everything fine in its time, or makes bad days to match good ones (7.14)—the similarities between these statements suggest that Qohelet is talking in all of them about a repeated divine action rather than a single event (unless bad days have been warehoused somewhere since the creation), and using 'making' in a sense broader than 'creating' or 'manufacturing' (which is wholly in line with, e.g., the use of the verb at the end of 3.14).

What it is that he has 'made' them is less clear. The word ישר has a basic implication of 'straightness' or 'evenness'. This use is most apparent when the term is applied to roads, but it can have other applications (e.g. Ezek 1.7, 23), and Job 33.27 associates sinning with 'twisting what was straight'. It is not clear that straightness in the sense of linearity is always the uppermost connotation, however, even in the case of roads, and Jer 31.9, for example, associates a road being ישר with people not stumbling on it, while in Ezra 8.21 the requirement seems to be for a safe road, free of bandits. The metaphor in Prov 14.12; 16.25, moreover, seems to be talking about a road that people consider 'safe' or perhaps 'right' (when it is not), and that latter idea may be what underpins the use at 2 Kgs 10.3, where Jehu invites the rulers of Samaria to see which of the sons of Ahab is הטוב וחישר and set him on the throne to lead them against him—the expression there means, perhaps, something like 'the best and most able/suitable', and at least seems to have little to do with physical or ethical 'straightness'. In the great majority of its occurrences, however, and almost always when it is applied to people, ישר means 'morally upright' or something similar, so it is interesting to note, therefore, that although G εὐθῆ, 'straight', and Hie, V *rectum* both retain the double sense of 'straight' and 'virtuous', σ' opts instead here for ἁπλοῦν, 'simple', 'uncomplicated', or 'without guile', which has probably been extrapolated directly from 'straight, even'.[11]

---

[11] This reading, from ms 252, is included in Field's *Auctarium*, but appears to have been overlooked by Schoeps, who, in 'Symmachusstudien III', 50, describes σ' as missing here, and argues from the *rectum* of V (and Jerome's use of σ') that Symmachus must have used a term denoting physical uprightness. His concern is to show that the curious reading of σ' at Gen 1.27, which has God create Adam 'in a different image, upright (ὄρθιον)' must have been derived from an interpretation of our verse in that way, reflected also in the Midrash Rabbah on 7.29. Responding, Salvesen, *Symmachus in Genesis*, 6-7, does not correct the oversight, but notes that ὄρθιος has exclusively a physical sense, that the Midrash appears to understand ישר in a moral sense (it is, at least, not explicitly a physical one), and that *rectum*, which can have both senses, probably just translates the Hebrew, with no need to postulate mediation by σ'. Whether or not Symmachus was influenced by ideas about Adam's posture in Genesis—and Salvesen notes the appearance of such ideas in a range of early Christian and Jewish literature—he does not

The only other use of ישר in the book is in 12.10, although it is pointed there as a noun rather than an adjective. Naturally, that verse presents difficulties of its own, which we shall consider later, but it certainly uses ישר to qualify the verb כתוב, and hence the character of Qohelet's composition. Although we cannot wholly exclude the possibility that he is being said to write 'uprightly', it is not clear what it would mean to talk in that way about the act of composition, rather than about the author or content. The previous verse, 12.9, moreover, has used תקן of Qohelet's activities, and that verb seems to mean 'straighten' in 1.15 and 7.13, so would correspond well with an idea that 'straightness' is something that the epilogue associates with Qohelet's writing. We have reason to suppose, therefore, that Qohelet himself might here be using a sense of ישר that is related to straightness, but that does not have a specific ethical nuance. If our construal of עשה is accurate, furthermore, it would be curious if he did mean 'upright': Qohelet very clearly does not believe that all people are virtuous, let alone that God makes each of them so.

If we draw Genesis back into our reckoning at this point, we find that it is no more illuminating on this question. T does suggest that the text is talking about the creation of Adam as virtuous, and it is not impossible that such an idea might have been held much earlier, but the biblical accounts of creation make no such suggestion. If that is what Qohelet is suggesting, then it is a fresh theological claim that can hardly be considered an obvious allusion to Genesis; if we insist that he is referring to Genesis, on the other hand, then he is unlikely to be using ישר with the sense 'upright'. Whether there is an allusion here or not, I think it is likely that σ' is on the right track, and that Qohelet is trying to say not that God makes humans upstanding, but that he makes them ישר in the way that a road might be—even, untwisting, and safe to pass along. There is no English word that captures that precisely, but the essential point is that God makes humans free of obstacles and complications. This is probably the implication of ישר in 12.10 as well: Qohelet writes truths without complications.

7.29 and it is they themselves that have sought a lot of plans] Lit. 'and/ but they, they have sought'. Note the similar use of המה in contrasts at 3.18 and 4.2: it clarifies and emphasizes the points of contrast, indicating here, I think, that Qohelet is interested less in the difference between 'making ישר' and

appear to have derived that understanding from this verse, or even specifically to have connected the two verses. It is possible, of course, that Symmachus is responding here to some other idea or ideas, such as the speculations reported in the Midrash Rabbah to Gen 8.1, that Adam was created 'androgynous' (the Greek word is used), with two conjoined bodies representing both male and female (an extrapolation from Gen 5.2). In that case, ἁπλοῦν might counter the idea that he was διπλόος, but there is a danger of reading too much into a term that very comfortably suits a notion of humans developing their own complications only after they have first been created.

'seeking חשבנות' than in the fact that it is God who does one and humans the other. Although, in pursuit of such a sense, several patristic citations of G (and the Armenian version, see Gentry) turn πολλούς, 'many', into πονηρούς, 'evil' (cf. λογισμοὺς πονηρούς at Ezek 38.10; 1 Macc 11.8), there is nothing to suggest that seeking a חשבון is something that Qohelet regards as inherently bad or wicked—he has been doing it himself, after all—and the related מחשבות in Gen 6.5, sometimes mentioned in connection with this verse, are only evil there because they are specified as such: God himself has מחשבות (e.g. Mic 4.12). If the preceding ישר actually meant 'upright' or 'virtuous', then it might indeed be the case that the context implied a similar specification in this verse, but even then it would be an implication, not a specific nuance of חשבנות.

The renderings of V and σ' are each interesting. In Hie *et ipsi quaesierunt cogitationes multas*, 'and they themselves seek many plans/thoughts',[12] Jerome essentially followed G, which is in turn close to M. The majority reading of V *et ipse se infinitis miscuerit quaestionibus*, 'and he tangled himself up in an infinite number of investigations', is more interpretative, and understands the point to be not that humans are acting sinfully, but that they are creating difficulties for themselves. The fragment of σ' that is preserved suggests something similar, and may have influenced V: περιειργάσαντο πολυπραγμοσύνην means something like 'they took pains about curiosity', or less positively, 'they meddled with meddling'. Indeed, a variant *et ipsi...miscuerint*, with the plural like Hie and σ', is found in Theodulphian manuscripts of V, and surely has some claim to be more original than the unexpected reading with a singular subject.

All the versions translate in terms of 'many' חשבנות, which is the natural sense of רבים (assuming that חשבנות is masculine, despite its -ות ending), but Fox, following Ginsberg, suggests that we should take רבים instead to mean 'great', and translates 'great solutions', claiming that 'It is not so much the quantity of the sought-for answers that exasperates Qohelet as their qualitative "greatness"'. It is doubtful, however, that רב can connote 'qualitative' as opposed to 'quantitative' greatness, or that biblical Hebrew had any idiom comparable to a 'big idea' or a 'grand solution' in English: it means that there were numerous חשבנות, not that they were ambitious. The text does not specify, however, whether each person sought many חשבנות, or each sought one חשבון, with the 'many' representing their collective efforts. That might have been implicit in the sense of חשבון intended by the author, and, if so, the fact that Qohelet sought only a single חשבון might make us lean towards a collective effort. It is perhaps more likely, though, that the text was ambiguous from the outset, and that the author was not concerned to be specific. In either case, we

---

[12] When the passage is cited in *Aduersus Jouinianum* 1, 29, with *cogitationes malas*, 'bad' instead of 'many' thoughts (PL 23, 262), this is probably a simple error in the transmission of the text, coinciding with the Greek patristic citations, rather than a further interpretative development.

should avoid following V too closely in its image of each person tangled up in countless questions.

8.1 Who is like the wise man?] Lit. 'Who (is) as the wise man?'. There are some significant problems in the text here. M has מי כהחכם, 'who is as the wise man', which involves an exceptional, unsyncopated writing of the article as -ה after -כ.[13] Most manuscripts of G, on the other hand, have τίς οἶδεν σοφούς, 'who knows wise men?' (which a few manuscripts have converted to 'who knows wisdom?'). Each of those readings is represented, at least partly, in manuscripts of the S tradition, by ܡܢܘ ܐܝܟ ܚܟܝܡܐ *mnw ᵓyk ḥkym*ᵓ, 'who is like the wise man?', and ܡܢ ܝܕܥ ܠܚܟܝܡܐ *mn ydᶜ lḥkym*ᵓ, 'who knows the wise man?'.

It seems clear that the reading in G is the result of an early, inner-Greek corruption. The reading of α' is attested as τίς ὧδε σοφός, 'who (is) thus a wise man?', and this was probably the original reading of G (so, e.g., McNeile, 164; Goldman; Gentry): its οἶδεν has arisen from assimilation of ὧδε to the following verb, after which σοφός has been corrected to σοφούς in order to make it the object (since τίς is clearly the subject). In that case, the G translator and Aquila seem to have read מי כה חכם, interpreting כה not as -כ with a subsequent article, but as כה, 'so, thus'. This is presumably also how σ' τίς οὕτως σοφός reads the text (which may have influenced V *quis talis ut sapiens*, 'who is of such a type as the wise man?', if that is not just a development of Hie). Goldman's claim that S and Hie support M's construal needs some qualification: S, as we have seen, presents a mixed picture, while Hie *quis ut sapiens*, 'who as a wise man?', may be drawn from the fuller *quis ita ut sapiens*, which is offered as a translation in the text of his commentary and more closely resembles G* (Jerome himself differentiates his reading from that of G as he knew it, *quis nouit sapientes*, 'who knows wise men', but he does not state his source, and may be drawing on α', σ', or perhaps even La, rather than the Hebrew).

In any case, it seems clear that there were two different construals of the sequence כהחכם in the Hebrew text tradition, as כ-ה-חכם with an article and as כה חכם with an adverb. If we look at the first of Qohelet's questions in isolation, then considerations of sense favour the former: כה is not a general word meaning 'so' in biblical usage (as a lot of modern translators and commentators seem to assume; cf. *NEB* 'who is wise enough', i.e. 'so wise as to...'), but means 'thus', 'like this', 'as follows' (and sometimes 'here').

---

[13] The non-syncopation of the article has been linked with Phoenician usage by Dahood, 'Canaanite-Phoenician', 45-46, and it is often observed that many of the other examples are to be found in the biblical books usually regarded as late. Syncopated and non-syncopated forms of כהיום are used to differentiate meaning (cf. GKC §35 n; J-M §35 e), but it is not generally easy to see any particular rhyme or reason to other cases.

It is adverbial, in other words, and would seem to have no proper place in a non-verbal sentence. Aquila and the translator of G probably felt able to render using τίς ὧδε because the classical usage of ὧδε was very like that of כה in Hebrew, although it had subsequently developed the broader senses of 'here, hither', and, much more generally, 'so, in this way' (like οὕτως): see MM for examples. However, despite the attempts of, e.g., Fox, Seow, to understand כה in the same terms (and the apparent willingness of Symmachus to do so), there is no evidence elsewhere for a parallel development of that general sense in Hebrew. Goldman, having followed M in *BHQ*, has since also thrown in his lot with the Greek reading ('Le Texte massorétique', 85-89), but does not acknowledge the issue. More conscious of the problem, perhaps, Ehrlich wants to read 'who *here* is the wise man' (a translation adopted also by Lohfink in Lohfink, 'War Kohelet ein Frauenfeind', 260 n. 10—although not in his commentary—and by Ginsberg, *Studies*, 35); this takes כה in its occasional locative sense, but Ehrlich has accordingly to posit an imaginary context of confrontation. Breaking with both versions of the text, *BHS* makes the suggestion that G might reflect an original מי מוֹכיַח כהחכם, 'who reproves like the wise man?', which appears to come from Galling 1940. This, however, is wholly speculative, and there are no grounds for any other emendation, unless we perhaps tried to read ככה on the basis of Jerome's *ita ut*, which would not get us much further. All this seemingly pushes us toward the כ-ה-חכם of M, for want of any other option that demonstrably makes sense (and not really because it is the more difficult, as Lavoie, 'Qui est comme le sage?', 91, suggests).

Matters become more complicated when we cease to consider the first question in isolation, and try to read it alongside the second. For reasons outlined below, it is very unlikely that this second question can be understood as an affirmation that nobody other than the wise man is able to interpret something, and it far more probably asserts that nobody can interpret anything. It is a recognition of this that drives Fox and others to follow G here, giving a sense like Fox's 'Who is so wise, and who knows the meaning of anything?', which coordinates the questions, but which, as we have seen, seems unlikely to be a plausible rendering of מי כה חכם. The only way realistically to retain that reading, I think, would be to vocalize חכם as a verb, 'who is wise in that way?', which would run against the understandings of the versions, and raise its own question—'what way?'. Equally, though, it is hard to accept the meaning 'who is like the wise man?', commonly attributed to the M reading, whereby Qohelet is taken to be asking whether anybody else has the qualities manifested by the wise man (cf. Gen 41.38, 'can we find a man like this [כזה]?'). This cannot easily be related to the second question.

There is another option, however. Eaton suggests that כ- 'sometimes speaks of exact likeness to an ideal, and the M reading could be translated "Who is really wise ...?"'. More specifically, Schoors calls this a reading in terms of the *kaph ueritatis*, a term and concept deprecated in GKC §118 x, but used freely by J-M §133 g. Schoors does not offer a reason for his own translation, 'Who is like the truly wise man', but is either, perhaps, following the same line, or else drawing in the sense of 'special wisdom' from his reading of the preceding verses. If the former, then I suspect he is reading too much into the construction. What is usually cited as the key example of a *kaph ueritatis*, כאיש אמת in Neh 7.2, is probably to be read as suggesting not that Hanani was faithful in an exceptional way, but that he came closer than most to the model or ideal of a faithful man. This is in line with broader uses of the preposition to connote resemblance or approximation to something (for the latter, note especially the uses in Exod 11.4; Ruth 1.4; 2.17). If we were to apply the same sort of understanding to our text here, then Qohelet would not be asking 'who is exceptionally wise?', but 'who is close to being "the wise man"?', and the need for the preposition is explained by the distinction between that and 'who is the wise man?'. An English equivalent to the construction might be 'who seems like a wise man?'. Because the question might also imply 'who is (as good) as the wise man?', however, I think it is very possible that the text was intended to be ambiguous. Indeed, were it not for the particular resonances of מי יודע in the second question, the whole verse could be read as a paeon to the wise man, and it has often been taken that way.

Whether we adopt this approach or not, accepting the reading of M also means accepting the determination of החכם (and it is worth noting that M has no article in Neh 7.2). '*The* wise man' is a formulation typical of the book. Syncopation elsewhere with prepositions means that it is not always possible to say for sure whether an article was originally intended, but Qohelet also prefers '*the* fool', so we can say with some certainty that the singular substantive is determined in 2.14, 16 (twice); 6.8; and 8.17, and the plural in 9.1; M also points with an article in 7.19 and 9.11. In the probable exception at 9.15, the reference is to a particular individual, and something similar is likely to be true in the difficult 7.7. At 7.4, 5 and 8.5, the non-determination has probably been influenced by the use of the specific expression 'heart of a wise man/wise men'. In other words, when Qohelet wants to talk about a typical or model wise man, he generally calls him '*the* wise man', which is rather unusual and distinctive. Proverbs, in contrast, clearly prefers '*a* wise man' (and in the three cases where חכם is in fact determined, at 11.29; 16.21; 24.23, the article is indicated only by the pointing); elsewhere, the use of החכם is adjectival in Jer 9.11, and all other uses with an article are references to specific wise men and women in the plural (such as the wise men of Egypt in Exod 7.11). Most of the time, this habit makes no difference, but I think the usage is important here: Qohelet is not suggesting that nobody is wise, but he questions whether anybody actually embodies this ideal, model 'wise man'. It is interesting to wonder whether the non-syncopation of the article in the textual tradition reflects an awareness of the need to preserve the distinction.

8.1 And does anyone know how to interpret something that is said?] Lit. 'And who knows an interpretation of a word?'. The expression 'who knows' was discussed in the notes to 2.19, and we have encountered it since at 3.21 and 6.12. It is not confined to Ecclesiastes, though, and in all other occurrences it expresses doubt that anyone knows. It seems likely to have that sense here as well, therefore, and that seems compatible, on the face of it, with a common understanding that Qohelet is affirming the uniqueness of the wise man: nobody else can interpret what they can interpret. The problem with that understanding lies in its implication of 'nobody *else*': this is not what the expression means elsewhere, it is not a normal connotation of מי, and it could only possibly be justified by a strong steer from the context. As noted above, there is some small scope for ambiguity here, if one reads an implied 'who else' in the first question, and then carries that over. It is more natural, however, and more in line with other usage, to suppose that Qohelet is affirming 'nobody knows', including the wise man.

The word פשר is found frequently in the Aramaic of Daniel in connection with the interpretation of dreams (e.g. 2.5-9, 24-26; cf. פתר in Gen 40-41), but in the Qumran scrolls it is a term associated especially with the interpretation of, and commentary on, texts. In the biblical commentaries found there, indeed, פשר הדבר is a very common expression meaning something like 'the interpreted reference of the expression is to (על or ל-)' (see, e.g., 1QpHab x, 9; xii, 2, 12; 4QpIsa^b [4Q162] ii, 1; 4Qpap pIsa^c [4Q163] ii, 4), or 'the interpretation of the expression is that (אשר)' (e.g. 4QpIsa^b [4Q162] i, 2). In the light of such usage, it is hardly surprising that G makes clear its understanding that דבר means 'word' or 'speech' by using ῥήματος: it uses ῥῆμα otherwise only at 1.1 and 8.5. All the other ancient versions share this understanding, and although דבר could in principle mean 'thing', G's interpretation accords with the usage in the book more generally. The Qumran evidence effectively excludes Graetz's suggestion that the term here means 'compromise'—a sense associated with later uses of the hiph'il of פשר to denote the cooling of hot water—although that understanding is also adopted in *b. Berakhot* 10a and *b. Sotah* 13b, so has a certain antiquity.

G λύσιν, 'solution', also reflects, however, the same lack of grammatical determination found in M, and Qohelet is apparently not talking about '*the* (proper) interpretation' of anything, or, indeed, about any specific דבר. Without wishing to read too much into it, this does make it unlikely that Qohelet can mean, as Gordis puts it, 'the true, underlying meaning', which is a sense implicit in such renderings as RSV 'the interpretation of a thing', or Gordis' own, more ambitious 'the meaning of events'. As Pinker, 'Aspects of Demeanour', 402, observes, this also tells against the idea that 8.1a is talking about interpreting 8.1b—a possibility which Crenshaw, among others, considers. Hertzberg refers to the discussion in GKC §125 c of 'indeterminateness for the sake of amplification', which arguably presents no more than a list of cases in which exegetes have felt that there should be an article where there is none, and which certainly offers little justification for his understanding of דבר to refer to the following sentence: 'Who can understand a saying such as this...'. Fox (cf. Fox and Porten, 'Unsought Discoveries', 32-33) goes rather in the opposite direction, using the lack of determination to justify a sense 'something' or 'anything', and paraphrasing 'No one is so wise as to understand the meaning of anything'. That depends in part, of course, on construing the earlier part of the verse according to a reading that has been rejected here, and also on a very general understanding of פשר, but in addition it pushes an absence of grammatical determination into becoming a positive assertion of indeterminacy, and I doubt that the context demands that sense. What Qohelet is saying seems to be closer, in fact, to 'Who can offer/is aware of an explanation of something that has been said?'

Jones, 'Qohelet's Courtly Wisdom', 213-15, and Lavoie, 'Qui est comme le sage?', 107-9, both emphasize the divinatory connotations of פשר in Daniel and at Qumran, where it commonly 'denotes unraveling the mystery of a prophetic oracle' (Jones, 214). It is indeed likely that we should take account of this in our understanding of just what Qohelet means here: the 'interpretation' or 'explanation' to which he refers is not merely a clarification or explication, but more properly an exposition of hidden truths, represented symbolically in dreams or texts. I am not wholly persuaded that the term necessarily carries so much technical baggage that we must see a reference here specifically to some form of mantic wisdom, so that Qohelet is praising the ability of the wise to interpret oracles or suchlike in particular—although that is not impossible, and is perhaps a further implication of G's ῥήματος. I suspect that he is, however, using a term that deliberately conveys a nuance of academic, scholarly activity, which at once affirms the cleverness of the wise and constrains the application of their wisdom. The Hebrew does not even necessarily imply the ability to produce one's own interpretations, merely the knowledge of how something has been interpreted.

Ibn Ezra offers an interesting reading, which places יודע more precisely in parallel with כהחכם by assuming elision of a second -כ, so that the sense is then, 'and who (is like the one who) knows...?' Such an elision would be extremely harsh, however, and if we wanted to find such equivalence, it would be easier to follow Kamenetzky, who conjectures (239) that the כה should simply be deleted as a corrupt duplicate of the following הכ.

Noting other places where it has sometimes been suggested that a verb should be read instead of the noun דבר, Pinker, 'Aspects of Demeanour', 415, claims that 'it is impossible to exclude' reading a piʻel infinitive here (which is true enough), and then that, if we do so (for some unstated reason), an adjective would fit better than the noun פשר (which is questionable). He proposes, therefore, that we should emend the word to שפר and take שפר דבר to mean 'speak nicely'. Pinker does not note that שפר is indeed used of 'pleasing speech' in Numbers Rabbah, at least according to Jastrow, *Dictionary*, but nor does he acknowledge that it appears only once in biblical Hebrew, at Gen 49.21, where the sense is obscure (and it is probably not an adjective). The reasons proposed for the emendation are not compelling, and the emendation itself may not offer the sense he wants.

8.1 A person's wisdom will light up their face] The literal meaning of the Hebrew is not in doubt, but the implication is less clear. In a number of passages, most famously Num 6.25, God is asked to make his face 'shine upon' people (or in Dan 9.17 his sanctuary), using the same verb as here, and in Ps 80.4 (ET 80.3) simply to 'make his face shine'. The context of such uses suggests that the expression means 'show favour to' or 'be gracious towards'. Gordis extrapolates from them a sense here of '*appearing* gracious...whatever may be one's real feelings', and Pinker, 'Aspects of Demeanour', 416, speaks of the 'pleasant demeanour' that can convince a judge or jury, while others have seen a claim that wisdom makes people genuinely benevolent. The expression in this sense, however, seems only to be applied to God, and whatever we read into its use historically, it is a form of solar imagery that could probably not have been used of people in general (see, e.g., Smith, *Early History*, 153).[14] A similar expression that *is* applied to humans uses the 'lightening' or 'brightening' of the eyes to describe animation, either in the sense of being alive (cf. Prov 29.13) or as the result of respite (Ezra 9.8) and sustenance—physical (1 Sam 14.27) or spiritual (Ps 19.9 ET 19.8). In Ps 13.4 (ET 13.3), moreover, it is opposed to being asleep in death, and probably has some nuance of wakefulness or alertness as well. Of course, the 'sparkling' of eyes might be an idea distinct in itself, but something comparable seems to be in mind in Sir 13.25-26, where the state of a person's heart is linked to the state of their face, and לב טוב פנים אורים, 'a good heart (gives) a lit-up face'—in contrast, pain is linked with מחשבת עמל, perhaps 'laborious thinking'. In the Midrash Rabbah, 8.1 is associated with an idea that Adam was created with a beauty that is described in terms of light and luminescence (Aaron, 'Shedding Light', doubts that he was actually supposed to have had a body that emitted light). It is unlikely that Qohelet is evoking any such tradition, and although it is not impossible that some implication of beauty is involved in the Ben Sira text, other interpretations in the Midrash seem to envisage 'lighting' of the face as something that might express embarrassment, intoxication, or excitement.

---

[14] It is not surprising that such imagery is associated in Babylonian literature with the sun god Šamaš, and the other associations of that deity with divination provide a slender basis for the attempt of Jones, 'Qohelet's Courtly Wisdom', 215-17, to find here a continuing reference to divination—as does his observation that Daniel is said to have light in him (not in his face; Dan 5.11,14) in connection with his ability to interpret dreams.

318   ECCLESIASTES

The most intriguing usage, though, is at Qumran, where we find references to another idiom—making knowledge 'shine' in human hearts (4QShir^b 18 II, 8; 1QS IV, 2)—but also places where God or his agents are said to 'light up the faces' of humans. In 1QH^a XI (Sukenik III), 3 and XII (Sukenik IV), 5, it is difficult to discern what this might mean, but in XII (Sukenik IV), 27 the speaker declares ובי האירותה פני רבים ותגבר עד לאין מספר, 'and by me you have lit up the faces of many and strengthened countless times', while 1QSb (1Q28b) IV, 27, using the same verb, speaks of serving as a light for the world 'with knowledge' and 'illuminating the face of many' (להבל בדעת ולהאיר פני רבים): *DCH* associates these references with enlightenment and teaching, although we should note the link with 'strengthening' as well. In short, although we do not know for certain what this idiom means, it probably evokes ideas of animation and/or intellectual enlightenment.

8.1 but the strength of their face will be dimmed] M ישנא is usually considered to be a form from the verb שנא/שנה which has meanings related to the concept of 'change'—it is the verb used in Sir 13.25, which we looked at in the last note, for the heart 'changing' the face. Sir 12.8 talks of somebody 'changing their face' apparently with the connotation of (falsely) putting on a sad or gloomy expression or turning pale (cf. the uses in Aramaic at Dan 5.6, 9, 10 etc., and in 1QapGen II, 12—although I am not sure why Goldman considers this, or the general sense 'alter', a specifically Aramaic nuance). M vocalizes as a pu'al, but it is sometimes suggested that it should be read as a pi'el instead (so, e.g., Ginsberg, *Studies*, 35, 'fierceness darkens his face'). This seems to be how Jerome parsed it in both Hie and V, which have the strong man changing his face, while the pi'el is presumed by those who would emend to ישנאו (see below), who variously believe that the strength of face changes that face or the man himself.

Whatever the vocalization, this is almost undoubtedly the intended verb,[15] and it is the one that has been read by Hie, V, T. However, G μισηθήσεται shows that the translator has read יִשָּׂנֵא, a niph'al from שׂנא, 'hate' (the G variant found in one manuscript, τιμωρηθήσεται, 'will be punished', is unlikely to reflect the M reading, as Gentry suggests), and this is the reading followed by

---

[15] The suggestion in Müller, 'Das eblaitische Verbalsystem', 217, that the verb here should be linked with *HALOT*'s III שנה, is picked up by Schwienhorst-Schönberger, who offers it as the basis for an alternative translation, 'und die Härte seines Antlitzes hellt sich auf', 'and the hardness of his face brightens'. This suggestion was first made long ago, in fact, in Eitan, *Contribution*, 10 n. 10, and is considered but rejected as unlikely in Emerton's review of possible instances of the root in Hebrew, 'The Meaning of *šēnā* in Psalm CXXVII', 25-31. Although there is plausible evidence for the root with the sense 'exalt', it is very uncertain that it was ever used in Hebrew with the meaning 'be bright' that is attested in Arabic, and the apparent use of I שנה to denote the lessening or dulling of brightness (see below) would sit uncomfortably with such usage.

S ܢܣܛܢ‎ *nstnʾ* as well. This enables an understanding 'someone shameless/ audacious in their face will be hated', which apparently also vocalizes עז as an adjective, rather than as the noun of M. That is not obviously appropriate to the context, but is, nevertheless, an understanding specifically commended in a discussion of this text in *b. Taʿanit* 7b, which links it to Prov 21.29, and 'hating' underpins one of the interpretations offered in the Midrash Rabba (see Ginzberg, 'Die Haggada', 37-38), so G and S probably reflect a more widely known interpretation. As de Rossi notes, some fifteen of Kennicott's manuscripts have ישונה or ישנה, which favour 'change', and I am aware of no manuscripts that point the word as 'hated', but this is the understanding of the Codex Graecus Venetus, which has either found that reading or overruled its source.

The passage in Proverbs 21 is one of several which speak of 'the strong of face', or, using the cognate verb, of 'strengthening one's face'.[16] In Deut 28.50 and Dan 8.23 the context suggests that the expression is referring to ruthlessness (although Dan 8 juxtaposes it most immediately with an ability to solve riddles: the ruthlessness is picked up in 8.24, the cunning in 8.25). In Prov 7.13, the context is very different, but the implication similar: the woman seizes the youth, kisses him, and then speaks to him with boldness, confidence or perhaps without hesitation (RSV 'with impudent face'). Proverbs 21.29 is difficult, but probably contrasts the willingness of the wicked to rush forward with the greater consideration that the upright give to where they are going. Generally, then, 'strength of face' seems to be associated with a willingness or inclination to act without pause for thought or mercy, which can be a good or bad thing from the point of view of those who possess it—strength of purpose, perhaps, but also rashness. The point here is apparently, therefore, that wisdom somehow 'changes' a person's boldness or self-confidence. The uses of the verb with 'face' in Sir 12.8 and 13.25 suggest a certain neutrality—it may mean just 'alter one's expression or demeanour'—but the Aramaic uses in Dan 5 refer to a change in the colour or splendour of the face (probably 'paling'), and in Lam 4.1 the qal has a specific reference to the 'dulling'

---

[16] Prov 21.29 in fact uses the hiphʿil of the verb with בפניו, so the wicked man does something 'with' his face, and in Prov 7.13 the woman העזה פניה, with the face either as the object of the verb or, in effect, an accusative of respect. Deut 28.50 has גוי עז פנים and Dan 8.23 a מלך עז פנים, so both are using the adjective. Lavoie, 'Qui est comme le sage?', 114-15, apparently regards use of the verb rather than the noun, and of a preposition in Prov 21.29, as sufficient grounds to reject a connection, but what the various passages demonstrate is that we are dealing not with a fixed cliché, but with an idea that can be expressed in similar but slightly different ways. Having rejected the relevance of Lam 4.1 for understanding the verb, on the grounds that it is not used in connection with a face there, Lavoie goes on to argue for a sense 'force' for עז without examining any of the places where it is used directly of faces.

of gold (// יועם). The evidence is rather slight, to be sure, because the verb is rather rare, but after a reference to 'lighting up', I think it is likely that a contrast is intended. There is certainly little or no evidence to suggest that the Hebrew might refer to 'increasing' the strength of the face, and to 'change' someone's ruthlessness or rashness might most naturally be understood as diminishing it, whether or not that nuance was explicit in the verb.

The construal of the sentence by M is not syntactically problematic: the construct nominal expression עז פניו is simply the subject of the passive (puʻal) verb. Goldman would prefer, however, (like G) to read the adjective עַז rather than M's noun עֹז, so that the subject would be 'one who is strong of face': he offers the translation 'but the arrogant will give himself away'. The understanding of the verb in that translation is based on Sir 13.25, where he thinks the changing of the face 'is to be understood as a revelation of internal feelings', but this reads the whole sense of that verse into the verb alone.[17] As for the vocalization of עז, it may be true that the versions read an adjective, but it is also largely irrelevant: they are vocalizing the same consonantal text on the basis of their own interpretations of the sentence as a whole. In the cases of G and S, this has been shaped by their understanding of the verb's meaning. In the case of Hie *fortis*, 'the strong man', and V *potentissimus*, 'the most powerful man', on the other hand, Jerome's construal of the sentence has arisen from his parsing of the verb as active, not passive, and his consequent understanding that עז must be the subject and פניו the object, hence Hie *fortis faciem suam commutabit*, '(even) the strong man will change his face' (which becomes past tense in most manuscripts of V). That is actually a perfectly legitimate reading, with only the existence of the established idiom עז פניו telling against it and in favour of M. It is true, as McNeile, 76, points out, that we never find this idiom elsewhere with the noun (a fact that may also have weighed with the versions), but if it can be used with both the adjective and the verb, it is hard to see that the use with a noun could be considered in any way problematic (cf. Schoors, who nevertheless adopts Goldman's understanding). In this case, it seems to me that the vocalization in M offers the best construal, and there are no good reasons to read it in any other way.

---

[17] Schoors adduces Sir 12.18 as evidence for this sense, noting the NRSV translation 'Then he will shake his head, and clap his hands, and whisper much, and show his true face (ישנא פנים)'. I doubt that such an understanding is correct, however. The description of the sinner in Sir 12 consistently involves a contrast between what he shows on the outside and feels on the inside, and 'changing the face' in 12.8 is part of his tut-tutting over an accident he has caused himself, which actually involves the concealment of his real feelings. If NRSV sees a sudden revelation of his real identity, it is perhaps because his clapping of hands has been interpreted as celebration—but it is hard to see that sense in the shaking of his head or his whispering.

If there is a difficulty, indeed, it lies in the very fact that there is so much ambiguity in this sentence, and scope for so many readings: it is rare for the versions to be so at odds with each other when they all apparently share the same text.[18] I think there is a good chance, therefore, that the verb was originally written with ה, which would significantly have limited the options, and that the writing with א is an early but secondary change in the orthography, which introduced some of the ambiguity.[19] It is possible, furthermore, that the text has changed in more serious ways. Goldman also discusses the intriguing emendation suggested by Allgeier, 5-6, and picked up by Galling 1940 and *BHS*, which deals with the peculiar אני at the start of v. 2 by taking it to be the remnants of a suffix that became detached from an original ישנאנו (יְשַׁנֶּאנּוּ), will change him/it'. Goldman's principal objection to this, that there is no sign in G either of the אני or of any suffix, has weight, but is not definitive: the detached pronoun is awkward enough to have dropped out (and is, curiously, attested in one Greek manuscript—see below), while graphic confusions between י and ו are common. My own objection is simply that there is a better explanation for the אני, which facilitates the reading of 8.2 (see the note there).

The emendation has found relatively few followers, but Fox does adopt it in his translation 'while the impudence of his face changes it', concerning which Schoors observes that, if the suffix is supposed to refer to פנים, we should expect it to be plural. Rose, *Rien de nouveau*, 243, emends, but reads a different verb, the rare (and somewhat controversial) III שנה of *HALOT*, enabling him to claim that the strength of his face 'elevates' the man, or earns him promotion. Seow also accepts the emendation, but takes the earlier אדם to be the subject and translates 'so that one changes one's impudent look'; he presumably takes the literal meaning to be 'and the strength of his face, he changes it'. Were that the intended sense, however, then the unmarked change of subject from חכמה to אדם would be extremely awkward if both statements are to be linked in such a way (we might anticipate a הוא), and it is difficult to see a satisfactory reason for the word-order. Although Rose's reading has some merits, the only natural reading with ישנאנו would be 'and the strength of his face will change him', which makes no obvious sense in the context (or at all, really). The ambiguities of the statement and the awkwardness of אני do leave open the possibility that some other word once stood after the verb,

---

[18] It is worth pointing out, however, that not all of the many proposed readings are legitimate. Longman's 'The wisdom of a person brightens his face and changes its stern expression', for instance, apparently takes the preceding חכמה to be the continuing subject, without explaining why it should take a third-person feminine verb in the first clause, as expected, but a third-person masculine one in the second.

[19] Although it rarely leads to such problems of sense, the treatment of *lamed-he* verbs as though they were *lamed-aleph*, often just with respect to particular forms, is not itself uncommon; see GKC §75 rr; J-M §79 l.

preserved only in a corrupt form as that pronoun, but it is hard to read a suffix on ישנא, and the difficulties are not so great that we need to seek some other emendation.

That has not discouraged Pinker from once again pursuing a very different reading. In 'Aspects of Demeanour', 416-17, he suggests that פניו is an error for פימו or פיו, so that what will change is 'the forcefulness of his mouth'. Such an error is quite possible, but this would carry more conviction were 'strength of face' not an established idiom.

Introduction to 8.2-9

Power and Powerlessness

(8.2) Watch out for the anger of a king, and concerning an oath by God, (8.3) do not be hasty. Leave him, do not hang on at a dangerous word, for he may do anything he wants. (8.4) Because a king's word is power, then who will say to him, 'What are you doing?' (8.5) One who obeys a command will experience no dangerous word or time of judgment.

The heart of a wise man knows:

(8.6)   that for every matter there is a time and judgment,

   that the human's harm weighs heavily upon him,

(8.7)   that he does not know what is going to happen,

   that when it happens—who is going to explain to him?

(8.8)   There is no human who governs the wind, so as to restrain the wind.

And there is no governing death's day—

and there will be no mission into battle,

nor will wickedness save whoever resorts to it.

(8.9) I observed all this when I applied my mind to every activity that is done beneath the sun, at the time when human had power over human to hurt him.

Although they are not nearly so prominent as has sometimes been suggested, sayings about kings, and admonitions about behaviour in their presence, are a staple of ancient advice literature, and have been influential upon ideas about the nature and origin of that literature. Even where the principal audience for a text was located firmly within the scribal class of a country, however, it is unlikely that most who heard such advice would have found themselves in regular contact with a monarch, and many may never have encountered one at all. It is important to appreciate, therefore, that the theme very commonly serves as a vehicle for discussing power, the exercise of power, and relationships to power:[1] if we simply read the advice literal-mindedly as a manual for would-be courtiers, we might as well declare that, say, the advice about sowing in Eccl 11.6 is relevant only to farmers. Such a warning may be all the more necessary, indeed, in the case of Ecclesiastes. If this book really is a provincial product of the Persian or Ptolemaic periods, as seems probable, then advice about kings would have been of literal use to almost nobody who received it: kings were distant in every sense, and it is highly likely, therefore, that the author intended his audience to extrapolate something more general from the warning and associated advice that he presents in 8.2-5.

That something could lie simply in the area of human authority and governance: anybody with a boss might conceivably worry about making them angry, which seems to be the key concern of 8.2-5. Most bosses have bosses, however, and the unrestricted, unquestioned authority that is depicted in those verses really does seem likely to have been possessed only by those who genuinely were at the very top of any hierarchy, and beyond the reach of any other authority. It is interesting to observe, then, that Qohelet returns directly to the topic of authority in 8.9, and curiously but specifically stresses that his observations were made 'at the time when' humans had power over humans—as though there were any time when they did not. Between those points, the theme has been

---

[1] This often takes the form of advice about behaviour in the presence of a king, but many works show a particular interest also in the character and behaviour of kings; the Egyptian *Merikare*, for instance, can reasonably be described as a *Fürstenspiegel*, as perhaps can Prov 31.1-9. The two perspectives co-exist among the various sayings about kings in Proverbs, and are found together in, e.g., Prov 25.2-8. A Hellenistic counterpart can be found in numerous literary treatments of kingship and the ideal king, which may have influenced the later book of Wisdom (cf. Reese, *Hellenistic Influence*, 71-89).

the wise man, and 8.6-8 seems concerned not directly with power so much as with the limits of human knowledge and control. I take Qohelet here, in fact, to be using the advice about the king not just to evoke a literary convention, but to suggest that human relationships with human power are indicative of the broader human situation in the world. Beyond the god-like king, there is a king-like God, who promises a more unavoidable judgment.[2] Qohelet will not call God a tyrant, and is careful to emphasize the worldly setting, but he intends us to understand, I think, that the experience of humans living in God's world is like the experience of humans subject to the dangers and decisions of an untrammelled human king—only without the opportunities to foresee and to escape approaching trouble. This will open the way for him to talk more directly about divine judgment and punishment in 8.10-17.

At the same time, these verses present ideas about wisdom, and what it is to be wise, in the light of the account that ended ch. 7. Much here is difficult, but Qohelet sets a tone that will characterize many of his comments on the topic from this point onwards, in which wisdom is by no means condemned, but its limitations are emphasized. The conventional-sounding advice in 8.2-5 imagines a royal court in which the king's anger can at least be avoided, through observation and flight, or through obedience, and there is, perhaps, a role for wisdom in this strictly human context. The wise man knows, however, that, in God's world, judgment will always come, and that what will happen can be neither predicted nor explained, leaving humans powerless in the face of death. We have at least as much to fear in God's world as in the royal court, but wisdom brings a recognition that whatever wise behaviour might save us in the court will be of no use when we are dealing with that

---

[2] For a more direct analogy of behaviour before a king with behaviour before God, see, e.g., Sir 7.4-5. The blurring of boundaries here between royal and divine has been observed by a number of scholars, who have tended, however, to understand it in terms of royal divinity. So, for instance, Jones, 'Qohelet's Courtly Wisdom', 222, speaks of 'the king's functional divinity', and Lohfink sees a reference to Ptolemaic claims of divine kingship. Pinker, 'Qohelet 8,5-7', proposes, very differently, that these verses disguise (for fear of the secular authorities) a call to religious obedience as a call to obey the king, and this recognizes, I think, that religious and secular relationships are both in play, although it also makes too much of the idea that different audiences might read the text in completely different ways.

world. The wise man knows, in other words, that what might work in the context of human power will have no effect in the context of divine power, but can understand the character of that divine power from a knowledge of human power.

8.2-5A

(8.2) Watch out for the anger of a king, and concerning an oath by God, (8.3) do not be hasty. Leave him, do not hang on at a dangerous word, for he may do anything he wants. (8.4) Because a king's word is power, then who will say to him, 'What are you doing?'
(8.5a) One who obeys a command will experience no dangerous word or time of judgment.

Commentary

The broader function here of this advice has been discussed above, in the introduction to 8.2-9. Taken in itself, though, it is a sort of counterpart to the advice in 4.17–5.6, about behaviour with respect to God: humans should be wary of the power that a king has to harm them without facing any repercussions, and should consequently avoid both his anger and any unnecessary entanglements. When Qohelet concludes by remarking that obedience to commands, or 'a commandment', will avoid reprimand and 'a time of judgment', these are statements that can, certainly, be read solely within the context of a court setting. The religious associations of such vocabulary are strong enough, however, to evoke the broader comparison with our relationship to God, which I take to be Qohelet's real concern.

There are several difficulties in the text, most of which do not greatly affect the meaning overall, even if they have given rise to different understandings of precisely what Qohelet is advising.

8.2-3] The Hebrew text begins with the words 'I' and 'face', from which it is difficult to extract any sensible meaning. My translation is based on an emendation. This problem cannot be entirely disconnected from another, concerning the division of the text. The Masoretes end 8.2 after the reference to an oath, probably understanding 'watch out...because of an oath'. They then vocalize the first verb in 8.3 in an uncommon way to avoid producing a contradiction at the start of the verse. None of that is impossible, but the Greek translator and Symmachus divide the text after that verb instead, which offers the smoother and more natural reading on which my own translation is based. The 'oath by God'—literally 'oath of God'—is probably an oath made to the king (see the notes for examples), and Qohelet's point in 8.2 is that one should not undertake such oaths lightly. In 8.3, his advice is then to get away rather than try to stand one's ground 'at a bad word' or perhaps 'in a bad situation': the implication is that anyone in this situation should make their excuses and leave as soon as they perceive that the king has become angry with them, rather than try to tough it out.

8.5a] Qohelet suggests that obedience will allow people to avoid the sort of rebuke or condemnation from which they are supposed to flee in 8.3, and might seem to strike a slightly discordant note after what has preceded (many scholars, accordingly, have seen quotations, editorial additions or a dialogue here and in the verses that follow; there is a valuable survey and discussion in Lavoie, 'Sagesse de cour royale', 210-15). Presumably, though, Qohelet's point is to emphasize that, although the king may be dangerous and all-powerful, he is not arbitrary: one can avoid the need to flee from punishment if one simply does not incur it. The vocabulary is not specifically religious, and Irwin, 'Ecclesiastes 8:2-9', 130, observes the problems that have been caused for commentators who assume here that the reference must be to obeying God. It can have religious overtones, however: 'judgment' will certainly be a divine judgment in 11.9, and 'command' is used of God's commandments in the epilogue, at 12.13. His use of it may in itself indicate Qohelet's intention to talk about our relationship with God by talking about our relationship with secular power.

My translation again rests on a division of the text different from that of the Masoretes. They read in 8.5 two statements set in parallel, with a chiastic structure: 'someone obeying a command will not know a dangerous word, while time and judgment the heart of a wise man will know'. On the face of it, this has a certain elegance, and makes a well-balanced saying—which is probably what has led to a construal of the text in such terms. The Greek keeps its options more open, but the reading is undoubtedly earlier than the Masoretes themselves. On this usual understanding, Qohelet is adding to his statement that obedience will avoid punishment a further statement that one who is wise will be able to discern 'time and judgment'—meaning that in some way that person will be able to speak or act properly before the king.

There are, in fact, some text-critical issues around 'time and judgment', which should probably be read 'time of judgment' (see the note), but the problem with this understanding should be clear anyway: if we take the statement about the wise person strictly in parallel with the statement about the obedient one, the most natural sense is: 'the obedient will *not* know punishment, but the wise *will* know time and judgment'. To avoid the implication that the wise will be judged, we have to understand the implications of 'know' differently in each statement ('encounter' in the first, 'be informed about' in the second), and we have to make 'time and/of judgment' refer to something other than being judged, in a context where it supposedly stands in parallel with a reference to punishment. Looking further afield, moreover, we may observe that the same 'time and/of judgment' is about to come up again in 8.6, where it is set beside human harm and expressed in a way that seems consciously to allude to 3.1 and 3.17. Some commentators have put much effort into finding in that verse a reference to something other than judgment, because they appreciate that if Qohelet uses 'time and/of judgment' there to talk about judgment, then it is unlikely to have a different implication in this verse, just a few words away.

The elegant chiastic statement in M, then, conceals some significant problems, and requires us to assign new meanings to words which are used differently elsewhere in the book. I think it is significantly easier to acknowledge that the tradition behind M has got it wrong here. If we take 'time and/of judgment' instead as the second thing or things that the obedient person will not know, then this has an additional benefit: it frees 'the wise will know' to become the hook upon which the various statements in 8.6-7 will be hung, as things which the wise know. As we shall see, it is otherwise very difficult to construe those statements.

Notes

8.2 watch out for the anger] Or 'face': I take the original to have been אפי מלך where M has אני פי מלך, and אפי can have both meanings. We have already encountered the stray אני which is to be found at the beginning of this verse: see the note at 8.1. Three basic approaches have generally been taken to this: (1) it should be read as it stands, either with the following שמור to give a sense 'I watch', or as a response to the questions asked at the beginning of 8.1; (2) it is a fragment of, or an ellipsis for a statement meaning 'I say'; (3) it is an error, and should be deleted or emended.

The first of these (1) is adopted in Hie *ego os regis custodio* and V *ego os regis obseruo*, 'I watch the mouth of the king'. It also underpins the interpretation that is attributed to R. Levi in the Midrash and found in much subsequent Jewish interpretation,[1] while it has been accepted by a few modern commentators, including Hitzig and Stuart. It generally involves the assumption that שמור has arisen through a misunderstanding of a participle written שמר, but Goldman notes that it could be read without alteration as an infinitive standing in place of a finite verb, and supposes that אני has been added to the existing text enabling it to be read that way (so that the subsequent אל תבהל has to be read as part of a separate clause, and not linked problematically with God). It is certainly not impossible that the word has been added for some such reason, but if, on the other hand, אני is original, then it is very unlikely that it was meant to be construed with שמׁ(ו)ר, not least because the word-order obscures such a connection.

The other interpretation, that אני provides an answer to the questions in 8.1a, has been proposed by Beentjes, who believes that the very fact of there being two questions makes it less likely that they are rhetorical, and that Qohelet associates אני with his royal *persona*, which is appropriate to what follows ('Who is like the Wise', 305-6; see also Kamano, *Cosmology*, 181-82). If it is intended as an answer, however, then the intervention of 8.1b is awkward, to put it mildly, while the lack of any explanation or elaboration is at least surprising. Under this heading, we might also put the recent suggestion of Heim, which does not see a response to the questions, but a simpler declaration 'me': Heim believes that Qohelet has been speaking in a woman's voice since 7.27, and now marks a return to his 'normal' voice.

The second approach (2) lies behind the rendering of σ' ἐγὼ παραινῶ ῥήσεις βασιλέως φύλασσε, 'I commend words of the king; keep...',[2] and represents the most popular modern understanding of אני. This is not least, perhaps, because if the expression can be taken as an ellipsis, then there is no need to emend the text. If we are to justify reading 'I say' or 'I said' here,

---

[1] That Jewish tradition is perhaps the source of Jerome's understanding. Goldman notes a similar interpretation, attributed to R. Yossi BeR. Bun in *y. Sanhedrin* 16b (he cites it as 21b, as does Gordis). Both see a reference to the words of God at Sinai, and paraphrase אני שמור פי as אשמור...אני פי. A similar interpretation is offered by Rashi, while Rashbam generalizes the reference to mean 'I observe the commands'.

[2] The first two words are corrupt in the principal Greek sources, but can be restored from the Origenic manuscripts and a catena, which all show the influence of σ'; see Marshall, and Labate, 'Catena Hauniense', 61.

however, then it seems important to offer some analogy to such a usage, and although scholars have pointed to many examples of elision elsewhere in biblical Hebrew, the only one that comes close to what is presumed here is to be found in the rather more distant context of *b. Qiddušin* 44b, cited by Gordis. There R. Nahman bar Isaac says that he quotes R. Abin as a source without using a patronymic to distinguish between two different rabbis with that name, and begins אנא לא רבי אבין ברבי חייא ולא רבי אבין בר כהנא, lit. 'I not R. Abin by R. Hiyya or R. Abin bar Kahana...', which requires us to supply a verb. The usage appears to be unique, and the text is very possibly corrupt, but in any case, the verb to be supplied is not 'I say' or 'I declare': the context demands something more like 'I cite...as', and this is not a true parallel to what is proposed for 8.2. More generally, Qohelet simply does not speak in this way. In 7.23 he reports his own words, but elsewhere he uses אמרתי to talk about conclusions that he has reached (2.2; 6.3; 8.14; 9.16) or about conversations in, or with, his heart (1.16; 2.1, 15; 3.17, 18)—אמרתי אני is generally reserved for the latter, although it is found at 9.16. Nowhere does Qohelet preface any sort of admonition by declaring 'I say', and it is difficult to see anything about this advice in particular that might drive him to do so—let alone to use an obscure ellipsis that he has managed to avoid in all those other places.

Finally (3), the identification of אני as an error, offers the opportunity to avoid the contortions of the other two approaches, but sacrifices any sort of certainty. The suggestion of *BH³* is that the versions have read an accusative marker את, which should perhaps be read rather as a second-person pronoun (cf. Spohn, and on the spelling, see the note 'you' at 7.22), while *BHS* commends simply reading the accusative marker, supposedly with the versions (among recent commentators, this is adopted by, e.g., Krüger, Köhlmoos). This is a little misleading: as Goldman notes, the versions (in fact, just G, S and possibly T) do not show any positive sign of having read את—they simply do not express any equivalent to אני, which may alternatively have been absent from their source-texts or omitted as unintelligible.³ Other proposals include seeing אני as an error for אל (Renan), for בני (Kamenetzky, 239), or for אנא/אנה (Durell), or else as a corrupt doublet/detachment of characters from the preceding word (Seow, but see also the note at 8.1).

Perhaps the most interesting suggestion, however, draws on a passage from *Ahiqar* that is sometimes cited for its close similarity to what Qohelet is saying here. In that, Ahiqar says: חזי קדמתך מנדעם קשה [על] אנפי מ[ל]ך אל תקום זעיר כצפה מן ברק אנת אשתמר לך, 'When something difficult confronts you, do not stand still in the presence of a king: his anger is quicker than lightning, you must take care of yourself' (Cowley, 215, l. 101; *TAD* C1.1 l. 85). This uses

---

³ So T, for example, has הוי זהיר ית פמך על גזירת מלכא, 'be careful with your mouth concerning the decree of the king': there is no equivalent to אני, but also no direct reflection of the object-marker or of a reading אָתְּ = אתה.

the expression אנפי מלך, 'the face of the king', and a number of scholars have suggested that this is what originally stood in the text of 8.2 (e.g., Whitley; Ginsberg, *Studies*, 34-35; Dahood, 'Qoheleth and Recent Discoveries', 311; Michel, *Untersuchungen*, 94 n. 25; Pinker, 'Aspects of Demeanour', 417). As it is usually proposed, the attractiveness of the suggestion is offset by the need to explain why Qohelet would use an Aramaic expression here, but there is another way to look at the matter. Whether he was originally talking about either the face or the anger of a king (cf. Prov 30.33), and whether or not he was aware of the saying found in *Ahiqar*, our author could certainly have used the Hebrew equivalent of אנפי, which is אפי. The cognate verb אנף is nasalized in Hebrew, and the nasalized form of the much more common Aramaic noun, as used in *Ahiqar*, is found at Dan 2.46; 3.19: it would have been familiar to Jewish copyists, and is, in fact, the usual form in the Qumran texts. Consequently, it would be surprising neither if an original אפי מלך were to be copied accidentally as אנפי מלך, nor if a subsequent copyist were to mistake this for אני פי מלך (perhaps especially if his text had the defective spelling שמר subsequently, so that what he was writing did not seem like nonsense).[4] In the end, I think this is the only way to make sense of the text: no good meaning can be extracted from אני as it stands, and other emendations that have been proposed are either too drastic or else inherently implausible. It resolves, moreover, the apparent tension between 8.2-4 and 8.5: royal anger should provoke flight, but it can also be avoided in the first place.

8.2 concerning an oath by God] The expression שב(ו)עת יהוה is used in Exod 22.10 of an oath made between neighbours to give a solemn assurance that one has not damaged the property of the other, and in 2 Sam 21.7 it refers to the oath between David and Jonathan that prevents David from killing Jonathan's son (cf. 1 Sam 20.15-17). In 1 Kgs 2.42-43, where Solomon accuses Shimei of breaking his 'oath of God' and of disobeying the royal commandment not to leave Jerusalem, it is not clear that Shimei has actually made any such oath, and by killing him, as David has urged him to do, Solomon actually gets around an earlier oath made to Shimei by David (cf. 2 Sam 19.23; 1 Kgs 2.8). All the same, the story seems to illustrate the use of such oaths to regulate the relationships between kings and others, and the context suggests that we are dealing with that sort of oath here: Qohelet is not repeating his earlier advice about vows made to God (5.3-4), but warning against making in haste

---

[4] The *plene* שמור is used in M^L, and so is found in the key critical editions from *BH*[3] onward, but it was formally identified principally with eastern texts; cf. Baer, 81, and the apparatus to this verse in *BH*[3]. The Masorah of M^L itself, however, identifies שמור *plene* as the reading of the western tradition, שמר defective as that of the eastern (the reverse is true when the word recurs at 12.13); see *BHQ* 42*; Ginsburg, *Introduction*, 235. Such confusion is not uncommon; see, the notes at 4.1. The defective spelling is by no means rare and is found as early as ms Sassoon 1053.

any solemn undertaking to the king (so Fox), or perhaps against breaking such an undertaking. There is nothing here to suggest that Qohelet is referring to some contemporary problem of Jews forced to swear allegiance by a foreign deity, as Schöpflin, 'Political Power', 26, suggests.

On the expression על דברת, see the note at 3.18 (where Bartholomew's interpretation of it here is also addressed). Qohelet does not use it as a simple equivalent to על דבר, and the meaning 'because' here would be inconsistent with his other usage. An insistence on that sense, however, has led many commentators to suppose that Qohelet must be talking about behaviour that is grounded in an oath between the listener and the king or, as Hertzberg, Kohlmoos and Goldman suppose, an oath made to the king by God (the ambiguity is emphasized in Krüger, 'Meaningful Ambiguities', 67-68, and Asurmendi, 'Power in Qoheleth and the Prophets', 137). That latter possibility is considered by Crenshaw also, who speaks of 'subjective' and 'objective' genitives, but there is no reason to suppose that שבועת אלהים might mean anything different from שבע(ו)עת יהוה, and if the author wished to talk about an oath uttered by God, it seems unlikely he would have picked something so close to a technical expression used of oaths made by calling on God.

8.3 do not be hasty. Leave him] The accents and punctuation of M break the sentence in 8.2 at אלהים, but G reads אל תבהל with the preceding ועל דברת שבועת אלהים (as Jerome observes in his commentary),[5] and S seems to do likewise. This construal appears also to be represented in σ' καὶ παραβῆναι ὅρκον θεοῦ μὴ σπεύσῃς, 'and to break an oath of God do not hurry', which has influenced a number of G manuscripts. If we do not follow G, then the ועל דברת שבועת אלהים of 8.2 has to be treated as either a secondary specification of the initial verb ('watch...especially in a matter of an oath of God') or as causal ('watch...because of an oath of God'): the latter requires, of course, either that the conjunction is explicative (so Lauha) or that על דברת can mean 'because', which Gordis assumes—but which is far from certain, as we have

---

[5] Jerome's citation of G here is unusually problematic. He says that it reads *et de iuramento et de uerbo dei ne festines a facie dei ambulare*, 'both concerning the oath and concerning the word of God do not hasten to walk away from the face of God'. G in fact says καὶ περὶ λόγου ὅρκου θεοῦ μὴ σπουδάσῃς ἀπὸ προσώπου αὐτοῦ πορεύσῃ, 'and concerning a word of an oath of God, do not hurry: from his face/presence you will go'. Jerome is clearly paraphrasing to clarify the sense, but he presents the reading as though it had καὶ περὶ ὅρκου καὶ (περὶ) λόγου. One manuscript of the commentary does lack the second *et* (= καὶ, 'and'), but the transposition of the nouns occurs in all witnesses and is likely to be original. In the G tradition, this transposition is found in only one late manuscript, probably coincidentally. The La for the verse is preserved as *os regis custodiet verbo iuramenti dei ne festinaveris*, 'the mouth of a king will pay heed to the word of an oath of God. Do not hurry...', so that is not obviously the source of Jerome's reading, although it in itself displays an interesting independence from G. See Berger, 'Notice', 140; Leanza, 'Le tre versione', 93-94.

already seen. Provan seemingly combines both: 'obey the king's command, (especially) because of the oath of God', glossed as 'because you took an oath before God'.

Following the arrangement of M also requires us to find an explanation for what seems like a contradiction: 'do not hasten from him, go!' M itself deals with the problem in most manuscripts by pointing אל תבהל as niph'al, so that it can mean 'do not be terrified (of him)' (cf. Gen 45.3), and the sentence thus becomes an admonition against becoming rooted to the spot. This reading is still accepted by a few modern commentators (and lies behind the RSV, 'be not dismayed'), but none of the other versions—not even T—followed such a vocalization, and all reflect the pi'el, which Qohelet used in 5.1 and 7.9. De Rossi and Ginsburg, *Writings*, note a number of later Hebrew manuscripts and editions which also point the word as pi'el.

The alternative now more commonly adopted to avoid the contradiction, involves reading מפניו תלך as constructed with אל תבהל, to yield a sense such as 'do not hasten your going from him'. This is complicated, inasmuch as when בהל is used with another verb to mean 'hasten to do something', it is elsewhere constructed with ל- and an infinitive, as we should expect (pi'el Esth 2.9; hiph'il Esth 6.14). We might conceivably take תלך as a final clause ('hurry, that you might go'), although it is hard to see why this would be preferred to the infinitive, especially given the ambiguity that it introduces. Schoors, however, talks of 'an asyndetic object clause', and if this is supposed to be, as it were, a substantivized אשר clause without the אשר, then we should also observe that when בהל is constructed with a substantive, it always, as an intransitive verb, takes a preposition (pi'el 5.1 על-; 7.9 ב-; niph'al Prov 28.22 ל-; hiph'il 2 Chr 26.20 מ-). Certainly, אל תבהל...על אשר תלך would be ugly, but it is a very considerable stretch to suppose that אל תבהל...תלך could simply stand in its place without being almost incomprehensible. This is not a natural reading of the text, or anything like it, but is simply an attempt to retain the Masoretic interpretation at any cost, which creates awkwardness in 8.2, and in 8.3 requires either an unlikely reading of the verb as niph'al, or the acceptance of an unnecessarily difficult construction with that verb. Although Fox and Longman are rare amongst modern commentators in doing so, it is a great deal easier to go with G on this point, even if it is then also necessary to understand that Qohelet is consistently advising flight, rather than advocating persistence, followed by flight only when things get bad.

Rudman, 'Qohelet's Use of לפני', 148, seeks a different way around the contradiction, by understanding מפניו תלך as a sort of play on the more familiar expression הלך לפני, which he understands in terms of serving somebody. Qohelet's expression would correspondingly mean the opposite, and the injunction would be 'do not…be disobedient'. Whether or not הלך לפני means what he wants, however, and even if we allow the play upon it, this translation involves understanding the preceding אל to qualify both תבהל and תלך, despite the lack of a conjunction and despite the fact that תעמד then gets its own אל.

8.3 do not hang on] Lit. 'do not stand' (cf. G μὴ στῇς) or 'do not remain' (cf. σ' μὴ ἐπίμενε). Commentators have tended to assign special meanings according to their understanding of the context, so that Ginsburg, for example, thinks of standing up in protest, Gordis of persistence, and Waldman of joining a conspiracy (see below). Following אל תבהל and לך, however, it seems hard to believe that the principal implication of תעמד is anything other than standing still or stopping (cf. Gen 19.17; 1 Sam 20.38; Jer 4.6). S has a conjunction here (which Kamenetzky, 236, thinks was in its source-text), as do Hie, V, and many later Hebrew manuscripts (see de Rossi, Miletto). This may have developed independently as a facilitation in each of those traditions but, although probably secondary, may equally have reached them as a common and early Hebrew variant.

8.3 at a dangerous word] The דבר רע is often understood to be a 'bad business' (V *in opere malo*), and commentators who take Qohelet to be commending obedience here correspondingly believe him either to be saying that one should not delay in fulfilling a command 'even in an unpleasant situation', or to be advising against involvement 'in a conspiracy' against the king. To be sure, when kings themselves talk of 'bad things' or 'bad words', they unsurprisingly tend to be referring to attacks, rebellions, or conspiracies, and Waldman, 'The *dābār raʿ* of Eccl 8:3', presents a selection of such references to suggest that Qohelet is talking about a conspiracy. It is difficult to see, however, that from anything but a royal perspective the term has any particular significance of that sort.

Elsewhere in the Bible, דבר רע is used variously of a defect in a sacrificial animal (Deut 17.1), bad things to be avoided in the Israelite camp (Deut 23.10), harm arising from poison (2 Kgs 4.41), and the speech or behaviour of the wicked (Pss 64.6 ET 64.5; 141.4)—a range that should discourage us from imbuing the term with any very specific meaning. Qohelet, however, will use it again in 8.5, which promises that the obedient will know no דבר רע, and when the uses are separated by fewer than twenty words, it is unlikely that he intends each to be understood in a completely different way (so Ginsburg). This is a problem for any interpretation in terms of 'bad affairs' or 'conspiracies', because he simply cannot promise that obedience will enable one to avoid such things; indeed, on most such readings, he is already saying here that one must be obedient when one encounters them. Even sooner, furthermore, Qohelet will be using דבר in 8.4 with reference to the king speaking, so it may not be merely the translation technique of G that has apparently led it to read a reference to speech here (ἐν λόγῳ πονηρῷ, cf. Hie *in uerbo malo*, 'during a painful word') and in 8.5 (ῥῆμα πονηρόν).

Such a reference has been understood by more modern readers as well, and דבר רע was translated in terms of speech by, e.g., Ewald, Hitzig and Ginsburg. The principal difficulty for such a reading is the use of the preposition -ב after עמד, although this is a difficulty also for other interpretations. In the great majority of such uses, -ב marks the location at which one stands (e.g., Gen 19.17; Exod 32.26; Num 22.26; Deut 10.10), occasionally with an implication of persistence (cf. Isa 47.12: 'stand in your enchantments'), but that does not really suit any of the usual understandings of בדבר רע. It has sometimes been suggested, therefore, that עמד ב- might mean 'enter into' or 'embark upon', even though that sense would seem incompatible with the normal senses of the verb. Most of the passages cited in support (by, e.g., Delitzsch, Schoors) are ones in which such a meaning could be entertained, but is not necessary: they can be—and usually are—understood quite naturally with עמד meaning 'stand' (Jer 23.18, 22; Pss 1.1; 106.23). The sole exception is 2 Kgs 23.3, which says that 'all the people stood in the covenant' just made by Josiah, but this is a specific allusion back to Deut 29.9-11 (ET 29.10-12), which can hardly sustain the general claim.

It seems much more likely that the -ב is temporal or circumstantial here (cf. 1 Chr 23.30; Ps 134.1), and that Qohelet is using an expression similar to that found in Mal 3.2, which asks who will endure and who will stand when (-ב) God appears, literally 'in his appearance'. Accordingly, I understand the דבר רע to be something said by the king that will potentially bring harm (contrast דבר טוב, 'speaking good', in Num 10.29; Esth 7.9, which means saying something to the benefit of someone), and 8.5 suggests that it is the sort of thing that might be faced by somebody who has disobeyed him. In the light of 8.4, this is unlikely just to be a rebuke: Qohelet's point there is that no-one can restrain a king from acting, and it seems more likely that he is talking about a condemnation, or a command that someone be punished.

8.3 he may do anything he wants] The claim כל אשר חפץ עשה is made of God in Pss 115.3; 135.6 and by God in Isa 46.10; there are comparable expressions in Jon 1.14 and Prov 21.1. Hurvitz (in 'History of a Legal Formula') notes the use of similar clauses in legal documents, where they express the rights of a purchaser over what they have purchased, and he argues that it became an equivalent of the earlier 'did what was good in his eyes' (found in, e.g., 2 Sam 10.12), which was adopted only after about 500 BCE. It is interesting to note that in Prov 21.1, the point is not that the king is all-powerful, but rather that he is completely under the control of God.

8.4 because a king's word] Or possibly 'when a king has spoken'. G καθὼς and Hie *sicut*, 'as', appear to reflect כאשר rather than M באשר (cf. McNeile, 147). See the note on 'when' at 4.19. S ܐܝܟܢ *'ykn'*, 'how', 'in what way', also reflects כאשר (cf. Kamenetzky, 223, 236), and that is the reading of a number of Hebrew manuscripts cited by de Rossi. On the other hand, σ' διὰ τὸ (var. τὸν) λόγον βασιλέως ἐξουσιαστικὸν εἶναι, 'on account of the word of a king being powerful', more probably represents באשר, as does the very paraphrastic T.

What seems a minor difference has a significant effect, in fact, on how the rest of the clause has been construed in the different versions, because while באשר naturally promoted an understanding 'since a word of a king (is) powerful', כאשר led to the expectation of a verbal clause 'just as a king speaks powerfully', which is why S translates דבר using a participle, and Hie has *sicut dixerit rex potestatem habens*, 'just as a king has spoken having power'. For α', ἐλάλησε, 'he has spoken', is attested in Syh, suggesting both that Aquila probably read כאשר as well, and that Hie may have drawn on his reading. These past tenses suggest that Aquila and Jerome are tying the words to what follows, and understanding 'When a king has spoken in power, then who will say to him…'. The understanding in G may be similar, although the textual tradition is in disarray. Most manuscripts have λαλεῖ, 'speaks', out of position after ἐξουσιάζων, 'being powerful' (in the use of which Vinel, 'Le Texte Grec', 299-300, rather tenuously sees a Solomonic allusion), but in some very important witnesses it is missing altogether, probably because the way that G construes the sentence makes it unnecessary; Syh notes, indeed, that 'Origen did not mention the λαλεῖ in the (manuscripts) of Ecclesiastes'.[6] It is difficult to say for sure whether באשר or כאשר is original, or whether דבר should be read as a noun or a verb, but it is easier to see an identification of דבר with the subsequent שלטון than to read שלטון either as an adjective characterizing the king (cf. G) or as the content of the speech, so the understanding in M is to be preferred here.

8.4 What are you doing?] Or 'what are you going to do?' In many contexts, the form of the verb would most naturally suggest a future tense, and the future is accordingly used here by G. The present and aorist tenses, however, are both widely attested as variants in the G tradition—the latter notably in the hexaplaric *O*-group manuscripts, which often align the Greek more closely with the Hebrew. Elsewhere, while the participle used by S might also carry a future implication, Jerome opts for the present tense in Hie and V, and T uses a perfect. These differences need not reflect variants in the Hebrew. The same question is used in Job 9.12; 35.6; Prov 25.8; Isa 45.9, and the context does not suggest future action in at least the first and last of those, because the yiqtol is quite commonly used in this sort of question with reference to action in the present (see J-M §113 d and, e.g., Gen 32.30; 37.15). G's future tense is a reflection of its translation technique, rather than of a limitation in the original.

8.5a one who obeys a command] The article on G ὁ φυλάσσων leads McNeile, 147, to suppose that the translator found השומר, perhaps after reduplication of the preceding ה. This may, however, be another feature of the translation technique: Yi, 242-43, notes that the Greek habitually has an article where a participle acting as a substantive takes an object, but never when it does not. The article is omitted in hexaplaric texts, aligning the Greek more closely with the Hebrew.

---

[6] On this, see Gentry, 'Special Problems', 135-38, and Marshall, and Gentry, 'Relationship', 78-79; the other note to the text there means that the reading of θ' was λαλεῖ.

Kohlmoos, who thinks that Qohelet has been speaking of obedience to an ideal king, claims the verb can refer as readily to that king as to the listener, and that he is being depicted as obedient to the Law. This is true in principle, if a bit of a stretch, but the construction here introduces a conditionality that sits uncomfortably with her interpretation overall: we are supposed to obey a king who only *may* be obedient himself. There is no clear reference here, moreover, to the Law, and if Lavoie, in 'Sagesse de cour royale', 220-21, cannot demonstrate beyond doubt that Qohelet is talking about a royal command, he at least shows there is no good reason to see a religious reference.

8.5a will experience no dangerous word] As most commentators observe, ידע here seems to mean 'have experience of' or 'be acquainted with', as at, e.g., Isa 53.3; cf. σ' ὁ φυλάσσων ἐντολὴν οὐ πειραθήσεται πράγματος πονηροῦ, 'one keeping a command will experience no evil deed', which has undoubtedly influenced V *qui custodit praeceptum non experietur quicquam mali*, 'who keeps a commandment will not experience anything of evil', and which is explained by a scholion in one Greek manuscript, to the effect that 'to know' an evil means 'to suffer' one (ms 248: τὸ παθεῖν τί πονηρὸν γινώσκειν εἶπε ῥῆμα πονηρόν). Among the exceptions, Hitzig thinks the point is that a dutiful servant will not realize that the דבר רע is bad, and McNeile, 77, that he will refuse to countenance evil, taking that to be the sense of ידע in Ps 101.4 also. It is unlikely that the latter is possible, but Hitzig's solution is not unattractive, and has been echoed more recently in Schöpflin, 'Political Power', 27 (who sees a double meaning). This suggestion, though, that the obedient will obey the king blindly, in a 'my country, right or wrong' sort of way, is less simple than it sounds: if we construe the verse as I propose, דבר רע sits alongside עת ומשפט, and that understanding of ידע does not suit both; if we construe it more traditionally, on the other hand, such a statement seems simply out of place, and bears no relationship to the next clause, with which it is supposed to stand in parallel.

The דבר רע is taken as 'anything bad', or as an action, by σ', V, T, with other versions opting to see it in terms of speech (G uses ῥῆμα). Either is possible, of course, although I think the use in 8.4 makes speech much more likely (cf. the note at 8.3), and that the danger here involves the response that a king will make to disobedience. Speech is implicit also, perhaps, in the notion of judgment which follows, so there is no need to establish parallelism between the two ideas by emending עת to פתגם, as Rose, *Rien de nouveau*, 248, chooses to do—and there is no text-critical basis for regarding עת with suspicion.

8.5a or time of judgment] Lit. 'and time of judgment'. Setting aside Rose's objection to it (discussed in the last note), there are two problems involved in understanding ועת ומשפט here. The first is that G καιρὸν κρίσεως, 'a time of judgment', shows no knowledge of the conjunction before משפט which is found in the other versions (although not in some Hebrew manuscripts: see de Rossi, and another instance in Lavoie and Mehramooz, 'Le Texte hébreu et la traduction judéo-persane', 499-500). This conjunction was probably absent from its source-text, as McNeile, 147, supposes, and it may well be that M reflects assimilation to the expression in the next verse, where G *does* have a conjunction (which shows that it is not treating them as a hendiadys here, as Schoors supposes, even were that consonant with the translation technique; cf. Fox). In practice, of course, this makes little difference to the interpretation offered by those commentators (like Ginsburg, Delitzsch, Gordis, Schoors) who take עת ומשפט to be a hendiadys meaning the same as עת משפט. Either way, it seems unlikely that we should understand 'time *and* judgment' here.

The bigger question, although it has attracted little discussion, is the place of ועת ומשפט in the verse as a whole. M divides the text to make a chiastic, two-part saying: '^AOne obeying a commandment ^Bwill not know ^Can evil word | and | ^C'time and judgment ^B'will know ^A'the heart of a wise man'. This has the consequence that the objects of each verb 'know' are not only juxtaposed, but joined by a conjunction on עת that easily leads them to be read as a single sequence, and that could just as easily have been omitted to prevent such a misreading. It also, more significantly, creates a curious pairing: what does the fact that obeying a command avoids a דבר רע (which clearly refers back to vv. 2-4) have to do with the fact that a wise man's heart knows עת ומשפט (which is just as clearly picked up in vv. 5b-8)? The meaning of the phrase עת (ו)משפט has been somewhat debated in itself, and we shall look at it in the next verse. Suffice it to say, though, that the context there makes it very unlikely that Qohelet is using the same expression here to talk about an understanding of court procedure or of anything that would naturally correspond to obeying a command. This division of the words also has Qohelet appear to say that the wise man 'knows' עת ומשפט, a difficulty that I noted in the commentary above. This is so unlikely a thing for him to say (especially in the light of what is about to come) that many commentators have supposed that it must be secondary, or a quotation from the views of others.

Although, then, this saying might be an ingenious, if rather forced, attempt to make a transition from one discussion to the other, I think that it is more probably the result of a misunderstanding, which has been induced by the curious structure of what follows. Seow has correctly identified this structure, which we shall discuss below, but has tried to treat עת ומשפט as a 'nominative absolute' construction, meaning 'as for time and judgment', rather than connecting the phrase with שומר מצוה לא ידע: if that were the true intention, then the initial conjunction would be even more misleading and unnecessary. The transition between discussions, such as it is, lies merely in the use of עת ומשפט as catchwords. In any case, though, the mis-division is early, and clearly underpins not only the Masoretic punctuation, but the understanding of T. On the other hand, G, σ', Hie can all be read either way.

8.5B-9

(8.5b) The heart of a wise man knows:

(8.6) that for every matter there is a time and judgment,

that the human's harm weighs heavily upon him,

(8.7) that he does not know what is going to happen,

that when it happens—who is going to explain to him?

(8.8) There is no human who governs the wind, so as to restrain the wind.

And there is no governing death's day—

and there will be no mission into battle,

nor will wickedness save whoever resorts to it.

(8.9) I observed all this when I applied my mind to every activity that is done beneath the sun, at the time when human had power over human to hurt him.

Commentary

These verses present two short lists. The first, in vv. 6-7, is ostensibly of some important things that wise people will know, although it becomes clear that certain limitations of knowledge are among these. The second, in v. 8, is concerned with human powerlessness to control the wind or the timing of death: the second half of the verse is difficult, but its purpose is probably not to extend this list, so much as to emphasize that no intervention will be possible. The theme throughout seems to be that humans face judgment for their actions, but have no way to predict or understand it. Perhaps correspondingly, they have no control over the death that will come to them sooner or later, and no way to resist it.

Qohelet has very carefully not stated that he is talking about divine judgment, but the events here are presented as unavoidable, in a way that the anger of the king was not in 8.2-5. In 8.8, furthermore, the initial claims draw on the political and military vocabulary of human rule: death will be subject to no human governance or armed action. It seems curious, therefore, that Qohelet finishes by characterizing his observations as derived from his study of activities in the world 'at the time when human had power over human to hurt him'—an expression that probably describes not some particular historical period, but the stage in the existence of each human when the power to which they are most obviously susceptible is simply the power of other humans. I take the implication to be that the things Qohelet is telling us here, which he believes the wise should know, are not dogmas, but understandings that the wise can extrapolate from human experience, as Qohelet himself has done. From the purely human-to-human context, including conventional warnings about the danger of royal power, we can understand what it means to be subject to judgment and death in a context that each of us will inevitably inhabit eventually, which transcends the mundane, and is subject to no human ingenuity or control.

8.5b] On the way that I have divided the text, see the commentary and notes on 8.5a. Qohelet will use the same expression, 'the heart of a wise man', in 10.2, where it is contrasted with the heart of a fool. Here, it would be possible also to understand 'a wise heart' (a translation attributed to August Knobel by Delitzsch, although I have not found it in his commentary); cf. 1 Kgs 3.12. As ever in the book, 'heart' is a reference to the mind and not specifically the emotions, so if the expression is not simply synonymous with 'the wise man', it perhaps has the implication that the following are things that the wise comprehend, or have come to realize.

8.6] 'Time and judgment' acts as a catchphrase to link this verse with the last, but it also harks back to 3.1, and especially to 3.17, where Qohelet declared that 'God will make a judgment—as there is a time for every matter—and about everything that is done there'. There is little reason to doubt that Qohelet is talking similarly here about the certainty of divine judgment, although, principally to solve the problem that such a sense poses for traditional understandings of 8.5, many commentators have tried to find a different meaning (see the notes). Such attempts generally result in a reading that there is a proper time and process for everything, or some such, which fits rather poorly with what follows. The implications of 'the human's harm' are less clear cut: the text leaves open the possibility that Qohelet is talking either about the bad things humans have themselves done (for which they know they will be judged, perhaps), or about something bad done to humans. In the context, I am inclined to think that the former is more likely, making Qohelet's broader point that humans are oppressed by the weight of their wrongdoing, knowing that something will happen because of it, but not knowing what.

Michel, 'Qohelet-Probleme', 92, argues that here and in the following verses Qohelet reinterprets terms like 'time' and 'judgment' that have been used in 8.2-5, showing that he has cited conventional advice and is now 'correcting' it. A change of perspective would not be inappropriate at this point of the monologue, but—more general issues about citations in the book aside—it is not clear to me that any such reinterpretation is evident, unless one sets out specifically to understand these terms differently.

8.7] On the tenses here, see the notes. The point is that humans do not know what will happen, and when whatever it is does actually happen, nobody will be able to inform them or explain it.

8.8] The items here are either still things that the wise know, more loosely constructed with the clause in 8.5, or separate observations set in parallel with it. In either case, they pick up the issue of inevitability: humans are powerless to resist what is going to happen to them. The first item is a simple analogy: humans will have no more control than they have over the wind (and the wind will further furnish Qohelet with analogies for human ignorance in 11.4-5, as well as making an appearance in 1.6, and in Qohelet's various expressions about wishing for, or working in the wind). Although it introduces a more sinister note, this is probably true of the second as well: the problem is not that humans cannot each change the time they will themselves die, but that death (perhaps personified here) is an uncontrollable force. The third item presents greater problems, and has been read in various ways (see the notes). Among the most popular of these is the idea that one cannot be discharged from a war, but it is more likely that this item should be read with the last: one cannot go into battle (or perhaps send out a rescue party) against the inevitable. Finally, the last statement, which claims in effect that 'their wickedness will not save the wicked', again seems to offer not an analogy to the problem of inevitability, but something closer to the statement about missions into battle. There is no fighting death, or perhaps either the wind or death, and even the wicked will have no control, however much of their wickedness they deploy. The claim also evokes the issue of judgment with which Qohelet began here, without addressing it directly.

8.9] On the relevance of the last clause, see above. With his references to ch. 3, and his analogies with human impotence against the wind and death, Qohelet has drawn out ideas of divine judgment and cosmic forces. He seems concerned here, on the face of it, to clarify that all these statements are to be read in the context of human society and human rule, but the implication is that this human setting, where we are at the mercy of the more powerful, offers a model for understanding the human condition more broadly. The same word 'time' that was just used in 8.6 appears again here, and since it was linked with judgment in that verse, and in the earlier verses evoked there, it seems possible that some such connotation is present here as well. I think it is more likely, however, that the force of the noun is very weak here, and the point is to specify not a period, but a situation. A slightly looser translation might be 'at the point when it's other humans who have power over humans to hurt them', and I take the broader point to be, 'these are the realities of human existence, as I could tell even just from looking at what happens to humans when it's humans exercising power'.

We have already encountered the verb in 2.19; 5.18; and 6.2, where it was used of controlling property or having the power to enjoy it. It is used of exercising power over people in Neh 5.15; Esth 9.1; and (in the hiphʿil) Ps 119.133, in each case with some connotation of gaining the upper hand, or 'lording it' over them. Although it picks up related words in 8.8, therefore, we should possibly not see it as an entirely neutral term for being 'in charge' or 'in control', as it can be in Aramaic and later Hebrew: some nuance of abuse may be present when humans are the object. The Hebrew can also imply either that one human is hurting another by 'ruling over' them in this way, or, in principle, that the humans doing the ruling are hurting themselves. Few commentators have adopted the latter reading, and it is not clear that the ambiguity is intentional, but Qohelet is conceivably implying that those in charge will themselves pay a price when it is their turn to be judged.

Notes

8.5b The heart of a wise man] Or 'a wise heart'. As I noted at 8.1, Qohelet prefers '*the* wise man', and this would be the only clear exception. That might push us toward 'wise heart' (so Lavoie, 'Sagesse de cour royale', 223), but in 7.4-5 he also talks about 'the heart of wise men', which points the other way. The ancient translations have all opted for 'wise man' here, but the sense is not much different either way.

8.5b knows] The two occurrences of ידע in 8.5 are both pointed the same way in most manuscripts of M, as yiqtol. G, however, renders the first with the future γνώσεται, and the second with a present tense, γινώσκει. Aitken, 'Rhetoric and Poetry', 62, sees deliberate stylistic variation, but it is not unlikely that the translator has read the second differently (as a participle or perhaps, as Podechard thinks, qatal). BHQ suggests that the Hebrew should actually be pointed as a participle (without noting that it is, in fact, pointed that way by a few late manuscripts, some of which actually have a *plene* יודע; see de Rossi and Ginsburg, *Writings*). Goldman thinks that M's reading is 'a harmonization with the following vv. 6-7'. G might support this, but his recruitment also of V, Hie, S and T in favour of this position is problematic: there is no such differentiation in Hie or S, and, while there are differentiations of tense in V and T, these are linked to broader, interpretative distinctions which include the use of different verbs. I think that the majority pointing in M, moreover, is tied up with its chiastic construal of 8.5, rather than with what follows (there is no verb in 8.6, and the ידע of 8.7 is actually pointed as a participle). There are several plausible readings of the consonantal text, none of which is strongly indicated by the context, and the most that can be said of all this, I think, is that G does not commit itself to the chiastic construal. Its change of tense, with the consequent lack of symmetry, might even suggest that the translator took this to be the start of a new sentence, as I do.

8.6 that[1]...8.7 that[2]] In vv. 6-7 we have four statements, each of a similar length (6-5-5-6 words respectively), and each introduced by כי. The connections between them are not self-evident, and because כי can have a range of meanings, the particle is rarely translated the same way each time. Seow notes the variation in Crenshaw's commentary, which is illustrative of the problem (I have italicized his renderings of כי):

> *Indeed*, for everything there is a time and procedure, *but* the evil of human beings is heavy on them. *For* nobody knows what will happen, *because* who can tell him when it will be?

It is not uncommon for a single word in one language to require differentiated translations in another, and the problem here lies not in the variety itself, but in the ambiguity. If we compare two other versions (also italicized), that becomes obvious:

> *for* every matter has a time and procedure. *Truly* man's misfortune weighs heavy upon him, *for* he does not know what will happen, *for* who can tell him when it will happen? (Fox)
>
> *For* everything has its proper time and procedure, [∅] man's evil being so widespread. *Indeed*, man does not know what the future will be, *for* when it happens, who will tell him? (Gordis)

If three perceptive exegetes, with a similar understanding of most of the expressions involved, relate the statements to their context and to each other in such completely different ways, what chance would any normal reader have to determine the relationship intended? This is not a problem limited to modern readers, and after some carefully differentiated conjunctions in Hie, Jerome resorts in V to translating only one of the four כיs at all: it seems likely that even readers earlier than his time and fluent in Hebrew would have struggled. As the ET of Delitzsch's commentary puts it:

> by such monotonous repetition of one and the same word, the author also elsewhere renders the exposition difficult, affording too free a space for understanding the כי as confirming, or as hypothetical, and for co-ordinating or subordinating to each other the clauses with כי.

If we are not to attribute to the author a certain carelessness, or even a desire to confuse, then it is important to consider the possibility that these statements were never intended to relate to each other directly, but that they are each connected separately to the ידע לב חכם that precedes them—a connection that has been obscured because M has already given that clause an earlier object. Seow (who has been followed by Miller) sees rightly, I think, that what we have here is a list of things that the wise man knows (or perhaps that he should know).

8.6 for every matter there is a time and judgment] As Lohfink observes, Qohelet seems to be alluding to his own words, and לכל חפץ יש עת is especially reminiscent of עת לכל חפץ in 3.1 and 3.17. It is in the latter that we also find a reference to divine judgment, ישפט האלהים, connected to the idea that 'there is a time', and it is difficult to resist the conclusion reached by most commentators, that Qohelet is correspondingly talking about divine judgment when he uses משפט here. G, and probably α', θ' (see Marshall), accordingly have καιρὸς καὶ κρίσις, 'a time and a judgment' (contrast καιρὸν κρίσεως in the previous verse), and Hie the corresponding *tempus et iudicium*; that understanding is found in S and T as well. σ', however, has ὅτι παντὶ πράγματί ἐστι καιρὸς χρείας καὶ τρόπος, 'as for every deed there is a time when it is needed, and a custom', which has undoubtedly influenced V *omni negotio tempus est et oportunitas*, 'for every business there is a time and an opportunity'. This probably takes משפט in the rather different sense found in, e.g., Judg 13.12; 18.7; 2 Kgs 17.33; Sir 35.5, where it refers to the lifestyles or customs of groups or of individuals, although Jerome stretches this somewhat.

This and other possibilities have been picked up by some modern commentators too. Schoors, for instance, takes potentially similar uses of משפט in 1QS III, 17, where it is associated with divine control, and in CD-A XII, 15, where it is not, to move from an idea that these 'have a deterministic flavour' through to a claim that משפט can mean 'destiny', and that this is the 'plain meaning' of the text here. Schoors appeals to Niehr's study of the root, which understands a usage seen here and in Isa 28.26; Prov 28.5; Jer 8.7; Job 32.9 to culminate at Qumran in a sense 'Plan der Schöpfung', 'plan of creation'.[1] That is anyway somewhat different from 'destiny', but it is questionable whether Niehr has identified any special usage: משפט probably means 'rightness' or 'what is right' in Isa 28.26 and Job 32.9, and possibly in Prov 28.5, but it has no connotation of any underlying scheme, plan, or divine preference. In Jer 8.7, where it is interestingly linked to birds' knowledge of their seasons and ability to keep to the time (עת) when they are supposed to appear, the reference is to God's judgment, for the imminence of which the people show no corresponding instinct. In fact, it is not impossible that משפט does mean a 'plan' in Exod 26.30, which refers to the revealed design of the tabernacle, and in 1 Kgs 6.38, where the plan is of the Temple, and this may be behind the claim of *DCH*, that משפט here means 'a proper measure' (a sense which might also suit Jer 10.24)—although it is important to be clear that, as the use in Lev 19.35 suggests, any 'plan' is a matter of measuring, not of making determinations about the future. It is difficult to extrapolate from such a specific context, but along with Isa 28.26 and Job 32.9 these texts do affirm that משפט can very occasionally be used to talk about a model or template of 'correctness' to which something should conform, and which may be taught or discerned (see also, e.g., Pss 25.9; 112.5).

This is obviously relevant to the influential suggestion of Gordis (picked up by, e.g., Crenshaw, Fox), that משפט here must mean 'the proper procedure', for which he cites Isa 28.26, comparing 1 Kgs 5.8 and Isa 40.14. The first of these, as we have already noted, is such a use of the noun in the sense 'correctness', and the verse talks about how God has taught the farmer למשפט so that he knows how to plant and harvest his crops correctly. Accordingly, to be sure, we may acknowledge that למשפט means something like 'in the proper

---

[1] Niehr, *Herrschen und Richten*, 302. Schoors cites p. 337, which speaks more broadly of integration into a deterministic framework.

way', but the 'way' part of that comes from the -ל, not the משפט: adverbial expressions can describe the way that something is done, but the something does not thereby become inherently a procedure. Similarly, in 1 Kgs 5.8, the officers each act כמשפטו, 'according to his custom', or perhaps in this context 'his duty', but 'custom' is no more here a procedure than is 'correctness' in Isa 28.26. In other words, although משפט here could probably mean that there is a proper way for everything to happen,[2] there are no grounds to suppose that it could mean there is a proper way to do everything. So, to take the meanings suggested along these lines in Lavoie, 'Sagesse de cour royale', 224, we might allow that there could be a reference here to knowing 'the custom to adopt', but there is no justification for 'the conduct to pursue'.

It is doubtful, however, that we need to reach even for that unusual usage. A reference to judgment is strongly suggested both by the links with ch. 3, and by the fact that משפט is associated with justice or judgment everywhere else that it is used in the book (3.16; 5.7; 11.9; 12.14—all, it so happens, translated in such terms by Gordis). Requiring this to be an exception would take a more compelling reason than any that has been offered.

8.6 the human's harm weighs heavily upon him] Lit. 'the human's trouble/evil is much upon him'. In Gen 6.5, God's perception that רבה רעת האדם בארץ leads to his decision that he must blot out the creatures he had made, and although there is no particular reason to see an allusion to that passage here, the similarity of Qohelet's רעת האדם רבה does lend some weight to the supposition that he is talking about something bad done by humans, as in 7.15, rather than something done to them. On the other hand, as Whybray points out, Qohelet uses רעה elsewhere regularly to talk about problems which affect humans; cf. 2.21 (רעה רבה); 5.12, 15; 6.1 (רעה...רבה); 10.5; 11.2, 10. Rashi reads the preceding כי as 'when', so the harm is specifically the punishment meted out at judgment.

It is not clear that we can use the accompanying עליו to shed any light on the problem. Fox points to רע עלי in 2.17, where it expresses Qohelet's perception that something is bad, but here we are dealing with רבה עלי, the only close parallel to which is in 6.1: in that verse, it seems to indicate a quantity or amount with which humans struggle to cope (see the note). I take the sense to be similar here, but the question is then whether humans are struggling with the weight of their own evil (in the face of judgment), or with some other trouble. Commentators who take it to be the latter tend either to see a continuing reference to a royal tyranny, or to think that the trouble lies in what Qohelet goes on to describe: human ignorance. To see a specific allusion forward to that ignorance, however, requires a particular understanding of

---

[2] This is the understanding of Gorssen, 'La Cohérence', 303, who suggests that משפט here is the proper condition of every situation in which a human might become involved.

the relationship between the כי clauses (cf. Fox's version above), which is effectively a way of shaping the context to fit the interpretation, not the interpretation to fit the context. Whether it is deliberate or not, there is an ambiguity here that cannot be resolved by reference either to the wording or to the context, and I have tried to retain that to some extent in my translation. The ancient versions offer a mixed picture: S ܒܝܫܬܐ ܕܒܪܢܫܐ *byšth dbrnš'*, 'evil/bad thing of a human', is probably no less ambiguous than the Hebrew, but σ' ἡ γὰρ κάκωσις τοῦ ἀνθρώπου πολλὴ κατ' αὐτοῦ, 'for the κάκωσις of the human is great on him', leans toward suffering: κάκωσις is typically used of oppression or affliction. This has probably influenced Jerome, who uses *afflictio/adflictio*, 'affliction', in Hie and V—his commentary associates the problem with human ignorance of the future. On the other hand, T clearly identifies the רעה with human evil. We cannot assess the opinion of G, because the translator clearly read a different text (G is γνῶσις τοῦ ἀνθρώπου πολλὴ ἐπ' αὐτόν, 'the human's *knowledge* is much upon him', and Jerome attributes the same reading to θ'). In an early instance of text criticism, Jerome explains the graphical similarity of ד and ר which has led G to reflect דעת, 'knowledge', rather than רעה, evil', and he notes that θ' has the same (the error may have been influenced, of course, by the reference to knowledge at the start of 8.7). Especially in view of 6.1, it is highly unlikely that G has the more original reading, but it is interesting to note that, maybe coincidentally, a few late Hebrew manuscripts also have דעת; see de Rossi.

8.7 he does not know] Cf. אינם יודעים in 9.5 and אינך יודע in 11.5, 6. The construction more generally was discussed in the note 'but the sea is never filled' at 1.7. G ὅτι οὐκ ἔστιν γινώσκων, lit. 'for not is one knowing', translates the participle with a participle, but σ' prefers the more elegant ὅτι οὐκ ἐπίσταται, 'for/that he does not understand'.

8.7 what is going to happen, that when it happens] Both here and in 10.14, M has מה שיהיה, but there are considerable problems around the original tense of the verb in that other verse: see the note. In this verse, V and S read a reference both to the past (where M has מה שיהיה) *and* to the future (where it has כאשר יהיה): respectively *praeterita et uentura*, 'things past (of which he is ignorant) and things future (which nobody can tell him about)'; ܠܡܐ ܕܗܘܐ ܘܡܢ ܢܗܘܐ *lm' dhw' wmn' nhw'*, 'what has happened and what will happen'. Hie is *quia nescit quod futurum est sicut enim erit quis annuntiabit ei*, 'since he does not know what is to be, for as it will be, who will tell him?', which corresponds to M, but in the body of the commentary Jerome gives another version, closer to V and S: *quia nescit quid factum sit et quid futurum sit post eum, quis annuntiabit ei*, 'since he does not know what has been done, and what is to be after him, who will tell him?' He claims to be offering 'now' (*nunc*) a word-for-word translation of the Hebrew, so that we may know there to be a second meaning, which he paraphrases as *nec ea quae praeterierint, scire possumus, nec ea quae futura sint, ita ut sunt futura, cognoscere*, 'we are able neither to know things that may have been in the past, nor to understand things that may be in the future, as they are future'.

All this is confusing, but it appears to suggest that Jerome knew two versions of the text, one in Hebrew, which he translates and offers as the text of Hie, and the other probably in Latin (although it is true that de Rossi notes a few late Hebrew manuscripts with שהיה, and it is not impossible that he had found two different readings in Hebrew). The latter gives a reference to past and future that he perhaps assumes would be familiar to his readers (and he will return to a version of it in V).[3] It is noteworthy that, as in S, the past/future version presented by Jerome includes a reference to 'after him', and it seems likely that S has drawn its reading from a similar source—perhaps ultimately a Greek text that has conflated this verse, with its future tense, and 10.14. It is not likely that σ' has been a significant influence here, as Goldman suggests in a confusing note, but like S and V, its reading τίς γὰρ τὰ ἐσόμενα ἀναγγελεῖ αὐτῷ, 'for who will tell him the things to be', does not reflect the -כ of כאשר.

It is not clear whether these versions are based on a text that actually had אשר for כאשר, not least because it is not clear what the function of כאשר is supposed to be here—and it may have been ignored deliberately.[4] This very common expression (כ- + אשר) is used to co-ordinate things, so we find it, for instance, applied to events or behaviours that are 'just as' they had been commanded or predicted (e.g. Gen 7.9; 41.54; Jer 17.22) or 'just as' they have been seen or heard (e.g. 2 Kgs 2.19; Jer 26.11). It is also employed (often with כן) to set up similes and analogies (e.g. Judg 1.7; Isa 66.20; Jer 19.11; cf. Eccl 5.14), but such co-ordination can be temporal or circumstantial (cf. 4.17; 5.3). In this verse, it is very widely understood to mean 'how', but that is essentially a guess from context, and it is hard either to reconcile such a translation with the normal usage or to find any analogous use that makes כאשר equivalent to

---

[3] In his later *Dialogus aduersus Pelagianos*, 2.5 (PL 23, 541), Jerome cites the text as *nemo scit quid futurum sit quia sicuti est quis annuntiabit ei?* This is similar to Hie, but if the text is accurate, it introduces a *present* tense 'as it is, who will tell him?', which makes a different distinction between two time periods. Immediately before this, however, his citation of 2.17 is very paraphrastic, so we should perhaps not put too much weight on it.

[4] They clearly did not, at least, have באשר, which Kennicott notes in four manuscripts, and which is likely behind the ἐν ᾧ of Codex Graecus Venetus. Gentry notes a plus after αὐτῷ in mostly hexaplaric manuscripts of G: ἐν τῷ ἐσομένῳ μετ' αὐτόν, 'in what will be after him'. That aligns this verse to 6.12 and 10.14, and the μετ' αὐτόν resembles a translation of מאחריו at 10.14 attributed to the Three (see my note there). The ἐν, however, does not come from that verse, and seems too awkward simply to be an adaptation to context (one manuscript has just τὸ ἐσόμενον, which provides a much easier fit). In its fuller form, therefore, this reading has conceivably incorporated another, earlier rendering of באשר.

אֵיךְ. Schoors tries to paraphrase as 'what it will be like', presumably understanding כאשר to mean 'like what', but it is hard to treat אשר as some sort of free-standing pronoun (we would need 'as what, it will be', rather than 'as what it will be'), even if we are willing to disregard uses of כאשר elsewhere.

To the extent that כאשר can have a temporal nuance, Seow's understanding, 'no one can tell them when it will happen', is more plausible, but, again, such a use is outside the normal scope of the term. It is far more likely that Qohelet is saying, in effect, 'when it does actually happen, nobody will tell him what is happening', and this accords with the word-order, which places the כאשר clause before the מי.

8.7 who is going to explain to him?] Or 'who will inform him?' See the note at 6.12. The verb is used absolutely in this sense at Gen 41.24.

8.8 who governs] Lit. 'having authority over': שליט is an adjective here. Although only the ש of שליט is preserved in Hebrew, Sir 9.13 appears to have used a similar construction: איש שליט ל- with an infinitive, in an expression that means 'a man who has the power/authority to kill' (ὃς ἔχει ἐξουσίαν τοῦ φονεύειν). Substantival uses, and the usage in Aramaic, suggest that the implication is of authority rather than capacity: the point is not that humans are physically incapable or have insufficient strength. The object of the control is expressed using -ב (cf. similarly ביום, below), which is rendered using ἐν πνεύματι in G: the Greek accordingly takes on a sense of being 'powerful in spirit'. α' seems to have used a simple dative τῷ πνεύματι (see Marshall: the citation is not explicit), while ms 788 records for σ' a genitive πνεύματος, which suggests that Symmachus may have construed the clause a little differently.

8.8 wind[1, 2]] Or 'spirit', 'life-breath': it is impossible in English to capture the potential ambiguity of the Hebrew. G elsewhere differentiates the two senses (cf. the note 'wind' at 1.6), so may understand 'spirit' here, perhaps in the way that Hie, V *spiritu* / *spiritum* makes this a matter of the life-breath (and Jerome speaks of our inability to hold this back at death, as does T). Because it fits well with what follows, some modern commentators have also preferred this meaning (e.g., Sacchi; Barolín, 'Eclesiastés 8:1-8', 16). The difficulty with it is that the רוח is not released, as it were, only at death, and so if it is understood just in those terms, the claim might be taken to mean that humans are unable to hold their breath. It is noteworthy also that there is no possessive pronoun here: the claim is about 'the רוח', not '*their* רוח', which would have made a reference to breath unambiguous. With most scholars, therefore, I take the primary implication here to be 'wind', and Qohelet's first statement to be, in effect, setting a point of comparison for the next: the lack of control over death is as undeniable as the fact that no human can control the wind. It is very possible, though, that Qohelet intends the claim to be ambiguous, with a secondary implication becoming clear as soon as he goes on to talk about death.

Irwin, 'Ecclesiastes 8:2-9', 130, makes the interesting suggestion that רוח here has the sense 'anger', and that the reference here is to the anger of the king. That sense is certainly possible, although in passages like Prov 29.11 the noun probably connotes something broader, like 'temper', but the interpretation belongs to Irwin's broader understanding, that the same court setting is presumed throughout 8.2-9, and it is difficult to demonstrate such a setting after 5b.

8.8 so as to restrain the wind] Despite the certainty with which *BHS* describes this as an addition, there is no text-critical evidence to support that opinion (which has likely been derived from Galling's 1940 commentary).

8.8 governing] M does not repeat the adjectival שליט here, but has instead the noun שלטון, so the literal sense is 'there is no governor over/in the day'. This variation is generally supported by the other versions, but most manuscripts of G have a second participle ἐξουσιάζων, as though translating שליט again, while the noun ἐξουσία, although accepted as G* by Rahlfs and Gentry, is found in relatively few, and could well reflect assimilation towards a text like M. If the noun is indeed secondary in G, the most likely explanation for the second participle would be that שליט was repeated accidentally in the source-text.

8.8 death's day] Most manuscripts of G lack an article here, and Goldman supposes that it was lacking in the original translation, which would imply a reading יום מות in the source-text. This is affirmed somewhat by the lack of an article in G's equivalent to במלחמה (see below), which serves as a parallel to 'day of death' in the G text. In 7.1, the only other place where the expression occurs, Qohelet uses an article, and if יום מות is, in fact, the original reading here, which is very possible, then there may be a personification of death involved (cf. Seow's discussion of the 'battle'). That would make it clearer that Qohelet is claiming nobody can control the appearances of death, rather than that nobody has power to control the time of their own death—but I think that this is probably the sense anyway. I have tried to avoid coming down on the side of one reading or the other in my translation.

8.8 there will be no mission] The point is either that one cannot go out to fight death, or, perhaps, that no rescue-mission will be sent. משלחת appears elsewhere in the Bible only at Ps 78.49, where it refers to a group of angels 'sent' by God to destroy, although it is used similarly in Aramaic to refer to an angelic emissary in 1QapGen VI, 13, 15 (cf. I, 26?). In *m. Baba Meṣiʿa* 7:9 (cf. *b. Baba Meṣiʿa* 93b) it is used of incursions by wild animals on a flock, and Numbers Rabbah 14 uses it of a 'mission' on which somebody has been sent. All the evidence suggests, then, that the word refers either to raiding parties or to missions of a more general sort. Rashbam, accordingly, thinks of soldiers being sent to battle the angel of death, and Desvoeux (135, 275) of embassies that cannot be sent in a time of war.

Among the ancient versions, σ' has οὐδε ἔστι(ν) παρατάξασθαι εἰς πόλεμον, 'there is no drawing up in battle-order for war', which must presumably express the idea that humans will be unable to prepare for death, and which also understands משלחת in terms of a military mission or formation. T, on the other hand, has a reference to weapons that suggests the translator saw a link with the noun שֶׁלַח (cf. Kamenetzky, 224). This link is pursued by Ibn Ezra and more recently both by Ehrlich and by Cohen, 'Studies in Hebrew Lexicography', 183, who cite the declaration in the Midrash Rabbah to Deut 9, that no man can make weapons that will save him from the angel of death. The other versions and subsequent commentators, however, have generally rejected the established uses of the noun, and derived the sense of משלחת directly from one of the many uses of the verb שלח. Correspondingly, they have usually also understood it to be a 'sending' of some sort—usually a 'sending-away' or 'discharge'—rather than as someone or something 'sent'.

Gordis is a notable exception, since he sees an ellipsis here for 'sending (stretching out) of the hand', as in Isa 11.14 משלוח ידם, which he believes (questionably) to be an expression of control. If that were the sense of the noun, Qohelet would be saying something like 'there is no conquest by battle', and Gordis' interpretation is hardly satisfactory, but the -ב of במלחמה is awkward for other interpretations as well: were the 'sending' something like the 'discharge from war' that RSV and many others would like, we might expect מן (במלחמה never means 'in time of war', although see below on the text), while we should not expect a preposition at all if the reference were to 'ending' a war (so Thilo: 'Man kann einen einmal begonnenen Krieg nicht nach Belieben abbrechen', 'One cannot break off a war once it has begun').

Among the other suggestions that have been made, Kuhn, *Erklärung*, 43, emends the text to מלחשת, derived from לחש, which he takes to be a word for a protective amulet; the suggestion is picked up in Galling 1940 and gives a reasonable sense, but it involves a speculative emendation to a word that is not known ever to have existed. Zimmermann, 'Aramaic Provenance', 42, avoiding emendation but switching languages, notes the Aramaic use of שלח for undressing, and thinks that the reference is to taking off armour in battle. This would be more plausible if armour were actually mentioned or if the verb ever had that connotation in particular, but such a reference does not, in any case, have any clear connection with the context. Midrash Rabbah and Rashi understand a different sort of ellipsis, and speak of 'sending' someone to fight in one's place: this suggestion has also been made more recently by Seow, who argues that there is an allusion to a practice of people being paid to fulfil the military obligations of the wealthy. Since he rejects 'discharge' on the grounds that discharges or exemptions were, in fact, permitted (cf. Deut 20.1-8), then it seems strange that Seow should go on to find a reference to an actual practice, which would similarly make Qohelet's claim false.

This discrepancy does, however, raise an interesting question: should we be treating what Qohelet says here as a general statement about wars or battles, or is this third statement with אין talking more specifically about the 'day of death', as Symmachus and others suppose? If we presuppose the former, then it is clear that many of these proposals are, in fact, counter-factual, although it is the more patent absurdity of a claim that 'there is no mission in war' that has driven most commentators in the first place to reject the attested meanings of משלחת. If, on the other hand, we take Qohelet to be talking solely about the human inability to fight death, then those meanings seem entirely appropriate to the martial context, and are to be preferred to speculative translations of the noun based on no other usage.

The slightly unusual form of משלחת has attracted a certain amount of attention, and Dahood, 'Canaanite-Phoenician', 46, adduces a number of parallels to support his claim that it is a Phoenician formation; Piotti, 'Le Teorie Aramaica', 351-52, supplies a number of counter-examples from Hebrew.

8.8 into battle] Or 'in the day of battle': it is difficult to establish the original reading. Apart from the article τῷ, which is presumably drawn from the vocalization attested in M, Rahlfs' reading ἐν τῷ πολέμῳ, 'in the war', is based entirely on Hie *in bello*: the manuscript tradition here overwhelmingly supports a reading ἐν ἡμέρᾳ πολέμου, 'in a day of war', which is also the meaning of S. It seems very likely that the translator found ביום מלחמה in his source-text: it is most unlikely that he is just harmonizing with the earlier 'day of death' (so Salters, 'Observations on the Septuagint', 171), or rendering more explicitly a sense that is implicit in the Hebrew of M, as Schoors suggests: both would be seriously out of step with his usual translation technique. At most, it is possible that the reading resulted from a secondary harmonization, very early in the course of the text's transmission, but that is hardly a simpler explanation.

The question is then, of course, whether we should regard this ביום מלחמה or the במלחמה of M as the earlier reading. Goldman, rightly, hesitates between the two, and it is possible to see both, on the one hand, how the G reading might have emerged from a doubling of the במ (McNeile, 147), perhaps under the influence of the preceding ביום, and, on the other, how the M text could have appeared when a scribe's eye skipped to the second מ. On my understanding of the text, the variation makes little difference, although the G reading might facilitate some interpretations of the preceding משלחת.

There are no grounds for emending or giving a different sense to מלחמה itself, although Dahood, 'Canaanite-Phoenician', 211, has suggested that it should be understood in terms of a root *mlḥ*, which expresses sharpness in Ugaritic and cleverness in Arabic: with the final ה omitted, מלחם would then be an abstract noun in the plural, meaning 'cleverness'. Ginsberg, *Studies*, 29-30, thinks that an Aramaic בקברא, 'in the grave', got corrupted to or was misread as בקרבא, 'in war', and then translated accordingly into Hebrew. Dahood says that 'the present reading does not yield sense', and Ginsberg asks (30) 'Is there any other *plausible* explanation of the Hebrew במלחמה?', but few scholars seem to have shared their belief that the usual reading or understanding is somehow intolerable, and Piotti, 'Le Teorie Aramaica', 354-57, provides a detailed rebuttal of their proposals.

8.8 wickedness] Some interpreters have long been uncomfortable with a statement 'wickedness will not save its owners', because, as Fox puts it, this 'is a warning that no one would need'. Graetz accordingly proposed an emendation to עשר, 'wealth', which has been adopted by many and suggested tentatively as the proper reading in *BHS*. Others have tried simply to re-interpret the text as it stands. Dahood, 'Phoenician Background', 277-78, notes that 'the wicked' are paired with the rich in Isa 53.9, and that the sense 'wealthy' for רשע would fit better in Job 24.6 and Prov 11.7. Citing Ibn Ezra, who came to the same understanding on other grounds, he concludes that we must also read that sense here—even though it would open the floodgates to confusion in many more verses if רשע could indeed connote 'wealth'.

A different approach is taken by Rose (in *Rien de nouveau*, 253-54), who leaves the consonantal text as it stands, but vocalizes the verb as niph'al and the subject as 'a wicked man' (rather than 'wickedness'), then takes את as a preposition rather than as marker of the object. The result is a reading 'and the wicked man will not escape with his peers', which is fine except that it invents a new meaning for בעל. To change the meaning of the clause, there is really no option other than to emend the text, and there is no text-critical basis on which to do so: the versions fully support M here.

8.8 whoever resorts to it] Or 'its possessor(s)'; cf. Prov 1.19. The expression is similar to that used in 7.12 and, e.g., Prov 16.22. On the rendering in G, see the corresponding note at 5.10; σ' here has <τὸν> ἔχοντα αὐτήν, 'the person having it'; cf. 5.10, 12; 7.12. As usual, the form בעליו is probably to be understood as a plural serving as a singular, although it is marked in S here as plural, and a plural sense cannot be excluded for the Hebrew. The sense of the noun in conjunction with other nouns is discussed in the note 'in having a tongue' at 10.11, and uses such as that in Prov 1.19 suggest that there is a similar scope even when the nouns are not compounded directly. In 7.12 the case was rather different, both because the wisdom concerned was specific wisdom rather than wisdom in general, and because the situation was not tied to such a specific context. Although there is undoubtedly an echo here, therefore, the verses do not together constitute some general claim that 'wisdom will save the wise, but wickedness will not save the wicked'.

Given the scope of בעל, it hardly seems necessary to suppose, with Dahood, that it is here a dialectal form of פעל, and that the reference is to those 'working evil'.[5] That scope does allow, however, a broader understanding, and the expression could be rendered as 'anyone prone to it' or similar (cf. RSV 'those who are given to it'). This is almost equivalent to 'wickedness will not save the wicked', as I observed in the commentary, but I am also inclined

---

[5] See Dahood, 'Qoheleth and Northwest Semitic Philology', 361-62; 'Hebrew–Ugaritic Lexicography I', 303. Whitley adopts a similar view, but makes a connection with Ugaritic uses of *b'l* rather than with פעל.

to think that the reference in this context is to specific actions rather than inherent character, and have translated accordingly.

8.9 I observed all this] G, S have an initial conjunction, which Vinel thinks may have originated through reduplication of the preceding ו in G's source-text. It probably was a Hebrew variant (McNeile, 147), but the same preceding ו could as well have led to its loss elsewhere in the tradition—if it did not simply drop out as redundant. It makes little difference to the sense whether we read it or not. Gentry reports an unattributed but plausibly hexaplaric (σ'?) reading in ms 788, ἄπαντα ταῦτα συνεῖδον, 'I understood all these things', which makes את כל זה plural.

8.9 I applied...the sun] This is very close to 1.13 אשר כל על...לבי את נתתי נעשה תחת השמים, and there is probably a deliberate echo of previous sayings; see also, for instance, 4.13 השמש תחת נעשה אשר הרע המעשה. S in fact has a plus, 'set my heart *to knowing*', which is a reminiscence of 1.17; cf. 7.25.

A number of later Hebrew manuscripts (see de Rossi, Miletto) have אל rather than את, so that Qohelet 'gives to his heart to know', which is an obvious error.

The verb ונתון is an infinitive absolute, apparently serving as a continuation after ראיתי (cf. וראה in 9.11, and GKC §113 z; J-M §123 r), and probably expressing a circumstance associated with the first verb rather than a simple sequence of events.

8.9 at the time when] M עת אשר has no close biblical parallel, but is probably to be understood as an equivalent to the expression עת ש- found in *m. ʿOrlah* 1.2, where עת שבאו אבותינו לארץ מצאו means 'At the time when our ancestors entered the land, they found' (so Ginsberg). The lack of an article should not be taken necessarily to imply, therefore, that Qohelet is talking about 'a' time or particular period when what follows was true (Sacchi, nevertheless, would read העת). G τὰ ὅσα (some manuscripts πάντα ὅσα), 'whatever things (with respect to which)', implies a reading את אשר (cf. 2.12), but M is supported by S, T, and α' καιρὸς ὡς ἐκυρίευσεν ὁ ἄνθρωπος, 'a time as the human lorded'. V *interdum*, 'sometimes', also probably supports M, but Hie has a simple conjunction *et*, which does not explicitly support either reading. It seems likely that the reading in G was found as a phonetic error in its source-text, rather than created in an effort to interpret or to avoid עת, as Euringer and some subsequent commentators have suggested— McNeile, 147, considers it an early variant.[6] The reading of σ' is attested as ἔστιν ὅτε ἐξουσίασεν ἄνθρωπος ἀνθρώπου εἰς κακὸν ἑαυτοῦ, 'it is when human rules human to his own hurt', which would seem to support M, but ms 788 adds two words, καὶ ὅσων, apparently corresponding to G τὰ ὅσα,

---

[6] Dahood, 'Canaanite-Phoenician', 51, unnecessarily offers two examples of עת being used as an 'accusative of time' (both without a subsequent relative). In passing, he asserts that Zapletal adopted the reading את, but that is not the case in either edition of his commentary.

which are difficult to integrate comfortably with the rest unless we assume that further text is missing. If this new reading is correct, it is possible that Symmachus attempted somehow to render both variants.

Krüger, 'Meaningful Ambiguities', 70, notes the possibility of reading the text without assuming 'at the time', either as a statement that 'there was a time when...' or as a nominal clause, 'a time when one man had power over another has (always) been detrimental for him'. The former, with an implied יש (cf. Ginsburg), involves a harsh ellipsis unless the עת is supposed to be equated with the preceding כל זה—although some such understanding presumably lies behind the assertion of V, that 'sometimes' one human rules over another to his hurt. Budde suggests that an original יש dropped out after שמש, and Michel, 'Qohelet-Probleme', 91, wants to read a 'unipolar' nominal clause which has dispensed with יש: he translates with 'es gibt', 'there is', but such a construction would probably have to be read as an exclamation, 'A time when...!'. The reading with a more regular nominal clause is not grammatically problematic, and although it is notably not the way that any of the versions have interpreted the text, it is a plausible construal. The main difficulty is that the construction would have to be taken as very loose, since strictly it would be the 'time' (presumably 'the occasion'), not the power, that is identified as harmful, and it seems unlikely that that is the intended point.

8.9 had power] Or 'has power'. In the absence of any other explicit indication, the tense of the verb has probably to be derived from the initial ראיתי, although the ancient translators have taken it in various ways. Joüon would read it as a participle, which would give a firmer indication of a present tense, but that is, of course, itself a matter of vocalization, and so is not explicit in the consonantal text.[7] The verb itself is שלט, which corresponds to the שליט and שלטון of the last verse: see the commentary.

8.9 to hurt him] Or 'to his own detriment'. M vocalizes לרע לו, as 'for harm to him' (cf. V *malum*, 'harm'; σ', above), but G, Hie, S, T all have verbal forms, and may have read or understood an infinitive—G, in particular, is unlikely to have switched from a noun to a verb for purely interpretative reasons, as Goldman suggests, and Yi, 21, thinks that the translator either read לרע as a hiph'il infinitive with syncopated ה, or encountered the reading להרע which *BHS* claims is to be found in one manuscript (although it is not clear which, or on what authority that claim is made).

The more significant issue is the reference of לו, which σ' εἰς κακὸν ἑαυτοῦ takes to be reflexive: the human doing the ruling is harming himself. This interpretation has attracted a minority of scholars, including Hitzig, and cannot be excluded on linguistic grounds: the Hebrew itself is ambiguous.

---

[7] Joüon, 'Notes de syntaxe', 225. The word is actually written שולט and pointed as a participle in Bodleian ms 2333; see Ratzabi, 'Massoretic Variants', 105, who thinks that T reflects the same reading. This reading is also noted elsewhere by Loevy, *Libri Kohelet*, 23.

Introduction to 8.10-17

Invisible Justice

(8.10) And then I saw wicked people who approach and enter a holy place: they walk about and are praised in the city for having done so. This too is an illusion: (8.11) since no indictment of wrongful behaviour is brought swiftly, the heart of humans is therefore encouraged within them to do what is wrong— (8.12) because a sinner does what is wrong, but puts off for himself his death. For I know too that it will be well for God-fearers who fear before him, (8.13) but that it will not be well for the wicked person, and, like a shadow, he will not prolong life, who has no fear before God.

(8.14) There is an illusion that is perpetrated on the earth, that there are righteous people who have an experience fitting for the behaviour of the wicked, and there are wicked people who have an experience fitting for the behaviour of the righteous. I said that this too is an illusion, (8.15) but I commended enjoyment, that there is nothing good for the human beneath the sun, except to eat, drink, and enjoy; and it will accompany him in his work for all the days of his life which God has granted him beneath the sun.

(8.16) When I had set my heart to knowing wisdom, and to observing the work that is done on the earth, since furthermore by day and by night it saw no sleep with its eyes, (8.17) then I saw all the achievement of God, that a human cannot discover the achievement which has been achieved beneath the sun, on account of which that human will work hard to seek, but will not discover. And also, even if the wise man says that he is going to know, he will not be able to discover.

In 8.10, Qohelet appears at first glance to move dramatically away from the issues about human powerlessness and the limits of wisdom that preoccupied him in 8.1-9. The text is very difficult at points, but his concern now seems to be instead with problems surrounding divine justice: the wicked are not punished at once, encouraging humans to be wicked, even if that will not really be to their benefit, and there is sometimes, more broadly, no apparent correlation between what people deserve and what they get. When Qohelet in 8.15 brings this back to his commendation of enjoyment, however, it starts to become clear that human limitations are still the issue, and the following verses make this explicit. To be sure, the nature of the limitations has changed. In 8.1-9, the problem was essentially one of power: humans lack control, not only in the face of a powerful deity, but over nature and death. Here the problem is instead one of understanding: the concealment of divine reward and punishment, in particular, means that humans cannot use observation or experience to determine how they should behave in a way that would win them reward—it is all too easy to end up trying to emulate the wicked, when it is the wicked who seem to be doing well. Ultimately, humans can do no more than seek the one good that is guaranteed—pleasure in their life and work—because the very way that God works tends to obstruct any human understanding of his work. As Qohelet emphasizes in closing, even the wise, who might claim that they can gain some insight, will never be able to do so, and his own tireless efforts have revealed to him nothing but the futility of the project—an observation that ties the discussion to his broader, ongoing concern with the limitations of wisdom.

8.10-13

(8.10) And then I saw wicked people who approach and enter a holy place: they walk about and are praised in the city for having done so. This too is an illusion: (8.11) since no indictment of wrongful behaviour is brought swiftly, the heart of humans is therefore encouraged within them to do what is wrong— (8.12) because a sinner does what is wrong, but puts off for himself his death. For I know too that it will be well for God-fearers who fear before him, (8.13) but that it will not be well for the wicked person, and, like a shadow, he will not prolong life, who has no fear before God.

Commentary

Qohelet is making a single point in 8.10-13, but he expresses it in a complicated way. First, in 8.10, he reports his observation that the wicked walk about with impunity even in 'a holy place'—perhaps the temple—and receive praise for having done so. Typically, he concludes that this is another *hebel*, or illusion, but less typically he goes on to explain why. Broadly, the reason is that this situation embodies something that misleads humans: Qohelet expresses his own certainty that things will go better for the God-fearing than for the wicked, but he acknowledges that this is not what people actually see. Since wickedness is not identified instantly, the wicked seem actually to be doing well, and so another aspect or consequence of the illusion is that those who see them carrying on are driven to emulate them. The problem will be compounded in 8.14, when Qohelet observes another *hebel*, that people may be misled not only by this deferral, but by the fact that the righteous and wicked may seem each to receive the just deserts of the other. The basic issue, though, is similar to that spelled out in Mal 3.15, where the rebellious are taken to be blessed, because those who do evil seem not only to be supported, but to get away with it when they put God to the test.

We saw earlier that Qohelet probably understands divine judgment to consider the behaviour of individuals in the round, and his advice in 7.16-18 relies on that idea. We should not presume, therefore, that he wishes things were different, and that sins were identified by being punished instantly. What he draws out here, by comparing what he sees with what he 'knows' to be true, is a side-effect of the way judgment works, which creates problems because people cannot understand what is happening on the basis of their own observations. Accordingly, it would be a mistake, I think, to see here an attack on conventional ideas about retribution (e.g., Mazzinghi, 'Divine Violence', 552). As often, Qohelet is concerned not to protest or lament the realities of the human condition, but to describe the consequences that flow from human misinterpretation of the visible evidence. If there is a criticism here at all, it is not of God or of belief in judgment, but of people's willingness to jump to conclusions on the basis of limited and misleading data. I think his principal intention, though, is not to criticize anybody or anything, but to offer a vivid illustration of the way that human motives are governed by misperception.

Scholars have often been inclined also to see Qohelet's observations here as radical and unorthodox (Mazzinghi, 'Esegesi ed ermeneutica', offers a wide-ranging survey of the scholarship)—not least because many have chosen to excise the more 'conventional' 12b-13 as secondary, to take them as citations of an opinion with which Qohelet disagrees, or at least to treat them as standing in tension with the rest, rather than as the basis on which Qohelet interprets his observations (Sneed, 'A Note on Qoh 8,12b-13', is an honourable exception, and draws out the connections in a way with which I largely agree). It is hard to say, however, whether these verses would have been regarded as problematic by the original audience, who may not all have subscribed to the rose-tinted outlook of Ps 37.25, and its claim that the righteous do not suffer. Qohelet comes as close here as he ever does to the principal concerns of the book of Job, which likewise explores the ways in which humans, without the insights granted by its prologue to readers of that book, struggle to interpret the evidence of divine retribution. It would be wrong to presume that more simplistic statements on the subject somehow constituted the norm, and it seems likely that Qohelet is touching on a problem that was widely recognized, and doing so in a way that is far from theologically subversive.

8.10] This is another verse that is often regarded as among the most problematic in the book (there are very helpful surveys of the problems and of the scholarship in Debel, 'What about the Wicked?', and Lavoie, 'J'ai vu'). I take Qohelet's original point to have been that the wicked not only seem to enter even holy places with impunity, but also receive praise for doing so. That is not an uncommon understanding; it is not, however, what any of the ancient witnesses to the text actually say. Despite some other significant differences between them, all those witnesses refer to the burial of the wicked. The Greek, for example, means, 'Then I saw the wicked carried into tombs; and from a holy place, and they went and were praised in the city that they did so', while the Masoretic Hebrew text seems to say 'Then I saw the wicked buried, and they came, and from a holy place they went, and they caused it to be forgotten of themselves in the city that they did so' (or just possibly, 'caused those who acted rightly to be forgotten in the city').

Even if we can find any coherent sense in these statements, which is questionable, it is difficult to see how they are supposed to fit with Qohelet's point, which is drawn out more clearly in the next few verses: if it is the apparent survival of the wicked long beyond their sins that poses a problem, why does he begin by talking about their deaths? The only way really to retain this reference is to understand that the wicked are receiving funerals and burials that are better than those of the righteous (Fox even goes so far as to suggest that the corpses of the righteous are being neglected), or that they should not have been granted burials at all (so Weißflog, 'Worum geht es', citing Deut 28.26). The text itself, however, says nothing explicit of the sort, and if that was indeed Qohelet's point, he has left us not only to read a lot in, but also with an observation that still sits poorly in the context.

Accordingly, I have followed many other commentators here in adopting an emendation to the text that is speculative, in that it is supported by no actual witnesses, but very slight: this assumes that an original word *qrbym*, 'approaching', was mistakenly transcribed in an early copy of the text as *qbrym*, 'buried' or 'tombs', and that the subsequent differences between the witnesses arise from efforts to make sense of that new text, and/or further errors that may have been provoked by it, once the clear sense and structure of the sentence had been lost. Whether we adopt that emendation or not, there are other emendations or choices to be made, so it does not let us off the hook entirely, but it does supply the basis for an interpretation that makes much more sense.

If Qohelet is indeed saying that the wicked not only survive when they should not, but actually walk happily around on holy ground without penalty, he is presumably also suggesting that for them to walk around a holy place is different from walking around anywhere else: when they effectively present themselves and linger before God in such a way, the wicked consciously or unconsciously almost invite retribution—'tempt fate', as it were—and, when none comes, they leave safely with their reputations actually enhanced. Of course, although holiness is potentially dangerous, and concerns about ritual contamination have been much discussed by biblical scholars in other contexts, there is no actual biblical notion that the wicked will somehow be struck down instantly if they enter the temple or any other place that might be regarded as 'holy'—so Qohelet is talking about a perception, and not suggesting that they actually should have been struck down.

8.11-12] Although he will go on to talk about divine judgment, Qohelet is likely not, at the beginning of 8.11, talking specifically about the pronouncement of that judgment, or the carrying out of any sentence. Rather, he observes more generally that, when bad behaviour passes without immediate condemnation (perhaps on any side), people are naturally more willing to behave in that way, taking silence as affirmation (the wicked are praised, after all), or at least as permission. It is only in 8.12 that this is identified as a problem with the application of divine justice in particular: God's condemnation of such behaviour is expected to involve the death of the perpetrator, so when no thunderbolts descend, as it were, and the sinner carries on living, others fail to understand how dangerous the behaviour actually is. The text is difficult again at this point, and the extent of the sinner's continued sinning has probably become exaggerated by versions that import the notion of 'a hundred' (cf. RSV 'though a sinner does evil a hundred times', based on the Hebrew). It is likely that the original had no such specification, and the problem for Qohelet is not so much that sinners can keep sinning so long as they remain alive, but that the passing of any time obscures the causal connection between their behaviour and the punishment that, he believes, will eventually overtake them (a problem that is addressed more briefly in Sir 5.4). It is the invisibility of that connection which frees humans to believe either that bad behaviour cannot really be so bad, or that it will be allowed to pass without meaningful punishment.

Notes

8.10 And then] The combination בכן is common in later Aramaic for 'then', but in biblical Hebrew is found only elsewhere at Esth 4.16 (cf. also Sir 13.7): Schoors is right to point out that the evidence does not support classifying it as an 'Aramaism', and it is interesting to note, in fact, that T renders it analytically as ובקושתא, 'and in truth'. V does not render it at all. The rare uses elsewhere do not really support Eaton's contention that it must mean 'in such circumstances', which has been picked up by Garrett, 'Use and Abuse', 171.

8.10 who approach and enter a holy place] There is no 'who' in the original, but I read קרבים ובאים מקום קדוש and take this to be an asyndetic relative clause (cf. σ', V, below).

At this point, M and G diverge significantly. M קברים ובאו וממקום קדוש יהלכו has to be understood literally as something like '(I saw wicked people) buried, and they came, and from a holy place they were going/will go'. The reading of G is complicated, but it usually appears as: εἰς τάφους εἰσαχθέντας καὶ ἐκ τοῦ ἁγίου καὶ ἐπορεύθησαν, 'brought to tombs and out of the holy one and they went'. This reading may be in part the result of errors in the transmission of the Greek text, and it is generally supposed that G* had τόπου for τοῦ, so that there would, in fact, have been a 'place' equivalent to M וממקום. It seems likely also that the differences between M and G have resulted to some extent from a different vocalization of קברים: G seems to have understood קְבָרִים, 'graves', where M has קְבֻרִים, a passive participle of the verb, meaning 'buried'.

It is more difficult to judge what has happened in the case of ובאו / εἰσαχθέντας, where G itself now has a passive participle and lacks the conjunction found in M. It is usually suggested (cf. *BHS*) that the translator has understood a hophʻal here, which would give the appropriate causative nuance and also the passive voice, so many commentators have proposed the participle מוּבָאִים. If that reading was earlier, and a number of commentators take it actually to be original, then it is possible to see how a sequence קברים מובאים וממקום might have become the current M קברים ובאו וממקום through haplography of the initial מ and of the final ים (before ומ); for it to have happened the other way round is less likely—that would require duplication of characters at each end of the word (cf. Podechard).

Goldman proposes instead that the translator found יבאו, rather than a participle, and vocalized it as a (passive) qal or hophʻal written defectively. This is an elegant solution, but it struggles to explain the form of εἰσαχθέντας: Yi, 151, 167, lists some 26 places where the translator renders a finite verb form using a participle, but all of these are relative clauses, and only in 5.8b (נעבד → εἰργασμένου) is the relative clause asyndetic, unmarked by אשר or -ש; only in the particular circumstances of 1.11 and 10.14, moreover, has the translator used an aorist participle for a yiqtol. Given that he has also felt constrained exceptionally to supply a preposition in εἰς τάφους (it seems unlikely that was already in his source-text; cf. Yi, 139), something has clearly pushed him firmly towards this understanding.[1]

As for the other versions, Hie *et tunc uidi impios sepultos et uenerunt et de loco* translates the same text as M and understands it in the same way; T probably does the same, although it understands 'coming' in terms of being annihilated from the world. For the Three, we have no equivalents for the text up to קברים, but for α' (and θ', according to Syh) we then have (in Greek) καὶ ἦλθον, which corresponds to M. The reading of σ' is very interesting, however: οἳ καὶ ὁπότε περιῆσαν, 'who, even while they survived', has doubtless influenced V *qui etiam cum aduiuerent*, which means the same, and interprets the verb in terms of 'living'.[2] The habitual aspect implied by that interpretation also suits the reading of S, which has an active participle (ܘܐܬܝܢ *w'tyn*, 'and coming'). After that, α' and θ' ἐκ τόπου ἁγίου, 'from a holy place', corresponds to M וממקום קדוש, but with no initial conjunction, while σ' ἐν τόπῳ ἁγίῳ and V *in loco sancto*, 'in a holy place', seem to translate מקום קדוש or במקום קדוש, with no -מ, and, likewise, no initial conjunction.

The other versions support M וממקום קדוש in full, although G, of course, only supports it if we restore τόπου for τοῦ. Goldman, however, declines to do so: he believes an original ובמקדש became וממקדש, as reflected in the καὶ ἐκ τοῦ ἁγίου of the Greek manuscripts, with M then finally inserting מקום 'for the sake of enlarging the concept of "sanctuary"'. Before looking at his explanation for such a transformation, we should note that the only possible witnesses for his proposed ובמקדש are σ' and V, which are paraphrasing here and lack the conjunction; since they render מקום, moreover, then if they reflect

---

[1] When Lavoie, 'J'ai vu', 81, objects that an aorist passive might have been used to render a qal by pointing to just such a translation in the Greek of 1 Kgs 7.14 (3 Kgdms 7.2), he ignores the switch from main verb to participle, but is also, of course, citing the work of a very different translator—and he goes on to cite yet other Greek translators (of the Pentateuch and of Ezekiel) when trying to show that hophʻal forms of the verb might anyway have been translated using active verbs.

[2] We could just possibly read the verb περιῆσαν as an error for, or a strange writing of περιήεσαν, from περίειμι, 'go round' (cf. Wisd 8.18). This would be closer to M, and seems to be presumed by the translation in Lavoie, 'J'ai vu', 81. However, the same expression is found elsewhere as ὁπότε περιῆν, meaning 'in his/her lifetime' or 'while he/she was still alive': see, e.g., the first-century CE mortgage and loan documents, P. Oxy. 243.10 and P. Oxy 1282.20-21, 27, and the second-century P. Gen. 1.6, 4 and P. Phil. 11, 8. If Jerome has indeed drawn his understanding from σ', he has most likely interpreted the expression correctly in terms of this common technical or idiomatic usage.

a Hebrew reading with -ב at all, it must be one which has defied Goldman's process in order to have both the early 'in' and the later, secondary 'place'.[3] What he proposes, furthermore, is substantially more complicated than restoring τόπου for τοῦ in G, so if not an entirely speculative emendation, it is at least based on very slight evidence.

What motivates the change, according to Goldman, is an earlier corruption of an original קרבים, 'approaching', to קברים: a possibility that we shall come to below—I agree with him on this. On Goldman's understanding, though, the original text was the very different ובכן ראיתי רשעים קרבים יבאו ובמקדש, and the meaning 'And I have seen wicked men approaching (God); they come and… in the sanctuary'. This is, of course, very attractive in terms of the sense that it gives, but we should bear in mind that nothing after the uncontroversial ובכן ראיתי רשעים is actually attested in any ancient version or represents the clear basis of any ancient translation: it is all more-or-less plausible conjecture. In strictly text-critical terms, moreover, the only significant issues here are the 'in' of σ' and V, alongside their omission of a conjunction (with α' and θ'), and the admittedly difficult problem of reconciling ובאו with εἰσαχθέντας; all else arises from the exegetical problem of understanding how the burial of the dead might fit Qohelet's broader point.

In terms of the witnesses themselves, probably the simplest way to reconcile their readings is to suppose that a variant ובאים existed, which is attested directly in S. The same pressure that led to σ' interpreting in terms of 'while they were still living'—the fact that the dead do not travel of their own accord[4]—could well have underpinned the understanding of G here,

---

[3] In fact, a few late manuscripts noted by Kennicott, de Rossi and Ginsburg, *Writings*, do have ובמקום: it is not impossible that this variant was early and informed σ', but it more probably shows just an independent reaction to the same problems.

[4] An ingenious way around this problem is proposed by Ibn Ezra and picked up by Ginsburg: the wicked are dying and being buried, but then they 'come again', in the sense that they are replaced (cf. 1.4, where בוא and הלך are contrasted to give a sense of succession). Lavoie, 'J'ai vu', 99, traces the opinion back in part to Tobiah ben Eliezer. Other problems aside, though, this requires that וממקום קדוש mark the start of a lengthy new sentence, in which the subject ('those who do right'—see below) does not appear until the very end or in which ממקום קדוש יהלכו has to be considered a sort of relative expression in its own right. 'Going from a holy place', furthermore, then has to mean something like 'die righteous', an idea for which there is no evidence. Pinker, 'Doings of the Wicked', 17, no less ingeniously emends ובאו to ואוב, and understands the wicked to be frequenting graves, 'a necromancer', and a holy place. Even allowing the curious word-order that this requires, though, we might expect prepositions with the nouns if that were the intended reading. Pinker understands the observation more broadly to be about the wicked doing the right thing, and that being forgotten. More mainstream is the interpretation of, e.g., Levy and Schwienhorst-Schönberger, which takes ובאו

that the sense of the participle must be passive even if its form was qal, so it may well have read the same, and not an actual hoph'al. This reading ובאים was proposed as the original in Hertzberg 1932, and later accepted in Driver, 'Problems and Solutions', 230 n. 5, I think rightly. If we set out the readings that seem to be reflected in the various versions, it is possible to see how all of them might be related quite straightforwardly to such an original:

                ובאים מקום

σ'   ובאים מקום (or ובאו מקום: loss of final מ before initial מ, reading of י as ו).

G, S   ובאים וממקום: reduplication of ים as ום.

α', θ'   ובאו ממקום: movement of final מ to next word, reading of י as ו.

M, Hie, T ובאו וממקום: movement of final מ to next word, reduplication of י as ו ו.

Of course, rather than each being a separate, coincidental development, it seems more probable that, for instance, the reading in M was derived from the Hebrew found by α' and θ', and that errors have provoked further errors—but it is difficult to put the readings in order with confidence. In any case, this is significantly less complicated than trying to relate M and σ' to a putative hoph'al מובאים behind G, or to explain why G might have rendered יבאו with εἰσαχθέντας.

If ובאים was indeed the earliest reading, then that, in fact, favours the popular emendation of קברים to קרבים on grounds of sense: Qohelet would be claiming to have seen how wicked people 'approach and enter a holy place'; cf. Isa 5.19 (and קרב, of course, was Qohelet's own choice of verb for 'approaching' in the temple at 4.17). We have already noted that Goldman accepts that emendation.[5] There is no particular need to give קרבים a litur-

---

to mean 'they die' or 'they go to their rest'. As Debel, 'What about the Wicked?', 145, points out, however, when Qohelet uses 'coming' and 'going' with reference to birth and death, he uses בא of birth, as we might expect, and it should be noted also that the order 'burial' then 'departure' seems odd whatever beliefs we might take to lie behind such a statement (contrast 12.5).

  [5] Goldman himself cites Serrano, 'I Saw the Wicked Buried', who, citing Gordis in turn, traces the idea back to Rudolph. In fact, Rudolph, 'Review of G. Kuhn', 226, merely mentions 8.10 in a list of verses where Rudolph likes the emendations proposed in Kuhn, *Erklärung*, and, anyway, this suggestion had already been made some years before in Burkitt, 'Is Ecclesiastes a Translation?', 25. A much earlier alternative to קברים is reflected in *b. Giṭṭin* 56b, which commends reading the word (for exegetical purposes) as קבוצים, 'gathered, assembled' (cf. Neh 5.16). Although he shows knowledge of this passage (see below on 'and are praised'), Rashi does not himself commend that reading directly, but

gical connotation, but to have at least one active verb here, of course, also significantly eases the understanding of כן עשו (see below). It is much harder to see what קברים might have meant, on the other hand, and if ובאים is indeed original, then the parallel form of the two participles would have to belie different uses (and time periods, cf. σ'). The least problematic way, although it is ugly, would be to suppose that Qohelet is looking at 'buried wicked', and recalling how they used to behave, rather than looking at wicked people 'being buried'. This is close to the understanding of Bartholomew, who claims that 'the MT is a problem only if we fail to discern the change in temporal reference in the latter part of the verse', and translates 'they used to go in and out of the holy place'. On such a reading, however, it is hard to explain without emendation the shift from M's qatal (or even weqatal) ובאו to yiqtol יהלכו if both verbs are supposed to have the same habitual past-time reference, and not much easier if we emend to ובאים. That is a problem also for attempts to import an indefinite or unspecified subject, with reference to the funeral rites granted the dead (cf. Lavoie, 'J'ai vu', 100), or to visitation of their tombs—and there is no explicit reference to any reverence or respect for the wicked or their graves (as in Job 21.32, which Fox compares), which would be the only way to find a point to this in the context.

As for the 'holy place', M^L and other early manuscripts point מקום as construct, suggesting a literal sense 'place of the holy (one)'—although de Rossi and Ginsburg, *Writings*, do find the absolute ('holy place') in some later sources (it was reportedly the reading of the famous Hillel codex, as Ginsburg notes), and that is probably how it was read by the versions. This is surely not a cemetery, as, e.g., Gordis and Jastrow, *Cynic*, suggest, given the ritual impurity of corpses (cf. Pinker, 'Doings of the Wicked', 7), or a grave (so Reines, 'Koheleth VIII, 10', who deletes a preposition and has the wicked go to their grave), but nor is it necessarily a temple: when the expression is used (with the absolute) in, e.g., Exod 29.31; Lev 7.6; 16.24, it apparently

perhaps alludes to it in his citation of Joel 4.2. Such rabbinic recommendations are not, of course, proposals for emendation, but this would not be unattractive as an alternative emendation, and would yield a similar sense—although it is not clear why Qohelet might portray the wicked as acting collectively. Resistance to emendation here has been based almost entirely on the lack of support from the versions (so, e.g., Debel, 'What about the Wicked?', 147), and sometimes comes unusually close to suggesting that 'absence of evidence is evidence of absence'. It should be borne in mind both that key variants in the Qumran manuscripts of the book find no echo in the ancient versions, and that all our versions are relatively late, drawing on a textual tradition that was probably already somewhat narrowed. Although support in those versions can help to demonstrate the existence of a variant text, the absence of such support does not exclude the possibility of an earlier variation, even if, especially when early errors have generated a text that remains broadly comprehensible, we can only argue for it on grounds of sense or coherence.

designates only a place that has been sanctified, so that no contamination can be picked up. Such a place may be a part of the sanctuary in some such references, but Deut 23.15 (ET 23.14) conceives of the whole camp of the Israelites being 'holy'. Although Mt 24.15 talks of the abomination standing ἐν τόπῳ ἁγίῳ, 'in a holy place', furthermore, the underlying reference may be to the Jerusalem temple, but the language is explicitly a cryptic circumlocution. Such terminology might also have been applied regularly to synagogues (Seow notes several references, and cf. Montgomery, 'Notes', 243), although Lavoie, 'J'ai vu', 96, notes the very late attestations of such usage. It is not clear, however, that the author wishes to single out any specific location, and he may have chosen his words to avoid doing so. Whether or not Qohelet is thinking of the temple in particular, which does not seem unlikely, his point concerns the encounter of the wicked with the holy (so, in principle, in whatever places might be considered holy). There is certainly little basis for Schwienhorst-Schönberger's contention that Qohelet is drawing a distinction between the wicked and those whose righteousness consisted specifically in attending the temple.

It is worth noting the unusual translation 'place of prostitution', proposed by Desvoeux (136, 561-65), which he favours on the grounds that the wicked must be visiting a place that *should* attract public condemnation, and which he justifies by reference to the supposed use of קָדֵשׁ and קְדֵשָׁה in connection with cult prostitution. Whatever one makes of that usage, קדשה, at least, clearly is used of women acting as, or like, prostitutes in Gen 38.21-22 and Hos 4.14, while 2 Kgs 23.7 speaks of בתי הקדשים in the Temple, associated in some way with the worship of Asherah. If such a sense was still current, one might expect a plural קדשים or קדשות here as well (cf. Lavoie, 'J'ai vu', 95), and the pairing with מקום would seem odd in such a context—or even misleading, given the other biblical references to 'holy places'—but this is probably the only route to any understanding that the wicked were doing something visibly immoral, albeit a tenuous one. Ginsburg sees the interpretation as 'additional evidence that learned men may be ignorant of the laws of exegesis'.

8.10 they walk about] Despite the יהלכו of M, G has a conjunction then a past tense καὶ ἐπορεύθησαν, 'and they went': the conjunction is lacking in some manuscripts, but there is little reason to follow Rahlfs in taking it as secondary. A καὶ already precedes ἐκ τό(πο)υ ἁγίου, and a second καὶ leaves those words stranded without a verb—the wicked cannot be coming out of the holy place, so in G's account the holy place has to be a specification of the place from which they were brought for burial ('and [it was] from a holy place, and they went...'). The awkwardness affirms quite strongly that the translator found the conjunction in his source. Syh suggests that α' and θ' shared this reading, which seems to reflect והלכו rather than M יהלכו. S ܐܙܠܘ 'zlw, on the other hand, supports M, as do Hie and T. The reading and sense of σ' is harder to pin down (see Marshall), but although all except one of the attestations imply a past tense (which may be a product of the way σ' understands the context—see above, and cf. the *erant* of V), none reflects a conjunction, so σ' too probably supports M.

As regards the form and sense of the verb, Hie, S, T have all apparently just read it as the strong form of the qal, יַהֲלֹכוּ (cf. Job 41.11): this is straightforward because they all presuppose וממקום קדוש, so the wicked can just 'go' out of the holy place. If we adopt the reading קרבים ובאים מקום קדוש, however, as suggested in the last note for the preceding words, then there is no preposition -מ and the 'holy place' is somewhere that the wicked enter, rather than somewhere that they explicitly leave. This problem confronted Symmachus, and the various forms from ἀναστρέφω that are attested for σ' probably reflect an understanding that the wicked were 'going about' in the holy place, which is picked up more vaguely in V's assertion that they were simply there. This suggests that σ' has chosen to understand יהלכו instead as a pi'el (cf. Goldman, who notes the use of the verb for the pi'el of הלך at Ps 55.15 ET 55.14), which is also the way the verb is pointed in M, despite M's very different text (which is probably intended to suggest that the wicked were 'going about out of' the holy place). That reading as a pi'el is probably the only practical course: הלך does not mean simply 'leave' or 'exit' (cf. the note at 6.9), so we could not easily read 'they go in and come out', even were the shift from participle to finite verb form not so awkward, while an absolute statement that 'they went' or 'they go' would make little sense. If we wish to read a qal, then perhaps the sense might be 'go on (living)', which we discussed at 6.8-9. There are no grounds for the suggestion by *BHS* that we might read יְהֻלָּלוּ, a pu'al from הלל meaning 'they were praised'.

8.10 and are praised] Or perhaps 'and were forgotten'. For the next verb, M^L reads וישתכחו as a hithpa'el from שכח with the sense 'they forgot themselves' or, more probably, 'were/caused themselves to be forgotten' (the form is otherwise unattested, but cf. the hiph'il at Jer 23.27). T and S support at least the derivation from שכח, but G ἐπῃνέθησαν, Hie *laudati sunt*, V *laudabantur*, σ' ἐπαινούμενοι all mean that the wicked were 'praised', and suggest a derivation from שבח instead—a verb that is attested elsewhere in the hithpa'el at Ps 106.47 (cf. 1 Chr 16.35); although α', θ' ἐκαυχήσαντο, 'they boasted', is apparently pejorative, it is probably based on the same reading, and reflects an understanding similar to that of Beentjes, 'Who is like the Wise', 313, 'priding themselves (on having done so)'. De Rossi notes a number of later Hebrew manuscripts with וישתבחו, which may reflect the Talmudic recommendation (*b. Giṭṭin* 56b), subsequently picked up by Rashi, to read that here as an exegetical stratagem (with the preceding קבורים read as קבוצים, and the whole associated with the confiscation by Titus of the temple vessels). It appears as the K^e*thîbh* in two of these manuscripts, with וישתכחו as Q^e*rê*.

There is no way to choose between the two readings, one of which has arisen from the other through a ב/כ confusion, except on grounds of sense and context, and it is possible to construe either of them with what follows. I take 'praised' to be marginally more probable because, if what follows is construed in the way that I shall suggest, the praise or forgetfulness is grounded in the fact that the wicked have 'done thus': praise can be associated easily with their stated action of having entered a holy place. Unless, however, we believe that anybody might have condemned such an action, forgetfulness that they had 'done thus' would have to be a much looser reference equating 'done thus' with 'been wicked'.

8.10 for having done so] Lit. 'that they had so done'. There is no reason to suppose that any of the versions read a text other than אשר כן עשו, but interpretations of the Hebrew have broadly followed two quite different lines. The first and more common takes the subject of the verb still to be the wicked, and כן to be an adverb that usually means 'so' or 'thus' (although it can have a range of different nuances). The second, picked up in the Midrash and still popular among commentators, takes כן instead to be the adjective that means 'right' or 'correct', perhaps used as a noun to mean 'what is right', enabling the Hebrew to be taken as a reference to 'those who have done right', standing in opposition to the wicked. The plausibility of each interpretation, of course, depends to a great extent on how one reads what has preceded. Having understood the first part of the verse to be about the burial of the wicked, for instance, Fox can comment quite fairly that 'there is no antecedent action to which "thus" could refer', but that is not the case if we have understood the wicked to be approaching and entering a holy place.

Of the ancient versions, G, S, Hie, T have all opted for 'so' or 'thus', but σ' ὡς δίκαια πράξαντες, followed by V *quasi iustorum operum*, has opted for an interesting compromise: the wicked are still the subject, but כן is taken as a noun and they are being praised 'as if (they were) people who do good'. Without associating it with σ', Schoors notes the similar possibility of reading '(the wicked) were praised in the city because they had acted rightfully', so although reading כן as 'right(ness)' is a prerequisite for understanding a new reference to the righteous, that reading does not at all exclude a continuing reference to the wicked.

Neither approach can be ruled out, but it is important to observe that examples of כן meaning 'righteous' or 'righteousness' are quite rare, if the word ever really means that at all in biblical usage. Joseph's brothers describe themselves as כנים several times in Gen 42 (e.g. 42.11), as an affirmation that they are not spies, although it is not clear that they are thereby actively claiming any moral virtue (we might call them simply 'above board'), and in Prov 28.2 כן apparently serves as a noun to describe the order or stability of a land. Much more often, though, כן means 'right' in the sense of 'true' or 'correct', not 'virtuous', with לא כן serving to express the opposite—so in Num 27.7, for example, God affirms that the daughters of Zelophehad are saying 'the correct thing', while Jer 8.6 affirms that the people are not. Even when לא כן is paired with רעה in Jer 23.10, the problem is apparently that things are off course or out of kilter, not that they are wicked. For the implication of 'justice' or 'right', Seow curiously cites Judg 12.6, where the issue is the inability to pronounce a word 'correctly', 2 Kgs 7.9, where the lepers say that they are not 'doing the proper thing' by waiting to break the news about the disappearance of the Syrians, and Prov 11.19, where the text is difficult and the meaning unclear, but someone who is 'כן righteousness' stands in parallel with someone who 'pursues wrong'—perhaps implying that they are 'properly' righteous.

Of all these, only 2 Kgs 7.9 comes close to the sense proposed, although it hardly refers to moral virtue, and, at the very least, 'those who do כן' would clearly have been an odd and unusual way of talking about the righteous, in opposition to the wicked. There is nothing in the context to suggest that Qohelet might be talking about people who do something 'correctly', which would be easier to justify. Although it cannot be excluded altogether, then, we can surely say that a reference to the righteous here is far less likely than a common adverbial use of כן to mean 'so' or something similar. To be sure, narrowing the proper interpretation down that far does not deal with all the issues. Several commentators take אשר to refer to the city, which leads Longman, for instance, to translate 'they were praised in the city where they acted in such a way'—this is possible, although we might expect a resumptive בה in such a case (and Sacchi duly adds one). It is also not clear whether we should describe אשר as verbal complement (forgotten/praised *that*) or take it to have a causal force here (forgotten/praised *because*). Such questions, however, do not really affect the sense of the text, which I take to be that the wicked are praised for entering a holy place.

8.11 since] Although the general sense is clear, the overall construction of vv. 11-13 is complicated, and has been understood in different ways. The first problem concerns the role of אשר here: although there is a general understanding that it is causal,[6] does the clause that it introduces present the basis for Qohelet's preceding statement, that 'this too is הבל' (so, e.g., Fox), or for his subsequent claim about human hearts (so, e.g., Schoors)? To put that another way, is אשר enlarging on what has preceded, which is the way in which it normally works when used with a causative implication, or is it to be construed with the על כן that follows, creating an equivalent to the expressions על אשר...על כן in 1 Kgs 9.9 = 2 Chr 7.22 and יען אשר...על כן in Ezek 44.12, which both mean 'because (of what follows), therefore'?

Delitzsch makes the attractive suggestion that, in some sense, it does both, with the אשר functioning initially to offer an explanation of גם זה הבל at the end of 8.10, but then becoming antecedent when the על כן clause is added.

---

[6] A causal sense is rejected by Michel, who understands אשר to have an explicatory nuance at the start of both 8.11 and 8.12. It seems that he is not so much rejecting a notion of causation, however, as demanding that the clauses explain 8.10, rather than what follows them. See Michel, *Untersuchungen*, 224.

That may be too complicated an idea, but it does capture the important point that causation runs in different directions across a sequence of statements here, and that if we try to link the אשר only with what precedes or only with what follows, we may be setting up a false dichotomy. In particular, the statement about human hearts sits between two other statements that make similar points—sins are not condemned or punished swiftly—and if the first אשר clause elaborates on גם זה הבל,[7] the statements that follow both flow from that clause and explain it.

The principal objection to linking אשר with גם זה הבל is that Qohelet uses גם זה הבל as a concluding observation, not to initiate new points, and it is certainly fair to say that Wildeboer, Fox and others make too much of the idea that it is starting a new passage or section here. Again, though, it is important to look in both directions, and the fact that אשר might be elaborating on the nature of the הבל does not exclude the possibility that the הבל might in the first place characterize Qohelet's observations of the wicked.

8.11 no indictment...is brought swiftly] Lit. 'there is not an edict being done...speedily'. Since אין is not used to negate verbal clauses, נעשה must be read as a participle נַעֲשֶׂה, not the qatal נַעֲשָׂה found in M: cf. G οὐκ ἔστιν γινομένη ἀντίρρησις...ταχύ, 'there is no contradiction/response taking place...quickly', and differently σ′ διὰ γὰρ τὸ μὴ γίνεσθαι τὴν ἀπόφασιν... ταχέως, 'because of the judgment/response not happening...quickly' (also T, S). Ginsburg notes that there are a few other cases where אין seems to be construed with a main verb (he points to Exod 3.2, where a participle is, in fact, commonly understood, and to Jer 38.5; Job 35.15), but these are rare, and similarly rest on the M vocalization, or some parsing of it; he is not right, though, to suppose that any participle נעשה would have to be feminine, and would therefore fail to agree with פתגם—a consideration that might outweigh the normal usage (cf. Neh 5.18). This case is clear cut, then, but on the broader questions about the pointing of נעשה in M, see the note at 1.9. Mazzinghi, 'Esegesi ed ermeneutica', 179, claims that the ἀντίρρησις of G must be a borrowing from the language of Hellenistic philosophy, but the term is used quite generally, in a variety of contexts (cf. Vinel).

The pointing of the verse in M more generally, in conjunction with the vocalization of this verb, has long preoccupied many commentators, who observe that the accents as they stand in most manuscripts demand a sense like 'since a פתגם is not done, the work of evil is swift'—despite the fact that מהרה is never found as an adjective. A few manuscripts conform to the more common understanding of the structure; see Wickes, *Accentuation*, 139.

---

[7] Cf. Holmstedt, 'The Grammar of שׁ and אשר in Qohelet', 306-7, and *Relative Clause*, 379-80. Speaking of the clauses with אשר at the head of vv. 11 and 12, in the latter he says (380): 'In each case, the appositional clause provides an additional example...of what is called הבל at the end of Eccl 8.10. Technically, the אשר clauses are nominalized appositives that clarify the nature of the deictic זה in the phrase גם זה הבל.'

The noun פתגם is usually taken to have originated in the Old Persian *patigāma*, which was used of official edicts, and that is its sense in the only other biblical Hebrew use, at Esth 1.20 (see the Introduction, 68-69). It was taken up widely in Aramaic, however, where it developed a broad reference to all sorts of words and statements, sometimes (principally in later sources) even meaning just 'matter'. A פתגם, however, is never an action, and when in Dan 4.14 (ET 4.17), פתגם refers to a sentence that is to be carried out, this is a 'sentencing' as it is pronounced over someone who has been convicted, not the 'sentence' that is served by them in response. A similar distinction has to be observed in, e.g., the Targum Onqelos to Gen 18.25, where Abraham is urging God not to act in accordance with the sentence he has decreed.

It is a blurring of that very distinction, however, that underpins a common interpretation of this verse in terms of divine punishment, represented by, e.g., RSV 'Because sentence against an evil deed is not executed speedily'. It is difficult not only to find any parallel to such a sense of 'punishment' among the attested uses of פתגם in Hebrew and Aramaic,[8] but also to draw something so precise from the construct expression פתגם מעשה הרעה, which is literally just 'a פתגם (of) bad behaviour'.[9] If the use of עשה might be considered to affirm that an action is involved here, moreover, then we should recall that precisely the same verb is used with פתגם in Esth 1.20 of 'making' a decree, and it is broadly that sense which seems to be uppermost here. Other nuances are possible. In an Aramaic document from Elephantine (*TAD* A6.10.9), a severe פתגם directed against somebody seems to be a reprimand for disobeying instructions, and in Aramaic, פתגם is very often a response of some sort (e.g. Dan 3.16; Ezra 5.11). Literally, we have here something like 'a pronouncement of bad behaviour', but even without a preposition it is reasonable to think in terms of a rebuke *for* bad behaviour, which is the understanding behind G's translation (cf. σ' ἀπόφασιν περὶ τοῦ κακοῦ, 'sentence concerning the evil').

I think it is more natural here, however, to associate what Qohelet says with the praise for the wicked that he mentioned in the last verse: his concern is with the absence of anything to contradict that praise. Of course, he might well have a divine response in mind—nothing would identify bad behaviour so effectively as rapid divine punishment—but it seems unlikely that the expression can be confined only to that sense, and his emphasis is upon the fact that people hear only praise of the wicked. When פתגם is used in the construct with המלך at Esth 1.20, the sense is that of a 'subjective genitive'—it

---

[8] It is worth noting, however, that S here has ܬܒܥܬܐ *tb'ṯ'*, 'punishment' or 'retribution', despite the fact that ܦܬܓܡܐ *ptgm'* is used in Syriac. The rendering is interpretative.

[9] Ginsburg's objection that פתגם must be absolute because of the vocalization פִּתְגָם is weakened by the fact that the same vocalization is found in Esth 1.20, where it is obviously construct, and Gordis suggests that this 'permanent *kameṣ*' is linked to its foreign origin.

is the decree made by the king. We could plausibly suppose the same here, that Qohelet is talking about bad behaviour announcing itself, but an 'objective' announcement *of* bad behaviour is more likely, or just possibly a construction without a genitive at all: 'an announcement "bad behaviour"'.

8.11 wrongful behaviour] Even when it is used in the singular, מעשה usually has a collective sense, and especially in Qohelet's usage refers not so much to individual actions as to work in general (cf. 3.17; 4.3, 4; 8.9) or to the work and accomplishments overall of an individual (cf. 5.5; 7.13); see the note at 2.17. Especially in light of the way it will be used shortly, in 8.14, it seems more likely that Qohelet is talking in just such general terms here, rather than about particular deeds.

G has not read מעשה at all here, and ἀπὸ τῶν ποιούντων, lit. 'from those doing', points to the translator having found מעשי in his source text, which he interpreted as מֵעֹשֵׂי, a plural participle with a prefixed preposition -מ. On the basis of this reading, he understood Qohelet to be talking about a pronouncement 'away from' evildoers, or a refutation of them; cf. Hie *contradictio facientibus malum*, 'contradiction to those doing evil'; Cassian *Collationes* ii, 11, 4 *contradictio ab his qui faciunt malum*, 'contradiction of those who do evil'. This same reading is reflected in S and V, while T speaks of both the wicked and their wicked deeds, possibly reflecting a knowledge of both מעשה and מעשי. The sense offered by מעשי is not unattractive, and the reading is well attested in the versions, but it is likely to be secondary, not least because מהרה is unlikely to have been postponed until so late in the clause if it were not for the inseparable פתגם מעשה הרעה: G's פתגם מעשי הרעה, could easily have been interrupted. Goldman suspects an assimilation to the following plural, or to the עשה רע of 8.12.

8.11 the heart of humans is...encouraged within them] Lit. 'the heart of humans is filled in them'. The similar expression at Esth 7.5 may have some connotation of boldness or impudence (the Greek translation there has ἐτόλμησεν, 'dared'), as well as of getting it into one's head to do something. That seems appropriate here too (and in the comparable expression at 9.3, although see the note there). However, Rey, in 'Knowledge Hidden and Revealed', 258, discussing the promise by personified wisdom in Sir 4.17 that her student's heart 'shall be full of me' (ימלא לבו בי), thinks the expression, there and elsewhere, 'pertains to the capacity to think or know so intimately that a kind of unity exists between the thinker and the thing thought'. He translates the parallel clause אשוב אאשרנו as 'I will return to make him happy', which is how the Greek takes it, and it might be possible to apply such a meaning to Qohelet's usage (so that people are becoming intimately acquainted with wrongdoing). That would hardly do in Esther, though, and אשוב אאשרנו is more commonly understood as 'I shall return and direct him' (so *HALOT*, *DCH*): it seems more likely that the expression in Sir 4 is simply a causative counterpart to the uses elsewhere, and that Wisdom is promising to inspire and direct.

G renders the Hebrew literally, cf. Hie and Cassian *Collationes* ii, 11, 4, *repletum est cor filiorum hominis in ipsis* (Hie *eis*), 'the heart of the sons of man are full in them', although, rather than a form from πληρόω, which he normally uses for מלא, the translator has opted for ἐπληροφορήθη, which perhaps gives an implication more like 'completely filled'. However, α' διὰ τοῦτο ἐτόλμησε(ν), 'therefore he dares' (which has been picked up by the hexaplaric, *O*-group manuscripts of G), and σ' διατοῦτο ἀφόβῳ καρδίᾳ οἱ υἱοὶ τῶν ἀνθρώπων κακουργοῦσιν, 'therefore with fearless heart the sons of humans do evil', both show the same understanding that daring is involved, and Symmachus has doubtless influenced V *absque ullo timore filii hominum perpetrant mala*, 'without any fear the sons of humans perpetrate evils' (cf. Cannon, 195).

8.11 to do what is wrong] G is generally faithful in its representation of definite articles, but here and at the start of 8.12 it has τὸ πονηρόν where M simply has רע. This is also the same expression that the translator used for הרעה earlier in the verse, which does have an article, and so he may have been motivated in part by a desire to impose, perhaps for stylistic reasons as Aitken supposes, a consistency that is lacking in the Hebrew. Aitken, 'Rhetoric and Poetry', 63, 72, also suggests that the articles may have been added for the sake of rhythm, since at the end of v. 11 and in v. 12 τὸ πονηρόν falls at the end of a sequence that corresponds metrically to the end of a hexameter. It is alternatively possible, of course, that the source-text of G already had articles (cf. McNeile, 148, on 8.12), and a greater consistency of expression than M.

As noted at 5.1, Qohelet does not normally use רע in the sense 'evil', and the 'doing wrong' of the fools in that verse was implied to be inadvertent: a product of their incompetence, not of wicked intentions. I take the same to be probable here and in 9.3: Qohelet's language does not exclude wickedness, but the problem in this context is that people are imitating behaviour that is misguided or incorrect (in that they will presumably be judged harshly for it by God), not that they are becoming inherently wicked.

8.12 because a sinner] Wildeboer sets the אשר here in parallel with that at the start of 8.11, and understands this to be a second elaboration of the הבל introduced in 8.10. I take it rather to be an explanation of the statement that humans are emboldened to act badly. G, very differently, reads it as a relative pronoun: ὃς ἥμαρτεν, 'he who sinned', and this is followed by S ܡܢ ܕܚܛܐ *mn dḥṭʾ*. On this reading, חטא has probably been vocalized as qatal, rather than as a participle, and although Schoors says that it 'does not render the meaning of the Hebrew correctly', it is a legitimate construal of the consonantal text. V *attamen*, 'nevertheless', adopts a different understanding again, but is arguably more an attempt to clarify the argument than an actual translation of אשר.

8.12 does] In accordance with its understanding of the sentence as a whole, G again vocalizes עשה as qatal, rather than as the participle indicated by the pointing in M and read by the other versions (except, possibly, S).

8.12 but puts off for himself his death] It makes little difference to the overall sense, but my reading is based on an emendation of מאת ומאריך to ומותו מאריך. The text here must be considered corrupt, unless we are willing to allow two awkward and unparalleled usages in a row, each of which obliges us to understand an implicit noun.

For the first, the translator of G has read what he found in his source-text as מאז (surely not מעת, as, e.g. Euringer supposes), and rendered it as ἀπὸ τότε, 'from formerly', or 'from of old'. On the other hand, σ' ἁμαρτὼν (var. ἁμαρτάνων) γὰρ ὁ κακοῦργος ἀπέθανε(ν), 'for sinning, the evildoer died', has probably read מ(ו)ח: Jerome reports that α' and θ' shared that understanding. M has מאת (vocalized by Jerome as *maath*), apparently the construct form of מאה, 'a hundred' (cf. S), which has to be understood as 'a hundred times' (Hie, V) or 'for a hundred years' (T, cf. Rashi), even though there is no parallel to such an omission of the following noun.[10]

All the versions have then read ומאריך or, with a defective spelling, ומארך, but they have understood it in different ways. The hiph'il of ארך is characteristically used with ימים in the expression 'prolong (one's) days', with the sense 'stay long' or 'live long' (e.g. Num 9.19; Isa 53.10): it will be used that way in the next verse, 8.13. It is never used absolutely, but is also found with נפש in Job 6.11 and with אף in Isa 48.9 and Prov 19.11, where the meanings are 'be patient' and 'be slow to anger' respectively; in those uses, the implication is 'put off' or 'postpone', rather than 'prolong'. Finding no explicit object, σ' has translated ומאריך לו impersonally as μακροθυμίας γενομένης αὐτῷ, lit. 'forbearance having become for him', which Jerome understands as *longanimatate concessa ei*, '(despite) forbearance having been granted to him'. Jerome picks this reading up himself in V *et per patientiam sustentatur*, 'and is borne with patience', although he does not follow the broader understanding of σ', that the sinner eventually dies after being shown much patience. S and Hie also read the verb, but more literally as 'prolongs', and this probably lies behind the idea in T, that the sinner is granted an 'extension' (ארכא) by God, so that he has time to repent—T perhaps took God as the subject of the verb.

---

[10] Gordis thinks it might be an archaic absolute form, but does not explain why the author would use such a form. He also suggests that no noun has been omitted, but that we should understand מאת רע as 'a hundred evils', citing GKC §134 c, but that word-order is only legitimate if the form actually is absolute. The same problem confronts any attempt to read the form as multiplicative, 'a hundred times' (cf. GKC §134 r; J-M §142 q), leading Schoors to insist that מאת 'cannot be' construct while simultaneously acknowledging that the normal form מאה is found for the absolute in 6.3. Seow would re-vocalize מאת as a plural (presumably written defectively, as at Gen 5.4, 30), so that the sinner is doing 'the wrong of hundreds', but it is hard to find any analogous use—'hundreds', used absolutely, are only ever military units in biblical Hebrew—and that notion would be clearer were the expression definite.

G, however, reads a noun directly, and construes the Hebrew as מ-ארך, 'from a length', set in parallel with the מ-אי that the translator has already understood. This gives rise to the somewhat obscure rendering καὶ ἀπὸ μακρότητος, 'and from a length (to him)', which is possibly supposed to mean that the sinner has sinned for a long time and across a great distance.[11] None of the ancient versions follows what has been a popular course among modern commentators, which is either to understand ימים as implicit or to take מאריך לו as equivalent to מאריך ימים—perhaps because there is no parallel to either such use of the verb.

It is difficult to make sense of all this. McNeile, 148, suggests that מאת may have originated as a false start for ומאריך, or perhaps as מאד, and it is certainly the most suspicious element here, but the use of מאריך absolutely, or with an object understood, is hardly less problematic. To kill two birds with one stone, we might most economically suppose that the verb did originally have an object, and that מאת is itself a corrupt form of that object. If we are to identify the original, then we can probably begin by eliminating the מאו reflected in G, which is likely an attempt to make sense of the problematic מאת found in M. It accordingly offers a much easier reading, which has led some scholars (including Fox) to adopt it, but it is hard to see how either of the other attested readings—מאת itself and the מ(ו)ת of the Three—could have been derived from it. These both suggest that the מ and the ת are original, but they are distinct, and (*pace* Goldman) none of the Three would likely have linked מאת to מות.

Galling would restore ואת ימיו מאריך, which is graphically too distant from the evidence, but which does draw out an important point: if we are indeed dealing with an object of מאריך, we should not expect a conjunction before מאריך, splitting the clause. Galling is probably right, therefore, to move the ו from ומאריך to the end of the preceding word, and read it as a suffix pronoun, but it is simpler to read מותו, rather than his את ימיו. The most likely sense would then be 'putting off his death', with מות used in a way analogous to the uses of אף with the verb, and the text would likely mean 'because a sinner doing wrong (is) putting off his death for himself'.

The final change that Galling makes is the addition of a new conjunction to the object, marking the beginning of a new clause, which is entirely speculative, but attractive nonetheless. The loss of such a conjunction is not inexplicable, if we suppose that the loss followed the move of the existing ו to create ומאריך, after which it became necessary to read the remaining ומות as a verb (and natural to write it defectively as ומת): it is difficult to make sense of the consequent 'does evil and dies and prolongs'. This difficulty could motivate the elimination of an initial conjunction—perhaps on the assumption that it has been transposed with the מ, if it was not actually just lost as

---

[11] The G text is complicated by the fact that we find αὐτῶν in all the manuscripts, so that they actually say 'from *their* length'. This is almost certainly an inner-Greek error for αὐτῷ, 'to him'.

the result of such a transposition. I am inclined to think that Galling is right in this respect too, and that we should restore ומותו rather than just מותו—which is the reading presumed in my translation. It is possible also, of course, that he is right in this respect but wrong in the other, and that the conjunction now found on ומאריך simply migrated there from an original מות, which would be a more serious error but require less emendation. In that case, Qohelet would be talking about the man putting off 'death', not specifically 'his death'.

It seems in any case, though, to have been a reading without either an initial conjunction or a suffix that informs our main witnesses. The Three found one way to interpret מת ומאריך לו by retaining מת as a verb, while the tradition behind M (and ultimately G) either took מת as a writing of מאת—the simpler explanation—or introduced an א accidentally, under the influence of the מא in the next word. Whatever else happened, the rather forced readings that we find now seem likely to have originated in a simple error, compounded by efforts to correct or make sense of the problems that it created, and they underpin what appear to have been three quite different construals of the sentence in the early Hebrew tradition.

8.12 For I know too] כי גם is often translated 'though' (cf. RSV, and, e.g., Piotti, 'Osservazioni', 158-59), but the expression has no concessive force: see the note at 4.14. Jerome reports σ' as taking it asseveratively, *porro ego scio*, 'besides, I know', and he himself somehow understands Qohelet to be saying that it is on the basis of the forbearance shown to the sinner that he knows (Hie *ex hoc cognosco ego*, 'from this I know'; V *ex eo quod...ego cognoui*, 'from this, that..., I know'). I take the force to be explanatory. The הבל of v. 10 is not הבל simply because sinners are not identified or punished in time, but because this situation conceals what Qohelet knows to be the truth.

8.12 it will be well] The expression טוב ל- is used quite commonly to mean that someone is healthy (e.g. 1 Sam 16.16, 23) or prospering (e.g. Deut 5.33). היה is not usually used with it, but Qohelet needs a verb here to specify the future tense.

8.12 for God-fearers who fear before him] On the use of מלפני with ירא, see the note on 'before him' at 3.14. Although I observed there the possibility that the expression conveys some nuance of actual fear (cf. V here, *qui uerentur faciem eum*, 'who dread his face'), the statement here nevertheless seems on the face of it tautologous, leading translators and commentators to try to find some particular implication for אשר that will give it more point.

Presumably on the basis of the yiqtol verb, G offers the most radical of the ancient interpretations, understanding אשר to mark a purpose clause: the point is presumably that God protects the pious *so that* they can fear him. Modern commentators have mostly been less adventurous, but Staples, 'Vanity of Vanities', 152, takes אשר to substantivize its clause, and ingeniously links this to the preceding טוב, translating 'that which is profitable to those who fear God, is that they fear Him', and rendering the next verse in much the same way. Krüger, similarly, has 'it is good for the God-fearers that they fear

God'. Staples is given short shrift by Schoors, who says that his reading can be rejected 'off-hand', but Krüger's version, without the problematic equation of טוב with 'profit', seems very plausible. The main difficulty is that the same understanding of יהיה טוב cannot be carried over to the next verse, where the אשר clause does not so readily serve to identify what is 'not good' for the wicked: another clause intervenes if the verse is read that way.

Schoors himself, along with most other modern commentators, prefers to understand אשר here as 'because', and those commentators who take this approach generally adopt the same understanding in the next verse, so that it is, conversely, the lack of fear that leads to a lack of benefit there (cf. RSV). Indeed, it seems to be a perception that אשר must be translated that way in 8.13 which sometimes drives this approach. If we translate אשר as 'because' in either verse, however, we lock in a very specific basis for the fate of both parties, which is more precise than Qohelet's own words, and so I have retained 'who' while acknowledging that some causal implication may be present. This also holds open the possibility that Qohelet is talking about only those who are really God-fearing among the humans who might describe themselves as such (see, e.g., Michel, *Untersuchungen*, 222-23, which cites the support of Delitzsch and others for such a view).

Beentjes, 'Who is like the Wise', 315, notes the discrepancy in number between *those* who fear God here, and the contrasting '*one* who does not fear' in the next verse. His suggestion, that Qohelet is deliberately alluding to 3.14, is supported by the use in both verses of the construction with מלפני, but 3.14 seems to be talking about all humans, while this verse clearly is not. If there is a deliberate allusion, therefore, we should not push the relationship between the verses too far.

8.13 like a shadow] See the note 'as a shadow' at 6.12. G here has read בצל and Jerome's account of σ' provides no equivalent to the term at all, but the other versions support the כצל of M (Codex Sinaiticus and a few other sources, in fact, have a conflate ὡς ἐν σκιᾷ, corrected in Sinaiticus, possibly indicating that readings based on כצל were known in the Greek tradition as well). The position is awkward if the shadow is supposed to be an image of transience, and for that reason כצל cannot readily be construed as part of the clause negated by לא to mean 'and he will not prolong days like a shadow'. The position does lend some support, however, to the suggestion of Wise, 'A Calque', 256, that we should read בצל here, with G, and understand it in the sense 'because'. This makes the verse a simpler statement that the wise man will not enjoy good things because he does not fear God. At 6.12 and 7.12, we have already encountered Wise's idea that בצל is used in the book in the same, extended ways that 'in shadow' can be used sometimes in Aramaic, and I found his suggestion plausible in 7.12. Here I think it is less likely that he is right, since, even if it is very likely that in a few places the expression means 'with the help of', or something similar, it is harder to establish any use of it in Aramaic simply to mean 'because'. The only example that Wise cites (255) is in the *Genesis Apocryphon*, where the idea of protection or assistance is clearly present, and all Wise's examples, in fact, refer to something good happening through the agency of something, or usually someone: they do not suggest that 'in shadow' had become an all-purpose conjunction connoting cause, of the sort that would be required here to achieve his understanding. Joüon, 'Notes philologiques', 423, would simply emend כצל to כצדיק ('prolong days like the righteous'), and, as at 6.12 (see the notes there), Tur-Sinai, 'Dunkle Bibelstellen', 280, would read בשל ('does not prolong days because', like Wise). Both these suggestions give a good sense, but I do not see anything obviously problematic about the use of shadow as an image, and emendation seems unnecessary.

8.13 prolong life] Lit. 'prolong days'. See the note at 8.12, where the same verb is used. σ' paraphrases with οὐδὲ ἐν μακροῖς ἔσται χρόνοις; in line with Jerome's Latin rendering of it as *neque longo supererit tempore*, we might ourselves paraphrase σ' as 'he won't be around in the long term'.

8.13 who has no fear] The normal approach is to take the subject of יאריך to be the preceding רשע, who then acts as the subject of the אשר clause. Hence RSV 'it will not be well with the wicked, neither will he prolong his days like a shadow, because he does not fear before God' (cf. σ', as reported by Jerome, *quia non timuit faciem dei*, 'because he did not fear the face of God'). That, of course, leaves the clause with אשר at a considerable distance from the רשע, and separated from it by a verbal clause, leading scholars to suppose that אשר is acting as a freestanding conjunction, 'because', which goes some way beyond the 'weak causal sense' granted it by J-M §170 e.

G, however, understands אשר here to specify the subject of the previous verb: οὐ μακρυνεῖ ἡμέρας ἐν σκιᾷ ὃς οὐκ ἔστιν φοβούμενος, 'he will not lengthen days in shadow, who is not fearing'. This interpretation has been adopted also by Michel, *Untersuchungen*, 223, apparently independently, and he speaks of 'ein Subjektsatz', by which he is presumably saying that the clause with אשר serves as the subject of יאריך; this is essentially the way it is taken by Holmstedt too, who doubts that אשר can be used conjunctively in the way that is commonly supposed here ('The Grammar of שׁ and אשׁר in Qohelet', 304; *Relative Clause*, 379). Without taking sides in the more general controversies about אשר, it is possible to say both that this approach grants the text an elegance which it altogether lacks in the usual translation, and that the usual translation rests on assumptions about the scope of אשר that are at least open to question, and for which few analogous examples can be supplied.

8.13 God] This is the last of the few places in which Ecclesiastes uses אלהים without a definite article (the others are 1.13; 3.10, 11; 7.18; 8.2; and M points לאלהים without an article at 5.3). This is the only one of them, however, where Kennicott notes a large number of later Hebrew manuscripts which read האלהים, with the article. That is perhaps because the determined form appeared in the previous verse, but it is curious that the inconsistent usage has given rise to so little variation elsewhere.

8.14-15

(8.14) There is an illusion that is perpetrated on the earth, that there are righteous people who have an experience fitting for the behaviour of the wicked, and there are wicked people who have an experience fitting for the behaviour of the righteous. I said that this too is an illusion, (8.15) but I commended enjoyment, that there is nothing good for the human beneath the sun, except to eat, drink, and enjoy; and it will accompany him in his work for all the days of his life which God has granted him beneath the sun.

Commentary

Qohelet's previous observation, that the sinner may survive, addresses a subset of the more general problem raised here, that what people experience does not always correspond to what they *should* experience—at least if we believe that their behaviour should have a bearing on what happens to them. At this point, however, Qohelet does not simply insist again upon the reality of the divine judgment concealed by such situations, or admonish us to fear God. His reaction, instead, is to return to his commendation of enjoyment as the only real benefit for humans.

In the light of what he has said in the preceding verses, we should probably not take this to imply that Qohelet sees no role for the fear of God, or that he has suddenly given up on the reality of divine justice. The problem highlighted in 8.10-13 was, in essence, that humans are misled by their interpretation of a situation, and can effectively place themselves in peril by basing their behaviour upon what they see: we should not imitate the sins of the sinner, just because that sinner seems to prosper. His concern here is that, in the face of misleading evidence, we should not try to make such calculations at all, but to focus on the one thing that we can know will be good for us: the pleasure that we can find in living.

8.14] The verse does not say that 'the righteous' suffer the fate of 'the wicked' and *vice versa*: the Hebrew not only makes a distinction between (some) righteous and *the* wicked, or (some) wicked and *the* righteous, but also uses a construction and terminology that are unlikely to refer either to the ultimate end or to the continual experience of either group. The point is that bad things can happen to good people, and good things to bad—not that they inevitably or constantly do so.

8.15] The modern expression, 'eat, drink and be merry, for tomorrow we die' seems to be a conflation of this verse with Isa 22.13, which uses similar language (without 'be merry'), and which is cited in 1 Cor 15.32. It is not impossible that Qohelet is alluding to the verse in Isaiah (and so drawing in an implication of death), but that verse at the very least throws light on the potential connotations of his language: it depicts partying in the face of death by a people who have been called to sackcloth and repentance, but who choose to do the very opposite. The three verbs, eating, drinking, and enjoying, crop up together twice elsewhere, in Isa 65.13, where they similarly appear to describe celebrations (cf. 65.11), and in 1 Kgs 4.20, where Judah and Israel are said to 'eat, drink, and enjoy' during the prosperous reign of Solomon.

Niccacci, 'Qohelet o la gioia', 81, helpfully lays this verse out next to 5.17, 19, drawing attention to the similarities. It is worth noting also, however, the differences, and in particular the shift from finding happiness in our work, at 5.17, to finding a happiness now that will go with us in our work. It might be unwise to read too much into such details, but it might also not be too much to suggest that Qohelet is visibly moving on here, from his original perception that human reward can be found only in the pleasure to be gained from what we do, toward a broader conception of enjoyment as something that we can take with us into our endeavours. There is also a shift of tone: in both places Qohelet notes that God grants the days of each human life, but 8.15 has none of the concern to stress the brevity of life, which is an issue in both 5.17 and 5.19. In ch. 5, the discourse is of salvaging what we can from a terrible situation, but here, and in what follows, Qohelet is urging us to let go of our concern with issues that we can neither control nor understand.

Notes

8.14 There is an illusion…wicked] The second part is lit. 'that there are righteous (ones) who a reaching/touching/arriving thing (is) to them according with the behaviour of the wicked'. Jerome reports the interesting paraphrase of σ' for the first part as *est difficile cognitu quod fit super terram*, 'there is a thing difficult to know which is done on the earth', and the Greek reflected in *difficile cognitu*, 'difficult to know', is attested in two manuscripts as ἄπορον, 'something difficult', or 'something puzzling' (ἄπορον is also attested for σ' at the end of the verse). According to those same manuscripts (with the first two words added from a third), σ' goes on to say εἰσὶ δίκαιοι οἷς συμβαίνει κατὰ τὰ ἔργα τῶν ἀσεβῶν, 'there are righteous people to whom it happens according to the works of the impious', although other witnesses have παρανόμων, 'lawless', rather than ἀσεβῶν: Marshall considers that latter the more likely reading (while acknowledging that both are possible; cf. also Labate, 'Catena Hauniense', 59), and it would seem to be confirmed by the reading in the second part of the verse (see below).

It is possible that some text is missing (see the note 'and there are… righteous', below); the significant point here, however, is Symmachus' use of οἷς συμβαίνει, 'to whom it happens', which stands in contrast to G ὅτι φθάνει πρὸς αὐτούς, 'that (it) approaches towards them'. The translator of G has not only taken the second אשר to be a second 'that', rather than as a relative pronoun, but has taken the hiph'il of נגע in its common sense 'reach', 'stretch to', while Symmachus understands it in the terms of, e.g. Esth 9.26, where it connotes what has happened to somebody. α' probably uses the same verb as G, but with εἰς αὐτούς, 'to them', indicating more clearly that the event has actually reached the righteous, and many manuscripts of G have ἐπ(ὶ), 'upon' them, which is likely a correction intended to give that same sense (cf. 1 Thess 2.16), rather than a reflection of a Hebrew reading עלהם, as McNeile, 148, supposes. By retaining the common meaning of the verb (here and in the matching sentence that follows), and in its renderings of אשר, G arguably brings out the sense in Greek much less clearly than does σ' (and Vinel describes the translation as 'obscure'), but this is normal, and reflects the different translation strategies of each. I see no basis for the rather vague claim of Mazzinghi, 'Esegesi ed ermeneutica', 179-80, that the translator is somehow using obscurity to neutralize the provocative statements of the Hebrew, or to iron out contradictions (an idea that he uses, wrongly I think, to explain a number of actual differences between G and M elsewhere).

Hie, V treat מגיע itself as plural, to give a sense of 'things' happening (contrast Jerome's citation of the passage in *Dialogus aduersus Pelagianos*, 2.5 [PL 23, 541], *ad quos peruenit quasi opus impiorum / iustorum*), while G and σ' both take it as impersonal, translating with a main verb—which is the usual approach among modern commentators, cf. RSV, 'it happens'. The participle would seem a very curious choice for such a construction, however, and Qohelet notably only uses this verb elsewhere for the arrival of years (12.1), not for his depictions of the fates that befall people. I take the specific implication to be that righteous people may be affected by a circumstance that would more properly affect the wicked, rather than that they are constantly so affected, or that they meet the end that the wicked should meet. The participle is then serving as a substantive, functioning in a way similar to נפלאות, 'wonders', in Job 5.9 and elsewhere; its sense is similar to that of מה הגיע in Esth 9.26, but without any nuance of tense.

8.14 on the earth] Qohelet uses על הארץ to contrast the listener's position with that of God in 5.1, of walking 'on the ground' in 10.7, of rain falling 'on the ground' in 11.3, and, if the text of M is correct, of dust returning 'to the ground' in 12.7. The uses in 8.14, 16 and 11.2 stand out because they seem to serve as an alternative to his more common 'under the sun' or 'under the heavens' as a way to locate the phenomena he is talking about.

8.14 fitting for the behaviour] The preposition -כ is used in this verse rather as in Judg 20.10, where Gibeah is to be treated 'in accordance with' all the crimes that the inhabitants have committed, or Ps 7.9 (ET 7.8), where God will judge 'according to' righteousness. On מעשה, see the note at 8.11.

8.14 and there are...righteous] The second part of the observation matches the first in M[L], except that the אשר before מגיע is replaced by -ש. That distinction is lost in most later Hebrew manuscripts and editions, which have אשר again, but if original, it may be euphonic or stylistic, since it is hard to perceive any plausible difference in meaning. The general symmetry is preserved in G, Hie, S, T. In σ', however, which previously had εἰσὶ δίκαιοι οἷς συμβαίνει κατὰ τὰ ἔργα τῶν παρανόμων (see above), we now find καὶ εἰσὶ(ν) παράνομοι οἷς συμβαίνει ὡς πράξασι κατὰ τὰ ἔργα τῶν δικαίων, 'and there are lawless people to whom it happens as *to those acting according to the deeds of the righteous*'. It is not clear why Symmachus would have translated each statement so differently, so it is possible that he actually used ὡς πράξασι in both places and that the text attested for the first is faulty. There is a more blatantly interpretative change in V, which also spoils the symmetry: *et sunt impii qui ita securi sunt quasi iustorum facta habeant*, 'and there are impious people who are as safe as if they had the deeds of the just'.

8.14 this too is an illusion] The majority text of V has *et hoc vanissimum iudico*, 'and I judge this the vainest thing', while in the Theodulphian manuscripts we find the interesting *et hoc vanitas est et vanissimum iudicium*, 'and this is a vanity and the vainest judgment' (partially erased and emended in Kongelige Bibliotek, NKS 1 2°, and with a correction to *iudico* in Württembergische Landesbibliothek HB II). This latter apparently adds a more standard rendering of the formula (cf. *et hoc vanitas est* in 8.10) to Jerome's uncharacteristic and interpretative translation, which effectively singles out this instance of vanity (he only uses the adjective elsewhere at 11.10, the superlative nowhere). The *iudicium* is surely a secondary development from *iudicio*, though, because the reading appears to introduce an explicit criticism of divine judgment.

8.15 but I commended enjoyment, that] On the sense of the verb, see the note at 4.2. Duncan complains that translations like 'commend' lose the 'robust emphasis', and that we should speak rather of Qohelet actively 'praising' pleasure. That emphasis does not suit 4.2, however, and we do find the specific sense of commendation in later uses of the Aramaic cognate (e.g. twice in Genesis Rabbah 33.3), comparable to the way that we might talk colloquially of 'singing someone's praises'. Earlier, 11QtgJob xiv, 5 used it to render the pi‘el of אשר in Job 29.11, probably to give a similar sense (this is the closest we come to evidence that Qohelet might have meant 'consider fortunate' in 4.2). It seems more likely that much the same usage existed in Hebrew at this time than that Qohelet actively 'gave praise' to the dead and to pleasure, which is where the other biblical occurrences would lead us.

The conjunction is supported by all the versions, and although many commentators read it as 'then', or regard it as a sort of summarizing 'so' ('waw conclusivum'), it is only the apparent change of direction that drives such an interpretation: it is far more natural to read it as linking שבחתי with the preceding אמרתי, which is another verb of speaking in the qatal (cf. Lohfink). Qohelet issues simultaneously a condemnation of the הבל he has just described, and a commendation of שמחה. If the statements are in parallel, then the אשר here corresponds to the -ש on שגם in 8.14, providing a 'that' after the verb of speaking, and does not need to be understood as causal or explicatory. Qohelet is not, therefore, offering an explanation either of what drove him to his commendation of pleasure, or of what he understands pleasure to be (cf. Michel, *Untersuchungen*, 222), but putting that commendation into words and enlarging upon it.

8.15 nothing good…except to] There is no מן, and this is not, therefore, a type of 'better than' saying: Qohelet is not declaring these things to be better than anything else, but commending them as the only good things available.

8.15 it will accompany him in his work] The sense of לוה is not in doubt, although this is the only biblical use of the qal. It is less clear whether Qohelet intends a jussive or 'subjunctive' nuance here: Wright and Delitzsch both, for example, think that he may either be calling on humans to take their pleasure with them, or stating that it will go with them as a result of eating, drinking, etc. The ancient versions all seem to understand a simple future, however, and if such a nuance is present, it has not been marked clearly.

The idea of uniqueness in σ' ὃ μόνον συμπροσέσται (vars. περιέσται, προσέσται) αὐτῷ, 'which alone will remain with him' (on the reading, see Marshall, Gentry), is picked up in V *et hoc solum secum auferret de labore suo*, 'and this alone will he carry with him from his work'. Both align the expression with the preceding 'except', but although this may actually be

Qohelet's intention, it is not expressed explicitly in the Hebrew. For V's 'from his work' (found also in Hie), see the note at 5.14: Jerome clearly takes the point here to be similar. In contrast, α' has συνεισέρχεται, 'enters along with', and θ' probably συμπορεύεται, 'goes with', both followed by αὐτῷ, 'him'. The NJPS translation, 'in exchange for his wealth', apparently sees a *beth pretii* here; it gives a strange sense, and has not been adopted by others. The Midrash Rabbah commends reading בעולמו instead of בעמלו, presumably as an exegetical strategy: that reading is not attested as a variant.

8.15 all the days of his life] Lit. 'the days of his life'. T, S, and one of the Babylonian manuscripts collated by Miletto do actually have a word for 'all' (as does one of Kennicott's manuscripts), but they are each probably likewise just trying to bring out the apparent sense. Rather more of the later manuscripts add instead the מספר found in similar expressions at 2.3; 5.17; and 6.12. As for the possessive pronoun, its absence only in the standard text of V is puzzling, especially since Jerome used *diebus uitae suae*, 'for the days of *his* life' in Hie, and *in diebus uitae suae* appears as a variant in the Theodulphian manuscripts: it seems likely that it has simply dropped out elsewhere as redundant.

8.15 which] Gentry prefers ἅς to the ὅσας for which Rahlfs opted. The latter introduces a nuance of 'for as many days as'.

8.16-17

(8.16) When I had set my heart to knowing wisdom, and to observing the work that is done on the earth, since furthermore by day and by night it saw no sleep with its eyes, (8.17) then I saw all the achievement of God, that a human cannot discover the achievement which has been achieved beneath the sun, on account of which that human will work hard to seek, but will not discover. And also, even if the wise man says that he is going to know, he will not be able to discover.

Commentary

Qohelet set his heart to the task of 'knowing wisdom' back in 1.17, and searched for it along with his heart in 7.25. Apparently recalling his quest, he speaks now of a tireless, constant examination that led him to an understanding touched on already in 3.11: God has made it impossible for humans to discover what is really being done in the world. Realizing their own ignorance, humans will work all the harder to find out, but even the wise man who claims he will succeed is certain to fail. What Qohelet's investigation of wisdom has led him to believe, therefore, is that the way in which God runs the world makes it impervious to wisdom, whatever the claims or ambitions of the wise. As the previous verses have suggested, we are as powerless as the subjects of a despot, and unable even to discern what God is doing when he judges our fellow humans. When he now summarizes the conclusions of his study, therefore, Qohelet is making a point that is broader, but that is wholly in line with those observations.

Wisdom will receive a few more mentions in chs. 9 and 10, but this marks the end of Qohelet's particular focus upon it, which began in ch. 7. It also, more explicitly perhaps, marks an end to the quest that he undertook in 1.17. That quest began, we may recall, because his unsatisfactory attempt in 1.13-15, to use wisdom to understand all that was achieved in the world, led him to an examination of wisdom itself. Echoes of the vocabulary used in 1.14 draw us back to that much earlier point, and Qohelet is, in effect, conceding here that wisdom, the quality which he had so cultivated in himself and with which he had set out at first to understand the world, could never, in retrospect, have answered the questions that he posed. He does not claim, it should be emphasized, that wisdom is useless: the point is, rather, that wisdom simply cannot hope to achieve comprehension of a world that is incomprehensible to humans. To that extent, though, Qohelet is acknowledging that his own efforts, and his hopes of using wisdom to answer his questions, were futile from the outset. He was himself, perhaps, a wise man promising insights that he could not deliver.

As in 3.11, it is not entirely clear whether human ignorance is the deliberate result of divine action, or merely a side-effect. The previous analogy with despotism might seem to point one way, but the issue of divine justice points firmly in the other: Qohelet makes no suggestion that the way God judges and punishes has been formulated specifically to confuse humans.

8.16] The relationship between 'knowing wisdom' and 'observing the work' is not drawn out in the Hebrew. Simian-Yofre, 'Conoscere la sapienza', 326, takes them as equivalent, with 'observing' understood in a particular sense of investigating or experimenting, while Schellenberg, 'Qohelet's Use', 152, thinks that Qohelet is specifying in the second task what he means by the first: his concern is not with wisdom in general, but with the human endeavour for wisdom. I am more inclined to think that these are linked but essentially separate quests. Qohelet had set out to do both, and has, very broadly, discussed them separately, with wisdom coming to the fore only since ch. 7. He presents his conclusions now, however, as a sort of synthesis. In 8.17, to be sure, he creates a link by talking about humans 'working' to discover, but the initial 'work that is done on the earth' picks up a phrase, and a motif of investigating with the heart, that appeared very recently in 8.9, where there was no specific connection with wisdom, and it alludes more broadly to 1.13. It seems unlikely that he intends to endow it with a different, more specific significance here.

The expression about sleeplessness is awkward if we try to see it as a reference to humans in general or to Qohelet himself. The easiest reading of the Hebrew involves taking the heart as the subject, and I have adopted that reading here. If that is correct, then the heart is virtually personified, and characterized almost as a servant who has been sent off to accomplish a task, but that does not seem out of line with Qohelet's other references to his heart as a companion or partner in conversation.

8.17] In the midst of this complicated verse, it has been common to read a statement that the human will not discover, 'however much' he tries to do so. This reading seems to fit the context well, which has contributed to its popularity, and it can claim some antiquity: Jerome renders the text along these lines in his Vulgate translation. It is hard to find any basis for it in the Hebrew, however, and Qohelet's point is more probably that the difficulty of discovery will motivate the human to work even harder.

The language of seeking and finding has not been used since it appeared so prominently in 7.25-29, but 'seek' appears once in this verse, and 'find' three times, connecting the sceptical claims here with Qohelet's own, earlier quest.

Notes

8.16 When] G ἐν οἷς, 'in which', reflects באשר, not the כאשר of M (which I take to be the more plausible reading in context), and may be supported in that respect by Hie and S, although the matter is not clear cut. Two later Hebrew manuscripts noted by de Rossi also have באשר. The reading of σ' is complicated: ἐν οἷς διὸ ἔταξα, lit. 'in which therefore I set', is understood by Marshall to involve a rendering of both באשר and כאשר, but although double renderings are not in themselves especially unusual, the translation of alternative readings would be exceptional. Admittedly, we have just seen a possible case, also involving σ', at 8.9, but it seems more likely either that the attestation is faulty here, and has drawn in ἐν οἷς from G (those words are attested in only one manuscript, the others affirmed by a second and by the adoption of διὸ in place of ἐν οἷς by hexaplaric manuscripts), or, less probably, that Symmachus has introduced διὸ interpretatively. Marshall does also note that Field's *Auctarium* has incorrectly placed an unattributed reading ἔγνων here: it refers to the נתתי in 9.1.

8.16 wisdom] M does not have an article with חכמה here, but G has probably read one: there is little basis in the manuscripts for Rahlfs' omission of τὴν. The fact that T interprets this specifically as 'the wisdom of the Torah' might suggest that it too found an article. If the article is original, which is far from certain, then its purpose was perhaps to highlight the reference here to 1.17—this is, in particular, the wisdom that Qohelet set out back then to investigate—and it might have dropped out of M, if that purpose was not recognized, simply because it seemed odd.

8.16 that is done] On the problems that surround the vocalization of נעשה generally, see the note at 1.9. Here M reads qatal, but G τὸν πεποιημένον is a participle (cf. 1.9, 14; 2.17; 4.3; 8.17; 9.6): the perfect participle is rarely used elsewhere to render the qatal (cf. Yi, 169), but it is hard to say whether this is a matter of grammatical understanding or of stylistic preference.

8.16 since furthermore by day and by night it saw no sleep with its eyes] There is a general consensus that the overall structure of Qohelet's statement here is 'When I set my heart...then I saw...'. This statement about sleeplessness seems intrusive, therefore, and matters are made worse by the fact that it is difficult to give any meaningful sense in context to the כי גם which introduces it (see the note on 'even' at 4.14).

The most common approach is to regard the clause as a parenthetical expression of all the busy-ness on earth, in which the suffix pronouns refer to an indefinite subject—hence RSV 'how neither day nor night one's eyes see sleep'. This is probably how G has taken it (and, in passing, we may note with Vinel its interesting differential translations of ראה). However, that reading is not just clunky (since the pronouns could have been avoided altogether), it also introduces an idea that is both irrelevant to Qohelet's broader point and inherently implausible: even granting a degree of hyperbole, is Qohelet really claiming that nobody ever sleeps? The leading alternatives are simply to move the statement (Seow transfers it to the next verse), to replace the third-person pronouns with first-person ones (so that it is Qohelet himself who does not sleep; cf. Fox), or to treat כי גם as concessive, and the statement as pre-empting what follows ('even though he does not sleep...the human will not discover', cf. Gordis). Joüon, 'Notes philologiques', 423-24, shifts text around to create separate statements about human and divine work in vv. 16 and 17, and wonders whether the reference was originally to experiencing עני in the sense of 'worry' during the day, leading to sleeplessness at night; he also suspects כי גם might be a dittograph of ביום.

None of these is very satisfactory. It is questionable, furthermore, whether Gordis' suggestion is even possible, while Joüon seems simply to be re-writing the text to say what he wants. I take the suffix pronouns, in fact, to be referring back to לבי, not to Qohelet or to humans in general, and the implication of כי גם to be that Qohelet is adding a further specification: he set his heart to knowing, and then, when it had worked tirelessly, he finally saw. This imagery introduces the slightly odd idea of a heart that has eyes, but Qohelet does not really treat לב as a physical organ, and he shows no reluctance to personify his heart elsewhere.

8.17 achievement of God, that] As at 7.13, G (cf. Hie, V) has plural τὰ ποιήματα, 'the works', where M has singular מעשה. σ' καὶ κατέμαθον ὅτι πάντων τῶν ἔργων τοῦ θεοῦ, 'and I learned that from all the works of God', is also plural, but although possible, it is again less certain here than in 5.5 that this represents a Hebrew variant, and it may be interpretative; see the notes at 5.5; 7.13; 12.14.

The point may seem minor, but it plays into broader questions about the meaning of 8.16-17, and in particular the role here of כי. Broadly, this may be understood in one of three ways: (1) it introduces a secondary object of וראיתי, so that Qohelet sees 'all the work(s) of God (and) that'; (2) it introduces a specification of the whole work(s) of God, that they consist of preventing humans from seeing; and (3) that it just means something like 'surely' here, and introduces a conclusion reached from the observation, not a part of that observation. This third understanding, with כי meaning 'surely', has been advocated at length in Rudman, 'Eccl. 8:17a', largely on the basis that the first two are grammatically difficult. This difficulty derives from Rudman's observation that in all other instances where verbs of perception take a clause as a second object, the first object is the subject of that clause (e.g. Gen 1.4, 'God saw the light, that it was good'; and note the instance at Eccl 11.8). If that is a rule, then it excludes the first understanding, and Rudman would then further extend this case to readings of the clause as a specification, which Fox and others link to the apparently epexegetical use of a כי clause in Jon 3.10, 'God saw their works, that they repented of their evil way': here, he notes that 'their' becomes the subject 'they' in that clause. If Rudman is right that verbs of perception can never take as their second object a clause with a subject other than the initial object, then this does indeed seem to rule out all but the third understanding, and he has at least shown that there is no clear parallel for the usages presumed in the first two.

I think that Rudman is wrong about this, however. As a matter of grammar and syntax, verbs of perception can, of course, take more than one object, and כי clauses can serve as objects for such verbs, so there is nothing fundamental to exclude the possibility of a substantive and a כי clause acting as separate objects for the same verb. In 8.5-7, moreover, we have just seen multiple כי clauses associated with one verb. If substantives are regularly followed, in the examples that Rudman cites, by כי clauses that further describe or specify them, then that is simply because they are using the particular predicative construction that we encountered earlier in 4.4 (see the notes there). Jon 3.10 is not using quite that construction, and *does* have a subject for the clause that is not the same as the initial object: grammatically, it is irrelevant that they are linked by a possessive pronoun (although this might suggest that the writer was aiming for a similar effect), and that verse significantly undermines his claim. If such exceptions are rare, it is not because there is some rule involved, but because of a feature that we noted in connection with 4.4, that substantival objects and object-clauses are different in character, and tend to require slightly different senses of the verb; this makes it awkward to mix them except for effect (the same is true in English, where we would not often say 'I saw Smith and that Jones was right').

In Jon 3.10, the two objects are linked by the fact that 'they repented' is not a wholly separate object, but unpacks 'their works'. This makes it feasible to combine them, and something very similar appears to be going on in this verse, which is why most scholars have, rightly I think, adopted the second of the understandings outlined above. This has the advantage also of qualifying Qohelet's claim to have seen all the work of God, which would sit very uncomfortably with claims elsewhere (3.11 in particular), if it were left unqualified. Returning to the text, it should be noted that if Qohelet is referring to a particular aspect of divine activity—the setting of limits on human discovery—then it seems more likely that the singular would have been used, as in M, than the plural, so this interpretation favours that reading. We might also observe that Qohelet's only other use of כל מעשה was very recently in 8.9 (the expression will recur in the epilogue at 12.14); that use, in another concluding observation, was with reference to human work 'beneath the sun', and it seems likely that there is an intention here to match it, with a corresponding reference to the work of God.

8.17 a human...that human] Lit. '(a) human...the human'. M has האדם in both places, with an article, but there is almost no attestation of an article in manuscripts of G for the first use, and the witnesses are divided over the second. Rahlfs and Gentry both take the article to be original in the second instance, but not the first. It is not clear that we can draw a precise analogy with the problems surrounding determination of אדם in the expression כל (ה)אדם) at 3.13; 5.18; 7.2, as does Goldman, but in any case, if G did have a different reading in each place, that tends to affirm that the translator found אדם then האדם in his source-text. The tendency for such distinctions to be ironed out in transmission makes it more likely than not that this is the original reading, and, if so, Qohelet is speaking not of a generic human each time, but saying on the second occasion that the same human who could not discover will work hard to discover.

For the statement containing the first use, σ' reads οὐ δύναται ὁ ἄνθρωπος ἐξευρεῖν οὐδὲ ἓν ἔργον πρασσόμενον, '(from all the works of God) the human is able to discover not a single work that has been done', which does have an article, but which is also very interpretative.

8.17 on account of which] The very common understanding 'however much', with its conditional or concessive nuance, has been rejected by a number of recent commentators. Although it gives a nice sense in context (cf. RSV 'However much man may toil in seeking, he will not find it out'), it is very hard to find any basis for it in the Hebrew.[1]

The expression in M, בשל אשר, consists of the preposition -ב attached to של, which serves as a possessive counterpart to the relative -ש, and then אשר, so it means literally something like 'in of which that'. We do not find the expression elsewhere in biblical sources, although בשלמי, 'because of

---

[1] The defences of this reading often seem to involve a certain looseness, or even sleight of hand. Fox, for instance, says that 'the phrase [viz. בשל אשר] introduces a causal clause...rather than a final or result clause', but then he translates, 'for even if a man seeks arduously'. The phrase בשל אשר can indeed

whom?', and בשלי, 'because of me', in Jon 1.7 and 1.12 illustrate uses of ב- with של. In 4QMMT B 12, however, we do find בשל שלוא meaning 'so as not to', and in B 16; C 30 ש- בשל conversely means 'so that' (see Qimron and Strugnell, *Qumran Cave 4: V: Miqṣat ma'aśe ha-torah*, 47-48), while in a second-century CE letter,]ם לו שיבו בשל דבר לכל is translated by the editors (Milik, Vaux, and Benoit, *Les Grottes de Murabba'ât*, 164-66) as 'au sujet de tout ce qui lui revient de la part de', 'on the subject of all that is owed him by'—although the fragmentary context makes it difficult to establish the sense precisely. It is a reasonable supposition, held by many commentators, that the Hebrew functions as an equivalent to the Aramaic ד- בדיל, which with a verb means 'on account of the fact that', 'in order that', or 'with the result that'.[2]

Neither the Hebrew nor the Aramaic, though, ever means 'however much'—indeed, neither is ever clearly used with any concessive sense—while the Hebrew here is understood to have such an implication by none of the ancient versions. In line with the last of the senses just listed, 'with the result that', σ' διόπερ (= δι' ὅπερ), 'wherefore', and Hie *ut quaereret*, 'that he might seek', both apparently understand the fruitless search, or at least the fruitlessness of the search, to be a product of what has just been said: no person can discover, and therefore a person will seek but not discover. This is actually the least common meaning attested for the Aramaic expression, but it suits well the uses of ש- בשל in 4QMMT. The בד of T is variously written separately or as a prefix to the next verb, but almost always understood to be the prefixed בד-, 'when' or 'if', rather than 'because', so T understands בשל -ש to be pointing forward ('when a man works…he will not find')—or at least paraphrases in those terms.

It is G ὅσα ἂν μοχθήσῃ ὁ ἄνθρωπος τοῦ ζητῆσαι that is surprising here, however. The translator's only use of ὅσα ἂν outside 8.17 is at 9.10, where πάντα ὅσα ἂν εὕρῃ ἡ χείρ σου, 'all the things that your hand might find', is used for ידך תמצא אשר כל, but he uses ὅσος for אשר at 2.12; 3.14, 15; 8.9; 9.10; 11.5, in contexts where אשר either appears in connection with כל or else can

mean 'because' (see below), but it is *not* used like 'for' to introduce explanations. Conditional clauses, moreover, can be asyndetic or can have a conditional particle, but they cannot be introduced by a causative conjunction. Schoors, differently, may give considerable space in his discussion to the meanings of the Hebrew and Aramaic, but his actual defence of the traditional reading appears to consist solely of the fact that none of the attested senses is 'superior' to it. He does not point out that there is no attestation of a concessive sense, but does try to claim that 'since mankind will' amounts to much the same as his own 'however much mankind may'—which it does not.

[2] That they are equivalent is likely, but that they are identical in scope or use seems less certain. The attested uses of the Hebrew at Qumran are principally in final clauses, while the Aramaic at Qumran nearly always means 'because'; cf. Cook, *Dictionary of Qumran Aramaic*, 31.

be understood to mean 'the things that'. Accordingly, his probable intention here is 'whatever the man labours to find'. This most likely influenced S ܠܕ ܢܒܥܐ ܒܢܫܐ ܕܥܡܠ *kl dᶜml brnšʾ dnb*⁽ᵒ⁾, 'all at which a man labours to seek',[3] and the proportionality that can be inherent in ὅσα probably also inspired V *quanto plus laborauerit ad quaerendum tanto minus inueniat*, 'the more he has worked at seeking, the less he finds'. If the G translator found בשל אשר in his source-text, however, then he has effectively ignored בשל, which seems out of character. Matters are complicated by the fact that, a little later in this verse, we find ὅσα ἂν used again, this time where M has אם: Gentry, 'Propaedeutic', 154-55, defends that reading as G* very persuasively (taking it also to be the reading of θ′), and the reading has influenced S, but it is again hard to reconcile it with M (for which we should expect ἐάν).

It looks very much as though the G translator read a text that had two virtually parallel statements with אשר, which he understood as:

what the human strives to seek, then he will not find, and also
what the wise man claims to know, he will not be able to find

A case could be made that this is original, at least in part, but it is more likely that the first statement was re-construed in this way after בשל had dropped out or been misunderstood, and the second then assimilated to it. Further assimilation is visible in S, which omits the conjunction on 'he will not find' (and see below on 'he will not be able').

8.17 And also, even if] וגם אם has a conditional sense here, with an additive and probably a concessive nuance. I do not think the primary purpose is to contrast the claims of the wise man with the reality of limitations upon wisdom, so much as to clarify that *no* human is exempted. That nuance, however, might be considered a secondary implication of the context, and אם often has the sense 'though'. The idea of Schoors and others, that the words גם אם together constitute a 'composite particle', explicitly conveying such a concessive sense (and removing the additive force from גם), is harder to substantiate. In biblical Hebrew, these words only ever occur together elsewhere at 4.11, where no such suggestion is generally made, and they can be translated in exactly the same way here as there, according to the normal sense that each word has individually. Comparisons have long been made with an אף אם found in Phoenician, and the link is affirmed by Dahood, 'Canaanite-Phoenician', 48; Piotti, 'Usi Linguistici', 54, sees in it evidence for Phoenician influence on the Hebrew of the book. However, where that expression occurs (just once, it seems) in *KAI* 14.6 (*CIS* 3.6), it likewise appears to mean just

---

[3] It seems far more likely (*pace* Kamenetzky 225-26, 236) that both uses in the verse of ܕ- ܠܕ *kl d-*, 'all that', are renderings of ὅσα, than that the translator found כל at either point in a Hebrew source, or that ܘܟܠ *wkl*, 'and all', in the second is an error for ܘܐܦ *wʾp*, 'and also' (= וגם).

'also, if', and to involve simply the juxtaposition of two common particles. It seems unnecessarily speculative to speak here of a Hebrew composite formed under the influence of a Phoenician composite, rather than of the same need, simultaneously to express addition and condition, arising coincidentally in more than one text.

8.17 the wise man] The G tradition shows much the same hesitation over the article here as with the occurrences of 'human' earlier in the verse. Caution is needed when it comes to determination in Aramaic, but T גבר חכים would tend to support a reading without an article,[4] and it is possible that both traditions reflect a variant with חכם instead of החכם.

8.17 says that he is going to know] The Hebrew could also mean 'says that he knows', or 'claims to know', and this is a translation often adopted by commentators. The text, however, goes on to say that he is unable to discover whatever it is, not that he 'does not know', and the implication is surely that, when the wise man makes his claim, he has not yet discovered his inability. The claim, then, involves a statement of future knowledge, that he is 'going to know' (e.g. Barton) or 'intending to know' (Fox), and the infinitive with -ל is being used, as a number of times elsewhere in the book, with a prospective aspect (see, e.g., the note on 'and what is to be' at 3.15).

8.17 he will not be able] In light of the tendency that we saw above, for the statements about the human and the wise man to become assimilated, it is interesting to note that some manuscripts of G add a conjunction, bringing οὐ δυνήσεται, 'he will not be able', into line with καὶ οὐχ εὑρήσει, '*and* he will not find'; a conjunction is also found in a number of later Hebrew manuscripts (see Kennicott; Miletto).

---

[4] The relevant section of text is lacking from many manuscripts of T, which skip from the first דעתיד למהוי in the verse to the second. Knobel gives the missing text as: ולא ישכח ואף אן יימר גבר חכים במימריה למדע לא דעתיד למהוי, 'he shall not find out, and also if a wise man says to himself that he will know what will be'; cf. Knobel, 'Targum Qoheleth', 287-88; *Targum*, 44.

Introduction to 9.1-12

Death and Living

(9.1) For I put all this to my heart, and my heart saw all this, that the righteous and the wise and their works are in the hand of God. No human understands loving and hating: everything before them (9.2) is illusion, because the same things happen to each, to the righteous and to the wicked, to the good and to the bad, to the clean and to the unclean, to the person who sacrifices, and to the person who never sacrifices; as the good man, so the sinner, the one who takes an oath, as one who fears an oath. (9.3a-b) This is a problem in everything which is done beneath the sun, that the same things happen to all.

And also, the heart of humans is encouraged to do what is wrong, and mindlessness is in their hearts during their lives.

(9.3c) And the back of each is to the dead, (9.4) for when any associates with all the living, there is reassurance—since it seems to a live dog that he is better than a dead lion. (9.5) This is because the living may know that they will die while the dead know nothing at all. And there is no more recompense for them, for any memory of them is lost; (9.6) their love, and their hate, and their passion—each has already perished, and there is nothing which is theirs for them anymore, forever, in all that is done beneath the sun.

(9.7) Come on, eat your bread with pleasure, and drink your wine with a happy heart. For God has already accepted your work. (9.8) Let your clothes be white at all times, and let not oil be lacking on your head. (9.9) Experience life with a woman you love all the days of your life of illusion, which he has given you beneath the sun, all the days of your illusion, for that is what is yours in life.

INTRODUCTION TO 9.1-12   397

And in all the business at which you work beneath the sun,
(9.10) anything which your hand finds to do, do with all your
might. For there is no work, or plan, or knowledge, or wisdom
in Sheol, which is where you are going.

(9.11) Again, I observed beneath the sun that the fast do not own
the race, nor the mighty the battle; nor likewise the wise, food,
nor the intelligent, wealth, nor the knowledgeable, favour—that
timing and circumstance affect them all.

(9.12) Also, that no human knows their time, like fish which are
caught in a terrible net, or like birds caught in a trap. Like them,
humans are held ensnared, for when a terrible time will fall
suddenly upon them.

There is no sharp break here. In 9.1, Qohelet picks up a reference
to his heart's investigations from 8.16, while 9.3 shows the same
concern as 8.11 with the effect of human ignorance upon human
motivations and behaviour. I am not wholly persuaded by the
claims made in Wright, 'Ecclesiastes 9:1-12', about the key structural and summarizing role of these verses, but they do occupy
an interesting position. In ch. 8, Qohelet's concerns were initially
with human ignorance and the limits of wisdom, while in 9.13 he
will return more specifically to the strengths and weaknesses of
wisdom. In thematic terms, therefore, everything between 8.10 and
9.12 is a sort of diversion, in which Qohelet describes the effects of
human ignorance upon human behaviour with respect in particular
to problems caused by the invisibility of divine judgment. Qohelet
builds upon the problem to draw out issues of life and death here,
considering these in the light of some of his strongest statements
about divine determinism, but in doing so seems to move ever
further away from the questions about wisdom with which he
began, and which he intends to pick up again shortly.

It is probably this broader structural concern that leads the
author to bookend the discussion with explicit statements of human
ignorance in 9.1 and 9.12, but it is important also to observe that such
ignorance is genuinely presented as the basis of Qohelet's reasoning,
and is not used merely as an artificial link between themes. Correspondingly, the call to pleasure here evokes the earlier language
of pleasure being one's 'portion' in life, but Qohelet is no longer
arguing on the basis that we can find no other profit: his point now

is rather that our ignorance precludes any other course. When we can find no guidance from the fate of the living, and refuse to look to the dead, then we might just as well simply enjoy life as best we can—with clean laundry, scented oils, and a beloved companion. It is for that reason, perhaps, that pleasure is no longer presented only or mostly as something to be found in work and activity, but more broadly as a principle that can guide our choices, in a way that our faulty calculations of advantage cannot.

The Hebrew is very difficult at various points, but the discussion probably begins with the statement of another conclusion that Qohelet has reached through his investigations. According to this, humans who behave wisely or well do so at the direction of God: nobody really understands the choices that they make, because all they can see is that the same thing seems to happen to everybody, whatever moral or religious behaviours they have adopted. This is a fundamental problem, which misleads people into doing wrong or being foolish while they are alive, and it is exacerbated by the inclination of the living to look to the living (who may set misleading examples), rather than to the dead (whose lives and deaths, perhaps, may more easily be considered in the round). Humans do this because they find reassurance in it, sharing the belief of every living creature, however lowly, that it is better off than even the greatest of the dead, who have nothing more in the world—not even the knowledge of their own mortality, which the living at least have in common. Correspondingly, however, the dead lose any remaining stake that they might have had in the world: the choices that they made and the courses that they pursued are simply forgotten. Qohelet is not talking directly about an afterlife in 9.5-6, and his point is probably not that the dead might otherwise hang on to some benefit as they lie in their graves. Rather, he implies, nobody can expect their lives to set an example, or to make a lasting mark on a world that looks only to the living (cf. 1.11; 2.16). Gammie, 'Stoicism', 182, thinks that he is contradicting a Stoic position.

In the first part of this discussion, therefore, the initial problem is that humans can make no informed decisions about their behaviour for themselves, but a part of the explanation—that they seek models to emulate or reject only among the living—leads Qohelet to the rather different point that we can seek no recompense for our lives by anticipating some future influence upon others. What follows in 9.7-10 picks up both issues: there is nothing to be gained by worrying about our choices, and we should invest effort in enjoyment of our lives, not in our deaths. The language echoes motifs found as early as the Old Babylonian version of the Epic of Gilgamesh, where similar advice is offered to dissuade the hero from his pursuit of immortality. It is hard to say whether the author consciously drew on that or any other text in particular, but the purpose here is likewise to discourage us from seeking immortality—although not in the literal sense. By considering the matter alongside the question of choice, however, Qohelet draws in another argument. To be sure, the knowledge that we shall die—and be forgotten—should motivate us to live our lives to the full, but we are also enabled to do so by the realization that our actions should not be a source of concern to us: we can only do anything that we do because it suits God that we do it, and so everything has been, effectively, approved in advance. At the beginning of the discussion, Qohelet used this determinism to imply that the righteous can claim no virtue for themselves, when their behaviour is controlled by God, but by the end of 9.10 it has been presented as liberating.

Of course, this is in some sense the culmination of ideas presented much earlier, at the end of ch. 2 and in ch. 3, but it sits uneasily with Qohelet's continued insistence upon the reality of judgment, which is implicit even here in his ideas about humans being misled. In 11.9, he will offer advice to the young along rather the same lines—but also offer an explicit reminder that their behaviour will be subject to a reckoning. No real resolution is ever offered, although his various references to fear of God may suggest that Qohelet thinks in terms of a judgment based at least in part on attitudes and motivations. Both here and in 11.9, however, there seems to be some implication that Qohelet sees the prospect of judgment as irrelevant to the living of life. Yes, we shall be judged, and we should not set out deliberately to antagonize God, but at the same time we have no way to discern what it is that he actually wants us to do. Accordingly, it makes no sense to ruin enjoyment of our lives by worrying about everything that we do, especially when what we do is, by definition, in accordance with the will of God, whether it is good or bad. Clearly, being good brings no guarantee that our lives will be good, and even if we end up being punished, the worst we face may be a foreshortening of our already brief time in the world. If everyone ends up in the same place anyway, that may be a problem in the sense that nobody can tell what they should be doing, but it also suggests that nobody should worry too much about what they are doing.

That optimistic way of looking at things is both undercut and emphasized by 9.11-12, which are presented as a separate observation, but which serve as a sort of afterword to what has just been said, as well as offering points of contact with what will follow. Although they are linked by a theme of unpredictability and by their use of analogies, each verse makes a separate point. The first continues the idea, found already in the last chapter, that things do not always turn out for people the way that we might expect, but instead of presenting this in terms of good things happening to bad people, and *vice versa*, it expresses the problem in terms of unexpected outcomes: those whose intellectual qualities might seem to have earned them the good things in life, do not (always, by implication) get them. This is presented as analogous to the fact that fast runners do not always win their race, or the powerful their battle, which seems to exclude the notion of a simple reversal here: unless Qohelet has hares and tortoises in mind, the point is probably not that the slowest and weakest win when they do not deserve to, but that even the swift and mighty may have bad days, or may encounter others who are still swifter or mightier than they are. We should not, correspondingly, presume that the intelligent will always get what they might be deemed to deserve. Qohelet will shortly introduce us to a poor wise man, in 9.15, who illustrates that point (and we have already met a poor, wise child in 4.13).

The second point, made in 9.12, extends Qohelet's ideas about human ignorance. When we do not know the outcomes for us of our actions, we also remain ignorant of the time at which we shall die. This might in 9.7-10 have been presented as a further reason for us to enjoy life while we can, but now it offers Qohelet the opportunity for some sinister images instead: humans are like fish in a net, or birds in a trap, unable to escape, but also unable to predict when the hunter will return to slaughter them. That is hardly a circumstance that might provoke celebration, but just as 9.10 reminds us of the existence that awaits us in Sheol, so 9.12 similarly highlights the seriousness of a situation over which we have no control, and the duration of which we cannot predict. These reminders serve to make it clear that Qohelet is telling us to enjoy life not because things are wonderful, but because they are terrible. At the same time, though, they lend an impetus and urgency to the advice: we must run our race even when we know that we may lose it, and should never delay when we have no idea how close the end may be.

9.1-3B

(9.1) For I put all this to my heart, and my heart saw all this, that the righteous and the wise and their works are in the hand of God. No human understands loving and hating: everything before them (9.2) is illusion, because the same things happen to each, to the righteous and to the wicked, to the good and to the bad, to the clean and to the unclean, to the person who sacrifices, and to the person who never sacrifices; as the good man, so the sinner, the one who takes an oath, as one who fears an oath. (9.3a-b) This is a problem in everything which is done beneath the sun, that the same things happen to all.

And also, the heart of humans is encouraged to do what is wrong, and mindlessness is in their hearts during their lives.

Commentary

The most significant problem here is the meaning of Qohelet's claim in 9.1, that, literally, 'both love and hate, there is no human knowing', which has been understood in various ways. The recurrence of love and hate in 9.6, however, points away from the common idea that Qohelet is talking about people's ignorance of God's attitudes or motivations, because in that verse these are things that humans possess but lose at death, alongside the sort of passion that, according to 4.4, they invest in work. It is more probable that Qohelet is talking about the preferences that people display—what they 'love' to do and what they 'hate' to do. These preferences distinguish the various groups contrasted with each other in 9.2, but humans can have no insight into which are beneficial and which harmful, because the same thing happens to all these groups regardless of the activities they have chosen or rejected. The distinctions are variously ethical and ritual or religious, so the issue is one of relationship to God, and the point would seem more precisely to be that people are unable to understand how the different ways in which they choose to behave or interact with God actually affect what happens to them, since there seems to be only one outcome for everybody.

This serves as an explanation for Qohelet's first, very striking claim here, that the righteous, the wise and their actions are 'in the hand of God', which, in this context, is probably not specifically intended as a statement of determinism, but is a way of saying that they have no control of their own, and possess no insight of their own into what actions they should choose or reject in order to please or displease God. The following verse, 9.3, will enlarge upon this to pick up the point that a lack of any discrimination visible to humans can drive them actively to do what is wrong—a point similar to that made earlier in 8.11—but the issue is not initially that God actively manipulates the righteous and the wise so that they behave in particular ways, rather that they have no independent basis for their decisions. When humans cannot tell for themselves what it is that they ought to be doing, in ethical and religious terms, then what they will do, along with its consequences, is effectively at the discretion of God.

Again, though, the discourse is in terms not of divine action but of human perception—despite such assertions as Mazzinghi, 'Divine Violence', 553, that 'the concept of the existence of a retributive principle is debated' in these verses, or that 'Qoheleth seems to dispute the very action of God'. Everything here is about what humans perceive, and their subsequent actions; nothing directly about what God does or does not do. This framing of the claims about one thing happening to everybody also poses an obstacle to the attempts of, e.g., Michel, *Untersuchungen*, 166-83, or Sekine, 'Qohelet als Nihilist', 17-18, to see here a specific opposition to contemporary beliefs in an afterlife where the righteous and wicked are treated separately. Qohelet's affirmations in 9.5-6, 10, of course, suggest strongly that he holds no such belief himself. The 'problem' he outlines in these first few verses, however, is not a matter of what actually happens to the dead beyond death, but of the way in which the living react to a seeming lack of differentiation. Along the same lines, finally, it is important to emphasize that Qohelet does not, in fact, suggest that there is in reality no differentiation, or that the fate of individuals is actually unaffected by their moral qualities or religious practices—only that the limits of what they can discern seem to constrain their ability to change their fates by changing what they do. God may not be indifferent to human behaviour, but the way he works does not show humans how to behave (cf. Lavoie, 'Vie, mort', 76, who speaks of a creator whose attitude is not even pedagogical—although Lavoie does also see a deistic portrayal of divine indifference).

9.1] The verse begins with a symmetrical statement, but whereas 'all this' at the beginning is a reference to the preceding ideas, which Qohelet set himself to think about, 'all this' at the end describes the conclusions that he reaches. The distinction is rather lost in the M text, which is difficult and probably corrupt (see the notes), and in some other versions based on similar readings, but it is preserved in the Greek and Syriac. There are also problems in M at the end of the verse, and the beginning of the next, after *hbl* was mistakenly transcribed as *hkl*, turning 'vapour' into 'all'. Again, the original reading can be determined from other witnesses, but the error has made it difficult to find any reasonable sense in the Hebrew, and has contributed to what is certainly a mis-division of the Masoretic text.

These problems have made an already difficult text still harder to understand, but essentially Qohelet seems to be making a statement about the human inability to understand what consequences can flow from the adoption or rejection of particular behaviours—because, as 9.3 will point out, the same thing seems to happen to everybody. Humans do not make informed choices about what they do, so even the actions of the righteous and the wise are at the mercy of divine, not human decisions.

The appearance of 'the wise' here is striking, not least because they will not appear in the next verse, but the reference clarifies an important distinction. In 9.2 Qohelet is talking about behaviours, as represented by those who adopt them (and who all share the same fate). Here, however, he is talking about those who seek to understand those behaviours: the righteous who simply want to do right, and the wise who want to discern the behaviours that lead to the best outcomes. These classes are not mutually exclusive, although they are not the same, but they embody the different motives that might lie behind wishing to distinguish good behaviours from bad. With respect to the logic of Qohelet's point, the 'righteous' here are distinct from the 'righteous' of 9.2: these are the people who want to do what is right, while those are the people who are considered to be doing what is right by anyone trying to assess the various behaviours listed in that verse.

9.2] The problems with the M text persist into this verse, where it does not have a reference to 'the bad' which is found in other witnesses: it is difficult to establish whether the pair 'good'/'bad' is secondary or not (and I have included it myself only after much hesitation), but the isolated 'good' in M seems unlikely to be original. Most of the verse is simply another of Qohelet's lists, consisting of six pairs, and the elements of the list mostly relate to general patterns of character or behaviour (being good/bad, clean/ unclean, etc.). The last two, however, are presented slightly differently, and describe more specific activities: offering sacrifices and making oaths. These are, of course, the same activities that Qohelet mentioned at the beginning of ch. 5, where he associated sacrifice with the insecurity of fools and warned against oaths. It seems unlikely that this is accidental, and the repetition emphasizes that, although there may indeed be consequences for actions, perhaps of the sort that he spelled out earlier for oaths, the point here is that any such consequences are effectively invisible.

9.3a-b] The first part of the verse evokes 8.11, where Qohelet was making a similar point about the human inability to see what is happening, but ignorance now is associated not just with doing what is wrong, but with a lifelong state of confusion or stupidity. This rounds off Qohelet's initial point: such a state makes it impossible for humans to have real control over their own lives. The reference to living also facilitates the transition to his next comments, which will be about the attitudes of the living toward the dead, but it is the juxtaposition of the two which seems to have fuelled an early understanding that the last few words of 9.3 belong with this statement, and not with what follows in 9.4. This will be discussed below, but it lies behind what should be considered another mis-division of the text by the Masoretes.

It is important to note that in 8.11, the lack of a swift indictment for wrongful behaviour was presented explicitly as the reason for humans being encouraged to act wrongly. No such logical connection is offered here, and instead, Qohelet identifies the lack of differentiation itself as the primary problem. The human response is then added in a way that associates the two, but leaves open the possibility of understanding that response both as a consequence of the lack, and as the reason why that lack constitutes a problem affecting every action taken in the world. Qohelet's purpose is apparently not to criticize what humans do, but once again to describe a formidable obstacle to the human discernment of what is right and wrong. The absence of an explicit logical connection between the two points here does also, however, make it possible to take the statement about humans as the beginning of his next discussion, with which the reference to 'lives' also forges a connection. It is very possible, therefore, that 9.3b is acting as a bridge to that discussion, offering the general issue of human motivations as a way across to the particular issue of attitudes toward the dead.

Notes

9.1 I put all this to my heart, and my heart saw all this] M את כל זה נתתי אל לבי ולבור את כל זה apparently means 'all this I gave to my heart and to examine(?) all this'. The text is supported by T, and more broadly by Hie *omne hoc dedi in corde meo ut considerarem uniuersa*, 'I gave all this into my heart that I might consider all things'; Jerome acknowledges the influence of σ', which he reports here as *omnia haec statui in corde meo ut uentilarem uniuersa*, 'I set all these things in my heart, that I might winnow all things'.[1] In G, on the other hand, we find σὺν πᾶν τοῦτο ἔδωκα εἰς καρδίαν μου καὶ καρδία μου σὺν πᾶν εἶδεν τοῦτο, 'all this I gave to my heart and my heart saw all of this'—although the sequence πᾶν εἶδεν τοῦτο is curious, with the verb positioned intrusively. S has much the same, and is probably following G, but has a more normal word-order: ܗܢܐ ܟܠ ܚܙܝ ܘܠܒܝ ܒܠܒܝ ܝܗܒܬ ܗܠܝܢ ܟܠ ܕܝܬ *dyt kl hlyn yhbt blby wlby ḥzʾ yt kl hnʾ*, 'I gave all these into my heart, and my heart saw all this'.

Except perhaps for V, which is paraphrasing, none of the versions supports the deletion of the second את כל זה, which Sacchi views as secondary. There can be little doubt, though, that the reading in G and S is derived from a Hebrew text that had ולבי ראה את where M has ולבור את, although in G the εἶδεν has subsequently slipped into the wrong position.[2] Scholars do not

---

[1] I mentioned in the notes to 8.16 an unattributed reading ἔγνων, 'I knew', from ms 252, which Field, *Auctarium*, mistakenly attached to the נתתי of that verse instead of this, and attributed to σ'. It appears in Gentry's second apparatus, but Marshall, 364, denies that it is hexaplaric, and it seems likely that it is simply a gloss, attempting to explain the sense of the expression, rather than part of any translation.

[2] *BHQ* favours the reading ולבי ראה, citing S in support. While I agree with that in principle, a note of caution should be sounded about the basis of the reading in S, which may simply be a revision of G, rather than an independent witness to a Hebrew source-text.

agree, however, which reading is original. If it is ולבי ראה את, then the text in M probably appeared after the loss of אה before the graphically similar את, followed by a reading of י as ו in an attempt to make sense of לב יד. If ולבור את is the original, then, conversely, the other text probably emerged after dittography of the את. Neither change is inherently more likely than the other, so the matter hinges on questions of sense and syntax.

Here it is important to note that לבור is an otherwise unattested form: commentators who accept it as original generally read it as the infinitive construct with -ל of a verb בור, 'examine', or of the better attested ברר: on those, see the note at 3.18.[3] σ' probably understood the latter, rendering the verb's common implication of selection or purification in terms of winnowing, and that is probably the best route to any understanding that Qohelet is turning things over in his heart. If the verb itself might yield a satisfactory sense, however, the same cannot easily be said of its form. With the prefixed conjunction, the infinitive cannot simply be expressing purpose, as σ' takes it (and it is probably this difficulty that has led a few Hebrew manuscripts to drop the conjunction; see Miletto, 211). For the same reason, we can hardly just conjure up a הייתי before the verb to give '(I was) going to consider', as Wildeboer would like. Those who retain לבור, therefore, commonly resort to the idea that it is an infinitive consecutive, equivalent to a finite verb (cf. GKC §114 p; J-M §124 p), which is by no means impossible, although that usage is uncommon. On balance, however, it is difficult to see why we should adopt a reading that involves either a very rare verb, or a more common verb in a rare form and rare sense, which has to be understood as part of a rare construction. Gordis complains that the G reading 'is a case of leveling an unfamiliar phrase to the ordinary', but the fact that Qohelet's heart is said to 'see' things elsewhere (1.16; cf. 8.16) does more to affirm the plausibility of that reading than to undermine it.

On a more minor matter, it is worth noting the very large number of late Hebrew manuscripts listed by de Rossi as reading את לבי rather than אל לבי; cf. also Lavoie and Mehramooz, 'Le Texte hébreu et la traduction judéo-persane', 500. Galling 1940 prefers this, and in his 1969 edition he suggests reading אל כל זה נתתי את לבי—which Hertzberg had also proposed in 1932 and 1963, to give a construction closer to 1.13 and 8.16, where Qohelet sets his heart to things, rather than putting things to his heart. The emendation is not unattractive or implausible, but it is unnecessary, and there is little to support it: the Hebrew variant has itself probably emerged under the influence of that usage elsewhere, and is accordingly more likely to be secondary than is the current reading. Qohelet is probably just varying his expression, as often

---

[3] As Goldman implies, interpretations of the verb in terms of 'examining' here and at 3.18 constitute something close to a circular argument, with each adduced in support of the other. Fischer, *Skepsis*, 115, would simply emend it to לתור to get that sense.

(cf. Ogden, 'Qoheleth IX 1-16', 159). Some other, non-Hebrew witnesses (Hie, V, S, Syh, and a few mss of G) have 'in' my heart, but may have been influenced in this respect by σ', and in any case almost certainly reflect an interpretation of אל or εἰς as 'into', rather than a further Hebrew variant with בלבי.

9.1 their works] Or 'servants'. In Hebrew, עבד means 'servant' or 'slave', and that is presumably how T has understood עבדיהם when it talks about תלמידיהון דמשתעבדין להון, 'their disciples who serve them' (cf. Rashi: תלמידיהם משמשיהם הולכי אורחותם, 'their disciples, their servants, who walk in their ways'; Codex Graecus Venetus οἱ οἰκέται σφῶν, 'their household slaves'). G, however, has ἐργασίαι αὐτῶν, 'their works', which employs a term used in the Greek of Gen 29.27 for עבדה, 'work' or 'service'. Jerome reports the reading of σ', furthermore, as *opera eorum*, 'their works', and adopts the same wording in Hie and V.

The noun עבדה is not used in the plural, and the interpretation 'works' is likely to be connected with the fact that עבד in Aramaic can be read as either 'servant' or 'work' (which makes the consonantal text of S here ambiguous). With the text as it stands, however, it is hard to understand why so many of the versions should have opted to understand עבדיהם in one of its Aramaic senses rather than in the normal Hebrew one, which would serve perfectly well in this context—even if a sudden reference to servants seems a little odd. Something has pushed them in this direction, and the likeliest candidate is a reading slightly different from the consonantal text of M, so I think that these versions most probably found ועובדיהם, and took it to be a *plene* writing of the Aramaic term עובד, used as a loanword. Another, slightly more complicated possibility, is that they found the Hebrew עבדתם, 'their עבדה'. We can readily understand a shift from ועובדיהם to ועבדיהם, in M and the source-text of T, as the consequence of a careless change to a defective spelling, which altered the sense in a Hebrew context. Alternatively, and with a little less ease, we can understand ועבדיהם to be a corruption of ועבדתם, perhaps provoked in part by the preceding plurals, or by an expectation that another group of people should be listed here. Neither change, though, would be at all easy to explain in the other direction, suggesting that, if the versions were indeed led to understand 'works' by encountering either of these words, then 'works' was the sense originally intended.

Used in the singular or plural, עובד often refers to the work or activities of some individual or group taken as a whole, which fits the context very well here. It is used quite commonly in the Qumran texts, and almost exclusively with that meaning (see Cook, *Dictionary of Qumran Aramaic*). The use of עבדה, on the other hand, would give a similar sense, but probably add also a connotation of 'service': it very often refers to work undertaken as a duty, or by slaves and servants. Either word would imply that Qohelet is talking about the totality of what each person does, rather than about their single actions, so he is not depicting divine control as a sort of continuous puppet-show.

9.1 are in the hand of God] When all that Potiphar has is 'in the hand' of Joseph (Gen 39.6), it means that Joseph has control of it, and the work that is 'in the hand' of Ithamar (Exod 38.21; Num 4.28, 33) is work being done under his direction, just as the Israelites were 'in the hand' of Pharaoh (Deut 7.8), and later 'in the hand' of Moses and Aaron when they were led by them (Num 33.1). The very common notion of being put 'in the hand' of someone involves being defeated or enslaved (e.g. Lev 26.25; Judg 3.8; Jer 20.4), and when Prov 18.21 wants to stress the power of speech, it talks of death and life being 'in the hand of a tongue'. The expression essentially means that someone or something is in the charge of, and subject to, the control of somebody else. There are a few particular metaphors in which there is a stronger implication of direct control. In Jer 18.6, for example, Israel in God's hand is like clay in the hand of a potter, while in Prov 21.1 the king's heart can be turned in any direction, like a stream of water in God's hand. The expression generally connotes a less specific sort of control, however, and the point here seems to be neither that the wise and righteous are simple puppets, nor that they are subject to divine whim, but more broadly that they are not free agents.

Such ideas are found elsewhere, and 1QS XI, 2-3, speaks of righteous behaviour being in the hand of God, in connection with judgment, while 1QH[a] VII, 15-16, declares that no human can choose or fix their own path, because the purpose and impulse (יצר) of every spirit is in God's hand (the text goes on to talk about God's creation of individuals as just or wicked); 4Q423 frag. 5, 3 talks similarly of the יצר כל מעשה, 'the impulse of every creature', being in God's hand. What we do not find in biblical or other early Hebrew texts is any use of the expression specifically to denote divine protection, which is a sense that Levy seeks here, and when Michel, *Untersuchungen*, 180, suggests that Qohelet is quoting (in order to contest) a claim that the righteous dead are protected by God in an afterlife, the only parallel he cites is the equivalent Greek expression, used at Wisd 3.1 (Krüger notes that the expression recurs in 7.16, without any connection to the afterlife, so it does not have that necessary connotation even in Wisdom). Schwienhorst-Schönberger, 'Absoluten Tod', 212-13, picks up the possibility nevertheless, and discusses the idea that Qohelet is portraying the ignorance of humans as to what will happen to each of them after death.

That G originally read ἐν χειρὶ ('in [the] hand of') here is beyond reasonable doubt, but a number of manuscripts have ἐνώπιον, 'before', and Syh suggests that this was Origen's reading in the Hexapla. The consequences for understanding the marginal notes on the reading in Syh are explored by Gentry, 'Hexaplaric Materials', 24-25. Jerome affirms *in manu* (= ἐν χειρὶ) for σ', and this reading is attributed to both σ' and α' in Syh; θ' may have had ἐνώπιον. That word is not used elsewhere in the Greek Ecclesiastes, but ἐνώπιον τοῦ θεοῦ is a common enough expression elsewhere in the Septuagint, usually reflecting לפני אלהים. Graphic confusion in either Hebrew or Greek seems unlikely, and the variant probably entered the Greek tradition as an interpretative (perhaps anti-anthropomorphic) clarification.

9.1 No human understands loving and hating] Lit. 'both love and hate, there is no human knowing'. Other ways in which the construction of the sentence has sometimes been understood are noted in Michel, *Untersuchungen*, 167-68, but the usual construal takes 'loving and hating' as objects of 'knowing', moved forward for reasons of style or emphasis. Although it lacks a reference to קנאה, the pairing of love and hate here surely prefigures Qohelet's point in 9.6, that humans will lose all such emotions at death, and it is even structured similarly, with גם...גם. This construction means 'both... and', or in the negative, 'neither...nor': it aligns 'love' and 'hate', rather than differentiating them. Correspondingly, it is doubtful that גם...גם would, or could, be used to mean 'whether...or', so Qohelet is unlikely to be saying directly that humans do not know whether God loves or hates them, or whether God's power over them is a matter of love or hate—despite many translations in such terms.

This might effectively be his point all the same, though, if the claim is that humans simply have no insight into what Fox calls 'the divine psychology': when God's opinions and attitudes are unknowable, even the righteous and the wise can have no idea how he feels about them, or, as some scholars would have it, how he is planning to treat them when they die. If Qohelet is indeed talking about God's own love and hate, however, it is not clear why he presents the two nouns as though they were abstract concepts, with no possessive suffix: 'love and hate', or 'loving and hating', not 'his love and his hate'. An alternative line of interpretation accordingly understands Qohelet to be talking about a human ignorance of human relationships and emotions that exemplifies a much broader lack of understanding. This, of course, gives weight to the connection with v. 6: humans do not understand such things, but then lose them anyway at death. A few scholars (most notably Seow) have championed a third approach, which makes 'love and hate' instances of the 'works' that are in the hand of God, and although it is not clear why they should have been singled out, this approach cannot be dismissed outright just because it does not correspond to the understandings of the versions, as Schoors seems to imply.

My own understanding, however, is closer to the second interpretation, while taking the reference to be to something more specific than general human ignorance. As it is drawn out in the next verse and in what follows, Qohelet's main concern here seems to be that humans are baffled by the fact that people who are opposites seem all to share the same fate—a fact that seems to render the distinctions between them meaningless. I take him here most probably to be talking about those distinctions in terms of 'loving and hating': in English, we might say 'likes and dislikes'. On that reading, humans are unable to understand the point of humans loving to do one thing and hating to do another, when the different paths down which their preferences take them seem to lead everybody to the same place. 'Loving' and 'hating', though, are left undefined and follow a reference to divine control, which arguably encourages a different reading: that humans cannot understand God's likes and dislikes when he seemingly reacts in the same way to whatever choices humans make. Although 9.6 will resolve the ambiguity, it persists up to then, and may be deliberate: Qohelet could even be saying that humans cannot understand the very concept of 'likes and dislikes'—on anyone's part—when there is no evidence of real difference. Whoever's likes and dislikes are at stake, however, the problem is the same, and the alternative readings do not affect the point.

Despite the fact that ἄνθρωπος itself is present in all manuscripts, G ὁ ἄνθρωπος, 'the human', is under asterisk and assigned to α' in Syh, suggesting that Origen found it in the Hebrew but not the Greek, and borrowed the reading from Aquila. Marshall argues persuasively that the asterisk should refer only to the article, and that Origen found ἄνθρωπος instead of ὁ ἄνθρωπος, which is indeed the reading of a number of manuscripts and citations. If this is G*, then the translator would probably have found אדם in his text, not האדם, and the existence of such a variant might well be affirmed also by the absence of an article in one (ms 252) of the two Greek witnesses to σ' here.[4] In Isa 13.14, which employs a similar construction with אין, the equivalent איש has no article, so it is very possible that אדם was the original reading here, and that it was displaced by the more familiar האדם.

9.1 everything before them (9.2) is illusion because...to each] The text is difficult, and I follow the reading suggested in *BHQ*. M has here הכל לפניהם הכל כאשר לכל, which has generally been divided, in accordance with the Masoretic punctuation, into two parts. This makes for a variety of translations, and Ginsburg, for example, renders 'both [viz. love and hatred] are before them, both just as before all others', while Plumptre has '(no man knoweth either love or hatred) *by* all *that is* before them. All *things come alike to all*' (his italics indicate words that have to be understood). Although they see different references, however, the many commentators who follow M generally judge that הכל לפניהם qualifies what went or will go before in some way, while הכל כאשר לכל is a more general statement of constancy, identity or equality—although, of course, it might be objected both that it is simply a tautology, and that כאשר is not elsewhere constructed with -ל.

G is very different, reading τὰ πάντα πρὸ προσώπου αὐτῶν ματαιότης ἐν τοῖς πᾶσιν, 'all things (are) before them, vanity in all things (or: in them all)'. S has elements of both: ܟܠ ܕܩܕܡܘܗܝ ܗܒܠ, ܘܡܬܘܗܝ ܟܠ ܐܝܟ ܕܟܠ *kl dqdmwhy hblʾ kl ʾyk dlkl*, 'everything before them is vanity, everything is like everything'.

---

[4] This issue is discussed at length by Marshall. σ' is attested as προσέτι (προς τι and προς ετι[?] in the mss) δὲ οὐ φιλίαν οὐδὲ ἔχθραν ἐπίσταται ὁ(?) ἄνθρωπος, 'but besides, a/the human understands not love/friendship nor hatred/ enmity', rendered by Jerome as *et insuper neque amicitias neque inimicitias scit homo*.

These variations seem to have arisen in part because where M has the second הכל at the start of 9.2, G has read הבל instead. The lack of an equivalent to כאשר and the appearance of ἐν in G is harder to explain, but here the reading of σ' is enlightening: the first part is attested in Greek, τὰ πάντα ἔμπροσθεν αὐτῶν ἄδηλα, 'all things are obscure before them' (for the sources, see Marshall), and the second mostly just in Jerome's Latin, *propterea quod omnibus eueniunt similia* (ἅπαντα ὅμοια), 'because similar things happen to all'. Symmachus is paraphrasing at the end, but it seems that he read not only הבל, like the G translator, but באשר where M has כאשר. In 8.16 and 11.5, where M has כאשר, G has ἐν οἷς, 'in which', probably because the translator read באשר, as σ' does here. McNeile, 149, argues, therefore, that G was originally τὰ πάντα πρὸ προσώπου αὐτῶν ματαιότης ἐν οἷς τοῖς πᾶσιν, reflecting a Hebrew הכל לפניהם הבל באשר לכל. This explanation has been picked up by Goldman, who commends that text as the original Hebrew in *BHQ*, and it is certainly not difficult to see how the current text of M might have arisen after an initial misreading of הבל as הכל (cf. Crenshaw, 'Quantitative', 5).

The text of S, which seems to reflect both the original הבל and the הכל derived from it in M, is clearly a conflation of G and a text like that of M. Jerome's readings are more interesting. In Hie, despite commending σ', he offers *(non est cognoscens homo) omnia in facie eorum in omnibus (euentus unus)*, '(the human does not know) all things in the face of them; in all things there is one thing that happens', which effectively ignores הבל באשר / הכל כאשר. In V, on the other hand, *sed omnia in futuro seruantur incerta eo quod uniuersa (aeque eueniant)*, 'but all things in the future are kept uncertain for it because all things (happen equally)', the paraphrase presumes the readings of σ'.

Jerome's renderings draw attention to the various ways in which לפניהם has been understood. This expression has some of the ambiguity that 'lie before' has in English, and can connote what has been before, what will be ahead, or simply what is physically in front. The potential temporal reference has led some scholars variously to think in terms of predestination or ignorance of the future (see the discussion in Michel, *Untersuchungen*, 168-70), but I think that in this context Qohelet is talking more broadly about what people can see in front of them or in their experience—the evidence of their eyes. It is harder to say whether הכל indicates 'both' (i.e. the loving and hating) or 'everything' that is before humans. Lavoie, 'Vie, mort', 69-70 n. 3, argues for the former, but of the passages that he cites from elsewhere in the book, only 7.18 unambiguously uses כל to refer specifically to things that have already been defined, and that has כלם (in 3.19-20; 6.6; and 7.15 a more general understanding is possible). Strictly, the Hebrew here should be considered ambiguous in this respect, but it does not make a great difference to the sense whether we speak of confusion about loving/hating, or about everything in which loving/hating might play a part.

Gentry notes a gloss at this point in two fourteenth-century manuscripts of G, to the effect that absences of distinction are common to all things (including the opinions held by both the wicked and the good).

9.2 the same things happen] Lit. 'there is one happening for'. Repeated in 9.3, this is the same formulation used in 2.14-15 (see the notes there), and is similar to the statement about animals and humans in 3.19. As in ch. 2, Qohelet is probably not referring simply to death 'but rather what happens during life to the righteous and the wicked' (Wright, 'Ecclesiastes 9:1-12', 253)—although, of course, the notion likely includes the timing of death, which would presumably be taken as a key indicator of divine favour or disfavour. The problem is not that everybody is mortal and will eventually die, but that their qualities or behaviour seem to have no effect upon the length or quality of their lives.

Jerome reports σ' here as *propterea quod omnibus eueniunt similia iusto et iniusto*, 'because things that are alike happen to everyone, just and unjust', but the phrase he renders with *similia* is attested in Greek as well, where it is rather stronger: ἅπαντα ὅμοια, 'absolutely all things alike'. Symmachus draws out the point that all share the same experience, rather than the weaker idea that they may share some of the same experience. Marshall has been confused here by the introduction of a second 'all': ἅπαντα does not correspond to the dative *omnibus*, and so there are no grounds for presuming that it would have been preceded by the <εἰς> which he includes in his reading.

9.2 to the good and to the bad] It is not certain that we should read this pair here. In a list that otherwise consists entirely of pairs, M לטוב, 'to the good man', stands by itself between the pairs לצדיק ולרשע and ולטהור ולטמא. All the other versions except T include a matching 'bad' or 'evil', and the possibilities are, therefore, that: (1) the Hebrew originally had nothing here, but 'good' was added in error, and 'bad' (presumably ולרע) then added in some manuscripts to complete a pair; (2) the Hebrew originally had just 'good' here, and 'bad', again, was added to complete a pair; (3) the Hebrew originally had a pair 'good/bad', but the 'bad' dropped out in parts of the tradition.

Of these, (2) seems the least likely on grounds of style and meaning, although it would yield a striking sequence of words starting with ט, and there is a general consensus that (1) or (3) must be correct. Schoors has a point, that טוב appears later and should not appear twice, which would favour (1), but its appearance is in the second part of the list, after the shift away from forms with -ל, and the argument is not decisive, while explanations for the appearance of an isolated לטוב, perhaps as a corrupt doublet of ולטהור (so, e.g., Zimmerli) are not especially compelling. It is difficult to reach any firm conclusion, but words drop out more easily than they arise from nothing, and (3) is the easiest option to defend on the basis of the textual evidence alone. On the other hand, García Bachmann, 'Study', finds groups of five across 9.1-12: five things unavailable to the dead (in vv. 5-6), five imperatives (in 7-10), and five types of person (in vv. 11-12). If she has actually identified a deliberate structural feature here, then that would tell against the good/bad pair, which takes this list to six pairs.

A Hebrew variant ולטוב, is quite strongly attested among the Babylonian manuscripts (see Miletto) and fits more easily into the current context, where, after the first, all the other elements of the initial sequence have a conjunction. The form may have arisen for that very reason, of course, and there are grounds to suppose that M may already have added some conjunctions to the original. For G, Gentry accepts conjunctions at all the points where they are found in M, but the conjunctions are lacking before 'to the clean' and 'to the person who sacrifices' in a significant number of manuscripts, including the hexaplaric *O*-group, so that none of the pairs is joined that way to the preceding pair. T probably matches M, but this is a feature of S and V also, and of the La attributed to Philip Presbyter (see below). The witnesses to Hie present a mixed picture, but in his *Epistle* 108.27, Jerome presents the list as *iusto et impio, bono et malo, mundo ac immundo, sacrificanti et non sacrificanti*, so all the evidence suggests that he would not have used the conjunctions in Hie either. This reading without conjunctions between each pair has a good claim to be early, and stylistic considerations might suggest that it is original—there are no such conjunctions, after all, in the list of pairs at 3.2-8. The sense is unaffected either way, however, and we do not need to commit ourselves to a particular reading here: I have omitted them in translation largely because the list reads better in English that way.

In S the first three pairs are marked as plural: Kamenetzky, 202, rightly suggests that the seyame on each is secondary, but one very late manuscript of G (609) also reads plurals.

9.2 the one who takes an oath] G ὡς ὁ ὀμνύων, 'as one taking an oath' (cf. Hie *sic iurans*; S ܐܝܟ ܐܝܢܐ *'yk ymy'*), is equivalent to כנשבע, rather than M הנשבע, and *BHS* commends that form as original (so also, e.g., Sacchi). The equivalence of this pair is not expressed in the same way as the last, however, and *BHQ* is probably right to see the reading in G as an assimilation to what preceded. Interestingly, there is no equivalent to ὡς in the La cited by Philip Presbyter (*In historiam Iob*, 86D; cf. Vaccari, 'Recupero', 119), and possibly reflecting Jerome's revision, *bono & in malo, mundo & immundo, sacrificanti, & no(n) sacrificanti, illius qui iurat, & eius qui iusiurandu(m) timet*, 'to the good also in the bad, to the clean and to the unclean, to the one who sacrifices and the one who does not sacrifice, this man who swears and that man who fears oath-swearing'. The citation, however, also lacks an equivalent to ὡς ὁ ἀγαθός ὡς ὁ ἁμαρτάνων, 'as the good man so the sinner', and may be incomplete: in the *Epistle* cited in the last note, Jerome himself has *sicut bonus, ita et qui peccat, sicut qui iurat, ita et is qui iuramentum metuit*, which does match the Greek (as does Hie). V *sicut bonus sic et peccator ut periurus ita* (var. *sic*) *et ille qui verum deierat*, paraphrases to contrast 'the perjurer' with 'he who swears truth'.

9.2 fears an oath] If G τὸν ὅρκον, '*the* oath', is original, it probably reflects a reading השבועה with an article. Seow uses analogies with Akkadian usage to suggest that the reference here is to 'revering' an oath, with the implication that the preceding reference is to swearing an oath falsely. That seems unnecessary in the light of 5.3-5: the contrast is more probably between willingness and unwillingness to take the risks entailed.

9.3a-b this is a problem in everything] Many commentators have felt that Qohelet is talking not just about any problem here, but about what he believes to be the most basic and most fundamental problem, and this understanding is probably reflected in Hie *hoc est pessimum in omni quod factum est sub sole*, 'this is the worst in everything that has been done under the sun', and V *hoc est pessimum inter omnia quae sub sole fiunt*, 'this is the worst amongst all the things that are done under the sun'. It is possible that Jerome derived this, like so much else, from σ', and his commentary on the verse begins by commending Symmachus' translation of the second part. For this first part, however, we have only ἐν πᾶσι τοῖς συμβαίνουσιν, 'in all things that happen', which does not point clearly that way.[5] None of the other versions displays that understanding explicitly, and it is difficult to find any basis other than Hie, V for claiming that the Hebrew itself makes, or ever made this point.

Two approaches have been attempted, however. The first is simply to emend the text and read a definite article: זה הרע בכל would indeed yield the proper connotation of '*the* problem', and Fox, for instance, like many other commentators, has shown no reluctance to embrace the suggestion of Ehrlich that we do this. The other approach is to suppose that, as Ginsburg puts it, 'The preposition בְּ in בְּכל gives to רע the force of the superlative, making it stand forth prominently as evil in the midst (בְּ) of all other evils'. Dahood has tried both, claiming in one article that זה רע is simply a writing of זה הרע in the Phoenician style, so does not really even require emendation, and later in another that -בְּ here is being used comparatively.[6] The problem with the first is that we either have to make an emendation that finds support only in Jerome's potentially paraphrastic renderings, or to follow Dahood and conclude, by implication, that Qohelet would have had no way actually to

---

[5] Marshall rightly observes, against Field, that ms 252 does not have the ἐν, which he omits, but it is now attested by ms 788.

[6] Dahood, 'Canaanite-Phoenician', 41; 'Hebrew–Ugaritic Lexicography I', 300. In the first of these, Dahood claims that the reading זה הרע is indicated by the *paseq* placed between the words in M, which is entirely speculative, but would go anyway only to the understanding of the Masoretes. *Paseq* is used many ways and can be rather mysterious, but it seems more likely that it was intended here to ensure a recognition that רע is not serving as an attributive adjective, and that the words are kept properly distinct.

say '*an* evil'. Setting aside the whole question of whether -ב can be used to indicate a superlative or not, the problem with the second approach is that it has to take בכל אשר נעשה to be a reference to every *problem*. Apart from the facts that we might expect the plural if this is the 'problem among all problems done under the sun', and that this is precisely the way in which Qohelet speaks in 1.13 of 'everything', it is hard to see that the problem he is describing is in any sense something that is 'done'. Seow, curiously, translates 'this is the evil', while claiming that no emendation is necessary, but provides no explanation.

9.3a-b And also] The וגם here has provoked a surprising amount of discussion, with some scholars trying to attribute to it a concessive sense, or an explicit meaning 'therefore'; there is a helpful survey in Pinker, 'Qohelet 9:3b-7', 221-23. Whether or not it permits such construals of Qohelet's point here (which I doubt), וגם certainly does not push us towards them, and the difficulties that scholars find in the usual additive sense of the expression arise more from exegetical supposition than from any genuine ambiguity in its meaning. It is true that Qohelet leaves open the relationship between his two statements here, but that does not mean that there is no relationship, or that he has turned to a wholly separate problem. Pinker himself, who also rejects the Masoretic punctuation of this verse, believes nevertheless that וגם must mark the beginning of a new discussion, and I would accept the possibility, at least, that the loose logical construction here may indicate a transition (see the commentary).

9.3a-b the heart of humans is encouraged to do what is wrong] The language is similar to that of 8.11: in that verse, literally, 'the heart of humans is filled within them to do wrong'; here 'the heart of humans is filled with wrong'. Especially in the light of the corresponding contexts, I think the sense is likely to be similar in both (on which, see the note at 8.11). Rudman, 'Anatomy of the Wise Man', 468-70, argues, however, that in this verse רע does not have a specifically moral connotation, and should be associated instead with הוללות (which is also said to be in human hearts, although it notably does not 'fill' them). Rudman notes the further linking of the terms at 10.13, and takes Qohelet to be talking about the irrationality that fills human lives. Ogden, similarly, thinks that Qohelet is talking about 'painful thoughts'. Both are right, I think, that the connotations of רע are not strictly moral—here or elsewhere in the book—and for Qohelet it is likely that 'doing wrong' implies 'acting mistakenly' as much as, or more than 'acting wickedly', even if the mistakes are around behaviour approved or condemned by God. To that extent, there is a connection with הוללות, but it would be a considerable stretch to make the terms synonymous. Qohelet believes, I think, that humans are motivated *rationally* to behave wrongly, because they misconstrue the evidence, as well as having to contend with their irrational motivations. In any case, though, 'filling' of the heart is an idiom that connotes presumption or emboldening, as at 8.11 and Esth 7.5, and if we take into account the likely limitations of רע, then it is very unlikely that Qohelet is talking here about human hearts being inherently evil or malicious (as, e.g., Schüle, 'Evil from the Heart', 163-65, suggests).

Jerome renders σ' here as *sed et cor filiorum hominum repletur malitia et procacitate iuxta cor eorum in uita sua*, 'but also the heart of the sons of men is filled with badness and impudence next/according to their heart in their life'. For *procacitate*, we have the variants αὐθαδία / αὐθάδιας, 'wilfulness', in Greek. If Jerome is translating precisely, we should prefer αὐθάδιας, read as the genitive (cf. Marshall), and in that case Symmachus does not understand there to be two parallel statements here: the heart is filled with both qualities. In V, Jerome uses *iuxta cor* where the Septuagint has κατὰ τὴν καρδίαν and M כלב or כלבב: see 1 Sam 13.14; 1 Chr 17.19; Jer 3.15. There is a potential exception at 1 Sam 2.35, but there the construction is כאשר ב-, and the sense similar to a simple -כ. It seems very likely that he found κατὰ τὴν καρδίαν in σ' here, therefore, and correspondingly that Symmachus read כלבבם, which is why he has construed the sentence so strangely. That would also explain the choice of αὐθαδία (he prefers ἔννοιαν θορυβώδη and θόρυβος for הוללות at 7.25; 10.13): he has been forced to construe הוללות with כלבבם as 'wilfulness-according-to-heart'.

9.3c-6

(9.3c) And the back of each is to the dead, (9.4) for when any associates with all the living, there is reassurance—since it seems to a live dog that he is better than a dead lion. (9.5) This is because the living may know that they will die while the dead know nothing at all. And there is no more recompense for them, for any memory of them is lost; (9.6) their love, and their hate, and their passion—each has already perished, and there is nothing which is theirs for them anymore, forever, in all that is done beneath the sun.

Commentary

Interpretations have varied, but commentators have generally understood Qohelet to make a jump at the end of 9.3: humans are confused in life—then they die. The next verse, 9.4, is then read as a statement that it is better to be alive than to be dead, and that statement is associated with the fact that humans have 'hope' or 'confidence', and/or with their possession of at least some knowledge, even if it is only of their own mortality (9.5); the dead, in contrast, have nothing at all (9.5-6). In short, Qohelet is taken to be making a case that death is certain, life offers things that death will not, and therefore life should be enjoyed while it lasts.

That is a plausible message in itself, but the reading is achieved through some less plausible interpretations of what the text actually says in some key places. It also fails to supply any proper connection between Qohelet's contrasting of life with death and the issue of a single outcome for all, which is what he has been talking about in 9.1-2 and most of the way through 9.3. Both concerns come together when we consider the end of that verse, which has long been understood as an abrupt 'and afterwards: to the dead', meaning, 'and afterwards they die'. That way of putting it would be odd anyway, even if it were more certain that anything in the Hebrew could mean 'afterwards', but it is hard to see how this can be taken in any meaningful way as a consequence or continuation of Qohelet's words.

Reading the text rather differently, I understand it actually to be a continuation, and the addition of a new issue that takes the problem of a single outcome in a different direction. That problem lies not simply in the fact of death, but in the attitude of humans toward it: death removes whatever distinctions might have existed in life between the good and the bad or all the other groups that were listed in 9.2, but it does not itself erase their reality. What makes them meaningless is the attitude of the living, who ignore the dead and look to other living humans for reassurance because they are, effectively, in denial about their own mortality. Just as a dog, a lowly animal, may regard itself as better than the admirable lion, merely because it is alive and the lion dead, so people strip the dead of all value, and the distinctions between them of all meaning, by turning their backs on them and forgetting them. Of course, characteristically, this does not lead Qohelet to urge any change of attitude towards the dead, and the lesson he takes from it is that humans should embrace life with all the more vigour.

Earlier, in the commentary to 6.4-5, we encountered a speech by Andromache in the *Trojan Women* of Euripides, which touched on the equivalence of death and non-existence, and expressed a preference for death over a painful life. That preference is explained in the difficult line 638, restored in the recent Loeb edition (Kovacs, *Trojan Women*, 78) as ἀλγεῖ γὰρ οὐδὲν <τῶν ἀγεννήτων πλέον τεθνεώς τις, οὐδὲν> τῶν κακῶν ἠσθημένος, and probably to be understood as 'for one who is dead feels no more pain than the unborn, having no awareness of their troubles'. In the context of the present passage, Lohfink notes also the earlier words of Hecuba (lines 632-33), to which Andromache is responding: οὐ ταὐτόν, ὦ παῖ, τῷ βλέπειν τὸ κατθανεῖν·τὸ μὲν γὰρ οὐδέν, τῷ δ' ἔνεισιν ἐλπίδες, 'being dead is not the same, my child, as being alive (lit. seeing [light]), for the one is nothing, but hopes are possible in the other'. It is interesting to compare Ecclesiastes, but also important to note the very specific, and very different context of the statements in Euripides: amidst the slaughter after the fall of Troy, Andromache has just reported to Hecuba the death of her daughter Polyxena, and is contemplating her own future as a captive, with the situation provoking questions about which of them, in fact, is better off. This brings the discussion close, at points, to Qohelet's own concerns in ch. 6, but the general state of the dead and the living is incidental here, and the resemblances less telling. In particular, Qohelet is almost certainly not talking about the hope for improvement of their lot that Hecuba sees as possible only for the surviving Trojans, and which she is not attributing as a quality to all the living.

9.3c-4] The Hebrew at the start could be read 'after each, toward the dead', which is the basis of the understandings mentioned above. It is difficult, however, to make this mean what such understandings require, and a reading along such lines would probably have to be taken as a reference to what happens after people have died (which is how the Targum takes it). I have translated in the light of a similar sentence in Ezek 8.16, where the crucial word means not 'after' but 'back' (it can possess both senses). Qohelet's point, I think, is that the living choose to face away from the dead, and so away from any possible evidence of the ways in which human choices might ultimately affect outcomes, both because there is reassurance to be found in the company of the living, and because (or for the very reason that) the living see themselves as superior even to the greatest of the dead.

Dogs were used in herding (cf. Job 30.1), and, in the book of Tobit, Tobias travels with his dog (presumably for protection), so we should not overstate the idea that dogs would have been held in contempt by the book's original readers (on this, see especially Miller, 'Attitudes', which questions some of the more extreme claims that are still commonly made). When people refer to themselves as dogs, moreover, it is not always in a self-deprecating way: Goliath in 1 Sam 17.43 is jeering at David for coming at him with his shepherd's staff, as though to control a dog (or perhaps to play with one, using sticks), and Abner, in 2 Sam 3.8, is apparently protesting against being treated badly despite his loyalty (although his expression 'a dog's head' is rather obscure). To be sure, Hazael in 2 Kgs 8.13 does speak of himself as a dog, but even there his point seems simply to be that he is merely in service (just as dogs serve humans), not capable of being responsible for the actions against Israel that Elisha has just predicted he will carry out. This seems to be much the same implication that we find in the Lachish letters, where several times the writers ask their superiors formulaically, 'Who is your servant, a dog, that…?', not debasing themselves as contemptible so much as formally acknowledging their inferior status.

On two occasions in the Hebrew Bible (although the Septuagint also has it for the simple 'dog' of the Hebrew at 2 Kgs 8.13), we find the expression 'dead dog', used by someone to characterize their own insignificance: it stands by itself in 2 Sam 9.8, but in 1 Sam 24.15 (ET 24.14) David claims that Saul is hunting 'a dead dog, a flea'. This is a usage found in Akkadian as well: *CAD* (vol. 8, under *kalbu* §2 j) cites texts which speak of, for example, 'a dead dog, the son of a nobody', and 'a poor man, a dead dog'.[1] Someone who is 'a dog' or more especially 'a dead dog', then, is by convention themselves a nobody, of no significance (sometimes in a context of self-deprecation, although it is hardly an expression of 'self-loathing', as Forti, 'The Fly and the Dog', 252 n. 50, suggests). That association is surely what underpins the language here as well: the dog is not vile, but it is unesteemed and unimportant, in contrast to the much more terrifying and powerful lion—which preys on the flocks that the dog might guard. Of course, if the expression 'dead dog' was familiar to the author, as seems likely, then his choice of 'live dog' in this verse may be a nod towards it: this creature will be almost proverbially insignificant when it dies. That said, whether the saying is itself proverbial, as is sometimes suggested, is a matter entirely for speculation.

Fischer, *Skepsis*, 129-30, cites aptly the response of Achilles to Odysseus (in *Odyssey* 11.488-91), after the latter has urged him in Hades (where the νεκροὶ ἀφραδέες, 'insensate dead', dwell, ll. 475-76) not to regret his own death:

μὴ δή μοι θάνατόν γε παραύδα, φαίδιμ' Ὀδυσσεῦ.
βουλοίμην κ' ἐπάρουρος ἐὼν θητευέμεν ἄλλῳ,
ἀνδρὶ παρ' ἀκλήρῳ, ᾧ μὴ βίοτος πολὺς εἴη,
ἢ πᾶσιν νεκύεσσι καταφθιμένοισιν ἀνάσσειν

Don't play down death to me, O glorious Odysseus!
I would rather be attached to the earth as serf to another man
—one without property or much livelihood of his own—
than rule as king among all the rotted corpses.

---

[1] See also Hurowitz, 'ABL 1285 and the Hebrew Bible', 12, which notes the similar claim in a text attributed to Urad-Gula (K 4267/*ABL* 1285 obv. 14-15: 'I was a poor man, son of a poor man, a dead dog, a vile and restricted person. He lifted me from the dung heap'; cf. Parpola, 'The Forlorn Scholar', 261), and discusses (14) the links with biblical usage.

9.5-6] I take what follows to begin as an explanation not directly of the living dog's sense of superiority over the dead lion, but more broadly of the way that the living relate to the dead and to each other. It rapidly becomes, however, simply a statement about the dead, which picks up ideas from the preceding verses and from earlier in the book. The key point initially seems to be that the living can have an awareness of their mortality, while the dead lack any awareness at all. The specification here, that it is knowledge of their own inevitable deaths, should dissuade us from reading this merely as a claim that the living are somehow better than the dead because they have at least some knowledge.[2] I think the link is rather with the previous notion of reassurance: the living cling to others who are alive, rejecting the dead who can no longer share their foreboding of death. This cuts the dead off from the world completely. Once forgotten, they can gain or suffer nothing more from what they did in life, since the choices that they made, or the tasks which engaged their zeal (cf. 4.4), no longer have any place in the world. Rindge puts it nicely in 'Mortality and Enjoyment', 269: 'Qoheleth perceives death as a destroyer of memory, since the memory of a dead person vanishes among the living'.

Shortly, in 9.10, Qohelet will mention the existence of the dead in Sheol itself. Here, however, he is talking not about a passionless afterlife, but about what the dead have left behind—which involves nothing of themselves. The chapter began by observing the inability of living humans to discern the consequence of choices they or others have made, because all seem to meet the same end. To that, Qohelet has now added the problem that, huddling in their own company for comfort, they reject and forget the dead, whose own choices had consequences—but who are long gone. This compounds the ignorance of those who are alive, but Qohelet presents it from the perspective of the dead: their choices leave no mark on the living, and have gained the dead nothing. If there is a moral to be drawn

---

[2] Jerome reports a Jewish interpretation according to which a living teacher, however unlearned, is still better than any dead one, however good (he rejects this in favour of seeing Judaism as the dead lion, Christianity as the live dog). The interpretation in the Midrash tends to contradict this: Hadrian cites the saying to prove that he is better than Moses because he is still alive, but is proved wrong when a command he gives is broken swiftly, unlike a similar commandment from Moses, which is still kept after generations.

here, it is that the living, who already find it difficult to know what they should do, can act in no expectation that their choices will exert any influence after they have died upon those who are still alive: it is in the nature of the living to reject the dead and so cut them out. The absence of remembrance appeared as a problem back in 1.11, where it was linked to the fact that humans perceive novelty where none really exists. The context here is different, but the claim essentially the same: humans do not remember the past, or their forebears, and so no generation can really change the future, or consider the prospect of such a change to be a gain for them, made by their living or as a consequence of their actions. The claim is as open to challenge here, of course, as it was in 1.11, but it is important as a basis for what will come next: life should be lived, however out of our control it may actually be, because there is going to be nothing for us afterwards, either in this world or in Sheol.

Notes

9.3c And the back of each is to the dead] M ואחריו has a singular suffix pronoun, which is supported by T, but G καὶ ὀπίσω αὐτῶν, 'and behind/after them', S ܘܚܪܬܗܘܢ *whrthwn*, 'and their rears', and σ' τὰ δὲ τελευταῖα αὐτῶν, 'but their endings', all use a plural. If the pronoun refers to the preceding humans (plural), then it has to be regarded as distributive anyway (cf. Krüger; GKC §145 m), which is how I have translated, and the translations might just be interpreting in those terms as well. It is also possible, however, that there was a variant אחריהם with a plural suffix, and, if it is not just to be derived from G, this suspicion may be strengthened a little by the use of *et post haec*, 'and after these things', in both Hie and V: Jerome has not seen a reference to the humans, but translated as plural nevertheless.

As at 3.22 (see the note there), some scholars believe that the suffix is a 'petrified' form, and that אחריו means 'afterwards'—a claim for which there is little evidence, although Schoors has recently favoured such an understanding here to explain the lack of concordance. Almost all modern scholars, however, follow Jerome's understanding that the reference here is temporal, so that the clause means 'and afterwards—to the dead', with a verb like 'they will go' understood; cf. V *et post haec ad inferos deducentur*, 'and after these things they will be brought down to the underworld'. This is itself derived, perhaps, from his reading of σ' τὰ δὲ τελευταῖα αὐτῶν εἰς νεκρούς, 'but their endings (are) to (the) dead', which he renders interpretatively in Latin as *nouissima autem eorum ueniunt ad mortuos*, 'their last things, however, come to the dead'. It is hard to say whether this was a common early understanding: later, the Midrash Rabbah is silent on the issue, while T translates temporally, but takes אחריו to refer to the period after each human life (which is actually its probable sense in 3.22; 6.12; 7.14).

This is arguably, though, one of those interpretations that has established itself more by familiarity than by any inherent plausibility. Even if we accept the dubious proposition that אחריו might be adverbial, that sense would involve an extremely harsh ellipsis of the verb, and if the term can actually mean no more than 'after him', it is doubtful that the clause can yield such a sense at all: 'and after him/each to the dead' does not, by any stretch, mean 'and afterwards they die'—any interpretation would probably have then to be along the lines of T's account, which itself reads much in. It is not even true that, as Crenshaw puts it citing Wildeboer, 'the sentence breaks off like life itself': it would either be simply incoherent, or require us to understand a great deal that is unstated.

Seow declares that 'MT makes no sense as it stands', but rather than move the words to a different place in the text as he does (and take אחרי in the dubious sense 'finality'), I think it is less drastic to consider the possibility that אחרי here is not actually temporal at all. Although it is much overshadowed by the prepositional uses of אחרי to mean 'after' and 'behind', there is also a noun אחור which is used, sometimes in the plural with a singular meaning, to describe the back of something or someone, and which is not especially rare.[3] Ezek 8.16 illustrates one use of this in an expression that may help us to understand what Qohelet is saying here: it speaks of 25 men, אחריהם אל היכל יהוה ופניהם קדמה, 'their backs (were) to the temple of YHWH and their faces toward the east'. This is precisely analogous to the construction found here, אחרי + suffix + אל, so it would be difficult to deny that אחריו אל המתים could similarly mean 'his back is to the dead' (cf. also 2 Chr 4.4, with ה locale instead of אל); this is possibly, indeed, the way that S ܘܣܘܦܗܘܢ ܠܒܝܬ ܡܝܬܐ *wḥrthwn lwt myt'* understood it (although the noun can refer both to back parts and to last times), and it is probably the grammatical understanding reflected in σ' (which then, however, extends the sense of 'rear part'). Zimmermann, in 'Aramaic Provenance', 41-42, and in his commentary, actually comes to a similar understanding *via* his Aramaic translation theory, although his focus

---

[3] Despite the pointing in M, it seems likely that the אחרי used in 2 Sam 2.23 of a spear's 'end' (or 'butt'—it is not quite clear what is going on) should be associated with this, rather than with the preposition. Ehrlich, and Montgomery, 'Notes', 243, think that Symmachus has read that noun here, and Montgomery suggests translating M as 'his end is to (be with) the dead'. However, if this is indeed how Symmachus took the Hebrew, which is not unlikely, then both he and Montgomery are relying on two different connotations of 'end' in their own languages. There is nothing to suggest that the Hebrew noun (unlike the related אחרית) could be used to indicate finality. Siegfried actually supposes that Symmachus read אחריתו, and emends the text to that reading—a suggestion made more tentatively in *BH³* as well.

there is upon המתים, which he considers the result of a misreading. According to him, the original would have meant 'and his back is turned upon the events to come'.

There is also a clear implication in the passage from Ezekiel that the men, who could stand anywhere they liked to face East, are deliberately ignoring or rejecting the Temple (just as in English we might speak of 'turning one's back on something'), so that the expression is equivalent to the more common פנה ערף. This, I think, makes good sense in the context of the next verse: humans keep their backs toward the dead because it is in their engagement with life or with the living that they find assurance in their own value. There is no clear reason, on the other hand, for a reminder at this point of the obvious fact that they will eventually die, even if we could push the Hebrew to mean that.

Pinker, 'Qohelet 9:3b-7', finds a different way around the problems, by emending אחריו to ארחיו, 'his ways' (a variant form of, or error for the expected ארחתיו, since the plural is usually ארחות). This leads him to read what follows— in a way that is almost diametrically opposed to my own understanding—as a statement that humans are drawn to the dead through necromancy, and a corresponding polemic against that practice. Since the rest supposedly belongs to that polemic, however, the emendation is the only basis upon which to see any reference to necromancy, and a speculative correction to a form that must then itself be corrected clearly does not offer the strongest of supports.

9.4 for when any] Lit. 'for whoever it is that'. The verse consists of three parts. The first is either a question 'who will?', possibly with the implication 'nobody will', or a statement with an indefinite relative pronoun 'whoever will'. The second consists of the two words יש בטחון, 'there is confidence', and the third of a saying about a live dog and a dead lion. We shall come back to the precise meanings: the more immediate challenge is to understand how these parts fit together. The first and third are introduced by כי, which connects each to what has preceded, and this has clearly guided many of the ancient versions. G, σ', Hie, V have probably all taken the first part as a question providing an explanation for the preceding אחריו אל המתים of the last verse. Roughly, humans are going to die because nobody can stay connected to the living. The יש בטחון is then the start of a new, if related, statement that there is hope/confidence *that* or *because* a living dog is better than a dead lion.

T and S vary this, but none of the versions seems clearly to adopt an understanding that is more popular amongst modern commentators, and that is reflected in, e.g., RSV 'But he who is joined with all the living has hope, for a living dog is better than a dead lion'. This associates בטחון with מי אשר, so that the 'who' or 'whoever' of the first part is identified as the possessor of confidence. A variation is adopted by, e.g., Ginsburg and Lohfink, who take the question to extend only as far as the first verb, and then read אל כל החיים יש בטחון as 'there is confidence for all the living'; all else aside, however, we would expect to find יש ל- not יש אל to express possession, and that reading is not really tenable.[4] It does, however, highlight a problem that confronts any translation in terms of possession: the fact that we have no ל- here. Strictly, for a sense like that adopted by the RSV we should expect למי rather than מי, or more likely a לו after יש, and it is difficult to assume a simple elision of any such elements when the structure of the sentence can be understood so differently without them.

Since I doubt, however, that what Qohelet is saying makes any sense unless we associate יש בטחון with the previous clause, I think that the choice of the unusual expression מי אשר may be more significant here than commonly allowed. Elsewhere, this occurs only in Exod 32.33; Judg 21.5 and 2 Sam 20.11. The מי is interrogative in Judg 21.5 and an indefinite 'whoever' in the others, but in all three places the expression as a whole has a nuance that is more particular than 'whoever', and it is used of singling out members or sub-groups of a group: those individuals amongst the people who have actually sinned, those tribes among all the tribes of Israel that did not come to the assembly, and those amongst the passers-by that are on the side of David and Joab. The sense, in other words, is closer to the English 'whichever', and if Qohelet is employing that nuance here, then he is talking about 'any in particular of those humans'. The construction can accordingly be understood as loosely circumstantial or conditional: whenever any human does this, then there is a hope or confidence expressed in their action. I doubt that we can read it as a question on grounds of sense, unless, like Ginsburg and Lohfink, we impart a special meaning to the subsequent verb: it does not seem likely that Qohelet would be questioning whether anyone would choose not to be with the living.

Of course, on this understanding, I do not take the initial כי as adversative with, e.g., Schoors, who translates 'however'. We have already seen a number of cases where כי seems to have little or no force before מי (see the note on 'who...who' at 2.25), and we should not, perhaps, place too much emphasis on it here, but I think that Qohelet probably does intend it to be explanatory: people ignore the dead because it is more reassuring to engage with the living.

9.4 associates with] The K*ᵉthîbh* is יבחר, 'will choose' (which forms the basis of the interpretation offered in the Midrash Rabbah), and the Q*ᵉrê* יחבר, generally understood as a pu'al 'will be joined'. All the ancient versions have read the Q*ᵉrê*, although they seem to have read it as active, 'will join', rather than as passive. For σ', joining or being joined to the living is equivalent to living, and τίς γὰρ εἰς ἀεὶ διατελέσει ζῶν is a paraphrase, 'for who will keep on living for ever?' This has had a direct impact on one G manuscript

---

[4] The same objection can be levelled against other readings that attempt to break the verse at this point, such as Schoors' construal of the K*ᵉthîbh* as a niph'al (*The Preacher* I, 36), resulting in 'For who is it that is chosen? To all the living there is hope.'

(798): see Gentry, in 'Issues', 211, who also speculates (212) that the tense of the verb may have less directly influenced the common G variant with the future κοινωνήσει, instead of the more probably original present-tense κοινωνεῖ. Jerome discusses the reading of σ' in his commentary, and it clearly influences his own later version in V, where the question becomes a simple statement: *nemo est qui semper uiuat*, 'there is nobody who lives for ever'. G, Hie, S understand יחבר more literally in terms of association or engagement with the living, while T speaks of 'keeping to' all the words of the Law.

Most modern commentators have followed the versions and adopted the *Qᵉrê*, although a steady stream of them have tried to retain the *Kᵉthîbh*. For example, the reading of Lohfink and Ginsburg mentioned already takes יבחר as passive with the sense 'chosen', 'selected out', from which a sense 'excepted' or 'exempted' is then more questionably extrapolated. Such readings go back at least to Rosenmüller in 1830, who understood '*Nam quis est qui eligatur, ut scilicet non ad mortuos abeat*'—'For who is there who is selected, presumably not to go to the dead'. Not only do they not reflect the usual sense of the verb, however, they positively reverse it. In this respect, Elster's alternative proposal is less problematic: 'denn wer ist der wählen könnte, dem eine Wahl offen stände?', 'for who is there who could choose, for whom a choice is open?' Although the Hebrew might have a volitive nuance ('who *would* choose'), however, it is really not possible to insert an implication of possibility or impossibility like that.

In fact, I think the *Kᵉthîbh* can give a good sense, especially if we take אל כל החיים here to stand deliberately in contrast with אל המתים at the end of the previous verse: it would not be so difficult to construe what is said here in terms of making a choice 'toward' the living and keeping one's back 'toward' the dead—אל is quite often used in terms of attitude 'toward' somebody (e.g., Gen 3.16; 2 Kgs 16.11), or we could assume a pregnant construction 'choose (to face) toward'. If we take such an approach, however, the sense is not ultimately very different from that of the *Qᵉrê*, which, as we have seen, can claim much better attestation among the versions. If that *Qᵉrê* יחבר is vocalized as a puʿal, then the text is presumably talking about being joined 'with' the living, and if as a qal (the probable preference of the versions), then about uniting or associating oneself with them. The preposition אל is again interesting, however, since it is used in a particular way with this verb. Although the hithpaʿel is used in Dan 11.23 of reaching out to form an alliance, the sense of being joined or united seems to be expressed with a direct object (Hos 4.17) or with עם (2 Chr 20.36)—the אל in Gen 14.3 is used of the place *at* which forces are joined, not of their joining. When we do find אל marking an indirect object, it seems to connote not unity but touching or linking: so the creatures' wings touch each other in Ezek 1.9, 11 (qal) and in Exod 26.6; 36.10 (piʿel) curtains are clipped *to* each other around the tabernacle (contrast 26.9; 36.16, but cf. Exod 28.7, with variant על in 39.4). Sir 13.2 uses חבר אל of entering into a relationship with someone richer and more powerful, which it compares with a clay pot being smashed when it tries to do the same with an iron kettle, and this is wholly in accord with the impression that חבר אל in biblical Hebrew usage connotes not the unification of two things into one, but the bringing together of two things so that they join or touch while remaining distinct.

Again, this accords with an image of facing away from the dead and reaching out to the living, but it makes it very unlikely that Qohelet is talking simply about being part of all the living, or, in effect, 'alive'. Although the $K^e th\hat{i}bh$ and the $Q^e r\hat{e}$ might well, then, bring slightly different nuances of 'making a choice for' or 'associating with' to the same basic idea of opting to engage with the living rather than the dead, they are probably not interpretative but graphical variants: one has arisen from the other through metathesis, even if the original error and the subsequent survival of the new reading were both doubtless facilitated by the good fit to context. I have opted for the $Q^e r\hat{e}$ largely because there is simply no evidence that the $K^e th\hat{i}bh$ is as early, but believe, with the versions, that in the context it was more probably intended to be read as qal than as pu'al.

Dahood, 'Qoheleth and Northwest Semitic Philology', 361, offers a way to have one's cake and eat it by proposing that the consonants of the $K^e th\hat{i}bh$ can be read with the sense of the $Q^e r\hat{e}$ if we see בחר here as a variant form of פחר, 'gather', with an extended sense of 'associate with' attested only here and in 1 Sam 20.30. Even if we accept that possibility (as do *DCH* and *HALOT*), it is not clear, however, what is supposed to have deterred readers from reading the more common בחר, 'choose': this is at best a way in which we might have explained the reading of the versions if we did not have the $Q^e r\hat{e}$.

9.4 all the living] Qohelet used the expression in 4.15, but the need for כל here is unclear, especially if a simple contrast with המתים is intended. It may be no more than a way to signal that we should read 'living' and not 'life'.

9.4 reassurance] There has been much debate about whether בטחון refers to trust, confidence, or hope—or perhaps to something in which one places one's trust, confidence, or hope (Duncan: 'a trustworthy thing'). Even before looking at the evidence, however, we may reasonably wonder what commentators might actually understand such things to represent in this context. A few read much into the text to find something very specific, as when Rodríguez Gutiérrez, 'Mientras hay vida hay esperanza', sees a manifesto against martyrdom, in which only live resistance offers hope against Ptolemaic rule. Most keep it broader, and Gordis, for example, talks about 'hope, the possibility of an improvement even in the most wretched lot', but does not explain why the humans that Qohelet is discussing here might themselves consider their lot to be wretched (whether he himself does or not). His translation, moreover, draws out an ambiguity that often confuses the discussion in English, where there is a significant difference between saying that somebody has hope and that there is hope for them.

Even when there is an effort to be rigorous, in fact, the language and conceptualization of this area creates problems. Fox, who evokes the only other use of the noun at 2 Kgs 18.19 = Isa 36.4, draws a careful distinction between 'a feeling of hope or inner security' and 'something that one can rely on and be confident of'—which he takes to be the sense both here and in that passage. This enables him to characterize their awareness of coming death as the 'trustworthy...knowledge' that humans possess, but the Rabshakeh in 2 Kings is talking about a source of confidence (asking מה הבטחון הזה אשר בטחת), not confidence in a source, and his question is not about what Hezekiah finds 'trustworthy', but about what 'leads him to trust' in his ultimate safety— to possess, in other words, the very sense or expectation of security that Fox wants to exclude. In that verse, בטחון may not itself be the 'feeling' of confidence, but it is the foundation or excuse for confidence, not the object of confidence. Accordingly, if we really wish to read 9.4-5 in terms of 2 Kgs 18.19 and connect בטחון with the knowledge of death, as Fox proposes, then the sense has to be not that humans have that one piece of knowledge in which they can trust, but that their knowledge of coming death gives humans a basis for trust in their future. This would be wonderfully ironic or paradoxical, but I doubt it is the author's intention.

We probably have to look beyond the precise usage in that other text, therefore, and toward the broader use of cognate terms. These do indeed point to 'confidence' or 'security' rather than 'hope', despite the decision of G to translate the noun here as ἐλπίς, and it is difficult, indeed, to find any evidence of words from the root being used to indicate hope.[5] In particular, the verb בָּטַח is used both with an indirect object for trusting or having confidence 'in' someone or something (e.g. Judg 9.26), or absolutely of 'being confident' or 'feeling secure' (e.g. Prov 28.1; Amos 6.1), and the noun בֶּטַח is commonly used in adverbial expressions for living 'securely' (e.g. Prov 1.33). To be sure, Job 11.18 portrays hope as a basis for feeling secure, but there is nothing to suggest that בטחון might be used of a feeling that things will turn out for the best, whatever the odds, or even of a desire for them to do so: the term almost certainly refers to an expectation that things will be alright, or at least to a state of not worrying about them.

---

[5] For the suggestion that it can have this meaning in later Hebrew, commentators are generally reliant on Jastrow, *Dictionary*, which cites *y. Berakot* for that sense; the relevant passages are XII.E-F and XIV.A in Zahavy, *Talmud of the Land of Israel I*, 317-18. It is important to be aware, however, that the tractate is itself talking about this verse, which it understands in terms of the possibility that even the wicked may still avoid damnation if they repent—a possibility that remains open just so long as they are alive, but then is lost. Even if the sense of בטחון is not being bent to fit the interpretation by broadly equating it with תקוה, it means at most 'there is hope *for* the wicked', not that 'the wicked have hope', and is not a reference to the emotions or expectations of the wicked themselves.

I take Qohelet's point to be that these humans engage with the world of the living and ignore that of the dead because their mortality is a source of anxiety which they wish to avoid, and he makes no suggestion that they actually hope or expect not to die. Correspondingly, בטחון connotes not some false belief or complacency, but a refusal to confront the reality of their situation: we might say that they are 'in denial' about death. In view of 2 Kgs 18.19, it may be that בטחון specifies not that state of feeling secure, but more particularly its source or basis; the overall sense, however, would be similar in either case.

9.4 since it seems to a live dog that he is better than a dead lion] Lit. 'to a live dog he (is) good, more than the dead lion', but the Hebrew is often read as a simple 'better than' statement, 'a living dog is better than a dead lion'. Such readings are inherently problematic, as we shall see shortly, but commentators have sometimes found it difficult to see the purpose of such a statement in this context, and, more broadly, Qohelet elsewhere certainly does *not* view any life as better than death (cf. 4.2; 6.8). Crenshaw, 'Quantitative', 12, resorts to suggesting that this is an aphorism, expressing the feelings of 'a former widow who from necessity married a person of inferior social status to her previous husband'. It would certainly fit such a situation, but it is less clear why Qohelet would cite such an aphorism here.

In 4.6, 9, 13; 5.4; 6.9; 7.1, 2, 3, 5, 8 we have already seen plenty of examples of how Qohelet likes to express 'better than' statements, and we will see others in 9.16, 18. In all these cases, טוב or טובה stands first, followed by the thing that is better, then מ- or מן is followed by the thing that is worse—which is precisely what we should expect. In two places, both of which place the statements in a context of indirect speech, the elements are arranged slightly differently: 6.3 טוב ממנו הנפל places what is better at the end, while 7.10 uses a complicated verbal construction with היו instead of the usual non-verbal clause, and what is better stands before both the verb and טובים. There is a set order, in other words, that is only occasionally varied, and, accordingly, if Qohelet were simply setting out to say here that 'a living dog is better than a dead lion', which is precisely what V *melior est canis uiuens leone mortuo* understands, and which has been the essence of most subsequent translations, we should expect him to say טוב כלב חי מן אריה מת, or perhaps טוב לכלב חי הוא טוב מן האריה המת. M actually, however, reads הכלב החי מן האריה המת and, even setting aside any questions about definite articles or the -ל on כלב, it will be clear that this is structured very differently. Indeed, it is not even just a variation or extension of the common structure, with the dog simply brought forward before the טוב, or brought forward and then resumed by הוא (for which we would expect טוב הוא מן, not הוא טוב מן).

G ὁ κύων ὁ ζῶν αὐτὸς ἀγαθὸς ὑπὲρ τὸν λέοντα τὸν νεκρόν, we may note, reproduces the elements and order exactly (except that it gives the dog a definite article), and there are no grounds for supposing that any of the words in M have been altered or transposed. We have to ask, therefore, whether we can determine a good reason for such a standard 'better than' statement to have been expressed in such an exceptional way here, or else find a different way to understand the words that does more justice to that expression. One alternative reading is, in fact, suggested by σ' κυνὶ ζῶντι βέλτιον ἐστὶν ἢ λέοντι τεθνηκότι, which understands 'it is better for a living dog than for a dead lion', and apparently takes the הוא to be impersonal. This is the only one of the ancient versions, moreover, to engage with the -ל of לכלב, which we have mentioned but not yet discussed, and which σ' renders by using a dative—although in doing so it draws attention to the lack of any matching -ל on אריה: without that, the text construed in these terms would strictly mean 'it is better for a living dog than the dead lion would be', which seems unlikely to be the intended sense. A number of commentators follow this reading, with Fox, for instance, getting round the problem of the missing second -ל by claiming that it has been elided after the מן, and if we do go down this route, then the statement becomes not a declaration that the dog is better, but that it is 'better off'. That does, in fact, make more sense in the context.

The other main approach to the -ל of לכלב has been to treat it as 'emphatic', and Schoors has been amongst the keenest recent advocates of this position. The idea of an emphatic ל in Hebrew, at least as it is understood in modern commentaries, goes back to Paul Haupt, who in an 1894 article used this very verse as the starting-point for his argument that a prefixed -ל here and sometimes elsewhere might be not the common preposition -ל, but a particle attested in some other Semitic languages, and that its function was to add a certain emphasis or affirmation, as though we were to say 'Indeed, a live dog...', or 'Verily, a live dog...'.[6] The number of cases in which there is anything close to general acceptance of an 'emphatic' ל, however, is very

---

[6] Haupt, 'A New Hebrew Particle'. This idea is picked up in GKC §143 e and in *HALOT*, both of which also cite this verse as a prime example. The idea has generally received a cautious affirmation in principle (although Muraoka pointedly does not cover it in J-M), and in particular with respect to this verse, but many other uses and nuances have been attributed to the particle, and in practice the willingness of scholars to identify particular examples has varied enormously. Huehnergard's cautious review of the particle and its equivalents in other Semitic languages observes that opinions range from characterizations of the particle in biblical Hebrew as unusual through to Dahood's identification of some 75 instances in the Psalms alone. See Huehnergard, 'Asseverative **la* and Hypothetical **lu/law* in Semitic', 591. This is because it is rare for proposed cases to be inexplicable in any other terms, and so in Ps 89.19 (ET 89.18), for example, which is one of very few proposed instances that would present a direct parallel to the usage here—see Nötscher, 'Zum emphatischen Lamed', 379—the matter boils down to whether we think that ליהוה means the psalmist is saying that 'our shield is YHWH' or 'our shield belongs to YHWH', and likewise 'our king' in the second part (since the next verses talk about God's selection of a human king, I am inclined myself to doubt that we should understand 'is' there).

small, and to appeal to that particle in Eccl 9.4 is almost to argue in a circle: were it not for Haupt's insistence that לכלב must have a 'nominative' role here, we might never have heard of an emphatic ל in biblical Hebrew, and the plausibility of the particle's existence, at least with this function, would be much diminished without the support of this verse. To call the ל here 'emphatic' is not to explain it, therefore, so much as to say that it cannot reasonably be explained in terms of any normal understanding of the preposition -ל, and, correspondingly, the real question is whether we do in fact need to understand לכלב as 'nominative', and so to preclude such normal understandings.

In fact, doing so does not really solve all our problems. Rejecting the sort of understanding adopted by σ' and Fox, Schoors says that 'it is easier to parse הוא as the copula than as the subject of an impersonal clause'. That is, however, to ignore the position of the pronoun, which we should expect always to stand after the predicate טוב if it were simply a 'copula': its position *before* טוב suggests that it is, in fact, the subject of the non-verbal construction (cf. J-M §154 i-j), and that we should read this not as a tri-partite non-verbal clause, but as a bi-partite clause ('he [is] better than the dead lion') with לכלב חי preceding in some other function. One way to understand this is to take -ל as prepositional with the sense 'concerning' or 'as regards', so that לכלב is a *casus pendens*, and the sentence means something like 'as for a living dog, he is better than the dead lion'. This makes perfectly good sense, and the -ל does not need to be described as emphatic, since it can be more simply understood by analogy with the common uses of the preposition (Barton and McNeile recognize the possibility of describing it either way).

Especially given that the other variations of the 'better than' statement in the book are related to indirect speech, however, I think that we may do better still to look at a slightly different use of the preposition to indicate perspective or viewpoint, rather than simply subject matter. On that understanding, 'to a dog' would mean, in effect, 'it seems to a dog that' and the 'better than' statement would then be organized like that in Dan 1.15, where it is governed by נראה, with the subject before טוב. Although such uses of -ל commonly receive little attention in the lexica, they are not really rare, especially in aphorisms, and the only unusual feature here would be that the dog is perceiving something about himself, rather than someone or something else, which entails the use of the clause with הוא.[7]

---

[7] The usage is illustrated most economically by the various sayings in Proverbs where 'x is y *to* someone', e.g. Prov 20.17 where 'bread of deceit is sweet *to* a man' (cf. 13.19; 16.24), Prov 15.21 where 'folly is a joy *to* one who lacks sense (cf. 15.23; 21.15), or Prov 14.6 where 'knowledge is easy *to* one who understands'. BDB would presumably class these instances under its heading 1e for -ל, which includes the use of the preposition 'with words denoting what is pleasurable or the reverse' or 'to denote the subj. of a sensation or emotion', but it is difficult to limit the usage in that way: note such comparisons as Prov 10.23,

Whatever understanding of the -ל we adopt here, however, the fact that the versions other than M and σ' show no awareness of it does raise questions about the status of the reading. Ginsberg's suggestion that the preposition has migrated from the earlier כי מי is more ingenious than plausible, but it is not impossible that the ל arose from a reduplication מכלב, construed as כי לכלב, which would explain its absence in the source-text of G. It is more likely, however, to have dropped out there, perhaps to facilitate the reading of a simpler 'better than' statement', than to have emerged as an error in M: as we have seen already, removing it does not actually leave us with that simple 'better than' statement, and if the -ל does indeed indicate perspective, then it both explains the form of the sentence and brings the sentiment better into line with Qohelet's views elsewhere (b. Šabbat 30a complains that this directly contradicts 4.2). There are also, in fact, some other grounds for supposing that G's source-text has been altered: the Greek has an article with both nouns, corresponding to a reading החי, not the simple חי of M (and most likely σ'), and this is again most readily explained by alignment of the text to an expectation that it should mean 'the dog is better than the lion'. The more probably original mismatch between 'a dog' and 'the lion', of course, is a sign that it does not, but the text or interpretation that lies behind G may have been shared by, or been influential upon, most of the other versions as well.

The hexaplaric, O-group manuscripts of G have a curious addition here: the dog is living ἐν σκότει, 'in darkness'. Although it seems to locate the darkness slightly earlier, the fourth-century Ambrosiaster, *Quaestiones*, 39, cites the saying in Latin similarly as *spes est in tenebris melior est canis vivus leone mortuo*, literally 'hope is in darkness, better is the living dog than the dead lion', and interprets the darkness in terms of pagan ignorance. Although this reading is clearly quite early, it is hard to know where it has come from

---

where כשחוק לכסיל עשות זמה means 'doing wrong is like a game to a fool', Prov 25.13, where the faithful messenger 'is like the coolness of snow at harvest-time to those who send him', or Ct 1.13-14, where the beloved is a bag of myrrh or bunch of henna 'to me'. Under the same general heading, we should probably place uses like those in Gen 13.13 or 2 Sam 22.24, where guilt or innocence 'to' God refers to God's perception of behaviour (and -ל is being used rather like לפני), Ps 31.12 (ET 31.11), where the psalmist has become objectionable to his neighbours and acquaintances, Ct 6.9, where the woman is 'faultless to the one who bore her', or Esth 10.3 where Mordecai was 'great to the Jews' (// 'was pleasing to most of his brothers'). What unites these various examples is the use of the preposition to denote the holder of a perception, and there is no reason to suppose that this use is constrained by the specific nature of the perception itself. It is also clear that such expressions are used not only with words, but with non-verbal clauses, as in the first three examples cited above. Although it probably has a separate origin, I doubt that the usage can be disconnected entirely from similar uses of על/אל: cf. the note 'and it seemed mighty to me' at 9.13.

or what it signifies. It probably reflects a particular attempt to contextualize or understand the saying.

9.5 This is because] Lit. 'for'. I take the כי to be explanatory, and, although this is often taken to be the basis on which humans believe themselves to be 'better' than the dead, I think it refers back beyond the statement about the dog and lion to the more general point that the living reject the dead.

9.5 may know that] Despite the large number of participles in the book, Yi, 251, notes only two places where G renders a participle using the future: here and in 10.3 (if we treat חסר there as a participle rather than an adjective). Yi himself sees both verses as proverbial, and the translations as an attempt to capture a modal nuance, but that certainly does not work as an explanation here: the translator surely would not have understood the text as found in M that way, and even if he did, why would he then have used the participial γινώσκοντες in the parallel statement about the dead? It is possible that he might have wished to avoid using a second participle after οἱ ζῶντες, but since he could have employed a present indicative in that case, the future γνώσονται which dominates the manuscript tradition of G more probably suggests that he found ידע in his source-text.

The other ancient versions all support M יודעים, but McNeile, 149, suggests that G represents the earlier reading here, and that M has been influenced by the subsequent occurrence of יודעים. I think this is right: if the statements are supposed to be read as a contrast, then we would certainly expect the verb form to be the same in each, and that expectation makes M by far the easier reading, but G correspondingly more likely to be original. In fact, it makes very good sense to read ידע if we understand it as modal (J-M §113 l), without a very specific implication of tense, and this adds a further dimension to the contrast without greatly changing the sense: the living *may* know they will die, but the dead absolutely know nothing. The -ש on שימתו functions as a verbal complement, not as a relative pronoun, so the living know *that* they will die, not *who* will die.

9.5 the dead know nothing at all] Lit. 'the dead: there is not them knowing anything'.

9.5 and there is no more recompense for them] G, Hie and S probably reflect להם עוד rather than the עוד להם of M, and this is the order found when the same words occur again in the next verse. It is difficult to know whether these versions are aligning the expression to that verse—a possibility that McNeile, 149, raises—or whether they have preserved the original reading. There is no obvious change in the sense that might explain the variation in M, although it is possibly euphonic: commentators have long noted the particular assonance between שכר and the following זכרם, but the whole sequence seems polished.

The noun שכר was used in the expression יש להם שכר at 4.9, and is discussed in the notes there. As in that verse, G renders it here as μισθός, 'pay', but σ' uses ἐπικαρπία, which has more of a nuance of continuing revenue than does the κέρδος, 'gain', which it used at 4.9. Ginsberg speculates that שכר might have displaced an original שבר, 'hope' or 'confidence' (cf. Pss 119.116; 146.5), which would have been a counterpart to the בטחון of the previous verse; this is clever, but it is not clear how that would accord with the statement about forgetfulness.

9.5 for any memory of them is lost] Lit. 'their memory has been forgotten'. This is usually taken to mean that the living forget the dead, but Lohfink understands a reference to the fading consciousness of the dead themselves, that deprives them of any post-mortem reward. I doubt that is tenable, but Lohfink does also draw attention to a widespread understanding in the ancient Near East that the living can provide a continuing connection to the world for those who are in the underworld, which may be important for understanding the force of this statement.

9.6 and[1]...and[2]...each has already perished, and] The three nouns forming a list at the beginning of the verse are linked by the use of גם before each, so this is literally 'also their love, also their hate, also their passion'. A similar device is used to link verbal clauses at Isa 48.8 and adverbial expressions at Exod 4.10. Since the first גם is acting like the 'both' in a 'both...and' construction, it is not explicitly joining this verse to the last. Furthermore, it is striking that the final verb is singular אבדה, so the construction apparently emphasizes that each of the (feminine) nouns is the subject of that verb, rather than that they are all acting collectively as its subject (cf. Zeph 1.18 for a negative analogy). I have tried to bring that out in the translation.

The link with 9.1, if I have understood that verse correctly, suggests that Qohelet is talking not so much about personal relationships here, as about the attachments and strong feelings that differentiated the dead in life by causing them to act in certain ways.

9.6 passion] See the note at 4.4.

9.6 and there is nothing which is theirs] Lit. 'and there is not for them a portion'. On חלק, see the note 'what was mine' at 2.10; here and at 9.9, Qohelet speaks of a portion 'in' (-ב) rather than a portion 'from' (-מ) as at 2.10.

Some important G manuscripts have καὶ γε μερὶς (equivalent to וגם חלק) where M has וחלק: McNeile, 149, cites Hie in support, but *sed et* is from the start of the verse, not here. The reading is more likely an inner-Greek development (so Gentry, 'Issues', 205-6) than the reflection of a Hebrew variant, but is in any case secondary.

9.7-10

(9.7) Come on, eat your bread with pleasure, and drink your wine with a happy heart. For God has already accepted your work. (9.8) Let your clothes be white at all times, and let not oil be lacking on your head. (9.9) Experience life with a woman you love all the days of your life of illusion, which he has given you beneath the sun, all the days of your illusion, for that is what is yours in life.

And in all the business at which you work beneath the sun, (9.10) anything which your hand finds to do, do with all your might. For there is no work, or plan, or knowledge, or wisdom in Sheol, which is where you are going.

Commentary

This is the most famous of Qohelet's exhortations to pleasure, but, as we noted earlier, it also includes an important statement of his determinism. In the Introduction (77), furthermore, we observed the resemblances between these verses and a passage in the *Epic of Gilgamesh*: while there may be no direct link, it seems likely that Qohelet draws here on existing, perhaps widely familiar motifs: a number of the other works that we looked at in the Introduction (105-10) included similar themes (there seems no particular reason, though, to see lines from an old drinking-song behind it, as Loretz, '"Frau" und griechisch-jüdische Philosophie', 257-60, suggests; cf. Fischer, *Skepsis*, 138-46).

In *Gilgamesh*, the admonitions are intended to dissuade the hero from his pursuit of physical immortality, and, in part, the function of these verses is not dissimilar: Qohelet has just suggested that the dead can have no real effect on the world of the living, so it is better to focus on one's life than on one's posterity—just as it would be better for Gilgamesh to enjoy what he has, than to seek immortality. Qohelet also now draws in, however, his previous point that humans are not really in control of their own actions. Since what they do must be in accordance with God's designs, it must be 'good', in the terms of 3.1-8, so we should not worry that we are doing the wrong thing: what is important is that we should do *something*. Qohelet does not only point out again that it is only in the enjoyment of our actions that we can find anything that is really for ourselves (our 'portion'), but also introduces a note of urgency: we shall not have in Sheol what we have in life. The point has been put well in a very different context: 'If there's no great glorious end to all this, if nothing we do matters, then all that matters is what we do. 'Cause that's all there is. What we do. Now. Today.'[1]

The list of things absent in Sheol is interesting, because it does not include the commonplace pleasures of life, as outlined at the start of these verses (although Qohelet would surely expect those to be absent), but comprises 'work', the sort of 'plan' that figured heavily in 7.25-29, 'knowledge', and 'wisdom'. The last three are perhaps qualities associated with the first, but the 'plan' in particular is evocative more of the sort of intellectual quests that Qohelet has himself undertaken. In any case, though, this list seems to provide a motivation specifically for the advice to act or work: we should find pleasure because that is our portion, but throw ourselves into activity because at death we will lose the opportunity and capacity to do so, or perhaps to reflect on what we are doing. After speaking of his pleasure in work in 2.10, and after treating lifestyle and occupation together in 2.24; 3.13; 5.17-18; 8.15, Qohelet still juxtaposes the two, but now imposes a distinction by providing different reasons for his advice about each. We should probably not make too much of this, especially if the presentation has been shaped by a desire to echo admonitions known from elsewhere, but it does have the consequence that activity is not directly associated with pleasure or personal benefit: it is something to be done simply because we will not be able to do it later. This stands in contrast to Sir 14. 16, which is sometimes compared, but which comments that אין בשאול לבקש תענוג, 'in Sheol, there is no seeking pleasure', to motivate advice about generosity and taking pleasure in what one has while one is still alive. Equally, therefore, we should not blur the distinctions, as does, e.g., Ogden, 'Qoheleth IX 1-16', 163-64, which takes the things listed here as divine gifts that will be enjoyed as pleasures by the wise.

---

[1] Joss Whedon, 'Epiphany', Angel. Series 2. 27 February 2001.

9.7] Although some modern readers might be inclined to associate the drinking of wine here with luxury, bread and wine are presented elsewhere as staples (e.g. Judg 19.19; 1 Sam 10.3; Neh 5.15; Ps 104.14-15; see also the commentary at 2.3), and it is unlikely that Qohelet is advising his audience to eat or drink anything more than they would usually do. At this point, the advice is not to do something special or luxurious, but happily to do something normal. We can relax and enjoy our lives because God has already 'accepted' what we do, and so (although this probably does not exclude our being judged for it subsequently) it is inevitable, and there is no point in worrying about it. In 9.8-9, this will be stepped up, at least to the extent that having clean laundry, fragrant oils, and a loving partner goes beyond the bare minimum of taking care of ourselves, and the first items suggest that we should be treating every day as special, like a feast-day. There is no call here, though, to live a life of great luxury, and if some of this would surely have been beyond the reach of the very poor, that probably just reflects the nature of the anticipated audience.

9.8] On the use of oil, see the commentary at 7.1. Leithart, 'Solomon's Sexual Wisdom', 457, claims that 'bread, wine, oil, and joy are, in the Hebrew Bible, particularly associated with the festivities of the sanctuary (Deut 12:1-19; 14:23). So, Solomon's exhortation to eat, drink, and rejoice is, in part, an exhortation to enjoy the gifts of God offered directly at His house'. To be sure, Deut 12.17 and 14.23, talk about tithes of corn, wine, and oil, which are often treated together (usually with a further reference to animals, e.g., Deut 7.13) as a stereotypical way of describing the produce of the land. The terms are hardly uncommon elsewhere, however, and those passages actually use a different word, referring to freshly pressed oil.

It is not clear precisely how clothes would have been whitened in the author's own context. Mal 3.2 refers to *bryt mkbsym*, perhaps a plant-extract used by fullers, and *bryt* occurs also in Jer 2.22: in the latter it stands beside natron, but the context in Malachi suggests that it is something harsher. The Roman use in fulling of ammonia from urine is well known, and citing a Roman law from the third century BCE, Pliny the Elder (*Naturalis Historia*, 35.57) discusses the Greek and Roman use of various minerals and of fumigation by sulphur. Such techniques were probably used elsewhere. If the text here is referring to bright white clothes, then these would probably have been relatively expensive to purchase and maintain (cf. Brenner, *Colour Terms*, 244, 'out of the question for the underprivileged, at least as a daily practice'), but Qohelet may only be talking about keeping one's clothes freshly laundered (so Ginsberg, 'Quintessence', 58 n. 14, who notes later uses of the cognate verb for cleaning and polishing more generally). Although 'cleanness' may naturally be associated with purity, and the text has sometimes been read in such terms (as by T; see the survey in Lavoie, 'Bonheur et finitude', 318-19), it seems unlikely that any such implication is intended here, where the other actions commended have no such associations.

9.9] The same word in Hebrew is used for 'woman' or 'wife', and there has been some debate about which is involved here. That debate is likely anachronistic, importing a distinction between married and unmarried cohabitation ('living in sin') that would probably have been foreign to the author, and about which the Hebrew Bible as a whole has nothing to say. Our evidence is limited, but setting aside relationships involving adultery or slavery, it is likely that, in practical terms, any man and woman living together and having sex would have regarded themselves as married.[2] Although contractual obligations between families may have been involved in setting marriages up (or dissolving them), the marital state itself was not initiated by a declaration, or probably even by an exchange of vows. Accordingly, 'woman' or 'wife' is essentially a problem of translation. The original audience would doubtless have understood Qohelet to be commending marriage, not because of any moral presuppositions, but because that is what

---

[2] Probably our best insight into the practices of a near-contemporary Jewish community (although it is set in the past) comes from the book of Tobit, where Tobias' wedding to Sarah (7.12-14) consists of receiving her father's written permission to sleep with her, followed by his doing so. Given the circumstances in that story, doubtless the bare minimum was being done, but whatever other complications might more commonly have been involved in terms of dowries, contracts, ceremonies and celebrations, marriages (as elsewhere in the Hellenistic world) were essentially put into effect by cohabitation, licensed by the male family member with responsibility for the bride, if any, and were uncomplicated by the concerns of Christian sacramental theology.

the advice would have meant to them—indeed, 'experiencing life with a woman you love' might have seemed to them the very definition of marriage; the same is not true for a modern Western audience. I have opted for 'woman', in the end, simply to avoid importing a more specific modern notion, but it is just as important to avoid importing the modern distinction, and seeing some implicit rejection or discounting of marriage. Of course, those receiving the advice are assumed to be (heterosexual) men, but this may be just a convention (cf. similarly Prov 18.22), albeit a telling one: we should not see it as 'a clue that Qohelet's audience was exclusively male' (Crenshaw).

There are some significant problems in the text that follows. The clause 'which he has given you beneath the sun' is probably original, but is missing in some manuscripts and textual traditions. 'All the days of your illusion' is also missing in key sources, but this phrase, on the other hand, is very likely to be secondary—a corrupt duplication of what preceded. I have retained it in my translation, but with some reluctance.

9.10] This is the book's only direct reference to Sheol, the underworld—the Greek translation talks of 'Hades', the equivalent concept in Greek culture. Qohelet's characterization is in line with other biblical depictions of existence in that afterlife as something closer to sleep than to conscious living (see especially Ps 139.8; Isa 14.11; Ezek 32.18-32).

Notes

9.7 Come on, eat] Lit. 'go, eat'. As in the more formal לכה נא of 2.1, the imperative of הלך is often used with other verbs, and without any necessary implication of movement, to express encouragement or avoid an abrupt command (e.g., Gen 19.32; 31.44; 1 Sam 14.1; Ct 7.12). G picks this up with δεῦρο, 'here!', which can be used similarly. The form with paragogic ה is often found in such usage, but see, e.g., Gen 37.14; Judg 19.13. Qohelet is not advising specifically that we should 'go away and eat...', although it is possible that in this context of food and drink, the language might be taken as that of invitation: in Prov 9.5, Wisdom uses לכו in a similar context when she invites the uneducated to turn aside, eat her food, and drink her wine (cf. the invitation of the foreign woman at 7.18, with לכה). At the very least, though, there are no grounds to see 'a note of imperious exhortation...an urgent summons to action', as Eaton puts it.

The La *ueni comede*, 'come, eat', reflects G and is cited by Jerome in his commentary, where he opts himself to translate less literally with *uade et comede*, 'go and eat', instead (cf. V *uade ergo et comede*, with 'therefore' added). Gentry, 'Issues', 208-10 (which notes other citations of the La), puts this under the heading 'Jerome correcting Old Latin to Hebrew', presumably because *uade* is closer to לך than is *ueni*, but the conjunction is Jerome's own improvement to the style.

9.7 with pleasure] Lit. 'in pleasure'; σ' μετ' εὐφροσύνης, 'with pleasure', is a paraphrase, but we need to adopt the same slight shift in English to convey the sense.

9.7 with a happy heart] Lit. 'a good heart'. Schoors observes that when לב is used in conjunction with the cognate verb טוב, the reference is always to the effects of alcohol (Judg 16.25; 1 Sam 25.36; 2 Sam 13.28; Esth 1.10), and so there may be an encouragement here actually to cheer oneself with drink. The unattributed reading attested here in ms 788, ἐν σταθερᾷ πίστει, 'with unwavering trust', understands the Hebrew very differently, interpreting it in the light of the following clause. If it is hexaplaric (which is questionable), the source and paraphrastic character make σ' the most likely candidate.

9.7 already] ἤδη, 'already', is lacking in many witnesses to G, and this fact may have influenced the similar absence of any equivalent to כבר in S and V. It was present in Origen's text and in the translations of the Three (cf. Gentry, 'Hexaplaric Materials', 16-17). If original in G, its omission is difficult to explain as a simple error: Gentry supposes that it might have been considered redundant or that it was omitted before the similar-sounding syllable εὐδ-, but neither explanation is compelling. It is conceivable that ἤδη might have been left out on some theological basis, but also worth noting that omission of כבר through haplography in the Hebrew sequence כי כבר רצה is much easier to explain. We cannot exclude the possibility, therefore, that the omission goes back to G's source-text, and that ἤδη was restored from one of the other Greek translations. As Lavoie, 'Bonheur et finitude', 318, observes, כבר is always used temporally by Qohelet, and there is no need to adopt the suggestion of Zimmermann, that it might mean 'perhaps', as sometimes later in Aramaic (usually, anyway, expressing the possibility that something *will* happen).

9.7 accepted] רצה in the qal is used most often with God as the subject, and refers to divine pleasure or acceptance. σ' uses ἐξήτασεν, which has a more precise nuance of approving something after careful examination.

9.8 white] On the G variant λαμπρὰ, 'bright', which is found in some patristic sources, see Gentry, 'Hexaplaric Materials', 17-18. λευκά is certainly G*, and appears to have been the reading of the Three as well. S ܢܗܘܘܢ ܢܚܬܝܟ ܚܘܪܝܢ *nḥtyk nhwwn ḥwryn*, 'your garments, may they be white', curiously changes the word-order; cf. Kamenetzky, 227.

9.8 at all times] In principle, בכל עת could mean 'on every occasion', which has led various commentators to suppose that Qohelet is talking only about taking particular opportunities for enjoyment offered by God. In practice, though, that sense is only really possible in Esth 5.13, and other uses of the expression clearly mean 'always', so this interpretation is probably too restrictive. See, e.g., Pss 10.5; 34.2; 106.3; Prov 5.19 (// תמיד). In *b. Šabbat* 153a, cited and enlarged upon by Rashi, the point is taken to be that we must be prepared to die at any time.

9.8 let not] Several late Hebrew manuscripts have לא for אל; see Miletto.

9.8 be lacking on your head] Ambrose, in *De Institutione Virginis* XVII, 110 and *Exhortatio Virginitatis* x, 62-63 (PL 16, 332, 355) three times cites the La as *et oleum in capite (tuo) non desit*, 'and let oil not be absent on your head', which reflects G, and G in turn supports M. The *'from* your head' of Hie, V (*de capite tuo*), and S (ܡܢ ܪܝܫܟ *mn ryšk*) is probably just a looser translation that arises from the notion of absence, and it fits Jerome's use of *deficiat*, 'be wanting', 'disappear', instead of *desit*. Gentry, 'Issues', 211, suggests that this may have been influenced by σ' οὐ μὴ διαλιπέτω, which conveys the more specific sense 'let it not be absent for a moment'.

9.9 Experience life] Lit. 'see life'. All Greek manuscripts of G have καὶ ἰδὲ, 'and see', with an initial conjunction: Rahlfs' reading without it is based on Hie *uide*, although that reading is found also in Coptic, and Gentry's rejection of the conjunction in 'Issues', 220, was based on an *assumption* that the translator found no conjunction in his Hebrew source. Gentry has ultimately reversed that decision in his edition, and the conjunction is supported by S: Kamenetzky, 227, 236, thinks it may be the original reading of the Hebrew. I am inclined to consider it secondary, linking the advice more explicitly to the suggestions in 9.8, but it is impossible to say for sure whether it arose in the Hebrew (which seems likely) or very early in the G tradition—or, for that matter, to exclude the possibility that it is original.

There is no conjunction in σ' ἀπόλαυσον ζωῆς, 'take advantage of life', although that may be just a limitation of the note, but this translation has probably influenced V *perfruere uita*, 'enjoy life', and that in turn has exercised a strong influence over subsequent translations and commentaries. There is no reason to suppose, however, that ראה חיים itself has any connotation of finding or taking pleasure in life. That is merely an implication of the context.

9.9 a woman you love] There is no article in the Hebrew or in G, and so although it is possible that Qohelet is talking about 'the wife whom you love' (RSV), rather than just any woman, the scope of his admonition cannot be limited in that way on linguistic grounds. Of course, 'a' woman may be a woman who is to be married, as in passages like Gen 21.21, cited by, e.g., Whitley and Crenshaw, but we cannot just insert an article to read '(the) woman you love'. Even when it points to linguistic data, scholarly discussion of the point has clearly often been influenced by anachronistic moral judgments held by commentators themselves, or else imputed to Qohelet. For instance, Zimmermann, in 'Aramaic Provenance', 21, connects the absence of an article with his theory of a translation from Aramaic, which would not have used one, and Dahood, 'Canaanite-Phoenician', 211, sees a Phoenician usage. Neither makes a moral judgment itself, but both are making implicitly the same assumption that Torrey, 'Question', 155-56, also arguing for Aramaic, had earlier made explicit: 'No Hebrew moralist could possibly have failed to write האשה, "*the wife* whom you love"'. A number of commentators over the centuries·have taken a different approach, represented recently by Ogden and by Pahk, 'Syntactical and Contextual Consideration', which construes the subsequent relative clause ('which he has given you') as referring to the woman rather than to 'the days of your life of illusion'. This is hardly a natural reading, especially in the light of other references to God 'giving days' (5.17, 18; 8.15), but Pahk (376-77) further sees נתן אשה ל- as a 'typological expression' indicating matrimony, citing, e.g., Exod 21.4, and claims that the text must refer precisely to a wife. He goes on to suggest, in tones reminiscent of Torrey, and citing similar opinions, that only such an admonition would have been acceptable in the original social context of the book (on which, see the commentary).

Pinker, 'Qohelet's Views on Women', 187, draws attention to the fact that the form of the verb is qatal (he suggests that a participle might have been expected, but note the yiqtol תמצא in 9.10). I doubt that this specifically implies a long-term relationship, as he supposes, but Qohelet is apparently speaking in terms of a partner who has already been found, rather than of finding one in the future.

9.9 all the days of your life of illusion] σ' τῆς ἀβεβαίου σου, 'of your insecure (life)', is interestingly interpretative, and echoed in V *uitae instabilitatis tuae*. α' has the expected ἀτμοῦ σου, 'of your vapour'.

9.9 which he has given you beneath the sun] Or just possibly 'which have been given to you beneath the sun', which is the sense of G τὰς δοθείσας σοι ὑπὸ τὸν ἥλιον. The G translator is not averse to translating relative clauses with a participle, especially, it seems, when the verb involved is the qal of היה or the niph'al of עשה (see Yi, 100-101, 151-54, 167-71; Gentry, 'Issues', 220). For אשר נתן לו in the similar expressions at 5.17, 18 and 8.15, however, G has ὧν/ ᾧ/ ὅσας ἔδωκεν αὐτῷ, which retains a main verb and a formal relative clause. It is possible that the translator was trying to avoid an ambiguity here, since Greek does not differentiate between genders in the third person, and the woman could conceivably (although not very plausibly in context) have been taken as the subject of a simple ἔδωκε. In the light of that consistency elsewhere, however, and of his approach more generally, it seems likely that the translator would have rendered נתן here with δοθείσας, a passive participle, only if he had parsed נתן as a niph'al participle, or else understood it to have an impersonal subject, giving a periphrasis for the passive, rather than, like M, taken it as a main verb with the 'God' of 9.7 as its subject.

Apparently not noting such possibilities, McNeile, 150, regards the rendering as 'foreign to the style of the translation', and Goldman accepts that opinion, suggesting that τὰς δοθείσας σοι ὑπὸ τὸν ἥλιον, 'which have been given to you under the sun', has been supplied, wholly or in part, from one of the other Greek translations (which may have happened with the words that follow; see the next note). I think it is easier, however, to accept that the translator simply understood the verb in a way that differed from the understanding of M, even if it is less easy to explain why he should have done so. Although the passive plural participles *dati* and *datae* found in V and Hie, moreover, reflect the influence of G's reading, they might also be taken to suggest that Jerome was unaware of the reading presumed in M, and that G's understanding had a wider currency. Since M offers, however, what is surely the most natural reading of the consonantal text as it stands (not least because we should usually expect a participle to agree with ימי חיי, not כל), and since there is no obvious interpretative reason to exclude God as the giver of life only here, there is a strong possibility that the G translator was pushed to his understanding by a slightly different text with נתנם / נתנים. If so, that variant might have some claim to originality, with M reflecting assimilation to the expression used three times earlier, but there is no direct evidence of its existence.

In any case, there is no good reason to doubt the originality of the clause as a whole in G, and its absence in S and in a number of Hebrew manuscripts, noted by de Rossi, is probably the result of errors caused by the repetition of 'your הבל' (on which, see below). There are no clear grounds, at least, to suppose with *BHS* that it is an addition.

9.9 all the days of your illusion] Although many commentators emphasize the power of the repetition as a literary device, the wording actually changes here, from 'days of your life of הבל' (cf. 6.12) to 'days of your הבל' (cf. 7.15). Both use the sort of construction exemplified in the common use of x + קדשך to mean 'your holy X' (e.g. Exod 15.13), on which see GKC §135 n. It would be unwise to make too much of the switch, however, because there is a possibility that כל ימי הבלך is a secondary, corrupt duplicate of the earlier כל ימי חיי הבלך, which uses הבל more normally, as an attribute of ימי חיי. McNeile, 150, considers it 'a certainty' that the phrase was lacking from the early text used by G as its source, and Seow rejects it as a product of 'vertical dittography'.

Matters are complicated by the way in which repetitions in the text here tend to provoke errors, with copyists skipping over clauses in the way that we observed for some Hebrew manuscripts in the last note. McNeile's claim is contested in Gentry, 'Issues', 221-22, which spells out the evidence for G in detail. Gentry acknowledges that the πᾶσαι ἡμέραι ἡμέραι ἀτμοῦ σου found in the earliest text of Codex B (pre-instaurator), and in a few other early sources (usually without the repetition of ἡμέραι), is obviously a corruption of the α' reading, πᾶσαι αἱ ἡμέραι ἀτμοῦ σου, 'all the days of your vapour'. He points out, however, that the more characteristically G πάσας ἡμέρας ματαιότητός σου is affirmed by Syh and other witnesses to Origen's text, so the reading is at least that early, even if it is absent from other important manuscripts. Marshall notes that, according to one manuscript, 'the rest' have ἀτμοῦ for ματαιότητός (not ἀτμοῦ σου, as claimed in Field, *Auctarium*), and if that does accurately represent the readings of the Three, then this reading with ματαιότητός would be unlikely to have been restored from one of them to fill a gap. On balance, it seems likely that Gentry is right to believe that the phrase was omitted and restored, not always accurately, in the G tradition, but that it is G*.

McNeile also claims that the phrase is lacking from Hie, which is untrue (Hie and V have *omnibus diebus uanitatis tuae* and *omni tempore uanitatis tuae*, respectively), but it is certainly absent, along with the previous clause, from S and some later Hebrew manuscripts (cf. de Rossi), probably as the result of errors (and possibly errors or variants in the source-text of S, rather than in the Syriac tradition itself; cf. Kamenetzky 227, 236). Its absence from T is interesting, because T has that previous clause (as do certain of the Hebrew manuscripts, although potentially under the influence of T), but the evidence of the versions is too confused to point clearly in any single direction. It seems likely that, as later in the Hebrew tradition, some early Hebrew manuscripts had the phrase, and some did not; those that did not may variously have inherited the minus or created it afresh through omission. In any case, questions about its originality are not going to be answered using the textual evidence, which allows but does not demand that it might be an addition.

I am very sceptical about its originality myself, largely because Qohelet does not typically use such virtual repetitions of phrases straight afterwards, in order to specify or to modify them. While we should, of course, be wary of imposing too much consistency upon the book, I am inclined to think, accordingly, that the phrase probably did arise as a faulty variant of the preceding כל ימי חיי הבלך, which found its way into the text either by mistake or in an effort to embrace two known readings. I have retained it, however, both because there are no solid grounds on which to reject it, with the text-critical waters far too muddy for any reliable analysis, and because it was clearly known to many early readers of the text.

9.9 for that is what is yours] Lit. 'that is your portion'. Ginsburg, *Massorah* 3:71, lists היא as a *Kethîbh* associated with the eastern tradition, הוא as the western reading and the eastern *Qerê*; cf. Baer, 81; T-S D1.15, 2v 16. This is an attractive reading, potentially making the woman, rather than the vaguer notion of experience, the subject of the clause—but the variant may have arisen for that very reason.

9.9 in life] G here has ἐν τῇ ζωῇ σου, 'in *your* life', while M just has בחיים, 'in life'. Both are found as variant readings in the S and T traditions, while Hie and V support M—although it is important to note that Hie has no 'your' for the following עמלך / μόχθῳ σου either, so the absence may be translational. It is hard to say which is original, and Kaiser, in 'Determination', 259, has chosen to follow the Greek (although he does not do so in his short commentary). It seems marginally more likely, though, that 'your' was added unconsciously in a context where it appears frequently, than that it dropped out.

9.10 finds] The reading ἐφῖκται attributed to σ' by Field is found in none of the manuscripts, and the probable reading is ἐφικνεῖται; see Marshall. This verb has a range of meanings, and Symmachus probably intended to express the idea of a hand 'reaching out' to something. It can also have an implication of attainment or success, however, and so probably lies behind Jerome's rendering in V, *quodcumque potest manus tua facere*, 'whatever your hand is able to do'.

Similar expressions are used in Hebrew at 1 Sam 10.7; 25.8, both times indicating that one should act (or 'give') according to one's inclination. The accentuation of the verb here seems to have been debated by the Masoretes: see Ginsburg, *Massorah*, 4:439, and below.

9.10 with all your might] G ὡς ἡ δύναμίς σου reflects ככחך, not M בכחך. The -ב of M is supported by all the other versions, but בכח always means 'by' or 'with' power (e.g. Judg 6.14; Job 24.22; 26.12; Jer 10.12), so Qohelet would be saying 'do (it) with force' or 'forcefully'. That is not a bad sense, although since כח does mean power rather than enthusiasm, this might not be the best advice for every situation.

Many commentators, however, have understood the context to suggest 'do it with all the strength that you can', or 'to the best of your ability', an idea that is expressed with ככל כח in 1 Chr 29.2 and with ככח in Ezra 2.69. Goldman, accordingly, notes that 'The reading of G seems better', and adopts it in *BHQ*, as does Fox in his commentary. There is a danger here of simply selecting a text to accord with one's understanding of the passage, but the variant reflected in G does have the edge text-critically: it is easier to understand the assimilation of a rather uncommon form ככח to the common בכח than *vice versa*.

Joüon, 'Notes philologiques', 424, does not like either reading, and would emend speculatively to בחייך, 'in your life', to provide a counterpart for the subsequent בשאול. In sense, this corresponds to a much older interpretation. As a number of commentators have observed, the Masoretic accentuation in most manuscripts groups בכחך with the preceding לעשות rather than with עשה, indicating a reading 'whatever your hand finds to do with strength, do'; Wickes, *Accentuation*, 139, notes some exceptions, but this reading is in line with rabbinic interpretations of the passage. These take 'in your strength' to mean 'while you still have strength', and the verse accordingly to mean 'do whatever you can, while you can, for there is nothing to do after death' (for references, see Carasik, 'Exegetical Implications', 158). Carasik, 'Double Translation', 225-26, suggests plausibly that the addition in T of ארום בתר מותא ...לית, 'for after death there is not', is an attempt to combine this interpretation with a reading in terms of 'all your might', which is closer to G.

9.10 plan] On חשבון, see the note at 7.25.

9.11-12

(9.11) Again, I observed beneath the sun that the fast do not own the race, nor the mighty the battle; nor likewise the wise, food, nor the intelligent, wealth, nor the knowledgeable, favour—that timing and circumstance affect them all.

(9.12) Also, that no human knows their time, like fish which are caught in a terrible net, or like birds caught in a trap. Like them, humans are held ensnared, for when a terrible time will fall suddenly upon them.

Commentary

As discussed above, these verses offer afterthoughts to what has just been said. The first picks up in very different terms the ideas expressed in 8.10-17 and 9.1-3a, that bad things may happen to good people, and that humans are unable to discern the qualities of behaviour from its outcomes. The issue now, though, is not the problem of perception, but of the associated unpredictability: when things do not always seem to turn out as they should, people will not always get what they expect. There is, perhaps, also an acknowledgment that the preceding commendations, of pleasure and of throwing oneself into work, have to be understood in the context of a world where we will not always get want we want, or deserve, and have to play the hand that we have been dealt.

Unpredictability is also the theme of the second saying here, which picks up the warning that we are all headed for Sheol. As we shall see below, the imagery of traps and nets is not supposed to suggest that humans are like animals, wandering around and sometimes falling into traps. It is rather worse than that: we are in the trap from the time we are born, inescapably destined to die. We simply don't know when. If this seems gloomy, then a more positive way to look at both sayings is as offering further motivations to the previous advice: we should throw ourselves into life even when we know that not everything will produce the results we want, and not hang about, because we do not know how much longer we have left.

The sayings are linked by references to 'time', which makes it tempting to interpret one in terms of the other. Ogden, 'Qoheleth IX 1-16', 168, for instance, speaks of sudden and unpredictable death as the constraint that may prevent the powerful or wise seeing the 'natural reward' for their qualities. That idea is not unattractive, but it fits badly with the examples actually presented in 9.11: it is hard to imagine that Qohelet only has in mind such rare occurrences as, say, a wise man struck down just before he gets his food, or a runner dying before he can reach the finishing-line, and there is no strong indication of some more general claim that people may die before being able to claim the proper rewards for their talent. 'Time' serves as a catchword, but has a different sense in each verse, with 9.11 using it of bad timing, and 9.12 with reference to death, or perhaps more particularly to the moment when our captivity in the trap is due to end.

9.11] Given the determinism that he expresses elsewhere, it is unlikely that Qohelet understands what happens to people as entirely random, or the product of some fickle fate. The fact that God's plans overrule human expectations, however, means that the world will inevitably seem unpredictable from the human perspective. The word for 'time' or 'timing' in this verse and the next was the keyword in 3.1-8, but on both occasions here it probably has a more negative connotation, as noted above. The word for 'circumstance' also takes on quite a negative nuance in later Hebrew, and the point here is probably that anyone can be caught up in bad circumstances, rather than that anyone can be lucky or unlucky. As discussed above (and see also the notes), the observation is that someone fast may always meet someone faster on the day, and someone mighty lose to someone mightier: the world will not always meet our expectations.

Whether or not Greek gymnasia had been introduced to Palestine before the time of Ecclesiastes (see Lavoie, 'Temps et Finitude', 441), there is no particular reason to associate the racing here with Greek athletic ideals, as does Lohfink. Sport was hardly unknown earlier in the ancient Near East. The noun is found only here in biblical Hebrew, but the cognate verb means 'run', and the reference is most likely to races on foot—although the nature of the race is not important to Qohelet's point. There is a certain correspondence between this item and the next in the list: both involve winning victories through some sort of physical prowess. The remaining items are very different: not the winning of victories by the powerful on particular occasions, but the attainment of food, money and support by the wise and their ilk on a daily basis. It seems likely that Qohelet is making a secondary point within his more general one: just as it is true that the fast and powerful may not win, so it is true that the wise may struggle despite their own abilities, and this corresponds to his concern that wisdom is subordinated to circumstance—a concern that will become prominent very shortly in 9.13-18.

9.12] Commentators have generally been inclined to see the trapping described in this verse as itself what happens to animals and to humans at the 'bad time' which befalls them. That is a possible understanding of the Hebrew, but I think that the imagery is in fact more vivid, and that Hitzig puts it well: 'humans are imprisoned for the duration of their lives, and are like birds in a snare, waiting for the moment that the bird-catcher comes to wring their necks'.[1] It is true that in principle the word for 'time' used in this verse and the last could mean 'right time' or 'opportunity', and some commentators have been keen to emphasize that Qohelet is talking about a human ignorance that is more general than not knowing the time at which they are to die. In practice, however, the simile used here has strong overtones of death, which is certainly what awaits the fish and birds. To assume that they, and humans like them, are merely getting 'caught up' in fates or misfortunes of some kind is to dilute, and almost to ignore that imagery. If the language of snaring and trapping implies that death will follow, however, as in, for example, Prov 7.22-23 (which Fischer, *Skepsis*, 135-37, associates with this verse), it is not itself the language of death: the nets and traps here hold the fish, birds, and humans who will die, but they do not kill them (see the notes). According to Qohelet, what awaits us is not some unpredictable trap but the death that inescapably follows—we are already in the trap, and what we don't know is when the hunter will return to kill us.

---

[1] 'Die Menschen sind also gefangen während der Dauer ihres Lebens und gleichen den Vögeln in der Schlinge, die des Momentes gewärtig sind, dass der Vogelsteller komme um ihnen die Hälse umzudrehn.'

450   ECCLESIASTES

The verse is phrased in such a way that the existence of a hunter is implied by the nets and traps, but never stated: it is the 'time' that falls upon people. Although it has been suggested that this time itself is being represented as the hunter (see the notes), it is not clear, in fact, that the metaphor is supposed to encompass the action of some additional player, and Qohelet certainly does not picture the direct intervention of God to end lives. Barclay Burns, 'Personifications', 23-24, sees here and in 7.26 a conventional presentation of death, personified as a hunter (see the note at 7.26), but if such ideas have indeed influenced the imagery here, they have not prompted the author actually to depict that figure directly.

Notes

9.11 Again, I observed] On the use of שבתי, see the note at 4.1. There and at 4.7, the Hebrew is ושבתי אני וראה, but here we have שבתי וראה, with ראה pointed as an infinitive absolute in M. The infinitive is probably to be understood as a 'continuation' after שבתי (cf. ונתון in 8.9, and GKC §113 z; J-M §123 r), but it is also conceivable that an א has just dropped out from an original ואראה: the rendering is simply 'I saw' in the versions, but they handled an infinitive similarly in 8.9 (cf. Yi, 261-62), and perhaps also at 4.2 (although see the note there).

9.11 the fast...favour] Individual readings from σ′ are preserved for much of the list (although the first two are curiously not explicitly attributed in Gentry's edition), and show that Symmachus introduced verbs: τὸ φθάσαι δρόμῳ / δρόμον, 'winning (in) the race'; τὸ κρατῆσαι πολέμου τῷ σοφῷ, 'winning a battle to the wise man'; πορίσαι τροφήν, 'procuring food'. The second of these is unexpected: it is not the wise who fail to win battles in the other versions, and Marshall discusses at length the ways in which Symmachus or his source might have become confused. It seems more likely, though, either that there is an error in the single witness (ms 248) that records τῷ σοφῷ, or that τῷ σοφῷ is the beginning of the next clause.

In any case, however, the fact that τῷ σοφῷ is singular also stands out, particularly since this reading is found as an early and common variant in the G tradition. McNeile, 165, argues that it originated in a misreading of τοιϲϲοφοιϲ as τοιϲοφοι, but such an error is not especially likely, particularly in a context full of other plural nouns, and Marshall makes a more plausible case that the origin is actually to be sought in a corruption of Hebrew לחכמים to לחכם, which appeared in the translator's source-text. If he is right, then τῷ σοφῷ was G*, and σ′ potentially a second witness to the same variant. The reading τοῖς σοφοῖς, although it matches our text of M, would then be secondary in G, either a borrowing from α′ or θ′, for whom it is attested, or else simply an assimilation to the other nouns in the context.

Some commentators have been inclined to read the descriptions here as superlatives, so that, for instance, 'the race is not to the swiftest'; see especially Ellermeier, *Qohelet I.1*, 245. That is, I think, to read in a particular interpretation, and in effect to change the sense. It is in the nature of races that they are won by the fastest (at least the fastest on the day), and Qohelet's point need not be that the race is unfair, or the fastest runner somehow prevented from reaching the line—at least not explicitly so. A translation with superlatives rules out any broader understanding that the swift do not always prove, in fact, to be the swiftest, or the mighty gain victories that they might expect to gain, and this is more compatible with what is said analogously about the wise.

The verse does not use verbal expressions to make each point, but says literally 'not to/for (לֹא ל-) the swift people the race', and so forth. This excludes any modal or temporal nuance: Qohelet does not claim that the swift will lose, that they may lose, or that, in his experience, they have lost—and it is difficult to retain this openness in translation without significant paraphrase. The expressions most probably, in fact, imply actual or presumptive possession: things do not just fall into the laps of those who might deserve them, and are not inherently 'theirs'. Of course, that does not rule out the possibility that those who deserve something might get it—and the intelligent, for instance, are not actively prevented from becoming wealthy. Qohelet's point is rather that qualities and abilities do not by themselves guarantee particular outcomes, and those outcomes are susceptible to other factors.

The first two items in the list are linked only by a conjunction, but the subsequent ones by וגם. Qohelet uses גם to link items elsewhere (cf. 4.3; 9.6), but the inconsistency and the more emphatic וגם suggest that he is trying to do more than simply link them here. We may also note that the introduction of וגם corresponds to a shift away from people who are physically strong toward people who are intellectually so, and away from victories toward the necessities or desiderata of everyday life—there is no contest here for 'the' food, 'the' wealth, or 'the' favour, and the corresponding nouns are no longer determined. This is a list in two parts, differentiated by the wording as well as by content, and I think that וגם is actually intended to relate each item in the second part to the first part: just as the fast do not own the race…so likewise the wise do not own food, nor likewise the intelligent own wealth. I have tried to capture this sense, that the first two items are used as an analogy for the others, by translating the first וגם slightly differently.

9.11 the knowledgeable, favour] σ' is attested in Greek as οὐδὲ τῶν τεχνῶν τὸ εὔχαρι, 'nor what is favourable of the skills' (a dative τέχναις is suggested by the Syh note's ܠܐܘܡܢܘܬܐ *l'wmnwt'*, but that may well be an assimilation to G, as Marshall suggests). It is very tempting to suppose, however, that if the original reading of σ' was not actually τεχνιτῶν or τεχνίταις, 'of/to skilful people' (cf. V *nec artificum gratiam*, 'nor favour of the skilful'; Cannon, 196), then τεχνῶν / τέχναις has to be understood as equivalent: it is very difficult to see what would have led Symmachus to the sense 'skills'.

9.11 that timing and circumstance affect them all] Lit. 'time and occurrence happen to them all'. The 'all' could refer in principle to the race etc., but the expression of the preceding items slightly favours it referring to the various humans involved. There are also several ways to understand the initial כי: it is often translated as an adversative 'but' (cf. V *sed*), and it could equally be an explanatory 'because', but I have taken it to sit in parallel with the previous כי which follows וראה (cf. Hie *et*). No option in either case makes a significant difference to the sense.

Vinel notes the stylish *figura etymologica* in G ἀπάντημα συναντήσεται, literally something like 'coming together will happen' (cf. 2.14 συνάντημα ἓν συναντήσεται), although note the epistolary formula cited in MM, which uses ἀπαντάω of how things are going; σ' here opts for συγκύρησις, 'coincidence' or 'conjuncture'. Both translations try to draw out the connection of the noun with the cognate verb פגע, which is used in Hebrew and Aramaic of meeting or encountering people, possibly by accident (Exod 23.4), as well as of falling upon them aggressively. The noun itself is often translated as 'chance', but more often has the sense 'affliction' in Aramaic and later Hebrew—cf. the only other biblical use, at 1 Kgs 5.18 (ET 5.4), which talks about a פגע רע—and although it possibly (by no means certainly) has the more general sense 'fate' once in *Ahiqar* (Cowley, 215, l. 89; *TAD* C1.1 l. 184), there may be a more negative implication than is conveyed by 'chance'. It would also be unwise to press too far any notion of 'luck' here: the point is that outcomes depend upon the larger, uncontrollable context of endeavours, not upon, as it were, a throw of the dice.

9.12 Also that] Lit. 'that also'. Again, I take the כי to follow from the earlier וראה, and the גם, therefore, to be additive: this is a further observation, and what follows is essentially a new point. 9.11 stresses the unpredictability of human life when it is subject to chance or fate, and now 9.12 turns to the problem that humans have no ability to know when death will strike. The כי גם as a whole cannot easily be understood as concessive: when Gordis renders 'Though man does not know his hour', his 'though' is essentially an adversative 'but'. Equally, however, if the כי is explicative, then it is far from clear how 9.12 explains 9.11, and that reading would require us to take גם as an awkward emphatic 'even'.

9.12 knows] Where M has ידע pointed as a yiqtol, G has the aorist ἔγνω, lit. 'knew', at 9.12 and 10.14; contrast 8.5. It is difficult in each case to know whether the translator is vocalizing the verb as a qatal (cf. 10.15), or simply using a gnomic aorist (so Yi, 155), but *BHQ* presumes the former here, adducing the somewhat questionable support of T.

9.12 their time] Lit. 'his time/season'. σ' here uses τὴν εὐκαιρίαν ἑαυτοῦ, 'his opportunity', or 'his right moment', and so clearly does not interpret עתו as a reference to death. Contrast V *finem suum*, 'his end'.

9.12 a terrible net] Or possibly 'by a hook'. As we observed in the note at 7.26, there is some confusion around the terms מצודה/מצוד. In context, we should expect מצודה here (cf. Ezek 19.9) to mean much the same as מצוד in that verse, and the fact that it is vocalized differently from the noun מצודה found in Ezek 12.13; 13.21; 17.20 seems likely, moreover, to be a quirk of the pointing rather than an indication of some original distinction.

It is not clear precisely how the net is 'terrible'—רעה may mean no more than that it causes misery or is inescapable—but (in an interpretation picked up by Rashi) the Midrash and *b. Sanhedrin* 81b both suppose that the expression מצודה רעה as a whole refers to a fishhook. There is no particular reason to believe that is true, but it is hard to disprove, and it seems likely that it was knowledge of such a tradition that earlier led Jerome to translate using *hamo*, 'with a hook', in V, which likewise has no separate translation of רעה. Precisely the same explanation cannot be offered in the case of T, which itself has no equivalent to רעה, but which understands the fish to be caught בסריגתא. That probably does not mean 'with a hook', as the noun usually refers to wickerwork, and in the Targum Jonathan to Isa 24.18 סריגתא is used to translate פח (on which, see the note 'trap', below), so the targumist may have had his own idea that the מצודה רעה was a particular thing. These translations offer no support, in any case, to the supposition in Galling 1969 (cf. also Barclay Burns, 'Personifications', 24), that רעה is just a secondary duplicate of the רעה in לעת רעה.

9.12 or] Lit. 'and'.

9.12 caught] *BHS* claims that האחזות is often found pointed with daghesh in the ז, indicating secondary gemination, but Goldman notes also the absence of this in key manuscripts.

Marshall's attribution of the reading τὰ συλλαμβανόμενα to σ′ is somewhat affirmed by its similarity to Hie *colligantur*; both suggest 'collected together', or 'gathered up', rather than 'trapped'. This reading is not found as a note in any of the usual sources, but as a striking variant, principally in the hexaplaric *O*-group manuscripts of G. On this understanding, the image is not of multiple birds each trapped individually, but of a trap that holds them all at once—which is, perhaps, the most natural way to envisage the preceding fishing-net, but which does not correspond to the probable nature of the trap here (see below).

9.12 trap] Hos 5.1 sets a פח alongside a spread net, Hos 9.8 speaks of a fowler's פח on the roads of Israel (cf. Prov 22.5; Ps 142.4 ET 142.3), and in Prov 7.23 a bird rushes into a פח. The clearest indications of the trap's nature, however, come from Job 18.9, which speaks of a פח catching someone by the foot, and especially Amos 3.5, which implies not only that the פח was used to catch birds on the ground, but that it 'rose up' to trap something. This is a strong indication that we are dealing with a clap trap, the use of which in ancient Egypt is well attested. The Egyptian version typically consisted of a stand with two netted wings which could be pried apart, against the tension of twisted cords, and held open with a pin so that they lay flat on the ground. A bird which took the bait would loosen the pin, allowing the wings to fly up and trap the bird inside the net (there is a more complete description, and photographs of a surviving specimen, in Scott, 'An Egyptian Bird Trap'). Some of the descriptions of the Mesopotamian *ḫuḫāru* trap suggest that it might have been similar (see *CAD*). In any case, it is unlikely that when the bad time 'falls' on people, it is *falling* on them like a פח, as Fox suggests.

9.12 Like them] For כהם a number of the manuscripts noted by Kennicott and two Babylonian manuscripts noted by Miletto have בהם. There is no support for this reading among the ancient versions, and it has probably arisen under the influence of the previous word.

9.12 are held ensnared for when a terrible time will] Lit. '(are) ensnared for a bad time when it will (fall)'. This is commonly translated as though the snaring of humans is what happens to them when the bad times arrive, and that interpretation has an ancient pedigree. An unattributed reading κρατηθήσονται, 'they will be conquered/held fast', appears in the margin of Syh, followed by a repetition of ἐν παγίδι from the previous clause, but this has also found its way, without that repetition, into some manuscripts of G (including the hexaplaric O-group) as a second translation of יוקשים, to sit alongside παγιδεύονται, 'they are trapped'. Like Hie *corruent*, 'they will collapse (together)', this reading (possibly from the Three) takes the verb to be describing what will happen to humans at the bad time that is to come, and its understanding of the verb's sense may be derived from passages like Isa 8.15; 28.13.

Such a reading, however, is not necessarily implied by the Hebrew. The form of יוקשים has been much discussed: the context requires a passive sense, and it has commonly been construed as a puʿal participle without the initial -מ (it is given as an example of such in GKC §52 s); it has also been emended to a niphʿal participle by some scholars, or more simply read as a passive qal participle by others. There is no doubt, though, that the verb is a participle, which stands in parallel with the preceding נאחזים and אחזות. As such, it can mean 'humans are going to' without any particular durative connotation (cf. J-M §121 e), and this is probably how the anonymous author of κρατηθήσονται took it. In its very nuanced translation here, however, G uses participles for the first two verbs (θηρευόμενοι / θηρευόμενα, 'caught'), but then a present indicative παγιδεύονται, 'are entrapped', for יוקשים, and an aorist subjunctive ὅταν ἐπιπέσῃ, 'whenever it may fall upon', for כשתפול. The translator would have used the future tense if he intended 'will be entrapped', not the present, and so εἰς καιρὸν must mean 'until the time' (a common implication of the preposition), not 'at the time'. G says, therefore, that humans 'are entrapped until an evil time, whenever it may fall upon them suddenly'.

This seems no less plausible a rendering of the Hebrew, where לעת can similarly mean 'for a time' or 'until a time' (cf. 2 Chr 18.34; Esth 4.14; Job 38.23), as well as 'at a time'. Since no future context has been established for the participles, furthermore, and since any ambiguity could have been avoided by using yiqtol throughout if an event in the future of each creature or human were intended, G's understanding is arguably the more natural. The suggestion of Montgomery, 'Notes', 243, that לעת here represents agency, so that humans are snared 'by' an evil time, seems less plausible—not because it is grammatically problematic, but because it is difficult to find any parallel to the virtual personification of time that it entails. Montgomery himself points to the Syriac *Epistle of Mara bar Serapion*, which talks about things being forced by time, in the sense of contemporary circumstance, but even this distant source comes close to such an idea only at the very end, when Mara jokes that time seems to be repaying to him a debt of trouble that he had never lent to it. The ambiguity of the preposition might indicate that the author is leaving other readings open, but ultimately, we have to be guided by context, and 'until' offers an understanding of the imagery that does not ignore the distinction between being trapped and being killed.

9.12 fall upon] נפל is not generally used to mean 'befall', but the things that can 'fall upon' people include sleep (Gen 15.12; 1 Sam 26.12), terror (Exod 15.16; Job 13.11; Ps 55.5 ET 55.4; Jer 15.8; Dan 10.7), a great wind (Job 1.19), insults (Ps 69.10 ET 69.9), and the hand and spirit of God (Ezek 8.1; 11.5). Probably the closest analogy to this verse comes in Isa 47.11, when ruin (הוה) will fall upon Babylon, but it should be clear from the list as a whole that the verb means more than 'happen to', and that it generally conveys some sense of attacking or overcoming when used with such subjects. T takes it more literally, to conjure an image something like the sword of Damocles: in a single moment, the bad time is going to drop upon them from the heavens, where it has been waiting.

Introduction to 9.13–10.3

Wisdom and Folly

(9.13) This too have I seen: wisdom beneath the sun, and it seemed mighty to me.

(9.14) A small city, with few men in it, and a mighty king comes up against it, surrounds it, and builds mighty palisades against it. (9.15) Should he encounter in it a poor man, a wise man, then *he* would save the city with his wisdom—but nobody remembers that poor man, (9.16) and I say:

—Wisdom is better than strength—but the wisdom of the poor man is disdained, and his words not heard: (9.17) words of wise men only get heard when there is respite, away from the shouting of someone in charge of fools.

—(9.18) Wisdom is good beyond weapons of war—but just one person getting something wrong lets much good go to waste.

(10.1) When corpse-flies cause a stench, scented oil pours out fragrance: even a little is worth more than wisdom, more than a great deal of folly.

(10.2) The mind of a wise man inclines to his right, but the mind of a fool to his left, (10.3) so even on the road, as the obtuse man goes along, his mind is absent, and everyone says he's obtuse.

After an affirmation that wisdom is indeed powerful in the world (even if, as we have already seen, its scope is limited to action within that world), Qohelet's starting-point for this sequence of sayings about wisdom is a sort of story or hypothesis, in which he surmises that even a poor wise man would be able to save his city from the attack of a mighty king. Such a nobody, however, would never catch the ear of those who needed to hear his words, and

Qohelet draws as conclusions the claims that follow: wisdom beats might, but gets ignored or drowned out; it is better than weapons, even, but its benefits can be annulled by a single error.

He moves on from the imagery of warfare in 10.1, where the text is extremely difficult, but the point is probably that for the dead (who are no longer 'under the sun'), neither wisdom nor folly are as valuable as a perfume that will cover the stench of their corpses. It is not difficult to see a continuity of thought here: if wisdom is limited in life by the way that it can be ignored, it is of little practical use at all once life has ended. The relevance of 10.2-3, on the other hand, is less obvious. These verses present a humorous vignette of the fool, who stubbornly displays his idiocy by choosing to go left when everybody else goes right. I take the underlying imagery to be not of turning aside, but of picking a side of the street, so that this fool is, in our terms, like a driver on the wrong side of the road. It seems likely that Qohelet is simply using the mention of folly in 10.1 as a hook on which to hang this observation, in a context that has essentially returned to the loose, sentence-literature style that he began to use in ch. 7. In 10.4, which can itself be read as part of this sequence, he will initiate a digression, not in this style, that picks up from 9.17-18 the theme of bad leadership, before returning to wisdom and folly in 10.10. While 10.2-3 seem to sit between two larger discussions, therefore, they also prefigure that later sequence.

I am not sure that Qohelet's presentation of wisdom in 9.13-18 involves an anti-militarism (so Schwienhorst-Schönberger, *Nicht im Menschen*, 211) or some implicit anti-monarchism (Lavoie, 'La Philosophie politique', 325-26). Although they seem like good slogans for pacifism taken out of context, his comparisons of wisdom with military power are intended to compliment wisdom, not denigrate might, and 'better than' in this context means 'more effective than', not 'preferable to' in some moral sense. The primary issue that Qohelet raises here, however, is not the relative strength of wisdom, but the way in which that strength is dependent upon context: it might be the most potent weapon in the armoury, but it is useless if nobody thinks to use it—and it may be ignored for reasons as seemingly insubstantial as the social status of its possessor or the chaotic noise in the context where it is required. At the outset in 9.13, moreover, and then again in 10.1, we are reminded of the broader limitation of its power to the world of the living. Qohelet struggled with wisdom back in the first two chapters, when it could supply no answer to his questions and seemed, therefore, to have been a waste of his time, and it has engaged his attention more extensively since ch. 7. It is not, he has learned, a way to answer the big questions that lie beyond what can be discerned, and the personal acquisition of wisdom is neither straightforwardly a desirable thing, nor as easy as some have claimed. Here, though, he is more positive: within its limits, wisdom can be immensely helpful and powerful—but those limits are tight, and while wisdom might defeat an army, it can also lose out to something trivial.

9.13-18

(9.13) This too have I seen: wisdom beneath the sun, and it seemed mighty to me.

(9.14) A small city, with few men in it, and a mighty king comes up against it, surrounds it, and builds mighty palisades against it. (9.15) Should he encounter in it a poor man, a wise man, then *he* would save the city with his wisdom—but nobody remembers that poor man, (9.16) and I say:

—Wisdom is better than strength—but the wisdom of the poor man is disdained, and his words not heard: (9.17) words of wise men only get heard when there is respite, away from the shouting of someone in charge of fools.

—(9.18) Wisdom is good beyond weapons of war—but just one person getting something wrong lets much good go to waste.

Commentary

There are three ways to understand the story that Qohelet tells here. According to the first, a city was besieged by a king and saved by a poor wise man, whose efforts were subsequently forgotten. This is the most popular approach, although commentators disagree about whether it should be read as a parable or as a condensed account of some actual event. The second approach, favoured by fewer scholars, is to suppose that in the same context the wise man might have saved the city, but was forgotten, and was therefore unable to do so. The third, which was apparently the approach taken by the Septuagint translator, but which has had no recent impact, is to take the whole narrative as hypothetical: in the circumstances of such a siege, Qohelet suggests, a wise man would certainly be able to save the city—but it is also likely that he would be overlooked and ignored.

A case can be made for each of these approaches, and each also presents difficulties. For the first, the principal obstacle is that the whole narrative would lead up to a point that features nowhere else in the verses that introduce or follow it: Qohelet simply displays no other interest here in the fact that the wise man has been forgotten. The second makes better sense in this respect, but it rests on the assumption that the last verb in a long sequence must have a sense quite different from all the others: they talk about things that happened, while it declares that the wise man 'might' have saved the city. The third, finally, avoids both these problems, and actually conforms rather better to the prescriptions of the classical Hebrew verbal system (which Qohelet does not always follow), but it does require us to accept what would be an unusually long and complicated hypothetical statement, with a no less complicated resolution. Since the book hardly shows itself averse to complexity elsewhere, however, I take that to be the least formidable obstacle, and I think that the Greek translator has probably got it right here.

On such an understanding, Qohelet's basic purpose in these verses is to state his own belief that even human wisdom can be formidably powerful—powerful enough, indeed, that a poor man in a small city, perhaps the humblest of wise men, would be able to use it to withstand a mighty army. When he gives that example, however, he qualifies it immediately with the recognition that a man of such low status would, in practice, be unlikely to attract the attention of those in charge, or to realize whatever plan he had. The story exemplifies, therefore, both the potential of wisdom to make a difference and the reasons why it so often does not: it should be easy to heed the wise, but they will not always be heard, while the capacity for wisdom to win a war means nothing when a single mistake—in this case, the failure to listen to a poor man—can render it utterly useless. Following on from his comments about unpredictability, and before turning to some further qualifications of wisdom and folly in ch. 10, Qohelet presents wisdom as a glass cannon: it is powerful but fragile, capable of accomplishing much, but no less liable than anything else to the vicissitudes of the world.

As noted above and earlier in the Introduction (72-73), modern commentators have sometimes been inclined to find references here to historical events, or at least to biblical accounts of those events (there is a helpful summary in Lavoie, 'La Philosophie politique', 319). Earlier readings, however, tended to be more symbolic or allegorical in character. One such reading is attributed to his Hebrew teacher by Jerome, and according to this, the city is a person, beset by evil, who is saved by their wise and calm inner self—an inner self that is then promptly ignored again once the danger is over. Much the same reading is found in *b. Nedarim* 32b, which sees a struggle between the good and evil inclinations of the self, as does the Targum; it re-appears (alongside numerous other interpretations) in the Midrash Rabbah, and is cited by Rashi.[1] Jerome himself offers an alternative reading in terms of the Church, protected from the devil by Jesus, who is then ignored when the persecution has passed. Of course, all this reflects more general differences between modern and pre-modern approaches to exegesis, but it also reflects the lack of specific detail in the account (cf. Lauha, 'Kohelets Verhältnis', 397-98) which seems to invite us to read it as something more like a parable than an allusion to real events. If the reading commended here is correct, moreover, then the hypothetical character of the story effectively precludes any actual historical reference, beyond some very general allusions to ancient siege techniques.

9.13] There is no basis in the text for reading 'wisdom' here as an 'example of wisdom' (RSV), and that common understanding is based on an assumption that 9.13 serves merely as an introduction to the story in 9.14-15. Given the things that Qohelet will go on to say in 9.16-18, however, it seems reasonable to suppose that the verse serves as an introduction to his broader discussion of wisdom. If so, then it is progressively qualified. Qohelet puts no date on his observation, but his relationship with wisdom has already changed in the course of the monologue, and the initial optimism of his statement seems strange in the light of his earlier criticisms. Perhaps we should understand 'I once thought that…' here, but it may be more likely that he is simply offering a more nuanced critique: wisdom in the world *is* mighty, Qohelet maintains, to the extent that it has the power to save cities—unfortunately, its power can go to waste, because humans are not good at heeding it.

9.14-15] The basis of my reading here is outlined above and discussed in the notes: I take the story to be an account of what

---

[1] These and other appearances of the interpretation are discussed in Rüger, 'Hieronymus', who notes the influence of the good/evil inclination reading on midrashic understandings of 4.13-14 also, and references to the 'inner' and 'outer' self in the Pauline epistles.

would happen in the hypothetical situation of a great king encountering a small city with a poor, wise man in it, not as a story about something that Qohelet claims actually to have happened.

Links with the vocabulary of 4.13, and its 'poor and wise child' have not gone unnoticed by commentators, especially since some have been keen to see both this passage and that as political stories or parables. It is hard to know what to make of such links, however, and probably unwise to put too much weight on them when Qohelet may simply be trying to make similar contrasts in both places. Ramond, 'Y a-t-il de l'ironie', 626, does not take the story here in the same way that I do, but does present it intriguingly as a sort of sequel to 4.13, which draws out and connects the anticipated future of each character. In that spirit, it is tempting to see an affirmation here of 9.11: the wise child has become a wise man, but wealth, power, and status have eluded him, despite his potential. In any case, whether or not he would have agreed that 'the wisdom of God is to be found among the broken and the marginalized more often than among the secure and the powerful' (Joyce, 'The Poor Wise Man', 102), Qohelet does indirectly make the point in all three verses that wisdom is not the prerogative of the wealthy. This is not so strange or radical as Joyce supposes, and a link between wisdom and the upper classes is more a product of modern speculations about 'wisdom literature' than a presupposition of the texts themselves. Wisdom, to be sure, is often presented as a source of prosperity, but the corollary or conclusion, that the poor cannot be wise, is not typically drawn. While we should not ourselves conclude, therefore, from elite representations of the 'clever poor' (perhaps most notably the much earlier Egyptian work, *The Eloquent Peasant*), or from the biblical instance of the wise woman in 2 Samuel 14, that wealth and wisdom were entirely unconnected in people's minds, such instances do show that Qohelet's associations of wisdom with poverty are nothing new. Indeed, they might lead us to suspect that he is playing with an established literary trope, which happens to suit his corresponding assertions that the wealthy need not be wise (especially 2.18-19, but cf. also the foolish king of 4.13-14).

9.17] The observations on the story in 9.16 and 9.18 refer directly to wisdom and take the form of a comparison followed by a qualification: 'wisdom is better than…but…'. Here we have a comparison, but there is no 'better than', and no qualification, while the reference is not to 'wisdom', as such, but to 'words of wise men'. This statement, then, seems to stand outside the short sequence, and to pick up not the general theme—that wisdom is strong yet vulnerable—but the particular comment in 9.16, that the poor man's wisdom and words are not heeded. It does so, however, by claiming that the words of the wise *are* heeded, and if this is not to be read simply as a puzzling contradiction, then its point must lie in its statement of the circumstances that are needed for them to be heard.

'Words of wise men' is an expression that will be used again in 12.11, and it is found also in Prov 1.6 and 22.17 (cf. 24.23). It would be too strong to call it a technical term, but it is probable in 12.11, and possible here, that the author is making some allusion to the tradition of advice literature (see the commentary on 12.11-12). At the very least, he is generalizing away from the 'poor, wise man', to speak about 'wise men' or their words. The 'someone in charge of fools', however, is not necessarily an 'arch-fool'—or even foolish—so it is not clear that the purpose is to contrast wise and foolish speech. The vocabulary, moreover, does not convey any specific implication of volume, so the issue is probably not that the wise are (or should be) heard even when they speak more softly. I take the key point to be, rather, that wisdom gets a hearing only in a situation of calm (and so, in this context of a chaotic siege, with fools being ordered around, never gets a look-in).

9.18] 'One error' is literally 'one person doing what is wrong', and is often translated as 'one sinner'. The point here is not, however, that 'one rotten apple spoils the barrel' (which is rather the way in which the Targum takes it), and whether Qohelet is commenting on his story or merely extrapolating from it, the problem is not a moral one about evil undermining good, but that a huge benefit can be prevented or offset by just one person (such as the person in charge in 9.17) getting things wrong. The problem of bad leadership will be picked up in 10.4-10, which implies similarly that leadership can lead to 'great sins'.

Notes

9.13 This too have I seen: wisdom beneath the sun] In 2.24, גם זה ראיתי אני had כי following to introduce what it was *that* Qohelet saw, and this is essentially the way that 9.11-12 has also just been expressed following שבתי

וראה. It is unlikely, therefore, that the sentence here, without כי or any equivalent, can be treated as similar, and translated 'I saw *that* wisdom was under the sun' (as T understands; its loose rendering here is cited by Rose, *Rien de nouveau*, 404-5, as evidence for such a sense). It is also difficult, however, to make the sentence mean, 'I saw this to be wisdom under the sun', since Hebrew does not commonly use verbs of perception simply with two 'accusatives' to give that sense (see the note at 7.25). Because the word-order further prohibits 'I saw this wisdom' (as Podechard noted long ago), we are left with little option but to read 'I saw this too, wisdom under the sun'.

In view of what follows, many commentators have understood חכמה here to be not 'wisdom' in a general sense, but a specific instance or example of wisdom, and if that were indeed the intended meaning, we might compare Qohelet's use of גם זה repeatedly with הבל to suggest that something is a particular manifestation of הבל. That label generally follows his description of the something, however, and for the reader who has not yet encountered what will follow in this passage, it is hard to see that חכמה תחת השמש could imply anything other than 'wisdom in the world' more generally. As Fox, and earlier Joüon, 'Notes philologiques', 424, have observed, moreover, if this is an 'instance' of wisdom, then the גם would imply that it follows another instance of wisdom, but there is none in the text that precedes.

For them, indeed, and for a few other commentators (cf. also *BHS*), the context precludes חכמה in either sense. Jastrow had already asserted that, 'The word "wisdom" after "I experienced" is either misplaced, or is an error for "evil" which the context demands', and subsequent emendations have correspondingly involved the deletion of חכמה or its replacement by רעה.[2] There is no versional support for any such emendation, however, and no obvious explanation for how חכמה might have come to appear in the text here: the very difficulties that these scholars highlight tell also against the introduction of the word as a gloss or facilitation, and they suggest, perhaps, that it is not the text that we need to modify, but our understanding of its relationship with what follows.

Contextual considerations have also driven another understanding adopted by some commentators here, that Qohelet is claiming to have seen something 'concerning' or 'about' wisdom; so, e.g., Schoors, 'This too I observed under the sun about wisdom, and it was of great importance to me'. This might be accomplished by understanding חכמה as an 'accusative of respect', which would be fine, if not entirely natural, until we had to deal with the next clause, where גדולה surely has to refer to חכמה and not to זה (despite the translation

---

[2] Another correction, which takes חסר to have dropped out from an original reference to 'lack' of wisdom, is attributed to Zimmerli by Barucq (cf. also Lavoie, 'La Philosophie politique', 315 n. 2), although I can find it in no edition of Zimmerli's commentary. Barucq himself suggests reading חולה (cf. 5.2) instead of חכמה.

that Schoors offers).³ If we do not take חכמה as an accusative of respect, we have to attribute a new sense and usage to ראיתי, enabling it to take two objects with the meaning 'I saw x as a result of investigating y'. This seems to be Schoors' own preference, but, like the other approach, it forces us to overrule the obvious meaning of a grammatically straightforward sentence (and either the normal rules of agreement or the normal semantic range of the verb) in order to impose a sense based on our own understanding of the context.

9.13 and it seemed mighty to me] The sense (although not the tense) is affirmed by σ' καὶ μεγάλη δοκεῖ μοι, 'and it seems great to me' (on the attribution, see Marshall, and cf. V *et probaui maximam*, 'and I considered it very great'), but the construction with אלי to mean 'in my opinion' is unusual: Jon 4.1 provides a rare analogy. It is a sense more often connected with על (although the interchange between אל and על is such that we need hardly emend to על here, as, e.g., BHS and Zimmerli suggest), but it is interesting to compare Qohelet's apparent use of -ל a little earlier with the dog at 9.4 (see the note there), and וגדול ליהודים at Esth 10.3: that construction was probably intended, and אלי the result of blurred boundaries between אל and -ל. Ehrlich would just emend to לי, and is followed by, e.g., Galling 1969, and Driver, 'Problems and Solutions', 231: they may be right to suppose that the א has simply been duplicated from the end of the preceding היא.

The use of גדולה cannot be entirely disconnected from the appearance of גדול to describe the king and his siege works in the next verse, and I have translated accordingly. The word can, however, mean simply 'important' or 'significant' (e.g. Exod 18.22), and this is the nuance highlighted by commentators who take Qohelet to be talking about an instance of wisdom that he considered especially enlightening, or that made a deep impression on him. For that reason, it is hardly necessary to follow the suggestion of Driver, 'Problems and Solutions', 231, and emend to דגולה, giving the sense 'remarkable' (or whatever דגול actually means in its sole use at Ct 5.10).

9.14 A small city, with few men in it, and a mighty king comes up] Translations commonly take some expression of existence to be understood here, as in RSV 'there was a little city', or Schoors 'there was once a small city', but the curious abruptness of the text presumed by that understanding has received little discussion. If we do not read anything in, then the city and the men can be construed loosely as further objects of the preceding ראיתי, since there is no other verb available, and the association between the city and wisdom implied by such a reading may have given rise to the allegorical approach found in T (and in the other sources noted above).

G has apparently taken a different approach, and begins to translate the verbs after this point using subjunctives (contrast G ἔλθῃ with α' ἦλθεν, and in 9.15 G εὕρῃ with α', σ', εὗρεν; a number of G manuscripts have substituted

---

³ Isaksson, *Studies*, 99, who offers a similar understanding, does indeed allow that גדולה must refer to זה, but claims that זה here is feminine.

indicatives at various points). The translator's understanding has probably been influenced by contextual considerations (and perhaps by a different source-text in 9.15; see below), but more immediately he has construed בא and the series of verbs that follows not as simple perfects with waw conjunctive, but as narrative forms with waw consecutive. Understood that way, such verbs could have a range of meanings, but few would be appropriate to the context here (cf. GKC §112 pp n. 2), and the translator has rightly seen no reason for a simple future sequence (as at, e.g., Exod 6.6-8). Accordingly, he has taken them to be modal (cf. J-M §119 w), and understood Qohelet to be using a sort of asyndetic condition—perhaps not a formal conditional clause, but something more like the positing of a hypothetical situation.[4] Accordingly, he has apparently understood not 'there was', but 'suppose there were...' or 'suppose there had been...'. It would be difficult to blame the Greek translator for feeling, perhaps, that a past narrative should have employed narrative forms, not simple perfects, despite the shortage of them elsewhere in the book, and, as I have argued in the commentary, I think he has probably identified the proper sense, in which case the initial description in the Hebrew has probably to be understood as a sort of *casus pendens*. I have attempted in my translation, however, to keep open the alternative possibility of reading a simple narrative here.

The 'mighty king' stands in contrast to the poor wise man, rather in the way that the poor wise youth and the king were contrasted in 4.13-14, and there is no particular reason to suppose that Qohelet is using the expression as a title. G to be sure uses βασιλεὺς μέγας, which is not only a verbatim translation of the Hebrew, but also a title adopted by Ptolemaic and Seleucid

---

[4] Yi's explanation (184-85) is that the translator felt unable to use the indicative because, the events having been forgotten, they could not be 'related as a reality'. This seems convoluted and far-fetched, particularly since, on Yi's broader understanding, the translator did believe that the events had actually happened, but more generally because that is just not the sort of 'unreality' for which the subjunctive is employed. All the same, the translator's use of the subjunctive is sometimes striking, and does not correspond to the normal Greek uses of it in main clauses, at least outside Homer, only to express deliberation, exhortation or prohibition. We already encountered one seemingly exceptional use in 3.13, and will see another string of verbs in the subjunctive at 12.5, but in neither of those cases does it seem likely, in fact, that the translator intended a main clause to be read, and the same is probably true here as well: the curious Greek is a product of the translation technique, which inhibits the translator from adding a particle or conjunction where there is no Hebrew word, but permits him to imply that such a particle should be understood (cf. my note on 'If I found her, I would say' at 7.26). There are similar anomalous subjunctives at Ezek 3.20 and 33.14, 18-19, which Muraoka, in *Syntax*, §89 j, is reluctant to see as conditional sentences, but he does speak of 'pseudo-conditional sentences', and translates our passage as 'Suppose there was a small city...'.

rulers, leading Lohfink and others to see a particular reference (even though the title probably was not adopted until some considerable time after the book was composed). As Lavoie, 'La Philosophie politique', 323, notes in a useful summary, Herodotus described some Persian kings that way, and in 2 Kgs 18.19, 28, the Rabshakeh uses 'the mighty king' to refer to Sennacherib (which is grist to the mill of those who would associate the story here with that siege). It is doubtful, however, that the term would have been viewed as referring to any particular king or dynasty, and God uses it of himself in Ps 47.3 and Mal 1.14, with the context of both suggesting that, if the expression has any particular resonance at all, the implication is something like that of the modern concept 'superpower': 'mighty kings' are not mere local rulers, but the rulers of significant nations or empires, with a place on the world stage.

9.14 mighty palisades] There is very little doubt about the general sense, but it is difficult to establish the proper reading. M has מצודים, the same term that was used of trapping in 7.26, which is clearly related to the net just described as מצודה in 9.12. Interpreting allegorically, T speaks of the evil inclination building a sort of base against the heart, because it wants to catch the man it has invaded in the snares or nets of Gehenna, and so obviously sees a connection with those words. There may be a double translation here, though, and the base, or 'place for dwelling' (אתר למיתב) perhaps suggests an association with מצד as well—that noun is used of locations that have been naturally or artificially fortified to become defensive 'strongholds'. Understanding such an association himself, Heim thinks there is a wordplay involved, and that Qohelet is deliberately evoking 7.26—although the point in doing so is unclear.

The term that we would expect to see in this context, however, is מצורה (with ר not ד) or מצור, both of which can also be used of defensive positions or fortifications (and מצור can simply mean 'siege' as well), but which each appear in very similar contexts in Deut 20.19-20 and Isa 29.3 where they refer to something set up against a city in the context of a siege. The Septuagint text in both places translates using χάραξ, which is the same term adopted in G χάρακας μεγάλους here, and which refers in such contexts to stockades or palisades—barriers erected around the city under siege to control access and egress. Xenophon and Thucydides both use ἀποτείχισμα in a similar sense, and that is the translation attested here for σ' (variously as the singular or plural; cf. V *munitiones per gyrum*, 'ramparts in a circle around'). We can be in little doubt, therefore, that G and σ' are both based on a text with ר not ד,[5] and the same is surely true of Hie *machinam magnam*, 'great engine'—although Jerome has understood the Hebrew to mean something slightly different—and S ܡܠܩܘܡܐ *qlqwm'*, which is derived from the Greek

---

[5] Accordingly, there is no force in the argument of Vinel that G has used differential translations of the same term to create a link with the story of Jeroboam (cf. 1 Kgs 12.24; 21.12); see Vinel, 'Le Texte Grec', 300.

χαράκωμα, another word for 'palisade' related to χάραξ.⁶ It is harder to say precisely what word they read: מצורה has the plural מצורות, as we might expect, and מצור is always used elsewhere in the singular, so מצורים would be anomalous. The ἀποτείχισμα of σ', however, is singular, as is the reading of Hie, while the plural of G may be translational, given both the normal Greek usage (e.g. Demosthenes Περὶ τοῦ Στεφάνου 18.87, χάρακα βαλόμενος πρὸς τῇ πόλει, 'throwing up a stockade against the city'), and the collective character of מצור. There is some possibility that מצורים occurred as an irregular form, but I think it more likely that the translators found מצור. If this is original, then the plural of M most likely arose after מצור had been misread as מצוד, the singular of which did not then seem appropriate in the context.

Given that context, many commentators have long been inclined, in fact, to take G's reading as the earlier: it is commended by Döderlein, 181, as early as 1779 (earlier scholars appreciate the contextual problem, but Münster, for instance, understands there to be two separate roots with ד, and connects the term here with מצד, 'stronghold'). This has accordingly led them to see M's text as a secondary error, perhaps facilitated by the proximity of מצודה in 9.12 (see, e.g., McNeile, 80). As it happens, de Rossi does report מצורים in two Hebrew manuscripts. As Goldman points out, these are not of such quality to suggest that they are the sole outposts of the original Hebrew, and their readings may have themselves been driven by the context, but it seems likely that this reading was also found by the translator of Codex Graecus Venetus, which has πολιορκήματα μεγάλα, 'great siege-engines'. S notably has no equivalent to גדלים, but since it is alone among the versions in this respect, the word has probably just dropped out in the S tradition.

Barbour, *The Story of Israel*, 127, suggests that the textual evidence for emendation is 'very slight' (which does seem to understate it, when only T clearly supports M against the other versions), and she makes a case that, since traps and nets are used in Ezek 19.9 and Hab 1.14-17, these are part of the standard imagery of sieges, noting similar usages in other ancient sources. If that were true, it would enable us to retain מצודים, and to explain the versional readings as facilitatory, but it is important to note that, in all the examples Barbour cites, the 'trap' is part of a broader imagery, in which it is explicitly birds, animals, or fish being caught: 'trapping' is an element in such similes, and not in itself simply 'a stereotyped way of speaking about the experience of siege'. We would have to suppose, therefore, that such broader imagery is being implied or evoked, which is a more complicated proposition. The verb בנה might also be considered slightly odd, if nets or traps were

---

⁶ Accordingly, it is unlikely that the Syriac also means 'siege-engine', as Brockelmann suggests, although Goldman cites in favour of this sense an exposition of the word by Ephrem (who understands the term to mean a platform or tower raised against the city wall) that is quoted in Payne Smith.

the object: it would connote their manufacture rather than their deployment (cf. Ezek 27.5). Barbour is surely right to reject the suggestion of *DCH*, that מצד, 'stronghold', could have taken on the sense 'siege-works', but it seems simplest to suppose that the proper reading is preserved in G. If the figurative use of traps and snares has indeed led to a virtual equation of מצודים with מצור, then it makes little difference to the sense anyway.

In *b. Nedarim* 32b, the text is cited as מצודים וחרמים, the combination found in 7.26: it is unclear whether this actually reflects an alternative reading (cf. Strack, *Prolegomena*, 106) or simply an elaboration, but to the best of my knowledge it is found in no existing manuscripts of Ecclesiastes.

9.15 should he encounter in it] After the king has been the subject of a series of verbs with the same form, it would seem natural to retain him as the subject here. G and Hie certainly do so, and M is normally understood that way. It is also true, however, that if the king were literally to encounter anybody 'in' the city that he has been besieging, then it is probably too late for the city to be saved: nobody besieges a city if they can freely walk the streets. From that rather pedantic point of view, S, V, T all give an easier reading with a passive verb: the wise man is 'found'. This could suggest that they read a niph'al rather than a qal here, and, e.g., Galling 1969 would emend to ונמצא. Commentators have also suggested, however, that the qal could itself be read as passive (Driver, 'Problems and Solutions', 231, wonders if this is a defective writing of the passive participle, used often in later Hebrew), or the construction here understood as an impersonal 'there was found' (so, e.g., Hertzberg 1963)—of course, if those versions did not find a different Hebrew text, their reading of the existing text with a passive would presumably have been motivated by considerations of context.

Some commentators have gone further, and suggested that there is not even any real 'encounter' here, but that for the wise man to be 'found' in the city means little more than that he lived or happened to be there—'there was a wise man to be found in the city', we might say in English—so Jastrow, for example, translates simply 'And there was in the town a man...'. It is very questionable, however, whether the force of מצא can ever be reduced so much in Hebrew, and even in passages like Gen 2.20, where no helper is 'found' for the man, or Zeph 3.13, where no deceitful tongue is to be 'found' in the mouths of those left, the element of discovery or encounter is still present: no helper has been found among the many creatures just named, and nothing that they say will reveal the remnant to be lying.

If we insist on retaining that element, as the usage of the verb elsewhere suggests that we should, then reading it as impersonal or passive here does not change the basic facts that the man was found or met, and that, as Fox puts it, '*someone* did the finding': it merely opens up the possibility that this was someone other than the king, and that Qohelet is talking about the man having been found by, say, his fellow citizens, who only subsequently forgot him. The problem is that such an unmarked change of subject might seem surprising, especially after a long sequence of verbs with the same form: it is hard to see how readers might have been alerted to the fact that this sequence has been broken, and that they need to read just this verb with a rare passive implication or as impersonal, rather than as active.

Such a change would seem all the more surprising in view of the fact that it is with the next verb, ומלט, that Qohelet actually includes a personal pronoun that is best understood as clarifying the new subject (see below). In short, therefore, the matter comes down to whether or not we consider that readers would have felt compelled to understand a new subject for the verb because they would not have believed that Qohelet could be talking about the king actually encountering the man in the city. If we are less literal-minded, and allow that he might be speaking more loosely about the king coming up against a man who happened to be in the city as he besieged it, then it is far more natural to take the king as the subject of ומצא, as he has been of all the verbs so far, and that also relieves us of any need to emend the text or to posit any unusual use of the verb.

9.15 a poor man, a wise man] The absence of a conjunction between מסכן and חכם is reflected in G and S: in the other ancient versions (and in many manuscripts of both M and G, see de Rossi, Miletto) a conjunction has been introduced to facilitate the reading 'a man poor and wise', like the ילד מסכן וחכם of 4.13. That must be the sense, very broadly at least, but the simple juxtaposition of the terms makes it easier to read חכם as a noun, and the purpose is, perhaps, to ensure that both qualities are given their proper emphasis here. On the sense of מסכן, see the note at 4.13.

9.15 then he would save] After a series of subjunctives, G here suddenly uses a future indicative διασώσει, 'he will bring (the city) through safely' (contrast σ' ὃς περιέσωσεν, 'who saved from destruction'; σ' [and α'] had εὗρεν for the preceding G εὕρῃ). Despite the improbable claim of Yi, 184, that this 'may have been used as a variation of the aorist subjunctive', the shift is striking. It is just possible that the translator read וימלט in his source-text, rather than the ומלט of M, but it is more likely that he has read the same text as M and simply sees this as the apodosis of the conditional, hypothetical situation that has been sketched so far: *if* the king besieged the city and encountered the wise man, *then* the wise man would save the city. I think this is, essentially, the correct understanding, and that Qohelet illustrates his observation about wisdom being mighty by claiming that it would save a city in such circumstances—the problem is, as he will go on to say, that it might not be given a chance to do so.

If this is another in the sequence of verbs with waw consecutive, then of course it continues to have the same modal nuance, and what is curious is that many commentators have been inclined to see that nuance only here. Scott, for instance, has so far translated 'There was a small city...and a great king attacked it, surrounded it, and built great siege works against it', but now suddenly translates 'and he might have saved the city by his wisdom'. Even

Isaksson, who talks at length in *Studies*, 97-98, about the waw consecutive 'forms in this passage' and who argues for their potentiality, only actually translates this verb as 'potential'. It is surely much more likely that none or all should be taken this way—as the translator of G has understood—and in that case the issue is not that the wise man *might* possibly have saved the city *when* these things happened, but either that he *did* save the city *when* these things happened, or that he *would* have saved the city *were* these things to have happened.

The use of the personal pronoun הוא with the verb has given rise to a certain amount of discussion, and has led some commentators to read the verb as an infinitive or participle, with Ginsberg, *Studies*, 26-27, further taking the pronoun to be a misreading of the Aramaic verb הוא, 'was'. I take the most obvious reason for its use to be that Qohelet needs to avoid an ambiguity: it is not the king who will save the city, but the wise man who stood as the object of the last clause (so similarly Fox). In formal English, we might translate הוא here as 'the latter'. S ܘܫܘܙܒ ܗܘ ܡܣܟܢܐ *wšwzb hw mskn'* offers a further clarification: 'and that poor man saved', but Kamenetzky, 228, sees ܡܣܟܢܐ *mskn'* as a late addition to the text here, after someone had wrongly read the preceding ܗܘ *hū*, 'he', as *hāw*, 'that'.

9.15 but nobody remembers] The construction ואדם לא זכר, which finally breaks the sequence of narrative tenses, apparently means 'nobody remembers/remembered': אדם לא is not a set phrase, as Schoors implies, but אדם itself can be used to mean 'anybody' (e.g. Ps 105.14; Job 32.21).

G ἐμνήσθη σὺν τοῦ ἀνδρὸς is notable for the use of the genitive with σύν: the translator seemingly breaks with his habit of using the accusative when σύν represents את, but this verb usually takes the genitive (cf. Muraoka, *Syntax*, §26 c), and, if the genitive is original rather than (as seems very possible) a secondary assimilation to that usage, he has simply retained the proper construction at the cost of introducing a potential ambiguity.

9.16 the wisdom of the poor man is disdained] Although traditionally translated 'despise', in line with the standard lexica, בזה rarely has the nuance of dislike which that word carries in modern English: it is almost always used of belittling or of treating things as though they do not matter (2 Sam 6.16 is a possible exception). σ' here is attested as καὶ πῶς ἡ σοφία τοῦ πτώσεως κατεφρονήθη, 'and how the wisdom of the calamity was disdained', although πτώσεως seems likely to be an error for πτωχοῦ, 'poor man'. Since V *quomodo ergo sapientia pauperis contempta est*, 'how then is the wisdom of the poor man despised?', is probably based on this, Symmachus likely also took the sentence as a question expressing incredulity: 'wisdom is better than might, so why…?'.

9.17 words of wise men…someone in charge of fools] Lit. 'words of wise men are heard in respite from'. We encountered נחת at 4.3 and at 6.5: see the note at 4.3. Although sometimes translated as 'quiet' here, it is doubtful that the term has any particular connotation of 'low sound', and Qohelet uses it elsewhere in its usual sense of 'rest', 'ease' or 'lack of struggle'. It is correspondingly doubtful, therefore, that it can provide a direct contrast to the other term, זעקה, which is generally a cry of alarm, protest, or sorrow, and which can be loud (e.g. Ezek 27.28), but which can also refer simply to a verbal protest (e.g. Neh 5.6). Neither word would be an obvious choice to provide the sort of contrast that many commentators have long wanted to find here, between wise men speaking with quiet calmness (σ' μετὰ προσηνείας, 'with mildness', perhaps 'coaxingly') and some arch-fool yelling.

Indeed, it is also far from clear that מושל בכסילים means an arch-fool: the verb משל means to 'rule' or 'be in charge of'—and Qohelet will use the participle again in 10.4 to talk about 'someone who has power over you', or perhaps simply one's superior—but it generally takes an indirect object with -ב, rather than a direct object (which is an objection to Fox's idea that בכסילים should be understood as 'heard...among fools'—if that was the intention, the usage creates an ambiguity, and the word-order pushes readers to a different understanding). Correspondingly, a מושל בכסילים is in charge of fools, but need not be 'among' them: that is not the necessary force of the preposition here. The זעקה of such a person is presumably either their cry of frustration in dealing with such charges, or the shouting with which they attempt to corral them—perhaps both—but the setting that is being evoked is one of chaos and recalcitrance, that stands in contrast to the calm and ease implied by נחת.

A few scholars have shifted the point of comparison from 'the wise' and 'the one in charge' to the words and the shouting, by taking מושל as descriptive of the זעקה. Obviously, the construct relationship prevents us reading it simply as adjectival and attributive, but it is not impossible that this is some sort of fixed expression, otherwise unattested. So, Ginsberg correspondingly understands Qohelet to be talking about shouted orders, presumably understanding literally 'shouts of (the sort shouted by) someone in charge'. This is not implausible, but it does not greatly change the sense. Pinker, 'זעקת מושל', goes rather further in seeing a reference to the shouts of plaintiffs or supplicants, directed toward someone in charge, and this accordingly seems more of a stretch.

My own reading rests on a rejection of the idea that there is a formal contrast or comparison here at all. In 9.16 and 9.18, מן is used as a component of the 'better than' sayings, and obviously has a comparative function. In this verse, however, where there is no adjective, it can only be construed in that way with the participle, so that the words of the wise are 'heard more than' the shouting. This does not make sense unless we either import some unstated notion, like 'heard more (clearly) than', for which it is difficult to find any analogy, or seek some special nuance in the verb, and understand דברי...נשמעים in 9.17 to have a sense that is significantly different from ודבריו אינם נשמעים in 9.16. The latter course is pursued by, e.g., Schoors, who says that the poor man's words 'are no longer heeded', but that the words of wise men 'are to be heeded', while Whybray (following Lauha) understands the second use to mean 'worth hearing'. Joüon, 'Notes philologiques', 425, would achieve such a sense by emending to a hoph'al participle משמעים (while acknowledging that the stem is unattested elsewhere), but most of those translations rest on the possibility that the niph'al participle can have a gerundive implication (cf. GKC §116 e; J-M §121 i). Kroeber, rather differently, argues that the niph'al is 'tolerative' in the second use, and that the niph'al of שמע can act as the acoustic equivalent of the niph'al of ראה, which means 'seem': the words of the wise, therefore, 'sound' ('ertönen') calm, or as though they were at rest.

While none of that is impossible (although Kroeber goes on to add that words sounding this way are 'better' than what follows, which is a considerable stretch), it would be fair to suggest that we should only accept such a disjuncture between the two uses of the same word in quick succession if the context absolutely demands that we should do so, and that we should begin by supposing that נשמעים means much the same both times. If we do so, however, then we are forced back to the problem that 'heard more than' makes little sense. Accordingly, I think it is substantially easier to construe the -מ of מזעקת in a different way, and I take it with נחת: the cognate verb נוח is regularly constructed with מן to specify rest 'from' something (e.g. Deut 12.10; Esth 9.16). The point then is that the words are heard when one has respite from chaos, or, more broadly, when one is away from it: the word-order suggests that מזעקת is applied to נחת as a secondary specification.

The text itself is not in any serious doubt, but G differs from M and the other ancient versions in two important respects: where M has a singular מושל, G has a plural ἐξουσιαζόντων, 'those holding power', and where M has בכסילים, G has ἐν ἀφροσύναις, 'among follies' (a plural found nowhere else in the Septuagint), rather than ἐν ἄφροσιν, 'among fools'. The former probably represents a simple assimilation to σοφῶν / חכמים in the G tradition or G's source-text, balancing the two elements of what G does take to be a comparison (cf. Yi, 227; *BHQ*). For the latter, McNeile, 150, suggests that the translator found a defective writing of כסילים without the medial י and took it as a plural of כסל (cf. 7.25), but it could just be a curious scribal slip or series of slips (perhaps *via* a singular ἀφροσύνη). The other ancient versions support M in both cases, and σ' is attested as μᾶλλον ἢ κραυγὴ ἐξουσιάζοντος ἐν ἀνοήτοις, 'rather than the shouting of one holding power among fools'.

Some modern discussion of this passage has been complicated by a focus on the Masoretic accents. Gordis insists that these make Rashi's construal of the text (the words of the wise are 'heard with pleasure') 'unacceptable', and that they point to 'words of the wise spoken quietly', while Fox would move a disjunctive to achieve the same result. Whether or not the accents are so prescriptive, they only reflect, of course, the understanding of the Masoretes or their tradition, and it is not clear why we should wish to move them, rather than simply reject them. The position of בנחת means that it can be read in principle either as referring to something in the context or manner of the delivery of the words, or to the hearing of those words, and whichever way the Masoretes went, the other ancient versions have mostly opted to retain the position and the ambiguity, with only V explicitly opting for *audiuntur in silentio*, 'heard in silence'; σ' is attested simply as μετὰ προσηνείας, 'with mildness / softness', but the choice of term suggests that Symmachus linked it to the words rather than the setting.

9.18 Wisdom is good beyond weapons of war] The basic structure here is a 'better than' statement, but the Hebrew plays on the uses of טובה as an adjective describing wisdom at the beginning of the verse and as a noun 'goodness' at the end, to suggest that it is the benefits or advantages of wisdom that may be annulled. I have tried to retain this in translation.

Qohelet also maintains the link with the preceding story by comparing wisdom specifically now with כלי קרב, a term that may refer more generally to all of the kit and implements involved in warfare rather than specifically to weapons, although it seems to be used here as an equivalent to the more classical כלי מלחמה (as the lexica note, קרב is an Aramaic term, and other attestations in Hebrew are late). Ginsberg's suggested emendation to מכל יקר is both improbable and unnecessary. A reading (σκεύη) πολεμικά is assigned to α' by all three of the Greek manuscripts in which it appears, and so by Field, but Marshall argues that this does not suit the translation technique of Aquila, and assigns it instead to σ'.

9.18 just one person getting something wrong] Lit. 'one person doing what is wrong'. S ܘܡܢ ܚܕ ܕܚܛܝ *wḥṭyʾ ḥdʾ* uses a noun, 'one sin', although the other versions support the participle of M. Even if Qohelet is extrapolating some broader point, the context here demands that we understand him not to be talking about the baneful influence of someone who habitually does what is wrong ('a sinner'), but about the ability of an error (failing to remember the wise man) to offset the power of wisdom. The participle may have been chosen because the noun חטא (which *BHS* suggests reading here) is used more particularly for offences rather than mistakes (cf. 10.4).

9.18 lets much good go to waste] We first encountered the piʿel of אבד in 3.6, where it was used of letting something become lost: see the note there. I think the sense here is similar: the problem is not that the error actively destroys what is good, but that it cancels it out or, more specifically, prevents it from happening. However great the potential benefits of wisdom may be, just one error can stop that potential being realized. σ' here translates with ἀγαθὰ πολλά, 'many good things', which is probably the basis for V *multa bona*, and in S ܛܒܬܐ ܣܓܝܐܬܐ *ṭbʾ sgyʾtʾ* is marked as plural (although Kamenetzky, 202, would delete the plural marker seyame on both words as secondary). It is unlikely that this represents a Hebrew variant: טובה הרבה has been understood as collective, and translated as plural to draw out a perceived contrast between the single sinner and the many good things that will be undone.

10.1

(10.1) When corpse-flies cause a stench, scented oil pours out fragrance: even a little is worth more than wisdom, more than a great deal of folly.

Commentary

This verse has traditionally been understood in very different terms, and the RSV, for instance, reads on the basis of the Hebrew text:

Dead flies make the perfumer's ointment give off an evil odour;
so a little folly outweighs wisdom and honour.

On that understanding, the saying picks up 9.18 and presents an analogy between the power of a little folly and the capacity of dead flies to turn a scented oil bad. This makes sense, although it may not offer a very good analogy: ending up in a jar of oil would undoubtedly be bad for the flies,[1] but it seems unlikely that they would actually make the oil putrefy in any way. The Greek version, however, is different in key respects, not the least of which is that it makes a little wisdom more valuable than folly (and so, of course, equates wisdom with the flies). This is probably not an instance of one text replacing the thought of the other with a more conventional sentiment (so Bolin, *Ecclesiastes*, 83): both versions, and especially the 'less conventional' Hebrew, present serious difficulties of their own, and they have probably arisen as separate attempts to make sense of a text that had become corrupt. Trying to reconstruct an earlier version that could have given rise to both these readings inevitably involves some uncertainties, but it is significantly easier to explain both the current readings and the use of particular terms like 'pour out' or 'a little' if we understand the original intention

---

[1] In his *Muscae Encomium* 4, Lucian observes of the fly that σύντροφος δὲ ἀνθρώποις ὑπάρχουσα καὶ ὁμοδίαιτος καὶ ὁμοτράπεζος ἁπάντων γεύεται, πλὴν ἐλαίου· θάνατος γὰρ αὐτῇ τοῦτο πιεῖν, 'Living alongside humans, sharing food and table, it tastes everything except oil, for to drink that is death to it'.

to have been different. I think Qohelet's purpose is neither to counter nor to re-iterate the claim made in 9.18—assumptions which have probably contributed to the problems in the text—but to set the relative strengths and weaknesses of wisdom and folly in perspective: neither is of any use to the dead, for whom a little deodorant is of far more value. The use of scented preparations on a funeral bier is described in 2 Chr 16.14, which uses terms related to those used here.

Notes

10.1 when] The original structure probably involved the simple juxtaposition of two statements, lit. 'flies of death cause a stench; scented oil pours out perfume', although it is possible that they were joined by a conjunction. In either case, I take the first clause to be serving as conditional or circumstantial: the fine oil is used to mask the smell of death.

10.1 corpse-flies] The common understanding of the image here is that a quantity of perfumed oil or ointment may be spoiled by something as small as the corpses of dead flies, which transmit to it their own putrefaction (and this can then serve as an analogy for a little folly spoiling a lot of wisdom). M זבובי מות, literally 'flies of death', sits uncomfortably with this image, however, since it is not a natural way of talking about flies that are dead or dying, and Schoors' statement that 'though harsh, this construction is acceptable as denoting "dead flies"' is presented with no evidence beyond the similar assertions of others.

The few expressions that might be considered analogous, in fact, suggest that people or things 'of death' are typically deserving of death (2 Sam 12.5; 1 Kgs 2.26), harbingers of death (Prov 16.14), or themselves deadly (2 Sam 22.6; Ps 7.14 ET 7.13; cf. Job 18.13, which has a more explicitly mythological caste). Despite various attempts to find a way for the flies to be lethal here (which is actually the way G and T interpret), none of those really suits the context or the understanding that they must be dead for the image to work. This consideration has undoubtedly shaped the way that most of the ancient versions approached the text. Translating the expression backwards, as it were, σ' (followed by hexaplaric manuscripts of G) uses μυιῶν θάνατος, 'death of flies', and so preserves the noun (as does Hie *muscae mortis*), but G θανατοῦσαι, 'death-dealing', has provided a basis for S ܕܒܒ̈ܐ ܕܡܝܬܝܢ *dbb' dmytyn*, and V *muscae morientes*, which all treat the text as though there were a plural participle here rather than a singular noun.[2]

---

[2] The La may be reflected in Eucherius *Formulae* iv: *muscae moriturae exterminant oleum suauitatis*, 'flies that are about to die ruin aromatic oil'. See *CSEL* 31 p. 24 l. 25, and Vaccari, 'Recupero', 118.

10.1   477

It is just possible, in fact, that the reading in G originated as an error for θανάτου, with the σαι arising from a partial doubling of the subsequent σαπ (as McNeile, 165, suggests), or that the translator found a variant in his source-text, but it is more likely, as Goldman supposes, that he was bringing his translation into line with his understanding of the image. The versions do not really support emendation: if the translator of G did find זבובים מתים in his source-text, then that was more probably a facilitation itself than the original reading (despite the preference for it of McNeile, 80).

Nevertheless, some emendation is required here anyway, to deal with a further problem: the following verb יבאיש is singular, and so cannot agree with the plural 'flies'. A number of scholars, correspondingly, have sought to kill two birds with one stone by emending not the verb but זבובי מות. BHS recommends simply removing the י and the ו to read זבוב מת, 'a dead fly', and Dahood thinks likewise that M has arisen from a misinterpretation of the defectively written זבבמת. A more elegant suggestion is that we should simply re-divide to read זבוב ימות, and this has been advocated recently by Seow and Fox (the latter attributes it to Perles, *Analekten*, 43, but Perles himself credits Luzzatto, who suggests it on p. 78). Read as an asyndetic clause of circumstance or condition, 'if/when a fly dies', this seems to provide a very easy way around the problems. It does not really explain, however, why the ancient translators and copyists were so obviously determined to retain plural 'flies', despite the problems caused by this reading, rather than correct what might have seemed an obvious error. It also leaves us with an awkward text: as we shall see, M already has two yiqtol verbs juxtaposed without a conjunction, and this emendation would add a third, with the extra complication that ימות would either have to stand in a subordinate clause with the following יבאיש in the main clause, despite its similar form, or as the first element in an odd sequence: neither is impossible, but the elegance of the emendation would certainly not be matched by the elegance of the resulting Hebrew.

We shall return to the matter of agreement in the next note, where it will become clear that the problems in the Hebrew run rather deeper. My own translation, which is based on a different understanding of Qohelet's point here, takes זבובי מות to be a reference to carrion flies, perhaps associated with death in the way that the *zumbi kalbi* and the *zumbi mê* in Akkadian are flies associated with dogs and water respectively. Saracino, 'Ras Ibn Hani 78/20', draws attention to an expression *dbbm dġzr* in an Ugaritic text: *ġzr* is used as an epithet for Mot, the god of death, and so the expression is plausibly understood as 'flies of Death'. The text is difficult, but these flies are apparently associated with a sickness and are to be driven away. That understanding is not without rivals (cf. Bordreuil and Caquot, 'Textes', 346-50), but if Saracino is correct then this tends to affirm the association with death and disease, while perhaps providing a different origin for the term.

10.1 cause a stench, but scented oil pours out fragrance] Having taken the reference to be to the 'death of flies', σ' μυιῶν θάνατος σήψει ἔλαιον εὐῶδες μυρεψοῦ has a singular verb: this death 'will corrupt the fragrant oil of a perfumer'. T paraphrases heavily, but its single fly 'makes the wise man stink...and spoils the good name previously likened to anointing oil scented with fragrances' (cf. 7.1). The other versions all use a plural verb in accordance with their idea of 'lethal/dying flies', but, like σ', they all have only one verb, while M has two singular verbs: יבאיש יביע, 'will cause to stink (or will stink), will pour out'. There is no trace of this second verb in any of the ancient translations, except possibly T, which also has two verbs: מסרי, the first, clearly translates יבאיש, but if the second, מחבל, actually reflects יביע, then it must be a guess at the sense, and the whole clause to which it belongs may simply be interpretative (T sees a connection here with the fine oil of 7.1).

Conversely, G σαπριοῦσιν σκευασίαν ἐλαίου ἡδύσματος includes a word that, on the face of it, has no counterpart in M: the flies 'will cause to decay *a preparation* of aromatic oil'. Scholars have naturally sought to reconcile the differences between M and G by connecting σκευασίαν with יביע, and one popular approach, commended in *BHS*, is to assume that the Greek actually reflects a Hebrew word גביע, 'cup' or 'bowl'. This idea comes in two flavours. Seow, for example, cautiously represents the more traditional position that the Hebrew was initially translated using σκεῦος, originally a 'vessel', which was then itself corrupted in the Greek (S ܡܐܢܐ *m'n'*, which is equivalent to σκεῦος, is sometimes presented as evidence of the original form). Fox, on the other hand, adopts the simpler theory that 'the translator took "chalice" as a metonym for its contents', and employed σκευασία itself as an interpretative rendering (he thinks that S has simply misunderstood the rare σκευασία, and translated as though it were σκεῦος).

Goldman, however, has set out in some detail the objections to this approach in general, and these may be summarized as: (1) it is not easy to see how גביע became corrupted to the difficult יביע; (2) there are no grounds for thinking that גביע would have been translated using σκεῦος or σκευασία; (3) σκευασία is, on the other hand, a very plausible rendering of the subsequent רוקח. That last point is important, because if σκευασία is indeed G's rendering of רוקח or some related word, which seems very likely, this not only leaves יביע still without a counterpart, but also implies that ἡδύσματος cannot have been used for רוקח, despite its correspondence in position after 'oil', making it the spare word here in G. It may help us visualize the situation if we set out the likely correspondences:

יבאיש	יביע	שמן	רוקח	
σαπριοῦσιν		ἐλαίου	σκευασίαν	ἡδύσματος

In fact, ἡδύσματα in the Septuagint usually translates the Hebrew בשמים, 'spices', and the singular ἡδύσματος would naturally represent בשם, which is literally 'balsam', but which is used generally also of fragrance (as is the cognate Aramaic word). An equivalent is lacking in Hie, V, but it seems likely that σ' ἔλαιον εὐῶδες μυρεψοῦ also reflects that term here, and quite possible that the 'myrrh' attributed to α' by Olympiodorus is a rendering of it (see Marshall, although he argues himself that it corresponds to רוקח). S ܒܣܡ̈ܐ *bsym'* (variant ܕܒܣܡ̈ܐ *dbsym'*) probably just follows G, but it is striking to observe that T also describes the oil as 'spiced (or scented) with perfumes (בבושמין)', and so we have good reason to suppose that G is rendering a version of the Hebrew which was widely circulated over a long period, and which probably contained something like שמן ר(ו)קח בשם; Goldman prefers מרקחת to רוקח, but the general reference in either case would be to 'perfumed/perfumer's oil'. It is likely that שמן רוקח is a technical term (an apparent equivalent is found in Ugaritic: cf. *HALOT*), but the relationship between this phrase and בשם depends on context. In the source-text of G, which apparently lacked יביע, all three words have to be construed as an object of יבאיש, or rather of the plural יבאישו which the translator appears to have found. He correspondingly understood בשם to qualify שמן רוקח, as it does other nouns in Exod 30.23, and the whole expression, in context, to represent a particular item—hence, literally, 'a preparation of oil of spice/ aroma'. רוקח itself can be read either as a participle from the verb (so a 'perfumer') or as a substance (cf. יין הרקח, 'spiced wine', at Ct 8.2), and even with the plene spelling it can in principle be understood both ways: a variant pointing without the *pataḥ* (cf. רקח at Exod 30.25) is, in fact, to be found in at least a few eastern manuscripts which are late but which may preserve earlier Babylonian readings (see Ratzabi, 'Massoretic Variants', 106; Lavoie and Mehramooz, 'Le Texte hébreu et la traduction judéo-persane', 497). Goldman's מרקחת would point more directly to 'perfumer', but adds a further, unnecessary text-critical complication to what is already a complicated situation. In terms of the overall sense, the difference is minimal: the reference is obviously just to a particular sort of oil.

M does have יביע, and if the text originally had בשם as well, then יביע שמן רוקח בשם would most naturally have stood as a second clause, with בשם as the object of the verb: 'perfumed/perfumer's oil pours out fragrance'. This fits the verb well: there is very little reason (despite the incursions into Arabic of Driver, 'Problems and Solutions', 231-32) to suppose that נבע in the hiph'il could mean 'cause to ferment' or even 'cause to bubble', and only, indeed, in Prov 18.4 does the verb (in the qal there) ever have any direct connection with the flowing out of liquid, which was probably its original connotation. Everywhere else it is used figuratively of the rush or flow of speech, and that image seems quite compatible with a similar use here to characterize the flow of fragrance from an oil or ointment. In that case, יביע is not supposed to be coordinated with the preceding verb, and this would have been clear if the text originally had a plural יבאישו, agreeing with the זבובי מות. We can get a very sensible text (which, as we shall see, fits well with what follows) by reading both the יביע of M and the בשם indicated by G, made all the more so if we read יבאישו (admittedly the easier reading). It is difficult to see, on the other hand, either how יביע could be an error for בשם (or *vice versa*) especially given their relative positions in the text, or how one of these words might simply have arisen as an addition—Goldman does not explain why he commends in *BHQ* the simple deletion of יביע, which is not readily explicable either as a graphical error or as a gloss. If the text originally ran זבובי מות יביע יבאישו שמן ר(ו)קח בשם, which I consider likely, then the intended sense was 'flies of death cause a stench, perfumer's / anointing oil pours forth fragrance' (for a similar contrast between putrefaction and בשם as perfume, cf. Isa 3.24).

It is relatively unusual for a textual tradition to split in quite such a way that each part preserves different fragments of the original reading, and we should not normally treat reconstruction of the text as a matter of raiding ruins for bricks. If this is what has happened, it is also striking, moreover, that both M and G have ended up supporting the same general understanding, that Qohelet is talking about flies corrupting oil, even though they have different words. It would be easy to suppose that interpretative pressure has influenced the changes on both sides, but I think, in fact, that simple errors have made at least as great a contribution.

In G's source, a scribe has skipped over יביע in the sequence יבאישויביעשמנ, probably because of its resemblance to the word he has already written. As noted already, that loss compels a reading of שמן ר(ו)קח בשם as the object of יבאישו, and leads to flies corrupting oil. M is more complicated, because its text involves two changes from what I presume to have been the original: the losses of the final ו on יבאישו and of בשם. The former seems likely again to have been a simple graphical error, caused by the following י: any deliberate attempt to coordinate the verbs would surely have resulted in them both becoming plural, not singular. The accidental coordination of the verbs, however, now forces an interpretation of זבובי מות that allows it to be treated as singular, and to act as the subject, because שמן ר(ו)קח could not meaningfully be the subject of יבאיש. M has now, in effect, to be construed in much the same way as G, but it crucially still has יביע, and this makes בשם awkward: the text would seem to be asserting that the flies both corrupt and cause the oil to pour out scent. Its omission is probably interpretative, therefore, and reflects an attempt to make sense of the saying. Although it is conceivable that one or both is betraying a knowledge of the reading behind G as well, I am inclined to think that T and σ' each reflect here the same form of the text that lies behind M, but without that further loss of בשם, and that the lack in each of any clear equivalent to יביע is a result of their tendency to paraphrase, taking יבאיש יביע to represent a single concept: that understanding also enables them to deal with the awkwardness of בשם.

10.1 even a little is worth more than wisdom, more than a great deal of folly] Lit. 'precious more than wisdom, more than a great weight of folly, is a little'. The second part of the verse is a famous crux, and there are again some significant differences between the versions, at least in terms of their sense.

M יקר מחכמה מכבוד סכלות מעט presents a number of problems, but seems literally to say something like 'precious more than wisdom, than abundance/ honour (is) folly, a little' (not strictly 'a little folly' because מעט should stand in a construct relationship before the noun it qualifies).[3] G τίμιον ὀλίγον σοφίας ὑπὲρ δόξαν ἀφροσύνης μεγάλης, on the other hand, means 'a little of wisdom is precious more than glory of great folly'. Some commentators have hypothesized a very different Hebrew source-text for G, but its readings may be understood as an attempt to understand much the same text that we have in M as a counter to 9.18: the first מ- (on מחכמה) has been read as partitive (GKC §119 w, n. 2), and ὀλίγον (for מעט; the reading κἂν μικρά in some Greek manuscripts is from σ′) has then been read with it to give the meaning: 'a little bit of wisdom is more precious than...'. M does lack a direct equivalent to μεγάλης, and the general character of the G translation raises the possibility that it found רב or similar in its source: Goldman suggests that רב might have appeared through dittography of the לב at the start of 10.2, although it seems more likely that any such reading would have been a deliberate gloss. It is also possible, however, that δόξαν...μεγάλης is a deliberate double translation of כבוד, bringing out the senses of both honour and weight

---

[3] In 5.1, מעט appeared in the plural as an adjective or participle—a usage found also in Ps 109:8, but not apparently intended here, since it would not agree with סכלות. In Deut 26.5; 28.62, we find an expression במתי מעט, lit. 'in men of a little', but meaning 'few in number': this appears to be constructed on the same principle as the various other expressions with מתי which place it in a construct relationship with a noun that describes it, so speaks to the usage of that noun, rather than of מעט. Otherwise מעט seems to follow the expression it qualifies only in Isa 10.7 ('[Assyria intends to] cut off nations—and not just a few of them'), and in four other, late passages. However, in three of these, Ezra 9.8; Ezek 11.16; and Dan 11.34, the meaning is apparently temporal, 'for a short while', or at least adverbial, 'to a small extent'—God is unlikely to be describing himself as a 'small sanctuary' in Ezekiel, for example. That leaves only Neh 2.12 as a potential parallel to the common understanding 'a little folly' in this verse, and אני ואנשים מעט מעט there is probably to be understood as a positive equivalent to the similar appositional usage in Isa 10: Nehemiah is declaring the small size of his party ('I and some men—just a few'). When it is not being used as an adjective, then, or to qualify a verbal idea, מעט stands before the substantive that it describes, and only follows it, rarely and for effect, when the quantity is being added to the initial statement, as though an afterthought. To that extent, Krüger, 'Wertvoller', 65, may be right to distinguish the uses before and after a substantive by sense (although he over-generalizes the normal meaning), but the use after a substantive is, in practice, an unusual device, and not a typical usage. If we were to understand the text here in such terms, the sense would not be 'even a little folly is worth more', but 'folly is worth more—a little of it', presenting as an afterthought the quantitative claim that many commentators consider central.

that the noun can possess, in order to clarify the perceived contrast.[4] In any case, the reading of one מ- as partitive is a reasonable attempt to deal both with the difficult pair מחכמה and מכבוד, and with the position of מעט. S probably conflates the readings found in M and G,[5] but the other ancient versions also probably reflect a text close to M.[6]

Despite this broad consistency across the versions, however, many commentators have considered it desirable or even necessary to emend the text here. The word מכבוד, in particular, has been regarded with suspicion, since its prepositional prefix suggests that it should stand in parallel with מחכמה, but

---

[4] Although he is probably right to see this as an instance where G has exercised some freedom to bring out the sense, I doubt Yi is correct to suppose that the translator has produced ὀλίγον simply from the partitive מ- and then 'contextually interpreted מעט and rendered it by μεγάλης' (125 n. 307). That would be not just 'an example of freedom' but an extraordinary departure from his normal habits. For other possible double translations in G, see 4.17; 7.13. There is an unattributed marginal note to μεγάλης in ms 252: πολλῆς, 'much'. That reading is not attested elsewhere as a variant, and Marshall, 366, raises the possibility that it is a hexaplaric reading. It would greatly strengthen the case for a Hebrew variant with רב if there was also an equivalent in one of the Three.

[5] Most of the manuscripts read 'more precious than wisdom and than much (ܣܘܓ݁ܬ swgʾt variant ܣܓܝܐܘܬ sgyʾwt) glory is great (ܪܒܬܐ rbtʾ) folly', but the variant ܩܠܝܠ qlyl is found for ܪܒܬܐ rbtʾ at the end of the verse: this is equivalent to the מעט of M. Goldman suggests that ܣܘܓ݁ܬ swgʾt / ܣܓܝܐܘܬ sgyʾwt is probably derived from a Hebrew text which also had רב, albeit in a different position from the רב which he thinks was read or understood by G in its source-text. It seems no less likely, however, that we are dealing with an early or original conflation of the G and M readings, which sheds no separate light on the original form of the Hebrew. Furthermore, the 'great folly' attested by many of the Syriac witnesses at the end of the verse is probably a secondary revision of the text in the light of G, which has led, in effect, to the Greek μεγάλης being rendered twice. In short, the curiosities of the S reading may be significant for the origins and development of that version, but they offer no strong grounds for questioning the authenticity of M here.

[6] T is characteristically midrashic, but clearly based around much the same Hebrew. Hie *pretiosa est super sapientiam et gloriam stultitia parua*, 'a little folly is more precious than wisdom and glory', has a conjunction between מחכמה and מכבוד, but otherwise reflects the wording and order of the M text. This conjunction is found also in many Hebrew manuscripts (see de Rossi), in T, and in most manuscripts of S: it is plausibly regarded as an early variant, and Krüger believes it to be original, but it most likely emerged as a secondary facilitation. V *pretiosior est sapientia et gloria parua ad tempus stultitia*, 'More precious than wisdom and glory is a little folly at a time', may be ambiguous (if one allows *pretiosior* to be the predicate of *sapientia et gloria*: 'wisdom and glory are more precious…'), but is probably to be read similarly, with *parua ad tempus* introducing a note of caution rather than indicating a different word-order or a variant Hebrew reading.

it is joined to it by no conjunction (except where one has been added in many later manuscripts and editions, cf. de Rossi), and its usual sense of 'honour' seems out of place. In line with the view that this stich must be presenting a contrast between a little of one thing and a lot of another, as suggested by G, a number of attempts have been made to replace מכבוד with an expression of quantity either from a different root (*BHS* favours the rare למכביר of Job 36.31), or from the same root in its sense of 'weight' (so Fox 1987, taking יקר with the preceding stich as a further attribute of the oil, emends to תכבד, with the sense 'outweigh').

Indeed, it probably is necessary to replace or emend מכבוד in order to achieve that sense: there is little basis for Gordis' assertion that מכבוד can itself mean 'in abundance'; the usage of the noun would require a different construction, or at least a different preposition here. It also seems likely, however, that further emendations would be required. The final word מעט is not an adjective but a noun, meaning 'a little', 'a small amount' or 'something small'. As we noted above, it does not naturally stand after a noun as an attribute, so סכלות מעט means at best 'folly, a small amount (of it)' rather than 'a little folly', and normal usage would require מעט סכלות to yield that latter sense. As we also noted above, G probably reflects an appreciation of this problem, and T similarly avoids reading מעט attributively. In short, we really cannot take this stich to mean 'A little folly is more precious than much wisdom' without at least some emendation of the text, and even the expressions 'a little folly' and 'much wisdom' are individually problematic.

Rather than emend the text to suit that sense, we should, perhaps, first consider reviewing the sense to suit the text. The natural grouping of words in M would suggest, in fact, that מעט is itself the subject of the sentence: מחכמה and מכבוד סכלות are readily understood as distinct units, which most likely serve as parallel points of contrast, and simply grouping them in this way leaves מעט isolated, with no clear function other than as the subject. If we take it as such, the sense would be 'A little is more precious than wisdom, than glory/weight of folly'. Unless this is a general denigration of both wisdom and folly (even anything small is better than both), the reference of מעט would then have to be back to the oil or perfume of the previous stich. This understanding receives some support from the normal usage of יקר, which is associated with value and worth, rather than with efficacy: as many commentators have observed, it would seem a strange choice of word to describe the ability of something inherently undesirable, like folly, to outweigh wisdom.[7] In that case, the second stich should probably be understood to mean literally 'more precious than wisdom, than a great weight of folly, is a little', or

---

[7] As is often noted, terms cognate with יקר can be used of weight in Aramaic, but they never unambiguously have that force in biblical Hebrew, and it is not common in later usage. The word might conceivably connote 'weighty', but there is no reason to suppose it could mean 'heavy', without any nuance of 'valuable'.

less literally 'even a little is more precious than wisdom, than a great load of folly'. Wisdom, then, is ranked more highly than folly, but neither can offset the stench of putrefaction in the way that perfume can, and so neither is of any value in the event of death.

10.2-3

(10.2) The mind of a wise man inclines to his right, but the mind of a fool to his left, (10.3) so even on the road, as the obtuse man goes along, his mind is absent, and everyone says he's obtuse.

Commentary

There has been much discussion of the significance that has sometimes been attached to the left, 'sinister' side by various cultures, and Lavoie, 'Qohélet 10,2-3', 73-74, gives a useful summary of the various implications that have been attributed to the terms (he reaches the conclusion himself that both sides represent something bad, connecting the imagery with biblical injunctions against turning aside). Nobody, however, has actually demonstrated any very compelling reason to suppose that 'left' and 'right' would have had particular connotations of 'bad' and 'good' for the writer of Ecclesiastes or his original audience, and so the sense of 10.2 has remained rather obscure. The fact that Qohelet is talking about inclinations of the mind also rules out suggestions such as that of Garrett, 'Use and Abuse', 173, that the imagery is based on clumsiness attributed to using the left hand, and we really have no good cause to suppose that Qohelet is referring to anything other than sides or directions. The saying that follows in 10.3 is difficult for rather different reasons, but it too presents a mysterious image, this time of a fool whose folly is somehow obvious even as he simply walks along. Since the sayings are linked by a conjunction in the Hebrew, they are probably intended to be read together, and I think they shed light on each other. Outside a Monty Python sketch, it is hard to walk foolishly by oneself, and there is nothing inherently right or wrong about any preference for the right or left side. If we read the first clause as circumstantial, however, then Qohelet may simply be saying that when sensible people go to the right, the fool always goes to the left, demonstrating his perverse instincts even as he walks.

There may even be a more precise reference, although here we have to speculate a little. The choice of left or right would certainly have mattered in the context of a busy ancient street, where the flow of pedestrian and other traffic must have been governed by convention, and there is evidence for some very strict conventions by Roman times. The Romans themselves apparently preferred to keep to the left on a road, but if this is indeed the background to Qohelet's statements here, he is familiar with a place where the right was more normal. The fool, drifting to the left, is a self-evident nuisance—and one attractive way of reading the text, indeed, suggests that, far from realizing this, he blames everyone else for their stupidity when they get in his way.

10.2] We have no direct evidence for whatever traffic conventions would have been familiar to the original readers, but there is a description in the Mishnah (*Middot* 2.2) of access to the Temple Mount. According to this, pedestrians would usually enter the area on the right and leave on the left, with only those who wished to draw attention to their own problems going in the opposite direction. This is at least compatible with a preference for keeping to the right.

10.3] The text is uncertain here (see the notes), and in the translation I have adopted what seems, by a small margin, the most natural construal of the more likely reading. That reading, though, is ambiguous, and could arguably be construed as '(the fool) says "Everyone is a fool"'—which matches the understanding of Symmachus and the Vulgate by portraying the fool as believing that it is everybody else who has got it wrong. Masoretic texts have the fool or his heart actively declare to everybody that he is a fool, presumably by his choice of the left side, although their reading is also sometimes taken (less plausibly) to mean that he is talking not 'to' but 'about' everybody.

Notes

10.2 mind] Here and in the next verse, I have translated לב, lit. 'heart', as 'mind', to avoid the different connotation that 'inclinations of the heart' would have in English. Qohelet used the expression לב חכם at 8.5: see the note there.

10.2 inclines to his right...his left] Hie, V and some manuscripts of S have '*in* his right/left', but this is probably translational. According to context, the expressions לימינו and לשמאלו can in principle indicate either direction of movement (e.g. Neh 12.31, 38) or relative position (e.g. Ps 45.10 ET 45.9), while the preposition -ל itself, of course, could potentially be used to express many other meanings. Moreover, the formulation 'the heart of X to' has no corresponding verb, and one has to be understood. The consequent range of possibilities, combined with the absence of a clear steer from the context, has led commentators to envisage what is being said here in a variety of ways. We can constrain this to some extent, I think, by considering the likely implications of לב. When Krüger suggests, for example, that the wise and the fools have 'right-handed' and 'left-handed' understandings, leading them the right or wrong way, it is important to point out that לב nowhere else connotes 'understanding' in the sense of good or bad judgment, and seems to have no ethical nuance (cf. Lavoie, 'Qohélet 10,2-3', 68-69).

It is also important, though, to look at parallels to the particular construction of לב with -ל. Most commonly, this occurs in contexts where the heart is the object of a verb, and people, for instance, 'set', 'turn' or 'give' their heart to things, expressing notions like 'pay attention to' or 'worry about'. We do, however, encounter the expressions 'find the heart to' in 2 Sam 7.27 and 'hinder the heart to' in Num 32.9, which respectively express motivation and discouragement. These senses come to the fore in contexts where the heart is not directed, but acts as the subject. So, in Judg 5.9, which is the only other place where we find a non-verbal clause with -ל and with 'heart' as the subject, לבי לחוקקי is clearly a way of expressing favour and admiration for the commanders, and in 1 Chr 12.38 and 2 Chr 30.12 the expression '(be of) one heart to' indicates a unanimous desire. Neh 3.38, furthermore, uses ויהי לב לעם לעשות as a way of saying that the people were moved or motivated to work—and our non-verbal clauses are most naturally understood as equivalent to the sort of clause with היה used there. It is trickier to judge expressions that use other verbs with 'heart' as their subject, since the preposition may convey some nuance related to the particular verb, but we may note, e.g., Exod 35.29, in which the heart 'moves' people to act, or Exod 36.2, in which it 'lifts' them to do so (cf. 2 Chr 25.19). Typically, in fact, we can say that when the heart 'is toward' something (rather than being directed toward something), it favours it or wants to do it (we might use 'minded to'), and people are motivated to actions by their heart moving them toward those actions. In this context, correspondingly, the most probable sense of the expressions is that the wise and foolish 'favour' the right and left respectively, a statement that in 10.3 translates into their wishing to move toward, or travel on, their preferred side.

10.3 so] Lit. 'and' or 'but'. The conjunction is frequently left untranslated by commentators who interpret 10.2 and 10.3 as separate sayings, but is supported by all the ancient versions.

10.3 as the obtuse man] M^L has כשהסכל, with no vowel applied to the ה and a Masoretic annotation that ה יתיר—'the ה is redundant'. This implies a *Qᵉrê*, although it is not technically presented as such. Or 9879 handles it more formally, with כסכל given in the margin as *Qᵉrê*. Both approaches are found in later Hebrew manuscripts, although some just offer one word or the other (cf. Ginsburg, *Writings*). G and σ' both read an article, and כשסכל may be simply an assimilation of the determined form to the undetermined כסיל in 10.2. If so, it would be wrong to make too much of the distinction (and Crenshaw views it as merely 'euphonic'), but the point may be that this is the very fool whose heart inclines to the left. Another possibility is that the ה is orthographic, serving as a vowel-letter for the *segol*: see the note 'a power greater' at 6.10. This is the view of Bar-Asher in Garr and Fassberg, *Handbook*, 207-8, and is very plausible.

10.3 his mind is absent] M חסר is often read as an adjective (explicitly by, e.g., Schoors, *The Preacher* II, 347), a construal that aligns the expression here very closely with the idiom חסר לב, 'lacking mind' or 'lacking sense', found many times in Proverbs. That construal is supported by S ܚܣܝܪ *ḥsyr*, 'lacking', σ' ἀνόητος, 'senseless', and by V *insipiens sit*, 'he is unwise'. G, however, which usually reflects the translator's grammatical understanding in such cases, reads ὑστερήσει, 'will be lacking', and Hie *minuitur*, 'is diminished', is also a verbal form. In fact, we probably should read a verb here. The expression חסר לב, 'lacking heart' = 'lacking sense', is applied to people, as Ginsburg and others have pointed out, and like the similar expression חסר תבונות in Prov 28.16, it describes their lack of understanding, or of any capacity to understand. Were we to read an adjective here, however, then M would not say that the fool '(is) lacking his heart', but that 'his heart (is) lacking', and the adjective חסר is never elsewhere used intransitively in that way, to mean 'absent' or 'deficient': it always means '(is) lacking (something)'. The verb, however, can be used in precisely that way, and we need look no further than 9.8, where it is used absolutely of oil being deficient (cf. Deut 15.8).

The original form of the verb here is not, however, entirely obvious. As McNeile, 151, points out, the tense of G suggests that the translator in fact found יחסר, not חסר: as already noted at 9.5, this would otherwise be one of only two places where the translator possibly rendered a participle with a future, and it is likely, *pace* Yi, that in that verse too he found a yiqtol. The variation חסר / יחסר has apparently arisen either through haplography after the preceding ו, or through dittography of that character. The direction of change is difficult to establish beyond doubt, since the subsequent ואמר could be read as a weqatal form, in sequence with יחסר, if we were to take לבו to be the subject of both (an issue that we shall turn to shortly). It is simplest to suppose, however, that חסר is original. Loevy, *Libri Kohelet*, 23, notes a late variant חוכר, which is probably just a graphical error.

10.3 and everyone says he's obtuse] It is likely that attempts to understand this statement in various different ways have themselves influenced the transmission of the text. In particular, it is hard to believe that the usually conservative translator of G would have rendered the current text of M as καὶ ἃ λογιεῖται πάντα ἀφροσύνη ἐστίν, 'and what he thinks about is all folly' (a rendering largely followed by S), and there are reasons to suppose that we are not actually dealing with the original text of G here.[1] If there have been early developments in the G tradition, though, the texts of T ושולא אמרין דשטיא הוא, 'and all say that he is a fool', and of Hie *et dicit omnis insipiens est*, 'and he says everyone is a fool', point at the very least to the existence of a variant Hebrew text, which had הכל instead of לכל—and such a reading was probably to be found in the source-text of G as well.

I consider הכל more likely to be original. The only other witness that might support M's לכל is σ', the text of which was preserved in full by Jerome in Latin (subsequently influencing his translation in V), and can now be reconstructed also in Greek: ἀλλὰ μὴν καὶ ἐν ὁδῷ ὁ ἄφρων περιπατῶν ἀνόητος ὢν ὑπολαμβάνει περὶ πάντων ὅτι ἄφρονές εἰσίν, 'but truly even on a road, the fool walking along, himself without sense, assumes of everyone that they are fools'. Here, περὶ could possibly reflect a reading of -ל with a sense 'concerning' (which has been favoured by many modern commentators), but the tendency of σ' to paraphrase makes this far from certain. 'Says concerning', moreover, would be a desperately unnatural interpretation of the very common אמר ל-, which always means 'says to', whatever the possible connotations of the preposition taken by itself. Since אמר is used of speaking, and not generally of informing or indicating in some other way, then if we retain לכל, M's ואמר לכל סכל הוא really has to mean 'and he says to everyone that he is a fool'—even if many interpreters, and perhaps Symmachus, have sought various ingenious ways to attribute the meanings with הכל ('and he says "everyone is a fool"', or 'and everyone says "he is a fool"') to a text with לכל.

Of course, there are obvious attractions to the idea of a fool pushing against the flow, and muttering that it is everybody else who is stupid (or at least, as the Midrash Rabbah would have it, that everybody else is also stupid). As Fox and others have pointed out, however, the fool's heart has not yet been replaced explicitly as subject, and it would require considerable leeway in any reading with לכל to find an image other than of the fool's heart itself muttering

---

[1] Notably, אמר is rendered using λογίζομαι nowhere else in the Septuagint. It is probably simplest to assume that G originally had something like καὶ λέγει τὰ πάντα ἀφροσύνη ἐστίν, which became καὶ λογιεῖται πάντα ἀφροσύνη ἐστίν through an error (cf. McNeile, 165). Goldman supposes that the translator might have found a relative particle in his source-text, but it seems more likely that ἃ was introduced when the sentence was re-worked to better accommodate λογιεῖται: S is not an independent witness, and there is no other evidence for אשר. The rendering ἀφροσύνη (contrast 10.6) is probably original, and conditioned by an assumption that כל is 'everything', not 'everyone'.

aloud to everybody. This is an obstacle also to reading הכל but understanding 'and he says "everyone is a fool"'. Although it is not perhaps the most interesting, therefore—and is certainly not the only possible understanding—the most straightforward construal is that found in T, which has read הכל but taken it to be the subject of אמר, not part of the speech's content. Accordingly, I have adopted that here.

10.4-10c

Bad Leadership

(10.4) If the urge to assume authority comes over you, do not give up your place—for self-restraint will avoid great sins.

(10.5) There is a problem I have seen beneath the sun, looking like a mistake that has got away from whoever is in charge: (10.6) when the obtuse man has been set in many high places, then rich people will dwell in lowliness; (10.7) I have seen underlings on horses, and princes walking like underlings on the ground.

(10.8) Digging a pit, he might fall into it, and a snake might bite him when he breaks through a wall; (10.9) quarrying stones he might be carved up by them, when chopping timbers be endangered by them—(10.10a-c) if the blade takes a deflection and he messes up his own face—and yet he might command armies.

Commentary

An initial admonition against taking charge, which formally belongs with the preceding sequence of short sayings, marks the start of a digression which interrupts Qohelet's statements about wisdom in order to pick up another aspect of the story in 9.14-18: the failure of leadership that it reflects. He describes a problem that looks to him like an instance of whoever is in charge slipping up: the proper order of society has been undermined, because the fool (who is perhaps that person in charge) has been allowed to occupy the upper reaches, squeezing out even the rich. Correspondingly, the lowliest in status can be observed riding and princes walking, each taking the role of the other—although Qohelet does not claim that they actually have traded places, or that this exchange is universal. The problem in 10.5-7 seems essentially, then, to be that neglect, arising from folly at the top, can lead to a levelling-down of society. In 10.8-10, on the other hand, the issue is more probably that someone—perhaps even the obtuse man of 10.6 again—can be both accident-prone and powerful (although the text is so difficult, especially in vv. 9-10, that it is hard to be sure just what Qohelet is claiming). If we are supposed to draw some more general point behind the admonition in 10.4, therefore, it is perhaps that when bad leadership can cause great problems, and when even the most hapless seem not to be disqualified, nobody should volunteer potentially to become the sort of person who gets things wrong in 9.18 (which likewise uses the vocabulary of 'sinning' in Hebrew).

Given this general context, I doubt that we are supposed to see a reference to God in 10.5, or to understand that Qohelet is talking about consequences that flow from some divine error or oversight— and such a reference would, in any case, sit uncomfortably beside his characterizations of God elsewhere. An understanding like that is found very early, however: Jerome says that his Hebrew teacher understood the text to be talking about God, from whom errors *seem* to come (an interpretation of the 'looking like').

10.4] Qohelet's turn to a new topic is marked more formally in 10.5, when he declares, as often before, that he has seen something, so that 10.4 appears to belong to the preceding sequence, with its loose style reminiscent of sentence-literature. It is probably to be understood, however, in terms of the new topic, and so marks a point of transition at which the theme of what will follow adopts the form of what has gone before. Qohelet's 'I have seen' statements do not always mark a break (e.g., 2.24; 5.17; 8.9; 10.7). Ogden, 'Variations', 32, tries to link the verse thematically with what precedes, by talking about 'an irate, and thus foolish, ruler', and characterizing the advice in terms of wise and unwise behaviour, but that is to impose a link, not find one (and it has significant consequences for Ogden's own reading of 10.20 as an elaboration of the ideas in 9.17-18).

This verse begins, literally, 'if the spirit of the ruler/ruling should come up upon you', and in a line of interpretation that goes back at least to Rashbam, modern translations and commentaries have generally understood it, in fact, to be a free-standing admonition: you should stand your ground if you have incurred the anger of a ruler, since even great offences may be pardoned if he can be placated. RSV is fairly typical: 'If the anger of the ruler rises against you, do not leave your place, for deference will make amends for great offences'. There is no indication, however, of any such understanding among the ancient versions. Both Jerome and the Targum instead understood the situation to be that of an unhealthy 'inspiration', and the advice to be that one should resist the dominance of an evil, worldly spirit—although Jerome reports another Jewish interpretation, that one should not abandon one's existing virtues if promoted to a position of authority, and this is the sense presumed throughout the various interpretations offered in the Midrash Rabbah. Rashi later thinks in terms of a divine inspection: God's spirit comes upon a person to judge and punish them.

Broadly speaking, what differentiates these approaches is their understanding of what it is for a spirit to be 'upon' someone. The interpretation in terms of a ruler's anger leans on passages like Judg 8.3, where the spirit of the men of Ephraim 'slips off from on' Gideon, meaning that they cease to be angry with him, or 2 Chr 21.16, where God stirs up the 'spirit' of the Philistines and Arabs 'upon' Jehoram, causing them to invade Judah. The other interpretations see here the widely attested use of spirits being 'upon' people in the sense that those people are endowed with authority (e.g. Num 11.29; Isa 42.1) or inspired (Num 24.2; Isa 11.2; not always in a good way, cf. Num 5.14; 1 Sam 16.16). Sometimes, of course, it is difficult to say which sense is in play elsewhere: God occasionally stirs up the spirits of one group against another (e.g. 2 Chr 21.16; Jer 51.1, 11), which seems to mean, in essence, that he inspires an animosity. On the whole, however, it seems that inspiration is by far the more common implication, and that preponderance gives some weight to the earlier interpretations: the Hebrew may well be ambiguous in the first part of the verse, but, as the very witness of the versions shows, it is not most naturally read as a reference to some ruler being angry, any more than the close of the verse is most naturally read as a reference to some remission of sins.

It is more likely that 'the spirit of the ruler' here is, as Symmachus seems to suggest in his translation, a way of describing the urge to take control, which Qohelet believes should be avoided: anybody in the grip of such inspiration should sit tight if they want to avoid committing the disastrous errors to which it might lead them. The language may be playful, and the contrast with self-restraint associates this urge with other damaging passions (see, e.g. Prov 14.30). The 'ruler', incidentally, is not necessarily a king, and although the

Hebrew word is often used in a political sense, it can in principle refer to any exercise of authority (as perhaps in 9.17, where Qohelet spoke recently of ordering fools around).

10.5] The verse begins in much the same way as 5.12 and 6.1, which are both places where Qohelet uses the stories of individuals to illustrate what he takes to be much bigger problems. The main difference here, in formal terms, is that he qualifies his description of the problem using a preposition: what he sees is 'like' or 'as' an error (the word that Qohelet uses for 'error' was employed previously in 5.5, and implies inadvertence or carelessness). This qualification means that although he could be understood as saying directly that the following problems result from mismanagement (as when we might say in English that something 'looks like trouble'), he could also just be suggesting a resemblance—they just look to him very much like the sort of things that happen when someone in charge takes their eye off the ball.

10.6] Qohelet probably begins by talking about 'the obtuse man' rather than 'obtuseness' or 'folly' (see the notes). The first word of the verse could be vocalized to give a sense that the ruler has actually set this fool up (which is probably how Aquila took it), rather than that he has 'been set', and it may also have some connotation of permission: the fool has been allowed on to the heights. It is not wholly clear in any case, though, just what this means: the Hebrew term for 'heights' more often refers to the heavens (which is how the Targum understands it here), and it is difficult to identify any clear use of it simply to imply social status (see the notes at 5.7 on the similar issues surrounding 'high'). It is also hard to determine whether Qohelet is talking about 'many' heights or 'great' heights. The 'lowliness' of the rich, on the other hand, may be a reference to their degradation, but in the only other place where the noun is used (Ps 136.23) it refers to the poor condition of the Israelites before God rescues them, rather than specifically to some social position.

There is an obvious contrast between 'high' and 'low', therefore, but this is not self-evidently a description of society turned upside down, and several other factors strengthen a suspicion that something else may be at stake. In the first place, just as the initial verb could be vocalized to give more than one sense, so the final word in the verse can be vocalized to give more than one tense, and the ancient versions are almost unanimous in their support for reading it in a way that distinguishes the two verbs: the fool 'has been set', but the wealthy 'will sit'. Those very actors, moreover, make an unlikely pair: apart from the obvious fact that folly and prosperity are not opposites, which has provoked much ingenuity among commentators, we are presented with the singular fool occupying multiple positions, while multiple rich people are to occupy a single position.

I take the point to be not that the fool and the rich have simply traded their proper positions, but that in a situation where the fool has occupied all the high ground, even rich people will find themselves living in the low. It is tempting to speculate that there is a reference here to desirable property on the high ground of a city (cf. perhaps Isa 26.5-6), but in any case, the issue is one of displacement, not replacement. Qohelet will move on to specifics in the next verse, after another 'I have seen'. What he first identifies here is a more general issue, which apparently constitutes the 'problem' of 10.5: the fool has been allowed to squeeze out even the rich, pushing everybody into the same bad place.

10.7] This verse is more clearly a nod towards a much older and broader literary tradition of writing about 'the world turn'd upside down', which singles out specific reversals of status or instances of bizarre behaviour in order to exemplify a deeper social or cosmic malaise. The most famous examples come from Egyptian literature, where it has long been recognized as a particular *topos* (see Luria, 'Die Ersten werden die Letzen sein'). There are comparable descriptions, however, in some Mesopotamian texts and, closer to home, in the 'Balaam inscription' from Deir ʿAllā in the Jordan valley: the motif is most commonly associated with literary predictions, and it may have left a mark on Hebrew prophetic literature as well (see Weeks, 'Predictive and Prophetic', 40-42). We find a more tongue-in-cheek depiction in Prov 30.21-23, which begins with the image of a slave becoming king, but which does not reflect some genuine belief that the world will collapse when someone worthless gets a meal, or a rejected woman finds a husband.[1]

---

[1] Toy, *Proverbs*, comments that 'the tone seems to be humorous or whimsical', and McKane, in his own commentary, sees 'a species of satire'. Van Leeuwen, 'Proverbs 30:21-23', rejects this understanding as 'an imposition of modern social

The common understanding of these texts, that observations of the improbable or improper reflect some more basic, but less visible problem, is made explicit by Qohelet, who spoke in v. 5 of the problem or 'mistake' that they seem to represent. That mistake was characterized in the last verse as a sort of social levelling caused by the elevation of the fool, which has driven everyone into the same position, and now he adduces an example of that levelling: slaves or servants are riding, and princes walking. Again, this is not, we should observe, expressed in terms of a specific reversal, and Qohelet does not say that the servants are riding their masters' horses, or that princes are being treated like servants. The issue is not so much that people have traded places with each other, as that the visible distinctions between them have disappeared, and with them the proper ordering of society. Bickerman, *Four Strange Books*, 164, sees a reference to 'slaves who, becoming rich, mount horses', but it may be too precise to understand this as a disdain for social climbing: it is not clear even that the servants have ceased to be servants.[2]

10.8] There are marked resemblances to Pss 7.16-17 (ET 7.15-16); 9.16 (ET 7.15); 35.7-8; Prov 26.27; and Sir 27.26, which also feature people falling into holes that they have dug themselves, and Krammer, 'Ben Sira als Tradent', sees the transmission of a proverb in the wide distribution of this motif. In those other places,

---

attitudes and customs upon an ancient text' (600), principally because of its links to the tradition found in other texts. I think that, on the contrary, the humour lies in this very application of cosmic concerns to increasingly banal but unexpected events, and that the writer may indeed be satirizing the motif.

[2] Hurowitz, 'ABL 1285 and the Hebrew Bible', 16-17, sees a link with the complaint in a petition to the Assyrian king, that 'People pass my house, the mighty on palanquins, the assistants in carts, (even) the juniors on mules, (and) I on my feet!' (K 4267/*ABL* 1285, rev. 18-20; cf. Parpola, 'The Forlorn Scholar', 265). This embodies a similar assumption that people use transport befitting their social station. I am not convinced, however, that there is any real correspondence here either to the levelling observed by Qohelet, or to the reversal found in other texts. The name of the sender has been lost from the first line of the tablet, but, in his edition, Parpola attributes the petition with some certainty to one Urad-Gula, whose problems with the king are known from other texts, and although it does, to be sure, contain various literary allusions, this scholar's complaint is not that society is disordered, but that his fall from favour with the palace prevents him from assuming (or displaying) anything close to his proper place in society.

however, the point is that the digger may be, in Hamlet's words, 'hoist with his own petard', and in the Psalms the pit is explicitly a trap, created by the wicked man, or by enemies who then fall into it themselves. The reference to the biting snake has no such close parallel, although it is reminiscent of Amos 5.19, where a man escapes to his house after fleeing first a lion and then a bear, only to be bitten by a snake when he leans against the wall. By linking the two incidents, however, Qohelet makes it clear immediately that he is talking about accidents, and not about either carelessness or the ironic fate of those who dig holes to trap others: while it is just possible that someone might be able to spot and avoid a snake by dismantling a wall very tentatively, it would be hard to say that they were really at fault if they were unlucky enough to encounter one while working normally. What makes the incidents extraordinary here is that they are compounded—and in this respect, as elsewhere in these verses, my understanding differs from that of other commentators. I take this not to be a list of accidents that might happen to just anyone, raising issues of unpredictability or unpreparedness, but a sequence of accidents that illustrate the haplessness of someone who may exercise authority even when everything that can go wrong for them has gone wrong. Of course, social distinctions at the time might well have made it unlikely that a potential leader would actually have been digging his own ditches or cutting his own stones, but by depicting him as the unluckiest workman ever, Qohelet introduces an element virtually of slapstick.

10.9-10] Interpretation of these verses has long been influenced by a particular understanding of what is going on—a version of which is found as early as Jerome's commentary. According to this, the worker will suffer problems because the blade of his tool is blunt, not having been properly sharpened in advance, or has become blunt. He must get around this problem, the interpretation usually goes on, by becoming stronger or putting more strength into his blows. Influential though it has been, this understanding relies on attributing a series of meanings and nuances to words in the Hebrew that never elsewhere have such a sense, and the interpretation is ultimately self-supporting: each dubious translation stands only because of the other dubious translations around it. The specifics are discussed in the notes below.

More importantly, any moral that can be extracted from such a reading sits unhappily with Qohelet's other examples: holes and snakes are not avoided by proper preparation, nor the difficulties that they pose overcome by greater strength and perseverance. The reading fails, therefore, to explain the first part of what is obviously intended to be a coherent sequence. It also, in all probability, pushes the sequence too far. Verse 9 picks up from the first part of v. 8 the idea that people may be harmed by the object of their labour, not just incidentally in the course of their work, and suggests that it is the stones and wood that themselves harm the worker, perhaps even doing to him what he had intended to do to them. Since stones and wood are not actively aggressive, however, Qohelet has to explain his image at the beginning of v. 10: the damage is done because the surfaces resist the blade, causing it to jar or even to rebound. This explanation probably marks the end of the sequence itself, and the words that follow are unlikely to be about the exertion of physical strength: Qohelet uses instead a vocabulary that is strongly associated elsewhere with military or social status, and his point is that the worker may, in fact, go on to enjoy power or prestige. I take the final part of the verse to belong with what follows: it seems likely to have been the traditional interpretation that influenced the Masoretic division and punctuation.

Notes

10.4 If the urge to assume authority comes over you] Lit. 'if the spirit of one ruling comes upon you', or 'of ruling' (if we vocalize as the substantive found at Zech 9.10 and Dan 11.4; cf. Sir 13.12, and perhaps Job 25.2, where M points המשׁל as an infinitive, but the sense is likely 'rule' or 'power'). On the likely implications of a spirit being 'upon' somebody, see the commentary. Two of the versions paraphrase, with T talking of domination by the 'evil inclination', while σ' has (with the first two words retroverted from Jerome's rendering) ἐὰν πνεῦμα ἀρχοντικὸν ἐπέλθῃ σοι τοῦ τόπου σου μὴ ἐκστῇς, 'if a spirit of office comes upon you, do not give up your place'—which I take to be essentially the correct understanding. For a formal parallel to רוח המושׁל, see especially רוח הרעה in 1 Sam 16.23, which is an evil spirit, not the spirit of evil.

10.4 self-restraint] The term מרפא usually means 'healing', and when we find אין מרפא, it means that something is 'beyond healing' (e.g. 2 Chr 21.18; Prov 29.1). That sense is reflected in G ἴαμα here. There are several places, however, where 'healing' gives an odd or entirely inappropriate sense (most notably Prov 14.30; 15.4; Sir 36.28; perhaps Prov 12.8), and *HALOT, DCH* recognize two different words, I מרפא 'healing', and II מרפא 'calmness'. It is this second meaning that gives rise to σ' ὅτι σωφροσύνη παύσει ἁμαρτήματα πολλά (var. μεγάλα), 'for self-control will stop many/ great wrongs' (Jerome renders the noun as *pudicitia*, which is something like a modest reluctance or sense of propriety, and probably catches the intended nuance: the Greek and Latin words could both be used in other contexts of 'chastity'). The consistent spelling with א suggests that this מרפא should still be connected with רפא, 'heal', although ה / א confusions are sufficiently common that it might possibly be linked with רפה instead, and the hiph'il of that verb can come closer to the idea of disengaging or holding one's self back. S ܡܪܦܝܘܬܐ *mrpywt'*, 'loosening' or 'negligence', probably makes this connection, although in some manuscripts we find a variant ܐܣܝܘܬܐ *'sywt'*, 'healing'.

10.4 avoid great sins] The hiph'il of נוח is found in two forms in M, with distinct meanings. The first generally means 'give rest', occasionally with the nuance of sating anger (e.g. Ezek 16.42). The second is used of putting or leaving something somewhere, or leaving it alone; in the earlier part of this verse, Qohelet used it of 'leaving' one's place. The pointing in M links יניח here with the second form, which is the more likely in my view, but G καταπαύσει, 'put a stop to', reads it as though from the first, and this is probably the understanding of σ', Hie, V also. The two are indistinguishable in the consonantal text, so this is a matter of tradition or interpretation. There is no text-critical basis for the suggestion in *BHS* that we should read יניא, 'will frustrate', or 'restrain'.

S is again complicated: ܥܒܕܐ *'bd'*, 'works', is probably a secondary corruption, influenced by an interpretation of ܡܪܦܝܘܬܐ *mrpywt'* in terms of 'negligence'; in the variant text with ܐܣܝܘܬܐ *'sywt'* we find ܫܒܩ *šbq'*, 'leaves', instead, so that different manuscripts claim 'negligence works great sins' and 'healing remits great sins'. The variant text probably has to be taken as a whole, and we may be dealing with two different attempts to render the Hebrew (so Lane, 'Lilies', 489; contrast Kamenetzky, 199).

10.5 looking like a mistake] Lit. 'like a mistake'. On the meaning of שגגה, see the note at 5.5. G used ἄγνοια there, with a view to the context, but here has the interesting translation ἀκούσιον (which Jerome attributes to α' and θ' also): that term can be used of involuntary offences.

The prefixed -כ has been understood in various ways. Gordis, 'Asseverative Kaph', 178, argues that it should be translated 'I have seen an evil under the sun, indeed an error proceeding from the ruler', and many commentators have identified it as a *kaph ueritatis*, that is, a -כ that supposedly emphasizes the nature of what is being described (GKC §118 x; J-M §133 g), so that this would be 'truly an error'. We encountered something similar at 8.1, where -כ was probably used to speak of close proximity or approximation to a model, which is probably a better way to understand the *kaph ueritatis*, and which is broadly analogous to such English expressions as 'he seems like a nice man', or 'this looks like trouble'. Here, on the other hand, the question should not be approached without an eye to the broader syntactic context, and in several other places where -כ is used after ראה it clearly has the sense 'perceive something to look like something else': see Judg 9.36; 2 Sam 18.27; Jer 30.6. I have translated in a way that preserves the apparent ambiguity. If Qohelet does mean, though, that this looks like an error but is actually not, then he does not say so clearly, or say what it really is. If we are supposed to understand a statement of resemblance rather than of estimation, then the point would probably have to be that what follows is analogous to the sort of mistake that a ruler makes.

The text of σ' is attested as ἐν ἀγνοίᾳ, raising the possibility that Symmachus read -ב here, instead of -כ. It is no less likely, however, that he is paraphrasing, and that ἔστι κακόν...ἐν ἀγνοίᾳ ἐξελθὸν means 'there is an evil...(that has) gone out by mistake'. The reading בפתגמא דשלותא, '*in* a matter of error', is also found in the T tradition, where it is plausibly just a simple error, although it too could be based on such a variant in the Hebrew, and it is hard to say whether the -ב found in a number of Hebrew manuscripts (see de Rossi, Miletto) preserves such an earlier variant or simply reflects the influence of T.

10.5 that has got away from] Or 'that gets away from'. A variant pointing as yiqtol is attested in Loevy, *Libri Kohelet*, 23, but manuscripts of M usually point יצא as a participle (on the vocalization, see Schoors, *The Preacher* I, 98), and this is supported by σ' ἐξελθὸν and Hie, V *egrediens*. Marshall thinks that α' and θ' had ἐξερχόμενον, which would also support M, but this is a very speculative restoration based on what Jerome says, and it *presupposes* a participial form. The reading of G is complicated. Rahlfs and Gentry have ὃ ἐξῆλθεν, 'which went out', but although this is attested by Syh ܕܢܦܩܬ *dnpqt*, most manuscripts lack any relative pronoun, and *BHQ* apparently takes G* to have been ἐξῆλθεν. Even ὃ ἐξῆλθεν would suggest that the translator read יצא as qatal rather than as a participle, and without a relative that construal would seem all but certain. If just ἐξῆλθεν is G*, furthermore, then the translator apparently found a Hebrew text without -ש, in which the evil, 'like an error, went out from a ruler'. That is not impossible, but it is more likely that ὃ simply dropped out in G manuscripts through a simple error.

Goldman wishes to link this verse with v. 4, adopting the common understanding of the latter as an admonition against abandoning one's position in the face of a ruler's anger. On that reading, Qohelet now describes such an exit as an evil: 'There is an evil which I have seen under the sun: indeed, the inadvertence of leaving the ruler'. This is ingenious, but even if we accept that v. 4 should be understood in that way, it would seem strange to characterize running away either as 'an evil which I have seen under the sun', or as a שגגה. When he speaks elsewhere of seeing something bad beneath the sun, furthermore, in 5.12 and 6.1, this is a way in which Qohelet introduces a new topic.

Goldman does succeed, however, in drawing attention to the fact that יצא מלפני describes departure from the presence of somebody without any further nuance: it is only from the context that we appreciate a distinction between fire coming directly from God to consume a burnt offering in Lev 9.24, and simpler statements about, for instance, Cain leaving God's presence in Gen 4.16, or Mordecai leaving the king in Esth 8.15. It is clear that the expression need not specifically imply that what is leaving must also have been sent out. In that case, it is interesting to ask in just what way an inadvertent error might יצא מלפני someone, and I think the most probable image is of something slipping away without being noticed, so that it is no longer seen.

10.5 whoever is in charge] Lit. 'the one having power'. The Aramaic word שליט is used adjectivally to indicate that somebody has rights or authority, and as a substantive to describe rulers or officials of various sorts (see Hurvitz, *Lexicon*, 234-36). We have encountered both uses in Ecclesiastes, at 8.8 and 7.19, along with the cognate verb שלט in the qal at 2.19 and 8.9, where it was used of exercising authority, and in the hiph'il at 5.18 and 6.2, where it referred to God granting a capacity to enjoy what one has. It is not surprising, therefore, to find that G translates it as τοῦ ἐξουσιάζοντος, 'the one who has power', while the double translation in σ', τοῦ ἐξουσιάζοντος ἄρχοντος, 'the ruler in charge', equally avoids identifying this as a reference simply to the king or ruler of a land: the term emphasizes authority and capacity rather than status. Qohelet is saying that what he sees in the following verses looks very much like a blunder on the part of whoever is supposed to stop such things.

10.6 the obtuse man] The only reason to suppose that סכל might ever have meant 'folly', rather than 'fool', is to be found in 10.3, where G renders the term using ἀφροσύνη. We have already seen reasons to suppose, however, that the Greek has been re-worked to take account of an error in that passage, presumably without reference to the Hebrew, so its value as evidence is limited. In this verse, all the ancient translations understand a reference to a fool (including α', who has ἔδωκεν τὸν ἄφρονα, 'he has set the fool', and probably T, which speaks of 'foolish Edom'). M, however, points the word as הַסֶּכֶל, in contrast to the normal סָכָל. If this is intended to mean 'folly', as seems likely, then the interpretation may have been driven by perceptions that the parallel term עשירים is plural, and that it is difficult for one fool to occupy many high places. At the very least, those considerations militate against Schoors' idea (*The Preacher* I, 220), presented more cautiously in his commentary, that the versions each understood the Hebrew to be saying 'folly' but meaning 'fool', *abstractum pro concreto* as he puts it, and it is likely that 'fool' is the intended meaning (so similarly Salters, 'Textual Criticism', 58). Kamenetzky, 239, would improve the contrast by emending, speculatively, to מסכן, and Ginsberg, *Studies*, 36, believes that מסכן would have been the proper translation of an Aramaic original יהיב מסכנא, which has been misread as יהיב סכלא.

10.6 in many high places] M points במרומים with an article, but if it is supposed to be '*the* heights', we should expect an article on רבים also. Such a lack of agreement is found from time to time (cf. especially הגוים רבים in Ezek 39.27), but in this context it means that there is nothing in the consonantal text to indicate the presence of an article at all. Along with the simpler parallel בשפל (which is also pointed with an article in M), the lack of agreement has led some scholars to take רבים with ועשירים instead, so that Qohelet is talking about 'great/aged and rich' people, and Salters, 'Textual Criticism', 59, would even restore a ו- before רבים. Although it goes against the accents, such a reading or understanding might have underpinned the vocalization, but G has no article with either במרומים or בשפל, and it is simpler to suppose that none was originally intended. That means that we do not have to reject the 'many high places' of M, which is the easier understanding in the absence of a conjunction, but the text is ambiguous, and T seems to show an awareness of both the possible construals by translating רבים twice (cf. Carasik, 'Double Translation', 220-21). Kamenetzky, 239, would get around the problems by emending רבים to רכבים and placing it after עבדים in v. 7, to give servants 'riding' on horses: this is attractive, but drastic.

A different sort of discordance, the singular שפל *versus* the plural מרומים, has led a number of commentators to emend the text here. Ehrlich, for example, would read במרום מרבים for במרומים רבים, comparing the use of מרום מראשון in Jer 17.12 and taking the sense to be that the position is 'out of the reach of' the many; Galling 1940 (cf. 'Kohelet-Studien', 284) emends to במרום ונדבים and deletes ועשירים, so that the fool sits in a high place while it is nobles who are low; *BHS* regards במרומים רבים as the product of dittography, and would read just במרום. There is little versional support for emendation,[3] however, and although σ' does have the singular κείμενον ἄφρονα ἐν ὕψει μεγάλῳ, 'a fool set in a great height', which is followed (cf. Cannon, 197) by V *positum stultum in dignitate sublimi*, 'a fool placed in high dignity', this is most likely a paraphrase.[4] Both those versions, incidentally, take the characters in this verse as the objects of the preceding 'I have seen', which is why they are in the accusative.

As to the sense of מרומים רבים, it is hard to exclude the possibility that Qohelet is talking about 'great heights' rather than 'many heights', but that connotation of רב is less common, and the very use of the plural מרומים would seem to indicate that plurality is an issue here.

---

[3] The reading of α' here is attested as ἐν ὑψώμασι μεγάλοις, 'in great heights'. Marshall regards μεγάλοις as an assimilation to G, noting that α' elsewhere uses πολύς for רב (although cf. Ps 39[40].11), but, in any case, the noun is plural.

[4] Some manuscripts of S have a singular, but this is probably just through loss of the plural-marker seyame, which is attested in others.

10.6 rich people] The subsequent reference to rulers has led many commentators to suppose that 'wealthy' must have some connotation either of wisdom or of power in this context, and Barton talks about 'men of ancestral wealth, who were regarded as the natural associates of kings'. Some support for the latter may be found in 10.20, where מלך and עשיר stand in parallel, and Dahood, 'Qoheleth and Recent Discoveries', 314-16, talks at length about the political power of the mercantile class in the Phoenician city-states. It seems reasonable to assume that Qohelet did, in fact, associate wealth with power, much as people might in almost any era, but that does not mean that we should simply treat the term as a virtual synonym for 'ruler' here, and the choice of עשירים is no less striking simply because it could have implications beyond just the possession of money.

Looking to the contrast between foolish and wealthy which is often presumed here, Piotti, 'Il Rapporto', draws on associations of wisdom with wealth in Proverbs and elsewhere to suggest that these wealthy should be considered wise, and Schöpflin, 'Political Power', 31, suggests less cautiously that Qohelet must have considered all rich people righteous and 'blessed' by definition. Piotti does also make a case that its varied connotations enable 'wealthy' to stand in contrast to both the fool and the servant, but I think it is simpler to suppose that Qohelet does not actually intend to present the fool and the rich as opposites: see the commentary.

10.6 will dwell] Or 'will sit', 'will be located'. The clauses in 10.6-7 are often translated as though they all relate to the same situation in the same way: the idiot is set up, the rich sit down, servants ride, and princes walk. There is significant variation between them, however, and that begins straight away. In the second part of this verse, σ′ πλουσίους δὲ ταπεινοὺς καθημένους, 'but rich people sitting lowly', uses a participle, as in the first where it has κείμενον; cf. Hie *sedentes*, 'sitting' (V uses a construction with the infinitive *sedere*). However, the consonants ישבו have been vocalized as yiqtol in M, and also apparently by G καθήσονται, 'will sit', T, and S (if it is not just taking its cue from G). This is despite the fact that נתן was qatal in the first clause, and was read as such by the same versions—which might consequently have been expected to vocalize ישבו as qatal too. That they have not, would seem to suggest that they all see a distinction here between the setting up of the fool, which is something that has happened already, and the sitting of the rich in lowliness, which is something that will, or may, happen against that background.

This distinction between the clauses is reinforced, perhaps, by the other differences between them—the article on סכל but not on עשרים, the singular fool and plural wealthy, the plural heights and the singular lowliness—and this may have guided the vocalization. If the versions are right and we should read two different tenses here, then the first clause is best understood as circumstantial: note the similar changes of tense in, e.g., Amos 3.8 or Isa 40.8 ('When the grass has withered, the flower faded, then the word of our God will stand forever').

10.6 in lowliness] The noun שֵׁפֶל only occurs in biblical Hebrew here and at Ps 136.23 (although see 12.4 also). In both places, the term might mean 'low place', which would give a better parallel to מרום, and Jastrow offers some very slight evidence of it being used as a substitute for שפלה in later Hebrew. S ܒܡܘܟܟ bmwkkʾ, on the other hand, substitutes a word that explicitly connotes 'humiliation'.

10.7 underlings on horses] De Rossi notes that two Hebrew manuscripts have רכבים, 'riding', which would provide a parallel with הלכים, but which has probably been inserted for just that reason. T has the cognate רכבין here, and has probably inspired that addition, but it is the only ancient version to have a verb at all.

10.8 Digging] Or 'Someone digging'. The article in G ὁ ὀρύσσων is unexpected, since there is no corresponding article before καθαιροῦντα, and there is no article in M. McNeile, 165, suspects a doubling of the omicron, perhaps under the influence of ὁ ὀρύσσων in Prov 26.27 (which has had a significant influence elsewhere in this verse on manuscripts in the G tradition) or Sir 27.26, but it is not improbable that the translator, whether or not he found an article in his Hebrew text, is trying to impose here the understanding that only one actor is involved in the sequence that follows. That is an understanding which I share. Qohelet does not specify a subject (syntactically, the participle in each clause is the subject), and it is possible to see a series of potential calamities that may afflict different people: one thing may happen to someone digging a pit, another to someone else breaking through a wall, and so on. Indeed, this has become the most common interpretation of these verses, but it gives a much better sense, I think, to see a series of circumstantial clauses or protases, with וחילים יגבר serving as the apodosis. An initial article would have clarified this structure, and I suspect that G does, in fact, reflect the original reading: ה- could readily have dropped out before ח and under the influence of the subsequent participles, especially if the sequence was already being understood differently. It is also possible, however, that all the participles were indefinite from the outset, and even that Qohelet is referring back to the כסל of 10.6: the text could be translated 'if/when he digs'.

10.8 a pit] גוּמָץ (and a related verb גמץ) are known from Aramaic, but not used elsewhere in Hebrew. The discussions around its origin are helpfully summarized in Bianchi, 'Teologia della prova', 111-12, but the sense is undisputed.

10.8 might fall...might bite...might be carved up...might command] In the Hebrew, the yiqtol verbs could express a simple sequence of future tenses (he *will* do these things), and G translates accordingly, but they could also express the idea that these things happen repeatedly (whenever he digs a hole he falls into it), or a modal nuance (these things *could* happen). I think the last is in play here, and we should not translate the text as an assertion that anyone who digs a pit will fall into it, etc., as does the RSV. My translation, though, is intended more specifically to express a concessive/conditional construction: he *might* be unlucky, but he still gets to be in charge, or *even if* he is unlucky, he still does so. The Hebrew is probably not constructed directly that way itself (we might expect an initial conjunction, or a particle such as כי, cf. Hab 3.17-18); rather, I think, it makes the point principally through the contrast in sense between the last of these clauses and those that have gone before. Attempts to align its sense with those others make the last clause of the verse the climax of the sequence instead, contributing to what I consider to be the mis-division of the text.

10.8 into it] M בו is supported by all the versions, but a significant number of G manuscripts have εἰς αὐτόν, 'into it', rather than ἐν αὐτω, 'in it'. McNeile, 165, again suspects the influence of Prov 26.27; Sir 27.26, but it may just be that εἰς αὐτόν is better Greek here.

10.9 quarrying] The verb נסע may simply be used of pulling things up or out, but the similar use of the hiphʿil at 1 Kgs 5.31 (ET 5.17) is in connection with quarrying stones for the foundation of Solomon's temple, so the sense may be more technical here; cf. Bianchi, 'Qohelet 10,8-11', 112.

10.9 carved up] Elsewhere in biblical Hebrew, we only find uses of a verb עצב with reference to emotional, not physical, pain. This is essentially true in later usage as well, and can be extended to the various nouns that are related to the verb, and although it has associations with childbirth in Gen 3.16 and 1 Chr 4.9, even in those passages it seems likely that the connotation is of prolonged and difficult labour, rather than of physical pain or injury in particular. This restriction is picked up by G διαπονηθήσεται, which would classically refer to 'being worked hard', but is found in Hellenistic usage with a specific nuance of being upset or annoyed. A reference to actual harm or injury, though, would clearly fit the context much better, and the other versions have responded accordingly. Hie *dolebit* and S ܢܬܟܐܒ *ntkʾb* (var. ܢܬܟܟܒ *nttkb*) both employ verbs that can represent mental grief or anxiety, but that can also be extended to cover physical aches and pains. The attributions of the Hexaplaric versions are muddled here in Syh, but the readings μετατιθῶν λίθους σπασθήσεται ἐν αὐτοῖς, 'someone moving stones around will get a strain from them', and μετεωρῶν λίθους κακωθήσεται, 'someone lifting stones will be harmed', are probably to be assigned to α′ and σ′ respectively (see Marshall), and these both show a similar tendency. Jerome, indeed, groups them together when he discusses them in his commentary, and says that both translators understood *qui transfert lapides dilacerabitur in eis*, 'he who moves stones will be torn by them', commenting that *postea tormenta patietur*, 'later he will suffer agonies'—this interpretation probably comes from taking the verb σπάω, used by α′, in the sense 'tear apart'; Aquila himself more probably understood a reference to straining or wrenching a muscle.

It would not be impossible to go down the same route as all these, and to assume that Qohelet is employing עצב, 'grieve, be aggrieved', in a way that is simply not attested elsewhere. Even if we do so, however, that yields a sense that fits the context but seems very weak: straining oneself lifting a stone, or being damaged in some other vague and unspecified way, is simply not on a par with falling into ditches or being bitten by hidden snakes—and that is an argument also against the speculative emendation to יעצר, proposed by Kamenetzky, 293, which would have someone merely 'hindered' by carrying stones. The other option is to set aside עצב in the sense 'be aggrieved' altogether, and to look at some alternative meanings. Driver, 'Supposed Arabisms', 117, in fact distinguished three separate roots עצב, with the first meaning 'grieved', the second 'cut to shape' and the third 'toiled', while a later study by Kottsieper ('Die Bedeutung', 216-17) finds four: I 'form, shape'; II 'bind'; III 'be angry, aggrieved'; IV 'cut, pierce' (he acknowledges that the second is not actually used in biblical Hebrew). More recently *DCH* has also distinguished four, broadly along the same lines, but with different numbers, and with some particular instances classified differently—this verse is the only example it gives for 'cut', while Kottsieper would include 1 Kgs 1.6 as a metaphorical instance (*DCH* groups the apparent sense 'rebuke' there with the broader use 'grieve'). Without getting involved in the minutiae, we can recognize, at least, that several different potential meanings exist for עצב, and that we are not confined to ideas of 'pain' here—indeed, this was probably understood by T, where an interpretation of the verse in terms of idolatry has undoubtedly been influenced by the use of עצב as a noun in connection with images, and as a verb in relation to making images (cf. Jer 44.19), and the targumist has also managed to draw in the sense of 'binding'.

How far some of the distinctions would have been recognized by the original readers, however, is uncertain, and even if they have different origins, I am not convinced that the notions of cutting and of shaping, in particular, would have been regarded as distinct. If we are right to think that Qohelet is talking about quarrying, then his point is perhaps not simply that the worker may find himself cut or injured by the stones (which is the way Kottsieper understands the verb), but that they may do to him what he was trying to do to them: stones would have been cut to shape before being detached from the rockface, and the notion of 'forming' or 'shaping' might be uppermost. It is not clear whether the accident that Qohelet has in mind, however, is simply an implied but unstated encounter with a falling rock or a sharp edge, or whether he has in mind the same problem that will afflict the woodworker who comes next, in which case it may be his tool, rather than the rocks themselves directly, that causes the damage.

10.9 by them] We might expect בהם to match the subsequent בם if it were original, but since אבנים would usually be feminine (although cf. 1 Sam 17.40), it seems likely that it is an error for בהן, perhaps attributable to the 'masculine' form of אבנים (cf. Delsman, 'Inkongruenz', 30-31, who suspects the same has caused similar mismatches in 11.8 and 12.1). Both בם and בהם are found elsewhere in the book—the former in 3.12, the latter in 2.5; 8.11; 12.1—but it is impossible to say whether the variation is original.

10.9 chopping timbers] עצים can be any pieces of wood, including firewood (e.g. Zech 12.6), and it is easy to think in terms of somebody splitting logs with an axe here. The context of construction and deconstruction in the previous actions, though, suggests that Qohelet may have in mind something more like the timbers used in building (e.g. Lev 14.45), or perhaps the cutting down of trees (e.g. Deut 19.5). The verb used here, בקע, is used (in the pi'el) to describe the cutting of sticks in Gen 22.3, but also the chopping up of a wooden cart in 1 Sam 6.14, so it does not offer a clue to the nature of the 'wood'; since both the sticks and the cart are to be burned, however, it does perhaps imply 'chopping up' rather than the preparation of planks or beams. A significant number of Hebrew manuscripts have a conjunction before the verb, reading ובוקע,[5] and conjunctions are found also in S, Hie, V: this is probably a secondary facilitation, but the wide distribution suggests that it may have arisen early in the Hebrew text tradition.

10.9 be endangered] The verb סכן is not found elsewhere in biblical Hebrew with the sense 'be in danger' or 'be endangered', although this meaning is well-attested in later Hebrew and Aramaic, and it has been adopted here by G and Hie. Rather differently, S has ܠܐܐ ܒܗܘܢ *lʾ bhwn*, 'is tired by them', with a variant ܬܒܪܗ ܢܗܘܐ *tbrh nhwʾ*, 'it will be his/its breaking' (the reading ܬܒܪܗ *trbh* in the Leiden edition is surely a misprint, and the editor cites it elsewhere as *tbrh* when he suggests that it is an alternative rendering of the Hebrew).[6] It is difficult to judge T, which is paraphrasing extensively, but it probably renders in terms of 'burning', while V has *uulnerabitur*, 'will be wounded'. Driver, 'Problems and Solutions', 239, considers the last of these to have resulted from a misunderstanding of the verb as a denominative form from שכין, 'knife' (frequently סכין in later orthography), while Kottsieper, 'Die Bedeutung', 219-20, argues that this is, in fact, the intended sense, and that the text has to be understood in terms of a root סכן, 'cut'. That is, in fact, an old interpretation, proposed as a possibility by Mendelssohn and Haupt, among others. The existence of any verb with that sense is highly questionable, however, and it is unlikely that Jerome's translation is based on anything more than considerations of context, so although the meaning it offers is attractive, and would give a good parallel to the case of the worker with stone, there are no good grounds for adopting it. It is difficult to rely on T at all here, or to judge how far S is also guessing from context, so while the implication of endangerment cannot be said to have passed unchallenged, there are, equally,

---

[5] See de Rossi, who counts 32 in Kennicott, 43 amongst his own; the variant is very widespread; cf. also Ginsburg, *Writings*, and Lavoie and Mehramooz, 'Le Texte hébreu et la traduction judéo-persane', 504. Ginsburg, *Massorah*, 1:191 (cf. 4:219, where the chapter/verse reference is misprinted as '9.1'), notes Masoretic attestation of a form ובקע, with both the conjunction and defective spelling.

[6] Lane, 'Lilies', 489. Kamenetzky 192 n. 1 suggests that it arose as a gloss on 11.3 (although he too has a misprint, citing 11.8 instead).

no good reasons to reject it. The Midrash Rabbah associates the verb with the noun סכנת, used of Abishag in 1 Kgs 1.2, 4, so interprets it as connoting a benefit of some sort, and this understanding is picked up by Rashi.

10.10 if] I take the protasis of the condition here to follow the apodosis: the worker may be injured or endangered *if* the following happens (compare, e.g., God's statement in Gen 18.28, or Reuben's in Gen 42.37). The reversal of the usual order is presumably intended to allow the statements in 10.9 to stand in parallel with those in 10.8, and this clause then to offer an explanation of the circumstances. The verbs accordingly shift to the qatal, and the construction is similar to that in Ps 63.6-7 (ET 63.5-6), 'my mouth will praise you if/when I have remembered you'. The more common construal of this verse takes וחילים יגבר to be the apodosis, which is not difficult syntactically, but which rests on an assumption that those words describe a reaction to the failure of the tool.

10.10 blade] ברזל is the word for 'iron', but it can also be used to describe the iron part of a tool (as opposed to the wooden handle in Deut 19.5), which is used for dressing stone (Deut 27.5) or cutting wood (2 Kgs 6.5-6; Isa 10.34): we might alternatively speak of the 'head' of an axe or adze.

10.10 takes a deflection] The verb קהה is found in biblical Hebrew only otherwise in Jer 31.29-30 and Ezek 18.2, where it is used in the qal to describe the way in which teeth react to eating sour grapes (traditionally translated 'set on edge' in English). In later texts, we find קהה and the Aramaic קהי/קהא (cf. S ܩܗܐ *qhʾ* here) still used with reference to teeth and to sourness, but also with causative forms used of causing someone pain or refuting their arguments by 'setting their teeth on edge' (we might perhaps speak of 'drawing their teeth').[7] The verb is also used at times for כהה, indicating tiredness or weakness. Although often translated in terms of 'bluntness' (cf. Hie, V *retu[n] sum*), notably in Jastrow, *Dictionary*, there is little evidence that it ever had that meaning in particular, and citations by the lexica of the term with that sense in Aramaic and Syriac tend to rely on the assumption that Qohelet uses it that way in this verse; it is, of course, difficult to understand elsewhere that sour grapes in any sense actually 'blunt' teeth (let alone 'numb' them, as Bartholomew would have it).

---

[7] This leads Schoors to suppose that, since a piʿel is unlikely to be intransitive, we should read an impersonal expression here, equivalent to a passive: he translates 'if somebody has blunted the axe'. It is simpler just to vocalize as qal, which may have been the way in which the verb was taken by the other versions. Fassberg, 'The Shift', 125, sees this as an instance of the piʿel taking on the role of the qal in late biblical texts, but the Masoretic pronunciation might equally have been influenced by the subsequent use of the piʿel of כהה to connote growing dull in later Hebrew: there was some interchange between the verbs. In any case, the various interpretations in the Midrash Rabbah to this verse represent the verb using the niphʿal and the nithpaʿel, and nobody seems to have been interested in assigning a transitive sense to it.

Neither the verb nor the cognate adjective is 'widely attested in Postbiblical Hebrew for iron implements', as Seow suggests (apparently on the basis of Jastrow's entry), at least with reference to anything other than this verse. There is a usage in *y. Berakot* 63a, however, which is striking because of its similar context. R. Yannai describes how, when Pharaoh had arrested Moses and they tried to cut off his head וקהת ההרב מעל צוארו של משה ונשבר, 'then the sword bounced off Moses' neck and was broken', showing that his 'neck is like an ivory tower' (Ct 7.4); R. Abyatar adds that 'the sword flew off' the neck of Moses and on to the neck of the executioner instead, killing him. It is clear that קהה is to be understood in that passage, at least, in the sense of a blade taking a deflection or bouncing off a hard surface, and it is likely that G ἐκπέσῃ reflects a similar understanding of what Qohelet is saying here: the Greek verb can be used of 'failing', but also more specifically of 'missing' or 'going off course'. The Midrash and T here understand a reference to the toughness or impenetrability of a surface, drawing a comparison with 'a sky tough as iron' that lets through no rain or dew, and that is, perhaps, a counterpart to the notion of deflection: the best way to understand the various uses of קהה is not with reference to the sharpness or bluntness of a cutting-edge *per se*, but more directly to its failure. Whether it is describing the deflection of a tool from a hard surface, the reflexive withdrawal of teeth from an acidic juice, or, correspondingly, the ability of surfaces and substances to cause such deflections, קהה refers to the way in which an edge fails to penetrate and rebounds—which may be more to do with the nature of the surface than with any fault inherent in the edge. The distinction is important, because if it does not specifically indicate 'bluntness', then קהה does not support an interpretation of Qohelet's words here in terms of a failure to prepare the tool properly, and its inability to cut may be a wholly unforeseeable consequence of, say, hitting a knot in the wood.

10.10 and he messes up his own face] Lit. 'and he disorders a face for himself'. It is difficult to establish either the text or the sense here. The majority text of M reads והוא לא פנים קלקל, which is often understood as something like 'and he has not sharpened the edge'. Setting aside the meanings of the words themselves, however, this faces the problem that לא is in the wrong position to yield any such sense: the particle negates the expression that follows it, so this would have to mean 'and he has sharpened the non-edge', or 'what is not the edge' (cf. the uses of לא פנים at Jer 2.27; 18.17; 32.33 for 'what is not the face').[8] This is a problem even for those commentators who would read פנים

---

[8] Fox is unusual among recent commentators in paying due attention to this issue, which troubled an earlier generation more: Haupt treats the problem as serious enough to justify moving אם to the beginning of this clause; see Haupt, 'Crystal-Gazing', 87. Seeking to discount the position of לא, Driver, 'Problems and Solutions', 232, points to Ps 147.10 for an analogy. That verse, however, shows no more than the use of position to nuance the negation: the psalmist is

as equivalent to לפנים with a temporal sense (or actually emend it to לפנים), and Jerome recognizes this with his rendering *non ut prius* in Hie and V—although it is probably no easier to make the text say that the sword was blunt and 'not (sharp) as previously', as he would like, than to understand 'he had not sharpened (it) beforehand' with some modern scholars.[9]

Matters are complicated by the fact that לא is not represented at all in G or S, although we do, intriguingly, find some variants amongst G manuscripts (καὶ αὐτὸς ἑαυτῷ πρόσωπον and καὶ αὐτὸς αὐτοῦ πρόσωπον) which would seem to reflect והוא לו פנים, as, possibly, could Jerome's account of the text (in his comments on v. 9) as *et faciem eius turbauerit*. This, in fact, is the 'eastern' reading referred to in *BH³*, *BHS* (it is characterized as such by the Masoretes; see Ginsburg, *Writings*, and Baer, 81), and Euringer supposed that it was read by the translator of G, with an αὐτῷ subsequently lost after αὐτὸς early in the G tradition. Despite the suggestion to the contrary by McNeile, 151, this is no less plausible than the simple loss of לא in G's source-text or of an equivalent to it subsequently in the Greek, and even if the equivalents to לו entered the G tradition through hexaplaric influence rather than as G*, they have a reasonable claim to represent an early variant.

If we are to choose between לא and לו, however, or even to reject both, we need a clearer sense of the meaning offered by each variant, and the following words פנים קלקל offer little elucidation. Apart from those who see it as temporal, most modern commentators understand פנים to refer to the 'edge' of

not trying to say that God takes no delight in the strength of the horse or the legs of a man, but that he takes delight in something which is neither of those things. Although it does not explain what it takes to be the emphasis, GKC §152 e in fact takes this verse as an example of לא standing in a strange position in order to bring another word into prominence, and that is a fair, if somewhat vague way to characterize such usage more generally—although there may be other factors involved. In Num 16.29, for example, the position of לא is probably intended to show that fulfilment of the condition would directly deny the claim made by Moses in the previous verse, by simply negating a repetition of that whole claim. To be sure, the nuances and distinctions may be subtle or slight in such cases, but general Hebrew usage offers no licence at all for treating לא פנים קלקל as though it were simply equivalent to פנים לא קלקל.

[9] Emendation to לא לפנים is mooted in *BH³* and proposed more forcefully by Driver, 'Problems and Solutions', 232, citing Budde. It would be an awkward emendation, however, since an error in copying לא לפנים would more easily have resulted in לפנים than לא פנים, and it has no versional support. In any case, even if פנים is taken as equivalent to לפנים, there remains the problem that לפנים does not usually mean 'previously' or 'beforehand', but something more like 'in times past' (as Pinker, 'Qohelet 10:10', 182, observes). Acknowledging the difficulty (unlike, e.g. Seow), Driver points to Sir 11.7. There, however, the implication is not 'previously', but 'the first thing you should do is...'. Jerome's translation again suggests an awareness of the problem.

the tool—a reference that seems curious in light of the word's use elsewhere to describe faces and surfaces. The sole justification for that understanding, in fact, is a use of פנים in Ezek 21.21 (ET 21.16), where God is talking to the prophet about a sword prepared for slaughter. The imagery is a little unclear, but the prophet and God are apparently both somehow to direct the action of this sword by clapping their hands, and v. 21 talks about going to the right or the left אנה פניך מעדות, 'whatever way your face is set'. God is apparently addressing the sword itself at this point, but the expression may amount to no more than 'whichever way you are facing', and, as Driver observes, the sword is most likely personified (see Driver, 'Problems and Solutions', 232; Driver describes as 'impossible' the suggestion that פנים might denote the 'edge' of a tool or weapon, and I am inclined to agree). This is not strong evidence, therefore, that 'face' might mean 'edge', and if there really is any technical reference to a part of the sword in Ezekiel, then it is more probably to the tip than to the edge, since we naturally take the 'direction' of a sword to be the way it is pointing. In our current context, it seems more likely that פנים must refer to the face of the worker, to the surface which is being cut, or perhaps to the 'flat' of the cutting-blade.

As for the verb קלקל, most commentators have accepted a meaning 'sharpen', but this is likewise based on little or no direct evidence. In Jer 4.24 התקלקלו is used with 'hills' as the subject, in parallel with רעשים which is most commonly used of land shaking or quaking. In that context, therefore, an intransitive form of the verb appears to describe some sort of violent motion, or the effects of that motion. The precise meaning of קלקל is less clear in Ezek 21.26 (ET 21.21, coincidentally just a few verses after the sword that we have just been discussing). Here, it describes something that the King of Babylon does to arrows in a type of divination, as he chooses which path he is to take. Arrows can be used in various ways by diviners, but it seems most likely that the king is shaking marked arrows together in a quiver, with a view to selecting one of them at random—rather like shaking dice or shuffling cards (see Jeffers, *Magic and Divination*, 190-93). From the biblical evidence alone, it would be difficult to know whether we should take Jer 4 to suggest that 'shaking' is the primary sense in Ezek 21, or Ezek 21 to suggest that 'disordering' is the primary sense in Jer 4, but the later, quite common occurrences of קלקל and cognate nouns in both Hebrew and Aramaic point very strongly to the latter: they are used to express ideas of disarrangement and of damaging disorder.[10] Were it not for the fact that most commentators have been reluctant to find such a meaning in this verse, it would seem quite unproblematic to suggest that קלקל refers primarily to disordering, or to setting outside an

---

[10] With this understanding, it does not seem necessary to disassociate the mysterious הקלקל of Num 21.5 from this root, even if it is used (disparagingly) of food. Pinker, 'Qohelet 10:10', would actually use that word to understand the text here, in terms of a battle-axe that has been blunted, has no front, and is 'worthless'.

established order—words derived from this stem are used later of refuse heaps, indeed, and the late sense of the verb is not far, perhaps, from that of 'trashing' in colloquial usage.

In an effort to hold on to a contrast between bluntness and sharpening, however, some scholars have asserted a link between 'shaking' and 'sharpening' based on a presumed similarity between the movements involved (although the resemblance may not seem very striking to anyone who has actually used a whetstone), while others have looked to unreduplicated forms of קלל, which can connote insignificance but also swiftness—and so, perhaps, the supposedly swift motions involved in sharpening a blade. There has been particular interest in the קלל of Ezek 1.7 and Dan 10.6, which is used to describe bronze that gleams or sparkles, and which is commonly understood to mean 'polished' or 'burnished'—Haupt, 'Crystal-Gazing', 87-88, indeed, even reads this back into the קלקל of Ezek 21, and claims that the king of Babylon must have been 'polishing' his arrows in order to scry with them, even though arrowheads might seem a most peculiar choice for that form of divination. The merits of that claim aside, a simple equation of 'polishing' with 'sharpening' is problematic in itself, however, even if קלל in Ezek 1 and Dan 10 actually refers to polishing, and to find a meaning 'sharpen' for קלקל necessarily involves a speculative leap *via* loose associations with the uses of a different stem. This is very hard to justify when the meaning of קלקל elsewhere is not itself really in any doubt at all, and when 'sharpen' would fit no other occurrence of the word outside discussions of this passage.

It seems self-evidently more straightforward and less speculative to assume that Qohelet is talking about 'disordering a face' here—even if we then have to work out what he might mean by such an expression—and, in fact, this is precisely how G πρόσωπον ἐτάραξεν and S ܐܦܐ ܕܠܚ *'p' dlḥ* take it (the seyame of the latter seems likely to be secondary). It is very possible that קלקל פנים is an idiom, but the context suggests that, at least at one level, it refers to the effect of a blade on a surface that is to be cut or dressed. If we read the לא of M, then Qohelet is perhaps elaborating on the failure of the blow: the tool is deflected and smashes 'what is not a surface'. I think the variant לו gives a more satisfactory sense, however, if we treat it as reflexive: the blade is supposed to 're-arrange' a surface on the stone or wood, but instead re-arranges a face (or surface) on the worker wielding it. The lack of an article or possessive pronoun on פנים suits the possibility that Qohelet is playing on the idea of two different 'faces'. Of course, this could be just an idiomatic way of saying that the worker is given a fright, but the 'danger' is more probably of an actual injury, from a rebounding axe-head.

10.10 yet he may command armies] Or perhaps more generally 'may be/ become a man of power'. In line with the idea that Qohelet is talking about the failure of a blunt blade to cut, most commentators see here a reference to the need for the worker wielding a blunt tool to exert more force or improve his strength. Neither גבר nor חיל, however, is typically used in connection with physical strength, and there is nothing in וחילים יגבר, furthermore, that explicitly indicates doing or using 'more' of anything. The most striking parallel to the expression is found in Job 21.7, where Job is talking about the wicked, and complains that they not only survive but actually reach old age and live to see their children enjoy a life of security and prosperity: גברו חיל in that verse seems to sum up the achievement of wealth and status, in line with the common use of the verb to connote the attainment of power and advantage over or among others (cf. also Ruth 2.1 איש גבור חיל, used of Boaz; 1 Sam 9.1; 1 Kgs 11.28).

In the singular, חיל denotes worth or valour, often in a military context, but it can also be used of wealth or produce. On the concept of 'a man of חיל' more generally, see the note 'gentlefolk' at 12.3. Qohelet notably, however, uses the plural חילים here, and that is also reminiscent of an expression גבור חילים that occurs four times in 1 Chr 7, where the context is military, and the term apparently an indication of rank (vv. 5, 7, 11, 40); it is, perhaps, related to the earlier use of שר החילים to describe a military commander (e.g. 2 Kgs 25.23, 26; Jer 40.7), although the use of the latter still at 2 Chr 16.4 suggests that it has not simply displaced it. In fact, we may note that biblical Hebrew generally maintains a distinction between חיל in the singular and plural that is close to that between 'force' and 'forces' in English: only in Isa 30.6 (and then only if we accept the vocalization in M) does the plural refer to anything other than military forces. Ginsburg makes this point forcefully, and although few have followed his consequent insistence that there must be some literal reference to an army here (such as is found in T and in Rashi's interpretation), it does seem very likely that Qohelet is talking, at least figuratively, in military terms.

Taking חילים as the object, both M and G καὶ δυνάμεις δυναμώσει have vocalized the verb as pi'el with a causative sense, 'strengthen' (although the pi'el is otherwise attested only in Zech 10.6, 12) and this would most naturally mean something like 'he gives power to forces/armies', in both Hebrew and Greek. S ܘܡܣܓܐ ܚܝܠܐ *wqṭyl' msg'* probably reflects the same reading of the verb, but the sense, 'he increases the slain' is odd: the translator has perhaps found or understood וחללים instead of וחילים in his source (so Kamenetzky, 230). From the consonants alone, though, the qal might also be read, as in Job 21.7, where חיל serves as an 'accusative of respect' rather than as direct object. Jerome's use of ablatives to represent the noun in both Hie *uirtutibus corroborabitur*, 'it will be strengthened by virtues', and V *multo labore exacuatur*, 'it will be sharpened by much work', suggests that he understands it in that way here, although he uses passive forms for the verb itself (taking the blade to be the subject). T, although elaborating considerably, appears more certainly to have read יגבר as qal. Whether we see a reference to making forces strong or to growing strong in respect of forces, however, it is difficult to take this as either a literal or a metaphorical statement that the man should hit his log harder: the choice and combination of terms is evocative of a social or military power that resides in status, not of dynamic exertion. The subject of the verb is nominally the man who might be injured by the axe, or perhaps any of the individuals liable to suffer accidents in the preceding verses, but it is effectively indeterminate.

10.10D-15

WISE AND FOOLISH SPEECH

(10.10d) And it is profit that makes wisdom appropriate: (10.11) if a snake may bite without hissing, then there is no profit in having a tongue.

(10.12) The words of a wise man's mouth attract favour, but the lips of a fool consume him. (10.13) The first of the words of his mouth is obtuseness, and the last thing out of his mouth is terrible mindlessness, (10.14) yet the obtuse man makes many words.

No person knows what is going to be, and who is going to explain to him what will be, following him? (10.15) The effort of fools will weary him when he merely does not know how to reach a city.

Commentary

Qohelet returns to the general topic of wisdom and folly (and to the format of formally disconnected statements), but his theme is now more specifically the speech of fools. He begins with a claim that wisdom is of value only when it yields a profit or advantage—that it has a place only when it has a point—and this is supported by an analogy with snakes: if they can bite silently, then there is no advantage in possessing a tongue. This, of course, furnishes a loose connection with the preceding 10.8, where a snake bite is one of the risks faced by the worker, but it is the reference to a tongue, and hence to speech, that Qohelet is going to pick up here. The following verses, 10.12-13, establish the point that, while the wise man wins friends and favour through his speech, the fool actively destroys himself by talking nonsense. As the beginning of 10.14 observes drily, however, this does not prevent the fool from talking—a lot. The second part of that verse seems, on the face of it, to switch to a quite different point, recalling a claim made already in 3.22 and 6.12, that nobody can know what will come after them. It is followed, however, by a further statement about fools, the point of which is probably that their laboured explanations would exhaust even somebody just seeking directions to the city, and this offers a context for the more general claim of human ignorance: fools talk a lot, but in a world where nobody can answer the most important questions, fools cannot answer even the simplest.

The aphoristic quality of the material here suggests that the author may again be re-working sayings that were already in existence, or at least seeking a way to link clever sayings of his own. Correspondingly, we need to be wary of imposing a logical sequence that may never have been intended, and it is striking, for instance, that 10.12-13 do not really pick up the central implication of the preceding statements, even though they are tied to them not just by the theme of speech, but also by references to 'mouths' and 'lips' that correspond to the 'tongue' of 10.11. We might legitimately discern, however, a certain coherence overall: if there is no point to wisdom when it delivers no advantage, then, conversely, there is also no advantage in speech without wisdom, even when, or perhaps especially when, there is a lot of it.

It will be obvious from the verse-numbering that my understanding of the text in 10.10 does not correspond to the traditional division of units, and I do not follow what has become the most common interpretation of 10.11. Both of these points are discussed in the comments and notes below, but it is important to emphasize that in each case the usual understanding has been shaped by certain assumptions about the structure or sense of the text that have led to very unnatural, and arguably impossible construals of the Hebrew. These assumptions flow in part from the way that the first clauses of 10.10 have been understood, and from a desire to find a satisfactory conclusion to what has preceded. Considerable pressure has also been exerted, however, by a belief that 10.11 is about the uselessness of snake-charming in a situation where the snake bites before it can be charmed: this interpretation introduces a temporal element that seems to correspond to the ideas about sharpening blades in advance that I have already addressed above, even if it also seems to contradict or undermine those ideas.

10.10d] The difficulties that surround this clause result in large part from attempts, ancient and modern, to read it with the preceding verses, rather than with 10.11. The verb has been vocalized as an infinitive by the Masoretes, probably in support of interpretations that depend on seeing an identification (x = y) here, and other ancient versions apparently did not read it as a verb at all. Correspondingly, translations have tended to parse the clause in a way that yields 'wisdom (is) the advantage of doing something', or 'the advantage of doing something (is) wisdom', and to translate the verb in a variety of different ways according to their understanding of the context. This gives rise to, for instance, 'wisdom (is) profitable to direct' in the AV, and 'wisdom helps one to succeed' in the RSV. Few of the many suggestions that have been made, however, offer a good sense, and those that do are generally difficult to reconcile with the Hebrew. My own understanding is that the verb has its usual, well-attested sense, and that the consonants should be read not as an infinitive but as a main verb, which gives the possible senses 'wisdom makes profit suitable' or 'profit makes wisdom suitable'. Neither of these fits well with what has preceded, where Qohelet has shown no explicit interest in wisdom, but the second fits well with 10.11. Taking the two together, the point is that wisdom is relevant to a situation only insofar as there is something to be gained from it in that situation. Having a tongue is of no use to a snake when it bites, if it can do so without hissing—although that does not mean that it will never need its tongue. By analogy, the wise will not gain an advantage from their wisdom in everything that they do, even if it is of value for some things (like speaking, as Qohelet will go on to point out).

10.11] The noun translated as 'hissing' is associated with a verb that commonly means 'whisper', and that is later used often of whispering incantations. This may be the way in which some of the early translators understood the text here: the snake bites in the absence of any incantation that might ward it off or heal the bite. The ancient versions, however, do not reflect what has come to be the dominant interpretation of this verse, and which goes back at least to Rashi. According to this, the snake bites before it can be charmed, which makes the snake-charmer useless and illustrates a general point, perhaps that 'an unused skill is wasted' (Crenshaw) or 'that no one, *not even* the skilled man, can undo damage after the fact' (Fox).

In itself, such an interpretation is not implausible, at least in general terms. There are interesting accounts of snake-charmers in nineteenth-century Egypt, who were paid to draw snakes out of houses or to cast charms on individuals that would protect or immunize them from snakebites; see Toledano, *State and Society*, 233-35. It is this sort of immunization, perhaps, that the ancient renderings of this verse in terms of incantations had in mind. We should probably not think of snake-charming in the form of entertainment here, however, or of any attempt to control a snake directly. If people ever did 'whisper' to snakes in an effort to charm them, it was at best in some attempt at mimesis, because there would almost certainly have been no perceptible reaction. Snakes cannot even hear each other hiss: they have no outer ears or eardrums, and so although they can use the conduction of low-frequency vibrations through their jawbones and an inner ear to 'hear', it is unlikely that 'whispering' would have much effect.

Correspondingly, when Ps 58.5-6 (ET 58.4-5) refers to the deaf serpent that 'shuts its ear so as not to listen to the voice of whisperers', the point is probably not that the wicked are like some exceptionally obstinate snake, but that, like snakes, they are venomous and show no sign that they have even heard enchantments intended to control them.[1] If so, we should not presume that anybody would have expected 'snake-whispering' to work, let alone that it would have been a familiar activity. This probably explains why the same verb used of whispering and enchanting can be used, at least in later Hebrew, for the hissing of snakes itself, a usage that would offer great scope for confusion if the word could simultaneously be used of 'charming' snakes. It also explains why none of the

---

[1] Forti, 'Of Snakes and Sinners' (cf. her 'על הלחש'), takes this portrayal of the wicked as snakes, and the similar language in Ps 140, to explain the background to what Qohelet is saying here: the snake represents the wicked, and thus also the foolish, but the saying can be read either with what precedes, as an affirmation of the unstoppable damage done by fools, or with what follows, making the failed snake-charmer a fool himself. I am far from persuaded that the dangerously eloquent villains of those psalms would have been associated with the fools of 10.12-13, but it is interesting that both the psalmist and Qohelet use snake imagery associated with false speech to depict the uselessness of speech.

ancient versions gives any indication that it understands 'charming' as a possible meaning of the word here. Even if some understood the verse in terms of apotropaic incantations, others clearly took 'without whispering' to mean 'in silence': Jerome makes this understanding explicit, and it is essentially the understanding of the Targum and Septuagint as well (although it is not the snake that is silent in the former). In short, we have no good reason to suppose that 'whispering' could refer to the charming of snakes or was taken to do so by early readers: the term might refer here to protective incantations, but it is simplest to suppose that Qohelet is talking about the hissing of the snake itself.

A second problem with the common interpretation of this verse is that, if the concern of the verse is really with things being done too late, or with a crisis that comes too early, then it is remarkable that there is no explicit indication of time here. The Hebrew simply means 'without', and the sense 'not yet' has to be read in, with little or no support from usage elsewhere, in order to achieve that meaning. There are other objections that might be added (see the notes), but it involves much less speculation to suppose that the first half of the verse is talking about a snake that bites in silence, and the second about possession of a tongue, than to find a reference here to snake-charming. The point seems clear enough, and matches the understanding proposed above for 10.10d: the ability of a snake to bite in silence renders possession of a tongue redundant.

Since snakes do have tongues, however, and may hiss (although not all species do), the corollary is that any noise they make is irrelevant, and this foreshadows Qohelet's comments about the speech of fools. The link is reinforced, perhaps, by the way the second part of the verse is expressed: the 'owner of a tongue' may be anybody, not just a snake. A similar expression used by Ben Sira (8.3) implies not just the ability to speak, moreover, but a proclivity to do so, and if the same implication is intended here, then Qohelet is more directly preparing the ground for what follows by claiming that there is no advantage in being talkative. In that case, the image here provides different points of contact for what precedes it and for what follows: a tongue that is both as useless as wisdom when not needed, and as useless as the speech of those who lack wisdom.

On linguistic grounds alone, it is difficult to exclude absolutely the possibility that Qohelet is referring to protective incantations. If we were to understand such a reference, however, then it would be hard to see the point here: since the snake is biting *in the absence* of incantations, this hardly reflects on the usefulness or otherwise of the enchanter. Like the snake-charmer interpretation, such a reading makes sense only if we allow an unspoken implication 'not yet'—and even then, I would venture, the sense is a poor one.

10.12-15] After 'tongue' in 10.11, we have 'mouth' and 'lips' in 10.12, but these two verses only introduce Qohelet's point, which will be made explicitly in 10.13-14a. If a snake can bite in silence, then achievement need not depend on speech. More than that, though, speech can actually prove self-destructive, and so although the wise gain through what they say, fools actively harm themselves—and there is perhaps a vivid image here of their own lips swallowing them up. This is because everything they say is nonsense, but, regardless of that fact, they speak a lot.

In a world, then, where nobody knows the answers to the big questions, and where no speech can convey what is going to happen, fools respond at exhausting, laborious length even to the most trivial query. In part because there has been a strong tendency to think that 10.14 is talking about the ignorance of fools, commentators have generally seen no clear train of thought in these verses, and many have tried to re-arrange them, but there is a visible coherence of theme here. Qohelet is not merely attacking folly, and arguably, indeed, folly itself is not his primary target. The focus, rather, is on speech, and perhaps especially on the fact that outcomes depend on the quality, not the quantity of speaking: some things may be accomplished with no sound at all, and about some things there is nothing that can usefully be said, so an outpouring of foolish words achieves nothing except to the detriment of both speaker and listener. To that extent, these verses pick up points that Qohelet has made earlier, in 5.1-6.

10.15] I have translated a little loosely here, to bring out what I take to be the point. Some difficulties in the Hebrew make it hard to discern precisely what was intended, but I understand the 'him' to be the 'person' of the preceding verse, and the issue to be that it is a bad idea even to ask fools for directions (let alone, perhaps, to endure their opinions on more substantial areas of human ignorance). That is not to say that directions to a city were necessarily straightforward themselves, which is an assumption underpinning readings that take Qohelet to be saying, rather, that fools are too stupid to find their own way to the city. In *b. ʿErubin* 53b, R. Joshua b, Hananiah tells the tale of how he once asked a young boy at a crossroads what was the best way to reach the city to which he was travelling. The boy offered two alternative routes, but when the rabbi chose the road described as 'short but long', he found himself cut off from the town by smallholdings and orchards, which forced him to turn back. If an eminent sage freely confesses such a problem, it would seem difficult to assume that, even a few centuries before, finding one's way into a city would have been regarded as so easy that only a fool could not do it. The story also highlights the wearisome problems that can arise from confusing directions.

Notes

10.10d And it is profit that makes wisdom appropriate] The meaning of this clause ויתרון הכשיר חכמה has been much debated, and Schoors offers a long list of translations that have been proposed. In line with the traditional division of the text, these have generally sought to understand Qohelet's statement in terms of the preceding description of the worker and his risks, but a significant number of them make no sense even in the context of that reading, and many commentators are forced to offer a translation of their translation.[2] To the same end, various emendations have been proposed, including Hertzberg's proposal to read הכשרון ויתרון חכמה, 'Is there an advantage and profit for wisdom?', and, more recently, the attractive suggestion of Sandoval and Akoto, 'A Note on Qohelet 10,10b', that הכשיר is an error (by metathesis) for השכיר, with the original sense being, 'the advantage of the hireling is wisdom'. Pinker, 'Qohelet 10:10', 187, less plausibly emends חכמה to המכה, 'the one who smites', in pursuit of an understanding that its wielder has to be informed in advance of his axe's deficiencies. Whether any of those actually give a better sense in context is debatable, but none enjoys any versional support.

At the heart of the problem lie the form and meaning of הכשיר, with which the ancient versions clearly struggled already. The usual text of M has הַכְשִׁיר, but the Masoretes describe the י as superfluous, implying a reading הַכְשֵׁר, to be vocalized as the hiphʿil infinitive absolute of כשר (*BHS*, *BHQ* refer to this as a *Qᵉrê*, although it is not, strictly speaking, described as such in Mᴸ; see the Introduction, 189). The consonants הכשר probably lie behind σ′ προέχει δὲ ὁ

---

[2] Even then it is difficult to see how, for instance, Crenshaw extracts the sense 'Wisdom is useless if a person does not put it to work for some benefit' from his rendering 'and the advantage of skill is wisdom'.

γοργευσάμενος εἰς σοφίαν, 'but the one who busied himself with wisdom has an advantage',[3] which has vocalized them, however, as a participle with a definite article, and G τοῦ ἀνδρείου, 'of the manly/courageous one', which similarly understands a participle or, more probably, an adjective (cf. the later כָּשֵׁר) with an article.[4] S ܠܟܫܝܪ̈ܐ lkšyrʾ, 'for diligent/skilful men', imitates the Hebrew Kethîbh, but probably interprets it on the basis of G (the seyame found in the manuscripts, and hence the plural, are likely to be secondary). Hie *fortitudinis*, 'of strength', and V *industriam*, 'industry', both suggest that Jerome considered the word a noun, although they could be a loose rendering of the infinitive. T אכשרות has perhaps been coined specially with a sense 'making fit' or 'making diligent', and likewise may represent the infinitive.

Most of these probably reflect הכשר rather than הכשיר, and the interpretation of the consonantal text as a substantive has made it necessary for the versions to construe the clause as non-verbal, with חכמה as the subject and יתרון הכשיר as the predicate, or *vice versa*. This construal has been picked up by some modern commentators, and Fox translates 'the advantage of the skilled man is wisdom'; cf. also Bianchi, 'Qohelet 10,8-11', 114, which notes the proposal of Dahood, 'An Allusion', to take כשיר in that sense at Ezek 33.32. It probably fed back also into M's interpretation: if הכשיר is the proper reading, as seems likely (with הכשר explained readily as just a defective spelling of the same), it would be more natural to parse it as a main verb הִכְשִׁיר, rather than as an infinitive. Such a reading at least avoids the problem of, if this really were a non-verbal clause, the relationships between its component words would be unmarked and quite unclear—as demonstrated by the many diverse interpretations of the text in such terms.

For all the versions, however, the sense has been a complicating factor here, and the various renderings attested for the ancient translations are similar to those used elsewhere for the problematic כשרון (see the note at 2.21). It is not clear, however, that we have any good grounds on which to associate this verb with the difficulties that surround that noun. Although the verb itself is rare in biblical Hebrew, כשר is quite well known from later sources in both Hebrew and Aramaic, where it refers to suitability or legitimacy (often, but by no means exclusively, in ritual contexts), and where the causative stems are correspondingly used of making or pronouncing things fit.[5] The lexica tend

---

[3] The several witnesses actually have προσέχει / προσέχων, 'gives heed', which Marshall and Gentry emend, and ms 788 begins the clause with 'and', not 'but'.

[4] Fox does not note the reading of G, which provides a simpler alternative to his own expedient of reading the Aramaic adjective כשיר here: Hebrew sources seem to prefer the form without *yod*.

[5] In Aramaic, the stem develops a slightly broader sense of permission, and especially in Syriac it also takes on an intransitive sense 'be successful', which is connected with the broader usage of the verb in Syriac, but for which there is

to translate the other biblical uses at 11.6 and Esth 8.5 contextually, but the meaning 'be fit' is appropriate for the qal in both those places, and, making allowance for some variation in the nature of the 'fitness' concerned, there is little reason to suppose that the verb ever had any other sense in Hebrew. Unless we emend the text, therefore, or follow G by parsing the word as an adjective, there is correspondingly no basis for taking הכשיר to mean anything other than 'deeming/making fit', or something similar.[6]

The obvious difficulty, however, is that the most natural reading of the Hebrew therefore yields the sense either that 'profit makes/pronounces wisdom fit', or that 'wisdom makes/pronounces profit fit'—and it is not easy to see what either of these might mean in the context of the preceding verses. Matters are not noticeably improved in this respect by taking the verb with M as an infinitive, although Frendo, 'Broken Construct Chain', takes it as a substantive, interrupting a construct ויתרון חכמה, and translates 'but the advantage of wisdom is success'. Freedman's first example of such supposedly fractured constructions in 'The Broken Construct Chain' (to which

no evidence in Hebrew or earlier Aramaic. There is also little evidence that the verb can mean 'make successful' even in later usage. To be sure, in a medieval Aramaic version of Tobit (at 4.19), it is said that God יכשר אורחתך, which could mean 'will make your way successful'; other versions here, however, talk about God guiding or directing one's way, so the intention may have been 'will make your way suitable'; see Neubauer, *The Book of Tobit*, 8; Weeks, Gathercole, and Stuckenbruck, *The Book of Tobit*, 151.

[6] Backhaus, *Den Zeit*, 282-83, talks of the verb being used in the sense 'rechtmäßig / rechtzeitig einsetzen', 'to use lawfully / at the right time', and Schoors uses this to justify his translation 'it is an advantage to prepare one's skill in advance', noting that this is in line with the opinion of several other commentators. Although the verb can obviously be used in the sense of getting things into a state of 'fitness', however, it never has any temporal connotation of the sort supposed here, and neither scholar adduces any other use that would justify such an understanding. It is not impossible that the verb might be used of making a tool suitable for use, but that common interpretation is based on a particular understanding of the context, rather than on any analogous uses, and the verb does not have any implication of doing things in advance, the way that the English 'prepare' does. The extended sense of 'preparing' somebody by informing them of a fact (which lies behind the understanding in Pinker, 'Qohelet 10:10') is also absent from the Hebrew usage. It is not at all clear where all of the many other understandings, like Ginsburg's 'repair', have come from, but some are clearly based on a similar equivocation in other languages. Seow, for example, gives a sensible account of the usage, but then in his interpretation slips from 'making proper' to 'doing properly'—which is certainly not what the verb means—and in his translation goes from 'make suitable' (i.e. make appropriate) to 'It is an advantage to appropriate wisdom', even though the verb 'appropriate' has a quite different sense from the adjective 'appropriate' in English.

Frendo appeals) does involve reading a non-verbal clause between two words in a construct relationship at Isa 10.5 (offering the sense 'a staff—it is in my hand!—of my fury'), but, whatever one makes of that apparent tmesis, Freedman offers no instances analogous to what Frendo proposes, which is effectively that the predicate has been interpolated into the compound subject of a non-verbal clause ('the advantage—[is] succeeding—of wisdom'). It is not just the usual rules about construct relationships that seem to be broken there, and I doubt this reading is even close to possible.

In any case, the basic problem with all such readings lies not just in the constraints on the meaning of the verb, but in the apparent lack of anything preceding it that could be considered an instance of wisdom, even if the worker who becomes successful might conceivably exemplify 'profit' or 'advantage'. On the other hand, this clause makes very good sense when read with the following verse, and a statement that the suitability of wisdom is determined by the profit that it offers seems wholly in line both with the general usage of the verb and with the point that Qohelet will make about snakes. Despite its initial conjunction, therefore, I think the sense demands that we read this clause with v. 11.

10.11 a snake] Lit. 'the snake'. The noun is determined in M, but there is no corresponding article in many manuscripts of G. BHQ would correspondingly read נחש for M הנחש, but the grounds for the deletion are slim, and Gentry anyway considers the article original in G. There is little difference in sense either way, but 'a snake' is slightly more natural here in English.

10.11 without] The combination of בלוא with a following noun is found elsewhere only in Isa 55.1, 2 and Jer 2.11, but we find the spelling בלא more commonly: Lev 15.25; Num 35.22 (twice); Deut 32.21 (twice); 1 Chr 12.18, 34 (ET 12.17, 33); 2 Chr 21.20; Job 8.11; 15.32; 30.28; Pss 17.1; 44.13 (ET 44.12); Prov 13.23; 16.8; 19.2; Eccl 7.17; Jer 5.7; 22.13 (twice); Lam 1.6; Ezek 22.29. Some of these uses appear to represent fixed expressions: בלא משפט, for instance, occurs four times in works as diverse as Proverbs, Jeremiah and Ezekiel, always with the implication 'unjustly'. In Num 25.35, an infinitive is used instead of a noun, and 2 Chr 30.18 construes בלא with a following -כ and a passive participle, but the only use with a main verb is at Lam 4.14, where בלא introduces a clause of circumstance. This last use is exceptional grammatically, but catches well the general meaning: when something is, or happens בלא X, it means that X is absent from the situation, or is not a component of the circumstances. In effect, therefore, it means 'without' X.

In virtually no case is time involved, and this is not inherently a temporal expression. When it is combined with a word for time, however, the expression can take on the nuance 'before', and we see this in Lev 15.25, which is talking about a discharge that occurs before a woman's period is due (בלא עת נדתה) or after it should have ended, while in Job 15.32, a payment בלא יומו appears to be a payment made before it is due. Qohelet has already used such an expression in 7.17, when he talks about dying בלא עתך, 'before your time', and we find בלא עת used in a similar way in Sir 30.24 to express prematurity. In all these instances, however, we are dealing specifically with an idiomatic use of בלא *followed by a word for time*, and there is nothing in the Hebrew usage to suggest that בלא can be used temporally with any other words to mean 'before', despite the belief common among commentators that that is the case here. It is not, we may remark, translated temporally by any of the ancient versions.

There is, equally, nothing in any other usage to support an alternative understanding (expressed by, e.g., Seow) that 'without whispering' might mean 'immune to charming'—an interpretation apparently derived from Jer 8.17, where that is probably not, in fact, the sense (see below), but where the Hebrew is, in any case, different.

10.11 hissing] Segal notes a rhyme between נחש and לחש, but there is more generally in אם ישך הנחש בלוא לחש an assonance and a sibilance appropriate to the sense. The verb לחש is used in both Hebrew and Aramaic of whispering, sometimes with the special connotation of whispering incantations, which probably lies also behind the use of the cognate noun in Isa 3.3; the more difficult Isa 3.20 may refer to charms or amulets. 'Whispering' and 'enchanting' both persist in rabbinic literature as meanings of the verb, but in *Midrash Tanḥuma-Yelammedenu* Vayera 4 we find מה הנחש מלחש והורג אף המלכות מלחשת והורגת את האדם, 'As the snake hisses and kills, so the Kingdom hisses and kills the man', where the verb is used explicitly to refer to the hissing of snakes itself, which is an understandable extrapolation from the sense 'whisper'; cf. also, e.g., לחישתן לחישת שרף, 'their hissing is the hissing of a serpent' in the earlier *m. ʾAbot* 2.10, where a cognate noun is used. 'Hissing' is probably the sense in Jer 8.17 also, although the noun there has often been understood in terms of enchanting: the context is difficult, but the previous verse lays great emphasis on the snorting and neighing of the invaders' horses, so loud that it can be heard from Dan and makes the whole land shake; God declares that, in contrast, he is going to send serpents which will bite without even hissing. The passage exploits, perhaps, a natural fear of an injury that might seem to come without warning and out of nowhere, and if its reference is indeed to silence, then the image there is close to what I take to be Qohelet's image in this verse.

The ancient versions reflect different understandings. S ܠܘܚܫܬܐ *lwḥšt'* has the same 'whispering'/'incantation' ambiguity as the Hebrew, and G ψιθυρισμῷ means 'whispering'. Although T is very interpretative, it has clearly understood the sense 'whisper', but the Three, on the other hand, have all opted for a reference to incantation, or perhaps to chanting. This is the sense both of the awkward α′, θ′ ἐν οὐκ ἐπαοιδῷ, lit. 'in not incantation', and of σ′ ἀπούσης ἐπῳδῆς, 'incantation being absent' (Marshall discusses the apparent confusion in the manuscripts between the readings of α′ and σ′); the Greek could be understood in terms of protective or healing incantations, but possibly also as a reference to a chanting designed to soothe the snake. Very differently again, Hie, V have *in silentio*, 'in silence'. Jerome offers two interpretations in his commentary, both of which refer to biting 'in secret', so he has taken לחש to refer to the hissing of the snake (which I take to be the correct understanding); the second interpretation, however, speaks also of the victim remaining silent, and telling nobody, so he has perhaps seen a secondary reference to human whispering as well.

La is cited in Cassian, *Collationes* ii, 11, 6 and xviii, 16, 10, where the verse is rendered *si momorderit serpens non in sibilo non est abundantia incantatori*, 'if the snake bites not in hissing, there is no plenty for the enchanter'. This follows G closely, and is not a direct witness to the Hebrew, but it uses a word *sibilus*, reserved for whistling and hissing, especially of snakes, which indicates that G's ψιθυρισμῷ could have been read in such terms.

10.11 in having a tongue] Lit. 'for the owner of the tongue', or 'for someone characterized by their tongue'. It is also possible that the nuance is similar to that of איש לשון in Sir 8.3, which refers to someone talkative (who will only become more talkative if one argues with him); when this same expression is used in Ps 140.12 (ET 140.11) it stands in parallel with איש חמס, and so something more pejorative than 'chatty' is clearly intended. In the context of the psalm, which uses its own snake imagery, the 'man of tongue' is someone who uses his facility with words to stir up trouble and attack the innocent. This is perhaps how our passage is understood in *b. ʿArakin* 15b, where animals ask the snake what talent it has comparable to the abilities of the lion to kill with its paws, and the wolf with its teeth, to which the snake responds by talking about its mastery of the tongue (the story is presented a little differently in *b. Taʿanit* 8a, to suggest the uselessness of charms against snakes). בעל הלשון itself is found nowhere else, but Qohelet uses similar expressions at 10.20, where the 'owner of wings' is a bird or flying creature (cf. Prov 1.17), and in the more obscure בעלי אספות of 12.11; elsewhere, in 5.10, 12; 7.12; 8.8, he uses בעל to refer to people who possess something, or, perhaps, who are prone to it. This is representative of Hebrew usage more generally: בעל can express ownership, but, when compounded with other words, often serves only to indicate that someone has a close association or involvement with something (as we saw in the note at 5.10), or possesses it as a personal characteristic.[7] Hence, variously, a בעל אף is someone given to anger in Prov 22.24 and Sir 8.16 (an 'anger-person'), the בעלי חצים in Gen 49.23 are archers ('arrows-people'), the בעל משה of Deut 15.2 is a creditor

---

[7] There is a useful discussion in Desvoeux, *A Philosophical and Critical Essay*, 483-84, who says of בעל with 'abstracted objects' that 'it does not imply dominion, or possession, but only attachment; and even such an attachment as is often very like subjection'. He goes on to suggest, indeed, that the בעל of wisdom in 7.12 is not 'one that is *master* or *possessor* of wisdom; but one that is addicted to it'.

(a 'loan-person'), and those who are בעלי שבועה in Neh 6.18 are bound to Tobiah by an oath ('vow-people'). Much later, a lengthy list in *b. Menaḥ* 65a claims that those appointed to the Sanhedrin had to be בעלי of wisdom, fine appearance, good stature, mature age and magical incantations. As these examples suggest, the usage does not really specify at all the actual nature of the relationship between the בעל and the thing of which they are בעל, and so although the meaning is rarely in doubt, it is usually difficult to translate such expressions without a degree of paraphrase.

It will also be obvious, accordingly, that when it is linked to another noun, בעל is not a term that in itself expresses expertise, or mastery of some skill (although it occasionally does, especially in later Hebrew), so the בעל הלשון here is someone who has a tongue, uses a tongue, or is characterized by their tongue, but there is no specific implication that they are especially skilled in the use of their tongue, or, taking the more extended uses of לשון, that they must be an especially competent speaker or linguist. The very common translation 'snake charmer' is essentially, then, a guess from context: there is nothing in the Hebrew to exclude such a reference if we think this was a technical term or familiar idiom, but equally nothing in the general use of בעל that would push us towards such an understanding—we are simply dealing in some sense with a 'tongue-person' or 'tongue-creature'. Accordingly, we cannot use this second part of the verse to drive our interpretation of the first, or to resolve the potential ambiguities around the earlier לחש.

Jerome in Hie settles for *habenti linguam*, 'someone having a tongue', but in V *qui occulte detrahit* makes explicit his interpretation in terms of a slanderer 'who slanders secretly'. T also thinks Qohelet is talking about slander (which is the understanding of the expression in the Midrash Rabbah). The readings of the other versions have to be treated with some caution. Although G is attested in almost all manuscripts simply as τῷ ἐπᾴδοντι, 'for the enchanter', we have no reason to suppose that the translator found a text any different from that of M, and elsewhere, as was discussed at 5.10, G habitually adopts the distinctive translation παρά for בעל. There is, to be sure, potentially one other exception in 10.20 (although the text is difficult there, and we face similar problems), but even in that verse בעל is rendered separately. Accordingly, τῷ ἐπᾴδοντι is a very unexpected translation, which seems at odds with the translator's usual technique, and McNeile (166) takes it to have come from Symmachus. That origin is speculative: the free rendering is certainly suggestive of σ', but the readings of the Three are not attested here (we have only the first part of the clause καὶ οὐδὲν ὄφελος, 'and it's no use', which Gentry attributes to σ'), and τῷ ἐπᾴδοντι is compatible with the way all of them handled לחש earlier in the verse. McNeile also tries to restore the original as τῷ ἔχοντι τὴν γλῶσσαν, 'to him who has the tongue', basing this on 10.20, where the majority Greek text includes ἔχων. It is very possible, however, that the reading in 10.20 itself shows hexaplaric influence in this use of ἔχων (see the note there), so although McNeile's reconstruction is right to seek consistency between the two verses, it is also potentially built on sand. While acknowledging the possibility that the G translator broke with his usual habits for the sake of clarity, I am inclined to agree that the original reading has been lost, but I doubt it can be retrieved. G's other renderings of בעל might lead us to anticipate τῷ παρὰ γλώσσης. Unless, however, there is some vestige of that in the plus γλωσση, '(with) a tongue', found principally in hexaplaric manuscripts (and more likely a hexaplaric reading itself), any such reading has been entirely displaced.

In any case, τῷ ἐπᾴδοντι underlies the La *incantatori* attested by Cassian and noted above, and probably the ܒܠܚܘܫܐ *blḥwš'*, 'in an enchanter', of S. It is noteworthy that the latter uses a preposition that could be derived from the dative of the Greek, but gives a sense very different from the ל- of M: it is now a matter of the advantage to be gained from having an enchanter, rather than the advantage to be gained by that enchanter.

10.12 The words of a wise man's mouth attract favour] Lit. '(are) favour/attractiveness'. The noun חן is often difficult to translate, because it can refer both to the high esteem in which somebody is held (as probably at 9.11) and, less commonly, to a quality that gives rise to such esteem. In Prov 22.11 and Sir 6.5, 'lips of חן' is used to describe speech that wins friends (cf. Ps 45.3 [ET 45.2]), and the idea is probably similar here.

10.12 lips] The plural שפתות is found less commonly than the dual, and may be a late usage (cf. Pss 45.3 [ET 45.2]; 59.8 [ET 59.7]; Ct 4.3, 11; 5.13; Isa 59.3).

10.12 consume him] *HALOT* has three different verbs בלע, and *DCH* has four, but there are no passages in which it is really difficult to read a single verb בלע meaning to 'swallow', which has an extended, metaphorical sense of 'engulfing' or 'destroying' (especially in the piᶜel). As Schoors argues, it is questionable whether we need, therefore, to identify distinct homonyms.

G καταποντιοῦσιν, lit. 'throw in the sea' (but regularly used for בלע, e.g. 2 Sam 20.19; Lam 2.2, 5), is probably imitated by S ܡܛܒܥܢ *mṭbᶜn*, 'drown', while Jerome has opted for *praecipitabunt*, 'throw down', in both Hie and V, and these (along with the understanding in T) probably all reflect a vocalization of the verb as piᶜel. The pointing of the verb here in Mᴸ is as a piᶜel; *BHS* reports a qal תִּבְלָעֶנּוּ in oriental manuscripts, and although the source and reliability of its information is unclear, that would arguably suit the imagery better. The consonantal text can, of course, be vocalized either way, but the verb has in any case to be read as singular, despite the plural subject שפתות. Such mismatches are not uncommon, and the lips are perhaps being thought of as a single entity, but it is also possible, as Gordis suggests, that the attachment of a suffix pronoun has caused the ending to be suppressed.

That pronoun is most commonly read as a reference to the fool himself, but T speaks of everyone being destroyed, and some scholars argue that the 'him' is actually the wise man: strictly speaking, the Hebrew is ambiguous, but the fact that subsequent pronouns in the next verse clearly refer to the fool tend to support the view that it is talking about self-destruction.

10.13 folly] On סכלות, see the note at 1.17, where it is likewise paired with הוללות (cf. 2.12; 7.25).

10.13 the last thing out of his mouth] Lit. 'the end of his mouth'. There is a contrast between beginning and end here, as at 7.8, and many scholars speak of a merism: Qohelet is talking about the totality of what the fool says, not *just* about his first and last words. If we suppose that הוללות רעה is something worse than just סכלות, though, the nuance may be rather that the fool's speech gets increasingly bad, not simply that it is consistently bad from start to finish.

The στόματος, 'mouth', of G is lacking in some important manuscripts, and McNeile, 151-52, suggests that it may be secondary in both the Greek and the Hebrew, supplying a parallel for the preceding פיהו. This is speculative and improbable, even though the Hebrew is admittedly a little awkward, but if the original reading was indeed אחריתו, then the reference would be to the fool's fate, as it is in those Greek manuscripts.

10.13 terrible mindlessness] On הוללות (vocalized -וּת rather than -וֹת only here in M[L]), see the note at 1.17. G here has περιφέρεια πονηρά (the La translation *circuitus malignus*, 'evil circuit', is attested, see Marshall), and Jerome tells us that σ' had *tumultus*, which probably reflects θόρυβος; on these renderings, see the note 'mindless' at 2.2.

In Syh, the word ܒܝܫ *byš'*, representing G πονηρά, 'bad', is under asterisk: this would usually suggest that Origen found no equivalent to רעה in G, and added πονηρά to his Greek text on the basis of the Hebrew. When a word is supplied in this way from one of the other Greek translations, there is usually an attribution, and the absence of one here might suggest, as Marshall proposes, that Origen found it in some manuscripts of G but not others, and believed it originally to have been absent from G. That is a significant testimony, and so although πονηρά is absent from no extant manuscripts of G, we must consider it a strong possibility that the word was at least lacking in some early manuscript(s) considered reliable by Origen, and may have been absent from the original G translation. That would be a slender basis on which to suppose that רעה is itself a secondary addition, however, and we may note that הוללות is associated with רע in 9.3.

10.14 yet the fool makes many words. No person knows] There is a conjunction linking 10.14a to the preceding 10.12-13 in all the ancient versions except V (including σ' καὶ ἀνόητος πολλὰ λαλήσει, 'and a fool will speak many things'), but its omission in Jerome's translation has had a clear influence on subsequent interpretations and translations—the AV, for instance, renders והסכל quite implausibly as 'a fool also', while such disparate versions as Luther's Bible and the RSV omit the conjunction altogether. The point here is probably that the fool talks a lot, even though what he says is wrong.

The second part of the verse might be acting as a secondary reinforcement of the point, but is more probably setting up the further mockery of the fool's speech in 10.15. In order to facilitate a reading of 14b with 14a, however, a number of Hebrew manuscripts introduce a conjunction before לא (see de Rossi, and cf. the 'though' introduced at this point by RSV): this is reflected in none of the ancient versions, although T does make a new link using דילא, 'so that (a human does) not (know)', and some G manuscripts add a conjunction of their own.

The expression לא ידע האדם, lit. 'the human will not know', was used in 9.12; on the rendering of ידע by G, see the note on 'knows' at that verse. M points the verb as yiqtol here, but qatal in 10.15; G has ἔγνω in both places, and the translator probably made no such distinction.

10.14 what has been] M has a yiqtol מה שיהיה, expressing the future, 'what is going to be': the same expression was rendered τί τὸ ἐσόμενον by G in the similar statement at 8.7, but here most manuscripts have a past tense, τί τὸ γενόμενον, 'what has happened'; this is echoed in S ܕܗܘܐ ܡܐ *m' dhw'* and Hie *quid sit quod factum est*, 'what it is that has happened'. The few manuscripts of G that do have a future tense employ τὸ γενησόμενον, which is not found even as a variant in 8.7, rather than τί τὸ ἐσόμενον, and this is likely to be an adaptation toward the Hebrew: τί τὸ γενόμενον is most likely original. Goldman suggests that the past tense might be a contextual exegesis, but this would be out of character for G, and it is more likely that the translator found מה שהיה in his source-text.

Although slightly different, σ' τὰ προγενόμενα, 'the former things', is probably paraphrasing a past tense, as is V *quid ante se fuerit*, so only T supports the future tense found in M. The probability that the other versions read מה שהיה may be strengthened a little further by the fact that this reading is actually found in a few Hebrew manuscripts noted by de Rossi, and may have been resisted by the Masoretes (cf. Ginsburg, *Massorah*, 4:299). It is harder to say for sure whether מה שהיה or מה שיהיה is original, but it is difficult to see what would have motivated the change from future to past, unless it was a simple slip of the pen, while a change from past to future can be explained straightforwardly as a recollection of 8.7 (so McNeile, 155), or as an effort to avoid a difficult statement that the past is unknown (particularly, Goldman points out, when so much of it is recounted in scripture). As the more difficult reading, therefore, מה שהיה has the better claim—but it is also, correspondingly, harder to interpret.

Marshall notes a scholion to the reading of σ' in two Greek manuscripts: in full, that reading is τὰ προγενόμενα ἀλλ' οὐδὲ τὰ ἐσόμενα, '...the former things, but nor the things that will be', and the scholiast understands this to express human ignorance about things that existed before the world and things that will exist after the world. We need not go to quite such lengths, though. The point made so briefly here is not that no human has any knowledge of anything that has happened, but that 'the past' in a general sense is as inaccessible to humans as the future.

10.14 and who is going to explain to him what will be, following him?] Lit. 'and (about what) will be behind him, who will inform/explain to him?'. This is similar to questions asked already in 6.12 and 8.7 (see the note at 6.12), but Qohelet has not previously used מאחרי—a term that is not commonly used in a temporal sense, even in later Hebrew, outside the expression כן מאחרי, 'afterwards'. The only really comparable biblical use is at Deut 29.21 (ET 29.22), where 'the children who will arise מאחריכם' are the coming generation, but even this is little more than an extension of the usual uses for following someone or being behind something. G translates using the same term ὀπίσω, 'after' or 'behind', that it uses for plain אחרי, while the Three (or possibly just α' and θ', see Marshall) have a very neutral τὰ μετ᾽ αὐτόν, 'the things after him'. S ܡܢ ܒܬܪܗ *mn btrh*, however, observes the distinction, while T has מן סופיה, lit. 'from his end', and I have attempted both to preserve that distinction and to capture the probable nuance.

10.15 The effort of fools would weary him] On my understanding of the construction, and consequent 'would', see the next note. עמל is usually masculine, but the verb with which it is apparently supposed to agree, תיגענו, is feminine. Ehrlich, followed by Hertzberg and Goldman, accordingly emends the first part of the verse to עֲמַל הַכְּסִיל מָתַי יְיַגְּעֶנּוּ, lit. 'the business of the fool, when will it weary him?', and Fox (followed by Krüger) less drastically to עמל הכסיל מיגענו, 'the business of the fool wearies him'. Others have argued, on various grounds, that עמל is simply treated as feminine here, that עמל הכסילים is a compound expression to be read as feminine (Wright: 'fools-work'), or that the verb is actually a taqtul form, and so may be read as masculine (an idea discussed in detail and rightly rejected by Schoors, '*taqtul*'). Zimmermann, 'Aramaic Provenance', 40-41, naturally puts the problem down to careless translation from an Aramaic original in which the noun was feminine (cf Ginsberg, *Studies*, 24).[8] The ancient translations show no consciousness of a difficulty, and G κοπώσει (on which, see below) may simply render תיגענו, accepting the disagreement; if it did have anything different at all, the future tense suggests that this would have to have been ייגענו, which is a reading attested in Babylonian manuscripts (cf. Miletto), not Fox's מיגענו—but the variant may well be just a correction. In the end, it is probably simplest either to accept that עמל is treated as feminine here, or to suppose that some copyist has turned יי into תי as the result of a misunderstanding or moment of

---

[8] Pinker, 'Reconstruction', 78, offers a way to solve the problems by emending to הכסיל לימת ייגענו, which he translates 'the effort of the kesil in time will tire him'. The reconstruction is less straightforward than he supposes, but if we allow it in principle, it is not clear that 'for days' or 'for a season' would have the implication 'in time' that he desires, while the form ימות (from יום) is rare in biblical Hebrew. The emendation is inspired by Hertzberg's proposal: עמל הכסיל מתי ייגענו, 'the work of the fool: when will it tire him?', which is hardly more plausible.

distraction (and Sacchi, e.g., would accordingly just emend to ייגענו). There is simply no evidence of any alternative tense or meaning.

The issue is complicated, however, by the fact that commentators have traditionally, and naturally, understood the fools themselves to be the object of the verb: it is they who are wearied by their own work. On that understanding, there is then a second disagreement, since the suffix pronoun on תיגענו is singular, and the emendations proposed by Ehrlich and Fox both attempt to account for this by shifting the ם to another word and taking הכסיל as a single fool. Scholars who adopt this understanding but who do not emend the verb (or הכסילם itself) are obliged either to explain the ם in a different way (perhaps as enclitic, with a facilitatory or genitive י preceding; cf. Dahood, 'Canaanite-Phoenician', 194; Hummel, 'Enclitic Mem in Early Northwest Semitic, Especially Hebrew', 94), or, less problematically, to take the singular suffix as distributive, so that the fools are each wearied by their work (cf. GKC §145 m, where this is cited as an example).

The versions do not offer any easier route out of this second difficulty: Rahlfs has κοπώσει αὐτούς, 'will weary them', as the reading of G, which might justify emendation of the suffix to a plural, but the singular αὐτόν, adopted by Gentry, is well attested and more probably original: the plural has emerged in the G tradition as a consequence of the interpretation, although it is subsequently picked up by Hie, V (cf. the La of Cassian, *Collationes* XXIV, 24, 6: *labor...stultorum adfligit eos*, 'the labour of fools afflicts them'),[9] and perhaps by S ܠܗܘܢ *lhwn* '(is wearying) to them'. T simply makes the fool singular, and this development is found also both in some of the G manuscripts that have αὐτόν and in a few Hebrew manuscripts noted by de Rossi. Once again, it would probably be easier to accept the disagreement, and perhaps a distributive sense, than to find any strong basis for emendation—but it may be easier still to discard the assumption that הכסילים must be the antecedent of the suffix.

This assumption actually yields a rather poor sense, either that the fool wearies himself by getting lost, or that he gets lost because he has wearied himself. Neither meaning picks up anything in the immediate context, and neither offers any very telling insight: getting tired by work or being unable to find one's way (perhaps in an unfamiliar place) are hardly activities confined to fools. G μόχθος τῶν ἀφρόνων κοπώσει αὐτόν ὃς οὐκ ἔγνω seems instead to take the suffix as an antecedent to אשר, giving a sense like that of Barton's reading, 'The toil of fools shall weary him who knows not how

---

[9] The *adfligit* of Cassian and similar forms in Hie, V probably reflect the influence of a variant reading κακώσει, 'harms', for κοπώσει, which is found in many important manuscripts of G, but is clearly a secondary development in that tradition. Syh suggests that α' also read κοπώσει, and σ' a different form from the same verb (see Marshall).

to go to town' (cf. Heiligstedt, *Labor stultorum fatigat...eum, qui nescit ire ad urbem*). Such a Hebrew usage would not be impossible in principle, and would correspond syntactically to instances in Gen 30.18 and Song 1.6, where relative clauses pick up suffix pronouns (possibly also to Ps 103.2-5, although the relative clauses there may loosely pick up יהוה, rather than the suffix on יגמוליו). Whether it can be regarded as a natural way to introduce an indefinite subject, however, is another matter, and there is no obvious analogy for such a construction expressing '…him, that is, whoever does *x*'. Accordingly, I take האדם in the previous verse to be the antecedent of both אשר and the suffix (as it is of the suffix on מאחריו), but in that case the suffix serves, perhaps, to bridge the long gap between the noun and the relative clause, and might itself be taken to have a loosely antecedent function. On this reading, עמל is used, perhaps with some irony, to express the laborious efforts of fools to answer a simpler question.

10.15 when he merely does not know how] The Hebrew is compact, and I have added 'merely' to bring out the sense and the relationship with the previous verse. What the text says literally is just 'who will not know', with the implication 'when he does not know', and more broadly the sentence reads 'the labour of the fools will weary him when he will not know…'. As discussed in the last note, I take האדם in 10.14 to be the antecedent of the suffix on תיגענו or an original ייגענו, which in turn serves as the subject of ידע. The אשר is strictly, therefore, a relative pronoun picking up that suffix ('weary him who will not know'), but it is not uncommon for אשר to express circumstance in such uses. Many commentators give it causal force here, seeing their ignorance as the reason for their work exhausting fools. Either nuance is possible in principle (although I am less persuaded by the 'so that he does not' adopted by Crenshaw), and the relationship of the clause to what precedes can only be established according to an understanding of the meaning overall here; see the note on 'when' at 4.9.

Because the subject of ידע must be the same as the referent of the previous suffix, the text-critical problems that surrounded the suffix continue here. G has a singular verb ἔγνω, 'knows' or 'knew', but Hie, V *nesciunt*, 'do not know', is plural, as is the verb in Cassian, *Collationes* XXIV, 24, 6: *qui non cognouerunt ire in ciuitatem*, 'who have not known how to go into the city', and the ܝܕܥܘ *ydʿw*, 'know', of S. Confusingly, σ' is attested in Greek as οὐ γὰρ ἐπίσταται ἀπελθεῖν εἰς πόλιν, 'for he does not know how to go to a city', with a singular verb, but in Syh it has a plural verb ܡܦܣܝܢ *mpsyn*, '(they are not) acquainted with'—equivalent to ἐπίστανται. Marshall argues for the originality of the plural, on the basis that Jerome's readings might be based on σ', as often, and that it is easy to understand an assimilation to the singular of G, but harder to explain how the plural might have arisen secondarily. As the reading from Cassian shows, however, La might have been Jerome's source here, and so it is difficult to decide what σ' had originally, while the use of the plural also in both La and S raises the possibility that it was known in the

G tradition as well, even if not now represented in the manuscript evidence. In any case, though, the plural has most probably arisen through an interpretative alignment to the preceding 'fools', which understands the ignorance suggested here to be a manifestation of their folly.

The construction ידע ל- with an infinitive is used to give several different senses in the book (cf. 4.17; 6.8), but here it has much the same common implication as the use in 4.13, of knowing 'how to do' something. The verb ידע itself is pointed qatal in M, but G uses ἔγνω, as for the ידע pointed as yiqtol in the previous verse, and has probably read both the same way.

10.15 to reach a city] Commentators generally understand this expression to have implications beyond an obvious statement about finding one's way into a town, but disagree about the nature of those implications. For the most part, such an inability is seen as an expression of the fools' more general ignorance, either because this is some sort of idiom, or because towns and roads are so obvious that only a fool could miss them. Other suggestions have included, though, the reluctance of fools to seek the instruction available in Jerusalem (Geier), their failure to gain the wealth and social status associated with having a house 'in town' (Lohfink, cf. Leahy, 'The Meaning of Ecclesiastes 10:15'), and a satirical association of the fools with Essenes, who avoided towns (Graetz—Delitzsch comments *habeat sibi*, 'he can keep that!').

If the fools are indeed the subject here, despite the grammatical discordances, then the expression is likely to be derogatory. Even in that case, however, there are a couple of important points to bear in mind. The first is that the noun is indeterminate (in both M and G): this is 'a' city, not 'the' city, and analogies from other languages, like 'go into town', do not offer convincing grounds to overlook that fact. Not knowing how to get to, or into one's own town may indeed be indicative of a certain stupidity, but if that were true of getting to any town, there might be fewer sales of maps and GPS systems. That ties in to a second point, that the way into an ancient town may actually have been less straightforward than one might think: see the commentary, and note the acknowledgment of the potential difficulties by, e.g., Ibn Ezra and Rashi.

Zimmermann thinks that 'city' has arisen from a confusion in Aramaic between למתא, 'to town' and למי(א)תי, 'coming', and that the original suggested that he did not know whether he was 'coming or going'. For Pinker, 'Reconstruction', 79-80, it is evidence that the words belong with 10.16-17, and he makes a drastic emendation: אי לך עיר אשר כעלל אלה, 'woe to you, O city whose leader is as a child'. This is unnecessary, and although Pinker tries to show how individual words or letters might have been confused, he offers no explanation for the total transformation of one sentence into another that is presumed.

10.16-19

Inaction

(10.16) Woe to you, a city whose king is a manservant, and whose ministers eat in the morning. (10.17) Happy are you, a land whose king is a free man, and whose ministers eat on time, with strength, and are not shamed.

(10.18) With a lazy pair, the rafters will sag, but it is with lowliness of the hands that the house will leak.

(10.19) When it is for fun that they are laying on food, then wine will make living people happy, but it is the cost that worries everyone.

Commentary

This sequence begins with two declarations, in 10.16-17, that contrast the misfortune of a city ruled by the powerless with the fortune of a land whose king is beholden to nobody—those who are supposed to govern the former sit down early to eat because they cannot work, or have nothing to do. Status means nothing, we might say, if there is no real power. 'City' here provides a catchword link with the preceding 10.15: there is no other obvious continuity, and Qohelet appears to have moved on. In 10.18, a saying observes not just the risks incurred by laziness, but the actual damage done by powerlessness, and this perhaps picks up or extends that issue. Inaction, and the inability to act, do not merely stop things getting done but also offer no protection against erosion and decay. In the difficult 10.19, the issue is not power or capacity but money, and, more specifically, the concerns about cost that can inhibit or deter people from engaging in something that they know will make them happy.

It is this last saying, I think, which most clearly indicates the train of thought in these verses, such as it is. Each suggests, in a different way, that there is a penalty to be paid for inaction, whether that inaction is imposed by circumstance or by misplaced self-interest: a city will suffer, a roof leak or a pleasure be missed. This sets up the remarkable sequence that follows in 10.20–11.6, which develops the idea in 10.19 of caution leading to self-deprivation, but the initial concern here is with the costs incurred by doing nothing, rather than specifically with human choices to avoid or defer acting.

10.16-17] It is not immediately clear how it might be considered a bad thing for officials to eat in the morning, and so the contrast at the heart of these verses is obscure. This might be less of a problem were it not that in the Hebrew text some other points of contrast have been obscured, with each verse addressed to a 'land', and with the reference to shaming turned into an expression that has been widely understood as a reference to drinking alcohol, but that may simply be meaningless. The Greek text probably represents the original better in both cases, but interpretations of the Hebrew have fostered a common understanding that Qohelet is talking about royal courts in which officials over-indulge themselves all day, or else refrain from doing so.

One contrast that does remain unaffected by textual problems, however, is that between the two kings of vv. 16 and 17. The first of these is described using a term that can denote youth, but is often used of servants; the second can be interpreted as a reference to noble birth, but is more probably the Hebrew equivalent of an Aramaic term used of people and animals who are free, or of property that is unencumbered.[1] This suggests that Qohelet's point is about the

---

[1] It is interesting to observe that 10.17 became a focus for sermons about the restoration of the English monarchy after the end of the republic in 1660 and the return of the 'noble' Charles II. A number of these have, at least in part, an exegetical character. See especially Godman, *Filius Heröum*; Brunsell, *Solomons Blessed Land*; and Willan, *Beatitas Britanniae*. Godman (7-8) and Willan (29) examine the Hebrew phrase *bn ḥwrym* itself, and both mention the opinion of Vatable and others, that it literally means 'sons of white'; there is probably no connection, in fact, with the stem *ḥwr*, used of paleness—although there is a superficial resemblance to the name of the Solomonic official mentioned in 1 Kgs 4.8, *bn ḥwr*, which was borrowed by Lew Wallace for his famous 1880 novel, *Ben-Hur: A Tale of the Christ*.

different capacities of two different states: one is small—a city or city-state—and its king is a vassal (perhaps also a young one); the other is a country whose king is beholden to nobody, and whose officials are powerful. If so, it seems unlikely that eating in the morning is supposed to imply decadence, which would be a wholly different issue. It is harder to say for sure what it does imply. On the whole, rabbinic sources are positive about food in the morning, and *b. Baba Qamma* 92b, for instance, commends eating bread and salt early in the morning as a way to counteract a wide range of maladies (see similarly *b. Baba Meṣi'a* 107b). It is doubtful, though, that such food was treated as a proper meal. In a passage that is to be found both in *b. Šabbat* 10a and in *b. Pesaḥim* 12b, we find a discussion that assigns the proper times for the daily meal of different groups, qualified by a note that the meal may be postponed if something has been eaten in the morning. This note tends to affirm that such morning food is not a 'meal' in itself, and that picture conforms to the biblical description of eating in the wilderness, where manna, as bread, is available from morning onwards, but it is the quails in the evening that furnish the Israelites with their meal for the day (see Exod 16.12). The Talmudic list of times, furthermore, although it sets meals unexpectedly early for everybody, has gladiators, robbers and heirs eating before anyone else—gladiators presumably because they famously ate three square meals spread across the day, and robbers because they would have been working during the night.

In fact, the context of the list in *Šabbat* is a question about the time of day at which judges may finish sitting, which cites 10.17 in response before turning to mealtimes, and the point seems to be that, for most people, the daily meal falls at the time when they stop working, which is why heirs, with no work to do, settle down for an early morning meal. The most likely implication of the mealtimes in 10.16-17, therefore, is not that the city officials are indulging themselves too much, but that they are eating first thing a meal that should only be eaten after they have done a day's work, and so demonstrating (unless they are robbers) either that they are lazy or that they have been given too little to do. Kravitz and Olitzky, who understand the text in these terms, wonder if the image is of lazy adolescents.

10.18] The verse is commonly translated as two synonymous statements, hence RSV: 'Through sloth the roof sinks in, and through indolence the house leaks'. In the second part, however, it is unlikely that the noun can mean 'indolence', and it more probably refers to incapacity or a lack of power. Accordingly, the point is that laziness can lead to a lack of maintenance, but it is the actual inability or refusal to fix a problem (and perhaps literally the 'lowness' of one's hands) that causes real damage. The image is of a roof built on beams, which lets water in after the beams have sagged, and I think Qohelet is probably using this image to address an issue that was present in 10.16-17 as well: neglect is one thing, but real problems arise when those in charge are either too 'lowly' to reach the roof and do what needs doing, or consciously keep their hands down as the problems get worse. On the difficulties in the text, see the notes. My translation here is of the Masoretic reading, which is unlikely to be original in detail, but it is hard to pin down the best alternative. Most probably, I think, the author wrote matching expressions 'with laziness of hands' and 'with lowliness of hands', but the former could just have been 'with laziness'.

10.19] The meaning of the verse hinges to a great extent on the interpretation of the last verb, with most commentators taking the point to be that money solves any problem—perhaps a view attributed to those who are eating bread, drinking wine, and, by extension, enjoying the comforts of life. It is very unlikely that the Hebrew can have that sense, but even commentators like Fox, who more plausibly understand Qohelet to be saying that 'money keeps them all occupied', tend to understand that the context is one of luxury and feasting, about which Qohelet is expressing disapproval.

Such understandings are heavily influenced by an interpretation of vv. 16-17 in terms of shameful over-indulgence, and a belief that those verses set the broader context for this one (Lavoie, 'Qohélet 10,16-20', 194-95, discusses more generally the ways in which the perceived connections have affected interpretation). If it is hard to find any such reference to lavish feasting there, however, it is almost impossible here, and there are no good reasons to suppose that Qohelet is expressing disapproval of humans who seek happiness through food and drink. When Longman suggests, though, that Qohelet might be 'sincere in his praise of feasting, laughter, wine, and money', this arguably swings too far in the other direction: there is no explicit commendation here, any more than there is a condemnation, and Qohelet is telling us what people do, not what he thinks of it.

The point could be simply to state that humans find ways in which to have fun or be happy, notably through food and wine, but that these activities are peripheral to their main concern, which is money. That is not, however, something that has been a focus of the monologue for a long time now, and I understand the rather unusual construction of the Hebrew to imply a certain conditionality. Qohelet's assertion is not just that people can find pleasure, but that pleasure may be found specifically in meals laid on for that purpose—in the wine drunk at dinner-parties, we might say, rather than in the glass we might take with a more everyday meal. The observation he adds is then equally specific, and refers to the cost of such parties. It is not clear whether he means that worrying about the cost puts people off holding them, or that it detracts from the pleasure—and both alternatives are probably left open—but the former suits the context slightly better.

Notes

10.16 a city] Or perhaps 'a land'. G uses γῆ for ארץ in the next verse, but here has πόλις, 'city'. Such variation is untypical of the translator, and πόλις is, besides, an unlikely translation of M ארץ: it much more probably represents עיר, as in the previous verse.[2] G is probably supported by S ܡܕܝܢܬܐ *mdynt'*, which is not used elsewhere in the book for ארץ, and by the La *ciuitas/ciuitati*, which is attested in several places (see Marshall, Gentry).[3] On the other hand, although Jerome had earlier accepted the La reading in Hie, V has *terra*,

---

[2] Dahood, 'Phoenician Background', 280, advances the curious argument that this is evidence for the Phoenician origin of the book, since the Phoenician cognate of ארץ can mean 'city-state'. At most it could imply that the translator of G was familiar with such a usage, since there is nothing in the Hebrew itself to demand that ארץ have such a sense.

[3] Leanza, 'Le tre versione', 94, gives as the La version revised by Jerome *uae civitati ubi rex iuvenis est et principes eius mane comedunt*, 'woe to a city where the king is a youth and its princes eat in the morning'. In both M and G, the address is second-person, and the reference is literally to 'your' king and 'your' ministers. Neither 'your' is rendered in this (or in V), and the first is lacking in Hie and many citations of La. The absence seems likely to be translational, and is a feature of V in 10.17 also.

'land', here, which is in line both with M and with σ' γῆ (cf. also T, which talks about the land of Israel).

There are two ways to explain the variation: either 'city' has been read inadvertently from the previous verse, and displaced 'land' (as McNeile, 166, supposes), or 'land' has displaced 'city' because it offers a more obvious parallel and contrast to the next verse. It is difficult to be certain, but the latter seems to me more probable, not only because עיר in G's source-text might have acted as a catchword, linking this new series of sayings to 10.15, but also because it is very difficult to see what might have led a copyist to repeat 'city' from the previous verse, either in Hebrew or in Greek. The sort of alignment with 10.17 that might have led to the displacement of עיר, on the other hand, is probably visible in S, where 'city' has come to stand in both places.

10.16 a manservant] Since it apparently stands in contrast to the בן חורים of the next verse, commentators have rightly been inclined to suppose that נער must connote the status of the king here, and the noun is commonly used this way. It does not mean 'slave', however, and it would be fair to say that the usage elsewhere points to נער connoting something more precise than עבד: although הנערים in Job 1.15 are tending cattle, 'lads' are more generally depicted as personal servants or assistants (e.g. Esth 2.2), who often accompany their master (e.g. 2 Sam 13.17; Neh 4.16 ET 4.22), while Ziba, the נער of the house of Saul, in 2 Sam 19.18 (ET 19.17), is apparently a sort of steward, who has his own servants (עבדים).

T identifies the king here as Jeroboam, who is described as a נער in 1 Kgs 11.28, where he is certainly not an infant and is given a position of considerable responsibility, so although the noun can have an implication of youthful inexperience (cf. 1 Kgs 3.7; 1 Chr 22.5), age is not likely to be the issue here, so much as subordination—hence the contrast with בן חורים. The noun would anyway be a slightly odd choice for 'child'—except when qualified with קמן, it is more commonly used with reference to adolescents, when age is involved at all. That has not, of course, inhibited various attempts to identify the king here with Hellenistic monarchs who ascended the throne as children (see the helpful survey in Lavoie, 'Qohélet 10,16-20', 187-88). Schultz, 'Qoheleth and Isaiah', 58-59, compares the threat in Isa 3.1-3, to replace the rulers of Judah with נערים, the result of which, we may note, will be oppression and a collapse of the respect usually shown by the young for the old and the scoundrel for the man of honour.

10.16 ministers] The term שר is used of many different types of official or commander, and although it is often translated as 'prince', it connotes authority, not nobility or aristocratic birth. Schoors claims that the שרים are 'the social class closest to the king' here, but that is potentially misleading: to the extent that the two can be separated in an ancient context, שרים are holders of office, not members of a particular class. The term is often found alongside references to kings because it is שרים who serve those kings in military or other capacities, and Qohelet is most probably describing here the behaviour not of some aristocratic class in general, but of senior officials responsible for governance under the king.

10.16 eat in the morning] בבקר is supported by all the versions, and is rather specific: it means 'in the morning', and cannot be construed as 'until morning' or 'from morning onwards' (a common understanding which has surely been influenced by Isa 5.11).[4] Furthermore, the verb אכל here is the normal verb for 'eating' and although, of course, it can be used in the context of feasts, it bears no specific connotation of feasting or of over-indulgence. Interpretations that understand Qohelet to be talking about getting drunk in the morning or about all-day feasting, therefore, rest not on anything that is said explicitly in this verse, but on extrapolation from the difficult closing words of 10.17, on which see below.

10.17 Happy are you] אשרי followed by a noun or suffix is used as a fixed expression meaning 'happy is'. The Masoretes vocalize it here with a 'singular' אַ֫ךְ, rather than with אַ֫שְׁ, which would be expected were the word being treated as a plural construct—the way it is usually parsed; cf. Delitzsch's remarks and GKC §91 l. Rubin, 'Form and Meaning', discusses this and other uses with suffix pronouns, suggesting that the term was originally an adjective, only secondarily re-interpreted as a construct, and that this re-interpretation only consistently influenced the pointing of the two uses with a third-person masculine singular suffix in Prov 14.21 and 16.20. If so, the vocalization here is not an error, but an indication that the understanding of the term as a construct form was not universally shared or applied among the Masoretes.

10.17 a land] On the reading of S, see the note on 'a city' at 10.16.

10.17 a free man] The term חורים is used of a particular group or class, linked with elders in 1 Kgs 21.8, 11 and with another group, the סגנים, several times in Neh (e.g. 2.16; 5.7). It is difficult to identify the precise status of either group. We do not find the expression בן חורים elsewhere in biblical Hebrew, but in mishnaic Hebrew בן חורין is equivalent to, and possibly a calque on, an Aramaic term בר חירין. That term is used of people (and, by extension, animals or things) that are free or (very commonly) have been freed, so if the Hebrew is indeed equivalent to the Aramaic, Qohelet is talking not about the son of people in a particular social class, but about someone who is a free or freed man—presumably in contrast to the נער of the preceding verse. That would also suit the use of חור(י)ם in Sir 10.25, where the Greek renders it as ἐλεύθεροι, 'free men'.

---

[4] Here Dahood, 'Phoenician Background', 280-81, is unusually in tune with many other commentators, although few, probably, would subscribe to his opinion that 'from' is 'one of the normal meanings of *b*' (281). Dahood sees a similar usage at 11.6: see the note there on 'Sow your seed in the morning...'.

10.17 on time] Although it is not used in quite this way elsewhere, בעת seems to be serving as a counterpart to the בלא עתך of 7.17. G πρὸς καιρὸν seems to be original (a variant ἐν καιρῷ is largely confined to the hexaplaric *O*-group manuscripts), and, on the face of it, would seem to suggest that the translator read לעת (contrast ἐν οὐ καιρῷ σου in 7.17). The Greek expression, however, means 'for (only) a while' (see, e.g., Lk 8.13), so this translation may simply reflect an understanding that the rulers do not dawdle over their food, rather than a different source-text.

10.17 with strength] Gordis' claim that גבורה might mean 'self-control' is entirely speculative and rests on his understanding of the passage, not on any use of the word with that connotation elsewhere. The more common idea that this strength might be the vigour gained from eating food is easier to accept, but the expression cannot mean 'for strength' (as, e.g., RSV would have it): that sense is beyond the scope of -ב. V *ad reficiendum*, 'for refreshment' adopts this understanding, but is simply an interpretative paraphrase. Curiously, S has the unexpected ܒܟܫܝܪܘܬܐ *bkšyrwt'*, which employs the Syriac cognate of כשרון, while σ' μετὰ ἀνδραγαθίας (var. ἀνδρείας) uses a term close to the ἀνδραγάθημα that rendered כשרון in 5.10 (on the sense, see the note there). Given the character of those translations, it would be too much of a stretch to say that these readings are evidence of a text with כשרון, but they do suggest that the translators saw no reference to physical strength at all.

10.17 are not shamed] Or perhaps 'and do not tarry'. The text and the sense are uncertain. M has ולא בשתי, and although a noun שתי is found elsewhere in Hebrew only in connection with cloth or weaving (several times in Lev 13, as the Masorah notes, and in later usage), the שתי here has generally been associated with the verb שתה, 'drink'. S ܡܫܬܝ *mšty*, 'drinking', however, is the only ancient rendering of the Hebrew in such terms, and that may be simply because the translator was able to read שתי as a Syriac word: a noun ܫܬܝ *šty* is attested with the senses 'drink', 'drinking', and (vocalized differently) 'drinker'. G is very different: οὐκ αἰσχυνθήσονται, 'they will not be ashamed', makes no connection with שתה, but looks instead to the root בוש. Jerome probably takes his cue from this when he uses *non in confusione*, 'not in confusion' in Hie (he quite often uses *confusio* in his Vulgate translation where the Septuagint has αἰσχύνη), but V *non ad luxuriam*, 'not for extravagance', seems to be interpretative. He makes no reference to drinking in his commentary, and whether or not he has himself seen a link to בוש / בשת, he has certainly made no connection with שתה. Finally, both T and the Midrash see a reference here to weakness (T adds blindness as well), and likewise make no reference to drink. Each phrases its reference differently, with the Midrash reading ולא בתשישותו, 'and not in his weakness', and T ולא בחלשות, 'and not in weakness', but both may have connected שתי with the late verb תשש, 'be weak', and the related noun תשישות. This need not reflect a textual variant so much as exegetical manoeuvring in search of a counterpart to גבורה, but it does indicate again that an association with 'drinking' was far from obvious to most early readers.

Such a sense is more normally conveyed in Hebrew, moreover, by משתה, and although we do find שתיה, perhaps with a distinct nuance, in Esth 1.8 and sometimes in later Hebrew, it would not be unreasonable to suppose that these versions do not have 'drinking' simply because they did not recognize it as a possible meaning here.[5] In that case, we should take seriously the distinctive reading of G, with a verb. Although it is tempting to suppose that the translator simply took the characters בשת as the noun meaning 'shame', and then interpreted this to mean that the officials would not be shamed, such a paraphrastic rendering would be very untypical of G's translation technique. This account also fails to explain why the translator would have ignored the final י, discounted the probability that the -ב was another preposition after בגבורה, or transformed the noun into a verb after he had rendered the previous גבורה with a noun.[6] It seems more probable that he found in his source a consonantal text that itself contained a verbal form from בוש (the qal יבשו, the hiph'il יבישו, the polel יבששו, or the hithpolel יתבששו [cf. Gen 2.25]), even if this requires us to accept that a ת might have been introduced into the text of M or lost from the source-text of G. There is no easy way to account for such a change in either direction, and the reading must necessarily be uncertain, but since it is both far from clear that M actually makes sense, and unlikely that G is an attempt to make sense of it, then it is simplest to suppose that M is corrupt.

In the text represented by G, the verb stands in parallel with the preceding יאכלו, and it may have been the influence of the closer בגבורה that led to the loss of an initial י in M, and the subsequent difficulties. If we go down this path, then it seems worth noting the uses of בוש (or of a separate stem II בוש, according to *HALOT*) to express delay or hesitation, rather than shame. These uses are associated with the polel (Exod 32.1; Judg 5.28), and in this context they raise the possibility that Qohelet is saying 'eat on time...and do not tarry' (cf. G's πρὸς καιρὸν, noted above). They are also too rare, however, for us to place much weight on that possibility.

10.18 a lazy pair] On the possible ways to read this, see the commentary. M עצלתים appears to be a dual form of עצלה, the feminine of the adjective עצל, which is used substantively many times in Proverbs, and traditionally translated there as 'sluggard'. It should, in other words, describe a pair of things that are feminine as lazy, and this is how I think the consonantal text of M has to be

---

[5] That is not to say that no early readers understood the passage in terms of drink, and *b. Šabbat* 10a notably offers a paraphrase of בגבורה ולא בשתי as בגבורה, של תורה ולא בשתיה של יין, 'in the strength of the Law, and not in the drinking of wine', although it draws from the text a point about timing for study, not about drunkenness.

[6] These points are addressed to a limited extent by McNeile's supposition (152, 166) that G originally had a dative αἰσχύνῃ, 'in shame', based on a faulty Hebrew text with בשת, but there is no evidence of any such reading, and the supposed transformation of αἰσχύνη to αἰσχυνθήσονται would itself be very difficult to explain.

construed: the two things are the hands that will follow in the second part of the verse (so similarly GKC §88 b), and the sense is then 'with a lazy pair (of hands)...with lowliness of hands'. On that understanding, which is reflected in the pointing, the construction is a little strange (why defer 'hands'?), and the parallelism between the parts a little loose: we might expect 'with laziness' to match 'with lowliness', but the word in this form is unlikely to be derived from the noun עצלה / עצלות (Prov 19.15; 31.27)—despite attempts to understand it as an 'intensive' dual (e.g., Gordis) or even speculatively to treat the ים as a formation with enclitic מ (Dahood, 'Canaanite-Phoenician', 194-95; cf. Hummel, 'Enclitic Mem in Early Northwest Semitic, Especially Hebrew', 94). The reading as dual also, of course, presents the problem that adjectives are not normally used in the dual.

G ἐν ὀκνηρίαις speaks of 'hesitations', or perhaps 'acts of laziness', and is followed by Hie, V *in pigritiis*, which probably comes from the La (see Cassian, *Collationes* VI, 17, 1); S ܒܫܦܠܘܬ *bšplwt'* is suspicious—the same noun is used to render the cognate שפלות later in the verse—but T בחלשות and σ' διὰ ὀκνηρίαν also use nouns, albeit with a singular sense. The ancient translations have seemingly not, therefore, read עצלתים as an adjective describing hands, and while it is difficult to deny the possibility that they did read עצלתים and took it as a noun in its own right, all of them could certainly be understood as renderings of the noun עצלות (the use of plurals does not mean that they must have read the dual, as, e.g., Gordis, Schoors, and Lavoie, 'Qohélet 10,16-20', 193, assert—this may simply reflect their understanding of the ות- ending—but it does make it unlikely that they found עצלה). That lends weight to the possibility that we are dealing with an error here in M, and that the letters ים have appeared as duplicates of the ימ in ימך, the following word (so, e.g., Graetz). Another possibility (raised by Siegfried, Sacchi, and, more recently, Schwienhorst-Schönberger) is that they are all that remains of an original ידים, matching that of the second part, although this demands the slightly more complicated supposition that these fragments were eliminated from the traditions behind the versions, while becoming attached to the preceding word in M's tradition. Despite that greater complexity, I find this explanation more plausible for reasons of form and sense. Rose, *Rien de nouveau*, 445-46, suggests a modification, with ימין rather than ידים, which he thinks would offer better stylistic variation and a more credible reason for the error. That is neither necessary nor impossible. No restoration, however, can be made with any certainty, and I have settled in the end for translating M, which, despite its probable faults, offers a sense I consider close to the likely original.

10.18 rafters] We have encountered מקרה several times in the sense 'fate' or 'fortune', but the word here is apparently a homonym (pointed differently in M) that is otherwise unattested in biblical Hebrew. It is connected with קורה, used in several places of beams, and with the verb II קרה which is used of building from wood; McNeile, 83, suggests that the מ in the noun here has been pointed with daghesh to distinguish it from the pi'el participle of that verb (cf. Ps 104.3). The reference is probably not to a roof as such, although the word is sometimes translated that way, but to the beam work that supports a roof, and G, σ' use δόκωσις, which has precisely that sense (see Aitken, *No Stone Unturned*, 52-54).

10.18 sag] M points the verb as niph'al (and G uses the passive ταπεινωθήσεται, 'will be lowered'), although the sense seems to be similar to that of the qal in Ps 106.43 (neither stem appears elsewhere). σ' κατενεχθήσεται might mean 'will sink', but the verb can have a stronger sense of 'will be demolished'.

10.18 lowliness] The word שפלות is another term found nowhere else in biblical Hebrew, but it is used of humility or humiliation in mishnaic texts. S uses the cognate ܫܦܠܘܬܐ *šplwt'*, which refers to humility or weakness, but G renders it using ἀργία: this can be used of laziness, but it literally means 'lack of work' and could simply connote 'inaction' here. This seems in turn to have been rendered *segnitia* in the La (cf. Cassian, *Collationes* VI, 17, 1), and that term has a stronger sense of being slow or lazy, but in Hie and V, Jerome rejects G and the La in favour of *in infirmitate manuum*, 'in weakness of hands'.

This is probably a better understanding. Although the preceding עצלתים has led many commentators to expect another reference to laziness here, there is no reason to suppose that שפלות ever had that sense. Jastrow, *Dictionary*, assigns the sense 'lassitude' to the related Aramaic שפלותא in the Targum to Jer 49.24, but in that text it stands in parallel with 'grief' and 'labour pains', and it corresponds to M רטט, 'panic', so hardly implies 'laziness'. In Syriac ܫܦܠܘܬܐ *šplwt'* can be used to describe the weakness or infirmity of body parts, and שפלותא probably has a similar sense in the passage cited by Jastrow: it is the 'lassitude' of fear and exhaustion, not of indolence or sloth. Along with the Hebrew uses for 'humility', such usages suggest that we are dealing not with sloth again, but with an inability to act that is rooted in some actual incapacity—mental, physical, or socio-political. Related terms in Hebrew include the 'lowliness' that we encountered as something bad in 10.6, and a number of other words indicating physical lowliness or social abasement, so there may be a suggestion that these hands are too low or lowly actually to reach the roof.

10.18 leak] דלף occurs as a verb in Job 16.20, where it apparently refers to weeping, and the cognate noun is found in Prov 19.13 and 27.15, used to describe the annoying dripping of water through a roof on a rainy day; both accord with later Hebrew and with Aramaic usage. In Ps 119.28, however, the verb is used with נפש as a subject, and many commentators have considered it unlikely that the psalmist seeks strength from God because his self is 'dripping' from grief. This has contributed to speculation that there may be more than one verb דלף, and Dahood ('Canaanite-Phoenician', 212; 'Three Parallel Pairs') has noted that the Ugaritic *ydlp* stands in parallel with *ymk* in

KTU 1.2 IV 17 with reference to Yam's body. Dahood sees an architectural metaphor there, which he uses to justify a translation in terms of a house collapsing, and would transfer that sense to ידלף here. There is no good reason to make that speculative leap, however, when the context permits us more simply to understand the verb in terms of a sense attested elsewhere in Hebrew, despite the attempt of Greenfield, 'Lexicographical Notes I', 207-10, to follow Dahood here but retain the sense 'weep' in Job.

10.19 When it is for fun that] Lit. 'for fun' or 'for laughter'; on 'when', see below. This is the same noun that Qohelet used in 2.2; 7.3, 6, and G understands it as 'laughter' in every case. I have tried to draw out in translation the emphasis given to this qualification by the Hebrew word-order.

10.19 they are laying on food] Lit. '(they are) making food' or 'bread' (cf. Ezek 4.15); the verb is a participle. This and similar expressions can refer to providing a meal; see especially Gen 26.30 and the Aramaic Dan 5.1. Salters, 'Koh 10:19', 424, is probably right to reject an idea mentioned by Rashi and picked up by many subsequent commentators, that the reference is to laying on banquets, which is commonly expressed by עשה משתה. However, לחם can refer to meals of a more modest character (1 Sam 20.27), and it seems more likely that Qohelet is claiming that humans take pleasure in dining, than that he believes them either to enjoy the very act of preparing bread or food, or to make food solely for the purpose of pleasure.

There is no explicit subject for the participle, and some commentators, including Fox and Schoors recently, see a reference back to the officials of 10.16-17. More often, the reference is taken to be indefinite, 'they make food', in the sense 'food is made'; that understanding is explicit in S ܚܒܝܕܝܢ *ʿbydyn* 'are made', although the translator adds 'wine' and 'oil' as additional subjects (see below). This is less straightforward than it sounds, because, although main verbs with the third-person plural are frequently used that way, there are very few examples with a participle (cf. GKC §116 t; J-M § 155 f), and most of those are problematic.[7] There are no biblical analogies that would

---

[7] GKC talks of an 'undefined' and J-M of a 'vague' subject in the cases that they list, and the best known instance with a singular participle, in Isa 21.11, involves a vision of 'a man calling', with no periphrasis for the passive, or equivalence to an indefinite 'one'; much the same is true of the less clear-cut uses in Isa 30.24 and 33.4. These should probably not be grouped with texts which have a plural participle, and which are more plausibly linked, therefore, with indefinite, main-verb uses of the third-person plural. Even among those, however, examples cited from Isa 32.12 and Ezek 37.11 are clearly not of a genuinely indefinite usage, and in most cases there is some sort of antecedent, even if the connection is loose (cf. Exod 5.16; Ezek 13.7; 36.13; Neh 6.10); none of these means 'there are people who…', as GKC suggests, and none is readily taken simply as an equivalent to the passive. Jer 38.22 comes closest to such a sense, but even there the reference is not to 'people' doing something in a broad sense, but to the specific actions of

justify rendering 'people make food', and even to get to 'there are people who make food' we would need to assume a very harsh ellipsis of יש. We should not, furthermore, overlook the use of a participle in this clause, as against a yiqtol in the next: despite the temptation to take 'food' and 'wine' in parallel with each other, it is unlikely that we are dealing simply with two parallel statements. I consider it likely that the participle in fact stands in anticipation of חיים (on the sense of which, see the next note), and that technically, therefore, we should construe the first clause as an object of ישמח standing in *casus pendens*, followed by a 'waw of apodosis' (cf. J-M §156 l and, e.g., Exod 12.15), and then a new noun (חיים) in place of a suffix (cf. J-M §156 f). Literally that would mean 'those laying on food...wine will make (them) the living happy'. Although this could have a range of specific implications ('those who...', 'if/when they...'), I think a circumstantial sense fits best here, and avoids an awkward equation of living with laying on dinners.

10.19 then wine will make living people happy] The juxtaposition of 'food' with 'wine' has led some of the ancient translators to try to take them together as objects of עשים. As Goldman suggests, this was probably true of θ', and the influence of that reading on the G tradition may have led indirectly to the similar understanding in S, noted already, as well as the *panem et / ac uinum*, 'bread and wine', of Hie and V.[8] Jerome and θ' do not have, however, any equivalent to a third element, καὶ ἔλαιον, 'and oil', which is widely attested in the G tradition, and reflected in S ܘܡܫܚܐ *wmšḥ*': this presumably emerged under the influence of 9.7-8 or the many other biblical passages in which wine and oil appear together. In any case, once the nouns had been taken together, 'wine' could not be construed simply as the subject of the following ישמח, and ישמח חיים had to be read as a relative or purpose clause of some sort. This may have led to the emergence of a reading לשמח or ישמחו, if the readings of the versions do not just reflect an interpretative manoeuvre.

---

an enemy whose presence is implicit in the context. There are no uses that mean 'people (habitually) do something', or 'something is (habitually) done', and so little justification here for translations like the RSV 'bread is made for laughter'.

[8] For the οἶνος εὐφραίνει which is almost certainly G*, a number of manuscripts have οἶνον τοῦ εὐφρανθῆναι, which is likely hexaplaric. Only the reading of θ' is attested, and that only in Syriac, but Field and Gentry retrovert the Syh reading as καὶ οἶνος τοῦ εὐφρανθῆναι τοὺς ζῶντας, which is clearly close to this Greek variant. The Syriac could equally be retroverted, though, with an accusative οἶνον (cf. Marshall), which would be still closer, and in that case the sense would be '(they make bread for laughter) and wine for gladdening the living'. Like S, however, Syh does not actually have an infinitive, but a third-person plural ܕܢܚܕܘܢ *dnḥdwn*, and the sense originally intended might actually have been like that of Hie, V (which have *ut epulentur*, 'that they might feast'): they make bread and wine 'so that the living may be glad'.

Despite their differences when it comes to the wine, however, all the ancient translators support an understanding of חיים as 'living people', rather than as 'life', even though the Hebrew can in principle have either sense. Subsequent commentators have been more divided (cf. Lavoie, 'Qohélet 10,16-20', 196), but the pi'el of שמח is used of 'making *x* feel happy', not of 'making *x* pleasurable', so an application to 'life' here would require a certain poetic license, even if we did not have the similar expressions in Ps 104.15 and Judg 9.13, noted by Fox, which speak of wine making people (or gods) happy. On my construal, of course, a plural sense is affirmed by the form of עשים, but we should also note that there is no article here (the absence is affirmed by G), and that Qohelet tends to use one when he talks elsewhere about 'the living' collectively (cf. 4.2, 15; 6.8; 9.4, 5), as is normal in biblical usage. These other uses in the book refer to those who are still living, in contrast to their successors (4.15) or the dead (e.g. 9.5), and do not suggest that חיים, even without an article, is simply another way for him to say 'people' or 'humans'. Since 'being alive', as such, does not seem to be the issue here, the term may have been chosen to give a particular nuance: wine makes the living happy to be alive. Rather delightfully, and under the influence of the context, V *uiuentes*, 'the living', has become (the similar sounding) *bibentes*, 'drinkers', in some important manuscripts.

10.19 it is the cost that worries everyone] Lit. 'the money pre-occupies everyone' or perhaps 'the money makes everyone subject (to it)'. The fact that ענה can have various different meanings is a problem here as it was in 5.19; see the note there, and the helpful summary in Lavoie, 'Qohélet 10,16-20', 197-98, of the ways scholars have understood the verb here. I take the most probable sense to be much the same in this verse as in that, and, indeed, as in 1.13 and 3.10 also. G, however, has translated יענה as ἐπακούσεται, which instead means 'will listen to', or 'obey', and which understands the word in terms of I ענה, 'answer'. This causes some immediate problems. G καὶ τοῦ ἀργυρίου ἐπακούσεται σὺν τὰ πάντα does not make 'money' the subject of the verb, and although it is possible that 'wine' continues to be the subject (so *NETS*), it seems unlikely that the translator thought his text meant 'wine obeys money in all things'. Despite the συν, which is omitted from some manuscripts but almost certainly original, we probably have to take σὺν τὰ πάντα as the subject, therefore, to read 'and all things obey money'—which is also the sense of Hie *et argento oboediunt omnia* and V *et pecuniae oboedient omnia*. Jerome, probably following G in this respect, has essentially swapped the subject and object in order to avoid a meaningless statement that 'money obeys all'. Muraoka, *Lexicon*, 203, extrapolates a sense 'grant' (in response to a request) from Hos 2.22, and in *Syntax*, p. 57 n. 1, he applies that understanding to this verse, rendering 'it [= wine], when paid with silver, would provide everything', and glossing this as 'work as a panacea'. Even allowing the possibility that the verb might have such a meaning here, however, 'when paid with silver' seems a considerable stretch for καὶ τοῦ ἀργυρίου, especially with its conjunction, and it is unlikely that the translator would have taken the Hebrew to have any such sense. The reading of G is further complicated by the fact that some important manuscripts have a double rendering, ταπεινώσει ἐπακούσεται, 'will lower / humiliate, will listen to'. It is likely that ταπεινώσει reflects an understanding of יענה as a causative form from the ענה which means 'be wretched' and which is listed as II ענה in *HALOT* and *DCH*, III ענה in BDB. Although it is likely that ταπεινώσει entered the Greek text *via* a marginal gloss, therefore, as McNeile, 166, affirms, it is a gloss that offers a legitimate alternative translation of the Hebrew—and it is tempting to speculate that this is actually a hexaplaric reading, from α′ or θ′. Once situated in the text, however, ταπεινώσει makes that text even more difficult to understand, since it is hard to see how the same subject, whether it is 'money' or 'all', could serve for both verbs, which mean almost the opposite of each other. This, of course, affirms that ταπεινώσει originated in a translation that construed the clause quite differently, and probably had 'money' as its subject. More immediately, though, it raises problems for S, which tries to adopt the double rendering that it has found in G. S ܡܡܟܟ ܘܡܛܥܐ ܠܗܘܢ ܒܟܠ *mmkk wmṭʿ lhwn bkl*, 'subdues and leads them astray in everything', accordingly introduces not only a conjunction to link the verbs, but also a pronominal object 'them', which allows it to take money as the subject, and to read את הכל / σὺν τὰ πάντα in an adverbial sense.[9]

T finds a quite different way around the problems, by following an interpretation found also in the Midrash, and making 'money' the money spent by the righteous on behalf of the poor, which will bear witness for them in front of everybody in the world to come; this is based on a specific use of I ענה in legal contexts (cf. Exod 23.2). Finally, σ′ is attested, with some variants, as ἀργύριον δὲ εὐχρηστήσει εἰς πάντα, 'but money will do for everything', or 'but money will be useful for anything'. This translation is essentially contextual—bread and wine meet specific needs, but those, and everything else, can be met by money instead—and it gets around the problem that G's translation, in terms of obedience, seems to pick up nothing in the first part of the verse. Most subsequent commentators have pursued a similar line, and justified such an understanding by seeing here an extension of I ענה, 'answer', to mean 'answer to (a need)'—and those who have noted σ′ accordingly tend to assume that Symmachus was doing the same. Whether or not that is the case, however, it is difficult to find any other use of the verb which is remotely analogous, and to the extent that I ענה ever goes at all beyond the literal sense

---

[9] The rendering of the second verb is difficult to connect to either the Hebrew or the Greek, leading scholars to suspect that ܡܛܥܐ *mṭʿ* is a corruption of ܡܥܢܐ *mʿn*' (Kamenetzky, 230-31) or ܡܬܥܢܐ *mtʿn*' (McNeile, 166 n. 1), derived from the Syriac equivalent of ענה.

of 'reply', it is only into the area of listening or reacting (the meaning picked up by G); see Delekat, 'Zum hebräischen Wörterbuch', 40.[10] If we are to find a connection between the first part of the verse and the second, then it seems worth considering more closely the sense of הכסף. Qohelet elsewhere uses the noun *without* an article to talk about 'money' in a general sense (see 2.8; 5.9 twice), and in 7.12, I took the use of an article to suggest that Qohelet was referring specifically to the money associated with an inheritance that had already been mentioned. It would be reasonable to assume that the article is significant here also, and that Qohelet is using הכסף in the way that it is used at, e.g., Jer 32.9, to refer to the money expended on something just mentioned—its 'price'—which in this case would be the cost of laying on food and wine. Qohelet's point is then presumably that humans are discouraged from doing something they know would make them happy by their concerns about its cost. I think this is probably expressed using the hiph'il of ענה, 'occupy', since that is a verb favoured by Qohelet elsewhere, but ענה, 'be/make low' (cf. ταπεινώσει), could also provide such a sense, with the cost metaphorically subjugating people rather than pre-occupying them (so Delekat, 'Zum hebräischen Wörterbuch', 41). Of course, the interpretation of את הכל as 'everyone' or 'everything' will depend on the broader understanding adopted for the verse.

[10] Driver, 'Problems and Solutions', 232, cites Hos 2.23-24 as a potential analogy for such a use of 'answer', but those verses have, in fact, long been associated with readings of 10.19 in terms of 'occupy'; cf. Macintosh, *Hosea*, 72-73, 86-87.

10.20–11.6

Over-caution

(10.20) Even with someone close to you, do not curse a king, nor in your bedroom curse someone rich, for the birds of the sky will carry off the sound, and anything with wings will broadcast a speech.

(11.1) Send your bread out upon the water, for over the fullness of time you may find it: (11.2) give a piece to seven, and even to eight, for you do not know what misfortune may happen on the earth.

(11.3) If the clouds are full, they will pour rain on the earth, and whether a tree falls in the south wind or in the north, wherever the tree falls is where it will be. (11.4) Whoever keeps watch on the wind will never sow, and whoever keeps an eye on the clouds will never reap, (11.5) since nobody knows what the way of the wind is.

Like an embryo in the belly of a pregnant woman, just so you will not know what God does, he who will do everything.

(11.6) Sow your seed in the morning, then do not rest your hand until evening: for you do not know which will work, this or that, or if both of them together will be fine.

Commentary

The problem that Qohelet addresses in these verses is that of the human response to uncertainty, and they are punctuated with claims that 'you do not know'. Although there are a few difficulties in the text, the general sense of 11.3-6 is clear: what will be, will be, and if humans spend too much time worrying about what will happen, they will never actually do anything. It is better not to be paralysed by uncertainty, but to be as active as possible. Not all the farmer's seeds will flourish, but that is not a problem if enough are sown, and it will be a bigger problem if all the time is spent watching for perfect conditions.

Although they seem to relate to the same theme, it is less clear what Qohelet is saying in the first two verses of ch. 11 (the principal interpretations, and some less common ones, are helpfully reviewed in Lavoie, 'Qohélet 11,1-2'). The traditional view is that they commend charity or doing good: what we give to others will ultimately be returned to us. This might be affirmed by a rather similar Egyptian saying (see the Introduction, 77-78), that talks of throwing a good deed into the water, and finding it again when it dries—if, of course, the Egyptian saying is itself about charity rather than, as seems more likely, the resilience of goodness. As Fox points out, though, there are other passages in Egyptian literature which see generosity toward others as a useful insurance against the vicissitudes of life. Some commentators have also pointed to a much later story of a prince stranded on an island, who is saved by bread thrown into the river without any consciousness that he was there, and v. 1, at least, could similarly be read as enjoining a less deliberate sort of charity.

The principal difficulty with this reading lies in the nature of the initial imagery. Throwing things on to water of an unspecified sort is not self-evidently a good way to distribute them to others, and unless the bread (or 'food', if we construe the Hebrew word more generally) is as waterproof as the Egyptian good deed, throwing that on to water looks like a way simply of destroying it, or of feeding the fish.[1] As Magarik, 'Bread on Water', 269, puts it, 'one could at best retrieve soggy refuse'. There are broadly two ways to address this problem, one of which tries to understand the imagery differently, the other of which accepts the imagery but sees the outcome as potential rather than certain. Perhaps the most popular approach under the first heading, at least for more than a century, has been to

---

[1] This is how it is understood in a later Jewish folktale, examined in Börner-Klein, 'Transforming', which features a fish that has grown giant because of a youth's obedience to the advice. A few scholars have also thought that Qohelet is commending fishing, either using bread as bait, or simply fattening the fish one will later catch: Bishop, 'A Pessimist in Palestine', 40, recounts the experience of a friend who saw fish being fed with bread in the Kinneret.

assume that the bread is not being thrown directly on to water, but sent across it in ships, so that this is an admonition to trade, or perhaps to disperse one's goods across many ships. This rests, however, on a somewhat literal-minded reading of Prov 31.14, which compares with merchant ships the woman who forages far and wide for her bread (presumably to get the best bargains or the finest loaves). That verse does not imply that the ships themselves trade in bread, which is far too perishable for such trade, and it would be a considerable stretch to claim that Qohelet is talking about 'grain' or 'wealth' more generally here, even were 'finding' their merchandise again the normal aim of merchants. A very different suggestion (Homan, 'Beer Production') that nonetheless retains the imagery, simply sees here a reference to beer-making—although it is then quite unclear what point Qohelet is supposed to be making, unless it is that one should seek every pleasure in the face of uncertainty.

The second general approach is to embrace the absurdity or apparent futility implied by the imagery. Throwing it out on the water might seem a sure way to dispose of bread forever—but sometimes it might turn up again, and prove that even the most thoughtless or reckless deed can ultimately pay off. For scholars who take such an approach, the point is either that protecting oneself involves taking risks while spreading risk (not putting all one's eggs in one basket), or that actions are utterly unpredictable (Lavoie, 'Qohélet 11,1-2', 88, sees a juxtaposition in 11.1-2 of a senseless action that can have a good outcome, with a prudent action that brings no guarantee of success). Both understandings, however, rest on an assumption that, to use Qohelet's image, the bread may not always be found. This is potentially problematic because Hebrew does not distinguish 'you will find' from 'you may find' except contextually, and so the element of uncertainty that might guide one to such an interpretation is only present if one already accepts that interpretation. It is very uncertain, furthermore, that v. 2 presents a counterexample of a cautious deed that may go wrong, which would at least help to clarify the point. More fundamentally, of course, if we accept the imagery as it stands, then it is hard to say that there is ever a 'good' outcome, unless the bread has somehow survived an immersion of 'many days' to remain edible.

I am sure that we must indeed embrace the absurdity of the image, but also that we should accept its implications. I take both the first two verses of ch. 11 to involve images of bread, which in some sense represents one's substance or possessions. The advice that Qohelet offers in the first is to throw it in the water, with the hope or expectation of eventually finding it again once whatever bad times have passed; in the second, he commends giving most or all of it to others—there are probably eight pieces to the loaf (see below). We are to get things out of harm's way or to spread them around as a response to our uncertainty, but by doing so, in effect we lose them. The advice, in other words, is apparently to let our fear of loss lead us to create that loss for ourselves. This prefigures what is to come in the verses that follow, where a caution bred of conscious ignorance similarly provokes an unhelpful over-reaction. It also, though, suggests that Qohelet is being sarcastic in advising us to adopt the very strategies that he is caricaturing—perhaps even parodying more familiar sayings about insurance for the future, if the example known from Egyptian literature had counterparts in the author's own context.

If 11.1-2 are in essence a parody, the same is probably true also of 11.3, with its solemn statement of the obvious. Such an understanding also offers a way to interpret 10.20, which is linked to the verses that precede it by references to kingship and wealth, but otherwise has little in common with anything said in 10.16-19. It probably is true that cursing the king would not have been wise, although it is less clear that the wealthy would generally have worried about such things. The idea that birds might report curses uttered in private, however, takes such concerns to an extreme, and although the advice itself is not so inherently absurd as what follows, this bizarre image, and the underlying paranoia, can reasonably lead us to suppose that Qohelet sees an instance of over-caution in this behaviour as well. Krüger, 'Meaningful Ambiguities', 71, rightly asks 'whether one should regard this text as a serious advice or as a caricature of an overanxious self-censorship'. The more important question, though, is how 11.6 is supposed to relate to all this, falling as it does after Qohelet's rejection of such caution in vv. 4-5. The advice to sow all day clearly counters the idea in 11.4, that too much worrying may lead one never to sow or reap, and so the verse seems to stand firmly against worrying. At the same time, though, it advocates excessive caution of a different sort, and shows that Qohelet's advice here is more nuanced than a simple, implied exhortation to be bold. Rather, we should not let a knowledge of our own ignorance lead us either to take ridiculous precautions or to do nothing, but instead throw ourselves into activity. In doing so, we should be aware that some of what we do may fail, but can hope that some will also succeed. The sentiment partly echoes Qohelet's earlier admonition in 7.18: 'It is good that you grab this, and do not hold your hand back from that'.

10.20] Ginsburg's analogy with a passage from Juvenal seems appropriate:

> O Corydon, Corydon, do you think anything to do with a rich man is secret? Should the slaves stay quiet, then the horses will talk, and the dog, and the doorposts, and the marbles. Shut the windows, block any cracks with cloth, latch the doors, do away with any light, get everyone out of there, let no-one settle down nearby—even then, by the time the cock makes its second crow, the nearest tradesman will know it before daybreak, and he will be listening to what the pastry-chef, the cooks and the carvers think as well.
> (Juvenal, *Satires* 9.102-108; my translation)

The point expressed by both Juvenal and this saying is that some things just will not stay secret, whatever precautions one takes. For Juvenal, however, the underlying problem is that the affairs of the rich inevitably generate interest among those who work for them, while here it is that the rich and the powerful themselves might punish disrespect: the saying is addressed, by implication, to those who are neither rich nor powerful. Even allowing that the audience may have had to contend with political oppression and informants, there is perhaps more than a note of paranoia in the idea that birds will pick up and make public even words spoken privately at home—although the paranoia probably does not extend to implying that the birds might pick up one's thoughts, which is a very early understanding of the text, reflected in many translations (see the notes). This verse is very plausibly the source of our modern, much more innocuous expression 'a little bird told me'.

Another text with which analogies are sometimes drawn is to be found in the Aramaic version of *Ahiqar* (Cowley, 215, l. 98; *TAD* C1.1 l. 82). In the context of advice about not talking too much, and taking care over what one says, this claims that a word is like a bird, never to be recaptured once it has been released. The imagery and the point here, however, are very different.

11.2] Although numerical progressions are a common feature of Hebrew literary style, the particular choice of the numbers seven and eight has provoked much discussion. Writing anonymously in 1730, Jacques de Martin (in his 'Explication') made a clever suggestion that has largely been overlooked by subsequent commentators, but that gives a plausible explanation for the use of 'seven' and 'eight' here. Noting the Roman habit of scoring a round *quadra* loaf so that it could be torn easily, and the (rather obscure) reference in Hesiod's *Works and Days*, 442, to a quartered loaf that probably yields eight portions, he suggested that the 'seven or even eight' here was a reference to just such pieces: we might think in more modern terms of a pizza sliced four times to yield eight slices. In fact, since de Martin's time, numerous carbonized loaves of *panis quadratus*, actually decussated into eight slices, have been discovered at Pompeii and Herculaneum, and such loaves are illustrated in frescoes there, whole or torn into their constituent slices. It is hard to say for sure what styles of bread would have been familiar to Qohelet's audience, but there is no particular reason to suppose that such loaves would not have been known earlier and elsewhere in the Mediterranean world—and the pre-formed loaves merely reflect anyway what is a natural way of slicing or tearing a round loaf. If the reference here is to portions of the bread, therefore, Qohelet is not just using a random numerical progression, but saying, in effect, 'give most—or even all—of it'. If we are to take vv. 1 and 2 together, moreover, there may be a contrast intended between sea and land (= 'earth'), or even a further level of irony: safety is being sought in the notoriously dangerous sea, when the potential problems are on the relatively safer land.

11.3-4] The Greek and Masoretic texts understand 'If the clouds are full of rain, they will empty themselves upon the earth', which is a plausible reading of the text, although slightly less likely. It is also possible to understand a reference to the directions, south and north, rather than to the winds. The point in any case, though, is that these things are obvious, and watching for them will not alter them—but it will prevent one from getting on with anything more useful. Some commentators have found references to divination, but that seems an unnecessary complication in a context that is clearly agricultural, and in which farmers are watching for the wind and rain because such things affect their sowing and harvesting of crops (the agricultural issues are discussed in Whitwell, 'Variation', 85-86).

11.5] Context is also important, I think, for understanding this verse. The same Hebrew word can be used for 'wind' and 'spirit', and this has long provoked commentators to see an illustration of human ignorance, in a claim that we do not know how the spirit enters an embryo in its mother's womb. It is actually quite difficult to extract that sense from the Hebrew, however, and we may reasonably wonder, anyway, whether the author would have believed such a thing to happen: 'spirit' is associated with breathing (cf. 3.21; 12.7), and babies do not breathe in the womb. This is an idea that could only really find purchase in contexts where 'spirit' had become 'soul' (see the notes). The point is more probably that humans are as ignorant as embryos, and equally unable to see what is going on around them. The reference to the wind then belongs with the previous verse, with which it fits very neatly: watching the wind will not only prevent sowing, but will also accomplish nothing, since nobody can learn its movements.

11.6] The admonition is to sow all day, not just in the morning and evening, and this is itself an indication that, although he is still using the imagery of agriculture, Qohelet is talking about something more general: we should be in constant action, because we do not know which of our actions will accomplish what we want. In T and other early Jewish interpretation (cf. also the Christian, Coptic homily cited in Wright, 'Commentary', 275-76), 'morning' and 'evening' are understood to stand for 'youth' and 'old age', drawing in the imagery and issues that are about to follow in 11.7–12.2, and many modern commentators (e.g. Barton; Fredericks, 'Life's Storms', 104) have adopted that understanding. Their willingness to read the passage figuratively has not generally extended to adopting the other element of that earlier interpretation—which takes the sowing of 'seed' as a reference to procreation—but I think this understanding anyway tends to overwrite the imagery of the verse, and to underplay its distinctiveness from what follows: if anything, 11.7–12.2 are playing off the figure of a farmer's day in order to introduce a very different day/night contrast. It is possible, however, to go too far in the other direction, and to neglect the figurative aspect altogether. When Whitwell, 'Variation', 86, makes the point that repeated sowings on the same day would make no difference to outcomes in terms of the weather, then perhaps he has a point that we should treat the expression here as closer to 'day and night', or '24/7'—implying continuous action over an extended period. I doubt, though, that Qohelet is actively and literally commending the practice of repeat sowings, as Whitwell goes on to suggest. I am similarly unpersuaded by the assertion of Gorssen, 'La Cohérence', 286, that the general context here is economic, because Qohelet sees economic activity as a prerequisite to the enjoyment of prosperity. This is not advice aimed actually at farmers, but an agricultural metaphor used to make a more general point about human activity.

That point can be taken in more negative terms. Lavoie, 'Le Repos', 345-46, for instance, talks about the implied lack of connection between effort and result, and about the lack of control that goes with a reliance on luck or the hidden activity of God. Those issues are undoubtedly important to Qohelet, and implicit in what he says. Especially in the light of what follows, however, I doubt they are supposed to be at the forefront here. The uncertainty that can provoke foolish over-caution, or simple paralysis, can also drive us to action, and to undertake the work in which it is possible to find pleasure. Viviers, 'Nie 'n kans vat', 377, offers a pleasing summary (most of which is included in the title to the article) that can loosely be translated: 'Don't take a chance or avoid a chance, but take all the chances you get—for life is uncertain'. On the other hand, I think Ogden, 'Qoheleth XI 1-6', 227, entirely misses the point by talking about a recommendation that the farmer 'is to proceed on the basis of what information he is able to obtain, though with an eye to what conceivably could happen but over which he has no control': Ogden seemingly imports the idea that there may be *some* knowledge from the reference to 'finding' one's bread in 11.1, with which he associates supposed cognitive uses of the verb.

Notes

10.20 with someone close to you] Or possibly 'in your mind'. In Dan 1.4, 17, מדע is an intellectual skill or quality shared by Daniel and his friends, and in 2 Chr 1.10, 12 it is מדע, alongside wisdom, that God grants to Solomon at his request. The word is late, and probably inherited from Aramaic, but these uses accord with others in both Hebrew and Aramaic (see Hurvitz, *Lexicon*, 159-60), so it is surprising to find that most of the ancient versions understand the noun here to mean not 'knowledge' or some such, but 'mind' (Hie *mente*), 'thought' (V *cogitatione*), or 'consciousness' (G συνειδήσει; La *conscientia*, see Leanza, 'Le tre versione', 94; it need not have the moral connotations of 'conscience' imputed by Vinel and found in much NT usage). It seems more likely that the translators have felt compelled to make such a change because one does not curse 'in one's knowledge', rather than because they were familiar with such a use of מדע. Even so, as many commentators have acknowledged, 'mind' offers a strange parallel to the subsequent 'bedroom(s)', even if it seems pedantic to insist that thoughts, by their very nature, are unlikely to be overheard. Consequently, there have been numerous attempts either to emend the text (most famously, Perles, *Analekten*, 71-72, would read במצעך, 'on your bed'), or to understand it in a different way (see Lavoie, 'Qohélet 10,16-20', 200; and Piotti, 'La relazione', 81-84).

The versions impose some constraints on both approaches. Although they have had to shift its sense, none of them obviously reflects a consonantal text different from that of M, and none has recognized any alternative meaning that would avoid the problems: if מדע could refer to putting out the lights, the matrimonial bedroom (so Piotti, 'La relazione'), or even just to intimacy or repose (so Thomas, 'Note'), none of the ancient translators was apparently aware of such an option. There is another term מדע, however, that is quite well attested, and that gives an appropriate sense, even if it is pointed differently in M: it was suggested as a possible alternative in *BH³*, and is the reading advocated here by Zorell. We find this as מדע in Prov 7.4, where it stands parallel to 'sister', and as מודע in Ruth 2.1 *Qᵉrê*, where it refers to a relation, or member of one's extended family. A similar word מידע is used of close friends or intimates (e.g. Ruth 2.1 *Kᵉthîbh*; 2 Kgs 10.11; Ps 55.14 ET 13; Job 19.14), and מודע is found with that sense in 1QHᵃ xii, 9 (aligned with רע), so there may have been some interchangeability. These terms are pointed and usually parsed as hophʻal and puʻal participles of ידע, but they are used as substantives (cf. the מדעת of Ruth 3.2), and can also be linked with the Ugaritic and Akkadian terms that led Dahood, 'Canaanite Words', 210-11, to understand the meaning 'friend' here. A defective spelling of מודע may have been sufficiently unusual that the versions could be forgiven for overlooking it, or their interpretation might have been influenced by a desire to give much the same, locative sense to ב- in each of its uses here, but if we do understand 'close friend' or 'family member' then Qohelet is probably using the preposition with its nuance of doing something in company with somebody, or speaking with them (cf. Num 12.8). In short, then, we have to choose between a familiar word used with an unfamiliar meaning, or a rarer but attested word in its usual sense, and I have opted for the latter.

10.20 curse[1]] σ′ uses the same verb as in 7.21, 22, and λοιδορήσῃς has a more general sense of abusing or reviling; cf. V *detrahas*, 'disparage'.

10.20 your bedroom] M חדרי משכבך is plural, 'the chambers of your lying', and this is reflected in G ταμιείοις, 'chambers'—although the reading in most Greek manuscripts extends the plural to the next word as well: ἐν ταμιείοις κοιτώνων σου means 'in chambers of your lyings'. A singular is attested in S, Hie, V, T, as well as in a few Hebrew manuscripts (see de Rossi), perhaps because this provides a closer parallel to the preceding מדע, but more probably because, as Barthélemy, *Studies*, 556-57, suggests, they recognize that the plural of this noun is being used idiomatically for the singular (cf. Ezek 8.12). There is no need, therefore, to emend to the singular, as Driver, 'Problems and Solutions', 233, suggests.

10.20 the birds of the sky...something with wings] If it meant 'a bird of heaven' or something similar, עוף השמים would have to be an instance of those rare, mostly poetic constructions, in which a genitive expression is indeterminate despite the *nomen rectum* having a definite article (cf. J-M §139 b). Although it is frequently translated that way, however, this is a fixed expression which does have a determinate, collective sense, 'the birds of the sky'. In 1 Kgs 14.11; 16.4; 21.24, indeed, it even takes a plural verb, although Ps 104.12 has a singular, as here. The image is not of every bird in the world collecting together, Hitchcock-style, but nor is it of a sparrow on one's windowsill. As in the 1 Kings passages, where bodies are left outside for the birds, the point is presumably that the sound will be picked up by whatever birds are in the area.

The second expression, בעל הכנפים or בעל כנפים has no such collective usage, and has no exemption from the rules about determination of genitive expressions. That means that the *Qᵉrê* without an article (which is also the primary reading in many Hebrew manuscripts) is more likely to be original on grammatical grounds if Qohelet means 'a thing with wings', less likely if he means 'the thing with wings'. The various Greek readings that are attested tend to support the latter (although they are complicated, see below), but it is also more likely that an article was introduced to match the preceding expression than that one was lost. See also the next note. For the ways in which בעל is used, see the note at 10.11. The expression here probably means no more than 'one that possesses wings', which is the sense of the majority reading in G, ὁ ἔχων πτέρυγας, which may be derived, wholly or in part, from θ′.[2]

---

[2] Syh gives θ′ as, ܡܠ ܐܝܬ ܪ̈ܐܒܐ ܐܦ *whw dʿp' 'yt lh*—which probably represents καὶ ὁ ἔχων πτέρυγας. For G*, Rahlfs adopts ὁ ἔχων τὰς πτέρυγας, for which there is only very slight attestation, and Gentry ὁ τὰς πτέρυγας ἔχων. It is questionable, however, whether either of these is likely to have been the original reading of G: the translator habitually renders בעל using παρά (5.10, 12; 7.12; 8.8; 12.11), and we never find ἔχω at all elsewhere in the book—not even in 10.11, which is the only other place where παρά does not appear for בעל. As in that verse,

10.20–11.6   561

The reading of α' καὶ ὁ κυριεύων πτέρυγος, 'and the ruler of a wing', takes בעל inappropriately in its sense of 'master', and σ' is probably closer to the original sense with καὶ τὰ πτερωμὰ / πτερωτὰ ἀναγγελεῖ, 'and the winged thing(s) will announce' (on the attributions, see Marshall). Although this is the literal sense, however, the expression may be just another way of saying 'bird': that is surely the sense of בעל כנף in Prov 1.17, where nobody is likely to be using nets to trap insects or beetles.

10.20 the sound...a speech] Where M has את הקול, almost all manuscripts of G have τὴν φωνήν σου, 'your voice', and none have σὺν τὴν φωνήν, 'the voice', which is the reading adopted by Rahlfs and Gentry. We do, however, find σου τὴν φωνήν in a few witnesses, and just τὴν φωνήν elsewhere, principally in Origenic texts (cf. Hie *uocem*): as Gentry, 'Propaedeutic', 155-56, has suggested, these support Rahlfs' reconstruction, and show how the tradition has developed. On that reckoning, the original σὺν, which is in line with the translation technique of G but is awkward in Greek, has been read as a more familiar σου, and that, in turn, has been moved to its proper position in the majority text, with other texts simply eliminating the initial σὺν or σου. Rather more substantial difficulties, however, surround the note in Syh that σ' and θ' are 'likewise'. Gentry, followed by Marshall, makes the case that this note is based on a lemma which had τὴν φωνήν σου, rather than the τὴν φωνήν of Syh itself, but if that is really the case, then the translators themselves had that reading, and potentially support a Hebrew text with 'your voice', evidence for which might also be supplied by V *uocem tuam* and S ܡܠܟ *qlk*.

It is very interesting to note, therefore, that where M has דבר, again without 'your', all Greek manuscripts have λόγον σου, 'your word', which is once more supported by S, although not by any other versions. There may have been Hebrew variants involved in both cases (which would make the purported change of σὺν to σου coincidental), but there was clearly pressure at various points to make the text more precise. In any case, it is not clear why M את הקול is determined but דבר is not. If Qohelet is generalizing the statement, then this might be a further argument for בעל כנפים and against בעל הכנפים.

10.20 will broadcast] יגיד appears to be pointed in M as a jussive (cf. GKC §53 n), which is specifically supported by none of the versions and is improbable in parallel with יוליך. *BHS* accordingly commends vocalizing as

---

it is not impossible that the translator broke with his normal habits, but we might expect the original reading to have been something like ὁ παρὰ πτερύγων, which is not found anywhere. In those texts that have ἔχων, it appears variably before or after the noun, and those that have not simply taken up the reading of θ' in its entirety may have borrowed or independently introduced just the verb, in order to facilitate the reading of a text which was already corrupt—perhaps the meaningless ὁ τὰς πτέρυγας of Vaticanus (and hence of Swete's edition), which is found also in a few other manuscripts.

יַגִּיד; cf. also Schoors, *The Preacher* I, 89. Ginsburg, *Massorah*, 3:71, lists a *Qᵉrê* יגד (which he points יַגֵּד), and it may have been knowledge of this defective form that influenced the Masoretic pointing. The verb can signify informing and reporting in all sorts of contexts, but in the absence of any specified destination, I take the point here to be not that the speech will be conveyed directly to the rich man who has been insulted, but that it will become public knowledge—the sense is, therefore, close to that in, e.g., Isa 48.20.

11.1 Send your bread out upon the water] Lit. 'send your bread over/ upon the surface of the water'. The expression על פני המים is used in Gen 1.2; 7.18; Exod 32.20, and it appears without an article in Job 24.18; 26.10; Isa 19.8; Hos 10.7. It does not refer to any particular type of water (V *transeuntes aquas*, 'running waters', makes it more specific and injects an idea of the bread being carried away), nor does it obviously have any particular connotation of 'floating', as Seow suggests, although in this context it is noteworthy that Hos 10.7 uses the expression in a simile for destruction.

Segal notes the assonance of שלח לחמך, and of the subsequent המים... הימים. Pinker's emendation of the text to לחש חלמך, 'whisper your dream' (in 'Qohelet 11:1'), furnishes a connection with 10.20, but is entirely speculative, with no support in the versions. He does not say how the text might have been so transformed, but although a transposition of characters in the second word is plausible, a simultaneous change of לחש to שלח would be difficult to explain.

The noun לחם itself refers to bread, and I take that literal sense to be what Qohelet is talking about here, because I also take the next verse to be talking about portions of that bread. To be sure, the noun can be used more generally for food or meals, and in Prov 31.14 it describes food sought out by the woman from distant sources—although it is doubtful that the comparison with merchant ships made there licenses us to suppose that לחם would characteristically have been used more generally for goods transported that way.[3] There are no grounds on which to suppose that לחם is being used of seeds, either of the sort that are sown,[4] or of those that could be used to impregnate somebody.

---

[3] Zimmermann tries to get that sense from another direction, claiming that a translator has mistakenly rendered the term פרס that is generally used for 'a covering' but once, in the Targum to Ezek 27.7, for 'a sail', as though it were a homonym that can be used for pieces of bread or food. This is very thin: the Aramaic noun is not a regular term for a sail, let alone a way of talking about ships. The objections to the 'merchant ship' interpretation in general are set out persuasively and very thoroughly in Pinker, 'Qohelet 11:1', 625-29.

[4] An idea that Qohelet commends here sowing on ground that is sufficiently wet, is found principally in Jewish scholarship: see Pinker, 'Qohelet 11:1', 629-31. Differently, Lowth, *Lectures*, 1:222-23, crediting George Jubb with the idea, cites from Theognis and Phocylides an image of 'sowing in the sea' used as an analogy for assisting or befriending the wicked—which would make this an admonition to

11.1 for] As often, the value of כי has evoked much debate in 11.1-2, and there is a detailed discussion of that debate in Ellermeier, *Qohelet I.1*, 253-55. The key point in this verse is whether the expectation of 'finding' in the second part of the verse is supposed to provide the motivation for 'sending' in the first place, or whether the point is that if one 'sends' one may *yet* 'find' later (an interpretation often associated with Hertzberg and Lauha in particular). Michel, in *Untersuchungen*, 207-8, adds another option of reading כי simply as a way of adding a comment to the commands: he characterizes it as 'deictic/discursive', and would translate 'Laß dein Brot auf dem Wasser davonschwimmen—fürwahr/nun: du kannst es (trotzdem) nach einer Reihe von Tagen wiederfinden', 'Let your bread float on the water—indeed/now you find it again anyway after a series of days'. Of course, this is not really a lexical question about כי, but a broader issue about the meaning of the verse. All the same, it is important to be conscious that the use of כי to introduce motive clauses after imperatives is so very common that for an author to use it with any other sense in such a context, with no clear signal, might be deemed clumsy or even positively misleading. In fact, I share the view of many who prefer the concessive/adversative translation, that uncertainty is the issue here, but take the force of the כי to be 'you may do something so counter-intuitive as casting away your bread *because* you think it may work out for the best'. It provides a motive, but not strictly a cause.

11.1 over the fullness of time] Lit. 'in abundance of the days'. An English speaker can say 'she will return in three days', meaning 'she will return *on the third day from now*', or more broadly 'in many days' to mean 'after many days have passed', but that is not a typical Hebrew usage, and in Isa 24.22 it is notably מרב ימים that is used for 'after many days'. When ב- is used with an expression for a period of time, in fact, we would expect it to indicate 'within' or 'in the course of', and the preposition does not naturally mark the time that separates events. Rather than suppose, therefore, with Dahood, 'Review of Aartun', 282, that here ב- means 'after' (which would be exceptional, although Dahood claims the sense to be common), we should probably take it with

be liberal without hope of reward. It probably is true that in Isa 28.28 לחם refers to the plants or ears of grain from which bread will ultimately be made, even if the verse is somewhat obscure, and the same may be true in Isa 30.23. The latter, however, explicitly differentiates between seed that is sown and לחם that grows from the ground, while the former is concerned with the processing of harvested לחם, not with either seed that has been sown or with processed grain. The fact that לחם can very occasionally be used to describe generically the plants from which grain for making bread might be produced does not suggest that in this verse we can equate it with seeds or grains. More importantly, the verb used here is not otherwise used of sowing (unlike זרע in vv. 4 and 6), so it is far from clear that an audience would have read this admonition in such terms, even were the sowing of seed a possible reading in principle.

תמצאנו as a vaguer expression of context. Strictly, Qohelet is not saying that the bread will necessarily be found after a long time has passed, but that it will be found at some point or points in the course of a long time (not necessarily all at once); cf. G, and σ' ἐν γὰρ πολλοῖς χρόνοις, lit. 'for within many periods of time' (which also uses a familiar Greek expression to make it clear that this is not just a matter of 'days'). S notably uses -ܒ *l*-, 'at', instead, to make the point more precise.

In the G tradition, some manuscripts omit the article before 'days', to give a smoother πλήθει ἡμερῶν, 'plenty of days', rather than 'plenty of *the* days', but some others understand the expression differently to be a reference to the days of one's life and add σου, 'your', to make that sense clearer. This is also, essentially, the understanding of T, and such particularization draws attention to the unusual determination of the expression here in the Hebrew (contrast Isa 24.22; Zech 8.4). If there is a special nuance intended by this, I take it to be that Qohelet is talking not just about any period of 'many days', but about 'the many days (to come)'.

11.2 give a piece to seven, and even to eight] Lit. 'give a portion' or 'share': the Hebrew word is חלק, used elsewhere by Qohelet to talk about one's share in the world. The advice could be 'give a portion each to seven or eight', or 'give a portion, to seven or eight'—that is, give away many portions or give one portion to many. It is interesting to compare Ezek 16.33, where 'they give a gift (singular) to all prostitutes, but you have given your gifts (plural) to all your lovers'. Hebrew, like English, can use either the singular (distributively) or the plural in such expressions, and accordingly, the fact that חלק is singular does not preclude the possibility that Qohelet is talking about giving many portions, or force us to the view of Podechard and others, that just one portion is involved. Equally, though, there are no definitive grounds on which to reject that view. This is not just a matter of the sense of נתן, as Seow assumes when he does so, or, indeed, of -ל, but it is true that uses like that in Josh 14.4 and 15.13 tell against understanding the expression specifically as 'make a portion into seven or eight pieces', or 'give a portion by sevens or eights'. On my understanding that Qohelet is still talking about bread, the most natural way to read this is in terms of a portion of the loaf being distributed to each of seven or eight (people), but there is admittedly some slight ambiguity. If the reference were not to bread and the nature of the gift unspecified, the implication of חלק would be unclear: the range of the noun in biblical Hebrew is not such that we could easily understand 'give alms to', or even 'give a share (of your possessions)'.

As for the 'seven and...eight', T takes the numbers to refer to months, and reads the verse in the light of v. 6, as an admonition to sow portions of seed at different times of year. More modern commentators have noted other progressions from 'seven' to 'eight'—only Mic 5.4 (ET 5.5) in the Bible, but a number of times in other languages, especially Ugaritic (see conveniently

Cathcart, 'Notes', 512-13, and 'Incantations', 41-42; the latter cites and supplements the list in Dahood, 'Parallel Pairs', 345). This distribution hardly requires explanation in terms of 'Canaanite influence' (so Dahood, 'Canaanite-Phoenician', 212-13), and the appearance of the sequence in incantations and magical texts does not, I think, suggest that it could only be used in such contexts, or that we must accordingly read 11.2 in such terms (so Cathcart, 'Incantations', 45). In fact, the numbered items are very disparate within those texts, and seem to represent no simple convention, while it is not always clear whether the numbers are simply magical, expressions of a large quantity (of promised sons, e.g., in the passage from Keret cited by Cathcart, 'Notes', 513) or references to specific but now unknown traditions (such as the 'eight wives' of Baal in an Arslan Tash incantation).

More generally, we must treat with some caution the claim of GKC §134 s, that the 'collocation of a numeral with the next above it' can be used not only to express numbers that need not be specified exactly (as in Isa 17.6, where 'two or three...four or five' are used just as we would use such expressions in English; cf., e.g., 2 Kgs 9.32; Jer 36.23), but also 'to express merely an indefinite total'. In Prov 30.15-16, 18-19, 21-23, 29-31, which are often cited as classic 'numerical sayings', the larger number in each sequence corresponds to the number of items in the list that follows (cf. Prov 6.16-19; Sir 23.16; 26.28; 50.25-26; and probably 25.7-10). The same is not true in the sequences that begin the book of Amos—although the consistent 'three or four' surely does not represent an 'indefinite' number there—and Job 5.19 begins a list that is not completed (perhaps for effect). All the same, numerical progressions in the biblical literature do not typically use just random or 'significant' numbers: they are not all manifestations of the same device, but when not of the 'two or three' sort, they more commonly count items or refer to specific items, and it is reasonable to take seriously the idea that Qohelet has in mind something that would naturally be understood to consist of seven or eight items or parts. Against the notion that this is merely an example of a common rhetorical strategy, furthermore, we should note the exceptional use of וגם to link the numbers. As my translation suggests, I take this to imply more than just 'seven or eight', as though those were vague alternatives.

A reading attributed to σ' in ms 252 is listed by Gentry as πρώτοις for τοῖς ἑπτά. This is curious enough to make Field and Marshall speculate that this note is actually just a misattributed scholion, but we are perhaps intended in this case to supplement rather than replace τοῖς ἑπτά. In that case, Symmachus may have paraphrased the text here as 'the first seven (people you encounter)'.

11.2 what misfortune may happen] As it is usually understood, the construction with מה has parallels in, e.g., 1 Sam 26.18; 2 Sam 19.29; 1 Kgs 12.16; Esth 6.3. Essentially, מה itself functions as a pronoun, which is then qualified by a subsequent substantive (J-M §144 d sees the latter in terms of an 'accusative of limitation'). Here, therefore, the Hebrew is literally 'what may happen (as) a misfortune'. This may be related to the usage of מה without a substantive, in e.g. 2 Sam 18.29, but there is no particular reason to make a connection with Ct 8.4, where מה replaces the אם used in similar expressions at Ct 2.7; 3.5 to mean something like 'lest': doing so does not, anyway, permit us to make it mean 'whether' here, as Montgomery, 'Notes', 244, proposes.

Either because the translator is trying to match the word-order, or because he has understood the expression differently, G reads τί ἔσται πονηρὸν, which more naturally means 'what will be evil' (although Syh, like S, moves the noun in front of the verb to avoid that implication). If we are to take this as interpretative, the translator perhaps takes the point to be that we cannot know which of the portions might prove bad (and maybe, like T, understanding the verse in the light of 11.6).

11.2 on the earth] יבשת / יבשה is normally used for 'dry land' *per se*, and this same expression על הארץ will be used in the next verse with no such connotation. All the same, it is tempting to see some contrast with the preceding 'water', and we might note both that ארץ is the name given to יבשה in Gen 1.10, and that Jastrow, *Dictionary*, lists the sense 'dry land' (without direct citation) for later Hebrew.

11.3 If the clouds are full, they will pour rain on the earth] G understands 'full of rain', reading נשם with מלאו, which is probably the reading implied also by the Masoretic accents (G does not contradict M, as Gentry suggests). A misunderstanding of the Greek ἐὰν πληρωθῶσιν τὰ νέφη ὑετοῦ provoked by the word-order (which follows the Hebrew, as usual), probably underlies the muddled S ܐܢ ܥܢܢܝܢ ܕܡܛܪܐ ܡܠܝܢ *'n nmlyn 'nny mṭr'*, 'if clouds of rain are full', which, as Kamenetzky, 231, notes, has hardly been derived from the Hebrew. In Hie and V, however, Jerome takes נשם as the object of יריקו, so that the clouds 'pour out rain', and this reading has been preferred by many commentators, not least because an absolute use of ריק in the hiphʿil is otherwise unattested, and the qal is never used. It is the easier to justify for that reason, and I have adopted it here, but both understandings are likely possible, and there is little difference in sense. For G ἐκχέουσιν, 'pour out', α' and (according to ms 252) σ' read ἐκκενώσουσιν, 'empty out', which gives a slightly different image.

11.3 the south wind or in the north] Both nouns can be used either of the direction, or of the wind associated with that direction. Since 11.4 is clearly referring back to this verse, I take the reference to be to the winds, and correspondingly, I doubt that this is a merism for 'everywhere', as Fox suggests. Unlike G, where the Greek shares the ambiguity of the Hebrew, σ' in the first part uses ἐν μεσημβρίᾳ, 'in the south', which can only refer to the direction. S ܒܐܬܪܐ ܕܓܪܒܝܐ *b'tr' dgrby'*, 'in a northern place', likewise seems designed to exclude a reading in terms of the wind, and Syh has a similar expression ܒܕܘܟܬܐ ܕܓܪܒܝܐ *bdwkt' dgrby'*, 'in a northern position'.

11.3 a tree] σ' is attested as both the singular δένδρον, 'tree', and as the plural δένδρα: Marshall argues convincingly that the plural is more probably original, and this fits the verb that σ' goes on to use (see below). It seems likely that Symmachus is trying to emphasize the generality of the statement by talking about trees, rather than a single tree. G uses ξύλον, which, like the Hebrew עץ of M, can mean 'timber': in both versions, the statement could possibly be taken as a reference to a falling branch. McNeile, 84-85, accordingly suggests that Qohelet is talking about the use of a divination rod, a suggestion that has been picked up by, e.g., Barton and Crenshaw; the latter is cited in Tsukimoto, 'The Background', 39-40, which sees references to divination throughout this section (there is a helpful summary and critique in Bühlmann, 'Divination', 58-61; Bühlmann himself sees a form of meteorological divination here). The strangest version here is T, which makes no mention of wood or trees, but talks a lot about 'counsel', and so seems to have connected עץ with עצה, presumably as an exegetical strategy.

11.3 wherever the tree falls is where] Although it is generally taken as such by ancient and modern translators alike, if the sense of מקום ש- were really 'in the place where', then we should expect a preposition, as at 1 Kgs 21.19 or Hos 2.1, which both have במקום. Accordingly, that translation has to be justified by taking מקום as an 'accusative of place' (so Schoors, following Dahood), which is a usage rare outside certain constructions and fixed expressions (cf. GKC §118 d-h; J-M §126 h). In fact, however, when we find מקום אשר used in other (especially late) biblical texts after nouns (Gen 39.20; 40.3) or other locative expressions (Esth 4.3; 8.17; Ezek 6.13), it often serves simply as a relative expression meaning 'where'. So in Gen 39.20, for instance, Joseph is taken to 'the prison *where* ("the place [in] which") the king's prisoners are imprisoned', and in 40.3, that prison is 'where' Joseph himself had been confined, while the passages from Esther and Ezekiel talk about 'every (place)…where'. It seems likely that we are dealing with this idiom here, after the references to north and south, and that we should not construe the sentence as '(in) the place where the tree falls, there…', but as literally 'whatever/whichever the place (in) which the tree falls, there…'.

11.3 it will be] The word יְהוּא in M is difficult, but the various ways in which it has been explained come down to three possibilities: (1) it is a corrupt form of the pronoun הוא; (2) it is derived from the verb הוה, which is rare in biblical Hebrew, or from היה; (3) it is a conflation of the two, perhaps preserving variant readings in the tradition (so most notably Gordis; Seow sees such conflation in the vocalization). G has ἔσται, 'will be', which is often taken to indicate that the translator must have read a verb (so, e.g., Goldman), but in fact his normal practice is to use a form of the verb 'to be' when he recognizes הוא as a copula (see Yi, 76). σ' παρατεύξονται, '(they) will turn up', is, perhaps, more clearly suggestive of a verb, but the verbs used in the other ancient versions may likewise be translational, and so do not really tell us whether they read a pronoun or a verb, while the הוא found in a few Hebrew manuscripts (see de Rossi) is probably an attempt to correct יהוא. If we are in fact dealing with a verb, it is hard to say how we should parse it, and a number of ingenious explanations have been offered. Schoors, for instance, thinks that an apocopated yiqtol form יהי has received an 'otiant aleph', while Seow blames א-/ה- confusion and Fox notes that this could simply be the Aramaic יהוא (= יהוה)—a view adopted by Montgomery, 'Notes', 244, which proposes that the M pointing is intended to 'disguise a pronunciation which was identical with that of the Tetragrammaton'. Given the scope both for confusion between י and ו and for orthographic variation between final א and ה, there are a number of possibilities, although it does seem more likely that the form has arisen from a misunderstanding in the course of transmission, rather than from the pen of the author, as Schoors seems to suppose. I regard a corruption of הוא as the simplest explanation, but it really makes very little difference what we read: the only suggestion that makes any significant change to the sense is that of Hitzig, who wants to read a verb הוה meaning 'fall', and compares the הוא of Job 37.6. This has attracted little support, although *HALOT* does list such a verb (as הוא) for the passage in Job, noting a presumed Arabic cognate. If that is the intended sense here, however, then the text moves from stating the obvious through to outright tautology.

11.4 wind...clouds] T associates watching the wind with magical or divinatory practices, and observing the clouds with astrology. A similar claim, without reference to T, has been made by Tsukimoto, 'The Background', 36-38, which notes the evidence for meteorological divination in Mesopotamia. The obvious objection is that the observations here are linked to agricultural practices: the farmer watches the wind because it may affect his sowing, and the clouds because rain may ruin his harvest, not in order to make predictions of any more general sort.

11.4 sow...reap] The second verb (יקצור) is rendered consistently as future tense in G, but, for the first (יזרע), there is a hesitation in the manuscript tradition between present-tense σπείρει and future σπερεῖ. The future is more probably original, and Gentry ('Hexaplaric Materials', 19; 'Relationship', 83-84; cf. Marshall) argues that it was also the reading of the Three. It is interesting to note that the La associated with Jerome has a future *non seminabit*, 'will not sow', but that in Hie and V he uses the present tense *non seminat*, 'does not sow', which conforms to the text of Origen. The La text is preserved as *obseruans uentum non seminabit, et aspiciens in nubibus non metet*, 'observing the wind, he will not sow, and looking to the clouds he will not reap' (see Leanza, 'Le tre versione', 94).

11.5 since nobody knows] I read כאשר אין יודע. For M כאשר אינך יודע, G has ἐν οἷς οὐκ ἔστιν γινώσκων, lit. 'in which things there is not someone knowing' (or perhaps 'he is not knowing'), and the translator probably found באשר אין יודע in his source-text. This is partly supported by α' ἐν ᾧ οὐκ εἶ σὺ εἰδώς, 'in which you are not knowing': this also reflects באשר, like G, but supports the אינך of M (as does σ' ἐπεὶ μὴ οἶδας, 'since you do not know', which has read כאשר). Goldman finds the reading of G attractive, and thinks that it reflects a version with the sense 'He who watches the wind will not sow and he who looks at the clouds will not reap, for he does not know. Just as the path of the spirit in the bones inside the womb of the pregnant woman, so you cannot know the deeds of God who creates all things'. As Schoors notes, however, it is highly unlikely that מה can mean 'just as', and G itself has not attempted to reproduce any such construction.

Noting that α' supports G in one case and M in the other, we should treat the variation between G and M here as two separate problems, perhaps particularly since the confusion of באשר and כאשר is endemic: see the note at 4.17. In that respect, it seems likely that M has the better reading, since באשר makes little obvious sense. With respect to אין / אינך, however, the matter is less clear cut. M enjoys the support of all the other ancient versions, and אינך יודע is consonant with the same expression in v. 6, as well as with the uses of לא תדע in v. 2 and later in this verse: this is a context in which Qohelet is keen to emphasize what 'you' do not know. For that very reason, however, it is easier to see how an original אין might have been drawn up into this to become אינך than to see how the reverse might have happened: the loss of the final ך is not readily explicable as a graphical error, and corresponds to no obvious interpretative requirement. If Qohelet is explaining the statement in v. 4, it is also more logical: 'your' ignorance is not behind the failure of unnamed others. Since the 'you' has a general address anyway, however, both readings offer much the same overall meaning.

11.5 what the way of the wind is. Like] By switching from ἄνεμος, 'wind', in v. 4 to πνεῦμα, 'spirit', here, the translator of G signals that he understands רוח to have a different meaning; cf. Hie, V *spiritus*, but contrast σ' ἐπεὶ μὴ οἶδας πότε παρέσται ὁ ἄνεμος, 'since you do not know when the wind will be present', which clearly, and rightly I think, connects the clause to what has preceded, and not what follows. In G, this remains a vague reference to the 'way of the spirit', and the connection with the subsequent reference to a foetus is unclear. Jerome, however, states explicitly his understanding that this is to do with ignorance of the way that the breath or spirit enters a baby, which is matched by an ignorance of its physical development. This reading has been very influential.

The key issue here is the way in which the various elements of the verse are supposed to be correlated, or more specifically what is supposed to correspond to the clause introduced by כה. In Jer 19.11, 'so shall I break... just as one breaks' is expressed using כה...כאשר, and it is clearly possible to read here 'just as you do/one does not know...so you will not know'. It is also possible, however, to coordinate כה with a simple -כ when the analogy is with a substantive rather than with a clause (cf. Num 15.12), so that we could read 'just like limbs...so you will not know'. Jerome's interpretation involves a more complicated understanding 'just as you do not know the way of the breath as it enters a baby, and as you do not know how the bones and vessels develop..., so you will not know'. T similarly sees two expressions of ignorance coordinated with the כזה clause that follows them: just as one knows not how the spirit of life enters the body of a foetus, and just as one knows not whether it will be male or female, so one does not know God's work. (The distinction between male and female has perhaps been derived from the use of the rarer עצמים rather than עצמות, on which see the next note.) These readings presume ellipsis—'as you do not know...(and) as (you do not know)...so you do not know'—and that is explicitly acknowledged by some of the more recent commentators who construe the text this way (see especially Althann, 'Ellipsis', 92-94).

Many other scholars, however, have tried to find not two different analogies set in parallel, but a single reference to the spirit entering or affecting the body, and this leads them to delete the -כ or emend כעצמים to בעצמים, with just כאשר coordinated with כזה. That latter reading (giving the sense 'just as you do not know the way of the breath into...so you will not know') is found in a significant number of Hebrew manuscripts cited by Kennicott and de Rossi, but it is hard not to suppose that it arose as an attempt to facilitate just such an interpretation, and there is little force in Goldman's suggestion that it was, in fact, -כ that arose 'for theological motives'. Despite some claims to the contrary, furthermore, it is probably not what T read: the fact that the targumist compares two points of ignorance shows that he has read -כ, and his talk of spirit entering the body belongs to his interpretative expansion of the first, even if it draws on elements from the second in a sort of double rendering. The readings and issues are discussed at some length in MacNamara, 'How the Wind Blows', 67-68.

None of the other ancient versions, in fact, offers any basis for emendation, and we might reasonably wonder, anyway, whether Qohelet's contemporaries would have understood there to be 'breath' in a foetus. To be sure, the רוח is an animating 'breath of life' in 3.19 and 12.7, as in Gen 2.7 and Ezek 37.9-10 (where it is bestowed by the four winds), but, as something external that is merely lent to humans for their lifetimes, it is neither a soul nor Aristotle's innate πνεῦμα (which Aristotle takes to have been present within the foetus from conception, neither dependent on breathing, nor acquired from outside in the course of the pregnancy; see, e.g., Solmsen, 'Vital Heat'). It is doubtful that the human was supposed to possess רוח before being born, any more than after death. A reference to God's preserving רוח in Job 10.12 might shed some light on beliefs in this area, but that reference is set alongside references to God's achieving life and חסד for the speaker, suggesting that 10.12 has moved beyond the fashioning within the womb that was the focus of 10.9-10. It is not unreasonable to suspect that G's rendering, and the various interpretations based on God somehow insufflating or ensouling the foetus in our verse, have been informed by understandings and equivalences which were probably only just beginning to influence Jewish thought around the time Ecclesiastes was written (in the commentary on 3.20-21, I noted early uses of רוח to describe the 'spirits' of the dead, and the distinctions between those uses and the understanding in Ecclesiastes).

Be that as it may, if we retain the text as it stands, then it is undoubtedly awkward to set the clause with כאשר and the phrase with כ- in parallel with each other and then to coordinate them with the ככה clause, as Jerome tries to do—and Schoors offers cogent reasons for rejecting this construal, despite his earlier acceptance of it (in *The Preacher* I, 204). Rather than emending the text, though, I think it is simpler to take this awkwardness, along with the reference to רוח, as an indication that the first clause should belong, in fact, with what has preceded. What follows is then an analogy between the inability of the unborn child to know what is going on around it (reminiscent of 4.3) and the inability of the listener to know what God does. Fischer, *Skepsis*, 149, thinks that the previous sayings about the wind and the saying about the embryo are connected by a play on the different senses of רוח, which he tries to replicate by using the archaic German word *Odem* to translate it here.

11.5 embryo] Delekat, 'Zum hebräischen Wörterbuch', 49-52, makes a plausible case that עצמים rather than the more common form עצמות, is used to refer to limbs and joints rather than to bones (see, e.g., Judg 19.29). In the absence of any reason to suppose that this is a usual term for a foetus, and since he avoids speaking of a 'child', Qohelet is probably trying to emphasize the unconscious nature of what he is describing by speaking of its physical character rather than its identity: this is the flesh and bone that makes up the embryo. If it is not corrupt, S appears to have understood the text very differently: ܐܝܟ ܙܢܐ ܕܒܛܢܐ ܕܒܛܢܐ *'yk zn' dbṭnt' dbṭn'* means 'like the way of the pregnant woman who is pregnant' (or possibly 'like how the pregnant woman becomes pregnant'). There is a variant, with ܓܝܪ *gyr*, 'indeed', standing improbably in place of ܙܢܐ *zn'*, 'the way', which Kamenetzky, 200, takes to be a corrupt form of ܓܪܡܐ *grm'*, 'bones', but that (fairly drastic) emendation would still leave no direct equivalent to בבטן / ἐν γαστρί, 'in the womb/belly', which is presumably instead the basis of ܕܒܛܢܐ *dbṭn'*.

11.5 what God does, he who will do everything] On the use of the plural τὰ ποιήματα (cf. Hie, V, S) for the singular מעשה of M (cf. T), see the notes at 5.5 and 7.13. Here the variation is probably translational. The verb can be used, of course, to refer to making or doing, but in V Jerome renders *opera dei qui fabricator est omnium*, 'the works of God, who is the one who contrives all things', and that captures the probable sense here, of divine activity that results in earthly events. Those events are probably not supposed to be limited to involvement with the formation of the foetus, as a few scholars suggest.

11.6 Sow your seed in the morning, then do not hold back your hand until evening] Most manuscripts of G have ἐν ἑσπέρᾳ, 'in the evening', which corresponds to בערב, and not the εἰς ἑσπέραν, 'until evening' or 'for an evening', which Rahlfs and Gentry prefer, and which would be equivalent to M לערב. Since secondary assimilation to בבקר is more likely than differentiation, the -ל in M is probably the original reading (and is supported by T, Hie), but it is difficult to say for sure whether the double ἐν of the G manuscripts arose within the G tradition or reflects a Hebrew variant. S likewise has 'in' twice, but may have inherited this from the G variant rather than from a Hebrew source. σ' πρώϊμον...ἀλλὰ καὶ ὄψιμον, 'early...but also late' (which likely influenced the *mane...uespere*, 'at morning...at evening' of V), may also have read the same preposition in both places, but the Greek terms can be used in connection with early- and late-fruiting crops (cf. Exod 9.32), so something interpretative may be behind the rendering.

If we accept M, the change from one preposition (-ב on בבקר) to another (-ל on לערב) is itself hard to understand if, as many commentators maintain, Qohelet is indeed talking about sowing seed on distinct occasions, 'in the morning' and 'in the evening', an interpretation that is usually justified by taking the subsequent זה או זה / שניהם to refer to the two separate periods, or to the efforts expended within them. I suspect, in fact, that 'this or that' is actually a reference to different seeds (see below), but even if the reference is to the starting and finishing points of the activity, it hardly requires that the activity be confined to those points (leading Fredericks, 'Life's Storms', 103-4, to talk of separate 'morning' and 'until evening' shifts), and I take לערב to mean 'until evening' (as, e.g., McNeile, 85, who compares Job 4.20). This does not mean that בבקר must literally mean 'from morning' here and at 10.16, as Dahood, 'Phoenician Background', 280-81, suggests (cf. his 'Hebrew–Ugaritic Lexicography VIII', 392), but Dahood probably is right to doubt that the similar בבקר...ולערב in Gen 49.27 is talking about Benjamin devouring prey in the morning then separately sitting down to divide spoil in the evening. Both here and in Genesis, an action is described as starting 'in the morning', then its continuation is implied by the statement that an associated action goes on 'until the evening'. I think the use of -ב rather than -מ, though, imparts a particular nuance of starting early then continuing, which I have attempted to catch in my rendering of the conjunction.

Fox sees 'in the morning...in the evening' as a merism that 'includes the entire workday'—a reading that somewhat undermines the reasons that he gives for seeing two separate periods in the first place—but emphasizes that this must mean working 'whenever the opportunity or need arises', not solidly throughout the day. Even if that is a possible reading of the Hebrew, which is questionable, it is hardly, however, a sense demanded by the text: the expression אל תנח ידך is similar to the אל תנח את ידך found in 7.18, and I have translated accordingly, but it also implies 'give your hand no rest', and suggests that Qohelet is talking about working continuously through to the evening—compare σ' καὶ μὴ καταλιμπανέτω ἡ χείρ σου, 'and do not let your hand give up'.

In the note on the expression at 7.18, incidentally, we saw that many manuscripts had a plural 'hands', and the same is true here, although there is no support for such a reading in the ancient versions: see Miletto, 212-13. Codex Graecus Venetus has a plural in both places.

11.6 which will work] The problems surrounding the noun כשרון have already been encountered (see the note at 2.21), but in the notes at 10.10d, I found no good reason to associate the better-known verb with those problems, and the same is true here. The basic sense of the qal is 'be fit', which can have an implication of being 'proper' or 'useful' (Esth 8.5; Sir 13.4), and α′ here correspondingly renders εὐθετεῖ or εὐθετήσει, '(will) be suitable' or 'timely'.[5] G στοιχήσει is more nuanced: the verb originally meant 'be in a row' or 'walk in a line', but it came to mean 'be in line with' or 'conform to'. Vinel sees an implication of continuity, but I suspect that the translator is playing on the less literal sense, with its implication of 'fit', to evoke the more literal one. Mindful of the concerns already expressed about sowing in the wind, he is talking about which seeds will lie properly in the furrows prepared for them. In his commentary, Jerome explains Hie *quid placeat* in terms of 'which work *is pleasing* to God', while T speaks in terms of children who are chosen to be good or not. All of these translations are in line with the established senses of כשר.

By using ܢܟܫܪ *nkšr*, S matches the Hebrew with a cognate verb, but opens up a new sense: in later Aramaic and in Syriac the verb can mean 'prosper' or 'succeed' (although not normally in the ground stem). Jerome brings a similar sense to his translation in V, where he uses *oriatur*, 'grow', 'spring up', and this idea of 'succeeding' has dominated subsequent interpretations. If we are to translate in such terms, however, it is important to be clear that Qohelet is more probably talking about immediate than about long-term outcomes. The question is not, directly at least, which seed or sowing will result in a successful crop, but which will be 'fit for purpose'—a notion much closer to the normal sense of the verb. The problem outlined in v. 4 is that the sower may see their seeds blown away out of the shallow furrows and lost: the 'successful' sowing is one in which this does not happen, or the 'successful' seed is one which is not blown away. In the notes at 2.3, I observed that אי זה

---

[5] The future tense is attested in all the Greek witnesses, but Syh probably reflects the present tense. Both forms are found in manuscripts of G that have been influenced by the reading. Marshall argues that the present tense is more likely to be original, and the future an assimilation to the tense of G. The reading of σ′ here is more problematic. It is attested in several witnesses as εὑρήσει, 'will find', which makes little obvious sense in this context. Marshall points to the sense 'acquire wealth' listed in LSJ for the verb used absolutely, but that is based solely on Lev 25.47, where the translator is attempting to reproduce the Hebrew idiom נשג יד, and is an example of the LSJ tendency simply to translate words in the Septuagint on the basis of their Hebrew equivalent. It is likely that the reading is corrupt.

tends to retain some nuance of location, and this tends to affirm that Qohelet is talking not about the viability of each seed, but, as G understands, which seeds will lodge where they are supposed to.

11.6 this or that, or if both of them together will be fine] Three Babylonian manuscripts noted by Miletto have a second אז instead of ואם, which arguably gives a smoother and more consistent reading—although the variant has probably arisen for that very reason. G seems unexpectedly free in the second half of this: it is true, as Yi, 304-5, observes, that ἐπὶ τὸ αὐτὸ is equivalent to כאחד, but we might still have expected the closer ὡς εἷς, 'as one', a rendering used elsewhere in the Septuagint for כאחד (on כאחד itself, see Hurvitz, *Lexicon*, 136-39). There is also no reflection of the suffix pronoun in שניהם, which was rendered when the term occurred in 4.3. We need not suppose with McNeile, 152, that the translator read a different text, but it seems likely either that he relaxed his usual technique here for the sake of clarity, or that the text of G has been polished a little in the course of transmission. If Hie *quasi unum* (= ὡς εἷς) is La, that would lend some weight to the latter possibility, and the reading in Miletto's manuscripts suggest that somebody else similarly found the Hebrew itself awkward.

The Hebrew as we have it, though, does offer a reasonably lucid expression of a complicated idea, and the general meaning is not in question. What is less clear, is the reference of the 'this or that', which commentators generally link to the preceding 'morning' and 'evening'. Obviously, neither time is itself the subject of יכשר, so this link is usually envisaged more loosely in terms of a comparison being made between the morning and the evening sowing. Loose as it is in one respect, though, this seems too literal-minded in another. Expressions with זה...זה often refer simply to different actors or items within a larger group (e.g. 1 Kgs 22.20; Isa 6.3; Ps 75.8 ET 75.7), and I think that Qohelet is in fact pointing back to the collective 'seed' that has been sown, saying, in effect, 'you don't know if it is this seed that will be alright, or that one there, or both of them, which is why you should sow as much as possible'. Either reading is possible, and the sense is much the same.

11.7–12.2

Living Mindfully

(11.7) Also, daylight is sweet, and it is good for the eyes to see sunlight. (11.8) For even if a person lives many years, he may take pleasure in them all, while being mindful of the days of darkness, that they will be many. All that is coming is an illusion.

(11.9) Rejoice, young one, in your youth, and let your heart be good to you in the days when you are young: walk in the ways of your heart but amongst what is before you, while knowing that, for all these things, God will demand of you a reckoning.

(11.10) And put anger out of your mind, and let trouble pass away from your body, for youth and youthfulness are an illusion, (12.1) while being mindful of your creator,

> in the days when you are young,
>
> while the days of trouble have not yet arrived,
>
> and years approached of which you say 'I have no use for them';

(12.2) while the sun, the daylight, the moon and the stars have not yet darkened,

> and the clouds still recede after the rain.

Commentary

The first verse here picks up where the previous verse left off: we should sow from morning to evening for the reasons spelled out in 11.6, but also for the simpler reason that it is good to see daylight, especially when we face years of darkness ahead. This segue allows

Qohelet to approach a different theme, and also to abandon the format of discrete sayings which has largely dominated ch. 10, so although there is some continuity with what has preceded, as we shall see, these verses are better treated separately. The imagery of light, or rather of light dimming, is subsequently picked up in 12.2, closing this part of the discussion in turn, and separating it from what will follow.

The initial contrast between light and darkness, in 11.7-8, seems to suggest that Qohelet's concern is with life and death: light 'under the sun' and the darkness of Sheol. In 11.9–12.1, however, he offers advice to the young which is sustained through the following verses, and which contrasts youth with coming 'days of trouble'. These are not further specified, beyond the fact that they will be unwanted, but the apparent implication is that they are a period of adulthood in which it will be impossible to remain carefree, and in which life seems a burden. In connection with readings of what follows as an allegory, it is often assumed that Qohelet is talking about old age, in particular, but that is not made explicit. Indeed, given the possibility stated in 11.8, that someone might enjoy every year of a long life, it is not clear even that this period of trouble should be regarded as some inevitable phase of adulthood. In 12.2 Qohelet speaks further of a time when light fades; set in parallel with the 'days of trouble', as something else that still lies in the future for the young, this provides a contrast with the daylight that began 11.7. It is hard, though, to see it as a simple characterization of adulthood, or even of old age—it seems to evoke the situation of the dead, enduring their 'days of darkness', but more particularly to describe the actual slipping away of life. Qohelet appears, in fact, to be running two things together: a (potentially long) life that may be enjoyed before the years of death to come, and a youth that offers freedoms before any burdens of adulthood arrive. Indeed, he may even be sketching an analogy between the two, so that (perhaps commonplace) advice to enjoy one's carefree youth before one takes on responsibilities is used to make a more general point about enjoying life before the lights go out: death is to life as adulthood is to youth.

I am correspondingly suspicious of the idea, advocated recently in Spieckermann, 'Jugend—Alter—Tod', that Qohelet is delineating specific phases of life, and using this periodization as a framework for the recollection of other topics. Spieckermann does draw comparisons, however, with part of a text that is very interesting in this context: the 'Sixteenth Instruction', or section, of the Demotic instruction on Papyrus Insinger (17.4–19.5; there are translations in Lichtheim, *Ancient Egyptian Literature III*, 198-200, and Hoffmann and Quack, *Anthologie*, 256-59). This calls on its audience to enjoy life and not to hoard for the future, in the face of their ignorance about how long they will live, and what that future will bring. The passage within it that deals with old age begins by stressing how little pleasure is available to those over sixty, which is treated as the age to which most people might hope to live, and then points out (in the section that is of interest to Spieckermann) that humans 'lose' two-thirds of that sixty years: first (as children) they must learn about life and death, then (as teenagers) about how to live; in their twenties they will accumulate the possessions that enable them to do so, and it will be another ten years before they reach, at 40, the age when their 'heart takes counsel'. A very few ('one in a million') will be granted longer life, up to a hundred, but the point is that one can only really enjoy life in the period between maturity and senescence or death, during which, after dealing with the needs and demands of others, one should spend one's money: the dead won't take their savings to the grave, and should not leave them for someone else. Despite some obvious points of contact, the theme is not the same as that pursued by Qohelet here, but it is important to note that this instruction perceives life as building up to the point where one can enjoy it, long after youth—which may caution us against presuming that Qohelet's 'days of trouble' would necessarily have been understood by everybody as some unavoidable period of later life.

These verses are characterized by a repeated juxtaposition of elements concerned with 'doing this while bearing that in mind' (cf. Slemmons, 'Ecclesiastes 12:1-13', 302, who summarizes them differently as 'rejoice but remember'). In 11.7-8, this takes the form not of an admonition, but of a statement that someone may take pleasure in a long life while remembering the reality of a death to come, but 11.9 presents a direct admonition to follow one's heart while remembering that one's actions will be judged by God, and in 11.10–12.1 the advice is to be untroubled while staying mindful of one's creator. The Hebrew does not explicitly draw a comparison or contrast in those verses between what one should do and what one should bear in mind (which is why I have translated neutrally with 'while', rather than with 'and' or 'but'). This makes it all the more difficult, however, to understand what the relationship between the elements in each place is supposed to be. In 11.8, for instance, which seems to serve as a justification for the claim in 11.7, is the recollection of death supposed to be curbing the person's pleasure in life, or sharpening it? In 11.9, are the young supposed to moderate their ambitions, or simply, in line with Qohelet's deterministic outlook, anticipate a reckoning that they may be powerless to influence? In 11.10–12.1 many scholars have, with some justice, found it difficult to see any link at all between the admonitions to let trouble go, on the one hand, and to remember one's creator, on the other.

Such problems have sometimes fuelled efforts to emend the text, or to delete material as secondary, but it is hard to extract some simpler call for us to enjoy life or youth. Difficult though they are, the juxtapositions seem to be central to whatever it is that Qohelet is trying to say. It may be important also to note that *hebel* makes a return here, after it has played little role in the closing chapters of the monologue, and has not appeared, indeed, since 9.9, when Qohelet associated it with the span of human life. Now it is used in 11.10 to characterize youth, and in 11.8 either of death, or, more generally, of one's whole future. The immediate context suggests that, as in 9.9, it may have some particular nuance of transience, especially in 11.10, but it would be wrong, I think, to limit the sense merely to that nuance, and to a reminder that our days of youth and life are short. The broader context points a different way.

In the preceding 10.20–11.6, Qohelet's main concern was to mock the sort of carefulness that leads to loss or inaction, and here the recollections of death, judgment, and dependence on God could all likewise induce a paralysis that holds us back. To be sure, of course, Qohelet views these as realities that cannot be denied or avoided, but he has suggested throughout that they are also matters over which humans can exercise little control. The living of our lives is 'vapour', or 'illusion', largely because we lack that control, or any knowledge that might enable it, and the real workings of the world are hidden from us. Correspondingly, though, our ignorance should be liberating: if we cannot know what might actually affect our lives for better or worse, then there is no point in worrying about such things. If Qohelet here tells us not to worry while still remembering them, it follows, I think, that he must be telling us to remember them, but also to ignore them: we are not to deny the reality of our situation, but we are not to let our acceptance of that reality impede the enjoyment of our lives. If that alone were Qohelet's point, however, we might expect the clauses to be reversed: 'remember this, but do that'. The order as it stands implies a different sort of emphasis: 'do this, and (still) remember that'. We are to get on with our lives, but we are not to forget that our experiences are an illusion, and that there is a reality behind the curtain.

This is not a formal conclusion to the monologue, before the set piece that will follow, but it almost serves as one, and it picks up some significant threads. Most importantly, it brings together Qohelet's concerns with 'vapour' and with the need for humans to find pleasure in life, by suggesting that happiness must rest not on the ignorance of reality that has hitherto been at the heart of what Qohelet calls 'vapour', but on an acceptance of the facts. We will die and be judged, and we will never be more than God's creatures, but we should be happy all the same (presumably because, as Qohelet has recently been at pains to point out, there is nothing much we can do to influence what will happen to us). He does not put it in such complicated terms, or even, perhaps, work properly through the issues, but Qohelet seems to accept, moreover, that the human happiness he commends must rely on a willingness to ignore certain realities as much as it depends on a knowledge of them. To take the simplest case here, we must recognize the inevitability of death if we are to accept the importance of living in the present, but that recognition may also impinge on our happiness.

This psychological balancing act is perhaps portrayed as easier for the young (although not impossible, 11.8 suggests, for the old), mostly because being young is a sort of 'vapour' or 'illusion' in itself—short-lived, and shielded from the troubles of later life. For the first time, that is explicitly a good thing: 'vapour' now enables something that Qohelet commends, and, in the light of that, we may wonder whether he actually considers it bad that 'all that is coming is vapour', or even, indeed, whether the 'life of illusion' that he talked about back in 9.9 might not have been something rather positive—it was a divine gift, there, associated with the enjoyment of life. Qohelet is opposed to human decisions founded on ignorance or misunderstanding, and he continues to insist that the proper situation be remembered, but happiness is to be achieved by disconnecting our actions from that disquieting knowledge—at least for as long as we can.

11.7-8] The language here provokes comparison with a passage in Euripides, *Iphigenia in Aulis*:

μή μ' ἀπολέσῃς ἄωρον, ἡδὺ γὰρ τὸ φῶς
βλέπειν· τὰ δ' ὑπὸ γῆς μή μ' ἰδεῖν ἀναγκάσῃς. (IA 1218-19)[1]

Do not destroy me prematurely, for it is sweet to see the light: do not force me to look upon what's beneath the ground.

The characterization of life as 'seeing the light' may have been conventional (cf. 6.5; 7.11), and it seems likely, at least, that the original audience would, at this point, have seen a corresponding reference to death. The language, of course, ties in with Qohelet's more frequently expressed understanding that humans live 'under the sun', and when the darkness of 12.2 is set in contrast with this light, it also brings closure to a metaphor that Qohelet has used throughout (cf. Seow, 'Eschatological Poem', 213-14).

Busto Saiz, 'Estructura Métrica', understands these verses to comprise the first strophe of a poem that runs through to 12.7, and contains six strophes in all. Obviously, there are signs here of the parallelism that is usually associated with Hebrew poetry, but it appears only erratically, and if there is a rhythm to the language, that rhythm is not consistent. As elsewhere in the book, we should probably avoid labelling the text as 'verse', but recognize that it is, nonetheless, highly polished and stylized.

11.9] There has been no previous indication that Qohelet is presenting his words particularly as instruction to the young, and it is unlikely that his audience, up to this point, would have been driven to understand them that way by considerations of genre. Accordingly, when he now speaks specifically to the young, here and in the verses that follow, it seems likely that Qohelet is adopting a particular mode, and perhaps deliberately adopting the perspective of other works, like Proverbs 1–9, which present themselves that way throughout. This address to the young, therefore, should not be read back into the whole monologue. Qohelet

---

[1] The passage is cited by Plutarch (*Quomodo adolescens poetas audire debeat*, 17D.1) with λεύσσειν, 'gaze', instead of the βλέπειν found in manuscripts of the play, and this verb is preferred as more likely original in some editions.

may have adopted this mode because the young, with many years ahead of them, are in the best position to follow the advice offered here, but it seems more likely that he is trying to associate his more general admonitions to enjoy life while it lasts with the idea that the young should be encouraged to enjoy a carefree youth while they can.

The particular advice, before the reminder about judgment, is to 'let your heart be good to you…walk in the ways of your heart but amongst what is before you'. The first element is probably an invitation to be happy or cheerful, but it is phrased a little differently from the similar expression in 7.3, and there is perhaps a more specific nuance 'allow yourself to be happy': the heart, as mind, is depicted as in control of the way one feels. The heart also has 'ways' according to the second, which probably invites the young to pursue their aspirations, rather than simply do what they feel like at any particular moment: again, the heart in Qohelet's monologue *is* one's mind, not some mass of emotions separate from reason, and there is a danger here of importing distinctions that are alien to the text. Finally, 'walk…amongst what is before you' reads literally 'in the sight of your eyes', with the implication 'what your eyes see', and uses an expression that we met earlier in 6.9. I have translated it here on the understanding that it most likely has a similar sense in both places, and that Qohelet is presented as advising the young to pursue their aspirations, but to do so within the world as they find it. His point in 6.9 was directed against the wasting of life by those who find no satisfaction in what they already have, and here I think he is qualifying his advice about the 'ways of the heart' in similar terms: ambitions and aspirations can be a source of unhappiness when they become insatiable and unrealizable. If we are willing to permit a looser relationship with 6.9, then the point could alternatively be that the young should walk with the 'seeing' of their eyes, taking in the world as they pass it.

The way this is expressed does not make it likely, I think, that Qohelet is alluding deliberately to Num 15.39, and contradicting the demand there to obey the law, and 'not to seek out a path following your heart and your eyes'—although the clash of views has long been noted (see especially Kynes, 'Follow Your Heart', which also argues for a connection between 5.5 and Num 15.25). The difficulty has provoked much discussion, and led Rashi to regard the advice as ironic, but whether there really is such a contradiction depends in part on what one thinks Qohelet means here—and I doubt, myself, that he intends a Crowley-esque 'Do what thou wilt shall be the whole of the Law', or even the 'Fais ce que tu voudras' of Dashwood's Hellfire Club: this is not a call to Thelemism, but, at most, to the pursuit of one's considered aims. More importantly, though, the advice here has to be understood within the context of Qohelet's determinism, which does not allow, in principle, the possibility that we might choose to do anything that would be contrary to the divine will. Qohelet does not discuss the issues in this context, but the underlying assumption may be that of 9.7: if what we do is automatically accepted by God, then there is no point in looking beyond our own ideas about what we should do. If this contradicts ideas in Numbers (or even if it sets out deliberately to question the value of the Law as a route to safety, as Mazzinghi, 'Dieu te convoquera', 107-9, suggests), then that merely reflects a tension between deterministic and non-deterministic worldviews, which is evident also if we compare the admonition here with, say, Sir 5.2-3.[2]

Of course, this broader context is important also for understanding the reminder which follows, that God will judge. This appears, on the face of it, to impose a further cap upon the happiness and aspirations of the young, but I have discussed above the general role of such reminders in these verses, and suggested that they are not really intended to impose such limitations, so much as to draw out Qohelet's distinction between the human context, in which we must do the best with what we have, and the realities of a world that is largely beyond our comprehension. In the other cases, there

---

[2] Sir 5.2 in Greek reads 'Do not obey your spirit and strength to walk in the desires of your heart'; the Hebrew (in ms A) is a little different: 'Do not go after your heart and your eyes to walk in חמודות רעה'. The last phrase is usually understood to mean 'desires of evil', meaning 'evil desires', but Pinker, 'Nuanced View', 14, translates it 'the finery of the evil woman'. This is possible (although not, in context, very plausible), and Pinker combines with it the supposition that זנים in Num 15.39 is being used not figuratively, as commonly supposed, but literally, as a specific reference to sexual promiscuity. Accordingly, he understands 11.9 in terms of making oneself attractive to women while young, in order to find a wife, and 11.10 as advice to get out of a bad marriage. This would seem forced even if there were actually any specific reference at all to women or matrimony in the text, and when the interpretation rests on finding an allusion to other texts not normally interpreted in such terms, then it seems very tenuous indeed.

really is nothing much to be done about the things we are supposed to remember—the inevitability of death, and our createdness—so it is difficult to read them as encouragements to alter the way we behave. Qohelet has made it abundantly clear that humans struggle to understand the basis of divine judgment, while his determinism raises significant problems for the very concept, so it seems unlikely that he is now suddenly commending a modification of behaviour to ensure divine favour. That, nevertheless, is the way in which the text here is most obviously to be read, and is also the way in which it has usually been interpreted. This leads very many commentators to reject it as secondary, especially in the light of its resemblance to the view of the epilogue, at 12.14.[3]

It might be possible to suppose that Qohelet is actually speaking of a reckoning in terms of the advice he has given, and saying that God will judge the extent to which individuals have properly taken advantage of their lives (so, e.g., Gordis, Heim). That idea, however, is not presented elsewhere, and Qohelet more generally seems to believe that we should be enjoying our lives regardless of the roles assigned to us by God, not in order actually to please God. I prefer to think that this reminder, despite its more practical implications, should simply be treated like the others, not as an invitation actively to modify behaviour (or even to be conscious that our existence should be informed by some ethic, as Lavoie, 'Quoi de nouveau', 128, suggests), but as a recognition of reality. Dell' Aversano, 'משפט in Qoh 11:9c', similarly emphasizes that this is essentially just another reminder of death, and of the fact that God will ultimately annul whatever choices and distinctions we make for ourselves: for everyone, the sentence will ultimately be death (cf. also Mazzinghi, 'Dieu te convoquera', 107). All Qohelet's calls here are to find happiness and self-fulfilment: we are not to forget that what we do is subject to powers and constraints that are hidden from us, and perhaps the 'judgment' of God here comprises no more than the divine allocation of opportunities to us (cf. Sacchi), but that recollection is not supposed to deter or intimidate us.

---

[3] Lange, 'Eschatological Wisdom', 820, exaggerates by speaking of a 'near *opinio communis*' on the matter, but the opinion has been very widely held, and the 'gloss' often attributed to the (supposedly secondary) epilogist. As Mazzinghi, 'Dieu te convoquera', 103, points out, the resemblance could as readily imply that such an epilogist simply drew on 11.9.

12.1-2] After death and divine judgment, the final thing to bear in mind is one's creator, and that seems, on the face of it, to have more positive connotations—even if the advice is followed immediately by a description of bad things to come. An alternative sense that has been proposed, 'your good health', makes good sense, but fits even less easily into the sequence. Various explanations have been suggested, but I think that, while the reference is clearly to God, the emphasis here is probably on the createdness of the human ('that you *have* a creator'), and the subordination that it implies, rather than on God himself: the account of death that is coming will culminate at 12.7 in a virtual 'un-creation' of the human, which drives home the point that we are not the true owners even of the flesh that we inhabit, or of the breath that animates us (cf. Gilbert, 'La Description', 100). Thankful though humans may be for the opportunity of life, it is something that has been given, and that will be taken, by a power beyond their control—and they are to remember the existence of that power.

These verses end with an extended temporal construction, incorporating numerous elements. It is probably to be construed as 'Be carefree, while remembering your creator, during the days when you are young—before you experience worse times and before the time of darkness'. This construction is often taken to run on into the following 12.3-7, so that everything which follows is a description of the 'days of trouble', and such a reading facilitates traditional readings of 12.2 onward as an allegorical description of old age. It is true that the following verses seem themselves to contain further extended constructions, with 12.3-4b setting out the circumstances to a sequence of actions, and 12.6-7 employs a 'not yet' series, which is often taken as resumptive of the similar sequence in 12.1-2. There would, accordingly, seem to be a certain economy to be achieved in reading all these together as one extremely extended construction rather than as a series of separate constructions. Objections to such an approach can be levelled on grounds of style and imagery: in particular, 12.2 seems to pick up and close the image of light and darkness introduced by 11.7, while 12.3-7 involve very different images. The attempt, furthermore, of Lohfink, 'Grenzen', to find lexical coherence in 11.7–12.8, seems to result in a demonstration of some such coherence only across 11.7–12.3 (see especially the diagram on his p. 42), as does the similar attempt in Witzenrath, *Süß ist das Licht*, 5-7. A more definitive objection, however, is to be found in the way that 12.3 begins, with a reference to a 'day' on which certain events transpire, in contrast to the 'days' and 'years' of which 12.1 speaks: even were the switch from plural to singular not striking in itself, it would be difficult to read that 'day' as a comparably long period of time—despite various efforts to dilute its force (see the note). It seems more likely that, falling as they do in the closing verses of the monologue, these constructions are another display of the author's fondness for set-piece lists, which was so much on display in the opening chapters.

The images in 12.2 can be understood in broadly three ways: (1) Qohelet actually is talking about the weather, and evoking the image of a storm, a winter, or even an eschaton; (2) he is talking about a perception of the world as persistently dark, by the human who is reaching or has reached the end of their life; (3) he is talking about that human passing into death, in the way that the light of the sun, moon, and stars fades between day and night, and clouds dissipate after rain. The poetic character of the language here does not exclude any of these readings, but it is difficult to retain all the possibilities in translation, and I lean toward the second.

The first, however, has enjoyed some recent popularity, and is found in several forms. In a particular manifestation of the construal of 12.1-2 with 12.3-7, a number of commentators (notably Umbreit; Ginsburg; more recently Leahy, 'Ecclesiastes 12, 1-5'; Fredericks, 'Life's Storms') have understood 12.2 to set the scene for what will follow, with members of a household depicted as terrified in the face of a storm, which may itself serve as an image of death. Since there is nothing especially stormy here, however, beyond the mention of rain, then Loretz, *Qohelet und der alte Orient*, 192, arguably offers a more plausible contrast between the dark wintertime which is the end of human life, and the images of nature's renewal in 12.5— although it is not clear that we can really extend the image so far when, with the exception of a single, unrelated reference to eyes 'darkening' in 12.3, there will be no further references in what remains of ch. 12 to the seasons, the weather, light, or darkness.

Other scholars, as early as Jerome, have seen an association with the imagery of darkness found in prophetic texts like Isa 8.22; Ezek 32.7-8; Joel 2.2; and Zeph 1.15 (elsewhere, as Seow, 'Eschatological Poem', 213, notes, in the Balaam text from Deir ʿAllā), and it cannot be denied either that such imagery often has a threatening implication (as in Job 15.22-23, where the wicked man anticipates a 'day of darkness'), or that contrasts between light and darkness extend beyond any simple life–death dichotomy. Fox extends this into the imagery that follows, noting the silencing of millstones alongside the extinguishing of a candle in Jer 25.10-11, and it is clearly possible that our text is drawing upon well-established imagery, evocative of very bad things. This language is not always simply eschatological, however, or descriptive of 'the undoing of the created order', as Beal, 'C(ha)osmopolis', 296-97, puts it: Ezekiel 32, for instance, is threatening Egypt, not the cosmos (cf. Exod 10.22). Accordingly, we should be cautious of attempts to see some affirmation here of the many efforts to read what follows in eschatological terms. If Qohelet is indeed portraying the death of an individual as a sort of 'shrunken apocalypse', as Sherwood, 'Not with a Bang', suggests, or it is true that God's every eschatological judgment is demythologized and individualized, as Bauer, 'Kohelet', 575, puts it, then the effort is probably confined to this verse. It is not clear to me, furthermore, that such a move would necessarily, or even probably, constitute 'an ironical and polemical attack against the eschatological view of apocalyptic', as Mazzinghi, 'Qohelet and Enochism', 165-66, claims. Salvaneschi, 'Memento vivere', sees allusions to the primal chaos and the flood, linked to remembering one's creator, and so to a reversal of creation that is not so specifically rooted in eschatology. Whether or not one agrees, it would be hard to maintain that the text employs imagery here that is evocative solely of eschatological or apocalyptic language.

To my mind, the greatest obstacle to such readings is the limited scope of what is actually said by our text. The usual way to understand the last clause is in terms of clouds persisting even after rain, and perhaps themselves blotting out light from the sky, and that image of persistent, dreary cloud-cover (when 'everything seems painted gray on gray', as Haupt, 'On the Book of Ecclesiastes', 116, puts it) seems some way from any depiction of a violent thunderstorm, or even of deep darkness. It also tends to undercut any sense that a disaster is looming, or, indeed, that anything sudden is happening at all. This dullness accords much more easily with a reading in terms of what precedes rather than what follows, and it is not hard to see why many have read the description in terms of the times late in life that humans reject: the sun has now gone in, and the gloom foreshadows the darkness that is coming.

That understanding is close, I think, to the author's intention, but if Qohelet is talking about grey skies and cloud-cover that keeps returning, then the introduction of the rain merely complicates the imagery, and that idea of the clouds returning is suggestive more of broken weather than of perpetual gloom. If he is trying to suggest that there may be sunny spells even in these final days, this is a strange way to do it, and if not, he could easily have talked about the clouds staying, not 'returning'. It is particularly interesting to observe, therefore, that there is evidence for an early interpretation of this image in quite different terms, with the clouds departing after the rain—which is an idea quite compatible with the Hebrew. It would be possible to understand this departure, and not the presence of the clouds, as the intended point of comparison with the darkening of the sun, moon, and stars, and, in turn, with the closing of life. On that reading, darkness and gloom function poetically to conjure up the darkness which contrasts with the sunlight of 11.7. The point then, however, would not be simply that humans see the lights going out, and Qohelet would rather be using the same sort of image that lies behind our own talk of 'twilight years': humans fade, like the light of the sun at dusk or of the moon and stars at dawn, and dissipate like clouds that have emptied themselves. It is simpler, on the other hand, to understand the construction in a different way (as reflected in my own translation), so that the contrast is between a time when the heavenly bodies still shine and clouds disappear, and a time when neither of those things happens.

Notes

11.7 Also] The initial conjunction is omitted in S and V, and often left untranslated in more modern versions. How we deal with it depends on our understanding of the verse's function in the broader context. For those who see it simply as the start of a new section, the conjunction is either just a marker of the new theme (so, e.g., Seow) or an emphatic 'indeed' (so Schoors, citing Lauha). A good case can be made, however, for connecting the statement with what has preceded (so, e.g., Delitzsch), and I understand Qohelet to be introducing his new theme loosely as a secondary motive for the preceding advice: sow from dawn to dusk because you do not know, but because it is good anyway to see the sun.

11.7 sweet] On metaphorical uses of sweetness and bitterness in classical Hebrew, see King, *Surrounded by Bitterness*, Chapter 9 and esp. 322-29. Qohelet (who spoke of the woman as 'bitter' in 7.26) used מתוקה in an identical construction to describe sleep at 5.11, and appears to understand the sort of equivalence between 'sweet' and 'pleasant' that is commonplace in English. Some such equivalence is stated in Prov 16.24, but there and in other biblical uses the adjective retains a more direct connection with taste, even if it tends to imply 'desirable', and it never seems to become simply a way of saying 'pleasant' in later rabbinic texts. 4QInstruction, however, does talk about discovering 'what is bitter' and 'what is sweet' for a human (4Q416 frag. 1, 15; 4Q418 frag. 9, 16), meaning essentially what is good and bad, so it is a reasonable supposition that this extended sense would have been familiar around the time both Ecclesiastes and 4QInstruction were composed (they are generally considered close in date). Even were that not the case, though, we hardly need follow Pinker, 'Sweetness and Light', in understanding Qohelet here to be claiming that honey is 'light to the eyes' of farmers worn out by a day's work, and 'good for seeing with sunlight'—a reading that he achieves by swapping לעינים and וטוב.

11.7 daylight] Lit. 'the light'; האור has its own place in the list at 12.2, and although Qohelet is probably not trying to assert an existence of light distinct from the sun and other heavenly bodies (of the sort that has troubled readers of Gen 1.3; cf. Fox; Seow at 12.2), I take him to be talking about the general lightness of the sky as opposed to the bright disk of the sun itself.

11.7 it is good for the eyes] טוב can mean 'beneficial' or 'pleasing': the alignment with מתוק suggests that the latter sense is uppermost. Of course, pleasure and benefit are closely associated in Qohelet's thinking by this point, but Ellermeier, *Qohelet I.1*, 304, goes too far in the other direction when he renders 'glücklich sind die Augen, welche', 'fortunate are the eyes which (may see)' (a translation adopted also by Fischer, *Skepsis*, 150).

11.7 to see sunlight] Lit. 'the sun'. Qohelet used 'has not seen the sun' in 6.5 as a way of saying 'has not been born', and in 7.11 'those who see the sun' are the living (although the sun there is a mixed blessing). He will go on to draw a contrast with darkness, however, so although the expression has a connotation of 'living', it has not lost its literal sense. Several manuscripts of S assimilate the verse to 7.11: instead of just ܠܡܚܙܐ ܫܡܫܐ *lmḥzʾ šmšʾ*, 'to see the sun', they have ܘܡܗܢܐ ܠܡܢ ܕܚܙܐ ܫܡܫܐ *wytyr lḥzyy šmšʾ*, 'and an advantage to those who see the sun' (see Lane, 'Lilies', 482). Codex Graecus Venetus curiously has τὸν οὐρανόν here, suggesting the translator found השמים, although that variant is not attested by Kennicott or de Rossi.

11.8 For even if…he may…but will] There is general agreement that the initial כי אם does not mean 'except', but the force of the כי is uncertain, and G ὅτι καὶ ἐάν (lit. 'for and if', but probably to be understood as 'for even if') seems to reflect כי ואם (contrast ὅτι ἐάν in 4.10). Whether or not that is the original reading, it gives a good sense which I take to be the intended meaning: it is good to see the sun because, even if one finds pleasure in a long life, one will always be conscious of the darkness to come. This is essentially the reading not just of G, but of Ellermeier, *Qohelet I.1*, 303-6, Galling 1969 and Krüger, who likewise take the statements as indicative, not admonitory.

It is much more difficult, in fact, to find an admonition or admonitions here. Jerome reports the interpretation of Symmachus as *si annis multis uixerit homo, et in omnibus his laetus fuerit* (καὶ διὰ πάντων εὐφρανθήσεται), *recordari debet et dies* (καὶ μεμνήσθω [var. ἐμνήσθη] τῶν ἡμερῶν) *tenebrarum*, 'if a man should live many years and be joyful in all these, he ought to be mindful also of the days of darkness' (I have included the readings preserved also in Greek). This seems to have influenced Jerome's own rendering in V, which is very close, and it takes only the last clause as admonitory (cf. also α' μεμνήσθω / μνησθήτω); however, it involves, of course, understanding a conjunction before ישמח which would enable that to form part of the protasis; it also apparently ignores the כי. Most modern commentators prefer a double admonition, as in RSV 'For if a man lives many years, let him rejoice in them all; but let him remember'. On such a reading, the כי has, again, virtually no explicatory force, and even if it is viewed as emphatic, it is essentially redundant. This could be remedied by following Lauha in taking ישמח as indicative but יזכר as jussive (although Lauha himself does not give כי the explicatory force that such a reading would enable), but that would also involve treating the verbs differently, in an arbitrary way that finds no explicit cue in the text itself (see the discussion in Niccacci, 'Qohelet o la gioia', 90).

11.8 in them all] Despite the plural form שנים, שנה is usually feminine, so בכלם does not agree; cf. בהם in 12.1. This may just reflect a more general neglect of feminine forms, but see the notes 'from which' at 2.6 and 'by them' at 10.9.

11.8 be mindful of the days of darkness, that they will be many] יזכר takes two objects: a substantive (the days themselves) and a syndetic object clause introduced by כי (the fact that they will be many), but the effect is to specify the first in terms of the second—the man will be mindful that the days of darkness will be many. Because seeing the sun has just been used as an image of life, it is natural to see darkness, conversely, as an image of death, and many commentators understand a reference to Sheol. Krüger claims, however, that this makes the emphasis on number seem strange: what does it matter how long one is dead? His own solution is to see these as dark days within one's life, but this fits uncomfortably with the preceding idea that the man might take joy 'in them all', which Krüger accordingly renders rather vaguely as 'darüber', '(rejoices) over that'. The same consideration would make it difficult to see a more specific reference to old age, and Krüger is probably wrong to suppose that the emphasis on number demands any such reference. Death is not depicted by Qohelet as momentary, but as a state of existence that will last no less time than the living even of a long life.

11.8 All that is coming is an illusion] There is no particular reason to take this as one of the things of which the person should be mindful, and Schoors, for instance, has effectively to understand another כי before כל in order to do so. It is more likely a comment on the situation.

Hebrew, like English, can use the idea that something is 'coming' to talk about the future (e.g. Jer 7.32, 'the days are coming when'; Isa 41.22, 'the things coming' = 'the things to come'), but it is reasonable, with Seow, to demand an explanation for the use of this expression here, when Qohelet habitually uses יהיה for future events (e.g. 3.22 שיהיה). Noting 1.4; 5.14-15; and 6.4, Seow himself suggests that Qohelet tends to use בא of humans 'coming' into the world, and so sees a statement of human transience. This is a view adopted also by Lohfink, against which Schoors raises the likewise reasonable objection that we might then have expected Qohelet to use כל האדם.

Seow's argument leads him in addition to reject a common interpretation of the phrase simply in terms of what is to come after death (he cites Whybray's views as an example), and in that, I think, he is more likely to be correct: the tense of the verb (whether we read it as a participle or as qatal) here sits uneasily with an idea that it refers to a point even beyond what has been described, while הבל is something that Qohelet relates elsewhere to days or periods of life (6.12; 7.15; 9.9), but not directly to the condition of death. I think that the reference here is probably similar: 'what is coming' is the potentially long life and its experiences, rendered הבל from its outset by the certainty of the long death that will follow it.

Some of the ancient versions simply match the Hebrew: θ', for instance, is probably to be retroverted from Syh as πᾶν τὸ ἐρχόμενον ἀτμίς (or ἀτμός), 'all which is coming (is) vapour'; cf. G πᾶν τὸ ἐρχόμενον ματαιότης, 'all which is coming (is) vanity'—although it is noteworthy that both seem to have understood בא as a participle, cf. Hie *omne quod uenturum est uanitas*, 'all that is going to come is vanity'. Some, however, do offer their own interpretations. T sees הבל as what the human will have done, for which they will be punished, and V has the highly paraphrastic *qui cum uenerint uanitatis arguentur praeterita*, '(the many days in) which, when they will come, the past will be accused of vanity', which is a little reminiscent of T. Although he cites it in his commentary, and although both clearly see a reference to the afterlife, for once Jerome is not depending here on σ', which is attested as ἐν αἷς ἁπάσαις ἐλεύσεται τὸ μὴ εἶναι, 'in all those things which will come (is) non-existence', and which seems accidentally or interpretatively to have read כל as בכל (cf. the preceding בכלם). Interestingly, Theodulphian manuscripts of V have *omnia*, 'all things', rather than *praeterita*, which is closer to the original and perhaps derived from La.

11.9 young one, in your youth…in the days when you are young] Lit. 'in the days of your young-man-ness'. The Hebrew wording, with its two terms for the period of youth (בחורות, ילדות) is difficult to match precisely in English ('nonage', alas, has slipped out of use), and the translator of G has probably struggled for a similar reason: he uses νεότης twice because there is no other Greek word that could correspond to his initial νεανίσκε, 'young one', in the way that בחורותך corresponds to בחור in M. Correspondingly, we should probably not assume that he read a different text, and Aitken, 'Rhetoric and Poetry', 64-65, observes that the Greek achieves both alliteration and a certain symmetry of its own. S, on the other hand, has a more drastic alteration, which

11.7–12.2   591

Kamenetzky, 231-2, considers deliberate: ܒܝܘܡܝ ܛܠܝܘܬܟ ܥܕܪ, ܛܠܝܐ ܚܕܝ ܛܠܝܡ *bywmy ʿlymwtk ḥdy ʿlym*, 'in the days of your youth (= בימי בחורותך) rejoice, young one (= שמח בחור)'—the elements are re-arranged and there is no equivalent to בילדותיך. The purpose is, perhaps, to eliminate the ambiguity in the sense of the Hebrew (see below).

Both the Hebrew nouns are unusual: the only other biblical uses of ילדות are in v. 10 and in Ps 110.3, while בחורות, used also in 12.1, is possibly found in the form בחרים at Num 11.28 (although the Greek there reads the word as בחירים, 'chosen ones'). Their form may also be unexpected, and Seow suggests that we should read בילדותך and בחורתיך (cf. 12.1), which are the readings of the Van der Hooght text and hence of many older printed editions, rather than בילדותיך and בחורותך.[4] The evidence from the later Hebrew tradition that he cites in support may reflect no more than a similar instinct to correct the difficult text, and the בילדותיך of M[L], we may note, is attested in a text with Palestinian pointing that Diez Macho takes to have been copied from a seventh- or eighth-century original.[5] The 'feminine' form of בחורות may have been coined to avoid confusion with בחורים in its more common sense 'young men', which is commonly used alongside terms for women, and has a specific connotation of masculinity: Richter, 'Kohelets Urteil', 593, actually translates it as *Männlichkeit*, 'manhood', but age rather than sex is clearly the thought uppermost here.

The construction is straightforward, if slightly ambiguous. We do not need to assume with Hitzig and others that בילדותיך is equivalent to בימי ילדותיך, and that we are dealing therefore with an invitation to 'be happy while you are young': it is perfectly possible, and arguably more natural, to understand 'be happy with your youth', 'take pleasure in it', but both understandings are possible (and both, perhaps, intended).

11.9 let your heart be good to you] The qal of יטב was used with לב in 7.3 of the heart being cheerful, and Hie, V, T speak here of 'your heart' itself being good, or 'in goodness'; cf. σ′ καὶ ἐν ἀγαθῷ ἔστω, 'and may (it) be in good'. Although these readings are not noted in *BHQ*, they lend some support to a common suggestion that we should emend the hiphʿil וייטבך to the qal ויטב, without a suffix (so, e.g., Ehrlich, *BHS*; Sacchi would read qal וייטבך), which would give a more precise parallel to שמח. G καὶ ἀγαθυνάτω σε, however, means 'may (your heart) do you good', and supports M, as, probably, does S (although see the footnote below.). With the precedent of 7.3, and the easier, more common sense yielded by the qal (cf. Judg 18.20; 19.6 etc.),

---

[4] Issues in the spelling of בחורותך extend beyond the presence or absence of the yod, and variations in the numbers of waws (here and in 12.1) are discussed in Ginsburg, *Massoreth*, 4:196.

[5] See, Chiesa, *L'Antico Testamento*, 235, and my Introduction, 184. The reading for בחורתיך / בחורתך is not extant.

the understanding of Hie, V, T probably arose from a Hebrew textual variant based on a defectively written hiphʿil, in which the suffix had been discarded as an apparent error when the verb was read as the expected qal. This seems more likely than the alternatives, that a qal was mistakenly taken to be such a hiphʿil and a suffix added, or that the suffix arose through partial dittography of the subsequent לבך.[6]

Given the sense of the expression in the qal, however, it is very possible that Qohelet is talking about the heart 'cheering' one: I have translated using the more general sense of the hiphʿil simply because we cannot be certain that this nuance alone is intended—an issue that corresponds to broader questions about the role of the heart in this verse. Again, we should be wary of imposing more modern associations of the heart with spontaneity upon Qohelet's characteristic use of it to describe the mind and intellect, and this is most likely an admonition to make a conscious effort. Schwienhorst-Schönberger raises the interesting possibility that we should read the verb as consecutive upon the initial admonition, giving broadly the sense 'rejoice...and you will be happy...'. That seems to state the obvious a little too much, but if 'your heart will do you good' had some more general implication, such a reading might be entertained.

11.9 walk] Schoors suggested in *The Preacher* I, 94, that the imperative was supposed originally to be read as qal, comparing Jer 51.50, but he also noted that the piʿel of M gives a good sense, and has not raised the possibility again in his subsequent commentary. The consonantal text could, of course, be taken either way (if one read a qal of the strong formation), but G, at least, has probably read the verb as piʿel, with a specific implication of 'walking' (cf. the rendering at 4.15).

11.9 in the ways of your heart] Isa 57.17 uses וילך שובב בדרך לבו to mean 'but he kept on walking astray in the way of his heart', and we are probably to understand 'the ways of the heart' here similarly as those directions in which one is determined to go. The heart is the intellect, the disposition or the determination, however, not the seat of appetite or desire, and Qohelet's point

---

[6] Dahood, 'Qoheleth and Northwest Semitic Philology', 363, seeks to read the qal but to retain the suffix by seeing it as 'dative', yielding the sense 'let your heart be glad for you'. For anyone like Dahood, who feels compelled by the parallelism to read the qal, then this offers an easier explanation for the suffix—but not much. Although Dahood claims to have identified other examples, this would be, at best, a very unusual usage in Hebrew, where the so-called *datiuus commodi* is usually expressed with -ל (see GKC §119 s; J-M §133 d). At first glance, S ܘܢܛܐܒ ܠܟ *wnṭʾb lk*, 'be good for you', appears to support an understanding of the suffix as dative, but ܠܟ *lk*, 'for you', has probably arisen as a corruption of (the otherwise absent) ܠܒܟ *lbk*, 'your heart'. This may have caused the suffix to be dropped and the verb read as impersonal, but it is also possible that S had a source-text without the suffix, like that of σ'.

is unlikely to be, therefore, that young people should just go about thoughtlessly doing whatever they feel like at any given moment—the idea is closer to 'live your dreams'.

It is perhaps a concern about the undefined character of the 'ways' that lies behind the problems of the G tradition here. Almost all the Greek manuscripts have some form of the word ἄμωμος, 'blameless' or 'unblemished', as well as or in place of καρδίας σου, 'your heart', so that this becomes a reference to walking blamelessly or in blameless ways, and is interpreted as such by early commentators (cf. Vinel). The plus is under lemnisk in Syh (for the possible significance, see the note on 'already has been' at 1.9), and has no counterpart in any of the ancient versions that has not been derived from G: it seems almost certain to have originated secondarily, but it is harder to say for sure precisely in what form it originated, or whether it was present already in the source-text of G, as Goldman supposes. Gentry, 'Hexaplaric Materials', 20-22, argues that it was in fact an inner-Greek development, influenced by the frequent use of ἄμωμος in contexts like Pss 101.2 or 119.1, but that development could presumably have happened as easily in a Hebrew text as in a Greek one. As Gentry acknowledges, moreover, if ἄμωμος has simply been added, then it is also difficult to explain the absence in key witnesses of καρδίας σου, 'your heart'. It is significantly easier, in that respect, to suppose that it originally replaced καρδίας σου (or that a Hebrew תמים replaced לבך in the source-text), and this in turn means that תמים / ἄμωμος is unlikely to have slipped into the text after originating as a marginal gloss. In neither language is there any graphical or phonetic similarity, furthermore, that might have caused it to arise as a minor slip, and it more probably came into being as a deliberate alteration, as a trick of some scribe's memory, or as an educated guess at a passage that was illegible.

11.9 but amongst what is before you] Lit. 'in sight of your eyes'. On the sense of מראה, see the notes at 6.9 and the comments above. Formally, the phrase stands in parallel with 'ways of your heart', but that does not mean that it must likewise carry some implication of decision or desire, despite the claim of Ogden, 'Qoheleth XI 7-XII 8', 31, that Qohelet is talking about allowing 'one's observations of life...to direct one's path'. I take this second phrase to constrain the first, as though we were to say 'travel where your mind takes you, but not beyond what your eyes can see'. The issue, therefore, is not the same as in 2.10, where Qohelet sought to gratify his eyes and heart. Watson, 'Unnoticed Word Pair', draws attention to the many times that 'eyes' and 'heart' are paired in the Hebrew Bible, but his examples demonstrate also that the pairing has no single implication.

The Masorah parva note draws attention to the unique spelling מראי: substantives ending in הִ֣- sometimes take a י before a suffix even when the substantive is singular (GKC §93 ss; J-M §96C e), and this happens frequently with מראה. There is no suffix here, however, and Goldman discusses the possibility that the noun actually is intended to be plural. It seems more likely that this is simply an error or curious orthographic variation that has become fixed in the textual tradition—or some part of it: Ginsburg, *Massorah* 3:71 (cf. 4:457), lists מראה as a *Qᵉrê*, affirming מראי as the proper text but suggesting a Masoretic understanding that it should not be taken as plural. Kennicott and de Rossi note this more regular מראה in numerous manuscripts and printed editions, and, whichever we read, the singular sense is affirmed by the other versions, none of which use a plural noun here.

G is καὶ ἐν ὁράσει ὀφθαλμῶν σου, 'and in sight of your eyes', but some significant manuscripts have καὶ μὴ ἐν ὁράσει, 'and *not* in sight'. Goldman treats this with the anomalous ἄμωμος (see the previous note) as part of the same variant, which he thinks the translator found in his source-text, but it is doubtful that they originated together, and this μὴ, which is much less well-established in the manuscript tradition, may be a gloss inspired by the ἄμωμος. Again, there is no parallel in the other ancient versions.

11.9 and know that, for all these things] The conventional translation of the conjunction as 'but' reflects a particular understanding that Qohelet is seeking to place a limit on behaviour (a point made by Spronk, 'Prediker', 111-12). On my understanding, see the commentary. The attested reading of σ', γίνωσκον ὅτι περὶ πάντων τούτων, may not cover the conjunction, but if the otherwise difficult γίνωσκον is in fact a writing of γινώσκων, so that the sense is 'knowing that concerning all these', then Symmachus must understand it to imply 'and' or 'while'. None of the other ancient versions draws an explicit contrast. Fries, 'Freue dich', 107 n. 16, seeks an adversative sense of a different sort: we should know that God will judge *despite* everything. He rests this on an understanding that כי על כל always has such an implication, but it does not (even in Jer 2.34, where 'despite' is often understood), and there is, anyway, no reason to suppose that this sequence of common words constitutes a fixed expression with a specific meaning.

11.9 will demand of you a reckoning] Lit. 'will bring you to a reckoning'. For this expression (used also in 12.14) and similar, see especially Job 14.3; 22.4; 34.23; Ps 143.2; Isa 3.14. Such passages make it difficult to deny a reference to divine judgment here, but that has not stopped some scholars from trying. We have already reviewed other potential meanings of משפט at 8.6 (see the note there), and Gorssen, 'La Cohérence', 304, develops one of these, the idea of a 'proper way' for something to happen, in order to suggest that Qohelet is talking about youth as a particular condition that is given by God— an idea that is adopted by Schoors. That idea seems forced, however, not least because it is difficult to see any emphasis here on the *proper* or *customary* nature of such a condition, and Gorssen seems to be moving towards an idea of משפט meaning simply a 'state' or 'situation', which would be very hard to justify from other usage.

A little differently, and without offering an explanation, Staples translates 'God will bring you into the right order', presumably meaning that God will ensure that everything works out properly for the person. This avoids losing the specificity of משפט, although if the noun is being used in that sense, the Hebrew would more naturally mean 'God will bring you in the proper fashion' or 'properly'. The principal objection to such a reading, however, is that if Qohelet were trying to make such a point, he could have done so without using language that would certainly have implied to his readers that he was talking about divine judgment (and that was taken this way by all the ancient versions). Unless we are to suppose that the author somehow overlooked the possibility of people reading his words in those terms, there seems little point in rummaging for possible alternative meanings in his text. As Mazzinghi, 'Dieu te convoquera', 104, points out, moreover, it is difficult to assign some special sense to משפט here, when the very similar expression in 12.14 is clearly talking about judgment.

11.10 but] S, V do not translate the initial conjunction, probably because they see this as the start of a new sentence. So, similarly, RSV.

11.10 put anger out of your mind] Lit. 'put aside / remove anger from your heart'. On כעס, see the note at 1.18. Marshall argues that the reading παροργισμόν found in the text of G²⁵³ and in the commentary of Antiochus Monachus belongs to α' or σ'.

11.10 youth and youthfulness] The first noun ילדות is not problematic, and was used in the last verse, although Rose, *Rien de nouveau*, 476, sees in that fact a reason to believe that it is a corrupt form of a noun (attested nowhere else) ילהות, meaning 'anxiety' or 'affliction'. A variant ܕܛܠܝܘܬܐ ܕܛܠܝܘܬܐ ʿlymwtʾ dṭlywtʾ, 'youth of youngness', is found in the S tradition in place of simple ܕܛܠܝܘܬܐ dṭlywtʾ, 'of youth': Lane, 'Lilies', 482, notes that this is a double translation or assimilation to 12.1 (where ܥܠܝܡܘܬܟ ʿlymwtk, 'your youth', occurs).

The second noun שחרות is more difficult, not least because it is found nowhere else as a noun. In the ancient versions we find several renderings that are probably guesses. G opts for ἄνοια, the quality of being thoughtless or foolish, which the translator perhaps associates with youth; this is picked up in Hie *stultitia*, and S ܠܐ ܝܕܥܬܐ lʾ ydʿtʾ, 'non-intelligence' (a very literal reading of the Greek as α-νοια). Symmachus has opted for a paraphrase ἡ περὶ αὐτὴν σπουδή, lit. 'and the trouble concerning it', to give a sense something like 'youth and all the effort that goes with it', while Jerome in V opts for *uoluptas*, 'delight'. There are variant readings in the T tradition here: the version that stays closer to the Hebrew, however, offers a sense that is adopted also by Rashi and Rashbam, and is widely accepted by modern commentators, אוכמות סער, 'blackness of hair'.

That meaning in itself is clearly possible: the adjective שחר is used of black hair in Ct 5.11 (where the comparison is with the blackness of a raven), although uses in Lev 13.31-37; Ct 1.5; and Zech 6.2-6 may imply darkness of colour, rather than strictly 'blackness'. The evidence for 'dark-haired' meaning 'young' in later Hebrew is not, however, clear cut: the 'black-headed' (משחורי הראש) in *m. Nedarim* 3.8 are defined in terms of being male, not young, and the best indication that there might be a reference to youth is much later in *Genesis Rabbah* 59.1, where R. Meir sees a group who are all שחורי ראש, and promises them that they will reach old age if they do charitable works. In *b. Šabbat* 152a, the verse is interpreted in terms of a different sort of 'darkness': what one does in one's youth will darken one's face (make one blush) as one grows older (cf. Ct 1.5-6, where the reference is to being suntanned or sunburned).

An alternative accepted by some scholars, which yields a similar sense and is espoused by Ibn Ezra (although he also considers the possibility of 'dark hair'), is to connect שחרות with שחר, 'dawn', so that this is 'the dawn of life' (Seow). Less plausibly, *HALOT* also suggests a link with an Arabic word *šḥr*, used of the early part of youth (cf. Driver, 'Studies', 44-45), while Rose, *Rien de nouveau*, 476-77, associates שחרות with the verb שחר found in e.g., Prov 1.28; 8.17, which means 'seek': he takes the point to be that anxiety and a painful questing for answers will pass—an interpretation permitted by his previous emendation of ילדות, but hardly validated by his tenuous claim that such an understanding is reflected in the ancient versions.

12.1 your creator] Or perhaps 'your good health'. Although all the ancient versions see a reference to 'your creator' here, the form of בוראיך is problematic, and many commentators have felt that such a reference is inappropriate to the context. As regards the form, we have just discussed at 11.9 (see the note 'with your eyes open') the way in which substantives ending in ה־ sometimes take a י before a suffix even when singular (GKC §93 ss, §124 k; J-M §96 e). To be sure, it is striking that this phenomenon is found with terms referring to God as creator, like עשיך in Isa 54.5 or עשיו in Ps 149.2 (cf. Salvaneschi, 'Memento vivere', 34-36), and it is not impossible that such usage has influenced the form, but the י here is probably to be understood fundamentally in terms of that orthographic peculiarity, with ברא being treated as though it were a *lamed–he* verb (so, e.g., Gordis, Fox, Seow), rather than treated as a 'plural of majesty' (so Schoors and many others) or as agreeing with an implicit אלהים (Van der Wal, 'Qohelet 12,1a', 118). As with the מראי of 11.9, a variant spelling without the י is found in a very substantial number of manuscripts and early printed editions listed by Kennicott and de Rossi, but may be an assimilation to the regular form.

The proper sense is a more interesting matter. The midrash connects with this passage an early play on words that is attributed to Akavia ben Mahalalel and found in the Mishnah at *ʾAbot* 3.1: you must watch out for בְּאֵרְךָ, 'your well', בּוֹרְךָ, 'your pit', and בּוֹרַאֲךָ, 'your creator', these representing your origin (as a drop of liquid), your destination (the grave), and the one to whom you must ultimately give an account.[7] Schoors suggests that 'Rashi already had a problem with the phrase זכר את בוראיך', but there is no sign of that: he simply

---

[7] The order of the first two has been swapped in Midrash Qohelet, but is preserved correctly in another account at *Leviticus Rabbah* 38.1.

picks up this traditional exegesis that draws several parallel meanings. It is more recent commentators who have actively sought a meaning that might *replace* 'your creator', with many focusing on 'your pit' (grave)—against which Beal, 'C(ha)osmopolis', 294, rightly notes the use of בור with a different sense at 12.6—or on 'your well' (understood in terms of the imagery in Prov 5.15-18 to mean 'your wife' by, e.g., Haupt, 'On the Book of Ecclesiastes', 116).

It is not impossible, of course, that any of these words stood originally in the text, but it would seem arbitrary to emend that text when it makes good sense as it stands, and when there is no versional support for a change. Seow makes an interesting suggestion that the rabbinic exegesis actually picks up an intention of the author, and that we are supposed to hear several different words here (similarly Nel, 'Remember', 154 n. 4); this is attractive, but only really works if those different words were pronounced more like each other originally than they are with the Masoretic vocalization.

The lexica recognize a verb II ברא, represented in the hiph'il at 1 Sam 2.29, and apparently connected with בריא, 'fat'. The cognate ברי means 'healthy' in Aramaic, as does the Arabic equivalent, and בורי in later Hebrew is used of 'health' in the sense 'one's normal condition when not ill'. Busto Saiz, 'בוראיך (Qoh 12,1), reconsiderado', argues for that sense here, and Schoors suggests that it 'deserves serious consideration'. The admonition then would be to remember one's good health while one has it, and this is undoubtedly attractive as an understanding of 12.1 by itself. It would not fit well, however, with the other reminders in 11.7 and 11.9, which invite the audience to recall what they are *not* currently experiencing, rather than to take advantage of their current situation.

12.1 while...not yet] The expression עד אשר means 'until' in biblical usage, and we encountered it with that sense at 2.3. Correspondingly, when followed by a negation, it should mean 'until...not', as when 2 Sam 17.13 says 'until not even a pebble is to be found there'. In this verse and the next, however, and then apparently again in 12.6, the expression refers to the period before something happens. This usage is more like that of עד שלא in, for instance, *b. Megillah* 14a, עד שלא נכנסו ישראל לארץ, 'while Israel had not yet entered the land', in *b. Berakot* 17a, עד שלא נוצרתי, 'while I had not yet been created', or in *Genesis Rabbah* 58.1 (which is interpreting Eccl 1.5), עד שלא ישקיע הקדוש ברוך הוא שמשו של צדיק הוא מזריח שמשו של צדיק חבירו, 'while the Holy One, blessed be, has not yet caused the sun of a righteous man to set, he causes the sun of a fellow righteous man to rise'. With this sense, עד אשר לא is found already at Qumran: see 4Q265 7, II, 11-13, [עד] אשר לא הובא...עד אשר לא הובאה, 'while he had not yet been brought...while she had not yet been brought', and 4Q270 6, IV, 19, עד אשר לא [ישלי]מו א[ת ימ]יהם, 'while they had not yet completed their days'. Of course, it is often translated simply as 'before' (and Schoors even describes the לא as 'pleonastic'), but the expression commonly seems to have a particular nuance 'during the time when something that will happen has yet to happen'.

12.1 the days of trouble...years] σ' has πρὶν ἐλθεῖν τὰς ἡμέρας τῆς κακώσεώς σου, 'before the coming of the days of *your* trouble'. It seems likely that this reflects not a variant source but an understanding that ימי הרעה is determined (while שנים is not) because it is picking up the reference to רעה in 'your' body at 11.10. Although T talks about the days and years reaching 'you', there is no corresponding possessive pronoun in the majority text of any other ancient version. However, *adflictionis tuae*, '*your* affliction', is found as a variant in Theodulphian manuscripts of V, and the potential link with σ' gives it some claim to attention.

12.1 I have no use for them] On חפץ, see the note at 3.1. Although a few commentators try to find it here, Qohelet is not, apparently, using the word in the unusual sense that it had in that verse. However, σ' οὐ χρήζω αὐτῶν, 'I have no need of them', is evocative of the χρείας used there (cf. also 3.17 if that is not α'; 5.3; and 12.10 χρειώδεις), while α' (on the attributions here, see Marshall) actually uses πρᾶγμα, 'deed' (contrast 12.10 χρείας). G and θ', on the other hand, use θέλημα, 'will' or 'what one wills' (cf. Hie *uoluntas*), as G does in 5.3 and 12.10; cf. 8.3 (on the reading of θ' here, and on renderings of חפץ more generally, see Gentry, 'Relationship', 79-80). These translations do not take חפץ to have the sense 'pleasure' or 'delight' that is commonly attributed to it, and do not typically grant it that sense when they translate it in other texts—probably because that is not what the Hebrew word actually means, and the rendering 'joy' in *HALOT* is more than a little misleading. Qohelet is not talking about an inability to find pleasure during these times or to enjoy them in themselves, but is employing the same idiom that we saw in 5.3, which expresses contempt for them as useless or without value; see the note there. Accordingly, of course, there is no direct contradiction with the notion in 11.8, that one might rejoice in all one's days, but there would still be a certain tension if these bad years are supposed to be inevitable.

As in that verse, there is a mismatch in gender between the שנים and the suffix pronoun of בהם, that refers to them (cf. the notes 'from which' at 2.6 and 'by them' at 10.9), although Seow raises the (slim) possibility that the reference is back to the days of youth, making the claim that 'I *had* no pleasure in them'. There are no reasons to doubt the text, but it has undergone some development in the S tradition, where what was probably an original ܨܒܝ *ṣbyn*, 'desire', has become ܨܒܝܢܝ *ṣbyny*, '*my* desire', and the preceding ܠܝ *ly*, 'to me', has accordingly dropped out of some manuscripts as redundant; see Kamenetzky 200, 232.

12.2 the sun, the daylight, the moon and the stars] The elements of the list are joined together by conjunctions in M, and these are generally reflected in the other versions. In S, however, the conjunction before 'moon' has been replaced by -ܕ *d-*, so that the text reads 'the light of the moon'. In some manuscripts, -ܕ *d-* has also been added after the conjunction on the next word, so that the whole list reads 'the sun and the light of the moon and of the stars'. The change has presumably been provoked by a discomfort with the appearance of 'light' as an item in its own right (for my understanding of which, see the note at 11.7). Gordis, implausibly, tries to find a sense similar to that of S by treating the last three nouns as (what he calls) a hendiadys, and Whybray wants to take two of them to mean 'bright stars', but it is clearly problematic to treat segments of the list as distinct units when the list as a whole is so consistent in form.

12.2 have not yet darkened] The verb is singular and agrees with השמש, which is feminine here (contrast 1.5), and the other elements of the list are appended as additional subjects; this is a common construction, cf. GKC §146 f. Although my own understanding suggests that Qohelet has the fading of light in mind, there is no specific implication in the verb either of growing dark gradually or of going out suddenly, and the terminology is used elsewhere of lights being out (cf. Isa 13.10; Job 3.9; 18.6)—as though, we might say, they had simply not been switched on. All the same, the Greek translations render תחשך using, variously, active forms of σκοτάζω, 'become dark', or passive forms of σκοτίζω, 'make dark'. Largely on the basis of the Syh note (which does not, of course, give the Greek directly), Field thinks that α' had σκοτάσῃ, σ' πρὶν σκοτάσαι (for which there is Greek attestation, albeit misspelled, in the σκοτασει of ms 252), and θ' probably σκοτισθῇ. Basing himself in part on the detailed discussion in Gentry, 'Relationship', 77-78, on the other hand, Marshall believes that α' had σκοτίσῃ (despite the strange sense 'makes dark') and θ' σκοτάσῃ (he agrees with Field about σ').

The original reading of G here was probably σκοτισθῇ, 'be made dark', but in the next verse (for which variants from the Three are not preserved), G then seems to have σκοτάσουσιν, 'will become dark', for ושבו. This inconsistency has to be treated with some caution, because it is not at all improbable either that the verbs might have been confused or that the text in 12.3 has been influenced by a reading from the Three. If it is original, however, then Aitken, 'Rhetoric and Poetry', 62, is probably right to see a deliberate stylistic variation, particularly since the contexts of each verb are so different. It is interesting to observe a similar variation in Hie, perhaps inherited from La, between *tenebrescat* here and *contenebrescent* in the next verse (they both mean 'grow dark').

12.2 and the clouds still recede after the rain] I take the 'still' to be implicit. The ancient translators are in agreement that the reference here is to clouds returning *after* rain. It is not clear why Scott regards this as 'a meteorological absurdity', or that there is any real force to his claim that אחרי can, and here must, mean 'together with', but along with Seow, who accepts that translation (and looks to Ugaritic for the sense, like Dahood, 'Hebrew–Ugaritic Lexicography VIII', 392), it seems that Scott is treating ושבו as though it meant simply 'come' rather than 'return'. The image does seem odd and inappropriate, all the same, if we adopt the usual understanding that, after emptying themselves (cf. 11.3), the clouds are said to come straight back, so that the sky does not brighten, and the sources of light—the sun, moon and stars—remain obscured. The only real alternative to this normal understanding is found in σ', and is only apparent in the reading from ms 788, which adds a crucial last four words to the text known previously: καὶ πάλιν ἀναστρέψαι τὰς νεφέλας μετὰ τὸν ὑετόν εἰς τὸ μὴ εἶναι, 'and the returning again of the clouds after the rain *to non-existence*'. This suits very well the common uses of the Hebrew verb, since it can imply persistence (e.g. Prov 26.11), and essentially had that sense in 1.7, but can also connote withdrawal (e.g. Gen 8.3), and there is an echo of this understanding also in Jerome's commentary, which interprets symbolically, but likewise takes the image to be of clouds returning home, rather than persisting.

If we adopt this understanding, it seems simplest to construe only the first clause with the preceding עד אשר לא, and the intended distinction may be signalled by the switch from yiqtol to qatal: the darkening of the heavenly bodies is a future event ('not yet'), the dissipation of the clouds a continuing but temporary reality ('while still'); there is, at least, no sense of sequence here that would demand we read the verb with waw consecutive. While it is tempting, in fact, to say that this clause is governed by the עד אשר, but not by the לא, there is no clear evidence that עד אשר without a negation had undergone the extension of meaning that we noted above for עד אשר לא, and that might give an explicit 'still'. Symmachus has more likely kept the clauses in parallel, and read the dissipation of the clouds as a separate image of human dissolution.

12.3-8

Death

(12.3) On the day when the house-guards are disturbed, the gentlefolk contort themselves, and the women fall idle at the mill, for they have shrunk away, when the eyes in the ceiling-holes mist over, (12.4) and the doors are closed on the street—the voice of the woman at the mill will be low, but it will rise back up at the sound of a bird. Then all the women who take up the song will be downcast, (12.5) but even at their full height they will be afraid, and utterly terrified on the road.

But the almond will blossom, and the locust carry itself within, and the caper-berry split open, even when the human has departed for the home of his eternity, and the mourners have gone about in the street.

(12.6)   While the silver cord has not yet been snapped,

and the golden bauble been crushed,

or a pitcher been shattered at the spring,

and the windlass spun free over the cistern,

(12.7)   then the dust returns to the ground as it was,

and the breath returns to God, who gave it—

(12.8)   a complete illusion! says the Qohelet, it is all an illusion!

Commentary

These verses, often linked directly to 12.1-2, have been interpreted in many different ways since ancient times (there is a helpful overview in Debel, 'When It All Falls Apart')—but most famously as a description of old age, in which the various objects and actions described stand for the failure of bodily parts and functions, or more generally for problems that confront the old. This was the interpretation offered by the Targum, it is discussed by Jerome, and it is found, piecemeal, in *b. Šabbat* 151b-153a; cf. also Leviticus Rabbah 18. Because it came to be seen specifically as the intention of the author, and not merely as an exegetical stratagem, that interpretation survived into the age of critical scholarship in a way that most other symbolic readings did not, and it is still advocated by many commentators. Along the way, it attracted the interest of scientists and physicians as well as of exegetes, and the history of scholarship offers a rich source of insights into the physiological and gerontological understandings of those writers (see especially Schäfer, 'Hebraeorum Hippokrates'). This means that the precise details of the interpretation came to be very varied, but they are far from consistent even in the early sources:

		(reported by) Jerome	*b. Šabbat* 151b-153a	Midrash Rabbah	Targum
12.2	the sun	eyes	forehead	face	
	the daylight		nose		eyes
	the moon	nostrils	soul	forehead	cheeks
	the stars	ears	cheeks		pupils of eyes
	nor the clouds receded after the rain		diminished sight after weeping		eyelids weeping
12.3	the house-guards are disturbed	ribs			knees
	the gentlefolk contort themselves	legs	thighs	arms / ribs	arms
	the women…at the mill	teeth		stomach	teeth
	shrunk away			teeth	
	the eyes in the ceiling-holes	eyes		eyes/ part of the lungs	eyes

12.3-8   603

12.4	the doors are closed on the street	impeded from travel	orifices		impeded from travel	
	the voice of the woman at the mill will be low	jaws and feeble voice	stomach			
	will rise back up at the sound of a bird	sleeping lightly		wakefulness (fear of bandits)		
	the women who take up the song will be downcast	tone deafness		lips/ kidneys	lips	
12.5	at their full height they will be afraid	weakness on slopes	trepidation about slopes on the road		fear of remembering the past	
	utterly terrified on the road	fear of falling on the road		trepidation about slopes on the road		
	the almond will blossom	sacrum/atlas				
	the locust carry itself within	legs swollen with gout	buttocks	ankles	ankles	
	the caper-berry split open	sexual desire/capacity				
	the home of his eternity		place in the world to come	grave		
	the mourners have gone about in the street			maggots on the corpse	angels of judgment	
12.6	silver cord…been snapped		spinal cord		tongue	
	golden bauble been crushed		penis	skull		
	pitcher been shattered at the spring		stomach		gall	
	windlass spun free over the cistern		excrement		body (running to grave)	

This has not been the only approach to the text. Jerome noted it in his commentary,[1] but discussed also a contemporary Jewish reading that saw in these verses an address to Israel: the nation is to enjoy its youth before losing its glory, its leaders, and its guardian angels at a time of captivity, before its temple doors are closed, the Babylonians summoned by the call of a bird, and the singers of psalms silenced. Enemies will be afraid as they approach, recalling the fate of Sennacherib, but the almond rod of Jeremiah's prophecy will blossom, and God's love will deteriorate, like the caperberry; as humans retreat from the protection of God, there will be lamenting under siege. The Israelites are to rejoice, therefore, while they still have the silver cord of their glory, the golden band of the ark, and the law and the spirit in the temple: they are going to be forced to return to Babylon, from where Abraham came, and will be shattered, losing their gift of prophecy as it returns to its maker. That reading was still offered, alongside the gerontological interpretation, in the Midrash Rabbah. Jerome himself tended to favour a third way of reading the text, as an account of the coming eschaton, and a version of this had already been propounded by Gregory Thaumaturgos. That interpretation seems to have been widespread, and remained popular among Christian readers in the Middle Ages (see Leanza, 'Eccl 12,1-7'; Munnich, 'Traduire', 109-10); it has also found some more recent advocates.[2]

Each of these readings can be characterized very broadly as 'allegorical' or 'symbolic', but in practice none of them is consistently so. Although the women at the mill, for instance, typically stand for digestion in the gerontological reading, or for teeth becoming less effective as they become fewer, other references in 12.4-5 have usually been interpreted as more straightforward

---

[1] Jerome's use of Jewish sources in his commentary on these verses is affirmed in Ginzberg, 'Die Haggada', 44-49, who presents the Jewish parallels, and is discussed at length in Kraus, 'Christians, Jews, and Pagans'. The latter notes (194) that there is no evidence for the 'old age' interpretation in Christian sources before Jerome, so it is unlikely to have been mediated through such sources, and goes on to argue that Jerome was aware of the version of this interpretation that subsequently appeared in *b. Šabbat*. In his appendices, he offers tabulations of each element in the various Jewish sources which are rather fuller than mine.

[2] See the commentary on 12.1-2. Kruger, 'Old Age Frailty', has proposed, a little differently (although not very convincingly), that the account is talking about the old age of the cosmos, not of the human, and includes mythological references.

allusions to wakefulness (being roused by the sound of a bird) and to trepidation when faced with steep hills. 'Symbolism' is probably not the best way, moreover, to understand those interpretations that depend on similarities of sound between words, or on etymological speculation (e.g. the connection between the locust and legs—see the notes—or the linking of the windlass *glgl* with excrement *gllym*). In the Jewish eschatological interpretation cited by Jerome, literal references jostle alongside other elements that are not symbols so much as items that require further specification, like the doors (of the Temple), and the almond (rod of Jeremiah). The eschatological reading of Gregory Thaumaturgos similarly blends literal readings of darkness and terrified women with items that need some interpretation: the blossoming almond, for instance, is an analogy for the bloody time that will arise, and the locust is a swarm, representing the coming punishments. This inconsistency is troubling, and these various interpretations give the impression that we are dealing not with a text that has adopted a particular, highly symbolic mode of presentation, but with interpreters who switch arbitrarily between whatever modes of reading best facilitate the matches they seek. When so much freedom is granted—Fox, 'Aging and Death', 56, speaks of 'all this hermeneutical flexibility'—then the text itself imposes only limited constraint upon interpretation.

Such concerns have long pushed some interpreters to adopt what is, on the face of it, a very different approach, which treats Qohelet's descriptions essentially as literal, and seeks to identify what situation is to be envisaged as having given rise to the various behaviours and events. In practice, this need not change the overall understanding very much, and eschatological readings, in particular, can be achieved with little or no symbolic interpretation of the specifics—although they tend then not to be clearly distinguishable from readings that see something less extraordinary, like the coming of a storm or the onset of winter (see the commentary on 12.1-2). Of course, in the broader context, such readings often identify the more-or-less cataclysmic circumstances with old age or death, and so arguably just introduce symbolic interpretation at a different point of the analysis. On the other hand, symbolism in the text is not always acknowledged by scholars who retain an understanding of it as an account of old age, but one in which Qohelet is talking literally about, say, the inability of (old) women to mill, or the decrepitude of strong men in their later years (so, especially

Buzy, 'Le Portrait', but cf. also Gilbert, 'La Description'). It is not methodological concerns that pose the greatest challenge to all such non-literal readings, however, but the particularities of the account: even if we accept that 12.2 belongs here (which I myself do not), the behaviours and events of 12.3-4 offer a curiously narrow and selective depiction of the effects upon humans either of old age, or of an apocalypse or storm.

Yet another approach, which can also claim a long ancestry, takes the location in the household as its starting point. Theodore of Mopsuestia is said to have understood the description in these terms, with the text depicting a wealthy household in decline, its residents paralyzed by fear after the weakening of its guards, and neglecting the very activities upon which the survival of the house depends (see Jarick, 'Theodore and the Interpretation', 311-15). Apparently independently, Sawyer, 'The Ruined House', has more recently seen here the portrayal of a house that goes into decline with the death of its owner, and is slowly reclaimed by nature. A little differently, Witzenrath, *Süß ist das Licht*, 44-50, has also understood Qohelet to be talking about the ruin of a house—although Witzenrath identifies the house as an image for the human body. Probably the best known account along these lines, though, is that of Taylor, *Dirge*, in the nineteenth century, which sees in the descriptions here not a continuing state of fear, or a prolonged process of dilapidation, but a much more specific portrayal of a household over the days in which its owner dies, then is mourned and buried. This has been taken further in one direction by Anat (in 'הקינה על מות'), who tries to read the account itself as a metrical lament, but has also been taken up by Fox, who is willing, however, to admit the possibility of a symbolic purpose behind various of the details, in a way that Taylor decidedly was not; Fox believes both that eschatological images of general disaster are re-applied in these verses to depict what is a disaster for the individual, and that some items should be considered figures for aging or death (see especially his 'Aging and Death').

My own reading falls into this last category, and is similar in many respects to that of Taylor (although I by no means agree with him on every point). Correspondingly, of course, it is also broadly similar to that of Fox, although I believe that 12.1-2, 3-5, and 6-7 have to be treated as distinct, and that neither the possible allusions in 12.1-2 nor the possible use of figures in 12.6 can be used to justify a search for non-literal layers of meaning in 12.3-5. The descriptions in those central verses, I think, are intended to exemplify the effect of human dying upon humans, while the world carries on regardless, and not to evoke broader eschatological themes, or to encode references to human frailty. The sophistication of the text here lies in the way that it moves through a series of images—the darkness at the end of life, the household gripped by fear, then lamenting in a world of birds singing and trees flowering, the breaking of trinkets and pots—each of which functions in a different way by evoking, typifying, or symbolizing an aspect of death or continuity. We should avoid approaching the text with the sort of hermeneutical flexibility required to impose some single theme upon it, but, equally, we will not read it properly if we presume either that each part works the same way, or that the way any single part works cannot be confined to that part.

In any case, though, the very wealth of previous interpretations has presented me with a practical problem: my desire to retain some clarity in my discussion of these exceptionally difficult verses makes it impossible even to mention, let alone properly to discuss, all of the various identifications that have been proposed by previous commentators alongside the other issues that need to be covered. Even in a volume this size, moreover, limitations of space forbid a separate commentary on the symbolic readings—which would be a substantial (and worthwhile) undertaking in its own right. My engagement with other readings, therefore, is less thorough in this section than I should like, and those symbolic readings, in particular, are addressed in any detail only where they have played a role in shaping construals of the Hebrew or suchlike.

With all that said, we can turn to the text itself. After his imagery of darkness replacing light as life comes to a close, Qohelet brings his own monologue to an end with a series of powerful snapshots and metaphors that evoke the theme with which he began, setting the mortality of humans against the continuity of the world. Fisch, 'Qohelet: A Hebrew Ironist', 177, claims that 'Never was there a gentler poem on the approach of death', and it is true that death here is portrayed as something natural and normal: the dead person is never portrayed as suffering, and their only action, indeed, is to move from one home to another. At the same time, however, Qohelet depicts the reaction of others to a death, first directly, through physical descriptions of fear and grief, and then perhaps implicitly, in images that evoke the suddenness and shocking quality even of trivial accidents.

In vv. 3-5, he begins with something that is almost like a *tableau vivant*, capturing the moment of a death in the fearful and grief-stricken reactions of those present in the household, and the closing of its doors. The spell is apparently broken by the cry of a bird, and a wail of lament is taken up by the shocked mourners, initiating the movement of the deceased from the house in which they have lived and died, toward the house—the grave—in which the corpse will spend the rest of time. The text is difficult at points, but we are not told explicitly what has provoked the grief in the first part, and catch no glimpse directly of the dead person before they leave the house, so it is as though our gaze is drawn constantly to those who are reacting, away from the centre of their own attention, and the focus is upon the way death affects those who have yet to die—most particularly, the terror it inspires. Against this, Qohelet sets images of fruitfulness and fertility in nature—the blossoming of a tree, the locust that will be reborn as it sheds its skin, and a berry that splits open to release its mass of seeds. The world will carry on, he suggests, even as the human departs, literally and figuratively, to the grave.

The following 12.6-8 build up to a virtual repetition of the claim that introduced Qohelet's words. Before that, however, we are presented with another list in 12.6. The normal assumption, in line with the various symbolic interpretations, is that old age or death continue to be characterized here, in a series of images that evoke destruction, fracture, and release, probably by reference to everyday, almost meaningless accidents. Qohelet associates these with references to the fate of the body in 12.7: we shall return to the earth from which we were made, and release back to God the breath that has animated us. If we do not try to read allegorical significance into the objects mentioned, the message would seem to be that death is at once both an unremarkable, almost mundane event, and an annihilation, which snatches back the borrowed parts that gave us life. We can also understand the sequence, though, as a counter-part to the point made in 12.5, that nature will go on even as the human dies, but with reference now to the possessions that humans leave behind—their baubles, even their pots, will themselves be broken one day, but in the meantime will survive their owners. In any case, the reason for picking the particular items and accidents in 12.5 might be clearer were the Hebrew of that verse not so ambiguous and obscure at various points, but they are apparently intended to match the description of the human's physical dissolution, with objects that do not simply wear out and are in some sense destroyed themselves—the human death, conversely, is depicted as just another breakage, by which the whole is reduced to its parts. Humans are, in the end, no less constructed and destructible than the objects they use or possess, and they will last less long than some of those.

However we understand the specifics, these closing sequences affirm Qohelet's appeals to live life well, while we can. Death is as inevitable as it is unwelcome, and although he does not tell us actively to rage, rage against the dying of the light, he does expect us to find it fearful and terrifying: we should find pleasure in what we do before that shadow hangs over us. If they reinforce what has immediately preceded them, however, they also mark a return, in very different terms, to the ideas with which Qohelet started. In the first chapter, he distinguished human brevity from the permanence of the world principally by talking about that world and its endless processes. Now that distinction is drawn out, although never pronounced, through Qohelet's focus on finite humans, who go to their grave even as the plants and animals around them burst with vitality. These humans, moreover, are forced to surrender their very breath and flesh, because those belong to God and the world, not to them, and Qohelet does not need to point out that they can hardly be taking any profit with them. As he turns actually to depict the death and impermanence that have informed so many of his claims so far, therefore, Qohelet chooses not to provide a commentary by restating those claims. Should anyone have missed the connections, however, perhaps reinforced by the re-use of vocabulary from ch. 1 (so Zimmer, *Zwischen Tod und Lebensglück*, 137-39; Bundvad, *Time*, 63-64), his closing evocation of 1.2 drives the point home: it is the fact of death that must force us to re-evaluate our perceptions of life.

12.3] The reference is more probably to guards here than to servants in some more general sense, but we are dealing in any case with what must be a large and prosperous household. The 'gentlefolk' are members of a propertied, upper class, and we might think of them almost as aristocracy. Precisely what the guards are doing is unclear: the verb is connected with trembling, but also with doing obeisance. Most likely, what is implied is some physical expression of shock. The gentlefolk are bent in some way—the Hebrew probably does not indicate precisely how, but suggests that they are bending or contorting themselves—presumably in reaction to grief or fear. In the courtyard of the house, the normal milling has come to a stop, as the women who operate the mills shrink away, or more literally make themselves small (not 'few', as many translations suggest—that is a reading driven more by allegorical interpretations of the mills as teeth than by any consideration of how such mills worked; see the notes). Finally, eyes fill with tears as they peer down through a hatch in the ceiling into one of the rooms below. There is perhaps some slight implication that these are the eyes of women, but those who are beginning to weep remain unidentified, as does the sight beneath them—presumably a deathbed. The images here are of various people, caught at a single moment of grief, when the household is shocked by a death.

12.4-5] The doorway is a large, double door, through which the house would normally be entered from the street. If not already closed, it is shut now—perhaps symbolically—and we return to the women who had been milling in the courtyard. The text probably plays with different connotations of 'high' and 'low' in this verse and the next, but the sense initially is most likely that one of these women is speaking in hushed tones, or from a position of prostration. As the sound of a bird calling breaks the virtual silence, however, her voice rises, to begin the keening of the mourner. The text talks obscurely about 'daughters of the song', which I take to be a poetic way of describing the women who join her singing. One of the most difficult passages in the text then seems to talk of these 'daughters' as being prostrate, but suggests that they will be afraid (or perhaps 'see' something), even when they stand, and talks of terror on the road. It is difficult to be certain what is meant, and the text is unclear even if we try to understand the daughters in some other way, perhaps as birds, or to find some other subject for the verb. It is possible, indeed, that the author is trying to do something clever with his high/low contrasts, which later readers are simply missing—perhaps because we do not grasp all the implications of the terms. I think the most likely purpose of the statements, though, is to provide a transition between the essentially static depiction of the household at a moment of death, and the funeral which follows: the woman draws herself up to sing, as do those who follow her lead, but their fear persists, both as they rise and as they eventually take to the road. It is this fear of death by the living that seems central to Qohelet's presentation, and it is a fear that outlasts the immediate, paralyzing shock of any particular death.

The burial that follows is presented as a journey made by the human (each human?) to their new, eternal home, but, like the death itself, it is described principally in terms of what is going on around it: the flourishing of nature and the movement of the mourners through the streets. The women singing their lament provide a sort of continuity between the death itself, in the household, and this procession. In the Hebrew, 'mourners' is the participle of the verb used back in 3.4, which has a practical more than an emotional connotation: 'mourning' is something commonly done in the presence of a corpse prior to, and during its burial (e.g. 1 Kgs 13.29-30; 2 Sam 3.31; 11.26; Jer 25.33), or in the context of some analogous mourning over an event (e.g. Joel 1.13). It is sometimes connected with wailing (Jer 4.8; 49.3; Joel 1.13; Mic 1.8), and clearly in some cases also explicitly involves lamenting aloud, with addresses to the dead person (1 Kgs 13.30; Jer 22.18; 34.5). The Mishnah (*Ketubbot* 4.4) was later to declare that 'even the poorest man in Israel must provide no fewer than two flutes and one lamenting woman' for his wife's burial, and the idea of women who specialized in laments appeared much earlier, in Jer 9.16-17 (ET 9.17-18; note also the reference to both male and female lamenters in 2 Chr 35.25), so it is very likely that Jewish funeral rites in this period would have included female singing or keening, and that the singing women would have been among the 'mourners'. On the other hand, neither the participle nor the verb with which it agrees have a specifically feminine form, and we are probably supposed to envisage a larger group, perhaps containing many more than the deceased's household: Josephus (*Contra Apion* 2.27) declares that Jews were under an obligation to join any funeral procession that passed by them, and the funeral procession described in Luke 7.12 involves a large crowd.

The text does not really suggest that the dead person walks the street and sees their own funeral (so Dulin, 'How Sweet Is the Light', 269), but the active verb—the dead person is not 'carried' but 'goes'—matches the verbs used for the activities of nature, and draws out the contrast. We are apparently supposed to envisage a procession that moves through the streets, against a background of natural fertility: the almond tree blossoms, ready later to bear its fruits, the grasshopper carries within itself the next stage of its own development—pregnant, as it were, with the body that it will wear after its next moult—and the caper-berry splits open to release its mass of seeds. Segal speaks of interpretations along these lines as involving 'a countermovement of rebirth', but the point is more properly, perhaps, that the world simply carries on. The contrast that Qohelet drew in 1.4 is being illustrated here, not with an account of new lives, somehow replacing the dead, but by images of potential life, which show how the world will just continue, while the corpse rests in its grave.

The almond tree blossoms famously early, in March or even before (so Murison, 'The Almond', 335, suggests that it would have been especially connected with the spring), while the caper-berry ripens much later in the summer. The development of locusts is less fixed to any particular point, but would generally happen between those times of year, so we are presented here with phenomena that are likely to occur in sequence, rather than simultaneously. Pabst, 'Verständnis von Alter', 170-71, sees the cycle of seasons embodied in this, and presented in some way as an analogy to the life of the human (Schwienhorst-Schönberger, 'Buch der Natur', 540-41, also sees a cycle, but one from which human life is to be distinguished). That is an attractive reading, so long as we do not push it beyond the poetic and into the allegorical, but if we are to give weight to the seasonal differences, perhaps the more fundamental implication is that Qohelet cannot be describing the background to a single funeral. Unless their rites are supposed to stretch across months, 'the human' here has become not just the human who died in the house, but every human.

Spieckermann, 'Jugend—Alter—Tod', 205-6, sees images of life in the almond and the caper, but an image of destruction in the locust, underlining the transience and fragility of life and beauty. While that is an interesting idea, the order here tells against it, as does the singularity of the locust. Heim sees all the images as negative: he takes 12.3-7 to depict the siege of a city, during which locusts fatten themselves upon the blossoming almond, while the caper-berry spoils because it lies unharvested. As with Spieckermann, the reading hinges on the idea that the locust is a swarm of locusts feasting, which is unlikely to be the implication of the verb, but it also involves an improbable assumption that the caper is left alone to go to seed, by insects voracious enough to strip a tree. The overall interpretation, moreover, feels very forced, with the 'going round' of the mourners turned into 'the endless cycle of funeral processions as the siege claims one fatality after another'.

12.6] The allusions in this verse are obscure: there are some text-critical difficulties, but, more importantly, we lack a clear understanding of the vocabulary, and so of what is supposed to be happening in each case. It is also difficult to establish the relationships between the clauses and the significance of the temporal construction with which the verse begins. Castelio remarks *haec quatuor ego non intelligo*—'I don't understand these four'—but it is widely supposed, outside interpretations which simply see some continuation of an allegory from the preceding verses, that each item here evokes the damaging, destruction, or malfunction of an object. The items seem also to fall into pairs.[3] The second two concern accidents—or more probably the consequences of a single accident—during the collection of water; I think we are supposed to envisage a container breaking as it is lowered to a water-source, so that the rope runs free when it is wound back up.[4] The first two are harder to judge, but the images are most likely of jewellery, or something similarly precious and decorative, being damaged. Again, there may be a single incident involved, rather than two separate ones—perhaps the snapping of a necklace, and the crushing, or maybe just the release, of an ornament that falls from it.[5] It is likely,

---

[3] Pabst, 'Verständnis von Alter', 173, explores the possibility that there is just one image here throughout the verse: a chain snaps, having been slung over a bar above a well, with a container at one end and a ball, serving as a counterweight, at the other—with the consequence that all parts of the device fall and are broken. Although this is ingenious, Pabst concedes that the characterizations as 'gold' and 'silver' alone make it hard to sustain.

[4] Nel, 'Remember', having read 'your creator' in 12.1 as 'your well', meaning 'your wife', now correspondingly sees a reference to male impotence. If so, the imagery of smashing suggests a particularly nasty case.

[5] The considerable difficulties are discussed in the notes, but boil down to the facts that the reading of the first verb is uncertain, and the meaning of the second ambiguous, while the word rendered 'bauble' here (with appropriate vagueness, I hope) is used elsewhere only of decorative/structural features at the top of

at least, that both images involve the suspension of one object from another, brought to an end when one of the objects is broken. Both pairs are probably supposed to be aligned, furthermore, with the description in 12.7, where the body is released to the ground and the breath to God, so that the images convey rupture and separation, although it is possible too that they each correspond more precisely to the dissolution of the flesh, downwards, and release of the breath, upwards. Something should also be read, perhaps, into the juxtaposition of the precious and ornamental with the everyday and functional—if only that between them they represent some much broader range of objects and possessions.

There are no good grounds on which to suggest any further, more specific significance, and when Seow, for instance, proposes that we are dealing with the symbolic destruction of a lamp shaped like a tree of life, and with some funerary custom of smashing jars at the graveside, this is largely speculation. Less specifically, Gurlitt, 'Erklärung', 341-42, also sees a reference to a lamp, and conjectures that there are two separate images for the destruction of the intellect (the 'inner light') and of the body. It is not impossible, of course, that the author was drawing on imagery and resonances that were already well established, but about which we know little. Petronius wrote his *Satyricon* some centuries after Ecclesiastes was composed, but in a famous scene the wealthy freeman Trimalchio gives directions for his tomb (remarking, incidentally, that *ualde enim falsum est uiuo quidem domos cultas esse non curari eas ubi diutius nobis habitandum est*, 'it is clearly wrong for homes to be done up for the living, while not caring about those in which we are

columns and a lampstand, and in two linked place-names. The ancient versions offer a wide variety of understandings, none suggesting that they possessed any better information. Commentators have made much of the lampstand described in Zech 4, which uses one of the words found here, and some see the imagery in terms of a lamp, damaged when the silver cord from which it is suspended snaps. The lamp in Zechariah, though, is not suspended, and there is no obvious parallel to the arrangement proposed. The precious metals also lead those scholars thinking of a large lamp either to see here an object that could belong only to the extremely wealthy (if not to a temple or palace), or to understand this component of the imagery as a function of what is being symbolized (cf. Müller, 'Ambivalenz'). Especially in the light of the less precious objects which follow, I am more inclined to think that we should envisage things that are actually much smaller.

due to stay longer'). One of the things he wants carved on it (71.11) is a picture of a broken urn with a boy weeping over it, and, in a context that also includes puppies, we are probably supposed to see this as a vulgar, sentimental cliché (Murphy, 'Petronius', notes the link with Ecclesiastes). It would be wrong to presume that broken jars must commonly have been associated with death in the popular imagination, but it would also be wrong to exclude the possibility that there are allusions here to existing associations or expressions.

Beyond the problems that surround the particular items and events, there is a broader question about how we are to construe the sequence as a whole. Most commonly, the elements are all set in parallel, so that the 'while not yet' construction applies to them all: allegorical readings have often then taken 12.6 as further symbols of old age, but the images in that verse have also been read in terms of 12.7, as symbolic references to death. The similar temporal constructions in 12.1-2 qualified what had immediately preceded them ('be mindful…while not yet'), and it is common, furthermore, to read the construction here simply as picking up that sequence, so that the invitation throughout is to be mindful before the physical disintegration of the body (in old age and at death, or simply at death). This usual understanding envisages, in effect, a sequence of three lists, each introduced by 'while not yet', interrupted after the second by a further, lengthy sequence introduced differently by 'on the day when' in 12.3, and then resumed in 12.6. That is plainly not a simple proposition, even if we discount the additional complexity engendered by trying to incorporate separate ideas of 'while you are not yet old' and 'while you are not yet dead', and I have discussed the problems posed for it by 12.3 above, in my commentary on 12.1-2, where I rejected the idea of a single basic temporal construction across the whole of 12.1-7.

Although 'while not yet' in 12.6 obviously echoes the similar constructions talking about 'days' and 'years' in 12.1-2, therefore, it seems unlikely that it is intended simply to resume them after the account in 12.3-5 has transported us to the events of a single day (or, correspondingly, that we should insert a resumptive 'Remember him' here, as NIV does to force that reading, without any specific basis in the text). Indeed, 12.6-7 seem no longer even to be talking about periods of time at all, but about specific, instant manifestations of destruction and disintegration. This could be viewed in terms of a progressive intensification, and there does indeed seem to be a move onward from the earlier depictions of death as a loss of light and as something experienced only through the reactions of others. It is not necessary, however, to set that intensification within a single, encompassing syntactic structure, and it is reasonable to ask whether the 'while not yet' here, whatever it echoes, is in fact formally constructed with something other than the much earlier admonition in 12.1. Since the events in 12.3-5 are not things that happen *before* death, that would imply that it is something in 12.6-7 which will occur earlier, and, probably, that we should avoid reading 12.6-7 simply as a series of parallel events.

As it happens, there are reasons to suspect that the Masoretes broke up that series (see the notes), but they probably did so in order to read 12.6 in terms of an allegorical interpretation, within which there was no place for the obviously literal description of death in 12.7. Some such motivation might also have lain behind the probable reading of the Three, which again understands there to be a break between 12.6 and 12.7, but that reading can quite naturally be construed also as suggesting that the events of 12.7 occur when the events of 12.6 have not yet occurred: that the disintegration of the human, in other words, precedes that of the objects described there. That understanding is compatible with the Hebrew, although not compelled by it, and offers an attractive parallel to 12.5: nature will go on when the human has died, and the disintegration of the human body will match but precede that of objects left behind. These ideas take the closing verses back, therefore, to the issue with which Qohelet began his monologue, the impermanence of each human in a world that will continue without them.

I have adopted that understanding in my translation, largely because it avoids seeing the items in this verse, and their violent destruction, purely as rather curious symbols for death. I think it is important at the same time, however, to recognize that the 'while not yet' of 12.6 does echo 12.1-2, even if it is not a formal continuation of the advice there, and creates a continuity with the general points that Qohelet was making before his more specific account in 12.3-5. Accordingly, it keeps in play his concern that the prospect of death should drive us to live life well. Equally, there clearly is a symbolic as well as a literal dimension to the items described here: their continuation beyond the human may be the more explicit point, but it is surely not a coincidence that the 'death' of each item is evocative of the human death. By aligning them, Qohelet manages to imply something else about death itself: however important it may be to us, each death is, in the greater order of things, just another breakage—of something precious but trivial, or of something cheap but useful. If the Hebrew has been left open to be read in different ways, that is perhaps not because the author has overlooked (or even tried to impose) some ambiguity, but because he is trying to use the same words to imply a lot of different things, as he starts to bring the monologue to a close.

12.7] The idea of a return to dust appeared earlier in 3.20, and 3.21 raised a question about the destination of the human spirit or breath at death; Qohelet gives his own answer to that question here. In the earlier passage, the issue was that humans could have no knowledge of what actually happened after death, so when he appears to display such knowledge, there is, strictly, an incompatibility. Such tensions between what Qohelet asserts himself, however, and his claims about the limitations of human knowledge, are arguably a feature of the book, and there is no good basis for presuming, as do some commentators, that this verse must be a secondary, 'orthodox' gloss (cf. Müller, 'Weisheitliche Deutungen', 81-82).

The speech of the impious in the later Wisd 2.1-20 presents them as holding ideas about human life and the world that are similar to those espoused by Qohelet, although these lead them beyond enjoyment of life into oppression of the weak and a rejection of the righteous who condemn them. In that book, there is an even greater insistence upon the reality of divine judgment, but also a recognition, like Qohelet's, that what humans see may differ from that reality. Accordingly, although the speaker in Wisdom of Solomon insists that the souls of the righteous actually enjoy the protection of God, what the impious observe (2.2-3) is that humans will be extinguished at death, with the body turning to ashes, and the breath or spirit simply dissipating. Qohelet's account here is similar, to the extent that it envisages a disintegration. There is also, however, an emphasis upon the return of our constituent elements. This likewise asserts death's permanence, but it offers at the same time a reminder both of human dependence upon God for life, and of our relationship with the world: we merely borrow from these the parts that animate us and give us form. Like everything we leave behind, they do not really belong to us, and in our graves, we will be stripped back further even than to the nakedness with which we were born. As Qohelet returns to the declaration with which he started, therefore, he does so with an emphatic illustration of his initial point about 'profit'.

12.8] The virtual repetition of 1.2 brings us back to the point at which Qohelet began. As noted in the commentary on that verse, I am not sure that we should think in terms of what Anderson, 'Poetic Inclusio', calls a 'thesis/validation formula', and I also see no good reason to assume that these verses are secondary additions—although, of course, the third-person 'says (the) Qohelet' in each marks a transition into and out of the monologue, so they belong in part, at least, to the framework that contains it. My understanding of 1.2 was that it served as a deliberately general and provocative statement, which was immediately, and then progressively, explained and qualified. Here, I think, we see the mirror-image of that, and are invited to re-consider the claim, following all that we have heard. This is not a matter simply of proof, although the monologue may well have allayed any scepticism, but of complexity. What began, essentially, as a claim about the futility of certain human expectations, has governed Qohelet's discussion of the many other issues which his ideas and purported experiences led him to consider, and it is now repeated immediately after he has addressed the need to enjoy our temporary lives, while remaining conscious of all that will follow. Although the same basic point is at stake, furthermore, and Qohelet's attention remains upon the gap between what the world is, and the way humans are obliged to experience it, there is also now something more positive, or even liberating to be found in that. Qohelet's thought has not been static, and even if the 'editorial', framing function of the two statements is intended to set them in parallel, as contemporaneous reflections on the monologue, the audience has been led to a place where they are bound to take the second rather differently.

Notes

12.3 On the day when] Or 'on *a* day when'. Lauha speaks of ביום as an 'anacrusis', an unstressed expression standing outside the main sentence, while Fox, Seow, and many others play it down in a different way, taking it merely to expand upon the nature of the time described in 12.2, when the sun is dimmed. That is unlikely and arguably impossible, not least because 12.1-2 talk explicitly about days and years, not about the events of a single day, and although sometimes described as one (e.g., by Pabst, 'Verständnis von Alter', 164) -ש ביום / אשר ביום is not simply a temporal conjunction 'when'—nor, as Schoors suggests, does it 'practically function' as one. On the contrary, on each of the occasions when we find it used elsewhere in biblical Hebrew (ביום אשר: Deut 27.2; 2 Sam 19.20; Esth 9.1; Mal 3.21 ET 4.3; ביום ש-: Ct 8.8), it refers to a specific day or occasion, and that specificity is usually important (although the days are, of course, different days, and the use in Malachi does not justify the assertion of Seow, 'Eschatological Poem', 214, that Qohelet is probably referring to a similar 'great and terrible day'). The same is true of the uses at CD-A XVI, 4 (and parallels); 11Q19 XLIX, 11, 13-14 (the house is to be cleaned *the same day* the corpse is removed); and 11QT^a LVII, 2. It is also generally true of the places where ביום is used with an asyndetic relative clause (e.g., Num 30.6, 8, 9, 13, 15; Obad 11), even if some instances, like that in Gen 5.1, are often translated more loosely.

Although Jerome uses *quando* in V, therefore, and by doing so facilitates symbolic readings of the text, there are no good grounds for diluting the sense to 'when': the expression means 'on the/a day when', or sometimes even 'on the very day when'. In many of these cases, it precedes the action, and the construction is 'on the day when…(then)'. I take that to be the case here—which is why, after a long series of circumstances linked by conjunctions, בשפל קול הטחנה in 12.4 lacks a conjunction: it marks the start of the events that 'then' happen on the day when those circumstances are in place. G may have read the construction slightly differently: it switches from subjunctive to indicative in the clause where the women milling become few/small, and probably takes that as the first of the actions that 'then' ensue; it does not simply use future indicative and aorist subjunctive interchangeably in 12.2-3, as Gorton, 'From Hebrew to Greek', 410, avers, but first one then the other.

There is a Masoretic *S^{e}bîr* / *S^{e}bîrîn* annotation to ביום here, which reads it without the article (see Ginsburg, *Writings* and *Massorah* 3:326-7, and the note on 'when' at 4.17 for the significance of *S^{e}bîr*). This is the pointing found in the earliest printed edition of 1486–87, and it appears also to reflect the way G vocalized the text here. For the reasons of sense outlined above, we should generally expect an article, but we do not always find one (e.g. Josh 14.11), and the only other occurrence of ביום ש- itself, at Ct 8.8, attracts a similar *S^{e}bîr*.

12.3 house-guards] Lit. 'keepers' or 'guardians' of the house. The phrase is not found elsewhere, but Seow offers a detailed defence of this meaning, over against the view (of, e.g., Fox; Taylor, *Dirge*, 8; Sawyer, 'The Ruined House', 525) that this is just a general term for servants ('house-keepers'). That view depends largely on the references in 2 Sam 15.16; 16.21; 20.3 to ten concubines who are appointed by David to 'keep' the house (and with whom Absalom subsequently has sex in public). Those concubines are not supposed to be servants, however, and running the household would hardly have been a priority: they are the most expendable part of David's cortège when he flees, and so are left behind as guards—presumably not with any great expectation that they will keep out an army, but so that no-one can wander in and steal the furniture, and maybe in the misplaced hope that Absalom will be reluctant to confront them. The שמרי הבית are perhaps to be contrasted with the אנשי החיל, as the latter term may have some connotation of class (see below).

12.3 are disturbed] זוע has traditionally been understood in terms of physical trembling, which is a sense found sometimes in Aramaic and in later Hebrew, and which suits the needs of the gerontological interpretation to find shaky limbs or joints. This sense is largely confined in the Hebrew verb, however, to the reduplicating stems (e.g. 1QH^a XIV, 27; perhaps Hab 2.7). The other biblical use of the qal, in Esth 5.9, seems to have a rather different meaning: there, Haman is angry because Mordecai, sitting in the gate, does not rise in his presence ולא זע ממנו. Now clearly Haman expects to see some physical reaction, but it is unlikely that even he would expect Mordecai literally to shake with fear (and Jerome, in V, renders in terms of Mordecai not 'moving from the place where he was sat'). Earlier in Esth 3.2, 5, Haman had been angered by Mordecai's failure to bow down or grovel to him, and that essentially seems to be the issue here too, although it is now complicated by Haman's plot to kill the Jews. Herodotus (*Histories* 1.134.1) describes the Persian custom of obeisance to a social superior, and against that background Mordecai is disdaining to acknowledge Haman's rank. In Sir 48.12, the verb is used similarly in the context of Elisha's refusal to recognize any human authority over him, and in neither case is shaking as such the issue, so much as showing submission by giving a physical indication of one's fear or respect for someone.

The cognate noun זועה / זעוה is characteristically found in the expression נתן לזועה, which is used to describe God turning Judah and its inhabitants into something notorious, from which other nations will recoil in abhorrence and contempt (Deut 28.25; Ezek 23.46; Jer 15.4; 24.9; 29.18; 34.17; 2 Chr 29.8), although it can also refer sometimes to a state of being terrorized or even perhaps tortured (Isa 28.19; 1QS II, 6-7; IV, 12). The notion of 'shaking' does not really do justice to such usage, and it is obvious that something much more than physical trembling is involved, so in my translation I have followed the example of G σαλευθῶσιν, which can express both physical and emotional agitation.[6]

---

[6] Sawyer, 'The Ruined House', 525, also rejects the sense 'tremble', but prefers a sense 'move out', which can be justified from a few later uses of the verb. Sawyer's own understanding is of a house that has been ruined and progressively abandoned. This would work better if it were easier to assign to the subsequent והתעותו the sense of being 'ruined through lawsuits' that he gives to it: the forensic uses of that verb are all to do with perversion of justification or falsification of

12.3 the gentlefolk] We encountered the term חיל at 10.10: see the note there. The present expression, אנשי החיל is found in this precise form only also at 2 Kgs 24.16, where it is used of a class deported to Babylon, which is listed between the rulers and the craftsmen. Without the article it occurs at Gen 47.6; Exod 18.21, 25; Judg 20.44, 46; 2 Sam 11.16; Neh 11.6; Ps 76.6 ET 76.5; Isa 5.22; Jer 48.14 and Nah 2.4, while the singular occurs at Judg 3.29; 1 Sam 31.12; 2 Sam 24.9; 1 Kgs 1.42; 1 Chr 10.12; 11.22; 26.8, with related forms at Josh 8.3; Judg 18.2; Ruth 2.1; 1 Sam 9.1; 1 Kgs 11.28; 2 Kgs 5.1; 1 Chr 5.24; 8.40; 2 Chr 13.3; 17.13; 24.24. As we saw earlier, there is no particular reference to physical strength, while although in many places the context is military, the term does not seem simply to connote ability as a soldier, and there is sometimes no such connotation at all.

We should probably think of אנשי החיל as something like the propertied class from which military officers were drawn[7] and from which the best soldiers were notionally supposed to come, even if, by some point or in some contexts, to be a man of חיל held no stronger association with battle than does being a 'knight' in modern Britain—and Exod 18.21-22 notably offers a non-military account of the class ascending through a divinely ordained recognition of its piety and honesty. When Prov 31.10 asks who can find an אשת חיל, it is talking about finding a woman who can meet in her own realm the expectations placed on members of such a class, and not so long ago this might reasonably have been translated 'who can find a true gentle-woman?' It is difficult to translate such a culturally specific concept, especially at a time when our own terminology of class is changing rapidly in the West, but here I take the reference probably to be to those members of this wealthy household (potentially including women) who are not servants, and the expression to be in terms of their belonging to the upper class.

12.3 contort themselves] The verb עות was used in the piʿel and puʿal at 7.13 and 1.15 of things crooked or bent that cannot be straightened. Here we have the hithpaʿel, which we would expect to convey a reflexive sense, and so although the idea that they might have 'been bent' or 'become bent' cannot wholly be excluded, it is more likely that they are being depicted as bending themselves. I take the image to be an exaggerated one, of them either bowing forward or bending backward in grief or terror. Seow similarly, though, sees them as either cowering or convulsed in fear, and the text probably conveys only the fact that they are contorting themselves, not the detail of the postures that they adopt.

---

measures, and stand some way from the idea of ruin, even before we try to account for the hithpaʿel form. Without that support, there is no reason to understand the first clause in terms of servants moving out.

[7] Similarly, although on slightly different grounds, Sawyer, 'The Ruined House', 525: 'the wealthy, land-owning classes who were liable for military service'.

σ' καὶ διαφθαρῶσιν οἱ ἄνδρες οἱ ἰσχυροί, 'and the mighty men incapacitated', is interpreted by Jerome in his commentary as a reference to death, but the verb can be used of corruption, of ruination, or, as is most likely intended here, of physical disability (they are 'crippled', without the modern pejorative connotations of that term). α' uses πλανηθήσονται, 'will go astray': Marshall wonders whether Aquila has perhaps linked והתעותו with תעה, but he may simply be looking to the uses of the piʻel in, e.g., Amos 8.5; Job 8.3.

12.3 the women fall idle at the mill] Lit. 'those grinding cease'; a feminine participle is used for 'those grinding'. This is the only biblical use of the verb בטל, although it is well known in Aramaic, and in later Hebrew is sometimes used of neglecting work (see Jastrow, *Dictionary*). This implication may be picked up in G καὶ ἤργησαν αἱ ἀλήθουσαι, 'and the milling-women are idle'.

σ' καὶ καταργηθῶσιν αἱ μύλαι [var. οἱ μύλοι], 'and the mills are left unemployed', could also mean 'and the molars are unemployed', but the Greek is ambiguous, and it is not likely that Symmachus is actively translating into the terms of the gerontological interpretation, as Munnich, 'Traduire', 109, supposes: he does not do so clearly elsewhere. 'Mills' may be a loose rendering, but it is possible that he has read a noun here consistent with the noun understood by M in 12.4 (where we do not have the reading of σ'). So far as we know, the Hebrew itself is not ambiguous in this respect, as Bartholomew suggests.

12.3 for they have shrunk away] In the qal, מעט means 'to be few' (e.g. Lev 25.16) or 'to be small' (e.g. Neh 9.32) in biblical Hebrew, and although M points the verb as piʻel here, the gerontological interpretation has tended to favour the sense 'have become (too) few', since this can be associated with the loss of teeth in old age (Rashbam prefers the idea that they have diminished in strength). That makes for a difficult image, however, because domestic flour mills would not have required more than one, or at most two people to work them, and if we are supposed to think of multiple mills, the cessation of one would not necessitate the cessation of another.

In Aramaic and in later Hebrew, the verb is used seldom of number, and generally refers to reduction or diminution in size. The piʻel in *b. Ḥullin* 60b is used in a story to talk about the moon making herself smaller (than the sun), and in *b. Sanhedrin* 17a, God promises to add to the greatness of Eldad and Medad because they have 'made themselves small' by considering themselves unworthy of appointment among the elders. This accords with the use in Sir 3.18, where מעט נפש means 'make yourself small', that is, be humble, or perhaps self-deprecating. I take the literal meaning here to be similar, but the motivation different: the women are making themselves small out of grief or fear, not humility. If so, the vocalization in M may well reflect the original intention (although it may have been motivated coincidentally by the forms of the contiguous verbs, cf. Gordis; Fassberg, 'The Shift', 124-25).

The AV margin offers an interesting alternative: the women cease because 'they grind little', and Taylor has a similar understanding, but it is something of a stretch to make the verb mean 'have little', and a reference to physical posture would fit well with what has preceded.[8]

12.3 the eyes in the ceiling-holes mist over] Lit. 'are dimmed'. An ארבה is not a window as we would normally conceive of one, but an aperture or hatchway high on the wall or more probably in the roof: *m. Beṣah* 5.1 talks of lowering goods through one, and *m. ʾOhalot* 10 discusses such hatches at length in relation to the spread of impurities. Jastrow cites from *b. Niddah* 20b the witticism that someone happening on a truth is כסומא בארובה, 'like a blind man in (falling through?) a hatchway'. The purpose of the hatchway might be to collect rainwater, like the *compluuium* in a Roman house, and that would suit the use of the noun sometimes to describe hatchways in the firmament through which water can pour (Gen 7.11; 8.2; Isa 24.18; Mal 3.10), but Hos 13.3 speaks of smoke coming from one, and an additional or alternative use might have been as a chimney-hole. Jer 9.20 paints a sinister picture of death climbing into houses through the ארבות. The sense is well represented by G ἐν ταῖς ὀπαῖς and S ܒܟܘܐ *bkwʾ*, which both mean 'in the roof-holes' (cf. σ' αἱ ὁράσεις διὰ τῶν ὀπῶν, 'the eyes through the roof-holes'), and rather more loosely by the *foramina*, 'holes', used in Hie, V.

None of the versions offers any basis for the image found by some commentators, of women staring out of windows:[9] Qohelet is talking rather about looking down through holes or hatches in the ceiling, presumably on to a scene that is being played out below (and the reference does not imply that the house had a second floor, as Bartholomew suggests). It is less certain, however, who or what is doing the looking. After the previous reference to women milling, the feminine participle הראות could refer to a further group of women, but it is not clear in what sense they might be 'dimmed', unless it is from the perspective of someone looking at them while they are looking. It is simpler to suppose with many commentators that this is a way of saying 'eyes', and Kedar-Kopfstein, 'Semantic Aspects', 165, sees a substantival use of the participle with a literal sense 'the peering ones'. Such an interpretation is supported by two important considerations: (1) on every other occasion that the feminine participle of ראה is used in the Hebrew Bible, it is with reference to an eye or eyes (Gen 45.12; Deut 3.21; 4.3; 11.7; 28.32; 2 Sam 24.3; 1 Kgs 1.48; Prov 20.12; Isa 30.20; Jer 20.4; 42.2); (2) the verb חשך is used elsewhere of eyes to indicate an induced blindness (Ps 69.24 ET 69.23) or grief (Lam 5.17)—hence my 'misted', which is the equivalent metaphor

---

[8] Taylor, *Dirge*, 13; see also his 'The Dirge', 538-39. The latter is not a re-working of the book, but a detailed defence of Taylor's original argument in the light of commentaries published in the years that immediately followed it.

[9] See, e.g., Seow; Taylor, *Dirge*, 14-17; 'The Dirge', 539; Dahood, 'Canaanite-Phoenician', 213-15. For a detailed criticism of Dahood's reading, see Piotti, 'Osservazioni su alcuni paralleli', 121-23.

in English.[10] It is certainly true that we should expect an explicit reference to עינים here, but the noun has plausibly been left out either for reasons of style or to create a certain ambiguity suggesting that these are women's eyes.

12.4 and the doorway is closed] Lit. 'the (two) doors are closed'. The noun has a dual form, as often, and the meaning is well illustrated in Judg 16.3, where Samson takes the 'two doors' that belong to a single gate. The reference here is to one entrance, as in, e.g., Job 31.32—presumably the main entrance to the house. The ancient translations render as plural, either because they are into languages that lack or are reluctant to use dual forms, or because the translators have read the noun as plural: this gives an impression that all the doors in the street are being closed (and so a variant in S has 'all the doors *of* the street').

As for the verb, M points וסֻגְּרוּ as puʻal and S uses an ettaphal ܘܢܬܬܚܕܘܢ *wntthdwn*, so that in both the doors are the subject and the verb passive. However, G, V, Hie all have active verbs, probably reflecting a reading as qal. In these versions, those who were previously 'looking' might be taken as subject of the verb (cf. Munnich, 'Traduire', 107), but since no subject is clearly specified (unless it be the preceding ראות), the construction with an active verb could naturally be read in the Hebrew as impersonal anyway ('they shut the doors' = 'the doors are shut'), so this makes little difference to the sense, and Goldman does not explain why he regards M as 'better'.

BHQ is uncharacteristically misleading here. No reading has been preserved for α′ at this point, but *later* in the verse the reading of α′ is attested as καὶ κλιθήσονται πάντα τὰ τῆς ᾠδῆς (see below). In two manuscripts, this actually appears as καὶ κλεισθήσονται πάντα τὰ τῆς ᾠδῆς and Goldman speculates (although he presents it as a fact) that κλεισθήσονται ('will be shut') was originally the reading of α′ at this point, which has become entangled with the later reading—in which case, α′ would indeed support M, as the *BHQ* apparatus claims. Since α′ does use that Greek verb for סגר at Isa 22.22 this is not implausible, but it is far from certain, and any unqualified citation of α′ in support of M would seem hard to justify. Marshall regards κλεισθήσονται simply as an inner-Greek corruption of κλιθήσονται.

12.4 street] The noun שוק is used in this verse and the next, but elsewhere in biblical Hebrew only in Prov 7.8 and Ct 3.2. It is common in Aramaic, where it can refer to streets or markets, and it is the latter sense that has been

---

[10] There is no need to take the verb as a form from חשׂך, 'withhold', used intransitively, as Sawyer, 'The Ruined House', 526, suggests. Sawyer takes the point to be that women no longer show themselves at the windows, an image that anyway does not suit the sense of ארבה. It is interesting to note, though, that the verb is pointed that way in a late variant, where it also takes a subject האפות, in place of הראות, so that the reference is to women bakers (counterparts to the grinders) holding back. See Loevy, *Libri Kohelet*, 23. Driver, 'Problems and Solutions', 233, would derive it from the same verb, but translates 'cease, stop'.

picked up by G ἐν ἀγορᾷ, 'in the marketplace'. A שוק need not be a market, however, and it is unclear why Seow insists that the reference in this context must be to gates in the market, and the image of a street-bazaar that is closed, or why Dahood, 'Canaanite-Phoenician', 215, insists that it must be to a 'forum', which he takes to be a specifically Phoenician usage. The most we can say is that the noun probably points to the house being within a town or city (although a few manuscripts of G have managed to turn ἐν ἀγορᾷ into ἐν ἀγρῷ, 'in a field/countryside').

12.4 the voice of the woman at the mill will be low] There are several difficulties here. To begin with, M points בשפל as an infinitive construct, so the sense would be 'when the sound…is low'. This may be supported rather loosely by σ' ἀχρειωθείσης τῆς φωνῆς, 'the voice having been made useless'; however, G, S, Hie, V have apparently read שפל as a noun (cf. 10.6, although G renders it differently here as 'weakness'), even though this leads them to connect it problematically with the preceding clause, as an explanation for the shutting of the doors.

M then points the subsequent הטחנה as though it were a noun (although such a noun is found nowhere else in Hebrew, and is not certainly found in Aramaic either),[11] while the same other versions read it as a singular form of the feminine participle that appeared in the previous verse. It is difficult not to suspect that the awkward differentiation in M has been driven by allegorical considerations, which leave no scope for the re-appearance of a milling-woman in a different role, and with little or no other evidence that a noun טחנה actually existed, it is manifestly more natural to follow G and the others here: Qohelet is talking about the voice of a woman, not the sound of a mill (and that, incidentally, makes a lot more sense in the context, where it is desperately difficult to establish what significance a mill's pitch or volume might have).

It is harder to be sure about שפל. If the broader temporal construction is based on ביום ש- in 12.3, however, then a further temporal construction with -ב and an infinitive here would have to be either resumptive of that ביום ('on the day when…[and] when the voice…'), or, more awkwardly, represent a second period. Only the former is really practical: if ביום faces forward, as I

---

[11] Seow, 'Linguistic Evidence', 652, notes the apparent use of the term in one text from Saqqara: see Segal, *Aramaic Texts*, 35-36: text 20, line 5. Segal does indeed restore לטחנה, in a general context where some reference to milling would be appropriate, but the line in which it appears is very difficult, and the immediate context unclear. Segal justifies his translation 'mill' by referring to the supposed use of the term in Hebrew, more specifically in our verse, so there is an obvious circularity involved in appealing to that Saqqara text as evidence that this might be the sense in Hebrew. Although the verb from this root is used of milling in Syriac, the evidence for a noun 'mill' is slight there also, and the terms that we do find with this sense in Aramaic are generally derived from רחי.

have suggested it must, then the latter would give two protases, and it is not possible to distinguish two corresponding apodoses; if ביום faces backward to 12.1, on the other hand, and בשפל does not, then ויקום and what follows has to be construed as an apodosis to בשפל alone, breaking the whole passage apart (we cannot just treat ויקום as a continuation of the series, as though nothing had intervened, even if RSV and other translations try to do so). If the only way realistically to understand בשפל temporally, however, is as a redundant resumption of the earlier ביום, then we may reasonably ask why it has no conjunction, and why the author has chosen to break the series at this point alone.

I think it is more probable that בשפל marks a break, indicated by the very lack of a conjunction, and that we have a non-verbal clause here. In that case, the infinitive of M would not be impossible (lit. 'the voice is in being low'), but the reading of שפל as a noun is certainly simpler and more obvious. The point then is not that when one sound is low, someone or something rises up to another, but that a sound that has been low now rises up: the verse is structured around images of rising, on the one hand, and being brought down on the other.

12.4 but it will rise back up at the sound of a bird] Lit. 'will stand'. The G variant ἀναστήσονται is plural ('they will stand up'): it is probably a result of assimilation to the previous plural κλείσουσιν, but may have influenced the use of *consurgent*, 'they will arise' in V. The Hebrew verb is used of standing, and especially standing up, so the point here is that something 'low' gets back up—on to its feet, as it were. As a very occasional variant, ויקום is found pointed as a jussive ויקֹם, although it is unlikely that any jussive force can have been intended.[12]

It is not clear what could have given rise to σ' as it is attested in ms 252, καὶ παύσεται φωνὴ τοῦ στρουθίου, 'and a sound of the bird will cease', and this reading has provoked attempts to emend the text. Siegfried thinks that it reflects יקוד (without the -ל) in the sense 'sinks', and several commentators (e.g., Sacchi) use it to justify a reading ויקמל, 'is thin'. Not only is it unlikely, however, that Symmachus would have translated either of those verbs with παύσεται, it is also difficult to attach such meanings to them: קדד is used only of bowing one's head, while the rare קמל, as some critics have previously

---

[12] Some modern references to the variant are confusing, in part because ויקֹם is the form used in the text of Baer with which many late nineteenth- or early twentieth-century commentators would have been familiar—McNeile, 88, for instance, treats it as the normal reading, noting that it is 'printed ויקֹם in some editions'. Ginsburg, *Writings*, notes one manuscript; *BHS* claims two, and Baer himself discusses the reading, citing additional sources (69). Wright names two manuscripts with it (presumably those claimed by *BHS*); cf. Delitzsch. It is presupposed in some Masoretic notes.

observed, is used only at Isa 19.6 and 33.9 to describe something bad that happens to plants. Kamenetzky, 239, followed by, e.g., Podechard, would read וידום from דמם, 'cease' or 'be quiet', which is not subject to the same difficulties and would make excellent sense. The transformation of a ר into a ק or *vice versa*, however, is not easy to explain, especially if, as Podechard would like, one has also to account for the addition or loss of the subsequent -ל. The problems could always have been addressed more simply by assuming that φωνή should actually be a dative φωνῇ, and that reading has now been affirmed by ms 788 τη φωνη, which can only be read as dative. Symmachus perhaps thinks that the preceding sound 'rises back up' at the sound of a bird, and so 'ceases' to be low, paraphrasing accordingly, or simply stretches the meaning of the verb (implausibly) from 'stand' to 'stop' (as later did Sebastian Schmidt, whose translation *subsistet intra uocem auiculae*, 'stands still while a bird sings', is approved by Schelling). It can be risky to rely on σ' as a basis for emendation at the best of times, especially without complete information on its readings, and here the other versions offer no reason at all to change the consonantal text.

Even without reference to σ', however, Ginsberg, 'Koheleth 12:4', makes a double jump, offering ויקול קול and ויקל קול as alternative restorations, and deriving each from a verb meaning 'to fall' that is attested in Ugaritic but not otherwise in Hebrew (the ל of the verb, he explains, became wrongly attached to the next word, and the remaining ויקו or ויק restored as ויקום). This suggestion is accepted and enlarged upon in Loretz, *Qohelet und der alte Orient*, 190 n. 223 ('und der Vogelgesang verstummt', 'and the birdsong falls silent'), but is entirely speculative. Whether or not they emend the verb itself, some other commentators find the subsequent -ל problematic, often because, for the sake of parallelism, they want to make the bird the subject. Sawyer, 'The Ruined House', 526-27, simply rejects it, believing that it was added to enforce an interpretation of the text in terms of the old-age allegory, and emends the text (similarly Rose, *Rien de nouveau*, 484, who cites σ'). Less gratuitously, Ginsburg compares constructions in Pss 76.10; 132.8; Jer 49.14, where קום is used with -ל and a following noun X to mean 'arise in order to do X'—we might say that the -ל in those has something like the force of *causa* in Latin. Correspondingly, this would mean 'arise to make a sound', and that understanding is adopted by Taylor, *Dirge*, 19-20. Seow prefers to see the -ל as asseverative, or as a subject-marker, even though such a usage would just obscure the sense here. Apart from the awkwardness, the principal objection to all of these attempts, as Schoors observes, lies in the fact that צפור is a feminine noun, and so we should have not only to allow an awkward construction, but also to assume either an abnormal gender for the noun or a mismatch between noun and verb. Neither is impossible in this book, but such anomalies remain the exception rather than the rule, and should not just be disregarded.

It is true that it seems no less awkward suddenly to introduce an indefinite subject here, as is demanded by the traditional understanding (e.g. RSV 'one rises at the sound of a bird'), or by extensions of this, such as 'in the morning before the birds cheep', for which Haupt, 'Assyr. *lâm iççûri çabâri*', 144, argues. That imports into the supposed allegory a sudden literal statement about old age, and demands also a complete change in the type of discourse. As Fox notes, furthermore, קום is not the word that would normally be used for waking up or being startled (although it is, in fact, used of getting out of bed in, e.g., Gen 19.35; Ruth 3.14; Job 14.12.). Schwienhorst-Schönberger, 'Buch der Natur', 541-43, pursues the different (and more interesting) idea that the one who rises here is the human who 'goes' to their grave in the next verse, and that we are dealing with the expression 'get up and go' used in Gen 22.3 and elsewhere. Again, though, it is far from clear why, in that case, the subject is only specified for the second verb, and is left indeterminate at this point. Grammatically and stylistically, the simplest option by far is to assume instead that the first קול continues to be the subject—but then what does it mean to say that the sound of one thing 'rises to' the sound of another?

There are some special uses of קום with ־ל that deserve notice: we have already mentioned the first, noted by Ginsburg, where the sense is 'arise for the purpose of something', but in Ps 94.16 the expression apparently means 'stand up for', in the sense of being on somebody's side, while in Gen 23.17, 20; Lev 25.30; 27.19 the expression is used of land becoming or remaining somebody's property. *BHS* cites the last of these in support of a proposal to read ויקום לו קול—rather mysteriously, because in those terms the emended text would have to mean something like 'the sound of the bird will belong to it'. I doubt, however, that any of these uses offers an appropriate sense. Galling 1940 represents quite a long line of interpretation by taking the point to be that the voice of the elderly becomes 'high-pitched', but that, too, is unlikely: קום is used neither directly of transformation, nor of 'rising up' in a general way, as we might talk of a sound 'rising' to a certain pitch or volume. Salvaneschi, 'Memento vivere', 42, similarly cites Ezek 7.11 to support the idea of 'becoming' weak, like the breath of a bird, but the imagery of that verse, which began in 7.10, is of injustice 'growing up into' a rod of wickedness, like a plant, and the verb is not being used as functionally equivalent to a copula, as Salvaneschi suggests. It is possible that some similar metaphor is intended here, and that the low sound is depicted as 'growing' to become as loud as birdsong. The relative rarity and variety of usage suggests that the verb is probably not actually constructed with ־ל here, however, and supports the traditional understanding, that something here happens 'at a sound' (cf. לקול at Isa 30.19; Jer 51.16; Ezek 27.28; Hab 3.16), so the point is more probably that the woman's voice will 'rise' *when* the virtual silence is broken by a bird-call—that of a sparrow, according to G and σ'.

That said, it is not clear what exactly 'rise' implies. In the Aramaic text of *Ahiqar* (*TAD* C1.1.91), there is a saying that claims [ו]ה גבה קלה אף כרחמן מלך מן הו זי יקום קדמוהי, 'however merciful a king, his voice is still higher than that of one who stands up before him', but such an implication of authority would seem out of place here, and, as noted already, there is no specific evidence that the expression might indicate a change of pitch or volume. In view of the 'lowliness' with which the verb is clearly contrasted, it seems most likely that we are intended to think of the voice returning to its normal height: the woman stands up, and, if there is any reference to timbre or suchlike, her voice perhaps returns to normal as well.

12.4 the women who take up the song] Lit. 'the daughters of the song'. The expression has no close parallel,[13] and, setting aside translations driven entirely by allegorical interpretation, it has been explained variously as a reference to birds, songs (or their notes, cf. McNeile, 88), and singers:[14] the explanations naturally correspond to broader understandings of the context, and little or no external evidence can be offered for or against any of them, while the uses of בן and בת in connection with other nouns are themselves too varied to help us pin down the sense. Some earlier scholars, such as Ewald, saw here a reference to birdsong, but the interpretation 'birds' or 'songbirds' is essentially a modern one, which seems first to have been promulgated by Ginsburg, although it has since enjoyed a certain amount of support (and is described as 'beyond all doubt' by Driver, 'Problems and Solutions', 233). Understandings in terms of music, on the other hand, are certainly very early: 'songs' or 'singers' is the interpretation offered in *b. Šabbat* 152a, and T joins it with the allegorical interpretation 'lips' that is found in the Midrash. Some such understanding probably lies also behind α' καὶ κλιθήσονται πάντα τὰ τῆς ᾠδῆς, 'and all the things of song will decline'; this perhaps looks

---

[13] Seow, in particular, makes much of the use of בת יענה or בת היענה to indicate a particular species or type of bird (often understood to be the ostrich) in, e.g., Lev 11.16; Mic 1.8, especially because such birds are linked to lamentation in the latter passage. Unless one were to claim (as Seow does not) that בנות השיר is simply another term for such birds, or the name of an otherwise unmentioned species, it is not obvious how this might be relevant: we cannot simply move from the particular to the general in such matters, and claim that בנות השיר must be a term describing any songbirds. On the other hand, although the origin of בת יענה is mysterious in itself, it does at least provide a counterargument to a possible objection, that birds would not be characterized generically as female. Another expression sometimes invoked is *bnt hll snnt*, found in *Aqhat* ii 27, and translated by Dahood ('Canaanite-Phoenician', 215) as 'daughters of joyful noise, swallows'. The sense of the Ugaritic is far from clear cut, however, as Fox appears to acknowledge when he cites it in support of 'songstresses'—and if the reference really is to female singers who are also given an avian epithet, it probably confuses the issue more than it resolves it. Ginsburg claims one instance of 'son of singing' meaning a songbird in Syriac, which seems both slight and distant.

[14] The different understandings are not always distinct: 'songs' and 'singers' are often run together, while Delitzsch (whose attachment to the allegory leads him to several suspensions of sound judgment) wants the idiom to incorporate both humans and birds—all creatures with the power of song must stop singing to avoid disturbing the old man. So, similarly, Plumptre.

to Aramaic בת קל, which is used of the sound or tone of a voice (sometimes euphemistically for the voice itself),[15] and an interpretation in those terms would explain a rendering that seems unusually paraphrastic for Aquila (assuming his text did not lack בנות).

My own understanding lies in this area, but although I take the reference to be to singers, I think that this is neither a technical reference to a particular class (mourners, according to Fox), nor some sort of idiom, but a deliberate poetic image. As the song started by the milling-woman is picked up by others, it gives birth, as it were, to new singers and voices—the 'daughters' of that song.

12.4 will be downcast] Since בנות should clearly be feminine and is certainly the subject, the verb is a striking illustration of the way that the third-person feminine plural form of the yiqtol has vanished in the book. On the broader tendency for this to happen, especially in later Hebrew and especially when the verb precedes the subject, see GKC §145 p; J-M §150 c. Ibn Ezra notes a similar case in Esth 1.20, and suggests the rather fanciful possibility that כול (presumably understood as implicitly plural) is actually acting as the grammatical subject in both instances. Although there are undoubtedly recollections of 2.8 and of 2 Sam 19.36 involved also, it is tempting to suppose that the masculine form of the verb has contributed to the view of *b. Šabbat* 152a, that Qohelet is talking about male and female singers here.

Geminate verbs can take so-called 'aramaizing' forms, and Kautzsch, 'Die sogenannten aramaisierenden Formen', 776, has argued plausibly that occurrences of שחח in the yiqtol that have traditionally been understood as niph'al should, in fact, be understood as qal, so we should be wary of assigning any special nuance to them (cf. GKC §67 g; J-M §82 h; in favour of the niph'al, see the remarks in Wright, 251 n. 1). A number of commentators, however, have noted the use of תשח in Isa 29.4 with speech as the subject, and *HALOT* uses this to justify a sense 'utter low, muffled sounds'. This sense cannot be proved by that text, in which the reference is not to the pitch or volume, but to the subterranean origin of the speech, and although we cannot altogether exclude the possibility of such an extended meaning, the general implication of the verb is 'to be low'—often with a nuance of degradation or humiliation, sometimes, though, in the context of loss or mourning (cf. Pss 35.14; 38.7; Lam 3.20). That seems to fit well here as a claim that the women are prostrate, and there is no compelling reason to adopt Sawyer's re-vocalization יָשֹׁחוּ (= יָשִׂיחוּ; cf. Ps 69.13), which enables him to talk about 'chattering birds': שִׂיחַ would anyway seem an odd choice of verb to represent meaningless sounds.[16]

---

[15] On later uses of the term to signify an overheard remark that is treated as an omen, see especially Lieberman, *Hellenism in Jewish Palestine*, 194-99.

[16] 'The Ruined House', 527. Sawyer does not note that *b. Šabbat* 152a already makes an interpretative connection with שיח via the cognate noun: the deafness of the old man means that even songs will sound to him כשיחה / כשוחה (the texts

12.5 but] The first part of 12.5 is extremely difficult, and the meaning far from clear; it is possible also that the text is corrupt, although, if so, the damage is early—the ancient versions adopt different understandings, but they seem largely to have been wrestling with the same consonants. One minor exception to this is at the very start of the verse, where it seems likely that G καί γε, 'and indeed', reflects וגם, while an initial conjunction is suggested also by Hie, S and (emphatically) by Jerome's account of σ', which starts *et super haec etiam*, 'and beyond these also'. M and T have no conjunction. A variant reading in G omits the γε, leaving *only* the conjunction, but although that is almost certainly secondary, it is much harder to say whether M or G reflects the earlier reading. I am inclined to consider the conjunction original, because I take this to be a continuation from v. 4, but it could be just such an understanding, of course, that led to the secondary insertion of a facilitatory conjunction.

12.5 even at their full height they will be afraid] Lit. 'even from a height' (see below). The consonants יראו can be parsed as either from ירא, 'fear' (written defectively as יִרְאוּ) or from ראה, 'see' (יִרְאוּ). If, they are read as 'see', then מגבה has to be treated as an adverbial expression 'they will see from what is high'. If, on the other hand, the word is read as 'fear', then מגבה can either be read that way ('they will fear from on high'), or taken as the object of the verb, since the object of ירא is often marked with מן ('they will be afraid of what [or of someone who] is high'). Clearly, there is much scope here for confusion.

Most of the versions have understood 'fear', but G ἀπὸ ὕψους ὄψονται means 'they will see from a height', and Jerome gives the reading of σ' in Latin as *de excelso uidebunt*, which has the same sense.[17] Although יִרְאוּ, 'fear', is the majority reading of M, the pointing יִרְאוּ, 'see', is also found in a very substantial number of Hebrew manuscripts and printed editions: cf. de Rossi and Ginsburg, *Writings*. Taken quite literally, neither reading works much better than the other with what precedes and follows, and the text as it stands seems genuinely ambiguous—if it were really so obvious that 'the meaning required by the context...excludes the LXX reading', as Schoors claims, it is hard to see why the generally competent and thoughtful translator of G would have adopted it.

---

vary)—presumably meaning that they will sound simply like talk rather than music (Jastrow, *Dictionary*, understands 'low talk', 'whisper'). That line of interpretation is also picked up by Rashi.

[17] A number of Greek witnesses have εἰς τὸ ὕψος instead of ἀπὸ ὕψους, and McNeile, 167, believes that this reflects an attempt to make better sense—the women who are low would then be looking up. He speculates that the reading is from Theodotion. It does, in fact, appear as an unattributed marginal note on ms 252, where we find many hexaplaric readings, and although Marshall, 372, suggests that it probably just represents the G variant there, this does add a little weight to the possibility that it is itself hexaplaric.

It should be noted (with Kamenetzky, 232) that the reading of G and σ' has probably also involved reading מִגֹּבַהּ, 'from a height', rather than M מִגָּבֹהַּ, 'from (what is) high'; this reading is apparently reflected also in Hie *ab excelsis timebunt*, 'they will fear from heights', and S ܡܢ ܪܘܡܐ *mn rwm' ndḥl*, 'he will fear from a height', despite the fact that they read 'fear' and not 'see'. There is thus a second ambiguity—resolved in a number of Hebrew manuscripts by the plene spelling מגבוה.

To complicate matters yet further, it will be apparent from the reading just noted that S takes the verb to be singular, and this is in line with the interpretation of the text in *b. Šabbat* 152a, picked up by Rashi and Rashbam. Ibn Ezra reports suggestions that the ו- is paragogic, or that the subject of the verb is a man's legs, but these are apparently attempts to reconcile the text as it stands with such an interpretation, which is driven by the gerontological reading. It seems very likely that S itself (or possibly a source) has been influenced by that interpretation. McNeile, 89, and Gordis both take the ו- as dittographic and would emend to a singular, which is a possibility suggested also in the various editions of *BH* and by *BHS*. None of these cites S in support, which is probably wise, given the many problems shown by this version later in the verse, but all (along with scholars like Lauha, who simply assign the plural a singular sense) are most likely driven by the same allegorical concern, even if they do not put it in such terms. Gordis claims, for instance, that 'the entire context is in the singular', apparently ignoring the fact that vv. 3-4 have contained six subjects in the plural or dual, and only one in the singular, while the last verb was itself a third-person plural yiqtol: any 'singular' character for the context is to be found only in the supposition that Qohelet is describing allegorically the body-parts and actions of one typical person. We have no good grounds, therefore, to emend the verb to singular, but the ambiguity in the text remains a problem.

My translation is motivated by the following, rather diverse considerations—not all of which, I readily confess, carry the same weight:

(1) As the text stands, the בנות השיר are the only natural subject of the verb, having been the subject of a verb in the same form in the previous clause, linked to this one by גם (and perhaps originally by a conjunction as well). There is no reason to assume that Qohelet is now suddenly talking about 'they' with the implication 'people in general' (on the mismatch in gender between subject and verb, see the note on 'will be downcast' at 12.4).

(2) The ambiguity of the verb is unlikely to have been intentional, and if the author intended ייראו ('fear'), the problem has most likely been caused by a change in the orthography, the potential consequences of which were not noticed by the copyist responsible. It is probable, on the other hand, that an original יראו ('see') would always have been ambiguous, and so would have been avoided unless such ambiguity were intended. The very fact that we have a difficulty, therefore, tends to favour a meaning 'fear'.

(3) If מגבה is simply read as an expression of 'place whence', and if the בנות are women, 12.5 suddenly and mysteriously translates them to a high position from which they can look or fear (although it is not clear at what). Even if they are birds, for whom a height would be more explicable, there is a significant tension between the verses: Seow has to picture these birds swooping down in 12.4, but then still being sufficiently far up in 12.5 to be observing from a height. There are three ways to address this problem. The first is to take מגבה as the object of the verb, which pushes us toward 'fear' and leaves us with the traditional translation 'they fear a height'. In the terms of the gerontological interpretation, this is usually taken (literally) to mean that the elderly struggle with the prospect of climbing a hill, rather than that they are acrophobic, but outside those terms it makes little sense. It is unlikely that without an article the expression can mean 'they fear the high one', i.e. God, as Fox acknowledges even though he broadly favours that understanding,[18] while גבה means 'who/what is high', not 'who/what is *on* high', and it can hardly have a sense 'they are afraid of what is above them'. The second way is to understand the verb as modal: the בנות are not actually moved, and the point would be then that they would see or be afraid even if they were not low, but standing high above what is going on. It seems awkward, however, to treat only this verb in the sequence as modal.

The third and last possibility is admittedly a little more speculative, insofar as there is no precisely analogous usage, but it makes good sense in context. Since there is no obvious reason suddenly to introduce a hill, or to lift the 'daughters of song' above the ground (even if they are birds), it seems important to note that, although the cognate verb has a broader application, גבה as an adjective is used principally of people or objects that are 'high' in the sense of being tall, and, by extension, of arrogance or of rank (cf. 5.7). It is not used typically of things that are 'high above' or 'high up'. In general, the uses of the noun are similar: it refers to the height of objects or people, and again, by extension, to arrogance or rank—even in Job 22.12 גבה שמים seems to mean not 'high in the heavens' but '(at) the topmost point of the heavens', meaning at the top of their height, just as that same verse also talks about the uppermost stars in terms of their 'head'. To be sure, distinctions between height from head to foot and height above the ground are as difficult to maintain in Hebrew as in English, and in the later *Tosefta Sanhedrin* VII—where

---

[18] The lack of an article is noted also by Wright, 254 n. 1, in a critique of Hahn's earlier attempt to find such a meaning. Hahn himself goes on to suggest fancifully that 'the way' which will be mentioned is the way from earth 'zu dem Hohen, der im Himmel thront', 'to the high one, who is enthroned in heaven'; as Wright allows, the basic elements of this are not far from Ibn Ezra's idea, that the spirit thinks it will have to depart for a higher place, and fears the journey.

questions are forbidden from anybody מעומד לא מגבוה ולא מרחוק ולא מאחורי הזקנים, 'standing from (a position) high up, distant, or behind the elders'—מגבוה seems to have to mean something like 'from an elevated spot'. It is not unreasonable to suppose, however, that the expression here might mean 'from (their) height', and express an idea equivalent to the 'standing up' implied by יקום in the previous verse. In 1 Sam 16.7, indeed, the expression גבה קומתו seems to mean something like 'the height of his elevation', or 'his standing height'. It is more mundane than views from 'on high' might be, but I do not think it is hard to suppose that Qohelet is talking about the singers continuing to be afraid even after they have got back on to their feet and taken to the road.

12.5 and utterly terrified on the road] Lit. 'terrified with terror' (following α'). וחתחתים is pointed in M and usually read as a reduplicated form of חת, which itself refers to 'fear' as an emotion or reaction, but which is related to the חתית used in Ezekiel (26.17 and seven times in 32.23-32) of the terror caused in a population by various rulers and warriors. G adopts this understanding, but renders using θάμβοι, which can refer either to amazement or to an object of amazement, with an implication of awe more than of terror—having previously translated יראו as 'see', the translator perhaps assumes that extraordinary spectacles are somehow involved. The notion of fear is retained better in σ', the reading of which is given by Jerome in Latin as *et terror erit in uia*, 'and terror will be in the road' (not *error*: as Marshall notes, the editor has made a strange choice here among the variants for his text in the *editio princeps*). However, both Hie and V have *et formidabunt in uia*, 'and they will be frightened in the road', while S also has a verb. These might simply be considered loose translations, but we should not expect a paraphrase from α', which is attested here as τρόμῳ τρομήσουσιν ἐν τῇ ὁδῷ, 'with trembling they will tremble in the road'. All four versions seem to have found in the word a participle of some sort from חתת, while Aquila has more precisely read it as חת חתים (or חת התתים), and seen a construction like that of פחדו פחד in Ps 14.5 (cf. GKC §117 p-r; J-M §125 q). This gives a significantly smoother reading.

When חתחתים is taken as a noun, then if we have not taken מגבה as an object of יראו, the prefixed conjunction obliges us to treat it as the beginning of a new, non-verbal clause—'and terrors (are) in the way'—traditionally understood in the gerontological interpretation as a literal statement that old people are frightened to go out or to walk along the street.[19] That clause is abrupt to the point of ugliness, and fits badly into the surrounding context of verbal clauses. If we were to insist on reading a noun, therefore, it might

---

[19] It is probably this understanding of the passage that gave rise to a very much later use of חתחתים to mean 'obstacles', which is very unlikely to be the original meaning. See Sawyer, 'The Ruined House', 528. In a number of instances, the expression is actually 'obstacles in the road', indicating the origin of that usage as a citation from this verse.

be better to assume that the initial conjunction was an early error, introduced either through simple dittography or from an interpretation of מגבה as the object of ייראו—without it, חתחתים can be taken straightforwardly itself as the object of that verb (even if it is a little odd to fear terror),[20] and the stylistic problems avoided. The clause is sometimes read that way even when מגבה has in fact been taken as an object (cf. RSV 'they are afraid also of what is high, and terrors are in the way'); under those circumstances, though, it is probably better to follow certain older commentators and take וחתחתים as a second object of ייראו, even though this means that the -מ has to do double duty ('they fear what is high and terrors in the road').

The most straightforward approach, however, is to follow Aquila and the others in reading a verb here: חתחתים is not attested elsewhere except in discussions of this passage or in expressions derived from it, and it would not be astonishing if the word actually came into being either through an error in writing the simple participle, or, as I think likely, from faulty word-division: α' gives an excellent sense without requiring changes other than the insertion of a space and, perhaps, a correction of the spelling.

I have some sympathy with the suspicion of Strobel that, in this context full of ups and downs, וחתחתים might just be a corruption of something like התחתים (cf. Gen 6.16), so that the בנות would 'even from a height be afraid of things below on the road' (de Rossi reports a number of manuscripts and editions with just this reading; see also Ginsburg, *Writings*). Ibn Ghayyat linked the word with נחת, and saw a reference to 'descents', understanding the point to be that the old are afraid not only of heights in the road, but of pitfalls or potholes; cf. Vajda, 'Ecclésiaste XII, 2-7', 40. If we do wish to find some reference to 'a height' at all, though, then גבה and דרך alone would provide a contrast between 'above' and 'below'.

12.5 But the almond will blossom] G has translated this and the next two verbs using aorist subjunctives, which serve to differentiate the series from the preceding series of clauses (where G used the future indicative, which many manuscripts now substitute for the subjunctive, losing the distinction). Pabst, 'Verständnis von Alter', 164, speaks of a switch to consecutive forms in the Hebrew here, signalling a discontinuity with those clauses, but that construal is a matter of interpretation: the text itself 'signals' nothing of the sort. Hie, V simply continue to use the future, and no shift of tense is implied by S or T, so it is not entirely clear what G is trying to do. Yi, 160, discerns contingency—'they will see from heights...*when* the almond tree blossoms, etc.' (cf. *NETS*)—and is probably correct to understand that the translator has construed the verbs with the previous 'seeing'. I consider it more likely, though, that the point is slightly different: 'they will see both wonders in the

---

[20] Desvoeux, *A Philosophical and Critical Essay*, 541-43, assumes accordingly that the noun must indicate not terror, but something designed to cause terror, and ventures 'scarecrows'—an opinion that has enjoyed little subsequent support.

way, and *whether* the almond will blossom, etc.' This is not a very compelling interpretation of the Hebrew, but permits G to connect the various elements. On the translator's use of the subjunctive more generally, see my notes at 9.14.

With a definite article, the consonants שקד can be read either as the noun meaning 'almond' (the nut in Gen 43.11; Num 17.23; or the tree in Jer 1.11) or else as a qal participle from the verb meaning 'be watchful, awake' (cf. Jer 1.12).[21] The verb וינאץ, on the other hand, should only have one possible interpretation: 'will reject' or 'will revile'—a yiqtol from נאץ. In the M tradition, however, most manuscripts have ינאץ, but point the word as though it were ינץ—in effect ignoring the א, as commended in the Masorah Parva (cf. *BHQ* ויתיר א, 'and the א is superfluous'—ינץ is not presented formally as a *Q*ᵉ*rê*, although some commentators talk about it as such). That pronunciation derives the word from נצץ (or נוץ / ניץ according to some early grammarians), 'to blossom', and permits us to take שקד easily as 'almond'. Many of the ancient versions, and the great majority of commentators have followed the Masoretes in this respect, and my understanding of the subsequent clauses leads me to do the same. This is not simply a matter of theme, but of construction: if all the clauses are broadly parallel, we should expect an active, intransitive verb here with השקד as its subject. If an active form of the transitive נאץ were to be read, then we should have no object (unless, like Schoors, we were to invent our own—see below), while if the verb were to be construed as passive, perhaps puʻal (although that form is otherwise unattested), then not only would the clause be out of step with the others, but it would be unclear who would be doing the 'rejecting'. If it seems most likely on such grounds that ינץ was originally intended, the rise of ינאץ might be explained as the consequence of error or misunderstanding, but this is plausibly a matter of orthography. As we can see from the Qumran texts, א was once more widely used as a vowel-letter than it is in M, and although it was not normally used for 'e' sounds, there are some possible exceptions at Qumran (see Reymond, *Qumran Hebrew*, 46-47). These somewhat offset Seow's critique of Gordis and others on this score, while the relative rarity of such cases, and the existence of נאץ, might have prevented scribes subsequently from recognizing this as a *plene* writing.

---

[21] A late variant הַשּׁוֹקֵד, the participle, is reported by Loevy, *Libri Kohelet*, 23. There is a third, rather tenuous possibility. In a lengthy discussion of the clause, Desvoeux, *A Philosophical and Critical Essay*, 203-11, sees a connection with a verb שקד (found only as נשקד in Lam 1.14), which he translates as 'embraced' or 'close pressed', and he thinks that we are dealing here with a derivative meaning 'close union' (that is, sexual intercourse). Accordingly, he takes the point to be that, in old age 'the commerce of women shall be despised'—in other words, 'sex will be spurned'. The verb in Lamentations, if it is not actually a form from שקד, as the Greek translation there supposes, is far too obscure to form the basis for such a proposal.

It is apparently a reading וייאץ, without a knowledge of the M pronunciation, that leads Symmachus to the translation reported by Jerome in Latin as *et obdormiet uigilans*, now known in Greek from ms 788, καὶ ἀποκοιμᾶται γρηγορῶν, 'and one who is wakeful will fall asleep': plants cannot reject anything, so שקד must be someone wakeful, rather than an 'almond', and to reject one's wakefulness is to give it up (so, e.g., Goldman, Marshall). It is apparently this part and the next of the σ' rendering that leads a somewhat mystified Jerome to remark in his commentary that the Laodicean (Apollinaris), because he follows Symmachus here, can please neither Jews nor Christians: his reading of this verse is close neither to the Hebrew nor to the Greek text.[22] Both of those (or at least M and G as we have them), along with T and Jerome himself, understand the reference to be to an almond tree. Symmachus is not entirely alone, however: the text and sense of S are very difficult throughout this verse, but in one of two different renderings of this clause ܡܢܒܥ ܥܠܘܗܝ ܫܗܪܐ *wnbʿ ʿlwhy šhr* appears to mean 'wakefulness will shoot up upon him', and this clearly reflects a similar association of שקד with the verb and not the noun (although the translator has perhaps read an infinitive rather than a participle).[23] Modern commentators have not generally been inclined to find a reference directly to wakefulness, but Plumptre, for instance, notes the play on words in Jer 1.11-12, and thinks that Qohelet is alluding to insomnia by introducing the homonymous 'almond'. Anyway, because, like Symmachus, the translator of S is unlikely to have made such an association if he had had any reason to suppose that the reference here was actually to a tree, it seems improbable that either translator connected וייאץ with נצץ, although it is equally clear that this verb was, in fact, understood by G, Hie, and V.

It is unlikely that Jerome, at least, was actually aware of the reading וייאץ: if he was, he surely would not have been puzzled by σ'. It seems probable, therefore, that ינץ and ינאץ co-existed as variants in the manuscript tradition from a relatively early point before the Masoretes attempted, in effect, to merge them.[24] In different permutations with understandings of שקד as 'wakeful' or

---

[22] Kraus, 'Christians, Jews, and Pagans', 185-86, is surprised by Jerome's criticism of Symmachus here, given his more general tendency to favour σ', and especially since the readings of σ' can largely be justified in terms of the Hebrew text. Jerome is most likely just taking the opportunity for a dig at Apollinaris, whose views had only recently been anathematized.

[23] It is less clear where 'shoot up (or "gush") upon him' has come from. Lane, 'Lilies', 487-89, discusses this verse at some length, but here suggests only that a pronoun has been added for clarity, with the Hebrew otherwise 'taken literally'. It is difficult, however, to connect ܢܒܥ *nbʿ* to any established meaning of ינאץ or נצץ. Perhaps the rendering has been informed by a corrupt or mistaken reading of G ἀνθήσῃ as ἀναθήσῃ, 'run up' (which can also be used of plants)?

[24] I doubt it is possible that the author intended a play on words, as Seow suggests: even allowing for orthographic variation, the writing would tend to

'almond', they have subsequently each provided a basis for different lines of interpretation within the gerontological reading, and each can claim a significant part in the reception history of the book.[25] One clearly originated from the other, possibly as a simple error or matter of orthography, but also plausibly as a change motivated by some scribe's desire to clarify a reading he found ambiguous or misleading in terms of the way he understood the context, and our own understanding of that context is really the only basis on which to choose between them.

Accordingly, Taylor, *Dirge*, 31-33, opts for ינאץ as part of a counter-allegorical reading that is strongly influenced by the idea that we must have a list here of things that are either 'good' or 'bad'. Since Taylor sees an epitome of sadness in the idea that the almond either fails to charm or refuses to blossom (both of which stretch that verb somewhat), he arguably makes the passage more symbolic than do most of the allegorizers. Other commentators have also opted for some form of נאץ, 'despise', in a more literal sense, however, and so Podechard, for instance, speaks of the almond being rejected (cf. Seow, 'the almond becomes revolting'), while Schoors translates 'the almond tree spurns him' (reading a hiph'il, and apparently introducing 'him', which is in none of the versions; what he understands it to mean is unclear). For Gilbert, 'La Description', 105, this is, correspondingly, a statement about the disinclination of the old to eat, set alongside others about a lack of appetite for other small dishes—locusts and capers.

In his commentary, Olympiodorus attributes to 'another of the interpreters' the following translation of this and the next two clauses: ἀνθεῖ τὸ ἀμύγδαλον καὶ παχύνεται ἡ ἀκρις διανοίγεται ἡ κάππαρις, 'the almond blossoms and the locust grows fat; the caper opens up'. Since we already have different readings attested for parts of this in α' and σ', then if this is a reading from the Three, it must be θ', as Marshall points out.

The early allegorical interpretations of the clause in Jewish sources are in terms of the sacrum or atlas bone, respectively at the bottom or top of the spine signal one sense or the other. The word continued to cause a few problems in the text tradition, and de Rossi notes two manuscripts with ינץ, others in which the א has been added as a correction, and a number with the letters transposed to give ויאנץ (cf. Kennicott). Two relatively late manuscripts, he reports, try to point the word as a form from נאץ.

[25] It is worth mentioning also one interpretation that understands the verb quite differently, if only because it is so peculiar. Hahn looks to נצה in Job 39.13, which refers to the plumage of a bird, and thinks that we are dealing here with a form of a denominative verb derived from that noun. Accordingly, he translates 'und Schwingen bekommt der Wache', 'and the watchful one gets wings'—to be understood in terms of a butterfly emerging from a chrysalis. Coincidentally, that would suit very well my own interpretation of the next clause—but it is extremely far-fetched.

(the former is more probably meant), and derive from the use of the noun לוז as a word for both this bone and for nuts or trees that produce nuts. The idea is that this bone becomes more prominent as the flesh around it becomes thinner. The more familiar understanding, in terms of hair becoming white, is proposed by Jerome, who distinguishes it from that Jewish interpretation.

12.5 and the locust carry itself within] Lit. 'will bear itself' or 'be pregnant with itself'. The verb סבל is used in the qal of carrying something or bearing a load and several cognate nouns refer to burdens or carriers. It appears once in the pu'al, at Ps 144.14, where the reference is to cattle being pregnant. This is the only use of the hithpa'el, but we would generally expect that form to convey a reflexive sense, which is what has probably inspired G's translation in terms of the locust becoming fat (παχυνθῇ; the ταχυνθῇ attested for α' on ms 788 is likely an error for the same word)—we need not suppose that the translator is trying to capture the sense of both סבל and סכל as Goldman suggests: ויסתכל appears in some later Hebrew manuscripts (see de Rossi, Ginsburg, *Writings*), but there is no reason to suppose that the variant is ancient. Hie, V, and the anonymous Greek reading noted by Olympiodorus follow G (cf. also T 'swells'), but one of the renderings in S has ܘܢܣܓܐ ܩܡܨܐ *wnsg' qmṣ'*, 'and the locust grows' or 'multiplies' (the other lacks a verb): this seems to be more or less a guess, but it does avoid the problem that locusts do not actually grow fat.

The word for 'locust' here is חגב, which is found also at Lev 11.22; Num 13.33; Isa 40.22; 2 Chr 7.13. There are a lot of other terms in use as well, however, and it is impossible now to know how these each relate either to different species or to different points in the life-cycle of the locust; for a convenient overview, see Thompson, 'Translation of the Words for Locust'. Given the use of the verb at Ps 144.14, however, I think it is reasonable to understand that what Qohelet has in mind here is the development of the insect through its five flightless stages as an instar and final emergence in its fully developed state, which would have been familiar to ancient readers, at least in very general terms. At each stage, the locust goes through a process of eclosion, shedding the exoskeleton that it has outgrown, so that in a very real sense it does carry itself within itself.

Elsewhere, the verb has no particular implications that the load being carried is heavy or difficult to lift, and the common idea that the locust is 'dragging itself along' seems to have been derived solely from the requirement of the gerontological interpretation that some sort of impairment be involved. This is also undoubtedly the source of early Jewish exegetical attempts to identify חגב with various parts of the body, which in turn influence Whitley's implausible notion that we should look to Arabic here, and understand a reference to hip joints. Motivated by a different concern, to have a consistent reference to plants in the verse, Fox speculates that Qohelet is talking about some sort of tree (he no longer maintains his 1987 preference for Ginsberg's emendation to חצב, 'sea-onion'), and Seow makes a similar case. The fact that we can talk about 'locust trees' in English, however, hardly supplies evidence that a word for locust in Hebrew could also have been used of a tree, and there is no sign that any of the ancient versions or early interpreters were familiar with such a usage.[26]

Jerome's account of σ' lacks any equivalent to this clause: as Marshall observes, it is unclear whether Jerome accidentally omitted the line or simply did not find it—although we should also note a third possibility, that it has dropped out during the transmission of his commentary. Jerome himself claims that the noun here, which he transliterates as *aagab* (var. *haagab*), is ambiguous, meaning either 'locust' or 'ankle/heel' (*talus*), which facilitates gerontological interpretation of the verse as a reference to swollen feet. Since the Hebrew word for 'heel' is in fact עקב, that statement seems hard to justify, and whichever word he found in his text, it would unambiguously mean one thing or the other. It seems likely that he has misunderstood, or is explaining poorly, an interpretation based on the similar sounds of the two words: there is no ambiguity in the written text, but someone hearing that text read aloud might *hear* in it a reference to feet. In *b. Šabbat* 152a, a similar strategy is pursued, but using עגבות, 'buttocks', rather than עקב; in an attempt to link the two readings, Kraus, 'Christians, Jews, and Pagans', 204 n. 72, argues that Jerome or the Jewish tradition might have confused the two nouns, but these appear to be two distinct, albeit similar, interpretations.

The initial conjunction is omitted in the standard edition of V, but does appear early as a variant.

12.5 and the caper-berry split open] Or 'be fruitful'. The verb I פרר generally understood here is a common one, but it is used almost exclusively in biblical Hebrew (and later) with a sense that seems inappropriate to this context, of breaking or cancelling various sorts of compacts and commands.[27]

---

[26] The issue tends to get tangled up with the long-standing objection of some readers to the idea that John the Baptist in Mt 3.4 might actually have been eating locusts (even though the insects were widely consumed, and in some places still are). Any evidence for a contemporary 'locust tree' has proved elusive in that debate as well, and claims made for this text on that basis have little force. Such concerns, nonetheless, prompt Henslow, 'The Carob', to suggest that הגב may have been an error for חרב, 'carob' (although he does not clarify what the verb might then mean). The modern description of carob beans as 'locust' beans, on the other hand, appears simply to go back to interpretations of John the Baptist's diet (and the beans are also known as 'St John's Bread'); they bear no obvious resemblance to the insect, and despite many claims to the contrary, there is no clear evidence that words for 'locust' were used to describe them prior to such interpretations. The various North American trees called 'locust tree' are all similarly leguminous, and have derived their name in turn from the carob.

[27] The verb is not used intransitively in that sense, which makes it difficult to follow Provan's understanding that the caper 'does not keep its promise to be fruitful'.

In Prov 15.22 (where the verb should perhaps be hoph‘al, cf. Isa 8.10) and Job 5.12 it is used in connection with plans, in Isa 44.25 of omens, and in Ps 85.5 (ET 85.4) of anger, so there is some scope for using it without specific reference to relationships, and in those places the sense seems to be 'cancel' or 'prevent from happening' something that was intended or predicted. A much rarer sense 'split', 'divide' or 'shake' is usually attributed in the lexica to a separate verb II פרר, found in various forms at Isa 24.19; Ps 74.13; Job 16.12: this probably lies behind both a later use for 'crumbling' bread, and the conventional rendering of פרר in Greek using διασκεδάζω / διασκέδαννυμι (which connotes 'scattering') even when the sense of I פרר is required (e.g. Lev 26.15)—the homonyms do not appear to have been regarded as distinct.

M points ותפר here as hiph‘il, which would imply that the אביונה itself was doing the breaking, but G διασκεδασθῇ, 'is dispersed' (cf. Hie, V *dissipabitur*), and σ' διαλυθῇ, 'dissolved' or 'dispersed' (attested in Greek in Syh as present-tense διαλύεται), are both passive. These probably represent פרר in the hoph‘al (which Goldman would prefer to read, as it gives an intransitive sense). The suggestion by Perles, *Analekten*, 30, that they actually reflect an original הפרה (since פרר is found sometimes in rabbinic usage with a connotation of dispersal) is adopted by Fox, but is implausible: if they had found a form from פרה, it is difficult to see why the translators would not have rendered it with the primary sense of that verb, 'bloom', which would be far more obvious in this context, and which Perles himself considers the correct meaning.

The Greek version cited by Olympiodorus and mentioned above as probably θ', has διανοίγεται ἡ κάππαρις, 'the caper opens up', which takes II פרר in a different way, probably as a reference to the way that the seed-pod ('berry') of the caper splits open (the Greek verb is typically used of body-parts, which would be analogous). G and σ' may likewise have in mind the dispersal of the seeds within, and all three be thinking either in terms of II פרר, or of פרח, which has considerable overlap with פרר (cf. Jastrow, *Dictionary*), and which can be used in Aramaic of splitting open. On the other hand, α' καὶ καρπεύσει ἡ κάππαρις, 'and the caper will fruit / be fruitful', seems to take ותפר as from פרה, and probably reflects a variant ותפרה: we must suppose either that this variant arose through duplication of the following ה (and under the influence of the context), or that it is original, and that the ותפר of M arose from haplography.

Both readings are possible, although I have followed an understanding in terms of II פרר, which avoids emendation, and which gives a slightly better sense: since אביונה is a 'fruit' itself, it can hardly 'yield fruit'. It is true that פרה / פרי is occasionally used in later Hebrew and Aramaic with the sense 'grow' (cf. *b. Baba Batra* 18b, 19a, of a mustard leaf), but if we were to follow α', it would be better to adopt the sense 'be fruitful' (found famously in Gen 1.28). The most notable feature of the caper-berry is that it is packed with small seeds, which will be dispersed by birds, wasps, ants and lizards when the berry splits along its length after ripening, and so a reference to it splitting is also, in effect, a reference to its fruitfulness, and both readings point the same way. Lauha, who also sees images of fertility here, translates similarly with 'platzt', 'bursts', although he apparently understands a reference not to the berries, but to the flower-buds bursting open (see below).

What does not seem possible, at least outside the terms of an allegorical reading, is to take the verb in the sense of I פרר, although this lies behind most attempts to find here a reference to an appetite or desire that will 'fail' or 'be frustrated', in something like the way that plans will fail in Prov 15.22 and Isa 8.10. Whether or not that reading is plausible in terms of the verb, it is very doubtful that אביונה can have the required connotation. The noun itself features several times in a discussion about the caper bush and its products at *b. Berakot* 36a-b, where the concern is to establish which components constitute 'fruit': it is the pickled buds that are best known these days, but flower-buds (קפריסין, apparently from the Greek), leaves (תמרות) and berries (אביונות) are all harvested from the bush (צלף).[28] In this context, אביונה refers clearly to the caper-berry, as it does also in a shorter discussion at *m. Maʿaśerot* 4:6 (cf. *y. Maʿaśerot* 20a, b).[29]

The origin of the word is uncertain, but, of course, it bears a clear resemblance to (and may even be derived from) the word אביון, which is used of the poor and vulnerable in society, and which is itself often linked with the verb אבה. This is used principally in Hebrew of wishing or of being willing to do something (cf. אבי in Aramaic), and there is an interjection אבי used in a few places to mean 'would that!' The evidence does not bear out Jerome's claim that *abiona...ipsum ambiguum est, interpretaturque amor, desiderium, concupiscentia, uel capparis*, 'אביונה...is itself ambiguous, and can be interpreted as love, longing, desire or caper': as he goes on to make clear, indeed, he (or his informant) has derived this ambiguity from some tenuous etymologizing. So far as we can tell, a contemporary reader of Hebrew would only have seen possible references to 'need' in the sense of poverty,[30] to the caper-berry, or, at a considerable stretch, to a willingness or wish to do something (not 'for' something).

---

[28] For a great deal of information on the caper as a plant, and on the culinary and medical uses of its products, see Sozzi and Vicente, 'Capers and Caperberries'.

[29] There is a thorough review of the relevant passages, and a lot of details about capers, in Moore, 'Caper Plant', 56-61. This usage also casts doubt on the anyway rather speculative assertion of Dahood, 'Qoheleth and Recent Discoveries', 313, that our text might mean 'the caper (plant) becomes barren'. The somewhat earlier Todd, 'Caper-Berry', while well-informed in some areas, is flawed by its failure to recognize that the berry of the plant was (and is) commonly eaten—which drives Todd to deny that the word could refer to the berry at all.

[30] In two late manuscripts (see de Rossi) that plausibly preserve much earlier Babylonian readings, the word is, in fact, vocalized with *segol* under the א, suggesting such an understanding; cf. Ratzabi, 'Massoretic Variants', 107; Lavoie and Mehramooz, 'Le Texte hébreu et la traduction judéo-persane', 497.

It is the first of these, presumably, that has given rise to one of the translations in S, which speaks of poverty ceasing, and, in an extended sense, it is perhaps behind the rendering of σ', if this was indeed ἡ ἐπίπονος, perhaps 'suffering', 'toil'.[31] To be sure, we find in Ps 119.20, 174 the much more distant forms תאבה and תאבתי, which do indicate 'longing' (the verb תאב has that sense in Aramaic), and Rashi cites תאבתי to support his own translation 'desire': it is hardly likely that anybody would have made such a connection, however, if they were not driven to do so by the requirements of an allegorical interpretation. That is doubly true of the Midrash's association of אביונה with תאוה, 'desire', but the purpose of such interpretations is the elucidation of allegory, not the presentation of lexicographical data. The problems arise, as Moore, 'Caper Plant', 61, puts it, 'when modern scholars take this sort of etymologizing seriously. אביונה,"desire," from אבה, "to desire", is an etymological figment to support a haggadic exegesis'.

Another path to the much same conclusion has been *via* the idea that 'caper-berry' is intended literally, but that, since the berry functioned as an aphrodisiac or as a stimulant to appetite, a reference here to its 'failure' would be a reference to the end of any such desire. For the effects of the fruit, Moore himself ('Caper Plant', 63) cites in Greek the first-century CE *De Materia Medica* of Pedanius Dioscorides—a work that remained influential for many centuries—and comments that 'a drug which has these effects might very well be employed to stimulate sexual desire'. The effects noted, however, are benefits for the treatment of sciatica, palsy, hernia and convulsions, along with an ability to dry up menstrual blood and mucus: it is not at all clear how any of these might relate to the stimulation of desire, which is notably *not* mentioned in the long list from which Moore cites only a section. Although all sorts of plants are used for all sorts of purposes in early medical literature, there is no clear reference to the use of caper fruit as an aphrodisiac earlier than the late medieval Arabic compendium cited by Wetzstein in his essay at the end of Delitzsch's commentary (252), and any speculation about such a use is, again, derived from particular understandings of this passage, not from any external

---

[31] The use of ἡ ἐπίπονος by itself is odd, to say the least: the word is an adjective and is used in expressions like ἡ ἐπίπονος εὐνή (Lucian, *Demonax* 1), where it describes the rough outdoor sleeping arrangements of Sostratus; we do not expect it as a noun. Cannon, 199, makes the rather fanciful suggestion that Symmachus plays on the word to evoke the sorrowful condition of his own 'Ebionite' community, but the reading is in any case uncertain. Jerome represents it in Latin as *spiritus fortitudo*, which means something like 'the force of the spirit', or 'the strength of breathing', which would be a strange translation of ἐπίπονος; Marshall suggests plausibly that he had a corrupt reading ἐπίπνοος, 'breathed upon', 'inspired', but the ἡ would still be awkward. To confuse matters further, Syh has, in Greek, ΕΠΙΓΟΝΟΣ, 'born in addition', which makes no obvious sense at all. We probably have to accept that the reading is corrupt, and I suspect that a word has been lost.

evidence. Delitzsch himself observes, indeed, the lack of any reference to aphrodisiac properties in Pliny's *Naturalis Historia*, which discusses the caper twice (xiii, 44; xix, 48). The only sort of stimulation associated with capers in the ancient world is stimulation of the appetite for food: Plutarch (*Symposia* VI 2) speaks of capers, olives and other pickles being used as aperitifs because of their piquancy— they are not being employed as a sort of drug, as sometimes implied, and he is talking, in any case, about what may have been a very different culinary environment. If that were really the point here, then Qohelet's statement would be both curious and banal, as though we were to talk about a loss of appetite by saying 'the peanuts don't work anymore'.

12.5 even when the human has departed] Seow says of the כי here that 'It gives the reason for all the gloom', and it could, indeed, have an explanatory force if one were to share his view that, since 12.3, Qohelet has been describing the ruinous aftermath of a death. That is a minority view, however, which is difficult to sustain, and such an understanding of כי fits neither the translation adopted here nor, realistically, the traditional interpretation in terms of old age: none of these things happen *because* a human has died and been mourned. Leupold suggests that death is being depicted as 'a continuous act of dissolution', but that idea runs into the immediate difficulty that סבבו בשוק הספדים is not readily separated from הלך האדם אל בית עולמו, and one is hardly being mourned in the streets throughout that long process.

The suggestion does, however, draw attention to the importance of tense here, especially since the long chain of yiqtol/weyyiqtol forms appears now to have ended. M perhaps shares the view of Leupold, or is at least looking to understand the כי in similar terms, when it points הלך as a participle, while σ' ἀπελεύσεται γὰρ ὁ ἄνθρωπος, 'for the human will go out', probably reflects not a variant reading, but an attempt to deal with the problem in a different way: all these things will happen because the human *is going to* die. The future tense is used in Hie, V as well, probably under the influence of σ', and is found in most of the hexaplaric *O*-group of G manuscripts, which have earlier introduced ἐάν to facilitate an understanding 'if the human goes... then the mourners will...'. The original translator of G, on the other hand, most probably read a qatal here (so Yi, 248; there is no reason to take his aorist as gnomic), which would be difficult to explain as interpretative, but which accords with the subsequent וסבבו and is most likely the reading that was intended.

The switch from the yiqtols used of the almond, the locust and the caper hardly indicates that we are now dealing with events subsequent to the states of each, and I take the point to be that those things continue even during or after the death and funeral: the image, in other words, is of a natural world that continues, perhaps bursting with renewal and fertility, even after a death—and in that case, it is hard not to be reminded of the point with which Qohelet began, in 1.4. This is not specifically a contrast, however, and it is improbable that the כי should be regarded as adversative: the issue is not that the almond will do one thing, but the human another. Rather, if we have to label it, then the כי is most likely concessive or temporal, as in, e.g., Prov 6.35 or Hos 13.15: the world goes on even though the human has departed.

12.5 to his eternal home] Lit. 'the home of his eternity' or 'his home of eternity'; the Hebrew can mean both, but the versions slightly favour the former; cf. σ' *in domum aeternitatis suae*, cited in Latin by Jerome, who adopts the same wording in Hie and V (although *suae* is lacking in some V manuscripts). In the S tradition, the reading ܠܒܝܬ ܥܡܠܗ *lbyt ʿmlh*, 'to the house of his labour', clearly includes an error, and ܥܠܡܗ *ʿlmh*, 'his eternity', should be read (so Kamenetzky, 201: that reading is also attested by one manuscript cited in the Leiden edition). An unattributed reading cited by Gentry from ms 788 has the adjective αἰώνιον, reflecting a less literal rendering '(his) eternal (home)'.

After the lengthy discussions around העלם in 3.11 (see the notes there), it may be a surprise to discover how seldom the basic sense of עולם has been challenged here (although it has disconcerted some commentators for doctrinal reasons). Youngblood, however, does pick up the possible associations of the term with darkness in his 'Qoheleth's "Dark House"', and although he was the first fully to draw out the possible implications, Lavoie, 'בֵּית עוֹלָמוֹ dans Qo 12,5', 214, observes that he was not the first to make the link (see, e.g., Gray, *Legacy of Canaan*, 200, which renders 'his dark house'). Similar expressions with 'eternity' are found in various languages, however, and in many different ancient sources referring to the grave (Schoors provides a long list),[32] and although this phrase itself is not found elsewhere in biblical Hebrew, the notion of graves as 'homes' is to be found in Ps 49.12 (ET 49.11), while Isa 14.18-19 seemingly uses בית as equivalent to קבר (this may be the sense of the term in passages like 2 Chr 33.20 also). As Lavoie goes on to argue at some length, it is difficult to sustain the rendering 'darkness' in the face of such evidence. At most, perhaps, we might allow that the term in Hebrew potentially has a secondary resonance.

As for the preposition, אל is expected and makes good sense: Kennicott lists only two manuscripts with על, despite common confusion between the words. Ginsburg, *Massorah* 3:71, however, notes על as a *Qᵉrê* associated with the eastern tradition (cf. also T-S D1.15, 2v 14), and it duly turns up in one of the Babylonian manuscripts from which Miletto takes his list of variants. In the same place, Ginsburg lists the *plene* עולמו as another eastern *Qᵉrê*; this

---

[32] See also Jenni, 'Das Wort ʿōlām', 27-29; Hurvitz, 'Two Funerary Terms'; Lavoie, 'בֵּית עוֹלָמוֹ dans Qo 12,5', 217-22. Niehr, 'Zur Semantik', cites passages such as Ezek 26.20 to suggest more precisely that עולם might refer to the underworld, although the possessive suffix makes that sense difficult here.

spelling is very widely attested, and Goldman (42*) notes that the word is quoted plene in M^L itself by a Masoretic note to 10.3, which also reads על for אל.

12.5 the mourners have gone about] There is no need to understand סבבו in the sense 'surround (him)': the term can be used, like the English 'go around', of movement that is not necessarily circular (e.g. Isa 23.16). It is possible, though, that the reference is to the mourners (lit. those [who are] lamenting) walking around or surrounding the dead body as they sing their laments (a sense that is rejected for G by Munnich, 'Traduire', 107).

Hie, V, σ' (cited by Jerome) all have the future *et circumibunt in platea plangentes*, 'and those lamenting will go about in the streets'; see the previous note on 'even when the human has departed'. Kennicott notes four manuscripts that have וספדו here, so that the mourners 'mourn' in the streets, and such a reading presumably lies behind the καὶ πενθῶσιν of Codex Graecus Venetus.

12.5 in the street] *BHQ* notes that M^L בַּשּׁוּק is an error for בָּשּׁוּק, citing that latter vocalization in the other early manuscripts M^L34 (St Petersburg EBP. II B 34) and M^Y (Cambridge Add. ms 1753). Sassoon 1053 does appear to support M^L—although the dot with which it distinguishes *qameṣ* is set so unusually low that it may just be a stray mark on the surface. G has apparently not vocalized the expression with an article at all.

12.6 While the silver cord has not yet been snapped] Or perhaps 'fastened' ('knotted'?). On the construction with עד אשר, see the corresponding note at 12.1. The basic implication is the same here, but I have translated differently to draw out what I take to be the intended sense. More literally, we could render 'when not yet…then…'.

For the verb, M offers ירחק as *K^ethîbh*, ירתק as *Q^erê* (with some variations on this, see de Rossi). The former, pointed as qal, would mean 'is distant'; the niph'al of the verb is not otherwise attested, but if ירחק were read as niph'al, it might conceivably mean 'is removed' (cf. *HALOT*; this is presumably the basis of Heim's translation 'plundered'). The latter is from the verb רתק, which is used of 'knocking' in Aramaic and usually has that sense in rabbinic Hebrew, but refers to 'binding' with chains in Nah 3.10 and 1QH^a xvi, 35. Jastrow, *Dictionary*, notes an interesting use of the participle in Song of Songs Rabbah 4.4, where the מתאימות that appear in Ct 4.2 and 6.6 are identified as chains of gold emerging from a breast plate and appearing to be 'conjoined', which perhaps preserves that sense of binding. The mysterious רתקות at Isa 40.19 is likewise associated with silver chains and רתוקות / רתיקות at 1 Kgs 6.21 with gold ones, so it is not difficult to suppose that a form of רתק might have been used of a 'silver rope', especially when the noun חבל can itself be used of cords that bind (cf. Job 36.8; Prov 5.22).

The problem is, of course, that 'the silver cord has not yet bound / been bound' leaves us with an image that is both obscure and out of step with the images of damage or destruction that are usually understood to follow. Accordingly, Gordis tries to argue that we may be dealing with a 'privative' niph'al that reverses the sense, so that the cord here would be 'severed', not 'joined' or 'bound'—a suggestion that would carry more weight if there were any substantial reason to suppose that a niph‘al could be used this way (Bruns, 'Eccles 12:6a', 428, accepts the suggestion, but prefers 'untied'). Seow, very differently, thinks that רתק should be understood in the sense 'knock', and that, correspondingly, the cord has been 'broken' or 'crushed' by a blow. The verb, however, never has such a general implication of destruction elsewhere, and is generally confined to the sense of knocking at doors or lashing out with one's fist, so at most we could understand 'while the silver cord has not yet been punched / knocked'—which does not seem to advance our understanding very much.

Seow attempts to bolster his interpretation by reference to the other ancient versions, and these do, indeed, complicate the matter. Most envisage the cord being cut or snapped: so σ' has καὶ πρὶν ἢ κοπῆναι τὸ σχοινίον τοῦ ἀργυρίου, 'and before the silver cord is cut', Hie, V *rumpatur*, 'broken apart', and S ܢܬܦܣܩ *ntpsq*, 'severed'. In fact, Hie, V, S rendered ינתק using these same verbs in 4.12, and it seems likely that they read that term here. On the other hand, G has ἀνατραπῇ, which literally means 'is overturned', although the verb had acquired a more general sense of destruction. Given the habits of the translator, it is hard to understand why, if he too had read ינתק, he would have chosen not to use the verb that he used in 4.12 (where he rendered ἀπορραγήσεται), but instead to adopt a different verb with a similar connotation.[33] Goldman thinks that ἀνατραπῇ is probably an interpretative rendering of ירחק, but it is more likely still that the translator actually read ירתק, and understood it to mean 'knock over', rather in the way that Seow does: it is interesting to note that MM cites a use of ἀνατρέπω for 'knocking down' a door. It is harder to say what lies behind T, which interprets allegorically in terms of one's tongue being dumb, but it may have in mind Job 40.25, where Leviathan's tongue is restrained with a חבל, and this favours ירתק, in the sense of 'binding'. In any case, the versions would seem to be split between ירתק and ינתק, with only the K*ethîbh* of M favouring ירחק.

Most modern commentators favour an emendation to ינתק, in line with σ', Hie, V, S, and this emendation is attractive, insofar as it gives a good sense. For that very reason, though, it must also be regarded with some caution: the readings of those versions, or their sources, are very easily explained as an assimilation to 4.12, while it is conversely rather hard to work out how ינתק might have given rise to the more difficult ירחק or ירתק (as is well demonstrated by Goldman's tenuous and complicated attempt at an explanation).[34]

---

[33] McNeile, 168, in fact, speculates that ἀνατραπῇ is a corruption of ἀναρραγῇ or ἀπορραγῇ, but there is no manuscript support for this, and ἀνατραπῇ is graphically distant from ἀπορραγῇ, in particular.

[34] Confusion between ר and נ is unusual because the characters are generally very different sizes, although that might count for less if the writing were cramped for some reason. Delitzsch, *Die Lese- und Schreibfehler*, 112 (§111), lists this among only a few instances where ר has plausibly displaced נ in the text of M. An

The context does not offer much help. There has been a great deal of speculation about the nature of the cord, and it is often seen in connection with the item that follows, as the cord from which a golden lamp is suspended, while Seow thinks that it is a branch or shoot on a lamp that is shaped like a tree. Nothing in the text itself, however, implies any particular connection with lighting, or demands that this silver cord be connected physically to whatever Qohelet is talking about in the next clause. The noun חבל itself is used both of ropes strong enough to hold a human (e.g. Josh 2.15; Jer 38.6) or drag down a wall (2 Sam 17.13) and of the presumably finer cords used to attach hangings and curtains (Esth 1.6)—although it is not used of threads, and this is probably not an image of extreme fragility. In a number of places חבל is used not only of ropes that bind, but apparently of ropes or wires that trap, and in, e.g., Job 18.10; 2 Sam 22.6, a חבל is probably to be understood as a snare. There is, therefore, a wide range of potential references, even if it is unlikely that, in reality, the rather low tensile strength of silver would make it a practical material for the sort of purposes to which most ropes are put: unless the writer is thinking of a cord into which silver has merely been woven (cf. Exod 39.3), we must imagine either that the use here is simply metaphorical, or that the term is being applied to something like an item of jewellery or of decoration.

Were we to read ירתק and assume the former, Qohelet would probably be talking about a rope that is precious and somehow traps people (perhaps the lure of money, which is how Olympiodorus read it, or the constraints of financial responsibility), but that would seem out of place here. I think it likely, therefore, that he is talking about either the fastening (ירתק) or the breaking (ינתק) of something like a cord, necklace or bracelet, and that in either case the verb should be read as niph‘al. With all due caution, given the caveats expressed above, I have settled for ינתק in the translation, as it gives a sense more in line with the other verbs here, but the reading must remain uncertain.

12.6 the golden bauble been crushed] The meaning is again very uncertain, and I would not exclude the possibility that the verb refers to rolling (lit. 'running') away. The noun גלה is translated 'bowl' in the AV, and that translation has been used by most commentators since the seventeenth century, leading Henry James to use a literal 'golden bowl'—flawed and later symbolically smashed—in his novel of the same name. It is not, however, the understanding reflected in any of the ancient translations or adopted by the medieval Jewish commentators, and the evidence for any such sense is very thin. The translation rests principally on Zech 4.2-3, which speaks of a golden lampstand, one part of which is described as a גלה, and so potentially provides a parallel to the object mentioned here. That difficult passage, however, demands no more

alternative, rather easier emendation to יחרק, is favoured by, e.g., Hitzig, but that verb is used only of gnashing teeth in biblical Hebrew, and a resort to Arabic for a sense of cutting or tearing seems a little desperate.

than that the גלה be something set at the top of the lampstand: it is not clearly a functional component of the lamp itself, and the idea that it is a bowl derives mainly from speculative reconstructions of the lampstand.[35]

May, 'Two Pillars', includes as figure 10 one such reconstruction by Galling, which sets the lamps themselves around the edge of a large bowl. May himself offers illustrations of several bowl-shaped capitals and pillar-stands, which seem to fit well with another use of גלה, to describe part of the capital of a pillar in 1 Kgs 7.41-42 = 2 Chr 4.12-13 (in 2 Kgs 25.17, each capital is itself decorated with the lattice-work and bronze pomegranates, which are said here to decorate the גלה, suggesting that the גלה is the main part of the capital). This seems compatible with Zech 4, to the extent that the גלה in each passage is something that sits on top of a pillar or a stand. It is clearly possible, furthermore, that גלה could mean 'bowl' in both places. It is less clear, however, that we are *required* to think in terms of bowls: it is only the presupposition that גלה means 'bowl' that leads to the identification of bowl-shaped elements with that term. If the word גלה itself, furthermore, is related to words like גליל and גלגל, then a גלה is likely to have been round, but not necessarily bowl-shaped.

The single other use of the Hebrew word, in Judg 1.15 and Josh 15.19, is in relation to an upper and lower גלה, described as גלת מים: the terms are possibly place-names, and גלה in this context seems to indicate some sort of water-source or geological feature associated with water. This is not a usage found elsewhere, and it may have been specific to this location, but it forms the basis for the understanding of Rashi and other medieval Jewish exegetes, following *b. Šabbat* 152b, that the noun here refers to a spring or cistern, so by extension to the penis. In short, the limited biblical usage of גלה nowhere includes a clear reference to a 'bowl', in the sense of a container made to hold

---

[35] The traditional depiction of the lamp in Zechariah has been of lamps fed by oil contained in the גלה *via* pipes. Setting aside the practicalities of such a contrivance, there is no particular reason to suppose that the מוצקות are pipes, rather than some other sort of moulded fitting for the lamps. The main problem is a plethora of suffix pronouns in 4.2. If the גלה is on top of the מנורה (על ראשה), then it is difficult to see how the lamps are also subsequently on top of the מנורה (על ראשה), suggesting that in the second use, the pronoun refers back not to the מנורה but to the גלה itself. In that case, the same is probably true of the pronoun on עליה, and we are supposed to think of the lamps as set on top of the גלה, which is in turn set on top of the מנורה. In any case, despite the apparent allusion, it is difficult to reconcile the description with the traditional branched menorah of the tabernacle and the later Jerusalem Temple, unless we take the מוצקות to be equivalent to branches, and set in the top of the גלה (making it a sort of raised base). For what it is worth, the image of the menorah on the Arch of Titus shows the seven stems on top of a short column, which itself stands on the base of the lampstand, and all or part of this column could fit the description of the גלה in Zechariah: the shape is hard to describe, but it is rounded in several ways, without being at all bowl-like.

liquid, but suggests that the term was used in a restricted, perhaps technical way, of (possibly bowl-shaped or otherwise rounded) features found typically at the top of a stand or column, to which decorative or other items might be attached, and perhaps also of natural features regarded as analogous.

In later Hebrew and Aramaic, Leviticus Rabbah 32.8 offers interpretations of the גלה in Zech 4.2-3 in terms of similar words for 'an exile' and 'a redeemer' (cf. Qohelet Rabbah at 4.1), while Targum Jonathan uses גולחא to render it—a term used elsewhere for a type of cloak, but here perhaps just an imitation of the Hebrew. There is no evidence, however, for any general use of the term to mean 'bowl', and, as we shall see shortly, the early translators seem not to have understood it in this or any other single sense.[36] It is a reasonable supposition that the term had fallen out of use within a few centuries of Ecclesiastes being written, and was no longer understood. Moving beyond Hebrew, and much further back, the golden *gl* that appears in Ugaritic in KTU 1.14 II 19 and IV 2 does appear to have been a container of some sort, from which wine was to be poured out for libations: it might be a bowl, although we should really expect a drinking-horn or rhyton to be used for that purpose. If we wander even further afield, the Old Babylonian *gullu* ('bowl' according to *HALOT*) is similarly listed by *CAD* simply as '(a container)'. There is, however, an interesting term *gullatu*, which is used in Assyrian of pillar-bases, but which appears in a rather different context on an Old Babylonian text, as some sort of golden decorative element on a gold jug and on the plaque of a necklace; these elements can include precious stones, and are perhaps some sort of mounting. The relevance of these potential cognate nouns is questionable, of course, but they serve to highlight the uncertainty that surrounds, and has clearly long surrounded, the meaning of the Hebrew noun.

This uncertainty is compounded by the ambiguity of the verb ותרץ, which can be derived either from רוץ, 'run', or from רצץ, 'oppress' / 'break'. It is not very surprising to discover, therefore, that the ancient versions have come up with a striking variety of different interpretations. Perhaps the most imaginative is that of θ' καὶ δράμῃ ἡ χελώνη ἡ χρυσῆ, 'and the golden tortoise run' (cf. Hos 12.12, where גלים is rendered by χελῶναι: although the sense is not attested outside Syriac, גלא / גל had probably come to mean 'tortoise' or 'turtle' more widely in Aramaic); on the problematic presentation of that citation in Syh, see the discussions by Euringer and Marshall. Jerome's rendering in Hie and V comes a close second, though: *et recurrat uitta aurea* means 'and the golden ribbon run back'—the *uitta* is literally a headband (or 'fillet') worn by poets and others, which Jerome here associates with the soul fleeing upon death (cf. Codex Graecus Venetus στέφος, 'garland'). He has perhaps linked

---

[36] The claim by Schoors, that 'גלה denotes a bowl in Rabbinic Hebrew', cites Jastrow, *Dictionary*, but Jastrow notes only the use in Leviticus Rabbah, and his gloss, 'cup, bowl', is simply a reflection of the way Zechariah is usually translated, not attestation of a later usage.

גלה with גלגלת, 'skull', as has T with its reference to מוקרא דרישך, 'the cranium of your head', becoming broken—although Bruns, 'Eccles 12:6a', 429, thinks that he may have been influenced by the G reading (on which see below). Marshall discusses the puzzling reference to Syh by Middeldorpf, cited in Field, but the reading of α' is not in any real doubt: καὶ δράμῃ λύτρωσις τοῦ χρυσίου. It is harder to say, however, what this is actually supposed to mean.[37] Symmachus has the interesting καὶ θλασθῇ τὸ περιφερές, 'and the spherical thing been crushed', presumably thinking in terms of a golden ball or sphere (and probably of גלל, 'roll'), while S ܘܢܫܬܚܩ ܚܙܘܪ ܕܕܗܒܐ *wnšthq ḥzwr dhb'* could be understood in similar terms as 'and the golden apple / round knob crushed'—although the noun is used in the Syriac version to render הכפתור at Amos 9.1, and the translator here could similarly be thinking in terms of pillars. Finally, G καὶ συνθλιβῇ ἀνθέμιον τοῦ χρυσίου, 'and the flowerlet of gold been dented', probably understands גלה in terms of ornamentation: ἀνθέμιον is a diminutive of ἄνθος, 'flower', and is used of floral patterns or decorations.[38] There is little to commend the suggestion of Bruns, 'Eccles 12:6a', 429, that because a crater decorated with flowers is found in book 24 of the *Odyssey*, the translator must have been talking about such a mixing bowl here.

In the cases of σ', S, and G, there is at least some plausibility, although it is hard to say whether any is based on a confident understanding of the Hebrew rather than on extrapolation from other uses of the noun or on etymological speculation. To that extent, the specificity of G's ἀνθέμιον tells in its favour, although that noun can be used of decoration on pillars and the translator might simply be thinking of 1 Kgs 7.41-42.

---

[37] The noun λύτρωσις is used of redeeming a pledge or of release from an obligation, and Marshall supposes that Aquila has simply confused גלה with גאלה, which has much the same meaning as the Greek word; this would then perhaps be some sort of re-purchase of, or using, gold, but it is hard to see how he would believe that such a transaction could 'run'. The Greek noun is used in the Septuagint, however, to render גלה in Judg 1.15, presumably on the basis of just such a confusion. Typically, LSJ takes this to suggest that the noun might mean 'spring of water' in Greek, which it does not, but Aquila has probably borrowed the translation from this other passage to reflect the Hebrew, even though it results in the nonsensical 'and a redemption of gold has run'.

[38] As Caird, 'Towards a Lexicon I', 459-60, points out, there is no justification for the translation proposed in LSJ, 'the purest quality' (of gold), but it is possible, he suggests, that the translator of G means to talk about the attractiveness of wealth wearing off. LSJ does usefully cite an identification of the verb συνθλίβω with συνεπτυγμένον, suggesting that it could be understood in terms of metal being dented. Aitken, 'Rhetoric and Poetry', 62-63, notes how the different verbs in the verse have been coordinated by the use of compound forms with συν-, which may have influenced the choice.

As for the verb, M points וְתָרֻץ as if from רוּץ, and it has been understood that way also by α', θ', Hie, V. It really is difficult, however, to find any meaning for גלת הזהב that could allow it to act as the subject of a verb meaning 'run' or 'rush'—unless we are to go with Theodotion's tortoise, or, with rather more plausibility, to envisage Symmachus' ball rolling away, rather than being crushed. We are probably dealing rather with a form from רצץ, but the scope of that verb is more limited than sometimes assumed. It is twice used of crushing heads, once in the hiph'il (Judg 9.53) and once in the pi'el (Ps 74.14), and it is also used of breaking/broken reeds (qal 2 Kgs 18.21 = Isa 36.6; Isa 42.3; niph'al Ezek 29.7). In Gen 25.22, the hitpo'al is used of twins struggling while pressed together in the womb, and in Isa 42.4 (probably to be read as niph'al) the sense is probably of breaking under pressure. These particular uses, however, are entirely congruent with the most common sense of the verb, which is to mistreat or oppress somebody from a position of power over them: if there is one basic implication, it is of doing harm by (literally or figuratively) bringing down a heavy weight on someone or something—in Isa 58.6, indeed, the verb is used specifically of those who are yoked. רצץ does not have a general meaning of breaking or destroying, therefore, but a more particular sense of crushing, bending, or squashing, and whatever the גלת הזהב may be, it is something that must be capable either of exerting or of receiving such pressure.[39]

It might be possible to think in terms of a golden capstone that weighs down on somebody (rather as a silver rope might trap them), but, again, it is difficult to think of any significance for such an image that would suit the current context. I am inclined instead to believe that the first two images in this verse are about damage to items of decoration or jewellery, that the verb should be read as a niph'al תֵּרַץ (so, e.g., *BHQ*), and that σ', S, T, and especially G are probably all in roughly the right area when it comes to the sense of גלה here.

12.6 a pitcher been shattered at the spring] The noun מבוע appears elsewhere in the Bible only at Isa 35.7; 49.10, where it refers to water-sources in the wilderness, and it is not common in later Hebrew outside references to the biblical texts. It is used more widely in Aramaic, but there too seems generally to refer to springs rather than wells (inasmuch as the two can be distinguished). A כד (on the lack of determination here, see the next note) is a pitcher or pot, characteristically but not exclusively used for water, and the noun appears numerous times in Gen 24, where women are depicted as filling their כד at a spring and then carrying it on their shoulder. We need not assume that the pitcher has been broken specifically by dropping it on the spring itself

---

[39] Of course, this makes it difficult to sustain the image favoured by some commentators, of a golden lamp-bowl, which falls when the silver cord from which it is suspended snaps. If a metal bowl sustained any damage at all from such a fall, it would not in any meaningful way be 'crushed'.

(as Fox suggests): על is commonly used to designate a position beside water (as, indeed, at Gen 24.30). On the other hand, the specification would seem to exclude any idea that the pitcher has been smashed deliberately as part of a funerary rite, which is an idea pursued at some length by Seow; we have no reason to believe that such rites would have been carried out at springs, if they were carried out at all.

σ' here has καὶ συνθραυσθῇ, 'and pulverized' (Symmachus is perhaps making a connection with the subsequent reference to dust). Marshall thinks that α' and θ' probably used the same συντριβῇ, 'shattered', as G, but this may have been their reading in the next clause (see the footnote below).

12.6 and the windlass spun free over the cistern] Lit. 'run' or 'rushed', rather than 'spun free'. גלגל is used elsewhere in biblical Hebrew of chariot wheels (e.g. Jer 47.3). It can have this sense in Aramaic as well (cf. Dan 7.9), but both in later Hebrew and in Aramaic the noun can be used much more widely of objects that rotate. Such usage makes it hard to accept the suggestion of Dahood, 'Canaanite-Phoenician', 216-17, and 'Phoenician-Punic Philology', 464, picked up by Seow, that it refers here to another sort of vessel: whatever the use of cognate nouns in Akkadian, and perhaps Phoenician (although Dahood's evidence for that is very thin), there is no evidence for such a sense in Hebrew, and no reason to suppose that any early reader understood גלגל that way. Besides, that understanding would make this image not merely analogous to the previous one, but a virtual duplicate of it, and the rest of the list shows no inclination toward such redundancy. To be sure, a בור is not the same as a מבוע, and the noun can refer to pits of various sorts, but these include cisterns that have been dug out to contain water (cf. Jer 2.13; 38.6), and a vessel broken at a בור would naturally be understood in such terms.

Even for the majority of commentators who take גלגל to mean 'wheel', however, the last image tends to provide a context for this one, and Qohelet is understood to be talking about a wheel that serves in some way as a mechanism at a well or cistern or in an irrigation system (cf. *m. Pe'ah* 5.3). On such an understanding, the reference is most likely to what Isidore in his *Etymologies* (20.15) was later to describe using the similar Latin word *girgillus*: a horizontal bar fixed above a well which could be wound to raise or lower a container or leather bag on a rope—in other words, a winch or windlass.[40]

---

[40] Isidore himself links the Latin word with *gyrus*, but it is almost certainly a Semitic loanword, as suggested by Klein, *Etymological Dictionary*, 99, and so related to גלגל. Ms 788 attests a reading τροχιλέα, a word which, variously spelled, is used of pulleys in, e.g., Aristotle, *Mechanica* 853 b, but also of the roller on a windlass (see LSJ). The less technical G τροχός is more typically a wheel of some sort, but probably does not exclude that idea. The slightly confusing observations on this passage from ms 788 are presented without comment by Gentry: (to πηγήν) οἱ ο' καὶ συντριβῇ τροχιλέα ἐπὶ τῷ λάκκῳ· τὸ γὰρ συντριβῇ ἡ

Seow's objection, that buckets were typically lowered directly by hand has limited force: the use of a גלגל for this purpose is plentifully attested in early Jewish sources (see, e.g., m. ʿErubin 10.4 [cf. b. ʿErubin 104a]; m. Middot 5.4; b. Yoma 19a; 37a), and although, doubtless, not all wells or cisterns were equipped in this way, there is no reason to suppose that such a mechanism would have been unfamiliar at the time Ecclesiastes was written.

It is harder to say, though, what is actually happening here to this or any other sort of גלגל. M presents the verb as ונרץ, a niphʿal form from רצץ (having read the previous ותרץ as from רוץ), and its qatal form is striking in a context where the other verbs are all yiqtol. If we read it with a conversive waw, which is the normal construal, it seems likely to indicate a relationship between the two events here: the pitcher shatters, *then* the גלגל is crushed. Alternatively, we might understand it as parenthetical and circumstantial: the pitcher shatters *when* or *because* the גלגל is broken. The reading of G is very different: συντροχάσῃ, lit. 'has run together', takes the verb as active and connects it with רוץ (after G has read the previous ותרץ as from רצץ). Both versions have probably been influenced by a perception that Qohelet would not simply have repeated the same verb (even if there is a certain resemblance between ותרץ גלח and הגלגל ונרץ), but there is no shift of tense in G, and the translator seems actually to have found וירץ in his source-text.[41] M here is supported by Hie and V, but G by S and T (which has the body 'running' to its grave), and both variants are probably early.

ὑδρία ἐπὶ τὴν πηγήν ἐκ τῶν Ἀκύ(λα) καὶ θ' then (to the remainder of the verse) οὗτος οὐ κεῖται παρὰ τοῖς λοιποῖς. Since συντριβῇ ἡ ὑδρία ἐπὶ τὴν πηγήν is from G, what we can glean from these is apparently that a direct equivalent to this reading was absent from the texts of α' and θ', and that καὶ συντριβῇ τροχιλέα ἐπὶ τῷ λάκκῳ, 'and a pulley is shattered above the cistern', stands in its place. Evidence from the Catena Hauniensis had already suggested that α' and/or θ' read συντριβῇ, and associated this reading with G συντροχάσῃ (which Marshall took to be a misplacement). The second observation seems to affirm that the rest of the verse was not to be found in the texts of the Three, but, if I have understood this correctly, we would probably say rather that this second member of the pair seems to have displaced the first, at least in whatever tradition lies behind the catenist's observations. In any case, on this evidence, τροχιλέα would appear to be α' and/ or θ'.

[41] The variant συντριβῇ which McNeile, 152, notes, is probably not an equivalent for נרץ, but a simple repetition of the preceding verb (which may reflect hexaplaric influence—see the previous footnote). Aitken, 'Rhetoric and Poetry', 63, as well as noting the coordination of the verbs by the use of compounds with συν, comments on the *figura etymologica* in συντροχάσῃ ὁ τροχὸς, which tends to support the originality of that reading. He also observes, more speculatively, that 'the rhythm of the wheel rolling along is recalled in the very sound of the words themselves', but we should note that Jerome understands G to mean that the wheel is *in suo funiculo conuoluta*, 'tangled in its own rope'.

The G reading of the verb, which is preferred by Goldman, is less likely than that of M to have been motivated by any particular understanding of the context, and I have adopted it in my own translation, so that the image is not of the גלגל being crushed or snapped at the cistern, but of it running or rushing. The text could sustain an idea that Qohelet is talking about a wheel rolling or driven into a pit, but it seems more likely that we are supposed to envisage a winch spinning rapidly, without restraint. Precisely what it is doing depends in part on how we read the subsequent preposition, however, and here there is again a difference between M and G. In the latter, ἐπὶ (cf. Hie, V *super*, S ܠ *ʿl*), reflecting על, might simply be the result of assimilation to the previous preposition (probably in its source-text, but possibly during the transmission of G),[42] and that possibility makes M אל marginally the easier reading to defend. Whether אל also fits better with our reading of the verb as from רוץ— since things are more likely to rush 'towards' something than 'above' or 'over' it—depends on our understanding of what is being described.

In that respect, it is striking that כד is the only undetermined noun in this series, and the absence of an article is reflected in G* also (although the noun has acquired one in most manuscripts). The effect of this is to align הגלגל but not כד with the items that precede and follow, and, even if we have rejected M's verb, with its implication of a connection, it is tempting to suggest that this discrepancy was intended to subordinate one clause to the other. If the clauses were quite separate, furthermore, then this would be the only element in the list that certainly involves no explicit destruction: the rolling of a wheel or spinning of a windlass might well be evocative of descent at death—and Goldman sees a play on the common use of בור as an equivalent of Sheol— but both seem substantially different from the other images. Neither of these considerations is determinative, but they both make it very possible that we are dealing with, in essence, a single image. If הגלגל is indeed a windlass, then its 'running' could be understood as the cause or the consequence of a pitcher shattering, if that pitcher were attached to it: either the windlass has been released prematurely, and spins as the heavy pitcher plunges, or the pitcher has broken before being lifted, so that the windlass spins freely as it is turned, with no weight to constrain it. The order of clauses favours the latter (which would in turn support the על reflected in G), and that image also offers an analogy to what will follow—the departure in different directions of the dust and the liberated breath—but I have tried to keep all the possibilities as open as I can in my translation.

---

[42] Ginsburg, *Writings*, presents על הבור...על האלהים as a Masoretic *Sᵉbîr* (see the note on 'when' at 4.17 for the significance of the term), which tells against reading על in both places, but also suggests that some people may have done. If ἐπὶ τῷ λάκκῳ is indeed α' and/or θ' (see above), then this reading offers further evidence of a Hebrew variant with על.

12.7 then the dust returns] M points the verb as jussive, but unless we want to impart a jussive sense to the following תשוב as well, we should probably not assume that the Masoretes were consciously trying to give a sense 'let the dust return', even if that would give a very interesting reading. *BHS* would point it instead as וַיָּשָׁב, but such anomalous vocalizations are not uncommon (see GKC §109 k; J-M §114 l), even if they are difficult to explain. Delitzsch's idea that we are in some sense dealing with a subjunctive is rejected by Schoors (The Preacher I, 89), who wonders (28) whether the vocalization might simply be for consonance with the preceding verb. Interestingly, though, many Greek manuscripts at this point break the sequence of subjunctives governed by ἕως ὅτου μή, 'until not', using an indicative ἐπιστρέψει, 'will return', and Gentry, 'Hexaplaric Materials', 22-23, argues that this was the reading of the Three.[43] We should probably understand this reading as 'when the silver cord has not yet been broken...then the dust returns to the earth', which is essentially the understanding that I have adopted in my own translation, and it is possible that the Masoretic vocalization is trying similarly to mark a break in the sequence.

On the face of it, the structure of the text here tells against any such reading. After the first verb in 12.6, the clauses in 12.6-7 are all simply linked by -ו, and it seems that they should all stand in parallel. We have already seen, however, that the last clause in 12.6 is plausibly to be construed specifically in relation to the clause before it, and involves an irregularity in the determination of the nouns; there is further disruption ahead in the next clause, where the subject, for no necessary reason, will precede the verb for the first time, and itself receive the conjunction. The clauses are usually translated in a way that obscures these variations, but they make it hard to sustain any claim that the very regularity of the sequence obliges us to read each clause in the same way. Accordingly, I understand the conjunction here to be, in effect, a 'waw of apodosis' (cf. J-M §176), and if the Masoretic pointing reflects a similar distinction, then the jussive might be compared to that at the start of Mic 7.10, where a series of clauses in 7.9 governed by עד אשר, '(I shall tolerate) *until* (these things happen)', are followed by -ו and a jussive, marking a switch

---

[43] Gentry's argument rests not on a direct attestation, but on the fact that the marginal note in Syh must originally have reflected a distinction between the Three and Origen's text (not an agreement, as Field supposes). Matters are complicated, of course, by the possibility that the different forms of the verb in the manuscripts are merely orthographic variants, but there are many fewer variants with -ει for the first three subjunctives in 12.6. The Syh note does not address the second occurrence of ἐπιστρέψῃ, but it would be logical to suppose that the Three had the indicative here also, and that reading is, again, widely attested in the G tradition. It should be noted that some of the same witnesses have an indicative for the previous συντροχάσῃ as well; this seems more likely to be a consequence of confusion caused by the verbs that follow.

within the sequence to what will *then* happen once the condition has been fulfilled. In that case, the understanding behind M is probably 'be mindful while these things have not happened; then the dust will return...', with 12.7 referring to a point beyond the situation outlined symbolically in the preceding verses.

12.7 to the ground] G and T seem to support M^L על, but the Midrash Zuta and many later Hebrew manuscripts have אל, which was probably read by S also; see Kennicott, Ginsburg, *Writings*. The *in* of Hie, V is found in several citations of the passage by Augustine,[44] and has probably been taken by Jerome from La: it is doubtful, therefore, that it too can be treated as a direct witness to אל, as assumed by de Rossi. The two prepositions can be used without much distinction in later Hebrew, and not too much should be made of the difference, but it seems likely that the reading אל הארץ is a secondary assimilation to the following אל האלהים. If so, and if we do wish to find a distinction, then the use of על perhaps implies an image not of burial, so much as of dust settling on the surface of the ground.

It is more puzzling that in both Hie and V Jerome has *terram suam*, 'its ground', as though he were reading a suffix pronoun on אר־ץ, but this may just be interpretative: he is keen to make the point that bodies are made from dust by God, not created out of the bodies of parents.

12.7 gave] G has ἔδωκεν, 'gave', with no attested variants, but according to Gentry, ms 788 cites the plural ἔδωκαν as the reading of α', and ἔκτισεν, 'created', as the Septuagint reading. The readings seem likely to be confused (and 788 sometimes elsewhere swaps the Septuagint with the hexaplaric reading), but neither seems plausible in the context as it stands: ἔκτισεν may have originated as a theological gloss or a recollection of Amos 4.13, and ἔδωκαν simply as an error.

12.8 the Qohelet] On the determination of the epithet 'Qohelet' (which is reflected also in G), see the notes to 1.1. M had simply קהלת in 1.2, but most manuscripts have הקוהלת here: de Rossi notes two which have אמרה קהלת, cf. 7.27. The reading of α' is preserved in its entirety in Greek, and notably includes a transliteration of the word: ἀτμὸς ἀτμίδων εἶπεν κωελέθ τὰ πάντα ἀτμός. As in 1.1, Aquila clearly treats 'Qohelet' as a name, although the transliteration preserved for that verse is κωλέθ.

---

[44] *De Genesi ad Litteram* 10:9, *et conuertatur puluis in terram sicut fuit et spiritus reuertatur ad deum qui dedit eum* (CSEL 28.1, p. 305); *Epistulae* 166.9.26, *tunc conuertetur in terram puluis sicut fuit et spiritus reuertetur ad dominum qui dedit illum* (CSEL 44, 581); *Epistulae* 190.5.17, *et reuertetur puluis in terram sicut erat et spiritus reuertetur ad deum qui dedit eum* (CSEL 57, 152). Vaccari, 'Recupero', 117, thinks that these are all derived from Jerome's revision of the La, although there are obviously significant differences between them. Cassian *Collationes* viii, 25, which alludes indirectly to this passage, has *ad terram*.

12.8 It is all an illusion] In G, Hie, V, T, α', and most manuscripts of M, the declaration is shorter than in 1.2, lacking the repetition of הבל הבלים before הכל הבל. The words are repeated here in S and in some Hebrew manuscripts (see de Rossi), but that is probably an assimilation to the earlier verse.

12.9-14

Epilogue

(12.9) And something else which happened: Qohelet, a wise man, further taught the people knowledge, and he listened and examined. He perfected a great many sayings: (12.10) Qohelet tried to find words that would be valued, and a blunt writing of words that convey truth.

(12.11) The words of wise men are like goads, and like embedded spikes. Drivers have been presented from a single shepherd, (12.12) and beyond them, my son, be careful: there is much working on books without end, and much study is a wearying of the flesh.

(12.13) An end of speaking: all has been heard. Fear God and keep his commandments, for this is everything for the human: (12.14) that for everything they have done, God will demand a reckoning—even of everything unseen—whether good or bad.

Commentary

The relationship between the monologue and this epilogue (or perhaps 'afterword') was discussed in the Introduction (esp. pp. 37-39). In line with a number of recent commentators, I take these verses to be part of the original composition, and not an addition, or series of additions, to the book (which is how they were usually understood by the previous generation of commentators: Lavoie, 'Qohélet 12,11', 131-33, offers a handy summary of the many ways in which they have been subdivided and assigned to various hands). They begin by talking about Qohelet in the third person, however, and it is not his voice that we now hear. Indeed, while praising Qohelet, they also somewhat bury him: where the monologue presented itself as embodying the personal experiences, reflections and emotional reactions of that character, the epilogue talks of it as the intentionally painful work of a clever writer, and warns of reading too many such books. The very first thing we are told is that Qohelet was 'wise', or 'a wise man', and this is used to align his work with a more familiar, literary concept, 'the words of wise men'. Essentially, the fiction of the monologue is discarded, and Qohelet re-invented (or revealed) as a writer—a fact the epilogue feels should be advertised, even though nothing had been said about it by Qohelet himself. The audience, furthermore, now find themselves compared implicitly with sheep or cattle, prodded by what they have heard as though they had been prodded with sharp sticks. They are also for the first time addressed as 'my son', which was an address used in much ancient literature that adopted a conventional self-presentation as parental instruction, but one that was avoided by Qohelet himself, even when he addressed himself specifically to the young in ch. 11.

All this marks a significant change in the relationship which the text seeks with that audience, and in the way that they are supposed to understand what they have heard up until this point. To be sure, it seems likely that the original audience would from the outset have understood Qohelet's account of his experiences and observations to be fictional, but by essentially ripping the curtain open at the end like this, and telling them that they have let themselves be pushed about, the epilogue seems positively to disown what has gone before: the audience should not take it too seriously, or wear themselves out over such works, and all they really need to do is fear and obey God.

Despite its very different tone, it is not clear, however, that the epilogue actually disagrees significantly with what Qohelet has been saying. There is much vocabulary shared between the monologue and epilogue, and Segal has recently suggested (95-96) that the epilogue habitually takes terms used by Qohelet and 'reapplies them': his list includes, in particular, expressions like (to use his translations) 'fear God' (5.6), 'any man' (5.18), 'abide by commands' (8.5), 'admonish' (4.13), 'hearing/obedience' (4.17), 'judgment' (3.17), 'call to judgment' (11.9), 'no end' (4.8, 16), and individual words such as 'wisdom', 'knowledge', 'word', 'weary', 'everything good', 'bad', and 'deed'. Obviously, such correspondences do not all carry the same weight, and it is the concentration of religious terminology in 12.13-14 that has most often led people to see something very different in the epilogue. It would certainly be wrong, nevertheless, to exaggerate any difference at this level. More importantly, as I have argued myself elsewhere (in 'Fear God'), there is little or nothing here that the Qohelet of the monologue would have found objectionable, although the character presented to us in that monologue would probably not himself have spoken directly in terms of obeying divine commandments, and would doubtless have included something on pleasure and activity if he were epitomizing his own message. It is important to be clear that I do not think the epilogue is intended to be read as a sort of key, or interpretative guide to the monologue, as, for example, Shead, 'Ecclesiastes from the Outside In', argues. It is not presented as such, and if anything, might itself be summarized as 'never mind all that hard stuff, just do this'. Equally, though, it offers no direct contradiction to the hard stuff, and arguments about whether it affirms or rejects the content of the monologue seem to be missing the point.

For all that commentators have tended to focus on its religious message, the most extraordinary aspect of this epilogue is surely, in fact, its re-characterization of Qohelet and of the book. There is no clear parallel to this elsewhere in biblical literature, although Hos 14.10 does have something in common (cf. also Sir 50.27-29). The effort to align the monologue with other literature has often been read, of course, in positive terms (so, e.g., Vignolo, 'La scrittura'): the important point, though, is that this is not at all the way the monologue presented itself. Against Qohelet's own self-portrait as a man in search of answers for himself, he is now described here as a composer, and perhaps a collector, of words and sayings that would be valued by others. He is also a teacher of knowledge, although it is not clear whether the epilogist is trying to suggest that he actively taught, rather than that his work informed those who encountered it. Qohelet himself, of course, came to be rather ambivalent towards the wisdom and knowledge that seem to be praised here, and it is possible that the epilogue is merely trying to characterize him as an author of 'wise' literature, rather than to claim that this is the nature and background of the monologue itself (although Backhaus, 'Der Weisheit letzter Schluß', believes that there is a deliberate attempt here to assert its place in the Solomonic corpus). It reveals its own ambivalence, however, when it starts to talk about 'the words of wise men'. This is an expression that Qohelet used in 9.17, but here it seems more clearly to have the sort of technical sense that we find in Prov 22.17, where it serves as a title or description for the sayings that follow: the epilogist is talking about a class of sayings or a type of literature with which Qohelet's monologue is aligned (we have just been reminded, of course, that Qohelet himself was 'wise'), and he implies that there are many such books.

The text as a whole presents numerous difficulties, leading to a great variety of translations (there is a helpful overview in Auwers, 'Problèmes'), and the imagery that is employed in 12.11 is especially problematic. The point there seems to be, though, that the author of each work like this book creates sayings that affect their audience in the way that goads or spikes used by drovers are intended to affect their sheep or cattle. We should be wary, the epilogist goes on to suggest, of subjecting ourselves to the words of more than the one such writer whose work has already now been encountered (or, in the terms of the imagery, to prods from the tools or drovers employed by more than the one shepherd). The implication is that such literature, whatever its benefits, is painful by design, and much study, correspondingly, is physically exhausting. This does not actively condemn the monologue or works like it, but it cautions strongly against them, and suggests that to engage with them—as the audience has just done—is voluntarily to submit to being disciplined like an animal. There may be a positive aspect to that (Boda, 'Speaking', 270, observes that 'this sort of painful guidance has a larger protective purpose'), but, if so, the personal benefits are not advertised here. All this lays the basis for the epilogue to declare, in effect, that there has been enough talking (*dbr*), and to offer its own, simpler advice. Even that declaration seems pointed, after it is Qoheleth and the wise to whom all the words (*dbrym*) have been attributed in 12.10-11.

When we reach the end of Qohelet's account, then, we are reminded that it has actually been crafted by an expert in the manipulation of words, are told that we should not have enjoyed ourselves and would be better off avoiding too much engagement with such books, and are offered a less complicated recipe for life, expressed in rather different terms. We are also, arguably, insulted and patronized by an epilogist who is polite about Qohelet, but apparently unimpressed by the value of experiencing books like this. Even on the older view that the epilogue was added later to the book, perhaps in stages, this all seems very strange: by transmitting the book at all, the epilogist seems to encourage potential readers to ignore his own warnings about such books. If his views are more 'conventional' in some sense, moreover, why does he suggest not that Qohelet's opinions need revision or re-contextualization, but that any problems lie in their being painful and exhausting? If the epilogue is actually the work of the same author as the monologue, on the other hand, then it is no less strange, but it does at least seem explicable. In that case, as I suggested in the Introduction, we are dealing with something more like the 'parabasis' of Greek comedy, in which the storyline is suspended while the author addresses the audience in another voice, often with some commentary on the play. Classicists have argued about whether such devices break the 'dramatic illusion' (see, e.g., Bain, 'Audience Address in Greek Tragedy', 13), and it is far from clear that ancient audiences were expected to be gripped in the spell of a work. Equally, we should not overstate the extent to which even the dramatic closing lines of the monologue were expected to compel some belief in Qohelet's authenticity. With its polished sayings and its set-piece lists, the craftedness and essential artificiality of the monologue is on display throughout, so although we are invited to identify with Qohelet in his questing, it surely comes as no great surprise to be reminded that this is artifice. The suggestion that we have been prodded, perhaps even manipulated, is more brutal, but is dressed up in an imagery grotesque enough to soften the blow.

After the bleakness and drama of his final section, then, the author defuses the tension, and releases us from his work, by telling us, in a different voice, that his protagonist was really just one of many writers, and that we shouldn't take his words too much to heart. In doing so, however, he also seems to draw out a key lesson to be learned from the monologue: Qohelet's own engagement with the issues that he explored produced no positive answer to the question with which he began, caused him unhappiness at various points, and seems to have brought him little that he could not have had anyway. The monologue itself should hardly encourage us to follow his example, and, in this respect, the epilogue merely goes a little further: we have only pain to gain even from hearing about such things. This is hardly a serious warning—the author would not have written the book if he really believed it—but it is, according to one's taste, either the logical conclusion or a *reductio ad absurdum* of what has gone before.

12.9-10] The beginning of 12.9 is difficult, and has been understood in various ways. None is entirely satisfactory, but many commentators opt for a sense something like 'besides', marking a transition to the epilogue. I understand the point more specifically to be that the epilogue now tells us about something that Qohelet himself had failed to mention: his educational and literary activity—which may cause us, perhaps, to see him in a rather different light. The verse probably does not go on to portray Qohelet actually as a teacher of pupils or disciples, but talks in a very general way about 'the people' (which need not mean 'the nation' in particular, so should probably not be seen as a deliberate reference to Qohelet as King Solomon). The description seems to be of a man who passes on knowledge, but also sets out to acquire it through his interactions with others.

Although the general sense is clear, the details of what Qohelet is doing at the end of 12.9 and in 12.10 are again difficult to pin down, and it would be unwise to place too much weight on them as a picture of the way in which any ancient texts were actually created. Most probably, we are being told that he created and shaped his words out of things that he had seen and heard, polishing them so that they would attract admiration while also conveying truth. We should not extrapolate from this any idea that he was simply taking and arranging sayings from some existing corpus, although the text leaves open the possibility that he was not the originator of all that he wrote. What the epilogist clearly does not affirm here, however, is that Qohelet actually offers us the account of discoveries derived from explorations and experience which the monologue itself purports to be: 'listened and examined' would be the weakest of ways to describe that.

The writing to which Qohelet is said to have aspired is described here using the same word I translated in 7.29 as 'uncomplicated' (or at least a closely related one). Of course, anyone who has followed the text attentively up to this point might be entitled to express a little scepticism that Qohelet's words are characterized by some lack of complexity. It seems very possible, in fact, that the epilogue is being ironic, and perhaps deliberately mischaracterizing what has preceded, but if it is not, then some other nuance must be intended. The term is often used ethically of being 'upright', but that seems out of place as a description of the composition itself, while 'orderly' or 'in order', although favoured by some, has no basis at all in the usage elsewhere. We cannot be certain precisely what is being implied, but I consider it most likely that there is a connotation here of 'plain-speaking'. Seow, 'Beyond Them', 131-32, is right to reject the assumption that ancient readers were 'somehow suspicious of literary artistry', and I have myself remarked in another context that, 'Fine expression was inextricably linked with the presentation of truth in the ancient world, and beauty of language, not simple lucidity, was the goal of those texts that sought to embody some truth' (*Instruction and Imagery*, 60). Accordingly, we should not see some apologetic 'he wrote words that were fine but honest' in this (which is the understanding of the NEB, cited by Seow). The point is more probably not that Qohelet's words of truth are presented without complexity or sophistication, but that they are without compromise (and perhaps also, it is tempting to think, in a form closer to everyday speech than is most Hebrew literature). Correspondingly, I have gone with 'blunt'.

12.11-12] I take the epilogue to be saying here that the sort of discourse attributed to Qohelet is intentionally painful: now we have experienced the words of one writer, we should think twice before inflicting upon ourselves any more of the many books out there, and the physically exhausting study that goes with them. It presents the first part of this message, though, using imagery derived from the herding of cattle or sheep. Determining both the precise nature of this imagery, and the point at which it ends, has caused significant problems for interpretation of the passage.

Like many popular Victorian works on the Bible, *The People's Dictionary of the Bible*, edited by John Relly Beard and published in 1847, offered its readers insights into contemporary 'Oriental' life, and the anonymous writer of its article 'Goad' claimed to have lived in 'Eastern countries' for many years. He describes the typical grouping together of herds from one village or neighbourhood under the supervision of a head shepherd, who would direct the others, and the use of goads 'about three feet long, having a spike of iron at one or both ends, secured by iron ferrules': an illustration is supplied, and he notes also that most goads have been repaired at some point using nails, rather than their original spikes. Details in the account suggest that the writer had lived somewhat further east than Palestine, and his description, of course, is far from contemporary with Ecclesiastes, but it is not improbable that these are very much the sort of practices and implements that lie behind the imagery here. The article closes with an attempt to elucidate 12.11 in such terms: 'The words of the wise are as goads and as the nails fastened therein by the masters (or head herd-men) of assemblies of cattle, which are given (or distributed) by one of the shepherds'. My own understanding differs in a few respects, but is along very much the same lines: the epilogue envisages the words of the wise as like the sharp prods used to drive animals by a herdsman and his subordinates.

Interpretations of this imagery, however, have been influenced over the centuries both by confusion over the meaning of the term I have translated 'drivers' (an inelegant rendering that attempts to cover the possibility of their being either people or implements), and by attempts to see in the 'single shepherd' a reference to God. The former is discussed at length in the notes: the Hebrew expression, not found elsewhere, refers to people or things characterized by their relationship to flocks, assemblies, or collections of some sort. Scholars have often tried to find a parallel with the 'words of the wise', and identified them as parts of sayings-collections, or as the creators of such collections: that is awkward, and I think they are more probably to be associated with the goads and spikes—but no translation can be offered with any great confidence. Identifications of the shepherd with God are motivated by the use of such imagery elsewhere in the Bible (most famously Ps 23), and other uses of the imagery have sometimes led scholars to think alternatively in terms of particular kings or other individuals. This approach has played less of a role in recent studies (although it is still maintained by, e.g., Bartholomew), but it pushes interpretations in a particular direction, turning the statements here into a more general claim about inspiration, canonicity, or authorship. Where I take the epilogist to be warning against inflicting upon oneself the sharp prods of more than one author, the Midrash, for example, sees a warning against using non-canonical books. Whether such a claim seems appropriate at this point cannot be disconnected from broader understandings of the epilogue's nature and history, but there is also a question of tone involved: on such readings, 'approved' or 'inspired' literature is being characterized in what seems an extraordinary way.

More generally, indeed, many commentators have been inclined to reject or play down the negative implications of the shepherding imagery here, which is clearly a long way from the psalmist's making to lie down in green pastures. It is difficult, though, to reconcile any entirely positive reading of 12.11 with the warning in 12.12, and if the words of the wise are actually being commended by talking about them as prods and spikes, then that commendation is at best double-edged. No actual benefits are ascribed to reading them, while it is implied or even stated that they will bring pain and physical exhaustion. It seems perverse and eisegetical to claim, therefore, as does Gordis, that the epilogue here 'pays tribute to the stimulation ("goads") afforded by the writings of the "Wise" and the firm support ("fixed nails") that they give to human life'. I doubt that is how sheep or cattle feel about getting poked. There is also implicit in this imagery an unflattering, if playful, identification of human education with the rearing of animals (a point made by Lavoie, 'Qohélet 12,11', 149, who draws links with 3.18-21, as well as with 7.26; and 9.11-12). Even in a world where corporal punishment was a norm, most humans would not expect to be prodded with sharp-pointed instruments.

I think it is doubtful that education, as such, is really the issue here anyway—at least in any formal sense. 'My son', which is used suddenly in 12.12, is quite commonly described as a way that teachers spoke to their pupils or disciples (so, e.g., Lohfink, 'Les épilogues', 91), and taken sometimes, accordingly, as evidence that the epilogue must be the product of an educational environment. This is an idea based on a rather complicated assumption, that when 'my son' appears frequently in Proverbs 1–9, or occasionally in the later chapters of Proverbs, and in some of the instructional literature from other countries that bears comparison with Proverbs, we are hearing a sort of coded language, in which teacher/pupil interactions are being depicted as parent/child. That is to put things the wrong way round. Such literature adopts a conventional presentation of its content as teaching passed down from one generation to the next, typically from father to son, and to the extent that teachers might have used such literature at all, they merely got to play the role of the parent in any reading out of it to their students. I shall not repeat the point I have made often elsewhere, that the texts concerned were rarely designed for specifically pedagogical use, but it is important to be aware, anyway, that the father/son language is a literary convention, sometimes developed far beyond mere parental address (as in Prov 4), and that there is little or no evidence to suggest teaching was more generally understood or described in terms of a parental relationship. Teachers were not 'fathers' because they were teachers, nor pupils 'children' (even if education may often have been within the household). When 'my son' is used here, therefore, it is as an apparent allusion to, or borrowing from, a famous style of didactic literature, not an incidental revelation that the epilogue was written by a schoolmaster. There is probably another allusion to such literature in the use of 'the words of wise men', which appeared earlier in 9.17 (a fact that Lavoie, 'Qohélet 12,11', 135, takes to exclude any technical use here), but is found also in Prov 1.6, referring to compositions, and in Prov 22.17, as part of the prologue to a collection of admonitions (cf. Prov 24.23 also). By using these expressions together here, in the context of a warning against didactic literature, the epilogue is perhaps being satirical, and deliberately speaking like exactly the sort of work it is concerned about. 'My son' also, of course, asserts a relationship between speaker and audience that seems very different from that implied by Qohelet's own, more confessional tone.

12.13-14] 'This is everything for the human' could also be read 'this is every human', but in any case, the conciseness of the expression has long led to problems. Some word or concept clearly has to be understood, and many commentators have opted to suppose that the preceding commands represent 'the whole duty of humans'. With some others, I take the expression instead with what follows: judgment, with respect to their every deed, constitutes the totality of what humans can know or expect, and should motivate them to fear and obedience of God. The subsequent 'everything unseen' probably refers not simply to actions that humans have tried to conceal, but to the invisible dimensions of every action: God will be able to assess them with an insight that humans do not possess.

Of course, Qohelet himself previously commended fear of God (cf. 5.6; 7.18; 8.12-13), and always maintained the reality of divine judgment, however uncomfortably it sat with his determinism. The epilogist is saying nothing about those things that Qohelet could not have said himself. The idea of obedience to commands, on the other hand, only appears in 8.5, where the immediate context is not explicitly religious (although I think there is an implicit reference to God). Especially if we think of 'commandments' here, and of a reference to the Jewish law in particular (cf. Lange, 'Eschatological Wisdom', 819; Dunham, 'Intertextual Links', 40-41, sees more precisely a 'literary allusion' to Deut 13.4), then this strays into an area outside the scope of Qohelet's own discourse. It is hard to say whether that concept—even if mediated *via* the re-interpretation of law in Proverbs 1–9 (as suggested by Wilson, 'The Words of the Wise'; cf., more generally, Cox, 'When Torah Embraced'), or the similar ideas in Ben Sira and Baruch (noted by Sheppard, 'The Epilogue', but see Gilbert, 'Qohelet et Ben Sira', 162-71, and the response in Lohfink, 'Quintessenz')—could actually find any place in the worldview attributed to Qohelet. It would certainly sit uncomfortably, though, with his broader presentation of a universal message, and, even understood more generally, with his tendency to emphasize the distance between God and humans.

In this respect, the epilogist steps beyond what Qohelet himself would say, and perhaps translates his concepts into a more specifically Jewish context. If the epilogue actually were secondary, and late enough, we might even suppose that he places them in a canonical context, as Sheppard argues (a view that is strongly contested by Lavoie, 'Qohélet 12,12', which discusses the many variations on this idea). He does not, however, actively contradict the implications of Qohelet's own ideas, and the reference to judgment is even reminiscent of 11.9. As observed above, this is probably not the way that Qohelet himself would have been portrayed summarizing his own words, and there is notably no reference either to finding pleasure in life, which is an inference that Qohelet draws on many occasions, or to the concerns around 'vapour' which were prominent in much of the monologue. We are dealing here, however, not so much with a misrepresentation of his message as with a very selective and simplified representation, which arguably makes it sound closer to the ideas of, say, Deuteronomy, than it actually is.

It is this, in particular, that has encouraged many commentators to think in terms of the epilogue, or these verses at least, putting a consciously orthodox gloss on the book's message, as a secondary attempt to make it more acceptable to a certain audience. Whether any readers would actually have been persuaded by this to overlook all that had gone before is questionable, of course. It is also far from certain that Qohelet's own words would have been found so radical or objectionable by such readers as is often presumed, and where the nature of early disputes about the book is actually specified, there is no indication that some perceived lack of orthodoxy lay behind them. I doubt, therefore, that we can legitimately use the distinctions between Qohelet and the epilogist here as an argument for the secondary character of the epilogue. They are more important, perhaps, as a guide to the author's characterization of this epilogist, in contrast to Qohelet, as impatient with complexity or discomfort, and happy to leap on the simple and conventional. 'That's enough books and enough talking!', he tells us—before confidently declaring the only, rather uncomplicated thing that people need to worry about. We are probably no more supposed to warm to this rejection of anything hard than to Qohelet's own materialism and anxiety, but it offers a sharp contrast, and a very different tone with which to close the proceedings.

Notes

12.9 And something else...taught] As observed in the note at 2.15, the book uses יֹ(ו)תר with various implications, but generally with some connotation of superfluity, excess or advantage. This sense will be apparent in 12.12, where ויתר מהמה can be understood to mean 'and beyond these', but here in 12.9 matters are complicated by the use of -ש directly after יתר. I take this to be serving as a relative pronoun, but it has commonly been understood to substantivize the following clause (as in, e.g., 5.4; 7.18), with Qohelet taken as the subject of היה.

Taking that approach, Gordis draws attention to some rabbinic uses of יותר with a following ממה and -ש which have the sense 'and more than the fact that': these lead him to understand the point here to be that Qohelet was not just wise, but also taught the people knowledge—literally, 'more than (or, beside the fact that) Koheleth was a sage, he also taught the people knowledge' (so similarly Lavoie, 'Un éloge', 146, 148, 'Qohélet fut plus qu'un philosophe', 'Qohelet was more than a philosopher'). It is difficult to sustain any strict analogy with that later usage, however, in the absence of a מן here, and, as Schoors points out (*The Preacher* I, 138-39), the passages that Gordis cites are comparative, and do not convey the additive sense that he wants, of going beyond one thing to another.[1] Nevertheless, this may be how the difficult G

---

[1] So in *b. Yebamot* 113a יותר משהאיש רוצה לישא האשה רוצה להנשא (cf. *b. Ketubbot* 86a, *b. Giṭṭin* 49b which have ממה שהאיש), the point is not that a woman wants to be married *as well as* a man wanting to marry, but that she wants it *more* or *even more*. Conversely, Lohfink, 'Zu einigen Satzeröffnungen', 136-37, suggests that the preposition might be merely an instance of a later tendency to multiply prepositions, so that the construction in our verse could be treated as equivalent, but the מן is surely crucial to the expression of the comparative, and it is far from clear that ש- יתר could mean 'more (than)', as he would like; cf. Seow, 'Beyond Them', 128.

καὶ περισσὸν ὅτι ἐγένετο Ἐκκλησιαστὴς σοφός took the Hebrew, if we understand the Greek to mean 'and beyond (the fact) that Ecclesiastes was wise'; cf. Hie *et amplius quia factus est ecclesiastes sapiens*, 'and more than that Ecclesiastes had become wise'.

S simply imitates the Hebrew, but another way of understanding the text in this way is apparently offered by σ' ὑπερβάλ(λ)ον, which Marshall is probably right to see as part of an impersonal construction, 'it was exceeding that...'. Jerome has probably picked this up in the more paraphrastic V *cumque esset sapientissimus Ecclesiastes*, 'and since Ecclesiastes was very wise', but Symmachus was most likely attempting to make a deliberate connection with 2.15, where Qohelet himself earlier asked למה חכמתי אני אז יותר, with the apparent implication that his wisdom had been superfluous, or with 7.16, which warns against being excessively wise. It is possible, in fact, that G tries to keep this sense open as well, and the Hebrew itself can be taken in such terms, as a claim that Qohelet was excessively wise, even if it is hard to find a direct analogy (cf., perhaps, 2 Sam 14.15 ועתה אשר באתי, 'and it is now that I have come'). It is difficult, however, to see what the point of such a claim would be in this context.

The general understanding that underpins the suggestion by Gordis remains popular among modern commentators, but a number (at least as far back as Ewald 1837, 'Uebrig ist [zu sagen] dass', 'it is superfluous [to say]'; cf. Cheyne, *Job and Solomon*, 231, and Hengstenberg) have simply isolated -ש ויתר, in line with the Masoretic accents, which put a disjunctive *zaqeph gadol* on יותר, and taken it to mean: 'it remains (to be said) that...'. On the face of it, this explains both the presence of -ש and the absence of any מן, while providing a formal announcement that what follows should be read as an epilogue (cf. Dohmen, 'Der Weisheit', 13, 14, 'es ist nachzutragen, daß', 'it is to be added as an addendum, that'; Lauha even considers יתר a technical term for 'epilogue', with the -ש serving as equivalent to a colon). Again, though, there is no remotely analogous usage elsewhere, and the result seems unsatisfactory in context, because it leaves us with a limp statement that 'Qohelet was wise'. Indeed, if we are going to understand an implicit 'to say', then contextually we might better translate 'it is *superfluous* (to say) that Qohelet was wise' (a point made already, I find, by Hölemann, 'Die Epiloge', 44). As Margoliouth ('Ecclesiastes xii. 8-14', 122) put it long ago, in response to Cheyne, 'Considering that Ecclesiastes then lay before the intelligent world of Jewish readers, where was the need to add that he was a wise man?' Margoliouth's own proposal was to understand, 'And the more wise Qoheleth became, the more did he teach the people wisdom'—he claims both that this is no more speculative a reading than any other, and that it had been adopted by a number of earlier translations and commentaries. The former is probably not true: this construal goes beyond finding a new sense for -ש יותר, instead implying the existence of an implausible and wholly unattested construction of -ש יותר with עוד to mean 'the more...the more...'. If Margoliouth's solution is difficult, however, his objection to the more common readings is basically sound, and there are good reasons why we might seek at least to understand Qohelet's wisdom as the basis of his teaching, not as something itself singled out by the epilogue.

We could do so, perhaps, by associating ויתר here with the noun found in Jer 27.19, and commonly elsewhere, which is pointed יֶתֶר in M, but has a significant overlap of sense with יֹתֵר: this may connote either a remnant ('a last vestige') or a gain ('a bonus'). The -ש would most likely then substantivize the following clause, with יתר standing in a genitive relationship, to give 'a surplus/remainder of (the fact that) Qohelet was wise (is that)...'. It is also conceivable, though, that the -ש should be treated as causal (so Seow), to give the sense 'a bonus: because Qohelet was wise, he has...', or that ויתר should be treated as verbal. While they are all possible, however, none of these seems compelling, and I have opted, in the end, for what I consider a simpler construal of the text, taking -ש as a relative pronoun that qualifies יתר (probably to be read as the substantive), to give a literal sense 'an excess which existed'. We might translate that as 'and something more which happened (was) that Qohelet was wise' (cf. Heim, 'But there was more to him: Qoheleth was a wise man'), but to avoid that statement of the obvious, I think that we have to consider the relationship between קהלת חכם and what follows, as well as the implication here of עוד.

The meaning attributed to this עוד has varied according to understandings of the sentence overall, but I doubt it can suggest that Qohelet's teaching was something he did 'continually' during his lifetime, as Schoors argues, representing quite a common modern position (*The Preacher* I, 138; Loretz, 'Poetry and Prose', 161, makes this stronger, preferring 'incessantly'). In passages like Gen 46.29 and Ruth 1.14, עוד does not imply that the characters kept meeting up over a long period to weep, but that on a single occasion they wept repeatedly, or for a long time, and that is probably the sense intended in, e.g., Ps 84.5: עוד can certainly connote addition, repetition or duration, but there is nothing in such instances, cited by Schoors, to suggest that the word might in itself be used simply to characterize an action as habitual. Another common use is to mean 'still' or 'yet', and this implication was present when Qohelet himself used עוד in 4.13; 7.28; 9.5, 6. On the remaining use in 3.16, see the note there, but the probable sense was 'again', picking up a previous action, and עוד not infrequently refers to something that is 'further' or 'additional' (e.g. Esth 9.12, 'what is it that you seek beyond [your primary request]?'). That gives quite a lot of scope, but since we have already been told that we are receiving supplementary information, this last seems the most likely connotation here (cf. RSV, '...the Preacher also taught the people knowledge'). In that case, קהלת חכם has to be taken either as a sort of circumstantial clause ('Qohelet being wise'), or, more plausibly and elegantly, I think, as an extended subject for the verb, which is why I have translated it with 'Qohelet, a wise man' (we might alternatively translate 'wise Qohelet', although such usages are unusual). It should be noted, though, that עוד can qualify non-verbal clauses (cf. Judg 7.4; 18.24; Ruth 1.11; 2 Sam 1.9; 14.32; 1 Kgs 22.8), and it might be possible also, therefore, to defend a reading 'while Qohelet was still a wise man, he taught...', and even perhaps to see an implicit acknowledgment of the crisis faced by Qohelet in ch. 7. It is hard to say, however, whether such ambiguity is deliberate or even real: certainly, none of the ancient versions read the text that way.

The Greek text here is corrupt: although it seems all but certain that G originally read ἔτι ἐδίδαξεν, 'yet/still he taught', all extant manuscripts have ὅτι, 'that (he taught)', or variants on that (most have a preceding καὶ also, presumably introduced to make the clause parallel to the preceding ὅτι ἐγένετο Ἐκκλησιαστὴς). This ὅτι is picked up by Syh, suggesting that it was the reading of Origen, and has influenced S ܘܗܐ *dmlp* as well: Hie *adhuc docuit*, 'he yet taught', which does reflect ἔτι, is based either on the Hebrew or on an La translation that had an uncorrupted Greek source-text.

Ginsburg, *Massorah*, 4:486, notes a Masoretic observation in which it is assumed that ויתר is written plene as ויותר, both here and in 12.12: that reading, widely attested in Kennicott's manuscripts, was clearly present in texts used by the Masoretes, and Ginsburg considers the source of the comment early. Ben Naphtali is reported to have pointed למד with *metheg* under the ל (see Lipschütz).

12.9 the people knowledge] M connects למד and דעת with *maqqeph*, apparently suggesting that they constitute a single concept ('knowledge-teach someone'). That is found in Job 21.22 also, but it may be in part a response to the unexpected word-order here: when Hebrew uses two objects with למד, the person who is being taught generally precedes the thing that is being taught (as in English, 'teach someone something', not 'teach something someone'): cf. JM §125 u, GKC §117 cc, and examples in Deut 4.5, 14; Ps 94.10; Jer 9.19. The rule is not absolute (cf. Deut 11.19), and we should probably not make too much of this, but the Masoretic construal may have picked up a nuance of the original. As the extensive review of the usage in Lavoie, 'Un éloge', 154-56, shows, neither the verb itself nor the combination 'teach knowledge' have any particular implication of formal education or schooling, so the Hebrew does not oblige us to understand that Qohelet actually worked as a teacher or gave formal lectures.

The textual problems continue in the Greek, where the λαόν that we would expect to find as an equivalent of עם, 'people', enjoys very little support among the manuscripts (only some hexaplaric texts and one much later mixed text, although it is apparently reflected in Hie, S and Coptic). Most instead have ἄνθρωπον, 'human' (cf. Syh ܠܒܪܢܫܐ *lbrnš'*), giving a sense that Qohelet is teaching humanity as a whole, and not just 'the people'. The attractiveness of this reading has led McNeile (91, 153), and more recently Goldman, to propose not only that G in fact found האדם and translated it with ἄνθρωπον, but that a case could be made for the originality of האדם itself within the

Hebrew tradition. On that reckoning, λαόν is likely a hexaplaric reading which has displaced ἄνθρωπον in a few texts—one source (ms 252) attributes it to α' and σ'—and that is the assumption made in Gentry's edition. Rahlfs, however, explains the anomaly as a graphic confusion in the G tradition: ΛΑΟΝ has been misread as the common abbreviation ΑΝΟΝ (ἄν[θρωπ]ον). This is less simple an explanation, and it probably is true that G* was ἄνθρωπον. Whether it follows that the translator actually read האדם is less certain, and the evidence of α' and σ' leaves G as the only potential witness to such a reading, over and against M's העם.

In terms of the sense, it may not matter very much which reading we adopt. Although 'the people' in biblical usage is typically a reference to 'Israel' or the Jews, it can have a more general application, and in Isa 40.7, for instance, העם seems to be serving as an equivalent for 'all flesh' in the preceding verse, and humanity in general to be the subject; the עם of Isa 42.5 is likewise a reference to all humans. It is not impossible, in fact, that the G translator, while actually reading העם, tried to bring out some implication of 'all humanity' with ἄνθρωπον (it would not be an idea so readily associated with λαόν). If, on the other hand, he did find האדם, then that may itself have been an attempt within the Hebrew tradition to present a similar idea of Qohelet instructing humanity—although it is also possible that העם is the secondary reading, and was a deliberate change intended to make Qohelet sound more regal or Solomonic. If we stick with העם as original, however, the claim here is probably neither that Qohelet has taught only Jews (or Solomon's subjects), nor that his words have reached all humankind. Qohelet himself in 4.16 used העם with reference back to 'all the living' in 4.15, and the author would probably not be averse to the sort of usage found in Second Isaiah, but it seems unlikely that the epilogue is trying to portray Qohelet's teaching as worldwide and universal, while it shows no other interest in making him a strictly national figure. In Esth 1.5, the noun refers simply to 'all the people' in Susa, as it does to the inhabitants of Sodom in Gen 19.4, while Prov 29.2 is surely talking about the reactions of whichever 'people' are subject to the authority in question when it uses העם and then עם. Here, similarly, the reference is most likely to a group limited simply, if rather vaguely, by the context, which is whatever environment we are supposed to imagine for Qohelet's activity as a teacher. This is effectively equivalent to saying that 'Qohelet taught people knowledge', but I have retained the article to keep open the possibility of a more specific reference.

Lohfink, 'Der Weise und das Volk', draws attention to Sir 37.22-26, which distinguishes between the wise man who is 'wise for himself' and the one who is 'wise for his people' (whose name will live for ever). Both the general point and the sense of 'people' seem to be different here, however.

12.9 And he listened and examined. He perfected a great many sayings] The verb אזן is used in Hebrew of listening, but elsewhere appears only in the hiph'il. Since we have ואזן here, and not והאזין, we seem to be dealing, therefore, with a stem of אזן that is otherwise unattested, with another verb altogether, or with the noun אזן. G has opted for the last of these, as part of a broader construal of the sequence that is very distinctive, and that leads it to translate καὶ οὓς ἐξιχνιάσεται κόσμιον, 'and an ear will track out an arrangement'. It is doubtful that this represents a Hebrew text that is significantly different from the consonantal text of M: אזן and תקן have been taken as nouns (cf. Driver, 'Problems and Solutions', 234), where M treats them as verbs, while וחקר has been read as יחקר—this may reflect a Hebrew variant, but the two forms would have been all but indistinguishable in many hands, and the decision to read י rather than ו may have been a result of the construal, not a reading that provoked it.

In any case, the sense of G is somewhat implausible, and its understanding has been picked up by neither Hie *et audire eos fecit et scrutans composuit*, 'and he made them hear, and, probing, composed...', nor S ܘܐܨܬ ܘܒܕܩ ܘܬܩܢ *wṣt wbdq wʾtqn*, 'and he heard and searched out and arranged'. Both of these read וחקר with M, but the latter has a conjunction before the final word as well, which would be easier to dismiss as a free rendering if we did not have a partial reading from σ' or α' which shows the same feature: καὶ κατεσκεύασεν (παροιμίας), 'and he arranged (proverbs)'.[2] S and σ' are given to paraphrase, but it is not impossible that they found a Hebrew ותקן. Another partial reading is preserved for α', which has been picked up by the 'Lucianic', *L*-group of G manuscripts, and which again shows a preference for verbs over the nouns of G: καὶ ἠνωτίσατο καὶ ἠρεύνησεν, 'and he gave ear and searched after'. T likewise has verbs, for which it supplies separate objects. In short, therefore, there is little appetite among the versions other than G to address the difficulty of אזן by reading it as a noun. M vocalizes it instead as a piʻel, as probably have S, T and α'; at least, they have all taken it as equivalent to the hiphʻil. V is curious, in that Jerome apparently changes the sense altogether by reading *et enarrauit quae fecerit*, 'and he recounted what he had done', but this is probably an extrapolation from his understanding, expressed in Hie *audire eos fecit*, 'he made them hear', that the verb is causative and therefore requires that an object be supplied.

---

[2] Ascertaining the readings of α' and σ' was tricky before, but has been complicated by the evidence from ms 788 presented by Gentry. This supports the attribution of καὶ ἠνωτίσατο καὶ ἠρεύνησεν to α', attested elsewhere, but then follows this with καὶ κατεσκεύασεν παροιμίας, which is elsewhere usually attributed to σ' (but to α' by ms 252 also). As the reading of σ', 788 gives καὶ ἐνωτίσασθαι ἐποίησεν καὶ ἐξευρὼν συνέθηκε παροιμίας, 'and he caused to give ear and, finding, he put together sayings'. This is very close to the readings of Hie *et audire eos fecit et scrutans composuit prouerbia*, and V, which tells in favour of the attribution to Symmachus, but if this is σ', then καὶ κατεσκεύασεν παροιμίας cannot be. Marshall argues for its attribution to σ' on the grounds that α' usually prefers παραβολή for משל, but it is simpler to assume that 252 and 788 are correct, and that this clause is α'.

Many modern commentators have been content to follow the broad understanding that Qohelet is 'listening', even if the verb is being used in an abnormal stem (Dahood, 'Qoheleth and Northwest Semitic Philology', 364, sees the piʻel as a 'Canaanism'). I am inclined to do the same, although, if a ה has not just dropped out, and we are indeed dealing with an abnormal usage, then it is tempting to speculate that this is a colloquialism or neologism, intended to suggest that Qohelet heard or overheard things, so that he was not 'giving ear' in the deliberate way that would be implied by the hiphʻil. I doubt the sense can actually be stretched to 'collected' (so Lohfink, 'Les épilogues', 86-87), but some such idea is apparently in mind. A significant number of commentators, however, have preferred to discard the association with אזן, 'ear', altogether, and to see the verb here as the only attestation of a verb אזן, 'weigh', related to the proto-Semitic root *wzn* and otherwise reflected in Hebrew only in the noun מאזנים, 'scales'. That is not impossible, and it gives a nice image of Qohelet measuring and evaluating his materials, but to see a metaphorical use here of an otherwise unknown verb is surely no easier than assuming that Qohelet might have used a qal or piʻel instead of a hiphʻil. Although it looks like a modern suggestion, incidentally, the interpretation as 'weighing' appears to have arisen in medieval Jewish scholarship (some early advocates are listed in Lavoie and Mehramooz, 'Étude de quelques mots obscurs', 188-89), and was being cited or adopted in Christian commentary (often as the interpretation of Qimḥi) as early as the late sixteenth and seventeenth centuries (cf. le Mercier, Fischer, Geier). It probably arose initially through much the same sort of exegesis as did the talmudic interpretation in *b. Yebamot* 21a, picked up by Rashi, which links אזן with a later use of the noun in the dual to mean 'handles', and declares that Solomon made handles for the Torah.

As for the other verbs, חקר is, like אזן, attested nowhere else in the piʻel, and the pointing in M must be regarded with some suspicion: it has probably been influenced by the surrounding verbs, and there seems no good reason not to read a qal here (Fassberg, 'The Shift', 124-25, sees the piʻel as original, but suspects it was used under that influence). The verb is used of searching, but often also of examining or scrutinizing. The third verb, תקן, has already appeared in the qal at 1.15 (although see my comments there on the form) and the piʻel at 7.13, both times in the context of repairing or straightening what has been bent. On the broader sense in later Hebrew, see the note at 1.15: such a sense is probably in play here, and the implication is not just that Qohelet set the sayings out straight or disentangled them, but that he brought them into the best possible form. It is not clear that this is a reference to their arrangement in an order, as often assumed, and the point may be simply that he polished each of them to perfection. Shields, 'Ecclesiastes and the End of Wisdom', 126-27, argues that the sense here must be 'corrected', but although this might be supported by the later use of a cognate noun in the technical expression

תיקוני סופרים, it is some distance from the normal biblical usage, and offers only weak support for a subsequent claim that Qohelet disagreed with others (and sought but failed to find pleasing words—a failure that Longman also imputes to him). The relationship of תקן to the other verbs is complicated by the absence of a conjunction, which may have been a factor in G's odd reading of the sequence, and which leads Jerome to translate the second verb as a participle in Hie and V. As we have already seen, S and σ' do each have a conjunction, and if this has not just been supplied as a facilitation by the translators or their source-texts, it is possible that there was an original Hebrew ותקן. That reading is noted by de Rossi in about a dozen manuscripts, and it seems necessary at least to understand a conjunction if we are to see a sequence here. The strong support for the majority reading of M, however, and the greater likelihood that a conjunction has been added, not lost, mean that we should perhaps do without a sequence at all, and it is certainly difficult to read the current text as a simple sequence of three verbs each taking משלים as its object (so, e.g., Dohmen, 'Der Weisheit', 14). Herzfeld suggests that the first two verbs qualify the third adverbially; Ginsburg, who accepts that suggestion, translates, 'carefully and studiously composed' (the proposal is examined and rejected in Lohfink, 'Zu einigen Satzeröffnungen', 141-42). Fox, having preferred to read the variant with a conjunction in 1989, treats the first two verbs as circumstantial in the later edition of his commentary: 'having listened and investigated, he composed'. I am inclined myself to think that McNeile, 91, was right to suppose that those verbs refer to Qohelet's acquisition of knowledge, and only the third to his work with sayings, and this suggests that the omission of a conjunction was intended specifically to prevent a reading of the verbs as a single sequence: Qohelet teaches, but he also listens and investigates, and he composes sayings.

12.9 a great many sayings] The distinctive reading of G leads it to group הרבה with the next verse, so that Qohelet there will 'seek out many things in order to find'; Hie follows suit. On the confusion in the manuscripts over the reading of α' καὶ κατεσκεύασεν παροιμίας, 'and he prepared sayings' (formerly attributed to σ'; see n. 2), and on the subsequent corruption of παροιμίας into the remarkable παροιμιαστης (by assimilation to Εκκλησιαστής in the next verse), see Marshall, and my summary in the notes at 1.1. This word has often, in honest error, been misrepresented as Symmachus' rendering of the name in 12.10 (so, e.g., Lavoie, 'Qohélet 12,11', 140, although it seems invidious to single anybody out), largely because the index for the marginal readings has been placed incorrectly in that verse by the two manuscripts that attest παροιμιαστης—this is likely also the source of the corruption, as efforts were made to reconcile it with the new lemma. A third manuscript has the proper placement and the original παροιμίας. If it were ever actually a real word, which seems highly unlikely, παροιμιαστης would be equivalent to 'proverbizer', and would mean something like 'creator of proverbs' or 'aphorist', but this is an accident of transmission, not a deliberate interpretation of the name.

משלים is probably not a strict technical term, but it is true, as Seow, 'Beyond Them', 130, observes, that little of what we find in the monologue would normally be described this way. Seow himself thinks that we are simply being told Qohelet's work was 'typical of a sage', but it is also true that the word has a strong association with Solomon in particular (Prov 1.1; 10.1; 25.1; 1 Kgs 5.12), and Barton (citing Hitzig and Wildeboer), thinks there is a reference here to the Book of Proverbs, and an allusion to the identification of Qohelet as Solomon. That is surely too precise (see the comments in Sheppard, 'The Epilogue', 183-84), although a teasing hint along those lines would certainly accord with the character of that identification elsewhere. It seems very possible, though, either that the epilogue is describing something in Qohelet's background—part of the 'something else' which is distinct from the monologue—or that the monologue is deliberately being characterized in more conventional terms.

12.10 Qohelet tried to] Or 'sought', but the use of בקש with -ל and a following infinitive is well-attested in the sense of attempting to do something; see, e.g., Exod 2.15; Deut 13.11; Esth 3.6. The interpretations of this verse in *b. Roš Haššanah* 21b understand the attempt to have been unsuccessful. As already noted, G, Hie take הרבה with this verse, so that Qohelet seeks 'much', or seeks 'many ways' (*NETS*). Strikingly, S has ܣܓܝ̈ܐܬܐ *sgy"*, 'much, many', at the end of 12.9 and then ܣܓܝ *sgy* again at the start of 12.10: this does not preserve some original reading now lost in the other versions, but rather provides a vivid illustration of the influence on S of both G and the traditions behind M. On the supposed rendering of Qohelet's name by Symmachus here, see the last note.

12.10 words that would be valued] Lit. 'words of desire' or 'of usefulness'; see the discussion of חפץ in the notes at 3.1, 5.3 and 12.1. The expression אבני חפץ is used of precious stones (e.g. Isa 54.12; Sir 45.11), and ארץ חפץ in Mal 3.12 seems to describe a land that is 'blessed' and a 'delight' because its crops are protected from failure. Some scholars have sought in various ways to link the description here with Qohelet's use of חפץ in the sense 'matter' or 'affair', often inspired by the conclusion of Staples, 'The Meaning of ḥēpeṣ in Ecclesiastes', that the term is used in the book to mean 'the business of life'. So, e.g., Dohmen, 'Der Weisheit', 15, translates the expression here as 'Lebenslehren', 'teachings for living (everyday life)', while Pahk, 'Role and Significance', interprets it as 'the meaning of reality'—an understanding driven largely by the belief that there must be a reference here to what Qohelet actually investigated. Such analogies, however, favour the more common understanding that דברי חפץ are 'precious words', or 'words that give pleasure'—although such renderings can imply a sort of superficiality that is absent from the Hebrew. It is tempting to compare the Egyptian term *mdt nfrt*, 'perfect speech', which is used to describe the fine expression of fine ideas, much admired by the Egyptian scribes, and what we are dealing with here is the opposite of the idea found in 5.3 and 12.1, where to place no value at all on someone or something was described as having no חפץ in it.

The ancient translators struggled somewhat to express the sense. S ܗܒ ܠܬܐ ܓܝܪ ܒܨܐ *ptgmʾ dṣbynʾ*, 'words of will/pleasure', and G λόγους θελήματος, 'words of will' (cf. Hie *uerba uoluntatis*), probably come closest. G distinguishes the different senses of חפץ, and here employs the same rendering used at 5.3 and 12.1 (cf. θελήση for יחפץ at 8.3); the probable connotation is 'words that someone might want'. T is superficially very different, turning this into a statement about Solomon trying to judge people according to their inner thoughts, but probably also reads חפץ in terms of will or desire. Taking the other sense 'matter' or 'affair', α' instead has λόγους χρείας, 'words of use', and σ' (see Marshall for the attribution) the similar <λόγους> χρειώδεις, 'useful words'. This latter has probably influenced V *uerba utilia*, which means the same.

12.10 and a blunt writing of words that convey truth] Lit. 'and a writing straightly of words of truth'. M points וכתוב as a participle, וְכָתוּב, and this understanding is reflected also in G γεγραμμένον εὐθύτητος, 'a thing written of straightforwardness'. T is probably too loose to be helpful, but איתכתב, 'it has been written', might suggest that it likewise read a passive participle. Hie uses *et scriberet*, 'and that he might write', parallel to the preceding *inueniret*, 'that he might find', which implies that Jerome understood a second infinitive, likely reading the same consonants וכתוב as כְּתוֹב. However, S ܘܟܬܒ *wktb* (var. ܘܟܬܒܝ *wktby*) and σ' καὶ συνέγραψεν (cf. V *conscripsit*) both mean 'and he wrote', suggesting a main verb here, and de Rossi notes several Hebrew manuscripts with the spelling וכתב. There seem to have been two writings, therefore, which were each read in at least two ways: וכתוב as a participle or infinitive, and וכתב as a qatal or as a defective writing of וכתוב.

On balance, it seems unlikely that the qatal was intended, although some scholars have attempted to have their cake and eat it, by construing the likely original וכתוב as an infinitive acting as a main verb (Fox, who would read an infinitive absolute, cites a potential parallel for the same verb in a late Hebrew version of Tobit). Others have taken וכתוב as a participle, but not as an object of בקש or למצא, so that it begins a new clause: 'what is written (is)…', or some such; Lohfink sees a declaration that true sayings have been written in the book before us. Obviously, that reading has to confront the problem that the singular form does not agree with 'words', and has itself to be explained. Our most important clues to the intended reading, however, lie in the strong probability that דברי חפץ and דברי אמת are supposed to stand in parallel, and in the constraints upon different ways of achieving this. So, if כתוב is supposed to correspond to בקש, it is difficult to see why we should not have qatal כתב, and if to למצא, why we should not have לכתוב: in either case, the use of כתוב would simply obscure the connection, and make it harder to construe the sentence in the way meant by the author. This suggests that כתוב ישר דברי אמת as a whole must correspond to דברי חפץ, as a second object of למצא. If we then read כתוב as a participle, the likely sense is 'Qohelet tried to find fine words and something written uprightly'; this is how G takes it (cf. Niccacci, 'Qohelet o la gioia', 92 n. 115). If, on the other hand, we read כתוב as an infinitive (cf. McNeile, 92, who thinks an infinitive construct would be 'simpler' than the participle), then we get 'Qohelet tried to find fine words and a writing uprightly (of true words)'. Both might be understood in terms of Qohelet seeking to achieve a proper written expression of his words, with reference either to the product of his writing or to the act of writing itself. Although I think an infinitive is more likely to have been intended, since it excludes the possibility that Qohelet was looking for a book already in existence, we do not really, therefore, have to make a choice between the infinitive and the participle—and an original וכתוב would not have forced one.

Of course, the grammatical relationship between כתוב and the following ישר depends in part on the way we parse the verb. Commentators have generally preferred to see ישר as adverbial here (cf. σ' ὀρθῶς, 'straightly'; Hie *recte*, 'rightly'), but Fox reads ישר as the first element in a construct chain דברי אמת, serving as the object of כתוב, and compares קשט אמרי אמת in Prov 22.21. Bearing in mind our discussion of the corresponding adjective at 7.29, I also doubt that it is necessary to see a specific moral component in the use of the noun ישר here, and this is especially true if we follow the majority by taking ישר as adverbial. On my translation of the term, see the commentary. What Qohelet writes might or might not be 'upright', but if the noun stands in apposition to the verb, qualifying it adverbially—which I consider likely— then it must qualify the act of writing itself, and it seems unlikely that we are being told 'Qohelet tried to write virtuously', or that he produced material 'written virtuously'.

If we were to follow Fox, which is tempting given the obvious similarity between דברי אמת and the אמרי אמת of Prov 22.21 (and perhaps also the fact that in the next verse we will encounter דברי חכמים, cf. Prov 22.17), then the literal implication would be that Qohelet sought to write 'the straightness of words of truth'. Fox himself sees a superlative sense in both passages, and translates 'the most honest words of truth', but this is speculative: the קשט in Prov 22 is something taught from or about the אמרי אמת which will enable the hearer to use his own אמרים אמת, and so seems likely to be either some underlying truth that may be discerned from them, or their 'validity'. If we try to take ישר דברי אמת in the same terms, then the sense would most likely be the 'rightness' or 'integrity' of words of truth, and the broader point would be that Qohelet was trying to capture that quality in his writing. This seems a stretch, but the verbal link to Proverbs does at least raise the possibility that אמרי אמת is a technical term for the sort of aphoristic composition that appears in both books. Lavoie, 'Un éloge', 164, looks to Prov 16.13, where דבר ישרים is set in parallel with שפתי צדק, and to Ps 33.4, where 'the word of YHWH is upright', and while these seem less closely analogous, the parallel between

ישר and באמונה in the latter does bring out the 'straight-dealing' connotations of ישר. It is worth noting Prov 8.8-9 as well: there ישרים is used of wisdom's words, which are also 'straight' or 'straightforward' (נכחים), and contain no 'entangling' (נפתל) or anything 'perverse' (עקש).

12.11 goads...embedded spikes] As Koenen, 'Zu den Epilogen', 25, observes, there is something close to a play on words in the comparison between דברי and דרבנות; I am less persuaded by his further suggestion, that the spelling of משמרות with ש rather than ס is an attempt to evoke שמר, and ideas about 'keeping' God's words (cf. v. 13; similarly Lavoie, 'Qohélet 12,11', 140-41). The spelling with ס is, in fact, found in a few manuscripts, and also, incidentally, in an early account of agreements between ben Asher and ben Naphtali (see Lipschütz, 3); ס / ש variations are so common that it would be hard to say which writing is original here, and I doubt that in this instance the author or any subsequent copyist was trying to convey any such subtle point by the use of one letter rather than the other.

The noun דרבן is found in 1 Sam 13.21 among a list of farming tools, and is used also in later Hebrew. As the reference in 1 Samuel suggests, the implement would have incorporated a spike that needed to be sharpened or set, and it is this to which משמרה apparently refers, although the מסמרות of Jer 10.4 are simply nails, and that is the usual understanding of the noun in 2 Chr 3.9 also (although they must have been exceptionally large). The spike would have been fixed into the end of a stick, and this is the apparent sense of נטועים: the verb more often refers to planting, but is used of pitching tents in Dan 11.45, perhaps with the thought of driving in tent-pegs. Despite the -ות, משמרות here is apparently masculine; cf. מסמרים in Isa 41.7. Lowth, *Lectures*, 2:167-68, offers a rather different interpretation of the spikes: unlike the goads, which have an instant effect, they represent the deeper penetration of sayings into the mind, and he takes the image to be of pegs, built into the walls of a house, which offer both convenience and greater structural integrity. In his commentary on Isaiah, he makes a similar claim at 22.23, and cites a description of Near Eastern building practices in the seventeenth century by the traveller John (Jean) Chardin.[3] In Isaiah, however, the word used is יתד, and even were the interpretation possible there (it is very speculative), I see no reason to suppose that the item described here is just the same thing under another name. In any case, however we are supposed to envisage the goad and spikes, most scholars have seen a reference to actual implements of some sort (although Galling, 'Scepter of Wisdom', 18, prefers 'sceptres' to 'spikes'), and Baumgärtel, 'Die Ochsenstachel', has won no apparent support for his suggestion that Qohelet is talking about the wedges used to create characters in cuneiform script.

---

[3] See Lowth, *Isaiah*, 128. Lowth found the description, and the association with the passage of Isaiah, in Harmer, *Observations*, 1:191, which draws heavily on unpublished manuscripts by Chardin.

The participle נטועים literally means 'planted', and although an extension of the sense similar to that at Dan 11.45 is probably in play here, it seems doubtful that Qohelet has actually switched to a more benign image of tent-pegs, as Vílchez Líndez supposes, matching the inclination of a few other commentators, like Murphy and Wilson, 'The Words of the Wise', 180, to see two different aspects of wisdom represented (cf. the comments of Gordis, noted in the commentary above). Accordingly, σ' πεπηγότες is arguably a better match than G's literal rendering πεφυτευμένοι (also used by α' and θ'): it covers such uses and brings out the sense of fixing something in, or embedding it. It may be this, and perhaps the less precise connotations of his *defixi*, 'fixed', that has influenced Jerome in Hie and V to specify that the nails are fixed *in altum*, 'deeply'.

Rose, 'Verba Sapientium', 214, argues instead that Jerome found a text which had ומעלה after the participle, and translated it this way because he did not recognize an intended sense, 'plantation'. The original, according to Rose, compared the בעלי אספות to נטוע ומעלה, 'a plantation and a cultivation (of trees)': the missing word slipped out as parts of it were variously re-assigned to the preceding word, or rejected as apparent dittographs of the following word. Text-critically, this creates a complicated explanation for a reading by Jerome that requires little explanation at all, while the notion that a speculatively restored מעלה might mean 'plantation'—which is not a normal sense of the noun—is itself another speculation, built upon a single use in Ps 74.5.

12.11 drivers have been presented from] The expression בעלי אספות is obscure, but may be either another term for goads of some sort, or a reference to the drovers that used them (I have tried to translate in a way that could cover either). It came to be used occasionally in later Hebrew to refer to human assemblies (which is why T talks about the Sanhedrin here; cf., for instance, *b. Sanhedrin* 12a, and the Midrash Rabbah on Num 11), but that usage is clearly a borrowing from this verse, based on a particular interpretation of it—cf. *y. Sanhedrin* 10.1 (50b); *b. Ḥagigah* 3b; *t. Soṭa* 7.7. As we saw in the note at 10.11, בעל has a very wide range of meanings and does not specify closely the nature of the relationship between the בעל and any noun to which it is connected. The word אספה appears in the difficult Isa 24.22, where M points it differently, but is not otherwise known, and all we can deduce about אספות from its root is that the term should refer to gatherings or collections of some sort (the cognate verb is used of gathering both things and people/animals).

The ancient versions offer little additional insight. S has the curious rendering ܡܪܝ ܐܣܟܦܬܐ, *mry 'skpt'*, 'owners/masters of lintels', but this is either an attempt to read the Hebrew as a derivative of סף, or, more probably, the result of an attempt simply to transliterate it, with the resulting ܐܣܟܦܬܐ *'spt'* adjusted to a more familiar word (cf. Kamenetzky, 234). The readings of the Greek translators are difficult to establish. Rahlfs gives οἱ παρὰ τῶν συναγμάτων, 'those of the accumulations', as the reading of G, but there are several variants, and Marshall presents a strong case for supposing that this originated, in fact, as the reading of α'. G* was more probably Gentry's οἳ παρὰ τῶν συνθεμάτων, perhaps 'those of the compacts' if not just literally 'of the things put together' (this is a reading attested by Olympiodorus, but attributed by him to 'other books'). σ' was likely οἳ παρὰ τῶν συναχθέντων, 'those of the gathered'.[4] The use of παρά in all these translations does not suggest that they found a variant מבעלי, as *BHS* and Marshall suppose, since G characteristically uses that preposition to represent בעל (see the discussion at 5.10), and all we can really tell from these various renderings is that the Greek translators had no clearer sense of what בעלי אספות were than do modern commentators. Jerome is a little less literal, and although in Hie he renders *habentibus coetus*, 'by/for those having assemblies', which remains close to the Hebrew, in V he offers *quae per magistrorum concilium*, 'which through the council of masters (are given by one shepherd)'. This gives a more specific sense, in line with the later Jewish usage, but it involves effectively reversing the grammatical roles of the Hebrew words.

As Schoors has shown, the common scholarly interpretations of בעלי אספות (which are helpfully surveyed in Lavoie and Mehramooz, 'Étude de quelques mots obscurs', 191-93) can be boiled down to three main understandings: these are the collectors who put together collections of sayings, they are sayings or headings within such collections, or else they are the leaders of human schools or assemblies. Scholars who see a reference to people (as either collectors or leaders) generally then set these people in parallel with the preceding 'wise' and understand a repetition or ellipsis of 'words', so that Fox, for instance, translates 'and the [words of] masters of collections are like implanted nails', while Seow has 'like implanted pricks are (the words of) the mentors of the assemblies'. Driver, 'Problems and Solutions', 234, is an exception, in that he sees a further description of the words, which are now presented as 'rulers of assemblies' because they 'dominate the minds of those who hear them'.

Those who understand the בעלי אספות to be items within collections set them instead in parallel with the 'words of the wise'; hence Barton's 'The words of the wise are as goads, and as driven nails are the members of collections' (similarly, Wilson, 'The Words of the Wise', 176). The accents in M tend to encourage such a reading, placing a disjunctive *'athnaḥ* on אספות even though this then strands the final clause with נתנו: in the absence of any other explicit subject, this generally has to be taken as an asyndetic relative clause—'...are the בעלי אספות (that) have been given by one shepherd'. Like Driver, the Greek versions and Jerome, however, simply take וכמשמרות נטועים

---

[4] For θ', Syh suggests the unexpected ἀόρατοι, 'unseen', but this seems to have been misplaced, and that reading probably corresponds to G παρεωραμένῳ in v. 14.

as a secondary characterization of the דברי הכמים: the words of the wise are like goads *and* like embedded spikes. The בעלי אספות are then taken by G to be the subject of a new sentence. Unfashionable though it is, there is much to be said for such an approach, both because it provides a clearer syntax for the subsequent נתנו and because it avoids the difficulties inherent in both types of 'parallel' reading. If we set בעלי אספות in parallel with הכמים, we have to accept that there has been an ugly and unnecessary omission of דברי, which robs the second clause of its very subject. If we set it in parallel with דברי הכמים, on the other hand, then we have to explain how בעל could take on such an extended sense, referring to words or objects as parts within something, for which there is no clear parallel.[5] If we dispense with such parallelism altogether, however, then the בעלי אספות can be taken simply as the subject of נתנו (there is no sensible way to construe the expression with נטועים instead).

If a בעל אספות is something given, set, or appointed by a shepherd, then, what might it be? In Isa 24.22, אספה apparently refers to a crowd driven together as prisoners in a pit, and the verb can be used of gathering sheep together, perhaps especially at the end of a day (Gen 29.7). In a pastoral context, a בעל אספות might naturally be understood, then, as someone who has charge of such droves, although a בעל פיפיות is apparently a threshing-sledge in Isa 41.15, so it is not impossible alternatively that a בעל אספות might itself be some other sort of tool, or another way of describing the herder's goad/spikes. Rashi, indeed, sees a reference to 'fat-headed' nails (citing the *Teshuvot Dunash*), while Podechard takes אספה as equivalent to the אספים of 1 Chr 26.15, 17 and Neh 12.25, which are usually understood to be provisions or storerooms: the nails are being described as nails upon which stores could be hung. Montgomery, 'Notes', 244, speculates along these lines that the text has been misconstrued and that the עלי of בעלי was originally a reference to nails driven 'into the top' of a club. Strobel retains 'collections' (which he interprets as 'wisdom literature'), but emends בעלי to על ב-, 'in the yoke'. The logic of the imagery would seem to demand in any case, though, that we are to equate the shepherd, and not the בעלי אספות, with the wise men, and that the בעלי אספות stand in relation to the shepherd in the same way that their words stand in relation to the wise men: they are employed to goad and drive.

Margoliouth, 'Ecclesiastes xii. 8-14', 123, would also construe בעלי differently, but unlike Montgomery, he wishes to change the metaphor completely. According to him, the word is to be parsed as ב- with the construct plural form of עלה, 'leaf', and he translates 'like nails (or metal fasteners) fixed in

---

[5] In a footnote, Wilson (*loc. cit.*) claims, 'The following passages are considered sufficient to establish the use of *baʿălê* to mean "individual members of a (larger, specified) group": Gen 14:13; 49:23; Judg 20:5; 2 Sam 1:6; 21:12; Neh 6:18'. In not one of those passages, however, is it remotely probable that בעל conveys that sense.

the leaves of collected sayings'. This idea has been picked up by Allgeier and Buzy, but would only be marginally less implausible if the attested uses of עלה for book-leaves were much earlier, or if the composition of the epilogue were late enough for its author to have been familiar with codices, and their leaves—which is unlikely to have been true before the turn of the eras at the very earliest.

The verb does not pose such problems: נתן has a relatively wide range of meanings, related to the central idea of 'giving'. It is difficult to translate here, however, both because the precise sense of בעלי אספות is unclear, and because the original was intended to suggest, I think, that we have been 'given' Qohelet's words just as sheep are 'given' the goad—which is difficult to retain in English. The subsequent preposition is ambiguous, perhaps to maintain that same dual reference: מן could be the agent ('given *by*') or the source of the בעלי אספות ('given *from*', as, e.g., Gen 17.16). The sense is not greatly affected, but I think the latter is the more natural reading, and it fits the context better.

12.11 a single shepherd] It is doubtful that the epilogue is making any claim here for some single source of wisdom or inspiration behind all the different wise men and their sayings, although familiarity with the image of God as a shepherd has led many commentators to read it that way, while some others have seen a reference to Solomon or to other biblical/historical figures (there is a list in Lavoie, 'Qohélet 12,11', 145). Perrin, 'Messianism', 48-57, argues that the reference is to an authoritative, eschatological figure of David, but the sole basis for this claim is a description of such a figure in Ezek 34.23-24 and 37.24-25 as 'one shepherd' (the only other biblical uses of the expression). This misses the point of the Ezekiel passages, I think, that the one-ness of that shepherd is not part of a nickname, but a matter of importance in itself: there is only to be one such leader for all. The issue here is similarly, but coincidentally, one of singularity: the work of just one wise man (the spikes of just one shepherd) should be more than enough, and to engage with the multitude of other books available is to subject oneself to unnecessary pain—Taylor, 'On Some Verses of Qoheleth', 308, translates 'one and the same'. This is drawn out through the use of אחד here, and הרבה twice in the next verse, a juxtaposition which in itself raises problems for the suggestion of, e.g., Fox, and Lohfink, 'Les épilogues', 88, that אחד is serving merely as an indefinite article.

The reading of רעה as 'shepherd' is driven, of course, by the previous references to goads and spikes, so Galling is unusual in wanting to vocalize the consonants as 'friend' instead: he sees a collegial reference to another wise man. Ginsberg retains the imagery, but presents no evidence to support a proposed emendation to מרדע: a כמרדע חד is another sort of agricultural implement, associated with ploughing and sometimes understood to be an ox-goad, so this would mean '(given) as a sharp goad'. DeRouchie, 'Shepherding Wind', 12-14, connects the shepherd with the expression רעות רוח used in

1.14 and elsewhere, understanding it as 'shepherding' the wind, and suggests that God is being depicted as able to accomplish the control of the world that eludes humans.

G draws ויתר מהמה from 12.12 into this verse, apparently understanding the sense to be that the shepherd has given בעלי אספות—'and a surplus of them' (καὶ περισσὸν ἐξ αὐτῶν); we might say 'more than enough of them'.

12.12 and beyond them, my son, be careful] For מהמה, there is an oriental $Q^e r\hat{e}$ מהם: see the Introduction, p. 190. The Midrash Rabbah interprets the word in terms of מְהוּמָה, 'confusion', related to using books 'beyond' those in the canon—it mentions Ben Sira and a mysterious Ben Tagla, while a similar discussion in y. Sanhedrin 10.1 (50a), also in connection with this passage, mentions Ben Sira and Ben La'anah—but this is an exegetical stratagem, not attestation of a variant. I take the reference to be to the בעלי אספות, but the use of ויתר here, so soon after it began 12.9, has led some scholars to see the term as delimiting two separate sections of the epilogue (so, e.g., Shead, 'Ecclesiastes from the Outside In', 29, who translates both uses with 'and in addition to'; cf. his 'Reading Ecclesiastes "Epilogically"', 68-69). On that reading, the text is talking more generally about 'these things', with reference to the contents of the monologue or the first part of the epilogue. Whether or not the author intended to pick up the previous use, however, ויתר takes a different construction in each place, and cannot reasonably be supposed to have the same sense. If we are to break the epilogue into separate sections, moreover, it is far from clear that this would otherwise be the most obvious point at which to make that break. The relative rarity of יתר (on the spelling of which, see the note at 12.9) makes a simple coincidence unlikely, so there probably is some stylistic or other intention, perhaps connected with the author's switch from the rather bland and platitudinous statements of 12.9-10, via the colourful imagery of 12.11, to an unexpected warning here against the very sorts of books and study for which Qohelet has just been complimented. The הרבה of v. 9 is also picked up in this verse—twice—and it seems both likely that the author wishes us to see a connection, and very possible that his particular repetitions are supposed to mark a certain intensification, to match the change of tone. Boda, 'Speaking', 279, claims that the author uses the repetition of ויתר to create 'a sense of forward movement that reaches a feverish pitch in 12:12'.

In any case, though, where the absence of מן presented a difficulty for certain interpretations of 12.9, its presence here is an obstacle to translations of ויתר as 'in addition to' or suchlike: as we saw earlier, constructions with the preposition mean 'more than', not 'as well as'. Were we to choose not to adopt that understanding (which underpins my translation, and, differently, that of, e.g., Lavoie, 'Qohélet 12,12', 394-95), then we should have to construe the preposition, and divide the text, another way. Boda, 'Speaking', 272, presents cogent reasons not to take מן with the subsequent verb, which is the most obvious other option (pursued by Fox, who has 'of these things be wary'). It is worth noting, though, the proposal of Meek, 'Translating the Hebrew Bible', 335, which construes this whole passage differently. According to Meek, יתר is an emphatic adverb qualifying הזהר, and the sense is 'be well instructed from them, my son', but, issues of word-order aside, this is not an attested sense of the verb in the niph'al (as opposed to the hiph'il), while the construction of the passive with מן, although just used in the previous verse, would be unusual, and unlikely to yield the nuance that Meek seeks: the nearest parallel to what is proposed, in Ps 19.12 (ET 19.11), uses -ב, and מן would more likely imply 'be warned off them'.

Glasser, *Le Procès du bonheur par Qohelet*, 176, goes in yet another direction, by translating 'On en retire du profit', 'one profits from them'. This is not explained, but Lavoie, 'Qohélet 12,12', 392 (in the course of an extensive review), is probably right to suppose that Glasser is reading יתר as a substantive with the sense 'advantage': the cognate verb does not usually convey that sense. If he is not reading an impersonal verb, however, an ellipsis of יש is apparently presumed. Hahn in 1860 reached a similar conclusion more explicitly, by parsing הזהר as an infinitive, not an imperative, and understanding 'the profit from them is to be warned/instructed'; again, that is not impossible, but it is not a very natural construal, and the position of בני seems especially awkward (used vocatively, this usually stands at the head of a clause, between clauses, or straight after an initial imperative). Another older proposal, not picked up by Lavoie, is that of Ewald in 1867, who construed the preposition like Glasser and understood the verb like Meek, making this an admonition to learn from 'what remains over' ('was...erübrigt') from the sayings, that is, what proves itself useful. This does not strictly render מהמה twice (so Engelhardt, 'Der Epilog', 316), but the idea seems convoluted, and the proposed construction with the verb as unlikely as the senses presumed for both יתר and זהר.

We have already encountered זהר in the niph'al at 4.13, where it was something that the old king could not do. It is normally used absolutely, as there, and it is unlikely that it can take a direct object, despite the RSV's 'My son, beware of anything beyond these', which is the difficulty in Ewald's construal. McNeile does not fall into that trap, as Schoors supposes, but he does offer another popular (if improbable) interpretation, claiming that 'The writer means "besides (attending to) those (words of the wise), be warned, and be not led away by the multitude of books"' (93). Apart from the facts that this imputes an additive value to ויתר מן and imports a new verb, the words of the wise are too distant to be an obvious antecedent of המה. G seems to have gone down yet another route: after relegating ויתר מהמה to the previous verse, it declares υἱέ μου φύλαξαι ποιῆσαι βιβλία πολλα. This more naturally means 'my son take care to make many books' (which is, incidentally, the interpretation adopted by T), than 'my son, beware of making many books'

(*NETS*); σ' clarifies the point with <τοῦ> μὴ ποιῆσαι, '*not* to make'.[6] Whatever G intended, and even though such readings have been suggested sporadically by modern commentators, it is no more likely that עשות is serving as a verbal complement to הזהר than that יתר is its object. The verb does not mean 'beware' of something or of doing something, but 'be wary' or 'be alert'. In short, then, we probably cannot isolate ויתר מהמה as an introduction, nor take either the whole phrase or just מהמה as the object of הזהר. Of the various possibilities that have been canvassed, none seems simpler or more plausible than understanding the phrase to mean something like 'more than these' or 'beyond these', and taking the imperative to be a free-standing command without an object, 'be wary'. The expression is uncommon and probably late, but if we look to Esth 6.6 (יותר ממני, '[for whom would he want to do honour] *more than me*?'), the only other biblical passage in which יתר is followed by מן, and to Sir 8.13, which has אל תערב יתר ממך, 'do not stand surety *beyond yourself* (= beyond your means)', it is clear in both cases that the relevant expressions stand alongside a verb or verbal expression which has no direct object, and loosely qualify either the indirect object, or an object implicit in the idea of the verb. I take the use here to be similar, 'be wary (about things) beyond these', with the word-order designed to emphasize the beyond-ness. In context, we need not be cautious in some general way, but after the goads and spikes of just one shepherd (already experienced in this book), we should be wary of the many others that are out there.

12.12 There is much working on books without end] Qohelet used the expression אין קץ at 4.8, 16, but there and in Job 22.5; Isa 9.6, where it also appears, -ל is used to specify what it is that has no end. Here there is no such preposition (nor any textual evidence to support reading one), so we have either to take it as a composite noun serving as a predicate (cf. Fox: 'making many books is a thing-of-no-end'), or as a second, perhaps parenthetical, clause, 'the making of books is much—there is no end'. There is little difference in the sense, although the latter seems less speculative. Attempts to see a characterization of the making as 'pointless' here, rather than just 'endless', do make a difference (and rather more than Schoors allows), but it is difficult to sustain that understanding of אין קץ when the noun has no implication of purpose elsewhere.

The construal of this verse in Meek, 'Translating the Hebrew Bible', 335, has been noted above. Meek understands עשות to follow from the preceding imperative, so that one is not warned here, but instructed to 'make use of' many books. This is much the way that T takes it (cf. also perhaps *b. ʿErubin* 21b), and the case is made at greater length in Shields, 'Re-Examining'. There is no insurmountable obstacle to reading these Hebrew words that way, and

---

[6] On the τοῦ, see Marshall. The article is found in many manuscripts of G as well, and might be original—although, if so, that would suggest that G found לעשות (cf. McNeile, 156).

some points in favour (not least the fact that imperatives rarely end a clause). The principal difficulties are that this makes it harder to relate יגעת בשר to להג הרבה, and further strands אין קץ; it also relies on the construral of להג as an infinitive (which is likely but uncertain; see below).

Meek's rendering 'make use of' for עשות presents a more challenging problem. If we allow that עשה might have such a connotation in passages like 1 Sam 8.16, it is possible, in fact, that the epilogue is indeed not talking here about the creation, but about the consumption of books (and, taking it to be secondary, Michel, 'Vom Gott', 88, wonders if it is actually talking about the study of the monologue itself). To be sure, Meek himself argues that creation is precluded because one does not 'make' books in Hebrew, but 'write' them,[7] and this argument could just as well be turned against his own proposal: one usually 'reads' books in Hebrew, one doesn't 'use' them. A later and more thorough discussion in de Boer, 'A Note on Ecclesiastes 12:12a', is also guilty of rejecting 'write' (with somewhat stronger arguments), while failing satisfactorily to demonstrate that the verb can or must refer to the use or study of books. The ancient versions are of little help: all just reproduce 'make/do' except S, where ܠܡܟܬܒ *lmktb* shows the translator to have understood 'write', and T, where the contextualization suggests that the verb is understood in terms of study. Unless it represents some now long-lost idiom, there is, I think, a genuine ambiguity in the expression, which I have attempted to preserve in translation. The author may actually have intended to capture both senses, or to express some broader notion.

It is much less likely that עשות here means 'acquire', as Margoliouth, 'Ecclesiastes xii. 8-14', 124, proposes (see the note 'I put together' at 2.8), or, since the initial observation is about 'words', that the reference here is to doing accounts—as claimed by Rainey, 'Ecclesiastes', 149 (followed by Salyer, *Vain Rhetoric*, 140), and Gray, *Legacy of Canaan*, 201 ('in much casting of accounts there is no end, and much reckoning is a weariness of the flesh'). Each builds on an observation by Dahood, 'Canaanite-Phoenician',

---

[7] The point is taken up by Loretz, *Qohelet und der alte Orient*, 139 n. 25. Quite independently of this discussion, Fishbane, *Biblical Interpretation in Ancient Israel*, 31-32, claims that 12.9-12 should be read in the light of Mesopotamian colophons. I doubt this is right: a colophon typically describes the work of the copyist, not of a composition's author or protagonist, and is something more like the edition notice or copyright page in a modern book than its blurb. The analogy leads him, though, to compare the use of עשה here with that of the similarly general Akkadian verb *epēšu*: the form *uppušu* is used formulaically in colophons to describe some stage in the process of copying or checking the text (see *CAD* 4:232). This surely does not imply that the Hebrew verb must likewise have a technical meaning here, as Fishbane would like, but it both shows that such verbs might indeed be used to describe aspects of writing or the creation of texts, and reminds us that interactions with texts before printing were not confined simply to 'composing' them or 'reading' them.

219, which does not reach that conclusion, but notes the occurrence of *spr* and *hg* together in *Keret*, apparently with reference to being beyond counting. Rainey seeks further support in the fact that G uses βιβλία here (which is strictly a diminutive form) for ספרים, observing that MM includes some uses of that word for financial documents; he does not note that MM also introduces βιβλίον as 'the regular word for "book," "writing" in the Κοινή'.

12.12 study] The word להג is not used elsewhere in Hebrew, except in reference to this passage, and although BDB follows medieval Jewish scholars in connecting it with an Arabic root *lhj*, forms from which are used of attachment or perseverance,[8] it is questionable whether it is a real word: there are no potentially cognate forms in any language closer to Hebrew. The discussion of this passage in *b. ʿErubin* 21b acknowledges the problem implicitly, and presents two different interpretations: R. Papa is cited as connecting להג with לעג, 'mock', and seeing a condemnation of those who mock the words of the wise, while Rabbah rejects this in favour of a link with הגה, used of muttering, meditating, and speaking (as, later, Rashi does also). That latter verb is connected with books in Josh 1.8 (and probably Ps 1.2 also), and it is often associated with reading in later Hebrew. If the translators are not simply guessing from context, the same connection has probably been made by G μελέτη, 'exercise' or 'meditation' (cf. Hie, V *meditatio*) and S ܡܡܠܠܐ *mmllʾ*, 'speech', 'discourse', as well as by T, which talks about meditation on the Law.

Many recent commentators have followed suit, but there is greater agreement about the fact of a connection with הגה than about the precise nature of that connection. Dahood, 'Canaanite-Phoenician', 219, understands להג to be a defective writing of the noun הגה with a prefixed -ל serving to mark a dative, giving the sense, 'as for study', and others have broadly followed this line (Gray prefers to see the -ל as enclitic, marking a predicate), while understanding the final ה to have been lost through haplography rather than as a result of a particular orthography. G and S seem to have read a noun, although there is no indication that they took ל as 'dative': if they read it, they seem simply to have ignored it. The main alternative has been to view להג as the beginning of an infinitive from the verb הגה with להג(ו)ת—ל or possibly להגה—the end of which has been lost, again through haplography (so, e.g., Whitley). This may be how T construed the form, and it offers a better way to deal with the initial ל. On that reading, the literal sense is 'to study much'.

12.12 wearying] G uses κόπωσις for the Hebrew יגעת; this is a rare word, and Aitken ('Rhetoric and Poetry', 72) suggests that the translator may have invented it. Something similar could well be true, indeed, of יגעת itself, which has no other biblical attestation and may be a neologism. The Greek can

---

[8] This leads Hengstenberg to conclude that the warning is an admonition against 'desiring' other, foreign books.

suggest both labour and weariness, as can the ܠܐܘܬܐ *l'wt'* of S and the similar ליאות of T, but Hie *labor* reflects Jerome's understanding (drawn out in his commentary) that is very much in terms of physical work, while V *adflictio* makes study a bodily affliction. The Hebrew probably avoids the more common יגיע because that word more often connotes the products of labour than labour itself, so it is difficult to identify any specific nuance solely from the form. I suggested earlier, however, that in 1.8 the associated adjective יגע had a sense close to 'used up', and in the difficult 10.15, the verb apparently refers to something induced by 'the work of fools', not to work itself, so the usage in the monologue tends to favour an interpretation here in terms of 'tiring out' rather than 'labour'.

12.13 A last word, now all has been heard] Literally, 'An end of speaking, all has been heard'. Fox discusses a comparable Aramaic expression in Dan 7.28, where a report is brought to its end with the statement עד כה סופא די מלתא, 'up to here the last of the speaking', but, as e.g. Podechard observes, it is also important to note Sir 43.27, where קץ דבר means '(let) the last words (be)…', after an indication that more could be said (we might use 'suffice it to say'). Given its position, it seems unlikely that the statement here is intended to report that what has just been said marks the end of some speech or matter, like that in Daniel (although Hurvitz, 'Two Scribal Terms', supposes that סוף דבר did originate as a technical scribal expression with this sense, and is here used more loosely). Furthermore, for any similar sense, like 'the end of the matter', which is popular among translations and commentaries, we should expect סוף הדבר: the non-determination of the expression does not suggest that דבר is simply a way of talking about what has preceded.

The usage in Sir 43 does raise the possibility, however, that, if we are willing to see הכל נשמע as a subordinate clause, then the epilogue is characterizing what follows it as 'closing words'. Such an understanding lies behind, e.g., Delitzsch's 'Das Endergebnis, nachdem Alles vernommen (ist dies)', 'The end result, after all has been learned (is this)', or Podechard's 'Conclusion, tout ayant été entendu', 'Conclusion, everything having been heard'. The Hebrew, however, is more probably talking simply about bringing things to an end, not about presenting a summary: although the τέλος of G and πέρας (Gentry) or περασμός (Field, Marshall) of σ', θ' (the word has to be retroverted from Syh ܣܟܐ *sk'*) may have some implication of 'completion' or 'consummation', no such nuance is ever attached to סוף, which Qohelet used earlier in 3.11 and 7.2 to talk about the 'end' of God's actions, in contrast to the beginning, and about the 'end' of all humans. I take the point to be that the epilogist is just offering words with which to close, not explicitly attempting to sum up what has been said.

The ancient versions do not reflect a different consonantal text, but do include some curiosities here. Where M has נשמע, the main manuscripts of G have a singular imperative ἄκουε, 'listen!', so that G, as it stands, begins the list of admonitions with 'heed everything'. Goldman considers this the original rendering, and it is presented as such in the apparatus of BHQ. It seems more likely, however, that it results from an error in the Greek, whereby ἀκούεται, 'is heard' (the usual reading in Origenic manuscripts) was misread as a plural imperative ἀκούετε (which is the reading reflected in the text of Syh, and attested there as the reading also of α' and θ'). This was then made singular under the influence of the following singular imperatives.[9] Rather differently, Jerome, who in Hie had rendered *finis sermonis uniuersi auditu perfacilis est*, 'the end of the whole speech is easy to hear', adopts for V the curious *finem loquendi omnes pariter audiamus*, 'let us all equally hear the end of the speaking'. This reads נשמע as a first-person plural yiqtol form of the qal (as, interestingly, does Codex Graecus Venetus ἀκούσωμεν), rather than as a third-person qatal or participle in the niphʿal. Most distinctive of all is S, which starts the verse ܐܚܪܝܬܐ ܕܦܬܓܡܐ ܗܢܐ ܟܠܗ ܫܡܥ *ʾḥryth dptgmʾ bskh*, which must mean something like 'the last of the word (is) in its end'; the first two words are identical to the translation adopted for אחרית דבר in 7.8, while Kamenetzky, 234-35, is probably right to think that the second noun originated as a variant on the first, with a preposition then added to make sense of the clause. Although there is a variant with a relative, ܕܫܡܥ *dšmʿ*, the majority reading of S then follows this with ܫܡܥ *šmʿ*, which is probably to be read as an imperative 'hear', imitating the G manuscripts.

Other issues have contributed to the problems, of course, but translators and copyists seem to have been reluctant to read two short, peremptory clauses here, and many of the variants result, at least in part, from a desire to find a more continuous text. More recent commentators have not been immune to the same temptation, and particular attention has been paid to the role of נשמע. Most notably, a number of scholars have accepted Jerome's reading in V, which enables סוף דבר to be construed as an object, 'let us hear the end of a word', while Ewald reads נשמע as a participle with a gerundive meaning 'must be heard' (cf. נורא in Ps 76.8 [ET 76.7]; J-M §121 i), enabling him to reach much the same understanding through a different construal. Neither of these is very persuasive: gerundive uses of the participle are rare, while the proposed 'let us' mode of discourse is found in no general admonitions outside a handful of psalms, and would sit uncomfortably beside the imperatives that follow (cf. Dohmen, 'Der Weisheit', 17). Some other, related attempts to find continuity are quite impossible. Jerome implausibly tries to make הכל refer to the subject of the verb, 'all of us', and is followed in this by, e.g., Gietmann and Zapletal, while others, including Elster ('Das Ende der ganzen Rede lasset uns hören') and the AV, connect it instead with דבר, to speak of 'the whole matter'; neither would be good Hebrew.

---

[9] See McNeile, 153; Gentry, 'Hexaplaric Materials', 25-26. Goldman takes ἀκούεται to be a revision of G towards the Hebrew, but does not explain how G might originally have come to read ἄκουε.

Although not in M^L or other early manuscripts, the ס of סוף is often enlarged in Masoretic texts and early printed editions. Yeivin, *Introduction*, 47, suggests that the enlargement in this instance is the mark of a new section, although it is tempting to connect it rather to the fact that this verse was customarily repeated in reading as the final verse (see below), for which the סוף can serve as a reminder. We have come across similar enlargements of letters at 1.1 and 7.1, but this is the instance most commonly recognized in the Masoretic lists which Ginsburg collates in *Massorah*, 4:39-40: those others appear in one list and six lists respectively, while this one appears in all ten.

12.13 Fear God] The phrasing here, את האלהים ירא, is the same as at 5.6. S ܘܡܢ ܩܕܡ ܡܪܝܐ ܕܚܠ *wmn qdm mry' dḥl*, 'and from before the Lord, fear', is unexpected, therefore: it seems to be a rendering of ומלפני האלהים ירא. The conjunction has arisen because S reads this as the second command, but the expression is reminiscent of Qohelet's words at 3.14 and 8.12, where he spoke of fearing 'from before' God. It is difficult to exclude altogether the impossibility that this reflects a Hebrew variant, but its many other problems in this verse undermine the credibility of S as a witness here.

12.13 this is everything for the human] Lit. 'the human's everything'. As is often observed, on each of the other eighteen occasions when it occurs in biblical Hebrew (including instances at 3.13; 5.18; 7.2), כל האדם means 'every' or 'any' human. We should also expect the construction with זה to express a simple identification (perhaps with conclusive force, cf. Enns, 'Evaluation', 135-36), as when כי זה היום in Judg 4.14 explains 'for this is the day', or Ps 48.15 (ET 48.14) declares 'this is God'. The most obvious meaning of the text, therefore, is 'this is every human', but if זה refers to the conduct which has just been commended, then that makes no sense: people might in some sense 'own' or 'owe' actions, but they cannot 'be' actions, and in order for the Hebrew to mean something like 'this is for everyone', it would require a preposition, like English.

The difficulty has provoked a variety of responses among the ancient versions. In his commentary, Jerome apparently understands the clause to mean that fear of God and obedience to his commandments is what humans were made for (*ad hoc enim natum esse hominem*, 'for the human is born for this'). In both Hie and V, however, he has just *omnis homo*, 'all the human', or 'every human', which is equivalent to G πᾶς ὁ ἄνθρωπος, and simply renders the Hebrew *verbatim*. A more precise translation is offered by σ', which has τοῦτο γὰρ ὅλος ὁ ἄνθρωπος, 'for this is the whole human', and that perhaps has the nuance 'this is quintessentially human', in line with Jerome's understanding. More explicitly interpretative readings are offered by T, which speaks of חמי למהוי אורח, 'the proper way to be' of every human, and S which has the lengthy ܡܛܠ ܕܗܢܐ ܗܘ ܕܡܢ *mṭl dhn' hw dmn 'wmn' ḥd 'tyhb kl 'nš*, 'for this is what is from one maker given to every man' (a variant ܠܟܠ *lkl* for ܠܟ *kl* clarifies the syntax). Kamenetzky, 204, treats this as a misplaced gloss on 12.11, but it seems more likely to be an interpretative gloss on the statement here, which evokes 12.11 to explain the nature of the 'this'. In *b. Šabbat* 30b and *b. Berakot* 6b, the construct is taken to imply a particular sort of possession, and the point to be that the whole world was created for one human. More modern commentators have generally pursued one of two courses, either seeing ellipsis of a specific term, or understanding this to be a pregnant construction. Among the former, for instance, Ginsburg believes that we should supply ישמר on the basis of the preceding שמור (and translates 'for this every man should do'), while among the latter, Gordis offers a list of instances like that in Ps 120.7, where 'I (am) peace' means 'I am seeking peace', or Job 8.9, where 'we (are) yesterday' is used to emphasize the ignorance of humans who have lived such a short time. This leads Gordis himself to adopt a traditional rendering, 'this is the whole duty of man', provoking Fox to respond that 'the notion of "duty" is not really provided by context and supplying it seems rather *ad hoc*'. That is, in fact, a very fair criticism, which might well be levelled at both approaches: if a word has been omitted, or if some concept is supposedly implied, then the context gives us no clear indication of what that word or concept might be, and anything we supply is simply a guess.[10]

There is wide agreement, then, that the text must be making a claim about the obligation of humans to fear God, either because it is their duty or because it is in their nature, but no satisfactory explanation of the way it makes that claim. For that reason, it seems necessary to move away from the most obvious meaning of זה כל האדם, and to explore some other possibilities. In particular, despite the other uses of כל האדם, if we retain the translation 'every human', then we also retain the principal difficulty, that people can themselves not 'be' or 'consist of' their own behaviour. The most popular alternative, 'the whole human', championed by σ' and many others since, does not overcome that problem, but the usage of כל is not limited to those two senses, and it can have the much broader sense of 'everything'—as most famously exemplified in the declarations at 1.2 and 12.8, and in the claim at 3.1. This picked up in the rabbinic explanations of the passage at *b. Berakot* 6b and in the Midrash,

---

[10] Fox's own approach is interesting, but perhaps not so very different. He does not speak of a pregnant construction, but employs some of the same examples as Gordis to make a point that predicates do not necessarily imply simple identity in non-verbal sentences, but can instead characterize the subject in terms of its nature or content. This leads him to conclude that 'this', fear of God and obedience, is 'the substance, the "material" of every person. There should be no alloy.' That actually results in an understanding close to Jerome's, and it is not inherently implausible. The argument would be more persuasive, however, if our clause actually corresponded more closely to the examples offered. In clauses like 'I (am) peace' or 'I (am) prayer' (Ps 109.4), Fox takes 'peace' and 'prayer' to be the predicates, but on that analogy, זה כל האדם would be describing זה as כל האדם, not כל האדם as זה—in other words, the clause would have to mean 'the nature/content of this is everyone', not 'the nature/content of everyone is this'.

which understand כל to be a reference to 'the whole world', and the clause to refer to the value of humans (presumably understanding 'this is everything, the human').[11] Although it would be an unusual expression, 'the everything of the human' (as read by, e.g., Niccacci, 'Qohelet o la gioia', 79) is by no means impossible, and it not only offers the best fit here, but possibly picks up Qohelet's own claim and question in 1.2-3 by stating a limitation on what is available for humans. I am inclined also to believe, however, that the identity of the זה should be revisited: see the next note.

12.14 that] Discussion has long been complicated by questions about the originality of the various elements here, but it is generally assumed that 12.13b-14, as they stand, should be construed as an admonition followed by two motive clauses: 'fear and obey because this is כל האדם (and) because God will judge every deed'. It is possible, however, and arguably less clumsy, to read the second כי not as 'because' but as 'that'—taking it to substantivize the verbal clause that follows. In which case we can construe the text rather differently as 'fear and obey, because this is כל האדם: that God will judge for every deed'. On such a reading (which has been adopted most recently by Schoors), the כל of כל האדם in 12.13 is picked up by כל מעשה and כל נעלם, so that there is a continuity of vocabulary even if that first כל has to be understood in a different way. More importantly, this offers a better, and smoother, sense: humans should fear and obey God not for two very different reasons—because they *have* to, and because God is going to judge their actions—but for the single reason that such judgment represents the totality of what they can expect.

12.14 for everything they have done, God will demand a reckoning] Lit. '(for) every deed, God will bring (them) into judgment', but see below. Where M has 'every deed' in the singular, V *cuncta quae fiunt* and S ܗܠܠ ܕܟܠ ܥܒ݂ܕܐ *dlkl 'bd'* are plural. The former is probably translational, however, and the latter may have acquired the seyame which marks the plural secondarily. It is unlikely that they reflect an early Hebrew variant, although the manuscript of ben Uzziel's *Kitāb al-Khilaf* cited by Lipschütz for information about the pointing (ben Naphtali is reported to have pointed כל with *metheg*, where ben Asher has it instead under the מ of מעשה) does in fact have מעשי, as though this were 'all the deeds of God'. Kennicott finds that in one manuscript, and מעשיו in another, so the Hebrew manuscript tradition has not entirely resisted the same temptation to read a plural.

---

[11] Mention should be made here of the reading attributed to θ', σύπαντα τὰ ἔργα τοῦ ἀνθρώπου, 'all the deeds of the human'. Long known from Syh, where it is marked as equivalent to πᾶν τὸ ποίημα, 'every deed', in G, this is now found in Greek on ms 788. It introduces a reference to humanity that is completely absent from all other versions, and if it is intended as a clarification, seems wholly untypical of θ'. This leads Goldman to doubt the attribution (he calls it 'a targumic clarification'), but we should perhaps rather doubt the position: this may originally have been an attempt to render כל האדם, which takes כל in the sense 'every deed'.

Hie *quia omne factum*, however, is singular, while G πᾶν τὸ ποίημα is also singular, but presents a problem that is harder to judge: it has an article that is absent from the Hebrew of M, and the translator is usually scrupulous about such things. As Goldman notes, though, there is much confusion around the use of articles after כל/πᾶς elsewhere in the book, and it is difficult to say what usage is original. The translator might also have considered an article to be implicit after את, which is generally attached to a determined object (we may note that, for exactly the same Hebrew, G used πάντα τὰ ποιήματα in 8.17, but had πᾶν ποίημα in 8.9, where there is no את); there is also a strong possibility that he simply renders such expressions contextually (see below). In any case, σ' πᾶσαν γὰρ πρᾶξιν, 'because every action', affirms M in respect of both the number and the article (on the attribution, and the untypical usage, see Marshall). None of this really affects the sense, but the nuance of what follows is important.

The expression האלהים יבא במשפט is commonly understood as a reference to God bringing 'every deed' into judgment, but is similar to that used in 11.9, where the actor rather than the act is the object of the verb. This is also the case in Job 14.3, while the qal of the verb is used with במשפט in Job 9.32; 22.4; Ps 143.2; Isa 3.14 of entering into judgment with someone. In general, the expression 'bring into judgment' seems to represent something that one does to or with people rather than deeds, and it seems to refer to the act of accusing or interrogating, rather than to the passing of a sentence. Unless we are to suppose that the deeds are personified here, and in some sense stand in the dock themselves, then את כל מעשה cannot really be what God 'brings into judgment'. Ehrlich, and Joüon, 'Notes philologiques', 425, are provoked by this to make speculative and somewhat implausible emendations. More likely, the usage is rather loose here, and is either idiomatic (as when one might speak in English of prosecuting a crime, and even of bringing a murder to court, when it is the murderer who actually appears), or a use of the accusative to delimit the action—'God will bring (humans) to judgment *with respect to* every deed'. The latter understanding lies behind my translation, which is also informed, however, by a desire to avoid the impression that the Hebrew must be referring to some instantaneous trial of every action as soon as it has happened: the point is more probably that the individual will eventually be held to account for the totality of their actions, and, as at e.g. 3.11, מעשה is being used collectively. It may be similar considerations that lie behind G's variable renderings.

12.14 even of everything unseen] Lit. 'of everything unseen'. The על of M is often translated 'along with', taking כל נעלם to be something else that is judged, alongside כל מעשה. Many commentators have objected, however, that 'every deed' would seem to include the concept of 'every hidden thing', and McNeile, 94, for instance, claims that 'על cannot mean "together with" after the universal כל מעשה'. 'Cannot' may be too strong, but על marked the basis of judgment in the similar expression at 11.9 (cf. 3.17), and that is probably the way in which it is to be understood here. Accordingly, נעלם must describe something that may be a feature of any deed, and we should avoid taking it to indicate simply things that people have attempted to conceal. In Lev 5.2 and elsewhere, the word is used of impurity that is acquired unknowingly, and in 1 Kgs 10.3, that there was 'nothing hidden' from Solomon in the Queen of Sheba's questions obviously means that there was nothing obscure to him: concealment, as such, is not a necessary component of the sense. Given that the נעלם may be good or bad, the point is probably that every deed will be scrutinized at a level of detail beyond its clear and visible features, or placed in a context beyond human grasp. The point is not, then, that two separate categories will be judged, 'everything' and 'everything unseen', but that each deed, seen or unseen, will be judged in a way that takes account even of its unseen components or ramifications.

This may be the implication of G παντὶ παρεωραμένῳ, 'everything that has been overlooked', although the reading is complicated by a preceding ἐν in the Greek manuscripts (not noted in *BHQ*). This is more probably an inner-Greek error for ἐπὶ, which G used at 11.9, than a translation of a Hebrew variant with ב, and the error may have been facilitated by the preceding ἐν κρίσει. Although the reading of σ' has been corrupted in some sources, it was probably περὶ παντὸς παροραθέντος—similar to G in sense, as Jerome observes, but with the περὶ making it more explicit that this is the basis for judgment. Jerome takes these readings to imply judgment even of unwitting errors. For α' we just have κεκρυμμένῳ, 'hidden', and θ' is usually retroverted from Syh as ἀόρατοι, 'unseen' (the reading has been misplaced at 12.11); both are similar to Hie *de omni abscondito*, 'concerning everything concealed'. Jerome paraphrases, however, in V, which is usually found as *pro omni errato*, 'for every error', although there is some important support for a variant *pro omni reatu*, roughly 'for every offence with which one has been charged'. The former corresponds to the understanding of G and σ', and could reflect the broader influence of σ' on V, but in his commentary Jerome had distanced himself from that opinion, and *pro omni reatu* better corresponds to his summary of the verse there, in which he talks of long-postponed verdicts being delivered. There is a very different reading in S, which renders נעלם with ܕܟܣܐ ܘܓܠܐ *dksʾ wglʾ*, 'that is concealed and revealed', an alteration that has been inspired, perhaps, by the following 'good or bad', and that is most likely secondary.

12.14 whether good or bad] There is an ambiguity here, which I have tried to retain in my translation. The accents in M may indicate that the Masoretes interpreted this as a qualification of כל מעשה, not כל נעלם (so, e.g. McNeile, 94), and it seems unlikely, to be sure, that these final words qualify only the 'hidden aspects': the verse sets out what is to be judged ('every deed') and, almost parenthetically, the basis of the judgment (even the unseen aspects of every deed). The last part is then usually taken to express a further qualification, that the deeds will be considered whether they are good or bad, even if that seems redundant after the initial specification of '*every deed*'. B. *Ḥagigah* 5a reflects a certain embarrassment that the verse seems to suggest the potential condemnation even of good deeds, and this is picked up in the Midrash. However, in the only other occurrence of אם טוב ואם רע, at Jer 42.6, the reference is to God's pronouncements, and passages like Gen 24.50 suggest that this vocabulary can be used not just of inherent qualities, but of commendation and condemnation. After the conciseness of 12.13, it would not be astonishing if we were supposed to understand the expression here as characterizing not the qualities of each deed, but the purpose of the משפט: to discern or to pronounce whether each actor is good or bad. A similar understanding is expressed in the paraphrase which Jerome offers in his commentary, where he speaks of a sentence delivered to each according to whether their actions have been good or bad, and we might ourselves understand: 'For everything they have done, God will bring (the human) to a reckoning—looking even at the hidden aspects—of either "good" or "bad"'.

An unattributed hexaplaric rendering of this phrase, ἐάν τε ἀγαθὸν ἐάν τε κακόν, is found in two manuscripts, and is plausibly attributed to σ' by Marshall. It lacks a conjunction before the second ἐάν, which probably just indicates a preference for using τε...τε to indicate alternatives—and this is one of the grounds upon which the reading is assigned to Symmachus—but a number of later Hebrew manuscripts do have אם for ואם (see de Rossi; Ginsburg, *Writings*), and the variant might be early enough to have lain behind this rendering; in any case, אם...אם is an alternative form of the construction (e.g. 2 Sam 15.21).

12.14 (end)] At some point it became customary, when reading out Isaiah, the Book of the Twelve, Ecclesiastes, and Lamentations, to repeat the penultimate verse after the last verse, so as not to end on a threatening, inauspicious note. Corresponding to this practice, we find a mnemonic (סימן) in later manuscripts and printed editions, usually יֳקָק, but sometimes (as in, e.g., BM Harley ms 5711) יֳקָא. This is an acrostic, with the letters standing for the name of each book (ישעיה, תרי עשר, קהלת, קינות or איכה). It is not found in M^L, the extant portions of M^A, or the Cairo Codex of the Prophets, but does appear as יֳקָא after Isaiah (although not Malachi) in the early tenth-century Codex Babylonicus Petropolitanus (St. Petersburg, Russian National Library, Evr. I. B 3), with the mnemonic there glossed as describing 'the four books which we do not finish at the end' (see Strack, *Prophetarum Posteriorum Codex*, 53a).